MW00744809

"No other guide has as ... a pleasure to read." G...

". . . Excellently organized for the casual traveler who is looking for a mix of recreation and cultural insight."
Washington Post

★ ★ ★ ★ ★ (5-star rating) "Crisply written and remarkably personable. Cleverly organized so you can pluck out the minutest fact in a moment. Satisfyingly thorough."
Réalités

"The information they offer is up-to-date, crisply presented but far from exhaustive, the judgments knowledgeable but not opinionated." *New York Times*

"The individual volumes are compact, the prose succinct, and the coverage up-to-date and knowledgeable . . . The format is portable and the index admirably detailed."
John Barkham Syndicate

". . . An abundance of excellent directions, diversions, and facts, including perspectives and getting-ready-to-go advice — succinct, detailed, and well organized in an easy-to-follow style." *Los Angeles Times*

"They contain an amount of information that is truly staggering, besides being surprisingly current."
Detroit News

"These guides address themselves to the needs of the modern traveler demanding precise, qualitative information . . . Upbeat, slick, and well put together."
Dallas Morning News

". . . Attractive to look at, refreshingly easy to read, and generously packed with information." *Miami Herald*

"These guides are as good as any published, and much better than most." *Louisville* (Kentucky) *Times*

The Stephen Birnbaum Travel Guides

Canada
Caribbean, Bermuda, and the Bahamas
Disneyland
Europe
Europe for Business Travelers
Florida for Free
France
Great Britain
Hawaii
Ireland
Italy
Mexico
South America
Spain and Portugal
United States
USA for Business Travelers
Walt Disney World

CONTRIBUTING EDITORS

David Baird
F. Lisa Beebe
Frederick H. Brengelman
Valerie Brito
Kevin Causey
Peter Collis
Rebecca Day
Thomas de la Cal
Martha Fitzmaurice
Dwight V. Gast
Judith Glynn
Michael Hudec
Arline Inge
Donald A. Jeffrey
Jill Jolliffe
Robert Latona
Charles Leocha

Howell Llewellyn
Jan S. McGirk
Erica Meltzer
Jeanne Muchnick
Joan Kane Nichols
Clare Pedrick
Michael Perreca
Mark Potok
Allan Seiden
Frank Shiell
Richard Slovak
Melinda Tang
Paul Wade
David Wickers
Mark Williams
Peter Wise
Maria Emília Zino

COVER   Robert Anthony

MAPS   B. Andrew Mudryk

SYMBOLS   Gloria McKeown

A Stephen Birnbaum Travel Guide

Birnbaum's SPAIN/ PORTUGAL 1991

Stephen Birnbaum
Alexandra Mayes Birnbaum
EDITORS

Lois Spritzer
EXECUTIVE EDITOR

Laura L. Brengelman
Managing Editor

Kristin Moehlmann
Senior Editor

Ann-Rebecca Laschever
Julie Quick
Beth Schlau
Associate Editors

Julie Hassinger Marks
Assistant Editor

HOUGHTON MIFFLIN COMPANY / BOSTON 1990

Copyright © 1990 by Houghton Mifflin Company

All rights reserved.

For information about permission to reproduce
selections from this book, write to
Permissions, Houghton Mifflin Company,
2 Park Street, Boston, Massachusetts 02108.

ISBN: 0-395-55997-9
ISSN: 0749-2561 (Stephen Birnbaum Travel Guides)
ISSN: 1042-6353 (Spain and Portugal)

Printed in the United States of America

WP 10 9 8 7 6 5 4 3 2 1

Contents

GETTING READY TO GO

All the practical travel data you need to plan your vacation down to the final detail.

Sources and Resources

PERSPECTIVES

A cultural and historical survey of Spain's and Portugal's past and present, their people, politics, and heritage.

Spain

Portugal

THE CITIES

Thorough, qualitative guides to each of the 18 cities most often visited by vacationers and businesspeople. Each section, a comprehensive report of the city's most appealing attractions and amenities, is designed to be used on the spot. Directions and recommendations are immediately accessible because each guide is presented in a consistent form.

DIVERSIONS

A selective guide to 19 active and cerebral vacations, including the places to pursue them where your quality of experience is likely to be highest.

For the Experience

For the Body

For the Mind

DIRECTIONS

The most spectacular routes and roads; most arresting natural wonders; and most magnificent castles, manor houses, and gardens — all organized into 21 specific driving tours.

A Word from the Editor

I was a little slow in getting around to running away from home — to tell the truth, I waited until the summer after my 20th birthday — but when I finally decided to hit the road, I made up for lost time. Rather than head across town to Aunt Maude's, I decided to sulk along the southern coast of Spain, a decision that was among the very best I ever made.

One of the major contributors to the joys of that very special summer was the limited amount of cash I had in my pocket. I'd been traveling very much on the cheap (remind me to tell you about the several nights spent snoozing on the beach), so my first views of Spain and Portugal were often from the wrong side of a dining room tray.

I have the impression that in the course of about 3 months, I walked from Málaga (actually Torremolinos) to Barcelona. The truth is, I hitchhiked more often than not, took the bus when I felt I could spare the change, and worked as everything from a bartender (I served as vice president in charge of making dirty glasses clean) to fisherman (my highest rank was second net puller).

Above all, I developed a fondness for Spain and Portugal that I have never lost, and must say that I have waited with some extra eagerness to finally focus on a guide to the Iberian Peninsula. Spain and Portugal are at once a part of Europe, and yet very distinctive and distinct from the other members of the European community. They offer a combination of cultures and historic influences that have molded these countries in ways very different from their continental neighbors.

Just a brief turning of the pages of this guide will demonstrate the diversity that thrives in Spain between the Pyrenees and the Strait of Gibraltar. The idea that Spain is a single, homogeneous nation is one of travel's least justifiable assertions, and the atmosphere and ambience that thrive across this extremely variegated country are, in themselves, among the prime magnets that draw visitors. At least half a dozen distinct "nations" co-exist under the Spanish flag — each demanding strict attention — and one of the joys of traveling to and through Spain is the constant feeling of surprise and discovery.

In Portugal, a traveler first discovers, above all, that he or she is not visiting a suburb of Spain. Language, food, history, and music are all dramatically Portuguese, and despite its modest size, Portugal offers travelers tastes of its remarkable heritage that are both pungent and wonderfully pleasurable. We've also tried to make some sense of the often awkward relationship between these two legendary nations that somehow emerged from a singular, separate square of European real estate.

Once again, the opportunity to present a single corner of the European continent in great detail has been part of the pleasure of preparing this guide. It gives us the opportunity to deal with Spanish and Portuguese destinations in the sort of detail that they truly deserve, and to provide a modern traveler with the perspectives and insights that are required to do more than just superficially see two of Europe's most intriguing countries.

Such thorough treatment only mirrors an increasingly pervasive trend among travelers — the frequent return to treasured foreign travel spots. Once upon a time, even the most dedicated travelers would visit distant parts of the world no more than once in a lifetime — usually as part of that fabled Grand Tour. But greater numbers of would-be sojourners are now availing themselves of the opportunity to visit favored parts of the world over and over again.

So where once it was routine to say you'd "seen" a particular country after a very superficial, once-over-lightly encounter, the more perceptive travelers of today recognize that it's entirely possible to have only skimmed the surface of a specific destination even after having visited that place more than a dozen times. Similarly, repeated visits to a single site permit true exploration of special interests, whether they be sporting, artistic, or intellectual in nature.

For those of us who spent several years working out the special system under which we present information in this series, the luxury of being able to devote nearly as much space as we'd like to just a single country is as close to paradise for guide writers and editors as any of us expects to come. But clearly this is not the first guide to the glories of Spain and Portugal — guides of one sort or another have existed for centuries, so a traveler might logically ask why a new one is suddenly necessary.

Our answer is that the nature of travel to Spain and Portugal — and even of the travelers who now routinely make the trip — has changed dramatically. For the past 2,000 years or so, travel to and through Spain and Portugal was an extremely elaborate undertaking, one that required extensive advance planning. Even as recently as the 1950s, a person who had actually been to Madrid, Lisbon, the Algarve, or the Costa Brava could dine out on his or her experiences for years, since such adventures were quite extraordinary and usually the province of the privileged alone.

With the advent of jet air travel in the late 1950s, however, and of increased-capacity, wide-body aircraft during the late 1960s, travel to and around these once distant lands became extremely common. In fact, in more than 2 decades of nearly unending inflation, airfares may be the only commodity in the world that has actually gone down in price.

Attitudes, as well as costs, also have changed significantly in the last couple of decades. Beginning with the so-called flower children of the 1960s, international travel lost much of its aura of mystery. Whereas their parents might have been happy with just a superficial sampling of Barcelona or Estoril, these young people simply picked up and settled in various parts of Europe for an indefinite stay. While living as inexpensively as possible, they adapted to the local lifestyle, and generally immersed themselves in things European.

Thus began an explosion of travel to and through both Spain and Portugal. And over the years, the development of inexpensive charter flights and packages fueled the new American interest in and appetite for more extensive exploration.

Now, in the 1990s, those same flower children who were in the forefront of the modern travel revolution have undeniably aged. While it may be impolite to point out that they are probably well into their untrustworthy 30s and (some) 40s, their original zeal for travel remains undiminished. For them it's hardly news that the way to get from western Europe to the Costa del Sol is to head toward the Mediterranean, make a right, and then watch for the outline of the Rock of Gibraltar. Such experienced and knowledgeable travelers know precisely where they want to go, and are more often searching for ideas and insights to expand their already sophisticated travel consciousness.

Obviously, any new guidebook to Spain and Portugal must keep pace with and answer the real needs of today's travelers. That's why we've tried to create a guide that's specifically organized, written, and edited for this more demanding modern audience, one for whom qualitative information is infinitely more desirable than mere quantities of unappraised data. We think that this book and the other guides in our series represent a new generation of travel guides, one that is especially responsive to modern needs and interests.

For years, dating back as far as Herr Baedeker, travel guides have tended to be encyclopedic, seemingly much more concerned with demonstrating expertise in geography and history than in any analysis of the sorts of things that more frequently concern a typical modern traveler. But today, when it is hardly necessary to tell a traveler where the Pyrenees are, it's hard to justify devoting endless pages to historical perspectives. As suggested earlier, it's not impossible that the guidebook reader may have been to Spain and/or Portugal nearly as often as the guidebook editor, so it becomes the responsibility of that editor to provide new perspectives and to suggest new directions in order to make the guide genuinely valuable.

That's exactly what we've tried to do in this series. I think you'll notice a different, more contemporary tone to the text, as well as an organization and focus that are distinctive and more functional. And even a random reading of what follows will demonstrate a substantial departure from the standard guidebook orientation, for we've not only attempted to provide information of a more compelling sort, but we also have tried to present the data in a context that makes it particularly accessible.

Needless to say, it's difficult to decide precisely what to include in a guidebook of this size — and what to omit. Early on, we realized that giving up the encyclopedic approach precluded our listing every single route and restaurant, a realization that helped define our overall editorial focus. Similarly, when we discussed the possibility of presenting certain information in other than strict geographic order, we found that the new format enabled us to arrange data in a way that we feel best answers the questions travelers typically ask.

Large numbers of specific questions have provided the real editorial skeleton for this book. The volume of mail I regularly receive emphasizes that modern travelers want very precise information, so we've tried to address these needs and have organized our material in the most responsive way possible. Readers who want to know the most evocative sights around Seville or the best places to dine in Valencia will have no trouble whatever finding that data in this guide.

Travel guides are, understandably, reflections of personal taste, and putting one's name on a title page obviously puts one's preferences on the line. But I think I ought to amplify just what "personal" means. I don't believe in the sort of personal guidebook that's a palpable misrepresentation on its face. It is, for example, hardly possible for any single travel writer to visit thousands of restaurants (and nearly as many hotels) in any given year and provide accurate appraisals of each one. And even if it were possible for one human being to survive such an itinerary, it would of necessity have to be done at a dead sprint and the perceptions derived therefrom would probably be less valid than those of any other intelligent individual visiting the same establishments. It is, therefore, impossible (especially in a large, annually revised guidebook *series* such as we offer) to have only one person provide all the data on the entire world.

I also happen to think that such individual orientation is of substantially less value. Visiting a single hotel for just one night or eating one hasty meal in a random restaurant hardly equips anyone to provide appraisals that are of more than passing interest. No amount of doggedly alliterative or oppressively onomatopoeic text can camouflage a technique that is essentially specious on its face. We have, therefore, chosen what I like to describe as the "thee and me" approach to restaurant and hotel evaluation and, to a somewhat more limited degree, to the sites and sights in the other sections of our text. What this really reflects is a personal sampling tempered by intelligent counsel from informed local sources; these additional friends-of-the-editor are almost always residents of the city and/or area about which they have been consulted.

Despite the presence of several editors and a considerable number of writers, researchers, and local correspondents, very precise editing and tailoring keeps our text fiercely subjective. So what follows is the gospel according to the Birnbaums, and it represents as much of our own tastes and preferences as we can manage. It is probable, therefore, that if you like your cities stylish and your mountainsides uncrowded, prefer small hotels with personality to huge high-rise anonymities, and can't tolerate paella or fresh fish that's been relentlessly overcooked, we're likely to have a long and meaningful relationship. Readers with dissimilar tastes may be less enraptured.

I also should point out something about the person to whom this guidebook is directed. Above all, he or she is a "visitor." This means that such elements as restaurants have been specifically picked to provide the visitor with a representative, illuminating, stimulating, and above all, pleasant experience. Since so many extraneous considerations can affect the reception and service accorded a regular restaurant patron, our choices can in no way be construed as an exhaustive guide to resident dining. We think we've listed all the best places, in various price ranges, but they were chosen with a visitor's perspective in mind.

Other evidence of how we've tried to tailor our text to reflect changing travel habits is most apparent in the section we call DIVERSIONS. Where once it was common for travelers to spend a foreign visit nailed to a single spot, the emphasis today is more likely to be directed toward pursuing some athletic enterprise or special interest while seeing the surrounding countryside. So we've selected every activity we could reasonably evaluate and have organized the material in a way that is especially accessible. It is no longer necessary, therefore, to wade through a pound or two of extraneous prose just to find the very best crafts shop or the most picturesque *parador* within a reasonable radius of your destination.

If there is a single thing that best characterizes the revolution in and evolution of current travel habits, it is that most travelers now consider travel a right rather than a privilege. Travel today translates as the enthusiastic desire to sample all of the world's opportunities, to find that elusive quality of experience that is not only enriching but comfortable. For that reason, we've tried to make what follows not only helpful and enlightening but also the sort of welcome companion of which every traveler dreams.

I also should point out that every good travel guide is a living enterprise; that is, no part of this text is carved in stone. In our annual revisions, we refine, expand, and further hone all our material to serve your travel needs even better. To this end, no contribution is of greater value to us than your personal reaction to what we have written, as well as information reflecting your own experiences while using our book. We earnestly and enthusiastically solicit your comments about this guide *and* your opinions and perceptions about places you have recently visited. In this way, we will be able to provide the most current information — including the actual experiences of recent travelers — to make those experiences more readily available to others. Please write to us at 60 E. 42nd St., New York, NY 10165.

We sincerely hope to hear from you.

STEPHEN BIRNBAUM

How to Use This Guide

 A great deal of care has gone into the organization of this guide-book, and we believe it represents a real breakthrough in the presentation of travel information. Our aim is to create a new, more modern generation of travel books, and to make this guide the most useful and practical travel tool available today.

Our text is divided into five basic sections, in order to best present information in the most useful way on every possible aspect of a vacation in Spain or Portugal. This organization itself should alert you to the vast and varied opportunities available, as well as indicating all the specific data necessary to plan a successful visit. You won't find much of the conventional "swaying palms and shimmering sands" type of text in this guide; we've chosen instead to deliver more useful and practical information. Prospective itineraries tend to speak for themselves, and with so many diverse travel opportunities, we feel our main job is to highlight what's where and to provide basic details — how, when, where, how much, and what's best (and what's not) — to assist you in making the most intelligent choices possible.

Here is a brief summary of the five sections of this book, and what you can expect to find in each. We believe that you will find both your travel planning and en route enjoyment enhanced by having this book at your side.

GETTING READY TO GO

This mini-encyclopedia of practical travel facts is meant to be a sort of know-it-all companion with all the precise information necessary to create a successful trip through Spain and Portugal. There are entries on more than 30 separate topics, including how to get where you're going, what preparations to make before leaving, what to expect in the different parts of the countries, what the trip is likely to cost, and how to avoid prospective problems. The individual entries are specific, realistic, and, where appropriate, cost-oriented.

We expect you to use this section most in the course of planning your trip, for its ideas and suggestions are intended to simplify this often confusing period. Entries are intentionally concise, in an effort to get to the meat of the matter. These entries are augmented by extensive lists of specific sources from which to obtain even more detailed data, plus some suggestions for obtaining travel information on your own.

PERSPECTIVES

Any visit to an unfamiliar destination is enhanced and enriched by understanding the cultural and historical heritage of that area. We have, therefore, provided just such an introduction to Spain and Portugal, their pasts and presents, people and politics, architecture, literature, music and dance, and food and drink.

THE CITIES

Individual reports on the 18 Iberian cities most visited by tourists and businesspeople have been created with the assistance of researchers, contributors, professional journalists, and other experts on the spot. Although useful at the planning stage, THE CITIES is really designed to be taken along and used on the spot. Each report offers a short-stay guide within a consistent format: an essay introduces the city as a historic entity and a contemporary place to live and visit; *At-a-Glance* material is actually a site-by-site survey of the most important, interesting (and sometimes most eclectic) sights to see and things to do; *Sources and Resources* is a concise listing of pertinent tourism information, meant to answer a broad range of potentially pressing questions as they arise — from something simple like the address of the local tourist office, how to get around, which sightseeing tours to take, and when special events occur, to something more difficult like where to find the best nightspot, to see a show, to play golf, or to get a taxi; and *Best in Town* is our collection of cost-and-quality choices of the best places to eat and sleep on a variety of budgets.

DIVERSIONS

This section is designed to help travelers find the very best locations at which to pursue a wide range of athletic and cerebral activities, without having to wade through endless pages of unrelated text. This very selective guide lists the broadest possible range of activities, including all the best places to pursue them.

We start with a list of possibilities that offer various places to stay and eat, and move to those that require some perspiration — sports preferences and other rigorous pursuits — and go on to report on a number of more cerebral and spiritual vacation opportunities. In every case, our suggestion of a particular location — and often our recommendation of a specific resort — is intended to guide you to that special place where the quality of experience is likely to be highest. Whether you seek golf or tennis, Spain and Portugal's most stylish hotels or most esoteric museums, tours of spectacular resorts or epic shopping excursions, each entry is the equivalent of a comprehensive checklist of the absolute best in Spain and Portugal.

DIRECTIONS

Here are 21 itineraries that range all across Spain and Portugal, along the most beautiful routes and roads, past the most spectacular natural wonders, through the most historic cities and countrysides and the most idyllic islands. DIRECTIONS is the only section of the book that is organized geographically, and its itineraries cover the touring highlights of Spain and Portugal in short, independent journeys of 3 to 5 days' duration. Itineraries can be "connected" for longer trips or used individually for short, intensive explorations.

Each entry includes a guide to sightseeing highlights; a qualitative guide to accommodations and food along the road (small inns, castle hotels, country hotels); and suggestions for activities.

Although each of this book's sections has a distinct format and a special function, they have all been designed to be used together to provide a complete inventory of travel information. To use this book to full advantage, take a few minutes to read the table of contents and random entries in each section to give you an idea of how it all fits together.

Pick and choose needed information. Assume, for example, that you always have wanted to take that typically Spanish or Portuguese vacation, a walking tour through rural Iberia, but you never really knew how to organize it or where to go. Turn first to the hiking section of GETTING READY TO GO, as well as the chapters on planning a trip, accommodations, and climate and clothes. These short, informative entries provide plenty of practical information. But where to go? Turn next to DIRECTIONS. Routes and desirable detours are all clearly set forth. Your trip will likely begin or end either in Madrid or Lisbon, and for a complete rundown on these remarkable cities, you should read the Madrid or Lisbon chapter of THE CITIES. Finally, turn to DIVERSIONS to peruse the chapters on sports, hotels, antiques, and other activities in which you are especially interested, to make sure you don't miss anything along your chosen route.

In other words, the sections of this book are building blocks to help you put together the best possible trip. Use them selectively as tools, sources of ideas, a reference work for accurate facts, and a guide to the best buys, the most exciting sights and sites, the most pleasant accommodations, the tastiest food — *the best travel experiences* that you can have in Spain and Portugal.

PORTUGAL

GALICIA

Moncão
Valença
do Minho
Caminha
Viana do
Castelo
MINHO
Ponte de
Barca
Montalegre
Chaves
Bragança
Ponte
de Lima
Venda
Nova
TRAS-OS-MONTES
Macedo
de Cavaleiros
Barcelos
Braga
Mogadouro
Póvoa de
Varzim
Guimarães
Vila Real
Murça
Mirandela
Miranda
do Douro
Vila do Conde
Amarante
DOURO
Peso da
Régua
LEÓ
PORTO
Douro
Lamego
Douro
Douro
Ovar
UPPER
Murtosa
Vouga
Viseu
BEIRA
Aveiro
Mangualde
Gouveia
Guarda
Ciudad
Rodri
Tondela
Luso
Mondego
Seia
Buçaco
Oliveira
do Hospital
Belmonte
Covilhã
Coimbra
Figueira
da Foz
Lousã
LOWER
SERRA DA ESTRELA
Zêzere
BEIRA
A T L A N T I C
Marinha Grande
Leiria
Castelo Branco
Tagus (Taj
O C E A N
Batalha
Fátima
EXTREMADUR
Nazaré
Tomar
Abrantes
Castelo
de Vide
Cáce
São Martinho
do Porto
Alcobaça
Constância
Marvão
Peniche
Óbidos
Golegã
Caldas
da Rainha
Chamusca
Portalegre
Lourinhã
Santarém
Alpiarça
UPPER
SPAIN
Cartaxo
Almeirim
Torres
Vedras
Tagus
(Tejo)
Sorraia
Monforte
Mérida
Ericeira
A L E N T E J O
Mafra
Mora
Estremoz
Guadiana
Sintra
Montemor
o-Novo
Arraiolos
Elvas
Badajoz
Cascais
Estoril
LISBON
Palmela
Évora
Zafra
Sesimbra
Setúbal
L O W E R   A L E N T E J O
Moura
Santiago
de Cacém
Sado
Sines
Beja
Guadiana
Chança
ANDALUSIA
Odemira
Mira
Monchique
Serra de
Monchique
Castro
Marim
Ayamonte
Huelva
Portimão
Silves
A L G A R V E
Lagoa
Loulé
Tavira
Lagos
Albufeira
Faro
Vila Real
de Santo António
Sagres
GOLFO DE CÁDIZ

Miles
0   50
0   80
km

ESTREMADURA

BEIRA LITORAL

RIBATEJO

MADEIRA ISLANDS

Porto Santo
Vila Baleira
A T L A N T I C
Porto
Moniz
Madeira
O C E A N
São
Vicente
Santana
Pico
Ribeira
Ruivo
Machico
Brava
Santa Cruz
Câmara
Funchal
de Lobos
Ilhas
Desertas

0   Miles   30

CANARY IS.
(Spain)

LA PALMA
Los Llanos
Santa Cruz de la Palma
Fuencaliente

HIERRO
Valverde
Punta Restinga

LA GOMERA
Vallehermoso
Guía de Isora
San Sebastián de la Gomera

TENERIFE
Puerto de la Cruz
La Laguna
Orotava
Santa Cruz de Tenerife
Pta de Anaga

GRAN CANARIA
Las Palmas
Teide
Maspalomas

ATLANTIC OCEAN

FUERTEVENTURA
La Oliva
Puerto del Rosario
Gran Tarajal
Pta de Jandía

LANZAROTE
Tinajo
Teguise
Yaiza
Arrecife

AFRICA
SAHARA DESERT

0   25   Km   50   75
0   Miles   45

AZORES
(Portugal)

CORVO
Vila Nova do Corvo

FLORES
Santa Cruz das Flores
Fajãzinha
Lajes das Flores

FAIAL
Horta
Madalena

GRACIOSA
Santa Cruz da Graciosa
Praia

SÃO JORGE
Velas
Calheta

PICO
São Roque de Pico
Topo
Lajes do Pico

TERCEIRA
Angra do Heroísmo
Praia da Vitória

SÃO MIGUEL
Ribeira Grande
Ponta Delgada
Vila Franca do Campo
Povoação

SANTA MARIA
Vila do Porto

ATLANTIC OCEAN

Gap of c. 70 miles

0   25   Km   50   75
0   Miles   45

GETTING READY TO GO

When and How to Go

What's Where

 Spain and Portugal comprise what is most often referred to as the Iberian Peninsula, a 230,436-square-mile rectangle jutting out from Europe to the southwest. The rugged Pyrenees separate the peninsula from France and Andorra, its most immediate neighbors to the northeast, and the slender Strait of Gibraltar separates it from North Africa to the south. In the Mediterranean, to the east, are the Balearic Islands, which belong to Spain, and in the Atlantic, to the west, are the Canary Islands, which also are Spanish, and the Azores and Madeira, which are Portuguese.

In shape, Spain, the larger of the peninsula's two nations and the second-largest country in western Europe, resembles an armless torso. Of the 50 provinces in its 17 autonomous regions, many have their own distinct language and culture. In all, Spain covers some 194,883 square miles and has a population of 39 million people. Portugal, Spain's smaller neighbor — about one-fifth its size — tucks into the peninsula on the west. It covers some 35,553 square miles and has a population of about 10.2 million.

SPAIN

Running north to south, Spain comprises three main regions: the green and mountainous north, the dry, windswept *meseta,* or tableland, of the center, and the sultry, romantic south. Second only to Switzerland as Europe's most mountainous country, Spain — with an average altitude of about 2,000 feet above sea level — contains many of the continent's highest roads and villages. Mountains spring almost straight up from the coasts, leaving only narrow strips or estuaries along the shoreline. Much of the country is dry, and, since people cluster near water, wide empty spaces separate one inhabited area from another. The sharpest boundaries in Spain are those that set off dry land from damp.

The green and mountainous north stretches from the province of Galicia on Spain's western shoulder to the province of Catalonia on the east. The misty coastal region, with the North Atlantic on two sides, brings to mind Ireland, Wales, or the Scottish Highlands. It extends from the Basque mountain range — which abuts the foothills of the Pyrenees — west to the reaches above Portugal. In the Middle Ages, pilgrims from Europe crossed the Pyrenees over this shoulder of the Spanish torso to the holy city of Santiago de Compostela, a pilgrimage still made today. The heavily industrialized Basque region lies east of the coast and occupies part of the Cantabrian Mountains. The fiercely independent Basques, with their unique language and customs, are quite possibly the oldest surviving ethnic group in Europe, predating the ancient Iberian tribes of Spain. In the Basque region are the caves of Altamira, famous for their 13,000-year-old paintings. Nearby, in Navarre, is the town of Pamplona, famous for its yearly "running of the bulls." Farther east, Aragón is close to the tiny, snow-capped country of Andorra.

Catalonia, on Spain's eastern shoulder, borders the Mediterranean. Its coast, the

Costa Brava (wild coast), forms Spain's twisted, tortuous northeastern shoreline. Unquestionably the country's most rugged coast, as well as its shortest, the Costa Brava's jagged granite cliffs rise from the sea as though chewed out of the earth by some gigantic sea monster with serrated teeth. These cliffs shelter a plethora of bays, coves, inlets, beaches, and traditional whitewashed villages. Catalonia as a whole differs in character and history from the other regions of Spain. The Catalans, who have their own Provençal-like language and culture, are a progressive, vigorous, and businesslike breed whose efforts have made their region Spain's chief economic center and the most up-to-date and densely populated part of the peninsula. Barcelona, its cosmopolitan capital, is a major European commercial and industrial city.

The 2,000-foot-high *meseta,* its brown earth sometimes awash with golden wheat, dominates central Spain — to many people the real Spain. Here, in the geographic center of the country, is the *comunidad,* or province, of Madrid, surrounded by the expansive regions of New and Old Castile. It was on this austere, windswept plateau that the character of the traditional Spaniard was formed; here, under vast skies, the fictional Don Quixote, the Man of La Mancha, tilted at windmills. Its considerable altitude makes for a continental climate, with hot summers, cold winters, and a continual wind. The names of its cities evoke splendors — Madrid, the nation's capital; old-fashioned Toledo; Avila, city of soldiers and St. Teresa; Salamanca, with its university; the Roman aqueduct and fabulous castle of Segovia. On Spain's western edge is the province of Extremadura, which despite its wealth of wildflowers is a harsh land. Many have emigrated from here, beginning with Cortés and Pizarro, Balboa and de Soto. To the east is the Levante, the Mediterranean coast where the Phoenicians traded, and the city of Valencia, famous for its rice fields and its wonderful rice dish, paella. Surrounding the city is the most fertile land in Europe, a densely populated agricultural region where the aroma of orange trees is overwhelming. Murcia, a little farther south along the coast, is on the fringe of a desert.

There also are those who claim that the real Spain is Andalusia. The warm, romantic south of Spain has everything most people think of as Spanish: snow-capped mountains and massive coastal dunes; the flamenco, a flamboyant music and dance identified with the Gypsies of Granada and Seville; Spain's many famous matadors; the traditional whitewashed cottages, draped with orange blossoms, clinging precariously to rocky hillsides; and the stunning Moorish palace and garden complex, the Alhambra. Mountain ranges occupy large sections of the region. Much of the land is given over to the cultivation of olives, oranges, sunflowers, and grapes. The Costa del Sol, which extends along the Mediterranean coast on Andalusia's southeast, is Spain's answer to Acapulco and Rio de Janeiro. Formerly a dry, hilly land sprinkled with whitewashed cottages, the Costa del Sol has become one of Europe's most developed and most popular beach resort areas, a traditional retreat of the British from their damp, cold winters. The Costa del Sol extends from Almería, on the easternmost part of the southern Mediterranean coast, to Algeciras, 236 miles to the west. The 84 miles between Málaga, an important southern port, and Algeciras is the most developed (and crowded) resort area. Along this stretch, Swedish, German, French, Arabic, and English are more widely spoken than Spanish. Near Algeciras, at the very tip of Spain, is Gibraltar, which is not Spanish but British. From Algeciras, a ferry sails across the Straits to Ceuta, which is not Moroccan but Spanish.

CANARY ISLANDS: A cluster of seven major and six minor islands in the Atlantic Ocean, the Canary Islands lie about 65 miles off the northwest coast of Africa. The major islands are Gran Canaria, Tenerife, Fuerteventura, La Palma, Gomera, and Hierro. The charming villages of white cottages with red roofs sprinkled throughout the mountainous interior of these volcanic formations make the Canary Island archipelago inviting to travelers seeking unusual places of distinctive character.

BALEARIC ISLANDS: The Balearic Islands lie 90 miles southeast of Barcelona in the Mediterranean Sea. The major section of this archipelago consists of two pairs of islands: Majorca and Minorca, Formentera and Ibiza. Many smaller islands complete the archipelagic structure. The Balearic Mountains are thick with ancient fig and olive trees; the beaches are shaded by evergreens. The surrounding seas are exceptionally calm and clear despite the prevailing winds.

PORTUGAL

Portugal, to most people, means either Lisbon — the sophisticated capital, rich in monuments, museums, and churches — or the Algarve — the famed vacation area, with its congenial mixture of sea, beaches, luxurious hotels, and varied cuisine. However, beyond Lisbon's city limits and away from the southern shore lies a country of ancient towns, walled villages, and captivating scenery. Portugal's landscape encompasses a wide variety of contrasts — the lush green valley of the Minho River, the rugged mountains of the Trás-os-Montes region, the steep, hilly vineyards of the Alto Douro, and the Beira's flat coast. In the south, the pale gold wheat fields and olive and cork groves of the Alentejo give way to the cosmopolitan resorts of the Algarve, where beaches and imposing cliffs are washed by the warm waves of the Gulf Stream.

Portugal's Atlantic seaboard runs from the mouth of the Minho to the mouth of the Guadiana. The country's boundaries with Spain are marked less by rivers and mountains than by lack of people; for much of its length, the Spanish-Portuguese border is a wasteland. Portugal always has turned its back on its big brother, facing not toward Spain but west, toward the Atlantic. The destiny of Portugal — its history, economy, and climate — have been formed by the sea. Most people live along the coasts, and its greatest cities — Lisbon and Porto, both excellent ports — are located there. Two-thirds of the coast — from the north to just below Lisbon — is low and sandy. In the south, especially in the Algarve, there are sea marshes and sand banks, estuaries, beaches, and coves. Unlike Spain, much of Portugal is mild and moist. But the agricultural benefits of climate are mainly offset by poor soil.

Much of northern Portugal is mountainous. Minho, on the northwest, is, along with the area to the south around Porto, the original nucleus of the country, a land of rolling hills and soft, misty countryside. Trás-os-Montes, "behind the mountains," in the northeast, is isolated and sparsely settled. A little farther south, the Douro River slices through steep slopes whose neatly terraced vineyards produce port wine. The Beiras region is the heart of the country. Here the distinction between coast and interior is not so sharp. The area encompasses high pastures, charming forests and valleys, lagoons and beaches. High above the pretty valley of the Mondego River is the city of Coimbra, the seat of a famous university and the center of intellectual life.

The Tagus River bisects the country, dividing north from south. Its broad valley contains both small holdings and large estates, irrigated fields, extensive pastures, and half-wild herds of cattle. The Tagus, which begins in Spain, ends at last in an inland sea on the Atlantic coast. This is the site of Lisbon and its suburbs. The Alentejo, in southern Portugal, is a large area but sparsely settled, even on the coast. Inland is mainly flat, dry heath with a few oak groves, no shade, little water, and intense summer heat. A low range of mountains divides it from the southern coastal area, the Algarve. Here grow almonds, figs, oranges, olives, wheat, vegetables, and flowers. Fisheries dot the coast. The Algarve's warm eastern side is much like Spain's Andalusia, but its western coast is less sheltered from Atlantic storms. The wind continuously sweeps across Cape St. Vincent, the southwesternmost point on the Iberian Peninsula, close to where Prince Henry the Navigator watched his ships set off to circle the globe.

Portugal contains a number of architectural highlights: in the north, the extravagant mountaintop castle built by Fêrnando II between 1846 and 1850 in Sintra; the imposing marble monastery in Mafra, built in 1717 for King João V; the walled towns of Obidos;

and the ruins of Conimbriga, the most important Roman settlement on the Iberian Peninsula. Tomar, in central Portugal, offers the magnificent Convento de Cristo, a fortified castle and convent, and blends styles of architecture from the 12th through the 17th century. Other notable sites include Marvão, a medieval village; Elvas, where a 15th-century aqueduct still carries water to the town; Estremoz, whose artisans are famous for their pottery figurines of people and animals; and Evora, with its 2nd-century Roman temple.

AZORES AND MADEIRA: Two archipelagoes lie off the coast of Portugal, both consisting of the tips of volcanoes. Madeira lies some 560 miles southwest of Lisbon. Its main island, also called Madeira, has produced the wine called madeira for almost 400 years. With its semi-tropical climate, abundance of flowers, and beautiful scenery, the island easily earns its nickname, "Enchanted Island." Funchal, its main city, is a lively resort town. Farther out in the Atlantic are the Azores, according to legend the mountaintops of the lost colony of Atlantis. Warm and wet, with luxuriant vegetation, black beaches, and mountains shrouded in mist, these islands, well off the beaten track, warrant a visit by the more adventurous traveler.

When to Go

The decision about exactly when to travel may be imposed by the requirements of a rigid schedule; more likely there will be some choice, and the decision will be made on the basis of precisely what you want to see and do, the activities in which you'd like to participate, or events you'd like to attend, and what suits your mood.

There really isn't a "best" time to visit Spain or Portugal. For North Americans as well as Europeans, the period from mid-May to mid-September has long been — and remains — the peak travel period, traditionally the most popular vacation time. But it is important to emphasize that the Iberian Peninsula is hardly a single-season destination; more and more travelers who have a choice are enjoying the substantial advantages of off-season travel. Though many of the lesser tourist attractions may close during the off-season — roughly November to *Easter* — the major sites stay open and tend to be less crowded, as are the cities and the rest of these countries in general. During the off-season, Spanish and Portuguese life proceeds at its most natural pace, and a lively social and cultural calendar flourishes. What's more, travel generally is less expensive.

It also should be noted that the months immediately before and after the peak summer months — what the travel industry refers to as shoulder seasons — often are sought out because they offer reasonably good weather and smaller crowds. But be aware that near high-season prices still can prevail in many places during these periods, notably in certain popular resort areas such as Spain's Costa del Sol and Portugal's Algarve.

For some, the most convincing argument in favor of off-season travel is the economic one. Even during high season, Spain and Portugal are relatively inexpensive compared to other European destinations; during the off-season, getting there and staying there is even less expensive. Airfares drop and hotel rates go down in the late fall, winter, and early spring. Relatively inexpensive package tours become available, and the independent traveler can go farther on less, too.

The Iberian Peninsula is not like the Caribbean, where high and low season are precisely defined and rates drop automatically on a particular date. But many Spanish and Portuguese hotels reduce their rates during the off-season, and resort savings can be as much as 30% to 35%. Although some establishments in smaller towns may close

during the off-season in response to reduced demand, there still are plenty of alternatives, and cut-rate "mini-break" packages — discounts for stays of more than 1 night,
particularly over a weekend (when business travelers traditionally go home) —
are more common.

There are, however, some notable exceptions to this rule. In Spain, the general
tourism off-season is high season for skiers in the Pyrenees, the Picos de Europa, the
Sierra de Guadarrama, and the Sierra Nevada, meaning higher prices and crowds
everywhere there is snow. In Portugal, February brings *Carnaval* — hardly a time
when hoteliers need to drum up business. Particularly in the larger cities, other special
events and major trade show or conferences held at the time of your visit also are sure
to affect not only the availability of discounts on accommodations, but the basic
availability of a place to stay itself.

However, traveling in the dead of winter is not for everyone. While most of Spain
and Portugal does not suffer freezing temperatures, the rain, fog, and cold gray skies
in some regions are not always conducive to relaxed sightseeing. But Spain and Portugal have devotees who prefer to visit in each of the seasons, and it is clearly a matter
of personal choice.

In short, like many other popular places, Iberia's vacation appeal has become multi-
seasonal. But the noted exceptions notwithstanding, most travel destinations are decidedly less trafficked and less expensive during the winter.

CLIMATE: The travel plans of most North Americans visiting Spain and Portugal
traditionally are affected by the availability of vacation time and a desire to visit when
the weather is likely to be best — or most appropriate for a particular sport or activity.
The most common concerns about off-season travel have to do with questions of
temperature and rain. *(Please note that although temperatures in Spain and Portugal
are recorded on the Celsius scale, for purposes of clarity we use the more familiar
Fahrenheit scale.)*

Those planning on traveling during the high season should note that Spain's Costa
del Sol and Costa Blanca and Portugal's Algarve can be extremely hot throughout the
summer. During July and August, stores and shops in Madrid, Seville, and Córdoba
often close for the day in the early afternoon, when the heat becomes too intense. If
sightseeing is a priority, the months of May, June, and September may offer more
comfortable weather. In the coastal regions of both countries, mild weather is not
uncommon during February and November. Although winters on the Spanish *meseta*
can be piercingly cold and windy, in the summer the weather resembles that of the drier
parts of the southwestern US.

The basic distinction in climate on the Iberian Peninsula is the amount of rainfall,
which varies among the north, central, and southern regions. Contrary to a popular
"weather report," the rain in Spain, and Portugal, *does not* fall mainly on the plain.
Precipitation is not uncommon in any region, although the Portuguese climate generally is damper amd the more temperate of the two, due to the winds that blow off the
Atlantic. Farther east, however, it becomes drier, with almost no rain in summer, more
like the *meseta.* Although snow is common in the mountains of Spain (in some areas,
the skiing can be excellent), frosts are uncommon in Portugal and snow rarely falls.

The following chart lists average low and high temperatures in major Spanish and
Portuguese cities at different times of the year to help in planning.

Travelers also can get current readings and 3-day Accu-Weather forecasts through
American Express Travel Related Services' Worldwide Weather Report number. By
dialing 900-WEATHER and punching in either the area code for any city in the US
or an access code for any one of 225 major travel destinations around the world, an
up-to-date recording will provide current temperature, sky conditions, wind speed and
direction, heat index, relative humidity, local time, beach and boating reports or ski
conditions (where appropriate), and highway reports. For locations in Spain or Portu-

AVERAGE TEMPERATURES (in °F)

	January	April	July	October
Alicante, Spain	43–61	52–70	62–88	57–77
Barcelona, Spain	43–55	52–64	70–82	59–70
Burgos, Spain	30–43	39–50	54–74	45–61
Cádiz, Spain	48–59	55–68	68–81	54–72
Coimbra, Portugal	41–57	48–70	59–84	54–73
Córdoba, Spain	41–55	50–73	68–99	55–77
Evora, Portugal	43–54	50–66	61–88	56–72
Faro, Portugal	43–61	52–66	64–81	59–73
Lisbon, Portugal	46–57	54–68	63–81	57–72
Madeira Island, Portugal	57–64	59–68	64–75	64–75
Madrid, Spain	36–48	45–64	63–88	50–66
Málaga, Spain	46–63	55–77	70–84	61–73
Majorca, Balearic Islands	43–57	50–65	66–83	57–79
Pamplona, Spain	34–46	43–61	57–81	46–66
Porto, Portugal	41–55	48–64	59–77	52–70
Salamanca, Spain	32–46	39–63	57–86	45–66
Santarém, Portugal	41–58	49–69	61–87	54–75
Santiago de Compostela, Spain	41–50	46–64	55–75	52–70
Seville, Spain	43–59	52–75	68–97	57–79
Tenerife, Canary Islands	57–68	61–73	68–82	65–79
Toledo, Spain	36–50	46–66	66–91	50–70
Valencia, Spain	43–59	50–68	68–84	55–73
Zaragoza, Spain	36–50	46–66	64–88	52–68

gal, punch in the first three letters of the city. For instance, by entering BAR you will hear the weather report for Barcelona. For other locations in Spain, punch in GRA for Granada, MAD for Madrid, MAL for Málaga, ROT for Rota, SEV for Seville, or VAL for Valencia. For the weather in Portugal, punch in LIS for Lisbon or POR for Porto. This 24-hour service can be accessed from any Touch-Tone phone in the US and costs 75¢ per minute. The charge will show up on your phone bill. For a free list of the cities covered, send a self-addressed, stamped envelope to *1-900-WEATHER,* 261 Central Ave., Farmingdale, NY 11735.

SPECIAL EVENTS: Many travelers may want to schedule a trip to Spain or Portugal to coincide with some special event. For a music lover, a concert in a great cathedral or in a splendid natural setting may be an especially thrilling experience, and much more memorable than seeing the same place on an ordinary sightseeing itinerary. Golf enthusiasts may derive as much pleasure following Severiano Ballesteros and other international superstars from tee to green during a Spanish golf tournament as they would if they were actually playing on one of the country's championship courses. A folklore or harvest festival can bring nearly forgotten traditions alive or underscore their continuing significance in modern life.

Spain and Portugal have literally hundreds of fiestas or festivals each year, particularly from *Easter* through October. City and town squares are festooned with brightly colored arches and lanterns, houses are adorned with flags, and people of all ages dress in folk costumes handed down for generations to take part in parades, folk dances, singing, and fantastic fireworks displays. No one is a stranger and everyone is drawn into the merriment. Spanish fiestas include *gigantes y cabezudos* (giants and bigheads), pasteboard figures symbolizing rulers (giants) and the conquered (bigheads); the flower-strewn *Corpus Christi* processions held on the second Thursday after *Whitsunday* (also known as *Trinity Sunday*); *ferias,* traditional fairs honoring past gatherings of Gypsies and dealers who traded horses, donkeys, and mules; and *romerías* (pilgrimages), religious processions usually honoring a city's or town's patron saint.

The events that follow are the major ones, listed according to the months in which they usually occur. Where possible, we have indicated the exact dates for the festivities this year. However, for those events for which specific dates were not yet available as we went to press, and to guard against inevitable scheduling changes, it is best to check with the National Tourist Office of Spain or the Portuguese National Tourist Office for the exact dates of anything that may be of interest and for current schedules of festivals, fairs, and other events. Also keep in mind that some events, particularly festivals, may vary by a few days to several weeks from town to town and region to region; again, it's best to check with the tourist authorities for the most up-to-date information (see *Tourist Information Offices,* in this section, for addresses).

SPAIN

January

Epiphany: The day Spanish children traditionally receive their *Christmas* gifts. January 6.

Día de los Reyes: The Procession of the Three Kings. January 7.

La Puebla: Parades, bonfires, dancing, and the blessing of the herd in honor of St. Anthony. Majorca, Madrid, and Burgos. January 17.

Tamborrada de San Sebastián: One of Spain's great undiscovered festivals, highlighted by colorful parades, including the marches of the Basque pipe and drum corps in honor of the city's patron saint. January 20 is *St. Sebastián's Day,* and for 24 hours, beginning at midnight on the 19th, the Old Town is filled with young and old dressed as 19th-century soldiers, bakers, and chefs, all banging *tambores* (drums) in a surprisingly orderly fashion. San Sebastián.

February

Bocairente Festival of Moors and Christians: One week of parades, costumes, fireworks, and reenactments of the epic struggles between Moors and Christians, some of which are the most colorful, exuberant fiestas to be found anywhere in the world — the first of many similar celebrations held throughout the year. Lasting several days (the exact dates vary from town to town), these fiestas usually feature the "Moors" capturing a "Christian" stronghold, only to be ousted amid a deafening fusillade of "gunfire."

Fiestas de Santa Agueda: Ancient "women's liberation" festival. Women parade through the streets in traditional costumes, culminating in "wheel dancing" and the burning of male effigies. February 5. Zamarramala.

Carnavales de Cádiz: Spain's oldest and most popular carnival; the singing, wild music and dancing, and other madness goes on day and night. A fireworks display signals the end of the celebrations, and the next morning all that remains — besides a citywide hangover — are several tons of confetti and empty wine bottles. Held the week before *Lent:* February 8–12, this year. Cádiz.

La Endiablada: A pre-Christian religious celebration featuring dancing and parades of "devils" dressed in floral outfits carrying huge metal bells. Almonacio del Marquesado.

March

Barcelona to Sitges Antique Car Rally: A 13-mile "race" held in early March that features an international assembly of colorful antique automobiles. De Dion–Boutons and Daimlers, Panhards and Bugattis, Fords, Hispanos, and Rolls-

Royces compete as ladies and gentlemen, dressed in the style of the respective eras, "put-put" their way from Barcelona to Sitges.

Fallas de San José: One of Spain's great festivals, featuring a week of flower-bedecked processions, fireworks, bullfights, and all-out partying. Beginning on March 12, it ends at midnight on *St. Joseph's Day* (March 19), when a fantastic array of huge papier-mâché and wooden caricatures are set afire. The fiesta dates from the Middle Ages, when on the day of its patron saint the carpenters' guild burned the wood shavings accumulated during the year. Today, no one is immune to the papier-mâché lampooning — politicians, the church, the rich, and the poor all are fair game. Valencia.

April

Semana Santa: Nationwide *Holy Week* celebrations. Seville features more than 100 parades and the singing of *saetas* (strange laments); Cuenca offers a week-long festival of religious music and candlelight processions; and Chinchón stages a reenactment of the Passion of Christ in the Plaza Mayor. Bridges the months of March and April (March 30 through about April 6).

Feria de Sevilla: This week-long fair began in the 19th century as a rural livestock market, but it has gussied itself up considerably since then: Andalusia's high-stepping horses, in tassels and bells, go through their paces, and brightly costumed groups parade around town in flower-decked coaches. Through mid-April there are nightly *corridas* (bullfights), fireworks, amusements, and dancing in the streets. Seville.

St. Jordi's Day: On April 23, flower stands overflow with roses and bookstalls on Las Ramblas are bustling; this is the day for lovers, and the traditional gifts are a rose and a book, associated with St. Jordi, patron saint of Catalonia. Barcelona.

May

Fiesta de los Patios: This famous festival fills the city with visitors during the first 2 weeks of May, when everyone goes from one private patio to another admiring walls literally covered with gorgeously planted flowerpots; at the same time, public plazas are decked with flowers and flowered crosses. Prizes are awarded for the best displays. Córdoba.

Fiestas de San Isidro: Ten days (starting on May 10) of nonstop street fairs, festivals, concerts, special daily bullfights, and numerous theater, cultural, and sports events, all celebrating the *Day of St. Isidro,* Madrid's patron saint, on May 15. The fiesta also helps usher in Madrid's bullfighting season and features some of Spain's best bullring exhibitions. Madrid.

Salamanca Celebration of Assumption: Parade featuring traditional costumes followed by an assembly in Plaza Mayor and the performance of the mystery play *Loa* in front of the town church. May 24. La Alberca.

Feria de Nuestra Señora de la Salud: Feria for short, this annual fair follows the *Fiesta de los Patios* during the last week of May and is especially festive because of its location in the heart of town. *Casetas,* or the little private tents for entertaining, and the midway Ferris wheel, merry-go-round, and snack stands run the length of the Jardines de la Victoria. Flamenco contests, pop and classical concerts, ballets, parades, fireworks, and displays of Cordoban horsemanship also fill the streets with action. Córdoba.

Romería del Rocío: Whitsunday pilgrimage (Andalusia's most famous) to the shrine of El Rocío features decorated carts and wagons, singing, and the sounds of drums, flutes, and tambourines. On Monday, 50 men carry the Virgin's statue 9 miles to Almonte for consecration. El Rocío and Almonte. May 19–20.

Corpus Christi: Since 1950, beautiful woven carpets of carnations line the streets in Sitges during this annual celebration. The *National Carnation Show* is held on the same day, with over 2,000 pots containing nearly 300 varieties from various countries. Awards also are given to the most artistically decorated street. Also celebrated elsewhere throughout Spain with traditional processions, mystery plays, bullfights, and other festivities. May 30.

June

Festival of the Virgen del Carmen: Celebration honoring the patroness of sailors and fishermen. Murcia and Málaga. June 16.

Festival International de Música y Danza: Three weeks of first-rate performances featuring classical music, jazz, and ballet by international stars in the *Auditorio Manuel de Falla* and the gardens of the magnificent Alhambra. Granada.

Hogueras de San Juan: Nine-day festival featuring bonfires, the burning of effigies, parades, religious services, and fireworks. Alicante.

July

Festival of Spanish Classic Drama: Dramatic performances staged in a historic theater throughout the month. Almagro.

Festival of Medieval Theater: Excellent medieval plays, food, dancing, and bullfights during the first 2 weeks of July. Hita.

Fiesta de San Fermín: Spain's most popular celebration (made famous by Ernest Hemingway in *The Sun Also Rises*), in which over 100,000 natives and foreigners take part in wild parades and celebrations, wine tasting, bullfights, fireworks, and the much-acclaimed *encierros,* or "running of the bulls," through the town's streets. Pamplona.

San Benitiño de Lérez Festival: Regional celebration featuring Galician music and singing. Pontevedra.

Festival of St. James: Two-week celebration highlighted by the pilgrimage to the tomb of St. James the Apostle, Galecian folkloric shows and competitions, parades, concerts, fireworks, and the swinging of the *botafumerio,* the giant incense burner, in the great cathedral. Santiago de Compostela.

San Sebastián International Jazz Festival: A gathering of top international jazz musicians, held during the last 2 weeks in July in the pavilion at the *Anoeta Sports Complex* and the open-air Plaza de Trinidad in the Old Town. San Sebastián.

August

International Music and Dance Festival: Month-long annual event featuring symphony and choral concerts, chamber music, recitals, and classical and Spanish ballet. Santander.

Festival of the White Virgin: Seven days of parades, music, dances, and fireworks, highlighted by the *Dawn Rosary Procession* on the morning of August 5. Vitoria.

Asturias Day: This pilgrimage is colorfully highlighted by a parade of decorated floats accompanied by lively folk music. Gijón.

Semana Grande: The week-long celebration includes sporting and cultural events, fireworks, regattas, outstanding bullfights, and the running of "cardboard bulls." San Sebastián.

September

Grape Harvest Fairs and Festivals: These festivals are well noted for great merriment and massive consumption, not necessarily in that order. Usually held in mid-September (sometimes later, depending on the harvest) in the following towns and regions: Jumilla (in Murcia), Montilla (in Córdoba), and Requena (in Valencia).

Cádiz Grape Harvest Festival: Spain's top wine festival, dedicated to a country that exports the world-famous sherry of Jerez, featuring 5 days of parades, a livestock show, a flamenco festival, bullfights, and sherry drinking. Mid-September. Jerez de la Frontera.

San Sebastián International Film Festival: Week-long screenings of international films, during the second half of September, and one of the premier events of its type in Europe. San Sebastián.

Fiesta Nuestra Señora de la Merced: Festival honoring Barcelona's patroness, complete with parades and floats, cavalry bands, *sardana* dancing, swimming races across the Port of Barcelona, men building human pyramids and towers, theater, film, concerts, and bullfights. Barcelona.

October

Fiestas del Pilar: Decorated float parades, sporting events, and dance contests honoring the Virgin of the Pillar. October 12. Zaragoza.

St. Teresa Week: Evening carnivals (*verbenas*), parades of "giants," dancing, singing, and other appropriate merriment. Avila.

The Saffron Rose Festival: Celebrates local folklore and the gathering of the "saffron rose," from which comes the famous spice used in dishes such as paella. Consuegra, Toledo.

December

Alava Nativity Parade: Christmas Eve midnight mass and a bonfire. Labastida.

New Year's Eve: Crowds gather at the Puerta del Sol and eat a grape on the stroke of midnight to ensure a new year of good luck. Madrid.

PORTUGAL

February

Carnaval: Pre-*Lenten* festivities celebrated throughout Portugal. Typically held for 4 days, ending at midnight on *Shrove Tuesday.* February 9–13, this year.

April

Festa da Flor (Flower Festival): This annual 3-day festival at the end of April celebrates Madeira's botanic abundance with flower-decked floats and a parade of over 2,000 children carrying blossoms pieced together as a floral Wall of Hope. The festivities have a heavy folk flavor, with plenty of Madeiran music, singing, and dancing. Funchal, Madeira.

May

Festival of the Crosses: Celebrates the Miracle of the Crosses in early May, attracting thousands of visitors who take part in Minho folk dancing, a pottery fair, fun fair, eating, drinking, and fireworks. May 3–5. Barcelos.

Fatima Pigrimage: Thousands of pilgrims from all parts of the world converge on Fatima to honor the the appearance of Our Lady of Fatima in 1917. Religious ceremonies, processions, and masses are held on May 12-13 (and again on October 12–13). Fatima.

Festival of the Roses: A splendid display of roses on parade and one of Portugal's most popular folkloric celebrations. May 12–14. Vila Franca do Lima.

June

Grand International Fair of Santarém: Beginning the first Friday in June, 10 days of horsemanship and bullfighting heroics, handicraft and livestock exhibitions, folk dancing, singing, and fireworks. June 8–16. Santarém.

Festa do São António: Celebration honoring the birthday of St. Anthony, the patron saint of young lovers. Lisbon's Old Quarter comes alive on the eve:

Dances are held in streets festooned with colored lanterns, and throughout the night gallons of good, rough wine are drunk to wash down mountains of sardines roasted on open barbecues. The saint is a powerful matchmaker, so this is the night when the city's young girls hope to meet their future husbands. June 12–13. Lisbon.

Festas de São João: A Christian holiday with roots in pagan rites celebrating the summer solstice. Parties go on until all hours of the night, the *vinho verde* flows freely, and the aroma of festive food, including roast goat, invades the popular neighborhoods. Festivities include parades, fireworks, folk music, medieval dancing, and ancient customs, such as passing around leeks and throwing scented herbs and thistles into large bonfires to make divinations. June 23–24. Braga and Porto.

Festival de São Pedro: Nationwide celebrations honoring St. Peter, the patron saint of fishermen, includes a blessing of the ships; a display of regional products, handicrafts, and the famous *queijadas de Sintra,* delicious sweet cheese tarts, in Sintra and Lisbon; solemn processions and "Sword Dancing" in Ribeira Brava (Madeira); running of the bulls through the streets of Montijo, outside Lisbon; and *Cavalhadas de São Pedro* — a parade of masked riders, dating from the 15th century — through the streets of Ribeira Grande (San Miguel, Azores). June 28–29.

July

Festival of the Colete Encarnado: Open-air festivities the first week in July, featuring the parade of the *campinos* (Portuguese cowboys), running of the bulls, bullfights, fireworks, and folkloric exhibitions. July 5–7. Vila Franca de Xira.

Festa da Rainha Santa: This festival, held at the beginning of July in even-numbered years, commemorates the beatification of the saintly Queen Isabel in 1516. On a Thursday night, the statue of the saint from the altar of Santa Clara-a-Nova is carried to Largo da Portagem by a procession of penitents; all lights in the city are turned off when it arrives, the better to see the spectacular fireworks display over the river. Another procession returns the statue to the church on Sunday afternoon. Evora.

August

Festas Gualteriānas: A huge folk fair featuring regional foods and wines, religious parades, music, and costumed singers and dancers satirizing the Middle Ages. August 3–5. Guimarães.

Festas de Senhora da Agonia (Festival of Our Lady of Suffering): In mid-August, 3 days of colorful festivities attract pilgrims from the most varied parts of the country to take part in the grand procession. Other activities include fairs, music, dancing, and fireworks. August 17–20. Viano do Castel.

Festa do São Bartolomeu: This festival, held on the third Sunday in August, has evolved into a *cortejo de papal,* or "paper parade," in which people dress in paper costumes to satirize public personages and politicians. They follow a float carrying Neptune and Sirens to the beach, where they battle "pirates" from the sea; the battle ends with all the participants and some of the onlookers rushing into the water for a holy bath, a practice no doubt related to the old superstition that a dip in the sea can cast out the devil. Porto.

September

Festival of Our Lady of Boa Viagem (Good Voyage): Five days in mid-September of street fairs, amusements, running of the bulls, and other festivities. Moitas.

Feiras Novas (New Fairs): This popular celebration, dating from the 12th century, now includes a procession to Our Lady of Sorrows. Ponte de Lima.

October

> *Fatima Pigrimage:* Pilgrimages (also held earlier, in May) to honor the appearance of Our Lady of Fatima in 1917. Religious ceremonies, processions, and masses on October 12 and 13. Fatima.

November

> *Feira Nacional do Cavalo (Feira de São Martinho):* One of Europe's largest horse fairs, featuring daring exhibitions by Portuguese cowboys, parades, and various equestrian events, fireworks, and folk dancing. The horse show coincides with the *Feast of St. Martin,* which includes eating roasted chestnuts and drinking local wine. November 3–11. Golegã.

December

> *Festa do São Silvestre:* Wild *New Year's Eve* celebration featuring singing, dancing, and a harborfront fireworks display. Funchal, Madeira.

Traveling by Plane

 Flying is the most efficient way to get to Spain or Portugal, and it is the quickest, most convenient means of travel between different parts of these countries once you are there. (Cruise ships that call at Spanish and/or Portuguese ports generally function more as hotels for passengers cruising European waters, rather than as especially efficient transportation between individual destinations.)

The air space between North America and Europe is the most heavily trafficked in the world. It is served by dozens of airlines, almost all of which sell seats at a variety of prices under widely different terms. Since you probably will spend more for your airfare than for any other single item in your travel budget, try to take advantage of the low fares offered by either scheduled airlines or charter companies. You should know what kinds of flights are available, the rules and regulations pertaining to air travel, and all the special package options.

GATEWAYS: At present, nonstop flights to Spain and Portugal leave from Boston, Chicago, Dallas/Ft. Worth, Los Angeles, Miami, and New York. Additional connecting flights depart from some of the above cities and a few others as well. Nonstop or direct, nearly all of these flights land in major Spanish and Portuguese destinations.

SCHEDULED AIRLINES: *Iberia Airlines of Spain* operates nonstop flights to Madrid from Chicago, Los Angeles, Miami, and New York, as well as flights to Málaga and Barcelona from New York. Both *TWA* and *Pan American* fly nonstop from New York to Madrid; *TWA* also flies nonstop from New York to Barcelona. *American* flies nonstop from Dallas/Ft. Worth to Madrid.

TAP Air, the Portuguese national airline, and *TWA* both operate nonstop flights from New York to Lisbon. *TAP Air* flies from Boston nonstop to Porta Delgado in the Azores; the flight, which operates about once a week, depending on the season, continues on to Lisbon. *TAP Air* also flies once a week from Los Angeles to Terceira (in the Azores) and Lisbon, and at least twice a week from Newark to Lisbon.

In addition, *British Airways* offers connecting flights from the US through London's Heathrow Airport to Barcelona, Bilboa, Madrid, and Málaga in Spain, and Faro, Lisbon, and Porto in Portugal, among other Iberian destinations. *Air France* also offers connections through Paris, where, after changing planes, travelers may proceed to Lisbon, Madrid, Porto, and other Spanish and Portuguese cities. *KLM* offers connecting flights from Atlanta, Anchorage, Baltimore, Chicago, Houston, Los Angeles, New

York, and Orlando, via Amsterdam to Barcelona, Madrid, Málaga, Palma de Mallorca, and Valencia in Spain, and Lisbon and Porto in Portugal. *Sabena* flies from a variety of US gateways, with connections made in Brussels for flights to Barcelona, Madrid, Málaga, and Palma de Mallorca in Spain, and Lisbon in Portugal.

Tickets – When traveling on one of the many regularly scheduled flights, a full-fare ticket provides maximum travel flexibility (although at considerable expense) because there are no advance booking requirements: A prospective passenger can buy a ticket for a flight right up to the minute of takeoff — if a seat is available. If your ticket is for a round trip, you can make the return reservation any time you wish — months before you leave or the day before you return. Assuming the foreign immigration requirements are met, you can stay at your destination for as long as you like. (Tickets generally are good for a year, but can be renewed if not used.) You also can cancel your flight at any time without penalty. However, while it is true that this category of ticket can be purchased at the last minute, it is advisable to reserve well in advance during popular vacation periods and around holiday times.

No matter what kind of ticket you buy, it is wise to reconfirm that you will be using your return reservations. For instance, if you do not call the airline to tell them you will be using the return leg of your reservation, they (or their computer) may assume you are not coming and automatically cancel your seat. For further information, see "Reservations," below.

Fares – Airfares continue to change so rapidly that even experts find it difficult to keep up with them. This ever-changing situation is due to a number of factors, including airline deregulation, volatile labor relations, increasing fuel costs (due to such factors as unrest in the Middle East), and vastly increased competition. Before the Airline Deregulation Act of 1978, US airlines had no choice but to set their rates and routes within the guidelines of the Civil Aeronautics Board (CAB), and they could compete for passengers only by offering better service than their competitors. With the loosening of controls (and the elimination of the CAB), airlines now are engaged in a far more intense competition relating to price and schedule, which has opened the door to a wide range of discount fares and promotional offers. Intensifying the competitive atmosphere has been the creation of several new carriers offering fewer frills and far lower prices. These carriers seem to appear and disappear with dismaying regularity. They have, however, served to drive down fares from time to time and make the older, more entrenched carriers aware that they are in a genuine competition for travelers' dollars. As Europe, too, moves closer to the deregulation of airline fares, the price of intra-European travel is expected to decrease somewhat as well.

Perhaps the most common misconception about fares on scheduled airlines is that the cost of the ticket determines how much service will be provided on the flight. This is true only to a certain extent. A far more realistic rule of thumb is that the less you pay for your ticket, the more restrictions and qualifications are likely to come into play before you board the plane (as well as after you get off). These qualifying aspects relate to the months during which you must travel (and the days of the week), how far in advance you must purchase your ticket, the minimum and maximum amount of time you may or must remain abroad, your willingness to decide on a return date at the time of booking — and your ability to stick to that decision. It is not uncommon for passengers sitting side by side on the same wide-body jet to have paid fares varying by hundreds of dollars, and all too often the traveler paying more would have been equally willing to accept the terms of the far less expensive ticket. The ticket you buy will fall into one of several fare categories currently being offered by scheduled carriers flying between the US and Spain and Portugal.

In general, the great variety of fares between the US and Spain and Portugal can be reduced to four basic categories, including first class, coach (also called economy or tourist class), and excursion or discount fares. The fourth category, called business class (an intermediate between first class and coach, with many of the amenities of first class and more legroom than coach), has been added by many airlines in recent years. In addition, Advance Purchase Excursion (APEX) and "Eurosaver" fares offer savings under certain specific conditions.

In a class by itself is the *Concorde,* the supersonic jet developed jointly by France and Great Britain, which cruises at speeds of 1,350 miles an hour (twice the speed of sound) and makes transatlantic crossings in half the time (3½ hours from New York to Paris) of conventional, subsonic jets. *Air France* offers *Concorde* service to Paris from New York; *British Airways* flies from Miami, Washington, DC, and New York to London. Additionally, *British Airways* has an arrangement with *Enterprise Airlines* for connecting flights between Boston and New York for *Concorde* service. Service is "single" class (with champagne and caviar all the way), and the fare is expensive, about 20% more than a first class ticket on a subsonic aircraft. Some discounts have been offered, but time is the real gift of the *Concorde.* For travelers to Spanish or Portuguese destinations, this "gift" may be more or less valuable as compared to a direct flight when taking connections from London or Paris into account.

A first class ticket is your admission to the special section of the aircraft — larger seats, more legroom, sleeperette seating on some wide-body aircraft, better (or more elaborately served) food, free drinks and headsets for movies and music channels, and above all, personal attention. First class fares are about twice those of full-fare economy, although both first class passengers and people paying economy fares are entitled to reserve seats and are sold tickets on an open reservation system. An additional advantage of a first class ticket is that if you're planning to visit several cities within Spain or Portugal or elsewhere in Europe, you may include any number of stops en route to your most distant destination, provided that certain set, but generous, maximum permitted mileage limits are respected.

Not too long ago, there were only two classes of air travel, first class and all the rest, usually called economy or tourist. But because passengers paying full economy fares traveled in the same compartment as passengers flying for considerably less on various promotional or discount fares, the airlines introduced special services to compensate those paying the full price. Thus, business class came into being — one of the most successful recent airline innovations. At first, business class passengers merely were curtained off from the other economy passengers. Now a separate cabin or cabins — usually toward the front of the plane — is the norm. While standards of comfort and service are not as high as in first class, they represent a considerable improvement over conditions in the rear of the plane, with roomier seats, more leg and shoulder space between passengers, and fewer seats abreast. Free liquor and headsets, a choice of meal entrées, and a separate counter for speedier check-in are other inducements. As in first class, a business class passenger may travel on any scheduled flight he or she wishes, may buy a one-way or round-trip ticket, and have the ticket remain valid for a year. There are no minimum or maximum stay requirements, no advance booking requirements, and no cancellation penalties, and the fare allows the same free stopover privileges as first class. Airlines often have their own names for their business class service — such as Preference Class on *Iberia,* Navigator Class on *TAP Air,* Clipper Class on *Pan American,* and Ambassador Class on *TWA.*

The terms of the coach or economy fare may vary slightly from airline to airline, and, in fact, from time to time airlines may be selling more than one type of economy fare. Economy fares sell for substantially less than business fares, the savings effected by limiting frills and stopovers. Coach or economy passengers sit more snugly, as many as 10 in a single row on a wide-body jet, behind the first class and business class sections, and receive standard meal service. Alcoholic drinks are not free, nor are the headsets (except on *British Airways,* which does offer these free of charge). If there are two economy fares on the books, one (often called "regular economy") still may include free stopovers. The other, less expensive fare (often called "special economy") may limit stopovers to one or two, with a charge (typically $25) for each one. Like first class passengers, however, passengers paying the full coach fare are subject to none of the restrictions that usually are attached to less expensive discount fares. There are no advance booking requirements, no minimum stay requirements, and no cancellation penalties. Tickets are sold on an open reservation system: They can be bought for a flight up to the minute of takeoff (if seats are available), and if the ticket is round-trip, the return reservation can be made any time you wish — months before you leave or the day before you return. Both first class and coach tickets generally are good for a year, after which they can be renewed if not used, and if you ultimately decide not to fly at all, your money will be refunded. The cost of economy and business class tickets does not vary much in the course of the year between the US and Spain and Portugal, though on some transatlantic routes they vary from a basic (low-season) price in effect most of the year to a peak (high-season) price during the summer.

Excursions and other discount fares are the airlines' equivalent of a special sale and usually apply to round-trip bookings. These fares generally differ according to the season and the number of travel days permitted. They are only a bit less flexible than full-fare economy tickets and are, therefore, useful for both business travelers and tourists. Most round-trip excursion tickets include strict minimum and maximum stay requirements and reservations can be changed only within the prescribed time limits. So don't count on extending a ticket beyond the prescribed time of return or staying less time than required. Different airlines may have different regulations concerning the number of stopovers permitted, and sometimes excursion fares are less expensive during midweek. Needless to say, these reduced-rate seats are most limited at busy times, such as holidays, when full-fare coach seats sell more quickly than usual. Passengers fortunate enough to get a discount or excursion fare ticket sit with the coach passengers, and, for all intents and purposes, are indistinguishable from them. They receive all the same basic services, even though they have paid anywhere between 30% and 55% less for the trip. Obviously, it's wise to make plans early enough to qualify for this less expensive transportation.

These discount or excursion fares may masquerade under a variety of names, they may vary from city to city (from the East Coast to the West Coast, especially), but they invariably have strings attached. A common requirement is that the ticket be purchased a certain number of days — usually no fewer than 7 or 14 days — in advance of departure, though it may be booked weeks or months in advance (it has to be "ticketed," or paid for, shortly after booking, however). The return reservation usually has to be made at the time of the original ticketing and cannot be changed later than a certain number of days (again, usually 7 or 14 days) before the return flight. If events force a passenger to change the return reservation after the date allowed, the difference between the round-trip excursion rate and the round-trip coach rate probably will have to be paid, though most airlines allow passengers to use their discounted fares by standing by for an empty seat, even if they don't otherwise have standby fares. Another common condition is a minimum and maximum stay requirement; for example, 6 to 14 days or 1 to 6 days, but including at least a Saturday night. Last, cancellation penalties of up to 50% of the full price of the ticket have been assessed — check the specific penalty in effect when you purchase your discount/excursion ticket — so careful planning is imperative.

Of even greater risk — and bearing the lowest price of all the current discount fares — is the ticket where no change at all in departure and/or return flights is permitted, and where the ticket price is totally nonrefundable. If you do buy a nonrefundable ticket, you should be aware of a new policy followed by many airlines, regarding international flights, that may make it easier to change your plans if necessary. For a fee — set by each airline and payable at the airport when checking in — you *may* be able to change the time or date of a return flight on a nonrefundable ticket. However, if the nonrefundable ticket price for the replacement flight is higher than that of the original (as generally is the case when trading in a weekday for a weekend flight), you will have to pay the difference. Any such change must be made a certain number of days in advance — in some cases as little as 2 days — of either the original or the replacement flight, whichever is earlier; restrictions are set by the individual carrier.

In the past, some excursion fares offered for travel to Spain and Portugal came unencumbered by advance booking requirements and cancellation penalties, permitted one stopover (though not a free one) in each direction, and had "open jaws," meaning that you could fly to one city and depart from another, arranging and paying for your own transportation between the two. Although, for the most part, such excursion fares are no longer offered on flights between the US and the majority of European destinations, they still exist on flights between the US and Spain and Portugal, where they cost about a third less than economy — during the off-season. High-season prices may be less attractive. The ticket currently is good for a minimum of 7 days and a maximum of 6 months abroad.

There also is a newer and less expensive type of excursion fare, the APEX, or Advanced Purchase Excursion. As with traditional excursion fares, passengers paying an APEX fare sit with and receive the same basic services as any other coach or economy passengers, even though they may have paid up to 50% less for their seats. In return, they are subject to certain restrictions. In the case of flights to Spain and Portugal, the ticket usually is good for a minimum of 7 days abroad and a maximum, currently, of 2 months (depending on the airline and the destination); and as its name implies, it must be "ticketed," or paid for in its entirety, a certain period of time before departure — usually 21 days, although in the case of Spain and Portugal it may be as little as 14 days.

The drawback to an APEX fare is that it penalizes travelers who change their minds — and travel plans. The return reservation must be made at the time of the original ticketing, and if for some reason you change your schedule while abroad, you pay a penalty of $100 or 10% of the ticket value, whichever is greater, as long as you travel within the validity period of your ticket. But, if you change your return to a date less than the minimum stay or more than the maximum stay, the difference between the round-trip APEX fare and the full round-trip coach rate will have to be paid. There also is a penalty of anywhere from $75 to $125 or more for canceling or changing a reservation *before* travel begins — check the specific penalty in effect when you purchase your ticket. No stopovers are allowed on an APEX ticket, but it is possible to create an open-jaw effect by buying an APEX on a split ticket basis; for example, flying to Lisbon and returning from Madrid. The total price would be half the price of an APEX to Lisbon plus half the price of an APEX to Madrid. APEX tickets to Spain and Portugal are sold at basic and peak rates (peak season is around May through September) and may include surcharges for weekend flights.

There also is a Winter or Super APEX, which may go under different names for different carriers. Similar to the regular APEX fare, it costs slightly less but is more restrictive. Depending on the airline and destination, it usually is available only for off-peak winter travel and is limited to a stay of between 7 and 21 days. Advance purchase still is required (currently, 30 days prior to travel), and ticketing must be completed within 48 hours of reservation. The fare is nonrefundable, except in cases of hospitalization or death.

Note that Winter or Super APEX sometimes is confusingly called Super PEX by *Iberia*. At the time of this writing, *Iberia* offered Super APEX (or Super PEX) on transatlantic flights to most destinations in Spain during the off-season; this fare also may be available to some destinations during the high season. *TAP Air* also offers Super APEX fares on transatlantic flights to destinations throughout Portugal, but only during the off-season. *TAP Air* also offers a PEX fare, which unlike their Super APEX and APEX fares is offered only on intra-European flights to cities outside Portugal.

Another type of fare that sometimes is available is the youth fare. At present, most airlines flying to Spain and Portugal are using a form of APEX fare as a youth fare for those through age 24. The maximum stay is extended to a year, and the return booking must be left open. Seats can be reserved no more than 3 days before departure, and tickets must be purchased when the reservation is made. The return is booked from Spain or Portugal in the same manner, no more than 3 days before flight time. On most airlines (including *Iberia* and *TAP Air*), there is no cancellation penalty, but the fare is subject to availability, so it may be difficult to book a return during peak travel periods, and as with the regular APEX fare, it may not even be available for travel to or from Spain and Portugal during high season and may be offered only on selected routes. For instance, *TAP Air* stresses that this fare is offered on a space-available basis, and *Iberia* offers this type of fare only on flights from the US to Madrid or Barcelona.

Standby fares, at one time the rock-bottom price at which a traveler could fly to Europe, have become elusive. At the time of this writing, most major scheduled airlines did not regularly offer standby fares on direct flights to Spain or Portugal, although *Pan American* occasionally offers standby, depending on availability. Because airline fares and their conditions constantly change, however, bargain hunters should not hesitate to ask if such a fare exists at the time they plan to travel. Travelers to the Iberian Peninsula also should inquire about the possibility of connecting flights through other European countries that may be offered on a standby basis.

While the definition of standby varies somewhat from airline to airline, it generally means that you make yourself available to buy a ticket for a flight (usually no sooner than the day of departure), then literally stand by on the chance that a seat will be empty. Once aboard, however, a standby passenger has the same meal service and frills (or lack of them) enjoyed by others in the economy class compartment.

Something else to check is the possibility of qualifying for a GIT (group inclusive travel) fare, which requires that a specified dollar amount of ground arrangements be purchased, in advance, along with the ticket. The requirements vary as to the number of travel days and stopovers permitted, and the number of passengers required for a group. The actual fares also vary, but the cost will be spelled out in brochures distributed by the tour operators handling the ground arrangements. In the past, GIT fares were among the least expensive available from the established carriers, but the prevalence of discount fares has caused group fares to all but disappear from some air routes. Travelers reading brochures on group package tours to Spain or Portugal will find that, in almost all cases, the applicable airfare given as a sample (to be added to the price of the land package to obtain the total tour price) is an APEX fare, the same discount fare available to the independent traveler.

The major airlines serving Spain and Portugal from the US also may offer individual excursion fare rates similar to GIT fares, which are sold in conjunction with ground accommodation packages. Previously called ITX, these fares generally are offered as part of "air/hotel/car/transfer packages," and can reduce the cost of an economy fare by more than a third. The packages are booked for a specific amount of time, with return dates specified; rescheduling and cancellation restrictions and penalties vary from carrier to carrier. When available, these fares are offered to popular destinations throughout Spain and Portugal. At the time of this writing, this type of fare was offered to Spain and Portugal by *Pan American* and *TAP Air,* and although their offerings did not represent substantial savings over the standard economy fare, it is worth checking at the time you plan to travel. (For further information on package options, see *Package Tours,* in this section.)

Travelers looking for the least expensive possible airfares should, finally, scan the travel pages of their daily newspapers for announcements of special promotional fares.

Most airlines traditionally have offered their most attractive special fares to encourage travel during slow seasons, and to inaugurate and publicize new routes. Even if none of these factors apply, prospective passengers can be fairly sure that the number of discount seats per flight at the lowest price is strictly limited, or that the fare offering includes a set expiration date — which means it's absolutely necessary to move fast to obtain the lowest possible price. Unfortunately, special fare offers can come and go quickly, and may not be available precisely when you want to travel.

Among other special airline promotional deals for which you should be on the lookout are discount or upgrade coupons, sometimes offered by the major carriers and found in mail order merchandise catalogues. For instance, airlines sometimes issue coupons that typically cost around $25 and are good for a percentage discount or an upgrade on an international airline ticket — including flights to Spain and Portugal. The only requirement beyond the fee generally is that a coupon purchaser is required to buy at least one item from the catalogue. There usually are some minimum airfare restrictions before the coupon is redeemable, but in general these are worthwhile offers. Restrictions often include certain blackout days (when the coupon cannot be used at all), usually imposed during peak travel periods. These coupons are particularly valuable to business travelers who tend to buy full-fare tickets, and while the coupons are issued in the buyer's name, they can be used by others who are traveling on the same itinerary.

Given the frequency with which the airfare picture changes, it is more than possible that by the time you are ready to fly, the foregoing discussion may be somewhat out of date. That's why it always is wise to comparison shop, and that requires reading the business and travel sections of your newspaper regularly, and making calls to all airlines that serve your destination from your most convenient gateway. The potential savings are well worth the effort.

Ask about discount or promotional fares and about any conditions that might restrict booking, payment, cancellation, and changes in plans. Check the prices from other cities. A special rate may be offered in a nearby city but not in yours, and it may be enough of a bargain to warrant your leaving from that city. If you have a flexible schedule, investigate standby fares. But remember that, depending on your departure point, they may not work out to be the rock-bottom price. Ask if there is a difference in price for midweek versus weekend travel, or if there is a further discount for traveling early in the morning or late at night. Also be sure to investigate package deals, which are offered by virtually every airline. These may include a car rental, accommodations, and dining and/or sightseeing features in addition to the basic airfare, and the combined cost of packaged elements usually is considerably less than the cost of the exact same elements when purchased separately.

If in the course of your research you come across a deal that seems too good to be true, keep in mind that logic may not be a component of deeply discounted airfares — there's not always any sane relationship between miles to be flown and the price to get there. More often than not, the level of competition on a given route dictates the degree of discount, and don't be dissuaded from accepting an offer that sounds irresistible just because it also sounds illogical. Better to buy that inexpensive fare while it's being offered and worry about the sense — or absence thereof — while you're flying to your desired destination.

When you're satisfied that you've found the lowest possible price for which you can conveniently qualify (you may have to call the airline more than once, because different clerks have been known to quote different prices), make your booking. Then, to protect yourself against fare increases, purchase and pay for your ticket as soon as possible after you've received a confirmed reservation. Airlines generally will honor their tickets, even if the operative price at the time of your flight is higher than the price you paid; if fares go up between the time you *reserve* a flight and the time you *pay* for it, you likely will be out of luck. Finally, with excursion or discount fares, it is important to remember that when a reservation clerk says that you must purchase a ticket by a specific date, this is an absolute deadline. Miss it and the airline automatically may cancel your reservation without telling you.

■ **Note:** Another wrinkle on the airfare scene is that if the fares go *down* after you purchase your ticket, you *may* be entitled to a refund of the difference. However, this is possible only in certain situations — availability and advance purchase restrictions pertaining to the lower rate are set by the airline. If you suspect that you may be able to qualify for such a refund, check with your travel agent or the airline (although some airline clerks may not be aware of this policy).

Frequent Flyers – The leading carriers serving Spain and Portugal — including *American, British Airways, Pan American,* and *TWA* — now also offer a bonus system to frequent travelers. After the first 10,000 miles, for example, a passenger might be eligible for a first class seat for the coach fare; after another 10,000 miles, he or she might receive a discount on his or her next ticket purchase. The value of the bonuses continues to increase as more miles are logged.

Bonus miles also may be earned by patronizing affiliated car rental companies or hotel chains, or by using one of the credit cards that now offers this reward. In deciding whether to accept such a credit card from one of the issuing organizations that tempt you with frequent flyer mileage bonuses on a specific airline, first determine whether the interest rate charged on the unpaid balance is the same as (or less than) possible alternate credit cards, and whether the annual "membership" fee also is equal or lower. If these charges are slightly higher than those of competing cards, weigh the difference against the potential value in airfare savings. Also ask about any bonus miles awarded just for signing up — 1,000 is common, 5,000 generally the maximum.

For the most up-to-date information on frequent flyer bonus options, you may want to send for the monthly newsletter *Frequent*. Issued by Frequent Publications, it provides current information about frequent flyer plans in general, as well as specific data about promotions, awards, and combination deals to help you keep track of the profusion — and confusion — of current and upcoming availabilities. For a year's subscription, send $28 to Frequent Publications, 4715-C Town Center Dr., Colorado Springs, CO 80916 (phone: 800-333-5937).

There also is a monthly magazine called *Frequent Flyer,* but unlike the newsletter mentioned above, its focus is primarily on newsy articles of interest to business travelers and other frequent flyers. Published by Official Airline Guides (PO Box 58543, Boulder, CO 80322-8543; phone: 800-323-3537), *Frequent Flyer* is available for $24 for a 1-year subscription.

Low-Fare Airlines – In today's economic climate, the stimulus for special fares increasingly is the appearance of new airlines along popular routes. These tend to be smaller carriers that offer low fares because of lower overhead, non-union staffs, uncomplicated route networks, and other limitations in their service. On these airlines, all seats on any given flight generally sell for the same price, which is somewhat below the lowest discount fare offered by the larger, more established airlines. It is important to note that tickets offered by the smaller airlines specializing in low-cost travel frequently are not subject to the same restrictions as the lowest-priced ticket offered by the more established carriers. They may not require advance purchase or minimum and maximum stays, may involve no cancellation penalties, may be available one way or round-trip, and may, for all intents and purposes, resemble the competition's high-priced full-fare coach. But never assume this until you know it's so. A disadvantage to many low-fare airlines, however, is that when something goes wrong, such as delayed baggage or a flight cancellation due to equipment breakdown, their smaller fleets and fewer flights mean that passengers may have to wait longer for a solution than they would on one of the equipment-rich major carriers.

At press time, one of the few airlines offering a consistently low fare to Europe was

Virgin Atlantic (phone: 212-242-1330 in New York City; 800-862-8621 elsewhere), which flies daily from New York (Newark) to London's Gatwick Airport. The airline sells tickets in several categories, including business or "upper" class, economy, APEX, and nonrefundable variations on standby. Fares from New York to London include Late Saver fares — which must be purchased not less than 7 days prior to travel and range from $229 one way during the off-season to $299 during the summer — and Late Late Saver fares — which are purchased no later than 1 day prior to travel and range from $179 one way for off-season travel to $229 in the summer. Travelers to Spain and Portugal actually will fly beyond their destination, then have to take a second flight from London to Spain or Portugal, but still may save money. To determine the potential savings, add the cost of these transatlantic fares and the cost of connecting flights to come up with the total ticket price. Remember, too, that since Spain and Portugal are such popular holiday destinations with the British, ultra-low-priced package programs are frequently available from British-based tour operators and bucket shops.

In a class by itself is *Icelandair,* which always has been a scheduled airline but long has been known as a good source of low-cost flights to Europe. *Icelandair* flies from Baltimore/Washington, DC, New York, and Orlando to Copenhagen (Denmark), Glasgow and London (Great Britain), Gothenburg (Sweden), Helsinki (Finland), Luxembourg (in the country of the same name), Oslo (Norway), and Reykjavik (Iceland). In addition, the airline increases the options for its passengers by offering "thru-fares" on connecting flights to other European cities. (The price of the intra-European flights — aboard Luxembourg's *Luxair* — is included in the price *Icelandair* quotes for the transatlantic portion of the travel to these additional destinations.)

Icelandair sells tickets in a variety of categories, from unrestricted economy fares to a sort of standby "3-days-before" fare (which functions just like the youth fares described above but has no age requirement). Travelers should be aware, however, that most *Icelandair* flights stop in Reykjavik for 45 minutes — a minor delay for most, but one that further prolongs the trip for passengers who will wait again to board connecting flights to their ultimate destination in Spain or Portugal. (At the time of this writing, *Icelandair* did not offer connecting flights to Spain or Portugal; however, connecting flight options are available through other carriers.) It may be a better choice for travelers intending to visit other destinations on the Continent when taking both this delay and the cost of connections into account. For reservations and tickets, contact a travel agent or *Icelandair* (phone: 212-967-8888 in New York City; 800-223-5500 elsewhere in the US).

Intra-European Fares – The cost of the round trip across the Atlantic is not the only expense to consider, for flights between European cities can be quite expensive. But discounts have recently been introduced on routes between some European cities, and other discounts do exist.

Recent Common Market moves toward airline deregulation are expected to lead gradually to a greater number of such budget fares. In the meantime, however, the high cost of fares between European cities can be avoided by careful use of stopover rights on the higher-priced transatlantic tickets — first class, business class, and full-fare economy. If your ticket doesn't allow stopovers, ask about excursion fares such as PEX and Super PEX, APEX for round trips, and other excursion fares for one-way trips. If the restrictions that govern them allow you to use them (frequently the minimum stay requirement means staying over for at least 1 Saturday night), you may save as much as 35% to 50% off full-fare economy. Note that these fares, which once could be bought only after arrival in Europe, now are sold in the US and can be bought before departure.

It is not easy to inform yourself about stopover possibilities by talking to most airline reservations clerks. More than likely, an inquiry concerning any projected trip will prompt the reply that a particular route is nonstop aboard the carrier in question, thereby precluding stopovers completely, or that the carrier does not fly to all the places you want to visit. It may take additional inquiries, perhaps with the aid of a travel agent, to determine the full range of options regarding stopover privileges. Travelers might be able to squeeze in visits to Paris and Nice on a first class ticket to Barcelona or Lisbon, for instance; London and Amsterdam can be visited on a ticket to Madrid; and Madrid might only be the first of many free European stopovers possible on a one-way or round-trip ticket to a city in Eastern Europe or points beyond. The airline that flies you on the first leg of your trip across the Atlantic issues the ticket, though you may have to use several different airlines in order to complete your journey. First class tickets are valid for a full year, so there's no rush.

Both *Iberia* and its subsidiary, *Aviaco* (the Spanish domestic airline), offer PEX-like fares for round-trip travel within Spain. They usually cannot be bought more than 3 days before the flight, are available only on certain flights, and have varying minimum and maximum stay requirements, depending on the route. *Iberia* also offers discounted thru-fares between Spanish and other European cities; these thru-fares must be bought in the US and the restrictions are the same as those for an APEX fare. *TAP Air* offers PEX fares for travel within Portugal, and between Portuguese and other European destinations; these fares generally must be purchased upon arrival in Europe.

For travel within Spain, *Iberia* offers the "Visit Spain" airpass, which allows purchasers to fly *Iberia* or *Aviaco* to as many as 30 Spanish destinations on the mainland or in the Balearic Islands — and gives these passengers 60 days to complete the travel — all for one price. The pass must be bought in the US in conjunction with a transatlantic round-trip ticket to Spain (of which at least the eastbound portion must be aboard *Iberia*). Although the pass holders must choose the Spanish cities to be visited at the time of purchase (with an option to skip any city as long as the original sequence of remaining cities is maintained), reservations for specific flight dates need not be made in advance and pass holders have the flexibility to spend as much time as they wish (within the 60-day validity period) at each destination. For further information and current pass prices, contact *Iberian Airlines of Spain* (phone: 800-772-4642).

Taxes and Other Fees – Travelers who have shopped for the best possible flight at the lowest possible price should be warned that a number of extras will be added to that price and collected by the airline or travel agent who issues the ticket. In addition to the $6 International Air Transportation Tax — a departure tax paid by all passengers flying from the US to a foreign destination — there now is a $10 US Federal Inspection Fee levied on all air and cruise passengers who arrive in the US from outside North America (those arriving from Canada, Mexico, the Caribbean, and US territories are exempt). Payable at the time a round-trip or incoming ticket is purchased, it combines a $5 customs inspection fee and a $5 immigration inspection fee, both instituted in 1986 to finance additional inspectors to reduce delays at gateways.

Still another fee is charged by some airlines to cover more stringent security procedures, prompted by recent terrorist incidents. The 8% federal US Transportation Tax, which applies to travel within the US or US territories, already is included in advertised fares and in the prices quoted by reservations clerks. It does not apply to passengers flying between US cities en route to a foreign destination, unless the trip includes a stopover of more than 12 hours at a US point. Someone flying from Los Angeles to New York and stopping in New York for more than 12 hours before boarding a flight to Spain or Portugal, for instance, would pay the 8% tax on the domestic portion of the trip. Note that all of these taxes *usually* are included in advertised fares and in the prices quoted by airline reservations clerks.

Reservations – For those who don't have the time or patience to investigate personally all possible air departures and connections for a proposed trip, a travel agent can be of inestimable help. A good agent should have all the information on which flights go where and when, and which categories of tickets are available on each. Most have computerized reservation links with the major carriers, so that a seat can be reserved and confirmed in minutes. An increasing number of agents also possess fare-comparison computer programs, so they often are very reliable sources of detailed competitive price data. (For more information, see *How to Use a Travel Agent,* in this section.)

When making a reservation through a travel agent, ask the agent to give the airline your home phone number, as well as your daytime business phone number. All too often the agent uses the agency number as the official contact for changes in flight plans. Especially during the winter, weather conditions hundreds or even thousands of miles away can wreak havoc with flight schedules. Aircraft are constantly in use, and a plane delayed in the Orient or on the West Coast can miss its scheduled flight from the East Coast the next morning. The airlines are fairly reliable about getting this sort of information to passengers if they can reach them; diligence does little good at 10 PM if the airline has only the agency's or an office number.

Reconfirmation is strongly recommended for all international flights (though generally it is not required on domestic flights). Some (though increasingly fewer) reservations to and from international destinations are automatically canceled after a required reconfirmation period (typically 72 hours) has passed — even if you have a confirmed, fully paid ticket in hand. It always is a good idea to call ahead to make sure that the airline did not slip up in entering your original reservation, or in registering any changes you may have made since, and that it has your seat reservation and/or special meal request in the computer. Although policies vary from carrier to carrier, some recommend that you reconfirm your return flight 48 to 72 hours in advance. If you look at the back of your ticket, you'll see the airline's reconfirmation policy stated explicitly. If in doubt — call.

Every travel agent or airline ticket office should give each passenger a reminder to reconfirm flights, but this seldom happens, so the responsibility rests with the traveler. Don't be lulled into a false sense of security by the "OK" on your ticket next to the number and time of the return flight. This only means that a reservation has been entered; a reconfirmation still may be necessary.

If you plan not to take a flight on which you hold a confirmed reservation, by all means inform the airline. Because the problem of "no-shows" is a constant expense for airlines, they are allowed to overbook flights, a practice that often contributes to the threat of denied boarding for a certain number of passengers (see "Getting Bumped," below). Let the airline know you're not coming and you'll spare everyone some inconvenience and confusion. Bear in mind that only certain kinds of tickets allow the luxury of last-minute changes in flight plans: Those sold on an open reservation system (first class and full-fare coach) do, while excursions and other discount fares often are restricted in some way. Even first class and coach passengers should remember that if they do not show up for a flight that is the first of several connecting ones, the airline very likely will cancel all of their ongoing reservations unless informed not to do so.

Seating – For most types of tickets, airline seats usually are assigned on a first-come, first-served basis at check-in, although some airlines make it possible to reserve a seat at the time of ticket purchase. Always check in early for your flight, even with advance seat assignments. A good rule of thumb for international flights is to arrive at the airport *at least* 2 hours before the scheduled departure to give yourself plenty of time in case there are long lines.

Most airlines furnish seating charts, which make choosing a seat much easier, but there are a few basics to consider. You must decide whether you prefer a window, aisle, or middle seat. On flights where smoking is permitted, you also should specify if you prefer the smoking or nonsmoking section.

The amount of legroom provided (as well as chest room, especially when the seat in front of you is in a reclining position) is determined by pitch, a measure of the distance between the back of the seat in front of you and the front of the back of your seat. The amount of pitch is a matter of airline policy, not the type of plane you fly. First class and business class seats have the greatest pitch, a fact that figures prominently in airline advertising. In economy class or coach, the standard pitch ranges from 33 to as little as 31 inches — downright cramped.

The number of seats abreast, another factor determining comfort, depends on a combination of airline policy and airplane dimensions. First class and business class have the fewest seats per row. Economy generally has 9 seats per row on a DC-10 or an L-1011, making either one slightly more comfortable than a 747, on which there normally are 10 seats per row. Charter flights on DC-10s and L-1011s, however, often have 10 seats per row and can be noticeably more cramped than 747 charters, on which the seating normally remains at 10 per row.

Airline representatives claim that most aircraft are more stable toward the front and midsection, while seats farthest from the engines are quietest. Passengers who have long legs and are traveling on a wide-body aircraft might request a seat directly behind a door or emergency exit, since these seats often have greater than average pitch, or a seat in the first row of a given section, since these seats have extra legroom. It often is impossible, however, to see the movie from these seats, which are directly behind the plane's exits. Be aware that the first row of the economy section (called a "bulkhead" seat) on a conventional aircraft (not a widebody) does *not* offer extra legroom, since the fixed partition will not permit passengers to slide their feet under it, and that watching a movie from this first-row seat can be difficult and uncomfortable. A window seat protects you from aisle traffic and clumsy serving carts, and also provides a view, while an aisle seat enables you to get up and stretch your legs without disturbing your fellow travelers. Middle seats are the least desirable, and seats in the last row are the worst of all, since they seldom recline fully. If you wish to avoid children on your flight or if you find that you are sitting in an especially noisy section, you usually are free to move to any unoccupied seat — if there is one.

If you are overweight, you may face the prospect of a long flight with special trepidation. Center seats in the alignments of wide-body 747s, L-1011s, and DC-10s are about 1½ inches wider than those on either side, so larger travelers tend to be more comfortable there.

Despite all these rules of thumb, finding out which specific rows are near emergency exits or at the front of a wide-body cabin can be difficult because seating arrangements on two otherwise identical planes vary from airline to airline. There is, however, a quarterly publication called the *Airline Seating Guide* that publishes seating charts for most major US airlines and many foreign carriers as well. Your travel agent should have a copy, or you can buy the US edition for $39.95 per year and the overseas edition for $44.95. Order from Carlson Publishing Co., Box 888, Los Alamitos, CA 90720 (phone: 213-493-4877).

Simply reserving an airline seat in advance, however, actually may guarantee very little. Most airlines require that passengers arrive at the departure gate at least 45 minutes (sometimes more) ahead of time to hold a seat reservation. *Iberia* and *TAP Air* for example, may cancel seat assignments and may not honor reservations of passengers not "checked in" 45 minutes before the scheduled departure time, and they *ask* travelers to check in 2 hours before all international flights. It pays to read the fine print on the back of your ticket carefully and plan ahead.

A far better strategy is to visit an airline ticket office (or one of a select group of travel agents) to secure an actual boarding pass for your specific flight. Once this has been issued, airline computers show you as checked in, and you effectively own the seat you have selected (although some carriers may not honor boarding passes of passengers arriving at the gate less than 10 minutes before departure). This also is good — but not foolproof — insurance against getting bumped from an overbooked flight and is, therefore, an especially valuable tactic at peak travel times.

Smoking – One decision regarding choosing a seat has been taken out of the hands of many travelers who smoke. Effective February 25, 1990, the US government imposed a ban that prohibits smoking on all flights scheduled for 6 hours or less within the US and its territories. The new regulation applies to both domestic and international carriers serving these routes.

In the case of flights to Spain and Portugal, these rules do not apply to nonstop flights going directly from the US to Europe, or those with a continuous flight time of over 6 hours between stops in the US or its territories. Smoking is not permitted on segments of international flights where the flight time between US landings is under 6 hours — for instance, flights that include a stopover (even with no change of plane) or connecting flights. To further complicate the situation, several individual carriers are banning smoking altogether on certain routes. (As we went to press, this ban had not yet extended to carriers flying between the US and Spain and Portugal — for instance, both *Iberia* and *TAP Air* allow smoking on all transatlantic flights.)

On those flights that do permit smoking, the US Department of Transportation has determined that nonsmoking sections must be enlarged to accommodate all passengers who wish to sit in one. The airline does not, however, have to shift seating to accommodate nonsmokers who arrive late for a flight or travelers flying standby, and in general not all airlines can guarantee a seat in the nonsmoking section on international flights. Cigar and pipe smoking are prohibited on all flights, even in the smoking sections.

For a wallet-size guide, which notes in detail the rights of nonsmokers according to these regulations, send a self-addressed, stamped envelope to ASH (Action on Smoking and Health), Airline Card, 2013 H St. NW, Washington, DC 20006 (phone: 202-659-4310).

Flying with Children – On longer flights, the bulkhead seats usually are reserved for families traveling with small children. As a general rule, an infant under 2 years of age (and not occupying a seat) flies to Spain or Portugal at 10% of whatever fare the accompanying adult is paying. A second infant (without a second adult) pays the fare applicable to children ages 2 through 11. In most cases this amounts to around 50% of an adult economy fare and 67% of an adult APEX fare.

Although airlines will, on request, supply bassinets for infants, most carriers encourage parents to bring their own safety seat on board, which then is strapped into the airline seat with a regular seat belt. This is much safer — and certainly more comfortable — than holding the child in your lap. If you do not purchase a seat for your baby, you have the option of bringing the infant restraint along on the off-chance that there might be an empty seat next to yours — in which case many airlines will let you have that seat free for your baby and infant seat. However, if there is no empty seat available, the infant seat no doubt will have to be checked as baggage (and most likely you will have to pay an additional charge), since it generally does not fit under the seat or in the overhead racks.

The safest bet is to pay for a seat — this usually will be the same as fares applicable to children ages 2 through 11. You might have to do some number-juggling to determine the cheapest fare for the infant. Excursion fares, which usually are the least expensive, often do not have children's rates, whereas the higher-priced fares usually are the ones that offer discounts for children.

Be forewarned: Some safety seats designed primarily for use in cars do not fit into plane seats properly . Although nearly all seats manufactured since 1985 carry labels indicating whether they meet federal standards for use aboard planes, actual seat sizes may vary from carrier to carrier. At the time of this writing, the FAA was in the process of reviewing and revising airline policies with regard to infant travel and safety devices — it was still to be determined if children should be *required* to sit in safety seats and whether the airlines will have to provide them.

When checking in, and using either a bassinet or infant seat, request a bulkhead or other seat that has enough room in front to use it. On some planes, bassinets hook into a bulkhead wall; on others it is placed on the floor in front of you. Even if you do use a bassinet, babies must be held during takeoff and landing.

The entire subject of flying with children — including a discussion of car seats — is covered in a special supplementary issue of a newsletter called *Family Travel Times*, published by *Travel With Your Children (TWYCH)*. An annual subscription (10 issues) is $35, and the "Airline Guide" supplement is available separately for $10, or it will be included free with a subscription. Contact *TWYCH* at 80 Eighth Ave., New York, NY 10011 (phone: 212-206-0688). (For more information on flying with children, see *Hints for Traveling with Children*, in this section.)

Meals – If you have specific diet requirements, be sure to let the airline know well before departure time. The available meals include vegetarian, seafood, kosher, Muslim, Hindu, high-protein, low-calorie, low-cholesterol, low-fat, low-sodium, diabetic, bland, and children's menus. There is no extra charge for this option. It usually is necessary to request special meals when you make your reservations — check-in time is too late. It's also wise to reconfirm that your request for a special meal has made its way into the airline's computer — the time to do this is 24 hours before departure. (Note that special meals generally are not available on intra-European flights on small local carriers. If this poses a problem, try to eat before you board, or bring food with you.)

Baggage – Travelers from the US face two different kinds of rules. When you fly on a US airline or on a major international carrier, US baggage regulations will be in effect. Though airline baggage allowances vary slightly, in general all passengers are allowed to carry on board, without charge, one piece of luggage that will fit easily under a seat of the plane or in an overhead bin and whose combined dimensions (length, width, and depth) do not exceed 45 inches. (If you prefer not to carry it with you, most airlines will allow you to check this bag in the hold.) A reasonable amount of reading material, camera equipment, and a handbag also are allowed. In addition, all passengers are allowed to check two bags in the cargo hold: one usually not to exceed 62 inches when length, width, and depth are combined, the other not to exceed 55 inches in combined dimensions. Generally no single bag may weigh more than 70 pounds. Note that *Iberia* does not make a distinction between the measurements of the two bags, although the standard weight restriction applies. The weight restriction, however, may vary on some other European airlines, ranging from as much as 88 pounds permitted for first class passengers to as little as 50 pounds for economy class — so check with the specific carrier in advance.

On many European local or trunk carriers, including domestic services in Spain and Portugal, baggage allowances may be subject to the old weight determination, under which each economy or discount passenger is allowed only a total of 44 pounds of luggage without additional charge. First class or business passengers are allowed a total of 66 pounds. (If you are flying from the US to Europe and connecting to a domestic flight, you generally will be allowed the same amount of baggage as you had on the transatlantic flight. If you break your trip and then take a domestic flight, the local carrier's weight restrictions apply.)

Charges for additional, oversize, or overweight bags usually are made at a flat rate; the actual dollar amount varies from carrier to carrier. If you plan to travel with a bike, skis, golf clubs, or other sports gear, be sure to check with the airline beforehand. Most have procedures for handling such baggage, but you probably will have to pay for transport regardless of how much other baggage you have checked.

Airline policies regarding baggage allowances for children vary and usually are based on the percentage of full adult fare paid. Children paying 50% or more of an adult fare on most US carriers are entitled to the same baggage allowance as a full-fare passenger, whereas infants traveling at 10% of an adult fare are entitled to only one piece of baggage, the combined dimensions of which may not exceed 45 inches — 39 inches on *TWA*. Particularly for international carriers, it's wise to check ahead. Often there is no luggage allowance for a child traveling on an adult's lap or in a bassinet.

To reduce the chances of your luggage going astray, remove all airline tags from previous trips, label each bag inside and out — with your business address rather than your home address on the outside, to prevent thieves from knowing whose house might be unguarded. Lock everything and double-check the tag that the airline attaches to make sure that it is coded correctly for your destination: MAD for Barajas Airport in Madrid, Spain, or LIS for Portela Airport in Lisbon, Portugal, for instance.

If your bags are not in the baggage claim area after your flight, or if they're damaged, report the problem to airline personnel immediately. Keep in mind that policies regarding the specific time limit in which you have to make your claim vary from carrier to carrier. Fill out a report form on your lost or damaged luggage and keep a copy of it and your original baggage claim check. If you must surrender the check to claim a damaged bag, get a receipt for it to prove that you did, indeed, check your baggage on the flight. If luggage is missing, be sure to give the airline your destination and/or a telephone number where you can be reached. Also, take the name and number of the person in charge of recovering lost luggage.

Most airlines have emergency funds for passengers stranded away from home without their luggage, but if it turns out that your bags are truly lost and not simply delayed, do not then and there sign any paper indicating you'll accept an offered settlement. Since the airline is responsible for the value of your bags within certain statutory limits ($1,250 per passenger for lost baggage on a domestic flight; $9.07 per pound or $20 per kilo for checked baggage and up to $400 per passenger for unchecked baggage on an international flight), you should take some time to assess the extent of your loss (see *Insurance,* in this section). It's a good idea to keep records indicating the value of the contents of your luggage. A wise alternative is to take a Polaroid picture of the most valuable of your packed items just after putting them in your suitcase.

Considering the increased incidence of damage to baggage, it's now more than ever a good idea to keep the sales slips that confirm how much you paid for your bags. These are invaluable in establishing the value of damaged baggage and eliminate any arguments. A better way to protect your precious baggage from the luggage-eating conveyers is to try to carry your gear on board wherever possible.

Be aware that airport security increasingly is an issue all over Europe, and the Spanish and Portuguese take it very seriously. Heavily armed police patrol the airports, and unattended luggage of any description may be confiscated and quickly destroyed. Passengers checking in at a European airport may undergo at least two separate inspections of their tickets, passports, and luggage by courteous but serious airline personnel — who ask passengers if their baggage has been out of their possession between packing and the airport or if they have been given gifts or other items to transport — before checked items are accepted.

Airline Clubs – US carriers often have clubs for travelers who pay for membership. These clubs are not solely for first class passengers, although a first class ticket *may* entitle a passenger to lounge privileges. Membership (which, by law, now requires a fee) entitles the traveler to use the private lounges at airports along their route, to refreshments served in these lounges, and to check-cashing privileges at most of their counters. Extras include special telephone numbers for individual reservations, embossed luggage tags, and a membership card for identification. Two airlines that offer membership in such clubs are *Pan American* — the *Clipper Club,* yearly membership $150 (plus a one-time $25 initiation fee), spouse an additional $45; 3-year and lifetime memberships also available — and *TWA* — the *Ambassador Club,* single yearly membership $150, spouse an additional $25; lifetime memberships also available. However, such companies do not have club facilities in all airports; other airlines also offer a variety of special services in many airports.

Getting Bumped – A special air travel problem is the possibility that an airline will accept more reservations (and sell more tickets) than there are seats on a given flight. This is entirely legal and is done to make up for "no-shows," passengers who don't show up for a flight for which they have made reservations and bought tickets. If the airline has oversold the flight and everyone does show up, there simply aren't enough seats. When this happens, the airline is subject to stringent rules designed to protect travelers.

In such cases, the airline first seeks ticketholders willing to give up their seats voluntarily in return for a negotiable sum of money or some other inducement, such as an offer of upgraded seating on the next flight or a voucher for a free trip at some other time. If there are not enough volunteers, the airline may bump passengers against their wishes.

Anyone inconvenienced in this way, however, is entitled to an explanation of the criteria used to determine who does and does not get on the flight, as well as compensation if the resulting delay exceeds certain limits. If the airline can put the bumped passengers on an alternate flight that is *scheduled to arrive* at their original destination within 1 hour of their originally scheduled arrival time, no compensation is owed. If the delay is more than an hour — but less than 2 hours on a domestic US flight or less than 4 hours on an international flight — they must be paid denied-boarding compensation equivalent to the one-way fare to their destination (but not more than $200). If the delay is more than 2 hours after the original arrival time on a domestic flight or more than 4 hours on an international flight, the compensation must be doubled (not more than $400). The airline also may offer bumped travelers a voucher for a free flight instead of the denied-boarding compensation. The passenger can choose either the money or the voucher, the dollar value of which may be no less than the monetary compensation to which the passenger would be entitled. The voucher is not a substitute for the bumped passenger's original ticket; the airline continues to honor that as well. Keep in mind that the above regulations and policies are for flights leaving the US only, and do *not* apply to charters or to inbound flights originating abroad, even on US carriers.

In Spain and Portugal, each airline is free to determine what compensation it will pay to passengers who are bumped because of overbooking. European airlines often spell out their policy on the airline ticket, and many of these policies are similar to the US policy. Passengers involuntarily bumped may be paid twice the price of a one-way ticket (up to $400) if they reach their destination 4 or more hours late, or may be offered other negotiable compensation — such as a voucher for a free flight or a night's stay at a hotel — to make up for the inconvenience. However, don't assume all carriers will be as generous.

To protect yourself as best you can against getting bumped, arrive at the airport early, allowing plenty of time to check in and get to the gate. If the flight is oversold, ask immediately for the written statement explaining the airline's policy on denied-boarding compensation and its boarding priorities. If the airline refuses to give you this information, or if you feel they have not handled the situation properly, file a complaint with both the airline and the appropriate government agency (see "Consumer Protection," below).

Delays and Cancellations – The above compensation rules also do not apply if the flight is canceled or delayed, or if a smaller aircraft is substituted because of mechanical problems. Each airline has its own policy for assisting passengers whose flights are delayed or canceled or who must wait for another flight because their original one was overbooked. Most airline personnel will make new travel arrangements if necessary. If the delay is longer than 4 hours, the airline may pay for a phone call or telegram, a meal, and, in some cases, a hotel room and transportation to it.

■ **Caution:** If you are bumped or miss a flight, be sure to ask the airline to notify other airlines on which you have reservations or connecting flights. When your name is taken off the passenger list of your initial flight, the computer usually cancels all of your reservations automatically, unless *you* take steps to preserve them.

CHARTER FLIGHTS: By booking a block of seats on a specially arranged flight, charter operators offer travelers air transportation, often coupled with a hotel room, meals, and other travel services, for a substantial reduction over the full coach or economy fare.

Charters once were the best bargains around, but this is no longer necessarily the case. As a result, charter flights have been discontinued in many areas, but they still can be a good buy to some popular travel destinations, including Spain and Portugal. Charters are especially attractive to people living in smaller cities or out-of-the-way places, because they frequently leave from nearby airports, saving travelers the inconvenience and expense of getting to a major gateway to begin their Iberian trip.

Where demand persists, charter operators will continue to rent planes or seats from scheduled airlines (or from special charter airlines) and offer flights to the public directly through advertisements or travel agents. You buy the ticket from the operator or the agent, not from the airline owning the plane. With the advent of APEX and various promotional fares on the major airlines and the appearance of low-fare airlines, however, charter flights lost some of their budget-conscious clientele and suffered some lean years, especially on highly competitive routes with a choice of other bargains. At the same time, many of the larger companies running charter programs began to offer both charter flights and discounted scheduled flights (see below). Nevertheless, among the current offerings, charter flights to European cities are common, a sign that they still represent a good value.

Charter travel once required that an individual be a member of a club or other "affinity" group whose main purpose was not travel. But since the approval of "public charters" years ago, operators have had some of the flexibility of scheduled airlines, making charters more competitive. Public charters are open to anyone, whether part of a group or not, and have no advance booking or minimum stay requirements. Operators can offer air-only charters, selling transportation alone, or they can offer charter packages — the flight plus a combination of land arrangements such as accommodations, meals, tours, or car rental.

Though charters almost always are round-trip, and it is unlikely that you would be sold a one-way seat on a round-trip flight, on rare occasions one-way tickets on charters are offered. Although it may be possible to book a one-way charter in the US, giving you more flexibility in scheduling your return, note that US regulations pertaining to charters may be more permissive than the charter laws of other countries. For example, if you want to book a one-way foreign charter back to the US, you may find advance booking rules in force.

From the consumer's standpoint, charters differ from scheduled airlines in two main respects: You generally need to book and pay in advance, and you can't change the itinerary or the departure and return dates once you've booked the flight. In practice, however, these restrictions don't always apply. Today, although most charters still require advance reservations, some permit last-minute bookings (when there are unsold seats available), and some even offer seats on a standby basis.

The savings provided by charters vary, depending on their point of departure in the US and the countries to which they are headed (some governments do not allow charters to land at all; others allow them to undercut scheduled fares by a wide margin). As a rule, a charter to any given destination can cost anywhere from $50 to $200 less than an economy fare on a major carrier, with East Coast charters realizing a greater saving than those from the West Coast.

Some things to keep in mind about the charter game:

1. It cannot be repeated often enough that if you are forced to cancel your trip, you can lose much (and possibly all) of your money unless you have cancellation insurance, which is a must (see *Insurance*, in this section). Frequently, if the cancellation is made sufficiently far in advance (often 6 weeks or more), you may forfeit only a $25 or $50 penalty. If you cancel only 2 or 3 weeks before the flight, there may be no refund at all unless you or the operator can provide a substitute passenger.

2. Charter flights may be canceled by the operator up to 10 days before departure for any reason, usually underbooking. Your money is returned in this event, but there may be too little time to make new arrangements.

3. Most charters have little of the flexibility of regularly scheduled flights regarding refunds and the changing of flight dates; if you book a return flight, you must be on it or lose your money.

4. Charter operators are permitted to assess a surcharge, if fuel or other costs warrant it, of up to 10% of the airfare up to 10 days before departure.

5. Because of the economics of charter flights, your plane almost always will be full, so you will be crowded, though not necessarily uncomfortable. (There is, however, a new movement among charter airlines to provide flight accommodations that are comfort-oriented, so this situation may change in the near future.)

Bookings – If you do take a charter, read the contract's fine print carefully and pay particular attention to the following:

1. Instructions concerning the payment of the deposit and its balance and to whom the check is to be made payable. Ordinarily, checks are made out to an escrow account, which means the charter company can't spend your money until your flight has safely returned. This provides some protection for you. To ensure the safe handling of your money, make out your check to the escrow account, the number of which must appear by law on the brochure, though all too often it is on the back in fine print. Write the details of the charter, including the destination and dates, on the face of the check; on the back, print "For Deposit Only." Your travel agent may prefer that you make out your check to the agency, saying that it will then pay the tour operator the fee minus commission. It is perfectly legal to write the check as we suggest, however, and if your agent objects too vociferously (he or she should trust the tour operator to send the proper commission), consider taking your business elsewhere. If you don't make your check out to the escrow account, you lose the protection of that escrow should the trip be canceled. Furthermore, recent bankruptcies in the travel industry have served to point out that even the protection of escrow may not be enough to safeguard a traveler's investment. More and more, insurance is becoming a necessity. The charter company should be bonded (usually by an insurance company), and if you want to file a claim against it, the claim should be sent to the bonding agent. The contract will set a time limit within which a claim must be filed.

2. Note specific stipulations and penalties for cancellations. Most charters allow you to cancel up to 45 days in advance without major penalty, but some cancellation dates are 50 to 60 days before departure.

3. Stipulations regarding cancellation and major changes made by the charterer. US rules say that charter flights may not be canceled within 10 days of departure except when circumstances — such as natural disasters or political upheavals — make it physically impossible to fly. Charterers may make "major changes," however, such as in the date or place of departure or return, but you are entitled to cancel and receive a full refund if you don't wish to accept these changes. A price increase of more than 10% at any time up to 10 days before departure is

considered a major change; no price increase at all is allowed during the last 10 days immediately before departure.

DISCOUNTS ON SCHEDULED FLIGHTS: The APEX fare is an example of a promotional fare offered on regularly scheduled transatlantic flights by most major airlines. Promotional fares often are called discount fares because they cost less than what used to be the standard airline fare — full-fare economy. Nevertheless, they cost the traveler the same whether they are bought through a travel agent or directly from the airline. Tickets that cost less if bought from some outlet other than the airline do exist, however. While it is likely that the vast majority of travelers flying to Spain or Portugal in the near future will be doing so on a promotional fare or charter rather than on a "discount" air ticket of this sort, it still is a good idea for cost-conscious consumers to be aware of the latest developments in the budget airfare scene. Note that the following discussion makes clear-cut distinctions among the types of discounts available based on how they reach the consumer; in actual practice, the distinctions are not nearly so precise. One organization may operate part of its business in one fashion and the remainder in another; a second organization may operate all of its business in the same fashion, but outsiders — and sometimes the organization itself — would have difficulty classifying it.

Courier Travel – There was a time when traveling as a courier was a sort of underground way to save money and visit otherwise unaffordable destinations, but more and more this once exotic idea of traveling as a courier is becoming a very "establishment" exercise. Courier means no more than a traveler who accompanies freight of one sort or another, and typically that freight replaces what otherwise would be the traveler's checked baggage. Be prepared, therefore, to carry all your own personal travel gear in a bag that fits under the seat in front of you. In addition, the so-called courier usually pays only a portion of the total airfare — the freight company pays the remainder — and the courier also may be assessed a small registration fee.

There are over 4 dozen courier companies operating actively around the globe, and there are at least two travel newsletters that have sprung up for the purpose of publishing courier opportunities. One of these, called *Travel Secrets* (PO Box 2325, New York, NY 10108), lists more than 20 US and Canadian courier companies. The other, *Travel Unlimited* (PO Box 1058, Allston, MA 02135), lists 30 to 40 courier companies and agents worldwide. A particularly useful reference is *A Simple Guide to Courier Travel* by Jesse L. Riddle. Published by the Carriage Group (PO Box 2394, Lake Oswego, OR 97035; phone: 800-344-9375), it's available for $14.95, including postage and handling.

And for those traveling to Spain and Portugal, *Excaliber International Courier Inc.* flies to London, where you can catch a connecting flight to Iberian destinations. For information, contact *Excaliber*'s representative, *Way to Go Travel* (3317 Barham Blvd., Hollywood, CA 90068; phone: 213-851-2572). *Voyager*, another company, sends couriers to Madrid. For information, contact *Voyager* (74 Varick St., Suite 307, New York, NY 10013; phone: 212-431-1616). In addition, courier companies are listed in the yellow pages and, in general, are best used by folks with *very* flexible travel schedules.

Net Fare Sources – The newest notion for reducing the costs of travel services comes from travel agents who offer individual travelers "net" fares. Defined simply, a net fare is the bare minimum amount at which an airline or tour operator will carry a prospective traveler. It doesn't include the amount that normally would be paid to the travel agent as a commission. Traditionally, such commissions amount to about 10% on domestic fares and from 8% to 20% on international tickets — not counting significant additions to these commission levels that are payable retroactively when agents sell more than a specific volume of tickets or trips for a single supplier. At press time, at least one travel agency in the US was offering travelers the opportunity to purchase tickets and/or tours for a net price. Instead of making its income from individual commissions, this agency assesses a fixed fee that may or may not provide a bargain for travelers; it requires a little arithmetic to determine whether to use the services of a net travel agent or those of one who accepts conventional commissions. One of the potential drawbacks of buying from agencies selling travel services at net fares is that some airlines refuse to do business with them, thus possibly limiting your flight options.

Travel Avenue (formerly *McTravel Travel Service*) is a formula fee-based agency that rebates its ordinary agency commission to the customer. For domestic flights, an agent will find the lowest retail fare, then rebate 8% to 11% (depending on the airline selected) of that price minus an $8 ticket-writing charge. The rebate percentage for international flights varies from 8% to 25% (again depending on the airline), and the ticket-writing fee is $20. The ticket-writing charge is imposed per ticket; if the ticket includes more than eight separate flights, an additional $8 or $20 fee is charged.

Travel Avenue will rebate on all tickets including Max Savers, Super Savers, and senior citizen passes; if the customer is using a free flight coupon, there is an additional $5 coupon processing fee. Available 7 days a week, reservations should be made far enough in advance to allow the tickets to be sent by first class mail, since extra charges accrue for special handling. It's possible to economize further by making your own airline reservation, then asking *Travel Avenue* only to write/issue your ticket. For travelers outside the Chicago area, business may be transacted by phone and purchases charged to a credit card.

And for travelers seeking discounts on other travel services, *Travel Avenue* offers a similar net cost service, through which travelers can collect rebates on the cost of hotel accommodations and car rentals if the booking is made through *Travel Avenue*. Upon return home, you simply send *Travel Avenue* a copy of your receipt and they will send you a check for 5% of the total bill — returning part of their agency commission to the consumer. For further information, contact *Travel Avenue* at 641 W. Lake St., Suite 201, Chicago, IL 60606-1012 (phone: 312-876-1116 in Illinois; 800-333-3335 elsewhere in the US).

Consolidators and Bucket Shops – Other vendors of travel services can afford to sell tickets to their customers at an even greater discount because the airline has sold the tickets to them at a substantial discount, a practice in which many airlines indulge, albeit discreetly, preferring that the general public not know they are undercutting their own "list" prices. Airlines anticipating a slow period on a particular route sometimes sell off a certain portion of their capacity to a wholesaler or consolidator at a deep discount (usually executed by substantially increasing the applicable commissions). The wholesaler sometimes is a charter operator who resells the seats to the public as though they were charter seats, which is why prospective travelers perusing the brochures of charter operators with large programs frequently see a number of flights designated as "scheduled service." As often as not, however, the consolidator, in turn, sells the seats to a travel agency specializing in discounting — or is a travel agent himself. Airlines also can sell seats directly to such an agency, which thus acts as its own consolidator. The airline offers the seats either at a net wholesale price, but without the volume-purchase requirement that would be difficult for a modest retail travel agency to fulfill, or at the standard price, but with a commission override large enough (as high as 50%) to allow both a profit and a price reduction to the public.

Travel agencies specializing in discounting sometimes are called "bucket shops," a term fraught with connotations of unreliability in this country. But in today's highly competitive travel marketplace, more and more conventional travel agencies are selling consolidator-supplied tickets, and the old bucket shops' image is becoming more respectable. Agencies that specialize in discounted tickets exist in most large cities, and usually can be found by studying the smaller ads in the travel sections of the Sunday newspapers. They deal mostly in transatlantic and other international tickets.

Before buying a discounted ticket, whether from a bucket shop or a conventional, full-service travel agency, keep the following considerations in mind: To be in a position to judge how much you'll be saving, first find out the "list" prices of tickets to your destination. Then, do some comparison shopping among agencies, always bearing in mind that the lowest-priced ticket may not provide the most convenient or most comfortable flight. Also bear in mind that a ticket that may not differ much in price from one available directly from the airline may, however, allow the circumvention of such things as the advance purchase requirement. If your plans are less than final, be sure to find out about any other restrictions, such as penalties for canceling a flight or changing a reservation. Most discount tickets are non-endorsable, meaning that they can be used only on the airline that issued them, and they usually are marked "non-refundable" to prevent their being cashed for a list price refund. (A refund of the price paid for the ticket often is possible, but it must be obtained from the outlet from which it was purchased rather than from the airline.)

A great many bucket shops are small businesses operating on a thin margin, so it's a good idea to check the local Better Business Bureau for any complaints registered against the one with which you're dealing — before parting with any money. If you still do not feel reassured, consider buying discounted tickets only through a conventional travel agency, which can be expected to have found its own reliable source of consolidator tickets — some of the largest consolidators, in fact, sell only to travel agencies.

A few bucket shops require payment in cash or by certified check or money order, but if credit cards are accepted, use that option, which allows a purchaser to refuse to pay charges for services they haven't received. Note, however, if buying from a charter operator selling seats for both scheduled and charter flights, that the scheduled seats are not protected by the regulations — including the use of escrow accounts — governing the charter seats. Well-established charter operators, nevertheless, may extend the same protections to their scheduled flights, and when this is the case consumers should be sure that the payment option selected directs their money into the escrow account.

Among the numerous consolidators offering discount fares to Spain and Portugal (and Europe in general) are the following:

Bargain Air: 655 Deep Valley Dr., Suite 355, Rolling Hills, CA 90274 (phone: 800-347-2345 or 213-377-2919).

Maharaja/Consumer Wholesale: 393 Fifth Ave. 2nd Floor, New York, NY 10016 (phone: 212-391-0122 in New York; 800-223-6862 elsewhere in the US).

TFI Tours International: 34 W. 37th St., 12th Floor, New York, NY 10001 (phone: 212-736-1140).

Travac Tours and Charters: 989 Sixth Ave., New York, NY 10018 (phone: 212-563-3303).

Unitravel: 1177 N. Warson Rd., St. Louis, MO 63132 (phone: 314-569-0900 in Missouri; 800-325-2222 elsewhere in the US).

■**Note:** Although rebating and discounting are becoming increasingly common, there is some legal ambiguity concerning them. Strictly speaking, it is legal to discount domestic tickets but not international tickets. On the other hand, the law that prohibits discounting, the Federal Aviation Act of 1958, consistently is ignored these days, in part because consumers benefit from the practice and in part because many illegal arrangements are indistinguishable from legal ones. Since the line separating the two is so fine that even the authorities can't always tell the difference, it is unlikely that most consumers would be able to do so, and in fact it is not illegal to *buy* a discounted ticket. If the issue of legality bothers you, ask the agency whether any ticket you're about to buy would be permissible under the above-mentioned act.

Other Discount Travel Sources – An excellent source of information on economical travel opportunities is the *Consumer Reports Travel Letter,* published monthly by Consumers Union. It keeps abreast of the scene on a wide variety of fronts, including package tours, rental cars, insurance, and more, but it is especially helpful for its comprehensive coverage of airfares, offering guidance on all the options from scheduled flights on major or low-fare airlines to charters and discount sources. For a year's subscription, send $37 to *Consumer Reports Travel Letter* (PO Box 2886, Boulder, CO 80322; phone: 800-525-0643). Another source is *Travel Smart,* a monthly newsletter with information on a wide variety of trips with additional discount travel services available to subscribers. For a year's subscription, send $37 to Communications House (40 Beechdale Rd., Dobbs Ferry, NY 10522; phone: 914-693-8300 in New York; 800-327-3633 elsewhere in the US).

Still another way to take advantage of bargain airfares is open to those who have a flexible schedule. A number of organizations, usually set up as last-minute travel clubs and functioning on a membership basis, routinely keep in touch with travel suppliers to help them dispose of unsold inventory at discounts of between 15% and 60%. A great deal of the inventory consists of complete tour packages and cruises, but some clubs offer air-only charter seats and, occasionally, seats on scheduled flights. Members pay an annual fee and get a toll-free hot line number to call for information on imminent trips. In some cases, they also receive periodic mailings with information on bargain travel opportunities for which there is more advance notice. Despite the suggestive names of the clubs providing these services, last-minute travel does not necessarily mean that you cannot make plans until literally the last minute. Trips can be announced as little as a few days or as much as 2 months before departure, but the average is from 1 to 4 weeks' notice. It does mean that your choice at any given time is limited to what is offered and if your heart is set on a particular destination, you might not find what you want, no matter how attractive the bargains. Among such organizations offering discounted travel opportunities to Spain and Portugal are the following:

Discount Club of America, 61-33 Woodhaven Blvd., Rego Park, NY 11374 (phone: 800-321-9587 or 718-335-9612). Annual fee: $39 per family.

Discount Travel International, Ives Building, 114 Forrest Ave., Suite 205, Narberth, PA 19072 (phone: 800-334-9294). Annual fee: $45 per household.

Encore Short Notice, 4501 Forbes Blvd., Lanham, MD 20706 (phone: 301-459-8020 or 800-638-0930 for customer service). Annual fee: $48 per family.

Last-Minute Travel Club, 132 Brookline Ave., Boston, MA 02215 (phone: 800-LAST-MIN or 617-267-9800). As of this year, no fee.

Moment's Notice, 425 Madison Ave., New York, NY 10017 (phone: 212-486-0503). Annual fee: $45 per family.

Spur-of-the-Moment Tours and Cruises, 10780 Jefferson Blvd., Culver City, CA 90230 (phone: 213-839-2418 in California; 800-343-1991 elsewhere in the US). No fee.

Traveler's Advantage, 3033 S. Parker Rd., Suite 1000, Aurora, CO 80014 (phone: 800-548-1116). Annual fee: $49 per family.

Vacations to Go, 2411 Fountain View, Suite 201, Houston, TX 77057 (phone: 800-338-4962). Annual fee: $19.95 per family.

Worldwide Discount Travel Club, 1674 Meridian Ave., Miami Beach, FL 33139 (phone: 305-534-2082). Annual fee: $40 per person; $50 per family.

Generic Air Travel – Organizations that apply the same flexible-schedule idea to air travel only and sell tickets at literally the last minute also exist. The service they provide sometimes is known as "generic" air travel, and it operates somewhat like an ordinary airline standby service, except that the organizations running it offer seats on not one but several scheduled and charter airlines.

One pioneer of generic flights is *Airhitch* (2901 Broadway, Suite 100, New York, NY 10025; phone: 212-864-2000), which arranges flights to Europe from various US cities at very low prices. Prospective travelers register by paying a fee (applicable toward the fare) and stipulate a range of acceptable departure dates and their desired destination, along with alternate choices. The week before the date range begins, they are notified of at least two flights that will be available during the time period, agree on one, and remit the balance of the fare to the company. If they do not accept any of the suggested flights, they lose their deposit; if, through no fault of their own, they do not ultimately get on any agreed-on flight, all of their money is refunded. Return flights are arranged the same way. *Airhitch* cautions that, given the number of variables attached to the flights, they are suitable only for travelers willing to accept approximate destinations, although the time period will be the one specified and, for a majority of travelers, the place of arrival, too. At the time of this writing, fares to Spain and Portugal ranged from $160 or less one way from the East Coast, $269 or less from the West Coast, and $229 or less from other points in the US. Another of the company's programs, Target, offers greater certainty regarding destinations.

BARTERED TRAVEL SOURCES: Suppose a company buys advertising space for a hotel in a newspaper. As payment, the hotel gives the publishing company a number of hotel rooms in lieu of cash. This is barter, a common means of exchange among hotels, airlines, car rental companies, cruise lines, tour operators, restaurants, and other travel service companies. When a bartering company finds itself with excess hotel rooms (or empty airline seats or cruise ship cabin space, and so on) and offers them to the public, considerable savings can be enjoyed.

Bartered-travel clubs often offer discounts of up to 50% to members who pay an annual fee (approximately $50 at press time) which entitles them to select from the flights, cruises, or hotels that the club obtained by barter. Members usually present a voucher, club credit card, or scrip (a dollar-denomination voucher negotiable only for the bartered product) to the hotel, which in turn subtracts the dollar amount from the bartering company's account.

Selling bartered travel is a perfectly legitimate means of retailing. One advantage to club members is that they don't have to wait until the last minute to obtain room or flight reservations. However, hotel rooms and airline seats usually are offered to members on a space-available basis. Ticket vouchers are good only for a particular hotel and cannot be used elsewhere. The same applies to car rentals, cruises, package tours, and restaurants. Among the companies specializing in bartered travel, several that frequently offer members travel services to and in Spain and Portugal include the following:

> *IGT (In Good Taste) Services,* 1111 Lincoln Rd., 4th Floor, Miami Beach, FL 33139 (phone: 800-444-8872 or 305-534-7900). Annual membership fee is $48 per person.
>
> *The Travel Guild,* 18210 Redmond Way, Redmond, WA 98052 (phone: 206-885-1213). Annual membership fee is $48 per family.
>
> *Travel World Leisure Club,* 225 W. 34th Street, Suite 2203, New York, NY 10122 (phone: 800-444-TWLC or 212-239-4855). Annual membership fee is $50 per family.

CONSUMER PROTECTION: Consumers who feel that they have not been dealt with fairly by an airline should make their complaints known. Begin with the customer service representative at the airport where the problem occurs. If he or she cannot resolve your complaint to your satisfaction, write to the airline's consumer office. In a businesslike, typed letter, explain what reservations you held, what happened, the names of the employees involved, and what you expect the airline to do to remedy the situation. Send copies (never the originals) of the tickets, receipts, and other documents that back your claims. Ideally, all correspondence should be sent via certified mail, return receipt requested. This provides proof that your complaint was received.

If you still receive no satisfaction and your complaint is against a US carrier, contact the US Department of Transportation. Passengers with consumer complaints — lost baggage, compensation for getting bumped, smoking and nonsmoking rules, deceptive practices by an airline, charter regulations — should contact the Consumer Affairs Division, Room 10405, US Department of Transportation (400 Seventh St. SW, Washington, DC 20590; phone: 202-366-2220). DOT personnel stress, however, that consumers initially should direct their complaints to the airline that provoked them.

Travelers with an unresolved complaint involving a Spanish or Portuguese airline also can contact the US Department of Transportation. DOT personnel will do what they can to help resolve all such complaints, although their influence may be limited.

Although neither Spain nor Portugal has a specific government bureau that deals with airline complaints, consumers with complaints against Spanish or Portuguese airlines or other travel-related services can write to the tourist authority in the area of Spain or Portugal where the problem occurred (see *Sources and Resources,* in this section, for addresses). Outline the specifics in the native language of the country — Spanish for Spain, Portuguese for Portugal — in as much detail as possible. (Keep in mind, if a translator is required, that this correspondence could get expensive.) The agency will try to resolve the complaint or, if it is out of their jurisdiction, will refer the matter to the proper authorities, and will notify you in writing (in their own language) of the result of their inquires and/or any action taken.

The deregulation of US airlines has meant that a traveler must find out for himself or herself what he or she is entitled to receive. The Department of Transportation's informative consumer booklet *Fly Rights* is a good place to start. To receive a copy, send $1 to the Superintendent of Documents, US Government Printing Office (Washington, DC 20402-9325; phone: 202-783-3238). Specify its stock number, 050-000-000513-5, and allow 3 to 4 weeks for delivery.

To avoid more serious problems, *always* choose charter flights and tour packages with care. When you consider a charter, ask your travel agent who runs it and carefully check out the company. The Better Business Bureau in the company's home city can report on how many complaints, if any, have been lodged against it in the past. As emphasized above, protect yourself with trip cancellation and interruption insurance, which can help safeguard your investment if you or a traveling companion is unable to make the trip and must cancel too late to receive a full refund from the company providing your travel services. (This is advisable whether you're buying a charter flight alone or a tour package for which the airfare is provided by charter or scheduled flight.) Some travel insurance policies have an additional feature, covering the possibility of default or bankruptcy on the part of the tour operator or airline, charter or scheduled.

Should this type of coverage not be available to you (state insurance regulations vary, there is a wide difference in price, and so on), your best bet is to pay for airline tickets and tour packages with a credit card. The federal Fair Credit Billing Act permits purchasers to refuse payment for credit card changes where services have not been delivered, so the onus of dealing with the receiver for a bankrupt airline falls on the credit card company. Do not rely on another airline to honor the ticket you're holding, since the days when virtually all major carriers subscribed to a default protection program that bound them to do so are long gone. Some airlines may voluntarily step forward to accommodate the stranded passengers of a fellow carrier, but this now is an entirely altruistic act.

Traveling by Ship

 There was a time when traveling by ship was extraordinarily expensive, time-consuming, utterly elegant, and was utilized almost exclusively for getting from one point to another. Times have changed in many ways for ship travel; after a period when the very idea of seaborne transportation was almost completely sunk by the coming of swift, inexpensive jets, cruising has floated to very near the top of leisure travel options.

Alas, the days when steamships reigned as the primary means of transatlantic transportation are gone, days when Italy, France, Sweden, Germany, Norway, the Netherlands, and England — and the US — had fleets of passenger liners that offered week-plus trips across the North Atlantic. Only one ship (*Cunard*'s *Queen Elizabeth 2*) continues to offer this kind of service between the US and Europe with any degree of regularity; others make "positioning" cruises a few times a year at most. At the same time, the possibility of booking passage to Europe on a cargo ship is becoming less practical. Fewer and fewer travelers, therefore, set foot on Spanish or Portuguese soil with sea legs developed during an ocean voyage.

Although fewer travelers to Europe are choosing sea travel as the means of transport to their original specific destination, more and more people are cruising *around* Europe. No longer primarily pure transportation, ocean cruising currently is riding a wave of popularity as a leisure activity in its own right, and the host of new ships (and dozens of rebuilt old ones) testifies dramatically to the attraction of vacationing on the high seas. And due to the growing popularity of travel along coastal and inland waterways, more and more travelers — particularly repeat travelers — are climbing aboard some kind of waterborne conveyance once they've arrived in Europe, and see Spanish or Portuguese ports while cruising around the Mediterranean or take a ferry to one of the Spanish or Portuguese islands.

The only thing that's lacking from the cruising scene today is much of that old elegance — ships like *Cunard*'s *Sea Goddess I* and *Sea Goddess II* and *Sea Bourn Cruise Line*'s *Sea Bourn Pride* and *Sea Bourn Spirit* are notable exceptions — though most modern-day passengers don't seem to notice. Cruise ships seem much more like motels-at-sea than the classic liners of a couple of generations ago, but they are consistently comfortable and passengers often are pampered. Prices are reasonable, and cruises focusing on European ports generally last around 2 weeks. What's more, since the single cruise price covers all the major items in a typical vacation — transportation, accommodations, all meals, entertainment, a full range of social activities, and sports and recreation — a traveler need not fear any unexpected assaults on the family travel budget.

When selecting a cruise, your basic criteria should be where you want to go, the time you have available, how much you want to spend, and the kind of environment that best suits your style and taste (in which case price is an important determinant). Rely on the suggestions of a travel agent — preferably one specializing in cruises (see "A final note on picking a cruise," below) — but be honest with the agent (and with yourself) in describing the type of atmosphere you're seeking. Ask for suggestions from friends who have been on cruises; if you trust their judgment, they should be able to suggest a ship on which you'll feel comfortable.

There are a number of moments in the cruise-planning process when discounts are available from the major cruise lines, so it may be possible to enjoy some diminution of the list price almost anytime you book passage on a cruise ship. For those willing to commit early — say 4 to 6 months before sailing — most of the major cruise lines routinely offer a 10% reduction off posted prices, in addition to the widest selection of cabins from which to choose. For those who decide to sail rather late in the game — say, 4 to 6 weeks before departure — savings often are even greater — an average of 20% — as steamship lines try to fill up their ships. The only negative aspect is that the range of cabin choice tends to be limited, although it is possible that a fare upgrade will be offered to make this limited cabin selection more palatable. In addition, there's the option of buying from a discount travel club or a travel agency that specializes in last-minute bargains; these discounters and other discount travel sources are discussed at the end of *Traveling by Plane,* above.

Most of the time, the inclusion of air transportation in the cruise package costs significantly less than if you were to buy the cruise separately and arrange your own air transportation to the port. If you do decide on one of these economical air/sea packages, be forewarned that it is not unusual for the prearranged flight arrangements to be less than convenient. The problems often arrive with the receipt of your cruise ticket, which also includes the airline ticket for the flight to get you to and from the ship dock. This is normally the first time you see the flights on which you have been booked and can appraise the convenience of the departure and arrival times. The cruise ship lines generally are not very forthcoming about altering flight schedules, and your own travel agent also may have difficulty in rearranging flight times or carriers. That means that the only remaining alternative is to ask the line to forget about making your flight arrangements and to pay for them separately by yourself. This may be more costly, but it's more likely to give you an arrival and departure schedule that will best conform to the sailing and docking times of the ship on which you will be cruising.

Prospective cruise ship passengers will find that the variety of cruises is tremendous, and the quality, while generally high, varies depending on shipboard services, the tone of shipboard life, the cost of the cruise, and operative itineraries. Although there are less expensive ways to see Europe, the romance of a sea voyage remains irresistible for many, so a few points should be considered by such sojourners before they sign on for a seagoing vacation (after all, it's hard to get off in mid-ocean). Herewith, a rundown on what to expect from a cruise, a few suggestions on what to look for and arrange when purchasing passage on one, and some representative prices for different sailings.

CABINS: The most important factor in determining the price of a cruise is the cabin. Cabin prices are set according to size and location. The size can vary considerably on older ships, less so on newer or more recently modernized ones, and may be entirely uniform on the very newest vessels.

Shipboard accommodations have the same pricing pattern as hotels. Suites, which consist of a sitting room–bedroom combination and occasionally a private small deck that could be compared to a patio, cost the most. Prices for other cabins (interchangeably called staterooms) usually are more expensive on the upper passenger decks, less expensive on lower decks; if a cabin has a bathtub instead of a shower, the price probably will be higher. The outside cabins with portholes cost more than inside cabins without views and generally are preferred — although many experienced cruise passengers eschew more expensive accommodations for they know they will spend very few waking hours in their cabins. As in all forms of travel, accommodations are more expensive for single travelers. If you are traveling on your own but want to share a double cabin to reduce the cost, some ship lines will attempt to find someone of the same sex willing to share quarters (see *Hints for Single Travelers,* in this section).

FACILITIES AND ACTIVITIES: You may not use your cabin very much. Organized shipboard activities are geared to keep you busy. A standard schedule might consist of swimming, sunbathing, and numerous other outdoor recreations. Evenings are devoted to leisurely dining, lounge shows or movies, bingo and other organized games, gambling, dancing, and a midnight buffet. Your cruise fare includes all of these activities — except the cost of drinks.

All cruise ships have at least one major social lounge, a main dining room, several bars, an entertainment room that may double as a discotheque for late dancing, an exercise room, indoor games facilities, at least one pool, and shopping facilities, which can range from a single boutique to an arcade. Still others have gambling casinos and/or slot machines, card rooms, libraries, children's recreation centers, indoor pools (as well as one or more on open decks), separate movie theaters, and private meeting rooms. Open deck space should be ample, because this is where most passengers spend their days at sea.

Usually there is a social director and staff to organize and coordinate activities. Evening entertainment is provided by professionals. Movies are mostly first-run and drinks are moderate in price (or should be) because a ship is exempt from local taxes when at sea.

To prepare for possible illnesses, travelers should get a prescription from their doctor for pills, patches, or stomach pacifiers to counteract motion sickness. All ships with more than 12 passengers have a doctor on board, plus facilities for handling sickness or medical emergencies.

Shore Excursions – These side trips almost always are optional and available at extra cost. Before you leave, do a little basic research about the ports you'll be visiting and decide what sights will interest you. If several of the most compelling of these are some distance from the pier where your ship docks, chances are that paying for a shore excursion will be worth the money.

Shore excursions usually can be booked through your travel agent at the same time you make your cruise booking, but this is worthwhile only if you can get complete details on the nature of each excursion being offered. If you can't get these details, better opt to purchase your shore arrangements after you're on board. The fact is that your enthusiasm for an excursion may be higher once you are on board because you will have met other passengers with whom to share the excitement of "shore leave." And depending on your time in port, you may decide to forget about the guided tour and venture out on your own.

Meals – All meals on board almost always are included in the basic price of a cruise, and the food generally is abundant and quite palatable. Evening meals are taken in the main dining room, where tables are assigned according to the passengers' preferences. Tables usually accommodate from 2 to 10; specify your preference when you book your cruise. If there are two sittings, you also can specify which one you want at the time you book or, at the latest, when you board the ship. Later sittings usually are more leisurely. Breakfast frequently is available in your cabin, as well as in the main dining room. For lunch, many passengers prefer the buffet offered on deck, usually at or near the pool, but again, the main dining room is available.

DRESS: Most people pack too much for a cruise on the assumption that daytime wear should be chic and every night is a big event. Comfort is a more realistic criterion.

Daytime wear on most ships is decidedly casual. For warm-weather cruises, women can wear a cover-up over a bathing suit through breakfast, swimming, sunbathing, and deck activities, lunch, and early cocktails without a change; for men, shorts (with swim trunks underneath) and a casual shirt will be appropriate on deck or in any public room. (Bare feet and swimsuits usually are inappropriate in the dining room.) For travel in cooler seasons, casual, comfortable clothes, including a variety of layers to adjust for changes in the weather, are appropriate for all daytime activities. Also bring along a comfortable pair of rubber-sole, low-heel shoes or sneakers, as sloping gangways and wet decks can be slippery.

Evening wear for most cruises is dressy-casual. Formal wear probably is not necessary for 1-week cruises, optional on longer ones. There aren't many nights when it's expected. Most ships have a captain's cocktail party the first or second night out and a farewell dinner near the end of the cruise. Women should feel comfortable in hostess gowns, cocktail dresses, or stylish slacks. (To feel completely secure, you may want to pack one very dressy item.) Jackets and ties always are preferred for men in the evening, but a long-sleeve, open-neck shirt with ascot or scarf usually is an acceptable substitute. (For further information on choosing and packing a basic wardrobe, see *How to Pack,* in this section.)

TIPS: Tips are a strictly personal expense, and you *are* expected to tip — in particular, your cabin and dining room stewards. The general rule of thumb (or palm) is to expect to pay from 10% to 20% of your total cruise budget for gratuities — the actual amount within this range is based on the length of the cruise and the extent of personalized service provided. Allow $2 to $5 a day for each cabin and dining room steward (more if you wish), and additional sums for very good service. (*Note:* Tips should be paid by and for each individual in a cabin, whether there are one, two, or more.) Others who may merit tips are the deck steward who sets up your chair at the pool or elsewhere, the wine steward in the dining room, porters who handle your luggage (tip them individually at the time they assist you), and any others who provide personal service. On some ships you can charge your bar tab to your cabin; throw in the tip when you pay it at the end of the cruise. Smart travelers tip twice during the trip: about midway through the cruise and at the end; even wiser travelers tip a bit at the start of the trip to ensure better service throughout.

Although some cruise lines do have a no-tipping policy and you are not penalized by the crew for not tipping, naturally, you aren't penalized for tipping, either. If you can restrain yourself, it is better not to tip on those few ships that discourage it. However, never make the mistake of not tipping on the majority of ships, where it is a common, expected practice. (For further information on calculating gratuities, see *Tipping,* in this section.)

SHIP SANITATION: The US Public Health Service (PHS) currently inspects all passenger vessels calling at US ports, so very precise information is available on which ships meet its requirements and which do not. The further requirement that ships immediately report any illness that occurs on board adds to the available data.

The problem for a prospective cruise passenger is to determine whether the ship on which he or she plans to sail has met the official sanitary standard. US regulations require the PHS to publish actual grades for the ships inspected (rather than the old pass or fail designation), so it's now easy to determine any cruise ship's status. Nearly 4,000 travel agents, public health organizations, and doctors receive a copy of each monthly ship sanitation summary, but be aware that not all agents fully understand what this ship inspection program is all about. Again, the best advice is to deal with a travel agent who specializes in cruise ships and cruise bookings, for he or she is most likely to have the latest information on the sanitary conditions of all cruise ships (see "A final note on picking a cruise," below). To receive a copy of the most recent summary or a particular inspection report, contact Chief, Vessel Sanitation Program, Public Health Service, 1015 N. America Way, Room 107, Miami, FL 33132 (phone: 305-536-4307).

TRANSATLANTIC CROSSINGS: For seagoing enthusiasts, *Cunard's Queen Elizabeth 2* is one of the largest and most comfortable vessels afloat, having undergone a complete overhaul and refurbishing, from a replacement of its engines to a redecoration of passenger quarters. Each year, in addition to a full calendar of Caribbean and European cruises, plus a round-the-world cruise, the *QE2* schedules approximately a dozen round-trip transatlantic crossings between June and, usually, December.

The *QE2* normally sets its course from New York to Southampton, England (a 5-day trip), and then sails directly back to the US, although on a few of the crossings it proceeds from Southampton to Cherbourg, France, or to other European ports before turning back across the Atlantic. (Similarly, on some crossings, the ship calls at various East Coast US ports in addition to New York, thus giving passengers a choice of where to embark or disembark.)

For instance, this year the *QE2* will make a Mediterranean cruise that includes Spanish ports — Barcelona, Málaga, and Palma de Mallorca — before returning to Southampton and then continuing on its usual return trip. If this itinerary is not offered at the time you plan to travel, *British Airways* offers travelers the option of paying a supplement for an intra-European flight from Southampton or Cherbourg to Spain or Portugal; contact *British Airways* for details.

For those sailing to Europe on the *QE2* and flying home, another option for travel to Spain and Portugal is based on the validity period of the return ticket. Following the transatlantic crossing, passengers have a specified time — up to 35 days for first class passengers and 20 days for the less expensive fares — during which they can take a trip to Spain and Portugal via a separate round-trip ticket on *British Airways* from London to one of the following cities: Barcelona, Bilbao, Madrid, and Málaga in Spain; Faro, Lisbon, and Porto in Portugal. The intra-European round-trip fare is subject to the availability of discounts, and the traveler must return to London in time to leave for home within the 20 or 35 days specified.

Transatlantic crossings, however, do not come at bargain prices. Last year, the one-way, per-person cost of passage from New York to either Southampton or Cherbourg ranged from around $1,400 (for the least expensive, two-per-cabin, transatlantic class accommodations at the end of the season) to $8,925 (for one of the grandest travel experiences imaginable). *Cunard* brings a voyage aboard a luxury liner within reach of the less affluent traveler, however, by offering an air/sea package in conjunction with *British Airways.* The one-way ticket to Europe by sea includes an allowance toward return economy class airfare from London to any of 57 North American cities — a free flight home, in essence — provided certain length-of-stay restrictions are respected. The allowance can be applied to an upgraded air ticket if desired, and, if you want to splurge, you can even fly home on a specially reserved *British Airways'* supersonic *Concorde,* provided you make up the difference between the allowance and the *Concorde* fare (the shortfall at press time was $995).

Cunard now also is offering a particularly economical round-trip air/sea option for travelers with a flexible schedule. Special "standby" fares are available on some transatlantic crossings between the US and London (20 sailings were offered between April and December 1990) and include airfare on *British Airways* to a number of US gateways. The package cost (at press time, $1,195 to $1,950 — depending on dates of travel) includes a berth in a double-occupancy "minimum" room on the *QE2* and a one-way *British Airways* economy class ticket to or from London and Boston, Chicago, Detroit, Miami, New York, Philadelphia, or Washington, DC. For an additional $100 supplement charge, passengers may fly to or from other *British Airways* US gateways, including Anchorage, Atlanta, Houston, Los Angeles, Pittsburgh, San Diego, San Francisco, and Seattle. Although this fare is offered strictly on a space-available basis, confirmations are provided 3 weeks before sailing. To qualify for this fare, travelers must submit a written application and a $100 deposit to a travel agent or *Cunard;* full payment is due upon confirmation. For information, check with your travel agent or contact *Cunard,* 555 Fifth Ave., New York, NY 10017 (phone: 800-221-4770 or 800-5-CU-NARD).

Another interesting possibility for those who have the time is what the industry calls a *positioning cruise.* This is the sailing of a US- or Caribbean-based vessel from its winter berth to the city in Europe from which it will be offering summer cruise programs. Eastbound positioning cruises take place in the spring; westbound cruises return in the fall. Since ships do not make the return trip until they need to position themselves for the next cruise season, most lines offering positioning cruises have some air/sea arrangement that allows passengers to fly home economically — though the cruises themselves are not an inexpensive way to travel.

Among the ships that have been offering positioning cruises for a number of years are *Cunard*'s *Vistafjord* and ships of the *Royal Viking Line* and *Royal Cruise Line*. Itineraries and ports of call vary from year to year. Typically, the ships set sail from Florida or San Juan, Puerto Rico, and cross the Atlantic to any one of a number of European ports where the trip may be broken — including Barcelona, Lisbon, and Málaga — before proceeding to cruise European waters (for example, the Mediterranean, the Baltic Sea, the Black Sea, the Norwegian fjords). Passengers can elect to stay aboard for the basic transatlantic segment alone or for both the crossing and the subsequent European cruise. For information, ask your travel agent or contact the cruise lines directly (see below).

This year, *Cunard*'s Europe-based *Princess* will be making a positioning cruise from Ft. Lauderdale to Málaga. Four different air/sea packages are available for the European cruise portion, starting at $2,295 per person, including round-trip airfare from numerous gateways in the US and Canada. Upon arrival in Europe, passengers have the option to continue on additional sailings. Among the itineraries offered is a 10-day Canary Island sailing, including as many as nine ports of call. The trip begins in Málaga, Spain, and sails on to Morocco before heading south to the Canaries. *Cunard* also offers land-vacation extensions to this cruise in Spain. Travelers wishing to extend their Canary Island cruise, before or after they sail, can opt for a 2-night land package in Málaga, with excursions to Granada or Ronda; rates for this side trip begin at $465 per person. In addition, *Cunard*'s luxurious *Sea Goddess I* also makes a positioning cruise from St. Thomas in the Caribbean to Málaga in April, returning to St. Thomas in October. The transatlantic fare to Málaga starts at $4,400 and the return fare starts at $3,300 per person. (For more information on *Sea Goddess I* cruises, see "Mediterranean Cruises," below.)

This year, the *Royal Viking Sun*'s eastbound positioning cruise is a 12-day crossing from Ft. Lauderdale to Lisbon. The price of the cruise, ranging from $3,695 per person in a double cabin to $19,415 for an upper-deck suite, includes the cost of a 2-night pre- or post-cruise land package in either Ft. Lauderdale or Lisbon, as well as free return by air to eastern (but not central or western) US cities. After arriving in Lisbon, the ship proceeds on a 12-day Mediterranean cruise that can be tacked onto the transatlantic cruise. The *Royal Viking Sea* will be making a 20-day westbound crossing from Rome to Ft. Lauderdale, via Barcelona and Gibraltar; fares range from $5,370 to $16,970 per person double, including land package and airfare. For information, contact *Royal Viking Line,* 95 Merrick, Coral Gables, FL 33134 (phone: 305-447-9660 in Miami; 800-634-8000 elsewhere in the US).

Royal Cruise Line offers a 19-day transatlantic positioning cruise aboard the *Golden Odyssey* from San Juan, Puerto Rico, to Venice — travelers to Spain and Portugal can disembark at Málaga or Lisbon; prices range from $6,198 to $11,238. This year, *Royal Cruise Line*'s *Crown Odyssey* also will make a 20-day trip from Buenos Aires to Lisbon, calling at Cádiz, Spain. The cost of the cruise ranges from $6,724 to $16,854. For information, contact *Royal Cruise Line,* One Maritime Plaza, Suite 1400, San Francisco, CA 94111 (phone: 800-792-2992 or 415-956-7200 in California; 800-227-0925 or 800-227-4534 elsewhere in the US).

Sea Bourn Cruise Line's *Sea Bourn Pride* makes an 11-day transatlantic positioning cruise from Ft. Lauderdale to Lisbon. Fares range from $5,050 to $7,250. The *Sea Bourn Spirit* goes on 12-day positioning cruises from Ft. Lauderdale to Bordeaux — passengers can disembark in the Portuguese Azores, or opt to continue on any of several subsequent Mediterranean cruises that depart from Lisbon. Although you can call *Sea Bourn Cruise Lines* at 800-351-9595 for a brochure, for additional information and reservations you must contact a travel agent.

Sun Line's Stella Solaris will be making a 12-day positioning cruise between Ft. Lauderdale and Piraeus, Greece, this spring. Ports of call include Lisbon, Portugal, and Minorca, Spain, as well as ports in France and Italy. One-way fares begin at $2,235 to $4,233, and include return airfare from Piraeus to New York. For information, contact *Sun Lines,* 1 Rockefeller Plaza, Suite 315, New York, NY 10020 (phone: 800-445-6400 or 212-397-6400).

MEDITERRANEAN CRUISES: The Mediterranean Sea is one of the world's most popular and picturesque cruising grounds, busy with ships offering sailings of varying lengths from spring through fall. The Atlantic Ocean southwest of the Iberian Peninsula, where it laps the Canary Islands of Spain and Portugal's Madeira Islands, attracts almost as much pleasure-seeking cruise traffic. Thus, it's not difficult to find a cruise ship calling at Lisbon, Barcelona, Málaga, Las Palmas on Gran Canaria, Funchal, or some other Spanish or Portuguese port. Less easy to find is a cruise devoting its time exclusively to Spanish or Portuguese territory. Many Mediterranean cruises may begin in an Iberian port, such as Lisbon, but end elsewhere — Genoa or Venice or even farther afield. (The reverse itinerary also is common.) And many Canary Islands cruises call at a number of Moroccan ports or, even when cruising the islands alone, sail from and to a home base as far away as Southampton.

Among the cruises especially oriented to Spain and Portugal and their islands this year are several 6- and 7-day cruises aboard *Cunard's Sea Goddess I,* a yacht-like vessel (350 feet) less than half the size of the average cruise ship (it carries only 116 passengers). Its shallow draft allows it to visit Spanish island villages, with access to little-known beaches, as well as even more exotic ports of call. The *Sea Goddess I's* equally luxurious and exclusive sister ship, the *Sea Goddess II,* also offers cruises taking in Iberian ports. One 5-day Iberia/Morocco itinerary, beginning in Málaga, calls at Puerto Banus, Casablanca, and Funchal; fares start at $3,400 per person. Another itinerary offered this year is a 7-day Riviera cruise departing from Monte Carlo which includes Ibiza, Spain, as well as several other French ports of call. (For other Iberian cruises offered by *Cunard,* see above.)

Royal Cruise Line's Crown Odyssey offers several Mediterranean itineraries that feature calls in Spain and/or Portugal. The 12-day "Great Capitals of Europe" cruise starts in Venice and ending in London, and ports of call this year include Barcelona, Lisbon, and Porto, as well as major ports in France, Italy, and Yugoslavia. The smaller *Golden Odyssey* includes Iberian ports on a 12-day cruise departing from Lisbon and stopping in Málaga, Spain, as well as ports in France, Greece, and Italy. Fares for both cruises rane from $3,898 to $11,238. The *Golden Odyssey* also offers a "Magnificent Odyssey" cruise, a 21-day cruise calling at Santa Cruz de Tenerife, Funchal, Gibraltar, Palma de Mallora, and Barcelona. At the time of this writing, fares for the whole cruise ranged from $6,418 to $16,098. Other itineraries include "Mediterranean Highlights" and "Gala Mediterranean" cruises. For information, contact *Royal Cruise Line,* One Maritime Plaza, Suite 1400, San Francisco, CA 94111 (phone: 800-792-2992 or 415-956-7200 in California; 800-227-0925 or 800-227-4534 elsewhere in the US).

Another line, *Paquet French Cruises,* spotlights cuisine and wine on its European cruises. From Le Havre, France, the *Mermoz* makes a 10-day cruise taking in Barcelona and Cádiz in Spain, and Lisbon and Porto in Portugal. A visit to Casablanca in Morocco also is included. Besides shore excursions visiting wine cellars in the port and sherry regions, there may be lectures, wine tastings, and wine-related contests aboard ship. For information, contact *Paquet French Cruises* (1510 SE 17th St., Ft. Lauderdale, FL 33316; phone: 800-556-8850 or 800-999-0555).

Another Mediterranean cruise departing from Portugal is a *Royal Viking* 13-day sailing between Lisbon and Rome aboard the *Royal Viking Sun;* fares range from $3,850 to $12,430. Ports of call include Barcelona and Cádiz in Spain, as well as stops in France and Italy. For information, contact *Royal Viking Line,* 95 Merrick, Coral

Gables, FL 33134 (phone: 305-447-9660 in Miami; 800-634-8000 elsewhere in the US).

And for those who want to add a Mediterranean cruise onto the end of their visit to Spain, *Princess Cruises* offers a 13-day cruise aboard either the *Royal Princess* or the *Crown Princess* between Barcelona and Venice. Fares range from $3,640 to $9,190. The *Royal Princess* also makes a 13-day cruise from Barcelona to London, stopping in Lisbon and Vigo en route. For information, contact *Princess Cruises,* 10100 Santa Monica Blvd., Los Angeles, CA 90067 (phone: 800-421-0522).

Commodore Cruise Line's *Eurosun* makes 7-day cruises around Spain's Canary Islands. Departing from Las Palmas, the cruise also visits Morocco. A post-cruise 2-night stay in Barcelona or Seville is included in the package price, which ranges from $1,940 to $2,415. For information, contact *Comtours,* 30311 Clemens Rd., Cleveland, OH 44145 (phone: 800-248-1331 or 216-835-1480).

Other lines whose ships will be visiting ports in Spain, Portugal, or their islands this year are *Canberra Cruises* (c/o *Express Travel Services,* Empire State Building, Suite 7718, 350 Fifth Ave., New York, NY 10118; phone: 212-629-3630 in New York State; 800-223-5799 elsewhere in the US), with several cruises that include Spain and/or Portugal in their itineraries; and *Costa Cruises* (PO Box 019614, Miami, FL 33101-9865; phone: 305-358-7330), which offers several cruises that include ports of call in Spain and Portugal and their islands.

In addition, the *International Cruise Center* (250 Old Country Rd., Mineola, NY 11501; phone: 516-747-8880 in New York State; 800-221-3254 elsewhere in the US), general sales agent for several European lines, offers Canary Islands cruises (to and from Tilbury, England); per-person round-trip fares range from $1,679 to $3,565 during the off-season. (It also runs a ferry twice a week from Plymouth, England, to Santander, in northern Spain; fares range from about $232 to $248 for passage, plus $90 to $150 for a cabin.)

For this and other offerings, book well in advance in order to qualify for substantial "early bird" discounts. For further information, ask your travel agent or contact the cruise lines mentioned above directly.

FREIGHTERS: An alternative to conventional cruise ships is travel by freighter. These are cargo ships that also take a limited number of passengers (usually about 12) in reasonably comfortable accommodations. The idea of traveling by freighter has long appealed to romantic souls, but there are a number of drawbacks to keep in mind before casting off. Once upon a time, a major advantage of freighter travel was its low cost, but this is no longer the case. Though freighters usually are less expensive than cruise ships, the difference is not as great as it once was, and excursion airfares certainly are even less expensive. Accommodations and recreational facilities vary, but freighters were not designed to amuse passengers, so it is important to appreciate the idea of freighter travel itself. Schedules are erratic, and the traveler must fit his or her timetable to that of the ship. Passengers have found themselves waiting as long as a month for a promised sailing, and because freighters follow their cargo commitments, it is possible that a scheduled port could be omitted at the last minute or a new one added.

Anyone contemplating taking a freighter from a US port across the Atlantic should be aware that at press time, only one freighter line carried passengers on regular sailings to Spanish or Portuguese ports. Freighters of the *Yugoslav Great Lakes Line* sail monthly from Montreal, carrying 7 to 9 passengers to Lisbon, Portugal, and Valencia, Spain, as well as to ports in Italy and Yugoslavia. The complete itinerary takes from 35 to 40 days; prices to Spain or Portugal range from $2,900 to $3,400. For information, contact the line's general sales agent, *Freighter World Cruises* (address below).

Specialists dealing only (or largely) in freighter travel can help to arrange trips. They provide information, schedules, and, when you're ready to sail, booking services. Among these agencies are the following:

Freighter World Cruises: A freighter travel agency that acts as general agent for several freighter lines. Publishes the twice-monthly *Freighter Space Advisory,* listing space available on sailings worldwide. A subscription costs $27 a year, $25 of which can be credited toward the cost of a cruise. 180 S. Lake Ave., Suite 335, Pasadena, CA 91101 (phone: 818-449-3106).

Pearl's Travel Tips: Run by Ilse Hoffman, who finds sailings for her customers and sends them off with all kinds of invaluable information and advice. 333 E. 79th St., Penthouse S., New York, NY 10021 (phone: 212-734-6327).

TravLTips Cruise and Freighter Travel Association: A freighter travel agency and club ($15 a year or $25 for 2 years) whose members receive the bimonthly *TravLTips* magazine of cruise and freighter travel. PO Box 188, Flushing, NY 11358 (phone: 718-939-2400 in New York; 800-872-8584 elsewhere in the US).

■ **A final note on picking a cruise:** A "cruise-only" travel agency can best help you choose a cruise ship and itinerary. Cruise-only agents also are best equipped to tell you about a particular ship's "personality," the kind of person with whom you'll likely be traveling on a particular ship, what dress is acceptable (it varies from ship to ship), and much more. Travel agencies that specialize in booking cruises usually are members of the *National Association of Cruise Only Agencies (NACOA).* For a listing of the agencies in your area (requests are limited to three states), send a self-addressed, stamped envelope to *NACOA,* PO Box 7209, Freeport, NY 11520, or call 516-378-8006.

FERRIES: Numerous ferries link the Spanish mainland with the Balearic and Canary Islands and with Morocco. Nearly all of them carry both passengers and cars, and nearly all of the routes are in service year-round. Some operators may offer reduced rates for round-trip excursions, midweek travel, or off-season travel. While the trip across the Strait of Gibraltar is relatively brief, trips to the islands tend to be long, so a good many of the ferries travel overnight. Cabins as well as space for cars should be booked as early as possible, especially for crossings from June through September, when the boats can be crowded despite their greater frequency.

Spain's major steamship company, *Trasmediterránea,* services most of the routes, operating in conjunction with other companies on some of them. Its ferries to the Balearics operate from Barcelona and Valencia to Palma de Mallorca, Ibiza, and Mahón, Minorca, and also from Cádiz and Málaga to Palma. In addition, hydrofoil service recently has been added between Altea on the Costa Blanca and Ibiza and Formentera. Ferries to the Canary Islands operate from Cádiz or Málaga (via Cádiz) to Tenerife, Las Palmas, and Morocco. The trip from Cádiz to Tenerife takes a full day and a half and means spending 2 nights at sea, since it departs at 2 PM on Thursdays and Saturdays in summer (Saturdays only the rest of the year), and arrives at 8 AM on Saturdays and Mondays. A trip direct from Cádiz to Las Palmas (not offered during the off-season) is only an hour shorter.

The same company provides most of the inter-island ferry transportation in the Canaries, serving Puerto Rosario on the island of Fuerteventura, Valverde on El Hierro, Santa Cruz de la Palma on the island of La Palma, and La Gomera, besides Las Palmas on Grand Canary, Tenerife, and Arrecife on Lanzarote. The company also runs a year-round, passengers-only hydrofoil service between Las Palmas on Grand Canary and Santa Cruz de Tenerife on Tenerife. Inter-island service in the Balearics is between Palma de Mallorca and Ibiza and between Palma and Mahón. *Trasmediterránea* also provides a *Hydrojet* service from Palma to Ibeza and back; travel time is about 2 hours. The ferry departs twice daily from Palma, at 9 AM and 4 PM, and Ibiza at noon and 7 PM.

Trasmediterránea also is the major ferry operator to Morocco, connecting Algeciras with Tangier, Morocco (2½ hours), and with the Spanish enclave of Ceuta (1½ hours), farther east along the Moroccan coast; Almería and Málaga with Melilla, another Spanish outpost in Morocco; and Tarifa with Tangier.

For schedule and fare information, reservations, and tickets, contact your travel agent or *Trasmediterránea* (2 Calle P. Muñoz Seca, Madrid 28011; phone: 1-431-0700; or 2 Via Laietana, Barcelona 08003; phone: 3-319-8212). Reservations can be made for individual seats, 2- to 4-person cabins (singles are placed in double cabins for only a bit less than the double-occupancy price), and car space. Book at least 6 weeks before your projected trip, and much earlier if possible, although how far in advance reservations are accepted depends on the route and ferry in question.

Other, smaller ferry lines can be found plying the seas from mainland Spain to and among the islands and to Morocco. The National Tourist Office of Spain can provide information on some of them, although they generally do not have US representatives. One to be aware of is *Flebasa,* which operates from approximately mid-March through mid-November from the resort town of Denia, in the province of Alicante, and from Valencia to San Antonio Abad on Ibiza. Travel time is only 3 hours. The company also provides bus transportation from Alicante or Valencia to Denia at no extra charge.

Note that no ferries go from Portugal to the Madeiras, a frequent stop for cruise ships, or to the Azores.

Traveling by Train

 Perhaps the most economical, and often the most pleasant, way to see a lot of a foreign country in a relatively short time is by rail. It certainly is the quickest way to travel between two cities up to 300 miles apart (beyond that, a flight normally would be quicker, even counting the time it takes to get to and from the airport). But time isn't always the only consideration. Traveling by train is a way to keep moving and to keep seeing at the same time, and with the special discounts available to visitors, it can be an almost irresistible bargain. You only need to get to a station on time; after that, put your watch in your pocket and relax. You may not get to your destination exactly at the appointed hour, but you'll have a marvelous time looking out the window and enjoying the ride.

TRAINS AND FARES: While North Americans have been raised to depend on their cars, Europeans long have been able to rely on public transportation. As in other countries on the Continent, Spain and Portugal have relatively extensive railway systems; however, the track in both countries is broad gauge, not the narrow gauge used elsewhere in Europe (due to British influence and construction in the early days). Travelers crossing the Spanish border generally must change to another train, except on specially equipped *Talgos* trains, which can adjust their wheel base automatically to the standard narrow gauge and, therefore, may operate beyond the border into France. (As we went to press, the trains that run only on narrow-gauge tracks were gradually being replaced with these convertible models, and international-gauge track was being laid to allow other European trains to extend service into Spain.) Portuguese trains both operate within their own country and cross over into Spain.

In Spain, the government-owned and -operated *Red Nacional de los Ferrocarriles Españoles (RENFE),* known to the English-speaking world as *Spanish National Railways,* operates an 8,000-mile railway system. Most main lines radiate from Madrid, at the center of the country, like spokes of a wheel, so travel between the capital and large provincial cities, or between two smaller cities on the same spoke, is fast and frequent. In the case of towns on different spokes, it is sometimes faster and easier to go from one to the other by taking the long way around — via Madrid.

Most Spanish cities and towns have one train station, with the exception of Madrid, which has three, and Barcelona, which has four. In Madrid, the stations are Chamartín (the main station), Principe Pío (Norte) — also sometimes called Estación del Norte by residents — and Atocha. In Barcelona, the train stations are Barcelona Central Sants (the main station), Barcelona Terme-França, Plaça de Catalunya, and Plaça d'Espanya.

Unlike in many other countries, Spanish railway tickets are not purchased in the train station but in sales offices (some of which *may* be in a station, but not necessarily). *RENFE* sales offices (see below for more details) usually are centrally located in towns and cities. There also are auxiliary sales offices throughout Spain; tickets can be purchased at these offices, but other services, such as travel information, maps, and the like, will be more limited than at the main sales offices. Electronic vending machines dispensing tickets are increasingly common, particularly at auxiliary sales offices.

Although the main sales office in Madrid is closed for renovation until this summer, there is a *RENFE* sales office at the Madrid airport (Aeropuerto de Barajas; phone: 1-205-8544) with convenient hours: 8 AM to 8 PM, except Sundays and holidays, when it is open from 8 AM to 2 PM. The main sales office in Barcelona is at the main train station, Estación Barcelona Central Sants (phone: 3-250-4235). For information on other main and auxiliary sales offices in Spain, as well as locations for purchasing tickets in the US, see "Further Information," below.

Portuguese Railways, or *CP (Compañhia dos Caminhos de Ferro Portugueses),* operates trains connecting most of the main cities and towns in the country. It operates 2,500 miles of track, 700 stations, and has express trains that can travel at speeds up to 90 miles per hour.

Lisbon has four train stations. Santa Apolónia, the main station, is the departure point for trains bound north and northeast and for international trains making connections into Spain (and onward into France). Terreiro do Paço station actually is the landing stage for ferries crossing the Tagus River to Barreiro, as well as the terminus for trains serving the Algarve and other points south and southeast. Electric commuter trains for Estoril-Cascais and for Sintra leave from Cais do Sodré and Rossio stations respectively; other trains traveling up the western coast of Portugal to Figueira da Foz and Coimbra also leave from Rossio.

Porto, the second-largest city in Portugal, has two main stations: São Bento, in the center of town, and Campañha. Six express trains connecting Lisbon and Porto operate daily. One train, making only one stop, arrives at its destination in only 3 hours. Others make several stops and take 1 to 2 hours longer. Schedules are available at the train stations or through the Portuguese National Tourist Office. As in the US, tickets are bought at train stations throughout Portugal.

Some of the special trains you may encounter in Spain and elsewhere in Europe (excluding Portugal) include the *EuroCity (EC)* trains, which have ushered in a new phase of European train service. Introduced in May 1987, the *EC* network has by now all but replaced the *Trans-Europe Express (TEE)* trains, which provided the European Economic Community with fast, efficient, and luxurious train service between major cities since the 1950s. *EC*s currently are the prestige trains of Europe and maintain high standards. They use modern, air conditioned coaches, are punctual and clean, and travel at a minimum speed of 54 miles per hour (the average includes time for station stops). All *EC* trains also have dining facilities and bilingual personnel on board. Both first and second class service is offered, and supplements must be paid for all departures. The supplement includes the price of a reserved seat, which is obligatory on any *EC* border crossing but not on trips within one country. The *EC* network includes 200 connections within the 12 participating countries, including Spain.

If there are no *EC*s on a route, the next best trains are likely to be *InterCity (IC)* trains, which are similar to *EC*s in that they provide a high standard of service, have both first and second class cars, and generally require payment of a supplement. There are both national and international *IC* trains. Some, in fact, are former *TEE*s to which second class cars have been added in recent years to help curb high operating costs, a problem aggravated by low ridership. A great many more *IC*s already existed as part of the local rail network. Supplements must be paid to ride most continental *IC* trains, while reservations are obligatory only on those crossing borders. Another train of the same high quality is the *Trans-Europe Night (TEN)*, an overnight train with sleeping quarters. And joining other European countries in the addition of high-speed rail service, the *Spanish National Railways'* will be offering a speedy new service — called *Alta Velocidad Español (AVE)* — between Seville and Madrid — which will run at 186 mph (298 kph) and is scheduled to begin service late this year. Future plans include the addition of high-speed lines between Madrid, Barcelona, and the French border, between Madrid and Lisbon, and northwest connections to the French border at Irún.

These special trains are but a small part of Europe's highly developed rail service. International trains enter Spain from France at Perpignan-Figueres and Biarritz–San Sebastián. Express service from Paris to Madrid or Barcelona leaves every evening, arriving in the morning. The best of these trains are the *Talgos* (similar to the Europe-wide *EC*s) and *Electrotren* (similar to *IC*s elsewhere in Europe). These generally have first and second class cars and meal service. Those that make overnight trips also offer various sleeping facilities, which must be reserved well in advance during peak travel periods.

Hundreds of towns across Spain and Portugal are served by "regular" express and local trains. For travel within Spain, again the finest trains are the *Talgos, Electrotren,* and "expresos" (overnight trains with couchettes), which are somewhat slower. *Motorail* service connects Madrid with most major cities. Automobiles also can be transported by train between Madrid and many provincial cities (see "Auto-Expreso," below). Eurailpasses are accepted for travel in Spain, though advance seat reservations are necessary.

Portugal also is part of the Eurorail System, and daily service from London via Paris goes to Irún/Hendaye. Passengers for Porto must change trains at Pampilhosa. Paris to Lisbon takes 25 hours; Paris to Porto, an hour less. The trip from Paris to Porto is second class only, although sleepers and a mini-bar are available. The "Sud Express" between Paris and Lisbon has both first and second class carriages and dining and sleeping services in both classes.

In Portugal, the best trains are the *Rapidos.* These are comparable to the Europe-wide *IC*s, and offer a full range of services including lounges, restaurant cars, bars, diaper-changing facilities, and so on. More common are the *Inter-Regional (IR)* trains, which offer only basic amenities (only a few offer snacks and drinks) and make numerous local stops.

ACCOMMODATIONS, FARES, AND SERVICES: Fares on European trains are based on the quality of accommodations the passenger enjoys. You pay on the basis of traveling first class or second class, and on *EC, IC,* and other expresses such *Talgos* and *Electrotren* in Spain, first or second class, plus a supplement. Traditionally, seating is arranged in compartments, with three or four passengers on one side facing a like number on the other side, but increasingly, in the newer cars, compartments have been replaced by a central-aisle design.

Tickets can be purchased through travel agents or *FrenchRail Inc.* in the US and Canada (the North American representative of Spanish and Portuguese national railways), as well as at *RENFE* sales offices in Spain (see the end of this section for a list of some of the major offices) and train stations in Portugal. *RENFE* sales offices have both tickets and schedules, and the ticket agent will tell you the station from which your train leaves.

In Portugal, tickets, schedules, and departure information is available at train stations. In both Spain and Portugal, domestic and international tickets usually are sold separately. Be warned: In either country, ticket lines can be long. In order to save time, you may want to buy your rail tickets from *FrenchRail Inc.* offices before leaving the US — bookings require a minimum of 7 days for confirmation. Note that although *FrenchRail* sells tickets for both Spanish and Portuguese trains, they only will make overnight (couchettes or sleepers) reservations; all other reservations for both Spain and Portugal must be made on arrival.

Most of the international ticket and reservations systems are computerized and efficient. Fares vary from route to route, but short hauls always are more expensive per mile than longer runs. There is a $3 fee for European reservations made in the US (plus a $3 telex fee). Normally, reservations can be made up to 2 months prior to the travel date, and when making a reservation, you can ask for a window seat, as well as for a smoking or nonsmoking section. Reservations reduce flexibility, but they are advisable during the summer on popular routes. They also are advisable at any time of the year if it is imperative that you be on a particular train.

Spanish and Portuguese trains, like others in Europe, carry two basic kinds of sleeping quarters: "couchettes," the coach seats of a compartment converted to sleeping berths, and "wagon-lits," or sleepers, individual individual single or double bedrooms that compare favorably with the slumber coaches on transcontinental American trains. Second class couchettes have six berths per compartment (first class couchettes, which have four, are available only in France and Italy). The berth is narrow, with a pillow, blanket, and sheet provided. Single travelers generally — but not always — are booked into couchettes with others of the same sex; if it matters to you, make a specific request.

Couchettes cost a standard charge (around $15 per person if bought in the US) added to the basic first or second class fare. A private or semiprivate wagon-lit or sleeper is more expensive (anywhere from $30 and up, depending on your destination).

The wide range of dining facilities run the gamut from prix fixe menus served in dining cars or at your seat to self-service cafeteria-style cars and mobile vendors dispensing snacks, sandwiches, and beverages. In-seat and dining car lunch and dinner reservations either are made in advance or after boarding by visiting the dining car or through the train steward. If you're sure you will want to eat en route, it's a good idea to inquire beforehand exactly what meal service is offered on the train you'll be taking and whether advance dining reservations are required.

A standardized pictorial code has been designed to indicate the various amenities offered at many train stations. These may include showers, as well as restaurants, post and telegraph offices, exchange bureaus, and diaper changing facilities. In those cities that have two or more stations (see above), make sure you know the name of the station for your train.

Baggage often can be checked through to your destination or can be checked overnight at most stations. Some stations also provide 24-hour luggage lockers where you can temporarily free yourself of surplus bags, but these are becoming less common throughout Europe, as lockers are being eliminated due to bomb threats. It always is a good idea to travel as light as possible: Porters are in short supply at most stations, and self-service carts frequently are scarce as well.

Those planning driving routes should be aware that all European railways have some form of auto ferry — called *Auto-Expreso* in both Spain and Portugal. *Auto-Expreso* service is offered throughout Spain. In Portugal, this service is offered aboard all *Rapido* lines, and during the summer car-carrying service is available on additional routes. *Note:* The *Auto-Expreso* can be booked only in Europe, and it is quite popular with Europeans, especially during the peak summer months. Your best bet is to make reservations as soon as you get to Europe, the earlier the better.

RENFE's *Auto-Expreso* is available in three categories; the price is based on the length of the vehicle, the distance to be traveled, the route taken, and the number of passenger tickets purchased. Charges for trailers also are based on length, and motorcycles are transported at half the cost of mid-size cars. *Auto-Expreso* users can travel on a train other than the one transporting their car, which can be checked in and shipped up to 10 days before or 10 days after the travelers' rail trip, with the limitation that the starting point of car transport must be the same as that of the driver. Delivery and pickup of the vehicle usually is at the train stations, which have special areas for this purpose. Vehicles must be at the station 2 hours before the train departs, and delivery is made approximately 1 hour after arrival. Pickup and delivery of the vehicle can be arranged at other locations (such as your hotel) for an additional charge; this service must be requested at least 24 hours in advance. To take advantage of the reduced prices on "Blue Days" (see "Passes," below), the passenger's ticket and automobile ticket should be purchased at the same time. Fares also can be reduced if two or more successive routes or a round trip are made on Blue Days.

PASSES: Rail passes are offered by the Spanish, Portuguese, and most other European national railroad companies. They allow unlimited train travel within a set time period, frequently include connecting service via other forms of transportation, and they can save the traveler a considerable amount of money as well as time. The only requirement is the validation of the pass by an information clerk on the day of your first rail trip; thereafter, there is no need to stand in line — and lines can be very long during peak travel periods — to buy individual tickets for subsequent trips. Designed primarily for foreign visitors, these passes often must be bought in the US (or some other foreign location) prior to arrival in Europe. Although these passes can be among the best bargains around, be sure to look into the comparable cost of individual train tickets which — depending on the number of days you plan to travel — may work out to be less expensive.

The Eurailpass, the first and best known of all rail passes, is valid for travel through Spain and Portugal and 15 other countries — Austria, Belgium, Denmark, Finland, France, Germany, Greece, Holland, Hungary, Ireland, Italy, Luxembourg, Norway, Sweden, and Switzerland. It entitles holders to 15 or 21 days or 1, 2, or 3 months of unlimited first class travel, plus many extras, including some ferry crossings, river trips, lake steamers, and transportation by bus and private railroads, as well as scheduled *Europabus* services, and airport to city center rail connections. Since the Eurailpass is a first class pass, Eurail travelers can ride just about any European train they wish, including *EC*s, *IC*s, Spain's *Talgos,* and other special express trains, without paying additional supplements. The only extras are the nominal reservation fee and sleeper and couchette costs.

At the time of this writing, the prices for first class Eurailpasses were as follows: a 15-day pass cost $340; a 21-day pass cost $440; a 1-month pass cost $550; a 2-month pass cost $750; and a 3-month pass cost $930. A Eurailpass for children under 12 is half the adult price (children under 4 travel free) but includes the same features, whereas the Eurail Youthpass, for travelers under 26 years of age, is slightly different. The Youthpass is valid for travel in second class only. As we went to press, it was available in a 1-month version for $380 and a 2-month version for $500.

The Eurail Saverpass resembles the basic Eurailpass, except that it provides 15 days of unlimited first class travel for three people traveling together during peak season; two people traveling together qualify if travel takes place entirely between October 1 and March 31. Under these restrictions, each 15-day ticket costs $100 less than the 15-day Eurailpass.

Another option is the Eurail Flexipass, which can be used for first class travel on any 5 days within a 15-day period ($198), 9 days within a 21-day period ($360), or 14 days within a 30-day period ($458). All of these passes must be bought before you go, either from a travel agent or from the US offices of the French, German, Italian, or

Swiss railway companies. A Eurail Aid Office in Europe will replace lost passes when proper documentation is provided; a reissuance fee is charged.

Both the 7-day Eurailpass and the 9-day Eurail Flexipass can be combined with 3 to 8 days of car rental in both Spain and Portugal through *Hertz.* The program, marketed under the name *Hertz* EurailDrive Escape, starts at $229 per person (based on two people traveling together), and the car rental includes unlimited mileage, basic insurance, and taxes, as well as some drop-off options within most of the countries of rental. Reservations must be made in the US at least 7 days in advance by calling *Hertz* at 800-654-3001.

The Eurailpass is a bargain for those who are combining a visit to Spain and Portugal with sightseeing elsewhere on the Continent. But for those who will be traveling strictly within Spain and Portugal, these countries issue similar passes that allow unlimited travel for defined periods of time over the national transportation network, which are more economical for single-country travel.

RENFE offers a Tourist Pass (also called a Spanish Rail Pass), which is good for 8, 15, and 22 days, allowing unlimited trips within these time periods. At the time of this writing, the 8-day pass cost $125 for first class, $90 for second class; the 15-day pass cost $205 for first class, $145 for second class; the 22-day pass cost $240 for first class, $185 for second class. *Días Azules,* or Blue Days, are discount days for rail travel in Spain. There are presently 300 Blue Days a year, with up to 25% discounts on round-trip travel, 50% discounts for senior citizens and children age 7 to 14, as well as discounts on the *Auto Expreso* (see above). *RENFE* also offers a Spain Flexipass, which is valid for any 4 days in an 8-day period; as we went to press, the 4-day pass cost $99 for first class and $75 for economy class. As with the Eurailpass, these passes must be bought in the US.

Rail passes in Portugal include Tourist Tickets, which allow unlimited travel in any class and are good for 7, 14, and 21 days; as we went to press, prices were $76.50, $122, and $174.27, respectively. There also is a Family Ticket, which can be purchased for a minimum of three family members traveling a minimum of 150 kilometers (93 miles). One family member pays full fare (according to the type of train and the class) while other family members age 12 or older pay half fare, and children from 4 to 11 pay one-quarter fare. Children under 4 ride free in Portugal. To obtain the pass, you must provide passports and documentation indicating that the travelers sharing the pass are related.

TOURS: Special trains providing full-day or weekend sightseeing excursions for tourists are a very popular *RENFE* enterprise. In operation from May through October in most cases, these trains are an enjoyable way for travelers based in Madrid to visit several interesting Spanish towns. The *Tren Murallas de Avila* (Walls of Avila Train), for instance, leaves Madrid's Chamartín Station at 9:15 AM on Sundays and holidays bound for Avila, 70 miles northwest, where passengers take a guided motorcoach tour of the city, are left free for lunch and browsing, and then tour the walls before boarding the train back to Madrid for a 9:09 PM arrival. Other trains offering day trips are the *Doncel de Sigüenza* (Page of Sigüenza), which travels 80 miles northeast of Madrid to Sigüenza, a town in Guadalajara known for its cathedral, and the *Tren de la Fresa* (Strawberry Train), which follows the route once taken by the royal family to reach the country palace at Aranjuez, 30 miles south of Madrid in the midst of an area known for its strawberries.

Weekend trips (departing on Saturday mornings and returning Sunday evenings) range farther afield. The excursion aboard the *Ciudad Monumental de Cáceres* (Monumental City of Cáceres), visiting the Extremadura region, includes a stop at the Monastery of Guadalupe and a sightseeing tour of Trujillo and continues on to Cáceres for night sightseeing and an overnight stay, then a tour of the Carvajal Palace. (An alternate route takes in other towns of Extremadura, but both itineraries include a guided sightseeing tour of Cáceres.) The *Plaza Mayor de Salamanca*, named for the main square of the old university town that is its destination 125 miles northwest of Madrid, and the *Ciudad Encantada* (Enchanted City), which visits Cuenca, 100 miles east of Madrid, are other tourist trains that include overnight trips.

All of these excursions can be booked in Madrid at travel agencies or *RENFE* offices, and their prices are quite reasonable, from about $11 per person for the day trips to about $100 per person for the weekend trips, including round-trip transportation, sightseeing tours, and hotel accommodations (double occupancy) but no lunches or dinners (a picnic is included on the Cuenca excursion).

Two other tourist trains function as hotels on wheels and are thus in a class by themselves. The more famous one is the *Al Andalús Express*, or *Andalusian Express*, a luxury train made up of refurbished cars of the 1920s, with all the polished wood, decorative ground glass, damask drapes, and plush upholstery that its vintage implies in addition to the comforts of air conditioning, single and double sleeping compartments, shower rooms, a pub, piano bar, restaurant, gameroom, video collection, and discotheque.

This year, there are several itineraries offered aboard this historic train: In May, June, September, and October, the "Southern Journey" visits Seville, Córdoba, Granada, and Málaga, and versions range from 2 days to 15 days, depending on the amount of touring you wish to do en route. The all-inclusive price, including a reception, meals aboard the train, and sightseeing visits led by multilingual guides, is not inexpensive, however — as we went to press, per-person, double occupancy prices ranged from $690 for the 2-day excursion to $4,400 for the 15-day "City Splendor Mountain Retreat" package. An overnight from Málaga to Seville, which includes dinner, breakfast, and on board accommodations (but no touring on arrival) ranges from $290 to $390. The "Northern Journey," offered in July and August, visits such cities as Barcelona, Pamplona, Burgos, León, Santiago de Compostela, and Logroño. Various itineraries range from 3 days to 10 days. At the time of this writing, per-person double occupancy prices ranged from $950 for the 3-day version to $2,580 for the 10-day "Renaissance Towns" to Fjord Isles (which includes a chauffeured tour of the island of La Toja).

Later this year, passengers will be able to buy a combination ticket, including a trip aboard Spain's new high-speed train from Madrid to Seville (described above), where they transfer to the *Andalusian Express* for one of the "Northern Journey" itineraries. Also available will be a special World Heritage Tour visiting 16 sites on UNESCO's World Heritage List. Information on current tours and departure dates and reservations are available in the US through any of the three *Marsans International* offices in the US: 3325 Wilshire Blvd., Suite 508, Los Angeles, CA 90010 (phone: 213-738-8016); 1680 Michigan Ave., Suite 1026, Miami Beach, FL 33139 (phone: 305-531-0444); 19 W. 34th St., Suite 302, New York, NY 10001 (phone: 212-239-3880).

The second hotel on wheels is the *El Transcantábrico*, which also uses veteran, although less swank, rolling stock and operates on the narrow-gauge tracks of the *Ferrocariles Españoles de Vías Estrechas (FEVE)* line across the north of Spain. Excursions on this tourist train run from May through September and are a week long, leaving on Saturdays from León and heading northeast to Aranguren in the vicinity of Bilbao, then turning around and heading due west to cross nearly the entire Cantabrian coast and terminate at El Ferrol. (The trip can be taken in reverse on alternate Saturdays.) En route, stops are made at historic landmarks, tiny Cantabrian fishing ports, cities such as Santander and Oviedo, and in areas of outstanding scenic beauty, such as the Picos de Europa, at 8,700 feet the highest range in the Cordillera Cantábrica, yet only 20 miles from the sea. At the time of this writing, the fare for the 625-mile journey, including airfare between the US and Spain, was $1,650 per person double occupancy, including meals and sightseeing with multilingual guides. For information and reservations, contact *Marsans International* (address above).

RENFE also offers a variety of SpainRail Tours aboard modern, first class *Talgo* trains. Tour groups are accompanied by English-speaking guides and the tours generally last around 8 days; for current offerings, contact *RENFE.*

FURTHER INFORMATION: Particularly if Spain and Portugal are only a part of a more extensive trip through Europe or even farther afield, you may want to consult additional sources before finalizing plans. Both the *Eurail Traveler's Guide* (which contains a railroad map) and the *Eurail Timetable* are free from Eurailpass (Box 10383, Stamford, CT 06904-2383), as well as from the Eurail Distribution Centre (Box 300, Succursale R, Montreal, Quebec H2S 3K9, Canada). The *Eurail Guide* ($14.95) by Kathryn Turpin and Marvin Saltzman is available in most travel bookstores; it also can be ordered from Eurail Guide Annuals (27540 Pacific Coast Hwy., Malibu, CA 90265; add $2 per book for postage and handling). *Europe by Eurail* by George Wright Ferguson is available from Globe Pequot Press (PO Box Q, Chester, CT 06412; phone: 203-526-9571). Both of the latter two guides discuss train travel in general, contain information on the countries included in the Eurail network (the Saltzman book also discusses Eastern Europe and the rest of the world), and suggest numerous sightseeing excursions by rail from various base cities.

You also may want to buy the *Thomas Cook European Timetable* ($19.95), a weighty and detailed compendium of European international and national rail services that constitutes the most revered and accurate railway reference in existence. The *Timetable* comes out monthly, but because most European countries switch to summer schedules at the end of May (and back to winter schedules at the end of September), the June edition is the first complete summer schedule (and October the first complete winter schedule). The February through May editions, however, contain increasingly more definitive supplements on upcoming summer schedules, which can be used to plan a trip. The *Thomas Cook European Timetable* is sold by some travel bookstores and by the *Forsyth Travel Library* (PO Box 2975, Shawnee Mission, KS 66201-1375; add $3 for airmail postage; Kansas residents add 5½% sales tax). You also can order it by phone and pay by credit card by calling 800-367-7984 or 913-384-0496.

Following are the addresses for the national railway offices in Iberia and North America that sell tickets and passes and make reservations:

FrenchRail Inc. (US representatives of *RENFE* and *CP*)
- *Beverly Hills:* 9465 Wilshire Blvd., Beverly Hills, CA 90212 (phone: 213-451-5150).
- *Chicago:* 11 E. Adams St., Chicago, IL 60603 (phone: 312-427-8691).
- *Coral Gables:* 2121 Ponce de Leon Blvd., Coral Gables, FL 33134 (phone: 305-445-8648).
- *New York:* 610 Fifth Ave., New York, NY 10020 (phone: 800-848-7245 or 212-582-2816)
- *San Francisco:* 360 Post St., San Francisco, CA 94108 (phone: 415-982-1993).
- *Canada:* 150 Stanley St., Montreal, Quebec H3A 1R3, Canada (phone: 514-288-8255); 55 University Ave., Suite 600, Toronto, Ontario M5J 2H7, Canada (phone: 416-862-2227); 409 Granville St., Suite 452, Vancouver, British Columbia B6C 1T2, Canada (phone: 604-688-6707).

Portuguese National Railway Headquarters (Caminhos do Ferro Portugueses, CP)
- 20 Calçada do Duque, Lisbon 1294 (phone: 1-346-3181). Other offices are at trains stations throughout Portugal.

Spanish National Railways (Red Nacional de los Ferrocarriles Españoles, RENFE)
- Chamartín Station, Final de Agustín de Foxas/N Madrid 28036 (phone: 1-733-7616 or 1-733-1124).

RENFE Main Sales Offices

- *Algeciras:* 12 Augustín Balsamo, Algeciras 11203 (phone: 56-664164 or 56-651155).
- *Alicante:* 1 Explanada de España, Alicante 03002 (phone: 65-212441 or 65-219867).
- *Almeria:* 1 Alcalde Muñoz, Almeria 04004 (phone: 51-231822).
- *Barcelona:*
  Barcelona Central Sants (phone: 3-490-0202).
  617 Ave. Diagonal, Barcelona 08028 (phone: 3-322-9953).
  318 Calle Balmes, Barcelona 08006 (phone: 3-209-6165).
  Additional branch offices are located throughout Barcelona.
- *Benidorm:* 1 La Rioja (phone: 65-852960).
- *Cádiz:* Plaza de Sevilla (phone: 56-264302).
- *Córdoba:* 10 Ronda de los Tejares, Cordoba 14001 (phone: 57-475884).
- *Gijón:* 3 Asturias (phone: 85-347313).
- *Granada:* 63 Reyes Católicos, 18010 (phone: 58-223119).
- *Huelva:* Ave. de Italia (phone: 55-246666).
- *Irún:* At the train station, Estación *RENFE,* (phone: 43-612515).
- *La Coruña:* 3 Fontán, La Coruña 15004 (phone: 81-221948).
- *Madrid:*
  44 Alcalá, Madrid 28014. (*Note:* As we went to press, this office was closed until this summer.)
  Nuevos Ministerios, Paseo de la Castellana, Madrid 28046 (phone: 1-555-9268).
  63 Paseo de las Delicias, Madrid 28045 (phone: 1-228-6083).
  Aeroperto de Barajas (phone: 1-205-8544).
  Paseo de Recoletos (phone: 1-733-6300).
  8 Ave. Ciudad de Barcelona (phone: 1-501-3333).
  Additional branch offices are located throughout Madrid.
- *Málaga:* 2-4 Strachan, Málaga 29015 (phone: 52-213122).
- *Murcia:* 4 Barrionuevo, Murcia 30001 (phone: 68-212842).
- *Palma de Mallorca:* 9 Plaza de España, Palma de Mallorca 07002 (phone: 71-758817).
- *Salamanca:* 11 Plaza de la Libertad, Salamanca 37002 (phone: 23-212454).
- *San Sebastián:* 1 Camino, San Sebastián 20004 (phone: 43-426430).
- *Santander:* 25 Paseo de Pereda 39001 (phone: 42-212387).
- *Seville:* 29 Zaragoza, Seville 41001 (phone: 5-421-7998).
- *Tarragona:* 40 Rambla Nova, Tarragona 43003 (phone: 77-235294).
- *Toledo:* 9 Silleria, Toledo 45001 (phone: 25-221272).
- *Valencia:* 24 Calle Javita, Valencia 46003 (phone: 63-514874).
- *Valladolid:* Estación de Valladolid–Campo Grande (phone: 83-301217).
- *Zaragoza:* 13 San Clemente, Zaragoza 50001 (phone: 76-226598 or 76-226787)).

In addition, auxiliary offices can be found in, among other towns, Aranjuez, Avilés, Burgos, Cartagena, Lugo, Pamplona, and Pontevedra. For a list of these and other branch offices, contact the Spanish National Tourist Board (see *Tourist Information Offices,* in this section).

Finally, although any travel agent can assist you in making arrangements to tour Spain and/or Portugal by rail, you may want to consult a train travel specialist, such as *Accent on Travel,* 1030 Curtis St., Suite 201, Menlo Park, CA 94025 (phone: 415-326-7330 in California; 800-347-0645 elsewhere in the US).

Traveling by Bus

 Going from place to place by bus may not be the fastest way to get from here to there, but that (and, in some cases, a little less comfort) may be the only drawback to bus travel. A persuasive argument in its favor is its cost: Short of walking, traveling by bus is the least expensive way to cover a long distance. On average, a bus ticket between two cities in Spain or Portugal costs about two-thirds of the corresponding train fare. For this amount, it is possible to travel comfortably, if not always speedily, and at the same time enjoy an equally scenic view.

Buses also reach outposts remote from railroad tracks, for those so inclined. While train service in Spain and Portugal is more limited than it is in some another European country, a map of the bus routes is not much different from a road map: If the way is paved, it's certain that a bus — some bus — is assigned to travel it. The network of express buses — those traveling long distances with few stops en route — is only slightly less extensive. Because of this, Spain and Portugal are particularly well suited to bus travel.

Particularly in Portugal, bus travel is the most economical way to travel. In Portugal, the buses are run by numerous small regional lines, all of which come under the auspices of *Rodoviaria Nacional, EP (RN;* 86 Avenida Columbano Bordalo Pinheiro, Lisbon 1000; phone: 1-726-7123). This company can offer information on service to most cities and towns throughout the country and bus stations are located just about everywhere. The main bus terminal in Lisbon is at 18-B Avenida Casal Ribeiro, Lisbon (phone: 1-545439). Schedule and fare information can be obtained at the terminal, through the Portuguese National Tourist Office in the US or Portugal, or through travel agents.

The public bus service in Spain also is well developed, but is best for short day trips. Buses go from Madrid to many cities and towns throughout the country. In Spain, the buses are run by several privately owned companies, and tickets are purchased in the bus station. There are bus stations in all major cities, including several in Madrid; the busiest are Estación Sur de Autobuses at 17 Calle Canarias; 11 Paseo de la Florida; 18 Avenida de América; Estación del Norte; and 29 Paseo de la Florida. There are three stations in Barcelona; the busiest is Plaça de l'Universidad.

For schedule information, purchase the government-sponsored *Horario Guía,* a guide listing routes and timetables for buses, as well as trains and airlines in Spain. Updated monthly, it is available at newsstands. Although printed in Spanish, essential destination, arrival, and departure information is quite clear.

BOOKING: Reservations are not usually necessary on most local bus routes, which run on established and published schedules. As many rural lines are very crowded (since buses usually are the main form of transport for local residents), you may want to inquire about the possibility of making a reservation in order to ensure a seat. Tickets usually are bought on the bus and are valid for only that day and that ride. For long journeys, however, travelers must purchase tickets at the bus station before they leave (similar to riding *Greyhound* buses in the US, for example). When you buy your ticket, ask about any discounts available.

SERVICES: Buses are not equipped for food service, but on long trips, as in the US, they do make meal and rest stops. If you plan to spend some time traveling around Spain or Portugal by bus, it's not a bad idea to bring some food aboard to eat en route, though you're probably better off waiting until you reach a stop in a town or city where you can eat more comfortably at a restaurant. Toilet facilities are likely to be provided only on the newer buses on long-distance trips, and air conditioning is the exception rather than the rule — particularly on rural routes. If taking a motorcoach *tour,* however, you can expect special amenities such as air conditioning, toilets, upholstered and adjustable seats, and reading lamps.

FOR COMFORTABLE TRAVEL: Dress casually in loose-fitting clothes. Be sure you have a sweater or jacket (even in the summer) and, for when you disembark, a raincoat or umbrella is a must, particularly in the north during the winter (December through March). Passengers are allowed to listen to radios or cassette players, but must use earphones. Choose a seat in the front near the driver for the best view or in the middle between the front and rear wheels for the smoothest ride.

BUS TOURS: Many American tour operators offer motorcoach tours, however, one company *Gray Line,* an affiliate of *Rodoviaria Nacional, EP* (*RN;* address above) specializes in bus tours of Spain and Portugal. Among the numerous itineraries offered in Portugal are several in the vicinity of Porto, as well as Lisbon and surrounding areas. Tours in Spain include 1-day trips between Madrid and Toledo; 4-day tours visiting Avila, Madrid, Salamanca, and Segovia; 4-day tours visiting Córdoba, Granada, Seville; and other tours of southern Spain in the Costa del Sol. For further information on all-inclusive motorcoach tours offered by US tour operators, see *Package Tours,* in this section.

Traveling by Car

There are few places in Spain or Portugal that cannot be reached by train or bus or a combination of the two, yet many visitors are not in these countries long before they wish they had a car. Driving certainly is the most flexible way to explore out-of-the-way regions of Spain and Portugal. Trains often whiz much too fast past too many enticing landscapes, tunnel through or pass between hills and mountains rather than climb up and around them for a better view, and frequently deposit passengers in an unappealing part of town. Buses have a greater range, but they still don't permit many spur-of-the-moment stops and starts. In a car you go where you want when you want, and can stop along the way as often as you like for a meal, a photograph, or a particularly appealing view.

Spain and Portugal are ideally suited for driving tours. Distances between major cities usually are reasonable, and the historical and cultural density is such that the flexibility of a car can be used to maximum advantage. A visitor can cover large amounts of territory or spend the same amount of time motoring from village to village while exploring the countryside. (See DIRECTIONS for our choices of the most interesting driving itineraries.)

Travelers who wish to cover these countries from end to end can count on a good system of highways to help them make time. Travelers who wish to explore only one region will find that the secondary and even lesser roads are well surfaced and generally in good condition, although farther off the beaten track, this may not always be the case. Either way, there is plenty of satisfying scenery en route.

But driving isn't an inexpensive way to travel. Gas prices are far higher in Spain and Portugal than in North America, and car rentals seldom are available at bargain rates. Keep in mind, however, that driving becomes more economical with more passengers. Because the price of getting wheels abroad will be more than an incidental expense, it is important to investigate every alternative before making a final choice. Many travelers find this expense amply justified when considering that rather than just the means to an end, a well-planned driving route also can be an important part of the adventure.

Before setting out, make certain that everything you need is in order. Read about the places you intend to visit and study relevant maps. If at all possible, discuss your intended trip with someone who already has driven the route to find out about road conditions and available services. If you can't speak to someone personally, try to read about others' experiences. Automobile clubs (see below) and the Spanish and Portuguese national tourist offices in the US can be a good source of travel information, although when requesting brochures and maps, be sure to specify the areas you are planning to visit. (See "Roads and Maps," below.)

DRIVING: A valid driver's license from his or her own state of residence is required for a US citizen to drive in either Spain or Portugal. In addition, an International Driving Permit (IDP), which is a translation of the US license in 9 languages, is required in a number of countries, including Spain, where a US citizen is required to have an IDP in order to drive a rented car. While Spanish regulations are not always enforced and foreign drivers are known to have driven in Spain without incident using just their regular license, it's not recommended. A US citizen driving in Portugal needs only a valid driver's license from his or her state of residence; however, an IDP is strongly recommended.

You can obtain your IDP before you leave from most branches of the *American Automobile Association (AAA)*. Applicants must be at least 18 years old, and the application must be accompanied by two passport-size photos (some *AAA* branches have a photo machine available), a valid US driver's license, and a fee of $5. The IDP is good for 1 year and must be accompanied by your US license to be valid.

Proof of liability insurance also is required and is a standard part of any car rental contract. (To be sure of having the appropriate coverage, let the rental staff know in advance about the national borders you plan to cross.) If buying a car and using it abroad, the driver must carry an International Insurance Certificate, known as a Green Card (*Carte Verde* in Spain; *Cartão Verde* in Portugal). Your insurance agent or carrier at home can arrange for a special policy to cover you in Europe, and automatically will issue your Green Card.

Contrary to first impressions, Spanish and Portuguese drivers tend to be skillful and disciplined. Also contrary to first impressions, rules of the road do exist. Driving in Spain and Portugal is on the right side of the road, as in most of Europe. Passing is on the left; the left turn signal must be flashing throughout the entire process and the right indicator must be used when pulling back to the right; it's also a common practice to flash your headlights to signal the driver in front what you're doing. On mountain roads, get used to flashing your headlights at night and beeping your horn when rounding blind curves during the day; traffic going up usually has priority over traffic coming down, though signposts may indicate who has the right of way and at what times. In most larger cities, honking is forbidden (except to avoid accidents); flash your headlights instead. Also, don't be intimidated by tailgaters — everyone does it, in both Spain and Portugal.

According to law, those coming from the right at intersections have the right of way, as in the US, and pedestrians, provided they are in marked crosswalks, have priority over all vehicles. Unfortunately, however, this is not always the case. Exceptions are priority roads, marked by a sign with a yellow diamond on it; these have the right of way until the diamond reappears with a black bar and the right of way reverts to those coming from the right. In many areas, though, signposting is meager, and traffic at intersections converge from all directions, resulting in a proceed-at-your-own-risk flow.

Pictorial direction signs, generally found on the newer roads in Spain and Portugal, are standardized under the International Roadsign System, and their meanings are indicated by their shapes: Triangular signs indicate danger; circular signs give instructions; and rectangular signs are informative. Driving in European cities can be a tricky proposition, since many of them do not have street signs at convenient corners, but instead identify their byways with plaques attached to the walls of corner buildings.

These often are difficult to spot until you've passed them, and since most streets don't run parallel to one another, taking the next turn can lead you astray. Fortunately, most European cities and towns post numerous signs pointing the way to the center of the city, and plotting a course to your destination from there may be far easier. Look for the signs that read CENTRO (it's the same word in both Spain and Portugal). Also note that highway signs showing the distance from point to point are in kilometers rather than miles (1 mile equals approximately 1.6 kilometers; 1 kilometer equals approximately .62 mile). And speed limits are in kilometers per hour, so think twice before hitting the gas when you see a speed limit of 100. That means 62 miles per hour.

Spanish speed limits are 60 kph (37½ mph) in town for all cars. Outside town, the speed limit is 120 kph (75 mph) on *autopistas,* or toll highways (designated by the letter A), 100 kph (62½ mph) on *nacional,* or main roads (designated by the letter N), and 90 kph (56 mph) elsewhere unless otherwise marked.

Portuguese speed limits are somewhat slower, on main roads outside town speed limits are generally 90 kph (56 mph) for cars or 70 kph (44 mph) for cars towing trailers, with a minimum on highways of 50 kph (31 mph) and a maximum of 120 kph (75 mph).

Keep in mind, when touring along scenic roadways, that it is all too easy to inch up over the speed limit. And use alcohol sparingly prior to getting behind the wheel. Both Spain and Portugal have specific laws pertaining to drinking and driving and, as in other European countries, they are most zealous in prosecuting those who commit infractions under the influence. If you've been drinking, do as the natives do and walk home, take a cab, or make sure that a licensed member of your party sticks strictly to soft drinks or seltzer water *(acqua minerale).* Police also have the power to levy on-the-spot fines for other violations such as speeding, failure to stop at a red light, and failure to wear seat belts (required by law).

Traffic congestion is at its worst on main roads, particularly those radiating from major cities. Look for signs pointing out detours or alternative routes to popular holiday destinations. Service stations, information points, and tourist offices often distribute free maps of the alternate routes, which may be the long way around but probably will get you to your destination faster in the end.

■**Note:** Pay particular attention to parking signs in large cities, especially those indicating "control zones," where an unattended parked car presents a serious security risk. If you park in a restricted zone, unlike in the US (where you chance only a ticket or being towed), you may return to find that the trunk and doors have been blown off by overly cautious security forces. In Spain, it's more likely that you'll return to find one of the car's wheels "clamped," a procedure that renders your car inoperable and involves a tedious (and costly) process to get it freed.

Roads and Maps – Western Europe's network of highways is as well maintained as any in North America, with a system comparable to the American highway system: expressways, first class roads, and well-surfaced secondary roads. Three decades ago, a pan-European commission established standards for international European routes, called E roads. Most European maps note E route numbers together with national route numbers. Single-country maps generally use only a national number.

Spain and Portugal each maintains its own highway system. In general, the majority of main roads in Spain have recently been widened and repaved, and a lot of money currently is being spent on overall road improvements. The Portuguese are doing much the same types of improvements. Coastal roads tend to be foggy in the morning, and in the north of Portugal traffic can be very heavy. This is partly due to the ongoing construction of the autostrada (main highway) presently under way, which has been extended to link Lisbon and Porto. (At the time of this writing, the estimated completion date for the final work was sometime this year.) There also is another new road that links Lisbon to the Algarve, which makes traveling south fast and easy. However, pay special attention in Portugal, because there is a tendency to forget to paint signals or lines on repaved roads.

Except for stretches of free autoroutes in the vicinity of cities, most of the autoroutes (designated by A on pan-European maps) are toll roads, and they are fairly expensive. They save time, gas, and wear and tear on the car, but they obviously are not the roads to take if you want to browse and linger along the way. The other main roads (designated by N) and the secondary, or regional (designated by D), are free, well maintained, and much more picturesque, while minor roads have their own charm.

Be aware that in recent years, numerous changes have been taking place in the numbering of European roads. Many N roads have become D roads, some merely changing their prefix from N to D, some changing numbers as well. Another recent development is a new Europe-wide road numbering system. The European designations, prefaced by an E, appear together with the individual country's road numbers; so, for example, autoroute A1 in Spain could also be called E5, but Portugal's A1 would have a different E number. Both designations appear on Michelin's newest maps, but expect discrepancies between the old and new numbers to appear on maps and in guidebooks and brochures for some time to come.

Three particularly good sources of current information on Spanish and Portuguese roads and routes are the atlases, maps, and guides published by Michelin, Rand McNally, and Freytag & Berndt. All Michelin publications — the red and green guides, as well as road maps (by far the best for visitors touring) — are available in bookstores and map shops throughout the US and all over Europe, and also can be ordered from Michelin Guides and Maps (PO Box 3305, Spartanburg, SC 29304-3305; phone: 803-599-0850 in South Carolina; 800-423-0485 elsewhere in the US). A new edition of each Michelin map appears every year; if you're not buying directly from the publisher, make sure that the edition you buy is no more than 2 years old by opening one fold and checking the publication date, given just under the black circle with the map number. A particularly good map of Spain and Portugal is Michelin's *No. 990,* which is on a scale of 1 cm:10 km. It outlines scenic routes in green, highlights national parks and interesting sights, and includes insets of both the Canary and Balearic islands.

Rand McNally atlases and maps are available in most bookstores or can be bought directly from the following Rand McNally retail stores: 444 N. Michigan Ave., Chicago, IL 60611 (phone: 312-332-4628); 150 E. 52nd St., New York, NY 10022 (phone: 212-758-7488); 595 Market St., San Francisco, CA 94105-2803 (phone: 415-777-3131).

Freytag & Berndt's excellent series of 28 road maps ($8.95 each) cover most major destinations throughout Europe, including a map of the Iberian Peninsula. As the publisher is Austrian, this series is best ordered from either one of the Rand McNally bookstores listed above or the travel sources listed in *Books and Magazines,* in this section.

Another good source for these and just about any other map available is *Map Link* (25 E. Mason St., Santa Barbara, CA 93101; phone: 805-965-4402). You may want to order their excellent guide to maps worldwide, *The World Map Directory* ($29.95). If they don't have the map you want in stock — they have over 40 maps of Spain and Portugal — they will order it for you.

Road maps also are sold at gas stations throughout Europe. Stateside, some free maps can be obtained from the national tourist offices. The National Tourist Office of Spain distributes a smaller, free map of Spain, with insets of Bilbao, Barcelona, Madrid, Seville, Valencia, and Zaragoza. The Portuguese National Tourist Office has a free map of Portugal that, in addition to all road information, identifies gas stations that sell unleaded gas. *Avis,* the car rental company (see below), offers "Personally Yours," a travel packet complete with maps and interesting places to see and things to do while driving through Spain and Portugal.

The *American Automobile Association (AAA)* also provides several useful reference sources, including an overall Europe planning map, regional maps of Spain and Portugal, the 600-page *Travel Guide to Europe* (the price varies from branch to branch), and the 64-page *Motoring Europe* ($5.95). All are available through local *AAA* offices (see below). Another invaluable guide, *Euroad: The Complete Guide to Motoring in Europe,* is available for $8.80, including postage and handling, from *VLE Limited,* PO Box 547, Tenafly, NJ 07670 (phone: 201-567-5536).

Automobile Clubs and Breakdowns – Most European automobile clubs offer emergency service to any breakdown victim, whether a club member or not; however, only members of these clubs or affiliated clubs may have access to certain information services and receive discounted or free towing and repair services.

Members of the *American Automobile Association (AAA)* often are entitled automatically to a number of services from foreign clubs. With over 31 million members in chapters throughout the US and Canada, the *AAA* is the largest automobile club in North America. *AAA* affiliates throughout the US provide a variety of travel services to members, including a travel agency, trip planning, free traveler's checks at some locations, and reimbursement for foreign roadside assistance. They will help plan an itinerary, will send a map with clear routing directions, and will even make hotel reservations; these services apply to traveling in both the US and Europe. Although *AAA* members receive maps, brochures, and other publications for no charge or at a discount (depending on the publication and branch), non-members also can order from an extensive selection of highway and topographical maps. You can join the *AAA* through local chapters (listed in the telephone book under *AAA*) or contact the national office, 1000 AAA Dr., Heathrow, FL 32746-5063 (phone: 407-444-8544).

Through its association with the *International Touring Organization* (in France) the *AAA* is affiliated with automobile clubs in both Spain and Portugal that supply travel information, road maps, touring and restaurant information, towing, and limited emergency road service to members with a valid *AAA* membership card. In Spain, contact the *Real Automóvil Club de España* (10 Calle José Abascal, Madrid 28003; phone: 1-447-3200); in Portugal, contact the *Automóvel Club de Portugal* (24 Rua Rosa Araújo, Lisbon 1200; phone: 1-563931, 1-553711, or 1-553593).

If you break down on the road, the first emergency procedure is to get the car off the road. Some roads have shoulders that are narrower than those to which you're used, so make sure you get all the way off, even if you have to hang off the shoulder a bit. The universal signal for help is raising the hood, and tying a white handkerchief or rag to the door handle or radio antenna. Don't leave the car unattended, and don't try any major repairs on the road.

Motor patrols in both Spain and Portugal usually drive small cars painted a uniform color, and emergency call boxes are located on many major routes. On secondary roads in Spain, emergency phones may be posted with phone numbers of local garages providing towing and basic repair services, although on rural routes, these boxes are rare.

For breakdown assistance in Spain, motorists also can call the *Real Automovil Club de España* at 91-441-2222; they will direct you to the nearest service station. The National Tourist Office of Spain also can provide a map of garages throughout Spain.

Aside from these options, a driver in distress will have to contact the nearest service center by pay phone. And, although English is spoken in Spain and Portugal, if language is a barrier in explaining your dilemma, the local operator should be able to connect you to an English-speaking international operator for assistance. (For further information on calling for help, see *Mail, Telephone, and Electricity* and *Medical and Legal Aid and Consular Services,* both in this section.) Car rental companies also make provisions for breakdowns, emergency service, and assistance; ask for a number to call when you pick up the vehicle.

Gasoline – In Spain and Portugal, gasoline is sold by the liter, which is slightly more than 1 quart; approximately 3.8 liters equal 1 US gallon. Regular or leaded gas generally is sold in two grades in both Spain and Portugal — called *gasolina normal* or *gasolina super* in both countries. Diesel (called diesel) also is widely available, but unleaded fuel (called *gasolina sin plomo* in Spain; *gasolina sem chumbo* in Portugal) is only now being introduced in Europe and may be difficult (or even impossible) to find. At least until all European gas stations sell unleaded, your safest bet is to rent a car that takes leaded gasoline.

Gas prices everywhere rise and fall depending on the world supply of oil, and an American traveling overseas is further affected by the prevailing rate of exchange, so it is difficult to say exactly how much fuel will cost when you travel. As gas prices are considerably higher in Spain and Portugal, it is not difficult to predict that it will cost roughly twice as much as you are accustomed to paying in the US. At the time of this writing, gas cost an average of about 80 pesetas or 130 escudos (about 90¢) per liter, or about 304 pesetas or 494 escudos ($3.40) per US gallon.

Particularly when traveling in rural areas, fill up whenever you come to a gas station. It may be a long way to the next open station. (Even in more populated areas, it may be difficult to find an open station on Sundays or holidays.) You don't want to get stranded on an isolated stretch — so it is a good idea to bring along an extra few gallons in a steel container. (Plastic containers tend to break when a car is bouncing over rocky roads. This, in turn, creates the danger of fire should the gasoline ignite from a static electricity spark. Plastic containers also may burst at high altitudes.)

Considering the cost of gas in Spain and Portugal relative to US prices, gas economy is of particular concern. The prudent traveler should plan an itinerary and make as many reservations as possible in advance in order not to waste gas figuring out where to go, stay, or eat. Drive early in the day, when there is less traffic. Then leave your car at the hotel and use local transportation whenever possible after you arrive at your destination.

Although it may be as dangerous to drive at a speed much below the posted limit as it is to drive above it — particularly on major highways, where the speed limit is 75 mph — at 88 kph (55 mph) a car gets 25% better mileage than at 112 kph (70 mph). The number of miles per liter or gallon also is increased by driving smoothly. Accelerate gently, anticipate stops, get into high gear quickly, and maintain a steady speed.

RENTING A CAR: Although there are other options, such as leasing or outright purchase, most people who want to drive in Europe simply rent a car. Travelers to Spain and Portugal can reserve a rental car through a travel agent or international rental firm before leaving home, or from a local company once they are in Europe. Another possibility, also arranged before departure, is to rent the car as part of a larger travel package (see "Fly/Drive," below, as well as *Package Tours,* in this section).

Renting is not inexpensive, but it is possible to economize by determining your own needs and then shopping around among car rental companies until you find the best deal. As you comparison shop, keep in mind that rates vary considerably, not only from city to city, but also from location to location within the same city. It might be less expensive to rent a car in the center of a city rather than at the airport. Ask about special rates or promotional deals, such as weekend or weekly rates, bonus coupons for airline tickets, or 24-hour rates that include gas and unlimited mileage.

Rental car companies operating in Europe can be divided into three basic categories: large international companies; national or regional companies; and local companies. *Avis, Budget, Hertz,* and other international firms maintain offices in most major European cities. Because of aggressive local competition, the cost of renting a car can be less expensive once a traveler arrives in Europe, compared to the prices quoted in advance from the US. Local companies usually are less expensive than the international giants.

Given this situation, it's tempting to wait until arriving to scout out the lowest-priced rental from the company located the farthest from the airport high-rent district and offering no pick-up services. But if your arrival coincides with a holiday or a peak travel period, you may be disappointed to find that even the most expensive car in town was spoken for months ago. Whenever possible, it is best to reserve in advance, anywhere from a few days in slack periods to a month or more during the busier seasons.

The best guide to sorting through the options may be to contact the local tourist board, which usually can provide recommendations and a list of reputable firms.

Renting from the US – Travel agents can arrange foreign rentals for clients, but it is just as easy to do it yourself by calling (usually toll-free) the international divisions of the following car rental firms:

Avis: Has 150 locations in Spain and 26 in Portugal. Call 800-331-1084.

Budget: Has over 27 locations in Spain and 16 in Portugal. Call 800-527-0700.

Dollar Rent-a-Car (known in Europe as *Eurodollar*): Has several locations in major Portuguese cities including Faro, Lisbon, and Porto. Call 800-421-6878.

Hertz: Has 104 locations in Spain and 20 in Portugal. Call 800-654-3001.

National (known in Europe as *Europcar*): Has 110 locations in Spain and about 30 in Portugal. Call 800-CAR-EUROPE.

All of these companies publish directories listing their foreign locations, and all quote weekly flat rates based on unlimited mileage with the renter paying for gas. Some also offer time and mileage rates (i.e., a basic per-day or per-week charge, plus a charge for each mile, or kilometer, driven), which generally are only to the advantage of those who plan to do very little driving — the basic time and mileage charge for a given period of time is lower than the unlimited mileage charge for a comparable period, but the kilometers add up more quickly than most people expect.

It also is possible to rent a car before you go by contacting any of a number of smaller or less well known US companies that do not operate worldwide. These organizations specialize in European auto travel, including leasing and car purchase in addition to car rental, or actually are tour operators with a well-established European car rental programs. These firms, whose names and addresses are listed below, act as agents for a variety of European suppliers, offer unlimited mileage almost exclusively, and frequently manage to undersell their larger competitors by a significant margin.

Comparison shopping always is advisable, however, because the company that has the least expensive rentals in one country may not have the least expensive in another, and even the international giants offer discount plans whose conditions are easy for most travelers to fulfill. For instance, *Budget* and *National* offer discounts of anywhere from 15% to 30% off their usual rates (according to the size of the car and the duration of the rental), provided that the car is reserved a certain number of days before departure (usually 7, but it can be less), is rented for a minimum period (5 days or, more often, a week), and in most cases, is returned to the same location that supplied it or to another in the same country. Similar discount plans include *Hertz*'s Affordable Europe and *Avis*'s Supervalue Rates Europe.

Note: Avis also offers two helpful free services for customers traveling in Spain and Portugal, as well as in other European countries: the "Know Before You Go" US hot line (phone: 212-876-AVIS); and a Europe Message Center, which will take messages for customers traveling in Europe. The first service provides travelers with tourist information on Spain and Portugal (as well as Austria, Belgium, Denmark, France, Germany, Great Britain, Ireland, Italy, Luxembourg, Holland, and Switzerland). Topics may range from questions about driving (distances, gasoline prices, and license requirements) to queries about currency, customs, tipping, and weather. (Callers then receive a personal letter confirming the information discussed.)

Avis's Europe Message Center operates like any answering service in that it will take phone messages any time day or night for *Avis* customers. *Avis* renters are given a telephone number in Europe that they can leave with anyone who wants to contact them while they are touring; if your rental car comes with a car phone, *Avis* will give this number to callers (with your permission). The tourers themselves can call a toll-free number to pick up messages or leave word for family, friends, or business colleagues. To utilize the service, a renter picks up his or her car at an *Avis* outlet in Europe, and then simply calls the Message Center and registers with the rental agreement number. It's even possible to leave an itinerary — which can be altered later if necessary — making messages easy to leave and/or pick up. For Message Center service, customers in Spain and Portugal can call 0-753-696029 in London.

There are legitimate bargains in car rentals if you shop for them. Call all the familiar car rental names whose toll-free numbers are given above (don't forget to ask about their special discount plans), and then call the smaller companies listed below. In the recent past, the latter have tended to offer significantly lower rates, but it always pays to compare. Begin your comparison shopping early, because the best deals may be booked to capacity quickly and may require payment 14 to 21 days or more before picking up the car.

> *Auto Europe,* PO Box 1097, Camden, ME 04843 (phone: 207-236-8235; 800-223-5555 throughout the US; 800-458-9503 in Canada). Offers rentals at over 15 locations in Spain and in Coimbra, Faro, Lisbon, and Porto in Portugal.
>
> *Cortell International,* 17310 Red Hill Ave., Suite 360, Irvine, CA 92714 (phone: 800-228-2535 or 714-724-1003). Offers rentals at over 100 locations in Spain and 15 in Portugal.
>
> *Europe by Car,* One Rockefeller Plaza, New York, NY 10020 (phone: 212-581-3040 in New York State; 800-223-1516 elsewhere in the US), or 9000 Sunset Blvd., Los Angeles, CA 90069 (phone: 800-252-9401 or 213-272-0424). Offers rentals in over 20 Spanish cities and in Faro, Lisbon, Porto, and Praia de Rocha in Portugal.
>
> *European Car Reservations,* 349 W. Commercial St., Suite 2950, East Rochester, NY 14445 (phone: 800-535-3303). Offers rentals in 13 cities in Spain and in Faro, Lisbon, and Porto in Portugal.
>
> *Foremost Euro-Car,* 5430 Van Nuys Blvd., Suite 306, Van Nuys, CA 91401 (phone: 818-786-1960 or 800-272-3299 in California; 800-423-3111 elsewhere in the US). Offers rentals in Barcelona, Madrid, Málaga, and Seville in Spain and in Faro, Lisbon, and Porto in Portugal.
>
> *Kemwel Group Inc.,* 106 Calvert St., Harrison, NY 10528 (phone: 800-678-0678 or 914-835-5555). Offers rentals at 18 locations in Spain and in Estoril, Faro, Lisbon, and Porto in Portugal.
>
> *Meier's World Travel, Inc.,* 6033 W. Century Blvd., Suite 1080, Los Angeles, CA 90045 (phone: 800-937-0700). In conjunction with major car rental companies arranges economical rentals throughout Spain.

One of the ways to keep the cost of car rentals down is to deal with a car rental consolidator, such as *Connex International* (983 Main St., Peekskill, NY 10566; phone: 800-333-3949 or 914-739-0066). *Connex*'s main business is negotiating with virtually all of the major car rental agencies for the lowest possible prices for its customers. For example, at the time of this writing, rates for a subcompact car in some parts of Europe — including Barcelona, Madrid, Málaga, Seville, and Terremolinas in Spain and 20 cities in Portugal — were as low as $89 a week with unlimited mileage — comparable deals available from other major car rental companies run substantially higher. (*Connex* also can offer significant numbers of other travel services, varying from hotel accommodations to sightseeing programs.)

Local Rentals – It long has been common wisdom that the least expensive way to rent a car is to make arrangements in Europe. This is less true today than it used to be. Many medium to large European car rental companies have become the overseas suppliers of stateside companies such as those mentioned previously, and often the stateside agency, by dint of sheer volume, has been able to negotiate more favorable rates for its US customers than the European firm offers its own. Still lower rates may be found by searching out small, strictly local rental companies overseas, whether at less than prime addresses in major cities or in more remote areas. But to find them you must be willing to invest a sufficient amount of vacation time comparing prices on the scene. You also must be prepared to return the car to the location that rented it; drop-off possibilities are likely to be limited.

Once overseas, local branches of the National Tourist Office of Spain and the Portuguese National Tourist Office may be able to supply the names of Spanish and Portuguese car rental companies. The local yellow pages is another good place to begin. (For further information on local rental companies, see the individual reports in THE CITIES.).

In Spain, *Atesa* is a national car rental company with offices throughout the country. For information, contact *Atesa* (243 Paseo de la Castallana, Madrid; phone: 1-315-1349; or 18 Calle Nicolas Estebañez, Las Palmas; phone: 28-277308), or look for locations at airports and metropolitan centers throughout Spain. *Ital Rent a Car,* also with branches throughout Spain, is represented in the US by *Tour Directions* (70 W. 36th St., New York, NY 10018; phone: 800-423-4460 or 212-564-3236).

In Portugal, major national car rental companies include *Olivauto* (21 Avenida João 12-D, Lisbon; phone: 1-893588) and *Auto Algarve Internatinal, Ltd.* (150 Rua Do Alprotel, Lisbon; phone: 1-24672).

Also bear in mind that *Hertz* offers a rail-and-drive pass, called EurailDrive Escape, which is valid throughout all the countries that are included in the Eurail network, including Spain and Portugal (For further information on rail-and-drive packages, see *Traveling by Train,* above.)

Requirements – Whether you decide to rent a car in advance from a large international rental company with European branches or from a local Spanish or Portuguese company, you should know that renting a car rarely is as simple as signing on the dotted line and roaring off into the night. If you are renting for personal use, you must have a valid driver's license, as well as an IDP if renting in Spain, and will have to convince the renting agency that (1) you are personally credit-worthy, and (2) you will bring the car back at the stated time. This will be easy if you have a major credit card; most rental companies accept credit cards in lieu of a cash deposit, as well as for payment of your final bill. If you prefer to pay in cash, leave your credit card imprint as a "deposit," then pay your bill in cash when you return the car.

If you don't have a major credit card, renting a car for personal use becomes more complicated. If you are planning to rent from an international agency with an office near your home, the best thing to do is to call the company several days in advance, and give them your name, home address, and information on your business or employer; the agency then runs its own credit check on you. This can be time consuming, so you should try to have it done before you leave home. If planning to pay for your rental car in cash, it is best to make arrangements in advance — otherwise you must bring along a letter of employment and go to the agency during business hours (don't forget to take the time difference into account) so that your employer can be called for verification.

In addition to paying the rental fee up front, you also will have to leave a hefty deposit when you pick up the car — either a substantial flat fee or a percentage of the total rental cost. (Each company has a different deposit policy; look around for the best deal.) If you return the car on time, the full deposit will be refunded; otherwise, additional charges will be deducted and any unused portion of the deposit returned.

If you are planning to rent a car once in Spain or Portugal, *Avis, Hertz,* and other

US rental companies usually *will* rent to travelers paying in cash and leaving either a credit card imprint or a substantial amount of cash as a deposit. This is not necessarily standard policy, however, as *Budget,* some of the other international chains, and many Spanish and Portuguese companies will *not* rent to an individual who doesn't have a valid credit card. In this case, you may have to call around to find a company that accepts cash.

Also keep in mind that although the minimum age to drive a car in both Spain and Portugal is 18 years, the minimum age to rent a car varies with the company. Many firms have a minimum age requirement of 21 years, some raise that to 23 or 25 years, and for some models of cars it rises to 30 years. The upper age limit at many companies is between 69 and 75; others have no upper age limit or may make drivers above a certain age subject to special conditions.

Costs – Given all the competition, the price charged for a rental car changes continuously, rising and falling according to the level of renter traffic. The rate your friend paid last December may have been higher than the one you'll pay in May, and a super-bargain rate may be withdrawn as soon as the advertiser moves some cars off the lot and onto the road again. Nevertheless, there are some constants governing pricing in the international car rental market.

Finding the most economical car rental will require some telephone shopping on your part. As a *general* rule, expect to hear lower prices quoted by the smaller, strictly local companies than by the well-known international names, with those of the national Spanish or Portuguese companies falling somewhere between the two.

If you are driving short distances for only a day or two, the best deal may be a per-day, per-mile (or per-kilometer) rate: You pay a flat fee for each day you keep the car (which can be as low as $25), plus a per-mile charge of 12¢ to 40¢ — or 7¢ to 25¢ per kilometer — or more. An increasingly common alternative is to be granted a certain number of free miles or kilometers each day and then be charged on a per-mile or per-kilometer basis over that number. Flat weekly rates also are available, and some flat monthly rates that represent a further saving over the daily rate — however, even these longer-term rentals still will not be inexpensive.

A better alternative for touring the countryside may be a flat per-day rate with unlimited free mileage; this is certainly the most economical rate if you plan to drive over 100 miles (160 km) a day. (*Note:* When renting a car in Spain or Portugal, the term "mileage" may refer either to miles or kilometers.) Make sure that the low, flat daily rate that catches your eye, however, is indeed a per-day rate: Often the lowest price advertised by a company turns out to be available only with a minimum 3-day rental — fine if you want the car that long, but not the bargain it appears if you really intend to use it no more than 24 hours for in-city driving.

Other factors influencing cost include the type of car you rent. Rentals are based on a tiered price system, with different sizes of cars — standard, subcompact, compact, mid-size, large, and luxury — often listed as A (the smallest and least expensive) through F, G, or H, and sometimes even higher. The typical A car available in Spain or Portugal is a two-door subcompact or compact, often a hatchback, seating two or three adults (such as a small Ford, Fiat, Renault, or Peugeot), while the typical F, G, or H luxury car is a four-door sedan seating four or five adults (such as a Mercedes or BMW). The larger the car, the more it costs to rent in the first place and the more gas it consumes, but for some people the greater comfort and extra luggage space of a larger car (in which bags can be safely locked out of sight) may make it worth the additional expense, especially on a long trip. Be warned, too, that relatively few European cars have automatic transmissions, and those that do are more likely to be in the F than the A group. Cars with automatic shift must be requested specifically at the time of booking, and they cost more (anywhere from $5 to $10 a day than the same model with standard shift) and consume more gas. Similarly, cars with air conditioning are likely to be found in the more expensive categories only.

Electing to pay for collision damage waiver (CDW) protection will add considerably to the cost of renting a car. You may be responsible for the *full value* of the vehicle being rented, but you can dispense with the possible obligation by buying the offered waiver at a cost of about $13 a day. Before making any decisions about optional collision damage waivers, check with your own insurance agent and determine whether your personal automobile insurance policy covers rented vehicles; if it does, you probably won't need to pay for the waiver. Be aware, too, that increasing numbers of credit cards automatically provide CDW coverage if the car rental is charged to the appropriate credit card. However, the specific terms of such coverage differ sharply among individual credit card companies, so check with the credit card company for information on the nature and amount of coverage provided (also see *Credit and Currency,* in this section). Considering that repair costs for a rental car have become a real headache of late, and car rental companies are getting away with steep fees (up to the full retail price of the car) for damage to their property, if you are not otherwise covered, it is wise to pay for the insurance offered by the car rental company rather than risk traveling without any coverage.

Overseas, the amount renters may be liable for should damage occur has not risen to the heights it has in the US. In addition, some European car rental agreements include collision damage coverage. In this case, the CDW supplement frees the renter from liability for the *deductible* amount — as opposed to the standard CDW coverage, described above, which releases the driver from liability for the full value of the car. In Spain and Portugal, this deductible typically ranges from $1,500 to $2,500 at present, but can be more for some luxury car groups. As with the full the cost of waiving this liability — anywhere from $10 to $25 a day — is far from negligible, however. Drivers who rent cars in the US are often able to decline the CDW because many personal automobile insurance policies (subject to their own deductibles) extend to rental cars; unfortunately, such coverage usually does not extend to cars rented for use outside the US and Canada. Similarly, CDW coverage provided by some credit cards if the rental is charged to the card may be limited to cars rented in the US or Canada.

When inquiring about CDW coverage and costs, you should be aware that a number of the major international car rental companies now automatically are including the cost of this waiver in their quoted prices. This does not mean that they are absorbing this cost and you are receiving free coverage — total rental prices have increased to include the former CDW charge. The disadvantage of this inclusion is that you probably will not have the option to refuse this coverage, and will end up paying the added charge — even if you already are adequately covered by your own insurance policy or through a credit card company.

Additional costs to be added to the price tag include drop-off charges or one-way service fees. The lowest price quoted by any given company may apply only to a car that is returned to the same location from which it was rented. A slightly higher rate may be charged if the car is to be returned to a different city in the same country, and a considerably higher rate may prevail if the rental begins in one country and ends in another.

A further consideration: Don't forget that all car rentals are subject to Value Added Tax (VAT — known in Spain and Portugal as IVA). This tax rarely is included in the rental price that's advertised or quoted, but it always must be paid — whether you pay in advance in the US or pay it when you drop off the car. There is a wide variation in this tax from country to country: In Spain, the VAT rate on car rentals is 12%; in Portugal, it's 17%.

One-way rentals bridging two countries used to be exempt from tax, but that is no longer the case. In general, the tax on one-way rentals is determined by the country in which the car has been rented, so if your tour plans include several countries, you should examine your options regarding the pick-up and drop-off points. Even if you intend to visit only one country, you still might consider a nearby country as a pick-up point if it will provide substantial savings. For instance, for a tourer planning to explore Portugal, there's a financial incentive (particularly for long-term rentals) to pick up his or her rental car in Spain, and then drive across the border (at a 5% cost saving).

Some rental agencies that do not maintain their own fleets use a contractor whose country of registration determines the rate of taxation. An example is *Kemwel Car Rental Europe,* whose one-way rentals from most countries are taxed at the Danish rate, 22% — rentals in Spain and Portugal are taxed at the standard rate, 12% and 17%, respectively. *Kemwel*'s special programs offer savings to clients planning on touring throughout Europe (particularly where the tax rate is higher), and allow travel agents to earn commissions on CDW fees and on VAT. The SuperSaver Plus and UniSaver Plus tariffs offer inclusive rentals in 24 countries throughout Europe and the Middle East. These programs offer full insurance coverage (with a $100 deductible) and all European VAT, plus unlimited mileage. Rates start at $79 per week and are available in some 35 cities across Europe, including Barcelona, Madrid, and Lisbon. If part of a fly/drive packge (see below) booked through *Kemwel,* rates are as low as $39 per week. Bookings must be reserved and paid for at least 7 days before delivery of the car, and the vehicle must be returned to the *Kemwel* station from which it originally was rented. For further information, contact *Kemwel Group Inc.,* 106 Calvert St., Harrison, NY 10528 (phone: 800-678-0678 or 914-835-5555).

Rental cars usually are delivered with a full tank of gas. (This is not always the case, however, so check the gas gauge when picking up the car, and have the amount of gas noted on your rental agreement if the tank is not full.) Remember to fill the tank before you return the car or you will have to pay to refill it, and gasoline at the car rental company's pump is always much more expensive than at a service station. This policy may vary for smaller, regional companies; ask when picking up the vehicle.

Finally, currency fluctuation is another factor to consider. Most brochures quote rental prices in US dollars, but these dollar amounts frequently are only guides; that is, they represent the prevailing rate of exchange at the time the brochure was printed. The rate may be very different when you call to make a reservation, and different again when the time comes to actually pay the bill (when the amount owed may be paid in cash in foreign currency or as a charge to a credit card, which is recalculated at a still later date's rate of exchange). Some companies guarantee rates in dollars (often for a slight surcharge), but this is an advantage only when the value of the dollar is steadily declining overseas. If the dollar is growing stronger overseas, you may be better off with rates in the local currency.

Before you leave the lot, check to be sure the rental car has a spare tire and jack in the trunk. Also check that you have extra lightbulbs for the headlights, required by law in Spain. In addition, particularly for extensive touring, you may want to pick up the following equipment: a first-aid kit; a flashlight with an extra set of batteries; a white towel (useful for signaling for help, as well as for wiping the car windows); jumper cables; flares and/or reflectors; a container of water or coolant for the radiator; and a steel container for extra gasoline.

Fly/Drive – Airlines, charter companies, car rental companies, and tour operators have been offering fly/drive packages for years, and even though the basic components of the package have changed somewhat — return airfare, a car waiting at the airport, and perhaps a night's lodging in the gateway city all for one inclusive price used to be the rule — the idea remains the same. You rent a car *here* for use *there* by booking it along with other arrangements for the trip. These days, the very minimum arrangement possible is the result of a tie-in between a car rental company and an airline, which entitles customers to a rental car for less than the company's usual rates, provided they show proof of having booked a flight on that airline.

Slightly more elaborate fly/drive packages can be found listed under various names (go-as-you-please, self-drive, or, simply, car tours) in the independent vacations sections of tour catalogues. Their most common ingredients are the rental car plus some sort of hotel voucher plan, with the applicable airfare listed separately. You set off on your trip with a block of prepaid accommodations vouchers, a list of hotels that accept them (usually members of a hotel chain or association), and a reservation for the first night's stay, after which the staff of each hotel books the next one for you or you make your own reservations. Naturally, the greater the number of establishments participating in the scheme, the more freedom you have to range at will during the day's driving and still be near a place to stay for the night. The cost of these combination packages generally varies according to the size of the car and the quality of the hotels; there usually is an additional drop-off charge if the car is picked up in one city and returned in another. Most packages are offered at several different price levels, ranging from a standard plan covering stays in hotels to a budget plan using accommodations such as small inns or farmhouses. Airlines also have special rental car rates available when you book their flights, often with a flexible hotel voucher program. For information on available packages, check with the airline or your travel agent.

TAP Air and the *Kemwel Group* offer a variety of fly/drive packages in Portugal. The round-trip transatlantic flight must be on *TAP Air* and the car reservation must be made at least 7 days prior to travel. Pick-up and drop-off locations include Estoril, Faro, Lisbon, and Porto, and the car must be returned to the city in which it orginally was rented (or a $50 drop-off fee is charged). Although the typical car included is a subcompact, upgrades and extensions of the car rental also are available. Other features included depend on the package version chosen. For further information, contact the *Kemwel Group Inc.,* (106 Calvert St., Harrison, NY 10528; phone: 800-678-0678 or 914-835-5555) or *TAP Air.*

Less flexible car tours provide a rental car, a hotel plan, and a set itinerary that permits no deviation because the hotels all are reserved in advance. The deluxe European car tours packaged by *AutoVenture* (425 Pike St., Suite 502, Seattle, WA 98101; phone: 800-426-7502 or 206-624-6033), which can be bought in either a self-drive or chaffeured version, are of this variety. *Avis* offers less deluxe car tours with its Personally Yours program. You must book at least 2 weeks in advance to receive this planned itinerary service. For information on other packagers of car tours, see *Package Tours,* in this section.

LEASING: Anyone planning to be in Europe for 3 weeks or more should compare the cost of renting a car with the cost of leasing one for the same period. While the money saved by leasing — rather than renting for a 23-day (the minimum) or 30-day period — may not be great, what is saved over the course of a long-term lease — 45, 60, 90 days, or more — amounts to hundreds, even thousands, of dollars. Part of the saving is due to the fact that leased cars are exempt from the stiff taxes applicable to rented cars. In addition, leasing plans provide for collision insurance with no deductible amount, so there is no need to add the daily cost of the collision damage waiver protection (an option offered by rental car companies — see above). A further advantage of a car lease — actually, a financed purchase/repurchase plan — is that you reserve your car by specific make and model rather than by group only, and it is delivered to you fresh from the factory.

Unfortunately, leasing as described above is offered only in Belgium and France, and the savings it permits can be realized to the fullest only if the cars are picked up and returned in these countries. While leased cars can be delivered to other countries there is a charge for this service, which can be as high as $350 in the case of Spanish and Portuguese cities, to which must be added an identical return charge. If you don't intend to keep the car very long, the two charges could nullify the amount saved by leasing rather than renting, so you will have to do some arithmetic.

It is possible to lease a car in countries other than Belgium and France, but most of the plans offered are best described as long-term rentals at preferential rates. They differ from true leasing in that you will pay tax and collision damage waiver protection (though it may be included in the quoted price), and the cars usually are late-model used cars rather than brand-new.

One of the major car leasing companies is *Renault,* offering leases of new cars for 23 days to 6 months. The cars are exempt from tax, all insurance is included, and there is no mileage charge. *Renault* offers the following pick-up/drop-off options: free pick-up/drop-off in the following French cities: Bayonne, Bordeaux, Calais, Lyons, Marseilles, Nice, Paris, Pau, Perpignan, Rennes, Strasbourg, and Toulouse; charges between $50 and $230 in Amsterdam (Holland), Brussels (Belgium), Frankfurt (Germany), London (Great Britain), and Zurich (Switzerland), and several even more expensive locations elsewhere on the Continent. Pick-up and drop-off alternatives for those primarily touring Iberia include Barcelona, Bilbao, Madrid, Vigo. *Renault* does not offer the service in Portugal; however, cars can be picked up in Spain, driven into Portugal, and returned in Spain. For further information and reservations, ask your travel agent or contact *Renault USA,* 650 First Ave., New York, NY 10016 (phone: 212-532-1221 in New York State; 800-221-1052 elsewhere in the US).

Peugeot also offers a similar leasing arrangement, called the "Peugeot Vacation Plan." In accordance with the standard type of financed purchase/repurchase leasing plan, travelers buy a new car in France, drive it for anywhere between 22 and 175 days, then sell it back to *Peugeot* for a guaranteed price (the original price minus the actual charge for usage). The tax-free "purchase" includes unlimited mileage, factory warranty, full collision damage waiver coverage (no deductible), and 24-hour towing and roadside assistance. Pick-up and drop-off locations and charges are similar to *Renault*'s. For instance, the car can be picked up and dropped off at the airport in Madrid; however, there is a $440 charge for this service. *Peugeot*'s "European Delivery" program is a full-purchase program, including shipment of the car to the US, as discussed below. For further information, contact *Peugeot Motors of America* (1 Peugeot Plaza, Lyndhurst, NJ 07071; phone: 201-935-8400). Some of the car rental firms listed above — *Auto-Europe, Foremost Euro-Car,* and *Kemwel Group* — also arrange European car leases.

BUYING A CAR: If your plans include both buying a new car of European make and a driving tour of Europe, it's possible to combine the two ventures and save some money on each. By buying the car abroad and using it during your vacation, you pay quite a bit less for it than the US dealer would charge and at the same time avoid the expense of renting a car during your holiday. There are two basic ways to achieve this desired end, but one, factory delivery, is far simpler than the other, direct import.

Factory delivery means that you place an order for a car in the US, then pick it up in Europe, often literally at the factory gate. It also means that your new car is built to American specifications, complying with all US emission and safety standards. Because of this, only cars made by manufacturers who have established a formal program for such sales to American customers can be bought at the factory. At present, the list includes Audi, BMW, Jaguar, Mercedes-Benz, Peugeot, Porsche, Saab, Volkswagen, and Volvo, among others (whose manufacturers generally restrict their offerings to those models they ordinarily export to the US). The factory delivery price, in US dollars, usually runs about 5% to 15% below the sticker price of the same model at a US dealership and includes the cost of shipping the car home. All contracts except BMW include US customs duty, but the cost of the incidentals and the insurance necessary for driving the car around Europe are extra except, again, BMW's plan.

One of the few disadvantages of factory delivery is that car manufacturers make only a limited number of models available each year, and for certain popular models you may have to get in line early in the season. Another is that you must take your trip when the car is ready, not when you are, although you usually will have 8 to 10 weeks' notice. The actual place of delivery can vary; it is more economical to pick up the car at the factory, but arrangements sometimes — but not always — can be made to have it delivered elsewhere for an extra charge. For example, Jaguars must be ordered through a US dealer and picked up at the factory in Coventry, England, although they also can be dropped off for shipment home in any number of European cities. For information, write to *Jaguar Cars,* 555 MacArthur Blvd., Mahwah, NJ 07430 (phone: 201-818-8500).

Cars for factory delivery usually can be ordered either through one of the manufacturer's authorized dealers in the US or through companies — among them *Europe by Car, Foremost Euro-Car,* and *Kemwel Group* (see above for contact information) — that specialize in such transactions. (Note that *Foremost Euro-Car* serves all of the US for rentals and leasing, but they arrange *sales* only for California residents.) Another company arranging car sales abroad is *Ship Side Tax Free World on Wheels BV,* 600B Lake St., Suite A, Ramsey, NJ 07446 (phone: 201-818-0400).

Occasionally an auto manufacturer offers free or discounted airfare in connection with a European delivery program. This year, Mercedes-Benz has a program including discounted round-trip airfare ($500 for two economy fare seats or one business class seat) from any US gateway served by *Lufthansa, Pan American,* or *TWA,* to Stuttgart (where the buyer picks up the car), plus a 1-night stay at the local *Ramada* or *Hilton* hotel, and 15 days' free comprehensive road insurance. For details, contact *Mercedes-Benz of North America,* 1 Mercedes Dr., Montvale, NJ 07645 (phone: 800-458-8202).

The other way to buy a car abroad, direct import, sometimes is referred to as "gray market" buying. It is perfectly legal, but not totally hassle-free. Direct import means that you buy abroad a car that was meant for use abroad, not one built according to US specifications. It can be new or used and may even include — if made for use in Ireland or Great Britain — a steering wheel on the right side. The main drawback to direct import is that the process of modification to bring the car into compliance with US standards is expensive and time-consuming: It typically costs from $5,000 to $7,000 in parts and labor and takes from 2 to 6 months. In addition, the same shipping, insurance, and miscellaneous expenses (another $2,000 to $5,000, according to estimates) that would be included in the factory delivery price must be added to the purchase price of the car, and the considerable burden of shepherding it on its journey from showroom to home garage usually is borne by the purchaser. Direct-import dealers do exist (they are not the same as your local, factory-authorized foreign car dealer, with whom you are now in competition), but even if you use one, you still need to do a great deal of paperwork yourself.

Once upon a time, the main advantage of the direct import method — besides the fact that it can be used for makes and models not available on factory delivery programs — was that much more money could be saved importing an expensive car. Given today's exchange rates, however, the method's potential greater gain is harder to realize and must be weighed against its greater difficulties. Still, if direct importing interests you, you can obtain a list of those makes and models approved for conversion in this country, and of the converters licensed to bring them up to US specifications, by contacting the Environmental Protection Agency, Manufacturers' Operations Division, EN-340-F, Investigations/Imports Section, 401 M St. SW, Washington, DC 20460 (phone: 202-382-2505).

If you have special problems getting your car into the US, you might consider contacting a specialist in vehicle importation, such as Daniel Kokal, a regulatory consultant with *Techlaw,* 14500 Avion Parkway, Suite 300, Chantilly, VA 22021 (phone: 703-818-1000).

Package Tours

If the mere thought of buying a package for travel to and through Spain and Portugal conjures up visions of a race through ten cities in as many days in lockstep with a horde of frazzled fellow travelers, remember that packages have come a long way. For one thing, not all packages necessarily are escorted tours, and the one you buy does not have to include any organized touring at all — nor will it necessarily include traveling companions. If it does, however, you'll find that people of all sorts — many just like yourself — are taking advantage of packages today because they are economical and convenient, save you an immense amount of planning time, and exist in such variety that it's virtually impossible not to find one that fits at least the majority of your travel preferences. Given the high cost of travel these days, packages have emerged as a particularly wise buy.

Aside from the cost-saving advantages of package arrangements, Spain and Portugal are ideally suited to package travel. The reason is that, essentially, they are roam-and-do destinations distinct from, say, the Caribbean, where most visitors go to a single island for a week or two of vacation and unpack everything until they're ready to return home. To be sure, many visitors to Spain and Portugal do seek out a single city or area — such as the Algarve or the Costa del Sol — for a concentrated visit, booking themselves into a hotel, apartment, house, or villa that serves as a stationary base from which they make regional tours and visits. But the bulk of North American travelers want to explore as much of Spain and Portugal as possible within the restrictions of time and travel funds available. Hence the popularity — and practicality — of package tours.

Hundreds of package programs are on the market today. In the US, numerous packages to Spain and Portugal are offered by tour operators or wholesalers, some retail travel agencies, airlines, charter companies, hotels, and even special-interest organizations, and what goes into them depends on who is organizing them. The most common type, assembled by tour wholesalers and sold through travel agents, runs the gamut from deluxe everything to simple tourist class amenities or even bare necessities. Fly/drive and fly/cruise packages usually are the joint planning efforts of airlines and, respectively, car rental companies and cruise line operators. Charter flight programs may range from little more than airfare and a minimum of ground arrangements to full-scale escorted tours or special-interest vacations. There also are hotel packages organized by hotel chains or associations of independent hotels and applicable to stays at any combination of member establishments; resort packages, covering arrangements at a specific hotel; and special-interest tours, which can be once-only programs organized by particular groups through a retail agency or regular offerings packaged by a tour operator. They can feature food, music or theater festivals, a particular sporting activity or event, a commemorative occasion, even nature study or scientific exploration.

In essence, a package is just an amalgam of travel services that can be purchased in a single transaction. A package (tour or otherwise) to and through the Iberian Peninsula may include any or all of the following: round-trip transatlantic transportation, local transportation (and/or car rentals), accommodations, some or all meals, sightseeing, entertainment, transfers to and from the hotel at each destination, taxes, tips, escort service, and a variety of incidental features that might be offered as options at additional cost. In other words, a package can be any combination of travel elements, from a fully escorted tour offered at an all-inclusive price to a simple fly/drive booking allowing you to move about totally on your own. Its principal advantage is that it saves money: The cost of the combined arrangements invariably is well below the price for all of the same elements if bought separately, and particularly if transportation is provided by charter or discount flight, it could cost less for all its elements than just a round-trip economy airline ticket on a regularly scheduled flight. A package provides more than economy and convenience: It releases the traveler from having to make individual arrangements for each separate element of a trip.

Lower prices are possible through package travel as a result of high-volume purchasing. The tour packager negotiates for services in wholesale quantities — blocks of airline seats or hotel rooms, group meals, busloads of ground transport, and so on — and they are offered at a lower per-person price because of the large quantities purchased for use during a given time period. Most packages, however, are subject to restrictions governing the duration of the trip and require total payment by a given time before departure.

Tour programs generally can be divided into two categories — "escorted" (or locally hosted) and "independent." An escorted tour means that a guide will accompany the group from the beginning of the tour through to the return flight; a locally hosted tour means that the group will be met upon arrival in each city by a different local host. On independent tours, there generally is a choice of hotels, meal plans, and sightseeing trips in each city, as well as a variety of special excursions. The independent plan is for travelers who do not want a totally set itinerary, but who do prefer confirmed hotel reservations. Whether choosing an escorted or independent tour, always bring along complete contact information for your tour operator in case a problem arises, although US tour operators often have Spanish or Portuguese affiliates who can give additional assistance or make other arrangements on the spot.

To determine whether a package — or, more specifically, *which* package — fits your travel plans, start by evaluating your interests and needs, deciding how much and what you want to spend, see, and do. Gather whatever package tour information is available for your schedule. Be sure that you take the time to read the brochure *carefully* to determine precisely what is included. Keep in mind that travel brochures are written to entice you into signing up for a package tour. Often the language is deceptive and devious. For example, a brochure may quote the lowest prices for a package tour based on facilities that are unavailable during the off-season, undesirable at any season, or just plain nonexistent. Information such as "breakfast included" (as it often is in packages to Spain and Portugal) or "plus tax" (which can add up) should be taken into account. Note, too, that prices quoted in brochures almost always are based on double occupancy: The rate listed is for each of two people sharing a double room, and if you travel alone, the supplement for single accommodations can raise the price considerably (see *Hints for Single Travelers,* in this section).

In this age of erratic airfares, the brochure most often will *not* include the price of an airline ticket in the price of the package, though sample fares from various gateway cities usually will be listed separately, to be added to the price of the ground arrangements. Before figuring your actual cost, check the latest fares with the airlines, because the samples invariably are out of date by the time you read them. If the brochure gives more than one category of sample fares per gateway city — such as an individual tour-basing fare, a group fare, an excursion or other discount ticket, or, in the case of flights to Spain and Portugal, an APEX, Winter, or Super APEX fare — your travel agent or airline tour desk will be able to tell you which one applies to the package you choose, depending on when you travel, how far in advance you book, and other factors. (An individual tour-basing fare is a fare computed as part of a package that includes land arrangements, thereby entitling a carrier to reduce the air portion almost to the absolute minimum. Though it always represents a savings over full-fare coach or economy, lately the individual tour-basing fare has not been as inexpensive as the excursion and other discount fares that also are available to individuals. The group fare usually is the least expensive fare, and it is the tour operator, not you, who makes up the group.) When the brochure does include round-trip transportation in the package price, don't forget to add the cost of round-trip transportation from your home to the departure city to come up with the total cost of the package.

Finally, read the general information regarding terms and conditions and the responsibility clause (usually in fine print at the end of the descriptive literature) to determine the precise elements for which the tour operator is — and is not — liable. Here the tour operator frequently expresses the right to change services or schedules as long as equivalent arrangements are offered. This clause also absolves the operator of responsibility for circumstances beyond human control, such as floods or avalanches, or injury to you or your property. While reading, ask the following questions:

1. Does the tour include airfare or other transportation, sightseeing, meals, transfers, taxes, baggage handling, tips, or any other services? Do you want all these services?
2. If the brochure indicates that "some meals" are included, does this mean a welcoming and farewell dinner, two breakfasts, or every evening meal?
3. What classes of hotels are offered? If you will be traveling alone, what is the single supplement?
4. Does the tour itinerary or price vary according to the season?
5. Are the prices guaranteed; that is, if costs increase between the time you book and the time you depart, can surcharges unilaterally be added?
6. Do you get a full refund if you cancel? If not, be sure to obtain cancellation insurance.
7. Can the operator cancel if too few people join? At what point?

One of the consumer's biggest problems is finding enough information to judge the reliability of a tour packager, since individual travelers seldom have direct contact with the firm putting the package together. Usually, a retail travel agent is interposed between customer and tour operator, and much depends on his or her candor and cooperation. So ask a number of questions about the tour you are considering. For example: Has the agent ever used a package provided by this tour operator? How long has the tour operator been in business? Is the tour operator a member of the *United States Tour Operators Association (USTOA)?* (All members of *USTOA* must be bonded, meet certain basic financial levels of capitalization, and have been under the same management for at least 3 years. A list of members is available upon request; also offered is a useful brochure, *How to Select a Package Tour.* Contact the *USTOA,* 211 E. 51st St., Suite 12B, New York, NY 10022 (phone: 212-944-5727). Also check the Better Business Bureau in the area where the tour operator is based to see if any complaints have been filed against it.) Which and how many companies are involved in the package? If air travel is by charter flight, is there an escrow account in which deposits will be held; if so, what is the name of the bank?

This last question is very important. US law requires that tour operators place every charter passenger's deposit and subsequent payment in a proper escrow account. Money paid into such an account cannot legally be used except to pay for the costs of a particular package or as a refund if the trip is canceled. To ensure the safe handling of your money, make your check payable to the escrow account — by law, the name of the depository must appear in the operator-participant contract, and usually is found in that mass of minuscule type on the back of the brochure. Write the details of the charter, including the destination and dates, on the face of the check; on the back, print "For Deposit Only." Your travel agent may prefer that you make your check out to the agency, saying that it will then pay the tour operator the fee minus commission. But it is perfectly legal to write your check as we suggest, and if your agent objects too strongly (the agent should have sufficient faith in the tour operator to trust him to send the proper commission), consider taking your business elsewhere. If you don't make your check out to the escrow account, you lose the protection of that escrow should the trip be canceled or the tour operator or travel agent fail. Furthermore, recent bankruptcies in the travel industry have served to point out that even the protection of escrow may not be enough to safeguard your investment. Increasingly, insurance is becoming a necessity (see *Insurance,* in this section), and payment by credit card has become popular since it offers some additional safeguards if the tour operator defaults.

■ **A word of advice:** Purchasers of vacation packages who feel they're not getting their money's worth are more likely to get a refund if they complain in writing to the operator — and bail out of the whole package immediately. Alert the tour operator or resort manager to the fact that you are dissatisfied, that you will be leaving for home as soon as transportation can be arranged, and that you expect a refund. They may have forms to fill out detailing your complaint; otherwise, state your case in a letter. Even if the availability of transportation home detains you, your dated, written complaint should help in procuring a refund from the operator.

SAMPLE PACKAGES TO SPAIN AND PORTUGAL: There are so many packages available to Spain and Portugal that it's probably safe to say that just about any arrangement anyone might want is available for as long as it is wanted. The keynote is flexibility. Some packages include one or both of the countries, while others explore only a selected region or visit only major cities such as Madrid or Lisbon.

Nevertheless, those seeking the maximum in structure will find that the classic sightseeing tour by motorcoach, fully escorted and all-inclusive (or nearly), has withstood the test of time and still is well represented among the programs of major tour operators. Typically, these tours begin in a major city and last from 1 to 2 weeks, if exploring Spain or Portugal alone, and anywhere from 10 days to 3 or 4 weeks if visiting both. A good many tour operators also offer at least one package that rounds out a visit to Spain and/or Portugal with a trip across the Strait of Gibraltar to Morocco, sometimes exploring that country in depth, sometimes going no farther than the port city of Tangier.

Hotel accommodations in these packages usually are characterized as first class or better, with private baths or showers accompanying all rooms, although more than a few tour packagers offer less expensive alternatives by providing more modest lodgings. Breakfast almost always is included, whereas the number of lunches and dinners may vary considerably, and meals include wine (or other alcoholic beverages) only when the tour literature clearly states so. Also included are transfers between airport and hotel, baggage handling, tips to maids and waiters, local transportation, and sightseeing excursions and admission fees, as well as any featured evening entertainment, personal expenses for laundry, incidentals and souvenirs, and tips to the motorcoach driver and to the tour escort, who remains with the group from beginning to end — almost everything, in fact, except round-trip airfare between the US and Spain or Portugal (which generally is shown separately).

Andalusia and its Mediterranean shore, the Costa del Sol, are by far the areas most frequently visited on escorted tours of Spain, a good many of which take in these popular areas alone, either making a long, narrow loop starting and ending in Madrid or beginning in Madrid and ending in Málaga, where participants board a plane for their flight home. Tours with more time to spare may broaden the loop to include such cities as Barcelona and Valencia en route to or from Andalusia. Some packages avoid Andalusia entirely, however, and focus their attention elsewhere.

Among these are the 12-day "Castilian" tour from *American Express Travel Service* (branches throughout the US), which circles north from Madrid, passing through Avila, Valladolid, and Burgos, the regions of Navarre and Aragón, and the principality of Andorra before winding up with visits to Barcelona and Valencia; and the "Northern Spain" package from *Melia International* (450 Seventh Ave., Suite 1805, New York, NY 10103; phone: 212-967-6565 in New York State; 800-848-2314 elsewhere in the US), an 8-day tour available from May to October, covering Madrid, Lugo, La Coruña, Santiago de Compostela, Rias Bajas, La Toja, Vigo, Puebla de Sanabria, and Madrid. A 5-day tour from *AIB Tours* (3798 Flagler, Coral Gables, FL 33134; phone: 305-442-0246; 800-232-0242 in Florida; 800-242-8687 elsewhere in the US) visits Salamanca, Madrid, and Lisbon. *Melia* also offers a 12-day tour of Spain and Portugal, available from May to October, covering Madrid, Bodajoz, Lisbon, Seville, Torremolinos, Granada, and Córdoba; or an 8-day tour, available from April to November, covering Madrid, Badajoz, Lisbon, and Mérida. Numerous other Iberian itineraries also are offered.

Andalusia and the Costa del Sol also figure prominently on combined Spain-Portugal trips, which frequently begin in Lisbon, cut across the Alentejo Plains and the Spanish border to Seville, then make their way around Andalusia and the coast before turning north to Madrid for departure. The same itinerary in reverse — Madrid to Lisbon — also is common, as is a full circle, Lisbon to Lisbon or Madrid to Madrid. In this case, the northern link generally is via the Portuguese city of Coimbra, the Beira Mountains, and the Spanish cities of Salamanca and Avila, although the 16-day "Pousadas and Paradors" tour offered by *Maupintour* (PO Box 807, Lawrence, KS 66044; phone: 800-255-4266), circling counterclockwise from Lisbon to Lisbon, plots a different course, substituting the Spanish regions of Extremadura and Castile for Andalusia as the southern link of the itinerary and returning to Lisbon via Galicia and the far north of Portugal. The same package also deviates from the norm by scheduling the majority of overnights in the government-run *pousadas* of Portugal and *paradores* of Spain, accommodations more commonly found on fly/drive packages (see below) than on escorted tours.

When packaged on its own, Portugal, a small country, tends to break down into two regions at most, north and south, with tours of either beginning in Lisbon. *Abreu Tours* (317 E. 34th St., New York, NY 10016; phone 212-661-0555 or 800-223-1580) offers a 7- or 11-day "Northern Portugal" escorted motorcoach tour. Other tour operators with packages to both areas include *Skyline Travel Club* (666 Old Country Rd., Suite 205, Garden City, NY 11530; phone 516-222-9090 or 800-645-6198) which offers a 13-day "Portuguese Sun Seeker" motorcoach tour (with travelers staying in *paradores* or *pousadas*) that explores the south and includes the Algarve, while the 11- or 15-day "Best of Portugal" itinerary covers the rest of the country. *Mill-Run Tours* (20 E. 49th St., New York, NY 10017; phone: 212-486-9840 in New York State, 800-MILL-RUN elsewhere) offers tours throughout Portugal, including the Azores and Madeira, as well as selected destinations in Spain.

Examples of escorted, highly structured packages are those offered by *Olson Travelworld,* which offers two itineraries to Spain and Portugal: "Casbah and Castinets," a 22-day tour that takes in Lisbon, Cascais, Fatima, Seville, Madrid, Toledo, Córdoba, and the Costa del Sol; and "Connoisseur's Iberia," a 17-day deluxe tour of Gibraltar, Spain, and Portugal. For information on these and other European itineraries, contact *Olson Travelworld,* 100 N. Sepulveda Blvd., Suite 1010, El Segundo, CA 90245 (phone: 213-615-0711 in California or abroad; 800-421-5785 in California; 800-421-2255 elsewhere in the US).

Globus-Gateway offers numerous first class tours of Europe, including a 17-day Spain-Portugal-Morocco tour; a 14-day Spain-Portugal-Tangier itinerary; a 23-day "Treasures of France, Spain, and Portugal" tour; a 10- or 12-day "Sunny Spain" tour; and individual packages in Spain only. *Cosmos,* a budget tour operator affiliated with *Globus-Gateway,* offers numerous tours of Europe, including 12 multi-country grand tours, and 23 regional tours of the Continent. Iberian itineraries include a 15-day

Spain-Portugal-Morocco tour and a 12-day "Best of Spain and Portugal" package. Bookings for both agencies must be made through travel agents; however, both agencies can be contacted for information at 95-25 Queens Blvd., Rego Park, NY 11374 (phone: 800-221-0090) or 150 S. Los Robles Ave., Pasadena, CA 91101 (phone: 818-449-2019 or 800-556-5454).

Abercrombie & Kent (1420 Kensington Rd., Oak Brook, IL 60521; phone: 708-954-2944 in Illinois; 800-323-7308 elsewhere in the US) offers all-inclusive package tours that take care of just about everything — right down to a traveling bellhop to handle your baggage. These tours, which are grouped under the heading "Great Britain and Europe Express Tours," include packages to Spain, and as the name implies transportation is mainly via rail.

Trafalgar Tours offers more than 50 first class motorcoach itineraries of the Continent, plus a group of budget-conscious "CostSaver" tours that cut costs by scheduling a number of nights in good or select tourist class hotels. Among the regular itineraries is a first class, 14-day, 8-city, motorcoach tour of Spain and Portugal. Bookings are made through travel agents, but you can contact *Trafalgar Tours* directly at 21 E. 26th St., New York, NY 10010 (phone: 212-689-8977 in New York City; 800-854-0103 elsewhere in the US).

TWA Getaway Tours (phone: 800-GETAWAY) also offers a wide variety of escorted motorcoach tours throughout both Spain and Portugal. Another tour operator offering a wide range of similar packages throughout Europe, including Spanish and Portuguese destinations, is *Travcoa* (PO Box 2630, Newport Beach, CA 92658; phone: 714-476-2800 abroad; 800-992-2004 in California; 800-992-2003 elsewhere in the US), which offers a lineup of packages, for 18, 26, or 29 days, that include all meals.

Not to be discounted is *Thomas Cook,* the best known of all British tour operators. Its name is practically synonymous with the Grand Tour of Europe, but *Cook*'s tours span the world, with itineraries ranging from deluxe to moderate, including some of the budget variety as well. Among the packages to Iberia are a 14-day escorted motorcoach tour visiting Spain's Costa del Sol, Madrid, Málaga, Salamanca, and Seville, and Fatima, Lisbon, and Viseu in Portugal. Other tour and stay-put packages also are offered. This company is a wholesaler, and you can book a tour directly through any of its offices in major cities in North America or through travel agents. *Thomas Cook*'s headquarters are at 45 Berkeley St., Piccadilly, London W1A 1EB (phone: 71-499-4000).

Less restrictive arrangements for travelers who prefer more independence than that found on escorted tours are listed in the semi-escorted and hosted sections of tour catalogues. These may combine some aspects of an escorted tour, such as moving from place to place by motorcoach, with longer stays in one spot, where participants are at liberty but where a host or hostess — that is, a representative of the tour company — is available at a local office or even in the hotel to answer questions and assist in arranging activities and optional excursions.

Another equally common type of package to Spain and Portugal is the car tour or fly/drive arrangement, often described in brochures as a self-drive or go-as-you-please tour. These are independent vacations, geared to travelers who want to cover as much ground as they might on an escorted group sightseeing tour but who prefer to do it on their own. The most flexible plans include no more than a map, a rental car, and a block of as many prepaid hotel vouchers as are needed for the length of the stay (the packages typically are 4 or 7 days long, extendable by individual extra days or additional package segments), along with a list of participating hotels at which the vouchers are accepted. In most cases, only the first night's accommodation is reserved; from then on, travelers book their rooms one stop ahead as they drive from place to place, creating their own itinerary as they go. When the hotels are members of a chain or association — which they usually are — the staff of the last hotel will reserve the next one for you.

In other cases, there may be a choice of reserving all accommodations before departure — usually for a fee. Operators offering these packages usually sell vouchers in more than one price category; travelers may have the option of upgrading accommodations by paying a supplement directly to more expensive establishments.

Another type of fly/drive arrangement is slightly more restrictive in that the tour packager supplies an itinerary that must be followed day by day, with a specific hotel to be reached each night. Often these plans are more deluxe as well.

The car tours packaged by *AutoVenture* (425 Pike St., Suite 502, Seattle, WA 98101; phone: 206-624-6033 in Washington or abroad; 800-426-7502 elsewhere in the US) feature overnight stays in hotels that are elegant converted castles or manor houses or old and distinctive country inns. Many of its itineraries, 6 to 14 days in length, cover Spain (but not Portugal) and can be bought in either a self-drive or chauffeured version.

British Airways Holidays (phone: 800-AIRWAYS), a subsidiary of *British Airways,* offers a variety of fly/drive and fly/rail packages, including a choice of mix-and-match independent holiday options with accommodations ranging from inexpensive inns to deluxe hotels. Similar structured self-drive car tours also are offered by *Iberia* and *TAP Air.*

A further possibility for independent travelers is a "stay-put" package, such as the popular Spanish and Portugal city packages. These appeal to travelers who want to be on their own and remain in one place for the duration of their vacation, although it is not unusual for travelers to buy more than one package at a time. Basically the city package — no matter what the city — include round-trip transfer between airport and hotel, a choice of hotel accommodations (usually including breakfast) in several price ranges, plus any number of other features you may not need or want but would lose valuable time arranging if you did. Common package features are 1 or 2 half-day guided tours of the city; a boat cruise; passes for unlimited local travel by bus or train; discount cards for shops, museums, and restaurants; temporary membership in and admission to clubs, discotheques, or other nightspots; and car rental for some or all of your stay. Other features may include anything from a souvenir travel bag to tasting of local wines, dinner, and a show. The packages usually are a week long — although 4-day and 14-day packages also are available, most packages can be extended by extra days — and often are hosted; that is, a representative of the tour company may be available at a local office or even in the hotel to answer questions, handle problems, and assist in arranging activities and option excursions. A similar stay-put resort package generally omits the sightseeing tour and may offer some sort of daily meal plan if accommodations are in hotels; accommodations in apartment hotels with kitchenettes are a common alternative.

Almost all tour operators with programs to Spain and Portugal list Madrid and Lisbon city packages in their literature. The 3- and 6-night Madrid and Lisbon packages offered by *American Express Travel*'s travel agency (call 800-YES-AMEX or contact the nearest office of *American Express Travel*) are examples of the many such packages available. Travelers can choose from 6 different itineraries, such as the "Best of Spain" 10-day, 5-city packages; the "Iberian Sun Seeker" 14-day, 7-city package; the "Iberian-Moroccan Holiday" 17-day, 11-city tour; and "Independent Tours," with a 3-night minimum stay in Lisbon or Madrid.

Among tour operators with similar packages to Madrid (as well as Barcelona, and other Iberian destinations) are *Ibero Travel* (109-21 72nd Rd., Forest Hills, New York, NY 11375; phone: 800-654-2376 in New York State; 800-882-6678 elsewhere in the US), *Petrabax Tours* (97-45 Queens Blvd., Suite 505, Rego Park, NY 11374; phone: 718-897-7272 in New York State, 800-367-6611 elsewhere), *Marsans International* (19 W. 34th St., Suite 302, New York, NY 10001; phone: 212-239-3880 in New York State; 800-223-6114 elsewhere in the US), and *Sun Holidays* (26 Sixth St., Suite 603, Stamford, CT 06905; phone: 203-323-1166 in Connecticut; 800-243-2057 elsewhere in the

US), all with 3-night packages, and *Spanish Heritage Tours* (116-47 Queens Blvd., Forest Hills, NY 11375; phone: 718-520-1300 or 800-221-2580), with a 6-night package. *Petrabax* and *Marsans International* also offer 3-night packages to Seville, and the latter also has a 3-night package to Granada. Packages to the Portuguese city of Porto (as well as Lisbon) are offered by *Mill-Run Tours* (3 nights) and *Abreu Tours* (3 or 6 nights); they also have 3- or 6-night packages based on a choice of Estoril or Cascais, Lisbon's seaside suburbs, while *Spanish Heritage Tours* has a 6-night package based in Estoril. *TWA Getaway Tours* (phone: 800-GETAWAY) offers numerous city packages throughout Europe, including Madrid and Lisbon. *British Airways* Holidays (800-AIRWAYS) also offers city packages to Barcelona and Madrid.

The Spanish resort areas most frequently found on combination city/resort packages are on the Costa del Sol, particularly Torremolinos and Marbella, and the islands of Majorca (the capital, Palma de Mallorca, is the usual choice for hotels) and Ibiza in the Balearics and Gran Canaria and Tenerife in the Canary Islands (where Las Palmas and Puerto de la Cruz, respectively, are the main hotel sites). A third island of the Canaries, Lanzarote, is available on some programs. The Algarve, Portugal's southern coast, is the most common destination for resort packages in Portugal; the island of Madeira and various islands of the Azores also are offered by many tour packagers. Besides the tour operators mentioned above, so many others offer packages to one or more of these resorts (often in combination with cities or other resorts) that it's best to consult a travel agent or, since many of these packages are run in conjunction with *Iberia Airlines* (see *Iberia*'s "Spain and Beyond" catalogue of tours), directly with that airline. *TAP Air* collaborates with *Abreu Tours* (address above), *Cavalcade Tours* (450 Harman Meadow Blvd., Secaucus, NJ 07096; phone: 201-617-8922 or 800-356-2405), and several other tour packagers to offer a large selection of combined air/land packages. (They don't publish a tour catalogue, however.) For information, contact *Abreu Tours, Cavalcade Tours,* or your travel agent.

A good example of a stay-put vacation is the resort package offered by *Club Med* (40 W. 57th St., New York, NY 10019; phone: 800-CLUB MED), which operates its own resort villages around the world and has four resorts in Spain, the main one being at Don Miguel in the south near Marbella, and one in Portugal, in Da Balaia in the Algarve near Albufeira.

Special-interest tours are a growing sector of the travel industry, and programs focusing on food and wine are prominent among the packages of this sort. One thing to note is that they tend to be quite structured arrangements rather than independent ones, and they rarely are created with the budget traveler in mind. Also note that inclusive as they may be, few food and wine tours include *all* meals in the package price. This is not necessarily a cost-cutting technique on the part of the packager; rather, because of the lavishness of some of the meals, others may be left to the discretion of the participants, not only to allow time for leisure, but also to allow for differing rates of metabolism. Similarly, even on wine tours that spend entire days in practically full-time tasting, unlimited table wine at meals may not always be included in the package price. The brochures usually are clear about what comes with the package and when. For information on current offerings, check with your travel agent.

Among the various food and wine tours are *Bacchants' Pilgrimages'* tours of vineyards and wine cellars. Included are winery-hosted luncheons, picnics, dinners in three-star restaurants, and other luncheons and dinners in restaurants of lesser renown. This year's itineraries will include a tour to Spain and/or Portugal. Bookings are through travel agents or *Bacchants' Pilgrimages* (345 California St., Suite 2570, San Francisco, CA 94104; phone: 415-981-8518).

For groups of 10 or more travelers, *Travel Concepts* offers a variety of custom-designed food and wine tours throughout Europe. Although there is no pre-planned itinerary in Spain or Portugal, they can design one for individuals or groups. For information, contact *Travel Concepts,* 62 Commonwealth Ave., Suite 3, Boston, MA 02116 (phone: 617-266-8450).

There also are special-interest packages catering to travelers particularly interested in the arts. For example, *Dailey-Thorp* (315 W. 57th St., New York, NY 10019; phone: 212-307-1555) offers tours for music and opera lovers, focusing on European musical events. This year's offerings include a music and opera tour in Spain, visiting Barcelona, Granada, Madrid, and maybe a visit to Lisbon, depending on concurrent performances.

Other tours also visit major cities each year to enjoy the cultural attractions. For instance, art enthusiasts will enjoy *Prospect Art Tours'* 5- to 15-day packages visiting key museums and private galleries and art collections throughout Europe. Among their itineraries are a variety of eclectic tours to Spain and Portugal. For information, contact *Prospect Art Tours* (454-458 Chiswick High Rd., London W45TT; phone: 44-81-995-2151 or 44-81-995-2163) or their US agent, *The British Connection* (Suite 240, 2490 Black Rock Turnpike, Fairfield, CT 06430; phone: 203-254-7221).

The prehistoric cave art of northern Spain can be explored on *Past Time Tours'* 14-day package. The tour includes educational lectures and a look at some of the world's most intriguing prehistoric ritual art and symbols. For information, contact *Past Time Tours,* 800 Larch La., Sacramento, CA 95864-5042 (phone: 916-485-8140).

Currently, there are no ski packages to Spain, though there are resorts in northern Spain where it is possible to enjoy a skiing holiday. Those interested will have to do some investigation and book through a knowledgeable travel agent or on their own. (For a start see *Sensational Spanish Skiing,* DIVERSONS.) Ironically, *Adventures on Skis* (815 North Rd., Westfield, MA 01085; phone: 413-568-2855 in Massachusetts; 800-628-9655 elsewhere in the US) offers golfing tours to Spain and Portugal, but no ski packages.

Golf courses in many European countries are a fairly new addition; however, the courses in Spain and Portugal have been around for quite some time. Among the companies offering golf tours to Spain and Portugal are the following:

Adventure Golf Holiday, 815 North Rd., Westfield, MA 01085 (phone: 800-628-9655 or 413-568-2855). Offers packages to Portugal's Algarve.

Adventures in Golf, 29 Valencia Dr., Nashua, NH 03062 (phone: 603-882-8367). Offers custom-designed golf holidays in Spain and Portugal.

Fourth Dimension Tours, 1150 NW 72nd Ave., Miami, FL 33126 (phone: 800-343-0020 or 305-477-1525). Arranges group (of 20 or more) tours to Spain's Costa del Sol and Portugal's Algarve.

Golf Intercontinental/Marsans, 19 W. 34 St., New York, NY 10001 (phone: 212-239-3880 in New York State; 800-223-6114 elsewhere in the US). Offers a 7-day self-drive tour through Spain and Portugal — for serious golfers only.

Golfing Holidays, 231 E. Millbrae Ave., Millbrae, CA 94030 (phone: 415-697-0230). Has packages to golf courses in Costa del Sol and Madrid in Spain and the Algarve and Lisbon in Portugal.

Golfpac Inc., Box 940490, 901 N. Lake Destiny Dr., Suite 192, Maitland, FL 32794-0490 (phone: 800-327-0878 or 407-660-8277). Designs custom golf packages to Spain and Portugal including a rental car or transportation by motorcoach.

Grasshopper Golf Tours, 407 Hill Ave., Glen Ellyn, IL 60137 (phone: 708-858-1660). Designs custom golf packages for individuals or groups; although this company specializes in Portugal, they also can arrange play on Spanish greens.

InterGolf, PO Box 819, Champlain, NY 12919, or 4150 St. Catherine St. W., Suite 390, Montreal, Quebec. H3Z 2Y5, Canada (phone: 514-933-2772 in Canada; 800-363-6273 in the US). Offers self-drive golf package tours through Spain, and offers several escorted motorcoach and sightseeing itineraries in Portugal.

ITC Golf Tours, Box 5144, Long Beach, CA 90805 (phone: 800-257-4981 or 213-595-6905). Arranges custom golf packages anywhere and any way you want it — including Spain and Portugal.

Perry Golf, 5584 Chamblee Dunwoody Rd., Atlanta, GA 30338 (phone: 800-344-5257 or 404-394-5400). Has fly/drive golf packages to Spain's Costa del Sol and Portugal's Algarve.

Petrabax, 97-45 Queens Blvd., Rego Park, NY 11374 (phone: 800-367-6611 or 718-897-7272). Offers individual or group packages to Spain's Costa del Sol.

Value Holidays, 10224 N. Port Washington Rd., Mequon, WI 53092 (phone: 800-558-6850). Offers packages to Spain's Costa del Sol and Portugal's Algarve.

Wide World of Golf, PO Box 5217, Su Vecino Court, Carmel, CA 93921 (phone: 408-624-6667). Offers a 10-day golf package to Portugal, including courses in the vicinity of Lisbon and the Algarve.

As already mentioned, *Adventures on Skis* (address above) also offers golfing tours of Iberia. Information about many more golf packages can be obtained from a travel agent or from the appropriate tourist authorities (see *Sources and Resources,* in this section, for addresses).

Horseback riding holidays are the province of *FITS Equestrian* (2011 Alamo Pintado Rd., Solvang, CA 93463; phone: 800-666-FITS or 805-688-9494) and *Equitour* (Bitterroot Ranch, Rte. 66, Box 1042, Dubois, WY 82513; phone: 307-455-3363 in Wyoming; 800-545-0019 elsewhere in the US). The choices — not for beginners — include up to 15 days of riding on a purebred Andalusian mount through the villages and countryside and along the beaches of Andalusia or on the wide dirt roads of Castile, and 8 days discovering Portugal on the back of the country's Lusitano breed. Both companies also offer riding holidays in Extremadura — again only for experienced riders. Accommodations generally are in small hotels or inns.

Fisherfolk might enjoy the opportunity to fish for tuna in the Portuguese Azores that's offered by *Fishing International* (Hilltop Estate, 4010 Montecito Ave., Santa Rosa CA 95404; phone: 800-950-4242 or 707-542-4242). Other enticing packages include salmon fishing in Spain. These week-long packages include accommodations in a small country inn and breakfast daily, and the opportunity to exchange fish stories about the one that got away.

And for marksmen interested in trying their hands at shooting red-legged partridge in Spain, *Frontiers International* (PO Box 161, Pearce Mill Rd., Wexford, PA 15090; phone: 412-935-1577 in Pennsylvania; 800-245-1950 elsewhere in the US) offers two deluxe 3- and 4-day shooting packages in La Mancha. Accommodations are in a gracious manor house; all meals, cocktails, tips, and even shotgun shells are included. Assistants clean, carry, and load your gun, and guests also can enjoy riding the estate's fine Spanish mounts.

Special-interest tours for practitioners and spectators of other sports include many biking and hiking tours of varying levels of difficulty. For the names and addresses of their organizers, see below.

Camping and Caravanning, Hiking and Biking

 CAMPING AND CARAVANNING: Spain and Portugal welcome campers, whether they come alone or with a group, with tents or in recreational vehicles — generally known in Europe as "caravans" (a term that technically refers to towable campers as opposed to fully motorized vehicles, known as "minibuses" or "minivans"). Camping probably is the best way to enjoy the countryside. And, fortunately, campgrounds in Iberia are plentiful.

Where to Camp – Caravanning is extremely popular with European vacationers, and many parks cater more to the caravanner than to the tent dweller. Some campgrounds have minimal facilities, and others are quite elaborate, with a variety of amenities on the premises. Most sites are open from about *Easter* through October.

Directors of campgrounds often have a great deal of information about their region, and some even will arrange local tours or recommend the best restaurants, shops, beaches, or attractions in the immediate area. Campgrounds also provide the atmosphere and opportunity to meet other travelers and exchange useful information. Too much so, sometimes — the popularity of the European campgrounds causes them to be quite crowded during the summer, and campsites frequently are so close together that any attempt at privacy or getting away from it all is sabotaged. As campgrounds fill quickly throughout the season, and the more isolated sites always go first, it's a good idea to arrive early in the day and reserve your chosen spot — which leaves you free to explore the area for the rest of the day. (Whenever possible, try to call ahead and arrange a "pitch" in advance. At the height of the season, however, if you do not have advance reservations, you may be lucky to get even a less desirable site.)

In some communities, it is possible to camp free on public grounds. As the local police or local tourism information office about regulations. To camp on private property you first must obtain the permission of the landowner or tenant — and assume the responsibility of leaving the land exactly as it was found in return for the hospitality.

Spanish and Portuguese campgrounds generally are well marked. Still, it's best to have a map or check the information available in one of the numerous comprehensive guides to sites across the Continent. It may not be easy to find camping facilities open before June or after September, so a guide that gives this information comes in particularly handy off-season.

In the US, maps, brochures, and other information for campers are distributed by the National Tourist Office of Spain and the Portuguese National Tourist Office. The Portuguese office offers a brochure in English; unfortunately, a much more comprehensive guide, *Guía de Campings,* is published only in Spanish. A variety of useful publications also are available from American and European automobile clubs and other associations.

The *American Automobile Association (AAA)* offers a number of useful resources, including its 600-page *Travel Guide to Europe* and the 64-page *Motoring Europe,* as well as a variety of useful maps; contact the nearest branch of *AAA* or the national office (see *Traveling by Car,* in this section). In addition, the *Automobile Association of Great Britain (AA)* publishes a comprehensive guide, *Camping and Caravanning in Europe* ($12.95), which lists about 4,000 sites throughout Europe, inspected and rated by the *AA,* and provides other information of interest to campers. It is available from the *AA* (Farnum House, Basingstoke, Hampshire RG21 2EA, England). Another useful book, *Camper's Companion to Southern Europe,* which gives camping information for Spain and Portugal, is out of print. Look for it in your local library.

The French international camping organization *Fédération Internationale de Camping et Caravaning* issues a pass, called a *carnet,* that entitles the bearer to a modest discount at many campgrounds throughout Europe, including Spain and Portugal. It is available in the US from the *National Campers and Hikers Association* (4804 Transit Rd., Bldg. 2, Depew, NY 14043; phone: 716-668-6242) for a fee of $23, which includes membership in the organization as well as camping information.

Necessities – For outdoor camping, you will need a tent with flyscreens (the lighter and easier to carry and assemble the better); a sleeping bag; a foam pad, air mattress, or one of the new combination self inflatable mattresses; a waterproof ground cloth; a rain poncho (which, in a pinch, can double as a ground cloth); a first-aid kit (including sunscreen and insect repellent); sewing and toilet kits (including a roll of toilet paper in a plastic bag); a backpack stove; matches; nested cooking pots and cooking utensils; a canteen; a three-quarter ax (well sharpened and sheath-protected); a jackknife; and a flashlight with an extra set of batteries. If you want a campfire, you may want to pick up some supplies (and wood or charcoal) en route to the campground (though some campgrounds do sell bundles of firewood) — particularly where there is little wood, as in the desert. Be aware, however, that fires are prohibited in many areas, especially during the dry season.

If you have room bring (or pick up on arrival) a compact Coleman lantern (with extra mantles, fuel, and a funnel) or battery-powered light (with extra batteries); if not, candles will do. You can make a simple windscreen that also will reflect and amplify candlelight using aluminium foil, which also is useful for campfire cooking. Small Coleman-type lanterns that will take either candle inserts or lamp oil are another alternative; these are more practical than the standard lanterns, as they are designed for backpackers and the glass is protected by a metel sheath for safe transport.

For the backpack stove, consider a Mountain Safety Research (MSR) or similar model, which — unlike most stoves, which run only on white gas (which is hard to find in some parts of Europe) — also works with kerosene or alcohol. No matter what kind of camp stove you choose, however, it still is a good idea to bring along extra fuel. A stove helps out when you're knee-deep in the mud of a rainy day, and in-camp cooking is a great way to help stretch your travel funds.

Also include a canteen and/or plastic containers for water. Unless you are told that the campground where you are staying provides purified water, you should use it only for washing (don't even brush your teeth with it). In such cases, use only bottled, purified, or boiled water for drinking. To purify tap water, either use a water purification kit (available at most camping supply stores) or bring the water to a full, rolling boil over a camp stove. Unless deep in the wilderness, it is inadvisable to use water from streams, rivers, or lakes — even purified.

Keep food simple. Unless backpacking deep in the wilds, you probably will be close enough to a store to stock up on perishables. Staples such as sugar, coffee, powdered milk, rice, and other grains, and a basic assortment of spices can be carried along. Dehydrated food has become quite popular among both hikers and campers, but it can be expensive. Keep in mind, particularly in wilderness areas, that accessible food will lure scavenging wildlife, which may invade tents and vehicles. As a basic safety precaution, it is advisable to hang all foodstuffs from a tree some distance from your sleeping area. Bring along an extra waterproof stuff sack (available in a variety of sizes in camping supply stores) and some rope for this purpose.

Most experienced campers (particularly hikers and bikers; see below) perfer to bring their own tried and true equipment, but camping equipment is available for sale or rent throughout Spain and Portugal, and rentals can be booked in advance through any number of outfitters. The *AAA* and some of the other above-mentioned guides to camping and caravanning contain lists of outfitters, and the national tourist offices in the US can supply information on reliable dealers.

Recreational Vehicles – Known in Europe as caravans (or minibuses or minivans), recreational vehicles (RVs) will appeal most to the kind of person who prefers the flexibility in accommodations — there are countless campgrounds throughout Spain and Portugal and a number of them provide RV hookups — and enjoys camping with a little extra comfort.

An RV undoubtably saves a traveler a great deal of money on accommodations, and if cooking appliances are part of the unit, on food as well. However, it is important to remember that renting an RV is a major expense; also, any kind of RV increases gas consumption considerably.

Although the term "recreational vehicle" is applied to all manner of camping vehicles, whether towed or self-propelled, generally the models available for rent in Spain and Portugal and nearby countries are either towable campers (caravans) or motorized RVs. The motorized models usually are minivans or minibuses — vans customized in various ways for camping, often including elevated roofs — and larger, coach-type, fully equipped homes on wheels, requiring electrical hookups at night to run the TV set, air conditioning, and kitchen appliances. Although most motorized models are equipped with shift, occasionally automatic shift vehicles may be available for an additional charge.

Towed vehicles can be hired overseas, but usually are not offered by US or international companies. At present, however, the only type of motorized caravan rented in Spain and Portugal is a van or minibus with an elevated roof. These are available from international and Spanish or Portuguese car rental companies in the major cities (see *Traveling by Car,* earlier in this section), although you will probably have to do some calling around to find one. However, you can rent other types of RVs in France and drive them across the border into Spain (see list below). In this event, inform the rental company of your plans.

If you are planning to caravan all over Europe, make sure that whatever vehicle you choose is equipped to deal with the electrical and gas standards of all the countries on your itinerary. You should have either a sufficient supply of the type the camper requires or equipment that can use more than one type. When towing a camper, note that nothing towed is covered automatically by the liability insurance of the primary vehicle, so the driver's Green Card must carry a specific endorsement that covers the towed vehicle.

Whether driving a camper or towing, it is essential to have some idea of the terrain you'll be encountering en route. Only experienced drivers should drive large campers, particularly in northern Spain, where the terrain can be quite steep.In fact, grades sometimes can be too steep for certain vehicles to negotiate, and some roads are off limits to towed caravans. Also be aware that mountain passes and tunnels crossing the borders into France and Andorra sometimes are closed in the winter, depending on altitude, road grade, and severity of the weather. Your best source of information on weather and road conditions are the French, Spanish, or Portuguese automobile clubs. Car tunnels, or "piggyback" services on trains, usually bypass those summits too difficult to climb, but they also impose dimension limitations and often charge high fees. The *AAA* guides noted above provide detailed information on the principal passes and tunnels, as do tourist offices.

As mentioned above, only customized vans (minibuses or minivans) are available in Spain or Portugal; however, rentals of RVs in neighboring France (or other nearby countries for those planning to do more extensive touring in addition to visiting Iberia) are available. Among companies offering minivan and/or RV rentals for Iberian camping are the following:

Auto-Europe, PO Box 1907, Camden, ME 04843 (phone: 207-236-8235 in Maine; 800-223-5555 elsewhere in the US). Offers minibus rentals in over 15 cities in Spain and in Coimbra, Faro, Lisbon, and Porto in Portugal.

Avis Rent-A-Car, 6128 E. 38th St., Tulsa, OK 74135 (phone: 800-331-1084, ext. 7719). Offers minibus rentals at over 150 locations in Spain and 26 in Portugal; larger RVs can be rented at locations in France and driven over the border into Spain. Arrangements must be made through the US office.

Connex, 983 Main St., Peekskill, NY 10566 (phone: 800-333-3949). Rents minibuses in Spain and Portugal and motorized RVs in Germany.

Europe by Car, One Rockefeller Plaza, New York, NY 10020, or 9000 Sunset Blvd., Los Angeles, CA 90069 (phone: 212-581-3040 in New York State; 800-223-1516 elsewhere in the US). Rents RVs in Belgium and Germany.

Foremost Euro-Car, 5430 Van Nuys Blvd., Suite 306, Van Nuys, CA 91401 (phone: 800-252-9401 in California; 800-423-3111 in the US). Rents RVs in Germany.

Kemwel Group, 106 Calvert St., Harrison, NY 10528 (phone: 800-678-0678 or 914-835-5555). Offers minibus rental in 18 cities in Spain and Estoril, Faro, Lisbon, and Porto in Portugal.

The general policy with the above agencies is to make reservations far enough in advance to receive a voucher that will be used to pick up the vehicle at the designated location in Europe. (Early reservations also are advisable as the supply of RVs is limited and the demand great.)

Among the French companies offering RV rentals in France — which by special arrangement may be driven over the border into Spain and then Portugal — are the following:

FCI Location, Zone Industrielle de Sant-Brendan, Quentin 22800, France (phone: 33-96-74-08-36). Rents motorized RVs in France.

Trois Soleils, Maison Trois Soleils, 2 Route de Paris, 67117 Ittenheim, France (phone: 88-69-17-17 for reservations; 30-69-06-60 for the Paris branch). Rents motorized RVs, as well as some basic campers in France; pick-up and drop-off locations include Bordeaux, Montpelier, Paris, and Strasbourg.

As in the US, numerous smaller, local companies that rent both motorized and towable campers are to be found throughout Europe. For minivan and minibus rentals in Spain and Portugal, ask at local car rental companies and tourism offices.

For information on how to operate, choose, and use a recreational vehicle, see *Living on Wheels* by Richard A. Wholters (Dutton; currently out of print; check your library or bookstore). You also might want to subscribe to *Trailer Life,* published by *TL Enterprises* (29901 Agoura Rd., Agoura, CA 91301; phone: 800-234-3450 or 818-991-4980). A 1-year subscription costs $12; $9 for members of the Good Sam Club, which provides discounts on a variety of services for RV owners and which also is run by *TL Enterprises.*

Another useful resource is the complimentary package of information on RVs offered by the *Recreational Vehicle Industry Association (RVIA).* It includes a catalogue of RV sources and consumer information; write to the *Recreational Vehicle Industry Association* (Dept. RK, PO Box 2999, Reston, VA 22090; phone: 703-620-6003). The *Recreational Vehicle Rental Association (RVRA),* an RV dealers group, publishes an annual rental directory, *Who's Who in RV Rentals;* send $5 to the *Recreational Vehicle Rental Association* (3251 Old Lee Hwy., Suite 500, Fairfax, VA 22030; phone: 703-591-7130).

Finally, you may want to subscribe to *Trailblazer,* a recreational vehicle and motorhome magazine. A year's subscription costs $24; write to *Trailblazer,* 1000 124th Ave. NE, Bellevue, WA 98005.

Organized Camping Trips – A packaged camping tour abroad is a good way to have your cake and eat it, too. The problems of advance planning and day-to-day organizing are left to someone else, yet you still reap the benefits that shoestring travel affords. Be aware, however, that these packages usually are geared to the young, with ages 18 to 35 as common limits. Transfer from place to place is by bus or van (as on other sightseeing tours), overnights are in tents, and meal arrangements vary. Often there is a kitty that covers meals in restaurants or in the camps; sometimes there is a chef, and sometimes the cooking is done by the participants themselves.

The *Specialty Travel Index* is a directory for special-interest travel and an invaluable resource. Listings include tour operators specializing in camping, as well as myriad other interests that combine nicely with a camping trip, such as biking, ballooning, diving, horseback riding, canoeing, motorcycling, and river rafting. The index costs $5 per copy, $8 for a year's subscription of two issues. Contact *Specialty Travel Index*, 305 San Anselmo Ave., Suite 217, San Anselmo, CA 94960 (phone: 415-459-4900).

Among such packages are the camping tours of Europe offered by *Autotours* (20 Craven Terrace, London W2, England; phone: 44-71-258-0272), which range from 3 to 10 weeks. Recent itineraries included camping in Spain and Portugal; all their packages depart from London. Himalayan Travel (PO Box 481, Greenwich, CT 06836; phone: 800-225-2380) also offers a variety of camping tours throughout Europe, including Spain. In addition, a number of packagers listed below under "Hiking" and "Biking" also may offer these pursuits in combination with camping — it pays to call and ask when planning a trip.

HIKING: If you would rather eliminate all the gear and planning and take to the outdoors unencumbered, park the car and go for a day's hike. By all means, cover as much area as you can by foot; you'll see everything in far more detail than you would from the window of any conveyance. For information on suggested hikes throughout Spain and Portugal, see *Great Walks and Mountain Rambles* in DIVERSIONS.

Trails abound in Spain and Portugal. Preliminary information on where to hike is available from the Spanish and Portuguese tourist offices in the US, and local tourist authorities often distribute information sheets on popular trails in their respective regions upon request. There are other sources for those intent on getting about on their own steam; however, as material on hiking in these countries may be difficult to find in the US, you may want to contact an organization such as the *Sierra Club* (see below) for information.

One particularly useful set of guidebooks is the *Walking Through* series, which covers ten different European cities, including Barcelona, Madrid, and Seville. These guides are available from VLE Limited (PO Box 444, Ft. Lee, NJ 07024; phone: 201-585-5080), for $3 each, or $2.50 each if ordering two or more, and also may be found at select bookstores.

Another useful walking guide is *Landscapes of Madeira* (Hunter; $9.95) by John and Pat Underwood. Also for those wandering Spanish byways is *Trekking in Spain* (Lonely Planet; $11.95) by Marc Dubin. Both books are available from travel and major bookstores.

For those who are hiking on their own, without benefit of a guide or group, a map of the trail is a must. Particularly helpful for those heading out afoot are the Topographical Series for Spain and Portugal maps, which are on a detailed scale of 1:200,000: There are 102 of these maps for Spain ($10 each) and 174 of Portugal ($8 each). They are available from *Map Link* (25 E. Mason St., Santa Barbara, CA 93101; phone: 805-965-4402).

Even those tourist offices that do not have literature on hand (or have little in English) can direct you to associations in their countries that supply maps, guides, and further information. For long visits, membership in a local club is suggested.

To make outings safe and pleasant, find out in advance about the trails you plan to hike and be realistic about your own physical limitations. If hiking at high altitudes — such as in the Pyrenees — keep in mind that it is easy to underestimate the challenge of the grade combined with the thinner air. Choose an easy route if you are out of shape. Stick to defined trails unless you are an experienced hiker or know the area well. Whether heading out for a short jaunt or a longer trek, particularly in more remote areas, let someone know where you are going and when you expect to be back. If the hike is impromptu, leave a note in or on your car.

All you need to set out are a pair of sturdy shoes and socks; jeans or long pants to keep branches, nettles, and bugs off your legs; a canteen of water; a hat for the sun; and, if you like, a picnic lunch. It is a good idea to dress in layers so that you can add or remove clothing according to the elevation and weather. Make sure, too, to wear clothes with pockets or bring a pack to keep your hands free. Some useful and important pocket or pack stuffers include a jackknife, waterproof matches, a small first-aid kit, a map, and a compass. You also might want to tuck in a lightweight waterproof poncho (available in camping supply stores) in case of unexpected showers. In areas where snakes are common, include a snakebite kit.

■ **A word of warning:** It is particularly important to wear socks, long pants, and long-sleeve shirts when hiking in wooded areas due to the danger of Neuro Borreliosis, which is spread through the bite of the deer tick and other ticks. First diagnosed years ago in Europe, this disease recently has become familiar to Americans as Lyme Borreliosis (also known as "Lyme Tick Disease"). A strong insect repellent designed to repel ticks also may be helpful. The initial symptoms of this disease often are a swelling and/or a rash, generally accompanied by flu-like symptoms — such as fever and aching muscles. Readily curable in the early stages through antibiotics, if left untreated it can lead to serious complications. For information on precautions and treatment, contact the *Lyme Borreliosis Foundation*, PO Box 462, Tolland, CT 06084 (phone: 203-871-2900).

Organized Hiking Trips – Those who who prefer to travel as part of an organized group should refer to the January/February issue of *Sierra* magazine for the *Sierra Club*'s annual list of foreign outings. The *Sierra Club* offers a selection of trips each year, usually about 2 weeks in length. Hiking tours of southern Spain (and the Balearic Islands) and Portugal occasionally are offered. One recent package was a hiking tour of the northern two-thirds of Portugal, exploring national parks, vineyards, small villages, and castles en route. Other trips combine hiking with biking, and there also are walking tours. Some are backpacking trips, moving to a new camp each day; others make day hikes from a base camp. Overnights can be in small hotels, inns, farmhouses, guesthouses, or campgrounds and mountain huts. For information, contact the *Sierra Club*, Outing Department, 730 Polk St., San Francisco, CA 94109 (phone: 415-776-2211).

American Youth Hostels (AYH; see address below) also sponsors foreign hiking trips, though fewer than its foreign biking trips. As with the *Sierra Club*, the itineraries offered vary from year to year, usually ranging from around 15 to 52 days. For information on upcoming offerings, contact the *American Youth Hostels* (address below; see *Hints for Single Travelers,* in this section, for membership information.)

Mountain Travel, a company specializing in adventure trips around the world, offers a great variety of trips, ranging from easy walks that can be undertaken by anyone in good health to those that require basic or advanced mountaineering experience. Its trips take in the Pyrenees, and an itinerary for advanced hikers and climbers this year is a trek in the mountains of Spain. There's also a 17-day hike designed for moderate to experienced hikers in the Picos de Europa, the highest peaks in the Cantabrian range, led by two English-speaking tour guides. Low-elevation walking tours and expeditions that include easy day hikes, boating excursions, and visits to beaches and archaeological sites, such as "The Other Spain," are also available. This particular 18-day moderate hike includes a day's trek in the Picos de Europa, a taste of the Basque Country, and a hike through an ice cave, and finishes with a trip home via sleeper train to Barcelona. All make excellent alternatives for those who aren't in exceptional physical condition. Note that *Mountain Travel* also designs special itineraries for independent travelers. For information, contact *Mountain Travel,* 6420 Fairmont Ave., El Cerrito, CA 94530 (phone: 415-527-8100 in California; 800-227-2384 elsewhere in the US).

Other companies that offer hiking tours in Spain and Portugal include the following:

Alternative Travel Groups, 1-3 George St., Oxford, England OX1 2AZ (phone: 800-527-5997). The motto of this company is "The best way to see a country is on foot." Among their numerous itineraries worldwide are walking tours in Spain and Portugal.

Country Cycling Tours (140 W. 83rd St., New York, NY 10024; phone: 212-874-5151). Also offers several walking tours.

Himalayan Travel, PO Box 481, Greenwich, CT 06836 (phone: 800-225-2380). Offers hotel-to-hotel walking tours in Spain.

Wilderness Travel, 801 Allston Way, Berkeley, CA 94710 (phone: 415-548-0420 or 800-247-6700). Offers a wide range of hiking tours throughout Europe, including Spain and Portugal, similar to those offered by *Mountain Travel,* above.

An alternative to dealing directly with the above companies is to contact *All Adventure Travel,* a specialist in hiking and biking trips worldwide. This company, which acts as a representative for numerous special tour packagers offering such outdoor adventures, can provide a wealth of detailed information about each packager and programs offered. They also will help you design and arrange all aspects of a personalized itinerary. This company operates much like a travel agency, collecting commissions from the packagers. Therefore, there is no additional charge for these services. For information, contact *All Adventure Travel,* PO Box 4307, Boulder, CO 80306 (phone: 800-537-4025 or 303-939-8885.)

BIKING: For young or energetic travelers, a bicycle offers a marvelous way of seeing a country. Throughout Spain and Portugal there is an abundance of secondary roads that thread through picturesque stretches of countryside. Biking does have its drawbacks: Little baggage can be carried, travel is slow, and cyclists are exposed to the elements. However, should a cyclist need rest or refuge from the weather, there always is a welcoming tavern or comfortable inn around the next bend.

Besides being a viable way to tour Spain and Portugal — and to burn calories to make room for larger portions of regional food — biking is a great way to meet people. Remember, however, that although many natives of these countries do speak some English, this is less likely to be true in rural areas, so pack a good copy of a foreign phrase book if your command of the native language is not up to par. (For a list of helpful terms and basic expressions, see *Useful Words and Phrases,* in this section.)

Road Safety – While the car may be the bane of cyclists, cyclists who do not follow the rules of the road strike terror into the hearts of drivers. Follow the same rules and regulations as motor vehicle drivers. Stay to the right side of the road. Ride no more than two abreast — single file where traffic is heavy. Keep three bicycle lengths behind the cycle in front of you. Stay alert to sand, gravel, potholes, and wet or oily surfaces, all of which can make you lose control. Wear bright clothes and use lights or wear reflective material at dusk or at night, and, above all, even though European cyclists often don't, always wear a helmet.

Choosing, Renting, and Buying a Bike – Although many bicycling enthusiasts choose to take along their own bikes, bicycles can be rented throughout Europe. Long and short rentals are available; however, in Spain and Portugal, particularly in rural areas, it is recommended that you check ahead. Almost all European trains have facilities for bike transport at nominal fees.

As an alternative to renting, you might consider buying a bicycle in Europe, often for less than you might pay in the US. However, the bicycle may take some getting used to — seats especially need breaking in at first — and if you bring it home, it will be subject to an import duty by US Customs if its price (or the total of all purchases made abroad) exceeds $400. When evaluating this cost, take into account additional charges for shipping. Those planning to buy a bicycle, be it in the US or Europe, should consider a good-quality, lightweight touring bike that has the all-important low gears for climbing hills and riding against the wind. Particularly if you're riding primarily in hilly or mountainous regions, you may want to look at one of the specially designed mountain bikes. A European bicycle purchased in the US should have proof-of-purchase papers to avoid potential customs problems. Bike shops in major cities that rent and sell bikes sometimes also sell used ones — a particularly economical option that may be even less expensive than a long-term rental.

A bicycle is the correct size for you if you can straddle its center bar with feet flat on the ground and still have an inch or so between your crotch and the bar. (Nowadays, because women's old-fashioned barless bikes are not as strong as men's, most women use men's bicycles.) The seat height is right if your leg is just short of completely extended when you push the pedal to the bottom of its arc.

To be completely comfortable, divide your weight; put about 50% on your saddle and about 25% each on your arms and legs. To stop sliding in your seat and for better support, set your saddle level. A firm saddle is better than a soft springy one for a long ride. Experienced cyclists keep the tires fully inflated (pressure requirements vary widely, but always are imprinted on the side of the tire; stay within 5 pounds of the recommended pressure). Do not use top, or tenth, gear all the way; for most riding, the middle gears are best. On long rides remember that until you are very fit, short efforts with rests in between are better than one long haul, and pedal at an even pace.

The happiest biker in a foreign country is the one who arrives best prepared. Bring saddlebags, a handlebar bag, a tool kit that contains a bike wrench, screwdriver, pliers, tire repair kit, cycle oil, and work gloves, a bike repair book, a helmet (a rarity among European cyclists), a rain suit, a water bottle, a flashlight with an extra set of batteries, a small first-aid kit, and muscles that have been limbered up in advance.

Bicycle shops exist in most metropolitan areas, so you should be able to replace or add to gear; however, because tires and tubes are sized to metric dimensions in Spain and Portugal, when riding your own bike, bring extras from home. Seasoned bikers swear that the second day of any trip always is the worst, so keep this in mind and be ready to meet the mental and physical challenges ahead.

Airlines going from the US (or elsewhere) to Europe generally allow bicycles to be checked as baggage and require that the pedals be removed, handlebars be turned sideways, and the bike be in a shipping carton, which some airlines provide, subject to availability — call ahead to make sure. If buying a shipping carton from a bicycle shop, check the airline's specifications and also ask about storing the carton at the destination airport so that you can use it again for the return flight. Although some airlines charge only a nominal fee, if the traveler already has checked two pieces of baggage, there may be an additional excess baggage charge of $70 to $80 for the bicycle. As regulations vary from carrier to carrier, be sure to call well before departure to find out your airline's specific regulations. As with other baggage, make sure that the bike is thoroughly labeled with your name, a business address and phone number, and the correct airport destination code.

A good book to help you plan a trip is *Bicycle Touring in Europe,* by Karen and Gary Hawkins (Pantheon Books; $8.95); it offers information on buying and equipping a touring bike, useful clothing and supplies, and helpful techniques for the long-distance biker. Another good general book is *Europe by Bike,* by Karen and Terry Whitehall (Mountaineers Books; $10.95). The *International Youth Hostel Handbook, Volume One: Europe and the Mediterranean* ($8.95 plus $2 for postage) is a guide to all the hostels of Europe to which *AYH* members have access; a map of their locations is included. (For information on joining *American Youth Hostels,* see *Hints for Single Travelers,* in this section.)

Detailed maps will infinitely improve a biking tour and are available from a number of sources. Detailed Michelin maps (1:200,000) covering Europe, including Spain and Portugal, are available from Michelin Guides and Maps, PO Box 3305, Spartanburg, SC 29304-3305 (phone: 803-599-0850).

One of the best sources for detailed topographical maps and just about any other type of map (of just about anywhere in the world) is *Map Link* (25 E. Mason St., Santa Barbara, CA 93101; phone: 805-965-4402). Their comprehensive guide *The World Map Directory* ($29.95) includes a wealth of sources for travelers afoot, and if they don't stock a map of the area in which you are interested (or the type of map best suited to your outdoor exploration), they will order it for you. But it is likely that they'll have something to suit your needs — they stock numerous maps of Spain and Portugal, including a wide range of topographical maps. Particularly useful is the detailed Topographical Series of Spain and Portugal which includes a wealth of incredibly detailed information particularly useful for outdoor explorers on wheels and afoot; they cost $10 each for any of the 102 Spanish maps, and $8 each for any of the 174 Portuguese maps.

An additional source of maps and other information useful to cyclists is the local tourist authorities (see *Tourist Information Offices,* in this section, for addresses), which can often offer recommendations on popular scenic and historical routes.

Biking Tours – A number of organizations offer bike tours in Spain and Portugal. Linking up with a bike tour is more expensive than traveling alone, but with experienced leaders, an organized tour often becomes an educational as well as a very social experience which may lead to long-term friendships.

One of the attractions of a bike tour is that shipment of equipment — the bike — is handled by the organizers, and the shipping fee is included in the total tour package. Travelers simply deliver the bike to the airport, already disassembled and boxed; shipping cartons can be obtained from most bicycle shops with little difficulty. Bikers not with a tour must make their own arrangements with the airline, and there are no standard procedures for this (see above). Although some tour organizers will rent bikes, most prefer that participants show up with a bike with which they are already familiar. Another attraction of *some* tours is the existence of a "sag wagon" to carry extra luggage, fatigued cyclists, and their bikes, too, when pedaling another mile is impossible.

Most bike tours are scheduled from May to October, last 1 or 2 weeks, are limited to 20 or 25 people, and provide lodging in inns or hotels, though some use hostels or even tents. Tours vary considerably in style and ambience, so request brochures from several operators in order to make the best decision. When contacting groups, be sure to ask about the maximum number of people on the trip, the maximum number of miles to be traveled each day, and the degree of difficulty of the biking; these details should determine which tour you join and can greatly affect your enjoyment of the experience. Planning ahead is essential because trips often fill up 6 months or more in advance.

Among the companies specializing in biking tours to Europe and offering trips in Spain and Portugal are the following:

Butterfield & Robinson, 70 Bond St., Suite 300, Toronto, Ont. M5B 1X3, Canada (phone: 416-864-1354). Offers a number of first class, sophisticated bike trips throughout Europe, including an 8-day biking tour of northern Spain and Portugal. Bikes are provided, though you can take your own, and there are many departure dates for each itinerary. Tours are rated at four levels of difficulty.

Cycle Portugal, PO Box 877, San Antonio, FL 33576 (phone: 904-588-4132 or 800-245-4226). Offers a variety of tours in Portugal, including a 9- or 14-day "Valleys and Vineyards" tour of the Minho wine country; a 13-night "Castles and Corktrees" tour of the Alentejo province; an 8-night "Coasting to the Algarve" tour, beginning in Lisbon and ending in Faro; and a more extensive 14-day Spain and Portugal "Iberian Odyssey" tour.

Easy Rider Tours, PO Box 1384, E. Arlington, MA 02174 (phone: 617-643-8332). Offers an 8-day tour of the central plains of Portugal and a 14-day tour from central Portugal to northern Spain.

Eurobike, PO Box 40, DeKalb, IL 60115 (phone: 815-758-8851). Offers a 14-day hotel-to-hotel biking tour from Porto, Portugal, to Santiago de Compostela, Spain.

Hundreds of other organizations sponsoring biking tours have sprung up in response to the explosion of interest in this form of travel.

The *American Youth Hostels (AYH)* and its local chapters or councils also sponsor a variety of biking tours to Europe each year. You don't have to be a youngster to take an *AYH* trip; membership is open to all ages. The catalogue includes trips for teens and explains the custom trips for adults offered (groups design their own itineraries). *AYH* tours are for small groups of 9 or 10 participants and tend to be longer than average (up to 5 weeks). Departures are geared to various age groups and levels of skill and frequently feature accommodations in hostels — along with hotels for adult groups and campgrounds for younger groups. The *Metropolitan New York Council of American Youth Hostels* is an affiliate with a particularly broad tour program of its own, and is a good source of camping, hiking, and cycling equipment. For information on current offerings, contact your local council, the national organization (PO Box 37613, Washington, DC 20013-7613; phone: 202-783-6161), or The *Metropolitan New York Council of American Youth Hostels* (891 Amsterdam Ave., New York, NY 10025; phone: 212-932-2300).

The *International Bicycle Touring Society (IBTS)* is another nonprofit organization that regularly sponsors low-cost bicycle tours overseas led by member volunteers. Participants must be over 21. A sag wagon accompanies the tour group, accommodations are in inns and hotels, and some meals are included. For information, send $2 plus a self-addressed, stamped envelope to *IBTS* (PO Box 6979, San Diego, CA 92106-0979; phone: 619-226-TOUR). The *Sierra Club* also occasionally includes a bike tour to Spain and/or Portugal in its European offerings. For news about upcoming free-wheeling events, contact the club's Outing Department (address above).

You also may want to investigate the tours of the Continent offered by the *Cyclists' Touring Club (CTC),* Britain's largest cycling association. In addition to offering organized tours (including Spain and Portugal), *CTC* has a number of planned routes available in pamphlet form for bikers on their own and helps members plan their own tours. The club also publishes a yearly handbook, as well as magazines. For information, contact the *CTC* at Cotterell House, 69 Meadrow, Godalming, Surrey GU7 3HS, England (phone: 44-4868-7217).

The *League of American Wheelmen* (6707 Whitestone Rd., Suite 209, Baltimore, MD 21207; phone: 301-944-3399) publishes *Tourfinder,* a list of organizations, nonprofit and commercial, that sponsor bicycle tours of the US and abroad; the list is free with membership ($25 individual, $30 family) and can be obtained by non-members for $5. The *League* also can put you in touch with biking groups in your area.

Preparing

Calculating Costs

$ After several years of living relatively high on the hog, travel from North America to Europe dropped off precipitously in 1987 in response, among other considerations, to the relative weakness of the US dollar on the Continent. Many Americans who had enjoyed bargain prices while touring through Europe only a couple of years before, found that disadvantageous exchange rates really put a crimp in their travel planning.

But even though the halcyon days of dollar domination seem over for the present, discount fares and the availability of charter flights can greatly reduce the cost of a European vacation; package tours can even further reduce the price. What's more, Spain and Portugal are two of Europe's less expensive destinations, which is part of the reason these countries always have been popular with both first-time and seasoned travelers. They also are places where the competition for American visitors works to inspire surprisingly affordable travel opportunities.

Although most travelers have to plan carefully before they go and manage their travel funds prudently, in general, a holiday in Spain and Portugal still is a good value. While their major cities — like our own — suffer from a relatively high cost of living, travel in the surrounding countryside still is very reasonable (and sometimes even inexpensive), depending on your choice of accommodations and means of transport.

In Spain and Portugal, estimating the cost of travel expenses depends on the mode of transportation you choose, the part or parts of these countries you plan to visit, how long you will stay, and in some cases, what time of year you plan to travel. In addition to the basics of transportation, hotels, meals, and sightseeing, you have to take into account seasonal price changes that apply on certain air routings and at popular vacation destinations, as well as inflation, price fluctuations, and the vagaries of currency exchange. So while the guidelines in this book will remain useful, costs for both facilities and services may have changed somewhat in the months since publication.

DETERMINING A BUDGET: A realistic appraisal of your travel expenses is the most crucial bit of planning you will undertake before any trip. It also is, unfortunately, one for which it is most difficult to give precise, practical advice. Travel styles are intensely personal, and personal taste determines cost to a great extent. Will you stay in a hotel every night and eat every meal in a restaurant, or are you planning to camp or picnic amidst Iberia's picturesque and peaceful countryside, thus reducing your daily expenses? Base your calculations on your own travel style, and make estimates of expenses from that. If published figures on the cost of travel always were taken as gospel, many trips would not be taken. But in reality, it's possible to economize. On the other hand, don't be lulled into feeling that it is not necessary to do some arithmetic before you go. No matter how generous your travel budget, without careful planning beforehand — and strict accounting along the way — you will spend more than you anticipated.

When calculating costs, start with the basics, the major expenses being transportation, accommodations, and food. However, don't forget such extras as local transportation, shopping, and such miscellaneous items as laundry and tips. The reasonable cost of these items usually is a positive surprise to your budget; such extras as drinks served with imported liquors and airport departure taxes are definite negatives.

Package programs can reduce the price of a vacation in Spain and Portugal, because the group rates obtained by the tour packager usually are lower than the tariffs for someone traveling on a freelance basis; that is, paying for each element — airfare, hotel, meals, car rental — separately. And keep in mind, particularly when calculating the major expenses, that costs vary according to fluctuations in the exchange rate — that is, how much of a given foreign currency a dollar will buy.

Other expenses, such as the cost of local sightseeing tours, will vary from city to city. Official tourist information offices are plentiful throughout Spain and Portugal, and most of the better hotels will have someone at the front desk to provide a rundown on the costs of local tours and full-day excursions in and out of the city. Travel agents also can provide this information. Special discount passes that provide tourists with unlimited travel by the day or the week on regular city transportation are available in many large cities. Tourist authorities, as well as railway offices, can provide information on current discount offerings (for offices in the US, see *Tourist Information Offices* and *Traveling by Train,* both in this section.) Entries in the individual city reports in THE CITIES also give helpful information on local transportation options.

For purposes of a rough estimate — if you spend every night in a moderately priced hotel and eat every meal in a moderately priced restaurant, you can expect to spend around $150 to $225 for two people per day. This figure does not include transportation costs, but it does include accommodations (based on two people sharing a room), three meals, some sightseeing, and other modest entertainment costs. The accommodations take into consideration the differences between relatively inexpensive lodgings in rural areas (about $35 to $60 per night for two) and moderate hotels in urban areas (about $70 to $100 per night for two). With the exception of major cities — such as Madrid and Lisbon — these averages should be about right for a room for two throughout Spain and Portugal. You can find places that are much less expensive, or places at which you spend more for a commensurate increase in quality of service and comfort.

Meals are calculated for inexpensive to moderate restaurants. The entertainment calculated in this daily expense figure includes one sightseeing tour and admission to one museum or historic site and/or one recreation — such as greens fees for a round of golf or rental of a mount for an afternoon ride in the countryside.

Slightly lower hotel rates can be expected in Europe during the off-season — late fall through early spring. Many hotels offer "mini-break" packages, that is, a discount for a stay of 2 or more nights, usually over a weekend; though these discounts may be in effect any time of the year, they are most common when demand is lowest. In large cities, seasonal price variations may be negligible — with the exception of a dramatic rise in the cost of accommodations and services during holidays. During the shoulder season months in spring and fall, prices generally are somewhat more reasonable even for luxury hotels, although, again, high-season prices may prevail in large cities and popular tourist areas.

You should be able to use these averages to forecast a reasonably accurate picture of your daily travel costs, based on exactly how you want to travel. Savings on the daily allowance can occur while motoring in rural areas; budget-minded families also can take advantage of the wide range of inexpensive accommodations. Campgrounds are particularly inexpensive and they are located throughout Spain and Portugal (see *Camping and Caravanning, Hiking and Biking,* in this section). For information on other economical accommodations alternatives, such as *pensiones, pensões,* renting an apartment, house, or cottage, and home exchanges, see the discussion of accommodations in *On the Road,* in this section.

Picnicking is another excellent way to cut costs, and Spain and Portugal abound with well-groomed parks and idyllic pastoral settings, particularly along the coast. A stop at a local market can provide a feast of cheeses, fish, and meats, crusty bread, fresh fruit, and perhaps a bottle of wine at a surprisingly economical price — especially when compared to the cost of a restaurant lunch.

In planning any travel budget, it also is wise to allow a realistic amount for both entertainment and recreation. Are you planning to spend time sightseeing and visiting local museums? Do you intend to spend your days skiing or horseback riding? Is daily tennis or golf a part of your plan? Will your children be disappointed if they don't take a guided tour of a Moorish castle? If so, charges for these attractions and recreations must be taken into account. General guidelines on the costs of these and other activities can be found in our DIVERSIONS chapters, as well in the *Sources and Resources* sections of the individual city reports in THE CITIES. Finally, don't forget that if haunting clubs, discotheques, and other nightspots is an essential part of your vacation, or you feel that one performance at the *Auditorio Nacional* in Madrid may not be enough, allow for the extra cost of nightlife. This one item alone can add a great deal to your daily expenditures, particularly in the large cities and major tourist areas.

If at any point in the planning process it appears impossible to estimate expenses, consider this suggestion: The easiest way to put a ceiling on the price of all these elements is to buy a package tour. A totally planned and escorted one, with almost all transportation, rooms, meals, sightseeing, local travel, tips, and a dinner show or two included and prepaid, provides an exact total of what the trip will cost beforehand, and the only surprise will be the one you spring on yourself by succumbing to some irresistible, expensive souvenir.

The various types of packages available are discussed in *Package Tours,* in this section, but a few points bear repeating here. Not all packages are package *tours.* They often are no more than loosely organized arrangements including transatlantic transportation, a stay at a hotel, transfers between hotel and airport, baggage handling, taxes, and tips, which leave the entire matter of how you spend your time and where you eat your meals — and with whom — up to you. Equally common are the hotel-plus-car packages, which take care of accommodations and local transportation. On such independent or hosted "tours," a tour company representative or affiliated Spanish or Portuguese travel agent may be available at a nearby office to answer questions, or a host may be stationed at a desk in the hotel to arrange optional excursions, but you will never have to travel in a group unless you wish to.

More and more, even experienced travelers are being won over by the idea of package travel, not only for the convenience and the planning time saved, but above all for the money that can be saved. Whatever elements you include in your package, the organizer has gotten them for you wholesale — and they are paid for in advance, thus eliminating the dismal prospect of returning to your hotel each night to subtract the day's disbursements from your remaining cash, when you should be enjoying a glass of sherry in peace in a *tapas* bar.

The possibility of prepaying certain elements of your trip is an important point to consider even if you intend to be strictly independent, with arrangements entirely of your own making, all bought separately. You may not be able to match the price of the wholesale tour package, but at least you will have introduced an element of predictability into your accounting, thus reducing the risk that some budget-busting expense along the way might put a damper on the rest of your plans.

Those who want to travel independently — but also want to eliminate the element of surprise from their accommodations budget — can take advantage of the hotel voucher schemes that frequently come as part of a fly/drive package. Travelers receive a block of prepaid vouchers and a list of hotels that accept them as total payment for a night's stay, and for those who may want to upgrade their lodgings from time to time, there often is another set of hotels that accepts the same vouchers with payment of a supplement.

With the independent traveler in mind, what follows are some suggestions of how to pin down the cost of a trip beforehand. But there are two more variables that will influence the cost of your holiday, whether you buy a package or do it all yourself. One is timing. If you are willing to travel during the less trafficked off-season months, when airfares are lower, you'll find many hotels' rates lower also (except in ski resorts in Spain). Keep in mind those periods between the traditional high and low seasons, generally referred to as the shoulder months (approximately late March to mid-May and late September to mid-November). Although costs are only a little lower than in high season, and the weather may not be as predictable, you won't be bucking the crowds that in peak months can force a traveler without a hotel reservation into the most expensive hostelry in town. Don't forget, however, to find out what is going on in any place where you plan to spend a good deal of your vacation. The availability and possible economy gained by off-season travel are negated if a major conference or other special event is scheduled at the time you plan to visit.

Another factor influencing the cost of your trip is whether you will be traveling alone or as a couple. The prices quoted for package tours almost always are based on double occupancy of hotel rooms, and the surcharge — or single supplement — for a room by yourself can be quite hefty. When shopping for a hotel room, you'll find that there are many more double rooms than singles. Don't expect a discount if you occupy a double room as a single, and don't expect single rooms to cost less than two-thirds (in some cases as much as 80%) the price of doubles.

■ **Note:** The volatility of exchange rates means that between the time you originally make your hotel reservations and the day you arrive, the price in US dollars may vary substantially from the price originally quoted. To avoid paying more than you expected, it's wise to investigate rates that are guaranteed in US dollars. Remember that you also can determine whether it's more economical to pay for services in US dollars before departure or in local currency once in Spain and Portugal.

TRANSPORTATION COSTS: In earlier sections of GETTING READY TO GO, we have discussed the comparative costs of different modes of transportation and the myriad special rates available through package tours, charter flights, train passes, car rental packages, and other budget deals. See each of the relevant sections for specific information. Transportation is likely to represent the largest single item in your budget, but the encouraging aspect of this is that you will be able to determine most of these costs before you leave, since most fares will have been paid in advance.

Airfare is really the easiest cost to pin down, though the range and variety of available flights may be confusing initially. The possibilities were outlined fully in *Traveling by Plane,* earlier in this section.

The most important factors in determining which mode of transportation to choose for traveling around Spain and Portugal are the amount of touring you plan to do and the length of time you will be abroad. If you intend to move about a great deal among cities, a pass allowing unlimited train travel is likely to be the most economical approach. A Eurailpass is valid throughout Spain and Portugal and much of the rest of Europe. For more information on economical rail options, see *Traveling by Train,* in this section.

Although driving provides maximum flexibility, renting a car anywhere in Europe is a substantial expense. Car rental prices do vary from city to city, as well as according to season (but don't expect rates to be as low as the deeply discounted bargain rates so often found in the US), the type of car you choose, and whether the car is rented independently or as part of a package deal.

If you want to drive through the countryside, you should look carefully into fly/drive arrangements versus rentals alone, and also compare the rates offered by some of the smaller firms specializing in car travel in Europe with the rates offered by the larger, more familiar international car rental companies. The latter all have discount plans, provided the car is booked a certain number of days before pick-up and the rental is for a minimum period of time. Look for the flat rate that includes unlimited mileage — usually the best deal. Also, when estimating driving costs, don't forget that the price of gas in Spain and Portugal averages more than twice the price you're accustomed to paying in the US, so be sure to take this substantial expense into account. This cost also provides a significant incentive to rent a car that delivers the highest possible mileage per gallon — or liter — of gas.

FOOD: Meals are a more difficult expense to estimate. If you rent an apartment, house, or cottage, or are camping out, you will be able to prepare some meals yourself. Depending on where you're staying, groceries can be more expensive than they are at home, but they certainly will be less expensive than eating out. Restaurant dining — particularly in the better establishments of major cities and prime tourist areas — is going to hit your purse, wallet, or credit card hardest.

Independent travelers eating all of their meals in restaurants should allow roughly $35 to $70 per day per person for food. This amount includes a full breakfast, because the standard breakfast that frequently is included in the price of accommodations — although in many areas it is posted separately from the price of the room — increasingly is "continental" (coffee and rolls or pastries); there is an extra charge for a full breakfast (which could be anything from bacon and eggs to zesty local fish dishes). Lunch and an average dinner are also included. The estimate for dinner is based on a fixed menu (at a fixed price) in a moderate, neither-scrimp-nor-splurge restaurant, which at least can include a tasty and occasionally imaginative food selection, but no cocktails before dinner. This also should cover taxes and gratuities, and perhaps a pitcher of stout or a carafe of local wine at dinner — but you won't be splurging. If ordering an à la carte dinner and the pick of the wine list in one of the major cities, be prepared for the tab to rise much higher, and if you're addicted to *haute gastronomie,* the sky is the limit.

All of this is no reason to forgo your trip, however — remember, it's *dining* that is going to hit your wallet hard. Those who are up to a steady diet of fast food can get by on a lot less. And there is some relief out in the countryside, where, at many *pensiones, pensoês,* and other small establishments, a substantial breakfast may be available (usually for a reasonable additional charge, if any), one apt to hold most folks straight through midday, though even travelers on a severe budget are advised not to skip lunch. If you stick to picnic lunches put together from the infinite variety of Spanish and Portuguese delicatessens and markets and finish off the day with a carefully chosen meal in a *tasca* or *taverna,* you will sacrifice nothing in experience and hold down the cost.

Most Spanish restaurants and *cafeterías* (cafés) offer a *menú del día* (menu of the day), often including salad, two entrées, bread, dessert, and wine, at a fixed price considerably lower than ordering à la carte. Ordering from the *menú,* one can eat well in a moderate restaurant for as little as $5. In Portugal, where eating out is generally even less expensive than in Spain, travelers will find these daily fixed price specials (known as *menu do dia*) an equally good if not sometimes better bargain.

Our restaurant selections, chosen to give the best value for money — whether expensive or dirt cheap — are listed in the *Best in Town* sections of THE CITIES and in the *Eating Out* sections of each tour route in DIRECTIONS.

ACCOMMODATIONS: There is a wide choice and a substantial difference in degrees of luxury among the expensive, moderate, and inexpensive Spanish and Portuguese hotels. Although room costs in Spain and Portugal cover a very broad spectrum, for the purpose of making an estimate, expect to pay about what you would in a major American city for equivalent accommodations. Figure on the high side, however, if you're visiting major tourism centers during high season, and slightly lower rates can be expected off-season.

Most expensive — as high as $300 to $500 for a double room — will be the "palace" hotels in the most expensive cities — such as Madrid. Rates at international hotels with a full complement of business services also tend toward the top of the scale. Generally, the member hotels of international chains in any given city are priced roughly equally. In the larger cities (such as Barcelona and Lisbon), this ranges from around $125 and up, although similar hotels elsewhere range from about $60 to $100 for a double. There is a big jump down from these international class hotels to those in the moderate category in the same city, and prices generally will be from about $20 to as much as $50 less per night.

There is no sacred edict stating that travelers must put up at deluxe hotels in Spain and Portugal, and in fact you might be missing a good deal of the Iberian experience by insisting on international standards and skipping wonderful smaller establishments. Hotels in the first class range usually are available at about one-third less than their deluxe counterparts. Second class hotels offer clean, comfortable accommodations and often are thoroughly charming, and in the even more inexpensive range are hotels that many will find perfectly adequate.

In rural areas, there are family-run hotels and inns that are being used more and more by tourists. Spanish *pensiones* and Portuguese *pensões* are low-cost guesthouses that, in many cases, offer home-cooked meals. You can spend the night in surroundings that may be homey or spartan but almost always are clean, and the prices are low, averaging about $15 to $25 per person per night. Although not always as easy to find in the larger cities, budget accommodations in central cities do exist, and, and, recognizing the need, travel agents, tour packagers, airlines and the National Tourist Office of Spain and the Portuguese National Tourist Office are doing what they can to make their wherabouts known.

At the other end of the scale are the government-operated *paradores* (Spain) and *pousadas* (Portugal): restored castles, monasteries, and monumental historic buildings that have been fitted out with modern facilities. These are often surprisingly affordable and unique to Spain and Portugal. Spanish *paradores* range from approximately $70 to $140 for a double room, breakfast, tax, and tip included (these rates vary little from low to high season). Portuguese *pousadas* range from about $50 to $100 in the off-season and from about $65 to $120 in the high season, tax, tip, and breakfast included.

There are two additional options for less expensive accommodations for anyone staying for an extended period of time in one place. One is renting an apartment or house, sometimes called a "self-catering holiday" or a "holiday let." These are available throughout Spain and Portugal and easily can be arranged through travel agents. The other is a home exchange, in which you and a Spanish or Portuguese family exchange houses for an agreed-upon period of time.

LOCAL TAXES AND SERVICE CHARGES: A sales tax or VAT (value added tax, known as IVA in Spain and Portugal) is added to both goods and services in many European countries. In Spain, the rate ranges from lows of 6% on food to a high of 33% on luxury articles; in Portugal, the general rate is from 17% on food to a high of 30% for luxury items. The VAT is buried in the prices of hotel rooms and restaurant meals, so you won't even notice it. It also is included in the amount shown on the price tag of retail goods. There is no escaping the tax on services, but for foreigners the tax on purchases frequently can be reimbursed. Another alternative is to have the goods sent directly to your home address — if the store is willing to do so. For a full discussion of VAT refunds, see *Shopping,* in this section.

A service charge, usually in the 10% to 15% range, is charged on restaurant and hotel bills in both Spain and Portugal. Nevertheless, there still are many situations not covered by the service charge — or where an additional gratuity is appropriate. For more on these, see *Tipping,* in this section.

■ **A note on our hotel/restaurant cost categories:** There are a great many moderate and inexpensive hotels and restaurants that we have not included in this book. Our *Checking In* and *Eating Out* listings include only those places we think are best in their price range. We have arranged our listings by general price categories: expensive, moderate, and inexpensive. The introductory paragraph of each listing explains just what those categories mean within the context of local prices.

Planning a Trip

123 Travelers fall into two categories: those who make lists and those who do not. Some people prefer to plot the course of their trip to the finest detail, with contingency plans and alternatives at the ready. For others, the joy of a voyage is its spontaneity; exhaustive planning only lessens the thrill of anticipation and the sense of freedom.

For most travelers, however, any week-plus trip to Spain and/or Portugal can be too expensive for an "I'll take my chances" type of attitude. Even perennial Gypsies and anarchistic wanderers have to take into account the time-consuming logistics of getting around, and even with minimal baggage, they need to think about packing. Hence, at least some planning is crucial. This is not to suggest that you work out your itinerary in minute detail before you go; but it's still wise to decide certain basics at the very start: where to go, what to do, and how much to spend. These decisions require a certain amount of consideration. So before rigorously planning specific details, you might want to establish your general travel objectives:

1. How much time will you have for the entire trip, and how much of it are you willing to spend getting where you're going?
2. What interests and/or activities do you want to pursue while on vacation? Do you want to visit one, a few, or several different places?
3. At what time of year do you want to go?
4. What kind of topography or climate do you prefer?
5. Do you want peace and privacy or lots of activity and company?
6. How much money can you afford to spend for the entire vacation?

Obviously, your answers will be determined by your personal tastes and lifestyle. These will dictate the degree of comfort you require; whether you select a tour or opt for total independence; and how much responsibility you want to take for your own arrangements (or whether you want everything arranged for you, with the kinds of services provided in a comprehensive package trip).

With firm answers to these major questions, start reviewing literature on the areas in which you're most interested. Good sources of information are airlines, hotel representatives, and travel agents. Also consult such other sources of general travel information as reliable, annually updated guidebooks and maps. Motor clubs often can be a good source for brochures and other information on Europe. There also are lots of useful little city guides available at newsstands and bookstores on the spot throughout Spain and Portugal.

Government departments and affinity clubs focusing on individual outdoor activities

— golf, fishing, hunting, boating, mountain climbing, hiking, biking, nature study, and other such special interests — also may be able to provide information on these sports. For information on wilderness trips, hiking, and biking, see *Camping and Caravanning, Hiking and Biking,* in this section, and for information on these and other activities, see the various sections of DIVERSIONS, as well as the individual city reports in THE CITIES.

In addition, the National Tourist Office of Spain and the Portuguese National Tourist Office, have locations in the US (see *Tourist Information Offices,* in this section). Stop at or write to any of these — all are ready resources for brochures, maps, and other information on both cities and the countryside.

Up-to-date travel information on Spain and Portugal is plentiful, and you should be able to accumulate everything you want to know, not only about the places you plan to visit, but also about the relevant tour and package options. And if you're visiting Spain or Portugal for the first time, make a special effort to read up on your destination's food, history, and culture. A good place to start is the section called PERSPECTIVES, but if you're planning an extended stay in a particular city or region, you'll probably want to do even more extensive reading.

You now can make almost all of your own travel arrangements if you have time to follow through with hotels, airlines, tour operators, and so on. But you'll probably save considerable time and energy if you have a travel agent make arrangements for you. The agent also should be able to advise you of alternate arrangements of which you may not be aware. Only rarely will a travel agent's services cost a traveler any money, and they may even save you some (see *How to Use a Travel Agent,* below). Well before departure time (depending on how far in advance you make your reservations), the agent will deliver a packet that includes all your tickets and vouchers and hotel confirmations, and often a day-by-day outline of where you'll be when, along with a detailed list of all your flights.

If it applies to your schedule and destination, pay particular attention to the dates when off-season rates go into effect. In major tourism areas, accommodations costs may be lower during the off-season (and the weather often is perfectly acceptable at this time). Off-season rates frequently are lower for other facilities, too, although don't expect to save much on car rental costs during any season. In general, it is a good idea to be aware of holiday weeks, as rates at hotels generally are higher during these periods and rooms normally are heavily booked. (In addition, service is apt to be under par unless more staff people are employed for the holidays, since the regular bellhops, maids, dining room personnel, and others will be trying to cope with a full house instead of being able to provide personal attention to individual guests.)

Make plans early. During the summer season and other holiday periods, make hotel reservations at least a month in advance in all major cities. If you are flying at these times and want to benefit from savings of discount fares or charter programs, purchase tickets as far ahead as possible. The less flexible your schedule requirements, the earlier you should book. Many hotels require deposits before they will guarantee reservations, and this most often is the case during peak travel periods. (Be sure you have a receipt for any deposit, or better yet, charge the deposit to a credit card.) Religious and national holidays also are times requiring reservations well in advance in Spain and Portugal.

Before your departure, find out what the weather is likely to be at your destination. Consult *When to Go,* in this section, for information on climatic variations and a chart of average temperatures in various Spanish and Portuguese cities. See *How to Pack,* in this section, for details on what clothes to take. And see *When to Go,* also in this section, as well as the individual city reports in THE CITIES for information on special events that may occur during your stay. The city chapters also provide essential information on local transportation and other services and resources.

While arranging a vacation is fun and exciting, don't forget to prepare for your absence from home. Before you leave, attend to these household matters:

1. Arrange for your mail to be forwarded, held by the post office, or picked up daily at your house. Someone should check your door occasionally to pick up any unexpected deliveries. Piles of mail or packages announce to thieves that no one is home.
2. Cancel all deliveries (newspapers, milk, and so on).
3. Arrange for the lawn to be mowed and plants watered at regular intervals.
4. Arrange for the care of pets.
5. Etch your social security number in a prominent place on all appliances (television sets, radios, cameras, kitchen appliances). This considerably reduces their appeal to thieves and facilitates identification.
6. Leave a house key and your itinerary with a relative or friend. Notify the police, the building manager, or a neighbor that you are leaving, and tell them who has your key and itinerary.
7. Empty the refrigerator and lower the thermostat.
8. If you use a computer with a hard disk, back up all your files onto diskettes and store them in a safe place away from the equipment.
9. Immediately before leaving, check that all doors, windows, and garage doors are securely locked.

To discourage thieves further, it is wise to set up several variable timers around the house so that lights and even the television set or a radio go on and off several times in different rooms each night.

Make a list of any valuable items you are carrying with you, including credit card numbers and the serial numbers of your traveler's checks. Put copies in your purse or pocket and leave other copies at home. Put a label with your name and home address on the inside of your luggage for identification in case of loss. Put your name and business address — *never your home address* — on a label on the outside of your luggage.

Review your travel documents. If you are traveling by air, check that your ticket has been filled in correctly. The left side of the ticket should have a list of each stop you will make (even if you are only stopping to change planes), beginning with your departure point. Be sure that the list is correct, and count the number of carbons to see that you have one for each plane you will take. If you have confirmed reservations, be sure that the column marked "status" says "OK" beside each flight. Have in hand vouchers or proof of payment for any reservation for which you've paid in advance; this includes hotels, transfers to and from the airport, sightseeing tours, car rentals, and tickets to special events.

Reconfirmation of reservations is strongly recommended for all international flights. Although policies vary from carrier to carrier, it's still smart to reconfirm your flight 48 to 72 hours before departure, both going and returning. This will not, however, prevent you from getting bumped in case the flight is overbooked. Reconfirmation is particularly recommended for point-to-point flights within Europe.

If you will be driving while in Spain and Portugal, bring your driver's license, International Driver's Permit (required in Spain and recommended for Portugal), and any other necessary identification, proof of insurance, maps, guidebooks, a flashlight with an extra set of batteries, and sunglasses; a small first-aid kit also is a good idea. If driving about for more than a day, upon arrival you may want to pick up emergency flashers, a container of water or coolant for the radiator, and a steel container for extra gas.

Finally, you always should bear in mind that despite the most careful plans, things do not always occur on schedule. If you maintain a flexible attitude at all times, and shrug as cheerfully as possible in the face of postponements and cancellations, you will enjoy yourself a lot more.

How to Use a Travel Agent

A reliable travel agent remains your best source of service and information for planning a trip abroad, whether you have a specific itinerary and require an agent only to make reservations or you need extensive help in sorting through the maze of airfares, tour offerings, hotel packages, and the scores of other arrangements that may be involved in a trip to Spain and Portugal.

You should know what you want from a travel agent so that you can evaluate what you are getting. It is perfectly reasonable to expect your agent to be a thoroughly knowledgeable travel specialist, with information about your destination and, even more crucial, a command of current airfares, ground arrangements, and other wrinkles in the travel scene. Most travel agents work through computer reservations systems (CRS) to assess the availability and rates of flights, hotels, and car rentals, and they can book reservations through the CRS. Despite reports of "computer bias," in which a computer may favor one airline over another, the CRS should provide agaents with the entire spectrum of flights available to a given destination and the complete range of fares in considerably less time than it takes to telephone the airlines individually — and at no extra charge to the client.

To make the most intelligent use of a travel agent's time and expertise, you should know something of the economics of the industry. As a client, traditionally you pay nothing for the agent's services; with few exceptions, it's all free, from hotel bookings to advice on package tours. Any money the travel agent makes on the time spent arranging your itinerary — booking hotels or flights, or suggesting activities — comes from commissions paid by the suppliers of these services — the airlines, hotels, and so on. These commissions generally run from 8% to 20% of the total cost of the service, although suppliers often reward agencies that sell their services in volume with an increased commission, called an override.

Among the few exceptions to the general rule of free service by a travel agent are the agencies beginning to practice *net pricing.* In essence, such agencies may return all of their commissions and overrides to their customers and make their income by charging a flat fee per transaction instead (thus adding a charge after a reduction for the commissions has been made). Sometimes the rebate from the agent arrives later, in the form of a check. For further information, see "Net Fare Sources" in *Traveling by Plane,* in this section.

Net fares and fees are a very recent and not widespread practice, but even a conventional travel agent sometimes may charge a fee for such special services as long-distance telephone or cable costs incurred in making a booking, for reserving a room in a place that does not pay a commission (such as a small, out-of-the-way hotel), or for special attention such as planning a highly personalized itinerary. A fee also may be assessed in instances of deeply discounted airfares. In most instances, however, you'll find that travel agents make their time and experience available to you at no charge, and you do not pay more for an airline ticket, package tour, or other product bought from a travel agent than you would for the same product bought directly from the supplier.

This system implies two things about your relationship with an agent:

1. You will get better service if you arrive at the agent's desk with your basic itinerary already planned. Know roughly where you want to go, what you want to do, and how much you want to spend. Use the agent to make bookings (which pay

commissions) and to advise you on facilities, activities, and alternatives within the limits of your itinerary. You get the best service when you are requesting commissionable items. Since there are few commissions on camping or driving/camping tours, an agent is unlikely to be very enthusiastic about helping to plan one. The more vague your plans, the less direction you can expect from most agents. If you walk into an agency and say, "I have 2 weeks in June; what shall I do?" you most likely will walk out with nothing more than a handful of brochures. So do a little preliminary homework.

2. Be wary. There always is the danger that an incompetent or unethical agent will send you to the place offering the best commissions rather than the best facilities for your enjoyment. The only way to be sure you are getting the best service is to pick a good, reliable travel agent, one who knows where to go for information if he or she is unfamiliar with an area — although most agents are familiar with major destinations throughout Spain and Portugal.

You should choose a travel agent with the same care with which you would choose a doctor or lawyer. You will be spending a good deal of money on the basis of the agent's judgment, so you have a right to expect that judgment to be mature, informed, and interested. At the moment, unfortunately, there aren't many standards within the travel agent industry to help you gauge competence, and the quality of individual agents varies enormously.

At present, only nine states have registration, licensing, or other form of travel agent–related legislation on their books. Rhode Island licenses travel agents; Florida, Hawaii, Iowa, and Ohio register them; and California, Illinois, Oregon, and Washington have laws governing the sale of transportation or related services. While state licensing of agents cannot absolutely guarantee competence, it can at least ensure that an agent has met some minimum requirements.

Perhaps the best-prepared agents are those who have completed the CTC Travel Management program offered by the *Institute of Certified Travel Agents* and carry the initials CTC (Certified Travel Counselor) after their names. This indicates a relatively high level of expertise. For a free list of CTCs in your area, send a self-addressed, stamped, #10 envelope to *ICTA,* 148 Linden St., Box 82-56, Wellesley, MA 02181 (phone: 617-237-0280 in Massachusetts; 800-542-4282 elsewhere in the US).

An agent's membership in the *American Society of Travel Agents (ASTA)* can be a useful guideline in making a selection. But keep in mind that *ASTA* is an industry organization, requiring only that its members be licensed in those states where required; be accredited to represent the suppliers whose products they sell, including airline and cruise tickets; and adhere to its Principles of Professional Conduct and Ethics code. *ASTA* does not guarantee the competence, ethics, or financial soundness of its members, but it does offer some recourse if you feel you have been dealt with unfairly. Complaints may be registered with *ASTA* (Consumer Affairs Dept., PO Box 23992, Washington, DC 20026-3992; phone: 703-739-2782). First try to resolve the complaint directly with the supplier. For a list of *ASTA* members in your area, send a self-addressed, stamped, #10 envelope to *ASTA,* Public Relations Dept., at the address above.

There also is the *Association of Retail Travel Agents (ARTA),* a smaller but highly respected trade organization similar to *ASTA.* Its member agencies and agents similarly agree to abide by a code of ethics, and complaints about a member can be made to *ARTA*'s Grievance Committee, 1745 Jeff Davis Hwy., Arlington, VA 22202-3402 (phone: 800-969-6069 or 703-553-7777).

Agencies that are members of the *National Association of Cruise Only Agencies (NACOA)* have demonstrated special knowledge in the selling of cruises. For a list of cruise-only agencies in your area (requests are limited to three states), send a self-addressed, stamped envelope to *NACOA,* (PO Box 7209, Freeport, NY 11520) or call 516-378-8006. Agencies that belong to a travel consortium, such as *Travel Trust International* (phone: 800-522-2700 in New York; 800-223-8953 elsewhere in the US), have access to preferred rates, as do the huge networks of *American Express* (phone: 800-YES-AMEX) and *Carlson Travel Network* (formerly *Ask Mr. Foster;* phone: 818-788-4118) travel agencies.

A number of banks own travel agencies, too. These provide the same services as other accredited commercial travel bureaus. Anyone can become a client, not only the banks' customers. You can find out more about these agencies, which belong to the *Association of Bank Travel Bureaus,* by inquiring at your bank or looking in the yellow pages.

Perhaps the best way to find a travel agent is by word of mouth. If the agent (or agency) has done a good job for your friends over a period of time, it probably indicates a certain level of commitment and competence. Always ask not only for the name of the company, but for the name of the specific agent with whom your friends dealt, for it is that individual who will serve you, and quality can vary widely within a single agency. There are some superb travel agents in the business, and they can facilitate vacation or business arrangements.

Once you've made an initial selection, be entirely candid with the agent. Budget considerations rank at the top of the list — there's no sense in wasting the agent's (or your) time poring over itineraries you know you can't afford. Similarly, if you like a fair degree of comfort, that fact should not be kept secret from your travel agent, who may assume that you wish to travel on a tight budget even when that's not the case.

Entry Requirements and Documents

A valid US passport is the only document a US citizen needs to enter Spain or Portugal, and that same passport also is needed to reenter the US. The principality of Andorra also requires only a US passport for entry. As a general rule, a US passport entitles the bearer to remain in Portugal for up to 60 days as a tourist and in Spain for up to 6 months. Resident aliens of the US should inquire at the nearest Spanish or Portuguese consulate (see *Tourist Information Offices,* in this section, for addresses) to find out what documents they need to enter Spain or Portugal; similarly, US citizens intending to work, study, or reside in these countries should address themselves to the appropriate consulate.

Vaccination certificates are required only if the traveler is entering from an area of contagion as defined by the World Health Organization, and as the US is considered an area "free from contagion," an international vaccination certificate no longer is required for entering either Spain or Portugal for a short period of time. Because smallpox is considered eradicated from the world, only a few countries continue to require visitors to have a smallpox vaccination certificate. You certainly will not need one to travel to Spain and Portugal or return to the US.

VISAS: Visas are required, however, for study, residency, or work, and US citizens should address themselves to the appropriate Spanish or Portuguese consulate. Visas of this type are available for stays in Spain or Portugal of up to 1 year. Note that although visas for study often are issued, it is much more difficult to get a visa to work in either country. The ready processing of a visa application also may be based on the duration of the visa you are requesting — visas for studying in Spain or Portugal for several months are likely to be processed more quickly than residency visas good for 1 year or longer. Proof of substantial means of independent financial support during the stay also is pertinent to the acceptance of any long-term–stay application.

Issuing tourist visas is a routine service provided by the Spanish and Portuguese consulates, though it is a good idea to apply well in advance. This is particularly important for travelers who live some distance from the nearest consulate and are applying by mail. Two items are necessary to apply for a visa: a valid passport and a completed visa form. (These forms may be obtained by sending a self-addressed, stamped envelope to the nearest consulate with a written request.) There is no charge for the issuance of visas. Application must be made at the Spanish or Portuguese consulate within your jurisdiction (see *Tourist Information Offices,* in this section, for addresses). Visas often are issued on the spot; however, if there is a backlog, you may have to return to pick it up a few days later. To avoid frustration and wasted time, it is a good idea to call ahead to check during what hours and days visa requests are accepted.

PASSPORTS: While traveling in Spain or Portugal, carry your passport with you at all times (for an exception to this rule, see our note "When Checking In," below). If you lose your passport while abroad, report the loss to the nearest US consulate or embassy immediately. You can get a 3-month temporary passport directly from the consulate, but you must fill out a "loss of passport" form and follow the same application procedure — and pay the same fees — as you did for the original (see below). It's likely to speed things up if you have a record of your passport number and the place and date of its issue (a Xerox copy of the first page of your passport is perfect); keep this information separate from your passport — you might want to give it to a traveling companion to hold or put it in the bottom of your suitcase. (For a complete list of US consulates and embassies in Spain and Portugal, see *Medical and Legal Aid and Consular Services,* in this section.)

US passports now are valid for 10 years from the date of issue (5 years for those under age 16). The expired passport itself is not renewable, but must be turned in along with your application for a new and valid one (you will get it back, voided, when you receive the new one). Delivery can take as little as 2 weeks or as long as a month, and anyone applying for a passport for the first time should allow at least 4 weeks for delivery — even 6 weeks during the busiest season — from approximately mid-March to mid-September.

Normal passports contain 24 pages, but frequent travelers can request a 48-page passport at no extra cost. Every individual, regardless of age, must have his or her own passport. Family passports no longer are issued.

Passport renewal can be done by mail, but anyone applying for the first time or anyone under 16 renewing a passport must do so in person at one of the following places:

1. The State Department passport agencies in Boston, Chicago, Honolulu, Houston, Los Angeles, Miami, New Orleans, New York City, Philadelphia, San Francisco, Seattle, Stamford, CT, and Washington, DC.
2. A federal or state courthouse.
3. Any of the 1,000 post offices across the country with designated acceptance facilities.

Application blanks are available at all these offices and must be presented with the following:

1. Proof of US citizenship. This can be a previous passport or one in which you were included. If you are applying for your first passport and you were born in the United States, an original or certified birth certificate is the required proof. If you were born abroad, a Certificate of Naturalization, a Certificate of Citizenship, a Report of Birth Abroad of a Citizen of the United States, or a Certification of Birth is necessary.
2. Two 2-by-2-inch, front-view photographs in color or black and white, with a light,

plain background, taken within the previous 6 months. These must be taken by a photographer rather than by a machine.

3. A $42 passport fee ($27 for travelers under 16), which includes a $7 execution fee. *Note:* Your best bet is to bring the exact amount in cash (no change is given), or a separate check or money order for each passport. (Note that families usually can combine several passport fees on one check or money order.)

4. Proof of identity. Again, this can be a previous passport, a Certificate of Naturalization or of Citizenship, a driver's license, or a government ID card with a physical description or a photograph. Failing any of these, you should be accompanied by a blood relative or a friend of at least 2 years' standing who will testify to your identity. Credit cards or social security cards do not suffice as proof of identity — but note that since 1988, US citizens *must* supply their social security numbers.

Passports can be renewed by mail with forms obtained at designated locations only if the expired passport was issued no more than 12 years before the date of application for renewal, and if it was not issued before the applicant's 16th birthday. Send the completed form with the expired passport, two photos, and $35 (no execution fee required) to the nearest passport agency office.

As getting a passport — or international visa — through the mail can mean waiting as much as 6 weeks or more, a new mini-industry has cropped up in those cities where there is a US passport office. The yellow pages currently list quite a few organizations willing to wait on line to expedite obtaining a visa or passport renewal; there's even one alternative for those who live nowhere near the cities mentioned above. In the nation's capital there's an organization called the *Washington Passport and Visa Service.* It may be the answer for folks in need of special rapid action, since this organization can get a passport application or renewal turned around in a single day. What's more, their proximity to an embassy or consulate of every foreign country represented in the US helps to speed the processing of visa applications as well. *Washington Passport and Visa*'s fee for a 3- to 5-day turnaround is $25; for next-day service the charge is $50; for same-day service they charge $75. For information, application forms, and other prices, call 800-272-7776.

If you need an emergency passport, it also is possible to be issued a passport in a matter of hours by going directly to your nearest passport office (there is no way, however, to avoid waiting in line). Explain the nature of the emergency, usually as serious as a death in the family; a ticket in hand for a flight the following day also will suffice. Should the emergency occur outside of business hours, all is not lost. There's a 24-hour telephone number in Washington, DC (phone: 202-634-3600), that can put you in touch with a State Department duty officer who may be able to expedite your application.

■**When Checking In:** It is not at all unusual for a Spanish or Portuguese hotel to ask you to surrender your passport for 24 hours. While we all get a little nervous when we're parted from our passports, the US State Department's passport division advises that it's a perfectly acceptable procedure. The purpose usually is a local requirement to check the validity of the passport and ascertain whether the passport holder is a fugitive or has a police record. Many hotels merely will ask that you enter your passport number on your registration card. If a hotel does take your passport, make sure it's returned to you the next day.

DUTY AND CUSTOMS: As a general rule, the requirements for bringing the majority of items *into Spain or Portugal* is that they must be in quantities small enough not to imply commercial import.

Among the items that may be taken into Spain duty-free are 200 cigarettes or 250 grams of tobacco, 1 bottle of wine, and 1 bottle of liquor; for Portugal the duty-free limits are 200 cigarettes or 250 grams of tobacco, 2 bottles of wine, and 1 bottle of liquor. Personal effects and sports equipment appropriate for a pleasure trip also are allowed.

If you are bringing along a computer, camera, or other electronic equipment for your own use that you will be taking back to the US, you should register the item with the US Customs Service in order to avoid paying duty both entering and returning from Spain and Portugal. (Also see *Customs and Returning to the US,* in this section.) For information on this procedure, as well as for a variety of pamphlets on US customs regulations, contact the local office of the US Customs Service or the central office, PO Box 7407, Washington, DC 20044 (phone: 202-566-8195).

Additional information regarding customs regulations is available from the National Tourist Office of Spain and the Portuguese National Tourist Office. See *Tourist Information Offices,* in this section, for addresses of offices in the US.

■ **One rule to follow:** When passing through customs, it is illegal not to declare dutiable items; penalties range from stiff fines and seizure of the goods to prison terms. So don't try to sneak anything through — it just isn't worth it.

Insurance

 It is unfortunate that most decisions to buy travel insurance are impulsive and usually are made without any real consideration of the traveler's existing policies. Too often the result is the purchase of needlessly expensive, short-term policies that duplicate existing coverage and reinforce the tendency to buy coverage on a trip-by-trip basis rather than to work out a total and continuing travel insurance package that might well be more effective and economical.

Therefore, the first person with whom you should discuss travel insurance is your own insurance broker, not a travel agent or the clerk behind the airport insurance counter. You may discover that the insurance you already carry — homeowner's policies and/or accident, health, and life insurance — protects you adequately while you travel and that your real needs are in the more mundane areas of excess value insurance for baggage or trip cancellation insurance.

TYPES OF INSURANCE: To make insurance decisions intelligently, however, you first should understand the basic categories of travel insurance and what they cover. Then you can decide what you should have in the broader context of your personal insurance needs, and you can choose the most economical way of getting the desired protection: through riders on existing policies; with one-time short-term policies; through a special program put together for the frequent traveler; through coverage that's part of a travel club's benefits; or with a combination policy sold by insurance companies through brokers, automobile clubs, tour operators, and travel agents.

There are seven basic categories of travel insurance:

1. Baggage and personal effects insurance
2. Personal accident and sickness insurance
3. Trip cancellation and interruption insurance
4. Default and/or bankruptcy insurance
5. Flight insurance (to cover injury or death)
6. Automobile insurance (for driving your own or a rented car)
7. Combination policies

Baggage and Personal Effects Insurance – Ask your agent if baggage and personal effects are included in your current homeowner's policy, or if you will need a special floater to cover you for the duration of a trip. The object is to protect your bags and their contents in case of damage or theft any time during your travels, not just while you're in flight and covered by the airline's policy. Furthermore, only limited protection is provided by the airline. Baggage liability varies from carrier to carrier, but generally speaking, for domestic flights, luggage usually is insured to $1,250 — that's per passenger, not per bag. For most international flights, including domestic portions of international flights, the airline's liability limit is approximately $9.07 per pound or $20 per kilo (which comes to about $360 per 40-pound suitcase) for checked baggage and up to $400 per passenger for unchecked baggage. These limits should be specified on your airline ticket, but to be awarded the specified amount, you'll have to provide an itemized list of lost property, and if you're including new and/or expensive items, be prepared for a request that you back up your claim with sales receipts or other proof of purchase.

If you are carrying goods worth more than the maximum protection offered by the airline, bus, or train company, you should consider excess value insurance. Additional coverage is available from airlines at an average, currently, of $1 per $100 worth of coverage, up to a maximum value of $5,000. This insurance can be purchased at the airline counter when you check in, though you should arrive early enough to fill out the necessary forms and to avoid holding up other passengers. Major credit card companies, including American Express and Diners Club, also provide coverage for lost or delayed baggage. In some cases, you must enroll in advance to qualify. Check your membership brochure or contact the credit card company for details (see phone numbers listed in *Credit and Currency,* in this section). Excess value insurance also is included in certain of the combination travel insurance policies discussed below.

■ **A note of warning:** Be sure to read the fine print of any excess value insurance policy; there often are specific exclusions, such as cash, tickets, furs, gold and silver objects, art, and antiques. And remember that insurance companies ordinarily will pay only the depreciated value of the goods rather than their replacement value. The best way to protect the items you're carrying in your luggage is to take photos of your valuables, and keep a record of the serial numbers of such items as cameras, typewriters, radios, and so on. This will establish that you do, indeed, own the objects. If your luggage disappears or is damaged en route, deal with the situation immediately. If an airline loses your luggage, you will be asked to fill out a Property Irregularity Report before you leave the airport. If your property disappears at other transportation centers, tell the local company, but also report it to the police (since the insurance company will check with the police when processing the claim). When traveling by train, if you are sending excess luggage as registered baggage, remember that some trains may not have provisions for extra cargo; if your baggage does not arrive when you do, it may not be lost, just on the next train!

Personal Accident and Sickness Insurance – This covers you in case of illness during your trip or death in an accident. Most policies insure you for hospital and doctor's expenses, lost income, and so on. In most cases, it is a standard part of existing health insurance policies, though you should check with your broker to be sure that your policy will pay for any medical expenses incurred abroad. If not, take out a separate vacation accident policy or an entire vacation insurance policy that includes health and life coverage.

Trip Cancellation and Interruption Insurance – Although modern public charters have eliminated many of the old advance booking requirements, most charter and package tour passengers still pay for their travel well before departure. The disappointment of having to miss a vacation because of illness or any other reason pales before the awful prospect that not all (and sometimes none) of the money paid in advance might be returned. So cancellation insurance for any package tour is a must. Although cancellation penalties vary (they are listed in the fine print in every tour brochure, and before you purchase a package tour you should know exactly what they are), rarely will a passenger get more than 50% of this money back if forced to cancel within a few weeks of leaving. Therefore, if you book a package tour or charter flight, you should have trip cancellation insurance to guarantee full reimbursement or refund should you, a traveling companion, or a member of your immediate family get sick, forcing you to cancel your trip or *return home early*. The key here is *not* to buy just enough insurance to guarantee full reimbursement for the cost of the package or charter in case of cancellation. The proper amount of coverage should be sufficient to reimburse you for the cost of having to catch up with a tour after its departure or having to travel home at the full economy airfare if you have to forgo the return flight of your charter. There usually is quite a discrepancy between the charter fare and the amount charged to travel the same distance on a regularly scheduled flight at full economy fare.

Trip cancellation insurance is available from travel agents and tour operators in two forms: as part of a short-term, all-purpose travel insurance package (sold by the travel agent); or as specific cancellation insurance designed by the tour operator for a specific charter tour. Generally, tour operators' policies are less expensive, but also less inclusive. Cancellation insurance also is available directly from insurance companies or their agents as part of a short-term, all-inclusive travel insurance policy.

Before you decide on a policy, read each one carefully. (Either type can be purchased from a travel agent when you book the charter or package tour.) Be certain that your policy includes enough coverage to pay your fare from the farthest destination on your itinerary should you have to miss the charter flight. Also, be sure to check the fine print for stipulations concerning "family members" and "pre-existing medical conditions," as well as allowance for living expenses if you must delay your return due to bodily injury or illness.

Default and/or Bankruptcy Insurance – Although trip cancellation insurance usually protects you if *you* are unable to complete — or begin — your trip, a fairly recent innovation is coverage in the event of default and/or bankruptcy on the part of the tour operator, airline, or other travel supplier. In some travel insurance packages, this contingency is included in the trip cancellation portion of the coverage; in others, it is a separate feature. Either way, it is becoming increasingly important. Whereas sophisticated travelers long have known to beware of the possibility of default or bankruptcy when buying a charter flight or tour package, in recent years more than a few respected airlines unexpectedly have revealed their shaky financial condition, sometimes leaving hordes of stranded ticketholders in their wake. Moreover, the value of escrow protection of a charter passenger's funds lately has been unreliable. While default/bankruptcy insurance will not ordinarily result in reimbursement in time to pay for new arrangements, it can ensure that eventually you will get your money back, and even independent travelers buying no more than an airplane ticket may want to consider it.

Should this type of coverage not be available to you (state insurance regulations vary, there is a wide variation in price, and so on), the best bet is to pay for airline tickets and tour packages with a credit card. The federal Fair Credit Billing Act permits purchasers to refuse payment for credit card charges where services have not been delivered, so the potential onus of dealing with a receiver for a bankrupt airline falls on the credit card company. You must, however, make your claim within 60 days of receiving your bill from the credit card company. What's more, do not assume that another airline automatically will honor the ticket you're holding if it was written by a bankrupt airline, since the days when virtually all major carriers subscribed to a default protection program are long gone. Some airlines may voluntarily step forward to accommodate stranded passengers, but this now is an entirely altruistic act.

Flight Insurance – US airlines have carefully established limits of liability for the death or injury of passengers. For international flights, they are printed right on the ticket: a maximum of $75,000 in case of death or injury. Although these limitations once were established by state law for domestic flights, each case currently is decided in court on its own merits — this means potentially unlimited liability. But remember, these limits of liability are not the same thing as insurance policies; every penny that an airline must pay in the case of injury or death may be subject to a legal battle.

This may make you feel that you are not adequately protected, but before you buy last-minute flight insurance from an airport vending machine, consider the purchase in light of your total existing insurance coverage. A careful review of your current policies may reveal that you already are amply covered for accidental death, sometimes up to three times the amount provided for by the flight insurance you're buying in the airport.

Be aware that airport insurance, the kind typically bought at a counter or from a vending machine, is among the most expensive forms of life insurance coverage, and that even within a single airport, rates for approximately the same coverage vary widely. Often policies sold in vending machines are more expensive than those sold over the counter, even when they are with the same national company.

If you buy your plane ticket with an American Express, Carte Blanche, or Diners Club credit card, you automatically receive life and accident insurance coverage at no extra cost. American Express automatically provides $100,000 in insurance to its Green and Gold cardholders, and $500,000 to Platinum cardholders; Carte Blanche provides $150,000; and Diners Club provides $350,000. Additional coverage can be obtained at extremely reasonable prices, but a cardholder must sign up for it in advance. With American Express, $4 per ticket buys an additional $250,000 worth of flight insurance; $7.50 buys $500,000 worth; and $14 provides an added $1 million worth of coverage. (Rates vary slightly for New York residents.) Both Carte Blanche and Diners Club also offer an additional $250,000 worth of insurance for $4; $500,000 for $6.50. Both also provide $1,250 free insurance — over and above what the airline will pay — for checked baggage that's lost or damaged. American Express provides $500 coverage for checked baggage; $500 for carry-on baggage; and $250 for valuables, such as cameras and jewelry.

Automobile Insurance – Public liability and property damage (third-party) insurance is compulsory in Europe, and whether you drive your own or a rental car you must carry insurance. Car rentals in Spain and Portugal usually include public liability, property damage, fire, and theft coverage and, sometimes (depending on the car rental company), collision damage coverage with a deductible. In your car rental contract, you'll see that for about $13 a day, you may buy optional collision damage waiver (CDW) protection. (If partial coverage with a deductible is included in the rental contract, the CDW will cover the deductible in the event of an accident, and will cost from $10 to $25 per day.) If the contract does not include collision damage coverage, you may be liable for as much as the full retail value of the car, and by paying for the CDW you are relieved of all responsibility for any damage to the rental car. Before agreeing to this coverage, however, check your own auto insurance policy with your own broker. It very well may cover your entire liability exposure without any additional cost, or you automatically may be covered by the credit card company to which you are charging the cost of your rental.

You also should know that an increasing number of the major international car rental companies automatically are including the cost of the CDW in their basic rates. Car rental prices have increased to include this coverage, although rental company ad campaigns may promote this as a new, improved rental package "benefit." The disadvantage of this inclusion is that you may not have the option to turn down the CDW — even if you already are adequately covered by your own insurance policy or through a credit card company. For more information on this confusing issue, see *Traveling by Car,* in this section.

Your rental contract (with the appropriate insurance box checked off), as well as proof of your personal insurance policy, if applicable, are required as proof of insurance. If you will be driving your own car in Spain and Portugal, you must carry an International Insurance Certificate (called a Green Card — *Carte Verde* in Spain; *Cartão Verde* in Portugal), available through insurance brokers in the US, or take out a special policy for this purpose at customs as you enter the country.

Combination Policies – Short-term insurance policies, which may include a combination of any or all of the types of insurance discussed above, are available through retail insurance agencies, automobile clubs, and many travel agents. These combination policies are designed to cover you for the duration of a single trip.

Two examples of standard combination policies, providing comprehensive coverage for travelers, are offered by *Wallach & Co.* The first, *HealthCare Global,* is available to men and women up to age 84. The medical insurance, which may be purchased for periods of 10 to 180 days, provides $25,000 medical insurance and $50,000 accidental death benefit. The cost for 10 days is $25; for 76 days and over, it is $1.50 a day. Combination policies may include additional accidental death coverage and baggage and trip cancellation insurance options. For $3 per day (minimum 10 days, maximum 90 days), another program, *HealthCare Abroad,* offers significantly better coverage in terms of dollar limits, although the age limit is 75. Its basic policy includes $100,000 medical insurance and $25,000 accidental death benefit. As in the first policy, trip cancellation and baggage insurance also are available. For further information, write to *Wallach & Co.,* 243 Church St. NW, Suite 100D, Vienna, VA 22180 (phone: 703-281-9500 in Virginia; 800-237-6615 elsewhere in the US).

Other policies of this type include the following:

Access America International: A subsidiary of the Blue Cross/Blue Shield plans of New York and Washington, DC, now available nationwide. Contact *Access America,* 600 Third Ave., PO Box 807, New York, NY 10163 (phone: 800-284-8300 or 212-490-5345).

Carefree: Underwritten by The Hartford. Contact *Carefree Travel Insurance,* Arm Coverage, PO Box 310, Mineola, NY 11501 (phone: 800-645-2424 or 516-294-0220).

NEAR Services: Part of a benefits package offered by a travel service organization. An added feature is coverage for lost or stolen airline tickets. Contact *NEAR Services,* 450 Prairie Ave., Calumet City, IL 60409 (phone: 800-654-6700 or 708-868-6700).

Tele-Trip: Underwritten by the Mutual of Omaha Companies. Contact *Tele-Trip Co.,* PO Box 31685, 3201 Farnam St., Omaha, NE 68131 (phone: 402-345-2400 in Nebraska; 800-228-9792 elsewhere in the US).

Travel Assistance International: Provided by Europ Assistance Worldwide Services, and underwritten by Transamerica Occidental Life Insurance. Contact *Travel Assistance International,* 1333 15th St. NW, Suite 400, Washington, DC 20005 (phone: 202-347-2025 in Washington, DC; 800-821-2828 elsewhere in the US).

Travel Guard International: Underwritten by the Insurance Company of North America, it is available through authorized travel agents, or contact *Travel Guard International,* 1145 Clark St., Stevens Point, WI 54481 (phone: 715-345-0505 in Wisconsin; 800-826-1300 elsewhere in the US).

Travel Insurance PAK: Underwritten by The Travelers. Contact *The Travelers Companies,* Ticket and Travel Plans, One Tower Sq., Hartford, CT 06183-5040 (phone: 203-277-2319 in Connecticut; 800-243-3174 elsewhere in the US).

WorldCare Travel Assistance Association: This organization offers insurance packages underwritten by Transamerica Premier Insurance Company and Transamerica Occidental Life Insurance. Contact *WorldCare Travel Assistance Asso-*

ciation, 605 Market St., Suite 1300, San Francisco, CA 94105 (phone: 800-666-4993 or 415-541-4991).

How to Pack

No one can provide a completely foolproof list of precisely what to pack, so it's best to let common sense, space, and comfort guide you. Keep one maxim in mind: Less is more. You simply won't need as much clothing as you think, and though there is nothing more frustrating than arriving at your destination without just the item that in its absence becomes crucial, you are far more likely to need a forgotten accessory — or a needle and thread or scissors — than a particular piece of clothing.

As with almost anything relating to travel, a little planning can go a long way. There are specific things to consider before you open the first drawer or fold the first pair of underwear:

1. Where are you going — city, country, or both?
2. How many total days will you be gone?
3. What's the average temperature likely to be during your stay?

The goal is to remain perfectly comfortable, neat, clean, and adequately fashionable wherever you go, but actually to pack as little as possible. The main obstacle to achieving this end is habit: Most of us wake up each morning with an entire wardrobe in our closets, and we assume that our suitcase should offer the same variety and selection. Not so — only our anxiety about being caught short makes us treat a suitcase like a mobile closet. This worry can be eliminated by learning to travel light and by following two firm packing principles:

1. Organize your travel wardrobe around a single color — blue or brown, for example — that allows you to mix, match, and layer clothes. Holding firm to one color scheme will make it easy to eliminate items of clothing that don't harmonize; and by picking clothes for their adaptability and compatibility with your basic color, you will put together the widest selection with the fewest pieces of clothing.
2. Use laundries to renew your wardrobe. Never overpack to ensure a supply of fresh clothing — shirts, blouses, underwear — for each day of a long trip. Businesspeople routinely use hotel laundries to wash and clean clothes. If these are too expensive, there are local, self-service laundries in most towns of any size — called *lavandería* in Spain and *lavanderia* in Portugal.

CLIMATE AND CLOTHES: Exactly what you pack for your trip will be a function of where you are going and when and the kinds of things you intend to do. A few degrees can make all the difference between being comfortably attired and very real suffering, so your initial step should be to find out what the general weather conditions — temperature, rainfall, seasonal variations — are likely to be in the areas you will visit.

Spain and Portugal are roughly parallel with the US; Madrid (sitting astride latitude 40°) and Lisbon (at 39°) are about even with Washington, DC. The climate generally is moderate to hot in Portugal, though damp and chilly in the winter months, while in Spain there is more variation among its three principal regions, north, central, and southern — mostly in amounts of rainfall, depending on the time of year. Residents of the US will find that the same wardrobe they would wear in the southern United States will, with a few adjustments, also be appropriate for most parts of Spain and Portugal in the same season.

However, anyone going to Spain or Portugal from the late fall through the early spring should take into account that while central heating is prevalent, interiors usually are not heated to the same degree they would be in the US. Thus, although there is no need to prepare for sub-zero winters, most people probably will feel more comfortable wearing heavier clothing indoors than they might at home — for instance, sweaters rather than lightweight shirts and blouses. Rain gear also is advisable, especially in northern Spain, where precipitation can be heavy during the winter months.

More information about the climate in Spain and Portugal, along with a chart of average low and high temperatures for different cities, is given in *When to Go,* in this section; other sources of information are airlines and travel agents.

Keeping temperature and climate in mind, consider the problem of luggage. Plan on one suitcase per person (and in a pinch, remember that it's always easier to carry two small suitcases than to schlepp one that's roughly the size of the *QE2*). Standard 26- to 28-inch suitcases can be made to work for 1 week or 1 month, and unless you are going for no more than a weekend, never cram wardrobes for two people into one suitcase.

FASHION: On the whole, Spain and Portugal are no more formal than North America, so be guided by your own taste. Wear what you would in any cosmopolitan American city. Attire more formal than a cocktail dress or evening pants for women and something as formal as black tie for men are necessary only for the most elegant occasions. A blazer or sport jacket, trousers, and tie will get a man into the finest restaurants anywhere, and sometimes even the tie is not *de rigueur.* For women, a dress or a suit will do in the same situations. Other diners may be more formally dressed, but you won't be turned away or made to feel self-conscious if you do not mirror them. By the same token, you won't feel you've overdone it if you choose to turn an evening at an elegant restaurant into something special and dress accordingly. If you're planning a number of more formal evenings during your trip, bring two or three changes of clothes. Bear in mind that coordinates also are a good way of providing a number of dressier options without adding to your luggage content.

Women should figure on a maximum of five daytime and three late afternoon–evening changes. Whether you are going to be gone for a week or a month, this number should be enough. For daytime activities, women might pack jeans or light slacks, blouses, one or two swimsuits (depending on where you're going), and a pair of comfortable shoes or sneakers. In warmer weather, include T-shirts and a pair of shorts; skirts and summer dresses are a cool choice for touring. In cooler weather, pack corduroy or wool slacs, a longer skirt which can be worn with turtlenecks, blouses, and sweaters, and a pair of boots, which will provide a number of comfortable alternatives. Low-heel pumps are appropriate for both dressier daytime and evening wear. Again, before packing, lay out every piece of clothing you think you might want to take. Select clothing on the basis of what can serve several functions, and accessorize everything beforehand so you know exactly what you will be wearing with what. Eliminate items that don't mix, match, or interchange within your color scheme. If you can't wear it in at least two distinct incarnations, leave it at home.

If you are planning to be on the move — either in a car, bus, train, or plane — consider loose-fitting clothes that do not wrinkle, although the recent trend toward fabrics with a wrinkled look is a boon to travelers. Despite the tendency of designers to use more 100% natural fabrics, synthetics are immensely practical for a trip and lately have improved immeasurably in appearance. As a general rule, perishable clothes — pure cotton and linen — are hard to keep up and should be left behind. Lightweight wools, manmade fabrics such as jerseys and knits, and drip-dry fabrics that can be rinsed in Woolite or a similar cold-water detergent travel best (although in very hot weather cotton clothing may be the most comfortable), and prints look fresher longer than solids.

Men also will find that color coordination is crucial. Solid colors coordinate best, and a sport jacket that goes with a pair of pants from a suit and several pairs of slacks provides added options. For travel in warmer weather, lightweight cotton shirts and a coordinating cotton sweater paired with casual slacks or chinos (and the sport jacket on cooler days) will suffice for many occasions; also bring along shorts and one or two bathing suits (again, depending on your destination). Include several shirts that can be used for both daytime and evening wear, and sneakers and/or loafers (include at least one pair of double-duty shoes that go with both casual and dressier attire). For touring in cooler weather, bring heavier slacks or corduroys, long-sleeve shirts or turtlenecks, a wool sweater, and a medium-weight jacket or coat. Hanging bags are best for packing suits and jackets.

Since a prevailing characteristic of Iberian weather is rain, a raincoat with a zip-out lining — and maybe even a hood — is a versatile choice. The removable lining affords adaptability to temperature changes, and the hood is better suited (and less cumbersome) than an umbrella for fine, misty rain, although a practical alternative is a rain hat that can be rolled up in a pocket or carry-on bag. If you do decide to take an umbrella, a compact telescoping model is best.

If your trip will encompass all parts of Spain and Portugal, layering is the key to comfort — particularly when touring in parts of the countryside where mornings and evenings can be chilly even when the days are mild. No matter where you are traveling in Spain or Portugal, however, layering is a good way to prepare for atypical temperatures or changes in the weather. For damp or unexpectedly cool days or for outings in the countryside, recommended basics are a T-shirt and lightweight cotton shirts or sweaters, which can be worn under another shirt and perhaps a third layer, such as a pullover sweater, jacket, or windbreaker. In cooler weather, substitute a lightweight wool or heavier cotton turtleneck for the lighter layers. As the weather changes, you can add or remove clothes as required, and layering adapts well to the ruling principle of dressing according to a single color scheme. Individual items in layers can mix and match, be used together or independently.

Among the layers, don't forget to include a warm sweater or jacket. This will not be needed to take the chill off air conditioned rooms (air conditioning is not the rule in Spain and Portugal), but even in a heat wave, it will be welcome for exploring caves or wine cellars. In fact, you probably will be tempted by the great variety of fashionable handmade garments available throughout Spain and Portugal to acquire more layers than you really need, so buy only the basics before departure.

If you are planning to be on the move — either in a car, bus, train, or plane, or aboard a boat — consider loose-fitting clothes that do not wrinkle, although the recent trend toward fabrics with a deliberately wrinkled look is a boon to travelers. Despite the tendency of designers to use more 100% natural fabrics, synthetics — particularly the new washable rayon blends — are immensely practical for a trip, and they have improved immeasurably in appearance lately. As a general rule, clothes in pure cotton and linen are the most perishable and hard to keep fresh-looking. Lightweight wools and manmade fabrics — such as jerseys and knits, and drip-dry fabrics that can be rinsed in Woolite or a similar cold-water detergent — travel best (although in very hot weather cotton clothing may be the most comfortable), and prints look fresher longer than solids.

Pack clothes that have a lot of pockets for traveler's checks, documents, and tickets. Then, if your bag gets lost or stolen, you will retain possession of the essentials. Men who prefer to keep their pockets free of coins, papers, and keys might consider a shoulder bag, useful for carrying camera equipment, as well as daily necessities.

And finally — since the best touring of Spanish and Portuguese monuments, churches, and countryside is done on foot — comfortable walking shoes are a must for both sexes, no matter what the season or the fashion. You will do a lot of walking up and down stairs, up and down hills, to distant archaeological sites and back. Even in the evening, when you anticipate walking no farther than to the nearest restaurant, women should avoid spike heels. Cobblestones are ubiquitous, and chunkier heels have a better chance of not getting caught — and ruined.

Your carry-on luggage should contain a survival kit with the basic things you will need in case your luggage gets lost or stolen: a toothbrush, toothpaste, all medications, a sweater, nightclothes, and a change of underwear. With these essential items at hand, you will be prepared for any sudden, unexpected occurrence that separates you from your suitcase. Also, if you have many 1- or 2-night stops, you can live out of your survival case without having to unpack completely at each hotel.

Other items you might consider packing are a flashlight with extra batteries, small sewing and first-aid kits (including insect repellent), binoculars, and a camera or camcorder (see *Cameras and Equipment,* in this section).

Sundries – If you are traveling in the heat of summer and will be spending a lot of time outdoors, pack special items so that you won't spend your entire vacation horizontal in a hotel room (or hospital) because of sunburn. Be sure to take a sun hat (to protect hair as well as skin), sunscreen, and tanning lotion, which is available in graduated degrees of sunblock corresponding to the level of your skin's sensitivity. (The quantity of sunscreen is indicated by number: the higher the number, the greater the protection.) A good moisturizer is necessary to help keep your skin from drying out and peeling. The best advice is to take the sun's rays in small doses — no more than 20 minutes at a stretch — increasing your sunbathing time as your vacation progresses. Also, if you are heading for a vacation on skis, do not underestimate the effect of the sun's glare off snowy slopes, especially in higher altitudes — your face and neck are particularly susceptible to a burning.

PACKING: The basic idea of packing is to get everything into the suitcase and out again with as few wrinkles as possible. Simple, casual clothes — shirts, jeans and slacks, permanent press skirts — can be rolled into neat, tight sausages that keep other packed items in place and leave the clothes themselves amazingly unwrinkled. The rolled clothes can be retrieved, shaken out, and hung up at your destination. However, for items that are too bulky or delicate for even careful rolling, a suitcase can be packed with the heaviest items on the bottom, toward the hinges, so that they will not wrinkle more perishable clothes. Candidates for the bottom layer include shoes (stuff them with small items to save space), a toilet kit, handbags (stuff them to help keep their shape), and an alarm clock. Fill out this layer with things that will not wrinkle or will not matter if they do, such as sweaters, socks, a bathing suit, gloves, and underwear.

If you get this first, heavy layer as smooth as possible with the fill-ins, you will have a shelf for the next layer — the most easily wrinkled items, like slacks, jackets, shirts, dresses, and skirts. These should be buttoned and zipped and laid along the whole length of the suitcase with as little folding as possible. When you do need to make a fold, do it on a crease (as with pants), along a seam in the fabric, or where it will not show (such as shirttails). Alternate each piece of clothing, using one side of the suitcase, then the other, to make the layers as flat as possible. Make the layers even and the total contents of your bag as full and firm as possible to keep things from shifting around during transit. On the top layer put the things you will want at once: nightclothes, an umbrella or raincoat, a sweater.

With men's two-suiter suitcases, follow the same procedure. Then place jackets on hangers, straighten them out, and leave them unbuttoned. If they are too wide for the suitcase, fold them lengthwise down the middle, straighten the shoulders, and fold the sleeves in along the seam.

While packing, it is a good idea to separate each layer of clothes with plastic cleaning bags, which will help preserve pressed clothes while they are in the suitcase. Unpack your bags as soon as you get to your hotel. Nothing so thoroughly destroys freshly cleaned and pressed clothes as sitting for days in a suitcase. Finally, if something is badly wrinkled and can't be professionally pressed before you must wear it, hang it overnight in a bathroom where the bathtub has been filled with very hot water; keep the door closed so the room becomes something of a steamroom. It really works miracles.

LUGGAGE: If you already own serviceable luggage, do not feel compelled to buy new bags. If, however, you have been looking for an excuse to throw out that old suitcase that saw you through 4 years of college and innumerable weekends, this trip to Spain or Portugal can be the perfect occasion.

Luggage falls into three categories — hard, soft-sided, and soft — and each has advantages and disadvantages. Hard suitcases have a rigid frame and sides. They provide the most protection from rough handling, but they also are the heaviest. Wheels and pull straps can rectify this problem, but they should be removed before the luggage is turned over at check-in or they may be wrenched off in transit. In addition, hard bags sometimes will pop open, even when locked, so a strap around the suitcase is advised.

Soft-sided suitcases have a rigid frame that has been covered with leather, fabric, or a synthetic material. The weight of the suitcase is greatly reduced, but many of the coverings (except leather, which also is heavy) are vulnerable to rips and tears from conveyor machinery. Not surprisingly, the materials that wear best generally are found on more expensive luggage.

The third category, seen more and more frequently, is soft luggage. Lacking any rigid structural element, it comes in a wide variety of shapes and sizes and is easy to carry, especially since it often has a shoulder strap. Most carry-on bags are of this type because they can be squeezed under the plane seat. They are even more vulnerable to damage on conveyor equipment than soft-sided bags, and as the weak point on these bags is the zipper, be sure to tie some cord or put several straps around the bag for extra insurance. Also be prepared to find a brand-new set of wrinkles pressed into everything that was carefully ironed before packing.

Whatever type of luggage you choose, remember that it should last for many years. Shop carefully, but be prepared to make a sizable investment. In fact, you might consider putting off the purchase of new luggage until you get to one of Spain or Portugal's major cities, where fine hand-crafted leather goods can be found.

It always is a good idea to add an empty, flattened airline bag or similar piece of luggage to your suitcase; you'll find it indispensable as a beach bag or to carry a few items for a day's outing. Keep in mind, too, that you're likely to do some shopping so save room for those items. If you're planning any extensive shopping, you might consider packing one of those soft, parachute-cloth suitcases that fold into a small envelope when not in use.

For more information on packing and luggage, send your request with a self-addressed, stamped, #10 envelope to *Samsonite Travel Advisory Service* (PO Box 39609, Dept. 80, Denver, CO 80239) for its free booklet *Lightening the Travel Load: Travel Tips & Tricks.*

SOME FINAL PACKING HINTS: Apart from the items you pack as carry-on luggage (see above), always keep all necessary medicines, valuable jewelry, and travel or business documents in your purse, briefcase, or carry-on bag — *not in the luggage you will check.* Tuck a bathing suit into your handbag or briefcase, too; in the event of lost baggage, it's frustrating to be without one. And whether in your overnight bag or checked luggage, cosmetics and any liquids should be packed in plastic bottles or at least wrapped in plastic bags and tied.

Golf clubs and skis may be checked through as luggage (most airlines are accustomed to handling them), but tennis rackets should be carried onto the plane. Some airlines require that bicycles be partially dismantled and packaged (see *Camping and Caravanning, Hiking and Biking,* in this section). Check with the airline before departure to see if there is a specific regulation concerning any special equipment or sporting gear you plan to take.

Hints for Handicapped Travelers

From 35 to 50 million people in the US alone have some sort of disability, and at least half this number are physically handicapped. Like everyone else today, they — and the uncounted disabled millions around the world — are on the move. More than ever before, they are demanding facilities they can use comfortably, and they are being heard. The disabled traveler will find that services for the handicapped have improved considerably over the last few years, both in the US and abroad, and though accessibility is far from universal, it is being brought up to more acceptable standards every day.

Spain and Portugal, countries of many hills and steps, have been comparatively slow in developing access for the handicapped. Both countries, however, do have services that will assist the handicapped traveler. Generally, only the best or newest hotels and restaurants are easily accessible to a person in a wheelchair, and unless you are on a special tour for the handicapped, you will need to rely mostly on taxis for transportation. Nevertheless, with ingenuity and the help of an able-bodied traveling companion, you can get around these fascinating countries well enough to thoroughly enjoy their varied delights. What the Spanish and Portuguese lack in facilities for the handicapped they more than make up for in willingness to help.

PLANNING: Good planning is essential: Collect as much information as you can about your specific disability and facilities for the disabled in Spain and Portugal; make your travel arrangements well in advance, and specify to all services involved the exact nature of your condition or restricted mobility, as your trip will be much more comfortable if you know that there are accommodations and facilities to suit your needs. The best way to find out if your intended destination can accommodate a handicapped traveler is to write or phone the local tourist association or hotel and ask specific questions. If you require a corridor of a certain width to maneuver a wheelchair or if you need handles on the bathroom wall for support, ask the hotel manager. A travel agent or the local chapter or national office of the organization that deals with your particular disability — for example, the *American Foundation for the Blind* or the *American Heart Association* — will supply the most up-to-date information on the subject. The following sources offer general information on access:

Access to the World, by Louise Weiss, offers sound tips for the disabled traveler abroad. Published by Facts on File (460 Park Ave. S., New York, NY 10016; phone: 212-683-2244), it costs $16.95. Check with your local bookstore; it also can be ordered by phone with a credit card.

Access Travel: A Guide to the Accessibility of Airport Terminals, published by the Airport Operators Council International, provides information on more than 500 airports worldwide — including the major airports in Spain and Portugal — with ratings according to 70 features, including accessibility to bathrooms, corridor width, and parking spaces. For a free copy, write to the Consumer Information Center, Access America (Dept. 563W, Pueblo, CO 81009), or call 202-293-8500 and ask for "Item 563W — Access Travel." To help travel agents plan trips for the handicapped, this material is reprinted with additional information on tourist boards, city information offices, and tour operators specializing in travel for the handicapped (see "Tours," below) in the *Worldwide Edition* of the *Official Airline Guides Travel Planner,* issued quarterly by Official Airline Guides (2000 Clearwater Dr., Oak Brook, IL 60521; phone: 708-574-6000).

Air Transportation of Handicapped Persons is a booklet published by the US Department of Transportation, and will be sent at no charge upon written request. Ask for "Free Advisory Circular #AC-120-32" from the Distribution Unit, US Dept. of Transportation, Publications Section, M-443-2, Washington, DC 20590.

Handicapped Travel Newsletter is regarded as one of the best sources of information for the disabled traveler. It is edited by wheelchair-bound Vietnam veteran Michael Quigley, who has traveled to 93 countries around the world. Issued every 2 months (plus special issues), a subscription is $10 per year. Write to *Handicapped Travel Newsletter,* PO Box 269, Athens, TX 75751 (phone: 214-677-1260).

Information Center for Individuals with Disabilities (ICID), Fort Point Pl., 1st Floor, 27-43 Wormwood St., Boston, MA 02210 (phone: 617-727-5540/1 or 800-462-5015 in Massachusetts only); both numbers offer voice and TDD (telecommunications device for the deaf) service. *ICID* provides information and referral services on disability-related issues and will help you research your trip. The center publishes fact sheets on vacation planning, tour operators, travel agents, and travel resources.

The Itinerary is a travel magazine for people with disabilities. Published bimonthly, it includes information on accessibility, listings of tours, news of adaptive devices, travel aids, and special services, as well as numerous general travel hints. A subscription is $10 a year; write to *The Itinerary,* PO Box 2012, Bayonne, NJ 07002-2012 (phone: 201-858-3400).

Mobility International/USA (MIUSA), the US branch of *Mobility International,* a nonprofit British organization with affiliates in some 35 countries, offers advice and assistance to disabled travelers — including information on accommodations, access guides, and study tours. Among its publications are a quarterly newsletter and a comprehensive sourcebook, *World of Options for the '90s: A Guide to International Education Exchange, Community Service, and Travel for Persons with Disabilities.* Individual membership is $20 a year; subscription to the newsletter alone is $10 annually. For more information, contact *MIUSA,* PO Box 3551, Eugene, OR 97403 (phone: 503-343-1284; voice and TDD — telecommunications device for the deaf).

National Rehabilitation Information Center, 8455 Colesville Rd., Suite 935, Silver Spring, MD 20910 (phone: 301-588-9284). A general information, resource, research, and referral service.

Paralyzed Veterans of America (PVA) is a national veterans service organization. Its members all are veterans who have suffered spinal cord injuries, but it offers advocacy services and information to all persons with a disability. *PVA* also sponsors *Access to the Skies,* a program that coordinates the efforts of the national and international air travel industry in providing airport and airplane access for the disabled. Members receive several helpful publications, as well as regular notification of conferences on subjects of interest to the disabled traveler. For information, contact *PVA/ATTS Program,* 801 18th St. NW, Washington, DC 20006 (phone: 202-USA-1300).

Royal Association for Disability and Rehabilitation (RADAR), 25 Mortimer St., London W1N 8AB, England (phone: 44-81-637-5400), offers a number of publications for the handicapped, including a comprehensive guide, *Holidays and Travel Abroad for the Disabled,* which covers all of Europe and provides helpful advice to the disabled traveler abroad. Available by writing to *RADAR,* the price, including airmail postage, is £3; *RADAR* requires payment in pounds sterling, so this should be sent via an international money order (available at the post office and at banks).

Society for the Advancement of Travel for the Handicapped (SATH), 26 Court St., Penthouse, Brooklyn, NY 11242 (phone: 718-858-5483). To keep abreast of developments in travel for the handicapped as they occur, you may want to join *SATH,* a nonprofit organization whose members include travel agents, tour operators, and other travel suppliers, as well as consumers. Membership costs $40 ($25 for students and travelers who are 65 and older) and the fee is tax deductible. *SATH* publishes a quarterly newsletter, an excellent booklet, *Travel Tips for the Handicapped,* and provides information on travel agents or tour operators who have experience (or an interest) in travel for the handicapped. *SATH* also offers a free 48-page guide, *The United States Welcomes Handicapped Visitors,* that covers domestic transportation and accommodations, as well as travel insurance and other useful hints for the handicapped traveler abroad. Send a self-addressed, #10 envelope to *SATH* at the address above, and include $1 for postage.

TravelAbility, by Lois Reamy, is a vast database with information on locating tours for the handicapped, coping with public transport, and finding accommodations, special equipment, and travel agents, and includes a helpful step-by-step planning guide. Although geared mainly to travel in the US, it is full of information useful to handicapped travelers anywhere. Previously published by Macmillan, *TravelAbility* is currently out of print, but may be available at your library.

Travel Information Service at Moss Rehabilitation Hospital is a service designed to help physically handicapped people plan trips. It cannot make travel arrangements, but it will supply information on travel accessibility for a nominal fee. Contact the *Travel Information Service,* Moss Rehabilitation Hospital, 12th St. and Tabor Rd., Philadelphia, PA 19141 (phone: 215-456-9600).

There also are organizations throughout Spain and Portugal that provide not only information for the disabled traveler, but in some cases an escort who will meet the traveler at the airport. You will need to write well in advance, however, to take advantage of such special services. Among these organizations are the following:

Spain: The National Institute of Social Services, Ministry of Labour, Health and Social Security, Nuevos Ministerios, Paseo de la Castellana, Madrid 28071, Spain (phone: 1-253-6000, 1-253-7600, or 1-233-7995). Information and escort services.

Portugal: Portuguese League for the Disabled, 380 Rua da Junqueira, Lisbon 1300, Portugal (phone: 1-1-648439). A nationwide organization dealing in information and services for the disabled.

Other good sources of information are the National Tourist Office of Spain and the Portuguese National Tourist Office. Although brochures specifically for the handicapped may not be in English, they sometimes offer a clipping service on articles about disabled travel in their countries, which also will be sent on request. (For the US addresses of these government tourist authorities, see *Tourist Information Offices,* in this section.)

Two organizations based in Great Britain offer information for handicapped persons traveling throughout Europe, including Spain and Portugal. *Tripscope* (63 Esmond Rd., London W4 1JE, UK; phone: 44-81-994-9294) is a telephone-based information and referral service (not a booking agent) that can help with transportation options for specific journeys throughout Europe; it also may be able to recommend outlets leasing small family vehicles adapted to take a wheelchair. And for general information, there's

Holiday Care Service (2 Old Bank Chambers, Station Rd., Horley, Surrey RH6 9HW, UK; phone: 44-293-774535), a first-rate, free advisory service on accommodations, transportation, and holiday packages throughout Europe for disabled visitors.

Regularly revised hotel and restaurant guides use the symbol of access (person in a wheelchair; see the symbol at the beginning of this section) to point out accommodations suitable for wheelchair-bound guests. The red *Michelin Guide to Spain and Portugal* (Michelin; $20.95), found in general and travel bookstores, is one such publication.

The *Canadian Rehabilitation Council for the Disabled* publishes a useful book by Cinnie Noble, *Handi-Travel: A Resource Book for Disabled and Elderly Travelers* ($12.95, $2 for shipping and handling, 50¢ each additional copy). This comprehensive travel guide is full of practical tips for those with disabilities affecting mobility, hearing, or sight. To order this book and for other useful information, contact the *Canadian Rehabilitation Council for the Disabled,* 45 Sheppard Ave. E., Suite 801, Toronto, Ontario M2N 5W9, Canada (phone: 416-250-7490).

A few more basic resources to look for are *Travel for the Disabled,* by Helen Hecker ($9.95), and by the same author, *The Directory of Travel Agencies for the Disabled* ($12.95). *Wheelchair Vagabond,* by John G. Nelson, is another useful guide for travelers confined to a wheelchair (softcover, $9.95; hardcover, $14.95). All three are published by Twin Peaks Press (PO Box 129, Vancouver, WA 98666; to order call 800-637-CALM). Additionally, *The Physically Disabled Traveler's Guide,* by Rod W. Durgin and Norene Lindsay, is helpful and informative. It is available from Resource Directories (3361 Executive Pkwy., Suite 302, Toledo, OH 43606; phone: 419-536-5353) for $9.95, plus $2 for postage and handling.

Also check the library for Mary Meister Walzer's *A Travel Guide for the Disabled: Western Europe* (Van Nostrand Reinhold), which gives access ratings to a fair number of hotels along with information on the accessibility of some sightseeing attractions, restaurants, theaters, stores, and more.

It should be noted that almost all of the material published with disabled travelers in mind deals with the wheelchair-bound traveler, for whom architectural barriers are of prime concern. For travelers with diabetes, a pamphlet entitled *Ticket to Safe Travel* is available for 50¢ from the New York chapter of the *American Diabetes Association* (505 Eighth Ave., 21st Floor, New York, NY 10018; phone: 212-947-9707). For those with heart-related ailments, *Travel for the Patient with Chronic Obstructive Pulmonary Disease* is available for $2 from Dr. Harold Silver (1601 18th St. NW, Washington, DC 20009; phone: 202-667-0134); the *American Heart Association* (7320 Greenville Ave., Dallas, TX 75231; phone: 214-373-6300) also provides a number of useful publications. For blind travelers, a wealth of additional information is available from the *American Foundation for the Blind* (15 W. 16th St., New York, NY 10011; phone: 212-620-2147 in New York State; 800-232-5463 elsewhere in the US).

Travelers who depend on Seeing Eye dogs should check with the airline they plan to fly and the appropriate Spanish and Portuguese authorities well before they leave. In general, the rules that apply to bringing any dog into these countries apply without exception to Seeing Eye dogs. Travelers to Spain need to acquire veterinary and rabies inoculation certificates, which can be validated at the nearest Spanish consulate. For Portugal, the same documents are required and should be issued within 1 year of departure. In addition, vaccination certificates for Portugal should include the date, type of vaccine used, name of manufacturer, and the serial number of the vaccine. These documents should be stamped by a veterinarian or notarized by the nearest Portuguese consulate. (See *Tourist Information Offices,* in this section.)

The *American Society for the Prevention of Cruelty to Animals (ASPCA)* also offers a very useful book, *Traveling With Your Pet,* which includes inoculation and quarantine requirements by country and territory. It is available for $5 (which includes postage and handling). Send check or money order to the *ASPCA* (Education Dept., 441 E. 92nd St., New York, NY 10128; phone: 212-876-7700). For helpful information and a general discussion of travel with Seeing Eye dogs, *Seeing Eye Dogs as Air Travelers* can be obtained free from *Seeing Eye* (Box 375, Morristown, NJ 07963-0375; phone: 201-539-4425).

PLANE: Advise the airline that you are handicapped when you book your flight. The Federal Aviation Administration (FAA) has ruled that US airlines must accept disabled and handicapped passengers as long as the airline has advance notice and the passenger represents no potentially insurmountable problem in the event that emergency evacuation becomes necessary. As a matter of course, US airlines were pretty good about helping handicapped passengers even before the ruling, although each airline has somewhat different procedures. Spanish and Portuguese airlines also generally are good about accommodating the disabled traveler, but again, policies vary from carrier to carrier. Ask for specifics when you book your flight.

Disabled passengers always should make reservations well in advance, and should provide the airline with all relevant details of their condition at that time. These details include information on mobility, toilet and special oxygen needs, and requirements for equipment that must be supplied by the airline, such as a wheelchair or portable oxygen. Be sure that the person to whom you speak understands fully the degree of your disability — the more details provided, the more effective the help the airline can give you. On the day before the flight, call back to make sure that all arrangements have been prepared, and arrive early on the day of the flight so that you can board before the rest of the passengers. Carry a medical certificate with you, stating your specific disability or the need to carry particular medicine. (Some airlines require the certificate; you should find out the regulations of the airline you'll be flying well beforehand.)

Because most airports have jetways (corridors connecting the terminal with the door of the plane), a disabled passenger usually can be taken as far as the plane, and sometimes right onto it, in a wheelchair. If not, a narrow boarding chair may be used to take you to your seat. Your own wheelchair, which will be folded and put in the baggage compartment, should be tagged as escort luggage to assure that it's available at planeside upon landing rather than in the baggage claim area. Travel is not quite as simple if your wheelchair is battery-operated: Unless it has non-spillable batteries, it might not be accepted on board, and you will have to check with the airline ahead of time to find out how the batteries and the chair should be packaged for the flight. Usually people in wheelchairs are asked to wait until other passengers have disembarked. If you are making a tight connection, be sure to tell the attendant.

Passengers who use oxygen may not use their personal supply in the cabin, though it may be carried on the plane as cargo when properly packed and labeled. If you will need oxygen during the flight, the airline will supply it to you (there is a charge) provided you have given advance notice — 24 hours to a few days, depending on the carrier.

Useful information on every stage of air travel, from planning to arrival, is provided in the booklet *Incapacitated Passengers Air Travel Guide.* To receive a free copy, write to Senior Manager, Passenger Services, International Air Transport Association, 2000 Peel St., Montreal, Quebec H3A 2R4 Canada (phone: 514-844-6311).

For an access guide to hundreds of airports worldwide, write for *Access Travel: A Guide to the Accessibility of Airport Terminals,* a free publication of the *Airport Operators Council International,* which includes detailed information on airports in Faro, Horta, Lisbon, Ponta Delgada, Porto, and Santa Maria, all in Portugal. (Currently, no listings are offered for Spanish airports.) The US Department of Transportation's *Air Transportation of Handicapped Persons* explains the general guidelines that govern air carrier policies. It is available free when requested in writing. For information on obtaining both of these publications, see the source list above.

The following airlines serving Spain and Portugal have TDD toll-free lines in the US for the hearing-impaired: *American* (phone: 800-582-1573 in Ohio; 800-543-1586 elsewhere in the US); *Pan American* (phone: 800-722-3323); and *TWA* (phone: 800-252-0622 in California; 800-421-8480 elsewhere in the US).

SHIP: Cunard's *Queen Elizabeth 2* is considered the best-equipped ship for the handicapped — all but the top deck is accessible. The *QE2* crosses the Atlantic regularly from April through December between New York and its home port of Southampton, England, sometimes calling at Cherbourg, France, and ports in Spain and Portugal. Handicapped travelers are advised to book reservations at least 90 days in advance to reserve specially equipped cabins.

GROUND TRANSPORTATION: Perhaps the simplest solution to getting around is to travel with an able-bodied companion who can drive. If you are accustomed to driving your own hand-controlled car and are determined to rent one, you may have to do some extensive research, as it is difficult in Spain and Portugal to find rental cars fitted with hand controls. If agencies do provide hand-control cars, they are apt to be offered only on a limited basis in major metropolitan areas and usually are in high demand. *Hertz,* for instance, rents hand-control cars in Madrid and Barcelona only; you need to call at least 7 days in advance (much earlier is advisable), and the availability of Class A and B vehicles is limited. The best course is to contact the major car rental agencies listed in *Traveling by Car,* in this section, well before your departure, but be forewarned, you still may be out of luck. Other sources for information on vehicles adapted for the handicapped are the organizations discussed above.

The *American Automobile Association (AAA)* publishes the booklet *The Handicapped Driver's Mobility Guide,* available free to members and for $3 to non-members. Contact your local *AAA* office, or send a self-addressed, stamped, 6-by-9-inch envelope to *AAA* Traffic Safety Department, 1000 AAA Dr., Heathrow, FL 32746-5063.

Another quite expensive option is to hire a chauffeured car. Other alternatives include taking taxis or using local public transportation; however, your mobility may be limited in rural areas.

BUS AND TRAIN: In general, bus travel is not recommended for travelers who are totally wheelchair-bound unless they have someone along who can lift them on and off or they are members of a group tour designed for the handicapped and are using a specially outfitted bus. If you have some mobility, however, you'll find local personnel usually quite happy to help you board and exit.

Train travel in Spain and Portugal also is not well adapted to wheelchairs, although timetables may specify which, if any, departures are accessible. On trains that cannot accommodate wheelchairs, depending on the type of train, wheelchair passengers sometimes can travel in the guard's van. Arrangements usually are made through the area manager in advance. For further information on this option, general accessibility, and for timetables, contact *FrenchRail Inc.,* the Spanish and Portuguese rail service representative in the US (addresses are listed in *Traveling by Train,* in this section), or ask for information at regional rail offices abroad.

TOURS: Programs designed for the physically impaired are run by specialists who have researched hotels, restaurants, and sites to be sure they present no insurmountable obstacles. The following travel agencies and tour operators specialize in making group and individual arrangements for travelers with physical or other disabilities. All of them have experience in travel to Europe. Because of the requirements of handicapped travel, however, the same packages may not be offered regularly.

Access: The Foundation for Accessibility by the Disabled, PO Box 356, Malverne, NY 11565 (phone: 516-887-5798). A travelers' referral service that acts as an intermediary with tour operators and agents worldwide, and provides information on accessibility at various locations. The firm also offers access to its audio/video travel library.

Accessible Tours/Directions Unlimited, 720 N. Bedford Rd., Bedford Hills, NY 10507 (phone: 914-241-1700 in New York State; 800-533-5343 elsewhere in the US). Arranges group or individual tours for disabled persons traveling in the company of able-bodied friends or family members. Accepts the unaccompanied traveler if completely self-sufficient.

Evergreen Travel Service/Wings on Wheels Tours, 19505L 44th Ave. W., Lynn-wood, WA 98036-5658 (phone: 206-776-1184 or 800-435-2288 throughout the US). The oldest company in the world offering worldwide tours and cruises for the disabled (Wings on Wheels) and sight impaired/blind (White Cane Tours). Most programs are first class or deluxe, and include a trained escort. *Evergreen* also offers a service called Evergreen Flying Fingers, for the deaf.

Flying Wheels Travel, 143 W. Bridge St., Box 382, Owatonna, MN 55060 (phone: 507-451-5005 or 800-535-6790 throughout the US). Handles both tours and individual arrangements.

The Guided Tour, 555 Ashbourne Rd., Elkins Park, PA 19117 (phone: 215-782-1370). Arranges tours for people with developmental and learning disabilities and sponsors separate tours for members of the same population who also are physically disabled or who simply need a slower pace.

Sprout, 893 Amsterdam Ave., New York, NY 10025 (phone: 212-222-9575). Arranges travel programs for mildly and moderately disabled teens and adults.

Travel Horizons Unlimited, 11 E. 44th St., New York, NY 10017 (phone: 212-687-5121 in New York; 800-343-5032 elsewhere in the US). Travel agent and regis-tered nurse Mary Ann Hamm designs trips for individual travelers requiring all types of kidney dialysis and handles arrangements for the dialysis.

Whole Person Tours, PO Box 1084, Bayonne, NJ 07002-1084 (phone: 800-462-2237 or 201-858-3400). Handicapped owner Bob Zywicki travels the world with his wheelchair and offers a lineup of escorted tours (many conducted by himself) for the disabled. Send a self-addressed, stamped envelope for a general tour brochure of foreign and domestic programs. *Whole Person Tours* also publishes *The Itinerary,* a bimonthly newsletter for disabled travelers (a 1-year subscrip-tion costs $10).

Hints for Single Travelers

Just about the last trip in human history on which the participants were neatly paired was the voyage of Noah's Ark. Ever since, passenger lists and tour groups have reflected the same kind of asymmetry that occurs in real life, as countless individuals set forth to see the world unaccompanied (or unencumbered, depending on your outlook) by spouse, lover, friend, or relative.

There are some things to be said for traveling alone. There is the pleasure of privacy, though a solitary traveler must be self-reliant, independent, and responsible. Unfortu-nately, traveling alone also can turn a traveler into a second class citizen.

The truth is that the travel industry is not very fair to people who vacation by themselves. People traveling alone almost invariably end up paying more than individu-als traveling in pairs. Most travel bargains, including package tours, accommodations, resort packages, and cruises, are based on *double occupancy* rates. This means that the per-person price is offered on the basis of two people traveling together and sharing a double room (which means they each will spend a good deal more on meals and extras). The single traveler will have to pay a surcharge, called a single supplement, for exactly the same package. In extreme cases, this can add as much as 30% to 55% to the basic per-person rate. As far as the travel industry is concerned, single travel has not yet come into its own.

Don't despair, however. Throughout Spain and Portugal, there are scores of smaller hotels and other hostelries where, in addition to a cozier atmosphere, prices still are quite reasonable for a solitary traveler. There are, after all, countless thousands of individuals who *do* travel alone. Inevitably, their greatest obstacle is the single supplement charge, which prevents them from cashing in on travel bargains available to anyone traveling as part of a pair.

The obvious, most effective alternative is to find a traveling companion. Even special "singles' tours" that promise no supplements usually are based on people sharing double rooms. Perhaps the most recent innovation along these lines is the creation of organizations that "introduce" the single traveler to other single travelers, somewhat like a dating service. If you are interested in finding another person to help share the cost, consider contacting the agencies listed below. Some charge fees, others are free, but the basic service offered by all is the same: to match the unattached person with a compatible travel mate, often as part of the company's own package tours. Among the better established of these agencies are the following:

Contiki Holidays: Specializes in vacations for 18- to 35-year-olds. Packages to Spain and Portugal frequently are offered. For information, contact *Contiki Holidays,* 1432 E. Katella Ave., Anaheim, CA 92805 (phone: 714-937-0611; 800-624-0611 in California; 800-626-0611 elsewhere in the continental US).

Cosmos: Offers budget motorcoach tours of Europe — including Spain and Portugal, with a guaranteed-share plan whereby singles who wish to share rooms (and avoid paying the single supplement) are matched by the tour escort with like-minded individuals of the same sex and charged the basic double-occupancy tour price. Contact the firm at any one of its three North American branches: 95-25 Queens Blvd., Rego Park, NY 11374 (phone: 800-221-0090 from the eastern US); 150 S. Los Robles Ave., Pasadena, CA 91101 (phone 818-449-0919; 800-556-5454 from the western US); 1801 Eglinton Ave. W., Suite 104, Toronto, Ontario M6E 2H8, Canada (phone: 416-787-1281).

Grand Circle Travel: Arranges extended vacations, escorted tours, and cruises for retired Americans, including singles. Membership, which is automatic when you book a trip through *Grand Circle,* includes discount certificates on future trips and other extras. Contact *Grand Circle Travel,* 347 Congress St., Boston, MA 02210 (phone: 617-350-7500).

Insight International Tours: Offers a matching service for single travelers. Several tours are geared for travelers in the 18 to 35 age group. Contact *Insight International Tours,* 745 Atlantic Ave., Boston MA 02111 (phone: 800-582-8380 or 617-482-2000).

Jane's International: This service puts potential traveling companions in touch with one another. No age limit, no fee. Contact *Jane's International,* 2603 Bath Ave., Brooklyn, NY 11214 (phone: 718-266-2045).

STI: Offers multi-country escorted tours ranging from 2 weeks to 52 days, including itineraries in Spain and Portugal. Contact *STI,* 8619 Reseda Blvd., Suite 103, Northridge, CA 91324 (phone: 800-525-0525).

Saga International Holidays: A subsidiary of a British company specializing in older travelers, many of them single, *Saga* offers a broad selection of escorted coach tours, cruises, and apartment-stay holidays, including packages, for people age 60 and over or those 50 to 59 traveling with someone 60 or older. Members of the *Saga Holiday Club* receive the club magazine, which contains a column aimed at helping lone travelers find suitable traveling companions. A

1-year club membership costs $5. Recent itineraries in Spain and Portugal included a tour of Spain's Costa del Sol and stay-put packages in Portugal. Contact *Saga International Holidays,* 120 Boylston St., Boston MA 02116 (phone: 800-343-0273 or 617-451-6808).

Singleworld: Organizes its own packages and books singles on the cruises and tours of other operators; it arranges shared accommodations if requested, charging a one-time surcharge that is much less than the single supplement would be. *Singleworld* actually is a club joined through travel agents for a yearly fee of $20, paid at the time of booking. About two-thirds of this agency's clientele are under 35, and about half this number are women. *Singleworld* organizes tours and cruises with departures categorized by age group. Contact *Singleworld,* 401 Theodore Fremd Ave., Rye, NY 10580 (phone: 914-967-3334 or 800-223-6490 in the continental US).

Travel Companion Exchange: Every 8 weeks, this group publishes a directory of singles looking for travel companions and provides members with full-page profiles of likely partners. Members fill out a lengthy questionnaire to establish a personal profile and write a small listing, much like an ad in a personal column. This listing is circulated to other members who can request a copy of the complete questionnaire and then go on to make contact to plan a joint vacation. It is wise to join as far ahead of your scheduled vacation as possible so that there's enough time to determine the suitability of prospective traveling companions. Membership fees range from $6 to $11 per month (with a 6-month minimum enrollment), depending on the level of service required. The membership package includes a travel newsletter for singles. A sample issue costs $4. Contact *Travel Companion Exchange,* PO Box 833, Amityville, NY 11701 (phone: 516-454-0880).

A special guidebook for solo travelers, prepared by Eleanor Adams Baxel, offers information on how to avoid paying supplementary charges, how to pick the right travel agent, how to calculate costs, and much more. Entitled *A Guide for Solo Travel Abroad* (Berkshire Traveller Press), it's out of print, so check your library. A new book for single travelers is *Traveling on Your Own* by Eleanor Berman; available in bookstores, it also can be ordered by sending $12.95, plus $2 postage and handling (per book), to Random House, Customer Service Dept., 400 Hahn Rd., Westminster, MD 21157 (phone: 800-726-0600).

The single traveler who is particularly interested in meeting the Spanish or Portuguese may want to consider one of two very different possibilities. One is *Club Med,* an organization that heartily welcomes singles. Of its more than 100 activity-oriented resorts in countries around the world, one is in Portugal and four are in Spain — and more than 90% of the guests at its resorts are European. Though the clientele often is under 30, there is a considerable age mix: the average age is 37. For details, contact *Club Med* (3 E. 54th St., New York, NY 10022; phone: 800-CLUB-MED) or call one of the two *Club Med Boutiques:* in New York, 212-750-1687; in San Francisco, 415-982-4200.

The other possibility is the United States Servas Committee, which maintains a list of hosts around the world who are willing to take visitors into their homes as guests for a 2-night stay. Servas will send an application form and a list of some 200 interviewers around the US for you to contact. After the interview, if you are accepted as a Servas traveler, you'll receive a certificate making you eligible to become a member. The membership fee is $45 for an individual, with a $15 deposit to receive the host list, refunded upon its return. For more information, contact the United States Servas Committee, 11 John St., Room 706, New York, NY 10038 (phone: 212-267-0252).

WOMEN AND STUDENTS: Two specific groups of single travelers deserve special mention: women and students. Countless women travel by themselves in Spain and Portugal, and such an adventure need not be feared. You normally will find people courteous and welcoming, but remember that crime is a worldwide problem. Keep a careful eye on your belongings while on the beach, or lounging in a park, or traveling on a bus or train; lock your car and hotel doors; deposit your valuables in the hotel's safe; and never hitchhike.

One lingering inhibition many female travelers still harbor is that of eating alone in public places. The trick here is to relax and enjoy your meal and surroundings; while you may run across the occasional unenlightened waiter, a woman dining solo is no longer uncommon. A book offering lively, helpful advice on female solo travel is *The Traveling Woman,* by Dena Kaye. Though out of print, it may be found in your library.

Studying Abroad – A large number of single travelers are students. Travel *is* education. Travel broadens a person's knowledge and deepens his or her perception of the world in a way no media or "armchair" experience ever could. In addition, to study a country's language, art, culture, or history in one of its own schools is to enjoy the most productive method of learning.

By "student" we do not necessarily mean a person who wishes to matriculate at a Spanish or Portuguese university to earn a degree. Nor do we necessarily mean a younger person. A student is anyone who wishes to include some sort of educational program in a trip to Spain or Portugal.

There are many benefits for students abroad, and the way to begin to discover them is to consult the *Council on International Educational Exchange (CIEE).* This organization, which runs a variety of work, study, and travel programs for students, is the US sponsor of the International Student Identity Card (ISIC). Reductions on train tickets, airfares, and entry fees to most museums and other exhibitions are only some of the advantages of the card. To apply for it, write to *CIEE* at one of the following addresses: 205 E. 42nd St., New York, NY 10017 (phone: 212-661-1414); 312 Sutter St., San Francisco, CA 94108 (phone: 415-421-3473); and 919 Irving St., San Francisco, CA 94122 (phone: 415-566-6222). Mark the letter "Attn. Student ID." Application requires a $10 fee, a passport-size photograph, and proof that you are a matriculating student (this means either a transcript or a letter or bill from your school registrar with the school's official seal; high school and junior high school students can use their report cards). There is no maximum age limit, but participants must be at least 12 years old. The *ID Discount Guide,* which gives details of the discounts country by country, is free with membership. Another free publication of *CIEE* is the informative, annual, 64-page *Student Travel Catalog,* which covers all aspects of youth-travel abroad for vacation trips, jobs, or study programs, and also includes a list of other helpful publications. You can order the catalogue from Dept. ISS — #15 at the New York address given above.

Another card of value in Europe, and also available through *CIEE,* is the Federation of International Youth Travel Organizations (FIYTO) card. This provides many of the benefits of the ISIC card, and will facilitate entry to certain "youth hotels" throughout Europe, including Spain and Portugal. In this case, cardholders need not be students, merely under age 26. To apply, send $10 with a passport-size photo and proof of birth date to *CIEE* at one of the addresses above.

CIEE also sponsors charter flights to Europe that are open to students and non-students of any age. Flights between New York and Madrid and Málaga (with budget-priced add-ons available from Chicago, Cleveland, Miami, Minneapolis, Phoenix, Portland, Salt Lake City, San Diego, Seattle, and Spokane) arrive and depart at least three times a week from Kennedy (JFK) Airport during the high season.

Youth fares on transatlantic flights currently are offered by most of the scheduled airlines flying to Europe. Although the situation may change in the future, at press time the youth fare was almost the same as the standard APEX fare, and there may be some substantial drawbacks: a 7- or 14-day minimum stay, no stopovers, notification of availability and payment in full 1 to 3 days before the flight, and the return may be left open only if this is arranged before the trip, and again may be subject to 24-hour notice of availability. This space available restriction means that if you really must be home by a certain date, you are better off opting for a different type of ticket. Discount fares vary from carrier to carrier. To find out about current discounts, contact the individual airlines. Also see *Traveling by Plane,* in this section, for more information on economical flight alternatives.

For extensive travel throughout Europe, there is a version of the Eurailpass restricted to travelers (including non-students) under 26 years of age. The Eurail Youthpass entitles the bearer to either 1 or 2 months of unlimited second class rail travel in 17 countries, including Spain and Portugal. In addition, it is honored on many European steamers and ferries and on railroad connections between the airport and the center of town in various cities. The pass also entitles the bearer to reduced rates on some bus lines in several countries. The Eurail Youthpass can be purchased only by those living outside Europe or North Africa, and it must be purchased before departure. Eurail-passes can be bought from a US travel agent or from the national railway offices of the countries in the Eurail network (for further information and addresses, see *Traveling by Train,* in this section).

Students and singles in general should keep in mind that youth hostels exist in many cities throughout Spain and Portugal. They always are inexpensive, generally clean and well situated, and they are a sure place to meet other people traveling alone. Hostels are run by the hosteling associations of some 60-plus countries that make up the *International Youth Hostel Federation (IYHF);* membership in one of the national associations affords access to the hostels of the rest. To join the American affiliate, *American Youth Hostels (AYH),* contact the national office (PO Box 37613, Washington, DC 20013-7613; phone: 202-783-6161), or the local *AYH* council nearest you. As we went to press, new membership rules and rates were in effect: Membership in *AYH* currently costs $25 for people between the ages of 18 and 54, $10 for youths under 18, $15 for seniors, $35 for family membership. The *AYH Handbook,* which lists hostels in the US, comes with your *AYH* card (non-members can purchase the handbook for $5 plus $2 postage and handling); the *International Youth Hostel Handbooks,* which list hostels worldwide, must be purchased ($10.95 each, plus $2 for postage).

Those who go abroad without an *AYH* card can get an *International Youth Hostel Federation* guest card (for the equivalent of about $18), as well as information on local youth hostels by contacting one of the following national associations: In Spain, *Red Española de Albergues Juveniles* (71 Calle José Ortega y Gasset, Madrid 28006, Spain; phone 1-401-1300); in Portugal, *Associação Portuguesa de Pousadas de Juventude* (46 Rua Andrade Corvo, Lisbon 1000, Portugal; phone: 1-571054). These associations also publish handbooks to hostels in their areas. In addition, the tourist boards also publish information sheets on hostels and on hosteling package holidays.

Opportunities for study in Spain and Portugal range from summer or academic-year courses in a language and civilization of a country designed specifically for foreigners (including those whose school days are well behind them) to long-term university attendance by those intending to take a degree.

Complete details on more than 1,700 available courses and suggestions on how to apply are contained in two books published by the *Institute of International Education* (IIE Books, 809 UN Plaza, New York, NY 10017; phone 212-883-8200): *Vacation Study Abroad,* $24.95; and *Academic Year Abroad,* $29.95. A third book, *Teaching Abroad,* costs $21.95. All prices include book rate postage; first class postage is $4 extra. IIE Books also offers a free pamphlet, called *Basic Facts on Study Abroad.*

The *National Registration Center for Study Abroad* also offers a publication called *The Worldwide Classroom: Study Abroad & Learning Vacations in 40 Countries (NRCSA),* which gives information on over 160 schools and cultural centers that offer courses for Americans (including several in both Spain and Portugal) with the primary focus on foreign language and culture. It is available for $8.50 from *NRCSA,* PO Box 1393, Milwaukee, WI 53201 (phone: 414-278-0631).

Those who are interested in a a "learning vacation" abroad also may be interested in *Travel and Learn* by Evelyn Kaye. This guide to educational travel lists and desribes a number of topics — everything from archaeology to whale watching — and provides information on organizations that offer programs in these areas of interest. The book is available in bookstores for $23.95; or you can send $26 (which includes shipping charges) to Blue Penguin Publications (147 Sylvan Ave., Leonia, NJ 07605; phone: 201-461-6918). *Learning Vacations* by Gerson G. Eisenberg also provides extensive information on seminars, workshops, courses, and so on — in a wide variety of subjects. The book is $11.95 in bookstores, or it can be ordered from Peterson's Guides (PO Box 2123, Princeton, NJ 08543-2123; phone: 609-243-9111; add $4.75 for shipping).

AFS Intercultural Programs sets up exchanges between US and foreign high school students on an individual basis for a whole academic year or a semester. For more information, contact *AFS Intercultural Programs,* 313 E. 43rd St., New York, NY 10017 (phone 800-AFS-INFO or 212-949-4242).

Work, Study, Travel Abroad: The Whole World Handbook, issued by the *Council on International Educational Exchange (CIEE),* is an informative, chatty guide on study programs, work opportunities, and travel hints. To obtain it, send $10.95 plus postage ($1 for book rate; $2.50 first class) to *CIEE,* 205 E. 42nd St., New York, NY 10017 (phone 212-661-1414).

Elderhostel is a network of schools, colleges, and universities that sponsors week-long study programs for people over 60 years of age on campuses throughout Spain and Portugal. Some of its programs are offered in cooperation with the *Experiment in International Living* (see below) and involve home stays. Contact *Elderhostel* (80 Boylston St., Suite 400, Boston, MA 02116; phone: 617-426-7788 or 617-426-8056). An informational videotape describing *Elderhostel's* programs is available for $5.

The University of New Hampshire, the original sponsor of *Elderhostel,* has its own program for travelers over 50; contact *Interhostel* (University of New Hampshire, Division of Continuing Education, 6 Garrison Ave., Durham, NH 03824; phone: 603-862-1147 weekdays, 1:30 to 4 PM eastern standard time). For more details about both programs, see *Hints for Older Travelers,* in this section.

If you are interested in a home stay travel program, in which you learn about European culture by living with a family, contact the *Experiment in International Living* (PO Box 676, Brattleboro, VT 05302-0676; phone: 802-257-7751 in Vermont; 800-345-2929 elsewhere in the US), which sponsors home stay educational travel. The organization aims its programs at high school or college students, but it also can arrange home stays of 1 to 4 weeks for adults in more than 40 countries, including Spain and Portugal. It is possible, after participating in the programs, to join supplemental travel/activities programs and tour these countries.

National Association of Secondary School Principals (*NASSP,* 1904 Association Dr., Reston, VA 22091; phone: 703-860-0200), an association of administrators, teachers, and state education officials, sponsors *School Partnership International,* a program in which secondary schools in the US are linked with partner schools abroad for an annual short-term exchange of students and faculty.

Another organization specializing in travel as an educational experience is the *American Institute for Foreign Study (AIFS).* Students can enroll for the full academic year or for any number of semesters. *AIFS* caters primarily to bona fide high school or college students, but its non-credit international learning and continuing education programs are open to independent travelers of all ages. (Approximately 30% of *AIFS* students are over 25.) Contact *AIFS,* 102 Greenwich Ave., Greenwich, CT 06830 (phone: 800-727-AIFS, 203-869-9090, or 203-863-6087 for summer programs; 203-863-6097 for foreign language programs).

Those interested in campus stays should know about the *U.S. and Worldwide Travel*

Accommodations Guide, which lists several hundred colleges and universities in Europe that offer simple, but comfortable, accommodations in their residence halls, primarily during the summer season. The accommodations vary from single and double rooms to full apartments and suites with kitchens, and the rooms can be booked by the day, week, or month. Prices range from $12 to $24 per night, with an average of about $18. An added bonus of this type of arrangement is that visitors usually are free to utilize various campus sport and recreation facilities. For a copy of the guide, which describes services and facilities in detail, send $11.95 to *Campus Travel Service,* PO Box 5007, Laguna Beach, CA 92652 (phone: 714-497-3044).

And there's always camping. Virtually any area along the coast in Spain and Portugal, as well as some sites around the countryside, has a place to pitch a tent and enjoy the scenery. There are numerous national parks, and many of the campsites have showers, laundry rooms, public phones, eating facilities, and shops. With permission, it's often possible to camp on private acres of farmland. (For more information, see *Camping and Caravanning, Hiking and Biking,* in this section.)

WORKING ABROAD: Jobs for foreigners in Spain and Portugal are not easy to come by and in general do not pay well enough to cover all the expenses of a trip. They do provide an invaluable learning experience, however, while helping to make a trip more affordable. Work permits can be obtained through the *Council on International Educational Exchange* (address above) only by students over 18 who are enrolled and working toward a degree in a US college or university and who have 2 years of college education in a foreign language or its equivalent to their credit. The permit allows them to work for 3 months at any time of year, but the students must find their own job. (Jobs as bilingual hotel, restaurant, and office workers are among those most commonly found.)

For a complete list of programs administered by Spanish and Portuguese institutions, contact the National Tourist Office of Spain and the Portuguese National Tourist Office in North America (see *Tourist Information Offices,* in this section, for addresses).

Hints for Older Travelers

Special package deals and more free time are just two factors that have given Americans over age 65 a chance to see the world at affordable prices. Senior citizens make up an ever-growing segment of the travel population, and the trend among them is to travel more frequently and for longer periods of time. No longer limited by 3-week vacations or the business week, older travelers can take advantage of off-season, off-peak travel, which is both less expensive and more pleasant than traveling at prime time in high season. In addition, overseas, as in the US, discounts frequently are available.

PLANNING: When planning a vacation, prepare your itinerary with one eye on your own physical condition and the other on a topographical map. Keep in mind variations in climate, terrain, and altitudes, which may pose some danger for anyone with heart or breathing problems.

An excellent book to read before embarking on any trip, domestic or foreign, is Rosalind Massow's *Travel Easy: The Practical Guide for People Over 50,* available for $6.50 to members of the *American Association of Retired Persons (AARP),* $8.95 for non-members (add $1.75 postage and handling per order, not per book). Order from AARP Books (c/o Scott, Foresman, 1865 Miner St., Des Plaines, IL 60016; phone: 800-238-2300). It discusses a host of subjects, from choosing a destination to getting set for departure, with chapters on transportation options, tours, cruises, avoiding health problems, and even handling dental emergencies en route. Another book, *The International Health Guide for Senior Citizens,* covers such topics as trip preparations, food and water precautions, adjusting to weather and climate conditions, finding a doctor, motion sickness, and jet lag. The book also discusses specific health and travel problems, and includes a list of resource organizations that provide medical assistance for travelers; it is available for $4.95 postpaid from Pilot Books (103 Cooper St., Babylon, NY 11702; phone: 516-422-2225). A third book on health for older travelers, Rosalind Massow's excellent *Now It's Your Turn to Travel* (Collier Books), has a chapter on medical problems; it is out of print but may be available in your library. (Also see *Staying Healthy,* in this section.) *Travel Tips for Senior Citizens* (State Department publication 8970), a useful booklet with general advice, also is currently out of print but may be found in libraries.

An ideal book for budget-conscious older travelers is *The Discount Guide for Travelers Over 55* by Caroline and Walter Weintz (Dutton; $7.95). Pilot Books features *The Senior Citizen's Guide to Budget Travel in Europe,* for $3.95, at the address above. You also may want to send for *101 Tips for the Mature Traveler,* a free publication available from *Grand Circle Travel,* 347 Congress St., Suite 3A, Boston, MA 02210 (phone: 617-350-7500, 800-221-2610, or 800-831-8880).

If you are traveling in the fall, winter, or spring, bear in mind that you will not always find central heating in public places in Spain and Portugal, and that even if your hotel has it, it may not warm your room up to the temperatures you're accustomed to at home. Bear in mind also that even in summer you will need something warm for the evening in many areas throughout Iberia, and there are areas where rainwear year-round is a good idea, too. However, remember that one secret to happy traveling is to *pack lightly.* (For further hints on what to bring and how to pack it, see *How to Pack,* in this section.)

HEALTH: Health facilities in Spain and Portugal generally are excellent; however, an inability to speak the language can pose a serious problem, not in receiving treatment at large hospitals, where many doctors and other staff members will speak English, but in getting help elsewhere or in getting to the place where help is available. A number of organizations help travelers avoid or deal with a medical emergency overseas. For information on these services, see *Medical and Legal Aid and Consular Services,* in this section.

Pre-trip medical and dental checkups are strongly recommended, particularly for older travelers. In addition, be sure to take along any prescription medication you need, enough to last *without a new prescription* for the duration of your trip; pack all medications with a note from your doctor for the benefit of airport authorities. It also is wise to bring a few common non-prescription over-the-counter medications with you: Aspirin or a non-aspirin pain reliever and something for stomach upset may come in handy. If you have specific medical problems, bring prescriptions and a "medical file" composed of the following:

1. A summary of your medical history and current diagnosis.
2. A list of drugs to which you are allergic.
3. Your most recent electrocardiogram, if you have heart problems.
4. Your doctor's name, address, and telephone number.

■ **A word of caution:** Don't overdo it. Allow time for some relaxation each day to refresh yourself for the next scheduled sightseeing event. Traveling across time zones can be exhausting, and adjusting to major climatic changes can make you feel dizzy and drained. Plan on spending at least 1 full day resting before you start touring. If you're part of a group tour, be sure to check the itinerary thoroughly. Some package deals sound wonderful because they include all the places you've ever dreamed of visiting. In fact, visiting all of them can become so hectic and tiring that you'll be reaching for a pillow instead of a camera.

DISCOUNTS AND PACKAGES: Since guidelines change from place to place, it is a good idea to inquire in advance about discounts for transportation, hotels, concerts, movies, museums, and other activities.

Many US hotel and motel chains, airlines, car rental companies, bus lines, and other travel suppliers offer discounts to older travelers. For instance, *TAP Air* offers senior citizen discounts on flights from Boston, Los Angeles, and New York to Portugal, which apply to senior citizens over age 60 and one traveling companion. Contact *TAP Air* for information on advance purchase restrictions, availability, and current fares.

Some of these discounts, however, are extended only to bona fide members of certain senior citizens organizations. Because the same organizations frequently offer package tours to both domestic and international destinations, the benefits of membership are twofold: Those who join can take advantage of discounts as individual travelers and also reap the savings that group travel affords. In addition, because the age requirements for some of these organizations are quite low (or nonexistent), the benefits can begin to accrue early. Among the organizations dedicated to helping you see the world are the following:

American Association of Retired Persons (AARP): The largest and best known of these organizations. Membership is open to anyone 50 or over, whether retired or not. *AARP* offers travel programs, designed exclusively for older travelers, that cover the globe; they include a broad range of escorted tours, hosted tours, and cruises, including tours and resort packages. Dues are $5 a year, or $12.50 for 3 years, and include spouse. For membership information, contact *AARP Travel Service,* 100 N. Sepulveda Blvd., Suite 1010, El Segundo, CA 90245 (phone: 800-227-7737 or 213-322-7323).

Mature Outlook: Through its *Travel Alert,* last-minute tours, cruises, and other vacation packages are available to members at special savings. Hotel and car rental discounts and travel accident insurance also are available. Membership is open to anyone 50 years of age or older, costs $9.95 a year, and includes its bimonthly newsletter and magazine as well as information on package tours. Contact the Customer Service Center, 6001 N. Clark St., Chicago, IL 60660 (phone: 800-336-6330).

National Council of Senior Citizens: Here, too, the emphasis always is on keeping costs low. This group offers a different roster of tours each year, and its travel service also will book individual tours for members. Although most members are over 50, membership is open to anyone, regardless of age, for an annual fee of $12 per person or $16 per couple. Lifetime membership costs $150. For information, contact the *National Council for Senior Citizens,* 925 15th St. NW, Washington, DC 20005 (phone: 202-347-8800).

Certain travel agencies and tour operators specialize in group travel for older travelers, among them the following:

Gadabout Tours: Operated by Lois Anderson, this organization offers escorted tours to a number of destinations, including Spain and Portugal. See a travel agent or contact *Gadabout Tours,* 700 E. Tahquitz, Palm Springs, CA 92262 (phone: 619-325-5556 or 800-521-7309 in California; 800-952-5068 elsewhere in the US).

Grand Circle Travel: Caters exclusively to the over-50 traveler and packages a large variety of escorted tours, cruises, and extended vacations. *Grand Circle* also publishes a quarterly magazine (with a column for the single traveler) and a helpful free booklet, *101 Tips for the Mature Traveler Abroad.* Contact *Grand Circle Travel,* 347 Congress St., Boston, MA 02210 (phone: 617-350-7500 or 800-221-2610).

Insight International Tours: Offers a matching service for single travelers. Several tours are geared for mature travelers. Contact *Insight International Tours,* 745 Atlantic Ave., Boston, MA 02111 (phone: 617-482-2000 or 800-582-8380 throughout the US).

Saga International Holidays: A subsidiary of a British company specializing in the older traveler, *Saga* offers a broad selection of escorted coach tours, cruises, and apartment-stay holidays, including packages, for people age 60 and over or those 50 to 59 traveling with someone 60 or older. Members of the *Saga Holiday Club* receive the club magazine, which contains a column aimed at helping lone travelers find suitable traveling companions (see *Hints for Single Travelers,* in this section). A 1-year club membership costs $5. Contact *Saga International Holidays,* 120 Boylston St., Boston MA 02116 (phone: 800-343-0273 or 617-451-6808).

Many travel agencies, particularly the larger ones, are delighted to make presentations to help a group select destinations. A local chamber of commerce should be able to provide the names of such agencies. Once a time and place are determined, an organization member or travel agent can obtain group quotations for transportation, accommodations, meal plans, and sightseeing. Groups of 40 or more usually get the best breaks.

Another choice open to older travelers is a trip that includes an educational element. *Elderhostel* is a network of schools, colleges, and universities that sponsors week-long study programs for people over 60 years of age on campuses throughout Europe, including Spain and Portugal. An informational videotape describing *Elderhostel*'s programs is available for $5. Accommodations are in residence halls, and meals are taken in student cafeterias. Travel to the programs usually is by designated scheduled flights, and participants can arrange to extend their stay at the end of the program. Elderhostelers must be at least 60 years old (younger if a spouse or companion qualifies), in good health, and not in need of special diets. For information, contact *Elderhostel,* 80 Boylston St., Suite 400, Boston, MA 02116 (phone: 617-426-7788 or 617-426-8056).

Interhostel, a program sponsored by the Division of Continuing Education of the University of New Hampshire, sends travelers back to school at cooperating institutions in 33 countries on 4 continents. Participants attend lectures on the history, economy, politics, and cultural life of the country they are visiting, go on field trips to pertinent points of interest, and take part in activities meant to introduce them to their foreign contemporaries. Trips are for 2 weeks; accommodations are on campus in university residence halls or off campus in modest hotels (double occupancy). Groups are limited to 35 to 40 participants who are at least 50 years old (or at least 40 if a participating spouse is at least 50), physically active, and not in need of special diets. For further information or to receive the three free seasonal catalogues, contact *Interhostel,* UNH Division of Continuing Education, 6 Garrison Ave., Durham, NH 03824 (phone: 603-862-1147 weekdays, 1:30 to 4 PM eastern standard time).

Hints for Traveling with Children

 What better way to be receptive to the experiences you will encounter than to take along the young, wide-eyed members of your family? Their company does not have to be a burden or their presence an excessive expense. The current generation of discounts for children and family package deals can make a trip together quite reasonable.

A family trip will be an investment in your children's future, making geography and history come alive to them and leaving a sure memory that will be among the fondest you will share with them someday. Their insights will be refreshing to you; their impulses may take you to unexpected places with unexpected dividends. The experience will be invaluable to them at any age.

PLANNING: The current generation of discount airfares makes flights to Spain and Portugal a good deal less expensive than a decent summer camp. It is necessary, however, to take some time beforehand to prepare children for travel. Here are several hints for making a trip with kids easy and fun.

1. Children, like everyone else, will derive more pleasure from a trip if they know something about their destination before they arrive. Begin their education about a month before you leave. Using maps, travel magazines, and books, give children a clear idea of where you are going and how far away it is. Part of the excitement of the journey will be associating the tiny dots on the map with the very real places they soon will visit. You can show them pictures of streets and scenes in Madrid, Barcelona, Lisbon, or other cities where they will stand within a month. Don't shirk history lessons, but don't burden them with dates. Make history light, anecdotal, pertinent, but most of all, fun. If you simply make materials available and keep your destination and your plans a topic of everyday conversation, your children will absorb more than you realize.

2. Children should help to plan the itinerary, and where you go and what you do should reflect some of their ideas. If they already know something about the sites they'll visit, they will have the excitement of recognition when they arrive and the illumination of seeing how something is or is not the way they expected it to be.

3. Learn the languages of the countries you will be visiting with your children — a few basics like "hello," "good-bye," and "thanks a lot." You need no other motive than a perfectly selfish one: Thus armed, your children will delight the Spanish and Portuguese and help break the ice wherever you go. (See *Useful Words and Phrases,* in this section, for a list of Spanish and Portuguese words and basic phrases.)

4. Familiarize your children with pesetas and escudos (see *Credit and Currency,* in this section). Give them an allowance for the trip, and be sure they understand just how far it will or won't go.

5. Give children specific responsibilities: The job of carrying their own flight bags and looking after their personal things, along with some other light chores, will give them a stake in the journey. Tell them how they can be helpful when you are checking in or out of hotels.

6. Give each child a diary or scrapbook to take along. Filling these with impressions, observations, and mementos will pass the time on trains and planes and help to focus their experiences.

One useful resource to which you may want to refer is the *Berlitz Jr.* instructional series for children, which includes an edition on Spanish. The series combines an illustrated storybook with a lively 60-minute audiocassette. Each book features a character, Teddy, who goes to school and learns to count and spell and speak Spanish phrases. The book/cassette package is available from the Aladdin Books division of Macmillan Publishing Company for $19.95, plus shipping and handling. To order, contact Aladdin Books, Front and Brown Sts., Riverside, NJ 08075 (phone: 800-257-5755).

No matter what the reading level of your children, there are books to prepare them for a trip. For the very young, try *Let's Learn About Spain,* by Sacha de Nisching and illustrated by Sylvie Rainard (Passport Books; $3.95), which has many games and puzzles, or *The Story of Ferdinand* by Munro Lest (Penguin; $3.95), a nicely illustrated version of the charming tale of Ferdinand the Bull. Slightly older children may enjoy

Take a Trip to Spain by Jonathan Rutland (Franklin Watts; $10.95), a book of photographs covering, among other things, bullfighting, fiestas, homes, money, and schools. *Welcome to Spain,* by Heather and John Leigh (Passport Books; $4.95), is beautifully illustrated by Joseph McEwan and covers things to watch for at festivals, music, dancing, and other fun in Spain.

David Macaulay's *Castle* (Houghton Mifflin; $14.95 hardcover; $6.96 paperback), which uses text and drawings to show how castles were built in the 13th century, is particularly suited to helping children learn about the castles they may see in Spain and Portugal; *Cathedral: The Story of Its Construction* (Houghton Mifflin; $14.95 hardcover; $6.95 paperback), by the same author, also is interesting and informative. For older children, see if you can find the highly regarded *City of Marvels,* by Eduardo Mendoza and translated by Bernard Molloy (Harcourt Brace Jovanovich; $19.95), the enthralling story of a Catalonian boy who travels to Barcelona in 1886 and is caught up in a web of intrigue.

These and other children's books can be found at many general bookstores and in libraries. An excellent source is *Eeyore's Books for Children* (2212 Broadway, New York, NY 10024; phone: 212-362-0634; or 25 E. 83rd St., New York, NY; phone: 212-988-3404).

And for parents, the *Travel With Your Children (TWYCH)* organization publishes a newsletter, *Family Travel Times,* that focuses on families with young travelers and offers helpful hints. Membership is $35 a year. For a sample copy of the newsletter, send $1 to *Travel With Your Children,* 80 Eighth Ave., New York, NY 10011 (phone: 212-206-0688).

Another organization that publishes a newsletter for families, as well as functioning as a "family travel club," is *Let's Take the Kids.* They are involved in various activities relating to family travel, including putting together tours and packages and running a "parent travel network," whereby parents who have been to a particular destination can evaluate it for others. This group occasionally organizes trips for single-parent families traveling together. Annual family memberships in the club is $35, which includes all club services. For information, contact *Let's Take the Kids* (2560 Barrington Ave., Suite 107, Los Angeles, CA 90064; phone: 800-726-4349 or 213-472-4449).

There's also a fairly new organization called *Just Me and the Kids Travel* (PO Box 249, Watkins Glen, NY 14891; phone: 607-535-2966), which puts together trips to popular family destinations for a single-parent family. A membership fee of $25 per family covers the costs of newsletters and travel updates. Another organization, *Parents without Partners* (8807 Colesville Rd., Silver Spring, MD 20910; phone: 301-588-9354) has had chapters (which operate individually) all over the country for many years, offering information for — and activities of interest to — single parents; contact the national office for information on local chapters.

In addition to books, audio cassettes may make Spain and Portugal come alive for children. The infectious rhythms of Spanish and Portuguese music are a lively introduction to these vibrant cultures. Be sure to include some flamenco music — after listening to the thrilling tones, children will particularly enjoy clapping along to a performance by dashing dancers.

PACKING: Choose your children's clothes much as you would your own. Select a basic color (perhaps different for each child) and coordinate everything with it. Plan their wardrobes with layering in mind — shirts and sweaters that can be taken off or put on as the temperature varies. Take only drip-dry, wrinkle-resistant items that children can manage themselves and comfortable shoes — sneakers and sandals. Younger children will need more changes, but keep it to a minimum. No one likes to carry extra luggage (remember that *you* will have to manage most of it!)

Take as many handy snacks as you can squeeze into the corners of your suitcases — things like dried fruit and nut mixes, hard candies, peanut butter, and crackers

— and moist towelettes for cleaning. Don't worry if your supply of nibbles is quickly depleted. A trip to a Spanish or Portuguese grocery store is fascinating sightseeing for little ones (and adults as well), and it's fun to try another country's snacks. Also, airports and train and bus stations are well stocked with such items.

Pack a special medical kit including children's aspirin or acetaminophen, an antihistamine or decongestant, Dramamine, and diarrhea medication. Do not feel you must pack a vacation's worth of Pampers. Disposable diapers — called *pañales desechables* in Spain, *fraldas descartaveis* in Portugal — are available in most drugstores (*farmacias* in Spain; *farmácias* in Portugal) and supermarkets (*supermercados* in both countries). A selection of baby foods also is available in most supermarkets, but in case you may not be able to find the instant formula to which your child is accustomed, bring along a supply in the 8-ounce "ready-to-feed" cans. Disposable nursers are expensive but handy. If you breast-feed your baby, there is no reason you can't enjoy your trip; just be sure you get enough rest and liquids.

Good toys to take for infants are the same sorts of things they like at home — well-made, bright huggables and chewables; for small children, a favorite doll or stuffed animal for comfort, spelling and counting games, and tying, braiding, and lacing activities; for older children, playing cards, travel board games with magnetic pieces, and hand-held electronic games. Softcover books and art materials (crayons, markers, paper, scissors, glue sticks, and stickers) ward off boredom for children of most ages, as do radio-cassette players with headphones. Take along a variety of musical and storytelling cassettes, extra batteries, and maybe even an extra set of headphones so two children can listen.

Advice: Avoid toys that are noisy, breakable, or spillable, those that require a large play area, and those that have lots of little pieces that can be scattered and lost. When traveling, coordinate activities with attention spans; dole out playthings one at a time so you don't run out of diversions before you get where you're going. Children become restless during long waiting periods, and a game plus a small snack — such as a box of raisins or crackers — will help keep them quiet. It also is a good idea to carry tissues, Band-Aids, a pocket medicine kit (described above), and moistened washcloths.

GETTING THERE AND GETTING AROUND: Begin early to investigate all available discount and charter flights, as well as any package deals and special rates offered by the major airlines. Booking sometimes is required up to 2 months in advance. You may well find that charter plans offer no reductions for children, or not enough to offset the risk of last-minute delays or other inconveniences to which charters are subject. The major scheduled airlines, on the other hand, almost invariably provide hefty discounts for children. (For specific information on fares and in-flight accommodations for children, also see *Traveling by Plane,* in this section.)

PLANE: When you make your reservations, tell the airline that you are traveling with a child. As a general rule, children under 2 travel free in a plane if they sit on an adult's lap — although on some carriers you will have to pay 10% of the adult fare. But it's much safer — and certainly more comfortable — to purchase an adjacent seat for a baby and bring an infant restraint which is then strapped into the airline seat with a regular seat belt. (The airlines do not provide infant seats, so you will have to bring your own. If you do not purchase a seat for your baby and bring the infant restraint along on the off chance that there may be an empty seat next to yours, you will have to pay to check it as baggage if an additional seat is not available.) There is no special fare for an infant, although discounts for children sometimes are in effect, and you can inquire about this when making a reservation — between the ages of 2 and 12, children generally travel at half or two-thirds of the adult fare.

If using one of these infant restraints, you should try to get bulkhead seats, which will provide extra room to care for your child during the flight. You also should request a bulkhead seat when using a bassinet (some airlines do provide bassinets) — again, this is not as safe as strapping a child in. On some planes, bassinets may hook into a bulkhead wall; on others it is placed on the floor in front of you. Even if you do use a bassinet, babies must be held during takeoff and landing. Request seats on the aisle if you have a toddler or if you think you will need to use the bathroom frequently. (Try to discourage children from being in the aisle when meals are served.)

Carry onto the plane all you will need to care for and occupy your children during the flight — formula, diapers, a sweater, books, favorite stuffed animals, and so on. (Never check as baggage any item essential to a child's well-being, such as prescription medicine.) Dress your baby simply, with a minimum of buttons and snaps, because the only place you may have for changing a diaper is at your seat. The flight attendant can warm a bottle for you.

Just as you would request a vegetarian or kosher meal, you are entitled to ask for a hot dog or hamburger instead of the airline's regular dinner if you give at least 24 hours' notice. Some, but not all, airlines have baby food aboard. While you should bring along toys from home, you also can ask about children's diversions. Some carriers have terrific free packages of games, coloring books, and puzzles.

When the plane takes off and lands, make sure your baby is nursing or has a bottle, pacifier, or thumb in its mouth. This sucking will make the child swallow and help to clear stopped ears. A piece of hard candy will do the same thing for an older child.

Avoid night flights. Since you probably won't sleep nearly as well as your kids, you risk an impossible first day at your destination, groggily taking care of your rested, energetic children. Nap time is, however, a good time to travel, especially for babies, and try to travel during off-hours, when there are apt to be extra seats. If you do have to take a long night flight, keep in mind that when you disembark, you probably will be tired and not really ready for sightseeing. The best thing to do is to head for your hotel, shower, have a snack, and take a nap. If your children are too excited to sleep, give them some toys to play with while you rest.

■ **Note:** Newborn babies, whose lungs may not be able to adjust to the altitude, should not be taken aboard an airplane. And some airlines may refuse to allow a pregnant woman in her 8th or 9th month aboard, for fear that something could go wrong with an in-flight birth. Check with the airline well before departure, and carry a letter from your doctor stating that you are fit to travel — and indicating the estimated date of birth.

SHIP, TRAIN, AND BUS: Children under 12 usually travel at a considerably reduced fare on ships. If you plan to travel by train when abroad, note that on some Spanish railways children under 3 travel free, provided they do not occupy a seat (under 4 in Portugal); children under 4 occupying a seat and from ages 4 through 11 also often travel at a lower fare. The Eurailpass, which is good for unlimited train travel throughout Europe, including Spain and Portugal, is half price for children ages 4 through 12. It must be bought before leaving the US, so plan ahead. Some regional bus lines also may have lower fares for children or family rates. For further information, see *Traveling by Ship, Traveling by Train,* and *Traveling by Bus,* all in this section.

CAR: Without a doubt, a car is the most flexible means of transportation with kids, since driving allows you complete independence in arranging your schedule and itinerary. Keep the car supplied with dried fruits, crackers, candy bars, bottled water, and facial tissue and/or toilet paper. You even may want to pick up a cooler so that you can picnic along the way.

ACCOMMODATIONS AND MEALS: Often a cot for a child will be placed in a hotel room at little or no extra charge. If you wish to sleep in separate rooms, special rates sometimes are available for families; some places do not charge for children under a certain age. In many of the larger chain hotels, the staffs are more used to noisy or slightly misbehaving children. These hotels also are likely to have swimming pools or gamerooms — both popular with most young travelers. Write to the hotel in advance to discuss how old your children are, how long you plan to stay, and to ask for suggestions on sleeping arrangements.

You might want to look into accommodations along the way that will add to the color of your trip. For instance, the many *paradores, pousadas,* and *pensões* in Spain and Portugal provide a delightful experience for the whole family and permit a view of Spanish and Portuguese life different from that gained by staying in a conventional hotel. Children will love them. Camping facilities often are situated in beautiful, out-of-the-way spots, and generally are good, well equipped, and less expensive than any hotel. For further information on accommodations options for the whole family, see our discussion in *On the Road,* and for information on camping facilities, see *Camping and Caravanning, Hiking and Biking,* both in this section.

For the times you will want to be without the children — for an evening's entertainment or a particularly rigorous stint of sightseeing — it is possible to arrange for a baby sitter at the hotel desk. Whether the sitter is hired directly or through an agency, ask for and check references and keep in mind, particularly in rural areas, that the candidates may not speak much, if any, English.

At mealtime, don't deny yourself or your children the delights of a new style of cooking. Children like to know what kind of food to expect, so it will be interesting to look up Spanish and Portuguese dishes in an encyclopedia of cookery. For example, *The Food of Portugal* by Jean Anderson (Morrow; $24.95) and *Foods and Wines of Spain* by Penelope Casas (Random House; $22.50) both are highly recommended (also see *Books and Magazines,* in this section, for more suggestions). Encourage your children to try new things and don't forget about picnics. Many grocery shops sell fresh bread, cheese, and cold cuts, and there's nothing lovelier than stopping at a beautiful site and eating lunch as you muse on the surroundings. (Note that although milk is pasteurized and water is potable in large cities, it's wise to stick to bottled water.)

THINGS TO REMEMBER: If you are spending your vacation traveling rather than visiting one spot or engaging in one activity, pace the days with children in mind. Break the trip into half-day segments, with running around or "doing" time built in; keep travel time on the road to a maximum of 4 or 5 hours a day. First and foremost, don't forget that a child's attention span is far shorter than an adult's. Children don't have to see every museum or all of any museum to learn something from their trip; watching, playing with, and talking to other children can be equally enlightening. Also, remember the places that children the world over love to visit: zoos, country fairs, amusement parks, beaches, and nature trails. Let your children lead the way sometimes; their perspective is different from yours, and they may lead you to things you never would have noticed on your own.

Staying Healthy

The surest way to return home in good health is to be prepared for medical problems that might occur on vacation. Below, we've outlined some things you need to think about before you go.

Obviously, your state of health is crucial to the success of a vacation. There's nothing like an injury or illness, whether serious or relatively minor, to dampen or destroy a holiday. And health problems always seem more debilitating when you are away. However, most problems can be prevented or greatly alleviated with intelligent foresight and attention to precautionary details.

Older travelers or anyone suffering from a chronic medical condition, such as diabetes, high blood pressure, cardiopulmonary disease, asthma, or ear, eye, or sinus trouble should consult a physician before leaving home. A checkup is advisable. A pre-trip dental checkup is not a bad idea, either.

People with conditions requiring special consideration when traveling should consider seeing, in addition to their regular physician, a specialist in travel medicine. For a referral in a particular community, contact the nearest medical school or ask a local doctor to recommend such a specialist. The *American Society of Tropical Medicine and Hygiene* publishes a directory of more than 70 travel doctors across the country. Send a 9-by-12-inch self-addressed, stamped envelope ($1.05 postage) to Dr. Leonard Marcus, Tufts University, 200 W. Boro Rd., North Grafton, MA 01536.

FIRST AID: Put together a compact, personal medical kit including Band-Aids, first-aid cream, antiseptic, nose drops, insect repellent, aspirin, an extra pair of prescription glasses or contact lenses (and a copy of your prescription for glasses or lenses), sunglasses, over-the-counter remedies for diarrhea, indigestion, and motion sickness, a thermometer, and a supply of those prescription medicines you take regularly. In a corner of your kit, keep a list of all the drugs you have brought and their purpose, as well as duplicate copies of your doctor's prescriptions (or a note from your doctor). These copies could come in handy if you ever are questioned by police or airport authorities about any drugs you are carrying, and also will be necessary to refill any prescriptions in the event of loss. Considering the essential contents of this kit, keep it with you, rather than in your luggage.

SUNBURN: Depending on when and where you're vacationing, the burning power of the sun can be phenomenal and quickly can cause severe sunburn or sunstroke. To protect yourself against these ills, wear sunglasses, take along a broad-brimmed hat and cover-up, and use a sunscreen lotion. When choosing a sunscreen, look for one that has a PABA (para-amino-benzoic acid) base. PABA blocks out most of the harmful ultraviolet rays of the sun.

Some tips on tanning:

1. Allow only 20 minutes or so the first day; increase your exposure gradually.
2. You are most likely to get a painful burn when the sun is the strongest, between 10 AM and 2 PM.
3. When judging if you've had enough sun, remember that time in the water (in terms of exposure to ultraviolet rays) is the same as time lying on the beach.
4. A beach umbrella or other cover doesn't keep all the rays of the sun from reaching you. If you are sensitive to sunlight, be especially careful.
5. As many ultraviolet rays reach you on cloudy days as on sunny days. And the sun is particularly strong when reflected off snowy slopes — as in the Pyrenees. Even if you don't feel hot, you still are exposed to rays.

If, despite these precautions, you find yourself with a painful sunburn, take a cooling bath, apply a first-aid spray, and stay out of the sun. If you develop a more serious burn and experience chills, fever, nausea, headaches, or dizziness, consult a doctor at once.

WATER SAFETY: Spain and Portugal are famous for their beaches, but it's important to remember that the sea, especially the wild Atlantic and the Mediterranean, can be treacherous. A few precautions are necessary. Beware of the undertow, that current of water running back down the beach after a wave has washed ashore; it can knock you off your feet and into the surf. Even more dangerous is the rip tide, a strong current of water running against the tide, which can pull you out toward the sea. If you get caught offshore, don't panic or try to fight the current, because it only will exhaust you; instead, ride it out while waiting for it to subside, which usually happens not too far from shore, or try swimming away parallel to the beach.

INSECTS AND OTHER PESTS: Mosquitoes, horseflies, and other biting insects can be troublesome. We recommend using some form of repellent against bug bites, especially for campers. Mosquitoes can be a terrific nuisance in some areas; vitamin B-1 or thiamine tablets may alter your body chemistry to help repel them. If you are at all susceptible to mosquito bites, you will be amazed at how quickly the vitamins can work — although they do not work for everyone. Discuss this strategy with your doctor before trying it. It still is a good idea to use some form of topical insect repellent. As many of the stronger, effective insect repellents have a pungent odor, you may want to try a relatively new alternative, Skin-So-Soft hand lotion, made by Avon. This orderless skin softener actually has been approved by the FDA as an effective insect repellent. For campers, burning mosquito coils containing pyrethrin or citronella candles is another effective precaution.

If you do get bitten — by mosquitoes or other bugs — the itching can be relieved with baking soda or antihistamine tablets. Should a bite become infected, treat it with a disinfectant or antibiotic cream. *Note:* Antihistamines should not be combined with alcohol or cortisone cream, or taken by those who will be driving.

If you are bitten and the area becomes painful or swollen and you develop flu-type symptoms, you may have been bitten by a tick carrying what is known as Lyme Borreliosis disease (or "Lyme Disease" in the US). Many Americans believe that this disease is unique to the US; however, it was first diagnosed in Europe — where it is called Neuro Borreliosis — and has been a problem there for years. Caution should be taken in all wooded areas.

Though rarer than insect bites, bites from poisonous centipedes, spiders, snakes, or sea creatures such as jellyfish can be serious. If possible, always try to catch the villain for identification purposes. In most cases — particularly if spasms, numbness, convulsions, or hemorrhaging occurs — consult a doctor at once. The best course of action may be to head directly to the nearest emergency ward or outpatient clinic of a hospital. Cockroaches, termites, and waterbugs thrive in warm climates, but pose little serious health threat.

FOOD AND WATER: Water generally is clean and potable throughout most of Spain and Portugal. Ask if water is meant for drinking, but if you're at all unsure, bottled water is readily available in stores. In general, it is a good idea to drink bottled water at least at the beginning of the trip. This is not because there is something wrong with the water as far as the residents are concerned, but new microbes in the digestive tract to which you have not become accustomed may cause mild stomach or intestinal upsets. Particularly in rural areas, the water supply may not be thoroughly purified, and residents either have developed immunities to the natural bacteria or boil it for drinking. You also should avoid drinking water from streams or freshwater pools. In campgrounds, water usually is indicated as drinkable or for washing only — if you're not sure, ask.

Milk is pasteurized throughout Spain and Portugal, and milk products (cheese, yogurt, ice cream, and so on) are safe to eat, as are fresh produce, meat, poultry, and fish. Because of Mediterranean Sea pollution, however, fish and shellfish should be eaten cooked, and make sure it is *fresh,* particularly in the heat of the summer, when inadequate refrigeration is an additional concern.

Following all these precautions will not guarantee an illness-free trip, but should minimize the risk. As a final hedge against economic if not physical problems, make sure your health insurance will cover all eventualities while you are away. If not, there are policies designed specifically for travel. Many are worth investigating. As with all insurance, they seem like a waste of money until you need them. For further information, also see *Insurance* and *Medical and Legal Aid and Consular Services,* both in this section.

HELPFUL PUBLICATIONS: Practically every phase of health care — before, during, and after a trip — is covered in *The New Traveler's Health Guide,* by Drs. Patrick J. Doyle and James E. Banta. It is available for $4.95, plus $2 postage and handling, from Acropolis Books Ltd., 80 S. Early, Alexandria, VA 22304 (phone: 800-451-7771 or 703-709-0006).

The *Traveling Healthy Newsletter,* which is published six times a year, also is brimming with health-related travel tips. For a subscription, which costs $24, contact Dr. Karl Neumann, 108-48 70th Rd., Forest Hills, NY 11375, (phone: 718-268-7290).

For more information regarding preventive health care for travelers, contact the *International Association for Medical Assistance to Travelers* (*IAMAT*; 417 Center St., Lewiston, NY 14092; phone: 716-754-4883), or write to the US Government Printing Office (Washington, DC 20402) for the US Public Health Service's booklet *Health Information for International Travel* (HEW Publication CDC-86-8280; enclose a check or money order for $4.75 payable to the Superintendent of Documents).

On the Road

Credit and Currency

It may seem hard to believe, but one of the greatest (and least understood) costs of travel is money itself. If that sounds simplistic, consider the fact that you can lose as much as 30% of your dollar's value simply by changing money at the wrong place or in the wrong form. So the one single objective in relation to the care and retention of travel funds is to make them stretch as far as possible. When you do spend money, it should be on things that expand and enhance your travel experience, with no buying power lost due to carelessness or lack of knowledge. This requires more than merely ferreting out the best airfare or the most charming budget hotel. It means being canny about the management of money itself. Herewith, a primer on making money go as far as possible overseas.

CURRENCY: The basic unit of Spanish currency is the *peseta* (abbreviated pta.). This is distributed in coin denominations of 1, 2, 5, 10, 25, 50, 100, 200, and 500 pesetas. Paper money is issued in bills of 100, 200, 500, 1,000, 2,000, 5,000, and 10,000 pesetas.

The Portuguese currency unit is the *escudo,* which is divided into 100 *centavos.* The escudo is abbreviated with a dollar sign, which takes the place of the decimal point in US currency. Coins are issued for 1, 2$50, 5, 10, 25, and 50 escudos. Bank notes are in denominations of 20, 50, 100, 500, 1,000, and 5,000 escudos.

Like all foreign currencies, the value of Spanish and Portuguese currency fluctuates daily in relation to the US dollar, affected by a wide variety of phenomena. As we went to press, the exchange rate for the Spanish peseta was 100 pesetas to US$1 (or US1¢ to 1 peseta); the exchange rate for the Portuguese escudo was 140 escudos to US$1 (or US1¢ to 1.4 escudos, or US70¢ to 100 escudos).

Although US dollars may be accepted in Spain and Portugal (particularly at points of entry), you certainly will lose a percentage of your dollar's buying power if you do not take the time to convert it into pesetas and escudos. By paying for goods and services in the local currency, you save money by not negotiating invariably unfavorable exchange rates for every small purchase, and avoid difficulty where US currency is not readily — or happily — accepted. *Throughout this book, unless specifically stated otherwise, prices are given in US dollars.*

There is no limit to the amount of US currency that can be brought into Spain or Portugal. There is likewise no restriction on the amount of traveler's checks (in dollars, escudos, or pesetas) that may be brought in, and these usually present no difficulties when you leave the country, since their US origin is obvious. To avoid problems anywhere along the line, it's advisable to fill out the customs form that will be provided on your flight to Spain or Portugal, on which you can declare all money you are bringing into the country — cash, traveler's checks, and so on. Although travelers usually are not questioned by officials about currency going into or out of these countries, the sensible course is to observe all the regulations just to be on the safe side. US law, however, requires that anyone taking more than $10,000 into or out of the US must report this fact on customs form No. 4790, which is available at all international airports. If taking over $10,000 out of the US, you must do this *before* leaving the US, and if returning with such an amount you should include this information on your customs declaration when you return.

FOREIGN EXCHANGE: Because of the frequent volatility of exchange rates, be sure to check the current value of Spanish and Portuguese currencies before finalizing any travel budget. And before you actually depart on your trip, be aware of the most advantageous exchange rates offered by various financial institutions — US banks, currency exchange firms (at home and abroad), or Spanish or Portuguese banks. Almost invariably, the best exchange rate offered for US dollars will be found in European banks.

For the best sense of current trends, follow the rates posted in the financial section of your local newspaper or in such international newspapers as the *International Herald Tribune.* It also is possible to check with your own bank. *Harold Reuter and Company,* a currency exchange service in New York City (200 Park Ave., Suite 332 E., New York, NY 10166; phone: 212-661-0826), also is particularly helpful in determining current trends in exchange rates; or check with *Deak International Ltd.* (for the nearest location, call 800-972-2192 in Illinois; 800-621-0666 elsewhere in the US). *Ruesch International* also offers up-to-date foreign currency information and currency-related services (such as converting Spanish peseta or Portuguese escudo refund checks into US dollars; see *Shopping,* in this section). *Ruesch* also offers a pocket-size *Foreign Currency Guide* (good for estimating general equivalents while planning) and a helpful brochure, *6 Foreign Exchange Tips for the Traveler.* Contact *Ruesch International* at one of the following addresses: 3 First National Plaza, Suite 2020, Chicago, IL 60602 (phone: 312-332-5900); 1925 Century Park E., Suite 240, Los Angeles, CA 90067 (phone: 213-277-7800); 608 Fifth Ave., "Swiss Center," New York, NY 10020 (phone: 212-977-2700); or 1350 Eye St. NW, 10th Floor and street level, Washington, DC 20005 (phone: 800-424-2923 or 202-408-1200).

In Spain and Portugal, you will find the official rate of exchange posted in banks, airports, money exchange houses, and some shops. The difference between the exchange rates offered in banks and in hotels varies from country to country — although generally you will get more local currency for your US dollar at banks than at any other commercial establishment. The convenience of exchanging money in your hotel (sometimes on a 24-hour basis) *may* make up for some of the difference in the exchange rate. Don't try to bargain in banks or hotels — no one will alter the rates for you.

Money exchange houses (called *casas de cambio* in Spain and *cambios* in Portugal) are financial institutions that charge a fee for the service of exchanging dollars into local currency. When considering alternatives, be aware that although the rate again varies among these establishments, the rates of exchange offered are bound to be slightly less favorable than the terms offered at nearby banks — again, don't be surprised if you get fewer pesetas or escudos for your dollar than the rate published in the papers.

That said, however, the following rules of thumb are worth remembering:

Rule number one is as simple as it is inflexible: Never (repeat: *never*) willingly exchange dollars for foreign currency at hotels, restaurants, or retail shops, where you are sure to lose a significant amount of your dollar's buying power. If you do come across a storefront exchange counter offering what appears to be an incredible bargain, there's just too much counterfeit specie in circulation to take the chance (see Rule number three, below.)

Rule number two: Estimate your needs carefully; if you overbuy you lose twice — buying and selling back. Every time you exchange money, someone is making a profit, and rest assured it isn't you. Use up foreign notes before leaving, saving just enough for airport departure taxes (which often must be paid in local currency), other last-minute incidentals, and tips.

Rule number three: Don't buy money on the black market. The exchange rate may be better, but it is a common practice to pass off counterfeit bills to unsuspecting foreigners who aren't familiar with the local currency. It's usually a sucker's game, and you almost always are the sucker; it also can land you in jail.

Rule number four: Learn the local currency quickly and keep abreast of daily fluctuations in the exchange rate. These are listed in the English-language *International Herald Tribune* daily for the preceding day, as well as in every major newspaper in Europe. Banks post their daily exchange rates, which might vary by a few cents — or even tenths of a cent — from a neighboring bank's posted rate. Rates change to some degree every day. For rough calculations, it is quick and safe to use round figures, but for purchases and actual currency exchanges, carry a small pocket calculator to help you compute the exact rate. Inexpensive calculators specifically designed to convert currency amounts quickly for travelers are widely available.

When changing money, don't be afraid to ask how much commission you're being charged, and the exact amount of the prevailing exchange rate. In fact, in any exchange of money for goods or services, you should work out the rate before making any payment.

TIP PACKS: It's not a bad idea to buy a *small* amount of Spanish and/or Portuguese coins and banknotes before your departure. But note the emphasis on "small," because, for the most part, you are better off carrying the bulk of your travel funds abroad in US dollar traveler's checks (see below). Still, the advantages of tip packs are threefold: You become familiar with the currency (really the only way to guard against making mistakes or being cheated during your first few hours in a new country); you are guaranteed some money should you arrive when a bank or exchange counter isn't open or available; and you don't have to depend on hotel desks, porters, or taxi drivers to change your money. A "tip pack" is the only foreign currency you should buy before you leave.

If you do run short upon arrival, dollars often are accepted at points of entry. In other areas, they either *may* be accepted, or someone may accommodate you by changing a small amount — though invariably at a less than advantageous rate.

TRAVELER'S CHECKS: It's wise to carry traveler's checks on the road instead of (or in addition to) cash, since it's possible to replace traveler's checks if they are stolen or lost; you usually can receive partial or full replacement funds the same day if you have your purchase receipt and proper identification. Issued in various denominations and available in both US dollars and Spanish pesetas or Portuguese escudos, with adequate proof of identification (credit cards, driver's license, passport), traveler's checks are as good as cash in most hotels, restaurants, stores, and banks.

You will be able to cash traveler's checks fairly easily in Spain and Portugal, but don't expect to meander into a small village and be able to get instant cash. Also, even in metropolitan areas, don't assume that restaurants, small shops, and other establishments are going to be able to change checks of large denominations. Worldwide, more and more establishments are beginning to restrict the amount of traveler's checks they will accept or cash, so it is wise to purchase at least some of your checks in small denominations — say, $10 and $20. Also, don't expect to change them into US cash except at banks and international airports.

When deciding whether to buy your travel funds in US or foreign denomination traveler's checks, keep in mind that the exchange rates offered by the issuing companies in the US generally are far less favorable than those available from banks both in the US and abroad. Therefore, it usually is better to carry the bulk of your travel funds abroad in US dollar denomination traveler's checks.

Every type of traveler's check is legal tender in banks around the world and each company guarantees full replacement if checks are lost or stolen. After that the similarity ends. Some charge a fee for purchase, others are free; you can buy traveler's checks at almost any bank, and some are available by mail. Most important, each traveler's check issuer differs slightly in its refund policy — the amount refunded immediately, the accessibility of refund locations, the availability of a 24-hour refund service, and the time it will take for you to receive replacement checks. For instance, American Express offers a 3-hour replacement of lost or stolen traveler's checks at any American Express office — other companies may not be as prompt. (Note that American Express's 3-hour policy is based on the traveler's being able to provide the serial numbers of the lost checks — without these numbers, refunds can take up to 3 business days.)

We cannot overemphasize the importance of knowing how to replace lost or stolen checks. All of the traveler's check companies have agents around the world, both in their own name and at associated agencies (usually, but not necessarily, banks), where refunds can be obtained during business hours. Most of them also have 24-hour toll-free telephone lines, and some even will provide emergency funds to tide you over on a Sunday.

Be sure to make a photocopy of the refund instructions that will be given to you by the issuing institution at the time of purchase. To avoid complications should you need to redeem lost checks (and to speed up the replacement process), keep the purchase receipt and an accurate list, by serial number, of the checks that have been spent or cashed. You may want to incorporate this information in an "emergency packet," also including your passport number and date of issue, the numbers of the credit cards you are carrying, and any other bits of information you can't bear to be without. Always keep these records separate from the checks and the original records themselves (you may want to give them to a traveling companion to hold).

Although most people understand the desirability of carrying funds in the form of traveler's checks as protection against loss or theft, an equally good reason is that US dollar traveler's checks invariably get a better rate of exchange than cash does — usually by at least 1% (although the discrepancy has been known to be substantially higher). The reasons for this are technical, but it is a fact of travel life that should not be ignored.

That 1% won't do you much good, however, if you already have spent it buying your traveler's checks. Several of the major traveler's check companies charge 1% for the privilege of using their checks; others don't, but the issuing institution (e.g., the particular bank at which you purchase them) may itself charge a fee. Thomas Cook checks issued in US currency are free if you make your travel arrangements through its travel agency, for example; and if you purchase traveler's checks at a bank in which you or your company maintains significant accounts (especially commercial accounts of some size), you also might find that the bank will absorb the 1% fee as a courtesy. American Express traveler's checks are available without charge to members of the *Automobile Association of America (AAA)* at some *AAA* offices in the US (the policy varies from state to state).

American Express, Citicorp, Thomas Cook, MasterCard, and Visa all offer traveler's checks, but not at all locations. Call the service numbers listed below to find a participating branch near you. Here is a list of the major companies issuing traveler's checks that are accepted widely in Spain and Portugal and the numbers to call in case loss or theft makes replacement necessary:

American Express: To report lost or stolen checks in the US, call 800-221-7282. From Europe, American Express advises travelers to call 44-273-571600 (in Brighton, England). Another (slower) option is to call 801-968-8300 in the US, collect; or contact the nearest American Express office.

Bank of America: To report lost or stolen checks in the US, call 800-227-3460. From Spain or Portugal and elsewhere worldwide, call 415-624-5400 or 415-622-3800 collect.

Citicorp: To report lost or stolen checks in the US, call 800-645-6556; from Spain or Portugal and elsewhere worldwide, call 813-623-1709 or 813-626-4444, collect.

MasterCard: To report lost or stolen checks in the US, call 800-223-9920. In Spain or Portugal, call the New York office at 212-974-5696, collect.

Thomas Cook MasterCard: To report lost or stolen checks in the US, call 800-223-9920. In Spain or Portugal, call the US office, 609-987-7300, collect, or 44-733-502995 (in England) and they will direct you to the nearest branch of Thomas Cook or *Wagons-Lits,* their European agent.

Visa: To report lost or stolen checks in the continental US, call 800-227-6811; from Spain or Portugal, call 415-574-7111 collect. In Europe, you also can call this London number collect: 44-71-937-8091.

CREDIT CARDS: There are two different kinds of credit cards available to consumers in the US, and travelers must decide which kind best serves their needs — although many travelers elect to carry both types. "Convenience" or "charge" or "travel and entertainment" cards — American Express, Diners Club, and Carte Blanche — are widely accepted. They cost the cardholder a basic annual membership fee ($40 to $65 is typical for these three), but put no strict limit on the amount that may be charged on the card in any month. However, the entire amount charged must be paid in full at the end of each billing period (usually a month), so the cardholder is not actually extended any long-term credit.

"Bank cards" also are rarely issued free these days (with the exception of Sears Discover Card), and certain services they provide (check cashing, for example) can carry an extra charge. But this category comprises *real* credit cards in the sense that the cardholder has the privilege of paying a small amount (1/36 is typical) of the total outstanding balance in each billing period. For this privilege, the cardholder is charged a high annual interest rate (currently three to four times the going bank passbook savings rate) on the balance owed. Many banks now charge interest from the purchase date, not from the first billing date (as they used to do); consider this when you are calculating the actual cost of a purchase. In addition, a maximum is set on the total amount the cardholder can charge, which represents the limit of credit the card company is willing to extend. The major bank cards are Visa and MasterCard, with Discover growing rapidly.

Note that some establishments you may encounter during the course of your travels may not honor any credit cards and some may not honor all cards, so there is a practical reason to carry more than one. Also keep in mind that some major US credit cards may be issued under different names in Europe. For example, MasterCard may go under the name Access or Eurocard, and Visa often is called Carte Bleue — wherever these equivalents are accepted, MasterCard and Visa may be used. The following is a list of credit cards that enjoy wide domestic and international acceptance:

American Express: Emergency personal check cashing at American Express or representatives' offices (up to $500 in cash for all cardholders; traveler's check limits depend on the type of card: up to $500 for Green cardholders; up to $1,000 for Optima cardholders; up to $4,500 for Gold cardholders; and up to $9,500 for Platinum cardholders); emergency personal check cashing for guests at participating hotels (up to $100), and, for holders of airline tickets, at participating airlines in the US (up to $50). Extended payment plan for cruises, tours, and railway and airline tickets, as well as other prepaid travel arrangements. $100,000 to $500,000 travel accident insurance (depending on type of card) if ticket was charged to card; up to $1 million additional low-cost flight insurance available. Contact *American Express,* PO Box 39, Church St. Station, New

York, NY 10008 (phone: 212-477-5700 in New York; 800-528-4800 elsewhere in the US; 801-964-6665 abroad; cardholders may call collect).

Carte Blanche: Extended payment plan for air travel (from $2,000 to $5,000, depending on credit line). $150,000 free travel accident insurance on plane, train, and ship if ticket was charged to card, plus $1,250 checked or carry-on baggage insurance and $25,000 rental car insurance. Medical, legal, and travel assistance available worldwide (phone: 800-356-3448 in the US; 214-680-6480, collect, from abroad). Contact *Carte Blanche,* PO Box 17326, Denver, CO 80217 (phone: 800-525-9135 in the US; 303-790-2433 abroad; cardholders may call collect).

Diners Club: Emergency personal check cashing for guests at participating hotels and motels (up to $250 per stay). Qualified card members are eligible for extended payment plan. $350,000 free travel accident insurance on plane, train, and ship if ticket was charged to your card, plus $1,250 checked and carry-on baggage insurance and $25,000 rental car insurance. Medical, legal, and travel assistance available worldwide (phone: 800-356-3448 in the US; 214-680-6480, collect, from abroad). Contact *Diners Club,* PO Box 17326, Denver, CO 80217 (phone: 800-525-9135 throughout the US for customer service; for lost or stolen cards, call one of the following 24-hour service numbers: 800-525-9341 in the US; 303-790-2433, collect, from abroad).

Discover Card: Created by Sears, Roebuck and Co., it provides the holder with cash advance at more than 500 locations in the US, and offers a revolving credit line for purchases at a wide range of service establishments. Other deposit, lending, and investment services also are available. For information, call 800-858-5588 in the US (if you can't reach this number by dialing directly, call an operator, who will be able to place the call).

MasterCard: Cash advances are available at participating banks worldwide, and a revolving credit line can be set up for purchases at a wide range of service establishments. Interest charges on any unpaid balance and other details are set by issuing bank. Check with your bank for information. *MasterCard* also offers a 24-hour emergency lost card service; call 800-336-8472 in the US; 314-275-6690, collect, from abroad.

Visa: Cash advances are available at participating banks worldwide, and a revolving credit line can be set up for purchases at a wide range of service establishments provided by issuer. Interest charges on any unpaid balance and other details are set by issuing bank. Check with your bank for information. *Visa* also offers a 24-hour emergency lost card service; call 800-336-8472 in the US; 415-574-7700, collect, from abroad.

In addition to the credit card services discussed above, a number of other benefits and/or details are set by the issuing institutions. For instance, some credit cards now offer the added incentive of "bonus" programs. Each time the card is used, the cardholder may gather either points with a monetary equivalent, which can be applied toward the total cost of selected purchases or travel arrangements, or a credit with a specific travel supplier such as frequent flyer mileage bonuses with an airline. When deciding on whether one of these cards provides the best deal, you should compare the potential value of these and other special programs with the variations in interest rates charged on unpaid balances and annual membership fees.

One of the thorniest problems relating to the use of credit cards abroad concerns the rate of exchange at which a purchase is charged. Be aware that the exchange rate in effect on the date that you make a foreign purchase or pay for a foreign service has nothing at all to do with the rate of exchange at which your purchase is billed to you when you get the invoice (sometimes months later) in the US. The amount American Express (and other convenience cards) charges is ultimately a function of the exchange rate in effect on the day your charge is received at an American Express (or other agency) service center, and there is a 1-year limit on the time a shop or hotel can take to forward its charge slips. The rate at which Visa and other bank cards process an item is a function of the rate at which the hotel's or shop's bank processed it.

The principle at work in this credit card–exchange rate roulette is simple, but very hard to predict. You make a purchase at a particular dollar versus local currency exchange rate. If the dollar gets stronger in the time between purchase and billing, your purchase actually costs you less than you anticipated. If the dollar drops in value during the interim, you pay more than you thought you would. There isn't much you can do about these vagaries except to follow one very broad, very clumsy rule of thumb: If the dollar is doing well at the time of purchase, its value increasing against the local currency, use your credit card on the assumption that it still will be doing well when billing takes place. If the dollar is doing badly, assume it will continue to do badly and pay with traveler's checks or cash. If you get too badly stuck, the best recourse is to complain, loudly. Be aware, too, that most credit card companies charge an unannounced, un-itemized 1% fee for converting foreign currency charges to US dollars.

No matter what you are using — traveler's checks, credit cards, or cash — plan ahead. That way you won't live through the nightmare of arriving in a small Spanish or Portuguese town on a Friday afternoon without any local currency. If you do get caught in this situation, you may have to settle for a poor exchange rate at a hotel or a restaurant. In this case, exchange just enough dollars to get you through the weekend.

Also, carry your travel funds carefully. You might consider carrying them (cash and traveler's checks) in more than one place. Never put money in a back pocket or an open purse. Money should be kept in a buttoned front pocket, in a money purse pinned inside your shirt or blouse, or in one of the convenient money belts or leg pouches sold by many travel shops. It may be quaint and old-fashioned, but it's safe.

SENDING MONEY ABROAD: If you have used up your traveler's checks, cashed as many emergency personal checks as your credit card allows, drawn on your cash advance line to the fullest extent, and still need money, have it sent abroad via the *Western Union Telegraph Company.* A friend or relative can go, cash in hand, to any of *Western Union*'s 9,000 offices in the US, where, for a *minimum* transfer fee of $12 (it rises with the amount of the transaction) plus a $25 surcharge, the funds will be transferred to a participating *Banco Español de Credito* in Spain or a *Banco Espirito Santo* in Portugal, *Western Union*'s correspondent banks in Spain and Portugal. (In Spain, the cities to which money can be wired via *Western Union* are Barcelona, Bilboa, Córdoba, Granada, Madrid, Málaga, Palma de Mallorca, Santa Cruz de Tenerife, Seville, and Valencia; in Portugal, they are Coimbra, Faro, Lisbon, and Porto.) When the money arrives in either country, you will not be notified — you must go to the bank to inquire. Transfers generally take anywhere from 2 to 5 business days, although the wait may be much longer in particularly remote areas. The funds will be turned over in local currency, based on the rate of exchange in effect on the day of receipt. For a higher fee, the US party to this transaction may use a MasterCard or Visa card to send up to $2,000 by phone by dialing *Western Union*'s toll-free number (800-325-4176) anywhere in the US.

American Express offers a similar service in Spain called "Moneygram," completing money transfers in as little as 15 minutes. The sender — who must be an American Express cardholder — must go to an American Express office in the US and can use cash, a personal check, money order, or an American Express Optima, Gold, or Platinum card for the transfer. Optima cardholders also can arrange for this transfer by phone. The minimum transfer charge is $25, which rises with the amount of the transaction; the sender can forward funds of up to $10,000 (credit card users are limited to the amount of pre-established credit line). To collect at the other end, the receiver must go to an American Express office in Barcelona, Madrid, or Marbella and present a passport as identification proof. For further information on this service, call 800-543-4080.

If you are literally down to your last peseta or centavo, the nearest US consulate (see *Medical and Legal Aid and Consular Services,* in this section) will let you call home to set these matters in motion.

Accommodations

 From elegant, centuries-old castle resorts to modern, functional high-rises and modest, inexpensive inns, it's easy to be comfortable and well cared for on almost any budget in Spain or Portugal. Admittedly, the Mediterranean coast is full of deluxe establishments providing expensive services to people with money to burn, but more affordable alternatives have always been available, particularly in the countryside.

In fact, those watching their wallets will be pleased to find a larger selection of accommodations in their price range than is the case either at home or in most other countries in Europe. Both Spain and Portugal have long been among the European destinations where the cost of living is lowest, and despite inflation and the recent decline in the strength of the US dollar, they continue to be so — particularly Portugal. At the lower end of the price scale, you will not necessarily have to forgo charm. While a fair number of inexpensive establishments are simply no-frills, "generic" places to spend the night, even the sparest room may have the cachet of once having been the nightly retreat of a monk or nun. And some of the most delightful places to stay are the smaller, less expensive, often family-run small inns, *hostales* and *pensiones* in Spain, and *pensões* in Portugal.

Once upon a time, such things as the superiority of New World plumbing made many of the numerous, less expensive alternatives unacceptable for North Americans. Today, the gap has closed considerably, and in Spain and Portugal the majority of the hostelries catering to the tourist trade are likely to be at least adequate in their basic facilities.

Our accommodations choices, which embrace the wide range of possibilities, are included in the *Checking In* sections of the individual city reports in THE CITIES and each tour route in DIRECTIONS. They have been selected for a variety of travel budgets, but the lists are not comprehensive; with some diligent searching, before you leave and en route, you can turn up an equal number of "special places" that are uniquely yours. Also consult the numerous brochures and booklets available free from the Spanish and Portuguese tourist offices in the US (see *Tourist Information Offices,* in this section, for addresses). Other publications can be purchased from the travel bookstores listed in *Books and Magazines,* also in this section.

ACCOMMODATIONS IN SPAIN: The annual *Guía de Hoteles,* issued by Spain's Secretaría General de Turismo, lists most of the hotels in the country (except for those that are not officially graded according to the government's star system of classification). Hotels are classified from 5 stars (the highest rating) through 1 star (the lowest) on the basis of the tangible facilities they possess — such things as the proportion of rooms with private baths and telephones, the number of elevators, public rooms, and bars, the existence of air conditioning, and so on. Since the rating does not take into account the quality of those facilities or such intangibles as the warmth of the welcome or the sprightliness of the service, it should be considered only a guide in choosing a hotel.

A very few superlatively appointed five-star properties, such as the *Ritz* and the *Villa*

Magna in Madrid and the *Meliá Don Pepe* in Marbella, have earned the equivalent of a sixth star and carry the designation *gran lujo* (great luxury). Hotels listed as *residencias* are without restaurants, generally offering breakfast only, although some may have cafeteria service. Classified separately, from 3 stars through 1 star, but also listed in the guide, are *hostales,* more modest accommodations that translate as inns or "hostels," but should not be confused with youth hostels, however, and *pensiones,* which are fewer in number and somewhat like boardinghouses. Both *hostales* and *pensiones* tend to be unassuming places, often run by a family that has inherited a large apartment or the entire floor of a building and converted it for this purpose. Hostels, too, will be listed as *residencias* if they do not serve meals other than breakfast; pensions may require guests to take full or half board.

Also listed in the guide are the *paradores,* a special group of state-owned inns discussed more fully below; motels, although the country has comparatively few; and numerous *hotel apartamentos* and *residencia apartamentos,* or apartment hotels (see "Apartment and Villa Rental" below for more information). Not listed are such accommodations for the shoestring traveler as *casas de huéspedes,* or guesthouses, and *fondas,* which are primarily eating places that also may have rooms for rent. Local tourist offices should have information on these, as they may on the many *camas* (beds), *habitaciones* (rooms), and *casas particulares* (private houses with rooms for rent — similar to bed and breakfast accommodations elsewhere on the Continent) that can be found in smaller towns and the countryside.

Also ask local tourist offices (or, in the US, the National Tourist Office of Spain) for information on staying in a monastery or convent. More than a few, particularly in the region of Castile-León (Old Castile) and along the pilgrimage route to Santiago de Compostela, open their doors to guests (men only or women only, and sometimes married couples), charging very low rates or, occasionally, a voluntary donation. (These are not to be confused with other monasteries, no longer functioning as religious houses, that have been turned into *paradores;* see below.)

The *Guía de Hoteles* can be bought in bookstores in Spain, but regional versions with the same information can be obtained in the US by visiting or writing the nearest branch of the National Tourist Office of Spain (where the full guide also can be consulted) and specifying the city or area of interest (e.g., Barcelona, Balearic Islands, Andalusia). The listing for each hotel includes its star category, address and telephone number, number of rooms, and amenities, along with the prices of double rooms with or without bath and of breakfast and other meals, if offered.

Even without any of the above guides in hand, however, it is not difficult for visitors in Spain to figure out where a particular hotel fits in the scheme of things. A blue plaque by the door of any establishment that has been classified clearly reveals what it is — H means a hotel, HR a *hotel residencia,* Hs a hostel, HsR a *hostal residencia,* P a *pensión* — as well as the number of stars attained. Inside, room prices appear by law in the individual rooms and sometimes are posted by the reception desk as well. The posted prices include service (which generally ranges from 10% to 15%) and Value Added Tax (6%, except in 4- and 5-star hotels, where it is 12%), so that receiving the bill at the end of a stay rarely is a shock. Breakfast may or may not be included in the posted rate, and if it is, there may be no reduction if it is not taken (ask, if this is not clear).

Note that many Spanish hotels keep complaint forms — *hojas de reclamaciones* — handy should guests require them. Because any written complaints must be filed with the proper authorities, most hoteliers are eager to resolve disputes before they are put into writing.

In Spain, a single room is a *habitación sencilla;* a double room is a *habitación doble,* and it has either *camas gemelas* (two twin beds) or *una cama de matrimonio* (one double bed). A room with a private bath is *con baño,* but anyone traveling on a shoestring should note that all rooms in the officially graded accommodations have a sink with hot and cold running water, so it's possible to forgo the luxury of a private bathroom and still not be totally without convenience. Single rooms are in short supply, but if a person traveling alone is given a double because no single is available, the charge should be 80% of its normal price. A third bed placed in a double room increases its price by 35%.

Rates in many hotels vary according to high and low seasons, and some have an intermediate season — known in travel parlance as the "shoulder season." The definition of high season varies according to the hotel and the locality, but remember that in the Canary Islands and in mountain ski resorts on the mainland, winter — generally November through April — is high season, whereas elsewhere on the mainland and in the Balearics, high season corresponds more conventionally to summer. *Christmas, Easter,* and any local festivals also command high season rates. (See *When to Go,* at the beginning of this section, for further information on seasonal variations.)

ACCOMMODATIONS IN PORTUGAL: Accommodations in Portugal are listed in a free pocket guide, *Portugal: Hotels,* available from the Portuguese National Tourist Office in the US. It includes hotels, classified, as in Spain, from 5 stars (the highest rating) through 1 star (the lowest); *estalagens* (*estalagem* in the singular), which are 5-star and 4-star inns, and *albergarias,* also inns, but all of 4 stars (historically, these were less sophisticated hostelries than *estalagens,* although there is little difference between the two today); and *pensões* (*pensão* in the singular), 4-star through 1-star boardinghouses that are generally more modest than all of the foregoing establishments, often occupying only part of a building otherwise devoted to apartments or offices. Some *pensões* require guests to take one or more meals besides breakfast. Others may not serve any other meals than breakfast. As in Spain, any hotel, inn, or pension that calls itself a *residência* (an R follows its name in the guide) serves breakfast but no other meals.

The same guide also lists Portugal's *pousadas* (see below), its few motels, and a variety of apartment hotels and other furnished apartments suitable for vacationers (see "Apartment and Villa Rental," below). Listings in the guide include the star category of each establishment, its address and phone number, and the number of rooms with and without private baths. Prices are not given, although the tourist office also distributes information sheets showing average room rates in high season and low season for each category of accommodation, apartments excepted. Generally, high season runs from April through October everywhere in Portugal but Madeira, where winter is the busy season accompanied by the highest prices.

As in Spain, establishments in Portugal have signs outside showing the category to which they belong and their star ratings. Room prices, which include a 10% to 15% service charge and 16% Value Added Tax (IVA), are posted in individual bedrooms, along with the prices of meals if they are offered. Note that the price of the room always includes a continental breakfast. A single room is a *quarto individual,* a double room a *quarto duplo,* or, more specifically, a *quarto com duas camas* (with twin beds) or a *quarto de casal* (with a double bed). Rooms with private baths are *com banho;* those without are *sem banho.* In most establishments, however, rooms that have no private bathroom do have a sink with hot and cold running water. When one person occupies a double room, the price of one breakfast is deducted from the room rate. When an extra bed is added to a room, the price increases by 30% in most accommodations, by 25% in apartment hotels and motels. Should there be any complaints, remember that hotels in Portugal, as in Spain, often have an official complaints book — *libro de reclamaçiñes* — in which guests may register serious dissatisfaction.

PARADORES AND POUSADAS: Both Spain and Portugal boast a network of state-owned inns — *paradores* in Spain, *pousadas* in Portugal — that are among the most interesting hostelries in Europe. Spain's system was born in 1926, when the country's Royal Tourist Commissioner came up with the idea of providing hotel accommodations in out-of-the-way areas where private investment lagged. The first *parador* opened in 1928 and occupied built-for-the-purpose premises in the Gredos Mountains of Castile. But it wasn't long before the need to create hotels merged with another item on the government's agenda — that of reclaiming abandoned castles, palaces, convents, and other historic structures and converting them to new uses. Thus, today's traveler can sleep in a 15th-century castle where Cortés lived before he left for Mexico or in another occupied by King Carlos V, stay at a monastery in the Pyrenees or in a convent within the confines of the Alhambra, choose the elegance of a Renaissance palace or the rusticity of a Muslim fortress. About half of the 86 *paradores* now in existence are in such old buildings, furnished with antiques or fine reproductions but complete with modern conveniences, while the rest are modern establishments that, however, can be anything from a mountain chalet to a house in the typically tile-roofed, whitewashed style of an Andalusian village.

All *paradores* are set in picturesque, though no longer necessarily remote, locations, and all have restaurants, many of them excellent, specializing in regional cuisine. Yet prices are reasonable. In the Spanish system of grading hotels, *paradores* are mainly 3- and 4-star establishments (a few 2- and 5-star places exist), with prices for a double room ranging from about $80 to $140 and varying little from low through mid to high season. They can be exceedingly intimate, with as few as 6 rooms, or comparatively large, with as many as 100; the largest, *Parador de San Marcos,* in León, has 258 rooms.

In 1940, Portugal took its cue from Spain and began its own network of *pousadas,* now 31 inns strong. While a smaller percentage of them are in actual historic buildings — such as those in the castles of Obidos, Palmela, and Estremoz or in the Lóios Monastery of Evora — all, as in Spain, are in scenic areas and in regional styles of architecture that complement their surroundings. Portuguese *pousadas* also tend to be smaller than Spanish *paradores,* ranging from 6 rooms to a maximum of 50 in the largest, the *Pousada de Santa Marinha da Costa,* near Guimarães. All have modern conveniences and restaurants. *Pousadas* are not given a star rating along with the rest of Portugal's hotels; instead, they are divided into three categories (B, C, and CH, corresponding to inexpensive, moderate, and deluxe historic building), with prices for a double room with continental breakfast ranging from about $50 to $100 in low season and from $60 to $120 in high season.

The above-mentioned publications, *Guía de Hoteles* and *Portugal: Hotels,* include *paradores* and *pousadas* among their listings, but the Spanish and Portuguese tourist authorities also distribute illustrated booklets — *Visiting the Paradores* and *Pousadas de Portugal* — that provide a somewhat better view of the background and attractions of the individual inns and, in the case of the *paradores,* details of the facilities at each. Prices are omitted, however, so ask for a rate sheet giving the average prices for inns in each category. Since both *paradores* and *pousadas* are very popular, reservations are strongly recommended, particularly during the high season. In the US, they can be made through travel agents or *Marketing Ahead* (433 Fifth Ave., New York, NY 10016; phone: 212-686-9213). Note that some travel agents will make reservations only for stays of 3 or more nights per establishment; for shorter stays you may want to contact the *parador* or *pousada* directly. In addition, several tour operators offer fly/drive packages featuring accommodations in *paradores* and *pousadas* (see *Package Tours,* in this section).

MANOR HOUSES AND FARMHOUSES: Travelers who prefer to stay in establishments that are less commercial than hotels, inns, or even *paradores* and *pousadas,* and who like to leave the beaten track and meet people as much 40 possible should investigate Portugal's *Turismo no Espaço Rural* (Tourism in the Country) program. This is a network of privately owned properties, from aristocratic 16th- and 17th-century manor houses to rustic farmhouses, that accommodate paying guests.

The program — which is like the *pousada* program in its origin as an attempt to preserve the country's artistic heritage through tourism — began in the early 1980s, when the owners of many of Portugal's finest old estates received low-interest government loans to restore their homes and open them to overnight visitors. Initially, the program was known as *Turismo de Habitação* (Tourism in Private Houses), and its properties, largely concentrated in northern Portugal, were the country manors of some of the nation's oldest families. Indeed, a number of the properties were (and are) not merely *solares* and *quintas* — manor houses and country mansions — but *paços*, a word indicating that, at some time in the past, a king slept on the premises. Given the success of the program, it rapidly spread to the rest of Portugal and grew to include other types of country properties. Thus, *Turismo de Habitação (TH)* was joined by *Turismo Rural (TR)*, which includes homes that are more modest than the manor houses but still characteristically regional in their architecture (they can be in the countryside or in villages), and by *Agroturismo (AG)*, which includes rustic farmhouses. The new name, *Turismo no Espaço Rural (TER)*, came into being to cover them all.

Whatever its classification, a house can offer as few as 1 or 2 double or single rooms or as many as 10, usually with private baths; at some properties, entirely independent apartments are available. Amenities can include swimming pools, tennis courts, gardens to walk in, and horses to ride. Prices range from anywhere from $35 to $100 and up (depending on the level of luxury) for two people per day, including breakfast; some of the houses also serve lunch and dinner, if requested — in which case guests may eat with other paying guests or even with the host family, since, in most cases, the owner continues to live on the property.

The Portuguese National Tourist Office provides a list of participating houses. Reservations are then made directly with the proprietors or through the central booking offices of three owners' associations in Portugal. One of them, the *Associação do Turismo de Habitação (Turihab)* (Praça da República, Ponte de Lima 4990, Portugal; phone: 58-942729), handles houses in the northern Minho region only (where the network of houses is thickest, however). The two others, representing properties throughout the country, are the *Associação das Casas em Turismo (ACT)* (Alto da Pampilheira, Torre D-2 8-A, Cascais 2750, Portugal), whose marketing arm, *PIT* (phone: 1-286-7958), books the properties, and the *Associação Portuguesa de Turismo de Habitação (Privetur)* (209 Rua Castilho, Lisbon 1000, Portugal), whose reservations are handled by a travel agent, *Seriasol Viajens e Turismo* (phone: 1-286-8232). Note that some houses do not belong to any association and, therefore, have to be booked directly. Note, too, that a minimum stay, 3 nights in the case of *Turihab*, 2 or 3 nights elsewhere, usually is imposed. Information on the program also is available from the *Direcção Geral do Turismo, Divisão do Turismo no Espaço Rural* (86 Avenida António Augusto de Aguiar, Lisbon 1000, Portugal; phone: 1-575015).

RELAIS & CHÂTEAUX: Most members of this association are in France, but the group has grown to include dozens of establishments in many other countries, including, currently, 12 in Spain and 1 in Portugal.

Relais & Châteaux members are of particular interest to travelers who wish lodgings reflecting the ambience, style and frequently the history of the places they are visiting. Some properties actually are ancient castles or palaces — dating back more than 1,000 years — which have been converted into hotels. Others — the *relais* — are old inns, manor houses, even converted mills, convents, and monasteries. A few well-known city and resort establishments are included, such as the *Marbella Club* in Spain, but most are in quiet country surroundings, and freqently are graced with parks, ponds, and flowering gardens.

Another group of members, *Relais Gourmands,* is composed of exceptionally fine restaurants. These establishments also may have rooms for rent, but the establishments are *not* rated on the basis of their accommodations (unless they also are designated as

Relais & Châteaux), so they may not match (or even come close to) the standards of room quality maintained by other *Relais* hotel members. There are no *Relais Gourmands* in Portugal, and the four *Gourmand* members in Spain also are *Relais & Châteaux* hotel members and offer both fine food and elegant accommodations.

Members of the *Relais & Châteaux* group often are expensive, though no more than you would pay for deluxe, authentically elegant accommodations and service anywhere in the world (and many are not all that costly). At the time of this writing, the least expensive double room cost about $150 per night — although prices ranged anywhere up to $500 for the most luxurious establishments. (Prices include service and tax; some include breakfast and dinner, but if meals are not included they can add to the cost considerably, since all *Relais & Châteaux* have good restaurants.) Accommodations and service from one *relais* or château to another can range from simple but comfortable to elegantly deluxe, but they all maintain very high standards in order to retain their memberships, as they are appraised annually.

An illustrated catalogue of all the *Relais & Châteaux* properties is published annually and is available for $5 from *Relais & Châteaux* (2200 Lazy Hollow, Suite 152D, Houston, TX 77063) or from *David B. Mitchell & Company* (200 Madison Ave., New York, NY 10016; phone: 800-372-1323 or 212-696-1323). The association also can provide information on member properties. Reservations can be made directly with the establishments, through *David B. Mitchell & Company,* or through a travel agency.

APARTMENTS AND VILLAS: Another alternative to hotels for the visitor content to stay in one spot for a week or more is to rent a house or an apartment (usually called a "flat" overseas). Known to Europeans as a "holiday let" or a "self-catering holiday," a vacation in a furnished rental has both the advantages and disadvantages of living "at home" abroad. It certainly is less expensive than staying in a first class hotel for the same period of time (although very luxurious and expensive rentals are available, too). It has the comforts of home, including a kitchen, which means potential saving on food costs. Furthermore, it gives a sense of the country being visited that a large hotel often cannot. On the other hand, a certain amount of housework is involved because if you don't eat out, you have to cook, and though some rentals (especially the luxury ones) include a cleaning person, most don't. (If the rental doesn't include daily cleaning, arrangements often can be made with a maid service.)

Some of the possibilities are listed in the accommodations guides published by the Spanish and Portuguese tourist authorities. In Spain, they include *hotel apartamentos* and *residencia apartamentos,* that is, apartment hotels with or without restaurants and with the facilities and services of hotels, including maid service, but with guestrooms equipped with kitchenettes; and *apartamentos turísticos,* or tourist apartments (more like the "holiday let" arrangements found elsewhere on the Continent), which are furnished rentals geared expressly to the short-term vacationer.

Both tourist apartments (rated from 4 keys through 1 key) and apartment hotels are listed in the regional hotel guides available from the National Tourist Office of Spain in the US, whereas the larger *Guía de Hoteles* lists only apartment hotels. Similarly, the choices in Portugal include a variety of apartment hotels (rated 4 through 2 stars) and tourist apartments (1st, 2nd, and 3rd categories, with the 1st category the highest), as well as tourist villages, or *aldeamentos turísticos* (deluxe, 1st, and 2nd categories), all particularly prominent in the Algarve. The above-mentioned *Portugal: Hotels,* distributed by the Portuguese National Tourist Office in the US, lists all three types, but the manor house program discussed above should also be considered as a source of rentals, since a number of properties have made independent apartments out of servants' quarters, wine cellars, stables, and other buildings on their estates. In addition, many tour operators regularly include a few rental packages among their more conventional offerings; these generally are available through a travel agent.

Certain companies in the US specialize in rentals of apartments, houses, cottages, and other propeties. They handle the booking and confirmation paperwork, generally for a fee included in the rental price, and can be expected to provide more information about the properties than that which might ordinarily be gleaned from a listing in an accommodations guide. Those listed below have a number of properties in Spain and/or Portugal; to get detailed data and to have your pick you should begin to make arrangements for a summer rental at least 6 months in advance.

At Home Abroad: Modest to luxurious houses (some with pools) and a few apartments on Spain's Costa del Sol and in Portugal's Algarve. Photographs of properties and a newsletter are available for a $50 registration fee. 405 E. 56th St., Apt. 6H, New York, NY 10022 (phone: 212-421-9165).

Blake's Vacations: Rents small villas on Spain's Costa Brava. 49-39 Dempster St., Skokie, IL 60077 (phone: 800-628-8118).

Coast to Coast Resorts: Handles modest properties throughout Spain. 860 Solar Building, 1000 16th St. NW, Washington, DC 20036 (phone: 800-368-5721 or 202-293-8000).

Eastone Overseas Accommodations: Handles a few apartments, but mostly villas and houses in northern Portugal and along the coasts of both Spain and Portugal. 198 Southampton Dr., Jupiter, FL 33458 (phone: 407-575-6991/2) or 556B Willow Turn, Mount Laurel, NJ 08054 (phone: 609-722-1010 in New Jersey; 800-544-3396 elsewhere in the US).

Europa-Let, Inc.: Rentals range from modest apartments to luxurious villas in Portugal's Algarve, north of Lisbon, and along the Spanish coast. PO Box 3537, Ashland, OR 97520 (phone: 800-462-4486 or 503-482-5806).

Hideaways International: Rents apartments, private homes, and villas in both Spain and Portugal. 15 Goldsmith St., PO Box 1270, Littleton, MA 01460 (phone: 800-843-4433 or 508-486-8955).

International Lodging Corp.: Flats, villas, and some country homes in the vicinities of Spain's Costa Brava, Costa del Sol, and Marbella, and Portugal's Algarve. 89-27 182nd Pl., Hollis, NY 11423 (phone: 718-291-1342).

Rent a Vacation Everywhere (RAVE): Moderate to luxurious villas and apartments on the Costa del Sol, plus properties on other Spanish coasts (Costa Brava, Costa Dorada, Costa del Azahar), on the island of Minorca, and in the Algarve. 328 Main St. E., Suite 526, Rochester, NY 14604 (phone: 716-454-6440).

Villas International (formerly *Interchange*): Besides apartments in Madrid and Barcelona and a few in Seville and Granada, the choices range from simple to moderate houses and apartments along Spain's eastern coasts and from modest to super-luxury properties on the Costa del Sol and in the Algarve. 71 W. 23rd St., New York, NY 10010 (phone: 212-929-7585 in New York State; 800-221-2260 elsewhere in the US).

HOME EXCHANGES: Still another alternative for travelers who are content to stay in one place during their vacation is a home exchange: The Smith family from St. Louis moves into the home of the Alemán family in Valencia, while the Alemáns enjoy a stay in the Smiths' home. The home exchange is an exceptionally inexpensive way to ensure comfortable, reasonable living quarters with amenities that no hotel possibly could offer; often the trade includes a car. Moreover, it allows you to live in a new community in a way that few tourists ever do: For a little while, at least, you will become something of a resident.

Several companies publish directories of individuals and families willing to trade homes with others for a specific period of time. In some cases, you must be willing to list your own home in the directory; in others, you can subscribe without appearing in it. Most listings are for straight exchanges only, but each directory also has a number of listings placed by people interested in either exchanging or renting (for instance, if they own a second home). Other arrangements include exchanges of hospitality while owners are in residence or youth exchanges, where your teenager is put up as a guest in return for your welcoming their teenager at a later date. A few house-sitting opportunities also are available. In most cases, arrangements for the actual exchange take place directly between you and the foreign host. There is no guarantee that you will find a listing in the area in which you are interested, but each of the organizations given below includes Spanish and Portuguese homes among its hundreds or even thousands of foreign listings.

Home Base Holidays: For $42 a year, subscribers receive four listings, with an option to list in all four. 7 Park Ave., London N13 5PG England (phone: 44-81-886-8752).

International Home Exchange Service/Intervac US: The $35 fee includes copies of the three directories published yearly and an option to list your home in one of them; a black-and-white photo may be included with the listing for an additional $8.50. A 10% discount is given to travelers over age 65. Box 190070, San Francisco, CA 94119 (phone: 415-435-3497).

InterService Home Exchange: An affiliate of *Intervac International,* this service publishes three directories annually which include more than 7,000 exchanges in over 30 countries worldwide, including Spain and Portugal. For $35, interested home-swappers are listed in and receive a copy of the February, March, and May directories; a black-and-white photo of your home may be included with the listing for an additional $10. Box 387, Glen Echo, MD 20812 (phone: 301-229-7567).

Loan-A-Home: Specializes in long-term (4 months or more — excluding July and August) housing arrangements worldwide for students and professors, businesspeople, and retirees, although its two annual directories (with supplements) carry a small list of short-term rentals and/or exchanges. $35 for a copy of one directory and one supplement; $45 for two directories and two supplements. 2 Park Lane, Apt. 6E, Mt. Vernon, NY 10552 (phone: 914-664-7640).

Vacation Exchange Club: Some 6,000 listings, about half of which are foreign, including 75 or so in Spain and about 12 in Portugal. For $24.70, the subscriber receives two directories — one in late winter, one in the spring — and is listed in one. For $16, subscribers receive both directories but no listing. 12006 111th Ave., Suite 12, Youngtown, AZ 85363 (phone: 602-972-2186).

World Wide Exchange: The $45 annual membership fee includes one listing (for house, yacht, or motorhome) and three guides. 1344 Pacific Ave., Suite 103, Santa Cruz, CA 95060 (phone: 408-476-4206).

Worldwide Home Exchange Club: Handles over 1,000 listings a year worldwide. For $20 a year, you will receive two listings yearly, as well as supplements. 45 Hans Place, London SW1X OJZ, England (phone: 44-71-589-6055).

Home Exchange International (HEI), with offices in New York, Los Angeles, London, Paris, and Milan, functions in a somewhat different manner since it publishes no directory and shepherds the exchange process most of the way. Interested parties supply *HEI* with photographs of themselves and their homes, information on the type of home they want and where, and a registration fee of $50. The company then works with its other offices to propose a few possibilities, and only when a match is made do the parties exchange names, addresses, and phone numbers. For this service, *HEI* charges a closing fee, which ranges from $150 to $450 for domestic or international switches from 2 weeks to 3 months in duration, and from $275 to $525 for switches longer than 3 months. Contact *Home Exchange International,* 185 Park Row, PO Box 878, New York, NY 10038-0272 (phone: 212-349-5340), or 22458 Ventura Blvd., Woodland Hills, CA 91364 (phone: 818-992-8990).

HOME STAYS: Although travelers taking advantage of Portugal's Tourism in the Country program (see above) often come away feeling they've been one of the family, neither Spain nor Portugal offers a formal "meet the Spanish" or "meet the Portuguese" program. If the idea of actually staying in a private home as the guest of a Spanish or Portuguese family appeals to you, check with the United States Servas Committee, which maintains a list of hosts throughout the world (at present, there are about 250 listings in Spain and 18 in Portugal) willing to throw open their doors to foreigners, entirely free of charge. The aim of this nonprofit cultural program is to promote international understanding and peace, and every effort is made to discourage freeloaders. Servas will send you an application form and the name of the nearest of some 200 interviewers around the US for you to contact. After the interview, if you're approved, you'll receive documentation certifying you as a Servas traveler. There is a membership fee of $45 for an individual, and there also is a deposit of $15 to receive the host list, refunded on its return. The list gives the name, address, age, occupation, and other particulars of the hosts, including languages spoken. From then on, it is up to you to write to prospective hosts directly, and Servas makes no guarantee that you will be accommodated. If you are, you'll normally stay 2 nights.

Servas stresses that you should choose only people you really want to meet, and that for this brief period you should be interested mainly in your hosts, not in sightseeing. It also suggests that one way to show your appreciation once you've returned home is to become a host yourself. The minimum age of a Servas traveler is 18 (however, children under 18 may accompany their parents), and though quite a few are young people who have just finished college, there are travelers (and hosts) in all age ranges and occupations. Contact Servas at 11 John St., Room 706, New York, NY 10038 (phone: 212-267-0252).

You also might be interested in a publication called *International Meet-the-People Directory,* published by the *International Visitor Information Service.* It lists several agencies in a number of foreign countries (37 worldwide, 18 in Europe) that arrange home visits for Americans, either for dinner or overnight stays. To order a copy, send $4.95 to the *International Visitor Information Service* (733 15th St. NW, Suite 300, Washington, DC 20005; phone: 202-783-6540). For other local organizations and services offering home exchanges, contact the local tourist authority.

RESERVATIONS: To the extent that you are able to settle on a precise itinerary beforehand, it is best to reserve accommodations in any major Spanish or Portuguese city or resort area, even if you are traveling during the off-season. To be sure of finding space in the hotel of your choice, several months before arrival is not too soon to make the booking. Hotel rooms in the larger provincial cities also should be reserved ahead year-round. Because many of them also are important meeting centers, even off-season travelers may find hotel space scarce and "Full" signs everywhere if a large convention is being hosted. Also keep in mind that larger hotels are the ones most frequently booked as 2- and 3-day stopover centers for the thousands of tour groups ranging the Continent, and the major cities may be busiest during the off-season or shoulder months due to the simultaneous presence of business and convention travelers and tourists.

The *paradores* and *pousadas* are the accommodations that fill up fastest in Spain and Portugal, so they should be reserved well in advance no matter what time of the year you intend to visit — 3 months or more beforehand is not too soon. For the rest, the need to reserve ahead (and how far ahead) varies, depending on the season, the region, the type of accommodations desired, and the traveler's own preference for the security of fixed reservations or the flexibility of an itinerary open to spur-of-the-moment decisions. In general, reservations are recommended practically year-round for visitors to Madrid, Barcelona, and Lisbon (January and February, the slowest months, would be the exceptions), particularly for travelers wishing to stay in specific hotels. Reservations also are recommended for anyone traveling to other large cities, the coasts, and popular tourist sites from May through September. The recommendation becomes most important for anyone visiting during July and August, when not only the Spanish and Portuguese but also most Europeans take their vacations, and at other busy holiday periods, such as *Christmas* and *Easter*.

At other times, travelers who prefer to give free rein to their wanderlust will find it possible to reserve rooms as they go in both countries, although they should keep an eye on the special-events calendar to avoid arriving somewhere blissfully unaware that it is already bursting at the seams. Don't count on visiting Seville from *Holy Week* through the *Feria de Abril* (April Fair), Valencia during the *Fallas de San José,* the Portuguese *Grand Prix* in Estoril (September), or Pamplona during the *Fiesta de San Fermín* and the running of the bulls in July unless space has been reserved *well* ahead of time. Remember, too, that in the Canary Islands and Madeira, as well as at mainland ski resorts, winter is the busy season, when hotel reservations are in order.

The simplest way to make a reservation is to leave it all to a travel agent, who will provide this service at no charge if the hotels in question pay a commission. The regional hotel guides distributed by government tourist offices often use a symbol to show which establishments pay such a commission — the larger and more expensive ones invariably do, and more and more budget hotels are beginning to follow suit. If the one you selected doesn't, the travel agent may charge a fee to cover costs, or you may have to make the reservation yourself.

Reserving a room yourself is not difficult if you intend to stay mainly in hotels that are members of chains or associations, whether European ones with US representatives or American ones with hotels overseas. Most international hotel chains list their toll-free (800) reservation numbers in the white pages of the telephone directory, and any hotel of a chain can assure reservations for you at sister facilities. Naturally, the more links in the chain, the more likely that an entire stay can be booked with a minimum of letters or phone calls to one central reservations system. If booking with primarily Spanish or Portuguese establishments, either a travel agent or the Spanish or Portuguese government tourist offices will be able to tell you who in the US represents the chain or a particular hotel.

Among the well-known international hotel chains or associations with properties in Spain and Portugal, particularly in major cities, are the following:

> *Best Western:* Has over 200 properties in Spain, and about 100 in Portugal. Call 800-528-1234.
>
> *Hilton International* Owned by the Ladbroke's gambling group of Great Britain, there is no proprietary connection with the US *Hilton* chain. Has 1 property in Barcelona. Call 800-445-8667.
>
> *Holiday Inn:* Has 1 property in Lisbon. Call 800-465-4329.
>
> *Inter-Continental:* Has 1 property in Madrid and 1 in Lisbon. Call 800-327-0200.
>
> *Minotels Europe:* Has 33 properties in Spain and 13 in Portugal. Call 800-336-4668.
>
> *Sheraton:* Has 1 in Palma de Mallorca, Spain, and 2 in Portugal: 1 in Lisbon and 1 in Porto. Call 800-325-3535.
>
> *Trusthouse Forte:* Has 2 properties in Madrid and 1 property in Portugal's Algarve. Call 800-225-5843.

Among the better-known Spanish chains are *Sol Hotels* with 23 properties in Spain and *Meliá Hotels* with 16 Spanish properties. Note that the *Meliá* and *Sol* chains offer a special voucher program, which guarantees rooms at three-, four-, and five-star hotels — which usually cost as much as $275 — for $98 per night for a double room. The vouchers are available in booklets of six for $588 and are available only from travel agents and tour operators in the US. For these voucher books and reservations, contact *Petrabax Tours* (97-45 Queens Blvd., Suite 505, Rego Park, NY 11374; phone: 718-897-7272 in New York State, 800-367-6611 elsewhere in the US). Reservations also can be made through these hotel chains' US representative, *Utell International* (10605 Burt Circle, Omaha, NE 68114; phone: 800-44-UTELL).

Among other large European chains who have a US office that will provide information and take reservations are *Pullman International,* a group of approximately 200 hotels, with 1 property in Spain (Madrid) and 2 in Portugal (Lisbon and Lagos). *Pullman* has a US representative(200 W. 57th St., New York, NY 10019; phone: 212-757-6500 or 800-223-9862). Reservations for all *Pullman* properties also can be made through *Utell International* (address above). *Novotel,* with approximately 238 3-star hotels throughout Europe, has 5 properties in Spain and Portugal. The *Hoteles Tryp* has a number of properties in Madrid and is represented in the US by *Bravo Tours* (182 Main St., Ridgefield Park, NJ 07660; phone: 201-641-0655 in New Jersey; 800-272-8674 elsewhere in the US).

Note, finally, that *Marketing Ahead* (433 Fifth Ave., New York, NY 10016; phone: 212-686-9213), the US reservations service for both the *paradores* of Spain and the *pousadas* of Portugal, also represents numerous other independent hotels in Spain and Portugal, and that there are several other stateside reservations services for individual Spanish and Portuguese hotels. The Spanish and Portuguese tourist offices should be able to tell you who in the US represents a particular property.

Hotels that are not represented in the US will have to be contacted directly. All the hotels entries in the *Best in Town* sections of THE CITIES chapters include phone numbers for reservations; phone numbers also are included in the *Checking In* sections of DIRECTIONS. If you choose to write rather than telephone, it's a good idea to enclose at least two International Reply Coupons (sold at post offices and banks) to facilitate a response and to leave *plenty* of time for the answer. Give full details of your requirements and several alternate dates, if possible. You probably will be asked to send a deposit for at least 1 night's lodging, payable by check or credit card; in return, be sure to get written confirmation of your reservation and a receipt for any deposit.

Nevertheless, if the hotel you want to visit has no rooms available on your chosen dates, take heart. The advice to make reservations early always is woven into every travel article; making a *late* reservation may be almost as good advice. It's not at all unusual for hotel rooms, totally unavailable as far as 6 months ahead, to suddenly become available a week to a day before your desired arrival. Cancellations tend to occur closer to, rather than farther from, a designated date. One possible strategy is to make reservations at another hotel so you won't be left high and dry, determine the cancellation penalties, if any, and check back with your first choice closer to your date of arrival. It also is true that hotels that report SRO status to travel agents may remarkably discover a room if you call directly (FAX is even better) close to your proposed arrival date.

There also is reason to believe that hotels increasingly are offering one rate to travelers working through travel agents and less expensive rates to clients who book directly. Even if you do use a travel agent, it sounds like a prudent course to double-check hotel rates if saving money is one of your prime travel concerns.

Some people prefer not to inhibit their wanderlust by making hotel reservations too far in advance. Although the advice still stands to reserve high-season hotel space well beforehand, and although the traveler must keep an eye on the special-events calendar to avoid arriving *anywhere* blissfully unaware that the place is already bursting at the seams, it is possible to travel in Spain and Portugal reserving as you go. Naturally, the best method is to call ahead to hotels in the next town on your itinerary before checking out of the one you're in because it allows you to alter your course if you don't turn up any vacancies. (Hotels usually will hold rooms on the strength of a phone call provided you arrive no later than expected.)

Though not all travelers would face the prospect of arriving in a strange city without a reservation with equal *sangfroid,* throughout Europe there are services that help book rooms for those who risk it. In Spain and Portugal, these services are located at airports and train stations. It is best to arrive at these counters as early in the day as possible; at the latest, be there when they open for the afternoon — even still there are no guarantees that you will find what you're looking for when your turn comes. Note that local tourist offices in Spain and Portugal, unlike those in some other European countries, do not book accommodations, although they can be expected to be helpful in providing information on rooms in the vicinity.

OVERBOOKING: Although the problem is not unique to Spain and Portugal, the worldwide travel boom has brought with it some abuses that are pretty much standard operating procedure in any industry facing a demand that frequently outstrips the supply. Anticipating a certain percentage of no-shows, hotels routinely overbook rooms. When cancellations don't occur and everybody with a confirmed reservation arrives as promised, it's not impossible to find yourself with a valid reservation for which no room exists.

There's no sure way to avoid all the pitfalls of overbooking, but you can minimize the risks. Always carry evidence of your confirmed reservation. This should be a direct communication from the hotel — to you or your travel agent — and should specify the exact dates and duration of your accommodations and the price. The weakest form of confirmation is the voucher slip a travel agent routinely issues, since it carries no official indication that the hotel itself has verified your reservation.

Even better is the increasing opportunity to guarantee hotel reservations by giving the hotel (or its reservation system) your credit card number and authorizing the hotel to charge you for that room no matter what. Although many European hotels have strict rules regarding refunds — which apply to both prepaid (written) and credit card (phoned in) deposits — it still *may* be possible to cancel if you do so before 6 PM (before 4 PM in some areas) on the day of your reservation. The best course is to check the establishment's policy when making the reservations, and if it does cancel under this arrangement, make sure you get a cancellation number to protect you from being billed erroneously.

If all these precautions fail and you are left standing at the front desk with a reservation the hotel clerk won't honor, you have a last resort: Complain as long and as loudly as necessary to get satisfaction! The person who makes the most noise usually gets the last room in the house. It might as well be you.

What if you can't get reservations in the first place? This problem often confronts businesspeople, who can't plan months ahead. The word from savvy travelers is that a bit of currency (perhaps attached discreetly to a business card) often increases your chances with recalcitrant desk clerks. There are less venal ways of improving your odds, however. If you are traveling on business, ask an associate at your destination to make reservations for you.

There is a good reason to do this above and beyond the very real point that a resident has the broadest knowledge of local hotels. Often a hotel will appear sold out on its computer when in fact a few rooms are available. The proliferation of computerized reservations has made it unwise for a hotel to indicate that it suddenly has five rooms available (from cancellations) when there might be 30 or 40 travel agents waiting for them in the computer. That small a number of vacancies is much more likely to be held by the hotel for its own sale, so a local associate is an invaluable conduit to these otherwise inaccessible rooms. Another efficient alternative is direct communciation with the hotel via a FAX machine, which can prove useful in arranging and confirming reservations.

Dining Out

For the North American abroad, no aspect of going native is as easy as exploring the cuisine and the rites of table according to the custom of the country. A nation, a region, or even a town can make an irrefutably individual declaration in the very way it brings together the products of the local farms and gardens. Wherever you go, stick to what is indigenous; nine times out of ten, the best cooking will be that closest to "home" — wherever you happen to be. Often your most personal view of a people will be at a table. By sticking to the native traditions, you will discover an intimate aspect of a nation's character and pride.

In non-English-speaking countries, such as Spain and Portugal, you will often have the frustrating experience of being presented with a menu that might be written in Martian, for all you understand. An excellent pocket-size guide available in bookstores is the Berlitz *European Menu Reader,* which will help you decode menus in 14 languages, including Spanish and Portuguese. It is available from Berlitz Publishing (866 Third Ave., New York, NY 10022; phone: 800-526-8047) for $5.95, plus about $1.50 postage and handling.

The sunbaked cooking of the Mediterranean derives its appeal from an array of flavorful ingredients simply prepared and presented. Olive oil, garlic, tomato, basil, wild thyme, and fish and shellfish of every description are the staples. *Bacalhau* dishes are more complex versions of and almost as famous as the Marseilles fish soup of saffron, garlic, tomato, and seafood called bouillabaisse. Not surprisingly, Mediterranean fish soup has many names: In Spain it is called *zarzuela;* in Portugal, a seafood bisque is called *sopa de mariscos.* Fish, in fact, is a staple of Portuguese cuisine, although variations include combinations of seafood and meat. *Bacalhau à moda da Pousada do Castelo,* for example, is a famous Portuguese dish made with codfish scrambled with eggs and olives, named after the *Pousada do Castelo* at Obidos, the very first of Portugal's *pousadas* to be built in a historic castle. Also try *carne de porco a alentejana,* a pork dish made with clams in a coriander sauce — a Portuguese favorite.

There is more to the kitchens of Spain and Portugal, however, than the Mediterranean Sea. The best and easiest entrée into the amenities of Spanish life would be a visit to a *tapas* bar, where the dozens of appetizers — from bits of sausage and cheese to stewed game birds and pickled vegetables — are downed with slices of the dry-cured ham called *serrano* and *copitas* (small wine glasses) full of *fino* (dry) sherry. Spanish cooking at its best is a matter of fresh ingredients simply prepared; two examples are the garlic soup of central Spain and gazpacho, made from the early ripening tomatoes, peppers, and other vegetables. The expensive golden spice, saffron, though not exactly a staple, appears with rice in the national chicken and rice dish *arroz con pollo* and in the traditional dish of shellfish and chicken on a bed of saffron rice known as paella.

But aside from a few comparatively rare gastronomic highs, your best meals will be found in the bistros and inns of Spain and Portugal, wherever the fare is simple and caters to local tastes. Seeking these places out will do much to enhance your enjoyment of a Spanish or Portuguese trip, for it is by an accumulation of these intimacies that you look into a nation's heart. For a more detailed discussion of culinary delights and customs, see PERSPECTIVES, and for our list of Spain and Portugal's finest restaurants, see *The Best Restaurants of Spain and Portugal,* DIVERSIONS.

Time Zones, Business Hours, and Public Holidays

 TIME ZONES: The countries of Europe fall into three time zones. Greenwich Mean Time — the time in Greenwich, England, at longitude 0'0' — is the base from which all other time zones are measured. Areas in zones west of Greenwich have earlier times and are called Greenwich Minus; those to the east have later times and are called Greenwich Plus. For example, New York City — which falls into the Greenwich Minus 5 time zone — is 5 hours earlier than Greenwich, England.

Portugal is in the Greenwich Mean Time zone — which means that the time in Portugal is the same as it is in Greenwich, England, and when it is noon in Lisbon, it is 7 AM in New York and Washington, DC. However, time in the Azores is 1 hour earlier than on mainland Portugal. Spain (including the Canary Islands) falls into the Greenwich Plus 1 time zone (or Central European Time) — which means that the time is 1 hour later than it is in Greenwich, England, and when it is noon in Madrid, it is 6 AM in New York.

Like most western European nations, Spain and Portugal move their clocks ahead an hour in late spring and an hour back in the fall, although in both cases the date of the change tends to be about a week earlier (in spring) and a week later (in fall) than the dates we have adopted in the US. For about 2 weeks a year, then, the time difference between the US and Spain and Portugal is 1 hour more or less than usual.

Spanish, Portuguese, and other European timetables use a 24-hour clock to denote arrival and departure times, which means that hours are expressed sequentially from 1 AM. By this method, 9 AM is recorded as 0900, noon as 1200, 1 PM as 1300, 6 PM as 1800, midnight as 2400, and so on. For example, the departure of a train at 7 AM will be announced as "0700"; one leaving at 7 PM will be noted as "1900."

BUSINESS HOURS: Throughout Spain and Portugal, most businesses and shops are open Mondays through Fridays from 9 AM to 1 or 2 PM, and then from 3 or 4 PM until 7 or 8 PM. Many shops also are open on Saturdays from 9 AM to 1 PM. In small towns and villages, shops may close on one weekday at 1 PM; others may skip the early closing and simply not open on Mondays (or another day of the week). Larger stores in shopping centers generally stay open through midday and may close as late as 9 PM.

Banking hours in Spain are weekdays, from 9 AM to 2 PM, usually without a break for lunch; on Saturdays banks remain open only until 1 PM (although they may not have Saturday hours during the summer). In Portugal, weekday banking hours are from 8:30 to 3 PM,; certain branches in Lisbon have late hours from 6 to 11 PM on weekdays. Most banks in both countries are closed on Sundays and public holidays, although major airport banks may be open 7 days a week.

Restaurant hours are similar to those in the US. Most restaurants are open all week during the high season and close 1 day each week during the off-season — the day varies from restaurant to restaurant. Hours in general also tend to be a bit later in summer, and they vary from city to city; check local listings in THE CITIES and DIRECTIONS.

PUBLIC HOLIDAYS: In Spain, the public holidays are *New Year's Day* (January 1); *Epiphany* (January 6); *St. Joseph's Day* (March 19); *Maundy Thursday* (March 28); *Good Friday* (March 29); *Labor Day* or *May Day* (May 1); *Feast of Santiago* (July 25); *Assumption Day* (August 15); *Spain's National Day* (October 12); *All Saints' Day* (November 1); *Constitution Day* (December 6); *Immaculate Conception* (December 8);

Christmas Day (December 25). Note that, as of this year, *Corpus Christi* (May 30) no longer is an official public holiday, although many businesses still may close for religious observances.

In Portugal, they are *New Year's Day* (January 1); *Good Friday* (March 29); *Liberty Day* (April 25); *Labor Day* or *May Day* (May 1); *Corpus Christi* (May 30); *Portugal's and Camões Day* (June 10); *St. Anthony's Day* (June 13); *Corpus Christi* (June 17); *Assumption Day* (August 15); *Republic Day* (October 5); *All Saints' Day* (November 1); *Restoration of Independence* (December 1); *Immaculate Conception* (December 8); *Christmas Day* (December 25).

For information on holidays celebrated throughout Spain and Portugal, see "Special Events" in this section, as well as in each of THE CITIES.

Mail, Telephone, and Electricity

 MAIL: Before you leave home, fill in a "change of address card" (available at post offices), which is the form you need to get the post office to hold your mail until your return. If you are planning an extended stay abroad, you can have your first class mail forwarded to your vacation address. There generally is no charge for this service. (Note that many post offices will need 2 to 3 weeks' notice to put this change of address into effect.)

There are several places that will receive and hold mail for travelers in Spain and Portugal. Mail sent to you at a hotel and clearly marked "Guest Mail, Hold for Arrival" is one safe approach. Spanish and Portuguese post offices also will extend this service to you if the mail is addressed to the equivalent of US general delivery — called *Lista de Correos* in Spain and *Posta Restante* in Portugal. This probably is the best way for travelers to have mail sent if they do not have a definite address. Have your correspondents print your last name in big block letters on the envelope (lest there be any doubt as to which is your last name), and as there often are several post office locations in major cities, it is important that the address and/or specific name of the office be indicated (not just the name of the city), in addition to the words *Lista de Correos* or *Posta Restante.* Be sure to call at the correct office when inquiring about mail. Also, don't forget to take your passport with you when you go to collect it. Most Spanish and Portuguese post offices require formal identification before they will release anything; there also may be a small charge for picking up your mail.

If you are an American Express customer (a cardholder, a carrier of American Express traveler's checks, or traveling on an *American Express Travel Service* tour) you can have mail sent to its offices in cities along your route; letters are held free of charge — registered mail and packages are not accepted. You must be able to show an American Express card, traveler's checks, or a voucher proving you are on one of the company's tours to avoid paying for mail privileges. Those who aren't clients must pay a nominal charge each time they inquire if they have received mail, whether or not they actually have a letter. There also is a forwarding fee, for clients and non-clients alike. Mail should be addressed to you, care of American Express, and should be marked "Client Mail Service." Additional information on its mail service and addresses of American Express offices in Spain and Portugal are contained in the pamphlet *Services and Offices,* available from any US branch of American Express.

US embassies and consulates abroad do not accept mail for tourists. They will, however, help out in emergencies — if you need to receive important business documents or personal papers, for example. It is best to inform them either by separate letter or cable, or by phone (particularly if you are in the country already), that you will be using their address for this purpose.

Post offices in Spain are open weekdays from 9 AM to 1 PM and from 4 PM to 8 PM. Some branches also are open on Saturdays from 9 AM to 12:30 or 1 PM. In Portugal, they usually are open Mondays through Saturdays from 9 AM to 5:30 PM.

As in the US, letters can be mailed in letter boxes found on the street, but it is better to mail them (and certainly packages) directly from post offices. In Spain, mailboxes are mustard yellow with a red stripe. In Portugal, the mailboxes are red and mushroom shaped with *correio* printed on them. Mail rates change frequently following the upward trend of everything else; stamps (*sellos* in Spain; *sêlo* in Portugal) can be bought at the post office and at authorized tobacconists (called *estanco* in Spain; *tabacaria* in Portugal).

Mailing a letter or package, however, is not as straightforward as in the US. Post offices have different windows for each step in the procedure (one window to buy stamps, another to weigh a package, and so on), and standing in line for service may take a while. Another possibility is that some of the better stores in Spain can arrange to mail your purchases directly for you.

Be advised that delivery from Spain and Portugal can be slow (especially if you send something any distance by surface mail) and erratic (postcards often are given lowest priority, so don't use them for important messages). Send your correspondence via air mail if it's going any distance, and to ensure or further speed delivery of important letters, send them registered mail or express or special delivery.

If your correspondence is important, you may want to send it via one of the special courier services: *Federal Express, DHL,* and other international services are available in Spain and Portugal. The cost is considerably higher than sending something via the postal services — but the assurance of its timely arrival is worth it.

If you're mailing to an address within Spain or Portugal, another way to ensure or speed delivery is to use the postal code. Including a postal code in an address will help to speed a letter to its destination, and since small towns in Spain and Portugal may have similar names, the postal code always should be specified — delivery of a letter may depend on it. Put it on the envelope immediately after the name of the town or city and on the same line. If you do not have the correct postal code, call the appropriate tourism authority (see *Tourist Information Offices,* in this section, for telephone numbers) — they should be able to look it up for you. Alternatively, you could call the addressee directly — if you have the telephone number — and although this will be costly, it may be worth it to ensure delivery of your correspondence.

TELEPHONE: If you are planning to be away for more than a month, you may be able to save money by asking the telephone company to temporarily suspend your home telephone service. You also can arrange to have your calls transferred to another number.

The Spanish and Portuguese telephone systems are not too different from our own. They include direct dialing, operator-assisted calls, collect calls, reduced rates for certain times of the day and days of the week, and so on. The number of digits varies considerably within the country, and to further confuse matters, a city code may be included in the digits quoted as the "local" number. If you dial a number directly and your call does not go through, either the circuits are busy or you may need to add or delete one or several digits. If you have tried several times and are sure that you have the correct number, have an international operator place the call — however, this will be more expensive than dialing directly. (To reach an international operator in the US, dial "0" for a local operator and ask him or her to connect you.)

It is easy enough to call Spain or Portugal from the US: Just dial the international access code (011) + the country code (34 for Spain; 351 for Portugal) + the city code (if you don't know this, ask the international operator) + the local number. For example, to place a call from anywhere in the US to Madrid, dial 011 + 34 + 1 (the city code for Madrid) + the local number; to call Lisbon, dial 011 + 351 + 1 (the city code for Lisbon) + the local number.

The procedure for making a station-to-station call from Spain or Portugal to the US (usually a more expensive proposition) is similar to the procedure described above. To call a number in the US from Spain or Portugal, dial 097 (the international access code) + 1 (the US country code) + the US area code + the local number. For instance, to call a number in New York City from Spain or Portugal, dial 097 + 1 + 212 + the local number.

To make a call from Spain to Portugal: dial 009 (the European international access code) + 351 (the country code for Portugal) + the city code + the local number. To make a call from Portugal to Spain: dial 00 (the European international access code) + 34 (the country code for Spain) + the city code + the local number.

For calling from one Spanish city to another, dial 9 + the city code + the local number; and for calls within the same city code coverage area, simply dial the local number. For calling from one Portuguese city to another, the procedure is the same, except that the city code is proceeded by 0, so you would dial 0 + the city code + the local number, or if making a local call, simply dial the local number. Note that Spanish and Portuguese telephone directories and other sources may include the 9 (in Spain) and the 0 (in Portugal), which should be used only for dialing within these countries; when dialing from the US, follow the procedure described above, *leaving off the 9 or the 0.*

If you don't know the city code, check the front of a telephone book (if calling within Spain or Portugal) or ask an opertor. To reach a local operator in Spain, dial 0; when in Portugal, dial 13. To reach an international operator in Spain, also dial 0 for a local operator who can connect you; in Portugal, dial 098 for an international operator (again, you also can dial 13 for a local operator who can connect you). For information on calling for help in the event of an emergency, see *Medical and Legal Aid and Consular Services,* in this section.

Making connections in Europe sometimes can be hit or miss — all exchanges are not always in operation on the same day. If the number dialed does not go through, try later or the next day. So be warned: Those who have to make an important call — to make a hotel reservation in another city, for instance — should start to do so a few days ahead.

Pay telephones in Spain and Portugal are located much as in the US — in restaurants, hotel lobbies, booths on the street, and at most tourist centers. A local call from a pay phone in Spain costs 10 pesetas, 20 escudos in Portugal. A useful tip: Coins are fed into a slot at the top of the phone box and automatically drop down as the price of your call increases. It pays to use more coins than you think you may need to avoid being cut off during your conversation. If you insert over 10 pesetas or 20 escudos (which is the minimum charge) any unused pesetas or escudos will be returned at the end of the call.

Although the majority of Iberian pay phones still take coins, phones that take specially designated phone cards are increasingly common in Portugal. Instituted to cut down on vandalism, the phone cards free callers from the necessity of carrying around a pocketful of change, and are sold in various escudo or centavo denominations. The units per card, like message units in US phone parlance, are a combination of time and distance. To use such a card, insert it into a slot in the phone and dial the number you wish to reach. A display gradually will count down the value that remains on your card. When you run out of units on the card, you can insert another.

In Portugal, pay phones that take phone cards generally are found in metropolitan areas and in major tourism areas, particularly on the coast. Phone cards can be purchased at post offices or at national phone company offices. Note that, as we went to press, pay phones that take phone cards had not yet been introduced in Spain, but it is likely that the Spanish will follow this Europe-wide trend in the near future.

A lot of digits may be involved once a caller starts dialing beyond national borders, but avoiding operator-assisted calls can cut costs considerably and bring rates into a somewhat more reasonable range — except for calls made through hotel switchboards. One of the most unpleasant surprises travelers encounter in many foreign countries is the amount they find tacked on to their hotel bill for telephone calls, because foreign hotels routinely add on astronomical surcharges. (It's not at all uncommon to find 300% or 400% added to the actual telephone charges.) A practice initially begun to cover the expense of installing phone equipment and maintaining multilingual personnel to run it around the clock, it now is firmly entrenched as a profit making operation for many hotels.

Until recently, the only recourse against this unconscionable overcharging was to call collect when phoning from abroad or to use a telephone credit card — available through a simple procedure from any local US phone company. (Note, however, that even if you use a telephone credit card, some hotels still may charge a fee for line usage). Now *American Telephone and Telegraph (AT&T)* offers *USA Direct,* a service that connects users, via a toll-free number, with an *AT&T* operator in the US, who then will put a call through at the standard international rate. A new feature of this service is that travelers abroad can reach US toll-free (800) numbers by calling a *USA Direct* operator, who will connect them. Charges for all calls made through *USA Direct* appear on the caller's regular US phone bill. (As we went to press, this service was available in Spain only when calling from special *USA Direct* telephones that can be found at some airports, hotels, and phone centers; the service was not yet offered in Portugal.) For a brochure and wallet card listing toll-free numbers by country, contact International Information Service, *AT&T Communications,* 635 Grand St., Pittsburgh, PA 15219 (phone: 800-874-4000).

It's wise to ask about surcharge rates *before* calling from a hotel. If the rate is high, it's best to use a telephone credit card, or the direct-dial service described above (if you are in Spain); make a collect call; or place the call and ask the party to call right back. If none of these choices is possible, make international calls from the local post office or special telephone center to avoid surcharges. Another way to keep down the cost of telephoning from Spain or Portugal is to leave a copy of your itinerary and telephone numbers with people in the US so that they can call you instead.

Frequent business travelers to Spain and Portugal may want to look into corporate membership in *AT&T*'s Language Line Service. By calling a US toll-free number, employees of member companies will be connected with an interpreter in any one of 143 languages and dialects, who will provide on-line interpretive services for $3.50 a minute. From the US, this service is particularly useful for booking travel services in Europe where English is not spoken or not fluently spoken — such as Spain and Portugal. Once in Europe — this number can be reached by using the USA Direct toll-free (800) number connection feature described above. As we went to press, *AT&T* had no plans to open membership to individual travelers, however, if you require such a service, it may be worth contacting them at the time you plan to travel. For further information, contact *AT&T* at the address above.

■ **Note:** For quick reference, you might want to get a copy of a helpful pamphlet, *The Phone Booklet,* which lists the nationwide, toll-free (800) numbers of travel information sources and suppliers — such as major airlines, hotel and motel chains, car rental companies, and tourist information offices. Send $2 for postage and handling to *Scott American Corporation,* Box 88, West Redding, CT 06896.

ELECTRICITY: The US runs on 110-volt, 60-cycle alternating current; Spain and Portugal run on 220- or 240-volt, 50-cycle alternating current. Note that in some remote areas of Portugal 110-volt current still may be in use. (Some large tourist hotels also *may* offer 110-volt currency for your convenience — but don't count on it.) The difference between US and Spanish and Portuguese voltage means that, without a converter, at 220 volts the motor of a US appliance used overseas would run at twice the speed at which it's meant to operate and would quickly burn out.

Travelers can solve the problem by buying a lightweight converter to transform foreign voltage into the US kind (there are two types of converters, depending on the wattage of the appliance) or by buying dual-voltage appliances, which convert from one to the other at the flick of a switch (hair dryers of this sort are common). The difference between the 50- and 60-cycle currents will cause no problem — the American appliance simply will run more slowly — but it still will be necessary to deal with differing socket configurations before plugging in. To be fully prepared, bring along an extension cord (in older or rural establishments the electrical outlet may be farther from the sink than the cord on your razor or hair dryer can reach), and a wall socket adapter kit with a full set of plugs to ensure that you'll be able to plug in anywhere.

One good source for sets of plugs and adapters for use worldwide is the *Franzus Company* (PO Box 142, Beacon Falls, CT 06403; phone: 203-723-6664). *Franzus* also publishes a useful brochure, *Foreign Electricity Is No Deep Dark Secret,* which provides information about converters and adapter plugs for electric appliances to be used abroad but manufactured for use in the US. To obtain a free copy, send a self-addressed, stamped envelope to *Franzus* at the above address; a catalogue of other travel accessories is available on request.

Medical and Legal Aid and Consular Services

MEDICAL AID ABROAD: Nothing ruins a vacation or business trip more effectively than sudden injury or illness. You will discover, in the event of an emergency, that most tourist facilities — transportation companies, hotels, and resorts — are equipped to handle the situation quickly and efficiently. Most towns and cities of any size have a public hospital, and even the tiniest of villages has a medical clinic or private physician nearby. All hospitals are prepared for emergency cases, and many hospitals also have walk-in clinics to serve people who do not really need emergency service, but who have no place to go for immediate medical attention. The level of medical care in Spain and Portugal, especially in the larger cities, generally is quite good, providing the same basic specialties and services that are available in the US.

Before you go, be sure to check with your insurance company about the applicability of your policy while you're abroad; many policies do not apply, and others are not accepted in Spain and Portugal. Older travelers should know that Medicare does not make payments outside the US. If your medical policy does not protect you while you're traveling, there are comprehensive combination policies specifically designed to fill the gap. (For a discussion of medical insurance and a list of inclusive combination policies, see *Insurance,* in this section.)

If a bona fide emergency occurs, the fastest way to get attention may be to take a taxi to the emergency room of the nearest hospital. An alternative is to dial the free national "emergency" number used to summon the police, fire trucks, and ambulances — 091 in Spain, 115 in Portugal.

Most emergency services send out well-equipped and well-staffed ambulances, although ambulances in Spain and Portugal may not be equipped with the advanced EMS technology found in the US and may provide only basic medical attention and be used mainly for transportation. Since ambulance dispatchers often are accustomed to taking calls from doctors only, state immediately that you are a foreign tourist and then describe the nature of your problem and your location. In Spain and Portugal, however, the ambulance dispatcher probably will not be bilingual, and unless you speak Spanish or Portuguese, he or she will be unable to determine the nature of the emergency, what equipment will be needed, or even where to send the ambulance. Travelers with little or no foreign language ability should try to get someone else to make the call. If the situation is desperate, an international operator may be able to make the call to the local emergency service and stay on the line as interpreter. To reach an international operator in Spain, dial 0 for a local operator who will connect you; in Portugal, dial 098 (or dial 13 for a local operator who can connect you).

Both Spain and Portugal have socialized medicine. There are two types of hospitals in Spain and Portugal: public and private. Medical services at *policlinicas* (the same word in both languages), or clinics which are for less serious medical matters, are free (or relatively inexpensive) for Portuguese and Spanish citizens, but foreign travelers will have to pay full fees for such service. There may not be an English-speaking health worker there, however, and you can't just walk in off the streets; you need to make an appointment. Although private local services are the preferred option, in an extreme medical emergency, US military hospitals on bases in Rota, Morón, Torrejon de Ardez, and Zaragoza in Spain, and Lajes in Portugal, may treat travelers (of any nationality) who are seriously ill or injured until their conditions are stabilized — assuming that the US hospital has the facilities for the treatment required — and then transfer the patient to other hospitals.

If a doctor is needed for something less than an emergency, there are several ways to find one. If you are staying in a hotel or motel, ask for help in reaching a doctor or other emergency services, or for the house physician, who may visit you in your room or ask you to visit an office. (This service is apt to be expensive, especially if the doctor makes a "house" call to your room.) Travelers staying at a hotel of any size probably will find that the doctor on call speaks at least a modicum of English — if not, request one who does. When you register at a hotel, it's not a bad idea to include your home address and telephone number; this will facilitate the process of notifying friends, relatives, or your own doctor in case of an emergency.

Dialing the nationwide emergency number (091 in Spain; 115 in Portugal) also may be of help. Callers often will be given the name of a general practitioner, since private doctors, usually specialists, may see patients upon referral only. For the seriously ill or injured traveler, however, it is best to see a private doctor. It's usually possible to find one without referral from a general practitioner through a US consulate (see addresses and phone numbers below) or directly through a hospital, especially if it is an emergency. If you already are at the hospital, you may see the specialist there, or you may make an appointment to be seen at his or her office.

In addition, though general practitioners deliver primary care, there is no violation of protocol in approaching a specialist directly. Call the appropriate department of a teaching hospital or the US Embassy (address and phone number below), which also maintains a list of doctors. Remember that if you are hospitalized you will have to pay, even in an emergency.

Emergency dental care also is available throughout Spain and Portugal (again, see the front page of the local telephone directory), although travelers are strongly advised to have a dental checkup some weeks before the trip to allow time for any necessary work to be done. Again, any US consul also can provide a list of English-speaking dentists in the area the consulate serves.

There should be no problem finding a 24-hour drugstore (called *farmacias* in both Spain and Portugal) in any major city. In Spain, a pharmacy is identified by a red cross and is part of a network within a city, so that there always should be a drugstore somewhere that is open. In Portugal, as there is no easily recognizable sign to identify a pharmacy, you will have to watch for the word *farmácia*. In many areas, night duty rotates among pharmacies, closed pharmacies generally will have a sign in the window telling you the location of the pharmacy staying open for 24 hours on that day. In both Spain and Portugal, the name and address follows the words *farmacia du servicos.* A call to the emergency room of the local hospital also may produce this information. In small towns, where none may be open after normal business hours, you may be able to have one open in an emergency situation — such as a diabetic needing insulin — although you may be charged a fee for this off-hour service.

Bring along a copy of any prescription you may have from your doctor in case you should need a refill. In the case of minor complaints, Spanish or Portuguese pharmacists may do some prescribing and *may* fill a foreign prescription; however, do not count on this. In most cases, you will need a local doctor to rewrite the prescription. Even in an emergency, a traveler will more than likely be given only enough of a drug to last until a local prescription can be obtained. As "brand" names vary in different countries, it's a good idea to ask your doctor for the generic names of any drugs you use so that you can ask for their equivalents should you need a refill.

Americans also will notice that some drugs sold only by prescription in the US are sold over the counter in Spain and Portugal (and vice versa). Though this can be very handy, be aware that common cold medicines and aspirin that contain codeine or other controlled substances will not be allowed back into the US.

Emergency assistance also is available from the various medical programs designed for travelers who have chronic ailments or whose illness requires them to return home. The *Medic Alert Foundation* sells identification emblems which specify that the wearer has a health condition that may not be readily apparent to a casual observer. A heart condition, diabetes, epilepsy, or a severe allergy are the sorts of things that these emblems were developed to communicate — conditions that can result in tragic errors if not recognized when emergency treatment is necessary and when you may be unable to speak for yourself. In addition to the identification emblems, the foundation maintains a computerized central file from which your complete medical history is available 24 hours a day by telephone (the phone number is clearly inscribed on the ID badge). The one-time membership fee, between $25 and $45, is tax deductible and is based on the type of metal from which the emblem is made — the choices ranging from stainless steel to 10K gold-filled. For information, contact the *Medic Alert Foundation,* Turlock, CA 95381-1009 (phone: 800-ID-ALERT or 209-668-3333).

International SOS Assistance also offers a program to cover medical emergencies while traveling. Members are provided with telephone access — 24 hours a day, 365 days a year — to a worldwide, monitored, multilingual network of medical centers. A phone call brings assistance ranging from a telephone consultation to transportation home by ambulance or aircraft, and in some cases transportation of a family member to wherever you are hospitalized. The service can be purchased for 2 weeks ($25), 2 weeks plus additional days ($25, plus $2.50 for each additional day), 1 month ($50), or a year ($195). For information, contact *International SOS Assistance,* PO Box 11568, Philadelphia, PA 19116 (phone: 800-523-8930 or 215-244-1500).

The *International Association of Medical Assistance to Travellers (IAMAT)* provides its members with a directory of affiliated medical centers in over 140 countries (over 500 cities, including 21 centers in Spain and 19 in Portugal) to call for a list of participating doctors. Participating physicians agree to adhere to a basic charge of around $30 to see a patient referred by *IAMAT.* A nonprofit organization, *IAMAT* appreciates donations; for $25, you will receive a set of worldwide climate charts detailing weather and sanitary conditions. Delivery of this material can take up to 5 weeks, so plan ahead. Contact *IAMAT,* 417 Center St., Lewiston, NY 14092 (phone: 716-754-4883).

The *International Health Care Service* provides information about health conditions in various foreign countries, as well as a variety of travel-related health services. A pre-travel counseling and immunization package costs $185 for the first family member and $165 for each additional member; a post-travel screening is $75 to $135, plus lab work. Appointments are required for all services. Contact the *International Health Care Service* (New York Hospital–Cornell Medical Center, 440 E. 69th St., New York, NY 10021; phone: 212-472-4284). *The International Health Care Travelers Guide,* a compendium of facts and advice on health care and diseases around the world, can be obtained by sending $4.50 and a self-addressed, stamped envelope to PO Box 210 at the address above.

Those who return home ill with a condition they suspect is travel related and beyond the experience of their regular physician should consider seeing a specialist in travel medicine. For information on finding such a specialist in your area, see *Staying Healthy,* in this section.

For a thorough description of the medical services in Spain's and Portugal's larger cities, see *Traveling Healthy,* by Sheilah M. Hillman and Robert S. Hillman, MD. Although it is out of print, it may be in the library.

Practically every phase of health care — before, during, and after a trip — is covered in *The New Traveler's Health Guide* by Drs. Patrick J. Doyle and James E. Banta. It is available for $4.95, plus $2.50 postage and handling, from Acropolis Books Ltd., 80 S. Early St., Alexandria, VA 22304 (phone: 800-451-7771 or 703-709-0006).

LEGAL AID AND CONSULAR SERVICES: There is one crucial place to keep in mind when outside the US, namely, the American Services section of the United States consulate. If you are injured or become seriously ill, the consulate will direct you to medical assistance and notify your relatives. If, while abroad, you become involved in a dispute that could lead to legal action, the consulate, once again, is the place to turn.

It usually is far more alarming to be arrested abroad than at home. Not only are you alone among strangers, but the punishment can be worse. Granted, the US Consulate can advise you of your rights and provide a list of English-speaking lawyers, but it cannot interfere with the local legal process. Except for minor infractions of the local traffic code, there is no reason for any law-abiding traveler to run afoul of immigration, customs, or any other law enforcement authority.

The best advice is to be honest and law-abiding. If you get a traffic ticket, pay it. If you are approached by drug hawkers, ignore them. The penalties for possession of hashish, marijuana, cocaine, and other narcotics are even more severe abroad than in the US. (If you are picked up for any drug-related offense, do not expect US foreign service officials to be sympathetic. Chances are they will notify a lawyer and your family and that's about all. See "Drugs," below.)

In the case of minor traffic accidents, it often is most expedient to settle the matter before the police get involved. If, however, you are involved in a serious accident, where an injury or fatality results, the first step is to contact the nearest US consulate (addresses below) and ask the consul to locate a lawyer to assist you. If you have a traveling companion, ask him or her to call the consulate (unless either of you has a local contact who can help you quickly). Competent lawyers practice throughout Europe, and it is possible to obtain good legal counsel on short notice.

The US Department of State in Washington, DC, insists that any American citizen who is arrested abroad has the right to contact the US embassy or consulate "immediately," but it may be a while before you are given permission to use a phone. Do not labor under the illusion, however, that in a scrape with foreign officialdom, the consulate can act as an arbitrator or ombudsman on an American citizen's behalf. Nothing could be farther from the truth. Consuls have no power, authorized or otherwise, to subvert, alter, or contravene the legal processes, however unfair, of the foreign country in which they serve. Nor can a consul oil the machinery of a foreign bureaucracy or provide legal advice. The consul's responsibilities do encompass "welfare duties" including providing a list of lawyers and information on local sources of legal aid, informing relatives in the US, and organizing and administrating any defense monies sent from home. If a case is tried unfairly or the punishment seems unusually severe, the consul can make a formal complaint to the authorities. For questions about Americans arrested abroad, how to get money to them, and other useful information, call the *Citizens Emergency Center* of the Office of Special Consular Services in Washington, DC, at 202-647-5225. (For further information about this invaluable hot line, see below.)

Other welfare duties, not involving legal hassles, cover cases of both illness and destitution. If you should get sick, the US consul can provide names of doctors and dentists as well as the names of all local hospitals and clinics; the consul also will contact family members in the US and help arrange special ambulance service for a flight home. In a situation involving "legitimate and proven poverty" — of an American stranded abroad without funds — the consul will contact sources of money (such as family or friends in the US), apply for aid to agencies in foreign countries, and in a last resort — which is *rarely* — arrange for repatriation at government expense, although this is a loan that must be repaid. And in case of natural disasters or civil unrest, consulates around the world handle the evacuation of US citizens if it becomes necessary.

The consulate is not occupied solely with emergencies and is certainly not there to aid in trivial situations, such as canceled reservations or lost baggage, no matter how important these matters may seem to the victimized tourist. The main duties of any consulate are administering statutory services, such as the issuance of passports and visas; providing notarial services; distributing VA, social security, and civil service benefits to resident Americans; taking depositions; handling extradition cases; and reporting to Washington the births, deaths, and marriages of US citizens living within the consulate's domain.

We hope that none of the information in this section will be necessary during your stay in Spain and Portugal. If you can avoid legal hassles altogether, you will have a much more pleasant trip. If you become involved in an imbroglio, the local authorities may spare you legal complications if you make clear your tourist status. And if you run into a confrontation that might lead to legal complications developing with a citizen or with local authorities, the best tactic is to apologize and try to leave as gracefully as possible. Do not get into fights with residents, no matter how belligerent or provocative they are in a given situation.

Following are the US embassies and consulates in Spain and Portugal. Note that mailing addresses may be different — so call before sending anything to these offices. (Note that we have included the phone number prefixes — 9 for Spain and 0 for Portugal — as you are most likely to dial these numbers once in these countries; if calling from the US, leave off the 9 or 0.)

Spain
Barcelona: US Consulate, 33 Via Layetana, Barcelona 08003 (phone: 93-319-9550).
Bilboa: 11-3 Avenida del Ejercito, Bilboa 48014 (phone: 94-475-8300).
Madrid: US Embassy, 75 Calle Serrano, Madrid 28006 (phone: 91-577-4000).

Portugal
Lisbon: US Embassy, Avenida das Forcas Armadas, Lisbon 1600 (phone: 01-726-6600).
Ponta del Gada: US Consulate, Avenida D. Henrique, Ponta del Gada 09406 (phone: 09-622216).
Porto: US Consulate, 826 Rua Júlio Dinis, Porto 4000 (phone: 02-63094).

You also can obtain a booklet with addresses of most US embassies and consulates around the world by writing the Superintendent of Documents, US Government Printing Office, Washington, DC 20402, and asking for publication #78-77, *Key Offices of Foreign Service Posts.*

As mentioned above, the US State Department operates a Citizens Emergency Center, which offers a number of services to American travelers abroad and their families at home. In addition to giving callers up-to-date information on trouble spots, the center will contact authorities abroad in an attempt to locate a traveler or deliver an urgent message. In case of illness, death, arrest, destitution, or repatriation of an American citizen on foreign soil, it will relay information to relatives at home if the consulate is unable to do so. Travel advisory information is available 24 hours a day to people with Touch-Tone phones (phone: 202-647-5225). Callers with rotary phones can get information at this number from 8:15 AM to 10 PM (eastern standard time) on weekdays; 9 AM to 3 PM on Saturdays. For emergency calls, from 8:15 AM to 10 PM weekdays, and 9 AM to 3 PM Saturdays, call 202-647-5225. For emergency calls only, at all other times, call 202-634-3600 and ask for the duty officer.

Drinking and Drugs

DRINKING: It is more than likely that some of the warmest memories of a trip to Spain or Portugal will be moments of conviviality shared over a drink in a neighborhood bar or sunlit café. Visitors will find that liquor, wine, and brandies in Spain and Portugal are distilled to the same proof and often are the same labels as those found at home. However, Spanish and Portuguese beer tends to be about 5% higher in alcoholic content than beer brewed in the US.

You'll want to try each country's specialties. Spanish and Portuguese beer and wine are favorites in the respective country's bars and cafés. Spanish beer (*cerveza*) is served ice cold in three varieties; regular, light (*dorada*), and dark (*negra*). Most Spanish bars, cafés, and *cervecerias* (taverns specializing in beer and wine) serve beer in bottles and on tap. *San Miguel* and *Aguila* are popular national brands, while others (*Cruz Campo* in Seville and *Alhambra* in Grenada) are sold regionally. Draft beer is *cerveza de barril.* Portuguese beer (*cerveja*) also is served cold in a *cervejaria,* or tavern. *Sagres* is a popular national brand, available in regular, light (*leve*), and dark (*preta*). Draft beer is called *cerveja fino.*

Spanish and Portuguese wines are as world-renowned as they are varied, with each region boasting its own specialty. The most famous Spanish wine is *jerez* (sherry), served either *manzanillas* (very dry) or *amontillados* (sweet) as an aperitif; or *fino* (dry) or *olorosos* (very sweet) as an after-dinner drink. Portuguese *vinho verde,* or green wine, is a clear and refreshing, light, young "white" wine (8% to 14% alcohol). *Calares,* a full, smooth red; *bucelas,* a dry, fresh white, and *sangría,* a red wine and brandy fruit punch, are other popular favorites. (For a more thorough discussion of Spanish and Portuguese beverages, see *Food and Drink,* PERSPECTIVES, and *Visitable Vineyards,* DIVERSIONS.)

Spanish and Portuguese bars and cafés open at 8:30 AM or earlier to serve coffee and breakfast, although alcohol generally is not served until at least 10 AM. Most remain open until midnight, but others may stay open until as late as 4 AM.

The legal age for drinking in Portugal is 18, though it is not strictly enforced. In Spain, there is no established minimum drinking age. The rule of thumb generally is at the discretion of the establishment — in some cases, the bartender.

As in the US, national taxes on alcohol affect the prices of liquor in Spain and Portugal, and, as a general rule, mixed drinks — especially imported liquors such as whiskey and gin — are more expensive than at home. If you like a drop before dinner, a good way to save money is to buy a bottle of your favorite brand at the airport before leaving the US and enjoy it in your hotel before setting forth. Both countries allow a liter or more of hard liquor or one bottle of wine to be brought in duty-free.

Visitors to Spain may bring in 1 bottle of wine and 1 bottle of liquor per person duty-free; the duty-free limit for entering Portugal is 2 bottles of wine and 1 bottle of liquor. If you are buying any quantity of alcohol (such as a case of wine) in Spain or Portugal and traveling through other European countries on your route back to the US, you will have to pass through customs and pay duty at each border crossing, so you might want to arrange to have it shipped home. Whether bringing it with you or shipping, you will have to pay US import duties on any quantity over the allowed 1 liter (see *Customs and Returning to the US,* in this section).

■ **A warning:** When setting off for an evening including some serious drinking, leave your car behind and make alternate plans for getting back to the hotel; otherwise choose a "designated driver" in your party who will stick strictly to soft drinks. Aside from the obvious danger in which you place yourself and others on the road, there are strict laws against drunk driving throughout Spain and Portugal, and they are zealously enforced — confiscation of the driver's license, high fines, and even imprisonment are common penalties.

DRUGS: Illegal narcotics are as prevalent in Spain and Portugal as in the US, but the moderate legal penalties and vague social acceptance that marijuana has gained in the US have no equivalents in either Spain or Portugal. Due to the international war on drugs, enforcement of drug laws is becoming increasingly strict throughout the world. Local narcotics officers and customs officials are renowned for their absence of understanding and lack of a sense of humor — especially where North Americans are involved.

Opiates and barbiturates, and other increasingly popular drugs — "white powder" substances like heroin and cocaine — are as pervasive a problem throughout Europe as in the US. The main drawback to buying any illegal drug (besides the obvious health hazards) is the inherent risk of getting locked up. Most European countries — including Spain and Portugal — have toughened laws regarding illegal drugs and narcotics, and these laws do not distinguish between types of drugs — possession of marijuana, cocaine, heroin, and other narcotics are treated with equal severity. Don't assume that you're safe in carrying even small amounts of controlled substances for "personal use" — particularly for foreigners, the maximum penalties may be imposed for possessing even *traces* of illegal drugs. There is a high conviction rate in these cases, and bail for foreigners is rare.

The best advice we can offer is this: Don't carry, use, buy, or sell illegal drugs. The dangers are clear enough when indulging in your own home; if taking drugs while traveling, you may not only endanger your own life but also put your fellow travelers in jeopardy. And if you get caught, you may end up spending your hard-earned travel funds on bail and attorney's fees — and still wind up in jail. There isn't much that the American consulate can do for drug offenders beyond providing a list of lawyers. Having broken a local law, an offender puts his or her fate in the hands of the local authorities.

Those who carry medicines that contain a controlled drug should be sure to have a current doctor's prescription with them. Ironically, travelers can get into almost as much trouble coming through US customs with over-the-counter drugs picked up abroad that contain substances that are controlled in the US. Cold medicines, pain relievers, and the like often have codeine or codeine derivatives that are illegal, except by prescription, in the US. Throw them out before leaving for home.

■ **Be forewarned:** US narcotics agents warn travelers of the increasingly common ploy of drug dealers asking travelers to transport a "gift" or other package back to the US. Don't be fooled into thinking that the protection of US law applies abroad — accused of illegal drug trafficking, you will be considered guilty until you prove your innocence. In other words, do not, under any circumstances, agree to take anything across the border for a stranger.

Tipping

Throughout both Spain and Portugal (as in most of the rest of Europe), you will find the custom of including some kind of service charge as part of a meal more common than in North America. This can confuse Americans not familiar with the custom. On the one hand, many a traveler, unaware of this policy, has left many a superfluous tip. On the other hand, travelers aware of this policy may make the mistake of assuming that it takes care of everything. It doesn't. While "service included" in theory eliminates any question about how much and whom to tip, in practice there still are occasions when on-the-spot tips are appropriate. Among these are tips to show appreciation for special services, as well as tips meant to say "thank you" for services rendered. So keep a pocketful of 100 peseta bills (or coins) and/or 100 escudo bills and 50 escudo coins ready, and hand these denominations out like dollar bills (100 pesetas equals about $1 US; 140 escudos equals $1 US).

In Spanish and Portuguese restaurants, the service charge (called *servicio incluido* in Spain; *servicça incluido* in Portugal) may appear in one of two ways: It either already is calculated in the prices listed or will be added to the final bill. For the most part, if you see a notation at the bottom of the menu without a percentage figure, the charge should be included in the prices; if a percentage figure is indicated, the service charge has not yet been added. To further confuse the issue, not every restaurant notes if its policy is to include service and at what point the charge is added. If you are at all unsure, you should feel no embarrassment about asking a waiter.

This service charge generally ranges from 15% to 20%. In the rare instance where it isn't added, a 15% tip — just as in the US — usually is a safe figure, although one should never hesitate to penalize poor service or reward excellent and efficient attention by leaving less or more. If the tip has been added, no further gratuity is expected — though it's a common practice in Spain and Portugal to leave a few extra coins on the table. The emphasis is on *few,* and the equivalent of $1 (about 100 pesetas or 140 escudos) usually is quite adequate.

Although it's not necessary to tip the maître d' of most restaurants — unless he has been especially helpful in arranging a special party or providing a table (slipping him something in a crowded restaurant *may* get you seated sooner or procure a preferred table) — when tipping is desirable or appropriate, the least amount should be the local equivalent of $5 (about 500 pesetas or 700 escudos). In the finest restaurants, where a multiplicity of servers are present, plan to tip 5% to the captain. The sommelier (wine waiter) is entitled to a gratuity of approximately 10% of the price of the bottle.

When eating at a self-service, take-out, or fast-food establishment where you pay at the cash register, generally no tip is necessary. There also is virtually no tipping in bars or cafés — unless you become something of a regular and care to offer the barman an occasional drink. It is not uncommon, however, to leave a few pence for a barmaid, and for those served at a table in a bar or cocktail lounge, a small gratuity — of a few hundred escudos or pesetas (depending on the tab) — is usual for the server.

In allocating gratuities at a restaurant, pay particular attention to what has become the standard credit card charge form, which now includes separate places for gratuities for waiters and/or captains. If these separate boxes are not on the charge slip, simply ask the waiter or captain how these separate tips should be indicated. Be aware, too, of the increasingly common, devious practice of placing the amount of an entire restaurant bill (in which service already has been included) in the top box of a charge slip, leaving the "tip" and "total" boxes ominously empty. Don't be intimidated: Leave the "tip" box blank and just repeat the total amount next to "total" before signing.

As in restaurants, visitors usually will find a service charge of 10% to 15% included in their final bill at most Spanish and Portuguese hotels. No additional gratuities are required — or expected — beyond this billed service charge. It is unlikely, however, that a service charge will be added to bills in small family-run guesthouses or other modest establishments. In these cases, guests should let their instincts be their guide; no tipping is expected by members of the family who own the establishment, but it is a nice gesture to leave something for others — such as a dining room waiter or a maid — who may have been helpful. A gratuity of $1 (about 100 pesetas or 140 escudos) per night is adequate in most cases.

If a hotel does not automatically add a service charge, it is perfectly proper for guests to ask to have an extra 10% to 15% added to their bill, to be distributed among those who served them. This may be an especially convenient solution in a large hotel, where it's difficult to determine just who out of a horde of attendants actually performed particular services.

For those who prefer to distribute tips themselves, a chambermaid generally is tipped at the rate of $1 per day — 700 pesetas a week in Spain, around 1,000 escudos a week in Portugal. Tip the concierge or hall porter for specific services only, with the amount of such gratuities dependent on the level of service provided. If you leave your shoes outside the room at night for a shine, give the hall porter a couple hundred of escudos or pesetas when you next see him. If you order from room service, 140 escudos (Portugal) or 100 pesetas (Spain) to the waiter for each delivery is sufficient. For other special services, such as personal deliveries, the tip depends on the service rendered, but in most cases, several hundred escudos or pesetas is more than sufficient.

Bellhops, doormen, and porters at hotels and transporation centers generally are tipped at the rate of $1 (100 pesetas or 140 escudos) per piece of luggage, along with a small additional amount if a doorman helps with a cab or car. Once upon a time, taxi drivers in Europe would give you a rather odd look if presented with a tip for a fare, but times have changed, and 10% to 15% of the amount on the meter is now a standard gratuity.

Tipping ushers in a movie house, theater, or concert hall used to be the rule, but is becoming less common — the best policy is to check what other patrons are doing and follow suit. Most of the time, the program is not free, and in lieu of a tip it is common practice to purchase a program from the person who seats you. Sightseeing tour guides also should be tipped. If you are traveling in a group, decide together what you want to give the guide and present it from the group at the end of the tour. If you have been individually escorted, the amount should depend on the degree of your satisfaction, but it should not be less than 10% and easily could be as high as 50% of the total tour fee. Museum and monument guides also usually are tipped, and it is a nice touch to tip a caretaker who unlocks a small church or turns on the lights in a chapel for you in some out-of-the-way town.

In barbershops and beauty salons, tips also are expected, but the percentages vary according to the type of establishment. Since the prices usually are quite a bit higher in expensive salons (particularly in metropolitan areas), no more than 10% is common; in less expensive establishments, a 15% or 20% tip is in order. (As a general rule the woman who washes your hair should get an additional small tip.) The washroom attendants in these places, or wherever you see one, should get a small tip — they usually set out a little plate with a coin already on it indicating the suggested denomination. Don't forget service station attendants, for whom about 50 pesetas or 70 escudos for cleaning the windshield or other attention is not unusual.

Tipping always is a matter of personal preference. In the situations covered above, as well as in any others that arise where you feel a tip is expected or due, feel free to express your pleasure or displeasure. Again, never hesitate to reward excellent and efficient attention and to penalize poor service. Give an extra gratuity and a word of thanks when someone has gone out of his or her way for you. Either way, the more personal the act of tipping, the more appropriate it seems. And if you didn't like the service — or the attitude — don't tip.

Shopping

Browsing through the department stores, boutiques, street markets, small shops, and crafts centers of Spain and Portugal undoubtedly will be one of the highlights of your trip. Visitors from the US may not be quite as enthusiastic about prices as they might have been a few years ago, as prices throughout Europe have risen dramatically. But there still is plenty of value left for the money and enough quality and craftsmanship to make many an item irresistible. To help steer visitors toward the best, several sections of this book are devoted to shopping. In THE CITIES, individual city reports include a list of specific stores and markets, as well as descriptions of special shopping streets where they exist. And sections in DIVERSIONS describe not only where to find antiques and other collectibles, but also — for those who have yet to experience a particularly stimulating form of acquisition — how to buy them at auctions.

HOW TO SHOP AND WHAT TO BUY: The goods are enticing, but even so, top-quality items are not necessarily less expensive in a fashionable boutique in the capital city of the country from wich they came than they are in an equally fashionable US store. To be sure, do some homework before you go and arrive prepared with a list of the things you want — as specific as possible, with brands or labels — and the cost of each in the US. In some cases, you will find it less expensive to buy abroad, but frequently it is not, and knowing the difference is crucial to a productive shopping foray. On arrival, it still is necessary to comparison shop as much as time permits, bearing in mind that articles can be less costly the closer you get to the point of manufacture, and usually least expensive of all at the factory that makes the item — if it sells to the public. Visitors will get a better price at small factories and shops, for example, than in major cities and towns.

On the whole, your eye and your fancy will be your guide. Note that the Spanish and Portuguese are particularly known for their colorful, hand-painted tiles, their lovingly sewn handicrafts, and their dazzling array of ceramics. The diversity of Spain's regions is particularly evident in the country's wide range of ceramic styles. Over 700 years of Arab influence is clearly evident in ceramic designs of the southern regions; wall plates are enameled and trimmed in 24-karat gold. Spanish porcelains, particularly the Lladró figurines, are collectors' items, and Spanish ceramic and porcelain tableware and giftware are well made and exported worldwide. Portuguese artisans mold earthenware and ceramics into works of art, as do modern Portuguese manufacturing plants, producing whimsical pottery, elegant porcelains, and gleaming crystal befitting any table.

Tiles are everywhere; on churches, restaurants, palaces, storefronts, homes, and shops. They capture the bright colors and sunny vistas that are so much a part of Spain's and Portugal's landscape and heritage. *Azulejos,* uniquely Portuguese tiles, can be found throughout the country. Handwoven rugs, both designer-quality and functional, as well as hand-made sweaters and intricate embroideries symbolizing a national pride lovingly worked at for centuries can be found throughout both countries. Leather goods are subtle, soft, and a good value. Majórica pearls, from Spain, carry a worldwide 10-year guarantee. Fine gold jewelry, by law, is 18 karat.

Fashion ranges from very basic handicraft sweaters and clothing to haute couture. Spain's designers have a flair for fashion and experiment with styling and color, and their clothes have emerged as strong rivals to French and Italian creators. Spanish fashion has become provocatively alluring, yet it keeps a classical line.

Both Spain and Portugal are excellent hunting grounds for antiques, with a wide range of dealers, auction houses, and non-commercial institutions that offer many items at bargain prices.

Budget travelers need not feel cheated by the limits of their purse. Flea markets abound to delight the poor, the thrifty, the just plain stingy, and admirers of bric-a-brac. Department stores are not as ubiquitous as they are in the US, but two Spanish chains, *El Corte Inglés* and *Galerías Preciados,* carry authentic Spanish souvenirs — that's where many Spaniards buy everything from cosmetics and toiletries to household furnishings, kitchenware, tableware, toys, school supplies, electronics, sporting goods, and clothing. There are no equally well known chains in Portugal, but in Lisbon, for example, there is *Centro Comercial das Amoreiras,* a post-modern complex rather like a mall in the US, with 300 shops; at the other end of the scale is the *Feira da Ladra,* or Thieves Market, which is a flea market well worth investigating. Other large towns and cities will have equally interesting, if more modest, venues for bargains and souvenirs.

VALUE ADDED TAX: Commonly abbreviated as VAT, this is a tax levied by various European countries, including Spain and Portugal, and added to the purchase price of most goods and services. The standard VAT (known as IVA in Iberia and ITE in the Canary Islands) in Spain is 12% on most purchases and 6% on food, with the higher rate of 33% applying to luxury goods such as watches, jewelry, furs, glass, and cameras (food and transportation exempt). In Portugal, the IVA is 17% (slightly higher in the Azores and Madeira), but only 30% on luxury items.

The tax is intended for residents (and already is included in the price tag), but visitors are required to pay it, too, unless they have purchases shipped directly to an address abroad by the store. If visitors pay the tax and take purchases with them, however, they generally are entitled to a refund under a retail export scheme that has been in operation in both countries for several years. In the past, returning travelers have complained of delays in receiving the refunds and of difficulties in converting checks written in foreign currency into dollars, but a new service — *Exencion del Inpuesto* In Spain, or *IVA Refund* in Portugal — has recently been introduced that greatly streamlines the procedure.

In order to qualify for a refund, you must purchase a minimum of 10,000 pesetas ($100 US) or 10,000 escudos (about $71 US) at one store (purchases from several stores cannot be combined). In most cases, stores will provide the appropriate refund forms on request. If the store does not have this form, it can be obtained at the refund office at the airport, which also can provide information on the procedure for submitting the paperwork to obtain the refund. Visitors leaving Spain or Portugal must have all of their receipts for purchases and refund vouchers stamped by customs; as customs officials may well ask to see the merchandise, it's a good idea not to pack it in the bottom of your suitcase. Refund checks are sent out within about 1 month of receipt of the vouchers, and refunds by credit card also generally appear on the cardholder's statement within 1 month of receipt.

A VAT refund by dollar check or by credit to a credit card account is relatively hassle-free. If it arrives in the form of a foreign currency check and if the refund is less than a significant amount, charges imposed by US banks for converting foreign currency refund checks — which can run as high as $15 or more — could make the whole exercise hardly worth your while.

Far less costly is sending your foreign currency check (after endorsing it) to *Ruesch International,* which will covert it to a check in US dollars for a $2 fee (deducted from the dollar check). Contact *Ruesch International* at one of the following address: 3 First

National Plaza, Suite 2020, Chicago, IL 60602 (phone: 312-332-5900); 1925 Century Park E., Suite 240, Los Angeles, CA 90067 (phone: 213-277-7800); 608 Fifth Ave., "Swiss Center," New York, NY 10020 (phone: 212-977-2700); and 1350 Eye St. NW, 10th Floor and street level, Washington, DC 20005 (phone: 800-424-2923 or 202-408-1200).

DUTY-FREE SHOPS: If common sense says that it always is less expensive to buy goods in an airport duty-free shop than to buy them at home or in the streets of a foreign city, travelers should be aware of some basic facts. Duty-free, first of all, does not mean that the goods travelers buy will be free of duty when they return to the US. Rather, it means that the shop has paid no import tax acquiring goods of foreign make because the goods are not to be used in the country where the shop is located. This is why duty-free goods are available only in the restricted, passengers-only area of international airports or are delivered to departing passengers on the plane. In a duty-free store, travelers save money only on goods of foreign make because they are the only items on which an import tax would be charged in any other store. There usually is no saving on locally made items, although in countries such as Spain and Portugal that impose VAT taxes (see above) that are refundable to foreigners, the prices in airport duty-free shops also are minus this tax, sparing travelers the often cumbersome procedures they otherwise have to follow to obtain a VAT refund.

Beyond this, there is little reason to delay buying locally made merchandise and/or souvenirs until reaching the airport. In fact, because airport duty-free shops usually pay high rents, the locally made goods sold in them may well be more expensive than they would be in downtown stores. The real bargains are foreign goods, but — let the buyer beware — not all foreign goods automatically are less expensive in an airport duty-free shop. You can get a good deal on even small amounts of perfume, costing less than the usually required minimum purchase, tax-free. Other fairly standard bargains include spirits, smoking materials, cameras, clothing, watches, chocolates and other food and luxury items — but first be sure to know what these items cost elsewhere. Terrific savings do exist (they are the reason for such shops, after all), but so do overpriced items that an unwary shopper might find equally tempting. In addition, if you wait to do your shopping at airport duty-free shops, you will be taking the chance that the desired item is out of stock or unavailable.

Duty-free shops are located in most major international airports throughout Europe. In Spain, there duty-free shops at airports in Alicante, Barcelona, Girona, Ibiza, Madrid, Mahón, Málaga, Palma de Mallorca, Seville, and Valencia. In Portugal, they are located at the Lisbon and Porto airports.

■ **Buyer Beware:** You may come across shops *not* at airports that call themselves duty-free shops. These require shoppers to show a foreign passport but are subject to the same rules as other stores, including paying import duty on foreign items. What "tax-free" means in the case of these establishments is something of an advertising strategy: They are announcing loud and clear that they do, indeed, offer the VAT refund service — sometimes on the spot (minus a fee for higher overhead). Prices may be no better at these stores and could be even higher due to the addition of this service.

Religion on the Road

 Spain and Portugal are predominantly Catholic and every town, right down to the most isolated village, has its own church. In larger, more heavily populated areas, some amount of religious variety is reflected in the churches of other denominations, Jewish synagogues, and an occasional mosque or temple.

The surest source of information on religious services in an unfamiliar country is the desk clerk of the hotel or guesthouse in which you are staying; the local tourist information office, an American consul, or a church of another religious affiliation also may be able to provide this information. If you aren't in an area with services held in your own denomination, you might find it interesting to attend the service of another religion. You also might enjoy attending a service in a foreign language — even if you don't understand all the words. There are many beautiful churches in Spain and Portugal, and whether in a large city cathedral or a small parish church, visitors are welcome.

Customs and Returning to the US

 Whether you return to the United States by air or sea, you must declare to the US customs official at the point of entry everything you have bought or acquired while in Europe. The customs check can go smoothly, lasting only a few minutes, or can take hours, depending on the officer's instinct. To speed up the process, keep all your receipts handy and try to pack your purchases together in an accessible part of your suitcase. It might save you from unpacking all your belongings.

DUTY-FREE ARTICLES: In general, the duty-free allowance for US citizens returning from abroad is $400, provided your purchases accompany you and are for personal use. This limit includes items used or worn while abroad, souvenirs for friends, and gifts received during the trip. A flat 10% duty based on the "fair retail value in country of acquisition" is assessed on the next $1,000 worth of merchandise brought in for personal use or gifts. Amounts over $1,400 are dutiable at a variety of rates. The average rate for typical tourist purchases is about 12%, but you can find out rates on specific items by consulting *Tariff Schedules of the United States* in a library or at any US Customs Service office.

Families traveling together may make a joint declaration to customs, which permits one member to exceed his or her duty-free exemption to the extent that another falls short. Families also may pool purchases dutiable under the flat rate. A family of three, for example, would be eligible for up to a total of $3,000 at the 10% flat duty rate (after each member had used up his or her $400 duty-free exemption) rather than three separate $1,000 allowances. This grouping of purchases is extremely useful when considering the duty on a high-tariff item, such as jewelry or a fur coat.

There are certain articles, however, that are duty-free only up to certain limits. Individuals are allowed 1 carton of cigarettes (200), 100 cigars, and 1 liter of liquor or wine if over 21. Alcohol above this allowance is liable for both duty and an Internal Revenue tax. Antiques, if they are 100 or more years old and you have proof from the seller of that fact, are duty-free, as are paintings and drawings if done entirely by hand.

To avoid paying duty twice, register the serial numbers of foreign-made watches and electronic equipment with the nearest US Customs bureau before departure; receipts of insurance policies also should be carried for other foreign-made items. (Also see the note at the end of *Entry Requirements and Documents,* in this section.)

Gold, gold medals, bullion, and up to $10,000 in currency or negotiable instruments may be brought into the US without being declared. Sums over $10,000 must be declared in writing.

Personal exemptions can be used once every 30 days; in order to be eligible, an individual must have been out of the country for more than 48 hours. If any portion of the exemption has been used once within any 30-day period or if your trip is less than 48 hours long, the duty-free allowance is cut to $25.

The allotment for individual "unsolicited" gifts mailed from abroad (no more than one per day per recipient) has been raised to $50 retail value per gift. These gifts do not have to be declared and are not included in your duty-free exemption (see below). Although you should include a receipt for purchases with each package, the examiner is empowered to impose a duty based on his or her assessment of the value of the goods. The duty owed is collected by the US Postal Service when the package is delivered (also see below). More information on mailing packages home from abroad is contained in the US Customs Service pamphlet *International Mail Imports* (see below for where to write for this and other useful brochures).

CLEARING CUSTOMS: This is a simple procedure. Forms are distributed by airline or ship personnel before arrival. (Note that a $5-per-person service charge — called a user fee — is collected by airlines and cruise lines to help cover the cost of customs checks, but this is included in the ticket price.) If your purchases total no more than the duty-free $400 limit, you need only fill out the identification part of the form and make an oral declaration to the customs inspector. If entering with more than $400 worth of goods, you must submit a written declaration.

Customs agents are businesslike, efficient, and not unkind. During the peak season, clearance can take time, but this generally is because of the strain imposed by a number of jumbo jets simultaneously discharging their passengers, not because of unwarranted zealousness on the part of the customs people.

Efforts to streamline procedures used to include the so-called Citizens' Bypass Program, which allowed Americans whose purchases were under $400 to go to the "green line," where they simply showed their passports to the customs inspector. Note, however, that as we went to press, this procedure was being abandoned at international airport terminals in the US. In a return to an earlier system, American citizens arriving from overseas now have to go through a passport check by the Immigration & Naturalization Service (INS) prior to recovering their baggage and proceeding to customs. (US citizens will not be on the same line as foreign visitors, however, though this additional wait does delay clearance on re-entry into the US.) Although all passengers have to go through this obligatory passport inspection, those entering with purchases under $400 may be spared a thorough customs inspection, although inspectors still retain the right to search any luggage they choose — so don't do anything foolish.

It is illegal not to declare dutiable items; not to do so, in fact, constitutes smuggling, and the penalty can be anything from stiff fines and seizure of the goods to prison sentences. It simply isn't worth doing. Nor should you go along with the suggestions of foreign merchants who offer to help you secure a bargain by deceiving customs officials in any way. Such transactions frequently are a setup, using the foreign merchant as an agent of US customs. Another agent of US customs is TECS, the Treasury Enforcement Communications System, a computer that stores all kinds of pertinent information on returning citizens. There is a basic rule to buying goods abroad, and it should never be broken: *If you can't afford the duty on something, don't buy it.* Your list or verbal declaration should include all items purchased abroad, as well as gifts received abroad, purchases made at the behest of others, the value of repairs, and anything brought in for resale in the US.

Do not include in the list items that do not accompany you, i.e., purchases that you have mailed or had shipped home. As mentioned above, these are dutiable in any case, even if for your own use and even if the items that accompany your return from the same trip do not exhaust your $400 duty-free exemption. It is a good idea, if you have accumulated too much while abroad, to mail home any personal effects (made and bought in the US) that you no longer need rather than your foreign purchases. These personal effects pass through customs as "American goods returned" and are not subject to duty.

If you cannot avoid shipping home your foreign purchases, however, the US Customs Service suggests that the package be clearly marked "Not for Sale," and that a copy of the bill of sale be included. The customs examiner usually will accept this as indicative of the article's fair retail value, but if he or she believes it to be falsified or feels the goods have been seriously undervalued, a higher retail value may be assigned.

FORBIDDEN ITEMS: Narcotics, most plants, and many types of food are not allowed into the US. Drugs are totally illegal, with the exception of medication prescribed by a physician. It's a good idea not to travel with too large a quantity of any given prescription drug (however, in the event that a pharmacy is not open when you need it, bring along several extra doses) and to have the prescription on hand in case any question arises either abroad or when reentering the US.

Any sculpture that is part of an architectural structure, any authentic archaeological find, or other artifacts may not be exported from Spain without the permission of the Spanish Ministry of the Interior; for information on items that might fall into this category, contact the Spanish customs office in Madrid (phone: 1-254-3200). In Portugal, such exportatation is regulated by the Ministry of Culture in Lisbon (phone: 1-732821 or 1-767022). If you do not obtain prior permission of the proper regulatory agencies, such items will be confiscated at the border, and you will run the risk of being fined or imprisoned.

Tourists have long been forbidden to bring into the US foreign-made US trademarked articles purchased abroad (if the trademark is recorded with customs) without written permission. It's now possible to enter with one such item in your possession as long as it's for personal use.

Customs implements the rigorous Department of Agriculture regulations concerning the importation of vegetable matter, seeds, bulbs, and the like. Living vegetable matter may not be imported without a permit, and everything must be inspected, permit or not. The exceptions include dried bamboo, beads made of most seeds, mushrooms, truffles, nuts, seeds, seashells, shamrocks, spices, straw articles, canned or processed vegetables, and some plants.

Other processed foods and baked goods usually are okay. Regulations on meat products generally depend on the country of origin and manner of processing. As a rule, commercially canned meat, hermetically sealed and cooked in the can so that it can be stored without refrigeration, is permitted, but not all canned meat fulfills this requirement. Be careful when buying European-made pâté, for instance. Goose liver pâté in itself is acceptable, but the pork fat that often is part of it, either as an ingredient or a rind, is not. Even canned pâtés may not be admitted for this reason. (The imported ones you see in US stores have been prepared and packaged according to US regulations.)

Customs also enforces federal laws that prohibit the entry of articles made from the furs or hides of animals on the endangered species list. Beware of shoes, bags, and belts made of crocodile and certain kinds of lizard, and anything made of tortoiseshell; this also applies to preserved crocodiles, lizards, and turtles sometimes sold in gift shops. And if you're shopping for big-ticket items, beware of fur coats made from the skins of spotted cats. They are sold in Europe, but they will be confiscated upon your return to the US, and there will be no refund. For information about animals on the endangered species list, contact the Department of the Interior, US Fish and Wildlife Service (Office of Management Authority, PO Box 27329, Washington, DC 20038-7329; phone: 202-343-5634), and ask for the free publication *Facts About Federal Wildlife Laws.*

For information about transporting plants or wildlife, write to *Quarantines,* US Department of Agriculture (Federal Bldg., Hyattsville, MD 20782), or get in touch with the Animal and Plant Health Inspection Service office nearest your home (check under the US Department of Agriculture listings in your telephone book).

The US Customs Service publishes a series of free pamphlets with customs information. It includes *Know Before You Go,* a basic discussion of customs requirements pertaining to all travelers; *International Mail Imports; Travelers' Tips on Bringing Food, Plant, and Animal Products into the United States; Importing a Car; GSP and the Traveler; Pocket Hints; Currency Reporting; Pets, Wildlife, US Customs; Customs Hints for Visitors (Nonresidents);* and *Trademark Information for Travelers.* For the entire series or individual pamphlets, write to the US Customs Service (PO Box 7407, Washington, DC 200440, or contact any of the seven regional offices, in Boston, Chicago, Houston, Los Angeles, Miami, New Orleans, and New York. The Customs Service has a tape-recorded message whereby callers using Touch-Tone phones can get more information on various topics; the number is 202-566-8195. These pamphlets provide great briefing material, but if you still have questions when you're in Spain or Portugal, you can contact the customs representative at the US embassy in either country (see *Medical and Legal Aid and Consular Services,* above, for addresses).

Sources and Resources

Tourist Information Offices

The National Tourist Office of Spain and the Portuguese National Tourist Office in North America generally are the best sources of travel information, and most of their many, varied publications are free for the asking. For the best result, request general information on specific provinces or cities in which you are interested, as well as publications relating to your particular areas of interest: accommodations, restaurants, special events, sports, guided tours, and facilities for specific sports. There is no need to send a self-addressed, stamped envelope with your request, unless this requirement is specified. Offices generally are open on weekdays during normal business hours.

The following is a list of the North American offices of the National Tourist Office of Spain and the Portuguese National Tourist Office:

National Tourist Office of Spain
Chicago: Water Tower Place, 845 N. Michigan Ave., Chicago, IL 60611 (phone: 312-642-1992).

New York: 665 Fifth Ave., New York, NY 10022 (phone: 212-759-8822).

Los Angeles: San Vincente Plaza Bldg., 8383 Wilshire Blvd., Suite 960, Beverly Hills, CA 90211 (phone: 213-658-7188).

Miami: 1221 Brickell Ave., Suite 1850, Miami, FL 33131 (phone: 305-358-1992).

Canada: 102 Bloor St. W., 14th Fl., Toronto, Ontario M5S 1M8, Canada (phone: 416-961-3131 or 416-961-4079).

Portuguese National Tourist Office
New York: 590 Fifth Ave., New York, NY 10036-4704 (phone: 212-354-4403).

Canada: 500 Sherbrooke St. W., Suite 930, Montreal, Quebec H3A 3C6 (phone: 514-843-9328); 4120 Yonge St., Suite 414, Willowdale, Ontario M2P 2B8 (phone: 416-250-7580).

The best places for tourist information in Spanish and Portuguese cities are listed in the individual reports in THE CITIES. Below is a list of Spanish and Portuguese tourist authorities in Spain and Portugal. The US offices above are best equipped to handle written or telephone inquiries from potential visitors on this side of the Atlantic. Once abroad, these local offices are good sources of specific information for their respective regions. Note that the telephone numbers given are for dialing from another city within either Spain or Portugal; when dialing these numbers from the US, disregard the preceding 9 for Spanish numbers, or the preceeding 0 for those in Portugal. (For further information on calling procedures, see *Mail, Telephone, and Electricity,* earlier in this section.)

IN SPAIN

ANDALUSIA
Algeciras: Avenida de la Marina (phone: 956-600911).
Almería: 4 Calle Hermanos Machado, Edificio Servicios Múltiples (phone: 951-230858 or 951-233549).
Baeza: Plaza del Pópulo (phone: 953-740444).
Benalmádena-Costa: Carretera de Cádiz, Km 229 (phone: 952-442494).
Cádiz: 1 Calderón de la Barca (phone: 956-211313).
Córdoba: 10 Calle Torrijos (phone: 957-471235)
Granada: 19 Casa de los Tiros (phone: 958-225990).
Huelva: 5 Vázquez López (phone: 955-257403).
Jaén: 10 Avenida de Madrid (phone: 953-222737).
La Linea de la Concepción: Avenida Veinte de Abril (phone: 956-769950).
Málaga: 5 Marqués de Larios (phone: 952-213445).
Ronda: 1 Plaza de España (phone: 952-871272).
Seville: 21 Avenida de la Constitución (phone: 95-422-1404).
Torremolinos: 517 Bajos de los Nogalera (phone: 952-381578).
Ubeda: Plaza de los Caídos (phone: 953-750897).

ARAGON
Canfranc: 3 Avenida Fernando El Católico (phone: 974-373141).
Huesca: 23 Coso Alto (phone: 974-225778).
Jaca: 2 Avenida Regimiento de Galicia (phone: 974-360098).
Teruel: 1 Tomás Nogués (phone: 974-602279).
Zaragoza: Torreón de la Zuda, Glorieta de Pio XII (phone: 976-393537).

ASTURIAS
Arenas de Cabrales: Carretera General (phone: 985-845284).
Cudillero: El Pitu (phone: 985-590118).
Gijón: 1 Marqués de San Esteban (phone: 985-346046).
Oviedo: 6 Plaza de Alfonso II El Casto (phone: 985-213385).

BALEARICS
Ibiza: 9 Bes (phone: 971-304304).
Mahón: 40 Plaza de la Esplanada (phone: 971-363700).
Palma de Mallorca: 10 Jaime III (phone: 971-712216); San Juan Airport, DP 07000 (phone: 971-260803).

BASQUE REGION
Bilbao: Alameda Manzarredo (944-236430).
Irún: Barrio de Behobia (phone: 943-622627).
San Sebastián: Miramar, Esquina a Andia (phone: 943-426762).
Vitoria: Parque de la Florida (phone: 945-131321 or 945-249564).

CANARY ISLANDS
Fuerteventura: 33 Calle Primo de Mayo, Puerto del Rosario (phone: 928-851400).
Grand Canary: Parque de Santa Catalina, Las Palmas (phone: 928-264623).
Lanzarote: Parque Municipal, Arrecife (phone: 928-811860).
La Palma: 57 Avenida Marítima, Santa Cruz de La Palma (phone: 922-411641).
Tenerife: 1 Avenida José Antonio, Santa Cruz de Tenerife (phone: 922-242090); Plaza de la Iglesia, Puerto de la Cruz (phone: 922-386000).

CANTABRIA
Santander: 1 Plaza Porticada (phone: 942-310708 or 942-310756).
Santillana del Mar: Plaza Mayor (phone: 942-818251).

CASTILE–LA MANCHA (NEW CASTILE)

Albacete: 1 Virrey Morcillo (phone: 967-215611).
Alcalá de Henares: 1 Callejón de Santa María (phone: 91-889-2694).
Aranjuez: Plaza Santiago Rusiñol (phone: 91-891-0427).
Ciudad Real: 31 Avenida Alarcos (phone: 926-212925).
Cuenca: 8 Calle Dalmacio García Izcarra (phone: 966-222231).
Guadalajara: Plaza Mayor (phone: 911-220698).
San Lorenzo de El Escorial: 10 Calle Floridablanca (phone: 91-890-1554).
Toledo: Puerta de Bisagra (phone: 925-220843).

CASTILE-LEÓN (OLD CASTILE)

Avila: 4 Plaza de la Catedral (phone: 928-211387).
Burgos: 7 Plaza Alonso Martínez (phone: 947-203125).
Ciudad Rodrigo: 2 Arcos de las Amayuelas (phone: 923-460561).
León: 3 Plaza de la Regla (phone: 987-237082).
Palencia: 105 Calle Mayor (phone: 988-720068).
Salamanca: 41 Gran Via (phone: 923-243730).
Segovia: 10 Plaza Mayor (phone: 911-430328).
Soria: Plaza Ramón y Cajal (phone: 975-212052).
Valladolid: 3 Plaza de Zorrilla (phone: 983-351801).
Zamora: 20 Calle Santa Clara (phone: 988-511845).

CATALONIA

Barcelona
   658 Gran Via de las Corts Catalanes (phone: 93-301-7443 or 317-2246).
   El Prat Airport, DP 08820 (phone: 93-325-5829).
Castelldefels: Plaza Rosa de los Vientos (phone: 93-664-2301).
Girona: 12 Calle Ciutadans (phone: 972-201694).
La Junquera: Autopista 17, Area de Peaje (phone: 972-540642).
Lleida: 11 Plaza de la Paneria (phone: 973-248120).
Olot: 33 Mulleras (phone: 972-260141).
Puigcerdà: Querol (phone: 972-880542).
Ripoll: Plaza Abat Oliva (972-702351).
Tarragona: 4 Fortuny (phone: 977-233415).
Valls: 1 Plaça Blat (972-601043).

EXTREMADURA

Alcántara: 21 Avenida de Méreida (phone: 927-390002).
Badajoz: 1 Pasaje de San Juan (phone: 924-222763).
Cáceres: 33 Plaza General Mola (phone: 927-246347).
Caya: Frontera Internacional (phone: 924-241253).
Mérida: Pedro M. Plano s/n (phone: 924-315353).
Plasencia: 17 Calle Trujillo (phone: 927-412766).
Trujillo: 18 Plaza Mayor (phone: 927-320653).
Zafra: Plaza de España (phone: 924-551036).

GALICIA

La Coruña: Dársena de La Marina (phone: 981-221822).
Lugo: 27-29 Plaza de España (phone: 982-231361).
Orense: 1 Curros Enríquez, Edificio Torre (phone: 988-234717).
Ponteverda: 2 Calle General Mola (phone: 986-850814).
Santiago de Compostela: 43 Rúa del Villar (phone: 981-584081).
Tuy: Puente de Tripes (phone: 986-601785).
Vigo: Las Avenidas (phone: 986-430577).
Villagarcía de Arosa: Juan Carlos I, Bajo (phone: 986-501008).

LA RIOJA

Logroño: 10 Calle Miguel Villanueva (phone: 941-257711).

MADRID

Madrid:

3 Plaza Mayor (phone: 91-266-5477).

2 Duque de Medinaceli (phone: 91-429-4951).

1 Calle Princesa, Plaza de España (phone: 91-241-2325).

Barajas Airport (phone: 91-205-8656).

DP Chamartín Station, 14 Calle Vestíbulo Puerta (phone: 91-315-9976).

MURCIA

Murcia: 4 Calle Alejandro Seiquer (phone: 968-213716).

NAVARRE

Estella: Palacio de los Duques de Granada (phone: 948-554011).

Olite: Plaza del Ayuntamiento (phone: 948-740253).

Pamplona: 2 Duque de Ahumada (phone: 948-220748).

Tudela: Plaza de los Fueros (phone: 948-821539).

VALENCIA

Alicante: 2 Explanada de España (phone: 96-521-2285).

Castellón de la Plana: 5 Plaza María Agustina (phone: 964-227703).

Valencia:

46 Calle de la Paz (phone: 94-352-2897).

Estacíon del Norte (phone: 94-352-2882).

1 Avenida Cataluña (phone: 94-369-7932).

Manises Airport (phone: 94-153-0352).

CEUTA

Ceuta: 1 Calle Muelle Cañonero Dato (phone: 956-511379).

MELILLA

Melilla: 20 Calle General Aizpuru (phone: 952-684013).

PORTUGAL

Caia: 4 Estrada Nacional, Elvas (phone: 068-64132).

Faro: At the airport (phone: 089-818582).

Lisbon:

86 Avenida António Augusto de Aguiar (phone: 01-575091).

Palácio Foz, Praça dos Restauradores (phone: 01-346-3643 or 01-346-3658).

Aeroporto de Lisboa (phone: 01-885974, 01-884248, or 01-893689).

Gare Marítima da Conde de Obidos (phone: 01-665018).

Gare de Estação dos Caminhos de Ferro, Largo de Santa Apolónia (phone: 01-867848).

Marvão: Rua Dr. Matos Magalhães (phone: 045-94263).

Porto: 43 Praça D. João I (phone: 02-201-3951, 02-313038, 02-313143).

Sagres: 8650 Vila do Bispo (phone: 082-64125).

Valença: Ave. de Espanha (phone: 051-23374, 051-23375, 051-22182).

Vila Real de Santo António: Posto Tourismo Fronteira (phone: 081-43272).

Vilar Formoso: 6350 Almeida (phone: 071-52202).

Spanish and Portuguese Embassies and Consulates in the US

The Spanish and Portuguese governments maintain a number of consulates in the US; one of their primary functions is to provide visas for certain resident aliens, depending on their country of origin, and for Americans planning to visit for longer than 60 days in Portugal or 6 months in Spain, or to study, reside, or work in these countries. Consulates also are empowered to sign official documents and to notarize copies or translations of American documents, which often is necessary for those papers to be considered legal abroad.

Listed below are the Spanish embassies and consulates in the US.

Embassy: 2700 15th St. NW, Washington, DC 20009 (phone: 202-265-0190).
Consulates:
- 545 Boylston St., Suite 803, Boston, MA 02116 (phone: 617-536-2506).
- 180 N. Michigan Ave., Suite 1500, Chicago, IL 60601 (phone: 312-782-4588).
- 151 Sevilla Ave., 2nd Floor, Coral Gables, FL 33134 (phone: 305-446-5511).
- 1800 Bering Dr., Suite 660, Houston, TX 77057 (phone: 713-783-6200).
- 6300 Wilshire Blvd., Suite 1431, Los Angeles, CA 90048 (phone: 213-658-6050).
- 2102 World Trade Center, 2 Canal St., New Orleans, LA 70130 (phone: 504-525-4951).
- 150 E. 58th St., 16th Floor, New York, NY 10155 (phone: 212-355-4080).
- 2080 Jefferson St., San Francisco, 94123 (phone: 415-922-2995).

Listed below are the Portuguese embassies and consulates in the US.

Embassy: 1900 L St. NW, Suite 401, Washington, DC 20006 (phone: 202-331-8222).
Consulates:
- 899 Boylston St., Boston, MA 02115 (phone: 617-536-8740).
- 1180 Raymond Blvd., Suite 222, Newark, NJ 07102 (phone: 201-622-7300).
- 628 Pleasant St., Suite 201, New Bedford, MA 02740 (phone: 508-997-6151).
- 630 Fifth Ave., Suite 655, New York, NY 10020 (phone: 212-246-4580).
- 56 Pine St., Providence, RI 02903 (phone: 401-272-2003).
- 3298 Washington St., San Francisco, CA 94115 (phone: 415-346-3400).

Sports

 Whether you're inclined toward watching a bullfight, catching an international soccer match, playing a round of golf on sun-drenched links, or skiing down a challenging slope in the Pyrenees, spectator and participatory sports are major activities in Spain and Portugal. Travelers who want to stay in shape, or just enjoy the excitement of watching tough competition, will find a great deal to keep them busy.

Barcelona, in particular, is busy preparing to host the Summer Olympic Games in 1992. This sports-minded city already boasts many major facilities, including the 120,000-seat *Camp Nou* soccer stadium, the largest in Europe. The southeast district of Montjuïc, Barcelona's sports and recreation area, has been designated the principal site for the *1992 Olympic Games* (July 25–August 9). The sports facilities within the *Anella Olímpica* (Olympic Ring) will include the main 70,000-seat *Olympic Stadium,* a new 17,000-seat domed *Olympic Hall,* smaller stadiums and sports halls, indoor and outdoor swimming pools, and practice fields, all within walking distance of one another.

BASKETBALL: Madrid plays host to some of the finest basketball in Europe. The city is represented by such teams as *Real Madrid* and *Estudiantes,* and also is the home of the Spanish National and Olympic squads. Recently, several National Basketball Association (NBA) teams from the US played exhibition games in Madrid as part of promotional tours and international tournaments, adding to the already growing popularity of the sport. For tickets to basketball games in Madrid, contact the *Palacio de Deportes* (99 Calle Jorge Juan; phone: 1-401-9100) or the *Polideportivo Magariños* (127 Calle Serrano; phone: 1-262-4022).

BICYCLING: Although many parts of Spain and Portugal are rather mountainous and thus a challenge to even the most fit cyclists, the mild climate, particularly in the spring and fall, provides the ideal environment, and the itinerary possibilities are inexhaustible. Visitors who pedal through the Spanish and Portuguese countryside will get to know parts of the countries that most people don't ever see. Bicycle rentals are available in both countries, though you may have to look for them. For information on bicycling itineraries in Spain and Portugal, see *Freewheeling by Two-Wheeler* in DIVERSIONS and *Camping and Caravanning, Hiking and Biking* in this section.

BULLFIGHTING: Most Spaniards view this centuries-old tradition as a highly skilled sport, a graceful *danse macabre* by matadors who flirt with death at every turn of their bright red capes, while animal lovers around the world regularly send angry letters to the Spanish government protesting what they say is an inhumane and unnecessary bloody spectacle. Many non-Spaniards find the Portuguese version more palatable, since the bull isn't killed in the ring. (Although others feel that it is more humane to kill the bull and put it out of its pain.) Portuguese bullfighting is more a demonstration of superb horsemanship than a purely primeval battle between man and beast. Nevertheless, sharp darts *do* penetrate the bull's hide, and the bullfighter *is* in constant danger, as are the tired old horses that take part.

The bullrings in Béjar, Campofrio, Zaragoza, and Seville are considered among the oldest in Spain, although those in Ronda and Seville are architecturally among the most interesting and have the greatest historical importance. Small towns and villages are not as sophisticated about their bullfights. In Chinchón, an hour's drive south of Madrid, the dirt-covered town square turns into an amateur bullring on Sundays during the summer. There, brave young boys practice their skills, and matadors past their prime test what's left of their agility and speed. The bulls, though not exceptionally large, still are dangerous.

Travelers with a taste for experiencing this particularly Spanish sport should check out the fights in Pamplona during the first week of July, when thousands of visitors come for the annual *Fiesta de San Fermín,* best known for its famous "running of the bulls" — highlighted in Hemingway's novel *The Sun Also Rises.* A variation on the traditional bullfight also is part of many festivals held throughout the year in the Portuguese Azore Islands. The bullfighting season in both countries generally lasts from late spring through the fall. For ticket information, contact the tourist office in the city you are visiting.

FISHING: With countless miles of sun-soaked Atlantic and Mediterranean coastline, unpolluted waters, and over 200 varieties of fish, Spain and Portugal are truly an angler's paradise, providing unlimited possibilities for those who wish to practice any one of the diverse aspects (deep-sea, river and lake, and underwater) of this sport. Deep-sea enthusiasts can wrestle year-round with swordfish, ray, tuna, shark, trout, and snapper, while freshwater anglers can cast for tench, salmon, carp, trout, pike, bass, barbel, and chub. For the best of Spain's and Portugal's prime places to wet a line, contact the *Spanish Fishing Federation* (3 Calle Navas de Tolosa, Madrid 28013; phone: 1-232-8353), the *Centro Português de Actividades Aquáticas* (45 Rua do Alto Duque, Lisbon 1495; phone: 1-616961), and see *Gone Fishing* in DIVERSIONS.

GOLF: Golf is very popular and is played at over 100 courses throughout Spain and Portugal. In Spain alone, the number of courses has quadrupled in the last two decades. The climate for golf in southern Spain and Portugal is ideal year-round; July and August are the hottest months, but nights often are cool. Spring and fall are best. In the wetter, cooler north, playing conditions are less predictable. American visitors will readily adjust to Spanish and Portuguese courses; both tend to be designed in the American mold — target golf, with fairly narrow fairways leading to greens surrounded by bunkers and trees. Spain and Portugal host several professional tournaments, including the *Spanish and Portuguese Open Championships* for men and women. For further information on tournaments, contact the *Royal Spanish Golf Federation* (9-5 Calle Capitán, Madrid 28020; phone: 1-455-2682 or 1-455-2757) and the *Direcção-Geral do Turismo* (86 Avenida António Augusto de Aguiar, Lisbon 1000; phone: 1-575091); also see *Great Golf* in DIVERSIONS.

HORSE RACING: Races are held on Sunday and holiday mornings between mid-September and *Christmas* at Madrid's *Hipodromo de la Zarzuela* track (Carretera La Coruña; phone: 1-207-0140). All bets are in 100-peseta (about $1) increments, and usually only the winner pays, although across-the-board and daily-double wagers are accepted at certain prize meets. There are no racing form hawkers or tipsters to help bettors handicap the races. Spain's other great public racecourse is the *Lasarte* track, run by the *Sociedad Hipódromo de San Sebastián* (2 Plaza de Zaragoza; phone: 43-421002). It is just outside the Basque city of San Sebastián on the North Atlantic coast, where the curves are tighter and the last few hundred yards before the finish line come on a slight downhill slope. This is where Spain's smart money goes in the summer. Meets are held on Sundays from July through the first week of September. For details on meets and feature races, check the local newspapers. There is no serious horse racing in Portugal.

HORSEBACK RIDING: It almost goes without saying that Spain is the land of the horse. It was here that the Moorish invaders crossed the Bab steeds of their North African homeland with the native Iberian stock. The purebred Andalusian, renowned for its sturdy legs, strong back, and agility, provided battle mounts for conquerors from Julius Caesar to Richard the Lionheart. Horseback riding has become such a popular pastime in Spain that numerous daily, weekly, and monthly tours are available. Though riding is somewhat less organized in Portugal, there are numerous stables stocked with Anglo-Arab and Lusitano horses from the luxuriant pinewoods of the Costa Verde to the almond groves and soft sands of the Algarve. For more information, contact the *Spanish Riding Federation* (8 Calle Monte Esquinza, Madrid 28010; phone: 1-419-0232 or 1-419-0233) and the *Direcção–Geral do Turismo* (86 Avenida António Augusto de Aguiar, Lisbon 1000; phone: 1-575091). For complete details on riding tours of Spain and Portugal, see *Horsing Around*, DIVERSIONS.

HUNTING AND SHOOTING: Spain and Portugal are game paradises, thanks to their variety of climates and ecosystems. Hunting, however, is subject to strictly enforced laws designed to protect wild animals. Therefore, only certain species in certain areas can be hunted during given times of the year, always provided that the hunter has a game license and a gun permit. Throughout the year, enthusiasts practice clay pigeon and target shooting at numerous well-equipped shooting clubs throughout the peninsula. Portugal's *Vilamoura Shooting Center,* in the Algarve, is Europe's largest. For complete information, contact the *Spanish Hunting Federation* (53 Avenida Reina Victoria, Madrid 28006; phone: 1-253-3495 or 1-253-0174) and the *Direcção–Geral do Turismo* (86 Avenida António Augusto de Aguiar, Lisbon 1000; phone: 1-575091).

PELOTA: This ancient sport, related to jai alai, developed from a simple rural game that consisted of hitting a ball against a wall with the hand. Part of the curious Basque culture, it initially was found in the French and Spanish Basque Country and the region of Navarre and later brought to other parts of Spain, as well as other countries. There are several versions of the sport, which is played in an enclosure of three (frontón), or four (trinquete) walls. The ball is hit with either the hand or some sort of hand-held instrument, which has given rise to the different versions. The most popular place to watch pelota is in San Sebastián's *Frontón de Anoeta*. From a spectator's point of view, the most exciting form of pelota is the very fast *cesta punta,* played with a curved wicker basket that whips the ball off the wall at lightning speeds. For further information, contact the *Spanish Pelota Federation,* 11 Calle Los Madrazo, Madrid 28014 (phone: 1-221-4299 or 1-232-3879).

SAILING: Spain and Portugal offer sailors a veritable paradise in which to practice their skills. Remote coves, strong and constant winds, and a wide range of full-service marinas make sailing simple. Visitors can rent anything from a dinghy to a sailboat (provided they are licensed to do so) or charter a luxury yacht complete with a captain and crew. The Spanish and Portuguese sailing federations, of which yachtsmen and clubs usually are members, organize official championships and regulate competitions and regattas. Both countries have numerous marinas, basins, and landing stages where sailors can moor their own vessels, as well as rented craft. For more information, contact the *Spanish Sailing Federation* (23 Calle Juan Vigón, Madrid 28003; phone: 1-233-5305 or 1-233-5304) and the *Sailing Federação Portuguesa de Vela* (Doca de Belém, Lisbon 1300; phone: 1-647324) or the *Direcção–Geral do Turismo* (86 Avenida António Augusto de Aguiar, Lisbon 1000; phone: 1-575091).

SCUBA DIVING AND SNORKELING: The crystal-blue waters surrounding Spain and Portugal hold a dazzling assortment of marine life. Almost every resort town along the sea has top-rate facilities offering scuba and snorkeling instruction, equipment sales, rental, and service, and instruction. For more information, contact the tourist office of the city, town, or region you are visiting.

SKIING: One of the most mountainous countries in Europe, with skiing available from January through May, Spain offers novice through advanced skiers the thrills of a lifetime — and once experienced, these hills will not soon be forgotten. There are excellent ski runs and many winter resorts equipped with modern facilities, offering the permanent gift of an ever-generous sun and marvelously blue skies. Among the Spanish mountains and ranges of greatest skiing interest are the Pyrenees, the Sierra Nevada, the Cantabrian Range, the Iberian Range, and the Gúdar Range. For information on the best places to ski in Spain, contact the *Spanish Winter Sports Federation* (32 Calle Claudio Coello, 28001 Madrid; phone: 1-275-8943 or 1-275-0397) and see *Sensational Spanish Skiing,* DIVERSIONS. Skiing in Portugal is relatively nonexistent, due to its mild winter temperatures and lack of both snow and dramatic mountain peaks.

SOCCER: Historically, soccer has had the reputation of being more violent in the stands than on the playing field, and nowadays many prefer to watch the game on TV from the comfort of their armchairs. But this reputation comes mainly from the rowdy supporters of a few teams and is not a true reflection of the game as a whole. If attendance records are a guide, soccer is one of the most popular sports in the world, and was called football long before Americans began to play anything remotely resembling it. Officially called "association football" and eventually "soccer" (through constant repetition of the abbreviation of "association"), the game is exciting, particularly when the *European Cup* and *World Cup* tournaments are in progress. The tough international competition shows what an entertaining, skillful sport soccer can be at its best.

Most medium-size towns in both Spain and Portugal have a soccer team of either professional or amateur standing. Among the more famous Spanish teams are *FC Barcelona,* the club with the biggest following, with fans numbering in the hundreds of thousands, and also the wealthiest, and *Real Madrid* (there's also a basketball team with the same name), while in Portugal the outstanding teams are *Beneficia FC, Porto,* and *Sporting Lisbon.*

Legend has it that football was born in 8th-century England, when victorious Saxons celebrated the defeat of a Viking raiding party by playing "kick the ball" with the head of the Viking leader. During the 1890s the game established itself internationally, partly as a result of Victorian Englishmen traveling abroad to study at European schools and universities. In 1904 the *Fédération Internationale de Football Associations (FIFA)* was founded, and included Spain among its original members. By 1929, Spain had joined an impressive array of countries that had established major national football leagues (Portugal established one in 1935). The Spanish established their standing that same year by defeating England, 4-3, in Madrid. *Beneficia,* arguably the premier Portuguese team, won the *World Cup* in 1930, 1931, 1933, and 1935. Spain, meanwhile, besides defeating the English (regarded until the First World War as masters of the sport), subsequently did well in both *Olympic* and *World Cup* competitions. In 1956, *Real Madrid* won the first *European Cup* final in Paris, and the team then proceeded to establish themselves as one of the aristocrats of European football. For the next 4 years, they dominated the competition, winning the cup against tough opposition an additional four times. In 1961, *Beneficia* broke *Real Madrid*'s supremacy and repeated their success the next year. Portuguese soccer teams have been floundering in international competitions recently. Spain's team, however, reached the quarter finals of the *World Cup* in 1986, and just missed reaching that round of the *1990 World Cup. Real Madrid* has won the *Spanish First Division League* for the last 5 years, while *Barcelona* (currently 2nd in the league), won the *Spanish FA Cup* last year.

The season generally runs from August to May, and games are played on the weekends, often in the evening or late afternoon to avoid the heat of the day — which the English blame for their first defeat by the Spaniards. For ticket information, contact the tourist office in the city or town you are visiting, and see the *Sports and Fitness* section of the individual reports in THE CITIES.

TENNIS: In both Spain and Portugal, tennis usually takes a back seat to golf, though Spain recently has seen an increased interest in the sport, especially following Arantxa Sanchez's win in the *1989 French Open Women's Singles Championship.* Many hotels and resorts in both countries have tennis facilities. Beginners and experts alike will find satisfaction: Racquets, balls, and courts are easily rented, and the single player should have no problem finding a partner. The actual tennis-oriented resorts and clubs, however, are concentrated in two main areas. In Spain, the majority of tennis facilities are along the Costa del Sol; in Portugal, the Algarve is foremost. Contact the *Portuguese Tennis Federation,* Estadio Nacional Caixias Oerias, Lisbon 2480 (phone: 1-419-5244 or 1-419-8472).

For complete descriptions of the best courts in Spain and Portugal, as well as further information on other sports mentioned in this section, see the individual reports in THE CITIES and entries on specific sports in DIVERSIONS.

Theater and Special Event Tickets

 The National Tourist Office of Spain and the Portuguese National Tourist Office also can supply information on the many special events and festivals that take place in Spain and Portugal, though they cannot in all cases provide the actual program or detailed information on ticket prices. In more than one section of this book you will read about events that spark your interest — everything from music festivals and special theater seasons to sporting championships — along with telephone numbers and addresses to write for descriptive brochures, reservations, or tickets. Since many of these occasions often are fully booked well in advance, think about having your reservation in hand before you go. If you do write, remember that any request from the US should be accompanied by an International Reply Coupon to ensure a response (send two of them for an airmail response). Tickets usually can be paid for by an international money order or by foreign draft. These international coupons, money orders, and drafts are available at US post offices and banks.

For further information, write for the *European Travel Commission*'s extensive list of events scheduled for the entire year for its 24 member countries (including Spain and Portugal). For a free copy, send a self-addressed, stamped (45¢), business-size (4 x 9½) envelope, to "European Events," *European Travel Commission*, PO Box 1754, New York, NY 10185.

Books and Magazines

Throughout GETTING READY TO GO, numerous books and brochures have been recommended as good sources of further information on a variety of topics. In many cases, these have been publications of the National Tourist Office of Spain and the Portuguese National Tourist Office and are available free through their offices both here and abroad. Others may be found in the travel section of any good general bookstore. If you still can't find something, the following stores and/or mail-order houses specialize in travel, though not in travel to any particular country or continent. They offer books on Spain and Portugal along with guides to the rest of the world and, in some cases, even an old Baedeker or two.

Book Passage, 51 Tamal Vista, Corte Madera, CA 94925 (phone: 415-927-0960 in California; 800-321-9785 elsewhere in the US). Travel guides and maps to all areas of the world. A free catalogue is available.

The Complete Traveller, 199 Madison Ave., New York, NY 10016 (phone: 212-685-9007). Travel guides and maps. A catalogue is available for $2.

Forsyth Travel Library, PO Box 2975, Shawnee Mission, KS 66201-1375 (phone: 800-367-7984 or 913-384-0496). Travel guides and maps, old and new, to all parts of the world. Ask for the "Worldwide Travel Books and Maps" catalogue.

Gourmet Guides, 2801 Leavenworth St., San Francisco, CA 94133 (phone: 415-771-3671). Travel guides and maps, along with cookbooks. Mail-order lists available on request.

Phileas Fogg's Books and Maps, 87 Stanford Shopping Center, Palo Alto, CA 94304 (phone: 800-533-FOGG or 415-327-1754). Travel guides, maps, and language aids.

Tattered Cover, 2955 East First Ave., Denver, CO 80206 (phone: 800-833-9327 or 303-322-7727). The travel department alone of this enormous bookstore carries over 7,000 books, as well as maps and atlases. No catalogue is offered (the list is too extensive), but a newsletter, issued three times a year, is available on request.

Thomas Brothers Maps & Travel Books, 603 W. Seventh St., Los Angeles, CA 90017 (phone: 213-627-4018). Maps (including road atlases, street guides, and wall maps), guidebooks, and travel accessories.

Traveller's Bookstore, 22 W. 52nd St. (lobby), New York, NY 10019 (phone: 212-664-0995). Travel Guides, maps, literature, and accessories. A catalogue is available for $2.

Travel Suppliers, 16735 Lake Forest La., Yorba Linda, CA 93686 (phone: 714-528-2502). Mail-order suppliers of books, maps, language aids, and travel paraphernalia from money belts and pouches to voltage and currency converters. A catalogue is available.

Librairie de France/Libreria Hispanica (French and Spanish Book Corporation), which specializes in language dictionaries and French and Spanish fiction and nonfiction, carries some Spanish-language guidebooks published in Spain. Of the company's two stores in New York, the one at 610 Fifth Ave., New York, NY 10020 (phone: 212-581-8810), has the greatest selection of travel material; the other is at 115 Fifth Ave., New York, NY 10003 (212-673-7400). In addition, *Luso Brazilian* specializes in Portuguese and Brazilian books, some in English translation. The store has a mail-order facility and can be reached at PO Box 170286, Brooklyn, NY 11217 (phone: 718-624-4000). *Lectorum* (137 W. 14th St., New York, NY 10011; phone: 212-929-2833) also specializes in Spanish books (although none in translation), including a variety of travel books and Spanish classics.

A subscription to the *International Herald Tribune* also is a good idea. This English-language newspaper is written and edited mostly in Paris and is *the* newspaper read most regularly and avidly by Americans abroad to keep up with world news, US news, sports, the stock market (US and foreign), fluctuations in the exchange rate, and an assortment of help-wanted ads, real estate listings, and personals, pan-European in scope. Published 6 days a week (no Sunday paper), it is available at newsstands throughout the US and in cities worldwide, including Spain and Portugal. Home delivery also is widely available, and you can have your subscription transferred to an address in Spain or Portugal. To subscribe, write or call the Subscription Manager, *International Herald Tribune,* 850 Third Ave., 10th Floor, New York, NY 10022 (phone: 800-882-2884 or 212-752-3890).

The New York Times, Wall Street Journal, USA Today, Los Angeles Times, and other US newspapers also can be bought in many of the larger cities and resort areas, at hotels, airports, and newsstands. Note that some papers may cost more than in the US, and some may be available a day or two after publication.

Sampling the regional fare is still likely to be one of the highlights of any visit. You will find reading about local edibles worthwhile before you go or after you return. *Gourmet,* a magazine specializing in food, now and then features articles on Spanish and Portuguese cooking and touring, although its scope is much broader than Spain and Portugal alone. It is available at newsstands throughout the US for $2.50 an issue or for $18 a year from *Gourmet,* PO Box 2886, Boulder, CO 80322-2886 (phone: 800-365-2454).

The cuisines of Spain and Portugal are almost as famous as that of their neighbor France. The *Spanish Olive Oil Institute* has a number of free books and other material, including *Cooking with Spanish Flair* and *Spanish Cooking* by Rose Cantrell, both available through the company's Spanish Commercial Office (attention: Elizabeth Aguirre, 405 Lexington Ave., 44th Floor, New York, NY 10174; phone: 212-661-4959). *The Food of Portugal* by Jean Anderson (Morrow; $24.95) is highly recommended, as is *Foods and Wines of Spain* by Penelope Casas (Random House; $22.50 hardcover). Also look for the Time-Life series of books on Iberian cuisine, including *Cooking of Spain and Portugal* and *Mediterranean Menus;* out of print, check the library. Also out of print, but well worth looking for are Barbara Norman's *Spanish Cookbook* (Atheneum) and *Food of Spain and Portugal* by Elizabeth Lambert Ortiz (Doubleday), both of which delve into the mysteries of authentic Iberian cooking. *Tapas* by Penelope Casas (Knopf; $24.95, hardcover; $12.95, paperback) covers Spanish appetizers and, in addition to recipes, includes interesting information on regional and cultural specialties. Jan Reed's *Wines of Portugal* (Faber & Faber;

paperback, $11.95) is a comprehensive and readable book, though somewhat technical on occasion.

Many books have been written about the rich and fascinating history and culture of Spain and Portugal. The inhabitants of the Iberian Peninsula were involved in wars with the Romans for 2 centuries before finally becoming a part of the Roman Empire at the end of the Second Punic War, in 218 BC. The Iberian tribes united and reconquered much of central and western Spain from 147 to 139 BC, but Rome triumphed again in 19 BC and held power until AD 414. Edward Gibbon's multi-volume, umpteenpage *The Decline and Fall of the Roman Empire,* if you want to plow through it, is a good overall source of information about these wars. An abridged version of the 18th-century English historian's work (Penguin Classics; paperback) is currently out of print, but check the library. Histories of the Roman period by writers much closer to the action, such as Suetonius — who wrote biographies of twelve of the Caesars — are all available in the classics department of a good bookstore.

The next major historical period begins with the expulsion of the Moors; the most famous of the Christian defenders was Rodrigo Díaz de Vivar — known as El Cid (the Lord Champion) — whose exploits were romanticized in *Poema del Cid* (ca. AD 1140), the oldest extant Spanish epic. The story is also told in a variety of contexts, including an opera written by Massenet in 1885. A translation of *The Poem of the Cid* by Rita Hamilton and Janet Perly is published by Penguin ($9.95) in a bilingual text (offering parallel English and Spanish texts on facing pages), and, of course, there is always the movie version, starring Charlton Heston and Sophia Loren. Finally, this period is nicely recounted in *Mohammed and Charlemagne* by Henri Pirenne; available in libraries or from Barnes and Noble Imports ($19.75).

The Age of Discovery, which began with Columbus's famous trip across the Atlantic, is marvelously documented in *The Discoverers* (Random House; $12.95, paperback) by Daniel Borstein, former Librarian of Congress. There are countless books about Columbus; among the best are *Christopher Columbus, Mariner* (Little Brown; $14.45 paperback) by Samuel Eliot Morison and *The European Discovery of America* (Oxford University Press), published in two volumes (1971 and 1974; $35 each), by the same author. This fascinating period of history — not only in terms of Spanish and Portuguese colonialism, but also of the countries they subdued in South, Central, and North Americ — is also well documented in *Portuguese Voyages to America in the 15th Century* (1965), another Morison book, and Bernal Díaz's eyewitness account of being a foot soldier during Cortés's conquest of the Aztec in Mexico (1519–1521) in his sometimes brutally honest memoirs *Historia Verdadera de la Conquista de la Nueva España.* The latter is available in an English translation, *The Conquest of New Spain* (Penguin; $5.95).

The most famous Portuguese of this period were King Henry the Navigator, the subject of E.D.S. Bradford's *A Wind from the North* (Harcourt, Brace, & Javonovich; out of print), and Vasco da Gama. Both are mentioned at length in the *Portuguese Seaborne Empire, 1415–1825* (Penguin; 1969) by C. R. Boxer (out of print; check the library). Last, Carmi House Press recently published the historical novel *The Alhambra Decree* by David Raphael, a well-researched and fascinating account of the expulsion of the Jews from Spain.

On the next great period in Iberian history, there is *The Spanish Armada* by Felipe Fernandez Arnesto (Oxford University Press; $12.95 paperback, $24.95 hardcover). A scholarly work, although rich and zesty, it draws on personal accounts of both English and Spanish sailors who took part in the famous naval battles. Dealing with both Spain and Portugal is *Inquisition* by Edward Peters (University of California Press; $12.95), a fascinating account that not only documents this turbulent and violent period but also discusses the historical context that led to the Inquisition. A companion volume of a sort is the autobiography *The Life of St. Teresa of Avila* (Penguin, $6.95, translated by

J. M. Cohen). Mainly the story of the saint's conversion in 1555, it is considered a literary masterpiece, the most widely read prose classic of Spain after Cervantes's *Don Quixote.*

In modern times, *Blood of Spain* by Ronald Fraser (Pantheon; $12.95) is a moving oral history of the Spanish Civil War; *Homage to Catalonia* (Harcourt, Brace, & Javonovich; $5.95) by George Orwell is an account of his experiences during this period. Novels on this period also abound, among them *Death in the Afternoon* (Macmillan; $16.95 hardcover), *The Sun Also Rises* (Macmillan; $6.95, paperback), and *For Whom the Bell Tolls* (Macmillan; $22.95 hardcover; $5.95 paperback) by Ernest Hemingway, which all offer an insider's perspective on 20th-century Spain.

Hundreds of titles exist on Spain's painters, musicians, and artists, though less has been written about Portugal's. A good place to start is E. H. Gombrich's classic *The Story of Art* (Phaidon Press; $42.80 hardcover, $35.40 paperback), which covers not only painters and sculptors but also architects. *Lives of the Artists* (Penguin Classics; $7.95, paperback) by the 16th-century Italian Giorgio Vasari covers the Renaissance period. More encyclopedic volumes are J. Lassaigne's *Spanish Painting: From the Catalan Frescoes to El Greco* (Vol. 1) and *Spanish Painting: From Velázquez to Picasso* (Vol. 2; Skira); published by Rizzoli, both are out of print. The *Hispanic Society of America* publishes the biography *Velázquez* by E. du Gué Trapier. Other fine works are *Goya: His Life and Work* by P. Gassier and J. Wilson (1971; with a complete catalogue) and *Goya, The Phantasmal Vision* by Jacqueline and Maurice Guillard (Clarkson N. Potter); *The Unspeakable Confessions of Salvador Dalí* by Dalí (Morrow; out of print); and *Dalí* by Dalí (Harry N. Abrams; out of print). *Picasso: His Life and Work* by R. Penrose (Gollancz) is just one of a multitude of books on the famous Spanish artist. On architecture there is Kubler's *The Art and Architecture of Spain and Portugal* (Pelican) and John Julius Norwich's *Great Architecture of the World* (Random House; out of print).

There also are a number of books on the life of Andrés Segovia. Through his singlehanded promotion and technical development of the guitar as a serious instrument, relegated to the parlor until his arrival, Segovia brought the guitar into the concert halls of the world. Out of print, but worth looking for in your library, is Segovia's autobiography, *Andrés Segovia, An Autobiography of the Years 1893–1920,* translated by W. F. O'Brien (Macmillan; out of print), which includes illustrations and portraits from this time.

Spain and Portugal have inspired much travel writing, some of it outstanding. H. V. Morton's *A Stranger in Spain* (Dodd, Mead; out of print, but check your library), describing a journey through Spain, is a classic. Also see V. S. Pritchett's *Marching Spain* (Hogarth Press, London; $19.88), an account of a 300-mile walk through Spain in 1927, when he was the first foreigner many Spaniards had ever met. *Roads to Today's Portugal* (Gava-Brown, 1983) by Nelson Vieira delves into the culture of that country, as, in its own way, does *Long Stays in Portugal* (David and Charles) by Roger W. Hicks and Francis Schultz. *The Spanish Temper,* also by Pritchett (Ecco Press; $8.95), is an impressive, potent account of living in Spain in the 1920s; *Spain* by Jan Morris (Penguin; out of print) is a particularly vivid and superbly written book about the country. Also out of print, but worth looking for in the library, is Hans Christian Andersen's *A Visit to Portugal 1866* (Bobbs-Merrill, 1973), a lively account of his travels there. Other books on Portugal worth looking for in the library include *I Like it Here* (C. Chivers, London) by Kingsley Amis, *The Mandarins* by Simone de Beauvoir, and the particularly enjoyable *They Went to Portugal* (G. Cape, London) by Rose Macaulay.

You could read about Spain and Portugal for a lifetime; in fact, were you to begin with the Romans and continue to modern times, you could occupy several lifetimes — and never have a chance to travel. *The* classic Spanish novel, of course, is *Don Quixote* by Miguel de Cervantes Saavedra, available in a number of translations, including Penguin's paperback version (abridged $4.95; unabridged $6.95), translated by J. M. Cohen. Another set of must-reads is the work of Portugal's most famous novelist, Eça Miroz, whose novels include *Osmaias* (available in English as *The Maias*), part of a series detailing the trials and tribulations of a Portuguese family, somewhat in the tradition of John Galsworthy's *Forsyte Saga.*

Genealogy Hunts

 Some of the most extensive pedigrees in the world are to be found in Spain, where many nobles or "grandees" can trace their genealogies to Roman times. Over the years, Spain has suffered a succession of invaders and civil uprisings, and these, plus the country's isolation on the Iberian Peninsula between the Pyrenees and the sea, have produced a unique race, proud, brave, and with a passion for exploration and conquering lands beyond the horizon.

Spain has been inhabited since the earliest times, and there has been little immigration into the country since the Christian kingdoms defeated and expelled the Muslim Moors in the 13th century after more than 400 years of domination by these North African warriors. At the time of the invasion, about AD 711, Spain was a collection of small kingdoms: León, Navarre, Aragón, Castile, and so on. It wasn't until 1492, under King Ferdinand and Queen Isabella, that Spain became a unified kingdom. Three hundred years later, Spain was a dominant world power and established numerous colonies, encouraging emigration to the southern, central, and western Americas.

It was only during the 20th century that those choosing to leave Spain were no longer content with settling in present or former colonies, and immigration to the United States again became substantial. Unfortunately, due to the tragic Civil War from 1936 to 1939, many records were destroyed, but far fewer than would be imagined in proportion to the overall destruction, even in areas of the fiercest fighting. Of the 19,000 parishes in Spain, only a handful lost their registers.

The Portuguese have a similar, though distinctive, history. The area that now is Portugal originally was inhabited by a tribe called the Lusitanians. In the 5th century, German Visigoths invaded the country but were conquered by the Moors 3 centuries later. In the 1st century AD, Portuguese Christians began to wage war against the Moors, and by the time the Moors had been ousted from the Iberian Peninsula, Portugal had declared its independence, which was recognized by Spain in 1143. Except for a brief period of Spanish rule, from 1580 to 1640, Portugal has the oldest fixed frontiers of any European country.

Few immigrants have settled in Portugal, but many have emigrated since the 1500s — for Portugal, too, was a major world power at this time — and settled in Portuguese colonies in South America (Brazil), Africa (Angola, Mozambique, Guinea, St. Thomas), India, and Asia (Macao). Of these, only Macao remains under Portuguese administration today. The Atlantic islands of Madeira and the Azores always have been considered an integral part of Portugal. During the 19th century, a great many Portuguese from these islands came to North America, settling chiefly in Massachusetts, California, and Hawaii.

Happily for contemporary ancestor-worshipers, both the Spanish and Portuguese have kept pretty good records, beginning as far back as the 13th century in some cases, and legitimate evidence of Iberian forebears — no matter how humble their origins — usually is yours for the searching. With a little digging around, you'll probably at least be able to visit the church where your great-uncle Julio married your great-aunt Celina before leaving for America, or the port where your grandfather waved good-bye to the Old Country, or the cemetery where your mother's family has been resting quietly for centuries.

While there is not much written on how to conduct research in Iberia, particularly in Portugal, if dig you must, try to do as much preliminary research as possible before your trip. One of the challenges of this sort of project is the need for creativity, since most people don't have convenient pedigree charts they can consult. Family Bibles are a good source, as are old letters, documents, photographs, or heirlooms, even anecdotes from the oldest members of your family (that's how Alex Haley began when he traced his own *Roots*). What follows is, hopefully, a helpful primer on how to tackle what may at first appear to be a daunting project.

To begin with, check your library and state offices for local published records, regional archives, and local history. The *US Library of Congress* (Local History and Genealogy Room, Jefferson Building, Washington, DC 20540; phone: 202-707-5537) and the *New York Public Library* (Division of US History, Local History and Genealogy, Room 315N, 42nd St. & Fifth Ave., New York, NY 10018; phone: 212-930-0828) both have extensive facilities for personal research; however, you may want to call ahead to find out if they have material relevant to your particular search.

There is a wealth of archival information in Spain to help you trace your family, though you'll probably run into a few dead ends in the process, particularly in regions where war-related destruction obliterated church and civil records. Time and patience are the keys where the information is neither centralized nor indexed. As more Mexicans, South and Central Americans, and others of Spanish descent become interested in learning about their origins, a praiseworthy attempt is being made to organize this information and make it more accessible.

Those wishing to trace their Portuguese ancestry may wish to join the *American-Portuguese Genealogical Society.* For information, contact Cecilia Rose (PO Box 644, Taunton, MA 02780; phone: 508-823-3330). This society has amassed a large number (65,000) of ancestral records — primarily on individuals who lived before the turn of the century — which are housed in the nearby Taunton Public Library (12 Pleasant St., Taunton, MA 02780; phone; 508-823-3570). Both are a good source of information on researching your Portuguese ancestry.

Another source of both Spanish and Portuguese information is the *Genealogical Society of the Church of Jesus Christ of Latter-Day Saints,* which has thousands of reels of genealogical records on microfilm, available for consultation in person at its headquarters (35 NW Temple St., Salt Lake City, UT 84150; phone: 801-240-2331) or through any of its branch libraries. Ruth Gomez de Scheirmacher (phone: 801-240-2881) will guide anyone who asks through the first steps to be taken in a search. Using the Mormons' index reels, you can, for a small fee, order from Salt Lake City the microfilm records of almost any Iberian town. The film should arrive at the branch library in about 6 to 8 weeks, and loans are renewable for 2-week periods up to 6 months. There is no charge for reviewing a film at the headquarters in Salt Lake City.

Look in your library for T. Beard and D. Demong's *How to Find Your Family Roots* (McGraw-Hill, 1977), which contains an excellent list of available genealogical resources. *In Search of Your European Roots* by Angus Baxter (Genealogical Publishing Co., 1985) has chapters on both Spain and Portugal, as does Noel Currer-Briggs's *Worldwide Family History* (Routledge & Kegan Paul, 1982). For general information, take a look at Jeane Eddy Westin's *Finding Your Roots* (J. P. Tarcher, distributed by St. Martin's Press). You also may want to subscribe to the excellent *Ancestry Newsletter,* edited by Robb Barr and published bimonthly by Ancestry Incorporated (PO Box 476, Salt Lake City, UT 84110; phone: 800-531-1790); a yearly subscription costs $12.

Constructing a family tree is a backward process: You need to start with your parents' dates and places of birth, their parents' dates and places, and so on, as far back as you can. It should be a considerable stretch since it's quite possible to trace back several hundred years. To obtain the relevant documents, make sure you have the exact names of each ancestor (remember, many immigrants' surnames were irrevocably, if unwittingly, changed through clerical misspellings at Ellis Island and other ports of entry), as well as the names of any family members closely related to the ancestor you are researching. You can request many different types of documents that contain information about a previous generation: for example, birth and death certificates, marriage licenses, emigration and immigration records, and baptism and christening records.

In Portugal, unless your ancestors were members of the aristocracy, parish records weren't kept consistently until about the early 16th century, though again, it may be possible to go back as far as 1390, when the writing of parish records first was promulgated by King Afonso IV. The Council of Trent (1545–63) was convened in northern Italy to reestablish discipline in the Catholic Church, and one of the ways it did this was by insisting that parish priests all over the world keep a register of church events. In Portugal, there was an almost 100% compliance with this edict. Although the registers are a little unorthodox, they almost certainly will have the personal observations of the local priest and details of baptisms and burials. Something to bear in mind in the case of Portugal, however, are three events that caused great destruction of records: the 1755 earthquake in Lisbon; the French invasions that devastated the provinces of Beira, Baixa, and Ribatejo; and the invasion of Alentejo by the Spanish.

Records of baptisms, marriages, and burials in Spain may precede 1570, while in the diocese of Solsona, near Saragossa, there are records as far back as 1394. The Spanish National Archives is a good place to start. It's crucial that you know beforehand the birthplaces of your ancestors, not just the port from which they left Spain. There are 11 different National Archives, based mainly on the divisions of what is now a united country. They are included in a list of sources at the end of this section.

REQUESTING RECORDS: Before about 1870, personal records — baptism, confirmation, marriage, and death — were kept, for the most part, only by parish churches. Thus, to obtain information on your family before 1865, you should begin by writing either to the parish priest or to the bishop holding territorial jurisdiction. Since about 1865, birth, marriage, death, and citizenship records have been kept by municipalities, so, after discovering where your ancestors came from, you must write to the local authorities. There are important archives (*Archivo Municipal* in Spain) in all the major centers, as well as in smaller towns and villages and in Mahón, in the Balearic Islands. Again, on the local level you will find civil registration (*registros civiles* in Spain; in Portugal, *registro civil*) as well as church registers (*registros de parroquia* in Spain; in Portugal, *registros paroquiais*).

It's worth noting that because of the close ties between Great Britain and Portugal and the number of British businessmen living in the country, there were Church of England (Anglican) churches in Lisbon and Madeira. Registers for the period from 1721 to 1890 are in the custody of the Bishop of London in England. Bear in mind also that in Portugal, records of the notorious Catholic Inquisition trials held in Lisbon, Coimbra, and Evora in particular (roughly from the 15th to the 18th century) often include very detailed personal biographies of the accused people. They all can be found in the Portuguese National Archives in Lisbon.

DIGGING DEEPER: Once you've done your basic research, you might want to turn to some older records or even use them as duplicates to verify information you've already accumulated. The following are some of the most readily available records by mail or in person.

Certificates of Family Genealogy – Write to the archives office in the town where your family member lived to obtain a certificate of your family genealogy, giving names, relationships, birth dates, and birthplaces of all living family members at the time of recording.

Emigration Records – Passenger lists (*listas de pasaejeros* in Spain; *listas de passageiros* in Portugal), passports (*pasaportes* in Spain; *passaportes* in Portugal), and other emigration records also can be helpful. Again, try the local archives of the province of the emigrant's birthplace or port of departure to obtain documentation of emigration.

In Portugal, passports were first issued in 1757. The records are in the District Archives and list name, date, place of birth, date of the voyage, and destination. Records of passports in Spain offer similar information, and this information is kept by the *Archiva de Gobernación* in Madrid. Spanish passports weren't issued until the end of the Civil War, in 1939.

Lists of passengers on sailings from the port of Seville, Spain (a major emigration port), to the Americas in 1509–1701 also are available. Unfortunately, these records may be of limited value, as most of the people on the list were functionaries of government or private business and eventually returned to Spain. These records can be found in the *Archivo General de Indias* in Seville.

Draft Records – In Spain, military records (*Cartilla militar*), dating from the 1600s, contain the complete personal records of every Spanish soldier and sailor. The lists have been published and indexed, and can be found at the Archives of the *Archivo Central del Ministerio de Marina* (Ministry of the Navy) and the *Archivo del Museo Naval* (Naval Museum).

Clerical Surveys – To obtain Catholic parish records in Portugal, write to the particular church or, if it is no longer in existence, the District Archives or the National Archives. The oldest parish register in existence is that of Nabainhos, near Gouveia, which started with a baptism in 1529. Other early ones include Cheleiros and Santiago. If you are writing to the parish priest, ask if he has a list of the names appearing on the tombstones (*pedras tumulares*).

In Spain, parish records go back to about 1650. A guide to the existing Spanish parishes was published in 1954 (*Guía de la Iglesia en España, Vol. 4*). Try the archives of the diocese in which the parish is located; duplicate records usually are kept by the bishop. If you don't know the exact diocese, write to the Spanish headquarters of the Catholic Church (Conference Episcopal Española, Oficina de Estadística y Sociologia, 4 Calle Alfonso XI, Madrid 28014). Be sure to give the name and province of the village in question and ask for the name of the diocese and the address of the diocesan office.

Census Registers and other Municipal Records – Civil censuses have been held frequently in Spain since the 1500s, though there is no official list. The most comprehensive census was called *Catastro del Marqués de la Ensenada,* completed in 1752. These records contain so-called real estate records (actually tax records; census takers were no fools even then) of heads of households, subtenants, or taxpayers and their residences along with the amount of tax assessed. Most of the records are in the various local archives in Spain. For information in Spain, write to the local municipal offices (*ayuntamientos*).

The Portuguese national archives (*Arquivo Nacional da Torre do Tombo*) are in a central office at Largo de São Bento, Lisbon 1200; Civil Registration Archives (*Conservatórias do Registro Civil*) are kept in Lisbon, as are the Property Registration Archives (*Conservatórias do Registro Predial*) and the National Identification Archives (*Conservatórias de Identicação Civil e Criminal*).

In Spain, the 11 main archives are *Archivo Histórico Nacional* (115 Calle Serrano, Madrid); *Archivo General de Indias* (Avenida de la Constitución, Seville); *Archivo General de Simancas* in Valladolid; *Archivo de la Corona de Aragón* in Zaragoza; *Archivo del Reino de Valencia* (22 Calle Alameda, Valencia); *Archivo General de Navarra* in Pamplona, Navarre; *Archivo Regional de Galicia* (San Carlos, La Coruña,

Galicia); *Archivo del Reino de Mallorca* (3 Calle Ramón Llull, Palma de Mallorca); *Archivo de la Real Chancillería* in Valladolid; *Archivo de la Real Chancellería* (17 Plaza Suárez, Granada); and *Archivo General del Ministerio de Asuntos Exteriores* in Madrid.

For those who would rather leave the digging to others, reputable genealogical societies in Spain and Portugal will do it for you for a fee. The *Instituto de Genealogía y Heráldica y Federación de Corporaciones* (Apartado de Correos, Madrid 12079) will provide those researching their ancestry in Spain with a list of qualified local genealogists for hire; a copy of the society's catalogue also may be found in many libraries. In Portugal, particularly if you or someone in your family is of noble descent and has been granted the right to use a coat of arms, the *Instituto Português de Heráldica* (20 Avenida da République, Lisbon 1000) may be able to provide information about your forebears. In the US, contact *Lineage* (PO Box 417, Salt Lake City, UT 84110; phone: 801-531-9297).

With the above information and a little patience, you should have a firm grasp for a lengthy climb up your family tree.

■ **In the Works:** The Spanish-government-run *Spain '92 Foundation* currently is collecting data on Spanish immigrants to the US, family names, ancestral origins, and other information pertinent to those seeking to learn about their roots in Spain. Next year, the plan is to offer this information to the US public, particularly in areas with large Spanish-American communities. For further information, contact *Spain '92 Foundation,* 1821 Jefferson Pl. NW, Washington, DC 20036 (phone: 202-775-1992).

Weights and Measures

When traveling in Spain and Portugal, you'll find that just about every quantity, whether it is length, weight, or capacity, will be expressed in unfamiliar terms. In fact, this is true for travel almost everywhere in the world, since the US is one of the last countries to make its way to the metric system. It may happen soon in the US, and your trip to Spain and Portugal will serve to familiarize you with what one day may be the weights and measures at your grocery store.

There are some specific things to keep in mind during your trip. Fruits and vegetables at a market generally are recorded in kilos (kilograms), as are your luggage at the airport and your body weight. (This latter is particularly pleasing to people of significant size, who instead of weighing 220 pounds hit the scales at a mere 100 kilos.) A kilo equals 2.2 pounds and 1 pound is .45 kilo.

Body temperature usually is measured in degrees centigrade or Celsius rather than on the Fahrenheit scale — a normal body temperature is 37C, not 98.6F, and freezing is 0 degrees C rather than 32F. Gasoline is sold by the liter (approximately 4 liters to 1 gallon). Tire pressure gauges and other equipment measure in kilograms per square centimeter rather than pounds per square inch. Highway signs are written in kilometers rather than miles (1 mile equals 1.6 kilometers; 1 kilometer equals .62 mile). And speed limits are in kilometers per hour, so think twice before hitting the gas when you see a speed limit of 100. That means 62 miles per hour.

The tables and conversion factors listed below should give you all the information you will need to understand any transaction, road sign, or map you encounter during your travels.

CONVERSION TABLES
METRIC TO US MEASUREMENTS

Multiply:	by:	to convert to:
LENGTH		
millimeters	.04	inches
meters	3.3	feet
meters	1.1	yards
kilometers	.6	miles
CAPACITY		
liters	2.11	pints (liquid)
liters	1.06	quarts (liquid)
liters	.26	gallons (liquid)
WEIGHT		
grams	.04	ounces (avoir.)
kilograms	2.2	pounds (avoir.)

US TO METRIC MEASUREMENTS

LENGTH		
inches	25.	millimeters
feet	.3	meters
yards	.9	meters
miles	1.6	kilometers
CAPACITY		
pints	.47	liters
quarts	.95	liters
gallons	3.8	liters
WEIGHT		
ounces	28.	grams
pounds	.45	kilograms

TEMPERATURE

$$°F = (°C \times 9/5) + 32 \qquad °C = (°F - 32) \times 5/9$$

APPROXIMATE EQUIVALENTS		
Metric Unit	**Abbreviation**	**US Equivalent**
LENGTH		
meter	m	39.37 inches
kilometer	km	.62 mile
millimeter	mm	.04 inch
CAPACITY		
liter	l	1.057 quarts
WEIGHT		
gram	g	.035 ounce
kilogram	kg	2.2 pounds
metric ton	MT	1.1 ton
ENERGY		
kilowatt	kw	1.34 horsepower

Cameras and Equipment

Vacations are everybody's favorite time for taking pictures and home movies. After all, most of us want to remember the places we visit — and show them off to others. Here are a few suggestions to help you get the best results from your travel photography or videography.

BEFORE THE TRIP

If you're taking your camera or camcorder out after a long period in mothballs — or have just bought a new one — check it thoroughly before you leave to prevent unexpected breakdowns or disappointing pictures.

STILL CAMERAS

1. Shoot at least one test roll, using the kind of film you plan to take along with you. Use all the shutter speeds and f-stops on the camera, and vary the focus to make sure everything is in order. Do this well before your departure so there will be time to have the film developed and to make repairs, if necessary. If you're in a rush, most large cities have shops that can process film in as little as an hour. Repairs, unfortunately, take longer.

2. Clean your camera thoroughly, inside and out. Dust and dirt can jam mechanisms, scratch film, and mar photographs. Remove surface dust from lenses and camera body with a soft camel's hair brush. Next, use at least two layers of crumpled lens tissue and your breath to clean lenses and filters, but as they are easily scratched, don't rub hard and don't use water, saliva, or compressed air. Persistent stains can be removed by using a cotton swab moistened with liquid lens cleaner. Anything that doesn't come off easily needs professional attention; a periodic professional cleaning also is advisable. Once your lenses are clean, protect them from dirt and damage with skylight or ultraviolet filters.

3. Check the lithium batteries for your camera's light meter, and take along extras just in case yours wear out during the trip.

VIDEO CAMCORDERS

1. If you haven't used your camcorder lately, use a "practice" videocassette to reacquaint yourself with the various shooting techniques — such as panning, zooming, and segueing (that is, transitioning without pause) from one scene to another. Practice fully before you leave; don't save it for the plane.

2. Clean and maintain your camcorder lenses with a soft, dry cloth. Don't use solvents such as paint thinner or chemically treated cloths. Once your camcorder lenses are clean, protect them from dirt and damage with inexpensive skylight or ultraviolet filters. If your camcorder's heads need cleaning, a recorded tape will tell you. A "snowy" tape is a sign that a head cleaning is needed. If a head cleaning doesn't improve the picture, the problem may lie elsewhere. In that case, take the camcorder to a professional for a check-up. Check the operation of each component on your camcorder, making sure that each feature performs correctly. If there's an internal problem, don't try to fix it yourself. You could void the manufacturer's warranty or, even worse, cause further damage. Even if all appears well at home, take a head cleaner along on your trip to make sure your videos remain clear and sharp.

3. Check the lithium batteries for your camcorder's light indicators, and take along extras just in case yours wear out during the trip. If you took along all your camcorder accessories, your carrying bag would get heavy and cumbersome, but there are a few "musts." Take extra nickel-cadmium (Ni-Cd) batteries so that you always have one or two power sources ready while another is recharging back at the hotel. You never know when a once-in-a-lifetime opportunity will present itself, and if you just used up your 45-minute allotment of power on a local festival, you'll have none left to shoot anything else. Remember that the more features you use, including reviewing what you've taped in the electronic viewfinder, the more battery power you will consume.

EQUIPMENT TO TAKE ALONG

Keep your gear light and compact. Items that are too heavy or bulky to be carried comfortably on a full-day excursion will likely remain in your hotel room, so leave them home.

1. Invest in a broad camera or camcorder strap if you now have a thin one. It will make carrying the camera much more comfortable.

2. A sturdy canvas or leather camera or camcorder bag, preferably with padded pockets (not an airline bag), will keep your equipment organized and easy to find.

3. For cleaning, bring along a camel's hair brush that retracts into a rubber squeeze bulb. Also take plenty of lens tissue, soft cloths, and plastic bags to protect equipment from dust and moisture.

STILL CAMERAS: Lenses and Other Equipment – Most single-lens-reflex (SLR) cameras come with a 50mm, or "normal," lens — a general-purpose lens that frames subjects within an approximately average angle of view. This is good for street scenes taken at a distance of 25 feet or more, and for full-length portraits shot at 8 to 12 feet.

Any lens from 35mm on down offers wide-angle capabilities, which in effect pull segments of the peripheral scene into the picture, and are especially handy for panoramas and landscapes. A wide-angle lens in the 20–28mm range is perfect for palace gardens. Where the normal perspective of a 50mm lens provides only a partial view of the magnificent Alhambra, a 20mm incorporates this Moorish palace above its lush gardens in one flowing scene. While a 50mm lens only provides a partial view of Lisbon from the ramparts of Castelo de São Jorge (St. George's Castle), taken from the proper perspective a 20mm lens captures the sweeping panorama of the city below. The wide-angle lens also is excellent for linking people with their surroundings because of its great depth of field — that is, sharp focus from foreground to background — that can focus pictures between 3½ feet and infinity. And it also can be valuable when there's very little space between you and your subject.

Wide-angle lenses are especially handy for panoramas, for cityscapes, and for large buildings or statuary from which you can't step back. For extreme closeups, a macro lens is best, but a screw-on magnifying lens is an inexpensive alternative. Keep in mind that wide-angle lenses have a tendency to distort when used very close to a subject, or when dealing with vertical lines. Tall trees or a high-rise hotel may seem to converge toward the top of the frame, for example. Once you're aware of these effects, you can use them to creative advantage.

Where a wide-angle lens extends normal perspective, a telephoto lens focuses on a portion of the overview, providing perspective in detail. Telephoto lenses, 125mm to 1,000mm, are good for shooting details from a distance and permit dramatic silhouettes of fishing boats against a setting sun, detailed portraits, floral design, and candids — although when choosing a lens, keep in mind that the weight of the higher ranges may prove difficult to support without a tripod (see below).

In addition to individual telephotos, a number of telephoto zoom lenses have become popular with travel photographers. Zooms offer the most versatility as they incorporate a range of focal lengths. A typical telephoto zoom — ranging from 70mm to 210mm, for example — allows you to frame a picture as you want it by choosing the most appropriate lens setting for the situation. That means carrying one lens with millimeter-to-millimeter variations from 70mm to 210mm. Also try a 35mm to 80mm. In general, beware of inexpensive models which can result in poor photographs.

The drawbacks of a zoom lens are its weight and a potential loss of clarity when compared with individual telephotos. This is less of a problem with the better lenses; and both problems are being eliminated by technological advances.

A 2X Teleconverter is a simple addition to a camera kit. Lightweight and easy to carry, the 2X doubles the focal length of various lenses, converting a 20mm into a 40mm, a 50mm into a 100mm, a 70mm to 210mm zoom into a 140mm to 420mm, and so forth. Though there is again a potential loss of clarity, and in low-lighting situations focusing may be somewhat more difficult due to the extra thickness of lens glass, the 2X is a versatile accessory that's easy to use.

While it may seem excessive, a small, lightweight tripod is a real asset in assuring picture quality. This is particularly true when the heavier telephoto lenses are used, or in situations where the available light is limited and shots will be made at speeds slower than 1/60 of a second. For sharp detail, closeups, night, or limited-light pictures while in Europe, a tripod is a must.

A small battery-powered electronic flash unit, or "strobe," is handy for very dim light or night use, but only if the subject is at a distance of 15 feet or less. Flash units cannot illuminate an entire scene (they're only effective up to about a dozen feet), and many museums and other establishments do not permit flash photography, so take such a unit only if you know you will need — and be able to use — it. (If you do violate these rules and take a picture in such a restricted area your film, and even your camera, may be confiscated.)

Subjects as varied as the interiors of Moorish castles, cathedrals, and wine cellars all become photographable with a flash. It also can provide frontal light for a backlit subject and additional light in a variety of dim situations, as it often is overcast in Iberia. If your camera does not have a hot-shoe, you will need a PC cord to synchronize the flash with your shutter. Be sure to take along extra batteries for the flash.

Film – Travel photographs are normally best in color. Good slide films are Koda-chrome 64 and Fujichrome 50, both moderate- to slow-speed films that provide satu-rated colors and work well in most outdoor light. For very bright conditions, try slower film, like Kodachrome 25. If the weather is cloudy, or you're indoors with only natural light, use a faster film, such as Kodachrome 200 or 400. There are now even faster films on the market for low-light situations. The result may be pictures with whiter, colder tones and a grainier image, but high-speed films open up picture possibilities that slower films cannot.

Films tend to render color in slightly different ways. For instance, while Kodachrome results in "warmer" tones and brings out reds and oranges, Ektachrome, a similar film, is "colder" and produces crisp, clear colors — particularly blues and greens. (It is also worth noting that Ektachrome generally can be processed at more photolabs than Kodachrome.) Fujichrome is noted for its yellows, greens, and whites. You might test films as you test your camera (see above) to determine your preference.

If you prefer film that develops into prints rather than slides, try Kodacolor 100 or 400 for most lighting situations. Vericolor is a professional film that comes in speeds of 160 and 400 and gives excellent results, especially for skin tones, but is particularly sensitive to temperature extremes which may cause color alteration. Bring it along for taking shots of people *if* you're sure you can protect it from extreme heat and cold. A newer all-purpose film with similar properties to Vericolor in terms of quality results is Ektar. It is not as sensitive to temperature changes as Vericolor, and comes in three speeds: 25, 125, and 1000. All lens and filter information applies equally to print and slide films.

If you are concerned about airport security X-rays damaging undeveloped film (X-rays do not affect processed film), store it in one of the lead-lined bags sold in camera shops. This possibility is not as much of a threat as it used to be, however. In the US, incidents of X-ray damage to unprocessed film (exposed or unexposed) are few because low-dosage X-ray equipment is used virtually everywhere. However, when crossing international borders, travelers may find that foreign X-ray equipment may deliver higher levels of radiation and damage film.

As a rule of thumb, photo industry sources say that film with speeds up to ASA 400 can go through security machinery in the US five times without any noticeable effect. Nevertheless, if you're traveling without a protective bag, ask to have your photo equipment inspected by hand. (Naturally, this is possible only if you're carrying your film and camera on board with you — a good idea, because it helps to preclude loss or theft or the possibility at some airports that checked baggage will be X-rayed with equipment more powerful than normally used for hand baggage.)

In the US, Federal Aviation Administration regulations require that if you request a hand inspection, you get it, but overseas the response may depend on the humor of the inspector. One type of film that never should be subjected to X-rays is the new, very high-speed ASA 1000 film; there are lead-lined bags made especially for it — and, in the event that you are refused a hand inspection, this is the only way to save your film. Finally, the walk-through metal detector devices at airports do not affect film, though film cartridges may set them off.

How much film should you take? If you are serious about photography, pack at least one roll of film (36 exposures) for each day of your trip. Film is especially expensive abroad, and any extra can be bartered away or brought home and safely stored in your refrigerator. (Processing also is more expensive abroad and not as safe as at home.) Nevertheless, if you don't bring enough, you should have no trouble getting any standard film in most places in Spain and Portugal; it's sold everywhere.

VIDEO CAMCORDERS: In general, camcorders are self-contained, automated, point-and-shoot devices, though for the more ambitious film-making traveler, 8mm video or movie cameras allow the operator a greater degree of control over the images recorded and superior image quality. What follows is a brief roundup of tips and suggestions for the beginning home moviemaker, and those travelers who need to brush up on their videotaping technique.

Your camcorder has some type of zoom feature, whether it's 4:1, 6:1, or all the way up to 12:1. For most people, that's enough. Although some models have a fixed lens, others, like 8mm video, provide you the option of adding a telephoto for close-up shooting or a wide-angle lens if you often find yourself not being able to fit all of what you want to shoot into the viewfinder. If you do decide to add a lens, check that the one you buy will fit your camcorder. You may be able to double up on your filters, though. As long as it's the same size, your camera filter should be able to fit on your camcorder lens. (See the discussion of filters below.)

Although the lux ratings of camcorders now are low enough to achieve some impressive videos in low-light situations, for good clarity and color saturation you should have an additional light (10 watts or higher) to brighten indoor shooting. Generally, the lights easily can be attached to the camcorder and come with the necessary accessories such as battery charger, battery pack, and light diffuser. All that can get fairly heavy, however, so you might want to leave your light at home. Most museums and churches prohibit the use of video lights — both for security reasons and because they can be harmful to paintings and stained glass, not to mention annoying to other visitors.

In general, Europe operates on 220 volt 50 Hz electric current, as opposed to the 110 volt 60 Hz current that is the standard in the United States (although 110 volt current also may be used in some areas of Portugal). To compensate for the difference, you'll need to make sure that the battery charger that comes with your camcorder is compatible with the current in the countries you're touring. Most chargers are compatible, but owner's manuals don't always spell this out. So if it's unclear, be sure to call the company and ask. If the charger is incompatible, you'll have to get a voltage converter. Even if your camcorder's charger is compatible with the current and voltage ratings in other countries, you'll need a plug adaptor kit to cope with the variations in plug configurations found in Europe. Voltage converters and adapter plug kits are available from some of the companies listed in *Books and Magazines* (above), specializing in travel paraphernalia; also see *Mail, Telephone, and Electricity,* in this section, for further information and sources.

You'll also be in for a shock if you try to play back your tape through a European TV set or VCR. Whereas the United States and Canada use the NTSC television standard, most European countries operate on the PAL standard. Still other European countries use the SECAM standard, so the chance of your playing back your video movies through a TV set in another country is unlikely. Because the various systems use a different number of lines-per-frame and frames-per-second, they are incompatible with each other. (For the same reason, if you send a tape of your sister's wedding to your brother in Spain, he won't be able to view it.) In order to review what you've taped, you'll either have to use the electronic viewfinder on your camcorder or have to take along a small portable NTSC TV to which you could connect your camcorder. For the same incompatibility reasons, however, you won't be able to view European telecasts with your portable. Although there are a few multiple-standard TV sets available, don't count on there being one in your hotel room.

Tapes – It usually is best to buy tapes before leaving home, as they probably will be lots more expensive near major tourist and resort areas. It also will be less confusing, since different countries have their own ways of labeling tape. Although the variations in recording and playback standards won't affect your ability to use the tape, they will affect how quickly you record. Because the tape moves slower in a PAL camcorder than in an NTSC camcorder, you will get less recording time from a European tape than is indicated on the label. So if you buy an E-160 tape designed for a PAL camcorder, you really will have only about 2 hours of recording time (T-120) on your NTSC camcorder.

If you do run out of tape while on your trip, you shouldn't have a hard time finding what you need. Most of the major tape brands — TDK, Sony, Memorex, Maxell,

BASF, Fuji, and Scotch — are available throughout the US, but when buying tapes abroad, you're bound to run into some unfamiliar names. Stick to what you know, if possible. When choosing, especially among unfamiliar brands, be sure that it is indeed the correct tape format — 8mm, VHS, Super VHS, Beta, and so on — for your camcorder.

Also, if an unknown brand is priced substantially below the rest, there's probably a reason. First of all, the image quality may be poor. Secondly, the few dollars you save in buying the least expensive videocassettes will mean nothing a few years from now when the tape is showing signs of wear. You also should be aware of the potential problem of low-quality tapes' damaging the heads of camcorders.

Because you'll want to keep your accessories to a manageable number — especially if you're using a full-size camcorder — you should use the longest-length tape possible for recording your trip. Depending on the tape speed of your equipment, the longest 8mm and VHS tapes generally run for 2 hours and VHS-C cassettes run for 20 minutes. VHS and VHS-C cassettes can record in the extended-play mode for 6-hour and 60-minute recordings, respectively, but extending the recording time reduces the picture quality substantially. It's best to record in the standard-play mode, because you'll get the best picture quality.

With the wide variety of grades and types of videocassettes on the market, it's easy to get confused about what kind of tape to buy for a particular application. Certain camcorders can record in stereo, so for those you'll want a hi-fi videocassette for better sound quality. If you have a Super VHS, Super VHS-C, or Hi Band 8mm camcorder, you'll want to buy the corresponding tapes for those high-end machines to achieve the best possible picture quality. A Super VHS-C videocassette will not improve your regular VHS-C video picture, however. Get a high-grade or professional quality tape for the once-in-a-lifetime videos that you plan to watch a lot. Before loading up on videocassettes for your trip, think about how much time you'll actually spend shooting, and about how many tapes you'll really want to view later. Plan on a tape for every other day of your vacation, or, if you intend to use your camcorder heavily, a tape for each day. Remember that you always can edit a tape, and even reuse it if you decide you don't want to keep it.

Your videocassettes generally are safe from the X-rays in airport detector devices, but the electromagnetic fields generated by those devices could cause dropouts in your tapes, which are recorded by an electromagnetic process. The lead-lined bags that protect against X-rays unfortunately don't protect against an electromagnetic field, so your best bet is to take your tapes along for a hand inspection. Because cassettes have been favorite carriers for terrorist explosives over the years, however, airport officials may insist that you put everything through the X-ray machine. If you don't have a choice, put them through and hope for the best.

FILTERS: For both Camcorders and SLR cameras, filters are important considerations. Take a skylight filter (1A or 1B) for each lens. There's no need to remove it, except to replace it with a different filter. Not only will it provide the filtration needed to combat atmospheric haze and ultraviolet light, but it also will protect the lens surface.

A polarizing filter goes one step beyond the skylight variety, cutting out reflections from non-metallic surfaces (water and glass, for instance) and penetrating haze for extra clarity and rich color saturation. It also will add impact to greens and blues in a landscape. While its effects are dramatic, it can be a difficult filter to use as it cuts back on light (it's a dark filter) and creates deep shadows. It will work well only under certain lighting conditions. In spite of these drawbacks, it remains an excellent filter for certain effects.

Unless you plan to experiment with the increasingly diverse range of specialty filters now available (diffraction, multiple image, and closeup, for instance), skylights and a polarizer are just about all you'll need. Stick to the high- to medium-priced glass filters (Hoya, Tiffen, or Vivitar, for example) to assure picture quality.

SOME FINAL TIPS

Get organized. A small, lightweight canvas camera bag with cushioning and Velcro dividers is perfect for carrying lenses, lens tissue, filters, rolls of film or tapes, and a strobe. It's amazing how compact camera equipment is when packed properly. For better pictures, remember the following pointers:

1. Get close. Move in to get your subject to fill the frame.
2. Vary your angle. Shoot from above or below; look for unusual perspectives.
3. Pay attention to backgrounds. Keep it simple or blur it out.
4. Look for details: not just a whole building, but a decorative element; not an entire street scene, but a single remarkable face.
5. Don't be lazy. Always carry your camera gear with you, loaded and ready for unexpected opportunities.

For Better Videos – Try to plan your movie with an introduction, a development, and a conclusion. Sometimes you can't help but get a video collage, but shoot with an eye — and an ear — toward how it's going to look and sound on a TV set. You're not just capturing a moment, as you do with still photography; you're telling a story.

1. To divide the tapes by country or region, use the camcorder's titling feature, if it has one, or shoot museum signs or some other kind of marker that indicates where you are. Use your fade in/fade out feature to provide smooth transitions.
2. Suppress your impulse to point and shoot and then find another object to shoot. Your viewers will need several seconds to focus on a subject and orient themselves to what they're seeing. Stay on each subject for at least 5 or 6 seconds — longer if the situation warrants.
3. Try not to shoot directly into strong, bright light as this may damage your camcorder. Your subject also is likely to appear as a silhouette because the camcorder will adjust for the brightest source. Some camcorders, however, do have backlight compensating features.
4. Vary your shooting techniques. Using the various buttons available at your fingertips, zoom in and out and pan from side to side to view your subject. If your subject is stationary, walk around (but hold the camera steady) to get a different angle. Your objective should be to create a smooth flow.
5. Your camcorder won't be welcome everywhere, although as they become more popular, they are increasingly accepted. In any event, before lugging your gear with you, check with the places you plan to visit.

■ **A note about courtesy and caution:** When photographing individuals in Spain and Portugal (and anywhere else in the world), ask first. It's common courtesy. Furthermore, some governments have security regulations regarding the use of cameras and will not permit the photographing of certain subjects, such as particular government and military installations. When in doubt, ask.

Useful Words and Phrases

Unlike the French, who tend to be a bit brusque if you don't speak their language perfectly, the Spanish and Portuguese do not expect you to speak their native tongues — but are very flattered when you try. In many circumstances, you won't have to, because the staffs at most hotels, as well as at a fair number of restaurants, speak serviceable English, or at least a modicum of it, which they usually are eager to try — and that means practicing with you. If you find yourself in a situation where your limited Spanish or Portuguese turns out to be the only means of communication, take the plunge. Don't be afraid of misplaced accents or misconjugated verbs — in most cases you will be understood.

Although there are several languages spoken throughout Spain, including *Gallego* (in the Galician region), *Catalan* (in Catalonia), and *Euskera* (in the Basque Country), the majority of the population is fluent in the most common language, Castilian Spanish. Castilian Spanish represents sounds quite predictably; pronunciation is straightforward, with only some minor dialect variations.

The list that follows is a selection of commonly used words and phrases to speed you on your way. Note that in Spanish and Portuguese, nouns either are masculine or feminine, as well as singular or plural, and that the adjectives that modify them must agree in both gender and quantity. Most nouns ending in *o* in the singular are masculine; the *o* becomes *os* in the plural. Most nouns ending in *a* in the singular are feminine; the *a* becomes *as* in the plural. Nouns may have other endings.

In Spanish, the letter *a* is pronounced as in *father.* The *e* is pronounced as in *egg* or *get.* The *i* is pronounced like the *ee* of *beet.* The *o* is pronounced as in *note.* The *u* is pronounced as in *lute.* The combination *ei* is pronounced like *ey* in *they; ai* is pronounced like *y* in *by; au* is pronounced like *ou* in *house.* In Spanish words, if there is no accent mark the vowel before the last consonant is stressed, with the exception of words ending in *n* or *s,* which are stressed on the second-to-last vowel (or syllable).

Spanish consonants are pronounced approximately as in English with these exceptions: The consonant *b* when beginning a word is pronounced somewhat like the English *b* with the lips slightly open for a softer sound; between vowels, it is pronounced like *v* in *lever.* The *h* always is silent, as in *hola* pronounced *ola.* The *j* is pronounced somewhat like the breathy *h* in *ha!* The consonant *c* preceding *e, i* or *y* in standard Castilian Spanish is generally pronounced *th* as in *then.* The same rule applies to the letter *z,* which is also pronounced as *th.* The *ll* in Spanish is pronounced *lya,* as in the English *million.* The letter *ñ* is pronounced like the *ny* in *canyon.*

Although, at first glance, Spanish and Portuguese spelling may appear similar, Portuguese pronunciation is substantially different and somewhat more difficult for the average English-speaking traveler. As a general rule, Portguese pronunciation does not represent sounds as consistently as Spanish.

The *a* is pronounced as the *a* in *watch.* The *e* in stressed syllables sounds like *eh,* as in English *pear* or *era.* Unstressed final *e* is pronounced like the *i* in *pin.* Like Spanish, the *i* in Portuguese is a simple vowel similar to the *i* in *pique.* Initial *i* before a vowel is pronounced like English *y* in *yet.* Stressed *o* also is a simple vowel pronounced as in *orb;* when written *ô* it is pronounced like the *o* in *mote.* Unstressed final *o* is pronounced like the *u* in *put.* The stressed *u* is pronounced as in *toot.* When vowels either bear a tilde (˜) or are followed by *m, n,* or *nh,* the pronunciation is nasal; that is, some air is emitted through the nose while the vowel is being pronounced. The French pronunciations of *dance* and *cent* illustrate this sound. As in Spanish, *ei* is "long a," *ai* stands for "long i," *ou* stands for "long o," and *au* has the vowel sound of *how.* As in Spanish, Portuguese words are generally stressed on the vowel preceding the last consonant. A nasalized vowel preceding a final vowel will be stressed.

Portuguese consonants are pronounced much like English with these exceptions: In Portuguese as in English, *c* always is hard before *a, o, u,* or a consonant, as in *car, core,* and *climb;* however *ch* has a soft sound like *sh* in *show.* (The letter *x* is also pronounced like *sh.*) *C* is soft when it falls before *e* or *i* or is marked with a cedilla (*ç*), as in *century.* The *s* following a stressed vowel is pronounced with a *z* sound, as in *rose.* The letter *i* is pronounced like *si* in *vision.* The letter *t* before a final unstressed *e* is pronounced like English *ch; d* in the same position is pronounced like English *i.*

These are only the most basic rules, and even they may seem daunting at first, but they shouldn't remain so for long. Nevertheless, if you can't get your mouth to speak Spanish or Portuguese, try your hands at it: With a little observation, you'll pick it up quickly and be surprised at how often your message will get across.

Greetings and Everyday Expressions

	Spanish	Portuguese
Good morning! (also, Good day)	*Buenos días!*	*Bom dia!*
Good afternoon/evening! (when arriving)	*Buenas tardes/noches!*	*Boa noite/tarde!*
Hello!	*Hola!*	*Ola!*
How are you?	*Cómo está usted?*	*Como vai?*
Pleased to meet you. (How do you do?)	*Mucho gusto en concerle.*	*Muito prazer em conhecê-lo (-la).*
Good-bye!	*Adiós!*	*Adeus!*
So long!	*Hasta luego!*	*Até logo!*
Goodnight! (when leaving)	*Buenas noches!*	*Boa noite!*
Yes	*Sí*	*Sim*
No	*No*	*Não*
Please	*Por favor*	*Por favor*
Thank you	*Gracias*	*Obrigado(a)*
You're welcome	*De nada*	*De nada*
I beg your pardon (Excuse me)	*Perdón*	*Perdão*
I don't speak Spanish/Portuguese.	*No hablo Español.*	*Não falo português.*
Do you speak English?	*Habla usted inglés?*	*Fala inglês?*
I don't understand.	*No comprendo.*	*Não compreêndo.*
Do you understand?	*Comprende?/Entiende?*	*Compreênde?/Entende?*
My name is . . .	*Me llamo . . .*	*Me chamo . . .*
What is your name?	*Cómo se llama?*	*Como se chama?*
miss	*señorita*	*menina*
madame	*señora* (married) *doña* (unmarried)	*senhora*
mister	*señor*	*senhor*
open	*abierto/a*	*aberto/a*
closed	*cerrado/a*	*encerrado(a)/fechado(a)*
entrance	*entrada*	*entrada*
exit	*salida*	*saída*
push	*empujar*	*empurrar*
pull	*tirar*	*puxar*
today	*hoy*	*hoje*
tomorrow	*mañana*	*amanhã*
yesterday	*ayer*	*ontem*

Checking In

I would like . . .	*Quisiera . . .*	*Queria/Costaria . . .*
I have a reservation a single room	*He hecho una reserva una habitación sencilla*	*Mandei reservar um quarto individual*

	Spanish	Portuguese
a double room	*una habitación doble*	*um quarto duplo*
a quiet room	*una habitación tranquila*	*um quarto tranquilo*
with bath	*con baño*	*com banho*
with shower	*con ducha*	*com chuveiro*
with a sea view	*con vista al mar*	*com vista para o mar*
with air conditioning	*con aire acondicionado*	*com ar condicionado*
with balcony	*con balcón*	*com varanda*
overnight only	*sólo una noche*	*só uma noite*
a few days	*algunos días*	*alguns dias*
a week (at least)	*una semana (por lo menos)*	*uma semana (pelo menos)*
with full board	*con pension completa*	*com pensão completa*
with half board	*con media pensión*	*com meia-pensão*
Does that price include	*Está incluido en el precio*	*O preço está incluido*
breakfast	*el desayuno*	*cafe da manhâ*
taxes	*los impuestos*	*as taxas*
VAT (Value Added Tax)	*IVA*	*IVA*
It doesn't work.	*No funciona*	*Não funciona*
Do you accept traveler's checks?	*Acepta usted cheques de viajero?*	*Aceitam cheques de viagem?*
Do you accept credit cards?	*Acepta tarjetas de crédito?*	*Posso pagar com cartão de crédito?*

Eating Out

	Spanish	Portuguese
ashtray	*un cenicero*	*um cinzeiro*
bottle	*una botella*	*uma garrafa*
(extra) chair	*una silla (adicional)*	*uma cadeira (mais)*
cup	*una taza*	*uma chávena*
fork	*un tenedor*	*um garfo*
knife	*un cuchillo*	*uma faca*
napkin	*una servilleta*	*um guardanapo*
plate	*un plato*	*um prato*
spoon	*una cuchara*	*uma colher*
table	*una mesa*	*uma mesa*
beer	*una cerveza*	*uma cerveja*
hot cocoa	*un chocolate caliente*	*um chocolate quente*
black coffee	*un café expreso*	*um café*
coffee with milk	*café con leche*	*café com leite*
cream	*crema*	*creme*
milk	*leche*	*leite*
tea	*un té*	*um chá*
fruit juice	*un zumo de fruta*	*um sumo/suco de fruta*
lemonade	*una limonada*	*um gasosa*
water	*agua*	*água*
mineral water (carbonated/ not carbonated)	*agua mineral (con gas/ sin gas)*	*água mineral (com gás/ sem gas)*

	Spanish	Portuguese
orangeade	*una naranjada*	*uma laranjada*
port	*oporto*	*vinho do Porto*
sherry	*jerez*	*vinho de Xerez*
red wine	*vino tinto*	*vinho tinto*
white wine	*vino blanco*	*vinho branco*
cold	*frío/a*	*frio/a*
hot	*caliente*	*quente*
sweet	*dulce*	*doce*
(very) dry	*(muy) seco/a*	*(extra) seco/a*
bacon	*tocino*	*toucinho*
bread	*pan*	*pão*
butter	*mantequilla*	*manteiga*
eggs	*huevos*	*ovos*
hard-boiled	*huevo duro*	*ovo cozido*
fried	*huevos fritos*	*ovos estrelados*
omelette	*tortilla*	*omelete*
soft-boiled	*huevo cocido pasado por agua*	*ovo cozido quente*
scrambled	*huevos revueltos*	*ovos mexidos*
honey	*miel*	*mel*
jam/marmalade	*mermelada*	*doce de fruta/mermelada*
orange juice	*zumo de naranja*	*sumo/suco de laranja*
pepper	*pimienta*	*pimenta*
salt	*sal*	*sal*
sugar	*azúcar*	*açúcar*
Waiter	*Camarero*	*Criado*
I would like	*Quisiera*	*Queria*
a glass of	*un vaso de*	*um copo de*
a bottle of	*una botella de*	*uma garrafa de*
a half bottle of	*una media botella de*	*uma meia-garrafa de*
a carafe of	*una garrafa de*	*uma jarra de*
a liter of	*un litro de*	*um litro de*
The check, please.	*La cuenta, por favor.*	*A conta, por favor.*
Is a service charge included?	*Está el servicio incluido?*	*E servico incluso?*
I think you made a mistake in this bill.	*Creo que hay un error en la cuenta.*	*Creio que se enganou na conta.*

Shopping

bakery	*la panadería*	*a padaria*
bookstore	*la librería*	*a livraria*
butcher shop	*la carnicería*	*o talho/açougue*
camera shop	*la tienda de fotografía*	*a loja de artigos fotográficos*
delicatessen	*ultramarinos*	*a salsicharia/lojade frios*
department store	*almacén*	*o grande armazém*
grocery	*la tienda de comestibles*	*supermercado*

	Spanish	Portuguese
jewelry store	*la joyería*	*a ourivesaria*
newsstand	*el quiosco de periódicos*	*o quiosquo la banca de jornais*
pastry shop	*la pastelería*	*a pastelaria*
perfume (and cosmetics) store	*perfumería*	*perfumaria*
pharmacy/drugstore	*la farmacia*	*a farmácia*
shoestore	*la zapatería*	*a sapataria*
supermarket	*el supermercado*	*o supermercado*
tobacconist	*el estanco*	*a tabacaria*
inexpensive	*barato/a*	*barato/a*
expensive	*caro/a*	*caro/a*
large	*grande*	*grande*
larger	*más grande*	*maior*
too large	*demasiado grande*	*muito grande*
small	*pequeño/a*	*pequeno/a*
smaller	*más pequeño/a*	*menor*
too small	*demasiado pequeño/a*	*muito pequeno/a*
long	*largo/a*	*comprido/a*
short	*corto/a*	*curto/a*
old	*viejo/a*	*velho/a*
new	*nuevo/a*	*novo/a*
used	*usado/a*	*usado/a*
handmade	*hecho/a a mano*	*feito/a à mão*
Is it machine washable?	*Es lavable a máquina?*	*Pode lavar-se à máquina?*
How much does it cost?	*Cuánto cuesta esto?*	*Quanto custa isto?*
What is it made of?	*De qué está hecho?*	*De que é feito?*
camel's hair	*pelo de camello*	*pêlo de camelo*
cotton	*algodón*	*algodão*
corduroy	*pana*	*bombazina*
filigree	*filigrana*	*filigrana*
lace	*encaje*	*renda*
leather	*cuero*	*cabedal/couro*
linen	*lino*	*linho*
silk	*seda*	*seda*
suede	*ante*	*camurça*
synthetic	*sintético/a*	*sintético/a*
tile	*azulejo*	*telha*
wool	*lana*	*lã*
brass	*latón*	*latão*
copper	*cobre*	*cobre*
gold	*oro*	*ouro*
gold plate	*lámina de oro*	*com banho de ouro*
silver	*plata*	*prata*
silver plate	*plata chapada*	*banhado a prata*
stainless steel	*acero inoxidable*	*aço inoxidável*
wood	*madera*	*madeira*

Colors

beige	*beige*	*bege*
black	*negro/a*	*prêto/a*

	Spanish	Portuguese
blue	*azul*	*azul*
brown	*marrón*	*castanho*
green	*verde*	*verde*
gray	*gris*	*cinzento/a*
orange	*naranjo/a*	*laranjado/a*
pink	*roso/a*	*cor-de-roso/-rosada*
purple	*morado/a*	*roxo/a*
red	*rojo/a*	*vermelho/a*
white	*blanco/a*	*branco/a*
yellow	*amarillo/a*	*amarelo/a*
dark	*oscuro/a*	*escuro/a*
light	*claro/a*	*claro/a*

Getting Around

	Spanish	Portuguese
north	*norte*	*norte*
south	*sur*	*sul*
east	*este*	*este*
west	*oeste*	*oeste*
right	*derecho/a*	*direita*
left	*izquierdo/a*	*esquerda*
Go straight ahead	*Siga todo derecho*	*Vá sempre em frente*
far	*lejos*	*longe*
near	*cerca*	*perto*
gas station	*gasolinera*	*estação de serviço*
train station	*la estación de ferrocarril*	*a estação dos comboios/de trem*
bus stop	*la parada de autobuses*	*a paragem do autocarro*
subway station	*estación de metro*	*estação de metrô*
airport	*aeropuerto*	*aeroporto*
tourist information	*información turística*	*informações de turismo*
map	*mapa*	*mapa*
one-way ticket	*un billete de ida*	*um bilhete/uma passagem de ida*
round-trip ticket	*un billete de ida y vuelta*	*um bilhete/uma passagem de ida e volta*
track/platform	*la vía/el andén*	*o cais/a plataforma*
first class	*primera clase*	*primeira classe*
second class	*segunda clase*	*segunda classe*
no smoking	*no fumadores*	*não fumadores*
gasoline	*gasolina*	*gasolina*
normal leaded	*gasolina normal*	*gasolina normal*
super leaded	*gasolina super*	*gasolina super*
unleaded	*gasolina sin plomo*	*gasolina sem chumbo*
diesel	*diesel*	*diesel*
tires	*los neumáticos*	*pneus*
oil	*el aceite*	*o óleo*
Fill it up, please.	*Llénelo, por favor.*	*Encha o depósito, por favor.*
Where is . . . ?	*Dónde está . . . ?*	*Onde éstão . . . ?*
Where are . . . ?	*Dónde están . . . ?*	*Onde são . . . ?*
How far is it to . . . from here?	*Qué distancia hay desde aquí hasta . . . ?*	*A que distância estamos de . . . ?*

	Spanish	Portuguese
Does this bus go to . . . ?	*Va este autobús a . . . ?*	*Este autocarro pára em . . . ?*
What time does it leave?	*A qué hora sale?*	*A que horas parte?*
Danger	*Peligro*	*Perigo*
Caution	*Precaución*	*Cuidado*
Detour	*Desvío*	*Desvio*
Do Not Enter	*Paso Prohibido*	*Entrada Proibida*
No Parking	*Estacionamento Prohibido*	*Estacionamento Proibido*
No Passing	*Prohibido Adelantar*	*Proibido Ultrapassar*
One Way	*Dirección Unica*	*Sentido Unico*
Pay Toll	*Peaje*	*Pedagio*
Pedestrian Zone	*Peatones*	*Pedestres*
Reduce Speed	*Despacio*	*Afrouxe/Devagar*
Steep Incline	*Fuerte Declive*	*Descida Perigosa*
Stop	*Alto*	*Alto*
Use Headlights	*Encender los faros*	*Acender as Luzes*
Yield	*Ceda el Paso*	*Dê Passagem*

Personal Items and Services

	Spanish	Portuguese
barbershop	*la peluquería*	*o barbeiro*
beauty shop	*el salón de belleza*	*o instituto de beleza*
dry cleaner	*la tintorería*	*o lavandaria a seco*
hairdresser (salon)	*la peluquería*	*o cabeleireiro*
launderette	*la lavandería*	*a lavanderia automática*
laundry	*la lavandería*	*a lavanderia*
post office	*el correo*	*correio*
aspirins	*aspirinas*	*aspirinas*
Band-Aids	*tiritas*	*pensos rápidos*
sanitary napkins	*unos paños higiénicos*	*pensos higiénicos*
shampoo	*un champú*	*um shampoo*
shaving cream	*espuma de afeitar*	*um creme de barba*
soap	*el jabón*	*um sabonete*
stamps	*sellos*	*selos*
tampons	*unos tampones higiénicos*	*tampões higiénicos*
tissues	*unos pañuelos de papel*	*lenços de papel*
toilet paper	*papel higiénico*	*papel higiénico*
toothbrush	*un cepillo de dientes*	*uma escova de dentes*
toothpaste	*pasta de dientes*	*pasta de dentes*
Where is the bathroom?	*Dónde está el baño?*	*Onde está o banheiro?*
The bathroom door will say:		
for the men's room	*Caballeros*	*Cavalheiros*
for the women's room	*Señoras*	*Senhoras*

Days of the Week

	Spanish	Portuguese
Monday	*Lunes*	*Segunda-feira*
Tuesday	*Martes*	*Terça-feira*
Wednesday	*Miércoles*	*Quarta-feira*

	Spanish	Portuguese
Thursday	*Jueves*	*Quinta-feira*
Friday	*Viernes*	*Sexta-feira*
Saturday	*Sábado*	*Sábado*
Sunday	*Domingo*	*Domingo*

Months

January	*Enero*	*Janeiro*
February	*Febrero*	*Fevereiro*
March	*Marzo*	*Março*
April	*Abril*	*Abril*
May	*Mayo*	*Maio*
June	*Junio*	*Junho*
July	*Julio*	*Julho*
August	*Agosto*	*Agosto*
September	*Septiembre*	*Setembro*
October	*Octubre*	*Outubro*
November	*Noviembre*	*Novembro*
December	*Diciembre*	*Dezembro*

Numbers

zero	*cero*	*zero*
one	*uno*	*um/uma*
two	*dos*	*dois/duas*
three	*tres*	*três*
four	*cuatro*	*quatro*
five	*cinco*	*cinco*
six	*seis*	*seis*
seven	*siete*	*sete*
eight	*ocho*	*oito*
nine	*nueve*	*nove*
ten	*diez*	*dez*
eleven	*once*	*onze*
twelve	*doce*	*doze*
thirteen	*trece*	*treze*
fourteen	*catorce*	*catorze*
fifteen	*quince*	*quinze*
sixteen	*dieciséis*	*dezesseis*
seventeen	*diecisiete*	*dezessete*
eighteen	*dieciocho*	*dezoito*
nineteen	*diecinueve*	*dezenove*
twenty	*veinte*	*vinte*
thirty	*treinta*	*trinta*
forty	*cuarenta*	*quarenta*
fifty	*cincuenta*	*cinquênta*
sixty	*sesenta*	*sessenta*
seventy	*setenta*	*setenta*
eighty	*ochenta*	*oitenta*
ninety	*noventa*	*noventa*
one hundred	*cien*	*cem*
one thousand	*mil*	*mil*

PERSPECTIVES

Spain

History

According to the old saying, "Europe ends at the Pyrenees," and it's true that throughout modern history, Spain has often found itself the "odd man out" among European nations. Yet once, for a brief, glorious period, it outshone every other nation in the West. Fresh from the Reconquest against the Moors, Spain emerged at the end of the 15th century to straddle the diplomatic stage like some new colossus: discovering a new world, becoming the greatest power on earth, and creating a breathtaking golden age of culture. Within 150 years, however, her empire was breaking up and her domestic affairs were a shambles. No wonder, then, if today Spain seems to live in the shadow of a great, and oft-remembered past.

As the cave paintings at Altamira and elsewhere attest, people have lived on the Iberian Peninsula since the Stone Age. (Scientists believe that the enigmatic Basques of northern Spain, with their unique language, may be direct descendants of prehistoric Pyrenean cave dwellers.) Early in its recorded history, the peninsula began to exert the special allure it has always held for foreigners. The first to arrive — probably from North Africa sometime around 3000 BC — were the people for whom the peninsula is named: the Iberians. Joining them, about 2000 years later, were Celts from northern Europe, the same people who inhabited Ireland, Scotland, and Wales.

In the course of time, remote Iberia became a final destination for many expanding Mediterranean civilizations, at least for those whose ships dared to pass through the Pillars of Hercules (the Straits of Gibraltar) and brave the certain dangers of the "Sea of Darkness" — the Atlantic Ocean. One people who dared were the seafaring Phoenicians. Around 1100 BC, they established trading cities along the coast, including Gadir (Cádiz) — Europe's oldest continuously inhabited city. Greek colonizers arrived about 5 centuries later, bringing with them the olive and the vine, which would become the two indispensable items of Spanish life.

A misguided invitation brought the Carthaginians. The Phoenicians had asked Carthage, then an emerging power, to assist them against Tartessos, a mysterious native civilization that — from a capital near the mouth of the Guadalquivir River — controlled most of present-day Andalusia. The Carthaginians not only agreed to help, they decided to stay and in no time were entrenched along the coast. Eventually, they took over the peninsula, which they named *Spania,* or the "land of rabbits." The Carthaginians, in turn, lost their hold to Rome in 218 BC, during the Second Punic War.

It took Rome 2 centuries to subdue the bellicose inhabitants of the newly named *Hispania;* one tribe, the Numantians, burned their own city and perished in its flames rather than surrender. In 147 BC, Viriatus the shepherd, one of Spain's (and Portugal's) great heroes, united neighboring tribes and managed to reconquer and control much of western and central Spain for 8 years. But Rome's legions eventually triumphed, and by 19 BC they had the peninsula firmly under control.

Hispania remained a vital colony for 4 centuries, providing Rome with minerals and food, as well as the emperors Trajan and Hadrian. In return, Rome gave the peninsula its first taste of political and cultural unity, an efficient administration, and a code of law. Commerce flourished. Córdoba became a center of intellectual life. Rome built aqueducts, bridges, and roads to serve other prosperous cities such as Itálica and Mérida. It gave its language, Latin, from which the languages of the peninsula — except the enigmatic Basque — derive, and eventually it gave its religion — Christianity.

Roman rule lasted until the arrival of the barbarians during the 5th century. Vandals and others invaded from the north in 409. Five years later, the Visigoths — semi-civilized and Christian — arrived, supposedly to help Rome fend off other barbarian groups. Like so many others, however, they remained — and ruled Iberia for the next 3 centuries, gradually assimilating with the Hispano-Roman population. Though originally followers of Arianism — a heretical form of Christianity — by 589 the Visigoths had converted to Roman Catholicism and adopted it as the state religion.

What eventually brought about the Visigoths' demise was their tradition of elective kingship, which encouraged a steady stream of pretenders to the throne. One such challenger, early in the 8th century, seems to have petitioned North African Muslims for help against his king, Rodrigo. As a result, an Arab-Berber army landed at Gebel-Tarik (Tarik's Rock — eventually corrupted to Gibraltar) on Spain's southern coast and smashed Rodrigo's army. Within a few years the Moors, as they came to be known, had swept across most of the peninsula.

Moorish Spain, called Al-Andalus (today's Andalusia) and centered at the caliphate of Córdoba, endured for nearly 800 years, reaching its height at the end of the 10th century. During that time, it made a profound impact, bringing a new culture, language, and religion to the European continent. While the rest of Europe thrashed about in feudal chaos, Moorish Spain flourished, becoming the most powerful and civilized kingdom in the West. Among its triumphs were new crops — such as oranges and figs — an efficient irrigation system, and expanded commerce. It also had the largest merchant marine in the Mediterranean.

The Moors were a cultivated people. Their scholars preserved and transmitted the wisdom of the ancients, and their architects left behind a wealth of beautiful buildings, including the one immortalized for Americans in Washington Irving's *Tales from the Alhambra.* They also were remarkably tolerant. Many Christians converted to Islam, though there was little pressure to do so. Those who didn't convert but did adopt Arab ways were known as Mozarabs. Jews, too, who had been persecuted under the Visigoths, could now live freely and prosper. The professions were opened to them, and some

Jews rose to fill the state's highest offices. Others became scholars, like the great Hebrew philosopher Moses Maimonides.

The one serious mistake the Moors made was neglecting to conquer the northern kingdom of Asturias. From this stronghold, in 722, the Visigothic noble Pelayo and his followers began the *reconquista* (the Reconquest). For the next 7 centuries, the defenders of Christian Spain waged a desultory and meandering war against the Moors, gradually regaining the land they had lost. In the process, they began to unify their country. They claimed St. James (Sant Iago) the Apostle as their patron; his shrine at Santiago de Compostela became the goal of Europe's greatest pilgrimage. Great romantic stories developed out of the Reconquest — of the Crusaders and especially El Cid, Spain's magnificent legendary hero, who captured Valencia in 1094.

Piece by piece, the kingdom of the Moors began to fall apart. In 1002, after the death of Al-Mansur, the last great Cordoban caliph, the caliphate shattered into some 20 small kingdoms. Then, in 1212, the Moors suffered their most stinging defeat yet at Las Navas de Tolosa. They were driven from Córdoba and Seville about 25 years later. By the middle of the 13th century, and for another 200 years, Moorish power was limited to the kingdom of Granada.

During this same period, the small Spanish states began to consolidate. By the end of the 11th century, for example, Alfonso VI was sole ruler of León, Castile, Navarre, and Aragon. Two centuries later, Aragon and Castile were the two largest and most important kingdoms. Aragon — which, turning outward to the Mediterranean, had set up a wealthy commercial empire — was quite different from crusading Castile. But then, in 1469, Castile's Isabella married Aragon's Ferdinand I and united the two kingdoms — creating a nation in one marital swoop. Each kingdom, however, continued to operate autonomously, and no one yet used the term *España* to designate the country as a whole.

For good or ill, the reign of the Catholic Monarchs (so called because of their religious fervor) was the pivotal point in Spanish history. Between them, Isabella and Ferdinand unified the country, instituted the Spanish Inquisition, expelled the Moors and the Jews, discovered a new world, and began an empire.

Their first significant act, in 1478, was to set up an institution to enforce the nation's religious "purity" — a dreaded court with one of history's most odious names: the Spanish Inquisition. Headed by the Dominican monk Tomás de Torquemada, its main victims were insincere Muslim and Jewish converts to Christianity. The Inquisition was to remain a feature of Spanish government for more than 350 years.

One year in the reign of the Catholic Monarchs stands out — 1492. In that year the kingdom of Granada — the Moors' final bastion and a dreamy remnant of Al-Andalus, complete with its fairy-tale palace, the Alhambra — finally surrendered. In the same year, the Catholic Monarchs gave both Muslims and Jews a choice — convert or leave, an edict that sent hundreds of thousands of skilled and able residents fleeing at a time when Spain needed them most. Another of that year's momentous events was the arrival at court of an adventurer named Christopher Columbus. After convincing the queen to sponsor his expedition, he set sail west for a shortcut to the Indies and found, instead, a new world. Within a few years, men like Vasco Núñez de Balboa, Ferdinand Magellan, and Hernando de Soto joined the ranks of explorers financed by the Spanish court.

The Catholic Monarchs were eventually succeeded, in 1516, by their grandson Carlos I of Spain, who was also the Holy Roman Emperor Charles V, heir to the Low Countries, Austria, and much of present-day Germany. He was the first of the Hapsburgs, a line that was destined to rule for nearly 2 centuries — and lead Spain from the pinnacle of power to the depths of despair.

Carlos's reign was the Age of the Conquistadores; Cortés landed in Mexico in 1519, Pizarro in Peru in 1532. Spain eventually laid claim to all of present-day Latin America (except Brazil), the southern part of the present-day United States from Florida to California, and the Philippines. Spanish fleets ruled the seas. Accompanying the explorers and conquistadores were Jesuit priests, members of a religious order founded in 1539 by Ignatius of Loyola to ignite the Counter-Reformation (a movement meant to keep Spain free from Protestantism, which was sprouting all over contemporary Europe) and to make converts, especially in the New World.

During his 40-year reign, Carlos spent just 16 years in Spain. Self-appointed defender of the Catholic faith against Protestants and Turks, he spent more on war than his treasure galleons could garner from the Americas. When he retired, the imperial crown went to his brother, and control of Spain and the Netherlands to his son, Felipe.

Felipe (Philip II), a much-maligned monarch, ruled from 1556 to 1598. He oversaw many of Spain's greatest triumphs and its most ignominious failures — victory over the Turks at Lepanto, the conquest of Portugal, the establishment of the capital at Madrid, and construction of the Escorial palace, as well as chronic warfare in the Netherlands and the disastrous defeat of the Spanish Armada in 1588, which put an end to Spain's hopes of remaining a great world power.

Ironically, just at the time Spain began to slip from political ascendency, its cultural Golden Age bloomed, with El Greco, Velázquez, Ribera, and other such artists, as well as immortal writers such as Cervantes, Lope de Vega, and Tirso de Molina. Their styles were unmistakably Spanish, from the picaresque in literature to the brooding mysticism of religious art.

This cultural explosion peaked in the 17th century, but European wars and a calvalcade of economic setbacks and weak kings left Spain in a pitiful condition. To make matters worse, this was the era of Francis Drake and other "seadogs" who delighted in "singeing the beard" of the Spanish king by capturing his treasure galleons. When the feeble-minded Carlos II became king at the end of the century, everyone knew the Hapsburgs' days were numbered.

Although Carlos had willed the throne to a grandson of Louis XIV, most of Europe spent years fighting the War of the Spanish Succession before the Bourbon dynasty, in the person of Felipe (Philip) V, settled in. Comparatively modern by Hapsburg standards, the new rulers finished the process started by Ferdinand and Isabella: unification of Spain. Hated by the provinces, the

Bourbons crushed regionalism and centralized with a passion in favor of Castile, especially Madrid, made Castilian the official language, and built grand avenues and imposing buildings.

New ideas, born of the Enlightenment, trickling in from France found their champion in Carlos III, whose reign (1759–88) offered hope for a revitalized Spain. But when the French Revolution erupted in 1789, Spanish nationalism was suddenly on a collision course with its proselytizing neighbor. Spain's hostility toward France deepened a few years later when the Spanish king was forced to step aside for Napoleon's brother, Joseph Bonaparte. This usurpation proved intolerable to Spaniards. On *dos de mayo,* May 2, 1808, they rose up against the French to launch the War of Independence (also known as the Peninsular War), a scene movingly depicted in Goya's magnificent painting *The Second of May.* Spanish guerrillas joined with British troops under the future Duke of Wellington to drive out the French.

After a brief flirtation with constitutional government in 1812, Spain reestablished the monarchy 2 years later in the person of the highly reactionary Ferdinand VII. For the remainder of the 19th century, Spanish politics were a continuing clash between the traditional ideas of aristocrats and peasants and the new, more liberal ideas of the emerging middle class. Both Carlist Wars — the first beginning in 1833, the second in 1874 — were expressions of this deep division. The army, which often sided with the liberals, became the ultimate arbiter of power, and so the great question became not who would control Spain, but who would control the army. Shifts in power were often brought about by the *pronunciamiento* (the Spanish version of the coup d'état).

The Spanish-American War in 1898 led to another crisis, for it meant the swift and humiliating loss of the last vestiges of empire. Spain had begun to lose its colonial grip during the Napoleonic Wars. Venezuela had declared its independence in 1811, and other South American countries soon followed its example. Yet Spain somehow held onto a belief in its imperial greatness. The economic and psychological malaise of the war's aftermath found bitter expression in the cultural movement known as the Generation of 1898. Some of modern Spain's great names belonged to it: Baroja, Unamuno, Machado, and Ortega y Gasset.

When the army suffered another disaster in 1921, this time at the hands of the Moroccan Berbers, General Primo de Rivera led a coup to prop up the wilting monarchy. His "benign" dictatorship lasted until 1930. A year later, the king was forced into exile and the Second Republic proclaimed. This unfortunate government — born amid mass enthusiasm — slowly disintegrated into near anarchy.

The stage now was set for the tragedy of the Spanish Civil War. In July 1936, right-wing generals, who had been plotting a revolt for months, decided to act. Led by a young general named Francisco Franco, the Nationalist rebels rose throughout Spain and captured about half the nation. Their supporters included most of the military and police, the Catholic church, landowners and other conservative groups, and the Falange, Spain's Fascist party. Supporters of the Republic, or Loyalists, included a larger slice of the general population: most of the workers and peasants, regional parties from

Catalonia and the Basque region, anti-clericals, socialists, Communists, and anarchists.

Unique to the Civil War (1936–39) was the passionate interest it aroused internationally (British statesman Anthony Eden nicknamed it the War of the Spanish Obsession). The Francoists received crucial aid from Germany and Italy, including combat units, and in 1937 a German bombing raid devastated Guernica, a town that had symbolized Basque independence for over 400 years. Left-wing groups and individuals from around the world rallied to the cause of the Loyalists. American writers, journalists, and intellectuals flocked to Spain to participate in the war and to report on it, among them Ernest Hemingway, who wrote about the conflict in his novel *For Whom the Bell Tolls.* The Loyalists also could count on the famed International Brigades, volunteers from a score of nations, including America's Abraham Lincoln Brigade.

Largely due to foreign aid and the Republic's internal strife, the Nationalists won in 1939. Generalísimo Francisco Franco had been named head of the Nationalist Government the previous year. During World War II, Spain remained neutral, much to Hitler's chagrin. Later, however, in the diplomatic world of post-war Europe, Spain was something of a Fascist pariah to the victorious nations. In reality, Franco's reign was essentially an old-fashioned military dictatorship that looked more to the glories of 16th-century Spain than to any Fascist ideology.

Spain's emergence from the diplomatic boycott began with an agreement allowing American military bases on Spanish soil. The United States exchanged ambassadors with Spain and granted it a large loan. By 1955, Spain was finally accepted into the United Nations. Now Franco — in theory just a guardian until the restoration of the monarchy — could concentrate on shoring up his regime and rebuilding a devastated economy.

Prior to 1969, the question on everyone's mind had been "After Franco, what?" Then, in that year, Franco named Juan Carlos, grandson of deposed King Alfonso XIII and heir to the throne, as his successor, not to assume power, however, until after Franco's death. The old general finally died in November 1975, and a nation eager for change began its great experiment with democracy.

Today, Spain is ruled by a parliamentary monarchy, but King Juan Carlos has proved to be no mere figurehead. In July of 1976, the new king named Adolfo Suárez as prime minister. Suárez swiftly introduced a political reform bill that was just as swiftly endorsed by parliament and the people, and in October 1978, a new liberal constitution was installed. When Suárez resigned in January 1981, the king presented him with a dukedom.

The following month, a group of army officers burst into parliament — the Cortes — and held it at gunpoint for almost 24 hours. The calm decisiveness of King Juan Carlos helped to cut short this attempted coup. Despite this ominous event, Felipe González, a socialist, was elected prime minister on November 28, 1982 — peacefully and with the army's acquiescence. Under Gonzalez's leadership, the Partido Socialista Obrero Español (PSOE) is in reality a European-style social democratic party, short on ideology and long on social programs.

The most far-reaching recent change has been the acceptance of regionalism. Spain, which began as a land of distinct regions, was not yoked into one nation until the 15th century; in many places strong regional feelings remain — often accompanied by distinct languages — as in the Basque areas, Catalonia, and Galicia. Now the development of the Autonomous Communities — a semi-federal arrangement — gives each of these regions a degree of self-government.

For one group, however, this may not be enough. The Basques have always been a fiercely independent people. These inhabitants of northern Spain and southern France share a language unlike any other in Europe and a history that goes back, many believe, to the Stone Age. Many Basques want complete independence, a country of their own to be named Euskadi ("collection of the Basques"). For the past 30 years, a terrorist organization, ETA (Euskadi Ta Askatasuna — "Euskadi and Freedom"), has been ferociously seeking this goal.

Paradoxically, along with this regional tendency, Spain also has been rekindling its romance with Europe, as shown by its membership in NATO and the Common Market. Now that the country is a full-fledged member of the European Community, it is no longer accurate to say that "Europe ends at the Pyrenees."

Nor is it accurate to look on Spain as an impoverished nation. During the 1960s and 1970s, the country experienced a rapid, dramatic upsurge of economic growth — an "economic miracle," albeit one accompanied by extensive urbanization that aggravated the problem of an already sparsely populated countryside.

Today, looking forward to the immediate future, Spain is approaching new heights of optimism. With Madrid living up to its EEC designation as 1991's Cultural Capital of the Year, the *1992 Summer Olympic Games* slated for Barcelona, a world's fair, *Expo '92,* taking over Seville, and the whole country set to join in commemorations of the quincentenary of Christopher Columbus's discovery of the New World, it would be hard to envision a nation tuned to a greater pitch of collective celebration. As far as the Spanish are concerned, their country is poised on the brink of a new era — just as it was 500 years ago, when Columbus set sail to meet and greet the world.

Literature

 From the beginning, Spanish literature has exhibited certain characteristics that have stayed with it through the centuries: a fierce individualism, a stern philosophy of life, a love for the tragic, tempered by lyricism, and the humorous, often satirical, rendition of everyday life. Spain takes its literature seriously; from Seneca to Lorca, Spanish writers have been paid the dubious compliment of paying for their opinions with their lives.

Spanish literature and language began with the Romans, who ruled Spain for 6 centuries after defeating the Carthaginians in 206 BC. One of Roman

Spain's most famous writers was the philosopher and dramatist Lucius Anna-eus Seneca (ca. 4 BC–AD 65). Born in Córdoba, Seneca advocated the Roman philosophy of Stoicism, which counseled strength of will and calm acceptance of both pain and pleasure. He left Spain early in life to become the tutor and then principal adviser to Nero, the infamous emperor. Learning that Nero had ordered his death for taking part in an alleged conspiracy, Seneca com-mitted suicide. Seneca's forte was melodramatic, bloodthirsty tragedy, writ-ten to be read aloud before the emperor's court. *Phaedra* and *Oedipus,* which are based on Greek legends, are among his most exciting works. His ethical essays, however, have proved more influential than his plays. In poetry, the master was Martial (ca. AD 40–104), born in Bilbilis, Spain. Sharp, witty satiric epigrams are his claim to fame.

Later, under Moorish rule the Spanish city of Córdoba became, after Byzantium, the second-most-important center of culture in the Western world. Many scholars believe that the Moorish *zejels* — brief love lyrics in colloquial Arabic — may have spawned the ballads of the troubadors of southern France, whose 12th-century creations underpin modern European poetry and even, perhaps, our whole concept of romantic love.

A truly Spanish national literature began during the medieval period (ca. 1000–1500) with folk epics — popular narratives in verse called *cantares de gesta* — that may have sprung from the Goths' love of epic songs. The most famous — *El cantar del mío cid* (ca. 1140) — celebrates El Cid, the great hero of the Christian Reconquest of Spain from the Moors.

Most medieval poetry consists of either the stories and songs of the min-strels or the devotional and didactic works of the clergy. Gonzalo de Berceo (1180–1246), the earliest Spanish poet of record, wrote in a learned lyrical form of the lives of the saints and the miracles of the Virgin. The most important prose work of the period, *La crónica general* (The General Chroni-cle — 1270, 1289), author or authors unknown, fuses world history with prose versions of the epics.

A dissolute genius and Spain's first humorist, Juan Ruiz, Archpriest of Hita (ca. 1280–1351), was the 14th century's literary giant. His poetic masterpiece, *Libro de buen amor* (Book of Spiritual Love), consists of both narrative and lyrical verses. The extent of its spirituality, however, can be deduced from the activities of its most famous character, Trotaconventos — a go-between for the archpriest's love affairs. The story is told in the first person; its author's distinctive personality suffuses this realistic view of Castilian life.

Due to Spain's geographic isolation and its peoples' fierce individualism, the Renaissance didn't arrive here until late in the 15th century. Some date it from 1469, when Ferdinand of Aragon married Isabella of Castile, a great patron of the arts. The century's greatest poet, Jorge Manrique (ca. 1440–79), wrote *Coplas por la muerte de su padre* (Verses on the Death of His Father), widely known through Longfellow's translation. A priest, Juan del Encina (1469–1529), earned the epithet "father of Spanish drama" for his plays on religious themes.

The century's best literary work, however, may be the prose drama *Celes-tina* (1499). It is attributed to Fernando de Rojas, a converted Jew who wished for anonymity because of the Inquisition's persecution. Celestina, a sagacious crone whom Calisto enlists to aid him in his suit for Melibea, is one of Spain's great literary characters.

Spain's Golden Age began in the 16th century. As the conquistadores seized gold from the New World, writers mined the spirit of the Renaissance. Garcilaso de la Vega (1501–36) — a nobleman who died fighting in France — commandeered Italian poetic forms, made them Spanish, and composed sublime sonnets to his dead beloved.

During the same century, Spain gave European literature the picaresque novel. The anonymously written *Lazarillo de Tormes* (1554), about a boy and his adventures serving various hardhearted masters, was the first of a genre that realistically depicts peripatetic rogues (*pícaros*) in the underworld.

The most important novelist, however — the master genius of Spanish literature — is Miguel de Cervantes Saavedra (1547–1616). The fourth child of a failed physician, Cervantes was rather a picaresque hero himself. At 22 he left home for Italy, and entered military service a year later. His left hand was crippled in a battle. In 1575, he was captured by pirates and sold into slavery in Algiers. After numerous attempts at escape, he was ransomed 5 years later. In 1584 he married and, needing money, began to write.

Cervantes's first novel, *La Galatea,* was published in 1585. Neither it nor his dramatic works were successful. After taking such jobs as purchasing agent and tax collector, he eventually wound up in debtor's prison. There he conceived and began to write his masterpiece, *Don Quijote de la Mancha* (Don Quixote). By 1603 he was living with his family in Valladolid. The first part of the book, published in 1605, was an enormous success. Unfortunately, Cervantes had sold all his rights to it for a paltry sum.

Don Quixote begins as a satire on the overblown romances of chivalry that were then so popular in Spain. Addicted to these romances, the impoverished nobleman Don Quixote sets forth with his materialistic servant Sancho Panza on a series of adventures; his aim is to revive the glorious ideals of honor and chivalry. Part Two, published 10 years after the first part, is an even richer work: Don Quixote has become more majestic and Sancho wiser.

Although some critics consider *Don Quixote* the quintessence of the picaresque, it is actually far more sophisticated than that simple genre. It has been called the first modern novel — a new fictional form that blends the real with the ideal, poetry with prose, romantic adventures with incisive literary criticism. Cervantes disliked the cynicism of the picaresque. Suffused throughout his work is faith in humanity. Cervantes's other major work is *Novelas ejemplares* (Exemplary Tales), a collection of stories, some of which are picaresque. In the dedication and prologue to his posthumously published *Persiles y Sigismunda* is the artist's moving farewell to the world. He died 4 days after completing it.

Félix Lope de Vega Carpio (1562–1635) is the Golden Age's dramatic giant. An orphan of modest means and little schooling, Lope wrote his first play at the age of 12. He chose to write drama because it was the only remunerative form of writing at the time. Lope wrote prodigiously — an estimated 2,000 plays of which 400 have survived. Many show the weaknesses that come with hasty writing. One of his best is *El caballero de Olmedo* (The Gentleman from Olmedo), about a nobleman who continues to visit his beloved despite repeated warnings that he may be killed. One of Lope's followers was Fray Gabriel Téllez, known as Tirso de Molina (ca. 1584–1648), who, in 1630, gave the world *El burlador de Sevilla* (The Seducer of Seville), the earliest known dramatic version of the Don Juan legend.

Literary critics call the 17th century the Age of Affectation. As Spain declined in power under incompetent Hapsburgs, the Renaissance style evolved into the baroque. Writers practiced *culteranismo,* a pretentious and obscure style and vocabulary designed for the elite. The champions of the worldly priest Luis de Góngora y Argote (1561–1627) changed the name of the style to Gongorism. Although for hundreds of years his poetry was scorned as too mannered, today Góngora has been revived and elevated to the rank of major Spanish poet.

The other well-known dramatist of the Golden Age is Pedro Calderón de la Barca (1600–1681). Although schooled in Gongorism, the well-educated Calderón knew that this type of literary subtlety would not work on stage. His play *La vida es sueño* (Life Is a Dream) is about a Polish prince who is imprisoned in chains by a fearful father. Its hero, Segismondo, now has become a symbol of moral choice.

The 18th century was the Age of Reason. French neo-classicism was the style in Europe and French Bourbon kings ruled Spain. Pedantry rather than artistry ruled Spanish literature. The best novel was the picaresque autobiography (1743) of a mathematics professor and soothsayer, *Vida de Don Diego de Torres Villaroel* (The Life of Don Diego de Torres Villaroel). In poetry and drama, the important figures were Juan Meléndez Valdés (1754–1817) and Leandro Fernández de Moratín (1760–1828), poet and playwright respectively.

During the first half of the 19th century, Europe turned from the objectivity and reason of classicism to the subjectivity and emotionalism of Romanticism. In Spain, Romanticism began in 1833 when Isabella II took the throne, ending the repression of the previous reign and allowing artists to return from exile. A popular literary movement — *costumbrismo* — dealt with local customs and expressed itself in satirical newspaper and magazine essays. Particularly outstanding were those written by the melancholic Mariano José de Larra (1809–37), who committed suicide. In drama, José Zorrilla (1817–93) achieved fame with *Don Juan Tenorio,* which added new touches to the old legend. Critics — and Zorrilla himself — condemned the play for its loose structure, but its popularity has not waned; it is still staged annually in Spain on *All Saints' Day.*

The leading Romantic poet was José de Espronceda (1808–42), a fighting political liberal and exile who once was jailed for his writings. His best work, *El estudiante de Salamanca* (The Student of Salamanca), is also based on the Don Juan legend. Another writer of the period, the post-Romantic dramatist José Echegaray (1832–1916), was the first Spaniard ever to win the Nobel Prize for literature (1904).

Around mid-century, the sketches of *costumbrismo* expanded into a new form of fiction, the regional novel. Countess Emilia Pardo Bazán (1852–1921) introduced the naturalism of Zola to Spain with a pair of novels about the degeneration of a noble Galician family. The Spanish novelist best known to

Americans is Vicente Blasco Ibáñez (1867–1928), whose most popular works, *Blood and Sand* and *The Four Horsemen of the Apocalypse,* are not his best. His masterpiece is a regional novel of Valencia, *La barraca* (The Cabin). The greatest novelist of the century, however, was not a regional writer. Benito Pérez Galdós (1843–1920), considered by many to be the Charles Dickens of Spain, composed a 46-volume series of historical romances, *Episodios nacionales* (National Episodes), on 18th-century Spanish life.

A crisis at the close of the century led to a new renaissance in the arts in Spain. After prolonged political and spiritual drifting, the country lost its colonies to the United States in the Spanish-American War of 1898. This loss of prestige brought artists together in a loose coalition called the Generation of 1898. One major prose stylist of the time was Ramón del Valle Inclán (1866–1936), whose four *Sonatas* are novels named for the seasons. Another great novelist was Pío Baroja (1872–1956), a Basque who wrote about life on the road. An important novel was *A.M.D.G.,* a violent attack by Ramón Pérez de Ayala (1881–1962) on Jesuit boarding schools, which he attended.

Many Spanish writers of the time gained international reputations. The author best known outside Spain was the Basque philosopher Miguel de Unamuno (1864–1936), whose greatest work is *Del sentimiento trágico de la vida en los hombres y los pueblos* (The Tragic Sense of Life in Men and Nations). The most important dramatist was Jacinto Benavinte (1866–1954). His tour de force, *Los intereses creados* (Bonds of Interest), is based on Italian masqued comedy. In 1922, Benavinte became the second Spaniard ever to win the Nobel Prize for literature.

This century's major literary figure, however, was Federico García Lorca (1898–1936), an Andalusian whose haunting blood-and-death poetry mirrored his life right up to its end, when Franco sympathizers dragged him from his home and murdered him in a cemetery. His most compelling work was *Romancero gitano* (Gypsy Romance). His drama is world famous, especially *Bodas de sangre* (Blood Wedding) and *La casa de Bernarda Alba* (The House of Bernarda Alba). The leading dramatist since the Spanish Civil War has been Antonio Buero Vallejo (b. 1916), who was imprisoned several years after the war. Originally a painter, two of his plays are about the lives of the great Spanish artists Goya and Velázquez.

An important Spanish literary style of the 20th century has been *modernismo,* a worldwide movement that focused on the nature of expression. An important modernist — and 1956 Nobel winner — was the poet Juan Ramón Jiménez (1881–1958), who also wrote a notable work of prose, *Platero y yo* (Silver and I), about his Andalusian wanderings with his donkey. Another Nobel-winning poet (1977) was Vicente Aleixandre (1898–1984), a romantic, sometimes surrealistic, writer whose works exhibit great stylistic freedom. The outstanding modernist philosopher was José Ortega y Gasset (1883–1955). He wrote *La rebelión de las masas* (The Revolt of the Masses) in 1930.

The outstanding novelist living today may be Camilo José Cela (b. 1916), the 1989 recipient of the Nobel Prize for Literature, whose *La colmena* (The Hive) captures the truth of gray, post–Civil War Madrid. Two contemporary novelists who have expertly described the spiritual emptiness of the times are Carmen Laforet (b. 1921) and Miguel Delibes (b. 1920). Laforet's first novel,

Nada (Nothing), about a lonely girl at the University of Barcelona, is the earliest Spanish existentialist narrative. Delibes's best novel is *Cinco horas con Mario* (Five Hours with Mario), a vulgar woman's interior monologue over her husband's dead body.

The years under Franco had a deadening effect on Spanish literature. With the coronation of King Juan Carlos and the end of censorship, many looked for a literary renaissance. It has been slow in coming. The first signs have appeared in poetry; the *novisimos* are a group of poets who deliberately have turned their backs on the social realism of the Franco years. In fiction, the most exciting news has been the work of young women novelists, such as Monserrat Roig. Drama, too, is beginning to experience a rebirth. Hopes are high that the long-awaited renaissance in literature is taking shape at last.

Painting and Sculpture

 Spanish painting and sculpture are rooted in the traditions of the Moors who ruled Spain from the 8th to 11th centuries. The Moorish domination and the resulting Catholic resistance to it left an inventory of art that contains a fanatical strain of religiosity and a strong flavor of individuality.

Subjects and styles have varied over the years. Illuminated manuscripts and church paintings are among the earliest works. Romanesque art shaped the 12th and 13th centuries and first showed the world Spain's expressive style and maturity. In Castile, many artists painted scenes from everyday life; in Catalonia, subjects were mostly Byzantine — portraying Christ and the Virgin in majesty. Altar fronts of wood — more economical than gold or silver — were either painted on a single panel or carved in relief.

Spanish sculptors have used various mediums. Polychrome (decorated in several colors) wood sculpture remained the traditional Spanish medium for altar reliefs and statues from the 15th to 20th centuries; unpainted wood (chiefly oak, walnut, cedar, or mahogany) served for choir stalls and lecterns. Alabaster was used for altars and tombs from the late Gothic to Mannerist periods. Marble was popular during the Renaissance and the 18th century. Stucco had a vogue during the 16th and 18th centuries because its ease of modeling appealed to Mannerist sensitivities.

In contrast to the balance and elegance of French art or the physical beauty and technical perfection of Italian, Spanish art is characterized by its realistic and expressive details. Spanish artists are famous for expressing both their philosophical and political views, as well as their personalities, on canvas. Spain has fostered some of Europe's most original artists: El Greco, Diego Rodríguez de Silva y Velázquez, Francisco José de Goya, Joan Miró, Salvador Dalí, and Pablo Picasso.

Each region of Spain has its own style — Moorish arches and cheerful hand-painted tiles in Andalusia, Roman remnants and ceramics in Castile-León; lovely fountains and landscaped public gardens in Valencia; enchanting *modernista* buildings and sculptures in Catalonia. But the greatest works of art are in the *Prado Museum* in Madrid. Here the visitor can wander for hours through the various stages of Spanish painting and sculpture, and drink in their glorious history.

THE FOURTEENTH AND FIFTEENTH CENTURIES

Artists of the 14th and 15th centuries cultivated Spain's Gothic style. They painted slender, spiritualized forms on great polyptychs and altarpieces, carved delicate, fantastic scenes, and sculpted fine work in cathedrals' porticoes and sepulchres. Thanks to French and English influence, they enlivened paintings with halftones and shading to add the illusion of a third dimension. Along with the usual subjects of Christ and the Virgin, so common to Romanesque art, they introduced scenes from the lives of the saints.

Under the influence of the Flemish painter Jan van Eyck, Gothic painting around the mid-1400s took on a slightly different form. His style, based on a refined glazing technique that made figures more realistic, inspired a generation of artists in the states attached to the kingdom of Aragon (Catalonia, Valencia, and the Balearic Islands). Works by two van Eyck-inspired painters, Luis Dalmau (1400–1445) and Bartolomé Bermejo (d. ca. 1490) are in Barcelona and Valencia museums. Another van Eyck pupil, Rogier van der Weyden (ca. 1399–1464), is often credited with Spain's complete entry into the Flemish sphere.

Artists flourished during this time; more and more names were added to the lists of masters. By the late 15th century, Fernando Gallego (ca. 1440–1507) had become one of the main figures in the Hispano-Flemish movement. Although at first look, his paintings seem to resemble the Flemish style, on closer scrutiny it is apparent that he also applied a sense of drama to his works. Two painters who worked for Queen Isabella, Juan de Flandes (1465–1514) and Michael Sittow (1469–1525), also stand out. Together they painted the *Polyptych of the Catholic Queen,* preserved in part in Madrid's Royal Palace.

It was at the end of the 15th century that the influence of the Italian Renaissance truly penetrated the Iberian Peninsula. Some artists, such as Fernando Yáñez de la Almedina, Luis de Vargas, Pedro Machuca, and Gaspar Becerra, copied the forms of their Italian masters. Oil on wood was the most common technique at first, then oil on canvas. Though religious works continued to remain popular, the end of the century also marked the beginning of great portrait work, inspired by the reign of Philip II.

After Spain's effective unification under Ferdinand and Isabella in 1469, the country underwent unparalleled expansion and material progress. The reconquest of Granada (the last Arab kingdom) and the voyages of Columbus were reflected in art. Spain was ready to snap its medieval bonds and fully absorb the achievements of the Italian Renaissance — its study of perspective, clarity of composition, and glorification of the human body.

THE SIXTEENTH CENTURY

The Italian influence, which began to appear around 1500, was brought to Spain by sculptors from Italy, and by Spanish, Flemish, and French sculptors who trained there. It first manifested itself in the funeral monuments of cardinals and kings, and initially found its greatest inspiration in the work of Leonardo da Vinci. Its effect was deepest in Valencia, a city that for geographic, political, and economic reasons maintained close ties with Italy. In 1506, in Valencia, two of Spain's great masters, Fernando Yáñez de la Almedina and Fernando de Llanos, began to paint the 12 panels on the wings of the cathedral retable, or altarpiece. Yáñez was the foremost Spanish painter of the High Renaissance. Known for treating sacred themes in a novel and imaginative way, he used his Italian training and his Spanish personality to transform his work into an expression of vital energy, as shown by his *St. Catherine, St. Damian,* and *Holy Family* paintings.

During the second third of the century, it was the Italian artist Raphael who stimulated Valencian painting. Spanish Raphaelism was headed by Vicente Juan Macip (1475–1550), whose masterpiece is the *Segorbe Retable* (1530). As in the Yáñez/Llanos style, he used sharp, vivid lines and concentrated on filling his canvas with massive figures that block out the background. His son, Juan de Juánes (1500–1579), also used lines like those of Raphael but became famous for his sweeter, more delicate forms, as evidenced by *The Last Supper,* his most popular work.

From about 1525 onward, the Renaissance gradually gave way to Mannerism, a reaction of the irrational against the rational. The classical, calm, and restful balance of the previous era was now replaced by self-conscious, artificial, and nervously stylized depictions of the unreal and the mystical.

Among Spain's greatest Mannerist painters was Luis de Morales (1520–86) from Extremadura. Morales became known for his plain, dark backgrounds, mystical elements, and versatility in painting the same subjects with many variations. Our Lady, for example, teaches the Christ Child to read or write, plays with him, or, wearing a wide-brimmed hat, holds him to her neck. His *Ecce Homo* series shows Christ as the man of sorrows, holding a reed, tied to a column, mocked, or carrying the Cross. Morales brought the Venetian manner to Spain, which emphasized sketchiness, effects at a distance, and colorism. One of his most personal creations is *The Penitent St. Jerome* (1569), in El Escorial.

Indeed, in the mid-1500s, the Real Monasterio de El Escorial — the monastery-palace built by Philip II — became a hotbed of Italian inspiration. Philip commissioned the first Italian artists to paint for his palace in 1567. Several Spaniards were also invited: Sánchez Coello (d. 1588) painted a *St. Catherine,* eight pairs of saints, and a *St. Sebastian;* Luis de Carvajal (1534–1607) painted other pairs of saints; and Juan Fernández Navarrate (d. 1579), called "El Mudo" because he was deaf, created several works (*Beheading of Santiago, Adoration of the Shepherds*) in the style of the Venetian Titian.

One of the most Italianized painters of the time was Pablo de Céspedes (1538–1608), whose treatment of anatomy and contrasts in lighting were influential. His foremost work is the *Altar of the Last Supper* in Córdoba's cathedral.

But perhaps the most famous 16th-century artist was Doménikos Theotokópoulos, known to the world simply as El Greco (1541–1614). Born in Crete and trained in Italy, he came to Spain imbued with the values of both the Byzantine and the Western worlds. He appeared on the Spanish scene around 1576, bringing with him the influence of Venetian art. El Greco's manner of lengthening human figures and his vibrant colors give his paintings their great religious intensity. By refusing to let himself be regimented, he became one of the world's most formidable geniuses, while still managing to maintain his artistic independence.

Although a good many of his figures are derived from Mannerist forms, El Greco broke with the lines and anatomical proportions of the Italians; his paintings combine spirituality and pomp, ecstasy and factual description. And although his coloring has Venetian origins, he added flashes of colors, achieved by dipping cloths in the pigments or by directly applying them with his fingers. El Greco painted not for painting's sake, but to use his art as a vehicle for his ideas. He eschewed tricks and careful finishing in favor of intense expression.

El Greco's *View of Toledo* is one of the most famous Mannerist paintings. Because he saw Toledo as a city of the spirit, he depicted it as a blossoming light-green landscape filled with petrified, ghostly white and blue-gray buildings, where violent, dramatic emotion charges the atmosphere. Most of El Greco's paintings are in Spain, including what many consider his masterpiece, *The Burial of the Count de Orgaz,* which can be seen in the Church of Santo Tomé in Toledo.

THE SEVENTEENTH CENTURY

The death of Philip II and the accession to the throne of Philip III in 1598 led to sweeping changes in Spain, which were reflected in the arts. From the reign of Philip III on, Spanish sculpture is almost entirely religious. After the first decade of the 17th century, allegory, mythology, and grotesques no longer had a place. There was very little tomb or portrait sculpture, and relief carving lost its importance. The Spanish artist became concerned instead with the devotional and spiritual. Glass eyes, eyelashes and wigs made of human hair, and even costumes of real fabric were widely used to facilitate the beholder's identification with the divine. This was an art meant to arouse people's piety.

It was also an isolated art. Unlike their Renaissance and Mannerist predecessors, the great sculptors of the baroque did not study in Italy but stayed at home. Influences from abroad reached them secondhand. This baroque era, a period that unfolded during the *Siglo de Oro,* or Golden Age, became known for its stern realism and contrasts of light.

The baroque had an ambivalent quality as well. It was in one way oriented toward heaven and in another, toward earth. Jusepe de Ribera, Velázquez, and Zurburán proclaimed the dignity of the individual — a particularly Spanish contribution to the style. No longer was the individual neglected in favor of the ideal, as had been the case with Mannerism. For Velázquez and Ribera, all people had spiritual value as human beings.

Between 1620 and 1650, still life, otherwise known as *bodegón,* paintings flourished. Valencia and Toledo became the main centers for this new style, and Francisco Ribalta (1555–1628) and Jusepe de Ribera (1591–1652) two of the main trend setters. For Ribera, like El Greco, the aim was spiritual. He was a fertile inventor of new themes, and was popular for painting biblical stories and portraits. Ribalta's famous *Vision of St. Francis* and Ribera's *Martydom of St. Bartholomew* are in Madrid's *Prado Museum.*

Painting and sculpture became a bit more somber from about 1640 to 1660. The loss of Portugal, the Catalan rebellion, and the death of the queen in 1644, had a sobering effect on the nation. Late baroque — a style rich in the imaginative and the theatrical — arrived after 1660, when Philip IV and his son Carlos II generously patronized the arts.

Francisco de Zurbarán (1598–1664) was one of the principal painters for the king and a follower of Ribera's style. Known in 17th-century Spain and far into 18th-century Spanish America for the immense spiritual power in his paintings, Zurbarán gave objects life, treating them with a refreshing tenderness and respect. His contribution to the baroque lies in the way he combined the haunting power of mysticism with realism and ascetic simplicity. During his lifetime, the Sevillian school of baroque sculpture was at its height, and some of the altars that he and other contemporary artists painted contained gilded images carved in wood.

But by far the greatest painter of the epoch was the Sevillian Diego Rodríguez de Silva y Velázquez (1599–1660). To many, he is the greatest painter Spain ever produced. Early in life, he was appointed court painter to the court of Philip IV. There he remained for most of his life, painting a marvelous collection of portraits of the royal family. In 1658, the king bestowed on him the title of Knight of St. James. Velázquez's popularity was due in large part to his use of light both to illuminate and to define the space around his figures and to his preoccupation with the character of his subjects. As a result, his canvases convey an aura of luminous realism. He carefully developed his compositions, using free, imprecise brushstrokes and subtle colors to relate the figures to each other and achieve a harmonious whole.

Among his masterpieces, all in the *Prado,* are *The Surrender of Breda, Philip IV,* and his most famous painting — which has a room to itself — *Las Meninas* (The Maids of Honor). This last, a group portrait of the family of Philip IV set within a complex interior, draws the viewer immediately into the scene. Through the use of mirrored images, Velázquez painted himself painting the little Infanta, her attendants, and her royal parents. In its brushwork and palette, its mastery of atmospheric perspective, and its sensitive portrayal of human nature, the canvas is the summation of a career.

The 16th century was also influenced by the style of Bartolomé Esteban Murillo (1617–82). Like his contemporaries, Murillo developed compositions on the basis of Flemish, French, German, or Italian prints. He also came under the influence of Ribera and Velázquez. What differentiates his work from others is the truthful and relaxed gestures of his figures. His *Family Group,* painted around 1660, shows how deftly the artist reached into the life of his people: Murillo's subjects are always strong and vitally human, the very essence of Spanish painting.

THE EIGHTEENTH CENTURY

Eighteenth-century painting focused on portraiture and frescoes. The main center was Madrid, followed by Seville, Valencia, and Granada. The greatest activity and the greatest influence of the time, however, came from one artist: Francisco José de Goya y Lucientes (1746–1828). The work of Goya represents an entire chapter in the history of Spain. His production was immense: some 500 paintings, 1,000 drawings, and more than 275 watercolors and lithographs. Because he worked during a critical moment in Spanish history — a period of transition from an optimistic era influenced by the Enlightenment to one marked by the failure and misery of the French invasion — he became the spokesman of the political and philosophical changes that took place beginning late in the 18th century. His work personified the very heart and soul of the people.

Goya's first paintings — mostly tapestry cartoons and portraits — were lighthearted and full of colorful optimism. But an illness in 1792 changed his life and his art forever. He became deaf, isolated from the world, and withdrawn within himself. The monsters, witches, robbers, prostitutes, and murderers that suddenly appeared in his work had a symbolic value that Goya used to attack the sociopolitical structure of his time. This same satiric intent showed up later when he began to paint portraits. In one of his most famous, *The Family of Charles IV,* the artist avoided symmetry and included himself at the easel, much as Velázquez had done in *Las Meninas.* The harmony of the figures and the warm colors make the painting a brilliant work. But what truly makes it noteworthy is Goya's depiction of the royal family as a remarkably unattractive and dull-looking group, a marked departure from the usual flattering royal portraits.

Two of Goya's other famous works are the *Clothed Maja* and the *Naked Maja,* painted around 1796–98. In both works, Goya's careful and glossy brushwork heightened the sensuous appeal of his mysterious subject — and prompted charges of obscenity. In marked contrast to these are two of the paintings that portray the artist's reaction to the invasion of Napoleon and his troops, *The Second of May* and *The Executions of the Third of May.* Out of his revulsion for war, Goya created works whose impact is as powerful today as it was then.

THE NINETEENTH AND TWENTIETH CENTURIES

The shadow of the great 18th-century painters reached into the 19th century, profoundly affecting the attitudes of its painters and sculptors. Some, such as Eduardo Rosales, developed a dark cast to their work; the work of others was airy and almost frivolous. Joaquín Sorolla y Bastida (1863–1923) brought a Mediterranean brightness to French Impressionism in his paintings of beaches bathed in light. Like his ancestors before him, he added Spanish touches to the currents of European art.

Twentieth century art turned to the influences of Paris. Famous Spanish members of the Paris School include Juan Gris (1887–1927), Joan Miró (1893–1974), Pablo Picasso (1881–1973), and Salvador Dalí (1904–89). José Gutiérrez Solana (1886–1945) and Ignacio Zuloaga (1870–1945), on the other hand, were known for their scenes of everyday life. Many of these men were responsible for a whole new movement in European art.

The greatest of all and the most influential artist of the 20th century was Pablo Picasso. Born in Málaga, Picasso attended the Barcelona Art School, where he proved himself an extraordinarily gifted young man. His landmark 1907 work, *Les Demoiselles d'Avignon,* with its flat planes, rigid geometric forms, and subdued colors, inaugurated the style known as Cubism. Thirty years later, following the tradition of Goya's anti-war paintings, Picasso painted *Guernica,* an enormous gray, black, and white mural, which depicts the bombing of a Cantabrian city sacred to the Basques during the Spanish Civil War. For many years the painting hung in New York, but in 1981, after negotiations with the post-Franco Spanish government, it was returned to its homeland. It now hangs, temporarily, in the Casón del Buen Retiro, an annex to the *Prado* in Madrid.

Cubism was the most significant of all the early-20th-century movements. Its aim — to show an object not as it is but in its totality as the mind's eye perceives it — complemented the evolution of abstract art. Aside from Picasso, the movement also numbered his countryman Juan Gris among its followers. Gris created familiar objects made of polychromatic abstract shapes. Touches of red and yellow, in honor of his native flag, added a political note.

Surrealism became the next step, further exploring the depth of unconscious thought. There is no moral constraint in Surrealistic art; it is dedicated wholly to the imagination. Joan Miró was one of the forerunners of this new movement. Primarily known for his painting of rounded, animal-like outlines in black, white, and red, he is said to have defined the term "surreal" as "more real than real." Although Miró may have defined the movement, it was Salvador Dalí who perfected it. By basing his paintings on dream consciousness, he was able to shock and challenge reality with his wild interpretations of life. Perhaps his best-known work is *The Persistence of Memory* (1931), with its bent and draped wristwatches.

After the Spanish Civil War, several schools of painting and sculpture developed. They included the Catalan group Dau al Set, formed by Joan Ponc, Antoni Tàpies, Modesto Cuixart, and Juan José Tharrats; the landscapes of Benjamin Palencia; and the neo-figurative group, which brought together Antonio Clavé, Pancho Cossío, Daniel Vásquez Díaz. The period's better-known sculptors include José Llimona, José Clará, Manuel Hugue, Pablo Gargallo, Angel Ferrant, and José María Subirachs.

Spanish art today remains defiant and individualistic, shaped by new values and new political developments. Few other countries are as rich in museums — more than 600 — and ornate expression.

Architecture

"Castles in Spain," we say, but Spanish architecture exults in more than just fabulous castles. From impressive Roman bridges to gorgeous Moorish mosques, from towering cathedrals to quiet hidden churches, a wealth of glorious buildings blankets the cities and countryside of Spain. This is a country where it's possible to see all the major European architectural styles — from Romanesque to modern — of the past 1,000 years and, in addition, something unique: an architecture formed from

Spain's sensuality and love of ornamentation, its physical isolation from the rest of Europe, and its 700-year subjugation by the Moors, an architecture that grandly fuses the richness of East and West.

The earliest architectural examples still extant in Spain — mainly bridges and aqueducts — date from the Roman occupation (206 BC–AD 414). Three bridges still stand as tribute to Roman builders — at Alcántara, Salamanca, and Mérida. The one at Alcántara, built by Emperor Trajan in AD 103, is a level roadway, 250 feet long, over six massive granite arches, with a portal over the central pier. The aqueduct at Segovia is even older — built during the reign of Augustus (27 BC–AD 14); composed of 2 tiers of granite arches, it spans a deep valley, 2,700 feet across.

The Romans were succeeded by the Visigoths, whose churches — characterized by the horseshoe arch — provide examples of the pre-Romanesque building style. San Juan Bautista, a stone basilica with three aisles at Baños de Cerrato, near Palencia, is the best example. It was built in 661 to house a sacred spring that is still visible today, neatly tucked away between two horseshoe arches.

Even during the Moors' reign, Galicia and Asturias in the north remained Christian; the architectural style forged by the Asturians used Visigothic designs. The best example is the Church of Santa María Naranco near Oviedo (842–50). Originally a royal hall for Ramiro I of Asturias, the church has outside steps that lead up to the nave. Arches, however, are rounded rather than horseshoe-shaped.

Christian refugees from the Muslim-occupied south migrated north, where they created a building style — part Christian, part Muslim — called Mozarabic. The Church of San Miguel de la Escalada (912–13), near León, is one of the most beautiful examples. Lovely marble columns topped by the palm-leaf capitals characteristic of Mozarabic design separate the five-bay nave from the aisles.

In the south, meanwhile, the Moors were building their own monuments to God and their rulers. The mosque begun in 785 in the magnificent city of Córdoba is their first significant design. Except for a Gothic chapel added after the Christians retook the city, the structure still looks like a 10th-century mosque with its arcade of horseshoe arches, voussoirs of alternating colors, forest of marbled columns, and filigreed walls and ceilings.

The most famous Moorish monument in Spain, however, is the Alhambra, a stunning complex of palace buildings that perches above Granada. Begun in the 13th century but built largely during the 14th century, it includes the lush palace of the Muslim kings, and features two richly decorated courts. The Court of the Lions is surrounded by an arcade of slender columns beneath arches interlaced with intricate geometric patterns.

Despite its beauty, the Alhambra suffered a demeaning fate after the expulsion of the Moors. For centuries, Christians consigned it to use as a debtor's asylum, hospital, and prison, before learning to value its voluptuous aesthetic appeal. Today, the lovely city of Granada itself has been declared a national monument. Written on its walls are these words of De Icaza, spoken by a blind beggar: "Alms, lady, alms! For there is nothing crueler in life than to be blind in Granada."

The Romanesque style, prevalent from 1000 to 1250, reflects the supreme importance of the Roman Catholic church in medieval life. The most celebrated example is the Cathedral of St. James at Santiago de Compostela, begun around 1075. Said to contain the saint's remains, this silver-gray granite sanctuary quickly became an important Christian shrine. Because the pilgrimage to Santiago was, during the Middle Ages, second only to one to Rome or Jerusalem, masses of travelers came this way, and other Romanesque pilgrimage churches were built. A surviving example is San Martín at Fromista, between Burgos and León.

In the Santiago cathedral, it is the interior that is Romanesque. One striking feature is the original Portico de la Gloria (Gate of Glory), with statues sculpted by Master Mateo in 1188. Other examples of the Romanesque are the cathedrals at Zamora, Tarragona, and Avila, the old cathedral at Salamanca, the collegiate church at Toro, and the Cistercian Abbey church at Meira.

Gothic architecture began in France around 1150. It didn't spread to Spain as quickly as to other countries, because of the Muslim occupation and the Spaniards' predilection for the Romanesque. Once it took hold, however, Spain was reluctant to give it up, and the style lasted until about 1600. Gothic building reached its soaring zenith in cathedrals with pointed arches, stone rib vaulting, flying buttresses, slender spires of great height, and massive amounts of stained glass. The best Spanish example is the Toledo Cathedral (begun in 1227), whose glory lies in the rich splendor of the high altar, the beautiful rose window, and the majestic nave. Paintings by two of Spain's greatest artists, El Greco and Goya, hang within.

Late Gothic is displayed in Seville's cathedral, constructed (1402–1520) on the site of the city's mosque, which was torn down to make room for it. Still surviving is the mosque's famous minaret, the Giralda (1172–82). Another late Gothic monument is Salamanca's New Cathedral, designed by Juan Gil de Hontañon and built from 1513 to 1560. Its style — called Plateresque because it resembles *platería,* or silverwork, an important Spanish craft at the time — illustrates the tendency in Spanish architecture toward excessive ornamentation. Other notable examples of Spanish Gothic are the cathedrals of León, Burgos, Barcelona, Segovia, and Girona, the churches of San Juan de los Reyes in Toledo (the 1477 masterwork of Juan Guas) and St. Paul's in Valladolid, and the Palacio del Infantado in Guadalajara.

Because of Spain's geographic isolation — surrounded on three sides by water and on the fourth by mountains — and the Catholic church's efforts to hold back the tide of humanism, the Renaissance arrived late. Early examples of Spanish Renaissance style still contain elements of the Plateresque in, for example, the ornamentation of the *Hostal de los Reyes Católicos* (1501–11), now a large luxury *parador,* or hotel, near the cathedral in Santiago de Compostela.

At the core, the very heart of Spain, stands El Escorial (1558–84), an enormous, austere, palace-monastery complex. Commissioned by Philip II to commemorate his victory over the French, it was designed by Juan de Herrera and built out of granite blocks from the neighboring Sierra de Guadarrama near Madrid. It is the best example of later, more classical Renaissance architecture. Although many have called it bleak and severe, Philip's aim for his palace was nobility without ostentation. The complex contains a palace, a church, a monastery, a mausoleum, a library, a museum, and 16 courtyards within its foursquare ground plan. Rising above are two bell towers and the high dome of the royal palace, which projects from the eastern façade.

Philip is also responsible, at least indirectly, for another example of late Renaissance architecture — Juan Gómez de Mora's Plaza Mayor in Madrid (1617–20). Once Philip had transformed the small, unimportant city at the center of Spain into its capital, it became worthy of this large, 4-story arcaded square reserved for pedestrians.

If Renaissance architecture did not fully capture the imagination and passion of Spain, the later baroque style, with its extravagant curved shapes, sensuousness, and feeling of movement certainly did. In Spain, it became known as Churrigueresque, after the talented Churriguera family of designers and builders. The most outstanding example is the Transparente, a masterpiece of sculpture and painting behind the altar of the Toledo Cathedral. Completed in 1732, it depicts the Last Supper, the Virgin Mary soaring to heaven, angels, and Christ seated on clouds. The vault above was broken through to allow daylight to illuminate it from behind.

Another marvelous example is the exterior of the cathedral of Santiago de Compostela, begun in 1738, while the only complete baroque cathedral is the Catedral Nueva in the lovely southern seaport of Cádiz, begun in 1722 by Vicente Acero. An important secular example, sometimes called the "Spanish baroque version of Versailles," is La Granja, the royal mountain palace retreat in the Sierra de Guadarrama.

The baroque culminated in the even more ornate rococo, a predominantly French style that is lighter and less sensuous than its predecessor. A leading illustration of the style is the white alabaster entrance portal to the Palacio del Marqués de Dos Aguas in Valencia (1740–44), a riot of decoration that includes nudes, lions, clouds, palm trees, drapery, twisted abstract shapes, and the Virgin and Child.

Following hard on the heels of baroque and rococo — and in reaction to their excesses — was neo-classicism, which represented a return to a pure, restrained, classic style that never had been popular in Spain. Examples are the main façade of the cathedral at Lugo (1769–84) and the interior of the cathedral at Zaragoza (1753–66).

During the 19th century, all styles were revived and little that was original was created. Churches were built in Romanesque and Gothic, public and civic buildings in classical style. One of the most important developments in architecture was new methods of construction. Engineers were using materials such as iron, steel, glass, and reinforced concrete, and mastering mass-production techniques.

At the end of the century, an architect with a unique style emerged to leave an indelible mark on modern Spain and stun the world. Antoni Gaudí (1852–1926) had been working in the neo-Gothic style in Barcelona, restoring medieval monuments, when he began experimenting with his characteristic parabolic curves in the portal arches of the Palacio Episcopal (Episcopal Palace) at Astorga (1887–1913). His masterwork, La Sagrada Familia (the

Church of the Holy Family) in Barcelona, was begun in 1882 as a neo-Gothic work.

Gaudí, who became principal architect of the church in 1891, completed various sections of La Sagrada according to his late employer's specifications. In 1893, however, he began incorporating his own designs into the transept façade depicting the Nativity. From World War I on, he devoted himself to the work. The first bell tower was finished in 1921. Five years later, the church still far from complete, Gaudí was struck and killed by a streetcar in front of the building on which he had labored for so long. His body was buried in the crypt. Work was renewed in 1950, using Gaudí's designs. It will not be finished until well into the next century.

La Sagrada is a far cry from its neo-Gothic origins. Gaudí's style is based on a combination of medieval Gothic, Moorish (his parabolic arch recalls the horseshoe arch), and his own rendition of Art Nouveau. Inspired by natural formations, Gaudí created a façade that has been compared to molten lava, melting snow, and a cake left so long in the sun that its frosting has melted; pointed arches hung with outgrowths like stalactites; and towers that appear modeled on dunce caps or on the towers dribbled atop a child's sand castle.

There are two other striking examples of his work in Barcelona, both built between 1905 and 1910 in the Art Nouveau style. One is Casa Batlló, a townhouse with slender, bony columns and a writhing ceramic roof; the other, Casa Milá, a large apartment block with a wave-like façade and balconies whose ironwork resembles seaweed. Gaudí professed two often-repeated principles: "Originality is a return to origins" and "There are no straight lines in nature."

Modern architecture, which developed in Germany between the world wars, did not produce any monuments of merit in Spain because Generalísimo Francisco Franco's totalitarian government preferred a more traditional style. The liberalization of Spanish society since Franco's death, however, has opened exciting possibilities. One of the most interesting new edifices is Madrid's 30-story Bank Building, designed by Francisco Sáenz de Oiza (1980), with cantilevered beams every fifth floor.

With the coming of *Expo '92* to Seville, permanent additions and changes are being made to that city's architectural landscape. Among them is the *Teatro de la Maestranza,* a new, 1,800-seat opera house located near the legendary Plaza del Toros on the city side of the Guadalquivir River. Reminiscent in design of the neighboring bullring, the theater is scheduled to open this May. Though many of the pavilions at *Expo* will be temporary buildings, Santa María de las Cuevas, the 15th-century monastery on the fairgrounds at Cartuja Island, is undergoing major renovations and will house the royal Spanish pavilion during *Expo* (and will serve as a cultural center thereafter). In addition, a group of Madrid architects are developing what ultimately may flower into an original — and wholly Spanish — style.

Traditional Music and Dance

Spanish music today is a composite of cultural influences that have shaped it over the course of 2 millennia. Long before the Phoenicians, Greeks, Romans, Visigoths, Jews, Moors, Indo-Pakistani Gypsies, Africans, and natives of the New World added their respective grace notes to the national repertoire, Spain had an indigenous tradition of music and dance that is depicted in several of its renowned prehistoric cave paintings. During the Middle Ages, music and dance were popular diversions at Spanish courts, and no fiesta, fair, or public celebration took place that didn't have its share of song and dance. Though flamenco is Spain's most famous musical form, national dances such as the *morisca* — which spread throughout Europe in the 15th century — the *jota,* and the *bolero* are also known beyond the country's borders.

The *jota, fandango, seguidilla,* and *bolero* share a common pattern, major variations residing in the complexity of the dancer's movements. The Aragonese *jota* debuted in the 18th century, gained widespread popularity during the early-19th-century War of Independence, and eventually spread across the entire Iberian Peninsula and to the Balearic and Canary islands. When the *jota* is rendered in a more sensuous Arabic style, it becomes the *fandango,* a word of Bantu origin. From the 15th to 19th centuries, Africans who were brought to Spain as slaves not only embraced the local dance traditions, but stamped upon them their own infectious rhythms, creating such lively dances as the *rumba flamenca.* Each Andalusian community gave the *fandango* its own local twists and turns; it became the *malagueña* in Málaga, the *granadina* in Granada, the *rondeña* in Ronda, and so on.

Similar to the *jota* and *fandango* is the *seguidilla* — born as a song form in the 15th century and reaching the pinnacle of its popularity in the 17th. Originating in La Mancha and developing regional variations as it spread, the dance's joy and exuberance were described by Cervantes in *Don Quixote* as "the gamboling of the soul, the frolicking of laughter, the restlessness of the body, and, finally, the quicksilver of all senses."

The *bolero,* derived from the *seguidilla,* was born in the Spanish *tablaos* (dance cafés) that enlivened the late 18th and early 19th centuries. "Boleros" and "boleras" were originally terms for the professional dancers who performed there. Metrically and rhythmically, the *jota, fandango, seguidilla,* and *bolero* are similar. All are dances for couples and, much like flamenco, are punctuated with interludes of guitar and song. Together, they represent the archetypal Spanish dance.

In Spain, one musical form outshines all others — flamenco. In its fullest sense, flamenco is more than just a song and dance; it is part of a world view that values freedom and movement over possessions, spontaneity over planning and routine. Artistically, it is a seductive blend of technical discipline and fierce passion ignited by the elusive *duende,* that electric moment when emotion finds its most poignant expression in the exquisite grace of a hand, the raspy trill of a voice, or the rapid-fire play of fingers across guitar strings.

Flamenco is the antithesis of rigidity. Thus any routine professional performance of the dance is a betrayal of its basic philosophy — live for the moment, when it comes. Where does this leave the tourist? More often than not, with facsimile flamenco, which, like an imitation gem, may be technically more perfect but lacks the fire and spirit of the real thing. Flamenco, the folk art, is as different from its professional alter ego as a genuine kiss is from one onstage.

A mixture of Byzantine Christian ritual, Jewish liturgical chants, the calls of the Muslim muezzin, and the half-breed Hindu heritage of the Gypsies, flamenco is a pliant art form that has assimilated disparate musical sources. As the ports of Andalusia thronged with New World commerce during the 16th and 17th centuries, people came from all parts of Spain and its overseas colonies to share the wealth, bringing their diverse musical heritages with them. Thus the folk traditions of the north as well as those of immigrants insinuated themselves into a nascent flamenco.

The catalyst that fused this hodgepodge into a coherent musicial tradition was the Inquisition. From the late 15th through early 19th centuries, this brutal attempt at religious conformity drove the nonconforming Jews, Gypsies, and Moors to seek refuge in the Andalusian hills. Here, in the solemn and moving rhythms of their various chants and songs, they described the terrors of persecution, gave voice to their pain, and found solace. Like the African-American's blues, their music was one of despair. It's possible that the very term "flamenco" is a mispronunciation of "felag" and "mengu," Arabic words for "fugitive peasant." Then, after some 200 years of incubation, flamenco emerged as a musical style in its own right in the 18th century, which saw the first recorded use of the word "flamenco" in the musical sense.

Though today dance is flamenco's most salient feature, first there was song and then the guitar. The *cante* (singing) expresses the fear of death, the enigma of sex, and the joy of existence. The voice must be gruff, gravelly, and as abrasive as the torment it laments. Though flamenco verse runs the emotional gamut from ecstasy to despair, anguish is its wellspring, the stuff of the *cante jondo* (literally, "deep song"), which is flamenco at its most moving and profound. It embraces two basic song forms, *soleares* — a Gypsy pronunciation of the Spanish *soledades,* meaning solitude or loneliness — and *siguiriyas.* The verses of the *cante jondo* speak of alienation, isolation — in short, the lot of the non-Christian in a virulently Catholic Spain.

> In the district of Triana,
> On the street of the Inquisition,
> They executed Curro Puya,
> The finest of our people.
> Look at the shame,
> You have made me bear,
> To go asking for alms from door to door
> To buy you freedom.
> The horsemen on the corners
> With torches and lanterns

Called out:
"Kill him! He's Gypsy!"
To my enemies
May God never send
The black sorrows of death
He has sent me.
Don't hit my father again!
Stop, for God's sake!
The crime you accuse him of
I myself have committed.

By the 18th century, the Gypsies had become flamenco's zealous custodians, allowing few payos (non-Gypsies) to witness it. Then in 1842, when Seville's first *café cantante* presented flamenco to a paying public, the face of flamenco changed forever. Though for Gypsies it remains an informal, impromptu form of expression, in today's *tablaos* or at *Carnegie Hall* it is, first and foremost, entertainment.

Early in the 20th century, the *tablaos* replaced the *cafés cantantes,* and the dance, originally a mere foil to the *cante* and guitar, moved center stage. Today's flashy footwork and provocative undulations repulse the purist, who would travel hundreds of miles to see the authentic Gypsy dance, which relies on the sinuous movements of arms, hands, upper torso, and head rather than the constant clicking of feet and castanets. *Flamenco puro,* in fact, doesn't use castanets because they restrict the grace and movement of the hands. Most flamenco song forms follow a set rhythm, or *compás.* Most common is the 12-beat rhythm with syncopated accent on the 3rd, 6th, 8th, 10th, and 12th beats. The guitar became a regular feature of flamenco in the 18th and 19th centuries. Before, the *compás* had been marked with *palmas* (hand clapping), feet tapping, or knuckles rapping on tables — a practice that continues today.

Every art form has its own language. In the case of flamenco, two key terms are *duende* and *juerga.* Originally, *duende* meant "spirit" or "demon," but its flamenco connotation is more elusive. The Granadan poet Federico García Lorca defines *duende* as the "black sounds" that emanate from human despair. More generally, it is that moment of self-abandonment when performer, music, and emotion become one. Since *duende* is capricious and spontaneous, it is rarely found where flamenco is routinely performed for wages.

Not all flamenco denotes doom and gloom. The *juerga* is a spontaneous flamenco event that may last hours or even days. By turns, everyone participates, if only by shouting encouragement or clapping in *compás.* No *juerga* is complete without its share of *cante intermedio* and *cante chico* songs. The former, though still moving, are less soul-wrenching than the *cante jondo* and include *fandango.* The *cante chico* highlights the sunny side of flamenco, featuring rhythms that are quick and contagious and verses that are light-hearted, often humorous. No wonder the spirited *bulerías,* accompanying *cante chico,* are among the most popular dances at any *juerga.*

Although it's hard to fix the number of song forms in the flamenco repertoire, estimates run from 70 to as many as 500. Among those most frequently found on professional programs are *bulerías, alegrías, farruca, tarantos, tien-*

tos, rumba flamenca, and, of course, *soleares* and *siguiriyas.* Most modern *tablaos* present the *cuadro flamenco* — a group of singers, dancers, and guitarists seated on stage and featured in turn as soloists (much like any *jota, fandango, seguidilla, bolero* — or jazz — performance). There are no leaps, no jumps, no aspirations to become airborne. And the dance, if authentic, is improvised.

Because flamenco melodies are often monotonous, the singers shrill, and the dancing arrogant, even contemptuous, and because flamenco is an intense art, fueled by reserves of deep-seated cultural passion, most people (including many Spaniards) consider it an acquired taste. Born and bred in Andalusia, flamenco's spiritual center still lies within an imaginary triangle marked by the towns of Lucena, Seville, and Cádiz, where the remaining Gypsies not only keep the fires of flamenco burning but consider it their exclusive possession — regarding with disdain and mockery all *payos* who presume to practice this singular art. Though the death knell has been rung for flamenco almost as many times as for the novel, it always springs back, renewed, revitalized, and a little bit different. The *Fundación Andaluza de Flamenco* (Palacio Pemartín, 1 Plaza de San Juan, Jerez de la Frontera) strives to keep flamenco traditions alive through exhibitions and its vast library of books, cassettes, and videotapes that chronicle all aspects of the art.

There are notable *tablaos flamencos* to be seen in Madrid, and Seville, too, has fine professional flamenco. But every August, flamenco can be seen in its proper cultural context in the towns and villages of Andalusia, which blossom with hundreds of flamenco festivals. The *April Fair* in Seville and the *Horse Fair* in Jerez de la Frontera every May also offer homegrown flamenco. All over Spain, *sevillanas,* Seville's flamenco version of the *seguidilla* of La Mancha, are danced in discos and special *sevillanas* clubs; in Seville itself, the clubs along Calle Salado in the Barrio Triana are the places to try to see *sevillanas.* Flamenco performances rarely begin before midnight, and do-it-yourself dance clubs usually catch fire around 1 or 2 AM.

Also part of the Spanish repertoire of musical offerings is the *zarzuela.* Developed in the 17th and 18th centuries, this national light opera, or operetta, is still popular today, though many foreigners find the language barrier a hindrance to their complete enjoyment. Heavily nostalgic and colorful, *zarzuela* is an unusual Spanish art form that takes a sentimental rather than tragic view of the past. From October to June, *zarzuelas* are staged at Madrid's *Teatro de la Zarzuela.*

Late in the 19th century, a movement arose to integrate the folk music and the classical music of Spain. A leading exponent was Manuel de Falla (1876–1946), a Spanish composer who achieved international fame. Among his best known compositions are the ballets *El amor brujo* (Love the Magician) and *El sombrero de tres picos* (The Three-Cornered Hat) and a nocturne for piano and orchestra, *Nights in the Gardens of Spain.*

One of the instrumentalists Falla wrote for was Andrés Segovia, the great Spanish guitarist, who died in 1987. Until Segovia's time, the guitar had not been considered an appropriate instrument for solo concerts, but his brilliant playing changed all that. Like so many fine Spanish musicians of the 20th century, Segovia delighted audiences all over the world with his music, a music rooted in the finest Spanish tradition.

Bullfighting

 There's a point in every bullfight that Spaniards call the "moment of truth." It happens just as the matador prepares to thrust his sword between the bull's shoulders. There will be a death — usually the bull's, but sometimes the bullfighter's.

It's also the moment of truth for hundreds of unsuspecting visitors. Many come away from their first bullfight full-fledged aficionados. The more faint-hearted bolt for the door. Animal lovers have been known to send angry letters to the Spanish government. Most Spaniards, however, see this centuries-old tradition either as a highly skilled sport or as a graceful dance performed by a matador who flirts with death at every turn of his cape.

Bullfighting began in Spain's southern and central regions sometime in the 12th century. Bullrings in Béjar, Campofrío, Zaragoza, and Seville are among the oldest in Spain, although those in Ronda and Seville are architecturally the most satisfying and have the greatest historical importance.

During King Philip III's reign, Madrid's Plaza Mayor, or main square, was used for bullfights. The seats of honor were the gold and black balconies of the 5-story red brick and stone buildings that surround the square. Various guilds decorated their balconies with velvet and damask canopies covered by coats of arms. A special section was allotted for the priests who heard the confessions of the men about to enter the bullring.

Today, the *Las Ventas* bullring in Madrid seats 50,000 and is open from mid-April through October. In May, during the *Feast of San Isidro*, Madrid's patron saint, bullfights take place daily.

Seats in most bullrings are sold in a wide range of prices; some are as low as about $3. Patrons buying *sol* (sun) — the cheapest seats — can expect to sit in glaring sunshine the entire time, while *sombra* seats — the most expensive — are in the shade, and *sol y sombra* seats strike a happy medium.

The bullfighting season generally lasts from late spring through the fall. The fights not to miss take place in Pamplona during the first week of July, when the entire town hosts thousands of visitors for the annual *Fiesta de San Fermín*, best known as a week-long, 24-hour drunken bash. In this northern town, visitors can see the best bullfighters and the most raucous bullfights. At 8 AM every day during the fiesta, six bulls race through the narrow, cobblestone streets to the bullring, challenged on the way by Pamplona's most daring — or most foolhardy — young men.

Small towns and villages are not sophisticated about their bullfights. In Chinchón, an hour's drive south of Madrid, the dirt-covered town square turns into an amateur bullring on Sundays during the summer. There, brave young boys practice their skills, and potbellied has-been matadors test their agility and speed. The bulls, though not exceptionally large, are still dangerous.

Bulls are expertly bred for the professional rings. To be chosen to fight, a bull must weigh at least 460 kilos (1,012 pounds) for the permanent, professional rings, less for the smaller rings, and be between 4 and 6 years old. (It will be checked after death to make sure it has at least six permanently developed teeth.)

The *corrida* (bullfight) always lasts about 2 hours and features six bulls. It always starts on time, to a blaring of trumpets and a flourish. A procession of mounted bailiffs, dressed in the uniforms of King Philip's court, opens the ceremony, followed by the matadors and their assistants.

Seated in the stands is the president, who has been officially elected to the post, or a delegate. He oversees the *corrida* and his word is final. Like a conductor with a baton, the president uses different colored handkerchiefs to cue the action. Resting a white one across the railing starts the parade and subsequent *corrida*. A red handkerchief signals that black *banderillas* be stuck into the bull, a green one signals that the bull be returned to the pen, and a blue one gives the bull another turn around the ring.

The president also awards trophies. Taking his cue from the cheering crowd, he will award the victorious matador one bull's ear, but whether he awards the second is solely up to him. Awarding the bull's tail happens rarely and only for an outstanding performance.

The drama begins when the bull charges into the ring, excited and confused — to be met by six *toreros* waving their capes. In its confusion the bull races about the ring in stops and starts. As it does so, its legs are checked and its performance judged to see if it is an equal match for the matador.

Prologue over, the first act begins when a husky *picador* carrying a long *puya* (spiked stick) gallops out on a padded horse. He must stay on the ring's periphery, outside the white circle painted on the ground. When the bull charges, horse and rider are often pushed against the boards. This is desirable since it makes it easier for the *picador* to thrust the *puya* into the *morrillo* (neck muscle) of the bull. This is the first sign of blood. The injury weakens the head, making for a better kill later in the *corrida*.

The stars of the second act are the three *banderilleros*, who each run at the bull with two barbed sticks (*banderillas*) and throw them into the open wound left by the picador.

Now at last, for the third and final act of this bloody drama, the matador, dressed in a dazzling mirrored costume, enters the bullring. The bull is easily enraged. The matador uses his *muleta* (red cape) to taunt it.

Deft use of the *muleta* is an art form. An inept bullfighter is often booed by a crowd well versed in the distinct variations of each move. The most popular move is the *natural*, in which the bullfighter flutters the cape within inches of the bull, awaits a charge that sometimes grazes his leg, then gracefully turns his wrist and body to face the bull as it returns for another charge. In addition to incredible courage, the ability to sense the bull's movements, speed, and idiosyncrasies is what distinguishes an excellent bullfighter from an unpopular bullfighter, or a dead bullfighter.

At last, trumpets sound to tell the bullfighter he has the customary 15 minutes in which to kill the bull. As the sword is withdrawn from the *muleta*, anyone can hear the hiss as the crowd draws in its breath. Slowly, the matador rises to his toes, raises the sword slightly above his head, and charges. He aims for a spot behind the bull's head. If his aim and thrust are successful, the bull drops to the ground. Sometimes the bull twirls in one spot before crumpling.

As the dead bull is dragged away by a team of horses, the matador either struts triumphantly around the bullring receiving cheers of praise and sometimes roses, or is booed out of the bullring for a bad fight in which the spectators believe the bull was not treated well. Whatever the outcome, the bullfight, for all its pomp and ceremony, remains a dangerous, possibly fatal, contest between fragile human beings and an animal formidable enough to have conquered lions and tigers with its horns.

Dining in Spain

 Sangría, paella, gazpacho, and *tapas,* those delectable Spanish contributions to the American table, are just teasers for the dining adventure that awaits the visitor to Spain. Although today's Spain boasts Michelin three-star restaurants — *Zalacaín* in Madrid, *Arzak* in San Sebastián — and trendy European-style establishments with menus that reflect the country's new internationalism, old Spanish hands needn't panic. Those venerable stucco and beam-ceilinged dining places found on every corner are still serving mountainous platters of *mariscos* (seafood), pots of nourishing *sopas* (soups), and bowls of comforting *cocidos* (stews). And the sidewalk cafés are still here, and the jewel-box pastry shops, and those cozy eateries and watering holes, the *taverna, tasca, bodega,* and *bar* — the neighborhood hangouts for coffee, wine, and *tapas* (snacks).

Those who love appetizers will adore the *tapas* bar. The word *tapa* (lid) came into use when bartenders kept flies out of wine glasses by covering them with a saucer or piece of bread and then placed a tidbit of free lunch on top. Although no longer free, *tapas* today cost only about $2 to $3 a plate. (For a larger portion, order a *ración.*)

Every *tapas* bar features the ultimate Spanish appetizer, a joint of prosciutto-like *jamón serrano* (air-dried mountain ham) to be razored out in paper-thin shavings. Ranged along the counter will be a dozen to 50 earthenware *cazuelas,* serving dishes filled with plump green olives and a mind-boggling assortment of sautéed or sauced seafood — crayfish, shrimp, clams, oysters, mussels, crab, squid, octopus, and roe — as well as cold fish, egg, and vegetable salads; cheeses and sausages; tripe and other varieties of meats; fried or marinated fish; and sea creatures such as snails and barnacles that fall into the "enjoy but don't ask" department.

Although Americans sometimes confuse Spanish and Mexican cuisine, the two are actually quite distinct — even though both use the potatoes, tomatoes, peppers, avocados, beans, and chocolate that 16th-century Spanish explorers discovered in the New World. Spanish-speaking travelers who learned the language in Mexico can be in for some linguistic surprises, though, such as discovering the very different meaning given the word *tortilla.* Unlike the sturdy maize pancake that Mexicans wrap around beans and meat, a Spanish *tortilla* is a deep-dish potato omelette that can be served warm at mealtime or sliced cold for snacks.

Spanish cooking, smoothed by fruity olive oils, doesn't call for the hot-pepper *salsa* of the Mexican kitchen. And despite a love affair with garlic, Spanish food is often as mild as American home cooking. (An exception is any dish labeled *al pil pil,* which means it comes in olive oil spiked with garlic and tongue-searing dried red peppers.) If anything, it's sweetness that runs through Spanish cuisine, thanks to the honey, almonds, hazelnuts, sesame, cinnamon, and aromatic spices introduced by the Moors.

The chance to drink reasonably priced Spanish wines, most of which never reach the United States, is a plus. Besides the fun of discovering young local wines — which change virtually from village to village — connoisseurs will appreciate the chance to taste the famous sherries from Jerez: the dry *finos* and *manzanillas,* the medium dry *amontillados,* and the sweet *olorosos.* Spain's greatest wines, aged red riojas from the north around Logroño compare with burgundies and bordeaux, while younger valdepeñas wines farther south are a popular "little" wine.

The Penedés region near Barcelona produces light reds and whites but is best known as the home of *cava,* Spanish champagne. A Common Market agreement forbids Spanish vintners from labeling their wine *champaña,* so they call it *cava* for the limestone caves where the wine is stored. In Barcelona, *champañerías* (champagne bars), offering dozens of *cava* bottlings, are in vogue. In the apple growing area of Asturias, *sidra* — dry, sparkling hard cider, quaffed in a restaurant or in a *sidería* (cider bar) — is the "wine" of choice, especially when downed with the local *fabada asturiana* (bean and sausage stew). Ice-cold *cerveza* (beer) is popular everywhere, as is mineral water: *agua con gas* (sparkling), or *sin gas* (without bubbles).

Spain's dining hours can be troublesome to the visitor with only a few days to adjust to the late hours of the Mediterranean, but understanding Spain's flexible restaurant options makes it easier to cope. Spaniards begin their day with a cup of the richest, most flavorful coffee in Europe — *solo* (black) or *con leche* (with milk) — along with *panecillos* (rolls) or a thick slice of *pan* (bread). For a continental breakfast, order a *café completo,* which most hotels include in the room price. There's an extra charge for a bacon-and-eggs American-style *desayuno* (breakfast).

In mid-morning the working population stokes up on *tapas* or sweet rolls at the local bar. This staves off hunger until the *comida,* the leisurely main meal of the day, which begins at 2 PM and lasts at least 2 hours. On weekends, whole families — toddlers to grandparents — settle around big restaurant tables for the afternoon meal. Travelers on the go, however, can grab a quick lunch by dropping into a bar for a *bocadillo* (sandwich), a hard roll filled with selections from the *tapas* platters. *Cafeterías,* American-style coffee shops for malts, burgers, and sandwiches, are now prevalent in Spain, and *auto-servicios,* self-service places, are handy for fast, if perfunctory, fill-ups.

Afternoon tea (*merienda*) fills up the *pastelerías* (sweet shops) late in the day, and by 7 PM the after-work crowd is three deep at the *tapas* bar, tossing back a *fino* (dry sherry) or a *caña* (beer by the glass) and spearing tidbits from shared plates. *Tapas,* too time-consuming for the home cook, are restaurant fare in Spain.

La cena (dinner) completes the culinary day. Most restaurants start serving at 10 PM, though some, especially hotel dining rooms, open earlier to accommodate tourists. If anyone is wondering how the Spanish can eat so much yet stay so slim, the answer is that they can't — and don't. The convivial folks around the bar at 7 o'clock are probably making a meal out of *tapas* before going home to a light supper (a good ploy for travelers, too). The late-night restaurant crowd usually turns out to be a mix of friends out for the evening, businessmen entertaining clients, Spanish travelers, and foreign tourists.

Spanish restaurant menus are à la carte; both lunch and dinner offer the same choices. A typical menu might categorize its offerings like this: *Entremeses* (starters) — either *tapas*-like appetizers or soup, generally *sopa de ajo* (chunks of ham and hard-boiled egg in garlic-chicken broth) or a cold tomato gazpacho. A listing for *verduras y ensaladas* (vegetables and salads) will feature *patatas fritas* (French fries) and seasonal vegetables served family style, while *tortillas* can be found listed under *huevos* (eggs); they can come with a variety of fillings — *jamón* (ham), *gambas* (shrimp), *chorizo* (sausage), but a *tortilla española* will be filled with potatoes and onions, while a *tortilla francesa* is a plain omelette.

The entries listed under *pescados* (fish) may be hard to figure out because so many of the fish come exclusively from local waters. But diners will always find old standbys like *merluza* (hake), *salmonetes* (red mullet), *lenguado* (sole), *trucha* (trout), and either *chiperones* or *puntillitos* (both baby squid). Meat and poultry dishes are generally grouped together under *carne y ave* or *asados* (from the broiler). For beef, look for *filete, solomillo,* or *entrecote* (tender beef filets — the word *buey* for beef is understood). *Puerco* (pork) is Spain's most plentiful meat, so *lomo* (loin of pork) is often a good bet. Many *pollo* (chicken) and *ternera* (veal) choices are offered as well.

Postres (desserts) invariably feature *fruta del tiempo* (fresh fruit) and *frutas en alimbar* (home-style canned fruits in syrup); *helados* (ice creams); flan, a small round cushion of caramelized custard, or one of its even richer relations such as *tocino de cielo;* and *quesos* (cheeses), notably the aged sheep's milk, *manchego,* which, accompanied by *membrillo* (quince jelly), is often served for dessert. Some restaurants, particularly *parador* dining rooms, dress up dessert menus with cookies and candies made by local nuns. Despite the wealth of rich honey-, nut-, and egg-based sweets — or because of them — Spaniards often finish off big meals with plain *zumo de naranja* (orange juice).

To dine at reasonable cost, choose the fixed-price, three-course *menú del día,* which the law requires all eating places — from checkered tablecloth *1 tenedore* (one-fork) *mesones* to white-tablecloth *5 tenedores restaurantes* — to provide. These meals will cost less than the restaurant's comparable à la carte selections. The fork rating, by the way, is based on ambience, service, and the range of menu offerings, not on the quality of the food.

Though many regional specialties have become countrywide, even worldwide favorites, nothing can replace the mystique of eating regional food on its home ground. The local cooking of Castile is king, for example, even in cosmopolitan Madrid, which has its full share of regional and international restaurants. This is the place to sample *cocido madrileño,* a stick-to-the-ribs stew served in three courses — the broth, then the meats, then the vegetables. Madrid and surrounding towns are also famous for *lechazo* (baby milk-fed lamb) and *cochinillo* (suckling pig), spit-roasted to crispy perfection outside, while the meat underneath melts on the fork.

Barcelona, Catalonia's seaside capital, has the best *zarzuela de mariscos,* a seafood stew of shrimp, mussels, prawns, squid, crab, and clams in a tomato-saffron sauce. And a wonderful light lunch is a heaping platter of grilled or sautéed mussels, crayfish, shrimp, barnacles, and crab, accompanied by country bread rubbed with fresh tomato, garlic, and olive oil. But unless money is no object, don't order *langosta* (rock lobster) or *bogavante* (clawed lobster). Lobster is sky-high throughout Europe.

For another Catalan specialty, try *romesco de peix* (fish stew) with its piquant *romesco* sauce, thickened with ground almonds and bread crumbs, and order one of the typical Catalan meat and fruit combinations such as *filet de bou amb fruits sec* (tenderloin of beef with dried fruit). And for the intrepid, there's the local way with snails, as in *conejo con caracoles* (rabbit-snail stew). The dessert of choice is *crema catalana,* creamy custard beneath a caramelized sugar crust.

If there's one thing Spaniards agree on, it's respect for Basque cooking. The word *vasco* (Basque) crops up in restaurant names everywhere. Many of the best cooks (including the owner of the three-star *Zalacaín*) come from Basque Country, which is known for its hundreds of all-male, members-only cooking clubs. It's hard to go wrong in any San Sebastián restaurant. Try the local fisherman's soup, *marmitako,* made with bonito, potatoes, peppers, and tomatoes. Order *bacalao a la vizcaina,* salt cod baked with dried sweet peppers. (Northern Spain shares the Portuguese passion for salt cod.) And, for those who feel daring, there's the popular Basque appetizer *angulas* (matchstick baby eels in a garlic-olive marinade).

The luxuriant rice-paddy country travelers notice along the east-central coastline should signal Valencia, and a stop for paella. This communal pan of creamy short-grained saffron rice, crusty from a wood-burning fire, is served all over Spain in varying delectable combinations of seafood, sausage, poultry and vegetables. But the Valencians invented it. Purists among them will declare that without snails, it's not the real thing.

Maybe it's Andalusia's balmy outdoor dining that captures gourmet fancies. Perhaps it's *tapas*-hopping in Seville or sampling sherry in Jerez or cooling off with an icy pitcher of sangria laced with orange slices. The surprising variety in gazpacho alone is worth exploring: In Seville, it's the familiar tomato and cucumber soup; in Córdoba, *salmorejo,* a thick tomato purée; in Málaga, white garlic-almond broth with sweet seedless grapes.

Andalusia's *pescadito frito* (deep-fried fish) — greaseless frying is an art form here — and its potato chips sizzling in vats of olive oil right on the street are typical southern treats. Andalusians will crunch on anything, even piles of deep-fried thread-like *chanquetes* (tiny whitefish). As befits the birthplace of the *corrida,* Andalusia also serves up a rib-sticking *rabo de toro* (bull-tail stew). Hearty *habas con jamón* (casserole of lima beans and mountain ham) is especially good in spring, when the local beans are soft and sweet. And *urta a la roteña* (a fish called *urta,* unique to Andalusian waters, in a tomato and red pepper sauce) is also worth trying.

The adventure of dining in Spain can reveal itself in the humblest, least expected spots. A case in point is the local *churrería* — a place to stop for the universal treat of hot chocolate and *churros* (crullers). Best on a brisk evening but irresistible anytime except when it's really hot, the slender bread-stick-length crullers are deep-fried in vats, often in the shop window, and served warm with cups of rich, hot chocolate for dunking. Little wonder that simple snacks like this can slip into so many visitors' gastronomic pantheons.

Portugal

History

For a country that prides itself on its *brandos costumes* (mild manners) Portugal has had a dramatic history. Though a minimum of bloodshed accompanied its 1974 coup (red carnations rather than bullets sprouted from soldiers' rifles), the factions that followed the "Carnation Revolution," the rulers who preceded it, and the clashes of the original prehistoric tribes all belie any idea of excessive mildness in the Portuguese character.

For several millennia, Portugal and Spain, which share the Iberian Peninsula, also shared a common history. The southern end of the peninsula was inhabited in Paleolithic times — no doubt by the same emigrants from Africa who settled elsewhere in southern Europe. By 3000 BC, Mesolithic peoples had settled in the north.

Recorded history, however, begins with three waves of invaders: the Iberians, who came from the eastern Mediterranean or northern Africa in the 3rd millennium BC and spread across the peninsula to which they gave their name; the Celts (the same people who inhabited Ireland, Scotland, and Wales), whose matriarchal, pastoral societies trudged south across the Pyrenees around 900 BC to settle north of the Douro River; and the Lusitanians, a patriarchal, warring society, who occupied the lands between the Tagus and the Minho rivers. Mythically, these Lusitanians, who were known to the Roman writers Polybius and Strabo, are considered the true ancestors of the Portuguese.

Around 1200 BC, more civilized visitors — the Phoenicians — explored the area on Iberia's western coast that would become Portugal's eventual homeland; Phoenician colonists from Carthage soon followed and, about 400 years later, so did the Greeks. During the 3rd century BC, the future country of Portugal shared the fate of most of western Europe: conquest by Rome. Hannibal, the Carthaginian general, had hired Lusitanian mercenaries to fight the Romans. To stop them, the Romans invaded Iberia in 212 BC. Hampered by fierce Lusitanian heroes like Viriatus, still revered in Portuguese (and Spanish) folklore, it took the Romans almost 200 years to conquer the peninsula, which they renamed Hispania; its southernmost portion — part of present-day Portugal — they named Lusitania.

The Romans founded several towns in Lusitania, including Bracara Augusta (Braga), Pax Julia (Beja), and Olisipo (Lisbon). This last, according to legend, was originally founded by Ulysses. Another town, Portus Cale — which became first Portucale and eventually the city of Porto (meaning port) — gave the country of Portugal its name.

As elsewhere in Europe, northern barbarians invaded as Rome grew weak. In AD 409, Suevians swept down from the Pyrenees and established a government seat at Braga. These were rather non-barbaric barbarians. In no time they converted to Christianity, which had arrived on the peninsula from Roman North Africa some 200 years earlier. Nor did they find it troublesome to live at peace with the Visigoths who ruled Hispania under Roman auspices.

The Moors — arguably the most civilized invaders of all — came to Spain in 711 to battle King Rodrigo and his Visigoths, decided to stay, and by the end of the decade had conquered most of the peninsula. In the western part of the peninsula, they did not adapt well to the climate — either political or meteorological — north of the Douro River, where resistance by the Visigothic chieftain Pelayo began almost immediately, and so they settled down instead in the Algarve (from the Arab *al-Gharb*, "to the west"), south of the Tagus River. There they reigned peacefully over Jews and Christians alike. Though the tolerant Moors allowed both to continue to practice their own religions, Christians in the south — like those in Spain — became so imbued with Islamic culture that they were known as Mozarabs.

But not all Christians. The Reconquest of the peninsula, begun in the north by Pelayo early in the 8th century, continued — on and off — for 5 centuries in Portugal, and even longer in Spain. The Christian kings of northern Asturias-León quickly retook Braga, Porto, Viseu, and Guimarães, cities that lay between the Douro and Minho rivers — an area that a 9th-century document calls for the first time *Provincia Portucalense,* Province of Portugal. For the next 200 years, this northern section of present-day Portugal acted as a buffer zone for the Christians struggling to regain the peninsula. By the late 11th century, Christian-held territory extended as far south as Coimbra.

Portugal's independence from Spain began in 1096, when Alfonso VI, King of Castile and León, awarded the northern county of Portucale — an area extending roughly from the Minho River down to the Mondego at Coimbra — to his son-in-law, Henry of Burgundy, the French nobleman and crusader, for helping to fight the Moors at Toledo. Henry died in 1112, leaving his wife, Teresa, regent for their young son, Afonso Henriques.

Some 16 years later, at the urging of the Portuguese, Afonso Henriques assumed his father's role of vassal to Castile and León. Not for long, however. After defeating the armies of his overlord, he triumphed over the Moors at a famous battle in Ourique. Then he supposedly saw a vision of the Cross in the heavens, and taking this as a sign, he proclaimed himself King of Portugal.

King Afonso Henriques and his Burgundian heirs continued the Reconquest southward, taking Lisbon in 1147, the Alentejo in 1225, and finally, in 1249, the Algarve, Portugal's southernmost edge. The nation's boundaries were now defined. King Afonso III transferred the court from Coimbra to Lisbon about 1260, and his son, King Dinis (who ruled from 1279 to 1325), made Portuguese the country's official language and, in 1290, established its first university (in Lisbon, but later moved to Coimbra). In 1297, the Treaty of Alcañices fixed the border with Spain.

When Ferdinand, the last king of the House of Burgundy, died in 1383, he left no legitimate male heir, only a daughter, Beatrice, and an illegitimate brother, João. Beatrice had married the King of Castile; as her consort, he would also be King of Portugal. The Cortes (Parliament) would not submit to Spanish rule, so they elected the brother, João of Avis, to the throne.

The new king reinforced his position by defeating the Spaniards at Aljubarrota in 1385. Aiding him was a contingent of English mercenaries. As a result, England and Portugal signed the Treaty of Windsor in 1386, which decreed perpetual friendship between the two countries. It is the longest unbroken alliance in the history of the west. To seal it, King João married Philippa of Lancaster, daughter of John of Gaunt, granddaughter of Edward III, and sister of Henry IV.

The marriage of João and Philippa heralded the beginning of Portugal's greatest age and produced four remarkable sons — Duarte, Pedro, Fernando, and Dom Henrique. One became king, one regent, one a crusader, and the fourth, Prince Henry the Navigator. The great Portuguese writer Luís de Camões called them the "wonderful generation."

In 1415 João I, three of his sons, and a fleet of over 200 ships seized the Moroccan town of Ceuta, a center of the spice trade. Inspired by this victory, Prince Henry founded a school of navigation in Sagres, at Portugal's southwesternmost point, 3 years later. Here on this windswept coast, the scientific-minded prince and his assistants collected information from returning sailors, charted the seas, drew maps, invented nautical instruments, and encouraged exploration.

And so the Age of Discoveries began — an age that would turn a small, rather insignificant country into ruler of one of the world's great empires. No wonder the Portuguese look back to this time with the longing and nostalgia they call *saudade*. Those intrepid explorers who set out from Portugal's Atlantic coast in quest of a route to India discovered Madeira in 1419 and the Azores in 1427, and rounded Cape Bojador in 1434. Their travels had led them to the farthest reaches known to Europe. Henry died in 1460, but Portuguese exploration continued. In 1482, Diogo Cão reached the mouth of the Congo River. In 1488, when Bartholomeu Dias rounded the Tempest Cape on Africa's southern tip, King João II quickly renamed it the Cape of Good Hope.

Four years later, Christopher Columbus discovered the New World; Spain had joined Portugal in the race for empire. To prevent future conflicts between the two nations, Pope Alexander VI drew a line just west of the Cape Verde Islands and divided the world between them. The following year, the Treaty of Tordesillas moved the line some 1,000 miles to the west, leading historians to believe that the Portuguese may already have known of Brazil's existence. Officially, Pedro Alvares de Cabral discovered Brazil in 1500, having been blown off course while following Vasco da Gama's route to India. Da Gama himself, probably Portugal's greatest explorer, reached Mozambique and then India in 1488.

Though Gaspar Corte Real discovered westward-lying Newfoundland in 1501, the then king, Manuel, encouraged eastward voyages. In 1510, Afonso de Albuquerque established a fort at Goa. From there, by 1515, the Portuguese commanded the Indian Ocean. Portuguese navigators continued to discover the rest of the world. Under Spanish auspices, the Portuguese Fernão de Magalhães (Ferdinand Magellan) set sail in 1519, landed in India 2 years later, and continued on to the Philippines. Although he was killed there, one of his ships completed the journey, becoming the first ever to circumnavigate the globe.

Under King Manuel, Portugal experienced its Golden Age. The empire garnered enormous wealth, most of it from the East Indies spice trade. The prosperous trade in gold, ivory, and slaves poured even more riches into the country. The arts flourished and people lived well.

But it was not to last. The empire was Portugal's strength, but it was also its weakness. Spices and pepper were brought to Lisbon for re-export to the rest of Europe. At the beginning of the 16th century, profits peaked. The Casa da India, the holding company largely owned and financed by the Portuguese crown, held a monopoly on the trade. As imports increased, the value of individual goods decreased; so did gold from Guinea, which was the medium of exchange. By 1560, Portuguese resources were taxed to the point where foreign investors were needed to keep the Casa da India in business.

To add to Portugal's troubles, King Sebastian and many of the nation's nobles died in 1578 in a battle against the Moors at Alcázarquivir in Morocco. The king's uncle, the aged Cardinal Henrique, assumed the throne. Two years later, the Hapsburg Philip II of Spain moved against the weakened empire. Once again the Spanish were in control.

Portugal, however, lived an autonomous existence under the Hapsburgs, who also controlled similarly independent kingdoms in Spain, Italy, and the Netherlands. But now that Portugal belonged to Spain, its colonies became prey to Spain's enemies. The Dutch attacked and acquired Portuguese colonies in Ceylon, Malacca, the East Indies, Africa, and parts of Brazil. Only Brazil eventually reverted back to Portugal. Another drawback of belonging to Spain was the heavy taxes Spanish wars extracted from Portuguese coffers.

In 1640, the Portuguese rose up against the Spanish and regained their complete independence. At the urging of Portuguese nobles, the Duke of Bragança (from an illegitimate line descended from the House of Avis) assumed the throne as King João IV of Portugal. The new ruler renewed the alliance with England, and enhanced the credibility of the Bragança line by marrying his daughter Catherine to Charles II of England. In 1703, Portugal signed the Methuen Treaty with its old ally, agreeing to import British textiles in exchange for exporting Portuguese wine, chiefly port. (This after-dinner wine, which English gentlemen traditionally sipped at table when the ladies retired to the drawing room, was no doubt one compelling reason for the durability of the Anglo-Portuguese alliance.) Shortly afterward, in 1706, João V, known as the Magnificent, came to the throne. The splendor of his reign, which lasted until 1750, was due to the steady trickle of Brazilian gold, discovered at the end of the 17th century, into Portuguese coffers, and the lavish application of gilt to the nation's churches. The sudden wealth also freed the monarchy from dependence on the Cortes and set it on an absolutist course.

In the world of late-18th-century Portuguese politics, one figure stands out — Sebastião José de Carvalho e Melo, Marquês de Pombal. Pombal, who held various ministerial posts under King José, eventually became the power behind the throne. His regime was notorious for anti-clericalism and the cruel treatment of its opponents. His leadership abilities, however, were more than welcome on November 1, 1775, the date of the catastrophic Lisbon earthquake. Combined with the fire and tidal wave that followed, the earthquake destroyed the city and killed 40,000 people. Pombal gained international fame with his directive to "bury the dead and relieve the living." Upon the death of King José in 1777, Pombal's dictatorship came to an end.

The early 19th century brought Napoleon's troops to Portugal in 1807, and the royal family escaped to Brazil to rule in exile. The French were defeated by Portuguese and British troops under the command of Sir Arthur Wellesley, later the Duke of Wellington, at Buçaco in 1810, but the royal family remained in Brazil as their country became a virtual British protectorate.

When João VI returned to Lisbon to rule, it was within the restrictions of the 1822 Constitution, which established a constitutional government with a limited monarchy. King João had left his son Dom Pedro in charge in Rio de Janeiro; Pedro promptly declared Brazil independent and himself emperor. When his father died, Pedro returned to Portugal — at British insistence — to urge a restructuring of the government that would give the sovereign more power. Having accomplished this (in the liberal Charter of 1826), Pedro returned to Brazil, leaving behind his young daughter Maria as queen under the regency of her uncle Miguel.

But Miguel was not to be trusted. His seizure of power and abolition of the charter prompted Pedro to return to Portugal again. There he led an expeditionary force to Porto in 1832. After a civil war in which liberals and conservatives battled for power, Pedro, with the help of the British, regained control in 1834. The middle class ruled as a liberal oligarchy for the rest of the century.

The 20th century began in turmoil: King Carlos was assassinated in Lisbon in 1908. Coups and counter-coups followed. In 1910, King Manuel II abdicated and fled to England. The liberals declared a republic and, in 1911, adopted a new constitution that established a parliamentary government. Afonso Costa became prime minister. Further struggles ensued as Portugal entered World War I on the side of the Allies, primarily to protect its African colonies.

This unpopular move resulted in Sidónio Pais taking over the government, provoking further turmoil until elections restored an orderly Democratic party majority in 1919. More and more, though, prime ministers came from the military. Anti-clericalism increased. Finances were a shambles. Finally, the right-wing military seized power in 1926. General António Oscar de Fragoso Carmona took control under a dictatorship and remained president until 1951.

In 1928, Dr. António de Oliveira Salazar, an economics professor from the University of Coimbra, became Minister of Finance and managed to pull the country out of its financial straits. He became prime minister in 1932. In 1933, a new constitution established Portugal's Estado Novo, or New State, and gave Salazar dictatorial powers. The New State, a repressive regime, suppressed individual rights, muffled the press, and outlawed political parties.

It's not surprising, therefore, that Portugal favored Franco during the Spanish Civil War. Afterwards, Portugal and Spain signed the Iberian Pact, thus forming an alliance between the two countries. During World War II, Portugal remained neutral, although it allowed the Allies to maintain bases in the Azores. More trouble followed the war, as the government became increasingly repressive, introducing censorship and encouraging the growth of a secret police force — the Polícia Internacional e de Defesa do Estado, or PIDE.

During the 1960s, the last shreds of empire crumbled. India seized Portugal's holdings there. Independence movements erupted in Angola and Mozambique. The young Portuguese sent to crush these movements sympathized with them instead. The fighting drained the economy and put great stress on the military.

Then, in 1968, after a blood clot formed in his brain, Salazar slipped into an irreversible coma, only to be succeeded by Marcello Caetano, who more or less followed Salazar's policies. And so dissatisfaction continued to grow until, on April 25, 1974, the so-called Young Captains staged a coup with flowers in their rifles — the *Day of the Red Carnations* — to oust Caetano and restore democratic principles to Portugal.

The changing winds of liberalism swept across the country and all the way out to the farthest limits of the empire. By the end of 1975, Portugal's African possessions had gained their independence. Foreign Minister Mario Soares traveled to Africa with the intention of organizing free elections. Instead, Cuban-inspired Marxist-Leninists took over the governments, provoking a massive emigration of some 750,000 *retornados* (refugees) from the colonies to Portugal, equivalent to about 10% of its population. Finally, after 2 years of jockeying for power between right and left, a new Portuguese constitution and elections ushered in a more moderate government (about 35% Socialist). Socialist leader Soares became prime minister in 1976.

In 1987, under Prime Minister Anibal Cavaco Silva, the moderate Social Democrat party won a parliamentary majority in a republican government presided over by Socialist President Mario Soares. Having joined the Common Market in 1986, Portugal now looks forward to the more complete integration of its economy with the rest of Europe, as is planned for next year.

Literature

 Saudade, a powerful sense of yearning and nostalgia, has long permeated Portuguese literature, as it does the Portuguese character. Because this literature is so rich in lyrical poetry and not often translated into English, a knowledge of Portuguese is useful for reading and appreciating it. Its greatest works, however, especially those of Luís de Camões, are available in English. Happily transcending the limitations of translation, these magnificent poems and stories tend to spring to life in English as easily as in their native tongue. Newer works also have become more available recently, as the success of Brazilian writers writing in Portuguese — among them Joaquim Maria Machado de Assis and Jorge Amado — has led to translations of the works of contemporary writers from Portugal as well.

From the very beginning, the great glory of Portuguese literature has been its lyric poetry. This literary tradition began shortly after the creation of the country at the end of the 11th century, when Henry of Burgundy brought French scholars with him to his court in the county of Portucale, the court into which Afonso Henriques, Portugal's first king, was born. Afonso's son, Sancho I (1154–1211), along with King Alfonso X of Castile and León (ca. 1226–84) and King Dinis I (1261–1325) of Portugal, created a body of Provençal-style poems written in Galician, the language of northwestern Iberia that foreshadowed both modern Spanish and modern Portuguese. Although the tradition began during the 12th century, only a few works survive from before 1200, one of them a brief verse said to be the work of Sancho I. About 2,000 of these songs — *cantigas de amor* (love songs), *cantigas de amigo* (songs of friendship), and *cantigas de maldizer* (satirical songs) — survive from the 12th and 13th centuries, however. Many of them were written by Dinis himself, the same king who founded the University of Coimbra during his reign and made the dialect of northern Portugal the official language of the entire kingdom.

During the 14th century, Portuguese literary efforts turned away from poetry and went into such prose works as detailed *livros de linhagem* (genealogical registers) and *cronicas* (chronicles). Though of greater interest as documentation than as literature, they remained the dominant literary form until the Galician troubador Macias o Enamorado (Macias the Enamored) briefly revived the tradition of Provençal poetry.

King Duarte (Edward) I (1391–1438) and his brother Dom Pedro (1392–1449) were the great patrons of prose writing during the 15th century. They used the essay as a literary form to write treatises on philosophy. They also created the position of royal chronicler. Among these chroniclers, Ferñao Lopes (1380–1460) was one of the best. He compiled a factual, well-documented history of the Kings of Portugal, distinguished by its vivid style.

The great voyages of discovery in the 16th century led to scholarly and personal accounts of the Portuguese conquests. Ferñao Lopes de Castanheda (1500–1559) and João de Barros (1496–1570) both published monumental histories of Portuguese expansion; Gaspar Correia (1495–1565) and Diego do Couto (1543–1616) wrote unofficial accounts of those years. Their histories — full of reported abuses of authority and generally unflattering accounts of Portuguese behavior in the colonies — were suppressed for centuries. Another personal account of years spent in the Orient, the widely read *Peregrinação* (Pilgrimage) of Ferñao Mendes Pinto (1510–83), earned its author, noted for his colorful exaggerations, the epithet "the father of all lies."

Earlier in the century, Gil Vicente (1470–ca. 1536), one of Portuguese literature's greatest figures and often considered Portugal's Shakespeare and the father of the modern play, had introduced drama to the court. His popular farces and religious dramas (*autos*), though still medieval in their stereotypical characters, were full of ribald wit.

Portugal's first Renaissance poet, Francisco de Sá de Miranda (1481–1558), wrote comedies and sonnets. A trip to Italy had resulted in his mastery of the Petrarchan sonnet form. At around the same time, the concept of *saudade* entered the literature — in the form of bucolic poems, a pastoral novel entitled *Livro das Saudades* (Book of Yearnings), and other works by Bernardim

Ribeiro (1482–1552), as well as in the lyric poetry of Antônio Ferreira (1528–69) and Diogo Bernardes (1530–1600).

Until this time, the literature of Portugal largely had been a reflection of other cultures. But with the appearance of Luís de Camões (1524–80), Portuguese literature came into its own. Camões, who is to Portugal what Dante is to Italy, lived a life full of suitably romantic incidents. After studying at the University of Coimbra, he fell out of favor with the king and was banished from court. Embarking on a military career, he lost an eye in a Moroccan campaign, then moved on to India and Macao where he was dismissed from an official post. When he set sail to return to Portugal, he was shipwrecked.

Having regained favor with the court under the patronage of King Sebastian, Camões published a work in 1572 named after Lusus, legendary ancestor of the Portuguese people. *Os Lusíadas* (The Lusiads), which chronicles the voyage of Vasco da Gama and retraces Portugal's history, is the country's great national epic. Along with his *Ten Songs* and *Sonnets, The Lusiads* ranks Camões among the most important figures of world literature.

Foreign influence returned to Portuguese literature with the Spanish domination of 1580 to 1640. During this period, Francisco Manuel de Melo (1611–66) wrote his histories, poems, and letters primarily in Castilian, but Portuguese was preserved in the letters of Antônio de Vieira (1608–97), a Jesuit missionary in Brazil. The most popular "Portuguese" work of the century, however, was *Lettres portugaises* (1669), a collection of letters in French reputedly written by a nun from Beja, Sister Marianna Alcoforado, and sent to her lover, the French Comte de Chamilly.

Despite their popularity, the authenticity of the *Portuguese Letters* was always doubtful, and in 1926 it was proved that their true author was Gabriel de Lavergne. Nevertheless, the letters, and the tale they tell of a passionate love affair, strongly influenced the epistolary novel, and provided the English Victorian poet Elizabeth Barrett Browning with the inspiration for her famous love poems, *Sonnets from the Portuguese.*

In spite of the Enlightenment, the 18th century was a largely uneventful period for Portuguese literature. While poet Pedro António Correa Garção (1724–72) was making a determined effort to eradicate the Spanish influence from Portuguese literature, Filinto Elísio (pseudonym of Padre Francisco Manoel do Nascimento, 1734–1819) was being influenced by nearby France to take an interest in neo-classical poetry and radical politics. Manuel Maria Barbosa du Bocage (1765–1805), of French descent, moved toward Romanticism with the Nova Arcadia group of poets' revolutionary and antireligious writing.

It was João Baptista da Silva Leitão de Almeida Garrett (1799–1854) who firmly implanted Romanticism in Portugal. A participant in the liberal revolution of 1820, he was forced into exile in Great Britain and France during the reaction to it. But on his return to Portugal, he entered politics, founded a national theater, and produced a prolific amount of verse, epic poetry, and drama that influenced a generation of writers. Alexandre Herculano de Carvalho e Araújo (1810–77), the other principal Romantic writer, was a historian and historical novelist. The Portuguese novel per se began with *Amor de perdição* (Love of Perdition) by Camillo Castello–Branco (1826–90) and was further developed by Julio Dinis (pseudonym of Joaquim Guilherme Gomes Coelho, 1839–71), who moved the form away from Romanticism toward realism.

Another prime mover was Antero Tarquinio de Quental (1842–91), an Azorean aristocrat and intellectual known especially for his darkly pessimistic sonnets. He became a Socialist, helped found the Portuguese branch of the International, and was the major inspiration for the so-called Generation of 1870, which included such writers as José Duarte Ramalho Ortigão (1836–1915) and José Maria de Eça de Queirós (1843–1900) and the poet Abílio Manuel Guerra Junqueiro (1850–1923). Ortigão and Eça de Queirós founded a satirical review, *As Farpas,* and Ortigão went on to write travel books, among them *John Bull* and *A Holanda.* Eça de Queirós's novels, all translated into English, had a tremendous impact in their day. His early works, *O crime do Padre Amaro* (The Sin of Father Amaro) and *O primo Basilio* (Cousin Basilio), are social commentaries on the clergy and the middle class.

In the spirit of *saudade,* many of the Generation of 1870 became disillusioned in later years (Quental committed suicide and Ortigão became *vencido da vida,* or "vanquished by life," another recurrent phenomenon among Portuguese writers) even as nostalgic poetry and historical fiction underwent a revival during the 1890s. Teixeira de Pascoais (1877–1952) developed the spirit of *saudade* into a literary theory he called *saudosismo,* a belief that Portugal's magnificent past would forever hold back its present and future.

Fernando António Nogueira Pessoa (1888–1935), on the other hand, had great faith in Portugal's progress, and with José Regio (the pseudonym of José Maria dos Reis Pereira, 1901–69) introduced Modernism to Portuguese literature. Pessoa, who grew up in South Africa and occasionally wrote poetry in English, also wrote under a variety of pseudonyms, each with its own distinctive stylistic personality. Though he only published one volume of poetry, *Mensagem* (Message), his work influenced Portuguese poets well into the 1940s and 1950s. Regio, also a playwright, was concerned with religious themes.

This century also saw the beginnings of regional writing, best exemplified by the works of Aquilino Ribeiro (1885–1963) about Beira, Miguel Torga (the pseudonym of Adolfo Correia da Rocha, b. 1907) about Trás-os-Montes, and Fernando Namora (b. 1919) about the Alentejo. The Portuguese presence in Brazil was explored by Ferreira de Castro (1893–1974), who based his social novels *Emigrantes* (Emigrants) and *A Selva* (The Jungle) on experiences in Brazil.

Among contemporary writers are Maria Teresa Horta, Maria Isabel Berreno, and Maria Fatima Velho da Costa. Known collectively as the "three Marias," they published *Novas cartas portugueses* (New Portuguese Letters) in 1972. With Sister Marianna Alcoforado's (1640–1723) 17th-century letters as its inspiration, the work is a compilation of letters, stories, and poetry about the repression of women in a male-dominated society. More recently, Maria Fatima Velho da Costa published the autobiographical *Missa in Albis.* Contemporary writers who have been translated into English include António Lobo Antunes, whose *Os cus de Judas* was published as *South of Nowhere,* and José Saramago, whose *Memorial do convento* came out as *Balthazar and Blinunda.*

Painting and Sculpture

Portuguese art has been so affected by certain national experiences, including foreign interventions, that it never established itself as a great school of national painting. Nevertheless, while few, if any, Portuguese artists' names are recognized beyond the country's borders, Portuguese painting and sculpture are rich in personality, combining the best techniques of Flemish, Italian, French, and Spanish art as a point of departure for its own. Compared to Spanish art — which overshadows it and with which it is too often confused — it is gentle and bright, a reflection of the warm spirit of the Portuguese people.

Little important sculpture has survived from the Roman and early medieval periods. Byzantine-style capitals carved with a few simple animals, birds, and people survive from the Romanesque period; they are located mostly in northern Portugal, the first part of the kingdom to be reconquered from the Moors. Because the Koran forbade representation of the human form and because the Moors were not expelled from all of Portugal until the 13th century, it was not until the advent of the Gothic that Portuguese sculpture began to develop in earnest. It manifested itself in funerary sculpture and in religious images, and was centered above all, in Coimbra, because of the availability of the easily worked local Ança stone. The finest monuments of Portuguese Gothic sculpture are the tombs of Dom Pedro I (1320–67) and his wife, the beautiful Inês de Castro, in the monastery church at Alcobaça. Also distinguished are the devotional figures of the Virgin and saints by the 14th-century Master Pero of Coimbra.

As for painting, although there are manuscript references to painters before the 15th century, little remains of their works. The arrival of Jan van Eyck in 1428 signaled the beginning of a Flemish domination that would last well into the 16th century. A royal marriage that linked Portugal and the Netherlands — including present-day Belgium — allowed Portuguese artists to train at Antwerp, while Flemish painters worked in Portugal or sent their works to Lisbon. The Age of Discovery also acquainted Portugal with the art of Africa, India, and the Orient, implanting influences that would last for hundreds of years. Due to Portugal's epic expansions overseas, both the 16th and 18th centuries were golden eras for Portuguese art. The reigning kings — Manuel I in the early 16th century and João V in the 18th — were both lavish spenders, commissioning the best foreign artists available, one reason why Portuguese art is so eclectic. Artists such as the French sculptor Nicolas Chanterene in the 16th century and the Tuscan painter-architect Niccolò Nasoni in the 18th century set styles that the Portuguese emulated.

Nuno Gonçalves (15th century) and Domingos António de Sequeira (19th century) — Portugal's most famous artists — rank as European old masters. Of the two, Gonçalves is considered the greater. His *St. Vincent Altarpiece,* composed of six wood panels representing the martyred St. Vincent, patron of Lisbon, is the major treasure of that city's *Museum of Ancient Art.* Sequeira, on the other hand — often compared to Goya — was a portraitist who used light to express the dramatic. An optimist, he painted with a strong sense of faith in life that is typically Portuguese.

THE FIFTEENTH CENTURY

The 100 years from 1450 to 1550 were fertile ones for Portuguese painting and sculpture. As the first great seapower in Renaissance Europe, Portugal could afford to commission the best foreign artists and send its own budding painters abroad. The period actually began when the Flemish artist Jan van Eyck came to Lisbon in 1428 to paint the portrait of a daughter of Dom João I, who married Philip the Good, Duke of Burgundy. Nuno Gonçalves appeared on the scene around 1450 with a Flemish style learned, presumably, from van Eyck. His most famous work, the six-panel polyptych known as the *St. Vincent Altarpiece,* attracted attention because of its twist on its Flemish roots. Gonçalves used yellow in places normally reserved for gold and accentuated the personalities of his subjects, rather than the precise indoor or outdoor setting, as was common in Flemish art. This attention to detail — the deep-set oval eyes, long nose, full lips, and slightly protruding jaw of the main figures — can also be found in many sculptures of this era. Today, the panels attract attention not only for their artistic merit, but also as a document of Portuguese society of the time. Among the crowd paying homage to the saint — a gathering of 60 or so, including many who have been identified, are Portuguese from all walks of life, from the king to fishermen, monks from Alcobaça, the Archbishop of Lisbon, a rabbi, Prince Henry the Navigator, and, possibly, Gonçalves himself.

By the time Dom Manuel came to the throne in 1495, Flemish painters and sculptors, attracted by visions of wealth, were swarming into Portugal. Multi-panel retables, or altarpieces, similar to Gonçalves's religious homage to St. Vincent, became the backbone of Portuguese art.

THE SIXTEENTH CENTURY

Throughout the 16th century, retables continued in popularity. Around 1510, Jorge Afonso (1508–40), premier painter of the High Renaissance, painted two of the most famous — the panels at the Convento de Cristo in Tomar and at the Convento de Madre de Deus in Lisbon. His works display the period's penchant for order and fascination with the human anatomy. His brother-in-law Francisco Henriques and son-in-law Gregório Lopes (1490–1550) carried on his tradition. In *Mass of St. Gregory,* a panel from the altarpiece of the Church of São João Baptista at Tomar, Lopes emphasized the dramatic emotions of his subjects, a group of chanting monks. Henriques, who is thought to have been Flemish by birth, is most famous for his 13-panel retable for the Church of São Francisco at Evora.

Another popular artist in the 16th century was Vasco Fernandes (1475–1541), called Grão, or "Great," Vasco. He also followed the Afonso style and is said to have painted the main retable of the Cathedral of Viseu (now housed in the *Grão Vasco Museum*), which shows the influence of Henriques's Evora pictures.

As for sculpture, it progressed from a medieval technique to a kind of architectural decoration. Manueline, which became the national style, displayed motifs from Portugal's heroic enterprise in navigation and discovery. During the last quarter of the 16th century, stone sculpture declined in importance and the majority of retables were made of gilt and polychromed (decorated in several colors) wood.

Painting also flourished in the form of illustrations of charts and atlases — a natural outcome of the intensive study of navigation launched by Prince Henry the Navigator and his brothers.

But by 1580, Portugal's reign as a supreme power had come to an end. The country's union with Spain (1580–1640) no longer afforded it a royal court to administer patronage or to send promising young painters to study in other countries. Traces of Flemish influence had already begun disappearing in the mid 16th century; the Portuguese art world began a long period of decline.

THE SEVENTEENTH CENTURY

Most art during this period, obviously and very naturally, was influenced by Spain. In sculpture and painting, Portugal entered its baroque phase (1590–1710). Baroque is characterized by grand, melodramatic, and expansive brushstrokes; light fused with everything, and colors that are strong and definite, in contrast to the uncertain in-between shades of previous styles.

With the great expansion of monastic churches that occurred between 1580 and 1640 came a demand for retables and images that continued until the end of the 18th century. Spanish rule in Portugal ended with the restoration in 1640, when João IV was proclaimed king, but generations passed before the ruined country and its court could again support artistic endeavors. The only notable Portuguese sculptor of the period, Manuel Pereira (1588–1683), spent most of his time in Madrid, where he could command better commissions.

THE EIGHTEENTH CENTURY

The discovery of gold in Brazil in the late 17th century brought wealth to the royal court, enabling art to flourish once again. João V (1706–50) called foreign artists to Portugal and sent promising young Portuguese to Rome. Most famous at the time was Francisco Vieira do Matos Lusitano, called Vieira Lusitano (1699–1783), who became the court painter in 1733 and set the tone for an intellectual art that reflects on the sentimental and the allegorical.

Unfortunately, the Lisbon earthquake of 1755 destroyed much of the best Portuguese art. Undaunted, the Portuguese began reconstruction under the Marquês de Pombal, who, like his forefathers, provided many commissions in sculpture and painting. Under Maria I (1734–1816), the statesman Pina Manique founded a Royal Academy of Design and sustained the Portuguese Academy in Rome, founded in 1791. Art was once again on the rise.

THE NINETEENTH AND TWENTIETH CENTURIES

Though Portuguese art had flourished in the 18th century, no single cohesive style had emerged — that is until the arrival of Domingos António de Sequeira (1768–1837), the portraitist who studied first in Lisbon and later in Rome. Sequeira brought to the art world a hopeful optimism: brighter colors, lighter shadows, realistic overtones — in sum, a pre-impressionistic style. His first works were mainly symbolic, such as the huge *Allegory of the Casa Pia,* which he painted in Rome in 1792 in honor of the intendant Pina Manique, the founder of his art school. But perhaps his most famous work is his portrait of the *Viscount of Santarém and His Family* (1805–10), which has often been compared to Goya's *Charles IV of Spain.* There is no evidence, however, that Sequeira ever visited Spain or saw Goya's work. Sequeira was Portugal's last great heroic artist. A staunch liberal, he painted stories that told of his dissatisfaction with politics, especially the French invasion of Portugal in 1807. His allegory of *Lisbon Sheltered by Junot* cost him 9 months in prison (1808–9). Eventually, like Goya, he sought voluntary exile. His last works, the *Ascension* and *Last Judgment of 1832,* were painted in Rome and tell of his obsession with religious meaning. Most of his works, like those of Gonçalves, are in the *Museum of Ancient Art* in Lisbon.

Today, a new revolution seems to be gaining speed in Portugal. Long inhibited by the rule of the Salazar government, which considered modern art subversive, Portuguese art once again is struggling to come into its own. Recent styles such as Impressionism, Cubism, Expressionism, and Futurism have all had their Portuguese adherents; still, there is no common ground that ties Portugal's art together, nor one great Portuguese master. Art is as eclectic as ever, as can be seen in the works of some of its most famous modern artists, Amadeo de Sousa Cardoso (1887–1918), José de Almada Negreiros (1893–1970), and Maria Helena Vieira da Silva (b. 1908), exhibited in Lisbon's *Centro de Arte Moderna.* Whether despite or because of its tumultuous history, Portuguese art, however, remains fascinating and enjoyable, the blend of hundreds of years of supremacy and struggle mixed with the perpetual optimism of its people.

Architecture

Along with influences from the outside world, a plethora of indigenous and invading cultures has contributed to the richness of Portuguese architecture. It reached its creative peak during the Manueline period, a time that, not surprisingly, coincided with the increased confidence (and coffers) of the Age of Discovery. Today, due to extensive remodeling over the years, most buildings exhibit a melange of historic styles. Still, certain characteristics have remained constant for almost 3 millennia: the use of a wide variety of local stone, uncomplicated ground plans, and simple architectural orders.

Not surprisingly in a practical country filled with granite and limestone, Portuguese architecture is founded on stone. Its earliest remains, dating from the 8th century BC, are the stone walls that surround the fortified hill towns of the northern *casteja* civilization. When excavated, many of these *castros* and *citanias,* like Briteiros and Sabroso, reveal both round and rectangular granite houses.

Much remains of the Roman presence — well-engineered roads, the bridges at Chaves and Ponte de Lima, aqueducts, and the still unexplained pink granite tower outside Belmonte. Left behind from Lisbon's Roman incarnation as Olisipo are numerous baths and ruins, including — beneath today's Baixa section — a theater built when Nero was Emperor of Rome. The ruins at Conímbriga, a Celtic city inhabited and fortified by the Romans, date from the 2nd century BC, and are among the most extensive on the Iberian Peninsula. The peninsula's best single Roman site, however, is the temple at Evora, built during the 2nd or 3rd century.

But the people who inhabited the peninsula during the next few centuries left little architectural evidence of their presence in the area that is Portugal today. The Visigoths built the Basilica of São Pedro de Balsemão near Lamego in the 7th century; Christians, under Moorish domination, built São Pedro de Lourosa near Oliveira do Hospital in the 10th century and rebuilt the Visigoths' São Frutuoso, near Braga, in the 11th century.

Present-day Portugal began to take shape late in the 11th century under the Burgundian dynasty. Alfonso VI of León and Castile had granted the county of Portucale to Henry of Burgundy, whose son, Afonso I, became Portugal's first king. This led, throughout northern Portugal, to an impressive number of churches built in the Romanesque style on the model of the Burgundian monastery at Cluny. Braga, Porto, Lisbon, Evora, and Coimbra all boast cathedrals from this period, though only the last two have remained relatively unaltered. Among smaller Romanesque churches, São Martinho de Cedofeita in Porto and São Salvador de Bravães on the Lima River are the best examples. Other outstanding Romanesque buildings include the *domus municipalis* in Bragança and the polygonal church — the Charola — built by the Knights Templar order in Tomar, and later surrounded by the convent-castle of the Knights of Christ.

The transition from Romanesque to Gothic began in the late 12th century, when Cistercian monks summoned from France by Afonso I built a monastery at Alcobaça. The rigidly simple architecture they used provides Europe's best example of the Cistercian style. During the next century, when the monks built the Cloister of Santa Maria de Celas in Coimbra, they used a much freer hand in the decoration of its capitals.

The Gothic style dominated Portuguese architecture until the 16th century, its austere local variation quite suited to the castles built during this increasingly militant time. Almourol, Guimarães, Leiria, Lisbon, Monsaraz, and Obidos provide examples. The fortress at Vila Viçosa was the first of many that also were built during this period.

In sacred architecture, the outstanding example of the Gothic style is the monastery Church of Santa Maria da Vitória in Batalha. This church marks a turning point, a moment when local architects used the international influences they had absorbed to develop a highly original national style. Begun during the late 14th century by Afonso Domingues, a Portuguese architect, it was taken over at the turn of the century by an architect named Huguet (or Ougete), who may have come from Ireland or France and introduced English and French influences to the design. Martin Vasques and Fernão d'Evora continued the work, and, with a flourish, the Spanish architect João de Castilho completed it. The use of golden limestone throughout the church gives an overall unity to the work of these numerous hands.

Castilho, Diogo Biotac, and the brothers Diogo and Francisco de Arruda were the principal architects of the Manueline style, a late Gothic phenomenon peculiar to Portugal. Though named for King Manuel I (who reigned from 1495 to 1521), the period actually extends from about 1490 to 1550. Highly decorative, exuberant, and characterized by the free use of nautical motifs, the Manueline style celebrates the Portuguese Age of Discovery. Waves, shells, ropes, and anchors cavort with such symbols as Prince Henry the Navigator's Order of the Garter and the King's Cross of Christ. Outstanding examples, in addition to the church in Batalha, include the Mosteiro dos Jerónimos (Hieronymite Monastery) in Belém, the Igreja Matriz do São João Baptista in Vila do Conde, the Igreja de Jesus in Setúbal, and the convent-castle of the Knights of Christ at Tomar.

The best examples of secular Manueline style are the wings that were added to Sintra's Palácio Real during Manuel's reign. The palace interior contains lavish examples of another characteristic of Portuguese architecture, the hand-painted ornamental tiles called *azulejos.* Those at Sintra were imported from Spain — where Moorish craftsmen made them — in the 16th century. Portugal began producing its own *azulejos,* based on Italian and then Flemish tiles, at about the same time.

Another peculiarly Portuguese phenomenon that flourished during the Manueline era are *pelhourinhos* (pillories). Introduced by the Romans, these were columns used for publicly displaying caged or chained criminals. Eventually, they became symbols of municipal authority, which burgeoned under King Manuel, and as a result, the Manueline versions are particularly numerous and elaborate.

Because Portugal remained in the grip of the Manueline style until well into the 16th century, the Renaissance architecture prevalent elsewhere in Europe arrived relatively late. Not until 1541, with the publication of Diego de Sagredo's textbook *Medidas del Romano,* was Renaissance neo-classicism formally introduced to Portugal. Its center was the university town of Coimbra, where the north portal of the Sé Velha (Old Cathedral) and its São Pedro chapel are among the best examples of Renaissance architecture in the country. Most Renaissance-style churches, however, including Coimbra's Sé Nova (New Cathedral) and the cathedrals at Leiria, Portalegre, and Miranda do Douro, were built later, when the neo-classical style had evolved into Mannerism.

Spanish Hapsburg rule in Portugal between 1580 and 1640 coincided with the construction of numerous religious buildings throughout the country. These combined Spanish monumentality with a neo-classicism that came from an interest in Palladian architecture. Filippo Terzi, an Italian architect who worked for the Hapsburgs, was responsible for the churches of São Roque and São Vicente de Fora in Lisbon, which were built at this time.

Baroque architecture, though it took its name from the Portuguese word for a misshapen pearl, *barroco,* originated in Italy during the 17th century. At the time, Portuguese wealth was being used to fight against Spain. The discovery of gold in the Portuguese colony of Brazil at the end of the century, however, resulted in money and materials for such projects as the palace designed by the German architect Johann Friedrich Ludwig for João V at Mafra, and the numerous churches decorated in gilded wood called *talha dourada.* Manor houses and country estates (called *solares* and *quintas* in Portuguese), which had long been a tradition in Portugal, also took a sumptuous turn. The royal palace at Queluz, with its formal gardens and lavish *azulejos,* is the most accessible.

Like the ill wind that blows somebody good, the devastating earthquake of 1755 gave Lisbon's city planners a clean slate. Under the Marquês de Pombal, José I's dictatorial chief minister, Eugénio dos Santos laid out the new Lisbon in a grid plan. The first buildings were in a rococo style that came to be known as Pombaline. The city's Praça do Comércio is the best example. When Pombal was dismissed upon José's death in 1777, rebuilding continued in a more neo-classical vein. Neo-classicism also extended to the north. It can be seen in the Cadeia da Relação (Law Courts) building and the Carrancas Palace in Porto, and in the Church of Bom Jesus do Monte near Braga, built atop a baroque staircase.

As elsewhere in Europe during the 19th century, architects in Portugal were seized with a passion for reviving historical styles. Given the diverse styles of Portugal's history, however, they produced forms seen nowhere else. The *Palace* hotel in Buçaco, for example, is neo-Manueline, and the *Campo Pequeno* bullfighting arena in Lisbon is neo-Moorish. Gustave Eiffel, the engineer responsible for the Paris tower that bears his name, designed the Dona Maria Pia railroad bridge in Porto, while his disciples were responsible for other engineering feats in Portugal — the Ponte de Dom Luís in Porto and the Elevador de Santa Justa in Lisbon.

During the 20th century, Portuguese architecture has continued to reflect European trends. Art Nouveau, in vogue at the beginning of the century, left its mark in Lisbon, Leiria, and Coimbra. The functional architecture that sprang up next is most pleasantly exemplified by the modern *Calouste Gulkenkian Museum,* designed by Alberto Pessoa, Pedro Cid, and Ruy Anthoguia, and begun in Lisbon in 1966. That year also saw the building of the Ponte 25 de Abril suspension bridge — the longest in Europe — connecting Lisbon to southern Portugal. After the 1974 revolution, the so-called *style méditerranéen* (Mediterranean style), ubiquitous in southern European resort communities, erupted all over the Algarve, site of an outbreak of intense tourism development. Even more recently, post-modernism arrived in the person of Tomás Taveira, who designed the colorful and controversial Amoreiras residential and industrial complex in western Lisbon.

Traditional Music and Dance

Just as the Portuguese are, generally speaking, less flamboyant than their Spanish neighbors, their signature musical tradition, the *fado* (from the Latin word meaning "fate"), is more subdued than the bold flamenco. While drawing upon the same wellspring of raw emotion, the tragic despair of flamenco becomes in *fado* an abiding melancholy. Though flamenco and *fado* seem to have much in common superficially — the coarse quality of the voice, the vocal glissandos and trills, the note of anguish — allegations of a common Moorish foundation are belied by the Algarve, the southernmost province of Portugal, where the Moorish presence was most prolonged but where there is no trace of a *fado* tradition.

First referred to formally in 1833, *fado* has been assigned various theoretical lineages. Most plausible among them deems it a blend of the African dance called the *lundum,* brought to Brazil by slaves and to Portugal by 18th-century sailors, and the more sophisticated *modinhas,* adaptations of the sentimental Italian operatic airs that were popular in Lisbon at about the same time. Originally a song form of sailors, it premiered in the dock areas of Lisbon and spread quickly through the city's Alfama, Mouraria, and Bairro Alto districts. Full of the loneliness and nostalgia of life at sea, the early *fados* were taught by sailors to their long-suffering wives, their prostitutes, their local vendors, and their neighbors. Until the 1830s, *fado* was strictly a working class diversion that chronicled the daily life of the Lisbon citizenry, commenting not only on love affairs but also on the popular figures of the day, political events, and, of course, scandals.

Ironically, it was a scandal that eventually made the art form upwardly mobile. During the first half of the 19th century, Maria Severa, an attractive, temperamental young prostitute whose mother was a Gypsy, had become Lisbon's most popular *fadista.* Succumbing to her numerous charms, the Count of Vimioso fell in love with her despite the profound discrepancy in their social standings. His persistent attentions to Maria and her art finally made *fado* respectable among the nobility. But Maria died young — at the age of 26 — prompting all *fado* singers of the time to don black to mourn her premature passing. Whether out of a lingering sentiment or its eminent suitability for the *fado* mood, the black costume remains to this day the traditional garb of the *fadista.*

The traditional themes of the *fado* continue to focus on *saudade,* a poignant yearning for the impossible that is akin to the Spanish *soledad.* Note the following *fado* verse:

> *I look at the earth and at the sky*
> *And everything reminds me of you.*
> *When I lost your love*
> *I lost every reason for living.*
> *There is only one truth*
> *Remaining in our love:*

> It is the image of "saudade,"
> Beautiful but covered with sadness.
> "Saudade" go away
> Depart from my tired heart
> Take it to a distant land
> This fado of mine.
> Written on the wind:
> At night my brother is the wind
> Trying to forget the storm
> As I long to forget
> This "saudade."
> But alas, I cannot.
> Come back, my love to me.
> The pain goes and gaiety returns;
> Love dies and friendship remains;
> Only this profound "saudade"
> Will not from my heart depart.
> Please come back, my love.
> Let me hold you in my arms.
> Why do you keep me distant,
> Knowing that I long to be near you?

Lisbon *fados* are the saddest of them all, bemoaning the sorrow and strife of life and love. When the lights dim in the capital's *fado* cafés, the time for the song has arrived. Typically, two guitars — one 12-stringed Portuguese and one 6-stringed Spanish — begin to play. The *fadista* (male or female) emerges from the shadows. If the singer is a woman, she will wear a black woolen shawl. True to tradition, she will clasp her hands in front of her, lean her head back, and close her eyes, retreating to the inner recesses of passion. If she is good, she will draw the audience in with her. Her throaty voice, singing in syncopated (2/4) time, matches the sad texture of the lyrics.

Unfortunately, *fado* has suffered much the same fate as flamenco. Those today who sing for love of art or from the agony of their souls are rare. Most often visitors will find those who sing for a salary, the emotional edge of their tired songs dulled by nightly repetition.

Unlike contemporary flamenco, *fado* is strictly a song form. Like flamenco, it also has its lighter side. The *fado corrido* from the Ribatejo, the bull-raising area along the Tagus River, is faster and more spirited than its Lisbon counterpart. And the more polished and lyrical *fado de Coimbra,* from the north's famed university town, is actually a romantic serenade that has little in common with its melancholy cousin from Lisbon.

Traditionally, many *fado* songs have taken their lyrics from Portuguese poets, although new lyrics are often written expressly for individual *fadistas.* Though *fado* is more melodic than flamenco, many visitors also consider its earthy vocals and exotic halftones an acquired taste. Many of Lisbon's *fado* houses are full-fledged restaurants that offer folk dancing and popular songs. "Before midnight," says a native *fado* connoisseur, "the *fado* they sing is fit only for tourists. After midnight, only for Portuguese." As Amália Rodrigues, the most famous *fadista* of all time, once sang so eloquently, "All this exists, all this is sad, all this is *fado.*"

Fado is not all there is to folk art in Portugal. Perhaps best known of all the Portuguese folk dances is the *vira,* a product of the northern Minho region. Though widely heard throughout the area extending from Porto to the country's northern border and running 30 miles inland from the coast, its two main focal points are Vila do Conde and Vila Nova de Famalição. Traditionally, the *vira* is a round dance for four couples, but any number may participate. Similar to waltz rhythm, the *vira*'s (6/8) time is frequently accentuated by the Minhotan women's wooden clogs.

A variation occurs in the fishing villages of Estremadura and, most notably, in Nazaré. Though the tempo here is also waltz-like, it's quicker and livelier. Another difference between the two versions of *vira* lies in the instruments played. The north favors the ukelele and fife; the south, the accordion. Both use the *bombo* (an earthenware pot) for percussion. A further difference lies in the chorus. Curiously, the Minhotan *vira* uses castanets, a custom not normally found in Portuguese folk music.

Bullfighting

 Bullfighting, or *tourada,* has taken place since the 17th century in Portugal. Today it is second only to soccer as the nation's spectacle of choice, although its use of sharp darts that penetrate the bull's hide, not to mention the risk taken by the bullfighter and the horse upon which he conducts his end of the fight, are not to everyone's taste.

Nevertheless, bloodshed is kept to a minimum. Unlike his Spanish counterpart, the Portuguese bullfighter does not kill the beast. A gory incident in which the Count of Arcos was mauled by a bull in the 18th century prompted the Marquês de Pombal, King José I's chief minister, to prohibit the practice. That act reflects the Portuguese attitude toward the bullfight as an elegant, dignified pastime. In fact, on the occasions when the bullfight is preceded by a *corrida de gala à antiga portuguesa* — a gala fight in the old Portuguese style — the ring assumes the pageantry of a fairy tale. Costumed and mounted musicians, footmen bearing the coats of arms of the noble old bullfighting families, brightly bedecked mules carrying baskets of darts to stick the bull, and white horses drawing coaches that carry the *cavaleiros* (horsemen) who will later engage the bulls on horseback, all parade around the ring.

A Portuguese bullfight, while it doesn't always include the *corrida de gala,* is customarily fought in 17th-century costume and divided into distinct segments. Like Spain's, it begins with a parade (*cortesia*): Horseback riders ceremoniously drive the bulls through the streets to the ring, where, to a trumpet fanfare, the cast of players enters the arena. First come the *campinos,* countrified bull handlers; next, the six *peões de brega* (capemen), wearing their glittering suits of lights, and the *forcados* — youths who will tackle the bull in the second half of the *tourada* — dressed in short jackets, breeches, white stockings, and green-and-red-tasseled stocking caps; and finally the mounted *cavaleiros,* the real stars of the spectacle. Dressed in plumed, tricornered hats, lace jabots, brilliantly decorated three-quarter-length coats, white breeches, and black boots, the *cavaleiros* bow gracefully to the *intelligente* (director of the bullfight) before circling the ring. Their high-spirited and skillful horses have plaited tails and manes. The high-backed saddles are heavily studded and decorated. At the sound of the bugle, all participants leave the arena and the segment ends.

Another bugle call sounds to signal the second segment. A lone *cavaleiro* returns. His horse stops short to gaze across the ring at a closed gate. It opens and the bull charges into the arena, its horns covered with leather sheaths called *embolados*. As the *peões de brega* toy with the bull, the *cavaleiro* sizes up his adversary. Then his task begins.

In a series of *sortes,* or strikes, he must plunge into the bull's neck muscle several darts — usually six, three long and three short — which release small flags upon impact. At the discretion of the *intelligente,* the rider can throw a seventh and shorter stick, but to do so he practically has to fall out of the saddle.

The *sortes* take different forms. The *sorte de gaiola* is a surprise strike: The bull charges directly from the gate past the gatemen to the *cavaleiro* — without benefit of a warm-up period — to receive its first dart, or *farpa.* The dart's length, about a yard, allows the *cavaleiro* to keep a certain distance as he swoops down on the bull. The usual encounter, however, after bull and *cavaleiro* have had time to assess each other during the cape play, is *poder-a-poder,* a frontal charge that ends with the placement of the *farpa.*

The shorter darts are called *bandarilhas,* and after the last one — just a few inches long — has been inserted, the *cavaleiro* rides victoriously around the ring to a cheering crowd — or a booing mob if he has not lived up to expectations. The *cavaleiro*'s circular saunter ends the segment.

Next, the eight-man team of *forcados* jumps over a barrier into the ring. Their role — as well as their costume — is based on the one played by servants of the original bullfighting nobility, who often turned the bull over to attendants before killing it. (*Forcados* are amateurs — unlike *cavaleiros,* who enjoy professional status.) Their leader taunts the bull, calling it names until it charges, at which time he lunges forward between the bull's horns and holds on tight, a maneuver called *pega de cara.* His mates then surround the bull, grab its tail, and dig in their heels until they bring it to a halt.

After the *forcados* jump back over the barriers, the bull is escorted out of the ring by a herd of bullocks gaily decorated with bells and bits of colorful material. Badly injured bulls are slaughtered; others are returned to pasture for breeding.

Variations liven up the customary *tourada.* The *cavaleiro* may perform tricks, or *adornos,* such as riding the bull's horns while carrying a dart in either hand, or breaking a dart to decrease the distance between rider and bull. Sometimes the *cavaleiro* will alternate with a *toureiro,* who enters the ring on foot, teases the bull with a cape, and pretends to kill it with a sword. (Actual slaughter of the bull can result in a heavy fine.) In some villages, such as in the Azores, the entire town participates in the bullfight; a roped bull is given the freedom of the streets, and local youths display their prowess in subduing it.

There are about 40 bullrings in Portugal, most in the center of the country.

Bullfighting, however, is most popular in the Alentejo and Ribatejo regions of southern Portugal, where fighting bulls and the specially trained horses used in the fights are bred. The best-known bullfighters appear at town festivals — in Santarém in June and Vila Franca de Xira in July — though the most famous arena is the *Praça de Touros do Campo Pequeno* in Lisbon, which seats 8,000 spectators. The season runs from *Easter* to October. *Touradas* take place on Sundays and occasionally Thursdays. During the month of June, when Lisbon honors Saint Anthony, its patron saint, there are bullfights at the *Campo Pequeno* every Thursday night from 10 o'clock on.

Dining in Portugal

When Vasco da Gama rounded the Cape of Good Hope late in the 15th century, he made world history — and forever altered the course of Portuguese cooking. He and his seafaring countrymen introduced pepper, cloves, curry, nutmeg, cinnamon, rice, tea, coffee, hot and sweet peppers, and a host of other savory foods to Portuguese larders. Portuguese cooks, in turn, added and blended these exotic ingredients into their fish and meat dishes, their soups, and their desserts. The result is a tasty, wholesome, and sometimes surprising cuisine that makes dining in Portugal both a pleasant experience and an adventure.

The foundation of Portuguese cooking consists of olive oil, garlic, onions, and salt and pepper. Potatoes, tomatoes, peppers, beans, and rice are its basic ingredients; coriander, cumin, and paprika its most popular spices. Parsley both flavors and decorates. It's a balanced cuisine: spicy, but not overtly spiked; savory, but not too seasoned; smooth, but not bland. And it's bold — the Portuguese, after all, have the audacity to combine potatoes and rice in the same dish and get away with it. Credit goes to the Moors for introducing honey, almonds, and eggs into the country's dessert diet.

The Portuguese love affair with the sea and its bounty is intense. Wherever people go along the coast, the aroma of sardines — cooking in earthenware charcoal grills outside corner *tascas* (taverns) — greets them, as does the sight of mounds of *mariscos* (seafood) in the window displays of *marisquerias* (fish restaurants). Of all fish, *bacalhau* (codfish) is dearest to the Portuguese palate. Portuguese fishermen have caught it off Newfoundland banks for over 500 years, and Portuguese cooks are reputed to have invented over 365 ways to prepare it. Codfish is so highly prized that it makes up the main course at *Christmas* dinner. Governments have been known to falter when cod is in short supply.

Caldeirada (fish stew), Portugal's bouillabaisse, is the second national seafood dish. Although its content varies from region to region and with the day's catch, a good *caldeirada* should include about nine varieties of fish and shellfish, including clams, mussels, squid, and octopus. Carnivores need not despair. Portugal's third national dish, *cozido à portuguesa* (Portuguese boiled dinner), is a stew made up of a hearty selection of meats, sausages, and vegetables.

Portuguese dining hours are more in tune with those of northern Europe than with the late schedules kept by neighboring Spain. Breakfast, *pequeno almoço,* is light, usually *chá* (tea) or *café* (coffee) *com leite* (with milk) or *sem leite* (without milk). Coffee shops serve a strong, flavorful *bica* (demitasse) and a creamy, machine-steamed *galão* (coffee and milk in a glass). Accompaniments can include *torradas* (toast) or *bolos* (sweet cakes) and cinnamon-covered *pastéis de nata* (egg and custard pastries). Lunch (*almoço*) is served between 1 and 3 PM. For travelers on the move, quick meals are available at *cervejarias* (beer halls), which specialize in *petiscos* (tidbits, or snacks, the equivalent of Spanish *tapas),* sandwiches, and simple meat and fish platters.

For *lanches* or *merendas* (afternoon snacks), artists head for the *café* (coffee shop), society women to the *salão de chá* (tea salon), and the general public to the *pastelaria* (pastry shop). This last offers a large choice — everything from sweet *pastéis* (pastries) to *croquetes* filled with cod, shrimp, chicken, and meat. By late afternoon, the *tascas* and *cervejarias* begin to fill up with the after-work crowd tossing down *imperiais* (glasses of draft lager), *cerveja preta* (dark beer), and *copos de vinho* (glasses of wine), both *tinto* (red) and *branco* (white), while munching on *caracois* (snails), *gambas* (prawns), *codornizes* (stewed quails), *polvo* (octopus), *bifanas* (miniature paprika-laced pork steaks), and *pregos* (steak sandwiches).

Restaurants serve dinner (*jantar*) between 7 and 10 PM, or even later in some cosmopolitan restaurants and modern shopping malls. Menus are à la carte, although many places carry a fixed-price, three-course *menu do dia* (daily menu) at reasonable rates.

A typical dinner starts with a selection of appetizers (*aperitivos*) such as *queijinhos* (fresh sheep or goat cheeses), a mild paté, and *azeitonas* (olives), along with mouth-watering bread: the rich *pão de milho* (maize bread), the wholesome, dark *pão de centeio* (barley bread), and the lusty, golden *broa* (yeast-based corn bread). Specialties may include *presunto* (smoked ham) from Chaves, Lamego, and Monchique; a plate of *amêijoas* (clams) in white wine, garlic, and parsley sauce; or *gambas na prancha* (grilled prawns).

The Portuguese excel at *sopa* (soup). The light *canja de galinha* (chicken and rice), the creamy *sopa de marisco* (shellfish), the nutritious *sopa de verdura* (vegetable), the heavy *sopa de grão* (chickpea), and the wholesome *sopa de feijão* (bean) are among the more common. Regional soups include the northern *caldo verde* (cabbage soup), the thick, breaded *açordas* from the Alentejo and Estremadura, and the cold, vinegary *gaspacho* soup of the Algarve.

A soup from Ribatejo called *sopa de pedra* (rock soup) contains beans, vegetables, and a stone. According to the story, whenever a certain roaming mendicant priest was refused a meal, he would simply light a fire, then fill a pot with water, put a stone in it, and set it to boil. As curious villagers approached, he slowly coaxed them into adding the ingredients necessary to make a real soup.

There's plenty of fish (*peixe*) on the menu, including boiled or batter-fried *pescada* (hake), grilled *linguado* (sole), and *salmão* (salmon), Tagus River *sável* (shad), *tamboril* (monkfish), ham-stuffed river *truta* (trout), *robalo* (sea bass), wine- or blood-stewed *lampreia* (eel) from the Minho and Tomar rivers, smoked *espadarte* (swordfish), *cherne* (stone bass), Algarve *carapau* (mackerel), and the ubiquitous sardine. Stewed, grilled, and stuffed *lulas* (squid), along with *santola no carro* (cold crab salad in a shell), are coveted seafood dishes, though *lagosta* (lobster) from Peniche is a luxury item for Portuguese and visitors alike.

Carne (meat) and *ave* (poultry) can be *assada* (baked), *grelhada* (grilled), *frita* (fried), *cozida* or *estufada* (stewed), and *recheada* (stuffed). In Portugal, where farmers feed their pigs chestnuts and acorns, *porco* (pork) is the most abundant and tasty meat. Each region has its pork dish: stewed in a copper pot with white wine, clams, and sausages in the Algarve; stewed in red wine in the Minho; and, from the Coimbra area, *leitão assado* (roast suckling pig). But the most interesting — and sublime — pork dish in Portugul is probably *carne de porco à alentejana* (pork and clams Alentejo-style), which means seasoned in a savory sauce of paprika, white wine, *pimentão* (sweet red peppers), garlic, oil, bay leaves, onions, and tomato paste.

Cordeiro (lamb) and *cabrito* (kid) dishes are best in the northern and central mountain regions. Steaks, not Portugal's forte, are still worth sampling when accompanied by the mushroom, cream, and mustard sauces used in the best restaurants. Especially good, however, are *bitoques,* thin beefsteaks cooked in butter and served with egg and French fries in hot earthenware dishes. Grilled *frango* (chicken) is becoming more and more popular, particularly in coastal areas, where chickens compete with sardines for space on outdoor grills. The waiter may ask if you want yours with *piri-piri* sauce. Be warned — *piri-piri,* made by mixing Angolan red peppers with oil and vinegar, may be the most tongue-searing sauce in the cooking almanac. Use it sparingly.

In Portugal, sausages are a staple — as appetizers, in stews and soup, and grilled. They come in several shapes, tastes, and sizes. The dry and garlicky *chouriço* is especially popular, and so is *linguiça,* its thinner cousin, sometimes cooked in alcohol to be eaten with bread in *fado* music houses. Smoked *paio* (pork sausage) is popular in the Alentejo, while *morcelas* (blood sausages) come mainly from the north. During the 15th century, at the time of the Inquisition, Jews, under duress and masquerading as Christians, invented *alheiras,* mixed-meat sausages disguised to resemble pork.

Sobremesa (dessert) is an ode to the Portuguese sweet tooth and the bane of cholesterol watchers. Some egg-based desserts such as *toucinho do céu* (bacon of the sky) require as many as 12 egg yolks, and the already rich flans (custard puddings) are thickened with eggs and caramelized. There are also sweets with amusing names such as *barrigas de freira* (nuns' tummies). These stem, apparently, from the 19th century, when the religious orders were banned and, in order to earn a living, nuns became cooks.

Other seductive desserts include *pudim Molotov,* a poached meringue with caramel or peach topping, golden *sonhos* (dreams), deep-fried batter puffs sprinkled with sugar and cinnamon, *arroz doce* (rice pudding), *doce de chila* (caramelized chila gourd), and *torta de amêndoa* (almond tart). For weight watchers, *fruta fresca* (fresh fruit), *melão* (melon) or *ananás* (pineapple) with razor-thin strips of *presunto* are lighter alternatives. *Queijo* (cheese) is another dessert option; the ones made from sheep's milk are the most coveted. The queen of Portugal's cheese is *serra,* a brie-like cheese from the central Serra da Estrela range. Following closely on its heels are the smooth *castelo branco* cheeses, the Alentejo's salty beja, and the semi-sharp and buttery *serpa,* brushed with paprika and oil.

Along with their love of a *boa mesa* (well-laid out table), the Portuguese love their wine. With its endless number of producers and labels, the country is like one huge wine cellar, and a tour of Portugal, where wine changes from valley to valley and from town to town, is a wine lover's dream. The traveler can discover young local wines and visit the shrine of the venerated port wine in the Douro Valley. This area is also the home of the superb Barca Velha reds and Monopólio whites and Portugal's best *vinhos espumantes* (sparkling wines): Lamego's Raposeira *brutos* (dry) and *semi-secos* (medium dry) bubblies.

The young, crisp *vinhos verdes* (green wines) from the Minho region, which are drunk chilled, go well with fish and shellfish. These wines have a lower alcohol content but higher acidity than more mature wines, however, so it's wise to resist the temptation to drink too much of them before going to bed. Other important demarcated-zone wines are the tart, white bucelas, grown on the sandy banks of the Tagus River east of Lisbon, the robust red dão wines from the upper Beira region, the fruity bairrada reds from the coastal areas near Coimbra, chilled colares reds and whites from the salty cliffs near Sintra west of Lisbon, the full-bodied and sweet muscatel from Setúbal south of Lisbon, and the light Algarve reds and whites. And then there are the fruity rosés — such as the Mateus rosé from Trás-os-Montes — so popular with tourists.

Portugal's after-dinner drinks are also unique. Liqueurs range from *medronho,* made from the smooth nectar of the arbutus-berry, to the bitter almond *amêndoa amarga* from the Algarve. The sweet cherry *ginginha* brandy from Alcobaça, west of Lisbon, is popular, as is the rougher *bagaço,* a clear brandy-like liquor distilled from grapes leaves and drunk chilled. Aged *aguardente velha* is a more refined, cognac-flavored spirit favored by connoisseurs and the well-to-do.

Part of the charm of dining in Portugal can be the history lesson consumed along with the meal. Consider, for example, *tripas à moda do Porto* (tripe in the style of Porto). Back in the 15th century, Prince Henry the Navigator, in order to provision an armada, commandeered almost all the meat in the city of Porto, leaving its citizens nothing but tripe. However, they immediately fashioned this into a delicious and spicy dish of tripe and beans. Today, culinary ingenuity and resourcefulness, together with the Portuguese flair for blending, still delight those fortunate enough to dine in Portugal.

THE CITIES

BARCELONA

Seeing a circle of men and women move in simple, slow steps to the music of flute and drum around a sun-drenched square on a Sunday afternoon provides an almost visceral understanding of Barcelona and its people. This regional dance, the *sardana* — once described by a poet as a dance "of people going forth holding hands" — is indicative of the sense of community and passion for music that is typical of Barcelona.

The *sardana* appears to happen spontaneously. People walking back from mass or a Sunday stroll begin to linger in the cathedral square. Seemingly from nowhere, a band gathers and begins to play what sounds like rhythmic dirges. People set aside purses, prayer books, and hymnals, then join hands to form large circles. Slowly, the circles revolve as the dancers step out the intricately counted measures on tiptoe, and soon they are caught up in the intensity of the music. They hold their hands high; some close their eyes. The music continues in melodic tones. Then, almost abruptly, the *sardana* is over. The dancers nod to their neighbors, gather up their belongings, and continue on their way home.

Witnessing this, you will see the soul of Barcelona, the strong communal feeling that tempers Catalonia's legendary individualism. Not only has Barcelona long been a great Mediterranean port and Spain's "Second City," but it also has long been the capital of the Catalan people, a stronghold of Catalan nationalism in more repressive times, the locus of Catalan representation vis-à-vis the government of Madrid in freer ones. There always has been a strong regional identity and pride here. After the death of Francisco Franco in 1975, the native Catalan language, no longer suppressed, quickly regained its place as the dominant one of the region. Streets and place names were changed back from Castilian to Catalan, and with the democratic constitution of King Juan Carlos, the region of Catalonia — encompassing the provinces of Barcelona, Gerona (Girona in Catalan), Lérida (Lleida), and Tarragona — was designated one of the country's 17 *comunidades autónomas* (autonomous communities).

Given its position across the Pyrenees from France, on the Mediterranean Sea south of the Costa Brava (literally, "wild coast"), Barcelona has a history and language that link it as much to France as to Spain. Catalan, the lilting language of the region, is derived from the French *langue d'oc,* or Provençal, and is spoken in French Catalonia as well.

The history of Barcelona dates back to 218 BC, when Hamilcar Barça, a powerful Carthaginian (and Hannibal's father), founded Barcino. The Romans developed the town, throwing up walls, parts of which can still can be seen. The Visigoths fought over it in the 5th century, the Moors in the 8th century, and in 801 it was the turn of Charlemagne, who included it in the Spanish March — a Frankish province serving as the dividing line between

Christian Europe and Muslim Spain. During the 9th and 10th centuries, local lords, the Counts of Barcelona, became strong enough to establish their independence and drive the Moors from the lands to the south, and by 1100 Barcelona had dominion over all of Catalonia. When Ramón Berenguer IV, a 12th-century Count of Barcelona, married an Aragonese heiress and became King of Aragon, the city became the capital of the combined Catalonian and Aragonese kingdom. It grew to be a major force in the Mediterranean before it was assimilated into the new Spain of Ferdinand and Isabella at the end of the 15th century.

At one point, it was said that "every fish in the Mediterranean wore the red and yellow stripes of the kingdom led by Catalonia." Barcelona was a major Mediterranean power, a force whose might can be felt even today in the medieval streets of the city's old Gothic quarter, the Barri Gòtic. During the 1400s, Barcelona rivaled Genoa and Venice in Mediterranean trade. But although Columbus (Colón in Castilian, Colom in Catalan) sailed from here on his historic voyage, the discovery of the New World proved disastrous for Catalonia. As trade moved from east to west, Seville, Cádiz, and other Spanish ports on the Atlantic rose in importance, and Barcelona declined.

Thereafter, the question of Catalan autonomy became a consistent theme in Barcelona's history, and the city and region often picked the wrong team in making a stand against the rest of Spain. They rose up against the Spanish crown during the Thirty Years War in the 17th century and failed in an attempt to set up an independent nation. In the early 18th century, they backed the Hapsburgs in the War of the Spanish Succession, prompting the victorious Bourbons to put an end to what Catalonian autonomy remained. Only in the late 19th and early 20th centuries did Barcelona begin to recoup. Success in industry fostered a cultural revival — the *Renaixença* — and a newfound sense of Catalan identity. Architects such as Antoni Gaudí and his contemporaries designed and raised buildings of astonishing creativity in new city quarters — in fact, Barcelona was as much a center of Art Nouveau as Paris or Vienna, but here the style was called *modernisme.* Catalan and non-Catalan artists such as Joan Miró, Pablo Picasso, and Juan Gris, attracted by the city's life and color and the spirit of its people, made it a meeting place. Political radicalism flourished, and Barcelona became the capital of a short-lived autonomous Catalan government set up in 1932. Then, during the Spanish Civil War, it became the seat of the Republican government from November 1937 until its fall to Franco's Nationalists in January 1939.

Today, Barcelona, the most European of Spanish cities, is big, rich, and commercial. Catalans are famous throughout Spain for their business acumen, and young people seeking commercial advancement are drawn here from all parts of the Iberian Peninsula. Barcelona is the publishing and literary capital of Spain, as well as its major port and second largest city (pop. 1,755,000). Government offices, boulevards, and fountains here are large and pompous exhibitions of civic pride; Catalans walk the city streets with a swagger and a confidence that boasts, "We are different, better educated, more culturally aware, and much better off than the rest of Spain." It is no coincidence that Barcelona has the highest literacy rate in Spain, and can claim to be the only city where the patron saint's day is celebrated with gifts of books to friends. "There's a bookshop and a bank on every block," they claim, and bellhops and shoeshine boys often are buried in books that on closer inspection turn out to be French, German, or English classics, rather than Spanish mystery novels.

The seaport atmosphere is felt throughout the city, but it is most apparent in the area closest to the waterfront. With all the charms of the rest of the city, the harbor remains a focal point: a place to watch the comings and goings of cruise ships and tankers; to hire motorboats or other pleasure craft for cruises along the coast; to photograph the 200-foot monument to Christopher Columbus and the replica of his caravel, the *Santa María;* or merely to be part of the bustle of the docks.

Barcelona has become a favored destination for Europeans who like their big cities to have more than just a cathedral and an art museum. Scores of good restaurants attest to the Barcelonan love of good food and the variety of the regional dishes. Chic designer fashion boutiques (the city police uniforms were designed by couturier Antoni Miró!) attract visitors, as do some of the finest modernist buildings in Europe, including not only the works of Gaudí but also the Palau de la Música Catalana, which attests to the Catalan love of music in this city where many people belong to choral societies and choirs, and the young usually join societies to learn regional dances such as the *sardana.*

Recent Catalan prosperity has restored the ancient, revamped the old, and forged the new. The prospect of playing host to the *1992 Summer Olympic Games* has accelerated Barcelona's already speedy face-lift. In preparation for the games, the city is spending over $100 million on the construction of 20 new hotels and is building a new, $150 million terminal at El Prat Airport. The technologically advanced terminal, capable of handling over 12 million passengers a year, is scheduled to be completed this June. These and other multibillion-dollar projects, however, are not geared to the requirements of the *Olympics* alone, but are designed to be permanent, expanding the city's tourism and sports facilities for the post-*Olympic* 21st century, referred to locally as "Barcelona 2000."

Still, if you are fortunate to be walking through the Barri Gòtic some evening at dusk, and hear voices softly singing a medieval madrigal as though the spirits of the past were alive, pause and savor the moment: You will have found the essence of Barcelona.

BARCELONA AT-A-GLANCE

SEEING THE CITY: There are excellent panoramic views of Barcelona, its harbor, the foothills of the Pyrenees, and the Mediterranean from the top of Tibidabo, a 1,745-foot hill on the northwest edge of the city. Covered with pines, it's topped with an amusement park, a church that is lit up at night, and, to celebrate the upcoming *Olympics,* a needle-like 800-foot-tall telecommunications tower, symbolic of Barcelona's perception of itself as "the city of the future." To get to Tibidabo, take the *FFCC* train to Avinguda del Tibidabo, change to the *tramvia blau* (blue tram), and take it one stop to Peu del Funicular, where you can take the funicular to the *Tibidabo Amusement Park.* Check the park's opening hours with the tourist office before setting out, however, because it's not open every day and it closes fairly early. At other times (or if you're interested more in the view than the park anyway), do as the locals do and get off after the tram ride and walk across the square to the smart but pricey restaurant, *La Venta* (Plaça Dr. Andreu; phone: 212-6455). Or stop for drinks at one of the bars (the *Mirablau* has panoramic picture windows). At night, the lights of the city below create a spectacular sight.

SPECIAL PLACES: The city's oldest buildings of historic and artistic interest are located in the Barri Gòtic, the old medieval heart of Barcelona, an area that is crisscrossed by alleyways weaving among ancient palaces, churches, and apartment blocks. When the walls of the old city were pulled down during the 19th century, Barcelona expanded north and west into the Eixample (Ensanche in Castilian — literally "enlargement"), a grid pattern of wide streets and boulevards. Avinguda Diagonal and Gran Via de les Corts Catalanes, modern Barcelona's major streets, cut across this chessboard, which is the city's special pride because of the unparalleled late 19th- and early-20th-century architecture found here, including Gaudí's most interesting works. To the south of the Barri Gòtic and the Eixample is Montjuïc, called the "Hill of the Jews" because a Jewish cemetery once was located here. This is the city's playground, a sports and recreation area and the site of the *1992 Olympic* complex. Buildings put up to house exhibitions for the *1929 World's Fair* still scale its slopes, and at the summit, a huge castle overlooks the sea.

BARRI GÒTIC

Catedral de Barcelona – Barcelona's cathedral, dedicated to Santa Eulàlia, the 4th-century Barcelona-born martyr who is the city's patron saint, is an excellent example of Catalan Gothic architecture. It was begun in 1298 on the site of an 11th-century Romanesque cathedral that one of the Counts of Barcelona, Ramón Berenguer I, had founded to replace an even earlier church damaged by the Moors. It was largely finished in the mid-15th century, except for the façade and two towers, which were not constructed until the end of the 19th century, although they follow the original plans. The interior is laid out in classic Catalan Gothic form, with three aisles neatly engineered to produce an overall effect of grandeur and uplift. The church is comparatively light inside, with the flickering of thousands of votive candles adding a cheery note, and on the saint's day, February 12, it is full of flowers.

In the enclosed choir are beautifully carved 14th- and 15th-century wooden stalls; the coats of arms painted on them, dated 1518, belong to the Knights of the Golden Fleece, who met here that year. The Grand Master of the group, Holy Roman Emperor Charles V, included the Kings of Hungary, France, Portugal, Denmark, and Poland in this "club," and Henry VIII of England had a stall on the emperor's right. Note also the *trascoro,* the white marble choir screen that forms the back of the choir, beautifully carved in the 16th century with scenes from the saint's life. Her remains are in an impressive white alabaster tomb in the crypt, which is down the stairs in front of the massive High Altar. Also buried in the church are the founder of the Romanesque cathedral, Ramón Berenguer, and his wife, Almodis, in plush-covered caskets on the wall to the side of the High Altar (look up). The chapel of St. Benedict (the third one beyond the caskets) is among the more notable of many in the cathedral; it contains the nine-panel Altarpiece of the Transfiguration by the 15th-century Catalan artist, Bernat Martorell. The fourth chapel before the caskets houses another of the cathedral's treasures, the 15th-century polychrome tomb of St. Raymond of Penyafort.

The adjoining cloister is a homey surprise. Reached through the cathedral, through the Santa Llúcia chapel, and through doors from the street, it is an oasis of greenery, full of palm trees and inhabited by numerous pigeons and a gaggle of geese who reside beside fountains and a pool. Off the cloister, in the chapter house, is the small *Museu de la Catedral,* containing, among other exhibits, *La Pietat,* a 15th-century painting on wood by Bartolomé Bermejo. The cathedral is open daily from 7:30 AM to 1:30 PM and from 4 to 7:30 PM; the museum is open from 11 PM to 1 PM. Admission charges to the enclosed choir and to the museum. Plaça de la Seu (phone: 315-3555).

Palau de la Generalitat (Palace of Government) – This 15th-century Gothic structure was the seat of the ancient Catalonian parliament and now houses the executive branch of Catalonia's autonomous government. Inside are a 15th-century Flamboyant Gothic chapel, the Chapel of St. George, with splendid 17th-century vaulting, the 16th-century Saló de Sant Jordi (St. George Room), in which the most important decisions of state have been handed down over the centuries, and other notable rooms. Unfortunately, this is a working building and is not at present open to the public, but arrangements can be made to see it, weekends only, by appointment. Contact the Protocolo (public relations) office. Plaça de Sant Jaume (phone: 301-8364).

Casa de la Ciutat (City Hall) – Like the Palau de la Generalitat across the square, this structure, also known as the Ajuntament, is another fine example of Gothic civil architecture. The façade on the square is 19th-century neo-classical, however. Walk along the Carrer de la Ciutat side to see the building's original 14th-century Flamboyant Gothic façade. Since this, too, is a working building and closed to the public, its interior, including the restored Saló del Consell de Cent (Chamber of the Council of One Hundred) and the Saló de Sesion (Session Chamber), can be seen on weekends and by appointment only. Plaça de Sant Jaume (phone: 302-4200).

Palau Reial Major (Great Royal Palace) – The former palace of the Counts of Barcelona, who later became the Kings of Aragon. Built in the 14th century, it actually is a complex of buildings, of which one large room, the Saló del Tinell, a magnificent banquet hall, is the nucleus. Legend has it that on his return from the New World, Christopher Columbus was presented to King Ferdinand and Queen Isabella here. The room is closed to the public unless there is a concert or exhibition; then it is worth the price of admission just to see it and the stylized painting of the Catholic Monarchs sitting on the palace's great steps, surrounded by the heroic Columbus and the American Indians he brought home on his return voyage. Plaça del Rei.

Museu d'Història de la Ciutat (Museum of City History) – The city's history museum, at the opposite end of Plaça del Rei, is housed in the Casa Clariana-Padellàs, a 16th-century Gothic merchant's house that actually was moved stone by stone from a nearby street and rebuilt on the present site. Begin a tour in the basement, where pathways thread through an actual excavated section of Roman Barcelona, past remains of houses, storerooms, columns, walls, and bits of mosaic pavement. Upstairs rooms contain paintings, furniture, and municipal memorabilia, including the 16th-century Gran Rellotge, one of the six clocks that have occupied the cathedral bell tower. The museum also incorporates part of the Palau Reial Major: that is, the 14th-century Capella de Santa Agata, which is bare except for the *Altarpiece of the Epiphany,* painted in 1465 by Jaume Huguet. Open Tuesdays through Saturdays from 9 AM to 8:30 PM, Sundays from 9 AM to 1:30 PM, and Mondays from 3:30 to 8:30 PM. Admission charge. Entrance on Carrer del Veguer (phone: 315-1111).

Museu Frederic Marès – Set up in another part of the Palau Reial Major, this is an important collection of medieval art, particularly medieval sculpture, donated to the city by the museum's namesake, a prominent local sculptor. The painted wooden religious statues, peculiar to this part of Spain, are outstanding. On the upper floors, a display of artifacts ranging from costumes and combs to pipes and purses invites visitors to discover what everyday life was like in old Catalonia. Open Tuesdays through Saturdays from 9 AM to 2 PM and from 4 to 7 PM, open mornings only on

Sundays; closed Mondays. Admission charge. 5-6 Plaça de Sant Iu (phone: 325-5800).

Museu Picasso – Housed in the beautiful 15th-century Palau Agüilar, which is of nearly as much interest as the master's works, this is not strictly within the Barri Gòtic, although it's quite near. A lovely Gothic-Renaissance courtyard opens to the roof, surrounded by tiers of galleries arcaded with pointed arches and slender columns. Lithographs and early works from the artist's years in Málaga and Barcelona (1889–1905) constitute most of the collection, but there are a few special pieces. One is the large exhibition of 44 variations of *Las Meninas,* the famous Velázquez painting in Madrid's *Prado.* Also notice examples of Picasso's warm and unpretentious ceramic work, including brightly painted plates and jugs. Open Tuesdays through Sundays and holidays from 10 AM to 8 PM; closed Mondays. Admission charge. 15 Carrer de Montcada (phone: 319-6310).

Palau de la Música Catalana – Also not far from the Barri Gòtic, although very distant from it spiritually, this is quintessential modernism, the Catalan variation on the Art Nouveau theme. Designed by Lluís Domènech i Montaner and built from 1905-1908, this concert hall is every bit as colorful as anything designed by the more famous Gaudí, but it's also less bizarre and, therefore, in the opinion of many, more beautiful — Gaudí himself is said to have likened it to what heaven must be like. The interior of the auditorium, topped by a stained glass dome, covered with mosaics, and rife with ceramic rosettes, garlands, and winged pegasuses, can be seen only by attending a performance. Those not wishing or unable to get tickets can amble in with the crowd and admire the foyer, itself a lovely space full of brick pillars that rise to ceramic capitals decked with ceramic rosettes. There's an elegant bar in the middle adorned with more stained glass. In summer, when there are no concerts, don't fail to walk by the equally colorful exterior. Carrer d'Amadeu Vives (phone: 301-1104).

EIXAMPLE

Passeig de Gràcia – Running from Plaça de Catalunya to Plaça de Joan Carles I, where it is cut off by Avinguda Diagonal, this is the widest boulevard in the grid-patterned enlargement that grew up in the 1860s and 1870s after Barcelona's old walls were torn down. Lined with boutiques, banks, hotels, cinemas, and art galleries, it links the Barri Gòtic to what once was the old village of Gràcia, and it provides a pleasant backdrop for a stroll. Characteristic of the street are the *fanals-banc,* combined lamp-posts and mosaic benches designed by the modernist architect Pere de Falqués and dating from 1900. Of much greater interest, however, are the modernist buildings located here, three of them in one block alone, between Carrer del Consell de Cent and Carrer d'Aragó, the so-called *mançana de la discórdia* or "block of discord." Locals, shocked by the clashing of avant-garde styles, gave it this nickname, a pun on the word *mançana,* which means both city block and apple — the reference to the mythological apple of discord is the sort of sophisticated joke Barcelonans enjoy.

Casa Lleó-Morera – On the corner of Passeig de Gràcia and Carrer del Consell de Cent, this is one of the three noteworthy modernist buildings occupying the "block of discord." Designed by Lluís Domènech i Montaner and built in 1905, at the peak of the Catalan modernist movement, it has stone balconies carved in flower designs and winged lions. The façade is monochromatic, but step across the street to see the ventilator on top, like an elaborate bonnet with a green, pink, and yellow flowered hat band. The ground floor is occupied by a *Loewe* boutique; upstairs the building houses the headquarters of the Patronat de Turisme. 35 Passeig de Gràcia.

Casa Amatller and Casa Batlló – Making up the remainder of the "block of discord," the Casa Amatller (41 Passeig de Gràcia) was designed by Josep Puig i Cadafalch in 1900 and has a Dutch look, with a stepped-gable front inlaid with tiles and green lacy shutters in its windows. It contrasts dramatically with its neighbor, the Casa Batlló (43 Passeig de Gràcia), which dates from 1904-1906 and is a typical design by

Antoni Gaudí, the leader of the modernist movement. With mask-shape balconies, sensuous curves in stone and iron, and bits of broken tile in its upper levels, it's a fairy-tale abode looking for all the world as though it were inhabited by giant mice. Casa Amattler is a library, so it's possible to tiptoe in, but Casa Batlló is closed to the public.

Casa Milá – Only a short way up Passeig de Gràcia, this apartment house, dating from 1906-1910, is regarded as the classic example of Gaudí's modernist architecture. Popularly known as La Pedrera (the "stone quarry"), it seems to be making an almost sculptural attempt to distance itself from the harsh, square lines of its turn-of-the-century neighbors. Notice the intricately swirling ironwork of the balconies, the melting, "soft" sinuousness of the building's horizontal lines as it wraps around the corner. The famous roof terrace has more strange formations covering the chimneys and ventilators. Conducted tours of the rooftop take place Mondays through Fridays at 10 AM, 11 AM, and noon and at 4 and 9 PM; Saturdays at 10 AM, 11 AM, and noon only. There is no charge — just turn up. There is no elevator, but the 6 flights of stairs are worth the effort to see details of doorknobs and banisters en route. 91 Passeig de Gràcia (phone: 215-3398 or 319-7700).

Fundació Antoni Tàpies (Antoni Tàpies Foundation) – Along with the Museu *Picasso* and the *Fundació Joan Miró* on Montjuïc, this is Barcelona's third, and newest, museum dedicated to a single artist. Opened in 1990 in a refurbished 19th-century modernist building designed by Lluís Domènech i Montaner, it houses a major collection of the still-living Catalan artist's works — paintings, drawings, sculpture, assemblage, ceramics — previously stored in warehouses and in private collections, including his own. There is also a research library and space for shows by other contemporary artists, but perhaps the main attraction is the huge Tàpies sculpture of metal wire and tubing on the roof of the building, taking up the entire width of the façade and adding 40-plus feet to its height. It's called *Cloud and Chair,* and you may love this bizarre construction or hate it, but if you're walking along the street, near Passeig de Gràcia, you certainly won't fail to notice it. Open daily from 11 AM to 8 PM; closed Monday. Admission charge. 255 Carrer d'Aragó (phone: 487-0315).

Parc Güell – Constructed between 1900 and 1914, this originally was planned as a real estate development by Gaudí and his friend Count Eusebio Güell, a noted Barcelona industrialist and civic leader. Only two plots of this garden city ever were sold, however (one to Gaudí himself), and the city purchased the propery in 1926. It now is a public park. Two gingerbread-style houses — entry pavilions intended as the porter's lodge and an office building — flank the entrance gate; between them a staircase sweeps up to a "hall" or "forest" of mock-classical columns that would have been the development's marketplace. They support a raised plaza covered with gravel and entirely edged with an undulating bench whose backrest is a mosaic quilt of colored ceramic tiles. This extraordinary outdoor space originally was meant to be a recreation center, which is more or less the function it serves today. Also within the park is the *Casa-Museu Gaudí* (Gaudí House-Museum), installed in the house in which the architect lived from 1906 to 1926 (it was designed by another architect, Francesc Berenguer); on display are personal objects, including his bed, and furniture designed by Gaudí and others — most interestingly, some of the original built-in closets from Casa Milá and a large sliding door from Casa Battló. The park is open during daylight hours; the museum is open from 10 AM to 2 PM and from 4 to 6 PM; closed Saturdays. Admission charge to the museum. Bus No. 24 up Passeig de Gràcia leads to the Carretera del Carmel entrance, which is close to the museum, and also not far from the main entrance (with pavilions) located at Carrer de Llarrad and Carrer d'Olot.

La Sagrada Familia (Church of the Holy Family) – Antoni Gaudí was killed in a tram accident in 1926 before he could complete this religious edifice, his most famous and controversial work. One of Spain's most extraordinary buildings (its full name is Temple Expiatori de la Sagrada Familia), it still is essentially a building site, unencumbered by a roof. Begun in 1884, the church originally was designed by Francisco del Villar in the neo-Gothic style. When Gaudí was commissioned to take over the project in 1891, he changed the design considerably. Of the two façades and eight towers that are complete, only the famous Nativity Façade, on the Carrer de Marina side, was finished when Gaudí died. Carved to suggest molten stone, it has four tall spires, blue-green stained glass windows, and a porch filled with sculpted figures, including the Virgin Mary, Joseph, and the infant Christ above the main portal. The Passion Façade, on the Carrer de Sardenya side, was begun in 1952. Still to come are a central dome, to rise more than 500 feet and represent Christ, along with several smaller domes representing the Virgin Mary and the Evangelists. Work continues slowly, and few expect the church's completion before the middle of the 21st century. Take the elevator (or the stairs) up the Nativity side to the dizzy heights of the spires for views of the city and close-ups of the amazing architectural details. Steps go even higher, but beware if you suffer from vertigo! The audiovisual show in the *Museu Monogràfic,* located in the crypt (which also was finished at the time of Gaudí's death), traces the history of the church, as do the architect's models. Open daily, June through August, from 8 AM to 9 PM; September through May, from 9 AM to 7 PM. Admission charge, plus an additional charge for the elevator (which keeps shorter operating hours than the site as a whole). Plaça de la Sagrada Familia; entrance on Carrer de Sardenya (phone: 255-0247).

MONTJUÏC

Fonts Lluminoses – These illuminated fountains, designed for the *1929 World's Fair,* look like Hollywood special effects. Colored lights play on jets of water that rise and fall to music broadcast by loudspeakers — all against a backdrop of the Palau Nacional, which was the Spanish pavilion for the same fair. It sounds like kitsch, but it's quite a show! The fountains are in operation in summer on Thursdays, Saturdays, and Sundays from 9 PM to midnight (with music from 10 to 11 PM), and in winter on Saturdays and Sundays from 8 to 11 PM (with music from 9 to 10 PM). No shows from January through March. Between Plaça d'Espanya and Montjuïc.

Poble Espanyol (Spanish Village) – Built for the *1929 World's Fair* and revitalized (as is everything else in the city) for the *1992 Olympics,* this is a 5-acre model village whose streets and squares are lined with examples of traditional buildings from every region of Spain, most of them re-creations of actual structures. There are a Plaza Mayor, a Calle de la Conquista, and a Plaza de la Iglesia, just as might be found in any Spanish town or city, and numerous restaurants, bars, and nightspots. A walk through "town" illustrates the diversity of Spanish architecture and offers a chance to see traditional artisans at work; their carvings, pottery, glass, leather, and metalworks are sold in the village's 35 shops. The grounds are open daily from 9 AM until the wee hours, closing at 2 AM Sundays and Mondays and at 4 AM the remaining days, but note that shops, restaurants, and other enterprises within the village keep their own, shorter hours. Admission charge. Avinguda del Marqués de Comillas (phone: 325-7866).

Museu d'Art de Catalunya (Museum of Catalonian Art) – The museum's home, the massive imitation Renaissance-baroque Palau Nacional that was the Spanish pavilion in the *1929 World's Fair,* has been undergoing a complete remodeling of its interior. Often referred to as "the *Prado* of Romanesque art," the museum contains a splendid collection of Romanesque panel paintings and sculpture, in addition to its chief treasure, a series of frescoes removed from small churches of the Pyrenees region. The museum also is renowned for its Gothic holdings, as well as for canvases by such greats as Velázquez, Zurbarán, and El Greco. Open from 9:30 AM to 2 PM; closed Mondays. No admission charge. Mirador del Palau, Parc de Montjuïc (phone: 223-1824).

Fundació Joan Miró (Joan Miró Foundation) – Set up in an ultramodern building designed by Josep Lluís Sert, the late Catalan architect, this is a light, airy tribute to

Catalonia's surrealist master, who also was an outstanding sculptor and weaver, as his *Tapis de la Fundació* demonstrates. Numerous painted bronze sculptures are displayed on terraces of the museum's upper level; in the galleries are works in various styles and mediums, including a haunting *Self Portrait*, which the artist began in 1937 and did not finish until 1960. The museum hosts frequent special exhibitions, and also has a library and well-stocked art bookstore. Open Tuesdays through Saturdays, from 11 AM to 8 PM; Sundays and holidays, from 11 AM to 2:30 PM. Admission charge. Plaça Neptú, Parc de Montjuïc (phone: 329-1908).

Museu Arqueològic (Archaeological Museum) – Exhibits include relics found in the excavation of the Greco-Roman city of Empúries nearby, various jewels and miniatures, and other remnants of Spain's prehistoric cultures, as well as a fine collection of Greek, Carthaginian, and Roman statues and mosaics. Open Tuesdays through Saturdays, from 9:30 AM to 1 PM and from 4 to 7 PM; Sundays, from 9:30 AM to 1 PM; and holidays, from 10 AM to 2 PM. Admission charge. Carrer de Lleida (phone: 423-2149).

Anell Olímpic (Olympic Ring) – Montjuïc has been designated the principal site for the *1992 Summer Olympics*, which are scheduled to take place from July 29 to August 9 of next year. The sports facilities within the Olympic Ring include the main, 70,000-seat *Estadi Olímpic* (Olympic Stadium), a complete restructuring of a stadium originally built for the *1929 World's Fair*. The opening and closing ceremonies and track and field events will be held here; tours begin at the Marathon Entrance between 10 AM and 3 PM on weekends (phone: 424-0508). Also within the ring are the new 17,000-seat domed *Palau d'Esports Sant Jordi* (St. George Sports Palace), by the Japanese architect Arata Isozaki; the *Piscines Municipals B. Picornell* (B. Picornell Municipal Pools), open-air pools with seating for 5,000; and baseball, rugby, and practice fields, all within walking distance of one another. There are numerous bicycle and jogging paths, too, and they are such popular exercise sites that it may seem the whole city is getting in shape for the *Olympics*.

Museu Militar (Military Museum) – From time immemorial there has been a fortress at the top of Montjuïc, and the castle occupying the spot today, built largely in the 17th century and expanded in the 18th, has been restored and pressed into service as a museum. The belvedere on the grounds provides stunning views of Barcelona — of the port below and across the city to Tibidabo. On display inside are military uniforms, toy soldiers, models of forts, and a collection of 17th- to 19th-century guns. The castle can be reached by road as well as aboard the Montjuïc *telèferic*, a cable car that takes over where the Montjuïc funicular leaves off (see *Getting Around*) and carries passengers up and over the *Parc d'Atraccions de Montjuïc* (Montjuïc Amusement Park) to the top of the mountain, where the castle, the belvedere, and a panoramic restaurant are located. The museum is open Tuesdays through Saturdays from 10 AM to 2 PM and from 4 to 7 PM, Sundays and holidays from 10 AM to 7 PM. Admission charge. The *telèferic* is in operation daily in summer, on Saturdays, Sundays, and holidays in winter. Parc de Montjuïc (phone: 329-8613).

ELSEWHERE

La Rambla – This is the city's favorite — and liveliest — promenade, brimming with activity. Originally a drainage channel, it runs from the harbor to Plaça de Catalunya, changing its name en route (Rambla dels Caputxins, Rambla de Sant Josep, Rambla de Canaletes, and so on). Traffic moves up one side and down the other, and in the middle is a wide, tree-lined pedestrian esplanade. A brisk 20-minute trot would cover it all, but the whole idea is to take it much more slowly, examining the flower stands, thumbing through the books at the book stalls, reading a favorite newspaper or magazine at a sidewalk café, or merely strolling and chatting with friends. Look for the sidewalk mosaic by Miró at the Plaça de Boquería; stroll to the nearby Mercat de Sant Josep (St. Joseph's market, better known as the Boquería); and be sure to visit the *Gran*

Teatre del Liceu, one of the world's great opera houses, at the corner of La Rambla and Carrer de Sant Pau. Don't be fooled by the drab exterior, as this is one of the world's largest and most majestic auditoriums. Tours are conducted September through June, Mondays through Fridays, from 11:30 AM to 12:15 PM. Admission charge. Also see Gaudí's first major work, the Palau Güell, 3 Carrer Nou de la Rambla (phone: 317-3974), a few steps off La Rambla and now serving as the *Museu de les Arts de l'Espectacle* (Museum of Theater Arts), open from 10 AM to 1 PM and from 5 AM to 7 PM; closed Sundays and holidays. Admission charge. Just off the port, the triangle between La Rambla and the Avinguda del Paral·lel, with its little alleyways, is known as the Barri Xinès, literally "Chinese district," but is actually the red-light district. At night, these dark side alleys are dangerous.

The Waterfront – Barcelona's historic seagoing tradition has made it one of the most important cities on the Mediterranean, one that today serves as a nearly compulsory port of call for major international cruise ships. But its industrial waterfront only lately has been cleaned up and reclaimed for the pleasure of the people. The Moll de la Fusta, the quay where the Barri Gòtic meets the harbor, now boasts a pedestrian promenade, palm trees, and park benches, as well as several outdoor restaurants and bars known as *chiringuitos.* Most locals consider most of these restaurants too expensive to patronize, so just stop in for a drink.

Monument a Colom (Columbus Monument) – At the harbor end of the La Rambla, anchoring one end of the Moll de la Fusta, this is the tallest tribute in the world to the noted explorer. It was erected in 1886 and consists of a statue of Columbus standing atop an orb atop a pillar, pointing seaward. Take the elevator to the top floor for an extraordinary view. Open late June to late September from 9 AM to 9 PM daily; the rest of the year, open Tuesdays through Saturdays from 10 AM to 2 PM and from 3:30 to 6:30 PM; Sundays and holidays from 10 AM to 7 PM. Admission charge. Plaça Porta de la Pau.

Museu Marítim (Maritime Museum) – The old low, stone buildings with the gables behind the Columbus Monument are examples of medieval Catalan industrial architecture. They were built in the 14th century as the Drassanes Reials (Royal Shipyards); ships that carried the red-and-yellow Catalan flag to the far corners of the world were launched from these yards years before Columbus's bold discovery. Fittingly, the city's *Maritime Museum* now occupies the yards. On display are old maps and compasses, ships' figureheads, models of ancient fishing boats, freighters, and other vessels, and a full-size reproduction of the *Real,* the galley that was Don Juan de Austria's victorious flagship in the Battle of Lepanto in 1571. Open Tuesdays through Saturdays from 9:30 AM to 1 PM and from 4 to 7 PM; Sundays and holidays from 10 AM to 2 PM. The admission charge also includes a tour of the full-size replica of the *Santa María* (see below) across the way. 1 Plaça Porta de la Pau (phone: 301-1871).

Santa María – This full-size replica of one of Columbus's caravels is anchored in the water not far from the *Museu Marítim,* just on the other side of the Columbus Monument. You can walk around in the belly of the ship and imagine how happy its crew must have been to finally sight land. Open daily, from 9 AM to 2 PM and 3 PM to sunset. Admission charge also gains entrance to the *Museu Marítim.*

Barceloneta – The lively "Little Barcelona" district is a long finger of land lying across Barcelona harbor, between the city and the Mediterranean. The Passeig Nacional, lined with bars and every kind of eating establishment imaginable, forms the area's waterfront promenade on the city side. Behind it, a grid of streets strung with laundry drying from balconies and encompassing a few leafy plazas stretches to the beach on the Mediterranean side, the Platya de la Barceloneta. The area is famous for its numerous tiny seafood restaurants — in summer, tables are put right on the beach and dining goes on into late evening. Somewhat to the north is Poblenou, a massive redevelopment zone that is the site of the 1992 Olympic Village. To reach Barceloneta, walk all the way around the waterfront past the Moll d'Espanya, take the subway to the Barceloneta stop and walk from there, take any of several buses, or take the Barceloneta *telèferic.*

Parc de la Ciutadella – This open space was created just over 100 years ago for the *Universal Exhibition of 1888.* It's popular with Barcelonans, not just for the park itself, but for the added attractions such as the zoo (phone: 309-2500) and the Palau de la Ciutadella, which houses the Parlament de Catalunya. Next door is the *Museu d'Art Modern* (phone: 319-5728 or 310-6308), devoted to Catalan artists little known outside the region. The museum is open Tuesdays through Saturdays from 9 AM to 7:30 PM, Sundays until 2 PM, and Mondays from 3 to 7:30 PM. No admission charge. The zoo is open from 10 AM to 5:30 PM daily. Admission charge.

■**EXTRA SPECIAL:** The Sierra de Montserrat lies 40 miles (64 km) northwest of Barcelona, in the geographical and spiritual heart of Catalonia. The many legends that surround Montserrat, which inspired Wagner's opera *Parsifal,* undoubtedly arose from the strangely unreal appearance of these impressive mountain peaks. Tucked within is the Benedictine monastery whose Marian shrine has attracted pilgrims for over 700 years. *La Moreneta* (The Black Madonna), a polychrome statue of the Virgin Mary, represents the spiritual life of the province and is central to Catalan unity. Legend has it that St. Luke carved the statue and presented it to St. Peter in Barcelona in AD 50. Actually, the tall, slim carving dates from the 12th century. The Virgin sits impassively in a small chamber above the main altar of the monastery's basilica, accepting pilgrims' reverential kisses on her out-stretched right hand, which holds a sphere of the world. The basilica is open daily from 8 AM to 8 PM. No admission is charged, but a donation is welcome. The monastery's famous *Escolania,* a boys' choir claiming to be the oldest choir in the world, sings at 1 PM each Sunday and on special occasions. There is also a museum at the site, open daily from 10 AM to 2:30 PM and from 3:30 to 6 PM. Admission charge (phone: 835-0251). From the monastery, paths and funiculars lead to the Santa Cova, the cave where the statue is supposed to have been found, and to the isolated hermitages of Sant Miguel, Sant Joan, and Sant Jeroni. The belvedere at the latter, 4,061 feet above sea level, provides views that stretch from the Pyrenees to the Balearic Islands and are as breathtaking as they are vertiginous.

SOURCES AND RESOURCES

TOURIST INFORMATION: Brochures, maps, and general information are available from the Patronat Municipal de Turisme de Barcelona (Barcelona Tourist Bureau), open Mondays through Fridays, from 9 AM to 2:30 PM and from 3:30 to 5:30 PM (35 Passeig de Gràcia; phone: 215-4477). There are also tourist information offices at 658 Gran Via de les Corts Catalanes (phone: 301-7443), open Mondays through Fridays from 9 AM to 7 PM and Saturdays until 2 PM; and in the Barri Gòtic (at the Ajuntament, Plaça de Sant Jaume; phone: 318-2525), open Mondays through Fridays from 9 AM to 9 PM, Saturdays until 2 PM. The information offices at the Moll de la Fusta (phone: 310-3716) and at Barcelona Sants Central Railway Station (phone: 250-2592) are both open daily from 8 AM to 8 PM, while the office at El Prat Airport international arrival hall (phone: 325-5829) is open Mondays through Saturdays from 9:30 AM to 8 PM, Sundays until 3 PM. The "Casacas Rojas," red-jacketed tourist guides who patrol popular areas such as the Barri Gòtic, the Passeig de Gràcia, and La Rambla, supply on-the-spot information from approximately mid-June to mid-September.

The US Consulate is at 33 Via Laietana (phone: 319-9550).

Local Coverage – The tourist offices provide good free maps and brochures. The weekly *Guía del Ocio* and monthly Barcelona city magazine, *Vivir en Barcelona,* both available at newsstands, provide comprehensive listings of museums, nightspots, restaurants, and other attractions, although not in English (the latter does include some information in English in high-season editions). Alternatively, dial 010 for Barcelona Information, a telephone "what's on" service where English-speaking operators occasionally can be found.

 TELEPHONE: The city code for Barcelona is 3. If calling from within Spain, dial 93 before the local number.

 GETTING AROUND: Airport – Barcelona's airport for both domestic and international flights is El Prat (phone: 325-5829), located 7½ miles (12 km) southwest of the city, or about 30 minutes from downtown by taxi; the fare ranges from about $15 to $20. Trains run between the airport and Barcelona Sants Central Railway Station, connecting with the subway lines, every 20 minutes; the trip takes 15 minutes and the fare is approximately $1. *Iberia's* shuttle (*Puente Aereo*) has flights to and from Madrid every hour throughout the day. There is an *Iberia* office at 30 Passeig de Gràcia (phone for domestic reservations: 301-6800; for international reservations: 302-7656; for information: 301-3893).

Boat – Ferries operated by *Trasmediterránea* leave Barcelona for the Balearic Islands daily in summer, less frequently in winter. The company is located at 2 Via Laietana (phone: 319-8212); departures are from the Moll de Barcelona pier near the Columbus Monument. *Golondrinas,* or "swallow boats," making brief sightseeing jaunts in the harbor (out to the breakwater and back) depart from directly in front of the monument from 10 AM to 8 PM in summer and from 10:30 AM to 1 PM and from 3 to 5 PM in winter. The trip takes only about 15 minutes; buy the ticket from the office at the water's edge (phone: 310-0342).

Bus – Although more than 50 routes crisscross the city, the system is easy to use, since stops are marked with a map of each route that passes there. The best deal for the visitor is *Bus Cien,* the No. 100 bus that constantly circles around 12 well-known sites such as the cathedral, the Sagrada Familia, and so on. The flat-rate half-day or full-day ticket (bought on the bus) lets you get on and off as often as you like, and also entitles the bearer to a discount at museums. The route operates only in high season, however, from approximately mid-June to mid-September. At other times, buy the 10-ride ticket (T-1, or Targeta Multiviatge) for 380 pesetas (about $3.50). It's valid on all buses as well as on the subway, the funicular to Montjuïc, and the *tramvia blau* (blue tram) to Tibidabo. (A T-2 ticket is good for the subway, the funicular, and the *tramvia blau,* but not for the bus.) Buy the ticket at the public transport kiosk in Plaça de Catalunya (where the *Guía del Transport Públic de Barcelona* also is available) or at any subway station. After boarding the bus (enter through the front doors), insert the ticket in the date-stamping machine. For city bus information, call 336-0000.

Long-distance domestic and international buses also serve the city. For information on tickets and departure points, phone 336-0000 or 241-1990.

Car Rental – Cars are useful for day trips outside Barcelona, but usually are more trouble than they are worth for touring within the city. All the major international and local car rental firms have offices at the airport.

Funiculars and Cable Cars – In addition to the funicular to Tibidabo (see *Seeing the City*), there is a funicular making the climb from the Paral-lel subway stop up to Montjuïc, where it connects with the Montjuïc *teleferic,* a cable car that swings out over the *Montjuïc Amusement Park* and makes one interim stop before depositing passengers at the castle, belvedere, and restaurant at the top. The funicular, cable car, and amusement park are in operation daily in summer; in winter, only on Saturdays, Sundays, and holidays. Both the T-1 and T-2 tickets are valid on the funicular, but neither is valid on the cable car, which requires an extra fare. Another *telèferic* connects Barceloneta with Miramar, at the foot of Montjuïc, making an interim stop at the Torre de Jaume I on the Moll de Barcelona. The trip is a spectacular one across the harbor — passengers swing out over the cruise ships and hang over the water as though in a slow-moving airplane. Rides begin at 10 AM in summer and 11 AM in winter; T-1 and T-2 tickets are not valid.

Subway – A "Metro" sign indicates an entrance to Barcelona's modern, clean subway system. There are four lines (*L1, L3, L4,* and *L5*), all easy to use. Individual rides cost 65 pesetas (about 60¢), but the 10-ride ticket (T-2, or Targeta Multiviatge) is a better buy for multiple trips; it costs 325 pesetas (about $3) at any subway station, and is valid on the funicular to Montjuïc and the *tramvia blau* as well, but not on the buses.

Taxi – Taxis can be hailed while they cruise the streets or picked up at one of the numerous *paradas de taxi,* taxi ranks, throughout the city. For *Radio Taxi,* call 300-3811. During the day, *Lliure* or *Libre* in the window indicates that a cab is available; at night, a green light shines on the roof. The city is divided into various fare zones, and fares generally are moderate.

Train – Barcelona is served by trains operated by *RENFE* (Spanish National Railways and by trains operated by *Ferrocarrils de la Generalitat de Catalunya* (*FFCC*). There are four railway stations, all undergoing long-term refurbishment as part of the *Olympic* face-lift. Local, national, and international departures constantly are being changed, so it is vital to check and double-check before any journey. The stations are Estació Central Barcelona Sants, at the end of Avinguda de Roma, the main station for long-distance trains; Estació de França, on Avingunda Marqués de l'Argentera; Estació Passeig de Gràcia, on Passeig de Gràcia at Carrer d'Aragó; and Estació Plaça de Catalunya. For fare and schedule information, contact *RENFE* at Barcelona Sants or call the 24-hour-a-day information service (phone: 490-0202).

SPECIAL EVENTS: Religious holidays and saints' days are occasions for numerous festivities in Barcelona. April 23 is the *Festa de Sant Jordi* (Feast of St. George), patron saint of Catalonia. Flower stands overflow with roses, and bookstalls on La Rambla are bustling, because this is the day for lovers, and its gifts are a flower and a book. Bonfires, fireworks, dancing, and revelry mark the nights before the feast days of *Sant Joan* (St. John) and *Sant Pere* (St. Peter), on June 23 and 28 respectively. On Thursdays from June through September, the Guardia Urbana (city police) don scarlet tunics and white plumed helmets for a riding exhibition at 9 PM at the Pista Hipica La Fuxarda, Montjuïc. September 11 is Catalonia's national day, *La Diada,* while September 24 is the *Festa de la Mercè* (Feast of Our Lady of Mercy), honoring the city's patron saint; the week building up to it is fun, noisy, exhausting, full of folk dancing, fireworks displays, and general gaiety, which includes teams of men forming *castellers* (human pyramids). *Christmas* is heralded by the 2-week *Fira de Santa Llúcia,* when stalls selling greenery, decorations, gifts, and the figures for *Christmas* crèches, are set up in front of the cathedral and the Sagrada Familia. One of the traditional figures on sale strikes an impudent pose — to say the least.

MUSEUMS: Barcelonans love museums, and the city has many more to be proud of than those listed in *Special Places.*
  Museu dels Autómates (Museum of Automatons) – A display of mechanical dolls and animals. Open only when the amusement park in which

it is located is open: Thursdays and Fridays from noon to 2 PM and from 3 to 5:45 PM; Saturdays, Sundays, and holidays from noon to 3 PM and from 4 to 7:45 PM. Admission charge to the park includes the museum. Parc del Tibidabo (phone: 211-7942).

Museu del Calçat Antic (Shoemakers' Museum) – Antique shoes, including 1st-century slave sandals and 3rd-century shepherd's footwear, and a collection of famous people's shoes. Open Tuesdays through Sundays and holidays from 11 AM to 1 PM. Admission charge. Plaça Sant Felip Neri.

Museu de la Ciència (Science Museum) – A popular, hands-on kind of place with changing exhibitions (e.g., "The Return of the Dinosaurs"); permanent rooms illustrating optics, the universe, mechanics, perception; and a planetarium. Open Tuesdays through Sundays and holidays from 10 AM to 8 PM. Admission charge. 55 Carrer Teodor Roviralta, off Avinguda del Tibidabo (phone: 212-6050).

Museu del Futbol Club Barcelona (Barcelona Soccer Museum) – Trophies and videos highlighting the local soccer club's illustrious history — one of the most popular attractions in town. Open Tuesdays through Fridays from 10 AM to 1 PM and from 4 to 6 PM, mornings only on Saturdays and holidays. Admission charge. *Estadi Camp Nou,* Carrer Arístides Maillol (phone: 330-9411).

Museu Monestir de Pedralbes (Pedralbes Monastery and Museum) – A 14th-century Gothic church known for stained glass windows, choir stalls, and an unusual 3-story cloister. Open Tuesdays through Sundays from 9:30 AM to 2 PM. No admission charge. 9 Baixada del Monestir (phone: 203-9282).

Museu de la Música – An odd collection of antique musical instruments. Open Tuesdays through Sundays from 9 AM to 2 PM. No admission charge. 373 Avinguda Diagonal (phone: 217-1157).

Museu Taurí (Museum of Bullfighting) – A collection of bullfighters' costumes — suits of light — and other memorabilia. Open daily from April through September from 10 AM to 1 PM and from 3:30 to 7 PM. Admission charge. 749 Gran Via de les Corts Catalanes (phone: 245-5803).

Palau Reial de Pedralbes (Pedralbes Royal Palace) – Mainly Italian antiques including fans, Murano chandeliers, and tapestries, housed in the former palace of Alfonso XIII; in 1990, a collection of ceramics, impressive for its range — from early Moorish and Catalan ware through 18th-century tiles and even contemporary designs — was moved here from the Palau Nacional on Montjuïc. Open Tuesdays through Fridays from 10 AM to 1 PM and from 4 PM to 7 PM, Saturdays, Sundays, and holidays from 10 AM to 1:30 PM. No admission charge. 686 Avinguda Diagonal (phone: 203-7501).

SHOPPING: Barcelona has been a textile center for centuries, and it always has been a good place to buy leather goods. Now, it's become a source of up-to-the-minute fashion as well, with bright, young designers coming to the fore. Fashion-conscious Barcelonans believe that their city has more in common with Paris than Madrid, providing them with contemporary chic right at home. Passeig de Gràcia and Rambla de Catalunya are lined with elegant shops selling leather goods, furs, accessories, and jewelry for men and women, as well as with boutiques carrying Spain's *moda joven* (young fashion). More boutiques are housed in shopping centers or indoor arcades, of which the best known is the *Bulevard Rosa* (55 Passeig de Gràcia), which has shops selling everything from clothing and hats to unusual jewelry and paper goods. Also located here is the government-sponsored *Centre Permanent d'Artesania* (phone: 215-7178 or 215-5814), where changing exhibitions of crafts by contemporary Catalan artists and artisans are held. What's on display is for sale, although it can't be taken away until the show closes. For crafts, however, don't fail to visit the *Poble Espanyol,* the model village on Montjuïc, where there are some 35 stores featuring pottery, carvings, glassware, leather goods, and other typical folk crafts made by artisans from every region of Spain. Also visit the Ribera-El Born quarter around the *Picasso Museum* on Carrer de Montcada, known as the artists' and craftsmen's quarter. There are two *El Corte Inglés* stores (Plaça de Catalunya; phone: 301-3256; and 617 Avinguda Diagonal; phone: 322-0012). Part of the Spain-wide department store chain, they're known for quality in everything from Lladró porcelain and leather gloves to other clothing, records, and books; best of all, they are open during the long Spanish lunch hour. In general, department stores are open from 10 AM to 8:30 PM; smaller shops close between 2 and 4:30 PM. All are closed — the sign says *Tancat* in Catalan — on Sundays.

As for the markets, a visit to at least one is a colorful must, whether the daily Boquería food market just off La Rambla, where the fresh, tempting produce puts big city supermarkets to shame, or one of the weekly meeting places for enthusiasts of coins, stamps, or bric-a-brac. Bargain hard at *Els Encants,* the flea market at Plaça de les Glòries Catalanes (Mondays, Wednesdays, Fridays, and Saturdays, dawn until dusk); spend Sunday mornings in Plaça Reial among the stamp and coin collectors (10 AM to 2 PM) or at Ronda Sant Antoni, leafing through old books (10 AM to 2 PM.) Plaça del Pi hosts an antiques market on Thursdays from 9 AM to 8 PM.

Artespanya – A high-quality choice of Spanish crafts, from handmade glass to tables and chairs. 75 Rambla de Catalunya (phone: 215-2939).

Jean Pierre Bua – Fashion by young designers, from Catalunya and elsewhere in Europe. Look for Roser Marcé's "modern classics" for men and women. 469 Avinguda Diagonal (phone: 439-7100).

Camper – Women's shoes and handbags, the latest in styles and colors. 248 Carrer Muntanyer (phone: 201-3188).

Adolfo Domínguez – Menswear from one of Spain's internationally recognized designers. 89 Passeig de Gràcia (phone: 215-7638).

Groc – The second-floor salon where trendy designer Tony Miró sells his chic and expensive ladies' evening and daywear. Will make-to-order in 15 days, but 20% is added to ready-to-wear prices. 103 Rambla de Catalunya (phone: 216-0089).

Jorge Juan – Well-priced women's shoes and handbags in distinctive designs. 125 Rambla de Catalunya (phone: 217-0840).

Loewe – A branch of Spain's best-known and most expensive purveyor of fine leather goods. 35 Passeig de Gràcia (phone: 216-0400).

Matrícula – The latest in men's and women's clothing and accessories from Yamamoto and Rifat Ozbek, among other names. 12 Carrer del Tenor Viñas (phone: 201-9706).

Margarita Nuez – Elegant women's clothing in the finest of fabrics. 3 de Josep Bertránd (phone: 200-8400).

Francesc Tasies i Ginesta – Handmade rope-soled espadrilles; an old-fashioned craft brought up to date by the use of contemporary colors and designs. 7 Carrer d'Avinyó (phone: 301-0172).

Tema – Fashions by Spanish designers Manuel Piña, Jesus del Pozo, and Jorge Gonsalves (a favorite of Queen Sofía). 10 Carrer Ferrán Agulló (phone: 209-5165).

Trau – Where society girls go for posh glad rags. 6 Carrer Ferrán Agulló (phone: 201-3268).

2 Bis – Amusing "popular art" pieces, including overweight terra cotta bathing beauties and papier-mâché infantas; also, some serious glassware and plates. Near the cathedral, at 2 Carrer del Bisbe (phone: 315-0954).

Vigares – A small, but good selection of leather goods at tempting prices (including riding boots for not much more than $100). 16 Carrer de Balmes (phone: 317-5898).

 SPORTS AND FITNESS: For the last few years, Barcelona has been busy preparing for its role as host to the *Summer Olympic Games* in 1992, and at press time, more than 100,000 volunteers from all over Spain were busy assisting the Barcelona Olympic Organizing Committee in its task. But the city already boasted many major facilities, including the 120,000-seat *Camp Nou Stadium,* Europe's largest, and the *B. Picornell Municipal Pools* on Montjuïc, before construction of the new Olympic Ring facilities began. Other possibilities for the sports-minded include the following:

Bullfighting – Catalans claim to abhor bullfighting and, in fact, most of the spectators in the arena are Spaniards who have moved to the area — or tourists. The gigantic *Plaça Monumental* (Gran Via de les Corts Catalanes) has fights on Sundays from April to late September at 5 PM (6 PM if it's very hot). Additional fights are on Thursdays in August. Advance tickets are available at 24 Gran Via de les Corts Catalanes, at the corner of Carrer d'Aribau (phone: 245-5803). The city's other bullring, *Les Arenes,* at the other end of the same avenue, is now used for pop shows and exhibitions.

Fitness Centers – *Squash Diagonal* (193 Carrer de Roger de Flor; phone: 258-0809) has a pool, sauna, and gym, in addition to squash courts. *Sport Dyr* (388 Carrer de Castillejos; phone: 255-4949) has four gyms, including weight room, sauna, and massage. A gym for women only (2 Avinguda de Roma; phone: 325-8100) also offers a sauna, a swimming pool, and a solarium, as well as aerobics sessions and beauty treatments.

Golf – There are several golf courses around Barcelona, including the *Real Club de Golf El Prat* (10 miles/16 km southwest of town near the airport; phone: 379-0278), which is the best course, used by the European pro tour; *Club de Golf Sant Cugat* (Sant Cugat del Vallès 12½ miles/20 km away and hard to find in the hilly suburbs to the west; phone: 674-3908); and *Club de Golf Vallromanes* (15½ miles/25 km along the Masnou-Granollers road; phone: 568-0362).

Jogging – Parc de la Ciutadella, near the center of town, has a good track. The paths surrounding Montjuïc also are popular jogging spots.

Soccer – The *Olympics* notwithstanding, soccer is the major passion. The *Futbol Club (F.C.) Barcelona* embodies the spirit of Catalonia, especially when the opponent is longtime rival *Real Madrid.* The world's greatest stars are signed up to play for the club, and infants are enrolled as club members from birth. More than 120,000 fans regularly attend home games, played at the *Estadi Camp Nou* (Camp Nou Stadium), which will also host the *Olympics* soccer final. *Espanyol,* the other, less popular, "major league" club in town, plays at *Sarrià Stadium.*

Swimming – Take a dip in the waters that will host the *1992 Olympic* swimming events at *Piscines Municipals B. Picornell* (on Montjuïc, near the main stadium; phone: 325-9281). Although the locals go to Barceloneta to the beach, the water is really rather polluted and it's not recommended to swim near the city.

Tennis – Courts may be available at the *Real Club de Tenis Barcelona* (5 Carrer de Bosch i Gimpera; phone: 203-7758) or *Real Club de Tenis de Turó* (673 Avinguda Diagonal; phone: 203-8012).

 THEATER: The city has a strong theatrical tradition in Catalan, but it still embraces foreign playwrights such as Shakespeare and Chekhov. At the *Teatre Lliure* (Free Theater, Carrer Leopold Alas; phone: 218-9251), Fabia Puigserver's cooperative troupe is so dynamic that language is no barrier when the works are familiar. The *Teatre Poliorama* (115 Rambla dels Estudis; phone: 3177599) hosts another Catalan troupe, the *Companiya Flotats,* led by Josep Maria Flotats, whose repertoire tends to be lighter, though still socially aware. Early this year, the company will move to the new national theater, part of the Plaça de les Arts complex being built near the Plaça de les Glòries Catalanes. Experimental theater can be seen in the impressive *Mercat de les Flors* (59 Carrer de Lleida; phone: 426-1875), the old Flower Hall built on Montjuïc for the *1929 World's Fair.* Higher up the hill, the *Teatre Grec* (phone: 243-0062), an open-air amphitheater, hosts a festival every June and July, with classic Greek tragedies and other works. Popular musicals and vaudeville-type shows are at the *Apolo* (59 Avinguda del Paral·lel; phone: 241-4006) and the *Victoria* (65 Avinguda del Paral·lel; phone: 241-3985). The sporting side of the *Olympics* begins in the summer of 1992, but Barcelona already has begun the cultural events. Many companies from around the world will be making an appearance. The *Gran Teatre del Liceu* (facing La Rambla with the box office at 1 Carrer de Sant Pau; phone: 318-9122) hosts opera and ballet with international stars as well as local favorite Montserrat Caballé (for more information, see *Special Places*).

 MUSIC: Barcelona is a music center year-round. From November through May, opera and ballet dominate, but there is a festival of some sort every month, from medieval music in May to the *International Music Festival* in October. Two new concert halls are under construction for 1992 in the Plaça de les Arts complex, located near Plaça de les Glòries Catalanes. The *Palau de la Música Catalana* (just off Via Laietana, at the corner of Carrer de Sant Pere Mès Alt and Carrer d'Amadeu Vives; phone: 301-1104) is a gem of Art Nouveau style by architect Lluís Domènech i Montaner. The *Orquestra Ciutat de Barcelona* (Barcelona Municipal Orchestra) can be heard here, among other groups.

 NIGHTCLUBS AND NIGHTLIFE: Barcelona has plenty of action, but beware while roaming through the most popular after-dark centers, since the city also has its share of muggers and purse snatchers. Be wary of thieves on motorcycles and minibikes, who snatch purses from pedestrians and out of cars parked or stopped at traffic signals. The city's pubs, bars, and cafés begin to fill up between 10 and 11 PM, but these establishments merely serve as a warm-up for the clubs and discotheques, which open even later and only kick into high gear at 1 or 2 AM. A Las Vegas–style nightclub, *Scala Barcelona* (47 Passeig de Sant Joan; phone: 232-6363) presents elaborate dinner shows and dancing. For flamenco, try *El Cordobés* (35 Rambla; phone: 317-6653), *Andalucía* (27 Rambla; phone: 302-2009), and *El Patio Andaluz* (242 Carrer d'Aribau; phone: 209-3375). Shows are continuous from 10 PM to 3 AM, but really get going after midnight, when the performers and the audiences are warmed up. Popular discotheques include *Bikini,* which features rock and Latin beats (571 Avinguda Diagonal; phone: 230-5134); the *Up and Down,* with loud music downstairs and a restaurant and a more "sophisticated" club upstairs (179 Carrer de Numancia; phone: 204-8809); and *Studio 54,* a weekends-only favorite, boasting lots of elbow room and the best light show in town (64 Avinguda del Paral·lel; phone: 329-5454). For hot jazz, try the live jams at *La Cova del Drac* (30 Carrer de Tuset, phone: 216-5642). The *Gran Casino de Barcelona* (Sant Pere de Ribes, 26 miles/42 km from the city near the seaside town of Sitges; phone: 893-3666). You have to be over 18, with a passport for identification, to enjoy the dining and gambling in a 19th-century setting.

BEST IN TOWN

 CHECKING IN: Barcelona always has been short on hotel space; not surprisingly, the drive now is on to double the number of beds available in time for the *1992 Summer Olympics.* By then, 5,000 new hotel rooms will have been added to the city's present 14,000-room-plus hotel capacity. These are meant not only to accommodate *Olympic* visitors, but also to serve as permanent expansions that will meet the demands of tourism into the 21st century. In an already noisy city, the sounds of construction are an added intrusion. When making reservations, ask for a quiet room. Expect to pay more than $350 a night for a double room at a hotel listed below as very expensive (a category that, in Barcelona, includes only the *Ritz,* in a class by itself), between $130 and $220 for a double room at a hotel listed as expensive, $80 to $130 at one listed moderate, and less than $80 at an inexpensive hotel. All telephone numbers are in the 3 city code unless otherwise indicated.

Ritz – Built in 1919, this deluxe aristocrat boasts a brand-new face, and once again lives up to its reputation for superb service in an elegant, charming atmosphere. A favorite meeting place — especially during afternoon tea, which is served in the lounge with a string quartet softly playing — this is the hotel of choice of many international celebrities. All 314 rooms have high ceilings and air conditioning. There also is a fine restaurant. 668 Gran Via de les Corts Catalanes (phone: 318-5200). Very expensive.

Avenida Palace – Polished brass and fancy carpets lend a tasteful, Old World atmosphere to this deluxe property. The 229 rooms are air conditioned, cheerful, and quiet, with color television sets and mini-bars. The public areas are adorned with sedate paintings, fine reproductions, and interesting antiques. The staff is well trained and extremely attentive. 605 Gran Via de les Corts Catalanes (phone: 301-9600). Expensive.

Condes de Barcelona – Modernist outside and modern inside, this is in a striking Art Nouveau building that was transformed into a luxury hotel only in the mid-1980s, and proved so popular that it already is undergoing an expansion. Its 100 air conditioned rooms and suites contain all the expected amenities (there will be a total of 180 rooms when the expansion is complete by *Olympics* gametime). The location in the heart of the Eixample is ideal, the *Brasserie Condal* restaurant, excellent. 75 Passeig de Gràcia (phone: 215-0616). Expensive.

Gran Derby – An apartment hotel, with 39 air conditioned suites and duplexes, each containing a sitting room, color television set, bar, and refrigerator. The very fashionable marble decor and the helpful staff make up for a somewhat inconvenient location away from the city center. 28 Carrer de Loreto. (phone: 322-3215). Expensive.

Gran Sarrìa Sol – Near Plaça de Francesc Macià, this is a favorite with businesspeople. All 314 rooms are air conditioned and have king-size beds. The Elite floor features its own concierge. 50 Avinguda de Sarrìa (phone: 410-6060). Expensive.

Hilton International – Brand new, with 300 rooms, including several executive floors, of which one is reserved exclusively for women. The business center, 15 meeting rooms, 1,000-seat ballroom for conferences, plus the health club confirm that this is aimed at the business market. 589 Avinguda Diagonal (phone: 419-2233). Expensive.

Majestic – A Barcelona classic affiliated with Best Western, with 360 air conditioned rooms endowed with color television sets, in-room English-language movies, built-in hair dryers, and mini-bars. There also is a gymnasium, sauna, and rooftop swimming pool. The location, in the heart of the Eixample (oppisite the *Condes de Barcelona*), amid restaurants, shops, and Art Nouveau buildings, couldn't be better. 70 Passeig de Gràcia (phone: 215-4512). Expensive.

Princesa Sofía – Big, bustling, and modern, this convention-oriented hotel has an indoor swimming pool, a gym, a sauna, and restaurants. It could be anywhere in the world, but is out near the university and the *Camp Nou Stadium.* The 514 air conditioned rooms, decorated in contemporary style, have large, tile bathrooms, direct-dial telephones, color television sets, and mini-bars. Plaça de Pius XII (phone: 330-7111). Expensive.

Ramada Renaissance – Previously the grand old *Manila* and now a big (210-room), imposing member of the international group, providing expected standards of comfort and service; the Renaissance Club rooms on the top 4 floors are the top accommodations, featuring Minitel computer terminals. Ideally located near the Barri Gòtic, it has 2 restaurants. 111 Rambla (phone: 318-6200). Expensive.

Calderón – Another long-time Barcelona favorite with the business crowd, but with a bright new image. The generously proportioned 244 rooms are air conditioned, and most have been equipped with the conveniences and services frequent business travelers expect. The rooftop swimming pool, sauna, and sun terrace command a splendid view of the city. 26 Rambla de Catalunya (phone: 301-0000). Expensive to moderate.

Colón – An old favorite in the Barri Gòtic, right in front of the cathedral. Clean, pleasantly decorated, it has 166 air conditioned, high-ceilinged rooms, including 10 on the sixth floor with terraces (3 of these — two doubles and a single — face the cathedral). 7 Avinguda de la Catedral (phone: 301-1404). Moderate.

Derby – Older sister to the *Gran Derby,* this is an elegant establishment done up in hushed colors, with diffused lighting and impressive wood trim and ornamentation. The 116 air conditioned rooms have private baths; those on the top floor have large terraces. The intimate piano bar adds an extra special touch. Affiliated with Best Western. 21 Carrer de Loreto (phone: 322-3215). Moderate.

Regente – This gem among Barcelona's smaller establishments is located on a quiet extension of La Rambla. The 78 rooms are comfortable, with private baths and color television sets, as well as smartly decorated: Door handles, wall panels, windows, and other fixtures reflect an Art Nouveau affinity. Rooftop pool, private garage, and cozy bar. 76 Rambla de Catalunya (phone: 215-2570). Moderate.

Gala Placidia – An economical apartment complex, it has 28 suites with sitting rooms (fireplaces, too), dining areas, and refrigerators, in addition to the small bedrooms. 5 Via Augusta (phone: 217-8200). Moderate to inexpensive.

Rialto – In the heart of the Barri Gòtic, this simple but stylish place has 128 rooms, all air conditioned. 42 Carrer de Ferrán (phone: 318-5212). Moderate to inexpensive.

Espanya – A budget hotel with an Art Nouveau dining room in a 19th-century building. It has antique plumbing, but it's clean, with 84 rooms on the edge of the Barri Gòtic. 9 Ronda de Sant Pau (phone: 318-1758). Inexpensive.

Gaudí – Renovated and rather bare, but handy for Montjuïc, the port, and the Barri Gòtic. There are 71 rooms; those on the top floor have great views of Montjuïc and the cathedral. 12 Carrer Nou de la Rambla (phone: 317-9032) Inexpensive.

Ginebra – Small, cheap, and clean, with air conditioning and showers, this 10-room hostelry is heavily subscribed in summer because of its price and handy location by Plaça de Catalunya. Fourth Floor, 1 Rambla de Catalunya (phone: 317-1063). Inexpensive.

Oriente – Right on the Rambla, so reserve a room at the back. Built in 1842, with fancy public rooms, its Old World charm has worn a bit, but its central location just about compensates. 140 rooms. 45 Rambla (phone: 302-2558). Inexpensive.

 EATING OUT: Catalans take pride in their regional cuisine, which is more sophisticated and closer to French cooking than that of the rest of Spain. Portions are generous and meals are quite frequent: Coffee and a pastry for breakfast, an omelette or a ham-and-cheese sandwich between 11 and noon, a late lunch, a round of *tapas* (see below) later in the day to take the edge off the appetite, and an even later dinner, beginning at 10 or 10:30 PM. (In the heat of summer, and on weekends, this could be 11 PM!) As Catalan self-pride has mushroomed, so have Catalan-style restaurants, exploiting the richness of the Mediterranean fish, as well as bountiful local orchards, fields, and vineyards inland. Try the *sarsuela,* a soup or stew of lobster, crayfish, squid, mussels, and whitefish of various types. The most basic Catalan dish is *escudella i carn d'olla,* a hearty stew of sausage, beans, meatballs, and spices. The ubiquitous caramel custard, *crema catalana,* made with eggs, milk, sugar, and cinnamon, usually concludes a meal. Check for the daily special — *menú del día,* usually a three-course meal with bread and wine — which restaurants are required to offer at a set price. Expect to pay $60 or more for a dinner for two in restaurants classified as expensive, $30 to $50 in the moderate range, and under $25 in the inexpensive places. All telephone numbers are in the 3 city code unless otherwise indicated.

Agut d'Avinyó – A favorite for both lunch and dinner, this beautiful multilevel restaurant in the Barri Gòtic has whitewashed walls, oak plank floors, and antique furnishings. Its traditional Catalan food — especially the duck with figs — is excellent. The award-winning owner-hostess, Mercedes Giralt, lends her considerable charm to it all. Closed Sundays, *Holy Week,* and the month of August. Reservations necessary. 3 Carrer de la Trinitat (phone: 302-6034). Expensive.

Beltxenea – When he opened it on the premises of the former *Ama Lur* restaurant, owner-chef Miguel Ezcurra was reviving the tradition of Basque cooking in Barcelona. His new approach to the typical dishes of northwest Spain makes a change from Catalan food. Fish in spicy sauce is a specialty. Open daily. Reservations necessary. 275 Carrer de Mallorca (phone: 215-3848). Expensive.

Eldorado Petit – Owner Luis Cruañas is a star in a city where eating is a serious pastime. Influenced by the simplicity of Italian cooking, he gave Catalan dishes a lighter touch, relying on the high quality of fresh, local produce. The result is a sophisticated restaurant, with dishes that constantly tempt even regular customers: delicate carrot and champagne soup; black rice, Palafrugell-style; rockfish filets with a tomato *coulis* and shallot vinaigrette; partridge stuffed with prunes and chestnuts; fresh roasted goose liver with sherry vinegar; all followed by homemade ice cream and petits fours. The Catalan white wines, rioja reds, and local sparkling *cavas* complement one of Spain's finest dining experiences. Closed Sundays and the first 2 weeks in August. Reservations essential. 51 Carrer de Dolors Monserdá (phone: 204-5506). Expensive.

Florián – Rosa Grau cooks while her husband, Javier, minds the front, where pictures line the walls. Pasta with sea urchin sauce, ravioli stuffed with four cheeses, and red mullet with black olives are examples of Rosa's flair with local products. Closed Sundays, *Holy Week,* 2 weeks in August, and *Christmas.* Reservations necessary. 20 Carrer de Bertrán i Serra (phone: 212-4627). Expensive.

Jaume de Provença – Innovative chef Jaume Bargues reacts well to what's available at the market. Frequent specialties include crab lasagna, sea bass stuffed with fresh salmon, and pigs' trotters with Roquefort cheese sauce. Closed Sundays and Mondays, *Holy Week,* and August. Reservations necessary. 88 Carrer de Provença (phone: 230-0029). Expensive.

Neichel – Strictly French, like the owner-chef, whose efforts have won two Michelin stars (there's no more highly rated restaurant in town) and a dedicated local following. The constant flow of inventive new dishes has put exotic little parcels of raw and smoked salmon with caviar, and salads of lobster with mustard vinaigrette on the menu along with more straightforward sea bass with a mousseline of truffles, monkfish in clam sauce, and pigeon with lentils and bacon. Add a selection of 30 desserts from the trolley, fine Spanish wines, and excellent service, and this is a place for a celebration. Closed Sundays, holidays, *Christmas* week, *Holy Week,* and the month of August. Reservations necessary. 16 bis Avinguda de Pedralbes (phone: 203-8408). Expensive.

Quo Vadis – Muted paneling, soft lights, and harmonious decor provide a pleasing ambience at this top establishment. Service is solicitous and the highly original international cuisine is excellent. Closed Sundays. Reservations advised. 7 Carrer de Carmen (phone: 302-4072). Expensive.

Reno – Another impressive kitchen that uses local recipes in a classic way, its specialties include sole with freshwater crayfish, hake with anchovy sauce, and roast duck with honey and sherry vinegar. The *Menú Reno* offers a sampling of the house's most popular dishes. Closed Saturdays in July, August, and September. Reservations advised. 27 Carrer de Tuset (phone: 200-9129). Expensive.

Azulete – Imaginative international dishes are served here, and the house, with its gardens and fountain, is a delight. The dining room of this former mansion is actually a glass-enclosed garden, with tables arranged around a decorative pool, surrounded by lush vegetation. Specialties include tiny medallions of pork, crowned with mushroom purée, and broiled *lubina* (sea bass) with fresh dill. For dessert, try figs with strawberry-scented honey. Closed Saturdays at lunch, Sundays, holidays, the first 2 weeks in August, and from *Christmas* through *New Year's.* Reservations advised. 281 Via Augusta (phone: 203-5943). Expensive to moderate.

Arcs de Sant Gervasi – One of Barcelona's newer favorites, in the bustling neighborhood near Plaça de Francesc Macià. Try the gratin of eggplant, ham, and tiny shrimp, or the slices of rare duck with zucchini mousse and sliced pears. Open daily. Reservations advised. 103 Carrer de Santaló (phone: 201-9277). Moderate.

Blau Mari – A chic new spot on the Barcelona waterfront, featuring fresh fish, seafood, and paellas. Open daily. Reservations unnecessary. Moll de la Fusta (phone: 218-9222). Moderate.

Brasserie Flo – The atmosphere is Parisian; the meat dishes, especially the barbecue, are outstanding. A favorite place for café society, in jeans or black tie, it's open late for the after-theater crowd. Open daily. No reservations. 10 Carrer de les Jonqueres (phone: 317-8037). Moderate.

Ca l'Isidre – The morning market determines the selection of standard-setting Catalan dishes in this Barcelona landmark, once a favorite of Joan Miró. There also is an intelligently stocked wine cellar. Only 10 tables, so reservations are essential and should be made *at least* 2 days in advance. Closed Sundays, holidays, *Christmas* week, *Holy Week,* and from mid-July to mid-August. 12 Carrer de les Flors (phone: 241-1139). Moderate.

Los Caracoles – At first glance this bustling, jovial place looks like a tourist trap, but the good solid Catalan cooking is most impressive. Try *los caracoles* (snails); the langostinos are fresh and delicious. Open daily. Reservations necessary (but, even so, you'll have to wait during rush hours). 14 Carrer dels Escudellers (phone: 302-3185). Moderate.

La Dorada – On an average day, this popular eatery serves 1,200 meals! The dining room is fitted with nautical relics, which complement the menu of mostly seafood dishes (and the recipes are more national than regional). Among the favorites are Galician scallops and *sarsuela* (seafood stew). Service is deft and, despite the crowds, never rushed. Closed Sundays. Reservations advised. 44 Travessera de Gràcia (phone: 200-6322). Moderate.

Senyor Parellada – Located near the *Museu Picasso,* this refined and ambitious restaurant serves traditional Catalan cooking at very reasonable prices. Try the *escalivada,* a cold salad of red peppers, onions, eggplant, and thin slices of cod; or breast of duck with tarragon vinegar. Closed Sundays and holidays. Reservations advised. 37 Carrer Platería (phone: 315-4010). Moderate.

Set Portes – Near the waterfront and a Barcelona favorite since it opened in 1836, it still retains its original decor and charm. Catalan cuisine, including great seafood and homemade desserts, is served in abundant proportions, and the large dining rooms are packed on weekends. Open daily. Reservations advised. 14 Passeig Isabel II (phone: 319-3033). Moderate.

La Bona Cuina – The decor looks a bit like a modernist parlor, with walls paneled in dark wood, lace curtains at the windows, and a huge Art Nouveau mirror, all gold swirls with a golden peacock on top, dominating the room. In the Barri Gòtic, behind the cathedral, it unabashedly caters to tourists, but delivers good food (Catalan, especially fish and seafood) and good value. Open daily. Reservations advised. 12 Carrer Pietat (phone: 315-4156). Moderate to inexpensive.

La Cuineta – Under the same management as *La Bona Cuina* and quite close by in the Barri Gòtic, this is set up in 17th-century wine vaults. Open daily. Reservations advised. 4 Carrer Paradis (phone: 315-0111). Moderate to inexpensive.

Can Costa – Only the freshest of fish and seafood is served at this delightful establishment, one of a number of restaurants side by side on the Barceloneta beachfront. The fish and vegetables are piled high on tables on the sidewalk, and guests walk past the hubbub of the kitchen to a large room open to the sea. In summer, the tables and benches spill out onto the sand. Open daily. No reservations. 12 Platja de Sant Miguel, Barceloneta (phone: 315-1903). Inexpensive.

Les Corts Catalanes – A wonderful vegetarian delicatessen, located 1 block from the Passeig de Gràcia, serving everything from vegetable lasagna to cheese or spinach empanadas (pot pies). Open daily. No reservations. 603 Gran Via de les Corts Catalanes (phone: 301-0376). Inexpensive.

Egipte – Very popular and definitely bohemian, serving students and artists. It's located behind the Boquería market, so order the dish of the day for the freshest food in town. Closed Sundays and religious holidays. No reservations. 12 Carrer de Jerusalén (phone: 317-7480). Inexpensive.

Quatre Gats – The third incarnation of the popular Barri Gòtic café. The original, which opened in 1897, was a hangout for artists and writers of the Catalan modernist movement, and Picasso had his first show here. There's café society ambience still: Art Nouveau lamps, wrought-iron and marble tables, potted palms, and candelabra on the baby grand. The menu is a limited one of unpretentious Catalan dishes (try the *Especial 4 Gats* salad for a new twist on diet food). Open daily. No reservations. 3 Carrer de Montsió (phone: 302-4140). Inexpensive.

 TAPAS BARS: The Catalans did not invent *tapas,* the Spanish equivalent of hors d'oeuvres; it's said the Andalusians did. But they've become as adept as the rest of the Spaniards at the *tapeo,* which consists of making the rounds of *tapas* bars, downing a drink at each, and sampling these delicious snacks — the Spanish version of the treasure hunt, some might say. Barcelona has numerous *tapas* bars, the most colorful of which are located along La Rambla and in the area surrounding the *Picasso Museum.* Some of the more popular choices are beyond this zone, however, including *Flish Flash,* well off the beaten tourist path (25 Carrer de la Ciutat de Granada; phone: 237-0990), where more than 70 types of tortillas attract a good crowd. *Jamón Jamón* (off Plaça de Francesc Macià at 4 Carrer del Mestre Nicolau; phone: 209-4103) serves what its name (which means "Ham Ham") implies — and it serves the best, from Jabugo. *Mundial* (1 Plaça Sant Agustín; phone: 331-2516) specializes in seafood. *Belvedere* (in a quiet alleyway off Passeig de Gràcia, 3 Passatge Mercader; phone: 215-9088) offers a nice terrace and a wide selection. At *Bodega Sepúlveda* (173 Carrer de Sepúlveda; phone: 254-7094), the proprietor's own wine accompanies cheese in oil and little salads. The *Cava de Olimpia* (10 Carrer de Loreto; phone: 239-1073), near the *Derby, Gran Derby,* and *Gran Sarrià Sol* hotels, takes its name from *cava,* the Spanish answer to champagne. It's part of a recent vogue of *xampanyerias* where corks are popped at reasonable prices.

BRAGA

Porto earns, Lisbon spends, Coimbra studies, and Braga prays. So goes the popular Portuguese saying, and the description fits Braga to a tee. With a reputed 300 churches and only 140,000 inhabitants, the city can boast one of the highest church-to-resident ratios in all Christendom. The capital of the northern Minho province, Braga has been Portugal's religious center and the home of its archbishops since the birth of the nation in the 12th century. At the height of the Church's power, not even the nobility was allowed to own land inside the city walls, and all industries centered around the Church's needs.

Today, the medieval walls have come down, the city's economic base has been diversified, and a sprawling, ugly metropolis is springing up around the old center. Yet despite these changes, the Old Quarter of Braga, with its ornate Renaissance and Manueline palaces, baroque churches, and narrow medieval streets, still charms the visitor and attests to the city's former glory.

The strategic location of Braga, in a fertile valley at the foot of three mountain ranges, always has made it ripe for occupation and development. The Goidelic Celts, also known as the Bracari, are believed to have founded the city and given it a name several thousand years ago. The Romans occupied it in 260 BC and made it the hub of five major roads, all leading to Rome. Through them Christianity and the first Bishops of Braga eventually came. The Suevians overran the city in AD 409, but were replaced in 585 by Visigoth invaders, who, in turn, were vanquished in 711 by a Moorish army. For more than 3 centuries, the Christians and the Moors jousted over Braga, until the Muslims were finally expelled at the end of the 11th century.

It was a Spanish king, Alfonso (VI of León and I of Castile), who, with the help of French Crusaders, succeeded in wresting this part of northern Iberia from the Moors. Thus, the bishops barely had returned to Braga when, in 1095, the king rewarded a French nobleman, Henry of Burgundy, with the hand of his daughter Teresa in marriage. The county of "Portucale" — not yet the kingdom, but a smaller entity to which Braga belonged — came as part of her dowry, and Henry became Count of Portucale. The new masters of Braga arrived with its first archbishop, a French prelate eventually canonized as St. Gerald, and work began on the cathedral. Later, in 1112, Henry granted a city charter to another archbishop, Dom Mauricio, making him Lord of Braga, a title the archbishops continued to hold until the late 18th century.

In the mid-12th century, when the Count of Portucale, Henry's son Dom Afonso Henriques, broke away from León and Castile and established the kingdom of Portugal, Braga's archbishops were his allies. They became the spiritual heads of the new nation and waged their own war against their Spanish arch-rivals in Santiago de Compostela and Toledo. But their energies ultimately were diverted southward to the business of driving out the Moors and, later, to evangelizing the new continents discovered by the Portuguese mariners of the late 15th century.

During the 16th century, a dynamic archbishop named Dom Diogo de Sousa used money from Portugal's new spice trade with India to embellish the city. Sousa imported artists from neighboring Spain, built a Renaissance palace, and commissioned the construction of new churches. The building boom came to an end soon after his death, however, as the same discoveries that had brought the country prosperity also drained it of manpower and cash. To make matters worse, the Portuguese king and a large part of the nobility perished in a disastrous campaign against Morocco in 1578, prompting Philip II of Spain to seize the opportunity to invade his neighbor and put an end to Portugal's Golden Age.

Independence returned to the nation in the 17th century, and the euphoria of that event, heightened by the religious zeal of the Counter-Reformation and by the flow of gold from Brazil, breathed new life into 18th-century Braga. Two prelates, Dom Rodrigo de Moura Teles — a midget of a man who made up in energy what he lacked in size — and Dom Gaspar de Bragança (son of King João V), used the newfound wealth to fund large construction projects. They turned Braga into the center of baroque art in Portugal (it was from the Portuguese word *barrôco,* meaning "rough pearl," that the style got its name). The Raio Palace and elegant Town Hall were built during this prolific period, as was the impressive staircase leading to the Bom Jesus Church. Braga artists also popularized the use of *talha dourada,* heavily gilded, carved wood, in church interiors. The archbishops were at the zenith of their power. They patronized the arts, dressed in satin and jewels, and even had their own private orchestra.

The social upheavals and revolutions that swept through Europe during the late 18th century, however, eventually reached Braga and eroded the power of the Church. In 1792, the archbishops were forced to give up their feudal title as Lords of Braga and to hand over control of the city administration to a growing bourgeoisie. In 1808, Napoleon's forces overran the city and sacked the churches. Finally, in 1910, church properties were confiscated by the first Portuguese Republic. Although some of these were later restored, the Church in Braga never regained administrative control of the city.

Today, Braga is enduring the growing pains of modernity, with all its motorized traffic and noxious fumes. Instead of cathedrals and chapels, industrial parks and shopping malls are going up. New industries, such as graphic design and the manufacture of auto accessories, are functioning alongside traditional crafts such as candlemaking and the fashioning of religious artifacts and vestments. Church institutions such as the Catholic University are being forced to compete with modern counterparts. And for the first time since the Inquisition, Roman Catholicism is being challenged by new religious sects such as the Mormons and Jehovah's Witnesses.

Yet despite the changes, Braga remains Portugal's Eternal City. Its numerous street altars and chapels are constantly lit with votive candles, and dozens of shops sell a vast assortment of religious artifacts to a constant influx of pilgrims from all over the world. *Holy Week* in Braga, a time of sumptuous processions and colorful religious pageantry, remains the most important event of the year, the most spectacular festival of its kind in Portugal. And the people of Braga — serious, hardworking, and contemplative — are considered the most religious in the country, so religious that it is said no citizen of Braga makes a major decision without lighting a candle and praying to any one of hundreds of saints, many of whom, incidentally, come from Braga.

BRAGA AT-A-GLANCE

SEEING THE CITY: For a spectacular view of Braga and its surroundings, leave town by Avenida João XXI and drive east 5½ miles (9 km) on N103-3 via Bom Jesus to the Monte Sameiro sanctuary and park. The reward for a climb up 265 steps to the lantern tower in the cupola of the Sanctuary to the Virgin at the park's summit is a breathtaking panorama of the Minho region. On a clear day, the Atlantic coastline can be sighted 20 miles to the west, and the Serra do Gerês and Serra do Marão peaks are visible to the northeast and southeast; closer are Braga itself to the west and the prehistoric city of Briteiros to the east. Feast on the marvelous view, then settle down to a meal on the ground at the *Sameiro* restaurant (see *Eating Out*), one of the area's best eating establishments. The sanctuary is open daily, from 8 AM to 8 PM; there is an admission charge for the tower.

The Torre de Menagem, in Braga on Largo de São Francisco, across from the tourist office, is also open to visitors. The crenelated tower, an 18th-century addition to the city's medieval fortifications and the only part of them to survive urban expansion, provides a nice view of the Old Town. It is open daily from 10 AM to noon and from 2 to 6 PM. Admission charge.

SPECIAL PLACES: Although Braga is a sprawling metropolis, the city center, which includes the historic section, is concentrated enough to explore on foot. Leave your car at the municipal parking lot on Praça Conde de Agrolongo, walk past the Torre de Menagem, and turn into Rua do Souto, a pedestrian walkway that is the site of the city's most elegant shops and picturesque outdoor cafés and which, together with Rua Dom Diogo de Sousa, cuts through the Old Town and religious heart of the city. Before this east-west parallel ends its trajectory at the Porta Nova arch, it passes several of the city's major landmarks: the Largo do Paço fountain and square and the former Archbishops' Palace to the north, and the Misericórdia Church and the cathedral to the south. Nearby, to the northwest, are the *Biscainhos Palace,* now a museum, and Braga's baroque Town Hall, on the Praça do Municipio, while to the southeast are two notable houses, the Casa dos Coimbras and the Casa dos Crivos, both on Rua de São Marcos, and the São Marcos Hospital, in the adjoining square, Largo Carlos Amarante. A 5-minute walk southeast from the hospital leads to the striking Raio Palace and, next door, the pre-Roman Fountain of the Idol; its cool and relaxing setting makes it an ideal place to unwind after a day's walking tour.

THE SÉ (CATHEDRAL) COMPLEX

Sé (Cathedral) – When the Portuguese want to point out the antiquity of something, they say it's "as old as the cathedral of Braga." Work on the Sé was begun in the 12th century by Henry of Burgundy and his wife, Teresa, at a site previously occupied by a 6th-century church destroyed by the Moors and, before that, by a Roman temple built in AD 43. The present building has undergone changes and additions over the centuries; the charming south door and the arching over the west (main) door are two of the most notable remnants of its early, Romanesque period. During the 16th century, the Gothic portico was added to the west door by Biscayan artists imported from Spain by Archbishop Dom Diogo de Sousa, who also rebuilt the apse in a Flamboyant ogival style. Archbishop Dom Rodrigo de Moura Teles was responsible for the 18th-century bell towers and the building's baroque façade. Several chapels line the cloister and courtyard of the cathedral. The plan was to incorporate the area where the courtyard stands as part of a five-nave structure so the Sé could compete with the cathedral in Santiago de Compostela, Spain. But financial restraints forced the archbishops to pare down their ambitions.

Before entering the cathedral, go around to the back (the Rua de São João side) to admire the elegant statue of Nossa Senhora do Leite (Our Lady of Milk, or the Madonna Suckling the Holy Child), standing under a lacework baldachin. Believed to have been sculpted by Nicolas Chanterene in the 16th century, it is actually only one of several statues of the Madonna on the cathedral grounds; some of them are surrounded by wax and plastic votive offerings in the shape of breasts. These are left by pregnant women imploring the Virgin to provide them with ample milk to nurse their babies, a practice that is possibly a holdover from Roman days, since the Roman temple originally on this spot was dedicated to Isis, the goddess of fertility and motherhood.

Upon entering the cross-shaped cathedral, a visitor sees a baptismal font carved in the ornate 16th-century Manueline style immediately to the left, and a chapel with the bronze tomb of the Infante Dom Afonso (a brother of Henry the Navigator), the work of 16th-century Flemish artisans, to the right. Still at the cathedral's west end, the *coro baixo,* or lower choir, is flanked by two magnificent 18th-century organs, richly decorated in brass, marble, and gilded wood, while the *coro alto* (raised choir), the gallery above it, contains 18th-century stalls in black wood that can be seen during the Treasury visit (see below). Look across the nave to the east end of the cathedral and the rib-vaulted chancel, its high altar carved in stone; above the altar is a statue of St. Mary of Braga, the patron saint of the city. To the right of the chancel is the Chapel of the Holy Sacrament, with a 17th-century polychrome wood altar representing the Triumph of the Church; to the left is the Chapel of São Pedro de Rates, the first Bishop of Braga, with 18th-century *azulejos,* glazed and painted tiles, depicting his life.

Tesouro (Treasury) – The cathedral's treasury — otherwise known as Braga's *Museum of Sacred Art* — contains religious objects dating as far back as the 10th century and is well worth a visit. There are rooms filled with gold and silver embroidered vestments and chalices from the 15th and 16th centuries, including a silver monstrance (a vessel used during mass) encrusted with 450 precious stones that belonged to Dom Gaspar de Bragança. Other treasures include a 10th-century Hispano-Arab (Mozarabic) ivory casket, a 17th-century silver reliquary cross, an iron cross said to have been used in the first mass celebrated in Brazil, a working 17th-century traveling organ, a 17th-century saddle embroidered in gold and silver used in Corpus Christi processions, and huge 17th- and 18th-century liturgical books. Most amusing are the giant platform shoes used by the diminutive archbishop Dom Rodrigo de Moura Teles, who was only 3'11" tall and needed the enormous heels to reach the altar. The treasury is open daily from 8:30 AM to 6 PM in summer (8:30 AM to 12:30 PM and 1:30 to 5:30 PM in winter) and can be seen by guided tours only. Both the tour (conducted in Portuguese) and the admission charge cover a visit to the cathedral's *coro alto* (for a close view of the organ cases and the choir stalls) and to the three chapels listed below (cathedral phone: 23317).

Capela dos Reis (Chapel of Kings) – This Gothic-style structure off the cathedral's cloister contains the tombs of the founders, Dom Henrique (Henry of Burgundy) and Dona Teresa. Teresa is buried beside her husband, although she took up with a

Galician count after his death; in the early 16th century, Dom Diogo de Sousa had her placed in the same tomb as her husband, but a later archbishop had it opened and the bones separated into adjoining tombs. The chapel also contains the embalmed remains of a 14th-century warrior archbishop, Dom Lourenço Vicente, who distinguished himself in the famous battle of Aljubarrota, where a small Portuguese force and British archers defeated a much larger Spanish army. For opening hours and admission information, see the Tesouro above.

Capela de São Geraldo (St. Gerald's Chapel) – The walls of this handsome Gothic chapel, located across the courtyard from the Chapel of Kings, are covered with *azulejos* depicting the life of St. Gerald, the first Archbishop of Braga. On December 5, the public brings baskets of fruit to the chapel as an offering to the saint. The tradition is said to derive from St. Gerald's first miracle — saving the life of a sick child by conjuring up fresh fruit in the middle of winter. For opening hours and admission information, see the Tesouro above.

Capela da Glória (Chapel of Glory) – Next to St. Gerald's Chapel is a third elegant Gothic chapel, this one built by Archbishop Gonçalo Pereira as his burial chamber. Vestiges of Renaissance frescoes and Mudéjar paintings can be traced on one of the walls. The archbishop's finely sculptured tomb is set on six sleeping lions, its sides bearing reliefs of the Crucifixion, the Apostles, the Virgin and Child, and a "theory of deacons" chanting the Litany of the Dead. The reclining statue of Dom Gonçalo looks up at an 18th-century ceiling of painted wood. For opening hours and admission information, see the Tesouro above.

ELSEWHERE

Igreja da Misericórdia (Misericórdia Church) – The Renaissance church next to the cathedral doesn't catch the eye, but its dazzling altarpiece does. The baroque wooden altar, intricately carved and gilded by Marcelino de Araujo, is considered one of the best — and certainly one of the most sumptuous — examples of *talha dourada* in Portugal. The two figures at the top, practically lost in this sea of swirls and lines, are Mary and her sister Elizabeth. Rua Dom Diogo de Sousa.

Antigo Paço Episcopal (Former Archbishops' Palace) – The former residence of the Archbishops of Braga is made up of wings from the 14th, 17th, and 18th centuries — although the latter burned at the end of the last century and was remodeled in the 1930s. The palace now serves as the city library and headquarters of the University of the Minho. Part of the 14th-century wing is used for university seminars and can be visited, as can the library reading room in the 18th-century wing, notable for its carved wood ceiling. The library houses over 300,000 volumes and is considered the second most important source of civil documents in Portugal, after Lisbon's Torre do Tombo. Its priceless parchments, some stored in wooden drawers inlaid with ivory in the Sala do Arcaz, date back as far as the 9th century and include detailed family genealogies, compiled during the Inquisition, of those persons who applied to enter church service. (Special permission is required to visit the rooms with these collections.) The lobby of the university rectory has a small but fine display of 17th- and 18th-century Portuguese tiles taken from various churches and homes in the region. The library is open Mondays through Fridays from 9 AM to noon and from 2 to 8 PM. No admission charge. Praça do Municipio (phone: 612234).

Chafariz do Largo do Paço (Largo do Paço Fountain) – In the picturesque square between the Archbishops' Palace and the cathedral stands a fountain built in 1723 by Archbishop Dom Rodrigo de Moura Teles to glorify his family. The fountain's basin is supported by angels and encircled by the city's six towers; a seventh tower, prominently displaying the Moura Teles family coat of arms, serves as a base for the Madonna, or St. Mary of Braga, the city's patron saint. Largo do Paço.

Arco da Porta Nova (Arch of the New Door) – The story behind this arch typifies the struggle between the church and the nobility for control of the city. In 1512, Archbishop Dom Diogo de Sousa had a door constructed to serve as the main gate to the city. In 1778, it was torn down and replaced by a wider structure on which, to the displeasure of the reigning archbishop, King José I placed his coat of arms. The situation was later resolved by the municipality, which simply added an episcopal hat on top of the royal coat of arms and encircled it with ecclesiastical tassels. Rua Dom Diogo de Sousa.

Palácio dos Biscainhos (Biscainhos Palace) – This nobleman's palace was built during the 17th century, but has undergone several alterations since then. It now serves as a museum, focusing on the lifestyle of the Portuguese nobility between the late 17th and the 19th centuries. Granite figures of pages welcome visitors to a spacious atrium leading to terraced gardens with interesting *casas de fresco,* or cool houses — large umbrella-shaped trees with square openings cut into them, which the nobility used to escape the hot sun. The Salão Nobre (Grand Salon) is lined with early-18th-century *azulejos* depicting the life of the leisure class (not always a life of ease, as can be seen in the painting on the ceiling portraying a missionary member of the household being burned at the stake in Japan in 1624). Several large rooms with ornate stucco ceilings contain elaborate Indo-Portuguese furniture, inlaid with ivory; handsome Portuguese, Chinese, and Dutch (Delft) pottery; glassware; silverware; and 18th- and 19th-century objets d'art. The salon of the Romantic period, with its rich reds and flamboyant furniture, is in sharp contrast to the more austere elegance of the neo-classical dining room, while the 18th-century bedroom is decorated in the Queen Dona Maria style, a period characterized by its emphasis on religious decoration. Open for guided tours (in Portuguese only) from 10 AM to 12:15 PM and from 1:30 to 5:15 PM; closed Mondays. Admission charge (no charge on Sunday mornings). Rua dos Biscainhos (phone: 27645).

Câmara Municipal (Town Hall) – The façade on this 18th-century building, attributed to the architect André Soares, is considered one of the best examples of baroque architecture in Portugal. Although its grand stairway is lined with tiles depicting the arrival in Braga of a new archbishop, Dom José de Bragança (the bastard brother of King João V), the building was constructed specifically as a town hall, demonstrating that secular power was already beginning to creep into the city. The reunion room drips with chandeliers, and its walls are hung with framed portraits of important religious and political figures. Open for short guided tours (Portuguese only) Mondays through Fridays from 8:30 AM to noon and from 2 to 5 PM. No admission charge. Praça do Municipio (phone: 613371).

Fonte do Pelicano (Pelican Fountain) – The water-spouting pelican at its center is the reason for this lovely baroque fountain's name. Originally in the Archbishops' Palace, it now graces a pleasant park in front of the Town Hall.

Jardim de Santa Bárbara (St. Barbara's Garden) – The 17th-century garden behind the Archbishops' Palace contains over 50 species of flowers, arranged in very original designs that do justice to Portugal's reputation as a nation with a collective green thumb. A 17th-century fountain sits majestically in the midst of this sea of colors, and the medieval wing of the Archbishops' Palace serves as a backdrop. Several stone arches from the interior of the palace, gutted by fire in the last century, have been placed in the garden along with Roman milestones retrieved from nearby archaeological sites. The setting is the most photographed in Braga. Always open; no admission charge. Rua Justino Cruz and Rua Eça de Queiros.

Casa dos Crivos (House of Screens) – The last of its kind in Braga. At one time there were dozens of such houses, with exterior grilles and screens of Moorish design. They were first built in the 16th century, during Dom Diogo's tenure, to allow cloistered nuns to look out onto the street without being seen. The present house dates from the 17th century. Restored inside, it is now open to the public as a gallery for exhibitions by local artists, which normally can be seen from 9:30 AM to 12:30 PM, from 2:30 to 6:30 PM, and from 9 to 11 PM. No admission charge. 45 Rua de São Marcos (phone: 76002).

Casa dos Coimbras (House of the Coimbras) – The handsome house and its chapel, built for Archbishop João Coimbra in 1525, are among the few remnants in Braga of the prolific and highly imaginative Manueline style of early-16th-century Portuguese architecture. Privately owned, they are not open to the public, but they can be admired from the street. The house, which has suffered some unfortunate remodeling, has retained its ornate Manueline windows. Rua de São Marcos.

Hospital de São Marcos (St. Marcos Hospital) – A functioning hospital known for its lively 18th-century façade by Carlos Amarante. At the top are large granite statues of martyrs and apostles. The figures are standing precariously on the ledge and gesticulating wildly, giving the impression that they are practically floating in mid-air. Largo Carlos Amarante.

Palácio do Raio (Raio Palace) – The 18th-century house was designed by André Soares, and is perhaps the finest example of a solar, or mansion, in Braga. Though the building — also called the Casa do Mexicano — is privately owned and cannot be visited inside, its best feature is the façade, an elegant blending of tile and stone, with the unusual shapes of the windows accentuated by the blue tiles surrounding them. Rua do Raio.

Fonte do Idolo (Fountain of the Idol) – Despite the Roman inscriptions, it is generally believed that the fountain dates from pre-Roman times. Some historians have suggested it was an immersion fountain and/or an altar for offerings to the Lusitanian idol Tongenabiago. The structure collapsed at one time; what remains is a high-relief section with a bust of a human over the water spout and a figure beside it holding a child on its lap. The figure is hidden behind a green iron gate, down some steps at 389 Rua do Raio.

ENVIRONS

Bom Jesus do Monte – No visit to Braga is complete without a tour of this spectacular sanctuary set on a densely wooded hill 3 miles (5 km) east of town via N103-3. The complex is composed of a monumental baroque staircase, begun in the early 18th century by order of Archbishop Dom Rodrigo de Moura Teles, leading up to a neo-classical church, begun in the late 18th century and finished in the early 19th. The staircase, decorated with allegorical sculptures, fountains, and chapels, is the *pièce de résistance* of the sanctuary, and should be climbed in order to appreciate fully its wealth of detail. Those not relishing a hike can take the funicular up (it takes 3 minutes to ascend 380 feet on a 40° incline) and walk back down the stairs. There is also a winding road leading up to the church.

The staircase is divided into three sections. The first part, the Sacred Way, is bordered with chapels presenting scenes from the Passion through the use of life-size terra cotta figures. The second set of stairs, the Stairway of the Five Senses, pays homage to the senses through the use of fountains and figures. Before climbing this section, note the columns on either side of the base, entwined with snakes covered with the water that pours out of their mouths and down their bodies. Stand back and gaze up the stairs: Note how the central granite sculptures blend to form the shape of a chalice. Moving up the stairs, there is Sight, with water gushing from its eyes; Smell, with water dripping from its nose; Taste, with water pouring from its mouth; Touch, with water flowing from its hand; and Hearing, with water coming from its ears. The final section, the Stairway of the Three Virtues, evokes Faith, Hope, and Charity by using more fountains and allegorical figures. It gives way to a lovely circular terraced garden and fountain surrounded by manicured lawns with geometric flower beds. (There is also an equestrian statue of a saint; it is traditionally held that if a woman circles the statue three times, she will be married within the year.) At the top of the stairway, facing the church, are statues of the men who condemned Jesus, fountains dedicated to the Four Apostles, and surrounding the main church, several chapels.

The Igreja do Bom Jesus (Good Jesus Church), designed by Carlos Amarante (who also designed the third staircase) and finished in 1811, contains an altar re-creating the final moments at Calgary with larger-than-life statues. Also of interest inside the church is the Altar das Reliquias (Altar of the Relics), practically buried under modern mementos from devoted pilgrims and tourists. Behind the church are several paths leading through grottoes and fountains to a small lake, where boats can be rented by the hour.

Those who have walked up the stairs may want to take the funicular down. Dating from the late 19th century, it is propelled by gravity and a tank of water — two carriages move in opposite directions at the same time, with the water in the carriage going down providing the weight to pull the other carriage up. It runs every half hour or when its 20 seats are filled and costs 50 escudos for the 3-minute ride. (For about $7, you can rent the carriage between scheduled runs for a private ride.) Bom Jesus is open from 8 AM to 8 PM daily.

Monte Sameiro – The Sanctuary to the Virgin at the summit of this green mountain is the most important center of devotion in Portugal after Fatima. Although the church itself (late 19th to early 20th century) is not particularly interesting, the view of the Minho region from the lantern tower of its cupola is breathtaking, and the size of the sanctuary grounds is also impressive. The courtyard outside the church is larger than a football field, and has held over half a million pilgrims at one time. (The main pilgrimages take place the first week of June and the third week of August.) A larger-than-life statue of Pope Pius XII, at the base of a staircase leading up to the courtyard, commemorates his visit in 1954, but the view up to the church from the stairway is obstructed by a large concrete stage used for outdoor masses. The woods and paths around the church are pleasant, and the *Sameiro* restaurant beside it (see *Eating Out*) is one of the best in the region. Monte Sameiro is located 5½ miles (9 km) east of town, 2½ miles (4 km) past Bom Jesus on N103-3. The sanctuary is open daily from 8 AM to 8 PM; there is a charge to climb the church tower.

Santa Maria Madalena – This granite church, which sits on the wooded heights of the Serra da Falperra, is one of the more unusual examples of baroque work in Portugal. André Soares, the same architect who designed the Raio Palace and the Town Hall in Braga, focused on its façade, playing with curving lines to give the building a sense of depth and movement. The church is normally open only on Sundays between 9 AM and noon (although longer summer hours are contemplated), but even when closed, the interior is visible through a grille in the door at the front entrance. The surrounding woods were once used by a local Robin Hood called Zé de Telhado (and, in fact, there is a Portuguese saint, Santa Marta da Falperra, who is the patron saint of thieves). The church is 3 miles (5 km) east of Braga on N309; it can also be reached from N103-3 by passing Bom Jesus and, less than half a mile before Monte Sameiro, taking the signposted turnoff to Serra da Falperra. Santa Maria Madalena is 2½ miles (4 km) from the turnoff.

Capela de São Frutuoso de Mortélios – The chapel of São Frutuoso, believed to have been constructed in the 7th century by Bishop Frutuoso of Dume, was damaged by the Moors in 711 and rebuilt in the 11th century. In the shape of a Greek cross, it is one of the few remaining examples of Byzantine art in Portugal, and despite an advanced state of disrepair — only one of the four naves that made up the cross is still attached to the cupola — it retains the aura and dignity of age. To visit, apply to the priest or sacristan at the adjoining church of São Francisco. St. Francis itself contains 16th-century stalls that were removed from the cathedral of Braga in the 18th century.

To reach São Frutuoso, 2½ miles (4 km) from Braga, take N201 northwest toward Ponte de Lima and turn right at Real.

■**EXTRA SPECIAL:** As elsewhere in Europe, whiling away the hours in a coffee-house is an important part of life in Braga. Of the several historic cafés in which to do as the natives do, the most famous is the 19th-century *Café Brasileira.* Its strategic location in the Largo do Barão São Martinho, by the entrance to fashionable Rua do Souto, makes it the city's informal salon. It is here that most of the intellectuals and artists traditionally have met and lingered over the latest news from Lisbon and Porto, and they still do. The marble tables and brass and copper fittings provide an Old World ambience; octogenarian waiters add timeless atmosphere. Patrons sit inside and stare out onto the street through large windows, which slide back in summer. Also recommended are the *Café Astoria* and the *Café Vianna,* in the arcade in front of the tourist office, both with 1930s decor and tables to sit outside in fine weather.

SOURCES AND RESOURCES

 TOURIST INFORMATION: The Municipal Tourism Board located in the center of town (1 Avenida Central, at the corner of Avenida da Liberdade; phone: 22550) offers advice and assistance in English. It is open daily, from 9 AM to 7 PM (except Saturdays from October through April, when it is open from 9 AM to 12:30 PM and from 2 to 5 PM, and on Sundays during the same months, when it is closed entirely).

Local Coverage – The *Correio do Minho,* the local newspaper with the largest circulation, publishes a daily agenda listing events and other pertinent information, such as exchange rates, the weather forecast, and the schedules of trains and buses departing for major cities in Portugal and elsewhere in Europe. The *Diário do Minho,* another local paper, is also available. Newsstands in the arcade in front of the tourist office sell major European newspapers, and magazines and the European editions of American news magazines, but not the *International Herald Tribune.* A comprehensive English-language pamphlet describing the city, entitled *Braga,* is published by the Municipal Tourism Board and distributed free. Pick it up at the tourist office (address above).

 TELEPHONE: The city code for Braga is 53. If calling from within Portugal, dial 053 before the local number.

GETTING AROUND: Most of the major sights of the city are easily accessible by foot. In any case, do everything to avoid driving in town during the rush hours (from 8:30 to 10 AM and from 5 to 7:30 PM), particularly on the Avenida da Liberdade. There is a municipal parking lot on Praça Conde de Agrolongo, on the north side of the Old Town, where a car can be parked for several hours for less than a dollar.

Airport – The local airport, 2½ miles (4 km) north of Braga at Palmeira, handles neither scheduled domestic nor international flights; it is used mainly by the *Braga Flying Club* (phone: 24530), which leases planes and pilots.

Bus – Service is reasonable, but buses do get crowded during rush hour and the frequency of their appearance drops off after midnight. Tickets are acquired on the bus (125 escudos — about 80¢ — within the city limits). The main bus station for long-distance arrivals and departures, the Central de Camionagem de Braga (Travessa da Praça do Comércio; phone: 27001). Among other companies, *Caima* provides comfortable, air conditioned express buses connecting Braga, Porto, and Lisbon; tickets can be reserved (38 Rua dos Chãos; phone: 77003 or 22061). *Abreu,* a travel agency (171 Avenida Central; phone: 613100), also handles reservations. The tourist office has lists of bus schedules to all destinations, and the *Correio do Minho* publishes a daily schedule of major runs.

Car Rental – *Avis* has a rental office beside the central bus station (28 Rua Gabriel Pereira de Castro; phone: 72520).

Taxi – There is a taxi stand in the Largo do Barão São Martinho, near the Municipal Tourism Board. You can also call for a cab (phone: 28019).

Train – The main train station, Estação do Caminho de Ferro (phone: 22166), on the west side of the city at the Largo de Estação, is a central rail hub for northern Portugal. The newspapers publish a daily schedule of trains to and from important destinations; the tourist office also has schedules.

 SPECIAL EVENTS: As is to be expected, *Holy Week* is the most important time of the year in Braga, a time when all commercial activity grinds to a halt and the city is transformed into a giant and sumptuous house of worship. Priceless gold and silver ecclesiastical relics are removed from church treasuries and paraded through town by the archbishop and his retinue, themselves clothed in diamonds and pearls. Balconies are decorated with luxurious drapes displaying the coats of arms of ancient families who fought in the Catholic armies to liberate Portugal from the Moors. The streets are festooned with lights and filled with the intoxicating smell of burning wax and incense. Daily processions vent the religious fervor of the populace: In one procession, hundreds of penitents dressed in the black habit of gravediggers carry torches and walk somberly in front of the image of the Lord to the slow, martial cadence of a funerary tune. Hooded men add a dark and mysterious note to the events. At one time, these masked men went around with large torches pointing out the houses of suspected sinners. That practice is a thing of the past, but *Holy Week,* with its grand religious manifestations, is a reminder that the spirit that made Braga the seat of ecclesiastical power and devotion in Portugal is alive and thriving.

From June 23 through 25, the city comes alive once again (and is again lit spectacularly) for the *Festas de São João* (Feast Days of St. John), a Christian holiday with roots in pagan rites celebrating the summer solstice. This is the time of year when the crops are beginning to blossom and the people of the Minho come out and rejoice. Parties go on until all hours of the night, the *vinho verde* flows freely, and the aroma of festive food invades the popular neighborhoods. Young women wear colorful regional dresses and ornate gold filigree, folk groups perform, and medieval dances are staged. Customs such as throwing herbs into large bonfires to make divinations or passing around pots of leeks with carnations attached to them, are reminders of the ancient origins of the festivities.

Both *Holy Week* and the *Festas de São João* draw many pilgrims and visitors, so advance hotel reservations are necessary for these periods. At any time of the year, however, Braga is probably playing host to some industrial fair, convention, or congress at the Palácio Municipal de Exposições e Desportos (in the park at the southern end of Avenida da Liberdade). A brand-new *vinho verde* fair, held here for the first time in fall 1988 and repeated in spring 1990, may become a regular event in even-numbered years.

MUSEUMS: In addition to those museums mentioned in *Special Places,* the *Museu Pio XII* and the *Museu Medina,* which share the same building, may be of interest. The former is the city's museum of antiquities, housing artifacts dating as far back as the neolithic period (albeit arranged in a haphazard way); the latter consists of a collection of paintings by 20th-century Portuguese artist Henrique Medina, in which his predilection for naturalist settings and young virgins is evident. The remains of a Roman swimming pool are in the courtyard. The museums share the same hours, from 10 AM to noon and from 3 to 6 PM (closed Mondays), but there are separate admission charges. 8 Campo São Tiago (phone: 23370).

 SHOPPING: Braga and its environs are known for their fairly large selection of moderately priced handicrafts — lace and embroidery, wicker and straw articles, earthenware goods, and religious artifacts. The best bargains can be obtained at the weekly Tuesday fair in the Palácio Municipal de Exposições e Desportos. For those unable to attend the fair, there is the shop at the tourist office, which carries all the regional goods, including the Minho's famed filigree jewelry, at prices only slightly above those of the manufacturer. Shopping malls, or *centros comerciais,* have made their appearance: They're largely restricted to Avenida da Liberdade, and are especially convenient because they stay open until midnight. Shoppers in search of quality, however, continue to patronize the stores on and around Rua do Souto. Stores are open Mondays through Saturdays, from 9 AM to 1 PM and from 3 to 7 PM.

Casa Eden – A large selection of hand-embroidered linen and bedspreads (a damask bedspread can cost anywhere from $200 to $300). English spoken. 140-144 Rua do Souto (phone: 22756).

Casa Fânzeres – The oldest religious artifacts shop in Braga both sells and restores religious objects. 132-134 Rua do Souto (phone: 22704).

Herdeiros de Francisco José Ferreira – Leather goods of quality — suitcases, briefcases, and ladies' handbags. 124 Rua do Souto (phone: 23886).

Ourivesaria Confiança – Fine silver and gold jewelry and repair work. 1 Rua do Souto (phone: 23187).

Sapataria Teresinha – Good-quality leather shoes made in the region. 84-86 Rua do Souto (phone: 22943).

Vadeca – Typical handmade *viola braguesa,* or *cavaquinho* guitars, from which the ukelele was developed. 15 Largo do Barão São Martinho (phone: 71045).

 SPORTS AND FITNESS: Braga has two major public sports facilities. The larger is the municipal sports complex (phone: 73363) that is part of the Palácio Municipal de Exposições e Desportos, in the Parque São João da Ponte at the southern end of Avenida da Liberdade. The other is Rodovia Recreation Park (Avenida João XXI; phone: 76803). Both have parking facilities and can be reached by public transport.

Boating – Small rowboats can be rented at the manmade lake above the Bom Jesus do Monte sanctuary.

Fishing – Numerous rivers, lakes, and beaches in the vicinity provide diverse fishing opportunities. The huge reservoir at Peneda-Gerês National Park is only 30 miles (48 km) away. The *Braga Amateur Fisherman's Club* (112 Rua dos Chãos; phone: 26060) can be of assistance.

Jogging – The best place to run is the Parque São João da Ponte, which has both green spaces and a track.

Soccer – *Sporting Clube de Braga,* a first-division team, has its own stadium, *Estadio Primeiro de Maio,* in the Parque São João da Ponte. The season runs from September to May, and major league games are played on Sunday afternoons.

Swimming – The Parque São João da Ponte has the largest public pool in town (phone: 24424), with restaurant and café service next door. The Rodovia Recreation Park sports complex has both an indoor pool (phone: 76803) and an outdoor pool (phone: 76703).

Tennis – There is a tennis club at the Rodovia Recreation Park (phone: 611753).

THEATER: The *Teatro Circo* (697 Avenida da Liberdade; phone: 22403) is the prime cultural site of the city, doubling as a theater and a movie house. Among the groups that appear here is the *Companhia de Teatro de Braga*, a young company performing largely classical plays by Portuguese greats such as Almeida Garrett. Two other cinemas are the *Cinema São Geraldo* (on Largo Carlos Amarante) and the *Cinema Avenida* (across the square from the tourist office). As elsewhere in Portugal, films are shown in their original language with Portuguese subtitles. The daily *Correio do Minho* publishes movie listings in its Roteiro section.

MUSIC: The Minho is Portugal's folklore center. On Saturday and Sunday evenings all summer long, regional folk groups, dressed in colorful costumes, take to the stage at the bandstand on Avenida Central, performing ancient songs and lively dances accompanied by small Minho fiddles, small Braga guitars, triangles, and bass drums. Keep an eye out for Braga's most famous group, the *Grupo Folclórico Dr. Gonçalo Sampaio.*

NIGHTCLUBS AND NIGHTLIFE: The choices are limited, but there's a certain variety nevertheless, and it all unfolds between 9 PM and 2 AM. Discotheques currently in vogue are the *Discoteca Club 84* (beside the *Turismo* hotel at Praceta João XXI; phone: 76482) and *Coreto* (15 Avenida Central; phone: 75814), a disco and pub catering to a younger and wilder set. The *Golden Bar* (in the *Turismo*) serves tropical drinks and late-night snacks, while the *Latino Bar* (in the Old Town, 5 Rua do Anjo) is a warm and cozy spot with soft music for the romantically inclined. *Café Tuarege* (Rua dos Congregados) exhibits artwork and draws an artsy crowd, and the *Pub John Lennon* (28 Rua do Raio) provides live music shows for the nostalgia crowd.

BEST IN TOWN

CHECKING IN: Accommodations in the city leave something to be desired, so demanding travelers head for the hills to the more deluxe rooms around the Bom Jesus sanctuary. In Braga, the larger commercial hotels, catering to the business community, are located in the newer part of town, while smaller establishments — of which there are too few for summer demand — are in the quieter and more picturesque historic center. Expect to pay $60 and up for a double room with continental breakfast in the expensive category, between $30 and $50 at a moderate property, and less than $25 at an inexpensive one. Reservations should be made at least a month in advance for summer traveling, and should be double-checked a week before departure. All telephone numbers are in the 53 city code unless otherwise indicated.

Do Elevador – Quite elegant, and tastefully done in classic Portuguese style. On the grounds of the Bom Jesus sanctuary, its plush, Old World decor and efficient service make it a favorite of Lisbon and Porto society. The 25 rooms with bath (which include a TV set on request) face a manicured garden and have a sweeping view of Braga. The posh dining room (see *Eating Out*) commands a similar view and serves fine regional specialties. Parque do Bom Jesus do Monte (phone: 676611). Expensive.

Do Parque – Also on the grounds of the Bom Jesus sanctuary, it has a turn-of-the-century look that has been retained despite refurbishing and modernization. The large sitting room is fashionably decorated in leather and wood; each of the 49 air conditioned bedrooms has a private bath, radio, and TV set. There is no restaurant, but meals can be taken at the sister *Elevador* hotel a few paces away. Parque do Bom Jesus do Monte (phone: 676548). Expensive.

Turismo – Modern, with 132 rooms, it is often billed as the city's best. Unfortunately, it's far too flawed to hold that title. It has all the conveniences, but the furniture is already falling apart, and its communications and air conditioning systems are erratic. A lively bar, rooftop pool, and a friendly (but overworked) staff are its greatest assets. Parking is available in front. Avenida João XXI (phone: 612200). Expensive.

Caranda – It has all the basic conveniences, although it's lacking in local character. There are 100 rooms, a simple restaurant, and a rooftop bar with a view of Bom Jesus. 96 Avenida da Liberdade (phone: 77027). Moderate.

João XXI – A smaller and more economical variation on the same theme as the *Caranda*. It has 28 rooms with bath, a dining room — and a dimly lit and noisy discotheque in the basement. Its greatest asset is its central location. 849 Avenida João XXI (phone: 22146). Moderate.

São Marcos – Friendly service and 13 modern, clean, and simple rooms characterize this *pensão*, which is ideally located in a quiet pedestrian street in the Old Town. As basic sleeping establishments go, it is the best pension in its category in Braga. No restaurant or bar service. 80 Rua de São Marcos (phone: 77177). Moderate.

Sul Americano – On the Bom Jesus grounds, adjacent to the church, this reliable, family-run hotel has 28 clean, simply decorated rooms, and a large dining room (with fireplace) serving regional fare. Parking nearby. Parque do Bom Jesus do Monte (phone: 676615). Moderate.

Dos Terceiros – Another *pensão* right in town, this one, with 20 rooms, is near the municipal parking lot and close to the Santa Bárbara Garden. No restaurant, but there is bar service. 85 Rua dos Capelistas (phone: 70466). Moderate.

Inácio Filho – The Portuguese antiques, 8 clean rooms, and perfect location (in the heart of the Old Town) make this *pensão* an attractive bargain. 42 Rua Francisco Sanches (phone: 23849). Inexpensive.

Casa Santa Zita – Run by a lay religious order, it provides functional and pleasant rooms at student rates. 20 Rua São João (phone: 23494). Very inexpensive.

Those wishing to get away from the conventional hotel circuit should note that Portugal's *Tourism in the Country* program — through which private homes take in paying guests — is particularly active in northern Portugal (see *Accommodations,* GETTING READY TO GO) and that many of the participating properties in the area are the very fine stately homes and manor houses belonging to the *Turismo de Habitação* network rather than the simpler houses of the *Turismo Rural* and *Agroturismo* networks. Among the participants in the Braga area is the *Casa dos Lagos,* a terraced house on the wooded hill at the entrance to Bom Jesus. The house has a cozy apartment with 2 double bedrooms, bathroom, sitting room, and kitchen. Contact Senhor Telmo da Silva Barbosa (phone: 676738), or write *Casa dos Lagos* (Bom Jesus, Braga 4700). Another participant, the *Casa da Pedra Cavalgada,* a 19th-century home a little over a mile northeast of Braga on N101, offers a self-contained area with 2 bedrooms and individual sitting rooms. Contact Dr. José Mariz (phone: 24596 or 28319), or write *Casa da Pedra Cavalgada* (Lugar do Assento, Palmeira, Braga 4700). Each is in the moderate price category. Reservations for most local *Tourism in the Country* properties — which generally require a minimum stay of 3 nights — can also be made through *Turihab, Associação de Turismo de Habitação* (Praça da República, Ponte de Lima 4990; phone: 58-942729).

 EATING OUT: The cooking of Braga is rich and heavy, and the portions are generous. Pork, kid, and cod are the staple main dishes, and of the three, pork is the most common. (Until recently, the killing of a pig was accompanied by much fanfare and ritual.) Pork is popular because it can be stored as ham or sausages, and consumed during the cold winter months. Two pork dishes found frequently are *rojões de porco,* or pork dumplings with maize, and *arroz de sarrabulho,* various meats stewed in pig's blood and rice. The *frigideiras de Braga,* flake pies filled with pork or other meat, are the traditional poor man's meal and are ideal for snacks and picnics. Roast *cabrito,* or kid, is in season during the early summer, and *bacalhau,* or dried salt cod, the most prized dish in the Braga repertoire, is consumed throughout the year — including at *Christmas* dinner. There are more than 300 ways to prepare cod — and each restaurant has its own recipe — but oven-baked codfish with cream is one of the better variations on the theme.

Braga is also known for its pastries. Not only are there more than 20 pastry shops — *pastelarias* — from which to choose, but most restaurants (in all categories) make their own pastries. Anyone with a sweet tooth should try the city's *pudim à abade de Priscos,* an extra rich pudding named after a corpulent prelate with a predilection for sweets. The recipe requires 15 egg yolks, in addition to port, lemon, and caramelized sugar.

Dining out in Braga, however, is not as popular as in other major Portuguese cities. Families tend to entertain at home, leaving restaurants for large celebrations, such as weddings and baptisms. The number of good restaurants is, therefore, limited, particularly in the expensive category. There are, however, several establishments on the Praça Conde de Agrolongo, near the municipal parking lot, serving simple, but tasty, dishes at modest prices for the merchant lunch crowd. A two-course meal for two, including regional *vinho verde* (green wine — referring to its age, not its color), brandy, and coffee, will cost $40 or more in any restaurant listed below as expensive, from $25 to $35 in a restaurant listed as moderate, and around $20 in an inexpensive one. All telephone numbers are in the 53 city code unless otherwise indicated.

Do Elevador – In the hotel of the same name, it offers elegant Old World charm, with views of box-hedged gardens and the Bom Jesus sanctuary. The set menu, changed daily, balances regional fare with continental dishes. The typical three courses include fish and meat and may not leave much room for more, although the richly laden dessert cart will still be a temptation. When it arrives, try the homemade almond cake (*bolo de amêndoa*). Open daily. Reservations advised. *Hotel do Elevador,* Parque do Bom Jesus do Monte (phone: 676611). Expensive.

Abade de Priscos – A simple, quaint restaurant upstairs, overlooking a tree-lined square beside the Catholic University. Good regional fare is served: Braga specialties and protein-rich dishes for the largely academic crowd that makes up its clientele. Closed Sundays. Reservations advised. 7 Praça Mousinho de Albuquerque (phone: 76650). Moderate.

Casa Cruz Sobral – What this ordinary-looking place lacks in decor and atmosphere, it makes up for in food and service. The owner and manager, António Sobral, son of the proprietor of the *Inácio* restaurant (see below), has taken the family recipes to a smaller locale next door, where he offers a traditional, seasonal menu, with special emphasis on roast meat. The *vitela assada à Cruz Sobral,* veal done in a wine-based onion sauce with copious amounts of garlic, parsley, and cumin, and the *sarrabulho com rojões à moda do Minho,* or pork with maize, are both tasty. Closed Mondays. Reservations unnecessary. 7-8 Campo das Hortas (phone: 22368). Moderate.

Conde Dom Henrique – The cook in this small, intimate restaurant prides himself on his fish dishes, particularly codfish and hake. On a quiet street in the Old Quarter of town, it is a favored lunch spot of city officials and intellectuals. The walls are covered with pictures of popular figures, such as the colorful watermen and brilliantly clad milk ladies who have largely disappeared from local life. Closed Mondays. Reservations advised. 17 Rua do Forno (phone: 28703). Moderate.

Inácio – The best and most popular restaurant in Braga proper. Family-run, it is decorated with regional artifacts, divided into three cozy dining areas, and has stone walls, wooden beams, and an open kitchen to give it a rustic look that goes well with the menu. Cured hams hanging from the ceiling of the bar are consumed as appetizers with dry port. Some dishes worth noting are the *cabrito no forno,* or roast kid, done over a wood fire, and the *lampreia com arroz* (lamprey with rice) — the fish is marinated in wine and its own blood, which is used later to make the rice sauce. (Preparing this dish is time-consuming and labor-intensive, so have your hotel call in advance to order it.) The wine cellar is well stocked with the best alvarinho green wines, as well as more modestly priced varieties such as Casal Garcia. Owner Claudionor Sobral and his very attentive staff oversee it all. Closed Fridays. Reservations advised. 4 Campo das Hortas (phone: 613235). Moderate.

Sameiro – Pilgrims visiting the shrine next door are not the only ones making tracks to this family-run restaurant beside the Sameiro sanctuary. Food connoisseurs as well are attracted by its excellent dishes and efficient service. The decor is as spartan as a monk's cell, but owner-chef Maria da Conceição has received several culinary awards for her regional cooking. Her wood-fired stoves add extra flavor to the dishes, which include such specialties as lamprey with mayonnaise and a soufflé of cod. The recipe for the squash-based *tarta de chila* is well guarded, but it appears from the taste to have been marinated in caramelized sugar, honey, and port. The house has its own green wine. Closed Mondays. Reservations advised. Monte Sameiro (phone: 675114). Moderate.

Casa Pimenta – A simple, family-run eating establishment that is a lunchtime favorite among local merchants and other businesspeople. Open daily. Reservations unnecessary. 24 Praça Conde de Agrolongo (phone: 22119). Inexpensive.

Lusitana – Small and bustling, and the best place in town for a snack. Despite its size, it manages to serve as a snack bar, tea shop, and pastry shop. Combination platters include a succulent veal stew, and the Braga *frigideiras* (meat pies) are house specialties. Eat indoors or outdoors on the small esplanade inside the Santa Bárbara Garden, but either way, if you plan to have lunch here, be sure to arrive before 12:30 PM to avoid the crowds. This is also the most popular hangout in town for the tea and pastry set, since the establishment makes its own sweets, including traditional local delicacies such as *fatias de Braga* (square cakes made of almonds, eggs, and sugar) and sweet Romeo and Juliet pastries, not to mention the ultra-rich *pudim à abade de Priscos.* Closed Mondays. 127 Rua Justino Cruz (phone: 28791). Inexpensive.

BURGOS

Lying between the Spanish *meseta* (plateau) and the foothills of the Cantabrian and Iberian cordilleras, about 150 miles (240 km) due north of Madrid and 95 miles (152 km) due south of the Atlantic coast at Santander (as well as half the way between Barcelona and Santiago de Compostela on Spain's east-west axis), is Burgos. It occupies a position that has made it an important crossroads for centuries, and thrives in a setting that — combining tableland and mountain, wheatfields and pine woods — is particularly characteristic of inland Spain. Although a relatively young city, dating from the 9th century, and a quiet and pleasant one, Burgos nevertheless boasts a rich and colorful history.

The earliest historic reference to Burgos was in 884, when Alfonso III of León chose the Castilian Count Diego Rodríguez Porcelos to build a castle and settlement on the Arlanzón River as an outpost for troops fighting on the Moorish frontier. By 950, Fernán González, another Castilian count, had grown powerful enough (through the consolidation of several small fiefdoms) to declare himself independent of the kingdom of León and establish the county of Castile, making Burgos his capital. When the county of Castile became the kingdom of Castile, Burgos became its capital, and remained so until 1087, when Alfonso VI moved his headquarters to Toledo.

Burgos is probably best known for its most famous native son, Rodrigo Díaz de Vivar, Spain's national hero, more commonly known as El Cid Campeador, a much romanticized hero who was born in the tiny village of Vivar, just north of Burgos, and became a legend of the Reconquest. Following his victory over the Moors in 1081, El Cid was expelled from Castile by Alfonso VI, who was jealous of the soldier's popularity and distrusted him, even though the hero was married to Doña Jimena, the king's cousin. As an exiled soldier of fortune, El Cid joined the forces of the Moorish King of Zaragoza, and subsequently fought *against* the same Christian forces he had once led. His sympathies soon switched again, and in 1094 he led 7,000 Christian knights to a stunning victory over the Moors at Valencia. The Moors, however, had their revenge in 1099, at Cuenca, where the legendary hero met his death. His brave widow held Valencia until 1102, when she burned the city before it was overrun by the Moors, then returned to Castile with her husband's remains.

El Cid was eventually immortalized in the great, anonymous 12th-century Castilian epic poem *El cantar del mío cid,* a tender but mostly fictional account of the often ruthless mercenary's exploits. Today, he and Doña Jimena are buried side by side in the Cathedral of Burgos, after centuries of peaceful rest in the Monastery of San Pedro de Cardeña, several miles east of town. A simple tombstone pays tribute to El Cid's loyal horse, Babieca, reputedly buried here. The hero's presence still pervades the city, as well as Spanish history and literature, and the striking statue of him in the Plaza de Miguel Primo de Rivera, sword thrusting, cape to the wind, bears an inscription that reads: "His death caused much mourning among Christians and great joy to his enemies."

While El Cid was making the name of Burgos known to the Moors of the medieval world, the city also was gaining equal renown among medieval Christians as a major stopping point for pilgrims on their way to the shrine of St. James in Santiago de Compostela. This great mass movement had begun in earnest in the 10th century, and as it grew, so did Burgos. The cathedral, begun and completed for the most part in the 13th century, became the city's focal point, and over the years has come to be recognized as one of the world's most important landmarks of Gothic architecture and sculpture. The cathedral is a living testament to the wealth of Burgos in the 13th century, when a powerful group of sheep farmers, known as the Mesta, generated an unprecedented amount of commerce by selling their merino wool, both locally and abroad. Burgos was a center of the wool trade, a fact that is recalled even by its name, which derives from the "burghers," or middle class merchants, who gave rise to the towns of the Middle Ages.

Burgos remained prosperous through the 16th century, and then began to decline. Only in this century did it return to the fore, this time infamously, as the capital of the Civil War regime of Generalísimo Francisco Franco. In 1936, the Nationalist (or Falangist) Party was spawned in Burgos, where it was said that "even the stones are nationalist," and soon after, again in Burgos, Franco was proclaimed head of the Spanish government and commander-in-chief of the armed forces. Yet despite adverse historical circumstances and its share of warfare, Burgos has retained a wealth of artistic relics that few Spanish cities or provinces can boast. The 13th, 14th, and 15th centuries were periods of extraordinary splendor, during which the construction of churches, monasteries, and homes grew under the influence of bishops and abbots and with the patronage of kings and noblemen. During the 15th and 16th centuries, the city achieved further spectacular development, thanks in part to its economic wealth, which attracted corps of painters, sculptors, and architects.

BURGOS AT-A-GLANCE

SEEING THE CITY: The best way to get a panoramic view of Burgos is to walk or drive up to the remains of the old castle, which is just above the cathedral. To reach it on foot, begin in Plaza de Santa María, just in front of the cathedral, take the steps up to the Iglesia de San Nicolás, and turn left onto Calle Fernán González; at the triumphal arch, take the stairs leading upward to the top. The castle is nothing but a ruin, having been blown up by departing Napoleonic troops in the early 19th century, but it's possible to climb carefully to the top of the walls (although it's not encouraged), then sit down and behold Burgos, majestically spread out below.

SPECIAL PLACES: The major sights are clustered in the Old Town, a relatively small area on one side of the Arlanzón River. Its central features are the arcaded Plaza Mayor (Plaza de José Antonio on some maps), just west of which, at the foot of the castle hill, is the impressive Gothic cathedral, which dominates the entire city. South of the cathedral is the Plaza del Rey San Fernando; from it, the Arco de Santa María, a massive gate with semicircular towers, opens onto the beginning of the Paseo del Espolón, one of the most beautiful and pleasant riverside promenades in Spain. Just in front of the gate, the Arlanzón is crossed by the Puente de Santa María (Santa Maria Bridge). The main sights of Burgos are within easy walking distance of this core, although most people will want to take public transportation to the Monasterio de las Huelgas and the Cartuja de Miraflores (Convent of Miraflores).

Cathedral – The cathedral in Burgos is the third-largest in Spain, following those of Seville and Toledo, but it was the country's first great Gothic cathedral. Begun in 1221 on the order of King Ferdinand III (the Saint) and Bishop Mauricio, who laid the cornerstone on July 20 of that year (curiously, no one knows which stone it is), the structure was largely designed by Master Enrique, who also built the Cathedral of León. The first mass was said 9 years later, although the church was not finished for several more centuries. Construction fell into two distinct periods, and two Gothic styles are evident. The main body of the church, mostly completed in the 13th century, is in a simpler Gothic style than that represented by such 15th-century additions as the two west front spires, by Juan de Colonia, or the Capilla del Condestable (Constable's Chapel), by Simón de Colonia. Both of these latter are wondrously Flamboyant Gothic. Yet while the cathedral's plan was originally based on French models, and both French and German architects collaborated in its construction, its design and decoration are in the finest Spanish tradition.

The difference between the two styles can be seen in the cathedral's main (west) façade, which faces Plaza de Santa María (from where it is also evident that the cathedral was built on sloping ground). The two towers bracketing the rose window date from the 13th century, while the lacy openwork spires above them are the masterpiece of the 15th-century architect from Cologne. The door in the main façade is known as the Puerto del Perdón (Door of Forgiveness), but before going inside, walk down to the Plaza del Rey San Fernando, from where a flight of stairs leads up to what is considered the most beautiful of the church's four entrances, the Puerta del Sarmentál, or Sarmental Door, in French Gothic style. (Note the tympanum, with carvings of each of the Four Evangelists writing at their desks.) The remaining splendid portals are the Puerta de la Coronería on the church's north side (Calle Fernán González), with a 13th-century bas relief of Christ in Judgment between the Virgin Mary and St. John, and, nearly adjoining it, the Puerta de la Pellejería, a 16th-century Plateresque design by Francisco de Colonia, Juan's grandson.

Inside, the cathedral stands as an overwhelming testament to the strength of the church. The massive columns rising to the vaulted dome at the crossing of the transept appear to stretch to the heavens, and the dome — colorless, opaque glass in an eight-pointed star shape amid ornate Plateresque stone carving — is as jewel-like as a giant rhinestone pin. In the floor under the dome is the tomb of El Cid and his wife, Doña Jimena, sandwiched between the 16th-century Renaissance Capilla Mayor (Main Chapel, or High Altar) and altarpiece (the Infante Don Juan, one of Alfonso X's sons, and other members of the royal family are in tombs at the foot of the altar) and the 16th-century Renaissance choir, with walnut stalls carved by Felipe Bigarny. Both the choir and the high altar are surrounded by a giant grille. The gilded staircase off to one side (north) here, a 16th-century Renaissance design by Diego de Siloé, is one of the church's treasures. So, too, is the series of extraordinarily expressive sculptured scenes around the back of the altar, depicting the death of Christ, the central ones also carved by Felipe Bigarny.

The cathedral has 19 chapels, not all of which are on view at any given time. Foremost among them is the octagonal Capilla del Condestable, behind the Main Chapel. A striking example of 15th-century Flamboyant Gothic, it contains a very ornate gilt altar, in front of which are the tombs, with Carrara marble effigies, of Don Pedro Fernández de Velasco, the Constable of Castile, and his wife, Doña Mencía de Mendoza y Figueroa; above them is a lovely star-shaped cupola of blue and purple stained glass. In the small room just off the chapel is a painting of Mary Magdalene, attributed to Leonardo da Vinci (it's behind closed cupboard doors — ask the attendant to open it). Another noteworthy chapel is the Capilla del Santísimo Cristo (the first to the right upon entering the church), which contains a much-venerated ancient figure of Christ, made by St. Nicodemus, according to legend; the figure of wood and buffalo hide, also known as the Christ of Burgos, has real hair, wears a skirt, and stands on five ostrich eggs. Two more chapels not to be missed are the Capilla Santa Tecla (directly across from the Santísimo Chapel), with an exceedingly lavish 18th-century gilt baroque altarpiece, by Alberto Churriguera, and the Capilla Santa Ana (next door to the Santa Tecla Chapel), with a wonderful 15th-century altarpiece by Gil de Siloé and Diego de la Cruz.

Also noteworthy are the cloister doors, beautifully carved. They lead into the 13th-century cloister, built on 2 levels, and adjoining chapel and chapter house, which function as the cathedral museum. Here the treasures include the 16th-century *Christ at the Column* sculpture by Diego de Siloé, considered a masterpiece of Spanish expressionism, and the silver carriage that transports the gold monstrance in the city's *Corpus Christi* procession. One of the cathedral's lighter facets is the famous 16th-century Papamoscas (Flycatcher), a clock with automated figures high up above the central aisle. On the hour, a figure to the right rings a bell causing the Flycatcher's mouth to open in a grimace (catching flies in the summer, hence the name). It's hard to see, especially if there's no gawking crowd gathered to direct the gaze, so stand just inside the main door of the cathedral, with your back to the door, and look way up to the left; the clock is set between the two arches of the clerestory windows. The cathedral is open daily, from 9:30 AM to 1 PM and from 4 to 7 PM. Admission charge to the cloister. Plaza de Santa María (phone: 204712).

Iglesia de San Nicolás – An unusual, mostly 15th-century Gothic church just up the stairs from the Plaza de Santa María, it has a magnificent altarpiece by Francisco de Colonia, dating from 1505. Carved in stone are some 48 scenes from the Bible and from the life of the saint, made up of hundreds of figures, some of them polychrome (decorated in several colors). On either side of the altar and on the sides of the church are haunting Gothic tombs. The church also contains some interesting 16th-century Flemish paintings. Don't spare the 100 pesetas for illumination — it's well worth it. Open Mondays from 9 AM to 2 PM and 5 to 9 PM, Tuesdays through Fridays from 6:30 to 8 PM, Saturdays from 9 AM to 2 PM and 6:30 to 8 PM, and Sundays and holidays from 9 AM to 2 PM and 5 to 6 PM. Calle Fernán González.

Arco de Santa María – When Burgos was a walled city, this was its main gateway, fed by the main bridge over the Arlanzón River. It dates from the 14th century (although there was an earlier, 11th-century gate here), and was remodeled in the 16th century. Pictured in its niches are some famous figures from local history: Count Diego Rodríguez Porcelos, the city's 9th-century founder, flanked by judges, on the lower level; Count Fernán González, the 10th-century founder of the County of Castile, flanked by the Holy Roman Emperor Charles V and El Cid, the city's mercenary hero, on the upper level. Plaza del Rey San Fernando.

Museo Arqueológico (Archaeological Museum) – Set up in the Casa de Miranda, a 16th-century mansion which features an elegant 2-story courtyard with a fountain in the center, the collection embraces finds from prehistoric times through the present day, and presents the changing ages in an easy-to-digest fashion through displays of burial sites, tools, jewelry, weapons, and household items. Roman artifacts include ceramics, weapons, glass bowls, and household items. There also is an interesting presentation on the region's Roman road system, complete with aerial photos that trace the old routes, and a small display of Visigothic items. The medieval section houses the Gothic tomb of Juan de Padilla, the Franciscan missionary, and an 11th-century Moorish ivory casket. Open Mondays through Fridays, from 10 AM to 1 PM and from 4:45 to 7:15 PM; Saturdays, from 11 AM to 1 PM. Admission charge. 13 Calle Miranda (phone: 265875).

Museo Marceliano Santa María – The museum occupies the former Augustinian Monastery of San Juan, now fully restored and converted into a palace of the arts. The upstairs houses 165 works by the local 19th- and 20th-century Impressionist painter, including portraits and colorful landscapes of the surrounding countryside. Downstairs is display space for the local art shows that are held here throughout the year; the exhibitions are set up around the enclosed arcades of the cloister, an interesting juxtaposition of modern art and Gothic vaulting. Open Tuesdays through Saturdays, from 10 AM to 2 PM and from 5 to 8 PM; Sundays, from 10 AM to 2 PM. Admission charge. Plaza de San Juan (phone: 205687).

Casa del Cordón – A fine example of secular, rather than ecclesiastic, Gothic architecture of the 15th century, it was built by the same Constable of Castile who lies buried in a chapel of the cathedral; it takes its name from the Franciscan *cordón* that is the decorative motif of its carved façade. The plaque next to the door identifies it as the building where, in April 1497, the Catholic Monarchs met Christopher Columbus after his return from his second trip to the New World. Beautifully restored, the building belongs to the bank that financed its restoration and is open to the public during banking hours, Mondays through Fridays from 9 AM to 2 PM. Plaza de Calvo Sotelo.

Estatua del Cid (El Cid Statue) – This statue of the Burgalese hero astride Babieca, his faithful steed, is so centrally located that visitors come upon it again and again as they explore the city. A contemporary work (1954) in bronze, it bristles with energy, as its subject certainly must have, and its assertiveness never fails to impress. Plaza de Miguel Primo de Rivera.

ENVIRONS

Monasterio de las Huelgas – What originally was a royal summer palace was converted into a Cistercian convent for nuns of aristocratic and royal lineage by Alfonso VIII and his English wife, Eleanor, in 1187. This eventually became one of the most important and powerful convents in Europe, and also served as a pantheon of the Castilian dynasty. The buildings and the artworks they contain reflect a wealth of changing architectural styles and influences from Romanesque and Mudéjar to Renaissance and Plateresque, although the church has a rather simple façade with a square tower. Inside, note the unique 16th-century revolving pulpit that allowed the priest to address both sides of the church, which is divided in two by a wall that turns out to be, when seen from the other side, a carved polychrome Renaissance-style altarpiece. This magnificent piece, surmounted by a 13th-century Deposition, is in the central nave of the church, where the tombs of the founders are also located. Tombs of other royal personages, as well as other wonderful altarpieces, are in the side aisles. Beyond are cloisters, rooms with stone ceilings carved Moorish-style, but with the castle of Castile as the main motif, a small room with a wonderful wooden *artesonado* ceiling, and, at the end, the *Museo de Telas Medievales* (Museum of Medieval Textiles). On display here, among other things, are garments found in the only one of the church's tombs left unsacked over the centuries, that of Don Fernando de la Cerda (1225–75), son of Alfonso X; included are his *birrete* (cap), his *saya* (tunic), his *manto* (cloak), and *cinturón* (sash), along with other articles. Also on display is the recently restored Moorish banner captured at the decisive Battle of Las Navas de Tolosa, in 1212, when Christian forces finally gained the upper hand against their Arab foes.

All of the above can be seen, unfortunately, only on a fast guided tour, which is conducted only in Spanish — it's worth it, but a pity. Open Tuesdays through Saturdays, from 11 AM to 1:15 PM and from 4 to 5:15 PM; Sundays and holidays, from 11 AM to 1:15 PM. Admission charge. Located in a residential district about 1 mile (1.6 km) west of the city center. Avenida del Monasterio de las Huelgas (phone: 201630).

Cartuja de Miraflores (Convent of Miraflores) – This is another sight out of town that should not be missed. In the mid-15th century, King Juan II gave the land here to the Carthusians to build a monastery, which he chose as the final resting place for himself and his second wife, Isabel of Portugal — parents of Queen Isabella of Castile. He died in 1454 and work on the church was carried out largely by their daughter, in the late Gothic style that came to be known as Isabeline; it was not finished until 1488. Visitors to the church pass through a grating into the Coro de los Hermanos (Brothers' Choir), with Renaissance choir stalls beautifully carved (1558) with reliefs of saints by Simón Bueras, then through the Felix Coeli Porta into the Coro de los Padres (Fathers' Choir), with Gothic choir stalls carved (1489) with arabesques by Martín Sánchez. Ahead, a wrought-iron grille surrounds the dual tomb of the king and queen, which consists of an intricately sculpted alabaster base in the shape of an eight-pointed star, with reclining figures of the monarchs on top. It hardly seems possible that this lacy extravaganza could have been carved in one lifetime, yet it was the work of the sculptor Gil de Siloé. He was called away from his work at the cathedral to do the job, and also completed the extraordinary exercise in filigree virtuosity against the adjacent wall — the tomb of the Infante Don Alfonso, Isabella's brother, who was "accidentally" dropped off the Alcázar walls in Segovia in 1468, allowing Isabella to become heiress to the Spanish throne. Even more astonishing is that the same Siloé, with the help of Diego de la Cruz, was responsible for the church's magnificent, immense wood altarpiece, whose sculptured, polychromed, and gilded biblical scenes are crowded with figures. Note the Last Supper, in the lowest row to the left, where it appears that the menu included the typically Castilian roast lamb (along with somebody's head on a platter); in the scene to the left of that is King Juan II (Queen Isabel is in a corresponding position to the far right).

Further treasures in the church include the *Annunciation* by Pedro Berruguete on the wall next to the Infante's tomb, the Flemish triptych on the wall facing the same tomb, and the Madonna with an unusually sweet-faced Child above the door marked Clausura. Open Mondays through Saturdays, from 10:15 AM to 3 PM and from 4 to 8 PM; Sundays and holidays, from 11:20 AM to 12:30 PM and from 1 to 3 and 4 to 6 PM. No admission charge. Located a little over 2 miles (3 km) east of the center, the monastery is best visited by car, taxi, or, in July and August, by bus, but it's easy to walk back, since the return is down a slight incline along a paved path the whole way — at a brisk pace it takes about 45 minutes to the city center. If walking *to* the monastery, just cross to the southern side of the river and follow Paseo de la Quinta east.

■**EXTRA SPECIAL:** There are promenades all along the river in Burgos, on both sides. The Paseo del Espolón, however, which runs from the Arco de Santa María to the Plaza de Miguel Primo de Rivera, is truly a treat. A walkway lined with park benches and topiary bushes, a parallel allée of sycamore trees, a sprinkling of fountains, a gazebo, and statues — along with a fair share of the milling citizenry — are all to be found here. Next to this, the river, with its wide grassy banks and overhanging willows, presents so bucolic a picture for a provincial capital that the visitor almost expects to see cows grazing at the water's edge. With such a place to carry it out, it's not surprising that the *paseo* — the communal stroll — is still an important part of Burgalese life, so why not join the crowd?

SOURCES AND RESOURCES

 TOURIST INFORMATION: There are two tourist offices in Burgos. The main Oficina de Informacion y Turismo (7 Plaza de Alonso Martínez; phone: 203125 or 201846) is open Mondays through Fridays, from 9 AM to 2 PM and from 4:30 to 6:30 PM; Saturdays, from 9 AM to 2 PM. A second office, the Asociación de Fomento del Turismo (1 Calle San Carlos; phone: 201844 or 208960), is open Mondays through Fridays from 8:30 AM to 2 PM and from 4:30 to 8 PM; Saturdays from 10 AM to 2 PM and from 4:30 to 8 PM; and Sundays from 11 AM to 2 PM. Both provide general information brochures on Burgos (in English), as well as a detailed city map.

Local Coverage – *Diario de Burgos,* the local Spanish-language daily newspaper, contains schedules of activities and events in and around the city.

 TELEPHONE: The city code for Burgos is 47. If calling from within Spain, dial 947 before the local number.

 GETTING AROUND: Walking is the easiest and most enjoyable way to get around in Burgos. Most of the major sights are within a relatively compact area. A car, taxi, or bus, however, will be useful for excursions to the sights in the environs and beyond.

Bus – Burgos has a good city bus system, with stops at or near the major sights and most hotels. A bus for the Monasterio de las Huelgas departs approximately every half hour from Plaza de Miguel Primo de Rivera, stopping at several bridges en route before turning away from the river; take the bus marked Barrio del Pilar. In July and August, there also is service connecting the center with the Cartuja de Miraflores approximately every hour; take the bus marked Fuentes Blancas from the same plaza. Burgos's main station for long-distance buses is at 4 Calle Miranda (phone: 205575), just across the river from the Arco de Santa María. There is daily service to León, Santander, Madrid, Soria, and San Sebastián; schedules are printed in the *Diario de Burgos,* and are often more convenient than those for the trains.

Car Rental – There are several choices: *Hertz* (10 Calle Madrid; phone: 201675); *Avis* (5 Avenida Generalísimo Franco; phone: 205813); and *Azteca* (Avenida General Vigón; phone: 223803).

Taxi – Taxis are available at stands throughout the city, or they can be flagged on the streets. To call a cab, try dialing 203055, 203088, or 262862, which correspond to centrally located cabstands at Plaza Santo Domingo de Guzmán, Calle Conde de Jordana, and Plaza de Vega respectively.

Train – The train station (Plaza de la Estación; phone: 203560) is across the river and at the end of Avenida Conde de Guadalhorce, a 15-minute walk from the cathedral. Burgos is on the main rail line connecting Irún and Madrid, with daily service to Pamplona, Vitoria, Bilbao, Valladolid, and other towns and cities. There also is less frequent service to Zaragoza, Palencia, León, and La Coruña. Tickets can be bought at the station or at *RENFE*'s downtown office (21 Calle Moneda; phone: 209131), open weekdays, from 9 AM to 1 PM and 4 to 7 PM.

 SPECIAL EVENTS: There are two particularly festive occasions that fill up the town. The first, *Corpus Christi,* in late May or early June, and *Curpillos,* the day following it, are marked by picturesque processions. (The banner captured at the Battle of Las Navas de Tolosa used to be paraded through town as part of the latter festivities, but since its recent restoration it no longer leaves the Monastery of Las Huelgas, where it's on display.) The second occasion, the *Feast Day of St. Peter and St. Paul,* on June 29, is an excuse for a week of celebration known as the *Fiesta de Burgos,* featuring parades, bullfights, sports competitions, and folkloric performances, and a host of other activities that can include anything from mime, ballet, and concerts to model airplane contests and fireworks. Detailed information on these events can be obtained from the tourist information offices.

 SHOPPING: Burgos is not known for any particular craft, food delicacy, or other product that might constitute the perfect souvenir, but it does have a variety of shops befitting its status as a solid provincial capital. The main shopping district spreads from the cathedral to the Plaza Mayor and up to Plaza de Alonso Martínez, including the streets between Calle Santander and Calle Lain Calvo. The major department store chain represented is *Galerías Preciadas* (two entrances: 4 Calle Almirante Bonifaz and 9 Calle Moneda; phone: 205846). In general, shopping hours are from 10 AM to 2 PM and 5 to 8 PM.

Con Rey – Costume jewelry with personality, mainly a Spanish one. 19 Calle Lain Calvo (phone: 260209).

Garden – One of the best clothing stores in town, selling everything from shoes to bags, belts, and overcoats, with departments for men, women, and young people. Plaza de Miguel Primo de Rivera (phone: 206990).

José Ruiz – A wide selection of shoes for men and women. 28 Plaza Mayor (phone: 260215).

Serrano – Another of the town's best shops for men's and women's clothing, but it's mostly for men and mostly British styles. This is where the Burgalese buy their Burberry's and Barbours. 4 Calle Santander (phone: 203668).

Vaquero – Handbags, wallets, briefcases, belts, umbrellas, plus cuff links and costume jewelry. 7 Calle Almirante Bonifaz (phone: 204791).

You – Men's and women's clothing, including cocktail dresses and formal wear, dressy and pricey. 15 Calle Vitoria (phone: 206444).

Zara – A budget clothing store (men, women, children); they do a land-office business, with price tags already converted into major international currencies, including US dollars. Corner of Calle Condestable and Calle Vitoria (phone: 201617).

 SPORTS AND FITNESS: The major public sports and recreation complex, *El Plantió* (Calle Vitoria; phone: 220001), has tennis courts and a municipal swimming pool. Open daily, from 10 AM to 9 PM.

Fishing – The most important fishing in Burgos and its surrounding areas is for river crayfish, which are abundant throughout the province. The Arlanzón yields trout and barbel.

 NIGHTCLUBS AND NIGHTLIFE: Nightlife in Burgos is best described as lively and very youth oriented, with most of the activity centered around the bars and cafés of the Old Town. Calle de la Llana de Afuera, behind the cathedral, is a center of activity, where the overflow bar and café crowds usually spill out onto the street. Popular discotheques include *Pentágono* (2 Calle

Conde de Jordana; phone: 202834); *Roma* (11 Calle San Pablo; phone: 265964); *La Finca* (Paseo de la Isla; phone: 234810); *Armstrong* (13 Calle Clunia; phone: 227266); and *Trastos* (9 Calle Huerto del Rey; phone: 246598).

BEST IN TOWN

 CHECKING IN: Burgos offers an excellent selection of hotels in various price ranges, most within a short walk of the cathedral. Expect to pay $85 or more for a double room at a hotel listed as expensive (more than $125 for the very expensive listing), $50 to $85 at a moderately priced hotel, and less than $50 at an inexpensive one. All telephone numbers are in the 47 city code unless otherwise indicated.

Landa Palace – The best in the Burgos area and one of Spain's best hotels, this hostelry is a world of its own. Set 2 miles (3 km) from the city center on the road to Madrid, it's a self-contained establishment (indeed, for some guests, Burgos begins to pale in interest) of 42 rooms and suites decorated with antiques, some of them in the stone tower of a 14th-century castle. An indoor/outdoor swimming pool is reached down a circular stone staircase, its indoor portion protected by soaring, skylighted Gothic vaulting, and the restaurant (see *Eating Out*) is a room of equally Gothic splendor. Carretera Madrid–Irún, Km 236 (phone: 206343). Very expensive.

Almirante Bonifaz – Noted for its high standards of comfort and service, it has 79 air conditioned rooms (with private baths, color television sets, radios, and telephones), a bar-cafeteria, even a bingo room. Centrally located, in the midst of banks and stores, it's a good choice for businesspeople as well as leisure travelers. 22 Calle Vitoria (phone: 206943). Expensive.

Condestable – One of the grand old dames of Burgos, a favorite with bullfighters (among others), also centrally located on one of the main business streets. Some of the 82 rooms retain the Old World elegance — ornate beds, overstuffed chairs, wallpaper that takes you back in time — that made the hotel's reputation; others have been modernized with off-white walls and modern furniture in blond woods. 8 Calle Vitoria (phone: 267125). Expensive.

Mesón del Cid – This Best Western–affiliated property occupies a lovely 15th-century house directly opposite the cathedral. The 30 rooms are well appointed, with a rustic, old-fashioned look and private bathrooms with brass fittings, but their biggest strength is that most of them are graced with an excellent head-on view of the cathedral's western façade. Only the public areas are air conditioned, there are a few steps to negotiate out front, and parking can be a problem, but the hotel will provide a garage for an added charge. The restaurant is a longtime Burgos favorite (see *Eating Out*). 8 Plaza de Santa María (phone: 208715). Expensive.

Cordón – The 35 rooms are large, comfortable, and clean, and the location is favorable. There is no restaurant, but some of Burgos's best eating places are just steps away. Staff members speak little English, which may or may not be a problem. 6 Calle de la Puebla (phone: 265000). Moderate.

Corona de Castilla – This modern facility offers 52 well-maintained rooms and a decent restaurant, but it is located across the river in a rather dull part of town, about a 10-minute walk from the cathedral. Ask for a room in the rear, which will be much quieter than one overlooking the street. 15 Calle Madrid (phone: 262142). Moderate.

Fernán González – Just across the bridge from the Arco de Santa María, overlooking the river. The 64 rooms are quiet and comfortable, the overall decor a medley of dark woods and fascinating antiques pleasantly tucked into virtually every nook and cranny. There's a dining room for guests, a somewhat old-fashioned space, plus a bright, beautiful à la carte restaurant — a blend of the modern with ancient stairways and balconies. 17 Calle Calera (phone: 209441). Moderate.

Conde de Miranda – Across the bridge from the Arco de Santa María and attached to the bus station, making it convenient for bus travelers (the area is safe at all hours). Nothing fancy, but the 14 rooms have private baths and offer simple yet comfortable furnishings. 4 Calle Miranda (phone: 265267). Inexpensive.

Norte y Londres – Centrally located, the 55 rooms here are clean and comfortable, offering lots of Old World charm and decor. Count on the friendly staff to provide good service. 10 Plaza de Alonso Martínez (phone: 264125). Inexpensive.

 EATING OUT: Among their other culinary treats, Burgos and the surrounding Castilian provinces are renowned for traditional lamb and pork dishes, especially *cordero asado* (roast suckling lamb) and *cochinillo asado* (roast suckling pig). For starters, try Burgos soup, a tasty broth made of chopped lamb and crayfish tails. Other local favorites include *olla podrida* (stew), *picadillo de cerdo* (finely chopped pork), fresh trout, sausages, *chanfaina a la cazuela* (hash), *caracoles* (snails), and *callos a la burgalesa* (tripe). Candied egg yolks are a well-known sweet. Dinner for two with wine will cost $60 or more in restaurants listed as expensive, $30 to $60 in moderate restaurants, and $30 or less at inexpensive ones. All telephone numbers are in the 47 city code unless otherwise indicated.

Casa Ojeda – Some say they've had the meal of their lives here, while others say the price is too high for the quality of the food. The establishment, however, going strong since 1910, is big enough to encompass all opinions: a traditional, regional restaurant upstairs, a popular and appealing *tapas* bar-*cafetería* downstairs, and a fancy-food store next door. The decor is charming, the ambience everything it should be, the experience worth the cost. Restaurant closed Sunday evenings (but the snack bar stays open). Reservations advised. Entrances at 5 Calle Vitoria and on Plaza de Calvo Sotelo (phone: 209052). Expensive.

Los Chapiteles – Enjoy *tapas* in the bar before settling down at one of the heavy, dark tables in the smartly rustic dining room. The menu is a regional one, stressing various grilled lamb and pork dishes. Closed Wednesdays and Sunday evenings. Reservations necessary. 7 Calle General Santocildes (phone: 205765). Expensive.

Landa Palace – Burgos's finest restaurant is in the hotel of the same name, 2 miles (3 km) from the center of town. It specializes in local Castilian dishes, and is perhaps best known for lamb baked in a wood-fired oven. But guests can choose from a full menu of other meat and fish dishes. The food is wholesome, the portions of good size, the service a study in Spanish exuberance — and the dining room itself is a lovely Gothic room with a 12-foot-high chandelier hanging from the center of the vaulted ceiling. Open daily. Reservations advised. Carretera Madrid–Irún, Km 236 (phone: 206343). Expensive.

Mesón del Cid – Within the splendor of the 15th-century building housing the *Mesón del Cid* hotel, this Burgos tradition features a downstairs bar and several dining rooms on the upper levels that convey a feeling of medieval rusticity, along with excellent views of the cathedral. The fare includes sumptuous salads, fish, and steaks. Try the *solomillo* (sirloin) or the chef's special *merluza* (hake). Closed Sunday nights and February. Reservations advised. 8 Plaza de Santa María (phone: 205971). Expensive to moderate.

Ribera del Duero – In the center of town, serving traditional Castilian fare in two elegant, antiques-filled dining rooms at the top of a beautiful winding staircase.

Closed Sundays and some holidays. Reservations necessary on weekends. Plaza Santo Domingo de Guzmán (phone: 208513). Expensive to moderate.

Mesón de los Infantes – Pleasantly tucked into a corner just downhill off the Plaza del Rey San Fernando, serving more fine Castilian specialties such as *olla podrida* and *lentejas medievales*, "medieval lentils." There are tables outdoors for summer dining. Open daily. Reservations advised. Calle de Corral de los Infantes (phone: 205982). Moderate.

Rincón de España – Another choice spot for fine regional cuisine, which is served in an elegant dining room decorated with ceramic tiles on a culinary theme, or, weather permitting, on the large, awning-covered terrace looking over at the cathedral. The service is pleasant, and though this has the perfect location to draw busloads of sightseers, it is packed with both locals and lucky visitors who happen on a good thing. Closed Mondays. Reservations necessary. 11 Calle Nuño Rasura (phone: 205955). Moderate.

Angel – Small, frequented by locals, it's up behind the cathedral, with its main dining room built against a section of the old city wall. Its own white stucco walls are accented with handsome wrought-iron lighting fixtures and coatracks, simple but attractive. Castilian cooking and fish dishes are the fare. Closed Sundays. Reservations advised. 36 Calle Fernán González (phone: 208608). Moderate to inexpensive.

El Buen Vantar – Also up behind the cathedral; pass the unpretentious bar and head downstairs to the dining room, which is actually outdoors, covered by an awning. This is a popular place with the lunchtime crowd, due to its picturesque setting, and also cool at night, when part of the awning is rolled back to reveal the stars. The food is regional, well prepared, and very reasonable — a find. Closed Mondays at lunch. Reservations advised. 41 Calle Fernán González (phone: 206116). Moderate to inexpensive.

Bonfin Self-Service – Located at the base of the stairs that descend from the west front of the cathedral. This cafeteria-style eatery has a wide range of entrée choices, as well as simple salads and sandwiches. A good choice for a quick meal between sightseeing stops. Open for lunch and dinner daily. No reservations. Calle Cadena y Eleta (phone: 206193). Inexpensive.

Hermanos Alonso – Simple food and surroundings, favored by the student crowd. The chicken, veal, and lamb dishes, all very good, are served in large helpings. Closed Thursdays. No reservations. 5 Calle de la Llana de Afuera (phone: 201711). Inexpensive.

 TAPAS BARS: Burgos has literally hundreds of *tapas* bars, as well as many cafés and restaurants that also serve *tapas. Casa Ojeda* (5 Calle Vitoria; see *Eating Out*) and *Bar La Cabana Arandina* (12 Calle Sombreria; phone: 261932), on a pedestrian street leading from Plaza Mayor, are considered by many to be the best *tapas* bars in town. Both offer huge selections, which include *boquerones, pinchos* of meat, fish, or mushrooms, calamari, mussels, sausage, *tortillas,* pickled vegetables, and much more. Another favorite is *Bodega Riojana* (9 Plaza de Alonso Martínez; phone: 260719), a crowded corner eatery with a counter and a few tables where an amazing variety of edibles is consumed, including some in miniature casseroles called *cazuelitas.*

COIMBRA

Sitting on the banks of the Mondego River, halfway between Lisbon and Porto, Coimbra is Portugal's third-largest city — and its most romantic. The greatest Portuguese poets — including Luís de Camões, who wrote the national epic, *The Lusiads,* during the 16th century — lived in Coimbra and immortalized their city, some carving their romantic verses on its very stones. Coimbra is the home of Portugal's oldest university, making the town teem with young people. Indeed, the romantic image of Coimbra is one of students in black capes hurrying through the nearly perpendicular streets around the ancient university as the cathedral bells toll them to class. Or of the same students, armed with guitars, serenading the young women — *tricanas* — of Coimbra under their balconies.

A popular local *fado,* or folk song, from the beginning of the century says that "Coimbra, to be Coimbra, must have three things — guitars, pretty girls, and black-caped students flitting through the streets." Luckily, as the end of the century approaches, the city remains true to itself, even though in a contemporary fashion. Today, the pretty girls bring out their ankle-length mantillas and colorful shawls only on special occasions, preferring jeans and other modern clothes. The black capes worn by the students since the Middle Ages almost disappeared after the end of the Salazar years, when all traditions came to be associated with the nearly half century of ultra-conservative dictatorship, but they are returning. As before, they are pinned with a colored ribbon identifying the student's course of study — dark blue for letters, light blue for science, red for law, yellow for medicine — with a tear at the border for each romantic conquest.

There is no serenading under the balconies today, but Coimbra *fados,* the sweet, nostalgic songs dedicated to love or to the river or to the city itself and sung only by men, are still heard in student cafés and at festivals, or whenever students with guitars gather on the steps by the Old Cathedral at night. Many *fado* singers, among them doctors, lawyers, and judges — graduates of Coimbra University — are better known for their singing than they are in their professions.

Coimbra has witnessed many romantic love stories. Perhaps the greatest of all was that of Dona Inês de Castro, acted out during the 14th century and beautifully told by Camões. Dona Inês, an aristocrat from Aragon, was loved by Prince Dom Pedro, whose father, King Afonso IV, wanted him to marry someone else. Nevertheless, the pair took up residence in a country house near Coimbra and had several children together. Fearing that her powerful brothers in Spain would usurp the Portuguese throne for her illegitimate children, King Afonso had her murdered. Pedro declared war on his father, but peace was soon established. After his father died, however, Pedro set Inês's body on the throne, forced all of the nobility to pay her obeisance, and executed two of her murderers by cutting out their hearts. In Coimbra, people believed that a spring gushed from the rocks where Inês was murdered, and that its waters were her tears.

Another woman well remembered in Coimbra was not sinner but saint — Isabel of Aragon, celebrated as Santa Isabel or the Rainha Santa (Saintly Queen). Isabel came to Coimbra in 1292 as the wife of Portugal's great King Dinis and devoted her life to good works. She is best known for the "miracle of the roses." In her efforts to help the poor, Queen Isabel often exceeded what the king thought necessary. One day, as she was taking alms to the poor, he angrily questioned her about what she was carrying in her mantle. When she opened it, the alms had turned to roses. Isabel lived out her last years in the Old Santa Clara Convent across the river, and is now buried in the New Santa Clara Convent. When her tomb was opened in 1612 on order of the bishop, her body was found intact, even though she died in 1336.

The university is the dominant force in the life of Coimbra. In 1290, 2 years before Isabel's arrival, her husband-to-be had founded a university — in Lisbon. In 1308, he transferred it to Coimbra. It moved back and forth several times until 1537, when it finally was permanently located in the heart of the city. The university became a renowned center for the study of philosophy, theology, law, and medicine, although it had its periods of stagnation, including one during this century, which prompted the dictator António Salazar, an alumnus and an ex-professor, to take action in the 1940s. Bent on having a really modern university, he tore down part of the historic Alta (Upper Town) surrounding the university — ancient narrow streets lined with 16th- and 17th-century houses and old churches — and to house his New University, erected some of the ugliest utilitarian buildings in Europe. Fortunately, the buildings in the adjoining Old University remain intact.

In the early days, only students, along with their servants, local nobility, and ecclesiastics, were allowed to live in the Alta section. Their lives and study habits were regulated by the ringing of the cathedral bells. There were strict rules for each class, particularly for the freshmen, who were often treated brutally and persecuted by the upperclassmen. Some of the ancient traditions persist. Students still live in *repúblicas* — houses passed down from one generation of students to another — where they share the household costs and chores. And they still celebrate the ancient ritual of burning their university ribbons at the end of the term in May to symbolize their moving to an upper class. The celebrations go on for a week, and include a famous serenade on the steps of the Old Cathedral.

The other dominant force in Coimbra life is the Mondego River, often called the river of poets because so many poems and songs have been written about it. But the Mondego — born in Portugal and not in Spain as most Portuguese rivers are — has done more than provide a romantic setting for the city. Long ago it made Coimbra an important port for trade with lands as far away as Phoenicia and Norway. Later, it was the dividing line between Christian and Moorish Portugal. Unfortunately, as it watered the fields and vineyards, it also brought destruction. Over the centuries, nearly 10 feet of silt finally buried a great part of the Baixa (Lower Town), where shopkeepers and artisans lived, and a good part of the Santa Clara area on the opposite bank. Old churches, convents, and other historic buildings disappeared forever before the Aguieira Dam tamed the river during this century.

Coimbra probably began as an Iron Age *castro* of Lusitanian and Celtic inhabitants on the Alta hilltop several hundred years before Christ. The Romans located their forum on the same hill, at the spot where the *Machado de Castro National Museum* now stands, and called their settlement Aeminium. The Visigoths brought Christianity, and when the bishopric was moved from the old Roman town of Conímbriga nearby, the name came with it, eventually to be shortened to Coimbra. Then, in 711, the Moors came. During their tenure, they built a set of walls around the hilltop city; one of its gates, the Almedina, still stands. The Christians recaptured the city, but in 987 the Moors again swept through and nearly razed it. The city was taken once more and held for good in 1064, under Ferdinand I, King of León and Castile.

Thus it happened that Coimbra became the capital of all the land between the Douro River to the north and Moorish-held territory to the south. Later, when Dom Afonso Henriques — son of Henry of Burgundy, to whom the Spanish king had given his Portuguese territory — defeated his mother and her Spanish allies and declared himself king of an independent Portugal, he, too, made Coimbra his capital — even though he had been born in Guimarães. In all, three medieval kings were born in Coimbra before Lisbon became the capital in 1260, and three more were born here after the transfer, because Coimbra remained a royal residence.

A good number of Coimbra's monuments date from the 16th and 17th centuries. Besides the permanent establishment of the university, the 16th century saw the arrival of the Jesuits (who remained strong until the mid-18th century) and of many other religious orders, who founded schools and put up notable buildings. A famous school of sculpture was born when the Frenchmen Nicolas Chanterene, Jean de Rouen, and others set up studios and proceeded to produce most of the statues and other stone carvings that now adorn the city's churches. The sculptors were influenced by the new methods and style of the Italian Renaissance, but they owed much of their art to the stone with which they worked — an exceptionally white, solid, granular limestone from the banks of the nearby Ança River.

The spate of building during the 17th century was brought about by the discovery of gold in Brazil, and it continued into the 18th century. Buildings dating from this time — such as the New Santa Clara Convent, the university library, and the Santo António dos Olivais church — were literally covered with Brazilian gold. Subsequently, Coimbra remained much the same until the 19th century brought a period of turmoil — the sack of the city by Napoleon's army during the Peninsular War and involvement in the War of the Two Brothers. In the latter, Coimbra sided with the liberal Pedro of Brazil, the victor, against his absolutist brother Miguel. There followed the suppression of all religious orders in Portugal, which drastically altered life as it had been on the banks of the Mondego. At the time of their suppression, the city had 33 monasteries, convents, and religious schools. Most became army installations.

The fame of its ancient university and its monuments draws hundreds of thousands of foreign and Portuguese visitors to Coimbra each year. Yet its aura of romance and beautiful buildings are not its only attractions. There are the bohemian student haunts, including the little *tascas* (eating houses) offering all kinds of snacks (from spareribs, ham omelettes, and grilled sardines to boiled pigs' feet). The picturesque, narrow streets in the Baixa, with laundry, bird cages, plants, and balconies hanging over them — and with picturesque names like Terreiro da Erva (Herb Square) and Rua dos Gatos (Street of the Cats) — are fun to explore. Strollers with time to browse may come upon a curio or antiques shop in a cul-de-sac or a little alleyway, or an old workshop where they still make, in the traditional way, the famous guitars — roundish in shape and light in sound — that typify the city. Better yet, those seeking to be at one with the spirit of the place will track down a Coimbra guitar in use, in the hands of a very soulful singer of *fado*.

COIMBRA AT-A-GLANCE

SEEING THE CITY: From the hilltop above the Vale do Inferno (Valley of Hell), off the highway leading into Coimbra from Lisbon — turn left at the Miradouro Vale do Inferno sign about 2½ miles (4 km) before town — there is a panorama of Coimbra with its old churches and university buildings clustered around the Alta hill, modern buildings and green gardens sloping down to the river, and, as a distant backdrop, the peaks of the Serra da Lousã and the pine forests of Buçaco. In town, the patio of the Old University affords an impressive view of the city's rooftops, old buildings, and narrow streets leading down to the river. All of the countryside surrounding the city can be seen from Penedo da Saudade (Place of Nostalgia), a high rocky cliff southeast of the center (take bus No. 3 from the tourist office). An isolated and romantic vantage point at the beginning of the century, it was a favorite haunt of students and poets, who carved verses on its stones. The place is still a nice garden with a view, but it is somewhat spoiled by encroaching modern construction.

SPECIAL PLACES: Coimbra is effectively divided into three districts. The Alta (Upper Town) is the university quarter, as well as the original site of the Iron Age settlement and of the castles and forts of the Romans, Moors, and Portuguese kings. The Baixa (Lower Town) is the part of the city that grew up by the river. Full of narrow streets and crowded with shops, banks, churches, cafés, and hotels, it is shaped roughly like a wedge, with the river on one side, Rua Ferreira Borges, Rua Visconde da Luz, and Rua da Sofia on the other, and Largo da Portagem at its point. Avenida Fernão de Magalhães is its main thoroughfare. The third district is the west bank of the Mondego, or the Santa Clara area, just across the Ponte de Santa Clara. Here, among other things, are the remains of an old convent associated with the saintly Queen Isabel and a newer one built as a replacement after it began to give way to Mondego floodwaters. The Santa Clara Bridge itself is not the first one to cross the Mondego. Parts of an 11th-century stone bridge can be seen from the present one when the water is low. It was torn down when the river silted up and caused the water level to rise too high for boats to pass under it.

The best way to see the sights is to take a taxi to the highest point of the Alta — the Old University — and walk down through its narrow streets, guided by one of the excellent maps available at the tourist office. To visit places beyond the Alta or the Baixa, it is necessary to use a car, taxi, or bus.

ALTA

Universidade Velha (Old University) – The entrance to the university is through the Porta Férrea (Iron Gate), a 17th-century triumphal arch surmounted by statues of King Dinis, who founded the university — originally in Lisbon — during the 13th century, and King João III, who during the 16th century donated his royal palace to house it. Inside the gate is the enormous University Patio, with a large statue of João III, looking very much like England's Henry VIII. (There is a large statue of King Dinis outside the university entrance in Praça Dom Dinis.) Beside the gate, to the left when entering, is a long, low palace wing that once contained suites for the princes and later served as the Colégio de São Pedro. Now serving as university offices, it has a beautifully carved 18th-century baroque door in its façade.

The baroque Biblioteca Joannina (Joanine Library), the university's — and the town's — pièce de résistance, is in the far left-hand corner of the patio. Its three halls dazzlingly decorated with carved and gilded wood, its precious rosewood and jacaranda tables, and the trompe l'oeil ceilings (to create an illusion of space) qualify it as one of the most beautiful libraries in the world (although the books are not well preserved). A portrait of King João V, who had the library built between 1717 and 1728, hangs at the back. Next to the library, facing the Porta Férrea entrance, is the Capela de São Miguel, the university chapel, with an ornate 16th-century Manueline doorway. The sumptuous interior contains an intricately carved 18th-century baroque organ decorated with gilt panels and Chinese lacquerwork, a Mannerist main altar, rococo altars in the side chapels, and walls covered with beautiful 18th-century tiles. Installed in an annex to the chapel is the *Museum of Sacred Art,* with gold and silver pieces, furniture, vestments, paintings, and sculpture.

The university's 18th-century clock tower stands in the right-hand corner of the patio, dominating the Coimbra skyline. Next to it, on the patio's right side, is the main part of the Manueline palace donated by King João III. An exterior double staircase in stone leads to a colonnade known as the Via Latina (Latin Way), because all who walked there in the Middle Ages, when the university was at its zenith, spoke Latin. From it, another staircase leads to passageways that look down on the Sala dos Capelos (Salon of Cardinals' Hats), which was, and still is, used for the awarding of degrees — it derives its name from the fact that those who presided at such ceremonies in the past were usually cardinals. Portraits of the Kings of Portugal and 17th-century carpet tiles (rectangular panels of tiles that resemble upright rugs) adorn its walls, which rise to a notable 17th-century paneled ceiling. To the right of the Sala dos Capelos is the Sala das Armas (Arms Room), where old arms and standards used in the ceremonies are on display; to the left is a long portico, from which there is a breathtaking view of the Old Cathedral, the Baixa, and the river. Downstairs again, a door at the end of the Via Latina opens to the Gerais, the cloister around which the old lecture rooms were located. The *Museum of Sacred Art* is open from 10 AM to 12:30 PM and from 2 to 5 PM; closed Mondays. The rest of the university opens daily at 9:30 AM. Admission charge to the museum. Praça Dom Dinis (phone: 35410 or 26088).

Aqueduto de São Sebastião (Aqueduct of St. Sebastian) – Though built during the 16th century to bring water to the Alta, it probably stands on the site of a more ancient Roman aqueduct. It originally had 20 arches, but part of it was torn down to make way for the New University. The main arch is topped with images of São Roque and King Sebastião, during whose reign it was built. Arcos do Jardim.

Jardim Botânico (Botanical Garden) – These pleasant gardens next to the aqueduct were begun by Prime Minister Marquês de Pombal during the late 18th century, and work on them continued into this century. Laid out on terraces and divided by tree-lined promenades and staircases, they contain trees and plants from all over the world. The terraces lead down to a large square with a lovely fountain; at the top, near the aqueduct, is an interesting fence of intricate 19th-century ironwork.

Museu Nacional de Machado de Castro (Machado de Castro National Museum) – Named after a major Portuguese sculptor of the 18th century, this is one of the most important museums in the country. It not only contains Portugal's finest collection of sculpture and gold and silver work, but it's housed in the former Paço Episcopal, or Bishop's Palace, which is itself a work of art. Lived in by the Bishops of Coimbra from the 12th century until 1910, when it was transformed into a museum, it is constructed around a large courtyard, with a double-arched verandah on one side facing a good view of the river, the houses of the Alta, and the dome of the Old Cathedral. Underneath it all, forming the foundation of the palace and part of the museum, is the cryptoportico — a series of vaulted underground passages and galleries built by the Romans beneath their forum, probably to serve as storerooms. One of the most interesting constructions of its kind in existence, it holds the museum's collection of Roman sculpture, inscriptions, and other objects found on the spot.

Later sculpture in the collection ranges from 14th-century works from the atelier of Master Pero (who also carved the tomb of Queen Isabel in the New Santa Clara Convent) to 16th-century Renaissance art by Jean de Rouen and his followers of the Coimbra school (including an entire chapel by Jean de Rouen and a *Last Supper* by Philippe Houdart), as well as baroque works by Cipriano da Cruz and Claude Laprade. The museum's gold and silver objects, collected from the cathedral's treasury and other churches, cover all periods from the 12th century to the 19th, including articles that belonged to the saintly Queen Isabel. Flemish and Portuguese paintings of the 16th and 17th centuries (Josefa de Obidos, a famous female painter of the 17th century, is represented), Oriental and Portuguese carpets, furniture, and a vast collection of faïence from the 16th century to the 19th are also on display. Open from 10 AM to 12:30 PM and from 2 to 4:30 PM; closed Mondays. Admission charge. Largo Dr. José Rodrigues (phone: 23727).

São João de Almedina – This church adjoining the museum once served as a chapel for the bishops. Founded during the 12th century, it was reconstructed during the late 17th and early 18th centuries. Its doorway came from an old west bank convent (Sant'Ana) that was virtually swallowed up by the river. Largo Dr. José Rodrigues.

Sé Nova (New Cathedral) – Begun by the Jesuits during the late 16th century and finished during the mid-17th century, this church became Coimbra's cathedral only after the Jesuits were expelled a century later. It is a severe building, both inside and out, yet a forerunner of the baroque style — note that the façade becomes livelier as it ascends, and the top part, finished last, is rococo. Most impressive inside are the intricately carved and gilded baroque main altarpiece and the choir stalls and baptismal font brought from the Old Cathedral. Also of note are the neo-classical organs and the 17th-century altarpiece in the side chapels. Largo da Feira.

Sé Velha (Old Cathedral) – Looking much like a fortress, festooned with merlons, this is considered the finest Romanesque church in Portugal. Its architects were French — Master Builder Robert and Master Builder Bernard — and its first stone was laid in the 12th century, during the reign of Afonso Henriques, Portugal's first king. The building has been modified since, particularly during the 16th century, and was totally restored during the 19th century. The portal in the west façade, decorated with columns, and the gigantic matching window above show signs of Islamic influence, while the north façade's main portal was, when added in 1530, one of the first signs of the Renaissance in Portugal. One of the most important works of Jean de Rouen, it has a carved medallion of the Virgin and Child over it.

Inside, the cathedral is dominated by the gilded wood altarpiece at the high altar, a,beautiful example of Flemish Gothic executed between 1498 and 1508 by the Flemish sculptors Oliver of Ghent and Jean of Ypres. To the right is the spectacular Capela do Sacramento (Chapel of the Sacrament), by Jean de Rouen. His beautifully sculpted life-size figures of Christ with the Apostles, Evangelists, and the Virgin are so filled with personality that they appear almost human. To the left is the Capela do São Pedro, with a retable showing a scene (*Quo Vadis*) attributed to Nicolas Chanterene. The cathedral also contains the tombs of medieval bishops and a Byzantine princess and, via stairs on the south side, a notable Gothic cloister, added during the 13th century. Open from 9 AM to 12:30 PM and from 2 to 5 PM; closed Mondays. Admission charge to the cloister. Praça Sé Velha.

Torre de Anto (Anto Tower) – This 9th-century tower in the city wall was once the home of the famous 19th-century poet António Nobre. It now houses the nonprofit *Casa de Artesanato da Região de Coimbra* (Coimbra Region House of Handicrafts), displaying and selling a host of local products — ceramics, handwoven rugs, basket-work, wrought-iron objects, woodcarvings, hand embroideries, and starched laces. Open Mondays through Fridays, from 9 AM to 12:30 PM and from 2 to 5:30 PM. 45 Rua de Sobre-Ripas (phone: 36592).

Palácio de Sub-Ripas (Sub-Ripas Palace) – Some of the city wall is incorporated into the lower part of this palace, which dates from the 16th century. It has a Manueline door and windows and walls covered with bas-reliefs and busts by Jean de Rouen of mythical and biblical figures, noblemen and ladies. Rua de Sub-Ripas.

Casa da Nau (Ship House) – This house in the shape of a ship, built at the time of Portugal's New World discoveries, is now a students' *república*. Rua Joaquim António de Aguiar.

Arco de Almedina (Almedina Arch) – The Moors built a wall around Coimbra, and this is the only survivor of its three gates (*medina* is Arabic for "city"). It is still the Alta's main entrance and exit, just down the fittingly named "step street," the Escadas de Quebra-Costas (Back Breaker Stairs), so called because of its nearly perpendicular incline.

BAIXA

Praça 8 de Maio (8th of May Square) – At the southern end of Rua da Sofia, the square is named for the date Coimbra was liberated from the absolutist forces of Dom Miguel during the War of the Two Brothers. The eight streets of the Baixa meet in the square, which is lined with well-preserved 17th- and 18th-century buildings. The Câmara Municipal (Town Hall), housed in a wing of the Mosteiro de Santa Cruz (Holy Cross Monastery), is also in the square, its façade adorned with Coimbra's coat of arms.

Igreja de Santa Cruz (Holy Cross Church) – This monastery church is one of the most important monuments in the country, not only because of its historical interest, but also because of the artistic merit of its carvings and tiles. The cornerstone was laid in 1131 under the patronage of Dom Afonso Henriques, Portugal's first king, who is buried here along with his son, Sancho I, Portugal's second king. The church was reconstructed during the 16th century, although traces of the original — by the Frenchman known as Master Builder Robert — can still be seen in the walls near the entrance to the present structure. The Manueline façade that was imposed on the medieval one incorporates statues of the Apostles and churchmen by Nicolas Chanterene and of the Virgin, Isaac, and David by Jean de Rouen.

Inside, the church has a starred dome in its enormous, vaulted ceiling and lovely 18th-century tiles lining the walls (those on the left illustrating the history of the Holy Cross, those on the right the life of Saint Augustine). The intricately carved stone pulpit, in a transitional, Gothic-to-Renaissance style, is one of Chanterene's most important works, and he also sculpted the tombs of the two kings behind the main altar — Afonso Henriques on the left and Sancho on the right. The magnificent 17th-century sacristy, inspired by the architecture of the Vatican, is decorated with paintings by some of Portugal's most famous artists, including Grão Vasco. Beyond are the chapter house, with an interesting Manueline door and 16th-century tiles, and the adjoining 16th-century Manueline Claustro do Silêncio (Silent Cloister), with a lovely Renaissance fountain and bas-reliefs attributed to Chanterene around three of its four sides. Open daily from 9 AM to noon and from 2 to 5 PM. Admission charge to visit the royal tombs, sacristy, chapter house, and cloister, but not for the church itself. Praça 8 de Maio.

Jardim da Manga (Manga Garden) – The garden, behind Santa Cruz and once one of its cloisters, contains a unique Renaissance fountain. Its waters, symbolizing the rivers of Paradise or the word of God spreading to all corners of the world, flow out from a central temple with a pointed dome. (The gargoyles jutting out from the dome represent demons fleeing God's word.) The four chapels surrounding the temple were probably designed by Jean de Rouen, who sculpted the figures in their altarpieces. Rua Olimpio Nicolau Rui Fernandes.

Igreja do Carmo (Carmo Church) – Part of a theological college founded during the 16th century, this church has a single domed nave with a coffered ceiling, an enormous gilt altarpiece in typical Portuguese style, side chapels with rococo altarpieces, and an adjoining cloister paneled in rococo tiles. The college, one of several along a street whose name means Street of Learning, was at one time one of the most prestigious institutions in the city. Rua da Sofia.

Igreja da Graça (Graça Church) – Another church founded during the 16th century as part of a school, it has a sober, classical façade. Inside are a high altar in mannerist style, with carved, gilt frames surrounding panels depicting the life of the Virgin, and side chapels with rococo altarpieces and interesting 17th-century tiles in carpet designs. The cloister is classic Renaissance. Rua da Sofia.

Praça do Comércio (Commerce Square) – Once known as Praça Velha (Old Square), this was the old marketplace where bullfights, *autos-da-fé,* and festivals were held. It is a large rectangle surrounded by shops and 17th- and 18th-century houses with lovely windows. There is a church at each end of the square and, in the center, a reconstructed pillory.

Igreja de São Tiago (St. James's Church) – People condemned to death by the Inquisition were buried in the cemetery of this early-13th-century church, which has two interesting portals with ornamental molding and intricately carved columns and capitals. The façade was restored during this century. Praça do Comércio.

Igreja de São Bartolomeu (St. Bartholomew's Church) – Probably the oldest church in Coimbra, dating from the 10th century — although the present building was put up during the 18th century; the original church was destroyed by a Moorish invasion, reconstructed during the 12th century, then torn down 6 centuries later to make way for a new one. Archaeological remains can be seen in the floor. The main altar is typical Coimbra rococo. Praça do Comércio.

Largo da Portagem – The large, busy square by the river, in front of the Santa Clara Bridge, is home to the tourist office. The statue is of Joaquim António de Aguiar, a 19th-century statesman born in Coimbra and known as the Mata Frades (Friar Killer), because he signed the proclamation expelling all religious orders from Portugal.

Parque Dr. Manuel Braga – This park is south of Largo da Portagem, with the river running along one side of it and Avenida Emídio Navarro along the other. Besides the gardens, laid out in patterns resembling the emblem and coats of arms of Coimbra, it has a bandstand in ornate ironwork and, at one end, the *Museum of Urban Transport* (open Mondays through Fridays, 9 AM to 12:30 PM and from 1 to 5 PM; admission charge), containing a large collection of old streetcars.

O Choupal – By the river at the north end of Coimbra, O Choupal was originally a grove of poplar trees (the translation of its name) planted to protect the riverbanks from floods. Most of the poplars have been cut down, but they've been replaced by eucalyptus, acacia, and other trees — as well as joggers. The park is more than a mile long and occupies the junction of the old and new courses of the Mondego — two have existed since a plan to control floods was put into practice at the end of the 18th century. Inlets of the river cross it, spanned by wooden bridges. At one time, the Choupal was a place for romance, meditation, and serenades, and though less idyllic today, it is still a pleasant place for walking.

SANTA CLARA AREA

Convento de Santa Clara-a-Velha (Old Santa Clara Convent) – A convent for Clarissa nuns once stood here, but all that remains is a church — and not all of it, since the structure is partially buried in silt. When the convent was completed in 1330, floods from the Mondego were already threatening it, and by the 15th century, water had reached the doors. Finally, in 1677, the nuns moved out to their new convent, Santa Clara-a-Nova, on a nearby hill. Both Queen Isabel, the Rainha Santa (Saintly Queen), who spent the last years of her life here, and Inês de Castro, who was murdered nearby, were buried at the convent before their bodies were moved elsewhere, the former to Santa Clara-a-Nova and the latter to the Monastery of Alcobaça, near Nazaré. The old church is a fine example of Gothic architecture, with three very fine rose windows. Rua de Baixo.

Portugal dos Pequenitos (Children's Portugal) – Interesting for adults, too, this is a wooded park containing reproductions of Portuguese houses from all provinces, of all of Coimbra's monuments, and of the principal monuments found throughout the country and its once far-reaching empire (Goa, Macao, Mozambique, Angola, and Guinea-Bissau). They're built on a small scale for children, most of them about 13 feet tall. Open daily, from 9 AM to 7 PM from April through September (to 5:30 PM in winter). Admission charge. Rua António Augusto Gonçalves (phone: 441225).

Convento de Santa Clara-a-Nova (New Santa Clara Convent) – This hillside convent was built during the 17th century — although the cloisters and other buildings were not finished until the 18th century — to keep the Clarissa nuns high and dry as their old convent began to succumb to the continuous flooding of the Mondego. The installation has been likened to a barracks, and in fact, since religious orders were suppressed during the 19th century, most of the convent buildings have been occupied by the army. Only the church and cloister can be visited. The church has a domed, coffered ceiling, sides decorated with ornate false chapels (serving as enormous, intricately carved and gilded frames for portraits), and a sumptuous domed altar flanked with gilded pillars. The remains of St. Isabel lie in the 17th-century silver and crystal urn behind the altar, which is also adorned with a statue of the saint and a bas-relief depicting scenes from her life. The most impressive sight in the church, however, is the magnificent 14th-century tomb, carved from a single block of Ançã stone, that the Saintly Queen had made for herself and in which she was originally buried. Located in the *coro baixo* (lower choir), it rests on six stone lions; pink, gold, and green carved statuettes of saints, Franciscans, Clarissa nuns, and other figures occupy niches on its sides; and on top is a reclining statue of the queen dressed in a nun's habit, complete with a pilgrim's staff and an alms bag such as those used by the pious on a pilgrimage to Santiago de Compostela. The actual pilgrim's staff that belonged to the queen can be seen in the *coro alto* (raised choir), which is a museum of religious objects and silver; the cloister, dating from the 18th century, is impressive for its size and massive architecture. Open from 9 AM to 12:30 PM and from 2 to 5 PM; closed Mondays. Admission charge. Calçada de Santa Isabel.

Quinta das Lágrimas (Estate of Tears) – A 19th-century *palacete* (little palace) stands on the site where Prince Dom Pedro and his beautiful mistress, Dona Inês de Castro, lived and where their tragic love ended in her murder. In the gardens at the back of the estate a spring gushes from the rocks into a wide pool. Local legend holds that the spring's waters are Dona Inês's tears and that the red spots on the plants growing there are her blood, the yellow ferns her hair. Verses by Luís de Camões, who immortalized the love of the unfortunate pair in *The Lusiads,* are carved in stone by the spring in this melancholy and haunted place, where even the tall cedars and their large, entwined roots appear ominous. Although the estate is privately owned, the gardens are open to the public daily (tip the caretaker). Off Estrada das Lages.

ELSEWHERE

Parque de Santa Cruz – An 18th-century archway off Praça da República (a gathering place for students, especially in the evening) is the entrance to this park. Beyond are fountains, pools, luxuriant vegetation, and paths lined with fragrant bay trees from Goa. An ornate portico with towers on both sides leads to a game area where, during the 17th and 18th centuries, girls played a ball game called *jogo de pela.* Also notable is the fountain, bedecked with statues of Triton and mermaids, at the top of a tall staircase that has pools and tile-backed stone benches on the landings. The park also has a large lake with a small island in its center and a terrace where drinks are served.

Mosteiro de Celas (Celas Monastery) – Founded in 1215 by King Sancho I's daughter, the nunnery was greatly modified later, particularly between the 16th and 18th centuries, and when the last nun died during the late 19th century, it was virtually abandoned. Today, only the church and cloister remain. Inside, the dark oak 16th-century choir stalls and Nicolas Chanterene's cloister door are noteworthy, and the cloister itself is of particular interest: Each of the 13th- and 14th-century capitals on the double pillars supporting the arches is carved with a different story from the lives of Christ and the saints. Largo de Celas (ring the bell at No. 23 for the caretaker).

Igreja de Santo António dos Olivais (Church of St. Anthony of the Olive Grove) – This is the only remnant of a Franciscan monastery that was founded during the 13th century and burned down 600 years later. Its name comes from St. Anthony of Padua, who taught here before going to Italy. Standing on the highest hill above Coimbra, the church, remodeled during the 18th century, is a typical sanctuary reached by a long flight of stairs flanked by chapels and representations of scenes from the Passion of Christ. The interior, covered with tile panels depicting the life of the saint, contains altarpieces from the 18th-century baroque Joanine period, as well as a sacristy richly decorated in gold leaf and finished with a painted, festooned ceiling. In the square at the bottom of the stairs is a small 16th-century chapel containing a Christ on the cross by Jean de Rouen. Rua Brigadeiro Correia Cardoso.

SOURCES AND RESOURCES

TOURIST INFORMATION: The Coimbra Tourist Office (Largo da Portagem, the main square in front of the Santa Clara Bridge; phone: 23886 or 25576) is open weekdays from 9 AM to 7 PM and on Saturdays and Sundays from 9 AM to 12:30 PM and 2 to 6 PM. Attendants offer advice and assistance in English as well as other languages and hand out excellent folders and maps in several languages. They will also make hotel, train, and bus reservations. Multilingual guides are available for about $50 for a half day of sightseeing, about $80 for a full day.

Local Coverage – The local daily newspaper is the *Diário de Coimbra,* published on Sundays as *Domingo.* The *Jornal do Coimbra* is a weekly. The *International Herald Tribune,* along with some of the British dailies and English-language news magazines, is available at newsstands in the better hotels. The newsstand near the *Tivoli* movie theater (Avenida Emídio Navarro) is another source of English-language newspapers.

TELEPHONE: The city code for Coimbra is 39. If calling from within Portugal, dial 039 before the local number.

GETTING AROUND: Coimbra is best seen on foot or by public transportation. Travel by car is difficult because of the narrow streets, horrendous traffic jams during rush hours, and limited parking space.

Airport – The very small local airport (phone: 94214) is in Cernache, 5 miles (8 km) southwest of town via the main highway to Lisbon. At present, no regularly scheduled flights land here.

Bicycle – The *Centro Velocipedico de Sangalhos* (23 Rua da Sota; phone: 24646) rents them, but travel by bicycle on Coimbra's crowded streets is not advisable.

Bus – Getting around by bus is fast and easy. There are no general maps of the routes, but each bus stop has a map. Among the most useful for tourists are bus No. 1, which goes to the Old University and the *Machado de Castro National Museum;* No. 3, to the Botanical Garden and Penedo da Saudade; No. 6, which goes over the river to the Santa Clara area, with the old and new Santa Clara convents and Portugal dos Pequenitos (from the latter, it is necessary to transfer to another bus to reach Quinta das Lágrimas); and No. 7, to Santa Cruz Park, the Celas Monastery, and the Santo António dos Olivais church. All leave from Largo da Portagem. Tourist passes allowing unlimited travel for 4 days or a week are available. The main bus station for long-distance buses is on Avenida Fernão de Magalhães (phone: 27081).

Car Rental – Six major companies operate here: *Hertz* (133 Avenida Fernão de Magalhães and 221 Avenida Fernão de Magalhães; phone: 37491); *Avis* (in the Coimbra A train station, Largo das Ameias; phone: 34786); *InterRent* (306 Avenida Fernão de Magalhães; phone: 33460); *Beira Centro* (in the *Oslo Hotel,* 23-25 Avenida Fernão de Magalhães; phone: 23664); *Hervis* (94 Rua João Machado; phone: 24062 or 33489); and *Auto Turistica Central de Coimbra* (23 Rua Dr. Manuel Rodrigues; phone: 29815).

Taxi – Coimbra's black-and-green taxis are metered and pick up riders anywhere. To call one, dial 28045. Rides are inexpensive; one from the tourist office to the Santa Clara area or the Santo António dos Olivais church, for instance, should cost less than $3.

Train – There are two railway stations: Coimbra A (phone: 34998), at Largo das Ameias, beside the *Bragança* hotel, and Coimbra B (phone: 24632), beyond Choupal Park at the junction of the Porto and Figueira da Foz highways. Regional trains to Figueira da Foz and Aveiro on the coast and to Luso and other towns in the mountains leave from the A station. Through trains to Lisbon, Aveiro, and Porto leave from the B station. A special fast train — the *Alpha* — connects Coimbra B with Lisbon (2½ hours), Aveiro, and Porto. Advance reservations are required.

SPECIAL EVENTS: The *Queima das Fitas* (Burning of the Ribbons) is a collective student letting-off-of-steam that goes on for a week at the end of the term in May and culminates when the 4th-year students burn their class ribbons in chamber pots and put on the wider ones of senior class members. (There is a 5th year of university study in Portugal.) The celebration begins at midnight on a Thursday with a serenade of *fado* and guitar music on the steps of the Old Cathedral. Each day thereafter is dedicated to a different faculty and a different class and ends with a musical evening by the riverside. There are balls, theatrical and sports events, and car races, plus a mock bullfight in Figueira da Foz on Sunday. The most colorful day, however, is Tuesday, when the actual burning of the ribbons takes place and the 4th-year students parade through the streets on top of flower-adorned cars. They are followed by freshmen with painted faces and funny clothes, 2nd-year students in black suits and gowns, and upperclassmen in top hats. Coimbra is very crowded, so anyone planning a visit at this time (the exact week varies according to the school calendar) should make hotel reservations far in advance.

Coimbra's other big event, the *Festa da Rainha Santa* (Feast of the Saintly Queen), commemorates the beatification of the saintly Queen Isabel in 1516 and takes place at the beginning of July of even-numbered years only. On a Thursday night, the statue of the saint from the altar of Santa Clara-a-Nova is carried to Largo da Portagem by a procession of penitents; all lights in the city are turned off when it arrives, the better to see the spectacular fireworks display over the river. Another procession returns the statue to the church on Sunday afternoon.

MUSEUMS: In addition to those mentioned in *Special Places,* museums of interest include the following:

Bissaya Barreto House Museum – Beautiful furniture and porcelain in a house once owned by the man who built Portugal dos Pequenitos. Open from 3 to 5 PM; closed Mondays and holidays. Admission charge. Arcos do Jardim (phone: 22468).

Museu Militar (Military Museum) – Weapons, uniforms, and photographs from military actions after 1850, housed in a wing of the New Santa Clara Convent. Open daily from 10 AM to noon and from 2 to 5 PM. Admission charge. Convento de Santa-Clara-a-Nova, Calçada de Santa Isabel (phone: 813959).

Museu Nacional da Ciencia e da Técnica (Science and Technology Museum) – One part is dedicated to the life and works of Madame Curie and another to Leonardo da Vinci. Open from 10 AM to noon and from 2 to 5 PM; closed Saturdays and Sundays. Admission charge. 23 Rua dos Coutinhos (phone: 24922).

SHOPPING: Coimbra has beautiful handicrafts, examples of which are exhibited and sold in the *Casa de Artesanato da Região de Coimbra* in the historic Torre de Anto (45 Rua de Sobre-Ripas; phone: 23886). Coimbra faïence, made as far back as the 12th century and revived during the 17th and 18th centuries, is being produced once again by several factories. The lovely, hand-painted pieces available in local shops run the gamut of local styles — multicolored Hispano-Arabic designs of the 15th century, Oriental designs of the 16th century, Delft-inspired blue and white designs of the 17th century, and pastel flora and fauna designs of the 18th century. Hand-embroidered bedspreads and tablecloths and wool and linen blankets are also worth buying, as are examples of traditional Coimbra wrought-iron work, artistic tinware, and basketry, still made in the same way they have been for hundreds of years. The tourist office can help to arrange visits to artisans in nearby villages for those with more than a passing interest in the local handiwork. Shops also carry some fine leather goods, footwear, stylish ready-made clothing, and jewelry. Rua Ferreira Borges, which leads north from Largo da Portagem, and Rua Visconde da Luz, its continuation, are the main shopping streets. Stores are open weekdays, from 9 AM to 1 PM and from 3 to 7 PM, and on Saturdays from 9 AM to 1 PM, while shopping centers are open daily from 10 AM to midnight. A big open-air market, selling everything from fish to video equipment, takes place daily from 6 AM to 2 PM at the end of Avenida Sá da Bandeira, near the Jardim da Manga.

Agata Joalharia – Fine jewelry, beautifully mounted at reasonable prices. 2 Escadas de São Tiago (phone: 22361).

Casa das Luvas Camisaria – Elegant fashions for men, one of the best in town. 112 Rua Ferreira Borges (phone: 24369).

Charles – A large selection of Portuguese-made, fashionable shoes for men and women. 113 Rua Ferreira Borges (phone: 23264).

Crislex – Home decorations, porcelain, and good crystal. 187 Rua Ferreira Borges (phone: 26801).

Loja das Artes Manuais – A good selection of all regional handicrafts. 1-9 Rua Fernandes Tomás (phone: 33136).

Jorge Mendes – Some of the finest copies of 15th- to 17th-century porcelains and ceramics in Coimbra; artisans can be seen making them in the workshop. 9 Praça do Comércio (phone: 25646).

A Nova Paris – Men's and women's fashions. 9 Rua Visconde da Luz (phone: 23642).

Patrão Joalheiros – One of the oldest and most respected jewelers in Coimbra, offering lovely Portuguese filigree, silver salvers, and silver tea and coffee services. 104 Rua Visconde da Luz (phone: 23096).

Renasçença – A big, upscale shop selling fashionable shoes and other leather goods. 104 Rua Visconde da Luz (phone: 35050).

Sociedade de Ceramica Antiga de Coimbra – A factory making (and selling) reproductions of old Portuguese ceramics, and the only one producing the special, pale flora and fauna designs typical of the 18th century. Open to visitors on weekdays. 2 Quintal do Prior (phone: 23829).

Ultimo Figurino – Ready-made clothing in classic styles. 50 Rua Ferreira Borges (phone: 23489).

 SPORTS AND FITNESS: Boating – Always a popular pastime on the Mondego. Pedal boats and kayaks can be rented in the Choupalinho park just across the Santa Clara Bridge. A kayak costs about $18 for a whole day including lunch and van transport 10 miles (16 km) up the river to Penacova, from which the person renting the kayak paddles it back down to Coimbra. Also for rent are *barcas serranas* — old wooden riverboats that were originally used for transporting goods down to the sea. Poled by a man standing in the prow, they hold four to six people and are available for 15 minutes, 30 minutes, or an hour.

Swimming – The municipal swimming pool is on Rua Dom Manuel, next to the *Estadio Municipal.*

 MUSIC: Coimbra's music is the *fado* — haunting, sweet ballads sung to the accompaniment of Coimbra guitars. Unlike Lisbon *fado,* which is sung by men and women, *fado de Coimbra* is sung by men only, and by students, lawyers, doctors, and others, rather than by professional entertainers. Coimbra *fado* grew out of the student custom of singing in the streets at night and serenading Coimbra girls; its themes range from unrequited love and homesickness to the city, the river, the university, and social issues. Some songs have become classics, among them the *Balada da Despedida* ("Farewell Ballad"), sung at graduation by medical students, and the *Balada de Coimbra* ("Coimbra Ballad"), which closes all serenades, including the beautiful and impressive midnight *serenata* on the steps of the Old Cathedral at the opening of the *Queima das Fitas* celebrations. Although Coimbra *fado* is normally sung only at such special celebrations or for private entertainment, it is possible to hear it in two places in the city. One is the *Diligência,* a very small, characteristic bar (on the narrow Rua Nova, off Rua da Sofia; phone: 27667), where the singing is spontaneous and often catch-as-catch-can. The other is the *Trovador* restaurant (Praça Sé Velha; phone: 25475), which presents *fado* on weekends and is somewhat touristy.

NIGHTCLUBS AND NIGHTLIFE: Neither very lively nor sophisticated, nightlife here tends to center around student activities or nights out with the whole family. There are, however, a number of pubs and discotheques for dancing. The biggest and best dance spot, open only Thursdays, Fridays, and Saturdays, is *Broadway* (in suburban Pedrulha, about 2 miles/3 km north of town; phone: 36330). It's not much to look at, but it has its own orchestra that plays typical dance music — foxtrot and Sinatra oldies — from 10 PM to midnight; after midnight, the loud disco music takes over. Three others, all closed Sundays, are *Scotch* (Quinta da Insua; phone: 813136), just across the Santa Clara Bridge in a nice old house, with a quiet bar, apart from the disco; *States* (Praça Machado Assis; phone: 27067), decorated in red, white, and blue with stars and catering to young people with lots of loud music; and *Coimbra B* (Monte Formoso; phone: 28919), small, but with two separate floors, a bar, and lots of flashing lights.

Quebra Costas (Escadas de Quebra-Costas; phone: 34724) is a small bar on the stairs in front of Praça Sé Velha; in summer, devotees stand on the stairs with their drinks, some with their guitars. *Sacristia* (phone: 24804), at the top of the stairs, is another small bar; it has live music at times, but people mostly just stand around and talk..Other pubs and bars include *Romisch,* a piano bar (102 Rua dos Combatentes; phone: 721721); *Briosa* (Rua Venancio Rodrigues; phone: 25663), decorated to look like an English pub; and *Café Forte Video Bar* (2nd Floor, 1 Avenida Lousã; phone: 721855), a modern bar whose forte is showing videos. Two more to try are *ETC* (51 Avenida Afonso Henriques; phone: 26933) and *Riverside* (Avenida João das Regras; phone: 811233).

BEST IN TOWN

CHECKING IN: Coimbra suffers from a definite dearth of good hotels, although several new hostelries are being built. Those that exist tend to be very old or purely functional. Most are right downtown, which makes them convenient for sightseeing, but noisy. A number of clean, comfortable pensions supplement the pickings. Expect to pay $60 to $80 for a double room with breakfast in a hotel listed as expensive, from $40 to $60 in the moderate category, and under $40 in an inexpensive place. Reservations for rooms during July and August, or during the *Queima das Fitas* celebrations in May, should be made at least a month in advance. All telephone numbers are in the 39 city code unless otherwise indicated.

Astoria – Built in the 1920s, in the style of that period: cupolas, arches, pillars, and wrought-iron balconies. The 64 rooms have baths and telephones; there is a television salon, a bar, and a restaurant serving typical regional dishes. The hotel is shaped like a triangle to fit between two streets that converge at Largo da Portagem, and is consequently a bit noisy (as well as a bit shabby now). 21 Avenida Emídio Navarro (phone: 22055). Expensive.

Dom Luís – Opened in 1988, it's on an high hill by the highway to Lisbon, across the river from Coimbra and a little over a mile (2 km) from the center of town. All of the 105 rooms and suites have private baths, telephones, mini-bars, and TV sets. A panoramic restaurant (food and service are good) and solarium with terrace on the roof, plus plenty of parking space, help to justify the distance. Banhos Secos (phone: 841510 or 813196). Expensive.

Bragança – Unpretentious and modern, it's on a busy street by the Coimbra A train station and the river. The 83 rooms, all with bath, are simple and functional. A bar, television room, private parking lot, and large restaurant serving Portuguese and French food are among the facilities. 10 Largo das Ameias (phone: 22171). Moderate.

Oslo – This simple, small place (30 rooms) on a busy street in the center of town, not far from the Coimbra A train station, has an upstairs bar and restaurant with a good view. 23-25 Avenida Fernão de Magalhães (phone: 29073). Moderate.

Almedina – A downtown *pensão* with 28 rooms, all with private baths. 203 Avenida Fernão de Magalhães (phone: 29161). Inexpensive.

Parque – An excellent *pensão* on the main avenue by Parque Dr. Manuel Braga, near the tourist office and the river. The 15 rooms are large and well furnished, but not all have private baths. Second Floor, 42 Avenida Emídio Navarro (phone: 29202). Inexpensive.

Among the local participants in Portugal's *Tourism in the Country* program — privately owned homes, even palaces, that take in paying guests (see *Accommodations,* GETTING READY TO GO) — is the *Casa dos Quintais,* a member of *Turismo Rural* set on a hill overlooking Coimbra about 4 miles (6 km) from downtown. The house, endowed with a swimming pool, has 3 double bedrooms with bath for rent and should be considered in the moderate category. To reach it, take the Lisbon highway south and turn left onto N110-2 toward the town of Assafarge. Contact *Casa dos Quintais,* Carvalhais de Cima, Assafarge, Coimbra 3000 (phone: 438305).

 EATING OUT: The food in Coimbra's better restaurants is imaginative and delicious, if a bit heavy for some tastes. Some typical dishes include *chanfana,* kid braised in wine; *lampreia à moda de Coimbra,* lamprey (eel) Coimbra-style; *leitão assado,* roast suckling pig; and the very special *boucho* — ox stomach stuffed with meats, sausages, and herbs and then roasted. Restaurants serving international cooking are also easy to find, as are many snack bars. Meals go down best with the fine, fruity Bairrada wines that have been made in the region since the 10th century. They tend to be somewhat tannic when very young, so it's best to drink them aged (1980 was a good year). Some names to look for are Frei João, Caves Aliança, Souselas, Porta Férrea, Angelus, and Fundação. Sweets made from old convent recipes are something else to try, though not only in Coimbra. As elsewhere in Portugal, when religious orders were suppressed during the 19th century, the nuns turned to baking in order to support themselves, and many of the confections still eaten today take their names from their convent of origin, such as *pastel de Santa Clara,* made of sugar, eggs, and almonds. Some other favorites are *arrufadas,* arc-shaped puff cakes, and *chilas,* made of squash. Expect to pay $30 and up for a meal for two with wine and coffee at a restaurant listed as expensive, from $20 to $30 in a moderate one, and less than that at an inexpensive one. Note that Coimbra's restaurants tend to be packed with families on Sundays. All telephone numbers are in the 39 city code unless otherwise indicated.

Dom Pedro – Decorated in classic Portuguese style, with interesting tiles on the walls and a fountain splashing in the middle of the room, this place serves well-prepared Portuguese and international dishes. Open daily. Reservations necessary. 58 Avenida Emídio Navarro (phone: 29108). Expensive.

Espelho d'Agua – An elegant, refined restaurant in a beautiful setting — it's in the middle of a garden, with a lovely, glass-enclosed terrace. Excellent Portuguese dinners are served — by candlelight in the evening. Open daily. Reservations necessary. Parque Dr. Manuel Braga (phone: 20634). Expensive.

Piscinas – Upstairs over the municipal swimming pool, but don't judge this place by its unprepossessing exterior. It has some of the best regional cooking in the city — the *chanfana* and *boucho* are delicious. Closed Mondays. Reservations essential on weekends. Piscinas Municipais, Rua Dom Manuel (phone: 717013). Expensive.

Trovador – Probably the best dining place in town (or at least the most expensive). The ambience is elegant, the service excellent, the food very good Portuguese and international fare. Near the Old Cathedral, so it's a good place to dine after sightseeing. Closed Mondays. Reservations essential. On weekends, there is *fado* music, and it's possible to drop in after 10 PM and listen to it over a drink. Praça Sé Velha (phone: 25475). Expensive.

O Alfredo – A typical Portuguese restaurant across the river, always full of people and noise. Good Portuguese food is served. Open daily. Reservations advised. 32 Avenida João das Regras (phone: 814669). Moderate.

Casa do Bacalhau – It serves codfish 20 different ways, quite a variety, even given the Portuguese penchant for codfish. The dining room is in typical regional style, with red-and-white checkered tablecloths and onions hanging from the ceiling. Open daily. Reservations advised. 43 Rua de Montarroio (phone: 233561). Moderate.

Crep's Grill Pierrot – Variety reigns here — pizza, plus French, American, and other Italian food. The decor is simple (pine furniture and blue sofas); there is a snack bar downstairs. Open daily. No reservations. 25 Praça da República (phone: 33569). Moderate.

Jardim da Manga – A self-service eatery, but its location allows diners to eat in a garden, since it is in the beautiful Jardim da Manga. Closed Saturdays. No reservations. Rua Olimpio Nicolau Rui Fernandes (phone: 29156). Moderate.

Joaquim dos Leitões – Another specialty spot, serving the typical roast suckling pig of the region. The dining room is also done up in regional style, its walls covered with tiles. Closed Saturday nights and Sundays. Reservations advised. 3 Rua do Arnado (phone: 33935). Moderate.

Lung-Wah – A wide variety of Chinese dishes served in Oriental-style surroundings. It's located in a hilltop area in the northern part of town. Open daily. Reservations advised. Monte Formoso (phone: 34443). Moderate.

Real das Canas – Under the same management as *Piscinas,* it's across the river in the Santa Clara area. The decor is simple, but the view of Coimbra from its windows is spectacular, and it serves good Portuguese food. Closed Wednesdays. Reservations advised. Vila Mendes, Santa Clara (phone: 814877). Moderate.

A Taberna – Very cozy, with a fireplace, it serves good Portuguese food in the main dining room and pizza in the restaurant downstairs. Closed Saturdays. Reservations advised. 86 Rua dos Combatentes (phone: 716265). Moderate.

O Verde Minho – In the eastern part of town, 10 minutes by car from the city center. Good Portuguese food and some special French dishes are served in a cozy atmosphere. Open daily. Reservations advised. Casal do Lobo (phone: 718163). Moderate.

A Pizzaria do Andre – Italian food, including pizza. Open daily. No reservations. 42 Travessa de Montarroio (phone: 36987). Inexpensive.

Ticino – Another plainly decorated place serving good Italian food. Open daily. No reservations. 120 Rua Bernardo de Albuquerque (phone: 718113). Inexpensive.

CÓRDOBA

The low-slung city of Córdoba sprawls along a sleepy, shallow stretch of the Guadalquivir River, 90 miles (143 km) upstream from Seville and 103 miles (165 km) northwest of Granada. For a traveler, it is the vital northern apex of the cultural, historical, and geographic triangle formed by the three great medieval Andalusian capitals, and of the three, it is Córdoba that best preserves its Moorish legacy. The city's incomparable treasure, the Mezquita or Great Mosque, is a forest of stone pillars and arches so vast that a full-blown cathedral, built by Christian conquerors who ripped out the heart of the mosque to accommodate it, seems lost in the shadowy aisles. Strange bedfellows, the mosque and cathedral are a fascinating expression of the amalgam of Moslem and Christian elements that is Spain.

The Mezquita, one of the greatest attractions in Spain, stands in the Judería, a quarter of the city where the pattern of narrow winding streets has not changed since Córdoba flourished as the capital of all Iberia under the rule of the opulent Umayyad caliphs, from the 8th to the 11th centuries. Judería, literally the Jewish district, is the name given to this intriguing Old Town, where Arabs and Jews once lived side by side. It still holds the former homes of two of the world's greatest thinkers, the Jewish philosopher-physician Maimonides and the Arab philosopher-mathematician AverroEs, a few blocks away from each other.

At the height of its splendor under the Arabs, who had wrested the territory from the Visigoths in 711, Córdoba was not merely the capital of all Iberia. It was also a city second in luxury and power only to glittering Constantinople. A pilgrimage to its Great Mosque is said to have equaled a journey to Mecca. Chroniclers of the day wrote of a city of half a million people, with 300,000 homes and palaces, 700 mosques, and hundreds of ritual baths. The same city that in Roman times had been home to Seneca the Elder and his son Lucius Annaeus Seneca, tutor of Nero, but which had declined under the Visigoths, became once again, under the Arabs, a center for scholars, scientists, and philosophers. It had the first university in Europe, a library with 400,000 hand-copied volumes, and legendary pleasure palaces. The silverwork and tooled leathers from its workshops were world famous. The tinseled silk veils produced for the caliph's wives were sheer enough to be drawn through the hoop of a silver earring.

The glory days of the Arabs in Córdoba lasted until 1031, when political infighting among the leaders led to the disintegration of the caliphate of Córdoba. Seville then became the capital of the Iberian Peninsula.

Today, Córdoba is a quiet provincial city of 290,000, its economy sustained by mining from the nearby *sierra* (mountains) and by agriculture from the surrounding *campiña* (plains). Conveniently compact, it has clearly defined old and new sections, which makes it an easy town to tour. Exploring its historic districts absorbs most of any visitor's time, but exploring its broad, tree-lined boulevards and up-to-date central core is a pleasant plus.

There are comfortable hotels, though too few of them, which leads too many visitors to make do with an afternoon stopover at the Mezquita on a trip between Seville and Madrid. Córdoba is worth a stay of at least 2 days, if only for the chance to drive out to the nearby excavations of the Medina Azahara, a country palace and royal city built by a 10th-century caliph. It takes time to browse Córdoba's famous flower-filled patios, to explore the Judería, to loll in Queen Isabella's gardens in the Alcázar, to watch the black-and-white cows grazing on the marshy river islands by the Roman Bridge. And those interested in Renaissance churches, palaces, and monuments will be occupied for several days. All the while, the romantic can fuel their dreams by sleeping and eating in centuries-old buildings that now serve as hotels and restaurants in the heart of the Judería. In Córdoba, if you so choose, you truly can live in the past.

CÓRDOBA AT-A-GLANCE

SEEING THE CITY: The bell tower of the Mezquita is the best place to take the measure of Córdoba. It's open every day, and though there's a fee to climb it in addition to the Mezquita's admission charge, it's worth it, especially because the tower affords a bird's-eye view of the Mezquita's roof with the cathedral rising out of it. Bordering the Mezquita to the north and northwest are the humble tile roofs of the Judería, enclosed on the west by restored Arab walls. The bridge near the foot of the Mezquita is the Puente Romano (Roman Bridge), leading over the Guadalquivir to the Torre de la Calahorra, a 14th-century fortress, and to working class suburbs on the south side of the river. Running west along the near riverbank are the golden walls and gardens of the Alcázar. They end near the Puente San Rafael, the city's main approach bridge, which feeds traffic into the major north-south avenues, Paseo de la Victoria and Avenida República Argentina. The big oblong green space enclosed by these two boulevards is the Jardines de la Victoria, a flower-filled park that holds the annual May fair. Farther north is the Plaza de las Tendillas, Córdoba's downtown hub; beyond, the residential El Brillante district rises gently toward the hills. North and east of the Mezquita are the beautiful Renaissance church towers, monasteries, and palaces that proliferated after the 13th-century Christian Reconquest, as well as 11 columns of an excavated Roman temple right beside the prizewinning modern white marble building that houses Córdoba's City Hall.

SPECIAL PLACES: Though its easygoing atmosphere is easy to love, Córdoba's casual attitude toward opening and closing times, especially for the less-visited attractions, can disrupt the best-made tourist plans. Be sure to check on hours and days of opening when you arrive, because they seem to change more frequently than in larger cities. Generally, summer hours are mornings from 9:30 or 10 AM to 1:30 or 2 PM and afternoons from between 4 and 6 PM to 7 or 8 PM. (Afternoon times begin earlier in winter.) Museums are closed on Sunday afternoons and Mondays. Because of the city's compact layout, all the sights below, except the Medina Azahara and others situated in the environs, are within walking distance of each other. Unless it's a terribly hot summer day, do it all on foot.

CITY CENTER

La Mezquita (Great Mosque) – This 1,200-year-old masterwork by a succession of caliphs covers so much ground that after the Reconquest, not even the construction of an enormous Catholic cathedral dead in its center could totally destroy the impact of its "forest" of pillars and red-and-white candy-striped Moorish horseshoe arches marching into the hazy distance. In fact, as seen from the Puerta de las Palmas (Palm Door), which leads into the mosque proper from the forecourt, the Patio de los Naranjos (Orange Tree Court), the phantasmagoric rows of columns stretching in every direction seem mercifully to screen out the florid cathedral in their midst. A sensible way to conduct a visit is to leave the cruciform Gothic-Renaissance church section for last and concentrate first on the ancient mosque.

Note that the now-murky mosque was originally open to light and air on all sides. When Abd-er-Rahman I built the first section in 785, on the site of a demolished Visigothic Christian church — which, in turn, had been built on the foundations of a Roman temple — each row of marble columns ran straight out to its own row of orange trees in the forecourt. It was only after King Ferdinand III conquered Córdoba in 1236 that the Christians closed in the mosque and lined the walls with Catholic chapels. Much later, in the 16th century, they tore out more than 60 of its columns to erect a proper cathedral in its heart. At the same time, the mosque's minaret was rebuilt as a bell tower.

Abd-er-Rahman I's original square mosque, 240 feet on each side, was enlarged on three occasions — in 848, 961, and 987 — as Córdoba grew in size and importance in the Muslim world. By the 10th century, it covered its present 6 acres. More than 800 pillars stood along its aisles, for the most part antique classical pillars, some left from the previous Visigoth Christian church and Roman temple on the site and others taken from structures as far away as Italy, France, North Africa, and Constantinople. Since these secondhand columns were of unequal lengths, the builders raised the brick and marble flooring of the mosque and "planted" the columns at various depths to maintain a uniform height (an average of 13 feet) on which to support the arches. This illusion of pillars growing right out of the floor combines with a profusion of leafy Corinthian capitals to underscore the forest image.

The addition made to the mosque by Alhakem II in 961 — the southwest corner, containing 10 rows of exquisite alternating rose and blue marble columns and the most dazzling of its holy shrines — represents the high point in caliphate art. Here, against the south wall, is the holy Mihrab, a glistening alcove indicating the direction of Mecca. Framed by an arch of golden and polychrome Byzantine mosaics that radiate outward like a sun, it was the repository of a bejeweled Koran copied by a caliph's own hand and anointed with his blood. A huge scallop shell of white marble, symbol of the goddess Venus, forms the ceiling of its inner dome. Just in front of it, on the site of a former *mihrab*, is the Mudéjar Capilla Villaviciosa (Villaviciosa Chapel), whose stalactite ceiling and plaster lacework are visible only through a locked grille.

The much-maligned cathedral — which even the Holy Roman Emperor Charles V, who authorized its construction, deplored after seeing how it had disfigured the mosque (he regretted the destruction of something "unique" to make way for something "commonplace") — has some magnificent details. Its 18th-century mahogany choir stalls by Sevillian sculptor Pedro Duque Cornejo are among Europe's most elaborate. Its 240-pound 16th-century monstrance (a vessel used during Mass) by Enrique de Arfe was first carried through the streets for the city's Corpus Christi parade in 1518. The big hanging lamp before the altar is a fine example of 17th-century Cordoban silverwork.

The Puerta del Perdón (Pardon Door), next to the bell tower on Calle Cardenal Herrero, is the main entrance to the mosque, although at present visitors enter at the ticket gate on Calle Magistral González Francés. Before going in, be sure to make a full circuit of its crumbling walls to see all the old mosaic-decorated entranceways (some long since blocked up). The plant-filled balcony near the Pardon Door is the outdoor chapel of the Virgen de los Faroles, whose lanterns (*faroles*) are aglow at night. The Mezquita is open daily from 10:30 AM to 1:30 PM and from 4 to 7 PM. Admission charge; there is a separate fee to climb the bell tower. Calle Cardenal Herrero (phone: 470512).

Judería (Jewish Quarter) – North and west of the Mezquita, Córdoba's Judería, the Old Town, is a medieval warren of whitewashed houses, some still standing from caliphate times. Many of these precious relics are now the residences of middle class and wealthy Cordobans, and the neighborhood is no longer Jewish or Arab. About a third of a mile of restored town walls, lighted till dawn, runs beside a moat and gardens along Calle Cairuán, at the neighborhood's western edge. A bronze statue of Seneca stands at the northern end of the walls, beside the Puerta de Almodóvar, a gate that once protected the city with an iron portcullis and is the principal western entrance to the Judería; farther south, a marble figure of AverroEs stands near a smaller entrance on Calle de la Luna.

Sinagoga (Synagogue) – Pass through the Puerta de Almodóvar and turn right down Calle de los Judíos to one of only three synagogues in Spain to survive the Inquisition. (Toledo has the other two, which are grander.) Note the niche where the holy scrolls were kept and the 14th-century Mudéjar plasterwork along the upper walls and balcony where the women were sequestered during worship. Open Tuesdays through Saturdays from 10 AM to 2 PM and from 4:30 to 8 PM; open mornings only on Sundays. Admission charge. Calle de los Judíos.

Museo Taurino y de Arte Cordobés (Museum of Bullfighting and Cordoban Crafts) – The city maintains this display in the 12th-century home of Maimonides (whose seated statue is nearby in the Plaza de Tiberiades). Most of the museum is devoted to bullfighting: room after room of posters, photos, swords, trophies, suits of light (jeweled suits for toreadors), and stuffed heads of bulls that were dispatched by such famous Córdoba-born *toreros* as Lagartijo, Guerrita, Manolete, and El Cordobés. Individual superstars have whole rooms devoted to their costumes (some bloodstained) and personal possessions, including their furniture. The crafts section of the museum, a small exhibit of fine Cordoban silver and leatherwork, is almost an afterthought. Open Tuesdays through Saturdays from 9:30 AM to 1:30 PM and from 5 to 8 PM; open mornings only on Sundays. Admission charge. Plazuela de Maimónides (phone: 472000).

El Zoco (Marketplace) – Across the street from the synagogue and adjoining the bullfighting museum is a 16th-century building complex surrounding a large cobblestone courtyard. Once an Arab *souk,* or marketplace, now it's a crafts market and, in summer, a setting for flamenco dancing. The artisans who work here with silver, ceramics, leather, and other materials, in ateliers provided by the city, welcome visitors to browse or buy. Open daily. Calle de los Judíos.

Calleja de las Flores (Alley of Flowers) – The loveliest lane in the Judería offers a postcard view of the Mezquita bell tower framed by flowers. It's just northeast of the Mezquita, reached from Calle Bosco off Calle Cardenal Herrero.

Casa del Indiano (The Indian's House) – Near the Puerta de Almodóvar and also known as the Casa de las Ceas, this was once a great Arab palace, but now only its 15th-century façade remains. Walk through the portal to see a small, upper-crust residential enclave of new Andalusian houses installed in the area once occupied by the palace proper. Calleja del Indiano.

Alcázar de los Reyes Cristianos (Fortress of the Catholic Monarchs) – Unlike the Alcázar of Seville, much of the beauty of this fortress is in its outer walls and three remaining towers rather than in the interior living quarters. Ferdinand and Isabella were in residence during the later stages of their conquest of Granada, but the Alcázar, begun by Alfonso XI in 1328 on the site of an older Arab fortress, has been a prison for most of its grim history. King Boabdil of Granada was held captive here, the local headquarters of the Inquisition was located here until the 19th century, and then the Alcázar became a provincial prison, which it remained until it underwent restoration after the Spanish Civil War. Upon entering the complex under the archway of the Torre de los Leones (Tower of the Lions), turn left into the clean-lined Gothic palace, where a few significant reminders of past glories are displayed, including a sword of Toledo steel that belonged to the 11th-century Castilian hero El Cid and an exquisitely carved marble sarcophagus with scenes of Roman Córdoba. Magnificent Roman murals from the 1st century line the walls of the royal salon, now used for concerts; down steep stairs are the crumbling walls of underground Moorish baths, with typical Arab star-shaped skylights.

The fortress's centerpiece, the Patio Morisco (Moorish Court), endowed with twin pools and an ivy-covered grotto, leads to the Arab-walled Alcázar gardens, a romantic spot filled with more pools, fountains, rose gardens, and orchards. At the far end, a statuary group re-creates the meeting here in 1492 when the Catholic Monarchs gave Christopher Columbus the go-ahead for his auspicious voyage. Before leaving the Alcázar, walk the ramparts and climb the three stone towers remaining from the original four: The Torre de los Leones is the oldest and most interesting because of its Gothic dome, but the other two, El Río (River) and Homenaje (Homage), also command sweeping views. The Alcázar is open daily from 9:30 AM to 1:30 PM and from 5 to 8 PM; gardens are lighted on summer evenings until midnight. Admission charge. Camposanto de los Mártires (phone: 472000).

Puente Romano (Roman Bridge) – Just along the river from the Alcázar and easily recognized by its 16 characteristic arches, this was built by the Roman emperor Augustus in the 1st century BC, although few traces of the original structure remain after centuries of destruction and rebuilding. The recently restored 16th-century triumphal arch, Puerta del Puente, guards the main Córdoba side of the bridge and is flanked by the Triunfo de San Rafael column, one of a dozen homages to the city's guardian archangel. Another statue of the saint (this one 17th century) stands at the bridge's halfway point, its base blackened by wax from candles burned by passing worshipers. What's left of the Arabs' old water-powered stone flour mills can be seen in the river, whereas the giant wooden waterwheel on the Alcázar side is a replica of one that used to scoop up river water to irrigate the fortress gardens.

Torre de la Calahorra (Calahorra Tower) – In the 14th century, King Henry II constructed this stone fortress at the south end of the Puente Romano to ward off attacks by his hated half brother, Peter the Cruel, who built the Alcázar of Seville. The well-preserved tower, designed in the shape of a cross, was erected over an old Arab fort. It's now a city historical museum with a slide show of Córdoba and Andalusia. Open daily from 10 AM to 6 PM. Admission charge. Puente Romano (phone: 293929).

Museo Arqueológico Provincial (Provincial Archaeological Museum) – Both the beautiful old multi-patioed 16th-century palace and its important collection, beginning with stones from neolithic times, are reasons to see this museum, a short walk northeast of the Mezquita. The history of Andalusia is written in its Roman and Moorish treasures. Some of the most appealing objects, such as the famous stylized bronze stag, come from the ruins of the Medina Azahara outside Córdoba. Open Tuesdays through Saturdays from 10 AM to 2 PM and from 5 to 8 PM; open mornings only on Sundays. Admission charge. Plaza Jerónimo Páez (phone: 471076).

Plaza del Potro – This famous square east of the Mezquita takes its name from the diminutive statue of a rearing colt (*potro*) atop the 16th-century fountain in its center.

The austere plaza, with its big, rough, gray paving stones, is walled in by the former Hospital de la Caridad (Charity Hospital) on one side and by an old inn, the *Posada del Potro,* on the other, and looks just as it must have when it rang with the cries of cattle traders and hummed with the gossip of travelers in the 16th and 17th centuries. Cervantes mentioned the big white *posada* in *Don Quixote* — it's where Sancho Panza endured the blanket toss. Now it functions as a cultural center, featuring a program of changing exhibitions.

Museo de Bellas Artes (Museum of Fine Arts) – The museum, with its blue-tile trim and black wrought-iron grilles newly restored, stands at the end of a manicured sculpture garden reached through the archway of the 15th-century Hospital de la Caridad. Goya's portrait of Queen María Luisa is the star of a creditable collection of statues and paintings, including works by such famous painters as Murillo, Zurbarán, and Córdoba's own Valdés Leal. Open Tuesdays through Saturdays from 10 AM to 2 PM and from 6 to 8 PM; open mornings only on Sundays. Admission charge. Plaza del Potro (phone: 473345).

Museo Romero de Torres – Most visitors are mystified as to why the entire frescoed building, part of the *Museo de Bellas Artes* complex, should be devoted to the works of the saccharine 1920s painter Julio Romero de Torres. Apparently Córdoba feels some affection for the man who grew up in the *Museum of Fine Arts,* where his father was the curator. His romantic portrayals of Gypsy women and especially his *Naranjas y Limones* (Oranges and Lemons), a portrait of a topless beauty, are the big draw. Open Tuesdays through Saturdays from 10 AM to 1:30 PM and from 4 to 6 PM; open mornings only on Sundays (in July, August, and September, closed all afternoons). No admission charge. Plaza del Potro (phone: 471314).

Plaza de la Corredera – This drab 16th-century plaza north of Plaza del Potro, entirely enclosed by brick-porticoed apartment buildings, faintly resembles Madrid's Plaza Mayor, but there's no other like it in southern Spain. Once the main square of Córdoba and the scene of bullfights, jousts, and races, it now comes alive as an outdoor market from early morning to 2 PM daily except Sundays.

Plaza de las Tendillas – The heart of downtown Córdoba, this is a huge square on a gentle hill, lined with banks, cafés, and shops. The figure astride the horse in the center of the fountain is Queen Isabella's vaunted general, El Gran Capitán, Gonzalo Fernández de Córdoba, who conquered the kingdom of Naples for the Spanish crown. At the northern end of the square, Avenida Cruz Conde leads down to the city's main shopping area; at the southern end, Calle Jesús y María leads to the Mezquita.

Cristo de los Faroles (Christ of the Lanterns) – Don't miss this towering 18th-century stone crucifix surrounded by wrought-iron lanterns in a stark, narrow square. It's particularly moving at night when the lanterns are lit. Inside the small, white church on the square — the Iglesia de los Dolores (Church of the Sorrows) — is Córdoba's most venerated virgin, the tearful, gold-crowned Virgen de los Dolores, displayed above the altar against a background of glowing blue light. Plaza de los Dolores.

Palacio-Museo de Viana (Viana Palace-Museum) – This enchanting ancestral palace of the Marqués de Viana, with a dozen breathtaking patios and 52 lavish rooms (of nearly 100) on view, is one of the best-kept and most efficiently managed attractions in Córdoba. A brochure in English describes a self-guided tour of its magnificent interconnected patio gardens, which are its star feature; a smartly uniformed guard leads visitors through the house itself, which is a complete museum of the aristocratic Andalusian lifestyle, fully furnished and decorated with the family's collections of china, silver sculpture, tapestries, paintings, equestrian trappings, swords, guns, coins, and tiles — just as though the family still lived there. Allow about 2 hours to see both house and gardens. Open from 9 AM to 2 PM (from 10 AM to 2 PM on Sundays); closed Wednesdays. Admission charge. Plaza de Don Gome (phone: 482275).

ENVIRONS

Medina Azahara – A dry, olive-dotted Sierra foothill 4 miles (6 km) west of Córdoba is the site of the extensively excavated and delightfully restored pleasure palace and city built by Abd-er-Rahman III for his favorite wife, Azahara, in 936. This archaeological mother lode, a place that once rivaled the Mezquita for beauty and mystery, runs down the hillside from the entrance at a small museum at the top. Clearly marked paths descend through a terraced town that once housed 20,000 royal retainers and served as the seat of Cordoban government for 70 years until Berber mercenaries, who had been called in to defend it, burned it to the ground. No expense was spared in laying out its royal palace, great mosque, 400 houses, army barracks, royal mint, gardens, fishponds, orchards, fountains, heavy fortifications, and ornate gateways, spread over 275 acres. The arches of the mosque, palace, and other buildings were supported by 4,000 ornamented columns of rose, azure, onyx, white, and mustard marble. After its destruction, the city was fair game for scavengers, so today its marbles are found in later palaces in Andalusia, including the Alcázar in Seville. The imposing early 15th-century Convento de San Jerónimo de Valparaíso (which can be visited by applying to the caretaker) on the mountain above the Medina also uses its stones. Nevertheless, there seem to be enough fragments left to keep restorers at work piecing the city together forever.

Excavation began in 1914 and proceeded fitfully until recent years, when the pace was stepped up. Much of what the visitor sees are foundations and ruined shells of buildings; but the magnificent, colonnaded Dar al-Mulk, or royal apartment complex, with delicate plasterwork, intricate stone carving, and majestic proportions, has already been roofed over and is being meticulously reconstructed. Medina Azahara (phone: 234025) is open Tuesdays through Saturdays from 10 AM to 2 PM and from 6 to 8 PM; open from 10 AM to 1:30 PM on Sundays. Admission charge. To reach the site by private car or cab, take Avenida de Medina Azahara out of town to the C431 highway. (Inquire at the tourist office for possible special bus service.)

Las Ermitas – Scattered in the hills 8 miles (13 km) northwest of town are a baker's dozen Christian hermits' cells known as Las Ermitas. Their existence may go back as far as the 4th century, although the hermits who occupied them to live a life of solitary self-sacrifice were organized into an order only in the 17th century. (They weathered even Córdoba's Moorish days, flourishing with the blessing of the Muslim caliphs.) The community finally died out in the 1950s, and the cells have fallen into disrepair, but the site is still evocative. The grounds are reached via Avenida del Brillante. (The tourist office can supply driving directions.) Admission by voluntary donation.

■ **EXTRA SPECIAL:** Don't be shy about gazing into Córdoba's flower-filled patios. It's a local custom. The gorgeous patios are considered an official asset of the city, which has built an annual 2-week festival around them (see *Special Events*). If the door to the forecourt is open, that's an invitation to look through the wrought-iron *cancela* (grille) into the family's private world, fragrant with geraniums, roses, carnations, orange and lemon trees, sweet basil, and jasmine. No two patio landscapes are alike; some of the most sophisticated are studies in greenery, masonry, and ceramics, rather than color. You'll find some outstanding beauties in the Judería around Plaza de Juda Levi, especially at 6 Calle Albucasis, where one of the most visited patios in town displays walls studded with pots of blazing geraniums. Take Calle Buen Pastor (be sure to stop at No. 2) and continue to Calle Leiva Aguilar. There's another cluster of prizewinners across from the Alcázar gardens, on Calle San Basilio and surrounding streets. Ask at the tourist office for a patio tour map.

SOURCES AND RESOURCES

TOURIST INFORMATION: The Oficina Municipal de Turismo (Municipal Tourist Office), in the heart of the Judería (Plaza de Juda Levi; phone: 290740), is open from 9 AM to 2 PM weekdays, 10 AM to 1 PM on Saturdays. A blackboard outside lists the city's principal sights and hours of opening, as well as special events. The Oficina de Turismo de la Junta de Andalucía, just west of the Mezquita (10 Calle Torrijos; phone: 471235), has information on all of Andalusia and is open from 9:30 AM to 2 PM and from 5 to 7 PM weekdays, 9:30 AM to 1:30 PM on Saturdays. Both offices have helpful English-speaking personnel, which is fortunate, because Córdoba lags badly in up-to-date tourist literature, especially in English. When buying a map or local guidebook, look for the one with the most recent printing date. Older maps and books, still being sold, show prominent streets and plazas with their names from the Franco era, which can add to the already considerable confusion caused by winding streets, many with hard-to-spot street names and house numbers. Since there is no satisfactory guidebook for the Mezquita (a lifelong study in itself), a local guide schooled in the subtle complexities of this fascinating structure is recommended. Licensed English-speaking guides can be hired at the entrance or at guide headquarters (2 Calle Torrijos; phone: 474274). A half-day bus and walking tour of the city (buses can't enter the Judería) is offered by *Viajes Vincit* (1 Calle Alonso de Burgos; phone: 472316).

Local Coverage – The local daily read by Cordobans is the *Córdoba*. The weekly *El Mercadillo,* also in Spanish, carries listings of theatrical and special events.

TELEPHONE: The city code for Córdoba is 57. If calling from within Spain, dial 957 before the local number.

GETTING AROUND: Airport – Córdoba's municipal airport, 5½ miles (9 km) from town, has an extremely limited flight schedule since most people arrive by bus, train, or car. For flight information, check with *Iberia,* 3 Ronda de los Tejares (phone: 471227 or 472695).

Bus – Green-and-white city buses cover the town. Tourists rarely use them, however, because it's possible to walk almost everywhere and taxi fares for Córdoba's short distances between sights are low. There is no central bus terminal for intercity buses and no central information number. The tourist office has up-to-date schedules; otherwise, for information on buses to Madrid and Barcelona, call 290158; for Seville, call 472352; for Málaga and Granada, call 236474.

Car Rental – Among the firms represented are *Avis* (at the airport and at 28 Plaza de Colón; phone: 476862); *Hertz* (at the airport and at the railroad station; phone: 477243); and *Europcar* (at the airport and at *Hotel Los Gallos Sol,* 7 Avenida de Medina Azahara; phone: 232011). Convenient parking for the Mezquita and the Judería can be found along the Paseo de la Victoria (a street attendant collects a small fee) or at the river at Plaza del Triunfo, where there's a guarded lot.

Horse and Carriage – A popular way to see the Judería, though coaches can't enter some of its alleyways. Drivers are entertaining guides. *Coches de caballo* are for hire around the Mezquita and the Alcázar.

Taxi – Call for a cab (phone: 470291) or hail one in the street.

Train – The railroad station is on Avenida de América. Tickets can be purchased downtown at the *RENFE* office (10 Ronda de los Tejares). For train information, call 478721.

 SPECIAL EVENTS: The famous *Fiesta de los Patios* fills the city with visitors during the first 2 weeks in May. Everyone goes from one private patio to another admiring walls literally covered with gorgeously planted flowerpots, and prizes are awarded for the best displays. At the same time, public plazas are decked with flowers and flowered crosses. This is followed by the annual *Feria de Nuestra Señora de la Salud* — *Feria* for short — held the last week in May. Córdoba's fair is especially festive because of its location in the heart of town: The lineup of *casetas,* private tents for entertaining, and the midway Ferris wheel, merry-go-round, and snack stands run the length of the Jardines de la Victoria; flamenco contests, pop and classical concerts, ballet, parades, fireworks, and displays of Cordoban horsemanship fill the streets with action; and the sounds of stamping and clapping ring out along with the twang of guitars from El Zoco, where Gypsies dance throughout the summer. Since May is also Córdoba's bullfight season, advance hotel reservations for this action-packed month are a must.

 SHOPPING: With prices on most goods generally high, the things to look for are local products, notably silver filigree jewelry and fine tooled leather. Silver shops with affordable filigree jewelry can be found around the Mezquita and especially along Calle Deanes, as can a jumble of souvenir stands selling toreador dolls, fans, caftans, brass trays, embossed leather wallets, handbags, and hassocks. Consider a stop at Córdoba's finest leather shop, *Meryan* (2 Calleja de las Flores; phone: 475902) — more like visiting a museum than shopping, unless you're prepared for a serious purchase. The artistic hand-embossed and tinted leather (*guadamecil*) goods are done in the Renaissance style (with some designs derived from classical paintings), the handwork is painstaking and magnificent, and prices on the larger pieces run into the thousands. Wander up and down the stairs in this centuries-old mansion, whose gardens once extended down to the mosque, to inspect leather chairs, chests, wall hangings, maps, picture frames, and even some wooden pieces, and ask to see the workshops surrounding the serene white marble patio. The more affordable leather bags and wallets that many visitors end up buying here are of excellent quality but not made by the shop. Silversmiths and leather workers are also among the craftsmen (there are woodworkers, weavers, ceramists, and others) selling their wares in *El Zoco,* the municipal crafts market opposite the synagogue in the Judería. The latest addition to this old complex is the avant-garde *Arte Zoco* cooperative art gallery facing Calle de los Judíos (phone: 204033).

For general purchases and boutique fashions, shop the Avenida Cruz Conde area off Plaza de las Tendillas. The city's major department store, *Galerías Preciados* (32 Ronda de los Tejares; phone: 470267), is another place for general shopping; it has a convenient cafeteria, too.

SPORTS AND FITNESS: Bullfighting – May is the season at the *Plaza de Toros* (Gran Vía del Parque), although there are occasional *corridas* during the rest of the year. Arrange for tickets through your hotel.

Golf – The *Club de Golf Los Villares* (5½ miles/9 km) north of town via Avenida del Brillante; phone: 474102) has an 18-hole course, a practice course, a restaurant, a swimming pool, and tennis courts. Visitors may use the facilities; reservations can be made directly or through the Patronato Provincial de Turismo (Provincial Tourist Office; 1 Calle Pérez de Castro; phone: 202377).

Horseback Riding – Try the *Club Hípico,* Carretera Santa María de Trassiera (phone: 271628).

Jogging – Beautiful suburban roads await guests of the *Parador de la Arruzafa* (see *Checking In*); for those staying in town, there's early-morning jogging in the Jardines de la Victoria.

Soccer – The *Club de Fútbol de Córdoba* plays at the *Estadio Arcángel* (Calle Venerable Juan de Santiago) — but Córdoba hasn't been proud of its home team lately.

Swimming – Short of a quick trip to the Costa del Sol, the best bet is to book one of the few hotels in Córdoba equipped with a pool. The great ones are at the *Meliá Córdoba* and the *Parador de la Arruzafa;* the pool at *Los Gallos Sol* is small for laps. The *Club de Golf Los Villares* also has a swimming pool (see above).

Tennis – The *Parador de la Arruzafa* has tennis courts for guests. Another option is the *Club de Golf Los Villares* (see above), which can be used by non-members.

 THEATER AND MUSIC: Plays (some by national touring companies), dance performances, and classical, flamenco, and pop concerts come to the recently refurbished, century-old *Gran Teatro* (Avenida del Gran Capitán; phone: 480237 and 480644). American and British films in original-language version are just about the only entertainment offered in English. In summer, the municipal orchestra gives Sunday concerts in the Alcázar gardens. Check the weekly *El Mercadillo* for listings or consult the daily newspaper.

 NIGHTCLUBS AND NIGHTLIFE: Except during the *Feria* in May, Cordobans stick pretty close to home at night. Nevertheless, count on finding life after dark in the center at Plaza Ignacio Loyola, off Avenida Menéndez y Pelayo, where, in fair weather, yellow and white café umbrellas sprout in front of the Iglesia San Hipólito. You can do your own *sevillanas* to live combos under orange and white polka dot paper lanterns at the crowded *La Caseta* (4 Plaza Ignacio Loyola; phone: 412967), which also offers dinner and *tapas,* flamenco shows, and disco. Go late for the shows — from 10 PM to 4 AM, although this lively spot is open earlier (closed Sundays). Or have snacks, wine, or beer at the contemporary little pubs, bars, and *bodegas* (liquor shops selling drinks) along the square. For disco, try the neon and red-plush ambience of *Contactos* (8 Calle Eduardo Dato; phone: 292466), or the sleek *Saint-Cyr* (4 Calle Eduardo Lucena; phone: 292440), in the basement of a downtown office building.

Bar hopping is a good way to end a day in the Judería. Join the neighborhood people at the hospitable bar in *Casa Rubio* (5 Puerta de Almodóvar; phone: 290064) or enjoy *tapas* and beer in its postage-stamp patio. Then cross the street (there's no number, but you'll see the sign), for the minuscule and impeccable *Casa Salinas* (phone: 290846), a longtime musicians' hangout, and munch the house specialty, *pescaítos fritos* — *tapas* of crisp fried fish. At the Calle de la Luna entrance to the Judería, Cordobans dance *sevillanas* within the 150-year-old, 3-foot-thick walls of *Mesón de la Luna* (Calle de la Luna) and at *Mesón Murillo* (just across the way). There's also a convivial crowd to be found at the venerable *Bar Mezquita* (24 Calle Cardenal Herrero), across from the front of the mosque.

BEST IN TOWN

CHECKING IN: Córdoba's charms are centered around the Judería, so try for one of the atmospheric hotels there. If they're all booked, don't despair — the city is so compact that even a hotel in the modern section is close to the center. But remember to book early for the month of May, when the *Patio Festival,* the *Feria,* and the bullfighting season make Córdoba's extremely tight hotel situation even tighter. The hotels noted are all air conditioned. Expect to pay from about $95 to $130 for a double room in those listed as expensive, from $65 to $95 in those listed as moderate, and from $30 to $65 in the inexpensive ones. All telephone numbers are in the 57 city code unless otherwise indicated.

Adarve – This white-on-white arcaded palace provides grace and comfort enough to please a caliph. An updated Moorish villa just across the street from the Mezquita, it has 103 rooms, but it seems much smaller and more intimate. The central courtyard, containing discreetly splashing fountains and one perfect orange and one perfect loquat tree, is enchanting. Some rooms have French doors opening onto the courtyard; others face the weathered walls of the mosque. There's a coffee shop, but for lunch and dinner, the *Adarve,* like its sister hotel, the *Maimónides,* uses the *Bandolero* restaurant (see *Eating Out*) adjoining the latter. There also is a garage. 15 Calle Magistral González Francés (phone: 481102). Expensive.

Husa Gran Capitán – An efficient international commercial property filled with tour groups. It's on the outskirts across from the railroad station (double window glass muffles the noise), but still only a short cab ride to the Judería and a comfortable haven when closer places are booked. It has 99 rooms, a restaurant, and a garage. 5 Avenida de América (phone: 470250). Expensive.

Maimónides – Across the street from the Mezquita (but on the opposite side from its glossier sister hotel, the *Adarve*), it is characterized by dignified but somber elegance, with Renaissance Spanish decor. There are 61 comfortable rooms; only breakfast is served, but the *Bandolero* restaurant is two steps across a narrow alley from the lobby (see *Eating Out*). Garage. 4 Calle Torrijos (phone: 471500). Expensive.

Meliá Córdoba – The city's "grand hotel" has an ideal location at the head of the Jardines de la Victoria, outside the Arab walls but just a 3-minute walk away, and only about 10 minutes on foot from the modern downtown area. It offers a big-hotel lobby and good concierge service, 106 well-appointed rooms, a cocktail lounge, the elegant *Restaurante del Palacio,* boutiques, and a large swimming pool in an exceptional garden setting. No garage, but street parking is generally easy to find except during the May festivals. Jardines de la Victoria (phone: 298066). Expensive.

Parador de la Arruzafa – The former garden of date palms (*arruzafa*) of Abd-er-Rahman I, first builder of the Mezquita, is the expansive country club setting of Córdoba's government-run *parador,* although the structure itself is of fairly recent vintage. Located 2 miles (3 km) from town, it has terraces overlooking spacious lawns and gardens leading down to a big swimming pool and tennis courts. Many of the 83 rooms have balconies. Cab service is available. Avenida de la Arruzafa (phone: 275900). Expensive.

Cisne – Simple but sparkling, this hostelry is near the railroad station, a short cab ride to the Judería; it has 44 rooms, and a restaurant. 14 Avenida Cervantes (phone: 481676). Moderate.

Los Gallos Sol – Just a short cab ride from the Old Town is a comfortable 7-story high-rise with upbeat, colorful decor, a token rooftop swimming pool, and a popular lobby cafeteria. Many of its 105 simple, tweedy rooms face a charming avenue; others have patio views. Old hands will recognize it as the former *El Cordobés,* once owned by the famous bullfighter but updated by new owners about a decade ago. 7 Avenida de Medina Azahara (phone: 235500). Moderate.

Albucasis – Close to the Mezquita, this delightful little newcomer occupies an old mansion that has been stylishly restored in Mudéjar fashion. Spotlessly clean, with friendly service, it has 15 rooms and a charming patio, and it's popular among visiting university staff. Breakfast only. 11 Calle Buen Pastor (phone: 478625). Moderate to inexpensive.

Boston – Tidy and comfortable, this little *hostal* of 40 rooms overlooks the hubbub of Plaza de las Tendillas. No restaurant. Reserve early. 2 Calle Málaga (phone: 474176). Inexpensive.

Marisa – A simple refuge with 28 rooms in a prime location across from the shrine of the Virgen de los Faroles at the Mezquita. Breakfast, but no restaurant. 6 Calle Cardenal Herrero (phone: 473142). Inexpensive.

El Triunfo – This 26-room *hostal,* right by the river at the foot of the Mezquita, is one of the best small hotels in the Old Town. A TV set blares in the tiny, crowded lobby during soccer season, the restaurant charges popular prices (see *Eating Out*), and European tourists keep it filled. Reserve early. 79 Calle Cardenal González (phone: 475500). Inexpensive.

 EATING OUT: Córdoba's most intriguing restaurants and *tapas* bars cluster around the Mezquita, although there are also some well-frequented places in the modern city that are convenient to hotels outside the Judería. As elsewhere in Andalusia, the local cuisine is Arab influenced, but here the Arab accent comes to the fore in dishes rich in almonds, honey, figs, candied fruits, oranges, pine nuts, and sweet, fragrant Arab flavorings. Then there are the dishes Cordobans say they originated, among them *salmorejo,* a thick, waterless tomato gazpacho. The city's most famous culinary contribution is *pastel cordobés,* sometimes called *tarta Manolete,* a flat, round pastry with a honey-sweetened *cabello del angel* (angel hair) pumpkin filling. It's on most dessert menus and in pastry shops. Be sure to taste the local montilla-moriles wines, ranging from dry white *finos* to sweet Pedro Ximenez dessert wines. The montilla-moriles wine country to the south produces twice as much sherry-like wine, made by the *solera* system, as is made in Jerez.

Expect to pay $55 or more for a 3-course meal for two with local wine at restaurants listed as expensive, from $25 to $55 at those listed as moderate, and under $25 at those listed as inexpensive. Restaurants in all categories have tourist menus that are relatively inexpensive. All telephone numbers are in the 57 city code unless otherwise indicated.

Mesón Bandolero – Rough brick arches, furnishings in tooled leather and old wood, tables set with hammered-brass service plates — this is a restaurant on a grand scale. It's set in an old palace where AverroEs lived, and it has, besides the lavish indoor dining rooms, a spacious canvas-shaded patio where songbirds in filigree cages sing among the four palm trees. The menu is elegant international, with local touches such as *rabo de toro* (oxtail stew), *ensalada de perdiz en escabeche* (marinated partridge salad), and *anguilas a pil-pil* (baby eels with garlic and oil). Next door to the *Maimónides* hotel. Open daily. Reservations advised. 8 Calle Medina y Corella (phone: 414245). Expensive.

Oscar – You'll be off the tourist track here at the city's leading seafood restaurant. Take a seat in the pocket-size plaza in front of the restaurant, inside at the *tapas* bar loaded with crab and rock lobster, or in dark, cozy dining rooms. Closed Sundays and August. Reservations advised. 6 Plaza de los Chirinos (phone: 477517). Expensive.

El Bosque – An indoor-outdoor suburban dining spot on the sloping road to the *Parador de la Arruzafa* (see *Checking In*). Well-heeled Córdoba congregates here — for a *copa* (glass of wine) while the lights of the city below are coming on, or for an elegant dinner later. Open daily. Reservations unnecessary. 134 Avenida del Brillante (phone: 270006). Expensive to moderate.

El Caballo Rojo – Consistently well-executed regional dishes, served by patient, red-jacketed waiters accustomed to foreigners, make this big, friendly place across from the mosque the most popular spot in Córdoba for first-time visitors. (It's also probably Andalusia's most famous restaurant.) Bypass the ground-floor bar and head upstairs to the bright dining rooms, where Andalusian specialties are displayed on a big buffet, and while sipping your complimentary aperitif of the local dry white montilla wine, ponder the choices: thick *salmorejo* (gazpacho), *sopa de ajo blanco* (milk-white garlicky gazpacho with chopped apples, raisins, and ground almonds), *rape mozárabe* (monkfish with raisins and brandy), *cordero a la miel* (lamb shanks in honey sauce). A 4-foot-high dessert trolley bears flan and other delights, but if you haven't tried *pastel cordobés,* this is the place. Open daily. Reservations advised. 28 Calle Cardenal Herrero (phone: 475375). Expensive to moderate.

Almudaina – Elegant Andalusian dining, in one of the intimate lace-curtained salons of a 15th-century palace or in the brick-lined, glass-roofed central courtyard. Try the *solomillo al vino tinto* (pork loin in wine sauce) or *merluza en salsa de gambas* (hake with shrimp sauce), and for dessert, order the chef's renowned tropical fruit sorbet or the *pudín de limón y almendras* (semi-frozen lemon-almond crème). The restaurant, across from the Alcázar, is owned by the well-respected *Ciro's* in the business section (see below). Closed Sunday nights. Reservations necessary. 1 Camposanto de los Mártires (phone: 474342). Moderate.

Azahar – Vaguely Arab in style, new and in vogue, it's often crowded with discerning locals. Roast meats are a specialty, but try the excellent *crema de cangrejos al brandy* (crab purée with brandy sauce). Open daily. Reservations necessary. 10 Avenida de Medina Azahara (phone: 414387). Moderate.

El Churrasco – When it comes to that one big meal in Córdoba, this low-key place gives the showier *El Caballo Rojo* a run for its money. Locals join tourists in this unassuming house on a Judería side street, tempted by the patio dining, the sumptuous *tapas* bar, and the signature dish, *churrasco* (charcoal-grilled pork loin in savory sauce), plus other grilled meat and fish dishes. Closed Thursdays and August. Reservations necessary. 16 Calle Romero (phone: 290819). Moderate.

Ciro's – It offers the same menu and the same prices as its sister restaurant, *Almudaina,* but in a sophisticated international setting that draws Córdoba's expense-account diners. Downstairs there's a lively informal café. Open daily. Reservations advised. Along the park at 19 Paseo de la Victoria (phone: 290464). Moderate.

El Burlaero – The modest outdoor dining court and cozy restaurant here are easiest to find by walking through *El Caballo Rojo* to the outdoor staircase in back and turning right up the stairs. A budget sleeper, this place serves simple, well-prepared Cordoban cooking, well suited to a light lunch. Open daily. Reservations unnecessary. The restaurant's front entrance is at 5 Calleja La Hoguera (phone: 472719). Moderate to inexpensive.

El Triunfo – The small restaurant of this *hostal* near the Mezquita is as good a buy as the rooms upstairs. Especially at lunchtime, its menu of *platos combinados* is a smart choice over the rival *mesones* that besiege you with handbills touting tourist specials; most of them are too cheap to be good. Open daily. Reservations unnecessary. 79 Calle Cardenal González (phone: 475500). Inexpensive.

EVORA

One of the oldest cities on the Iberian Peninsula, Evora is the Alto Alentejo's traditional capital, the capital of the Evora district, a "museum town," and a work of art all rolled into one. At the very least, it offers ample pleasure simply as a typical, delightful southern Portuguese city. It is untaxingly modest in size (approximately 50,000 inhabitants), and its Old City has pleasing places for strolling, provided visitors are sensibly shod for the cobblestones. All the emblems of the south are here: the glare of whitewash, bright splashes of geraniums and bougainvillea, tantalizing glimpses of cool, shaded courtyards, the evening air thick with swifts. The quintessential Alentejo town, in fact. But Evora has another dimension that is not nearly so common, even among the richly endowed towns of this historic region: The number of well-preserved historical buildings — over 30 of them classified as national monuments — is really exceptional for a city of its size.

Evora's earliest origins are lost in time, but all the archaeological clues indicate a city of extreme antiquity. It was already a fortified town of some importance when the Romans captured it from the Lusitanians during the 2nd century BC. Within a couple of centuries, it had become a prosperous imperial outpost, a *municipium* with the right to mint coins and a population that enjoyed most of the privileges of Roman citizenship. Just as it is today, Evora was a center of agriculture during the Roman era, noted for grain production. Pliny the Elder, who for a while held an official post in the region, referred to it, in his *Natural History,* as Ebora Cerealis.

At the beginning of the 5th century, as the Roman Empire crumbled, the city came under Visigothic rule. Then, in 713, it lay in the path of the Muslims sweeping up from North Africa and across the Iberian Peninsula. Under them, Evora grew considerably in military, economic, and cultural importance, so that the city described by the Moorish geographer Idrisi in 1154 is not much different — apart from its size — from the modern one. Evora, he said, is "large and populous, surrounded by walls, and with a strong castle and a mosque. The surrounding territory is of a singular fertility, producing cattle and all kinds of vegetables and fruit."

More than 400 years of Islam left an indelible imprint on the city's architecture and personality, but its most famous legend stems from the time of its recapture by the Christians. Several attempts had been made to win Evora back from the Moors, all of them unsuccessful or, like an assault in 1159, only briefly successful. Then, in October of 1165, a Christian warrior chief called Geraldo Sem Pavor (Gerald the Fearless — the epithet was a result of more than one celebrated feat of bravery during the Reconquest) scaled the walls under cover of darkness by driving lances into spaces in the masonry and using them as a ladder. After killing the surprised sentinels, Geraldo let in his men, took the castle, and conquered Evora. He presented his valuable prize to Portugal's first king, Afonso Henriques, who was engaged at the time in driving the Moors from the Alentejo, and in recognition of his feat was appointed *alcaide,* or governor.

Throughout the Middle Ages and the Renaissance, Evora grew steadily in importance and wealth, becoming a center of learning and the arts in the 15th and 16th centuries. It became a bishopric in 1540, and in 1559, Cardinal Henrique, who was later crowned king, founded here one of Europe's oldest universities (which was shut down in 1759 by Portugal's autocratic prime minister, the Marquês de Pombal, but reopened in 1975).

Evora's standing in the political and cultural mainstream had been strengthened by the accession of the House of Avis to the Portuguese throne during the late 14th century. In 1383 and 1384, the townspeople revolted against the Spanish-leaning regency of Queen Leonor, burned down most of the old castle, and proclaimed as Defender of the Realm the head of the Military Order of the Knights of Avis, who had their headquarters here. João I of Avis became king in 1385, and Evora, which had already been a seat of the early kings of the House of Burgundy, became one of the main residences of the new dynasty, remaining prominent for several centuries. João's rise to the throne also marked a turning point for the Portuguese nation. The defeat of Castilian forces at Aljubarrota in August 1385 set the stage for the country's golden age of independence and maritime expansion.

With Portugal poised for its greatest achievements, Evora became the scene of a decisive incident in the struggle for power between the monarchy and the nobility. In 1481, King João II summoned the *cortes* (a representative assembly of nobles) to Evora and extracted a new oath of obedience from this fractious group. When a conspiracy gathered against him, led by his ambitious brother-in-law, the Duke of Bragança, João had the duke arrested and, in 1484, executed — thus consolidating the power of the throne and investing it with an authority that was to be put to advantage in the approaching era. The square that served for Bragança's beheading, now the Praça do Giraldo, was later the arena where heretics and other victims were burned during the Inquisition, one of the skeletons in Evora's historical closet.

In 1637, during the unpopular Spanish monarchy, another grass-roots revolt — the so-called Manuelinho uprising — convulsed Evora and sent shock waves rippling throughout the kingdom. For 5 days, the townspeople ransacked the houses of the Castilian-appointed officials they hated and burned their belongings in a huge bonfire in the main square. This was the first major rebellion in Portugal against the Spanish domination, and just as Evora's ire had been instrumental 250 years earlier in bringing about a change in command, so it was again. Three years later, the Spanish monarchy was ousted and independence from Spain had been permanently secured.

Yet another disaster, the sacking of the city by the French in 1808 during the Peninsular War, left many buildings damaged and a number of works of art lost forever. Then a long period of provincial somnolence ensued, from which Evora seemed to awaken only in 1974, with the April 25th revolution that paved the way for a return to democracy in Portugal. The city became the center of the agrarian reform movement in which the Communist party made a partially successful attempt to create an alternative to the Alentejo's residual feudalism. The university was reopened, attention was paid to promoting the arts and preserving the city's architectural heritage, festivals were organized, and social services and infrastructure were improved. Evora, in short, moved into the 20th century.

But despite this undeniable development, the Alentejo's most famous city still retains a certain isolation from the outside world, afflicted by such trials as drought and an agricultural-social system out of touch with the realities of the European Community to which it now belongs. And Evora, for all its charms, is still no pleasure resort. Good hotel accommodations are limited in quantity; so are restaurants and other entertainment facilities. Nevertheless, advance booking will solve the room problem, and it is certainly true that whatever the city lacks in sophistication, it more than makes up for in other ways. For the native and the visitor alike, Evora is sort of a standing record in stone of the Portuguese nation.

EVORA AT-A-GLANCE

SEEING THE CITY: Early drawings show Evora rising out of the flat Alentejo landscape with the uncluttered simplicity of a child's sandcastle on a beach. Making some allowance for the inevitable urban sprawl, that image is remarkably like the view of the city seen today from the top of the Alto de São Bento, a 1,094-foot hill 2 miles (3 km) out of town on the road to Arraiolos. From this vantage point, the three towers of the cathedral dominate the skyline, and it is apparent that Evora still remains tightly enclosed by its nearly unbroken girdle of 14th-century walls. Legend has it that Evora's Christian reconqueror, Gerald the Fearless, had his castle here on the São Bento hill, but standing on it today is the 13th-century convent of São Bento de Castris, which is thought to be the first nuns' convent founded in Portugal. It has a fine 16th-century cloister, which unfortunately is not normally open to visitors (but you can try ringing the bell). Follow the little road past the convent up to the three ruined windmills for the view.

SPECIAL PLACES: Like all Alentejo towns, Evora is built on a hill. The cathedral occupies the highest point, and the rest of the Old City spreads out from it down to the encircling walls. The cathedral is thus a perfect reference point. It is nearly always visible if you crane your neck a bit, and practically everything there is to see lies within easy strolling distance of it. The old walled city — the "historical nucleus," as it is sometimes called — is divided into three sections: the Judiaria (Jewish Quarter), the Mouraria (Moorish Quarter), and the Zona Residencial dos Nobres (Quarter of the Nobles), but given the small size of Evora as a whole, it is easier to divide it into two simple parts: inside the walls and outside. In addition to nearly all the sights, the most worthwhile shops and restaurants are also within the inner city.

Besides the sights listed below, several prehistoric sites in the vicinity are worth a short excursion for anyone so inclined. The Alto Alentejo region was a center of the megalithic culture that flourished on the Iberian Peninsula between 4000 and 2000 BC, and there are a number of imposing dolmens and menhirs within easy reach. The tourist office publishes a folder giving the principal sites and their locations. The cromlechs, or religious circles, at Almendres and Xarez are particularly impressive.

IN THE CITY

Templo Romano (Roman Temple) – This structure is something of a trademark for Evora, and with good reason. It wears its age so gracefully that it looks as if it had been built just as it is for a romantic 19th-century stage set. Popularly called the Temple of Diana — although it was probably not dedicated to Diana at all — the temple is Evora's oldest surviving building, dating from the 2nd or 3rd century. It is also one of the best-preserved Roman temples on the Iberian Peninsula, thanks largely to the fact that it was bricked up in the Middle Ages and subsequently used as a storehouse. This practical use may have been inappropriate for such an elegant building, but it saved the structure from almost certain destruction. When the protective shell of bricks and rubble was removed in 1871, 14 of the 26 Corinthian columns that originally formed the peristyle were left standing. Twelve of the granite columns still have their Estremoz marble capitals. A large piece of the architrave remains in place, along with fragments of a frieze, but the rest has disappeared, perhaps incorporated into later construction in the area. Largo Conde de Vila Flor.

Cerca Velha (Old Walls) – The upper part of the city where the Roman temple stands is Evora's acropolis. It was once dominated by an old castle (the one that Gerald the Fearless took and that the angry populace of Evora largely destroyed in 1383–84), and was circled by Roman and Visigothic walls with a circumference of about 3,545 feet. Most of the old wall has disappeared, but some interesting fragments remain, including two of the five original gates: the Arco de Dona Isabel, a Roman archway opening onto Largo Alexandre Herculano, a block west of the Roman temple, and the twin towers that stand in Largo das Portas de Moura, on the southern side of the old perimeter. Bits of the old wall can also be seen incorporated into the façades of two palaces (neither is open to the public) in the former acropolis area: the Palácio dos Duques de Cadaval, across the square from the Roman temple, and the Solar dos Condes de Basto, behind the cathedral and near the old university.

Palácio dos Duques de Cadaval (Palace of the Dukes of Cadaval) – This rather severe, mainly 16th-century building, with two sturdy rectangular towers topped by Moorish-style battlements, was the palace of the Melo family, one of Portugal's oldest noble families. It includes part of a northwest section of the old castle, which King João I awarded to Martim Afonso de Melo in 1390 for his prowess in the Battle of Aljubarrota. The Duke of Bragança was held in the south tower before his execution by João II in 1484. Largo Conde de Vila Flor.

Solar dos Condes de Basto (Manor House of the Counts of Basto) – Originally a Moorish castle, this *solar* is one of Evora's oldest noble residences. It was given to the monks of the order of São Bento de Calatrava by King Afonso Henriques in 1167, after the city's reconquest from the Moors; it became crown property during the 13th century, and thereafter served as a royal residence on several occasions. It's now mainly a 15th- and 16th-century structure, but the base of the outer wall on the north side, facing Largo dos Colegiais, incorporates part of Evora's old wall. Largo dos Colegiais.

Sé (Cathedral) – This very imposing church, dating from the 12th and 13th centuries (consecrated in 1204), is not Evora's most beautiful building, although it is certainly one of its most interesting. Its plan is Romanesque, but in its structure and decorations, the building that rose was already Gothic, and additions made up to the 18th century left it with a mixture of styles. On several occasions the cathedral has lived up to its fortress-like appearance. It was from the terraces of this building that the townspeople supporting João of Avis for king in the late 14th century launched their incendiary assault on the old castle held by the unwanted regent, Queen Leonor. And it was in the cathedral's great naves that the townspeople took refuge during the height of the killing when the French were sacking the city during the early 19th century.

Part of the massive Romanesque-Gothic façade dates from the 12th century, but the two oddly dissimilar towers flanking the deeply recessed Gothic portal — one topped with a tile-covered cone, the other with a series of turrets — are from the 16th century. The Apostles standing guard on either side of the church entrance are 14th-century works, probably southern Portugal's first notable pieces of Christian sculpture. Inside, the three naves are the longest in Portugal. They are early Gothic (though the tasteless white pointing applied to the granite columns is modern), but the side chapels and transept date from the 16th century, and the splendid neo-classical chancel and high altar at the end are from the 18th century, designed by Johann Friedrich Ludwig, the German architect of the great monastery-palace at Mafra. The little polychromed stone statue of the Virgin set in a carved baroque altar at the beginning of the central nave is a 12th-century representation of Our Lady of O, the pregnant Virgin. Be sure to climb the stairs to the *coro alto* (above the west end of the central nave). The 16th-century carved wooden stalls are worth the effort: Panels behind the seats are full of vivid secular scenes of day-to-day country life in the Alentejo, as well as biblical scenes.

The early-14th-century cloister on the south side of the church is a magnificent example of the austere beauties of Evora's transitional Gothic. Its founder, a 14th-century bishop, lies in the carved marble sepulcher in a chapel in the cloister's southeast corner. The cathedral is open daily, from 9 AM to noon and from 2 to 5 PM. Admission charge to the cloister. Largo da Sé.

Museu de Arte Sacra (Museum of Sacred Art) – The collection, installed in the cathedral's south tower, contains fine ecclesiastical paintings, sculpture, vestments, gold, silver, and furniture. The ivory and polychromed stone figures of the 14th and 15th centuries are especially interesting — above all, the rare little ivory statue of the Virgin holding the infant Jesus, which opens up to form a triptych decorated with high-relief scenes from her life. The original head of this nearly unique figure is missing; the present wooden one dates from the 16th century. Open from 9 AM to noon and from 2 to 5 PM; closed Mondays. Admission charge. Largo da Sé (phone: 26910).

Museu Regional (Regional Museum) – In the former Bishop's Palace, a 16th-to-early-18th-century building next door to the cathedral, this museum — also known as the *Museu de Evora* — has an extremely interesting collection of archaeological pieces, paintings, and sculpture. Among several fine works is the series of 13 paintings on the life of the Virgin that once graced the high altar of the cathedral; an anonymous 14th-century Flemish work from the Bruges school, it alone would make the visit worthwhile. Another painting not to be missed is the little 16th-century Limoges enamel triptych of the Crucifixion. The museum's archaeological section contains several exquisite fragments that are tantalizingly evocative of Evora's antiquity. The 3rd-century marble relief of a maenad, her skirt twirling around her as she dances wildly, is particularly haunting. Open from 9 AM to noon and from 2 to 5 PM; closed Mondays. Admission charge. Largo Conde de Vila Flor (phone: 22604).

Biblioteca Pública (Public Library) – Just across from the museum, this is one of Portugal's outstanding libraries, with more than 500,000 manuscripts and 250,000 printed works, including a rare-book section containing over 500 incunabula (books printed before 1501), among other priceless early works. The collection is particularly noted for its codices connected with Portugal's maritime feats of the 15th and 16th centuries. Except for occasional exhibitions, the library's treasures are not on display. Visitors who wish to consult books must show their passports or other credentials to get a reader's card; the process normally takes 24 hours. Open Mondays through Fridays, from 9 AM to 12:30 PM and from 2 to 8 PM. Largo Conde de Vila Flor (phone: 22369).

Igreja e Convento dos Lóios (Lóios Church and Monastery) – The monastery building has become a state-owned inn, or *pousada* (see *Checking In*), but the church, although privately owned, is open to the public and can be visited. Dedicated to São João Evangelista (St. John the Evangelist), it was built in Gothic style between 1485 and 1491, but the main façade, with the exception of the Flamboyant portal, was rebuilt after the 1755 earthquake that destroyed Lisbon. The single Gothic nave is lined with 18th-century *azulejos* depicting the life of St. Lawrence Justinian (a 15th-century patriarch of Venice), some of them signed by Portugal's best-known tile maker, António de Oliveira Bernardes, and dated 1711. The church was founded by the nobleman Rodrigo Afonso de Melo to be his family's mausoleum. The chapterhouse belonging to the church has a particularly beautiful and curious doorway, with Manueline columns supporting two Moorish arches. Open daily, from 9 AM to noon and from 2 to 5 PM. Largo Conde de Vila Flor.

Universidade (University) – At the bottom of the hill, east of the cathedral, the Universidade do Espírito Santo (University of the Holy Ghost), to give it its full name, was founded by Cardinal Henrique for the Jesuits in 1559. The classical-baroque building is a notable piece of architecture with an especially handsome cloister, and it is profusely decorated with 16th-, 17th-, and 18th-century tiles. The university closed in 1759 when the Jesuits were expelled from Portugal by Prime Minister Marquês de Pombal; it reopened in 1975. There are no regular visiting hours, but most parts of the building can be seen upon request. Largo do Cardeal Rei (phone: 25572).

Largo das Portas de Moura – This small, picturesque square is a few blocks south of the university (walk along Rua do Conde da Serra da Tourega, following, more or less, the line of the old Roman wall). The two square towers on its north side mark the site of the south gate through the old wall. The Renaissance fountain in the center, built with funds donated by the people of the neighborhood and by Dom Jaime, Duke of Bragança, was inaugurated with festivities on November 4, 1556. On the square's south side is the verandah of the 16th-century Casa Cordovil. Six slender columns support Moorish arches and a little conical dome, forming a structure that, with its overtones of different cultures, manages to convey the essence of Evora's mixed history.

Igreja Nossa Senhora da Graça (Church of Our Lady of Grace) – The magnificent façade of this semi-ruined 16th-century church, one of the most striking examples of Renaissance architecture on the Iberian Peninsula, inevitably invites comparison with the architecture of Michelangelo because of its dramatic composition of triangles, circles, and columns. It was almost certainly designed by Diogo de Torralva, the architect of the Claustro dos Filipes in Tomar. The four heroically muscular but rather graceless figures supporting the spheres on the corners of the façade actually symbolize the four rivers of faith, but local people call them, ironically, the *meninos da Graça,* the children of Grace. The vault of the church collapsed in 1884, and most of the contents were taken to other churches, including the Church of São Francisco. The adjacent convent building is now occupied by the military. Rua da Graça.

Igreja de São Francisco (Church of St. Francis) – This 16th-century Moorish-Gothic church, about 2 blocks west of Nossa Senhora da Graça, has several outstanding architectural features, including a Gothic vault of unusual proportions over the single nave. But what everybody remembers it for is its curious Capela dos Ossos (Chapel of Bones). The walls of this macabre room are lined with bones and skulls laid out in intricate and sometimes ingenious patterns. The intention was to induce contemplation and instill a proper sense of mortality in the spirit of any Franciscan monk who might feel tempted toward frivolity. "We bones lie waiting here for yours," warns the Latin inscription over the door. The two mummified corpses hanging at the end of the chapel are said to be father and son, victims of an embittered wife's deathbed curse. (The lady's rather unusual malediction was that the flesh should never fall from their bones.) The chapel is open daily, from 9 AM to 12:30 PM and from 2:30 to 6 PM. Admission charge to the chapel. Praça Primeiro de Maio.

Jardim Público – Evora's charming public gardens are just south of the São Francisco church, enclosed by a section of the city wall. In the center is a fine old wrought-iron bandstand, where concerts are given in summer.

Palácio de Dom Manuel (Palace of King Manuel) – What was once a fine late-15th-century palace was sadly allowed to fall into ruin during the last century, and this restored fragment of the structure — the Galeria das Damas (Ladies Gallery) — is all that remains. Several kings lived here: Manuel I, João III, and the Spanish Philips. Many historic ceremonies also took place in the palace, including the momentous investiture of Vasco da Gama as admiral of the fleet that found the sea route to India in 1497. Exhibitions are now staged in its rooms. Jardim Público (phone: 25809).

Praça do Giraldo – A short walk up Rua da República leads to this square, named after the city's Christian liberator. It has been the geographic center and focal point of life in Evora since its beginnings as the forum of the Roman city. Until 1570, a triumphal arch stood at its northern end, where the parish Church of Santo Antão stands today. The Renaissance fountain in front of the church was built in 1571 (and paid for by the Cardinal-King Dom Henrique, the founder of the university), to replace an earlier one that was demolished along with the triumphal arch. The white marble benches ringing the fountain were placed there in 1970.

Igreja de Santo Antão (Church of St. Antão) – This rather sober church, built during the 16th century by the local architect Manuel Pires, is worth a look inside. It has some fine carved and polychromed altars and, on the front of the high altar, a very rare low-relief marble panel of the Apostles, dating from the 14th century. The piece was saved from the Templars Church of Santo Antoninho, the predecessor of the present church. Praça do Giraldo.

Cerca Nova (New Walls) – The approximately 9,840 feet of so-called new walls that once girdled the city are still nearly intact today, although much restored. The new walls were begun during the first half of the 14th century, in the reign of King Afonso IV, and were finished between 1384 and 1433, during the reign of King João I. Originally, there were 40 towers and 10 gates, but most of these have long since fallen prey to time and to cannibalization by stone-hungry builders. One that still remains much as it was during the 14th century is the tower guarding the Porta de Alconchel (Alconchel Gate), at the bottom of Rua Serpa Pinto. A good road, the Estrada da Circunvalação, follows the path of the walls all the way around the city.

OUTSIDE THE WALLS

Ermida de São Brás (Chapel of St. Blaise) – Built during the late 15th century, this is an excellent early example of the battlemented church that is so characteristic of the Alentejo region. Fourteen cylindrical buttress-turrets give the little building its unique, bellicose aspect. Inside, the green-and-white diamond-pattern tiles covering the barrel vault over the nave are from the 16th century. In 1490, a German historian named Munzer described his surprise at finding a huge crocodile hanging over the main door. It had been left there as an offering by Portuguese navigators after a successful voyage of discovery down the coast of Africa. Open daily, from 9 AM to noon and from 2 to 5 PM. Rua da República.

Aqueduto da Prata (Prata Aqueduct) – This outstanding work of engineering was built between 1532 and 1537, during the reign of King João III, to bring water from a spring at Graça do Divor, 11 miles (18 km) away. It cost quite literally a king's fortune at the time (over 700,000 *réis*), but Evora has always suffered a shortage of water, and King João's court spent a lot of time in the city. The road around the walls passes under the aqueduct at the point where it enters the city, but the most monumental section lies between the walls and São Bento de Castris, 2 miles (3 km) away on the road to Arraiolos.

■ **EXTRA SPECIAL:** Wander through the narrow streets and alleys of the Old City with a dictionary in hand, and you will discover wonderfully sonorous and evocative street names everywhere. Some commemorate local "celebrities" or simply local "characters" — Rua do Malbarbado (Street of the Unshaven One), Rua do Matamouros (Street of the Bully), Rua do Alfaiate da Condessa (Street of the Countesses' Tailor), and Rua da Ama do Cardeal (Street of the Cardinal's Maid). Residence near, or ownership of, an olive grove may have commended Manuel to posterity (Rua Manuel do Olival), and Master Resende de Alvaro (Rua Mestre Resende de Alvaro) may have won renown as a teacher, but the reasons for the immortalization of Beatriz de Vilhena (Rua Beatriz de Vilhena), the Cogominhos family (Travessa dos Cogominhos), or even the Dark Ladies (Rua das Morenas) are less obvious and probably long forgotten. Other names refer to features of the streetscape: Rua da Cozinha de Sua Alteza (Street of His Highnesses' Kitchen); Rua das Pedras Negras (Street of the Black Stones), an old street name often found in southern Portugal and Spain; and Rua das Casas Pintadas (Street of the Painted Houses), where Vasco da Gama's house is located — it has rooms decorated with frescoes of exotic wildlife (but is not open to the public). Some of the names may require a knowledge of Portuguese to appreciate their full flavor, but for beginners, this is a good way to pick up a little of the language, even if some of it might be a bit archaic.

SOURCES AND RESOURCES

 TOURIST INFORMATION: The Town Hall Tourism Department runs two information offices in Evora, both with English-speaking staffs. (The main one is at 73-74 Praça do Giraldo; phone: 22671; the other is on Avenida São Sebastião; phone: 31296, at the entrance to the city on the N114 from Lisbon.) Watch for a blue-and-white sign with a big "I". Both are open from 9 AM to 7 PM daily from April through October (to 6 PM off-season). Guides can be hired by writing in advance, addressing the query to Câmara Municipal de Evora, Departamento de Turismo (Praça de Sertório; Evora 4000; phone: 24101 or 27000).

Local Coverage – *Diário do Sul* is the leading daily regional newspaper. English-language newspapers such as the *International Herald Tribune* can be bought at *Tabacaria Paris,* a tobacco and stationery shop (19 Rua da República; phone: 24569). Although two or three locally published guidebooks, written by historians, are in print, their English translations tend to range from quaint to uproariously unintelligible. The best guidebook is probably Tulio Espanca's *Evora: Património Mundial,* but no English version was available at press time.

 TELEPHONE: The city code for Evora is 66. If calling from within Portugal, dial 066 before the local number.

 GETTING AROUND: The best way to see Evora is to walk. It is a small city, distances between places of interest are never very great, and the narrow streets make driving difficult if not impossible in the Old City. Parking spaces can usually be found in the squares, for those who do decide to drive across town.

Airport – The nearest is Lisbon's Portela de Sacavém (phone: 1-802060).

Bus – There is no inner-city bus service, but the national network, *Rodoviário Nacional,* serves Evora, with daily departures to Lisbon and points south. The buses are reasonably comfortable and inexpensive. Tickets should be bought in advance at the bus station (131 Largo da República; phone: 22121), or from *RN Tours–Viagens e Turismo,* a travel agency (131 Rua da República; phone: 24254).

Car Rental – *Europcar* is at 155 Rua Serpa Pinto (phone: 28815).

Taxi – Taxis are fairly plentiful. The best place to find one is at the city cabstands, especially the centrally located ones at Praça do Giraldo, Largo das Portas de Moura, and Largo Luís de Camões. To call a cab, dial 32220 or 32222. Taxis can be hired by the kilometer for tours in the surrounding area.

Train – The station (phone: 22125) is a little over a half mile south of the city. There are two or three trains a day to Lisbon (the trip takes about 3 hours) and also connections to Spain, the Lower Alentejo, and the Algarve. Those going to Lisbon should remember that trains do not cross the Tagus River. (The train takes passengers as far as Barreiro, on the south bank of the Tagus, from where they ferry across to the river station on Lisbon's Praça do Comércio; the price of the ride is included with the train ticket.)

SPECIAL EVENTS: Every second Tuesday of the month — June excepted — a market is held in the Rossio de São Brás outside the walls. These monthly markets are important events in all Portuguese country towns, and Evora's is especially so because it is held in a district capital. But Evora's biggest market gathering is the *Feira de São João* (St. John's Fair), held annually during the last 2 weeks of June. This major event is an enjoyable combination of country market, agricultural fair, and folk festival, and it draws huge crowds from all over the district. Open stalls sell everything from handicrafts to hair restorer, there is folk dancing and singing, and improvised restaurants serve tasty local dishes.

MUSEUMS: Evora's major museums, such as the *Museu de Arte Sacra* and the *Museu Regional* (also called the *Museu de Evora*), are discussed in *Special Places.* In addition, the following may be of interest:

   Museu de Arte Sacra (Sacred Art Museum) – Not to be confused with the *Museu de Arte Sacra* in the cathedral, this museum of religious art is an annex to the *Museu Regional,* and it's set up in the Igreja das Mercês (Church of Mercy). Open from 9 AM to noon and from 2 to 5 PM; closed Mondays; no admission charge. Rua do Raimundo (phone: 22604).

   Museu de Artesanato (Handicrafts Museum) – An excellent collection of local crafts — pottery, textiles, cork work, basketry, and so on — installed in the Celeiro Comun, a magnificent 18th-century building that was formerly a communal granary. Open from 10 AM to noon and from 2 to 5:30 PM; closed Mondays; no admission charge. 7 Praça Primeiro de Maio (phone: 22937).

   João Cutileiro – The studio of Evora's internationally known sculptor can be visited in the morning up to 12:30 PM; and, of course, his works can be purchased or commissioned. 13 Estrada de Viana do Alentejo (phone: 23972).

SHOPPING: This is the sort of provincial city whose inhabitants would probably do their shopping in Lisbon if they could. The local stores are fine for run-of-the-mill household needs; for travelers, the best buys are handicrafts. The main shopping streets are centered around Praça do Giraldo, with many of the most useful shops located on Rua 5 de Outubro and its side streets, as well as in the arcades that run the length of the east side of Praça do Giraldo and continue down Rua João de Deus to Largo Luís de Camões. The *Centro Comercial Eborim,* a modern shopping center (Rua Eborim; phone: 22260), has practically everything under one roof. The *Mercado Municipal* (Municipal Market; on Praça Primeiro de Maio), open every morning except Mondays, is not only the best place for fresh food and delicacies such as the excellent local cheeses and cured sausages, but also a colorful place to visit. Handicrafts, including good, brown-glazed oven pots, are sold from stalls outside, along with the omnipresent plastic goods. Two handicraft shops worth noting:

   Casa Silva – Typical painted *alentejano* furniture — one of the best sources for this increasingly rare work. 11 Rua do Cano (phone: 23456).

   Teoartis – Hand-painted tiles, original or reproduction, made to order and available from stock. 78 Rua 5 de Outubro (phone: 22736).

SPORTS AND FITNESS: Bullfighting – The *Praça de Touros* is just outside the walls, along the Estrada da Circunvalação. Several bullfights are held during the season, which runs from May to sometime in October, but programming is irregular. Check with the tourist office.

Soccer – The two local teams are not major league, but they have strong support, and, as everywhere in Portugal, soccer is the top spectator sport. The season begins in September and ends in May. Games are played on Sundays in the *Estádio Sanches de Miranda* (phone: 22200).

Swimming – An excellent complex of five municipal swimming pools (*piscinas municipais*) is set among lawns on the edge of town, 1¼ miles (2 km) from the city center. The facilities include an Olympic-size pool, a diving pool, a learners' pool, and two pools for children, plus two restaurants and a bar. The complex (phone: 32324) is open daily, from 9 AM to 8 PM (1 to 8 PM on Mondays, to allow for cleaning).

Tennis – Good clay courts can be rented at either of two sports clubs: *Lusitano Ginásio Clube* (Estrada das Alcaçovas; phone: 22844) and *Juventudes Sport Clube* (Estádio Sanches de Miranda; phone: 22200). Bring your own gear.

 THEATER: The *Teatro Garcia de Resende* (Praça Joaquim António de Aguiar; phone: 23112) is the biggest theater in the south of Portugal — the only one for miles around, in fact. It was built between 1881 and 1892 and destined rather snootily for opera, recitals, and concerts only, but it was not a great success. In 1975 the theater was handed over to the Centro Cultural de Evora, which since then has operated a theater school in it. Check with the tourist office for possible shows and concerts.

 MUSIC: The Câmara Municipal (Town Hall) sponsors classical music, jazz, and pop concerts, but there is no regular program. However, when something is going on, an attempt is made to publish the particulars as far in advance as possible, so check with the tourist office. The concerts take place in the *Teatro Garcia de Resende* (see above) and in other venues such as the Palácio de Dom Manuel, or even in old houses. Brass-band concerts take place in the Jardim Público in summer. Visitors interested in music should also ask about the possibility of taking in a performance of *cantares alentejanos* (Alentejo songs). *Cantares* are folk songs of remote origin, sung (chanted might be a better word) by groups of men. The singers stand together in a tight group or sometimes march along slowly, swaying in unison as they sing. The *Feira de São João* is a good occasion to hear them.

 NIGHTCLUBS AND NIGHTLIFE: Evora is the perfect place to enjoy the benefits of early nights without feeling like an old fogey. It has virtually no nightlife worth sampling, other than a few discotheques or the innocent pleasures of sitting on a café terrace or strolling through the town looking at the lighted monuments. Among the most popular discos are *Brown's* (54 Rua Serpa Pinto; phone: 20545) and *Slide* (135 Rua Serpa Pinto; phone: 28272).

BEST IN TOWN

 CHECKING IN: Accommodations are limited in quantity, but they range fairly widely in style, from luxury to plain, comfortable economy. At the expensive end of the scale — and there is only one luxury establishment in Evora — expect to pay from $90 to $115, depending on whether it is high season or low, for a double room with breakfast. In the moderate range, expect to pay from $40 to $65, and in the inexpensive range approximately $20 to $30. All telephone numbers are in the 66 city code unless otherwise indicated.

Pousada dos Lóios – This 32-room luxury establishment is one of the best of the state-owned *pousadas*. In the converted and restored Convento dos Lóios, built in

1485 by the nobleman Rodrigo Afonso de Melo, it occupies the site of Evora's old castle. Most of the rooms are in the old monks' cells, with period furnishings, but the essential modern services are adequate. There is an open-air pool and a restaurant serving regional food (see *Eating Out*). The location — next door to the Roman temple and right in the center of everything — is perfect. Largo Conde de Vila Flor (phone: 24051). Expensive.

Monte das Flores – This *estalagem,* or inn, occupies a converted farm 2½ miles (4 km) west of Evora on N114. The 17 rooms are all furnished attractively and comfortably in period rustic, and all have private baths. A pool and tennis courts are among the facilities; there's also horseback riding. The restaurant serves good regional dishes. Monte das Flores (phone: 25018). Moderate.

Planície – One of Evora's busiest hotels and generally considered the top establishment in its price range, it has 33 well-equipped rooms with baths. Spacious public rooms and a highly regarded restaurant add to the attractions. The location and service are first-rate. 40 Largo de Alvaro Velho (phone: 24026). Moderate.

Riviera – In line with all establishments in its *pensão residencial* category, it lacks a few of the regular hotel services — no restaurant or bar. But its 22 rooms do all have private baths and color television sets, and it is well located between the cathedral and Praça do Giraldo. 49 Rua 5 de Outubro (phone: 23304). Moderate.

Santa Clara – An unpretentious but first-rate modern hostelry in the heart of the Old City, west of Praça do Giraldo. The 30 rooms (with bath) are comfortably appointed, the service is attentive, and there is a large and very good restaurant. All things considered, the hotel offers unbeatable value. 19 Travessa da Milheira (phone: 24141). Moderate.

Vitória – A modern *albergaria* (another category of inn), it's comfortable and very well equipped, although without a restaurant. All 48 rooms have private baths, color TV sets, air conditioning, and phones. The location, about 300 yards outside the city walls to the south, means easy parking. Rua Diana de Lis (phone: 27174). Moderate.

Diana – A small, 15-room *pensão* in the center of town, modest but well regarded. The rooms are small, but all have baths and phone. No bar or restaurant. 2 Rua Diogo Cão (phone: 22008). Inexpensive.

EATING OUT: Portuguese from regions with more gastronomical cachet tend to look down their noses at Alentejo cooking as lacking variety and finesse. They may be right up to a point, because the spartan character of life on the great, dry, central plains is clearly present in the local food, and the region in general has never been known for the range and refinement of its culinary achievements. This is a virtue at times, but even if it weren't, there are more than enough good things to eat to keep a visitor from feeling homesick for a hamburger.

Bread — the heavy, crusty, delicious kind, with the ash from wood ovens still clinging to the bottoms of the huge loaves — is an important part of all meals, and even finds its way into the soup. The most basic of these, *sopa alentejana,* is in fact mostly bread and water. To make it, water is boiled with a lot of garlic and olive oil, then poured over slices of bread in a bowl. A poached egg is added just before serving.

Pork (*carne de porco*) and lamb or mutton (*borrego*) are the staple meats. In one of the few local dishes that have acquired a wider fame, *carne de porco à alentejana,* small pieces of pork are blended tastily with clams. Pork is also a basic ingredient in popular bean dishes such as the various versions of *feijoada alentejana,* a devastatingly substantial mixture of pork meats, fresh and cured, and white beans. Lamb and kid (*cabrito*) are most commonly eaten in stews (*ensopados*) or roasted in the oven (*assado no forno*). All meat dishes are inclined to be heavy in the Alentejo — and be warned that restaurant servings are never tailored to the needs of weight watchers.

Evora's desserts betray their Moorish and medieval convent background. The people of the Alentejo have inherited a collective sweet tooth, and their traditional sweetmeats (*doçaria*) tend to err in this direction. Most of the favorites, such as *queijo conventual* (convent "cheese") or *toucinho do céu* (bacon from heaven), have an egg base and are flavored with almond. The great Alentejo cheese, Serpa, made near the town of that name not far from Evora, is increasingly rare and difficult to find. The salty little cheeses made in Evora from cured sheep's milk are good as appetizers.

The best Alentejo wines are made in the Borba, Redondo, and Reguengos de Monsaraz areas east of Evora, and in Vidigueira, south of the city. The reds especially are good, rather heavy wines, and are almost always the product of cooperatives. The top wines from each cooperative are sold as *reservas*. Expect to pay from $40 to $60 for a dinner for two with wine at those restaurants listed below as expensive, from $30 to $40 in the moderate range, and under $25 in the inexpensive range. All telephone numbers are in the 66 city code unless otherwise indicated.

Cozinha de Santo Humberto – Humberto is the patron saint of hunters and this is one of the country's best dining places for game when it is in season (from October into January). At other times, it's famed for its *carne de porco à alentejana* and, for instance, for *arroz de pato no forno* (duck casserole with rice). Closed Thursdays. Reservations advised. 39 Rua da Moeda (phone: 24251). Expensive.

Fialho – Evora's most celebrated restaurant, serving genuinely traditional food — it's not unknown for gastronomes from Lisbon to drive out here for lunch, especially during game season. Little plates of delicious appetizers (*entradas*) precede the main meal. The *borrego assado* is justifiably renowned, and so is the *favada real da casa,* a monumental bean dish. In the game season, partridge, hare, and wild boar (*perdiz, lebre,* and *javali,* respectively) are specialties. The place is always thronged, and it's not large, so reservations are advised. Closed Mondays, but open throughout the day otherwise, with no break between lunch and dinner. 16 Travessa das Mascarenhas (phone: 23079). Expensive.

Pousada dos Lóios – The food here is not quite up to the standard of the *Fialho* or the *Cozinha de Santo Humberto,* but for those in search of something more international, the *pousada,* occupying a 15th-century monastery, could be worthwhile. The dining room itself, once the monks' refectory, is lovely, and in good weather, tables and chairs are set up around the equally lovely cloister. Open daily. Reservations advised. Largo Conde de Vila Flor (phone: 24051). Expensive.

Guião – One of Evora's top traditional eateries in the intermediate price range. It's large (3 rooms) and comfortable, with old-fashioned decor. The *borrego no forno* vies with *Fialho*'s. Closed Mondays. Reservations unnecessary. 81 Rua da República (phone: 23071). Moderate.

Luar de Janeiro – It leans less heavily on traditional regional fare than some of the other restaurants, and has good seafood. It's also convenient because it stays open late — until 2 AM. Closed Thursdays. Reservations unnecessary. 13 Travessa de Janeiro (phone: 24895). Moderate.

1/4 P'ras 9 – The odd-looking name actually means a quarter to nine. A relative newcomer to the Evora scene, it specializes in charcoal grills and seafood. The *açorda de marisco* (a difficult-to-describe mixture of bread and seafood) is excellent. Closed Wednesdays. No reservations. 9A Rua Pedro Simões (phone: 26774). Moderate to inexpensive.

A Gruta – On the basis of value for money, this has become one of the most popular restaurants in town in recent years. No frills, but the food is good. The specialty is oven-roasted kid. Closed Saturdays. No reservations. 2 Avenida General Humberto Delgado (phone: 28186). Inexpensive.

Martinho – A good, very popular place, where the specialty is a kid dish called *cabrito na canoa.* Open daily. No reservations. 24 Largo Luís de Camões (phone: 23057). Inexpensive.

GRANADA

Of all the fabled landmarks in the world, none stands in a more gorgeous setting than the magnificent Alhambra, the hilltop fortress-palace of the Nasrid kings, the last Muslim rulers of Spain. Snow-capped peaks of the nearby Sierra Nevada form a natural tapestry behind its golden walls, and below, a mosaic of Granada's Moorish-Christian towers spreads like a magic carpet over a fertile plain. Granada has much more to offer than the Alhambra alone, but even if visitors were to tour only the Alhambra's multitude of pleasures — for this is not a single building, but a complex of palaces, gardens, towers, gates, courtyards, and other structures whose exquisite decoration sums up the meaning of the word "arabesque" — the city would be worth the trip. This once-remote Arab stronghold, now just a 2-hour drive from the tourist-laden Costa del Sol, is Spain's second-biggest attraction after the *Prado* in Madrid.

In its Roman days and up through the early Muslim period, Granada languished on history's sidelines. But the city came into its own during the 13th century, when the Moors began to lose their grip elsewhere in Andalusia. Córdoba fell to Christian rule in 1236, Seville in 1248. But Granada, which had become the capital of the Nasrid kingdom of Granada (which included the present-day provinces of Granada, Almería, and Málaga) in 1238, would hang on under Moorish rule for approximately another 250 years. As the city became the last surviving Islamic capital in Spain, Moors by the thousands streamed into it, transforming it into a thriving center of artists and craftsmen. The royal Alhambra was their masterpiece. Through ensuing centuries, this wonder of the world cast its spell over writers, painters, and musicians, including the American author Washington Irving and two of Granada's most famous sons, the composer Manuel de Falla and the writer-poet Federico García Lorca.

The final triumph in the Christians' 781-year struggle to regain Moorish-held Spain took place on January 2, 1492, when the last Muslim king, Boabdil, handed over the keys to the city to Ferdinand and Isabella and rode tearfully off into the mountains with the queen mother, Ayesha. ("You weep like a woman for what you could not defend as a man" were her immortal words of consolation to her son.) The Catholic Monarchs installed their thrones in the Alhambra and set about remaking the city in the Christian image, creating the architectural mix that is still in evidence. Isabella ordered the construction of the cathedral and its Capilla Real, the finely wrought Royal Chapel, where the marble tombs of the royal pair, as well as her crown and jewel box, can be seen today. Muslim mosques were converted to Christian uses. Unfortunately, many fine Moorish buildings have been destroyed, but a walk through the twisted, narrow streets of the Albaicín, an old Arab neighborhood on a hill across from the Alhambra, gives a pretty good idea of what the city once was like.

Granada continued to flourish into the 16th century, then sank back into relative obscurity once again. Today, a city of about 230,000, it depends economically on its rich agricultural valley, as well as on nonindustrial enterprises such as banking, education, and tourism. A big boost to the latter will come in 1992. While the rest of Spain, and especially Seville, celebrates the 500th anniversary of Columbus's discovery of America, Granada will be celebrating the 500th anniversary of the Christian Reconquest as well. In the meantime, many museums and monuments are being renovated in anticipation of expanded world attention.

Sightseeing in Granada is delightful. The absence of heavy manufacturing sections and the existence of only a scattering of garish modern buildings in the busy downtown area confer a small-town, open-air feeling to the streets. And the large student population at the University of Granada keeps the town young. Then there are Granada's famous Gypsy women, those entrepreneurs in housedresses and sweaters pressing carnations and fortunes on passersby at the cathedral and on the Alhambra hill. Begging and wheedling are their chosen livelihood, and everyone seems to accept that. *Granadinos* shoo them off with a firm "no," but visitors don't get off so easily. "*Tu te vas a casar hombre alto*" (you will marry a tall man), they call to a passing tourist, grabbing her hand. And if you cross their palms with coins, they shout "*papel, papel*" (paper)! Your fortune, whether you want it or not, costs whatever the traffic will bear. (Only a "*vamos a la policía*" turns them off.) The Gypsy population played such a colorful part in history here that Granada is more accepting of their ways than Seville. Proposals to license them have come to nothing; posting official rates at the Alhambra has been suggested, though many *granadinos* say that wouldn't change a thing — nor would they want it to.

GRANADA AT-A-GLANCE

SEEING THE CITY: This is a city of many views, but the "postcard" picture of the Alhambra set against mountains that are snow covered most of the year is from Plaza San Nicolás in the Albaicín. Within the Alhambra walls, the Torre de la Vela in the Alcazaba (see below) affords a panorama of city, plains, and mountains.

SPECIAL PLACES: Granada is divided neatly into upper and lower towns. Two prominent hills facing each other across the narrow gorge of a river — the Río Darro — compose the upper city. On the southern hill are the Alhambra and the adjoining Generalife (the summer palace and gardens of the Nasrid kings). On the northern hill is the old Arab quarter, the Albaicín, now a fascinating residential district. An even taller satellite hill leads off from the Albaicín to the dusty Sacromonte Gypsy district, a warren of small white houses trailing out to a rocky mountainside pockmarked with abandoned Gypsy caves.

The main descent from the Alhambra is a narrow road, Cuesta de Gomérez, that drops directly down to the Plaza Nueva, where the lower city begins. The plaza is the eastern end of the principal east-west artery, Calle de los Reyes Católicos, which meets the principal north-south artery, Gran Vía de Colón, at the circular Plaza de Isabel la Católica. A much-photographed bronze statue of the enthroned Queen Isabella offering the Santa Fé agreement to Columbus graces this major intersection; the document, named for the nearby town where it was signed, authorized the epochal voyage to the New World. Calle de los Reyes Católicos then continues west, passing within a few short blocks of the cathedral, the Capilla Real, and other downtown sights, en route to Puerta Real, the hub of the city's business, shopping, and hotel and restaurant district.

Note that the opening hours listed below for Granada's monuments, churches, and museums are for the months of March through September; winter afternoon hours generally are shorter. Times are subject to change.

THE ALHAMBRA COMPLEX

Spain's last remaining fortress-palace built for a Moorish sovereign stands atop the Alhambra hill, girded by more than a mile of ramparts that appear in the distance like a golden shield. (To the medieval Arabs, however, the rust-colored local soil used to build the fortress gave it a more coppery tinge — the name Alhambra comes from the Arabic for "red fort.") Behind these walls is what amounts to a royal city, at the core of which is the Alhambra's crown jewel, the Casa Real (Royal Palace) — actually a series of three palaces leading from one to the other as if they were one building. Within their fountained courtyards and fanciful halls, whose scalloped mirador (balcony) windows frame vistas of the Albaicín and Sacromonte, the sultans conducted state business, housed their families and harems, and lived a fairy-tale lifestyle. Fierce leaders in treacherous times, their perquisites at ease included such niceties as sherbets made of snow brought to their tables by runners from the Sierra Nevada.

Mohammed ben al-Ahmar, a Nasrid sultan who moved his court here from the neighboring Albaicín hill in 1238, began the royal headquarters, but building continued under other rulers for much of the following century. Then, in 1492, the last Moorish ruler, Boabdil, surrendered the city to Ferdinand and Isabella, who raised their standard over the Alhambra and moved in. Their grandson, the Holy Roman Emperor Charles V, added a palace of his own in the 16th century, but during later centuries, the Alhambra was abandoned for long periods. Vagabonds and Gypsies built bonfires and stabled animals in it, and in the early 19th century, Napoleon's forces inflicted heavy damage on it. Washington Irving, writing about it in *The Alhambra* (1832) after a stint as an attaché in the US Embassy in Madrid (he was later Ambassador to Spain), finally focused world attention on this neglected treasure and started it on its long road to recovery.

Except for the limited use of marble in such features as pillars and fountains, the Moors had spun their magic out of perishable wood, plaster, and ceramics. Most of the present plasterwork veiling, colorful mosaic patterns, and *artesonado* (inlaid wood) ceilings are skillful reproductions based on descriptions, drawings, and remnants of the original designs. Restoration and excavation constitute an ongoing project, which accounts for the closing of areas from time to time. An Alhambra visit takes at least 1 full day (on the run), and it's wise to arrive at opening time, because as the day progresses, the lines of people waiting to walk through the palaces get longer — these famous rooms and courtyards are surprisingly small.

The main approach to the fortress is via the steep Cuesta de Gomérez and through the Puerta de las Granadas (Pomegranate Gate), which signals the entrance to the Alhambra's cool, elm-forested grounds. The gate, added by Charles V, is topped by three stone pomegranates, the symbol of Granada (although the city's name is of Arabic derivation and does not come from the Spanish word for pomegranate, *granada*). Visitors next pass through the Puerta de la Justicia (Justice Gate), a towering horseshoe arch erected by the original Moorish builders and completed with a statue of the Virgin after the Reconquest. This is the Alhambra's main entrance, leading to the Puerta del Vino (Wine Gate), where the ticket office is located. Beyond, bordering the Plaza de los Aljibes (Square of the Cisterns), are the fortifications of the Alcazaba and the Arab royal palaces (Casa Real). The Alhambra admission ticket includes visits to these two, as well as the Generalife, which is outside the Alhambra walls; Charles V's palace, which is within the walls, can be entered without paying any admission charge, although there is a separate charge for its museums.

Alcazaba – The oldest part of the Alhambra, this rugged medieval fortress had been part of the hill's defenses for centuries before construction began on the royal palaces across the square. Climb the most spectacular of its towers, the Torre de la Vela (Watch Tower), for a view directly down into the Plaza Nueva and out as far as the Sierra Nevada. When the Catholic Monarchs moved into the Alhambra, they hoisted their standard over this tower and installed a bell, which tolls each year on January 2 to commemorate the day in 1492 when the Moors lost their last foothold in Spain.

Mexuar – This is the first of the three palaces that make up the Casa Real. From the outside, it appears to be a simple stucco residence, but it was actually the headquarters of the sultan's ministers. The first main council chamber, the Hall of the Mexuar, was converted to a chapel in the 17th century (Chapel of Philip V), thus the coat of arms of Castile beneath the Moorish ceiling of marquetry and plaster restorations. The room is a tame introduction to the splendors of the Alhambra, but its dazzling mirador suggests the mesmerizing world to come, and the spectacle builds as visitors pass through another council chamber, the Cuarto Dorado (Golden Room), to the Patio del Mexuar, one of the palace's smallest but most admired spaces. Its intricate plaster-lace wall with twin tile-rimmed doorways under a deep *artesonado* overhang is actually the north façade of the next building, the Comares Palace.

Palacio de Comares (Comares Palace) – This was the royal palace proper, named for the stained glass that once decorated its windows. Its centerpiece is the Patio de los Arrayanes (Court of the Myrtles), graced with an oblong fishpond running its length between symmetrical myrtle hedges. The tower with the balconies at one end of the pool (to the right upon entering the patio) is a remnant of a seraglio that was partially destroyed to make room for Charles V's palace behind it. Opposite is the Torre de Comares, plainer because it was part of the Alhambra's fortifications. The Sala de la Barca (Hall of Benediction), which forms an antechamber to the latter tower, has a wonderfully intricate inlaid cedar ceiling, a re-creation of the original, which burned in the last century (the ceiling is shaped like an inverted boat, although the name of the hall comes from an Arabic word for "blessing," not from the Spanish *barca* for "boat"). Beyond, inside the tower, is the magnificent Salón de Embajadores (Hall of the Ambassadors), the Moorish kings' throne room. Perfectly square, and clothed in lacy plaster arabesques and brilliant mosaics, this is the largest room in all three palaces. Its domed *artesonado* ceiling is a geometric depiction of the firmament comprising more than 8,000 separate pieces of painted wood.

Palacio de los Leones (Palace of the Lions) – The final palace, built around the famous Patio de los Leones (Court of the Lions), was the royal residence. The court's 124 slim marble columns, each with a subtly different design carved into its capital, are said to represent a palm oasis in the desert (such as Granada seemed to the Moors after centuries in North Africa). In the center is a fountain, its basin supported by 12 gray marble lions, possibly representing the hours of the day, the months of the year, or the signs of the zodiac. At one time, it is said, water flowed from the mouth of a different lion each hour of the day. The lions no longer spout, but the fountain is filled, as are the four narrow channels (representing the four rivers of paradise) that run across the pebbled courtyard floor. The channels were designed to carry used household water from fountains in the living quarters surrounding the court, and on at least one occasion — when Boabdil's father ordered a mass beheading of suspected traitors belonging to a faction of nobles called Abencerrajes — the water ran red. The heads were thrown into the fountain of what came to be known as the Sala de los Abencerrajes, the room to the right upon entering the patio (it has a big rust stain in its fountain). Note the room's stalactite plasterwork ceiling with high inset windows, then go directly across the courtyard to the Sala de las Dos Hermanas (Hall of the Two Sisters), which has an even more extravagant dome. This room, named for two marble slabs set in the floor near the entrance, was reserved for the sultan's wife and inhabited at one time by Boabdil's mother, Ayesha. Off the room is the Sala de los Almeces (Room of the Windows), with the jewel-like Mirador de Lindaraja, or Mirador de Daraxa, the sultana's private balcony. The windows are low to the ground so the queen could gaze into her private cypress garden, the Patio de Lindaraja, from a couch of floor pillows. At the far end of the Court of the Lions is the Sala de los Reyes (Hall of Kings), surprising for its three 14th-century ceiling paintings done on leather by Christian artists.

Downstairs from the Court of the Lions, the Patio de Lindaraja leads to the sumptuous Sala de Baños (Royal Baths), where the sultan surveyed his women from balconies. Small, loosely fitted, star-shaped windows in the ceiling let in light and allowed steam to escape. Washington Irving's furnished rooms (open by special request), where he began his book about the Alhambra, are upstairs in the Patio de la Reja (Window-Grill Patio).

Alhambra Gardens – The Jardines de Partal (Partal Gardens), which occupy an area that once held the kitchen garden of the palace servants and contain the Torre de las Damas (Ladies' Tower), with a delicate porticoed mirador at its base, are passed upon leaving the royal palaces. From here, visitors can choose their own path among the lily pools, fountains, waterfalls, and flower beds that parallel the fortress wall and its succession of towers. Or, by following the fortifications to a footbridge across a narrow gorge, they can proceed directly to the Generalife. (This can also be reached from outside the Alhambra through a ticket gate at the parking lot off Avenida de los Alixares.)

Generalife – The Generalife — the word (pronounced Hay-nay-rah-*lee*-fay) derives from the Arabic for "Garden of the Architect" — was the summer home of the Nasrid rulers. Though the remnants of its simple white palace and pavilions are appealing, the main attractions are indeed the colorful terraced flower gardens, the pools, and the miradors from which the potentates could catch the country breezes while keeping an eye on the Alhambra below. Changes have been made by various proprietors, but many of the garden plans, fountains, and water channels are as they were. The sunken amphitheater was built in the 1950s to accommodate Granada's annual *International Festival of Music and Dance* (see *Special Events*); the maze of *caminos* (walkways), walled in by cypresses sheared and shaped into colonnades and arches, was replanted in the 1930s. The Patio de la Acequia (Patio of the Canal) within the palace walls, however, is an ancient plant-filled paradise with rows of fountain jets sending arcs of dancing waters over a long, narrow pool. Next to this is another original courtyard, the Patio de los Cipreses (Cypress Patio), where a sign next to a limbless cypress trunk proclaims the tree to be more than 500 years old and a witness to a stolen kiss between Boabdil's unfaithful wife and her lover. Running down the hillside is the Escalera de las Cascadas (Waterfall Staircase), with water running through channels cut into its stone banisters.

Palacio de Carlos V – The Holy Roman Emperor Charles V, who so loved Granada that at one point he planned to hold court here, built himself a grandiose Italianate palace right next to the delicate medieval Moorish palaces in the Alhambra. This majestic interloper, designed by Pedro Machuca, a student of Michelangelo, has been admired for its beautiful proportions and hated for its unsuitable location from the very start. The perfectly square exterior hides a spectacular circular 2-story courtyard open to the sky — a dome in the style of the Pantheon in Rome was originally intended. Inside are two museums. The *Museo Hispano-Musulmán* (Museum of Hispano-Muslim Art) contains fragments of original marble and tile from the Alhambra and other ancient city buildings, as well as jewelry and ceramics. Its most famous possession is the blue Jarrón de la Alhambra, a graceful amphora that was displayed for many years in the Sala de las Dos Hermanas. The *Museo Provincial de Bellas Artes* (Provincial Fine Arts Museum) contains painting, sculpture, and stained glass primarily by Granadan artists from the 15th to the 20th centuries. A prized work is a Limoges enameled portrayal of the Crucifixion that once belonged to Isabella's Gran Capitán, who conquered the kingdom of Naples. The *Museo Hispano-Musulmán* (phone: 226279) is open from 10 AM to 2 PM; closed Saturdays and Sundays. The *Museo Provincial de Bellas Artes* (phone: 224834) is open from 10 AM to 2 PM; closed Mondays. There is an admission charge to both museums (separate from the Alhambra's charge — see details below).

Parador San Francisco – Also within the walls of the Alhambra is the 15th-century Convento de San Francisco, founded by Ferdinand and Isabella and their temporary burial place while their mausoleum downtown was being readied. The convent is now a member of the government-run *parador* chain; non-guests are free to visit or dine in the restaurant.

Hours for the Alhambra complex are daily from 9:30 AM to 8 PM from March through September, and from 9:30 AMto 6 PM October through February. Visits to the illuminated complex can be made Tuesdays, Thursdays, and Saturdays from 10 PM to midnight, April through September, and from 8 to 10 PM Saturdays only the rest of the year. Admission to the Alhambra (phone: 227527), including the Alcazaba, is combined with admission to the Generalife (phone: 221342), and the ticket is good for 2 days, allowing the bearer to return to see unvisited parts of the complex. The *Parador San Francisco* (see *Best in Town*) and the Palace of Charles V can be seen without paying the admission charge, although there is a charge for the museums in the palace.

ELSEWHERE IN THE UPPER CITY

Casa-Museo Manuel de Falla – The composer's charming whitewashed house on the Alhambra hill has been kept as it was during his lifetime. A typical Granadan villa, or *carmen,* it has a bright blue front door and a garden awash with roses. De Falla's piano, furniture, manuscripts, photos, and mementos are on display. Open from 10 AM to 2 PM and from 4 to 6 PM; closed Mondays. Admission charge. Across from the *Alhambra Palace* hotel on Antequerela Alta (phone: 229421).

Albaicín and Sacromonte – These are Granada's oldest neighborhoods, dating back to medieval times. The Moorish rulers lived on the Albaicín hill before establishing their palaces on the hill across the way, and even after the Reconquest, Moors continued to populate this Old Quarter. Now a residential area in the early stage of gentrification, it can be reached by a fascinating walk from Plaza Nueva up the Carrera del Darro, which becomes Paseo del Padre Manjón before turning left up the Cuesta de Chapiz. En route, it passes several landmarks: El Bañuelo (Moorish Baths; 33 Carrera del Darro), officially visitable at no charge all day but sometimes closed anyway; the ornate 15th-century Casa de Castril (housing the *Museo Arqueológico,* open from 10 AM to 2 PM; closed Mondays; 41 Carrera del Darro); the 16th-century Convento de Santa Catalina de Zafra (43 Carrera del Darro); and, farther along on Cuesta de Chapiz, the Casa del Chapiz, a quintessential *carmen* serving as a college of Arab studies. Make a right turn at Camino del Sacromonte to climb the dusty streets, lined with sunbaked houses, into the Sacromonte Gypsy district, or continue along the Cuesta de Chapiz into the heart of the Albaicín. The long, steep road is rough going, especially on a hot summer day, but you can't go wrong by choosing any route either up or down through the neighborhood's narrow streets of red-roofed houses and walled gardens.

LOWER CITY

Capilla Real (Royal Chapel) – This Gothic-Plateresque treasure, downtown Granada's greatest attraction, is Ferdinand and Isabella's mausoleum. The cathedral beside it did not yet exist when the royal couple began their final resting place in 1504 — and because the chapel was not yet complete at their deaths (Isabella died before the year was out, her husband in 1516), the two were buried initially at the Convento de San Francisco (now the *parador*) at the Alhambra. They were moved when the new chapel was completed by their grandson and successor, the Holy Roman Emperor Charles V, in 1517. Visitors enter through the Lonja (Exchange House), an adjoining building on Calle de los Oficios, the narrow pedestrian street alongside the cathedral.

Note the graceful frieze on the chapel's façade, one of many decorative variations on the royal initials and crest that appear throughout the building. Inside, a wrought-iron *reja* (grille) crafted by Bartolomé de Jaén separates the nave of the cruciform chapel from the apse. Bronze figures on the grille's gilded Corinthian columns represent the Apostles; the royal coat of arms is centered above the lintel; and the band across the top shows scenes from the Inquisition. Behind the grille is an elaborate carved wood altarpiece, with scenes from the conquest of Granada, including Boabdil's farewell, along its base. To the right (as you face the altar) are the recumbent Carrara marble figures of Ferdinand and Isabella, sculpted by Domenico Fancelli of Florence in 1517; to the left are marble effigies of Juana la Loca and Felipe el Hermoso (Joan the Insane and Philip the Handsome — the parents of Charles V), sculpted by Bartolomé Ordóñez in 1520. Stairs at the royal feet lead to a crypt containing four lead caskets where the royal remains actually lie — plus a smaller one for a royal grandchild.

Isabella's prodigious collection of paintings, many by Flemish masters, as well as church vestments, Ferdinand's sword, Isabella's scepter, her ornate jewel chest, and her surprisingly dainty filigree crown are on display in the chapel's sacristy. Be sure to look above the exit doorway on leaving the chapel: There's a copy of a famous painting documenting Boabdil's surrender to Isabella, who is wearing the very same crown. Open daily from 10:30 AM to 1 PM and from 4 to 7 PM. Admission charge. Calle de los Oficios (phone: 229232).

Catedral – After the lush, dark intimacy of the Capilla Real, the cathedral's white interior, flooded with light from high stained glass windows, overwhelms with a stark grandeur. Begun in 1523, it was originally meant to be Gothic in style, but during the 150 years of its construction, under principal architects Diego de Siloé and Alonso Cano, a Renaissance church took shape. Given its highly built-up downtown setting, a helicopter would be useful to give an idea of this monumental building as a whole, but do walk around it, taking in Cano's 17th-century main façade, on the west along Plaza de las Pasiegas, and the Puerta del Perdón, a notably elaborate side entrance facing north on Calle de la Cárcel. The visitors' entrance at Gran Vía de Colón leads to the ambulatory around the golden Capilla Mayor, or chancel, where a 150-foot dome is ringed by a double tier of stained glass windows and by enormous scenes from the Life of the Virgin painted by Cano. Notice the polychrome figures at prayer on either side of the main arch: These are Ferdinand and Isabella, who commissioned the cathedral to celebrate the Reconquest but died before they saw a stone placed. Farther back in the nave are twin 18th-century organs, their pipes fanning out over the central aisle in the Spanish fashion. Numerous glittering side chapels grace the church, so be careful not to miss the extravagantly carved and gilded Capilla de Nuestra Señora de la Antigua (or Capilla Dorada) on the north wall. Even the gorgeous draped "damask" canopy above the Virgin is carved wood. Open daily from 10:30 AM to 1 PM and from 4 to 7 PM. Admission charge. Gran Vía de Colón (phone: 222959).

Alcaicería (Silk Market) – At one time, the old Moorish silk market in Granada covered an entire quarter and was among the most important markets in the Muslim world. It burned down in the 1800s, but a small part of it near the cathedral has been rebuilt as a tiny 3-street tourist bazaar crammed with gaudy souvenir shops and stands whose merchandise spills out into the paths of the shoppers. Reach it from Calle Zacatín.

Plaza de la Bib Rambla – This big, busy square, where the Moors once thronged for tournaments and horse shows, is now bright with flower stalls, and café tables and their umbrellas. All Granada pauses here, near the cathedral, for *tapas,* beer, or platesful of *churros* — long, skinny crullers just made for dipping into cups of thick hot chocolate.

Corral del Carbón (House of Coal) – A Moorish horseshoe arch leads into the gray stone courtyard of this building, which originally was an inn — the Grand Hotel of 14th-century Arab Granada — and subsequently a warehouse, a theater, and an apartment house. Now it houses Granada's branch of *Artespaña,* the government-run handicrafts company that has shops throughout Spain. 40 Calle Mariana Pineda (phone: 224550).

Monasterio de San Jerónimo (Monastery of St. Jerome) – The first monastery to be founded in Granada after the Reconquest, this huge establishment has both a private and a public cloister, the latter a magnificent space with double tiers of arcaded ambulatories surrounding an orange grove. The 16th-century monastery church, where Isabella's Gran Capitán was originally buried before the altar, is one of Diego de Siloé's greatest buildings. Open daily from 10 AM to 1:30 PM and from 3 to 6 PM. Admission charge. 9 Calle Rector López Argüeta (phone: 279337).

Iglesia de San Juan de Dios (Church of St. John of God) – Widely considered Granada's most beautiful place of worship because of its dazzling gilded chancel, this 18th-century baroque church is part of a complex that includes the 16th-century Hospital de San Juan de Dios. (The latter still functions as a hospital, but have a look at its frescoed courtyards and magnificent staircase with *artesonado* ceiling.) Open daily from 9 to 11 AM and from 6:30 to 9 PM. Calle San Juan de Dios (phone: 275700).

Nuestra Señora de las Angustias (Our Lady of Perpetual Sorrows) – This charming Renaissance church in the downtown shopping district honors the city's patron saint. The church's carved wood statue of the Virgin, bearing Christ in her arms, is carried through the city during *Holy Week.* Open daily from 8 AM to 1 PM and from 8 to 9 PM. Carrera de la Virgen (phone: 226393).

La Cartuja (Carthusian Monastery) – The daily routine of the monks is dramatically documented in the well-preserved refectory, capitular hall, and other common rooms of this great 16th-century religious center. The depictions of martyrdom, painted by a monastery friar, Juan Sánchez Cotán, are bloodcurdling. In contrast, the monastery church is enchanting. The sacristy, an 18th-century addition, is an airy surprise: White rococo plasterwork is paired with brown and white marble whose colors are swirled like a chocolate sundae. The interior doors are marvels in marquetry, and the polished cedarwood vestment chests lining the walls are inlaid with silver and mother-of-pearl. In the apse of the church are four statues surrounding a magnificent coral-colored marble altar — the folded and draped velvet and silk canopies are actually carved and painted wood. On the northern outskirts of town, about 10 minutes by cab (or take the No. 8 bus). Open daily from 10 AM to 1 PM and from 3 to 6 PM. Admission charge. Camino de Alfácar (phone: 201932).

SOURCES AND RESOURCES

 TOURIST INFORMATION: The Oficina de Turismo has an official home (10 Plaza de Mariana Pineda; phone: 226688), while a smaller office is off Plaza de la Bib Rambla (2 Calle Libreros; phone: 225990). Both offices are open from 10 AM to 1:30 PM and from 4 to 7 PM; closed Saturday afternoons and Sundays. An English-speaking staff can answer questions, but printed information in English is sketchy. At the Alhambra, on the other hand, information services are excellent. Visitors are provided with well-annotated maps of the Alhambra and Generalife, and there is a selection of books for sale. Tour guides for both the Alhambra and downtown attractions are headquartered in the ticket building at the Puerta del Vino entrance (phone: 229936).

Local Coverage – For those who read Spanish, three local papers — *El Ideal, El Día de Granada,* and the *Granada 2,000* — are sources of local and national news, information on entertainment and cultural events, and the *fútbol* scores. The weekly *El Faro* also contains an entertainment guide.

 TELEPHONE: The city code for Granada is 58. If calling from within Spain, dial 958 before the local number.

 GETTING AROUND: Those traveling by car won't have to park it for the duration of their stay, because Granada, unlike other ancient Andalusian cities, is fairly easy to navigate. Those without a car will find that the city's big red buses go everywhere, although except for hard climbs up the Alhambra and Albaicín hills, you'll probably prefer to walk anyway.

Airport – Granada Airport is 10½ miles (17 km) west of the city (phone: 446411). *Iberia* has an office in town (2 Plaza de Isabel la Católica; phone: 227592).

Bus – City bus routes are well marked at stops in the downtown area. The most useful ones for visitors are No. 2, which goes to the Alhambra and the Generalife, and No. 7, which goes to the Albaicín. Fare is 55 pesetas (exact change not required). Intercity buses depart from several terminals, depending on the line operating the service. The Alsina Graells Sur station (97 Camino de Ronda; phone: 251358), serving other points in Andalusia and Madrid, is the main one; the *Bacoma* line terminal in front of the train station (Avenida de los Andaluces; phone: 281883) is the departure point for buses to Murcia, Alicante, Valencia, and Barcelona. *Bonal* buses (Avenida de la Constitución; phone: 273100), go to the Sierra Nevada ski slopes.

Car Rental – *Avis* (31 Calle Recogidas; phone: 252358; and at the airport; phone: 446455), *Hertz* (46 Calle Recogidas; phone: 251682), and *Europcar* (Plaza de Mariana Pineda, Edificio Cervantes; phone: 295065) are among the firms represented.

Taxi – Hail one on the street or call *Radio-Taxi* (phone: 151461) or *Tele-Taxi* (phone: 280654).

Train – The train station is located some distance north of the center on Avenida de los Andaluces. Tickets can be bought there or at the *RENFE* office (at the corner of Calle de los Reyes Católicos and Calle Sillería). For all train information, call 271272.

 SPECIAL EVENTS: Granada's most unique celebration, the *Día de la Toma* (Day of the Capture), on January 2, commemorates the day in 1492 when the Muslim ruler, Boabdil, turned the city over to Ferdinand and Isabella, thereby completing the Christian Reconquest of Spain. Granada marks the day with a parade and the tolling of the Alhambra bell, as the flag of the Catholic Monarchs hangs from City Hall. On May 3, *Cruces de Mayo* (Crosses of May), there is dancing in the streets and plazas, which are bedecked with crosses covered with spring flowers, but this is only a prelude to a much bigger event, *Corpus Christi,* observed in May or June, when the church rolls out a glittering holy procession displaying the monstrance Isabella gave the cathedral and costumed *granadinos* ride horseback through downtown traffic. The fiesta goes on for 10 days, complete with bullfights, a flamenco festival, and a sprawling fair with blazing midway. In another vein, Granada's renowned annual *Festival Internacional de Música y Danza,* 3 weeks bridging June and July, is approaching its 40th anniversary and going strong (see *Theater and Music*).

SHOPPING: The booty includes ceramics, particularly the typical blue-and-white Fajalauza pottery (which took its name centuries ago from the city gate where the potteries clustered); marquetry items — boxes, trays, and other wooden objects inlaid with wood, shell, or ivory; woven rugs and blankets, some in the traditional style of the Alpujarra region; jewelry; copper pots; leather bags; and some of Spain's finest guitars, sold from stock or made to order (which may take anywhere from a week to several months). Crafts and souvenir shops are concentrated at a few popular tourist locations, so shopping is easy. Downtown, visitors browse the Alcaicería, off Calle Zacatín. In the vicinity of the Alhambra, fine craftsmen, as well as frankly-souvenir shops, line the lower section of the Cuesta de Gomérez approach. The Albaicín is also a good place for shopping. The two major nationwide department store chains both have branches in Granada: *Galerías Preciados* (13 Carrera del Genil; phone: 223581) and *El Corte Inglés* (97 Calle Arabial; phone: 292161). Note that on pleasant weekends, the promenade along Carrera del Genil turns into an outdoor bazaar, blossoming with booths selling paintings, leatherwork, ceramics, jewelry, and souvenirs.

Artespaña – The Granada outlet of the nationwide, government-operated company displays local and regional crafts and furniture in a handsome 2-story showroom at the rear of the courtyard in the Corral del Carbón. Calle Mariana Pineda (phone: 224550).

Eduardo Ferrer Castillo – The craftsman who taught most of the other guitar makers in Granada. 26 Cuesta de Gomérez (phone: 221832).

Cerámica Aliatar – Local designs in ceramics. 18 Plaza de Aliatar (phone: 278089).

Cerámica Arabe – A fine selection of typical Fajalauza platters and bowls (but the store doesn't ship). 5 Plaza San Isidro (phone: 277168).

Convento de Santa Catalina de Zafra – Cookies and sweet cakes made by the sisters, on sale year-round. Knock at the convent door when you're touring the Albaicín. 43 Carrera del Darro (phone: 226189).

Eduardo Ferrer Lucena – Fine craftsmanship in leather. 19 Calle del Agua, Albaicín (phone: 279056).

V. Molero Martínez – An outstanding shop for marquetry. 8 Calle Santa Rosalia (phone: 111356).

Antonio González Ramos – Another standout for marquetry objects. 16 Cuesta de Gomérez (phone: 227062).

Talabar – Elegant leather handbags and wallets. 2 Puente Verde (phone: 123851).

Tejidos Artísticos Fortuny – Handwoven bedspreads, rugs, and drapes. 1 Plaza Fortuny (phone: 224327).

SPORTS AND FITNESS: Bullfighting – Though the *corrida* has lost popularity here, the season of Sunday bullfights runs from mid-March to October, with daily events during *Corpus Christi* in May or June. The *Plaza de Toros* is on Avenida de Doctor Olóriz, near the soccer stadium. Tickets can be purchased downtown on Calle Escudo del Carmen behind the Ayuntamiento (City Hall) from 5 to 9 PM on the day of the bullfight.

Hiking – Follow the joggers to the Parque de Invierno (see below). Serious hikers can follow the route of the snow carriers who brought ice from the mountains to the Alhambra. The tourist office has trail maps.

Jogging – To jog along nearby mountain roads lined with olive groves, take the No. 2 bus beyond the Alhambra to Cementerio (the hilltop cemetery at the end of the line) for the entrance to the Parque de Invierno, the city's favorite outdoor recreation and picnic area.

Skiing – The ski slopes at Solynieve, the southernmost ski resort in Europe, are less than an hour's drive (about 20 miles/32 km) southeast of Granada along a well-tended mountain road. At 11,000 feet, Solynieve's snows never melt; up-to-date facilities include cable cars, chair lifts, ski shops, restaurants, and hotels, as well as the *Parador de Sierra Nevada* (phone: 480200), with broad terraces and cheery fireplace, bar, and restaurant, above the town. For bus transportation from Granada, call *Bonal* buses (phone: 273100); for highway conditions, call 480153.

Soccer – Consult the newspaper for game schedules during *fútbol* season at Granada's *Estadio de los Cármenes,* Avenida de Madrid.

Swimming – Because the city is so close to resort towns of the Costa del Sol, few of the hotels have pools. Those planning to swim have a choice of two hotels, *Los Alixares* and *Los Angeles,* both of which have pools for guests only. *Piscina Neptuno* (phone: 251067), part of the *Neptuno* sports complex downtown on Calle Arabial, has two pools open to the public.

Tennis – Courts are for rent at *Pistas Tenis Neptuno* (phone: 251055), part of the *Neptuno* sports complex on Calle Arabial.

 THEATER AND MUSIC: One of Granada's several cinemas, the *Cine Teatro Isabel La Católica* (Puerta Real), doubles as a theater for plays and other theatrical events — check the newspapers for what's on if your Spanish is up to it. Gypsy *zambras,* flamenco *tablaos,* and jazz are part of the music scene (see *Nightclubs and Nightlife*), as are classical concerts at the *Auditorio Manuel de Falla* (Paseo de los Mártires, near the Alhambra; phone: 228288). The auditorium, rebuilt after a fire and acoustically acclaimed, also is the principal indoor venue for the city's renowned *Festival Internacional de Música y Danza,* which runs from late June through early July. For the 3 weeks of the festival's duration, Granada is treated to a round-robin of daily performances not only indoors but also in the courtyard of the Palace of Charles V and in the outdoor theater at the Generalife. Among those doing the honors are ensembles such as the *Spanish National Orchestra* and the *Spanish National Ballet,* plus orchestras, ballet companies, chamber groups, and soloists from around the world. For an advance schedule of events, contact the festival office (21 Calle Gracia, Granada 18009; phone: 267442/43/44/45) or branches of the National Tourist Office of Spain in the US.

 NIGHTCLUBS AND NIGHTLIFE: Granada's biggest nighttime draw — and its biggest disappointment — are the *zambras,* Gypsy song-and-dance fests put on in cave dwellings hollowed out of the Sacromonte hill. Not so many years ago, the Gypsies danced for their own pleasure, but the shows have now deteriorated into tawdry commercial ventures complete with neon signs, barkers, cover charges, and women and children in tatty polka-dot ruffles stomping around to strident guitars. There's more emphasis on selling souvenir fans and castanets than on artistry, but the caves themselves are interesting — long, narrow rooms with rows of wooden chairs lined up against walls covered with copper pots and photos of legendary dancers. A nightclub bus tour run by *Viajes Meliá* (44 Calle de los Reyes

Católicos; phone: 223098) goes to several caves and is one way to see them; another is to have a taxi drive slowly along the Camino del Sacromonte while you choose one that intrigues you. Don't be tempted to wander around alone after dark in this impoverished neighborhood.

For something closer to a Seville-style *tablao* (flamenco song and dance performance), book the show at *La Reina Mora* (Mirador de San Cristóbal; phone: 278228 or 202006), in the Albaicín. *Jardines Neptuno,* a garden nightclub (downtown on Calle Arabial; phone: 251112), has flamenco and regional dance and song, while *El Patio* (downtown on Calle Pedro Antonio de Alarcón; phone: 209259) is the place to show your own flamenco style on the dance floor. Because it's near the university, Calle Alarcón — in the section from Calle Martínez de la Rosa to Callejón de Gracia — has wall-to-wall discotheques, jazz clubs, bars, and burger, pizza, and fried-fish places jammed with young people.

A more sophisticated disco scene prevails at the *Club Cadí* in the *Luz Granada* hotel (18 Avenida de la Constitución) and at *Granada-10* (13 Calle Cárcel Baja). Or try *Oxford 2* (25 Calle del Gran Capitán) or *Distrito 10* (5 Calle del Gran Capitán). Go late. The watering holes around the Campo del Príncipe provide nightlife or *tapas* nearer the Alhambra. Among them, the 2-story *Patio Rossini Quesería Bar* (15 Campo del Príncipe) is particularly charming. (Ask for a *tabla variada,* a cheese board that also includes pâtés, hams, sausages, and olives — priced by weight.) And don't fail to have at least one drink on the terrace of the *Alhambra Palace* hotel (2 Calle Peña Partida), with a view of the city lights glistening at your feet.

BEST IN TOWN

CHECKING IN: Choosing a hotel in Granada means deciding between the forested heights of the historic Alhambra hill and the "real life" of the city below. The hilltop choice offers rustic charm, inspiring views, a feeling of the distant Moorish past, and easy walking access to the Alhambra itself. A downtown hotel means a better acquaintance with Granada's Renaissance period and a greater selection of shops and restaurants. Either way, it's hard to go wrong. Fast, efficient transportation shuttles visitors freely between upper and lower Granada for a full range of sightseeing, shopping, and dining. Expect to pay $100 and up for a double room in a hotel listed as expensive, from $60 to $95 in a moderate hotel, and less than $60 in an inexpensive one. All telephone numbers are in the 58 city code unless otherwise indicated.

Alhambra Palace – A grand old baronial establishment on the Alhambra hill. This beet-red leviathan is an easy stroll to the Alhambra entrance, and many of its 121 high-ceilinged, old-fashioned (but air conditioned) rooms have a view of the city from token balconies. The huge lobby and lounges, with plaster curlicues and tiled dadoes aping the real Alhambra, provide a meeting place for locals and visiting dignitaries. The concierge and staff snap to attention when approached, and there's a palatial dining room with buffet and from-the-menu dining. 2 Calle Peña Partida (phone: 221468). Expensive.

Luz Granada – This 174-room businesspeople's hotel stands on the sweeping Avenida de la Constitución, somewhat out of the way for Alhambra-bound tourists. It offers the comforts of air conditioning, an international restaurant, an American-style cocktail lounge, boutiques, and a discotheque. 18 Avenida de la Constitución (phone: 204061). Expensive.

Parador San Francisco – Its 39 air conditioned rooms — within the very walls of the Alhambra — are the most sought-after accommodations in the government-run *parador* chain. Ferdinand and Isabella were originally buried in this former 15th-century convent, and one of the courtyards here has a monument marking the spot. The wait for rooms is from 6 months to a year, depending on the season, but cancellations do come up; ask for a room in the old wing. The restaurant serves Andalusian specialties (see *Eating Out*). In the Alhambra (phone: 221440). Expensive.

Princesa Ana – With a white marble and peach-colored interior, this recently built luxurious oasis has 61 air conditioned rooms and is down the street from the *Luz Granada* and a couple of blocks from the railroad station. Popular with European business executives. 37 Avenida de la Constitución (phone: 287447). Expensive.

Meliá Granada – The city's largest hotel, within a stone's throw of the downtown sights. There are 221 air conditioned rooms, a restaurant, cocktail lounge, coffee shop, and lobby boutiques. 7 Calle Angel Ganivet (phone: 227400). Expensive to moderate.

Los Alixares – The last hostelry up the Alhambra hillside above the Generalife is a charmless modern structure without Andalusian flavor, but it does have a swimming pool and sun deck, and European tour groups love it. The 148 air conditioned rooms (plus a restaurant) are a short cab or bus ride from downtown Granada. Avenida de los Alixares (phone: 225506). Moderate.

Los Angeles – This place requires a short — but steep — hike to the Alhambra. There may be no connection between the name and the hotel's resemblance to a deluxe LA motel, but the flashy balconies and big heated swimming pool fairly scream Hollywood. The 100 air conditioned rooms are furnished in a comfortable modern fashion. 17 Cuesta Escoriaza (phone: 221424). Moderate.

Kenia – A favorite with old Granada hands, this 16-room gem occupies a gracious old mansion at the foot of the Alhambra hill, near the Campo del Príncipe. The owner has furnished the lobby and parlor with family antiques, and each guest's plan for the day gets his personal attention. There's also a charming restaurant. 65 Calle Molinos (phone: 227506). Moderate.

Victoria – The silver dome and Parisian façade of this graceful dowager have been a landmark at the bustling Puerta Real for more than a century. The 69 air conditioned rooms were renovated, but the lavish period chandelier and potted palms in the tiny lobby remain, as does the aristocratic turn-of-the-century ambience that keeps the restaurant and bar popular with *granadinos*. Though the traffic is noisy, the downtown location is great, with easy bus access to the Alhambra. 3 Puerta Real (phone: 257700). Moderate.

Washington Irving – On the Alhambra hill. The building's namesake never actually lived in this century-old hostelry, but the roster of early travelers who have slept here is impressive. The somber lobby and spartan accommodations (68 rooms) need remodeling, but not the Mudéjar dining room, a treasure. The location, at a crossroad leading to the Alhambra entrance in one direction and up to the Generalife in the other, is hard to beat. 2 Paseo del Generalife (phone: 227550). Moderate.

Guadalupe – By the side of a steep road across from the upper entrance to the Generalife, this modest hostelry is high enough above the city to give guests a country feel. There are 43 air conditioned rooms and a small restaurant; bus to downtown. Avenida de los Alixares (phone: 223423). Inexpensive.

 EATING OUT: The fruitful fields and orchards surrounding the city, the game-rich mountains nearby, and the waters of the Mediterranean not far away make Granada's menus as notable for their prime ingredients as for the excellent food preparation. One of the most famous local dishes, for instance, is *habas con jamón,* a simple casserole of locally grown fava beans with ham. Most cooks won't use the prized ham from Trévelez, dried in the crisp Sierra Nevada air, but if you want to be your own judge in the ongoing contest between Trévelez lovers and aficionados of Seville's Jabugo ham, try slivers of Trévelez for *tapas,* with a fresh local wine (huétor, huescar, or albondón are names to note) or with one of the Jerez wines, plentiful here. Granada's tables are also laden with an outstanding selection of game, especially during hunting season, and with plenty of fresh seafood from the port of Motril. Then there's the famous local sweet tooth, derived, some say, from the Moorish delights that influence so much of modern Andalusian cooking. The city's convent kitchens are famous for their egg-yolk-based and sugared cookies and candies — some restaurants serve full platters purchased from the nuns. Expect to pay $45 and up for a three-course meal for two with local wine in any restaurant listed below as expensive, from $30 to $45 in a moderate one, and from $20 to $30 in an inexpensive place. All telephone numbers are in the 58 city code unless otherwise indicated.

Alacena de las Monjas – A sophisticated restaurant blending nouvelle cuisine niceties and old Arab recipes to produce an elegant dining experience that's hard to match anywhere. Tuxedo-clad waiters serve in the gleaming whitewashed cellar of a 16th-century house as guests nibble on crusty Arab breads and choose such dishes as *pimientos rellenos de bacalao en salsa de azafrán* (peppers stuffed with salt cod in saffron sauce) and *cordero Alacena de las Monjas* (lamb shank in a prune, carrot, and wine sauce), all more delicate than in the traditional Arab versions. An old Arab dessert, *cogollo de lechuga con miel de caña,* or hearts of romaine lettuce with orange slices in a burnt sugar sauce, is among the fascinating offerings, but there's also the house *tarta,* an airy cheesecake topped with honey and *crème anglaise.* Closed Sundays. Reservations necessary. 5 Plaza del Padre Suárez (phone: 272800). Expensive.

Baroca – Granada's business establishment favors the topflight international cooking here — salmon and avocado terrine, chef's salad, medallions of venison — but the local dishes are excellent, too. Closed Sundays and August. Reservations advised. 34 Calle Pedro Antonio de Alarcón (phone: 265061). Expensive.

Cunini – Pass through the long bar and choose your meal from the tempting fish market display. Well-heeled *granadinos* come here for the food, not for atmosphere or solicitous service (neither is to be found in this restaurant's plain, pine-paneled rooms). The menu lists almost a hundred fish and shellfish dishes, in addition to meats. For starters, try the *ensalada de hueva,* a cold fish roe salad, or the *pipirrana de chanquetes,* matchstick-size baby fish in tomato vinaigrette. Closed Sunday evenings. Reservations advised. 9 Pescadería (phone: 263701). Expensive.

Ruta de Veleta – This luxurious roadhouse restaurant on the way to Solynieve is worth the 4½-mile (7-km) trip. Feast on first-rate pheasant, partridge, roast suckling pig, and a cornucopia of other Spanish and international dishes, and enjoy the finest old rioja wines. Even the dining room ceiling, hung with row upon row of ceramic mugs in the typical blue-and-white floral pattern of Granada, is sensational. Closed Sunday evenings. Reservations advised. 50 Carretera de la Sierra, Cenes de la Vega (phone: 486134). Expensive.

El Corral del Príncipe – The outdoor tables crowded (especially on Sunday mornings) with homegrown yuppies mark the entrance to one of Granada's most spectacular eating places — a remodeled movie palace whose Andalusian interior is lavish with Moorish brass chandeliers and urns. The full range of Granadan cuisine is available. There's also a bar with lots of action, dancing on the former theater stage, and a late-night flamenco show. Open daily. Reservations advised. Campo del Príncipe (phone: 228088). Expensive to moderate.

Sevilla – Brigitte Bardot, El Cordobés, and Andrés Segovia have eaten here, and the menu is printed in three languages — you get the idea. But the food is tasty and authentic. Dine in one of the tiled dining rooms or on the narrow terrace, actually an alley, across from the frescoed walls of La Madraza, the old Arab university. Granadan specialties include *cordero a la pastoril* (spicy shepherds's lamb stew), *rape a la granadina* (monkfish in a shrimp, pine-nut, and mushroom sauce), and a dessert of *nueces con nata y miel* (the Arab-inspired nuts with cream and honey). Closed Sunday evenings. Reservations advised. 12 Calle de los Oficios (phone: 221223). Expensive to moderate.

Alcaicería – Three dining rooms with separate entrances grouped around a small patio are all part of the same restaurant in the silk market. The kitschy imitation of Alhambra tilework and plaster lace seems just right for this tourist enclave. English-speaking waiters help diners choose among the Granadan specialties. Open daily. No reservations. Placeta de la Alcaicería (phone: 224341). Moderate.

Casa Manuel – Ring the doorbell to gain admission to this old mansion in a neighborhood of elegant hillside residences. The walk down the long front hall to the dining rooms, the china-filled antique sideboards, and the informal, home-style cooking, with desserts baked by the owner's wife, make you feel more like a guest than a customer. Closed Sundays. Reservations unnecessary. Calle Blanqueo de San Cecilio, off Campo del Príncipe (phone: 229617). Moderate.

Chikito – Choose indoor dining in a historic building, once a meeting place for Federico García Lorca and the El Reconcillo band of intellectuals, or pick the restarant's shady outdoor café across the street. Shoppers and businesspeople keep both spots filled. Try the *zarzuela de pescado* (seafood casserole), or selections from the outstanding *tapas* bar. Closed Wednesdays. Reservations unnecessary. 9 Plaza del Campillo (phone: 223364). Moderate.

Los Manueles – Trévelez hams hang over the noisy bar in this friendly *taberna* in an alley off Calle de los Reyes Católicos. Spaniards and foreigners alike flock to the tile and wrought-iron accented dining rooms, seemingly untouched since the place opened more than 60 years ago. (The chef is set in his ways, too: He doesn't, for instance, serve after-dinner coffee — go to a *cafetería,* says he.) The menu runs to Andalusian specialties. Open daily — and great in summer when the tables spill outdoors. Reservations unnecessary. 4 Calle Zaragoza (phone: 223415). Moderate.

Mesón Antonio – Anyone in town from October through June should make a beeline for this homey eatery — and be hungry. After finding the humble house off Campo del Príncipe (even cab drivers have to inquire), go through the patio and upstairs to a simple dining room with an open kitchen. There, before cavernous wood-burning ovens, Antonio delivers sizzling platters of gratinée leeks, beef tongue in tomato sauce, and roast lamb, while his wife fries potatoes and stirs an intense seafood bisque at the range. Antonio also serves reasonably priced, fine old rioja wines. A bonus is that the couple speaks excellent English. Closed Sunday evenings and July, August, and September. No reservations. 6 Calle Ecce Homo (phone: 229599). Moderate.

Parador San Francisco – A leisurely three-course lunch in the *parador*'s spacious dining room — within view of the rose gardens and the Generalife hill beyond — is a delightful way to break a visit to the Alhambra. The menu is repeated at dinner. Reservations unnecessary. At the Alhambra (phone: 221440). Moderate.

Polinario – The buffet on the patio or a *bocadillo* (sandwich) and beer at the bar make for a quick lunch just outside the Alhambra. The cooking and ambience don't merit raves, but the location is convenient. Closed evenings. No reservations. 3 Calle Real de la Alhambra. Inexpensive.

LISBON

Lisbon is a bit like the heroine of an old movie who faces the gravest of perils in every reel — but emerges in the end still beautiful. During its more than 2,000 years of history, the city has undergone devastating earthquakes, plagues, fires, floods, invasions by barbarians, sackings, revolutions, and, more recently, the incursion of ugly urban development and pollution. But Lisbon remains beautiful, if a trifle faded and disheveled. At certain times of the day, the sun casts a golden reflection so intense that the broad expanse of estuary facing the city seems literally to live up to its popular name, Mar da Palha, or "Sea of Straw." And as the sun moves across the sky, the pastel buildings, tree-lined boulevards, cobblestone streets, and mosaic sidewalks of this city built in tiers on seven hills are bathed again and again in new perspectives of light.

Legend says that Lisbon was founded by Ulysses, who gave it the name Olisipo. Less romantic historians say that the ancient name was Phoenician in origin and that the city grew up gradually as a port town on the estuary of the Tagus River, where traders from many lands drew their boats to shore to sell their wares — or perhaps to raid. Gradually, safety-conscious inhabitants moved to the top of the hill where the old St. George's Castle stands today, and then, little by little, occupied the surrounding hills.

Over the centuries, many people came and went: Celts, Phoenicians, Carthaginians, Romans, Visigoths, and Moors, until the 12th century, when the city was taken by the Christian Portuguese. As Portugal built its vast empire during the 15th and 16th centuries, citizens from many diverse lands came to live in Lisbon. And when decades of dictatorship ended in 1974 and the country dissolved the remnants of its empire, a new wave of immigrants arrived from Angola, Mozambique, Timor, and the Cape Verde Islands.

More than 1.6 million people live in Lisbon and its environs today, and yet, in some ways, this westernmost capital of Europe is still a small town. The *lisboetas,* accustomed to foreigners, are tolerant of their visitors' ways, their dress, and their inability to speak Portuguese. They usually can give directions in English. Sometimes they will even drop what they are doing and take a visitor where he or she wants to go.

Lisbon has known moments of glory. The Romans, who arrived in 205 BC, made it, after Mérida in Spain, the most important city on the Iberian Peninsula, a place with baths, a theater, a 6-mile-long aqueduct (not the one standing today), and Roman roads stretching out in all directions. In their turn, the Moors, whose stay lasted from 714 to 1147, gathered their most brilliant thinkers, scientists, and writers at Aschbouna — as they renamed the city — and made it a renowned center of learning. Lisbon began to come into its own as Portuguese, however, only after its recapture from the Moors during the 12th century (Dom Afonso Henriques, Portugal's first king, and an army of crusaders from northern Europe besieged the castle for 17 weeks to accomplish that), and after King Afonso III's transfer of the court from Coimbra in 1260. By the 14th century, Lisbon had nearly 4 miles of walls, with 77 towers and 38 entranceways.

The city's greatest glory came during the 15th and 16th centuries. At a time when the world's seas were uncharted and darkness and superstition ruled people's imaginations, Lisbon was sending forth Portuguese caravels into the unknown, and her explorers were bringing the world's riches back from Africa, India, Brazil, and China. The Age of Discovery, as it is called, was ushered in by Prince Henry the Navigator (1394–1460), the son of King João I and his English wife, Philippa of Lancaster. During the early 15th century, Prince Henry established a school of navigation at Sagres, in southwest Portugal, and from there ships sailing under his authority explored the coast of Africa, making great strides in the study of geography, map making, and ship building. His contributions to the advancement of exploration led, at the end of the century, not only to the epochal voyage of Christopher Columbus, but also to the voyages of Bartholomeu Dias, who rounded the Cape of Good Hope in 1488, and of Vasco da Gama, who sailed out from Lisbon in 1497 and returned 2 years later after reaching the Indies. Portugal's so-called Spice Age had begun.

Trade with India, and later with Brazil — discovered by Pedro Alvares Cabral in 1500 — made Lisbon immensely rich. By the 16th century, the city was a great commercial and maritime power, the "Queen of the Tagus," ruling from one of the best harbors in Europe. Churches and palaces were built. In 1502, King Manuel I, wishing to erect a memorial to Portugal's explorers, began construction of one of Lisbon's greatest monuments, the Jerónimos Monastery in Belém, the Lisbon suburb from which Vasco da Gama had set sail. The ropes, anchors, and seaweed carved on this building (and on others of the period) are typical of the uniquely Portuguese decorative style that came to be known as Manueline.

But all was not joyful. Persecution of Jews began during the late 15th century, and the Inquisition was introduced during the early 16th century, to endure some 200 years. Thousands were tortured in the Palace of the Inquisition in the Rossio, and many others died in the *autos-da-fé* held in the public squares of the city. In 1580, Philip II of Spain annexed the country and became Philip I of Portugal; Spanish rule lasted until 1640, when the Spanish governor of Lisbon was deposed by a group of Portuguese noblemen. Lisbon then revived its profitable trade with the rest of the world, and a spate of new building began. This time, given the discovery of gold in Brazil during the late 17th century, the characteristic decorative element of the period was richly gilded baroque woodwork (it is possible that the name of the baroque style may have come from the Portuguese word *barroco*, meaning "rough pearl"). The reign of João V (1706–50) was known for its magnificence.

Then, on *All Saints' Day* morning, November 1, 1755, while most of Lisbon was at mass, one of the worst earthquakes ever known shook the city like a straw in the wind. Within minutes, two-thirds of Lisbon was in ruins. A 40-foot tidal wave rose on the Tagus and slammed into the city. Fires, begun by tapers lighted in the churches for the feast day and fanned by a violent windstorm, burned what the quake had left intact. As many as 40,000 people perished — causing philosophers, among them Voltaire, to conclude that this was not, after all, the most perfect of all worlds.

The prime minister, the Marquês de Pombal, quickly and efficiently set out to rebuild Lisbon on the rubble covering the valley floor between two of its hills. The stately plan of the city's classical squares and boulevards was traced out, and the straight lines and 18th-century proportions of the quarter called the Baixa — lower town — grew up in place of the previous medieval jumble. The Baixa's parallel streets are lined with nearly uniform, 5-story buildings.

Pombal is best remembered for this accomplishment, not for the reign of terror that he instituted against his enemies that made Lisbon a city of fear. Political turmoil marked the rest of the 18th century and the 19th. In 1908, King Carlos I and his son were assassinated in Praça do Comércio. In 1910, radical republicans overthrew the monarchy, forcing King Manuel II into exile. The political turbulence of the ensuing democratic republic gave way to dictatorship in 1926 and the rise to power of António de Oliveira Salazar, a professor of finance from Coimbra University, who ruled Portugal until 1968. He put the country's finances in order and kept Portugal out of World War II, but during the nearly half century he and his successor, Marcello Caetano, remained in power, Portugal was turned gradually into a police state.

On the 25th of April, 1974, a group of young officers staged a coup in Lisbon and helped set up a democratically elected government. It was a revolution in which few lives were lost, but it altered the face of the capital. As the streets became the scene of demonstrations by newly formed labor unions and political parties, once-pristine buildings and monuments were spray-painted with slogans, and mosaic sidewalks that used to be scoured daily became grubby. Up to this time, Lisbon had been the capital of the world's last colonial empire, but with the breakup of the empire following the revolution, nearly a million refugees poured into the city. The government housed some in hotels; others lived in shanties. Their crated belongings lined the banks of the Tagus.

Within a few years, the situation stabilized. The refugees were miraculously absorbed into the life of the city and helped make Lisbon a more dynamic place. The city's beauty began to reemerge from under the posters and slogans and grime. Many of the old buildings — the greater part of Lisbon's stock is from the late 18th and 19th centuries, with much plain, utilitarian architecture added during this century — are molding away from neglect. But some of the more important ones are getting a face wash and repairs. Post-modernist buildings, in glass and bright colors, mostly the work of architect Tomás Taveira, also have appeared.

Portugal joined the European Economic Community (Common Market) in 1986, bringing in new investment funds and new products for Lisbon's shelves. Anyone who knows the city, but has been absent for a while, will find that Lisbon today is not the same as it was even a very few years ago. Many of the streets in the Baixa are being closed to traffic and turned into pedestrian malls paved with cobblestones. Musicians entertain the strollers, and sidewalk artists sketch inexpensive portraits. Artisans offer jewelry, leatherwork, embroidery, and other wares from little stalls. There are many attractive open-air cafés and restaurants. Hotels have been renovated and more new accommodations for visitors seem to be added each year. The delights of Lisbon again are apparent; maybe that's why tourism is flourishing.

LISBON AT-A-GLANCE

SEEING THE CITY: A city built on hills frequently surprises visitors with lovely views that emerge without warning around unexpected corners. Lisbon is such a place. It has 17 natural balconies — called *miradouros* — from which to view the city. Foremost of these is the hilltop on which the ruins of St. George's Castle stand. All of the squares are laid out beneath: Praça do Comércio by the banks of the Tagus; the Rossio with its fountains and flower stalls; Praça da Figueira, the bustling market square; Praça dos Restauradores with its monument to Portugal's independence; the circular Praça Marquês de Pombal at the end of the broad Avenida da Liberdade; and beyond that, the lovely Parque Eduardo VII. On a clear day, it is possible to see the castles of Sintra far to the west. Another vantage point that's worth a pause is Largo de Santa Luzia, in the Alfama district, just downhill from the castle, between it and Lisbon's cathedral. Although the view from here — over the Alfama's red-roofed buildings down to the port — is less broadly panoramic than the one from the castle, the esplanade is charming, lined with *azulejos,* or glazed tiles, and endowed with flower beds and a trellis-topped colonnade. (For those who prefer not to walk, it's reached by one of Lisbon's picturesque, vintage *eléctricos,* or trolleys — the No. 28.) A third *miradouro* is the terrace on Rua de São Pedro de Alcântara, on the opposite hill across the city in the Bairro Alto. From here there is a picture postcard view of the castle, with the Alfama district spread down the slopes below its walls.

Another breathtaking view is from the bridge across the Tagus, known since the 1974 revolution as Ponte 25 de Abril, but previously named for Salazar, who built it in the 1960s. The third-longest suspension bridge in the world, it is particularly spectacular at night, when its cables, the ships in the river, and the city are all brightly lit. On the other side, there is a marvelous panorama of the Tagus estuary from the top of the statue of Cristo Rei (Christ the King), a gift to Portugal from Brazil. (Open daily from 10 AM to 6 PM; there is an admission charge, and an elevator takes visitors up.) Those without a car can cross the river by ferry from Praça do Comércio and take a bus from Cacilhas to the statue.

SPECIAL PLACES: In ancient times, and later under the Moors, Lisbon was contained within walls that surrounded the hill where St. George's Castle now stands. Today, that area is the Alfama, the oldest part of the city, where traces of the picturesque Judiaria (Jewish Quarter) and Mouraria (Moorish Quarter) still can be seen, along with Roman remains. The Alfama has been destroyed several times by earthquakes, but it always was rebuilt along the same plan, its tortuous, narrow streets spiraling down from the top of the hill to the Baixa below. The Baixa, to the west of the Alfama, is the main shopping and commercial district of Lisbon. Built after the earthquake in a grid fashion, it stretches northward from Praça do Comércio by the river to the top of the Rossio, one of the city's main squares, and includes such aptly named streets as Rua Aurea (its official name — confusingly, it's generally known and shown on most maps as Rua do Ouro, which means the same thing — Gold Street) and Rua da Prata (Silver Street), which are lined with fine jewelers and banks. Up the hill and west of the Rossio is the part of the Baixa known locally as the Chiado — not much more than 10 square blocks. This also is a popular shopping district dotted with coffeehouses and outdoor cafés, but a disastrous fire in September 1988 destroyed a great number of the shops — including two of Europe's oldest department stores — and other landmarks. Happily, most of the façades of the burned buildings remained standing after the flames were put out, even though the interiors were gutted, and recently announced rebuilding plans call for restoration of the district, rather than wholesale modernization. The plan, which includes turning the shell of one of the former department stores into an exclusive hotel and the other into a shopping and cultural center, is expected to take six years to complete.

Higher up is the Bairro Alto, or "high quarter," above and to the west of Praça dos Restauradores and the Rossio. At one time a wealthy (and later a seedy) residential district, it has been taken over by the avant-garde and become the center of nightlife in downtown Lisbon, with fine restaurants, typical *tascas* (taverns or small eating places), and *fado* houses, where sad Portuguese folk songs are sung. West of the Bairro Alto are the Madragoa and Lapa districts, residential areas where restaurants, government buildings, embassies, and several museums and art galleries also can be found. Modern Lisbon, with museums, the zoo, and new quarters, stretches to the north and east of the downtown area.

The Belém quarter is along the riverbank west of all of the above. Because it suffered very little in the 1755 earthquake, many of its fine palaces and monuments are still standing. Belém also is home to several museums, as well as many restaurants.

ST. GEORGE'S CASTLE AND THE ALFAMA

Castelo de São Jorge (St. George's Castle) – Built on one of Lisbon's highest hills, this castle with ten towers is considered the cradle of the city. An Iron Age *castro,* or fortified hilltop town, probably was located here, succeeded by Roman fortifications (Roman walls and other remains are being excavated), a fortress built by the Visigoths during the 5th century, and later, a Moorish fortified town. The present castle was built during the 12th century. Within the grounds are lovely gardens where peacocks roam free, the remains of an Arabian palace where the Kings of Portugal lived from the 14th to the 16th century, and a restaurant, the *Casa do Leão* (locals consider it overpriced for the quality of the food, although the locale is attractive). From the terrace on the south and west sides and from the walk around the towers, the views of Lisbon are extensive. Open daily from 9 AM to 9 PM (7 PM from October through March). No admission charge. Rua Costa do Castelo.

Alfama – This Old Quarter slopes downhill from St. George's Castle. A cobbled labyrinth with some streets so narrow that pedestrians must walk in single file, it is one of the most colorful spots in Europe. Its streets are overhung with balconies ablaze with scarlet geraniums and lined with little taverns decorated with strings of peppers, garlic, and cheese. By day, caged canaries on the balconies sing in the sun; at night, wrought-iron lamps light the scene; and on washdays, the buildings are strung with clotheslines and drying laundry. Although some medieval mansions and Moorish buildings exist, most of the houses date from the late 18th century, after the earthquake. The best times to see the Alfama are in the morning when the markets are open, late in the afternoon when the streets and squares are alive with people, or on a moonlit evening. The quarter stretches north to south from the castle to the banks of the Tagus, and west to east from the cathedral to the vicinity of the church of São Vicente de Fora.

Sé (Cathedral) – Lisbon's oldest church, built just after the Christian Reconquest of the 12th century, suffered enormous earthquake damage in 1755, but was rebuilt during the 18th century and restored during this one. It is a typical fortress-church of solid, massive construction, with battlements and towers. The plain façade is Romanesque, the ambulatory chapels and the cloister are pure Gothic, and the choir is baroque. In the *azulejo*-lined enclosure just inside the door is the baptismal font of St. Anthony of Padua, Portugal's patron saint, who was born here (although he spent much of his life in Italy), and in the chapel to the left is a *presépio* (Nativity scene) by Joaquim Machado de Castro. Relics of St. Vincent, patron saint of Lisbon, also are in the cathedral, but are brought out only on special occasions. There is a museum of religious vestments and ecclesiastical gold, currently closed for repairs. The cloister is open from 9 AM to 1 PM and from 2 to 4 PM; closed Mondays (cathedral open Mondays, however). Admission charge to the cloister. Largo da Sé (phone: 867652).

Museu-Escola de Artes Decorativas (Museum-School of Decorative Arts) – Located just around the bend from the Largo de Santa Luzia *miradouro* and housed in a 17th-century palace that survived the earthquake, this museum contains collections of Portuguese porcelain, silver, crystal, paintings, tapestries, and furniture, mostly of the 17th and 18th centuries. They're not arranged museum-style, but much more beguilingly as the furnishings of an aristocratic Lisboan home of yesteryear. The objects once were the property of Dr. Ricardo Espírito Santo Silva, who set up a foundation both to create a museum and to preserve the skills and tools of traditional Portuguese craftsmanship. The foundation runs a school and workshops for the reproduction and restoration of antiques — furniture, books, fabrics, and so on — adjacent to the museum, which visitors may tour. An appointment is required for the workshops (phone: 872429 or 872173). The museum is open Tuesdays through Saturdays from 10 AM to 1 PM and 2:30 to 5 PM. Admission charge. 2 Largo das Portas do Sol (phone: 862184).

Igreja de São Vicente de Fora (Church of St. Vincent Outside the Walls) – From Largo das Portas do Sol, follow the *eléctrico* tracks down Escadinhas de São Tomé and then up again to this church, which was built during the late 16th and early 17th centuries by Filippo Terzi and sports a mannerist façade. A remnant of an old monastery, it is notable for its cloisters, lavishly lined with 18th-century *azulejos*. Beyond, set up in the old monastery refectory, is the Panteão Real (Royal Pantheon), the mausoleum of the Bragança family, which ruled Portugal from 1640 to 1910. Most of the Bragança kings and queens, including Portugal's last monarchs, are buried here. Open from 10 AM to 5 PM; closed Mondays. Admission charge to the cloisters and pantheon also gains entrance to an ornate sacristy, lined with inlaid marble. Largo de São Vicente (phone: 876470).

Igreja de Santa Engrácia – Begun during the 17th century but not completed until 1966, when it also was restored, this church gave rise to a Portuguese expression, *"obras de Santa Engrácia,"* used to describe a seemingly never-ending task. The grandiose structure, with a baroque façade and an interior richly decorated in marble, now serves as the Panteão Nacional (National Pantheon), containing the tombs of three Portuguese presidents and three writers, as well as memorials to other famous figures — including Prince Henry the Navigator, Luís de Camões, and Vasco da Gama — who are not buried here. This is within easy walking distance of São Vicente, but on Tuesdays and Saturdays, you may be detained by the flea market that's set up on the street between the two. Open from 10 AM to 5 PM; closed Mondays. Admission charge. Campo de Santa Clara (phone: 871529).

Museu Militar (Military Museum) – Housed in an 18th-century arsenal (the huge, saffron-yellow building in front of the Santa Apolónia train station), it contains cannon, guns, swords, armor, and uniforms, as well as paintings, sculptures, coin collections, and other mementos of Portugal's wars. One room is dedicated to the discoveries of Vasco da Gama. Open Tuesdays through Saturdays from 10 AM to 4 PM; Sundays, from 11 AM to 5 PM. Admission charge. Largo dos Caminhos de Ferro (phone: 867135).

Igreja da Madre de Deus (Church of the Mother of God) – Although the convent complex here was founded in 1501, most of what is seen today was built during the 18th century. The church is resplendent with ornate, gilded baroque woodwork, oil paintings, and *azulejos,* but the church is only part of the attraction, because the *Museu*

Nacional do Azulejo is installed in the convent conplex, and it's a must-see for tile lovers. Exquisite examples of the art, both Portuguese and foreign, from the 15th century to the present, are displayed in rooms around two cloisters, one of them a small gem. In addition to its other treasures, the museum possesses a long tile frieze dating from approximately 1730 depicting a panorama of Lisbon before the earthquake. There's also a pleasant cafeteria, decorated with 19th-century kitchen tiles. Open from 10 AM to 5 PM; closed Mondays. Admission charge. Bus No. 13A from Praça do Comércio goes to the convent. Rua da Madre de Deus (phone: 814-7747).

Nossa Senhora da Conceição Velha – Built during the early 16th century on the site of Lisbon's ancient synagogue, this was completely devastated in the 1755 earthquake, but its original Manueline portal survived. The beautiful doorway, richly carved with limestone figures, was retained for the new church — which, however, has little of note inside. Rua da Alfândega.

Casa dos Bicos (House of Pointed Stones) – When it was built during the 16th century, this house belonged to the family of Afonso de Albuquerque, a famous Portuguese viceroy to India. The earthquake reduced the 4-story structure to only several feet of foundations, but it has been completely rebuilt. The façade is covered with pyramidal stones, similar to the Casa de los Picos in Segovia, Spain, and the Palazzo dei Diamanti in Ferrara, Italy. The house is now used as an art gallery and is open to the public only when there are special exhibitions. Rua dos Bacalhoeiros (phone: 877330).

BAIXA

Praça do Comércio – This impressive riverside square, laid out after the earthquake by the Marquês de Pombal, is edged on three sides by arcaded neo-classical buildings. It's also known as Terreiro do Paço (Palace Square), after the royal palace that stood here in pre-earthquake days, and, to the English, as Black Horse Square, after the bronze equestrian statue of King José I, a design by the 18th-century sculptor Joaquim Machado de Castro, standing in the middle. The triumphal arch on the north side of the square, leading to Rua Augusta and the rest of the Baixa, was finished during the late 19th century. The square was the scene of the assassination of King Carlos I and his son in 1908.

Rossio – Officially called Praça de Dom Pedro IV, after the 18th-century king who is the subject of the statue in the center, this is the heart of the city and the northern limit of the Baixa. As early as the 13th century, this was the city's marketplace, but like Praça do Comércio and the rest of the Baixa, it was destroyed by the earthquake of 1755; the square was then newly laid out by Pombal. On the north side is the 19th-century *Teatro Nacional de Dona Maria II,* standing on the site of a onetime royal palace that during the 16th century, became the seat of the Inquisition. The square is much cheerier now, graced with flower stalls, fountains, and open-air cafés.

Elevador de Santa Justa (Santa Justa Elevator) – This lacy gray iron structure reminiscent of the Eiffel Tower — and often erroneously attributed to Eiffel — was designed by Raoul Mesnier, a Portuguese engineer of French descent, and erected in 1898. It not only spares visitors' feet the climb from Rua do Ouro (Rua Aurea) to Largo do Carmo in the Chiado, but also provides a panoramic view of the city from the top, and as you exit, you pass under a flying buttress of the Igreja do Carmo. The elevator runs from 7 AM to 11 PM (from 9 AM on Sundays).

Igreja do Carmo (Carmo Church) – Built during the 14th century, this was an imposing, majestic structure that overlooked the city until it was largely destroyed by the 1755 earthquake. The shell, with Gothic arches and a Gothic doorway, remains, and is floodlit at night. The ruins have been turned into the *Museu Arqueológico do Carmo,* containing prehistoric, Roman, Visigothic, and medieval artifacts, as well as medieval sculpture, *azulejos,* and inscriptions. Open from 10 AM to 1 PM and from 2 to 5 PM (July through September, 10 AM to 6 PM); closed Sundays. Admission charge. Largo do Carmo (phone: 346-0473).

BAIRRO ALTO

Solar do Vinho do Porto – This comfortable bar run by the Port Wine Institute is the next best thing to a trip to Portugal's northern capital. It's stocked with all types and vintages of porto — the official name for port wine — which visitors can order by the glass. There are about 160 different kinds, so go early or, better, often. Open daily, from 10 AM to 11:30 PM. 45 Rua de São Pedro de Alcântara (phone: 323307).

Igreja de São Roque (Church of St. Rock) – This 16th-century church has a flat wooden ceiling painted to look like a vaulted one, but it's best known for the baroque Capela de São João Baptista, the fourth chapel on the left. The chapel was commissioned during the mid-18th century by King João V, designed in Rome and assembled there, blessed by the pope — and then dismantled, to be shipped to Portugal and rebuilt at its present address. The lapis lazuli, porphyry, marble, alabaster, ivory, and other precious and semi-precious building materials cost the king dearly, but the workmanship was impeccable, as can be seen in the *Baptism of Christ*, which looks like an oil painting but is actually an exquisitely fine mosaic. The *Museu de São Roque* adjoining the church contains paintings and liturgical objects and richly embroidered vestments. Admission charge to the museum, which is open from from 10 AM to 5 PM; closed Mondays. Church remains open after museum closes. Largo Trindade Coelho (phone: 346-0361).

NORTHERN AND WESTERN LISBON

Parque Eduardo VII (Edward VII Park) – Downtown Lisbon's largest green space is this formally landscaped park at the northern end of Avenida da Liberdade, just beyond Praça Marquês de Pombal. From the esplanade at the top of the park, the view extends over the lower town to the Tagus. In the northwest corner is the charming Estufa Fria (Cold Greenhouse), where lush tropical plants grow in abundance among streams, pools, and waterfalls. A slatted roof protects them from the extremes of summer and winter. Within the Estufa Fria is a hothouse, the Estufa Quente. Open daily from 9 AM to 6 PM (5 PM in winter); the Estufa Quente closes a half hour earlier. Admission charge (phone: 682278).

Museu Calouste Gulbenkian (Gulbenkian Museum) – When the Armenian oil tycoon Calouste Sarkis Gulbenkian died in 1955, he left most of his estate and his enormous art collection to Portugal, the country to which he had fled during World War II and where he spent the last years of his life. The result was the Calouste Gulbenkian Foundation, a modern building that houses not only this museum, but also auditoriums, a library, and exhibition space. Don't miss the museum, a repository of 50 years of astute collecting — 3,000 pieces including works Gulbenkian bought from the *Hermitage Museum* in the 1920s when the Soviet Union needed foreign currency. The treasures include fine European paintings, sculpture, 18th-century French furniture, Chinese vases, Greek coins, medieval ivories, illuminated manuscripts, Middle Eastern carpets and ceramics, and more. There also is a marvelous collection of small Egyptian pieces and a unique collection of Art Nouveau jewelry by René Lalique. Open June through November from 10 AM to 5 PM; closed Mondays (winter hours are the same except for Wednesdays and Saturdays, when the museum opens at 2 PM and closes at 7 PM). Admission charge. 45 Avenida de Berna (phone: 734309).

Centro de Arte Moderna (Modern Art Center) – In the gardens behind the *Gulbenkian Museum*, it has an impressive collection of 19th- and 20th-century Portuguese paintings and sculpture, including paintings by José de Almada Negreiros. A cafeteria overlooks the gardens. The hours are the same as those of the *Gulbenkian Museum*. Admission charge. Rua Dr. Nicolau de Bettencourt (phone: 734309).

Jardim Zoológico (Zoo) – Set in a 65-acre park, the zoo is home to some 2,000 animals, including an elephant who rings a bell for money. Other distractions include pony rides for children, rowboats, and a small train. Open daily, from 9 AM to 8 PM, from April through October (closes at 6 PM the rest of the year). Admission charge. Parque das Larangeiras (phone: 726-8041).

Palácio dos Marqueses da Fronteira – West of the zoo, on the edge of the Parque Florestal de Monsanto, is an interesting palace built during the second half of the 17th century and originally used by its aristocratic owners as a hunting lodge. It's notable for the great number of *azulejos* that cover its walls — both inside and outside in the formal gardens — many of them depicting historical events. The palace still is privately owned but open to visitors on Mondays and Wednesdays from 10 AM to noon and on Saturdays from 3 to 6:30 PM. Admission charge. 1 Largo de São Domingos de Benfica (phone: 782023).

Aqueduto das Aguas Livres – Built during the first half of the 18th century to bring water from Caneças (11 miles/18 km northwest of Lisbon) to a reservoir near the present-day Amoreiras complex, the Aguas Livres Aqueduct miraculously survived the 1755 earthquake and still supplies the city with drinking water. It consists of 109 stone arches, some of them underground, but an impressive stretch of it (with one arch 214 feet high) runs through the Parque Florestal de Monsanto and the Campolide section of town, and can be seen from the road (N7) that leads to Estoril and Sintra. With special permission, it is possible to visit the inside of the aqueduct, with its fountains and statuary; inquire at the tourist office.

Basílica da Estrela (Basilica of the Star) – Built by Queen Maria I between 1779 and 1790, it fulfilled a vow she had made while petitioning God to grant her a son. The dome is one of Lisbon's landmarks; the tomb of the founder is inside. This church reflects the style of the school of sculpture founded at Mafra by the Italian sculptor Alessandro Giusti, one of whose Portuguese pupils, Joaquim Machado de Castro, was responsible for the manger figures here. Open daily. Praça da Estrela.

Museu Nacional de Arte Antiga (National Museum of Ancient Art) – One of the most important of Lisbon's museums, this is housed partly in a 17th-century palace that once belonged to Pombal and partly in an adjacent 20th-century building. Although it contains numerous foreign works, such as a celebrated Bosch triptych, *The Temptation of St. Anthony,* the museum is most notable for its paintings of the Portuguese school, especially of the 15th and 16th centuries. The prize in this group — perhaps the most famous painting in Portugal — is the six-panel polyptych known as the *Panéis de São Vicente de Fora* (St. Vincent Panels), a masterpiece by Nuno Gonçalves, the most important Portuguese painter of the 15th century. The polyptych is precious not only for its artistic merit (and because it's the only Gonçalves painting still extant), but also because it constitutes a document of Portuguese society of the time. Also in the museum are sculptures; Portuguese, European, and Oriental ceramics; objects in silver and gold; jewelry, furniture, and tapestries; and the entire gilt-and-tile laden Saint Albert Chapel, an architectural leftover from a Carmelite convent that once occupied the spot. A tea garden overlooking the river is open in summer. Open from 10 AM to 1 PM and from 2:30 to 5 PM; closed Mondays. Admission charge. 95 Rua das Janelas Verdes (phone: 672725).

BELÉM

Mosteiro dos Jerónimos (Hieronymite Monastery) – One of Lisbon's great landmarks, this white marble monastery was founded in 1502 by King Manuel I to give thanks for the successful return of Vasco da Gama's fleet from the Indies and to commemorate all the great voyages of Portugal's explorers during the Age of Discovery. Because Vasco da Gama had sailed from Belém in 1497, to return 2 years later, the site of a small mariners' chapel here seemed a fitting one for the memorial, about which it is said that it was "built by pepper," since it was paid for by riches brought by the spice trade. The sea motifs — seashells, ropes, anchors, and other symbols — that are carved throughout in great profusion are the characteristic decorative elements of the Manueline style of architecture, a uniquely Portuguese style that represented a transition from Gothic to Renaissance and eventually took its name from the king, Dom Manuel. The monastery is considered the country's finest example of Manueline architecture: The two portals, the extremely slender columns and character-istic network vaulting of the church, and the richly sculpted 2-story cloister are excep-tionally beautiful. King Manuel I and several other monarchs are buried in the church, as is Vasco da Gama, whose tomb, just inside the entrance, is marked by a caravel. Opposite it, marked by a lyre and quill pen, is a monument to Luís de Camões, whose bones may or may not be inside (he died in Africa, and the wrong bones may have been brought back). The long galleries to the west of the monastery, neo-Manueline from the 19th century, contain the *Museu Nacional de Arqueologia e Etnologia* (open from 10 AM to 2 PM and from 2 to 5 PM; closed Mondays; admission charge) and, around the corner, the *Museu da Marinha* (see below). More modern annexes across the courtyard from the entrance to the latter contain its collection of real boats rather than models and the *Planetario Calouste Gulbenkian,* which has presentations several days a week (times are posted outside; admission charge). The monastery is open from 10 AM to 6:30 PM, July through September (to 5 PM the rest of the year); closed Mondays. Admission charge to the cloister. Praça do Império (phone: 617020).

   Museu da Marinha (Naval Museum) – In the 19th-century galleries attached to the monastery, plus a modern extension to handle the overflow, this museum contains small models of boats from all eras of Portuguese history, from the earliest caravels of the Age of Discovery to warships, trading ships, and submarines — along with naval uniforms and other marine paraphernalia. Real boats are exhibited in the hangar-like extension. Of them the late-18th-century *galeota,* or galley, built for the wedding of Crown Prince João (who became João VI) to a Spanish princess and rowed by 71 red-coated figures, is the star. Examples of traditional boats from various regions include a *rabelo* boat from the Douro River, a *moliceiro* from the Ria de Aveiro, and fishing boats from the Algarve. Open from 10 AM to 5 PM; closed Mondays. Admission charge. Praça do Império (phone: 612541).

   Museu Nacional dos Coches (National Coach Museum) – Probably the finest coach collection in the world, housed in a building that was once the riding school of the Palácio de Belém, formerly a royal palace and now the presidential palace. The collection contains coaches ranging from the 16th through 19th centuries, and although a few are simple (such as the first one as you enter, which carried Philip III of Spain when he came to claim the throne as King Philip II of Portugal), most are beautifully carved, gilded works of art suitable for transporting royal personages or their emissaries (note the three Italian-made 18th-century baroque extravaganzas used by the Por-tuguese Ambassador to the Holy See). Open from 10 AM to 1 PM and from 2:30 to 6:30 PM (closes at 5:30 PM from October through May); closed Mondays. Admission charge. Praça Afonso de Albuquerque (phone: 638022).

   Padrão dos Descobrimentos (Monument to the Discoveries) – On the river in front of the monastery, this is a modern monument, put up in 1960 to commemorate the 500th anniversary of the death of Prince Henry the Navigator. It's shaped like the prow of a Portuguese caravel, with the prince as a figurehead leading a sculptured frieze of the personages of the time seaward. Inside, besides exhibition space, there's an elevator to a belvedere on top, from where the view extends up and down the Tagus and over formally laid-out green lawns to the Mosteiro dos Jerónimos and the rest of Belém. Open Tuesdays through Sundays from 9 AM to 7 PM (to 6 PM October through February); opens at 2 PM on Mondays; admission charge to the belvedere. Praça do Império.

Torre de Belém (Tower of Belém) – This quadrangular, 5-story tower, which looks like a huge chess piece, stands on the banks of the Tagus, west of the Monument to the Discoveries. The Portuguese consider it a symbol of their brave past, and its image often is used on official papers. Built during the 16th century to protect the river from pirates (because land has been reclaimed from the river since then, the tower was at one time farther out, surrounded by water), it later functioned as a prison. This is another example of Manueline architecture, richly decorated with sea motifs, statues, stone tracery, and Moorish balconies. Inside is a permanent exhibition of 15th- and 16th-century armaments and navigational instruments. Visitors may climb to the top for a view of the Tagus from the outside terrace. Open from 10 AM to 6:30 PM (to 5 PM from October through May); closed Mondays. Admission charge. Off Avenida Marginal (phone: 616892).

Palácio Nacional da Ajuda – In the hills behind Belém, this former royal palace was built during the early 19th century and is full of furniture, paintings, sculpture, and objets d'art left much as they were when royalty still occupied the premises. The widow of King Luís, Maria Pia of Savoy, who died in 1911, was its last royal inhabitant, but the palace is still used occasionally by the Portuguese government for state dinners. Open from 10 AM to 5 PM; closed Mondays. Admission charge. Largo da Ajuda (phone: 637095).

ENVIRONS

Estoril – This seaside suburb about 15½ miles (25 km) west of Lisbon became internationally famous during World War II when both Allied and Axis spies were tripping over each other, notably at the *Palácio* hotel. Since Portugal was neutral, there was a gentlemen's agreement: Allied diplomats could play golf at the local clubs on certain days, Axis diplomats on others. Immediately after the war, Estoril became home for numerous members of Europe's exiled royalty, giving it a touch of glamour. The crowned heads are gone now, but Estoril, with its bars and cafés and its gambling casino, is still a glamorous place. Its large turn-of-the-century mansions, hidden away behind spacious lawns and gardens flanking winding, hilly streets and wide avenues, lend it a definitely Old World air. The Parque do Estoril, a lovely garden of stately palm trees and purple-red bougainvillea, faces the seaside esplanade and the beach. The modern, elegant *Casino Estoril* sits at the top of the park. The residential district of Monte Estóril is west of the park, tending to merge with Cascais. Estoril can be reached easily by train from Lisbon's Cais do Sodré station or via the beach highway (Estrada Marginal).

Cascais – Once a simple fishing village whose picturesque, brightly painted boats headed out to sea each morning, Cascais (pronounced Kash-ka-*ish*) evolved during this century into a beach resort and the home of thousands of European — especially British — expatriates and, like Estoril, deposed royalty and dictators. Today, the fast-growing town, just west of Estoril, makes its living largely from tourism, although fishermen remain and the sight of fish being auctioned off at the market (on weekday evenings) by the beach is worth seeing. Cascais has few monuments to detain sightseers: There is one important church, the Manueline Nossa Senhora da Assunção, notable for its 18th-century *azulejos* and for its paintings by Josefa de Obidos; the Citadel, a 17th-century military building; and the *Museu-Biblioteca Condes de Castro Guimarães,* with paintings, sculpture, furniture, and objets d'art set up in an old mansion (open 10 AM to 5 PM; closed Tuesdays; no admission charge). It has plenty of other distractions, however. The bullfights held on summer Sundays at the Monumental de Cascais attract many visitors. Water sports and sailing are available from its beaches; there are also riding stables, tennis courts, and golf courses in the vicinity. The town (and the coast around it) are famous for their seafood restaurants, many of which overlook the bay and the sea. There is no dearth of nightlife, either, as Cascais is full of bars and discos.

Along the coast west of town is the Boca do Inferno (Mouth of Hell), a set of rocky cliffs full of caves and smaller cavities through which the sea storms and rages — an awesome sight. Farther along the coast road, 5½ miles (9 km) from Cascais, is Praia do Guincho, an immense stretch of sand between two promontories where the wind howls (*guincho* means "shriek"), the sea is rough, and the undertow dangerous; it is popular with brave surfers. Still farther along is a headland, Cabo da Roca, the western-most point of continental Europe, where there is a lighthouse. Cascais can be reached by train from Lisbon's Cais do Sodré station.

Queluz – This town 7½ miles (12 km) northwest of Lisbon is known for its lovely pink rococo Palácio Nacional, where official guests of the Portuguese government usually are housed. The palace was begun in 1747 by the Infante Dom Pedro, who became Pedro III, consort of Queen Maria I, an unfortunate queen who lived here after going mad following Pedro's death and that of her oldest son. Designed by Mateus Vicente de Oliveira, a pupil of the architect of the Mafra Monastery, the royal residence took decades to finish and has been restored after being partially destroyed by fire in this century. Its rooms are filled with Portuguese furnishings and tapestries, Italian glassware and marble, Dutch tiles, Chinese screens, Austrian porcelain, and other exquisite antiques; its gardens are laid out to resemble those of Versailles (Queen Maria had been engaged to Louis XV), with fountains, statuary, and *azulejos*. Among the more striking rooms are the Throne Room, the Hall of Mirrors, the Hall of the Ambassadors, the Music Salon, and the Queen's Dressing Room. Chamber music concerts and other cultural events take place here during the summer. The palace is open from 10 AM to 1 PM and from 2 to 5 PM; closed Tuesdays. Admission charge (phone: 435-0039). Queluz can be reached by train from Lisbon's Rossio station.

■**EXTRA SPECIAL:** The beauty of Sintra, a town on the north slope of the Serra de Sintra about 17½ miles (28 km) northwest of Lisbon, has been sung through the ages, most notably by Portugal's most famous poet, Camões, in *The Lusiads,* and by Lord Byron, who called it a "glorious Eden" in "Childe Harold." The town has an enchanting setting, swathed in towering trees, dense ferns, and plants and flowers of every description brought by the Portuguese from all corners of their once far-flung empire — all kept green by water gushing from the rocks in springs and little waterfalls tumbling everywhere down the mountain. Mists from the nearby Atlantic often envelop its heights and lend it an ethereal and unreal air (as well as give it a pleasant climate in summer while, on occasion, obscuring its majestic views). Among the oldest towns in Portugal, it was occupied by the Moors, who built two castles, one of them winding around the side of the mountain from pinnacle to pinnacle and the other in the center of the present town. After Sintra was taken from the Moors in the 12th century, it became a favorite summer residence of the Portuguese monarchs. Over the centuries, they built the imposing National Palace in town on the site of one of the Moorish castles and the whimsi-cal, *Disneyland*-like Pena Palace on the very peak of the mountain, where it can be seen from as far away as Lisbon and the Arrábida Peninsula.

Sintra is very crowded in summer and on weekends. It can be reached by car on N117 and N249 or by train from the Rossio station. Those who come by train can take a taxi to visit the palaces that are located at some distance from the center; otherwise, the tourist office at Praça da República (phone: 923-1157) provides maps for those who want to walk. There also are horse-drawn carriages that take visitors sightseeing around town. Good restaurants and hotels abound, as do excellent shops selling handicrafts, especially rugs, porcelain, and straw goods. The Feira de São Pedro de Sintra, a market that takes place on the second and fourth Sundays of every month, sells everything imaginable. During the *Sintra*

Music Festival, held from mid-June to mid-July, concerts take place in the palaces and other public buildings.

The Palácio Nacional de Sintra, in the main square, was built on the foundations of a Moorish palace by King João I in the late 14th century and added to by King Manuel I in the early 16th century. Later, it received still further additions, making the enormous structure a survey of styles from Moorish through Mudéjar, Gothic, Manueline, and Renaissance to baroque. Outside, besides the twin conical chimneys that dominate the town, the most notable feature of the palace are the characteristic Manueline windows. Inside, its most important features are the *azulejos* facing its walls throughout, some of the finest to be seen in the country. One of the most interesting rooms is the Sala dos Brazões (Hall of the Coats of Arms), built during Manuel's reign; its ceiling is an octagonal wooden cupola whose painted panels show the coats of arms of the king, his 8 children, and the 72 noble familes of Portugal at the time. (The blue-and-white wall tiles depicting hunting scenes are from the 18th century.) In the Sala das Pêgas (Hall of the Magpies), the ceiling is decorated with 136 magpies — painted, so the story goes, on the orders of João I after his wife, Philippa of Lancaster, caught him kissing one of the ladies-in-waiting. (There were 136 ladies-in-waiting at court, and the idea was to put an end to gossip among them.) The largest room is the Sala dos Cisnes (Hall of Swans), so named because of the ceramic swans decorating it and the painted ones on the ceiling. The palace is open from 10 AM to 1 PM and from 2 to 5 PM; closed Wednesdays. Admission charge (phone: 923-4118).

The Palácio Nacional da Pena, standing on the highest peak above Sintra, is reached up a spectacular road of hairpin curves through beautiful parks and woods. After religious orders were expelled from Portugal in 1832, Ferdinand of Saxe-Coburg-Gotha, consort of Queen Maria II, bought a small 16th-century monastery that stood on this spot and commissioned a German architect, Baron Eschewege, to create a new medieval palace around it. Inspired by the Bavarian castles in his own country, the architect combined their styles with Moorish, Gothic, and Manueline elements to create a fantastic building complete with gold-topped domes, turrets, crenelated walls, parapets, and a drawbridge. The cloister and chapel of the monastery were preserved; the latter has a black alabaster and marble altarpiece executed in the 16th century by Nicolas Chanterene, although its stained glass windows are 19th-century German. The rooms of the palace proper are filled with furniture and ornaments of many different periods and are particularly noteworthy because they have been left much as they were when last occupied by the royal family, which fled into exile in 1910. The views from the palace verandahs are spectacular, and the Parque da Pena surrounding it, planted in the 19th century, also is impressive, containing plants and trees from all over the world. The palace is open from 9 AM to 6 PM (to 5 PM in winter); closed Mondays. Admission charge (phone: 923-0227).

Still another of Sintra's palaces, the *Palácio dos Seteais,* has been turned into a luxury hotel (see *Checking In*), but there are other sights to see, including the Castelo dos Mouros, or Moorish Castle, located off the same road that leads to the Pena Palace, about halfway up the mountain. It was originally built by the Moors in the 8th or 9th century and was restored after the Christian Reconquest of the 12th century and later by King Fernando I. It has five rather dilapidated towers, a keep, and long walls that undulate over a great part of the mountain. Elsewhere is the Quinta de Monserrate, a palace and park built by a 19th-century Englishman, Sir Francis Cook, about 2 miles (3 km) from Sintra via N375. The palace is an odd-looking, three-domed structure, but it is the wonderful gardens, landscaped on a steep slope, that are the prime attraction (open daily, from 9 AM to sunset; admission charge). Another sight is the Convento dos Capuchos, 4 miles (6 km) from town via N247-3. Built in the 16th century, it is a peculiar place in that the monks' cells are carved out of rock and lined with cork to keep out the damp. (Ring the bell and the caretaker will open the door.)

SOURCES AND RESOURCES

 TOURIST INFORMATION: Maps, brochures, shopping guides, listings of monthly events, and other information can be obtained from any of the Postos de Turismo (Tourist Posts) run by the Direcção-Geral do Turismo (Directorate General for Tourism), which is headquartered at 86 Avenida António Augusto de Aguiar. A tourist post is located at the same address (phone: 575091), but perhaps the most convenient one in downtown Lisbon is the one at Palácio Foz (Praça dos Restauradores; phone: 346-3624). Other branches are at Lisbon Airport (phone: 885974), at the Santa Apolónia train station (phone: 867848), and at the Alcântara boat dock (phone: 600756). English-speaking staff is available to answer questions and help make hotel reservations. It is possible to hire English-speaking guides through the tourist offices or by calling the guides union, the Sindicato Nacional da Atividade Turistica, Tradutores e Intérpretes (phone: 323298).

The US Embassy is on Avenida das Forças Armadas (phone: 726-6600).

Local Coverage – The leading daily is the *Diário de Notícias,* a morning paper. *Seminario* and *Expresso* are two of the most prestigious weekly papers. English-language newspapers and magazines are on sale at most newsstands.

 TELEPHONE: The city code for Lisbon is 1. If calling from within Portugal, dial 01 before the local number.

 GETTING AROUND: Although various sections of the city, such as the Alfama, are ideal for strolling, remember that Lisbon is built on seven hills; visitors probably will want to ride from one section to another. Parking is problematic, so public transportation and taxis are the best bet.

Airport – Lisbon's airport for both domestic and international flights, Portela de Sacavém (phone: 802060), is only 5 miles (8 km) northeast of the center, a 15- to 30-minute drive, depending on traffic. Taxi fare to most hotels should come to about $5. The *Linha Verde* (Green Line) express bus runs between the airport and the Santa Apolónia train station, stopping at major downtown points. *TAP Air Portugal* has a local address (3A Praça Marquês de Pombal; phone: 544080 or 575020). For information on *TAP*'s subsidiary, *Linhas Aéreas Regionais (LAR)*, which has flights to many cities as well as to Madeira and the Azores, call 887119 or 896102.

Boat – Ferryboats, carrying both passengers and cars, cross the Tagus every few minutes from the Praça do Comércio and Cais do Sodré for Cacilhas, Barreiro, and other points. There also is a river service to Cascais. Short cruises on the Tagus take place from April through October.

Bus – City buses and trams are run by *CARRIS (Companhia Carris de Ferro de Lisboa)*. Maps and other information can be obtained at the window at the side of the Santa Justa Elevator, just off Rua do Carmo. Bus and tram fares vary according to the zone; the basic fare is 100 escudos (about 65¢). Get on the bus by the front door, buy a ticket from the driver, and cancel it in the machine. Tourist passes for 7 days of unlimited travel by bus, tram, subway, ferryboat, and the Santa Justa Elevator can be bought at the Praça dos Restauradores and Praça Marquês de Pombal subway stations and at the Santa Justa Elevator. Lisbon's trams are not only vintage vehicles and picturesque in themselves, but many go through the more historic parts of the city, providing a cheap way to take a tour. Long-distance bus service is provided by *Rodoviária Nacional,* the state-owned bus company, whose terminal is at Casal de Ribeiro (phone: 545439).

Car Rental – Most major firms have offices in Lisbon and at the airport: *Avis* (12C Avenida Praia da Vitória; phone: 561177; at the airport; phone: 894836; at the Santa Apolónia train station; phone: 876887; at the *Alfa* hotel; phone: 726-3360; *Penta* hotel; phone: 726-5629; *Ritz* hotel; phone: 691521; and at the *Sheraton* hotel; phone: 575757); *Hertz* (10 Avenida 5 de Outubro; phone: 579077; at 10 Avenida Visconde Seabra; phone: 772944; and at the *Novotel* hotel, 1642 Avenida José Malhoa; phone: 726-7221). *Budget* (33 Avenida Fontes Pereira de Melo; phone: 560015; 124 Rua do Arsenal; phone: 320913 or 320861; and at the airport; phone: 801785 or 801738).

Elevator – The Elevador de Santa Justa takes passengers from Rua do Ouro (Rua Aurea) in the Baixa to Largo do Carmo in the Chiado. The Portuguese also refer to several streetcars that travel a steep route as "elevators," among them the *Gloria Elevator,* running from Calçada da Glória, on the west side of Praça dos Restauradores, to the Bairro Alto. The unlimited-travel tourist pass is valid on elevators; individual rides cost 22.50 escudos (about 15¢).

Subway – The underground system serving Lisbon is called the *Metropolitano.* A large "M" aboveground designates the stations — Rossio and Restauradores are the most central ones. The fare is 50 escudos (about 33¢ — or 40 escudos if bought in a machine) to any point. The unlimited-travel tourist pass is valid underground. Beware of pickpockets.

Taxi – Cabs are metered and inexpensive — a ride to almost any part of the city will cost less than $6. For trips outside Lisbon, a set rate per kilometer is charged beyond the city limits. Taxis can be hailed on the street or picked up at cabstands conveniently scattered around town. (Note that by law, passengers must get in and out on the sidewalk side, not the street side. Also by law, drivers may charge extra for luggage, but the regulation is vague and amounts are sometimes excessive.) To call a cab, dial 732756, 825061, or 659151.

Train – Frequent, fast electric trains connecting Lisbon with Belém, Estoril, and Cascais leave from the Estação Cais do Sodré (phone: 370181), by the river near Praça do Comércio. Trains to Queluz and Sintra operate from the Estação do Rossio (phone: 877092), just off the Rossio. (It's the 19th-century building with the charming, elaborately carved neo-Manueline façade just across from the side of the *Teatro Nacional.* Confusingly, it's hardly ever referred to by its real name, Estação Central, which is carved in neo-Manueline letters around its circular doors.) Trains for most of the rest of Portugal and elsewhere in Europe leave from Estação Santa Apolónia (phone: 876025), which is located along the river east of the Alfama district, not within walking distance of the center — take a bus or tram.) The station for trains to the Algarve is Estação Sul e Sueste (phone: 877179), on the east side of Praça do Comércio. These southbound trains actually leave from Barreiro, on the south bank of the Tagus, but tickets include the price of the ferry ride from the station. Trains between Lisbon, Porto, and Faro have air conditioned coaches with bar and restaurant service.

 SPECIAL EVENTS: In ancient times, the *Festas dos Santos Populares* (Feasts of the Popular Saints), held in June, were celebrations of the summer solstice, but they are now Christian rites in honor of Santo António (St. Anthony), São João (St. John), and São Pedro (St. Peter). The *Feast of St. Anthony,* June 13 and the night before, is a bit like *New Year's Eve* and *New Year's*

Day. Although most people associate St. Anthony (of Padua) with Italy, he actually was born in the Alfama in Lisbon, and people here make much ado about it. The Old Quarter comes alive on the eve: Dances are held in streets festooned with colored lanterns, and throughout the night gallons of good, rough wine are drunk to wash down mountains of sardines roasted on open barbecues. The saint is a powerful matchmaker, so this is the night when the city's young girls hope to meet their future husbands. Street stalls sell little pots of a spicy-smelling green herb called *manjerico,* each pot holding a message of advice or consolation for lovers. In the Baixa, neighborhood associations bedecked in traditional costumes parade down Avenida da Liberdade, each attempting to outdo the display of the others. For the *Feast of St. John,* on June 23 and 24, people make bonfires sprinkled with scented herbs and thistles and jump over them to show their daring, an ancient rite connected with fertility. The final celebration is the *Feast of Saint Peter,* on June 29. In little towns around Lisbon, such as Montijo, there is a running of the bulls and a blessing of ships on this day.

 MUSEUMS: In addition to those discussed in *Special Places,* Lisbon also has the following museums that may be of interest. Note that most museums are closed on Mondays, and that many that ordinarily impose an admission charge are free on Sundays.

Museu de Arte Popular (Folk Art Museum) – Furniture, paintings, ceramics, basketry, and other items illustrating the handicrafts, customs, and life of the various Portuguese regions. Open from 10 AM to 1 PM and from 2 to 5 PM; closed Mondays. Admission charge. Avenida Brasília, Belém (phone: 611282).

Museu da Cidade (City Museum) – Maps, engravings, and other objects telling Lisbon's history, set up in an 18th-century palace. Open from 10 AM to 1 PM and from 2 to 6 PM; closed Mondays. Admission charge. 245 Campo Grande (phone: 759-1617).

Museu Nacional do Teatro (National Theater Museum) – Costumes, scenery, drawings, programs, posters, and other theatrical memorabilia. Open from 10 AM to 1 PM and from 2:30 to 5PM; closed Mondays. Admission charge. 10-12 Estrada do Lumiar (phone: 759-1102).

Museu Nacional do Traje (National Costume Museum) – Changing exhibitions of Portuguese and foreign costumes, accessories, and fabric, in a lovely old suburban house located about a mile north of the *City Museum.* Open from 10 AM to 1 PM and from 2:30 to 5 PM; closed Mondays. Admission charge. 5 Largo São João Baptista, Parque de Monteiro-Mor, Lumiar (phone: 759-0318).

Museu Rafael Bordalo Pinheiro – Devoted to the works of the 19th-century caricaturist, ceramist, and painter of the same name. Open from 10 AM to 1 PM and from 2 to 6 PM; closed Mondays. Admission charge. 382 Campo Grande (phone: 759-0816).

 SHOPPING: The most important shopping area in Lisbon is the Baixa, the zone between the Rossio and the river, with the mosaic-paved, pedestrian street, Rua Augusta, as its backbone. Another shop-heavy street, Rua do Carmo, leads from this area to the part of the Baixa known as the Chiado, where many fashionable shops still are located, even though some of the more famous ones, along with two department stores, burned down when fire ravaged much of this area in 1988. The damaged blocks will be rebuilt, but at present shoppers either take the Santa Justa Elevator to the Chiado or make their way from Rua do Carmo to Rua Garrett, the backbone of the area, via temporary scaffolding erected over the debris. Antiques row also is located in this part of the city: Rua Dom Pedro V, in the Bairro Alto, is the heart of it, but shops also congregate along Rua do Alecrim, Rua da Misericórdia, Rua São Pedro de Alcântara, and Rua da Escola Politécnica. Shops in the downtown area are open Mondays through Fridays, from 9 AM to 1 PM and 3 to 5 PM, Saturdays from 9 AM to 1 PM; many *centros comerciais* (shopping centers) stay open until midnight. The most famous, with sophisticated shops of all kinds — more than 300 of them — is the *Centro Comercial das Amoreiras,* a post-Modernist complex (on Avenida Engenheiro Duarte Pacheco) with huge towers in pinks and greens and glass, designed by architect Tomás Taveira. At the other extreme is the *Feira da Ladra* (Thieves' Market), a flea market held Tuesdays and Saturdays (on Largo de Santa Clara) at the edge of the Alfama. Among the best buys in Lisbon are gold, silver, and jewelry — it is relatively inexpensive and the guaranteed content of the gold and silver make many pieces a bargain. There has been a renaissance in painting, tapestry making, and ceramics, with the accompanying opening of many new galleries. A revival in tile making, often in reproduction of 17th- and 18th-century designs, also has taken place, and many of the stores selling these wares will pack and ship. Rugs from Arraiolos and lace from Madeira, beautiful glass and crystal, copperware, fishermen's sweaters, and baskets are other good buys, along with fashionable clothing, shoes, and leather goods. Note that many of the shops below have branches in the *Amoreiras* shopping center.

Artesanato Arameiro – A wide variety of regional handicrafts — lace, rugs, ceramics, copperware, and filigree. 62 Praça dos Restauradores (phone: 320238).

Atlantis – Crystal tableware from Alcobaça. Centro Comercial das Amoreiras (phone: 693670).

Augustus – Elegant clothes for women. Centro Comercial das Amoreiras (phone: 693479).

Casa dos Bordados da Madeira – Embroidery and lace from Madeira and a wide selection of other Portuguese handicrafts. 135 Rua Primeiro de Dezembro (phone: 321447).

Charles – A very wide selection of shoes. 105 Rua do Carmo (phone: 320700) and 109 Rua Augusta (phone: 326584).

Charlot – Considered a very fashionable boutique, with designer labels from Portugal, Italy, and France. 28 Rua Barata Salgueiro (phone: 573665).

Diadema – Lovely gold and silver jewelry. 166 Rua do Ouro (phone: 321362).

Fábrica de Cerâmica Viúva Lamego – Makes and sells reproductions of old tiles; its bird and animal motifs are famous, but it also makes high-quality modern designs. 25 Largo do Intendente Pina Manique (phone: 521401).

Fábrica de Loiça de Sacavém – Fine porcelain in traditional and modern patterns. 57 Avenida da Liberdade (phone: 323902).

Galeria Comicos – A good gallery showing avant-garde paintings. 1B Rua Tenente Raul Cascais (phone: 677794).

Galeria Sesimbra – Lisbon's second oldest art gallery, known for hand-stitched Agulha tapestries, made from designs by leading contemporary Portuguese artists. 77 Rua Castilho (phone: 560291).

Galeria 111 – The longest established of Lisbon's art galleries, selling the best of today's Portuguese artists. 111 Campo Grande (phone: 767406).

Helio – Top-quality shoes for men and women. 93 Rua do Carmo (phone: 322725).

Joalharia Mergulhão – One of the oldest jewelers in the city. 162 Rua de São Paulo (phone: 346-0013).

Livraria Bertrand – An enormous selection of books. Corner of Rua Garrett and Rua Anchieta (phone: 320081).

Livraria Buchholz – A large stock of foreign books as well as Portuguese ones. 4 Rua do Duque de Palmela (phone: 547358).

Madeira Gobelins – Embroidery, woven tapestries, and carpets from Madeira. 40 Rua Castilho (phone: 563708).

Madeira House – Lisbon's oldest shop dealing in genuine Madeira embroidery and lace, it also sells less expensive embroidered linens. 131 Rua Augusta (phone: 320557).

New York – A classy shop with the latest in women's clothes. 206 Rua do Ouro (phone: 321764).

Ourivesaria Pimenta – Fine jewelry, watches, and silver. 257 Rua Augusta (phone: 324564).

Porfirios – For young and trendy dressers. 63 Rua da Vitória (phone: 368274).

Quintão – Beautiful handmade Arraiolos rugs that are works of art. 30 Rua Ivens (phone: 365837).

Rosa & Teixeira – A highly ranked tailor selling his own designs for men and women. 204 Avenida da Liberdade (phone: 542063).

Ana Salazar – Clothes by Ana Salazar, Portugal's most famous avant-garde designer for women. 87 Rua do Carmo (phone: 372289).

Sant'Anna – Reproductions of 17th- and 18th-century tiles, made in the shop's own factory. 95 Rua do Alecrim (phone: 322537). The factory, at 96 Calçada da Boa Hora, can be visited, but call first (phone: 638292).

Vista Alegre – The makers of Portugal's finest porcelain. 52-54 Rua Ivens (phone: 328612) and 18 Largo do Chiado (phone: 361401).

 SPORTS AND FITNESS: Bullfighting – Portuguese bullfighting, quite different from the Spanish version, is more a spectacle of horsemanship than a fight. Bulls are never killed in the ring here, and the fighting is done mostly on horseback, with the *cavaleiros* wearing magnificent 18th-century costumes as they ride against the bulls. After the horseman finishes with a mock kill, the *forcados* — eight young men dressed in brown pants, white shirts, cummerbunds, and tasseled caps — jump over the barrier and line up to wrestle the bull: the most popular part of the bullfight. Their leader taunts the bull to charge and when it does, the leader grabs it around the neck and they all wrestle it to the ground. Although there is a bullfight at *Easter,* the season begins in earnest in June and generally runs through September, with contests usually held on Thursdays, Sundays, and holidays. The most important fights take place in Lisbon at the *Praça de Touros do Campo Pequeno* (Campo Pequeno Bullring), a mosque-like structure with minarets all around its walls (Avenida da República; phone: 732093), and at the *Monumental de Cascais.*

Fishing – Boats for deep-sea fishing can be rented from local fishermen at Sesimbra, a fishing village 27 miles (43 km) south of Lisbon, or at Cascais.

Fitness Centers – *Health Club Soleil,* a chain, is in the *Sheraton* hotel (1 Rua Latino Coelho; phone: 553353); the *Palácio* (in Estoril; phone: 268-8184); the *Estoril-Sol* (in Cascais; phone: 286-8005); and at *Squash Soleil* (*Centro Comercial das Amoreiras,* Avenida Engenheiro Duarte Pacheco; phone: 692907).

Golf – The *Clube de Golfe do Estoril* (on Avenida da República in Estoril; phone: 268-0176) has 27 holes; caddies and clubs can be rented, and lessons by professionals are available. Also in the Estoril–Cascais area are the *Estoril-Sol Golf Club* (Estrada da Lagoa Azul; phone: 923-2461), with 9 holes belonging to the *Estoril-Sol* hotel; and the *Clube de Golfe da Marinha,* an 18-hole Robert Trent Jones course (in the Quinta da Marinha tourist development at Cascais; phone: 289881 or 289901). The British *Lisbon Sports Club* has an 18-hole course (at Casal da Carregueira, on the Belas–Sabugo road, about 15½ miles/25 km northwest of Lisbon; phone: 431-0077). The *Clube de Campo de Lisboa* (Lisbon Country Club; Quinta da Aroeira, Fonte da Telha; phone: 226-1802 or 226-1358) has 18 holes on the coast, 9½ miles (15 km) south of Lisbon.

Horseback Riding – Equestrians can be accommodated at the *Clube de Campo de Lisboa* (south of Lisbon; phone: 226-1802 or 226-1060); at the *Clube da Marinha* (at Cascais; phone: 289282); at the *Pony Club Cascais* (Quinta da Ricuda; phone: 284-

3233); and at the *Clube de Campo Dom Carlos I* (Estrada Areia, Praia do Guincho; phone: 285-1403).

Jogging – Attractive as it may seem, jogging in Lisbon's central Parque Eduardo VII is not recommended, especially alone or at night. Instead, run along the riverside between the Ponte 25 de Abril and Belém. Another good place is the fitness circuit in the *Estadio Nacional* (National Stadium) area on the outskirts of the city on the way to Estoril, where the track winds through pleasant pine woods. (But do not jog alone.) The park in Estoril and the seafront in Cascais are also good.

Soccer – This is Portugal's most popular sport by far, and it's ruled by a triumvirate of three top clubs: *Sporting* and *Benfica,* from Lisbon, and *Porto,* from the northern capital of Porto. Any game in which one of these teams takes part should be worth watching, as the rivalries are very intense. (Note that the crowds are not unruly here and there has been no hooliganism, as in some other parts of Europe.) The season runs from August until the end of June, and matches are played on Sundays at various stadiums; tickets can be obtained with the help of the hotel desk.

Swimming – The entire coast west of the city and south of it across the river is banded with sandy beaches, and many hotels have private swimming pools. However, water pollution has become a problem on some of the beaches between Lisbon and Estoril, so check first about possible health hazards. (Don't go in the water unless the blue safety flag is flying.) In Estoril, the *Tamariz* restaurant, on the beach, has changing rooms.

Tennis – Courts are available at Estoril's *Clube de Tênis* (Avenida Amaral; phone: 268-6669); at the *Clube de Campo Dom Carlos I* (Estrada Areia, Praia do Guincho; phone: 285-2362); and at the *Lisbon Sports Club* (Casal da Carregueira, 15½ miles (25 km) northwest of Lisbon near Belas; phone: 431-0077).

 THEATER: Classic and contemporary plays are presented year-round except during July at the *Teatro Nacional de Dona Maria II* (Praça Dom Pedro IV; phone: 371078). Performances take place in Portuguese, of course. The *revista,* or revue, a popular Lisbon tradition embracing topical sketches, satire, music, and dancing reminiscent of old-fashioned vaudeville, can make for a lively evening even for those who don't understand the language. The best revues are presented in small theaters in the rather ramshackle Parque Mayer theater district, just off Avenida da Liberdade.

 MUSIC: Lisbon's opera house, the *Teatro Nacional de São Carlos,* is near the Chiado district downtown (9 Rua Serpa Pinto; phone: 368408 or 368664). Built in the 18th century, it is one of Europe's prettiest, with an apricot-colored interior set off by touches of green and gold. The season runs from mid-December until May. Various ballet companies also perform at the opera house, but the *Gulbenkian Foundation Ballet Company,* sponsored by the foundation, is one of the best ballet companies in Europe at the moment, performing both classical and modern dance. Performances take place at the auditorium of the Gulbenkian Foundation building (45 Avenida de Berna; phone: 779131). Symphony and chamber music concerts can also be heard here and at the *Teatro Municipal de São Luís* (Rua António Maria Cardoso; phone: 327172).

 NIGHTCLUBS AND NIGHTLIFE: A good place to begin an evening with a pre-dinner glass of dry, white porto is *A Brasileira* (122 Rua Garrett), one of Lisbon's traditional old cafés. Take a seat at one of the tables outdoors and watch the world go by; the gentleman in bronze, occupying the bronze table, flanked by bronze chairs, is Fernando Pessoa (1888–1935), a Portuguese man of letters — this statue of him was placed here on the 100th anniversary of his birth. A second old café popular among the old guard is *Café Nicola,* on the Rossio.

Lisbon's popular *fado* houses — restaurants with *fado* music — are scattered throughout the old Alfama and Bairro Alto districts. *Fado,* which means "fate" or "destiny," is the name given to the anecdotal, satirical, sentimental, or occasionally happy songs performed, usually by a woman swathed in black (the *fadista*), to the accompaniment of one or more 12-stringed guitars. Although *fado* has become commercialized and many restaurants beef up their shows with folk dancing and popular music, a visitor may be lucky enough to be on hand some night when the singers and the musicians are in the mood to revive the real thing. Do not make a sound during the singing — neither the singers nor the spectators permit it. Some particularly good spots are *Senhor Vinho* (18 Rua do Meio à Lapa; phone: 672681), where the *fado* is pure; *O Faia* (54 Rua da Barroca; phone: 321923), one of the best known; *Adega Machado* (91 Rua do Norte; phone: 360095), fun because it offers spirited folk dancing; *Lisboa à Noite* (69 Rua das Gáveas; phone: 368557); and *A Severa* (51-61 Rua das Gáveas; phone: 364006). All are in the Bairro Alto, except *Senhor Vinho,* which is in the Lapa district west of the Bairro Alto. Those who are not dining should go after 10 PM. Reservations are essential.

The top discotheques are sometimes difficult to get into for all but regular customers (they're often frequented by local socialites), and many impose an expensive cover charge. Some of the best are *Banana Power* (52 Rua Cascais; phone: 631815), in the Alcântara dock area west of the center toward Belém; the *Fragil Bar* (128 Rua da Atalaia; phone: 369578), in the Bairro Alto; *Ad Lib* (18 Rua Barata Salgueiro; phone: 561717); *Stones* (1 Rua do Olival; phone: 664545); *Whispers* (35 Avenida Fontes Pereira de Melo; phone: 575489); *Trumps* (104-B Rua da Imprensa Nacional; phone: 671059), which has a huge dance floor; and *Springfellows* (Avenida Oscar Monteiro Torres), which is very fancy and on 3 floors. *Procópio* (21-21A Avenida Alto São Francisco; phone: 652851) is a bar with live music after 11 PM; *Loucuras* (37 Avenida Pedro Alvares Cabral; phone: 681117) also offers live music. African music — especially from Cape Verde — is heard all over town. *Clave di Nos* (100 Rua do Norte; phone: 368420), a restaurant with good food, has a good Cape Verdian band.

Bars to try in Estoril include the *Founder's Inn* (11D Rua Dom Afonso Henriques; phone: 268-2221); *Ray's Bar* (25 Avenida Saboia; phone: 269-0106), west of the center in Monte Estoril; and the *English Bar* (Estrada Marginal, Monte Estoril; phone: 268-0413). In Estoril, however, don't miss a night at the world-famous *Casino Estoril* (phone: 268-4521), a shiny, modern building in the Parque Estoril. It's open every day (to those over 21 endowed with a passport) from 3 PM to 3 AM, and has all the classic European and American games: roulette, baccarat, chemin de fer, blackjack, French bank, slot machines, bingo. The roulette stakes are higher than in Portugal's other casinos, and the slot machines sometimes spit out jackpots of more than $200,000. But gambling is only one of the attractions. The glittering restaurant-nightclub resembles the *Lido* in Paris, with balconies and a main floor seating 800 and the only really international show in the country.

Cascais has a spirited nightlife, with many bars and cafés such as the *John Bull,* an English-style pub at 32 Praça Costa Pinto (phone: 283319); *Tren Velho,* a converted train coach sitting beside the station (Avenida Duquesa de Palmela; phone: 286-7355); *Bar 21,* an attractive cocktail lounge (1A Travessa da Misericórdia; phone: 286-7518 or 286-4462); and *Cutty Sark* (6 Travessa da Ressureição). The list of popular discos includes *Coconuts* (7 Boca do Inferno; phone: 284-4109), with an outdoor terrace by the sea; *Julianas* (10 Avenida 25 de Abril; phone: 286-4052); and the very snooty *Van Gogo* (9 Travessa da Alfarrobeira; phone: 283378). For *fado* in Cascais, try *Forte Dom Rodrigo* (Estrada de Birre; phone: 285-1373), or *Picadeiro Maria d'Almeida* (Quinta da Guia, Torre; phone: 289982).

BEST IN TOWN

 CHECKING IN: A visitor's primary decision will be whether to stay right in Lisbon, to commute (with thousands of *lisboetas*) from Estoril or Cascais via the clean, inexpensive trains that run into the city about every 20 minutes, or even to stay in Sintra. Whichever your choice, a double room with a private bath will cost from $80 to $130 a night in a hotel in the expensive category, from $50 to $70 in the moderate range, and $30 to $40 in the inexpensive range. Reservations are necessary. All telephone numbers are in the 1 city code unless otherwise indicated.

LISBON

Alfa – A very modern 350-room luxury high-rise near the zoo and the *Gulbenkian Museum*. It has 3 restaurants (one with a panoramic view), a swimming pool, a sauna, shops, and a hairdresser. Avenida Columbano Bordalo Pinheiro (phone: 726-2121 or 726-4516). Expensive.

Altis – This 9-story ultramodern hotel of steel, glass, and concrete has 305 rooms, a nice view from its rooftop grill, and a heated indoor swimming pool. It's located about halfway between the Rossio train station and Parque Eduardo VII. 11 Rua Castilho (phone: 522496). Expensive.

Diplomático – Well situated near Parque Eduardo VII, it has 90 rooms equipped with air conditioning, mini-bars, and TV sets, plus a restaurant, bar, and private parking. 74 Rua Castilho (phone: 562041). Expensive.

Lisboa Plaza – Centrally located off Avenida da Liberdade, newly redecorated by a leading Portuguese designer, and elegant, this is family owned and operated. It has 93 air conditioned, soundproofed rooms (with mini-bars, TV sets, and all the rest), in addition to the *Quinta d'Avenida* restaurant; the bar, done in Art Nouveau style, is a popular meeting place. 7 Travessa do Salitre (phone: 346-3922). Expensive.

Lisboa Sheraton – One of the best of the chain in Europe, this 400-room high-rise offers comfortable accommodations, marble bathrooms, and elegant public areas and lounges. All rooms are air conditioned, and there is a heated, open-air swimming pool, plus several restaurants (including the 29th-floor *Panorama*), bars, shops, and a health club. It's located a bit away from the city center, a few blocks north of Praça Marquês de Pombal. 1 Rua Latino Coelho (phone: 575757). Expensive.

Meridien – A sparkling addition to Lisbon's complement of modern luxury hotels, it overlooks Parque Eduardo VII. The decor runs to chrome, marble, and splashing fountains, and the restaurants feature French cooking, hardly unusual in a hotel run by a subsidiary of *Air France*. 149 Rua Castilho (phone: 690900). Expensive.

Penta – Large, modern, and just a short cab ride from the center of town, beyond the *Gulbenkian Museum*. It has restaurants and bars, a disco, shops, a swimming pool on the grounds, and a shuttle service to the city center and the airport; the 592 rooms are fully equipped, with private baths, balconies, color TV sets, video, radio, and direct-dial telephones. 1600 Avenida dos Combatentes (phone: 740141). Expensive.

Ritz Inter-Continental – On a hill overlooking Parque Eduardo VII, next door to the *Meridien,* this luxury establishment is contemporary on the outside (built in the 1950s), but traditional within. The appointments are dazzling — silks, satins, and suedes — and some of its 260 rooms and 40 suites are furnished with reproductions of antiques. It has large public rooms and a lovely piano bar overlooking the park, fine shops, a tearoom, coffee shop, disco, and beauty parlor, as well as the *Grill Room* (see *Eating Out*), one of the most fashionable restaurants in Lisbon. Bedrooms are air conditioned, soundproofed, and equipped with mini-bars, TV sets, radio, and in-house movies; some have balconies overlooking the park. 88 Rua Rodrigo da Fonseca (phone: 692020). Expensive.

Tivoli – Well situated, with 350 rooms and suites. Because it's so convenient, right on the main avenue downtown, the lobby is a popular meeting place for businesspeople as well as tourists (and the excellent bar just off the lobby is a favorite of local journalists). There is a restaurant, plus a popular rooftop grill room, a small pool set in a garden, and tennis courts. 185 Avenida da Liberdade (phone: 530181). Expensive.

Flórida – Near Praça Marquês de Pombal, it has 120 air conditioned rooms with all the facilities (bath, telephone, TV set, radio); no restaurant, but there's a bar, a gift shop, and a hairdresser. 32 Avenida Duque de Palmela (phone: 576145). Expensive to moderate.

Príncipe Real – A small downtown hotel with a traditional flavor, located off Avenida da Liberdade in the vicinity of Parque Mayer and the Botanical Garden. There are 24 rooms, all with air conditioning and a TV set, nearly all with a balcony. The top-floor dining room has a swath of picture window looking across the city to St. George's Castle. 53 Rua da Alegria (phone: 346-0116). Expensive to moderate.

Rex – Modern, with 70 rooms, and on the edge of Parque Eduardo VII, near the more prestigious *Ritz* and *Meridien* hotels. All rooms have air conditioning, a TV set, and a radio; half have balconies overlooking the park. There are 2 restaurants (one with a panoramic view) and a bar. 169 Rua Castilho (phone: 682161). Expensive to moderate.

York House – One of the most attractive places to stay in Lisbon, although it is some distance west of the heart of the city, close to the *Museu Nacional de Arte Antiga*. Housed in a 17th-century building that was once a convent, this lovely, 45-room, antiques-filled *pensão* has a restaurant, and a nice bar with tables in the garden — a particular favorite of British visitors, writers, and embassy personnel. Across and down the street a bit, in an 18th-century house (No. 47) that once belonged to the writer Eça de Queirós, there's an equally old-fashioned and aristocratic 17-room annex to this small hostelry, making a total of 62 rooms (not all with private bath). 32 Rua das Janelas Verdes (phone: 662435). Expensive to moderate.

Dom Carlos – A comfortable place to stay at Praça Marquês de Pombal. The 73 rooms are air conditioned and equipped with private baths, TV sets, and mini-bars. No restaurant, but there is a breakfast room and a bar. 121 Avenida Duque de Loulé (phone: 539071). Moderate.

Eduardo VII – Not far from Praça Marquês de Pombal, it has 110 air conditioned rooms with private baths and other conveniences. There also is an excellent rooftop restaurant with a view of the city. 5 Avenida Fontes Pereira de Melo (phone: 530141). Moderate.

Flamingo – Small, conveniently located, with 39 rooms — some of them air conditioned. All have soundproofing, TV sets, and mini-bars. The hotel also has a good restaurant and a bar. 41 Rua Castilho (phone: 532191). Moderate.

Príncipe – Northeast of Parque Eduardo VII, it has 70 air conditioned rooms, each with a private bath, a TV set, and a telephone, plus a restaurant and bar. 201 Avenida Duque de Avila (phone: 536151). Moderate.

Senhora do Monte – Like the *York House,* this is an insider's inn. Small, located up in the old Graça quarter northeast of St. George's Castle, it has good views of

Lisbon from some of its 27 rooms (all with private baths). It's not the best location for access, but old hands swear by it. 39 Calçada do Monte (phone: 862846). Moderate.

Tivoli Jardim – On a quieter street behind its sister, the *Tivoli,* and therefore, a much quieter hotel. Modern, it has 120 rooms (each with a private bath and many with balconies), a restaurant, bar, snack bar, and car park. The service is first rate, and guests have access to the *Tivoli*'s pool and tennis courts. 7-9 Rua Júlio César Machado (phone: 539971). Moderate.

Dom Manuel – Modern and efficient (64 rooms, each with a private bath), and just around the corner from the *Gulbenkian Museum.* The rooms are small, but comfortably appointed, with air conditioning, TV sets, and video. There is a breakfast room and a bar, but no restaurant. 189 Avenida Duque de Avila (phone: 576160). Moderate to inexpensive.

Miraparque – In a quiet location facing Parque Eduardo VII, it has 100 rooms with private baths, a restaurant, and a bar. 12 Avenida Sidónio Pais (phone: 578070). Moderate to inexpensive.

Imperador – A *pensão* of 45 rooms with bath, located northeast of Parque Eduardo VII. 55 Avenida 5 de Outubro (phone: 574657). Inexpensive.

Insulana – In the Baixa, this exceedingly central, friendly *albergaria* (inn) has 32 rooms, each with a private bath. 52 Rua Assunção (phone: 323131 or 328013). Inexpensive.

Torre – This modern, attractive little place is a 15-minute taxi ride from the center of Lisbon, but convenient for sightseeing in Belém, where's it's right beside one of Lisbon's best known sights — the Jerónimos Monastery. There are 50 rooms with private baths, a bar, and a restaurant. 8 Rua dos Jerónimos (phone: 637332). Inexpensive.

ESTORIL

Atlántico – In the pleasant residential district of Monte Estoril, this is a modern spot on the sea (or rather, nearly on the sea, since the electric train tracks run between it and the beach). There are 175 air conditioned rooms (some with balconies overlooking the Atlantic), a terrace with a large saltwater swimming pool, an excellent restaurant, bar, nightclub, and billiards room. Estrada Marginal, Monte Estoril (phone: 268-5170). Expensive.

Lennox Country Club – A hillside *estalagem* (inn) standing in a garden setting overlooking the coast. There are 32 rooms with private baths, some in the main building, which was once a private home, and some in modern additions, plus a very good restaurant with excellent service, a kidney-shape, heated outdoor swimming pool, and a tennis court. The inn emphasizes golf — golfing memorabilia decorate it, there is a putting green, and free transportation is provided to courses in the area, as well as to area riding stables. 5 Rua Engenheiro Alvaro Pedro de Sousa (phone: 268-0424). Expensive.

Palácio – Imagine Allied and Axis spies peeping around pillars during World War II and the jewels of exiled royalty glinting in the light of crystal chandeliers; that's the essence of this gracious Old World hotel by the park. The public rooms are majestic, the staff the sort that seems to remember everyone who has ever stayed here, and the 200 rooms and suites, with traditional and contemporary furnishings, are air conditioned. In addition to the dining room, there is the adjoining, superlative *Four Seasons Grill* (see *Eating Out*). A heated swimming pool and cabanas are in the lovely gardens behind the hotel; the beach on the Atlantic is a 5-minute walk away. Temporary membership in the nearby *Estoril Golf Club* is available (hotel guests don't pay greens fees); there are tennis courts next door. Parque Estoril (phone: 268-0400). Expensive.

Anka Estoril – This modern property is near the park in front of the *Palácio*. It has 91 air conditioned rooms, some with balconies, a panoramic restaurant on the seventh floor, a bar, and a swimming pool. Estrada Marginal (phone: 268-1811). Expensive to moderate.

Cibra – Modern and freshly renovated, it has 90 rooms with private baths, a bar, a rooftop restaurant, and a swimming pool. It's also close to the beach. Estrada Marginal, Monte Estoril (phone: 268-1811). Expensive to moderate.

Grande – On a hill overlooking the sea in Monte Estoril, this is a modern establishment with 73 rooms with private baths (some with balconies), a bar, a restaurant, and a covered swimming pool. Avenida Sabóia, Monte Estoril (phone: 268-4609). Expensive to moderate.

Alvorada – Another modern hostelry, near the casino, it has 51 rooms, each with private bath and a balcony. There's no swimming pool, but there is a solarium on top, and the hotel is only 200 yards from the beach. Breakfast room and bar; no restaurant. 3 Rua de Lisboa (phone: 268-0070). Moderate.

Founder's Inn – British-owned and also known as the *Estalagem do Fundador,* it has 14 pleasant rooms with private baths, each furnished differently. The restaurant serves excellent English cooking; there's also a bar, with music, that's a local nightspot. A freshwater pool is on the grounds, which are on a hillside, set back from the beachfront. 11 Rua Dom Afonso Henriques (phone: 268-2221). Moderate.

Inglaterra – A charming, turn-of-the-century private home-turned-hotel, set in gardens near the *Palácio*. Inside, the 45 rooms (each with a private bath) are spare and contemporary, rather than old-fashioned in style; there's a bar, restaurant, and swimming pool. 1 Rua do Porto (phone: 268-4461). Moderate.

Lido – A very comfortable, modern hostelry in a quiet spot on a hillside away from the beach, but not far from the casino and park. The 62 rooms and suites all have private baths and balconies, telephones, and radios; there is a restaurant, a bar, a large swimming pool, a solarium, and a terrace with a view of the ocean. 12 Rua do Alentejo (phone: 268-4098). Moderate.

Pica-Pau – A good *pensão* in a nice old white-painted villa with a red tile roof, near the *Lido* and the *Founder's Inn*. The 48 rooms with private baths are completely modern; there is a bar, a restaurant, and a swimming pool. 48 Rua Dom Afonso Henriques (phone: 268-0556). Moderate to inexpensive.

Smart – Another *pensão*, in a very large old house. It has 16 rooms, most with television sets and private baths (the rest have washbasins), a breakfast room (no restaurant), and a garden with palm trees. It's not far from the beach. 3 Rua José Viana (phone: 268-2164). Inexpensive.

CASCAIS

Albatroz – A luxury property perched on the rocks at the water's edge. The location is choice, which is not hard to understand since the core of this hotel was built during the 19th century as a villa for the royal family. Between the original building and a newer balconied addition, there are 40 rooms with bath. An excellent restaurant (see *Eating Out*) and bar, both surrounded by windows overlooking the sea, and a swimming pool with plenty of room for sunbathing are further attractions. 100 Rua Frederico Arouca (phone: 282821). Expensive.

Baia – Right on the beach, in the heart of town, where the local fishermen tie up their painted boats. There are 85 rooms in this modern hotel, most with balconies; restaurant and terrace bar. Avenida Marginal (phone: 281033). Expensive.

Cidadela – Near the center of town, with 140 rooms and some apartments, each with its own seaview balcony. Facilities include a good restaurant, a bar, and a swimming pool set amid attractive gardens. Avenida 25 de Abril (phone: 282921). Expensive.

Estoril-Sol – The biggest on the coast, with 347 rooms and suites. It's east of town, between the center of Cascais and Monte Estoril, and is separated from the water only by the electric train tracks (an underground passage leads directly to the beach). The hotel is rife with facilities: an Olympic-size swimming pool, a children's pool, 5 bars, a large, panoramic rooftop restaurant, a disco, shops, a health club, sauna, squash courts, a bowling alley, and its own 9-hole golf course in lovely surroundings nearby. Parque Palmela (phone: 282831). Expensive.

Farol – A charming *estalagem* (inn) in a building that was once the private house of an aristocratic family. It's located by the sea, just west of the center along the road to Boca do Inferno and Praia do Guincho. It has 20 rooms with bath, a swimming pool, tennis court, bar, snack bar, and a restaurant that overlooks the water. 7 Estrada da Boca do Inferno (phone: 280173). Expensive.

Guincho – The waves crash on three sides of this restored 17th-century fortress that looks out to sea from a rocky promontory 5½ miles (9 km) northwest of Cascais. The location is spectacular, with beach on both sides, although walking on the beach is recommended more than going in the water, due to the treacherous undertow here, near the westernmost point of continental Europe. The 36 rooms and suites in this elegant establishment all have private baths, old brick-vaulted ceilings, telephones, mini-bars, and TV sets, and some have balconies. There is a bar and a panoramic restaurant (see *Eating Out*). Praia do Guincho (phone: 285-0491). Expensive.

Dom Carlos – This *pensão* in the center of Cascais occupies a restored house built in 1640, and the breakfast room and chapel maintain the decorations of that period. There are 18 rooms with private baths, a TV salon, and a garden with trees. 8 Rua Latino Coelho (phone: 286-8463). Moderate.

Equador – All the rooms in this very attractive 117-unit apartment-hotel are equipped with a kitchenette, bath, balcony, telephone, and radio. Set back and above the city center (but within walking distance), it has a restaurant, bar, swimming pools, a mini-market, sauna, solarium, disco, and gameroom. Alto da Pampilheira (phone: 284-0890). Moderate.

Nau – The location is convenient — in front of the train station and only 150 yards or so from the beach. Modern, it has 56 rooms with private baths and balconies, plus a TV room, a bar, and a restaurant with a terrace. 14 Rua Dra. Iracy Doyle (phone: 282861). Moderate.

Nossa Senhora das Preces – An *estalagem* (inn) close to the Boca do Inferno. It has 15 rooms, each with a private bath and telephone, 4 with terraces overlooking the sea. There are a swimming pool, a tennis court, and a bar, but no restaurant. 43 Rua Visconde da Gandarinha (phone: 284-0376). Moderate.

Valbom – An *albergaria* (inn) in the center of Cascais, near the train station, it's better looking inside than from the outside. There are 40 rooms with private baths; there's a bar, but no restaurant (breakfast is served). 14 Avenida Valbom (phone: 285801). Inexpensive.

SINTRA

Palácio dos Seteais – One of the loveliest and most romantic hotels in Europe. Built at the end of the 18th century for the Dutch consul in Lisbon, it was sold to the fifth Marquês de Marialva and was often visited by royalty. Marble gleams underfoot and murals line the walls of the public rooms; the 18 guestrooms are beautifully decorated with antiques, handwoven rugs, and tapestries, but no TV sets and no mini-bars to destroy the neo-classical illusion. Located just outside Sintra, the hotel does have a television lounge, a bar, and a well-known restaurant (see *Eating Out*) overlooking spacious gardens, a formal, windowed salon with views of the Sintra Valley, and a swimming pool and tennis courts. 8 Rua Barbosa do Bocage (phone: 923-3200). Expensive.

Tivoli Sintra – The best in town, this is situated off the main square of Sintra, right by the National Palace. The modern building has all the modern conveniences, along with traditional Portuguese touches in the decor. There are 75 air conditioned rooms with private baths, balconies, TV sets, and telephones. A highly regarded restaurant with a view (see *Eating Out*), lounges, bars, a hairdresser, and a garage are among the facilities. Praça da República (phone: 923-3505). Expensive.

Central – Short on rooms (only 11, all with private bath), it's long on charm, and it's on the main square, in front of the palace. There is a tearoom, a bar, and a pleasant restaurant with a terrace for lunch in the summer. 35 Praça da República (phone: 923-0963). Moderate.

Raposa – A small *pensão* near the center in a restored 200-year-old house. The 9 rooms (6 with private baths) are decorated in period style. Bar and tearoom, but no restaurant. 3 Rua Dr. Alfredo Costa (phone: 923-0465). Inexpensive.

Sintra – In São Pedro de Sintra, a 10-minute walk from downtown. This *pensão* has 13 rooms (10 with private baths), a swimming pool, TV room, and a breakfast room (no restaurant). Travessa dos Avelares, São Pedro de Sintra (phone: 923-0738). Inexpensive.

Portugal's *Tourism in the Country* program — a network of elegant old aristocratic estates and manor houses (categorized as *Turismo de Habitação* properties), simpler but still fine country homes (*Turismo Rural*), and farmhouses (*Agroturismo*) that take in small numbers of paying guests — is most active in the rural north, but travelers interested in this type of accommodation do have some choices in the Lisbon area. Among them is the charming *Casal de São Roque,* by the sea in Estoril. Built at the beginning of the century and furnished accordingly, it has 6 rooms for guests, 4 with private baths; the hosts will serve meals upon request. Contact Casal de São Roque (Avenida Marginal, Estoril 2765; phone: 268-0217). In the center of Cascais, there's the *Casa da Pérgola* (13 Avenida Valbom, Cascais 2736; phone: 284-0040), set in lovely gardens, offering a luxurious suite and 5 bedrooms with private baths.

Sintra has three properties. The *Quinta de São Thiago* (Sintra 2710; phone: 923-2923) is an imposing noble house several centuries old, surrounded by vast lawns with a swimming pool, near the *Palácio dos Seteais.* There are 7 double bedrooms, luxuriously furnished with antiques; the owners (an Englishman and his Spanish wife) serve meals on request. The *Quinta da Capella* (Estrada de Monserrate, Sintra 2710; phone: 923-0210) is another impressive old noble house surrounded by gardens, located beyond Seteais and the Quinta de Monserrate. One suite and 4 beautifully furnished bedrooms with private baths — or 2 independent apartments — are available. Finally, the *Vila das Rosas* (2-4 Rua António Cunha, Sintra 2710; phone: 923-4216) is a large, white 19th-century house with a red tile roof on the northern outskirts of Sintra; 4 double rooms with bath, a suite of 3 rooms with a private bath, and a cottage in the garden are available. In summer, breakfast is served in the cool wine cellar; other meals are served on request. The *Quinta de São Thiago* and the *Quinta da Capella* are in the expensive price category; the remaining three are moderate. Reservations for the above houses can also be made through certain central booking agencies (see *Accommodations,* GETTING READY TO GO).

EATING OUT: Portuguese food offers a surprising variety of tastes. Over the centuries, this seagoing nation's cuisine has come under the influence of far-flung countries in Asia, Africa, and the Americas, as well as neighboring Spain and nearby France. Lisbon's restaurants reflect this heritage (and all its regional permutations). Fish and seafood abound and usually are fresh and delicious. Those who want to splurge should order steamed lobster or grilled prawns, or dishes such as *arroz de marisco* (rice with shellfish). Stuffed crab and boiled sea spider (eaten by cracking it open with a wooden mallet) are flavorful, and codfish is a great local favorite — it's said the Portuguese have as many ways to prepare it as there are days in the year, one of the best being *bacalhau à Gomes de Sá,* named for a Porto restaurant owner. The best restaurants serve delicious smoked swordfish, sliced very thin, with lemon and capers, but for something uniquely Portuguese, sample the charcoal-grilled sardines sold in the street. Lisbon's meat is best grilled, but typical dishes such as *cozido à portuguesa* (a stew of boiled vegetables, sausages, and different types of meats, popular in the north) and *iscas à portuguesa* (thin slices of calf's liver marinated in wine, garlic, and bay leaves, and cooked in a shallow earthenware dish) are worth trying. Desserts, mostly based on eggs, sugar, and almonds, tend to be too sweet for some palates, but there are good cheeses — *queijo da Serra,* from northeastern Portugal, and Serpa, from the Alentejo, among the best. Wines from all over the country appear on the city's wine lists. The rule is to choose those that are more than 5 years old (except for northern *vinhos verdes,* which should be less than 2 years old, but which are not often found in Lisbon). Pungent, fruity bairrada wines, mellow, woody Dão wines, and flowery douro wines are all good. Bucelas is an excellent white from a small demarcated zone north of Lisbon.

Dinner for two, with a local wine, averages from $50 to $70 at restaurants listed below as expensive, from $30 to $50 at moderate establishments, and from $20 to $30 at inexpensive restaurants. Customary dining time is no earlier than 7:30 PM, but many restaurants close their kitchens at 11 PM. Lunch is served between noon and 2:30 PM. All telephone numbers are in the 1 city code unless otherwise indicated.

LISBON

Aviz – One of the best dining places in town. When the old *Aviz* hotel — where the multimillionaire Calouste Gulbenkian spent the final days of his life in Lisbon — was torn down, Chef Alberto Rapetti and some of his staff opened this restaurant just off Largo do Chiado, bringing with them all the elegance and flair that had made the old hostelry an international favorite. The decor is very Belle Epoque, the food excellent, and the service flawless. Closed Saturdays at lunch and on Sundays. Reservations advised. 12B Rua Serpa Pinto (phone: 328391). Expensive.

Casa da Comida – This discreetly elegant restaurant is in a converted house, with tables set around a charming enclosed garden and an adjoining period bar. The food is delicious and beautifully presented. Closed Saturdays at lunch and Sundays. Reservations advised. 1 Travessa das Amoreiras (phone: 685386). Expensive.

Chester – Although this attractive little spot near the *Ritz* specializes in steaks, it also has shellfish alive in tanks for the choosing and the fish is always fresh. Closed Sundays. Reservations advised. 87 Rua Rodrigo da Fonseca (phone: 657347). Expensive.

Clara – Very elegant and spacious, serving excellent regional Portuguese and international food — one of Lisbon's best. It's in an old house with gardens that are illuminated at night. Closed Sundays. Reservations advised. 49 Campo dos Mártires de Pátria (phone: 570434). Expensive.

Escorial – A famous dining place in a district, near Praça dos Restauradores, that's noted for seafood. Elegantly decorated, with a nice bar, and known for good service, it also serves excellent international cuisine. Closed only on the 1st of May — *Labor Day* in Europe. Reservations advised. 47 Rua das Portas de Santo Antão (phone: 346-3758). Expensive.

Gambrinus – Famous for fish and seafood, with numerous small dining rooms that fan out from the open blue-tiled kitchen. In the heart of the city, it usually is jammed with businessmen at lunchtime. Open daily. Reservations necessary. 25 Rua das Portas de Santo Antão (phone: 321466). Expensive.

Michel – The owner, a well-known cook on television in Portugal, specializes in nouvelle cuisine, Portuguese-style, although traditional French dishes also are served. Handsomely decorated, this is in the Alfama, just below St. George's Castle. Closed Saturdays at lunch and Sundays. Reservations necessary. 5 Largo de Santa Cruz do Castelo (phone: 864358). Expensive.

Ritz Grill Room – The restaurant of the *Ritz* hotel prepares unusually good food and is a fashionable gathering place for Lisbon businesspeople. Open daily. Reservations advised. 88 Rua Rodrigo da Fonseca (phone: 692020). Expensive.

Tágide – A beautiful staircase leads from the small dining room on the first floor to a second-floor dining area where picture windows afford a great view of the Tagus, a must for visitors who want to see the city and eat well at the same time. Portuguese and international dishes share the menu; the service is impeccable, yet pleasant. Closed Sundays. Reservations necessary. 18 Largo da Biblioteca Pública (phone: 320720). Expensive.

Tavares – Lisbon's oldest, it began as a café in 1784 and became a luxurious restaurant in 1861. After celebrating its 200th birthday, this city landmark had its gold leaf walls redone, its mirrors replated, its armchairs reupholstered, and more, so the light from its crystal chandeliers shines on a scene that's as opulent as ever, the haunt of businesspeople, government officials, and the like, and the perfect setting for excellent food and fine wine. Closed Saturdays at lunch and on Sundays. Reservations advised. 37 Rua da Misericórdia (phone: 321112). Expensive.

Conventual – The menu is based on old Portuguese convent and monastery recipes, some of which go back to the 17th century, and objects from churches decorate the premises. Typical dishes include *bacalhau com coentros* (cod with coriander) and *ensopado de borrego* (lamb stew). Closed Saturdays at lunch and Sundays. Reservations advised. 44 Praça das Flores (phone: 609196). Expensive to moderate.

Restaurante 33 – Good food and a pleasant atmosphere prevail in this well-appointed restaurant behind an elegant clapboard façade, not far from the *Ritz*. Closed Sundays. Reservations advised. 33 Rua Alexandre Herculano (phone: 546079). Expensive to moderate.

Sua Excelência – In the Madragoa quarter, near the embassy residences. Knock on the door to gain entry, and the attentive owner will read out the entire menu in English, if so desired. He serves a very good *açorda* (a sort of "dry" soup, or stew, a combination of seafood, bread, eggs, and coriander) and Mozambique prawns with a peppery sauce. Closed Tuesday evenings, Wednesdays, and the month of September. Reservations unnecessary. 42 Rua do Conde (phone: 603614). Expensive to moderate.

Caseiro – A good restaurant among the many near the Jerónimos Monastery in Belém. It is typically Portuguese, specializing in regional dishes and seafood, and attractively decorated. Closed Mondays. Reservations advised. 5 Rua de Belém (phone: 638803). Moderate.

Faz Figura – Overlooking the Tagus in the Alfama quarter, its wood paneling and leather chairs give it the atmosphere of an exclusive club, but there is also a verandah where diners can sit and watch the ships on the river. Fish and seafood, Portuguese and international dishes, are available. Closed Sundays. Reservations unnecessary. 15B Rua do Paraíso (phone: 868981). Moderate.

Gondola – A long-established Italian eatery near the *Gulbenkian Museum,* and a favorite with visitors. There's a lovely vine-covered garden for summer dining. Closed Saturday evenings and Sundays. Reservations advised. 64 Avenida de Berna (phone: 770426). Moderate.

Laçerda – Also near the *Gulbenkian Museum,* this small place used to be a butcher shop and is still devoted to meat (choose a cut from the hook by the door). Photos of celebrities who have dined here decorate the walls, and strings of garlic and onions hang from the ceiling. Closed Sundays. Reservations unnecessary. 36 Avenida de Berna (phone: 774057). Moderate.

Pap'Açorda – The entrance to this Bairro Alto bakery-turned-restaurant is through an old wood-paneled bar. Inside, there is a very attractive enclosed garden banked with green plants. The mixed fish grilled on a skewer is very good, but the specialty of the house is the porridgy seafood-bread-eggs-and-coriander mixture known as *açorda.* Closed Saturdays at lunch and Sundays. Reservations advised. 57 Rua da Atalaia (phone: 346-4811). Moderate.

Varina da Madragoa – An old tavern turned into a blue-and-white tiled restaurant, near Parliament. Good Portuguese food, including excellent *bacalhau,* or codfish. Closed Saturdays at lunch and Sundays. Reservations unnecessary. 36 Rua das Madres (phone: 665533). Moderate.

Bomjardim – Considered tops in preparing *frango na brasa,* chicken that's charcoal-broiled on a rotating spit and, if it's desired, accompanied by a fiery chili sauce (*piri piri*). This is one of Lisbon's most popular — and least expensive — culinary delights. There are two *Bomjardim* restaurants facing each other just off Praça dos Restauradores. Noisy and crowded at lunchtime; open daily. No reservations. 10-11 Travessa de Santo Antão (phone: 327424). Inexpensive.

Bota Alta – Traditional Portuguese cooking, served in a cheery bistro atmosphere. It's in the midst of all the Bairro Alto nightlife, and usually very busy. Closed Sundays. Reservations advised — or go early. 35-37 Travessa da Queimada (phone: 327959). Inexpensive.

Porto d'Abrigo – Although not imposing in appearance, this tiny eatery is one of Lisbon's culinary landmarks. Famous for its Portuguese specialties, it's usually very crowded at lunchtime. Closed Sundays. Reservations advised. 16 Rua dos Remolares (phone: 346-0875). Inexpensive.

Xico Carreira – In the picturesque, rather shabby theater district off Avenida da Liberdade, it's off the beaten track for most people and full of local color. A former bullfighter owns it; posters and mementos of the sport decorate it. Try the *bife a cortador* (a big grilled steak) or the *cozido transmontano* (boiled dinner of vegetables, sausages, and meats). Crowded at lunchtime. Closed Sundays. Reservations unnecessary. Parque Mayer (phone: 346-3805). Inexpensive.

ESTORIL

Casino Estoril – The glittering, balcony-lined restaurant here is known for its international show — at 11:30 PM every night, with stars such as Julio Iglesias and Dionne Warwick — but it's no less recommendable for food and service, both excellent. It has a long menu listing Portuguese and international dishes. Open daily. Reservations advised. Parque Estoril (phone: 268-4521). Expensive.

Choupana – On a cliff overlooking the sea a bit over a mile (2 km) east of Estoril, this specializes in seafood, but has a varied menu of other dishes as well. The dining room is large, panoramic, and air conditioned. Later at night, there is a show and music until all hours. Open daily. Reservations advised. Estrada Marginal, São João do Estoril (phone: 268-3099). Expensive.

Four Seasons Grill – A very elegant place for the finest dining in Estoril. The long menu of Portuguese and international dishes changes four times a year, according to the seasons, and when it does, so does the china, the decor, and the waiters' uniforms. It is run by the *Palácio* hotel, which is next door, and can be entered using either its own street entrance or the hotel lobby. Open daily. Reservations advised. *Hotel Palácio,* Parque Estoril (phone: 268-0400). Expensive.

English Bar – This brown-and-white building overlooks the water, with windows all around. It's cozily decorated in the English manner (and has a popular bar), but serves very good Portuguese and international dishes. Closed Sundays. Reservations unnecessary. Estrada Marginal, Monte Estoril (phone: 269-0413). Expensive to moderate.

A Maré – By the sea with a lovely panoramic view and a varied menu. There is a large air conditioned dining room and, in summer, an outside barbecue. Open daily. Reservations unnecessary. Estrada Marginal, Monte Estoril (phone: 268-5570). Expensive to moderate.

Ferra Mulinhas – Portuguese and Hungarian cooking. It's open only for dinner and is closed Tuesdays. Reservations unnecessary. 5A Rua Viveiro (phone: 268-0005). Moderate.

Garrafão – A fish and seafood spot with its own vivarium, on the outskirts of Estoril. Closed Thursdays. Reservations unnecessary. Amoreira (phone: 268-4195). Inexpensive.

CASCAIS

Albatroz – This outstanding restaurant — the dining room of the hotel of the same name — is set on rocks at the edge of the sea. It's known for a varied menu of well-prepared dishes, including good seafood, and the picture windows that surround it make it exceedingly fine for its views as well. Open daily. Reservations necessary. 100 Rua Frederico Arouca (phone: 282821). Expensive.

Baluarte – By the sea, with 2 air conditioned dining rooms featuring splendid views. It specializes in seafood, but also has a long menu of other Portuguese and international dishes. Open daily. Reservations advised. 1 Avenida Marechal Carmona (phone: 286-7198). Expensive.

Hotel do Guincho – The restaurant here, in a cliff-top hotel that was once a fortress guarding continental Europe's westernmost extremity, is surrounded by windows looking onto the crashing Atlantic. The location alone makes it a wonderful lunch or dinner spot for those on a day's outing along the coast, but the excellence of the food — with emphasis on seafood — and of the service would recommend it even without the view. Located 5½ miles (9 km) northwest of Cascais. Open daily. Reservations advised. Praia do Guincho (phone: 285-0491). Expensive.

João Padeiro – From its beginnings a number of years ago as a simple eatery, this has become one of the most renowned seafood restaurants in Cascais. Old stone grinding wheels and pieces from windmills decorate the 3 dining rooms most attractively. Closed Tuesdays. Reservations necessary. 12 Rua Visconde da Luz (phone: 280232). Expensive.

Muchaxo – In an *estalagem* of the same name, this is one of the most famous seafood spots on the Lisbon coast. The inn is by the sea, so there is a marvelous view over the water. Open daily. Reservations unnecessary. Praia do Guincho (phone: 285-0221). Expensive.

Pescador – A charming place near the fish market, it is decorated with a fishermen's motif. Fish and seafood are very good here. Open daily. Reservations unnecessary. 10B Rua das Flores (phone: 282054). Expensive to moderate.

O Batel – Nicely decorated in a rustic fashion, this is another good seafood restaurant, near the fish market. Open daily. Reservations unnecessary. 4 Travessa das Flores (phone: 280215). Moderate.

Beira Mar – One of the longest established of the seafood eateries near the fish market. Decorated with blue and white tiles, it serves international fare in addition to good seafood. Open daily. Reservations unnecessary. 6 Rua das Flores (phone: 280152). Moderate.

Burladero – By the bullring, it is large, air conditioned, and specializes in grilled meats. Closed for lunch on Wednesdays and Thursdays. Reservations unnecessary. Praça de Touros (phone: 286-8751). Moderate.

John Bull – A well-known English pub with a good little restaurant attached; international fare is served. Open daily. Reservations unnecessary. 31 Praça Costa Pinto (phone: 283319). Moderate.

O Pipas – A smart seafood spot in the center of town, near the fish market, it consists of a small air conditioned dining room decorated with wine barrels and hanging garlic and sausages. Open daily. Reservations unnecessary. 1B Rua das Flores (phone: 286-4501). Moderate.

A Taverna de Gil Vicente – This cozy little restaurant has a fireplace and features international cooking. Reservations unnecessary. 22 Rua dos Navegantes (phone: 282032). Moderate.

Galegos – Near the center of town, this simple place serves Portuguese and northern Spanish dishes. Open daily. Reservations unnecessary. 3 Avenida Valbom (phone: 282586). Inexpensive.

Lavagante – Seafood and Portuguese dishes are served in two plain, air conditioned dining rooms. The restaurant also has its own vivarium. Closed Mondays. Reservations unnecessary. 59 Rua Poço Novo (phone: 284-0154). Inexpensive.

QUELUZ

Cozinha Velha – The name means "Old Kitchen" — and this is the former royal kitchen of the National Palace at Queluz, now turned into a restaurant with consderable atmosphere. It has high stone arches, a 15-foot-long marble worktable, a walk-in fireplace, enormous spits, and walls lined with copper pots and utensils, many of them originals. Excellent food, combined with the splendor of the setting, make this an experience to remember. Air conditioned; open daily. Reservations necessary. Palácio Nacional de Queluz (phone: 950740). Expensive.

Poço – Large, with 3 air conditioned dining rooms where good Portuguese food is served. Closed Mondays. Reservations unnecessary. 33 Avenida da República (phone: 957737). Inexpensive.

SINTRA

Monserrate – The floor-to-ceiling windows of this air conditioned hotel restaurant afford a panoramic view of the valley below Sintra. The menu features international dishes. Open daily. Reservations necessary. *Hotel Tivoli Sintra,* Praça da República (phone: 923-3505). Expensive.

Palácio dos Seteais – An 18th-century palace makes a lovely setting for lunch on a sunny day, especially a leisurely Sunday, and especially when the restaurant has an adjoining garden terrace on which to indulge in after-dinner coffee. This very elegant restaurant, serving well-prepared Portuguese and international dishes, is located outside Sintra, in the hotel of the same name. Open daily. Reservations necessary. 8 Rua Barbosa do Bocage (phone: 923-3200). Expensive.

Cantinho de São Pedro – Also in São Pedro de Sintra, this rustic restaurant has 2 large dining rooms and a wine cellar. Try it for seafood, game, or one of the many French dishes on the menu. Closed Mondays and Thursday evenings. Reservations advised. 18 Praça Dom Fernando II, São Pedro de Sintra (phone: 923-0267). Moderate.

Dos Arcos – Typical Portuguese dishes are served in an attractive setting that includes a waterfall. In an old part of town, a 10-minute walk from downtown. Open daily. Reservations unnecessary. 4 Rua Serpa Pinto, São Pedro de Sintra (phone: 923-0264). Moderate.

Galeria Real – Above a gallery of antiques shops in São Pedro de Sintra, this is a lovely dining room, filled with antiques. The menu features Portuguese and French food. Open daily. Reservations unnecessary. Rua Tude de Sousa, São Pedro de Sintra (phone: 923-1661). Moderate.

Solar de São Pedro – Two large dining rooms with fireplaces and a menu of French and Portuguese selections keep this place busy. Closed Tuesday evenings and Wednesdays. Reservations advised. 12 Praça Dom Fernando II, São Pedro de Sintra (phone: 923-1860). Moderate.

Adega do Saloio – The rustic decor, the strings of onions and garlic hanging from the ceiling, the fireplaces, and the open kitchen tell visitors that this "countryman's winery" is aptly named. Meats, fish, and seafood grilled on the spit are the specialties. Located at the entrance to Sintra from Lisbon or Estoril. Closed Tuesdays. Reservations unnecessary. Chão de Meninos (phone: 923-1422). Moderate to inexpensive.

Portelinho – Small, air conditioned, with a bar, it serves a variety of Portuguese regional dishes at reasonable prices. Open daily. Reservations unnecessary. 66-70 Avenida Movimento das Forças Armadas (phone: 923-3857). Inexpensive.

MADRID

When King Philip II proclaimed Madrid the capital of Spain and all her colonies in 1561, he said that he chose it because of the "healthy air and brilliant skies" and because, "Like the body's heart, it is located in the center of the Peninsula." Philip was right. Madrid's air is delightfully dry and invigorating. Its "Velázquez skies" that so inspired the court painter are dramatically bright, with more than 3,000 hours of sunshine annually. As a result of Philip's proclamation, what had been an insignificant Castilian town of 17,000 suddenly burst into being as the cosmopolitan nucleus of the Spanish Empire — upon which, in those days, the sun never set. One of Europe's youngest capitals, Madrid grew fast, as if making up for lost time. A comment by a Spanish poet in 1644 continued to be true until just a few decades ago: "Each day, new houses are being built, and those that used to be on the outskirts are now in the middle of the town."

Today, the city has blossomed into a glamorous metropolis of 4.3 million, and it thrives on its own vitality. More than ever, it is ebullient, outgoing, fun-loving, proud, stylish, and creative, a city intensely lived in and adored by its varied mosaic of inhabitants. Throughout its history, a great proportion of its residents have been born elsewhere in Spain, a country of various and diverse cultures. Yet soon after their arrival, they feel "adopted" and become as genuinely *madrileño* as native sons and daughters.

According to a saying as meaningful to *madrileños* as the Cibeles Fountain, "the next best place after Madrid is heaven, but with a peephole for looking down at it." The city has a way of enticing foreigners as well. Visitors invariably feel at home in Madrid — much more so, of course, if they speak Spanish. Another popular saying, often seen on bumper stickers, boasts that Madrid is *"el pórtico al cielo"* ("the gateway to heaven"). The city is, in fact, the highest capital in Europe — 2,135 feet above the sea level of the Mediterranean at Alicante, affirmed by a plaque at Puerta del Sol.

Despite its high-tech, high fashion, streamlined skyscrapers up the Castellana, and its designation as the Cultural Capital of Europe for the year 1992 by the European Economic Community (EEC), Madrid still endearingly refers to itself as a "town," or *villa.* Its official name during the 16th century was the "Very Noble, Loyal, Heroic, Imperial, and Distinguished Village and Court of Madrid, Capital of Spain," or, simply, "Villa." The City Hall, for example, is Casa de la Villa, the modern concert-theater-exhibition center is *Centro Cultural del la Villa,* and the summer-long program of concerts, fairs, and entertainment is called *"Veranos en la Villa."*

Madrileños love to be out on the streets, where walking or strolling — the *paseo* — is an activity in itself, rather than just a means of getting somewhere. And they enjoy crowding together. In spring, summer, and fall, thousands of outdoor *terrazas* (cafés), set up on sidewalks and in squares and parks, teem day and night with convivial people chatting, eating, drinking, gossiping (locals love to gossip), and simply looking at each other. There's always eye contact and usually a friendly or witty greeting — *madrileños* also admire a quick wit — even to those who are just buying a newspaper.

Madrid's artistic-creative surge of the late 1970s and early 1980s — *la movida* — sparked a rebirth of indoor and outdoor café society. Stylish *madrileños* congregate at *terrazas* along Paseo de Recoletos and the Castellana from dusk until practically dawn. Crowded late-night, Spanish-style pubs, specializing in high-decibel rock or soothing classical music, line Calle de las Huertas, one of the liveliest streets in the old part of town. Amazingly, this street is also occupied by the early-17th-century Convent of the Trinitarias, where cloistered nuns live and embroider, and where Miguel de Cervantes is buried. In the typical old section of Lavapiés, entire families gather to eat, drink, and chat with their neighbors at simple restaurants with sidewalk tables. The *tertulia,* an age-old Madrid custom, brings experts and devotees together for informal discussions about their favorite subjects. Visitors will surely find *tertulias* about theater or literature at the *Café Gijón,* art at the *Círculo de Bellas Artes* lounge, and bullfighting and breeding at the bar of the *Wellington* hotel, to name a random few.

When it's time for the midday *aperitivo* around 1 PM (when stores, offices, and many museums close), thousands of *tapas* bars, *tabernas,* and swank cafés become jammed for a couple of hours until lunchtime, when they suddenly empty and the restaurants fill up. Around 4 or 5 PM (when the stores, offices, and museums reopen), the restaurants become vacant — it's customary to go somewhere else for coffee or cognac — and the bars and cafés are reactivated. They reach another peak when it's *aperitivo* time again, around 8 PM (as stores, offices, and museums close for the day), before dinner around 10 PM, when the restaurants fill up once more. Then it's time for a movie, concert, theater performance, jazz at a café, or simply a stroll.

Madrid boasts the longest nights of any Spanish city — even though in midsummer the sun doesn't set until almost 11 PM. Discotheques don't get started until 1 or 2 AM, and at many, the action continues until 7 AM. Then it's time for a typical Madrid breakfast of thick hot chocolate with *churros* (sticks or loops of crisp fried dough), elbow to elbow with others just beginning their day. Nevertheless, *madrileños* don't mistake their city for a vacation spot and are fully aware that it is indeed a place for hard work.

There are many Madrids. In fact, the city is sometimes referred to in the plural — *los madriles* — because of its various facets. In addition to nocturnal Madrid, daytime Madrid, and seasonal Madrid, there are different architectural and historical Madrids.

Not much remains of medieval Madrid (Madrid *antiguo*), particularly the Moorish one, and even less is known — although legends abound. In 852, the Emir of Córdoba, Muhammad I, chose the strategic ravine top above the Manzanares River (where the Royal Palace now stands) as the site for a fortified Alcázar (castle) to guard the route between Toledo and Alcalá de Henares against the reconquering Christians. The Moors described their settlement alongside the Alcázar as "a village bordered by the Manzanares

River on one side and the brilliant sky on the other." They called it Magerit (later mispronounced as Madrid by Castilians), meaning delicious and "plentiful flowing water," not for the meager water of the Manzanares, but for water from the nearby Sierra de Guadarrama. (This water from the Lozoya River continues to supply the city, and is also the brand name of a bottled mineral water).

Magerit began to grow, and the Moors built and rebuilt walls to enclose it, keeping up with its random expansion. Fragments of these old walls, as well as sections of underground passageways to the Alcázar, have been uncovered as recently as the 1970s — a major site can be seen at Cuesta de la Vega, near the Royal Palace. Other well-preserved remnants of medieval Moorish Magerit are the house and tower of the Lujanes family and the adjacent Periodicals Library building, both at Plaza de la Villa; the Mudéjar tower of the church of San Nicolás de los Servitas, slightly to the north of the plaza; the equally Mudéjar tower of the church of San Pedro el Viejo, on the site of what may have been the original mosque of the Moorish Quarter (La Morería), to the south of the plaza; and the Morería itself, a zone of winding alleys around Plaza del Alamillo.

In 1083, King Alfonso VI and his Christian troops reconquered Madrid and took up residence in the Alcázar. The *madrileño* melting pot expanded with the subsequent influx of Christians into what then became medieval Christian Madrid, and more walls were built to surround it.

The city really began to take shape when King Philip II of the Hapsburg House of Austria raised its rank to capital of Spain and moved the throne and court from Toledo. During his reign (1556–98) and those of his 17th-century successors, what is known as Madrid de los Austrias, or the Madrid of the Hapsburgs, was built. This is the charming and picturesque section of Old Madrid around the Plaza Mayor. As the nobility built mansions, the clergy founded churches, convents, monasteries, and hospitals, and merchants, artisans, and innkeepers set up shop. Hapsburg Madrid grew into a labyrinth of meandering narrow cobblestone streets and tiny squares lined with severe buildings of stone, brick, and masonry, topped by roofs that blended into a burnt-red "sea of tiles." The Spanish Empire was at its zenith, and the *siglo de oro* (Golden Age) of Renaissance literature flourished in Hapsburg Madrid. Streets, squares, and statues bear the names of Cervantes, Lope de Vega, Tirso de Molina, Quevedo, and Calderón de la Barca, all of whom lived here.

The city continued fanning southward, creating such delightful *barrios* (neighborhoods) as Lavapiés and Embajadores, lively with *tabernas, mesones* (inns), vendors, organ-grinders, and artisans. The authentically typical and uniquely *madrileño* personality of these barrios and their colorful people — defined by the word *castizo,* meaning purebred, or genuine — were the inspiration of many of the 18th- and 19th-century *zarzuelas* (traditional Spanish musical dramas), *La Verbena de la Paloma,* for example, that are presented outdoors during the summer at La Corrala, located in the heart of this other Madrid at Plaza Agustín Lara. (Lara, a Mexican composer who had never been to Madrid, wrote the city's unofficial anthem, "Madrid, Madrid, Madrid.") Anyone visiting Madrid during the first half of August should be sure to stroll around these *barrios castizos* to see *madrileños* of all ages bedecked in traditional costumes, dancing the graceful *chotis* in the streets, and enjoying the *verbenas* (fairs).

When the Hapsburg dynasty died out at the end of the 17th century, King Philip V, grandson of France's King Louis XIV, was the chief claimant to the throne of Spain. After a war of succession, he established the Bourbon dynasty as the legitimate heir to the kingdom. The Bourbon monarchs began the new century by setting out to create a splendid new European capital worthy of their neo-classical French models. When the Alcázar burned down, Philip V commissioned top architects (Spaniard Ventura Rodríguez and Italian Francesco Sabatini) to replace it with a grandiose palace comparable to Versailles. Systematic expansion to the east of old Hapsburg Madrid, with wide avenues and large squares laid out in geometric configuration, transformed Madrid into a model city of the Enlightenment — the Madrid de los Borbones, or Madrid of the Bourbons. The city's urban renewal, embellishment, and social progress culminated with the reign of *madrileno* King Carlos III, "the Construction King of the Enlightenment," known affectionately as the "King-Mayor." Carlos commissioned Juan de Villanueva to design the neo-classical *Natural Science Museum,* which later became the *Prado Museum,* and the adjacent Botanical Gardens. The exquisite tree-lined Paseo del Prado, with its Neptune, Apollo, and Cibeles fountains by Ventura Rodríguez, and the monumental Puerta de Alcalá (then marking the eastern end of the city) are among the legacies of Carlos III.

The steady progress of the city and the country foundered, however, in 1808, when Napoleon was encouraged to invade Spain because of the weakness of Carlos IV, the next Bourbon king. The French succeeded in the invasion after ruthlessly executing Spanish resisters on the night of May 2, a tragedy immortalized by Goya in his famous paintings now in the *Prado.* At the Plaza de la Lealtad on Paseo del Prado, a memorial obelisk with an eternal flame commemorates *el dos de mayo.*

Napoleon forced the crowning of his brother, Joseph Bonaparte, as King of Spain. "Pepe Botella" (Bottle Joe), as he was called (either for his drinking habits or for having put a tax on liquor), in his quest for open space for ongoing urban renewal, tore down picturesque chunks of Hapsburg Madrid, including much of the Retiro Park Palace and a church in the small Plaza de Ramales that contained the grave of Velázquez. But the Spanish War of Independence led to the expulsion of the French and the return to the throne of a Bourbon king, Fernando VII, in 1813.

In the last third of the 19th century, Romantic Madrid spread farther northward. Aristocratic palatial mansions graced the elegant Salamanca district, where today some of Madrid's finest shops and boutiques line Calles Serrano and Velázquez. Paseo del Prado extended north to become Paseo de Recoletos and, still farther north, Paseo de la Castellana. By the early 20th century, a transportation problem arose: There was no street connecting the new outlying districts of Salamanca and Argüelles. The solution was to chop through part of Old Madrid and construct a new thoroughfare, the Gran Vía.

The instability of the monarchy during the early 20th century led to further political upheaval. Alfonso XIII finally abdicated in 1931 to avoid a civil war.

But the Socialist Republican government's decentralization plan and reform measures aroused strenuous right-wing opposition, which resulted in insurrection and, in 1936, the Spanish Civil War. Madrid, which remained aligned with the Republican government, was blown to pieces at the hands of Generalísimo Francisco Franco's Nationalist forces. During the nearly 40 years of Franco's dictatorship, Madrid's spirit and creativity were stifled. Franco's death in 1975, the restoration of the monarchy, and the institution of a representative, democratic government brought about a dramatic multifaceted surge of activity ranging from construction to culture. As if making up for those 40 years of lost time, *madrileños,* with their newfound affluence and freedom of expression, have made their city one of Europe's most energetic and trendsetting, in art, fashion, music, and theater. The late mayor Enrique Tierno Galván inspired his fellow citizens with such an affection for the city's own traditions and lore, promoted the arts with such enthusiasm, and fomented the *movida madrileña* with such verve that he became a revered figure — so much so that after his death in 1986, a *zarzuela* was written about him.

With its new symphonic *Auditorio Nacional,* the revitalization of the *Teatro Real* into a new opera house, the *National Museum Queen Sofía Art Center,* and the expanding *Prado Museum,* Madrid is fast becoming a major cultural magnet. The city continues to spread outward, absorbing surrounding towns in order to meet the needs of a growing populace. Yet while it focuses its vision on the future, people still can hear organ-grinders in the streets of Old Madrid. There's no doubt that the city will live up to its EEC designation as 1992's European Cultural Capital of the Year — one more reason that this is an especially exciting time to see and savor its new vitality.

MADRID AT-A-GLANCE

SEEING THE CITY: For a wonderfully romantic view of Madrid, watch the sun set from the 25th-floor roof garden and pool of the *Plaza* hotel. The sharp "Velázquez sky," portrayed in the artist's famous paintings, is usually tinted with a golden hue. Looking over the "sea of tile" rooftops, visitors will see a fine view of the Royal Palace and, to the north, the distant Sierra de Guadarrama. The hotel's terrace and pool are open daily during the summer months. Admission charge. 2 Plaza de España (phone: 247-1200).

SPECIAL PLACES: The bustling Puerta del Sol, "kilometer zero" of the Spanish road network, and the Plaza de Cibeles traffic circle are two focal points at the heart of Madrid, which actually lies within the city's southwestern area. The Atocha railroad station and traffic circle mark the southern extremity of this zone, the Royal Palace and Parque del Retiro form its western and eastern borders respectively, and Plaza de Colón marks its northern limit. One major tree-lined avenue, with three names, bisects the entire city from top to bottom. Its southern section, between Atocha and Plaza de Cibeles, is called Paseo del Prado. From Cibeles north to Plaza de Colón, its name is Paseo de Recoletos. At Plaza de Colón, it becomes the long Paseo de la Castellana, which runs through modern Madrid to the north end of the city beyond Plaza de Castilla and the Chamartín railroad station. The two major east–west arteries are Calle de Alcalá and the Gran Vía; the latter angles northwest to Plaza de España.

For a basic overview, take a half-day motorcoach tour of the city with *Julía Tours* (38 Calle Capitán Haya; phone: 270-4300); *Pullmantur* (8 Plaza de Oriente; phone: 541-1805); or *Trapsatur* (23 Calle San Bernardo; phone: 542-6666). The best way to see Madrid, however, is by walking; many picturesque areas can be seen only on foot. Rest assured that, at least in the center of the city, things are much closer than they seem from the inside of a motorcoach or taxi. A good stroll, for starters, is from Puerta del Sol to Plaza Mayor, then downhill to Plaza de Oriente. Good maps of the city are provided free of charge at the tourist offices. Keep in mind that most museums close on Mondays, some close at midday, and smaller ones for the entire month of August.

Plaza Mayor – Oddly enough, this grandiose main square, which is closed to vehicular traffic, is easily missed if you don't aim for it and enter through one of the nine arched entryways. Built during the 17th century by order of King Philip III, it is the quintessence of Hapsburg Madrid — cobblestones, tile roofs, and imposing austere buildings. Before the king commissioned Juan Gómez de Mora to "straighten it out," the perfectly rectangular, perfectly flat plaza shared the irregularity of the surrounding architectural chaos. After its completion, the plaza became the stage for a wide variety of 17th- and 18th-century spectacles — audiences of over 50,000 witnessed hangings, burnings, and the decapitation of heretics, as well as canonizations of saints (such as St. Teresa and St. Isidro, Madrid's patron saint), jousting tournaments, plays (including those of Lope de Vega), circuses, and even bullfights. The 477 balconies of the surrounding buildings served as spectator "boxes" — not for the tenants, but for royalty and aristocrats. Today, the Plaza Mayor is still lively, but with tamer entertainment — strolling student minstrels (*la tuna*), other amateur musicians, artists, and on-the-spot portrait painters selling their works, as well as summer concerts and ballets, and outdoor cafés for watching it all. Myriad shops, many over a century old, line the arcades around the plaza. On Sunday mornings, philatelists and numismatists set up shop in the arcades, to the delight of stamp and coin collectors. Visitors can easily lose their sense of direction inside this vast enclosure, so it's helpful to know that the bronze equestrian statue of Philip III in the center is facing east (toward the *Prado Museum*). The legendary Arco de Cuchilleros entrance is at the southwest corner.

Puerta del Sol – This vast oblong plaza is the bustling nerve center of modern Madrid life. Ten streets converge here, including the arteries of Alcalá, San Jerónimo, Mayor, and Arenal. The name of the square, "Gate of the Sun" in English, comes from a long-disappeared medieval city wall carved with a sunburst. On the south side, the 18th-century Comunidad government building, originally the Central Post Office, is topped by a clock tower. At midnight on *New Year's Eve,* thousands gather here to hear the clock strike and swallow one grape at each stroke to ensure 12 months of good fortune during the new year. Near the curb in front of the building's main entrance, a famous (yet inconspicuous) emblem in the sidewalk marks "kilometer zero," the central point from which all Spanish highways radiate, and from which their distance is measured. Directly across the plaza stands the venerated bronze statue of the *Oso y el Madroño* (the bear and the madrona berry tree), the symbol and coat of arms of Madrid since the 13th century.

Museo Nacional del Prado (Prado Museum) – One of the world's supreme art museums, the *Prado* is a treasure house of over 4,000 universal masterpieces, most of which were acquired over the centuries by art-loving Spanish monarchs. The wealth of Spanish paintings includes famous works by El Greco (including the *Adoration of the Shepherds*), Zurbarán, Velázquez (including *The Spinners* and *Maids of Honor*), Murillo, Ribera (including the *Martyrdom of St. Bartholomew*), and Goya (including his renowned *Naked Maja* and *Maja Clothed*). On the ground floor, a special section is devoted to the tapestry cartoons designed by Goya for the palace-monastery at San Lorenzo de El Escorial (see *Extra Special*) and to his extraordinary *Disasters of War* etchings, which represent his thoughts and comments on Spain's War of Independence. Visitors also will find Goya's stunning *Second of May* and *Third of May* canvases. Vast rooms are devoted to Italians Fra Angelico, Botticelli, Raphael, Correggio, Caravaggio, Titian, Tintoretto, and Veronese. Other rooms display paintings by Flemish and German masters such as Rubens, van der Weyden, Hieronymus Bosch (including *The Garden of Earthly Delights*), Memling, Dürer, and Van Dyck. From the Dutch are works by Rembrandt, Metsu, and Hobbema. French art is represented by Poussin, Lorrain, and Watteau, and the English by Reynolds, Gainsborough, and Lawrence.

The neo-classical *Prado* building was originally a natural science museum, conceived by Carlos III, the Enlightenment "King-Mayor," who ordered its construction by architect Juan de Villanueva. In 1819, King Fernando VII converted it into a museum to house the royal art collection. A bronze statue of Velázquez stands before the main façade, a statue of Goya at the north façade, and one of Murillo at the south side. In addition to the main *Prado*, or Villanueva building, the museum also includes two annexes. One, the Casón del Buen Retiro, resembles a small Greek temple, and is just up a hill from the Goya statue. It was once the stately ballroom of the 17th-century Royal Retiro Palace complex, which was destroyed during the French occupation of Madrid. It now contains, up the stairs, the *Museum of 19th-Century Spanish Painting* and, on the other side, facing the Parque del Retiro, with a separate entrance, a wing devoted to Picasso's monumental *Guernica,* which portrays the horrors of the Spanish Civil War and the devastating bombardment of that Basque town. The other annex, the splendid Villahermosa Palace, is diagonally across Plaza Cánovas del Castillo (the square with the Neptune Fountain) from the main building. Its spacious interior has been redesigned to house a major portion of the vast Thyssen-Bornemisza Collection, which will be exhibited here on long-term loan, and which many consider the most important privately owned art collection in the world.

The *Prado* long ago outgrew the its walls. Thus, the main building recently underwent a major refurbishment program, opening some 2 dozen remodeled rooms to display works previously in storage or on loan to other Spanish museums. Expansion plans for additional exhibit space include the acquisition in the mid-1990s of the nearby 17th-century Salón de Reinos building, which currently houses the *Museo del Ejército* (Army Museum). Still in the planning stages is the final relocation of *Guernica,* and the drawings related to it, to the *National Museum Queen Sofía Art Center,* which is devoted to contemporary art.

The *Prado* collection is so vast that it is impossible to savor its wonders in a single visit. If time is limited, it is best to select a few galleries of special interest, or enlist the services of the extremely knowledgeable government-licensed free-lance guides at the main entrance. The guides are more readily available in the early morning, and their fee is about $15 per hour. Reproductions from the *Prado*'s collection, postcards, and fine arts books are sold at the shop inside the museum. There also is a bar-restaurant on the premises. The *Prado* is open Tuesdays through Saturdays, from 9 AM to 6:45 PM; Sundays, 10 AM to 1:45 PM. Closed holidays. One admission charge grants access to the main building and the annexes. Paseo del Prado (phone: 420-2836).

Palacio Real (Royal Palace) – The Moors chose a strategic site overlooking the Manzanares River to build their Alcázar, or castle-fortress. After the 11th-century Reconquest, Christian leaders renovated it and moved into it, and Philip II made it the royal residence after proclaiming Madrid the capital of Spain in 1561. During the reign of Philip V, Spain's first Bourbon monarch, the Alcázar was destroyed by fire on *Christmas Eve,* 1734. The king then commissioned top Spanish and Italian architects to construct a glorious new palace in neo-classical style on the very same rugged steep site. It took 26 years to build the colossus of granite and white limestone, with walls

13 feet thick, over 2,800 rooms, 23 courtyards, and magnificently opulent interiors. "King-Mayor" Carlos III finally became the first royal resident. The east façade faces the grand Plaza de Oriente; at the north side are the formal Sabatini Gardens; and down the slopes on the west side is the Campo del Moro — 20 acres of forest, manicured gardens, and fountains, now a public park. The palace's main entrance is on the south side, through the tall iron gates leading into an immense courtyard called the Plaza de la Armería (armory), a setting for the pageantry of royal occasions. The imposing structure at the courtyard's south end is just a façade — so far. Under construction for over a century, it eventually will become Madrid's Catedral de la Almudena, honoring the patroness of the city. Upon completion, it will be the oldest *new* cathedral in the world!

The palace is seen by guided tour, with different sections shown on different tours; both Spanish- and English-speaking National Patrimony guides lead the tours. Note that the King and Queen of Spain live in the Palacio de la Zarzuela, on the outskirts of Madrid, but the Palacio Real still is used for official occasions and is closed to the public at those times, which are not always announced in advance. Normally, opening hours are Mondays through Saturdays, from 9:30 AM to 5:15 PM; Sundays and holidays, from 9:15 AM to 2:15 PM. Admission charge. Plaza de Oriente (phone: 248-7404).

Plaza de Oriente – To the disappointment of Asian tourists, its name in Spanish simply means East (*oriente*) Square, because it faces the east façade of the Royal Palace (which also is sometimes referred to, in turn, as the Palacio de Oriente). Across the plaza from the palace is the *Teatro Real* (Royal Theater), which, after a major 2-year revamping of its interior, is scheduled to reopen this year as one of Europe's finest opera houses. In the center of the plaza stands the 9-ton bronze equestrian statue of King Philip IV, based on a drawing by Velázquez. Philip's horse is rearing up, supported solely by its hind legs, posing an equilibrium problem for Florentine sculptor Pietro Tacca. He consulted none other than the illustrious Galileo, whose solution was to make the front end of the statue hollow and the rear end solid.

Museu Nacional Centro de Arte Reina Sofía (National Museum Queen Sofía Art Center) – This gargantuan 18th-century building was Madrid's Hospital General de San Carlos until 1965. Following a tremendous reconstruction project, the building reopened in 1986 as a museum devoted to contemporary art, named in honor of the present Queen of Spain. A long-term program of continuous expansion within its own vast space is intended to position the center among the world's leading contemporary art galleries. In the planning stages is the permanent relocation of Picasso's *Guernica* from the *Prado*'s Casón del Buen Retiro annex. Important works from other contemporary art collections in Madrid also are being consolidated here. In addition to the permanent collection, there are extensive research facilities and workshops, plus a schedule of approximately 20 changing exhibitions per year. Open from 10 AM to 9 PM; closed Tuesdays. Admission charge. 52 Calle Santa Isabel (phone: 467-5062).

Plaza de Cibeles – Dominating Madrid's favorite traffic circle is the fountain and statue of the Greek fertility goddess Cibeles, astride her chariot drawn by two rather friendly looking lions. A Madrid custom requires that visitors "say hello to La Cibeles" upon arrival in town. Almost drowning out the vision of the Cibeles Fountain with its massiveness, the wedding-cake turn-of-the-century Palacio de Comunicaciones (now the city's post office) on the plaza is so imposing that *madrileños* often refer to it as "Our Lady of Communications." Both Cibeles and the monumental arches of the Puerta de Alcalá (Alcalá Gate) up the street at Plaza de la Independencia are 18th-century endowments of the Bourbon "King-Mayor" Carlos III. On the southwest side of Plaza de Cibeles is the Banco de España; on the northwest side, the Palacio de Buenavista, which houses the Ministry of Defense.

Parque del Retiro (Retreat Park) – During the early 17th century, it was a royal retreat and the grounds of both a royal palace complex and a porcelain factory, then on the outskirts of town. Now Madrid's public park, right in the city, the Retiro covers 300 peaceful acres of forest, manicured gardens, statuary, fountains, picnic grounds, and cafés. It is a delightful place for strolling, jogging, a horse-and-carriage ride, or a boat ride around the lake, which is overlooked by the huge semicircular monument to King Alfonso XII. Art exhibitions are held at the park's Palacio de Cristal, a 19th-century jewel of glass and wrought iron, and at the Palacio de Velázquez, named for its architect, not for the painter. During the summer, at 10 PM and midnight, classical and flamenco concerts are staged in the Cecilio Rodríguez Gardens (Menéndez Pelayo entrance), and the outdoor cinema (entrance on Alfonso XII) features Spanish and foreign (including US) films. The park's loveliest entrance is through the wrought-iron gates at Plaza de la Independencia, also referred to as the Puerta de Alcalá.

Plaza de la Villa – One of Madrid's most charming squares, its architectural diversity makes it especially interesting. Dominating the west side, the 17th-century neoclassical Casa de la Villa, also called the Ayuntamiento (City Hall), was designed by Juan Gómez de Mora, the same architect who planned the Plaza Mayor. Adding to the *madrileño* atmosphere, its carillon chimes the hour with *zarzuela* melodies and plays 20-minute concerts every evening. Along the back of the square is the 16th-century Plateresque Casa de Cisneros palace, built by the nephew and heir of the cardinal regent of the same name. On the east side are the old Periodicals Library, with a large Mudéjar doorway, and the massive medieval Lujanes Tower, one of the oldest in Madrid and full of legends (one of its prisoners was King Francis I of France). Separating these two structures, the tiny Calle de Codo (Elbow Street) angles down to the tranquil Plaza del Cordón, which is surrounded by historic noble mansions. The bronze statue in the center of Plaza de la Villa honors Admiral Alvaro de Bazán, who fought — as did Cervantes — against the Turks in the Battle of Lepanto in 1571. The City Hall's splendid museum collection is open to the public every Monday (except holidays), from 5 to 7 PM, with free tours escorted by guides from the Madrid Tourist Board. Plaza de la Villa (phone: 542-5512).

Museo de la Real Academia de Bellas Artes de San Fernando (Museum of the San Fernando Royal Academy of Fine Arts) – Housed in a splendid 18th-century palace just east of the Puerta del Sol, the academy's permanent collection comprises some 1,500 paintings and over 800 sculptures. There are works by El Greco, Velázquez, Zurbarán, Murillo, Goya, and Sorolla, to name a few, as well as by Italian and Flemish masters. The only painting of George Washington in Spain is here; the portrait commemorates the Treaty of Friendship between Spain and the US. Closed to the public for 12 years, the museum reopened in 1986 and is gradually regaining the international renown it deserves — not only for its permanent collection, but for prestigious scheduled exhibitions held throughout the year. Open Tuesdays through Saturdays, from 9 AM to 7 PM; Sundays and Mondays, from 9 AM to 2 PM; during the summer, 9 AM to 2 PM daily. Admission charge. 13 Calle de Alcalá (phone: 532-1546).

Convento de las Descalzas Reales (Convent of the Barefoot Carmelites) – Behind its stark stone façade is an awesomely opulent interior filled with an astonishing wealth of artistic treasures and ornamentation bestowed by kings and noblemen. Princess Juana of Austria, sister of Philip II, opened this convent of the Royal Barefoot Carmelite Nuns in 1559. It welcomed disconsolate empresses, queens, princesses, and *infantas,* including Juana's sister María, Empress of Germany. The grandiose stairway is a breathtaking example of *barroco madrileño,* every centimeter lavishly decorated with frescoes and carved wood. Art treasures include works by El Greco, Zurbarán, Titian, and Sánchez Coello, as well as Rubens tapestries. From the windows of the upper floor is a lovely view over the tranquil rooftop garden, where the cloistered nuns still grow their vegetables just as they have for centuries, unaffected by the bustling Gran Vía just 1 block north, or the gigantic *El Corte Inglés* department store practically alongside. Visitors are escorted by resident Spanish-speaking National Patrimony guides; tours in English should be arranged in advance through the *Office of Museums* (phone: 248-7404). Hours vary according to the season, and are limited because the cloistered nuns often use the museum sections in their daily life; in general, however, opening hours are Tuesdays through Saturdays, from 10 AM to 1:30 PM. The admission charge includes the tour. Plaza de las Descalzas Reales (phone: 248-7404).

Convento de la Encarnación (Convent of the Incarnation) – Built by order of Queen Margarita of Austria, wife of King Philip III, this Augustinian convent was blessed in 1616. Designed in the severe classical style by Juan Gómez de Mora, its façade gives no clue to the bounteous religious and secular art treasures inside. The dazzling reliquary room displays some 1,500 religious relics contained in priceless gold and silver urns and jeweled cases. Among them, a legendary vial contains the blood of St. Pantaleón, which is said to liquefy every year on his birthday, July 27. A contrasting neo-classical 18th-century church designed by Ventura Rodríguez is set back in the center of the convent façade, and a statue of Lope de Vega graces its peaceful front garden. Like the Descalzas Reales, this is an active cloistered convent, and individuals and groups must be escorted by resident guides; tours in English can be arranged in advance through the Office of Museums (phone: 248-7404). Open Tuesdays through Saturdays, from 10 AM to 1:30 PM. The admission charge includes the tour. Plaza de la Encarnación (phone: 247-0510).

Museo Municipal – Devoted to the history of Madrid, this fine museum will enhance any visitor's awareness of the city's evolution, culture, and personality. It is filled with art, furnishings, porcelains, photographs, engravings, and meticulously detailed maps and models of the city during the 17th, 18th, and 19th centuries. The museum building, declared a National Monument in 1919, was originally an 18th-century hospital, and its elaborately ornate Churrigueresque-style entrance is in itself a worthwhile sight. Open Tuesdays through Saturdays, from 10 AM to 2 PM and 5 to 9 PM; Sundays, from 10 AM to 2:30 PM. Admission charge. 78 Calle Fuencarral (phone: 522-5732).

Mercado Puerta de Toledo – What used to be Madrid's old Central Fish Market (*mercado*) has been transformed into a sparkling showcase of fine Spanish handicrafts, art, antiques, jewelry, fashion, and interior design — everything from soup to nuts, in fact, since the premises include *El Abanico Gastronómico,* a combined restaurant and store featuring fine foods and wines from every region of Spain. The market also is the setting for concerts, recitals, and art and photography exhibitions. Regularly scheduled video projections include a "bird's-eye view" of Madrid past and present. At the courtyard entrance is a functional Monument to Time: a giant sculptured combination sundial and lunar clock, considered the world's largest. The market is adjacent to the Puerta de Toledo, one of the ancient city gates, dominated by a 19th-century neo-classical triumphal arch. Joseph Bonaparte initiated construction of the arch; ironically, its completion celebrated the ousting of the French in the War of Independence, and the "welcome back" of Bourbon King Fernando VII. Open daily with dining, drinking, and entertainment going on into the wee hours. No admission charge. 1 Ronda de Toledo (phone: 266-7200).

Jardín Botánico (Botanical Garden) – The garden was designed in 1774 by Juan de Villanueva, the same architect who designed the *Prado Museum,* whose south façade it faces. Twenty manicured acres contain some 30,000 species of plants and flowers from Spain and throughout the world. Carlos III commissioned the project as part of his urban refurbishment program. By his order, therapeutic and medicinal plants and herbs were distributed free to those in need. Between the *Prado* and the entrance to the garden is the small Plaza de Murillo, which has a bronze statue of the 17th-century painter and the "Four Fountains" of mythological triton cherubs playing with dolphins. Open daily, from 10 AM to 7 PM (later in summer). Admission charge. On Paseo del Prado at Plaza de Murillo (phone: 420-3568).

Real Fábrica de Tapices (Royal Tapestry Factory) – Established early in the 18th century, this factory-museum continues to use authentic traditional techniques in producing handmade Spanish tapestries and rugs. In addition to the permanent collection, visitors can see the workshops and watch master artisans at work weaving tapestries from cartoons by Goya and other artists, knotting luxuriant rugs, or doing intricate restoration work. Rugs and tapestries can be purchased by special order, and they can even be custom-made from the customer's own design. Open Mondays through Fridays, from 9:30 AM to 12:30 PM; closed August. Admission charge. 3 Calle Fuenterrabía (phone: 551-3400).

Museo del Ejército (Army Museum) – Everything imaginable related to battle throughout Spain's history is here in an amazing array of over 27,000 items — uniforms, armor, cannon, swords (including one belonging to El Cid), stupendous collections of miniature soldiers, and portraits of heroines and heroes (such as Cervantes, when he lost his hand in the Battle of Lepanto). Downstairs, a curious collection of damaged carriages and automobiles whose illustrious passengers were assassinated en route recounts Madrid's turbulent political history. It's all chockablock within the vast and lavishly baroque interior of one of the two surviving buildings of the 17th-century Royal Retiro Palace complex (the other is the adjacent Casón del Buen Retiro, which the museum's pleasant bar overlooks). Whatever your interests, this is well worth seeing — while it lasts. Plans have been laid for the ever-expanding *Prado Museum* to take over this palatial building, and for the collection to be moved in the mid-1990s to a new venue at the Ministry of Defense complex in the Moncloa district. Open from 10 AM to 2 PM; closed Mondays. Admission charge. 1 Calle Méndez Núñez (phone: 531-4624).

Museo Arqueológico Nacional (National Archaeological Museum) – The star among the Iberian and classical antiquities is the enigmatic *Dama de Elche,* a dramatic Iberian bust of a priestess, or perhaps an aristocrat, estimated to have been sculpted during the 4th century BC. Also on display are basket weavings and funeral objects of early Iberians, as well as neolithic, Celtic, ancient Greek, Roman, and Visigothic artifacts and handicrafts. In the garden at the entrance is an underground replica of the famous Altamira Cave and its prehistoric paintings. Open Tuesdays through Saturdays, from 9:30 AM to 8:30 PM; Sundays and holidays, from 9:30 PM to 2:30 PM. The admission charge includes entrance to the *National Library* (see below), at the opposite side of the same building. 13 Calle Serrano (phone: 403-6607).

Biblioteca Nacional (National Library) – With over 4 million volumes, this is one of the world's richest libraries, truly a researcher's paradise. It was inaugurated in 1892 to commemorate the quadricentennial of the Discovery of America. Statues of Cervantes, Lope de Vega, and other illustrious Spaniards of letters stand at the classical columned entrance. Scheduled and seasonal exhibits of publications and graphics are held in the ground floor galleries. Open Tuesdays through Saturdays, from 10 AM to 9 PM; Sundays and holidays, 10 AM to 2 PM. The admission charge includes entrance to the *National Archaeological Museum* at the opposite side of the same building. 20 Paseo de Recoletos (phone: 575-6800).

Casa de Campo – Once the private royal hunting grounds, this 4,300-acre forested public park on the right bank of the Manzanares River is a playground for *madrileños* and visitors alike. It has a zoo (complete with a panda), picnic and fair grounds (important trade fairs and conventions are held here), and a giant amusement park, *Parque de Atracciones,* with rides and entertainment at an outdoor theater rife with a spirited carnival atmosphere. Other highlights include a concert stadium, an all-encompassing sports complex, a small lake, and the bullpens of La Venta de Batán (for bullfight practice and previews of the bulls). The park is easily reached by bus, metro, taxi, or the *teleférico* (cable car) that runs from Paseo del Pintor Rosales in Parque del Oeste (not far from Plaza de España). The zoo is open daily, April through September; Saturdays, Sundays, and holidays only, October through March. The amusement park is closed in winter and closed Mondays the rest of the year. Admission charge to attractions. Casa de Campo (phone: 463-2900).

Basílica de San Francisco el Grande – A few blocks south of the Royal Palace, this neo-classical church is one of the largest and most richly decorated in Madrid. Another project of King Carlos III, it was designed by the city's finest 18th-century architects. Six side chapels (the first on the left was painted by Goya) line its circular interior, which is topped by a cupola 108 feet in diameter. The museum inside the church contains a wealth of religious art. Museum hours are Tuesdays through Saturdays, from 11 AM to 1 PM and 4 to 7 PM; closed holidays. Admission charge to the museum. Plaza de San Francisco (phone: 265-3800).

■**EXTRA SPECIAL:** Some 30 miles (48 km) northwest of Madrid, the colossal monastery-palace of El Escorial symbolizes the grandeur of the Spanish Empire during its 16th-century Golden Age. King Philip II ordered its construction on a foothill of the Sierra de Guadarrama to commemorate Spain's victory over France at St.-Quentin, Flanders, and also to serve as a pantheon for his father, Holy Roman Emperor Charles V, and himself. It took more than 1,500 workmen 21 years to complete this extraordinary, austere monument designed by Juan de Herrera. The gray granite edifice, with hundreds of rooms and thousands of windows, is a sight never to be forgotten. The guided tour includes visits to the royal apartments, the museums (with paintings by Titian, Ribera, Velázquez, Tintoretto, Dürer, Lucas Jordan, and others), the library (with 40,000 priceless volumes and 4,700 manuscripts), the basilica, the royal pantheon with its tombs of Spanish monarchs, and the adjacent pantheon where their progeny are entombed. To reach the monastery-palace by car, take the N-VI national highway northwest to Guadarrama, then head south on C600; or take the more scenic country route, C505. There is frequent train and bus service between Madrid and the contiguous town of San Lorenzo de El Escorial, which is charming and well worth seeing. Open from 10 AM to 1 PM and 3 to 6 PM; closed Mondays. Admission charge (phone: 890-5903).

Nearby, to the north, is the Valle de los Caídos (Valley of the Fallen), a spectacular memorial to those who died in the Spanish Civil War. A huge basilica containing the tombs of soldiers from both sides has been hollowed into a mountain. Generalísimo Francisco Franco, who ordered the monument's construction, also is buried here. A granite cross stands 500 feet in the air atop the mountain peak. Open Tuesdays through Sundays, 10 AM to 6 PM. No admission charge, but there is a small parking fee (phone: 890-5611).

SOURCES AND RESOURCES

TOURIST INFORMATION: Information, maps, and brochures can be obtained from the Oficina Municipal de Turismo (Municipal Tourist Office, 3 Plaza Mayor; phone: 266-5477). Information on the city, the rest of the province, and all of Spain also is available from the tourist information office of the Comunidad de Madrid (Province of Madrid, 2 Duque de Medinaceli; phone: 429-4951), near the *Palace* hotel. Other information offices run by the province are at Torre de Madrid, Plaza de España (phone: 541-2325), at Barajas Airport, and at the Chamartín train station.

The US Embassy is at 75 Calle Serrano (phone: 576-3400 or 3600).

Local Coverage – *ABC* and *El País,* Madrid's most popular Spanish-language dailies, cover local, national, and international events. The *Guía del Ocio* ("Leisure Guide"), in Spanish, is the most complete weekly guide to restaurants, entertainment, culture, and sports.

TELEPHONE: The city code for Madrid is 1. If calling from within Spain, dial 91 before the local number.

GETTING AROUND: Airport – Aeropuerto de Barajas, 10 miles (16 km) from downtown Madrid, handles both international and domestic flights. It is about a 20-minute taxi ride from the center of the city, depending on traffic; the fare will run about $15. (Note that taxis charge an additional 50¢ for picking up passengers at the airport, as well as another 25¢ per bag. There also is a 50¢ surcharge for all rides at night (11:30 PM to 6 AM) and all day on Sundays and holidays. Public buses run every 15 minutes between the airport and the air terminal in the center of the city under Plaza de Colón; the buses are yellow and are marked "Aeropuerto." The main *Iberia Airlines* office is at 130 Calle Velázquez (phone for domestic reservations: 411-1011; phone for international reservations: 563-9966).

Bus – Excellent, inexpensive bus service is available in Madrid. Signs clearly marking the routes are at each bus stop. There are both regular buses (red), costing 65 pesetas (exact change not required), and microbuses (yellow), which cost slightly more — they have upholstered seats and air conditioning and do not allow standees (so they won't stop if all seats are taken). Individual bus tickets are bought from the driver. Discounted "bonobus" passes, good for ten rides, cost 410 pesetas, and can be bought at the *Empresa Municipal de Transportes* (*EMT*) kiosks on the east side of Puerta del Sol and the south side of Plaza de Cibeles; upon boarding the bus, insert the pass into the date-stamping machine behind the driver. For information on the city bus system, call *EMT* at 401-9900. Madrid has no central bus station from which long-distance buses depart, but the Estación Sur de Autobuses (17 Calle Canarias; phone: 468-4200), serving Andalusia and other points south, is the largest of several.

Car Rental – All major international and Spanish firms are represented. Agencies in the city include *América* (23 Calle Cartagena; phone: 246-7919); *Atesa* (59 Gran Vía; phone: 247-0202; and 25 Calle Princesa; phone: 241-5004); *Avis* (60 Gran Vía; phone: 247-2048; and 57 Paseo de la Castellana; phone: 441-0579); *Europcar* (29 Calle Orense; phone: 445-9930; and 12 Calle García de Paredes; phone: 448-8706); *Hertz* (88 Gran Vía; phone: 242-1000; and 46 Calle Doctor Fleming; phone: 457-1772); and *Ital* (31 Calle Princesa; phone: 241-9403).

Subway – Madrid's metro is efficient and clean and in operation from 6 AM to 1:30 AM. Stops along all ten lines are clearly marked, and color-coded maps are easy to read. Tickets are purchased from machines and inserted into electronic turnstiles, or they're bought at pass-through booths. (Do not discard the ticket until the end of the ride.) Discounted ten-ride tickets also are available (410 pesetas); buy these at metro stations. For subway information, call 435-2266.

Taxi – Metered cabs are white with a diagonal red line. If a cab is available, it will have a windshield sign that says *libre* and an illuminated green light on its roof. Fares are moderate. Taxis can be hailed on the street, picked up at cabstands, or summoned by phone: *Radio-Teléfono Taxi* (phone: 247-8200); *Radio-Taxi* (phone: 405-1213); *Tele-taxi* (phone: 445-9008).

Train – The two major stations of the *RENFE* (Spanish National Railway) are Chamartín at the north end of Madrid and Atocha at the south end. Both serve long-distance trains, as well as commuter trains to surrounding areas (*cercanías*). West of Plaza de España, a third station, Principe Pío (also called Estación del Norte), serves some lines to northern Spain. *RENFE*'s main city ticket office is located at 44 Calle de Alcalá (phone: 429-0518 for information; 429-8228 for reservations). Tickets also can be purchased at the train stations and at *RENFE's* Nuevos Ministerios and Recoletos stations.

On Saturdays and Sundays from May through October, *RENFE* operates a series of tourist trains offering 1- and 2-day excursions to nearby places of interest. Museum entrance fees, guided tours, motorcoach sightseeing, and, in some cases, meals are included in the cost of the transportation; hotel accommodations are included in the 2-day packages, which travel to more distant destinations. The specially named 1-day excursion trains head for Aranjuez (*Tren de la Fresa,* or "Strawberry Train"); Toledo (*Ciudad de Toledo*); Avila (*Murallas de Avila*); Sigüenza (*Doncel de Sigüenza*); and the Piedra River and Monastery in Aragon (*Monasterio de Piedra*). The cost is approximately $15–$20, with discounts for children under 12. Trains departing on 2-day excursions, leaving Saturday mornings and returning Sunday nights, make trips to Cáceres (*Ciudad Monumental de Cáceres*); Burgos (*Tierras del Cid*); Cuenca (*Ciudad Encantada de Cuenca*); Valladolid (*Cuna del Descubrimiento*); Salamanca (*Plaza Mayor de Salamanca*); Soria (*Camino de Soria*); Zamora (*Románico de Zamora*); and Palencia (*Camino de Santiago Palentino*). Prices range from about $60 to $120, depending on the train and choice of hotel. Reservations should be made in advance at *RENFE* offices or through one of the many travel agencies scattered throughout Madrid. (Check the list of destinations for additional cities upon arrival in Madrid, because the innovative tourist train idea has been so successful that new destinations are added each season.)

 SPECIAL EVENTS: Madrid has a distinctive, exuberant way of celebrating Spain's national holidays, as well as its own year-long calendar of local fairs and festivals. *Madrileños* go all out for *Carnaval* frolic, frocks, and parades in February, ending on *Ash Wednesday* with the allegorical *Entierro de la Sardina* (Burial of the Sardine). The *International Festival of Theater and Film* is held in April. On the *Second of May,* at Plaza 2 de Mayo in the Malasaña district, processions and events commemorate the city's uprising against the massacring French, which Goya portrayed so dramatically. But even more *madrileño* are the *Fiestas de San Isidro* — 10 days of nonstop street fairs, festivals, concerts, special daily bullfights, and more, all in celebration of Madrid's patron saint, whose feast day is on May 15. (This age-old tradition of picnics and merrymaking at the Meadows of San Isidro alongside the Manzanares River also was depicted by Goya.) On June 13, the *Verbena de San Antonio* (St. Anthony's Fair) takes place at the shrine of San Antonio de la Florida, with outdoor singing and dancing and traditional drinking from the fountain. It's also customary to throw pins into the holy water; young "spinsters" dip in, and their chances for acquiring a mate depend on the number of pins that stick in their hands.

Madrid is extra-lively during the summer, despite the mass exodus by summer vacationers. During July, August, and early September, the city government presents *Veranos en la Villa* (Summers in the "Village"), 2-plus months of countless cultural events featuring international superstars and local talent — ballet, symphonic music, opera, jazz, rock, pop, salsa, *zarzuelas,* films, and many diverse exhibitions — in open-air and theater settings throughout the city. Fitting in neatly with all this are colorful *verbenas* (street parties) honoring the feast days of three of Madrid's most popular saints: San Cayetano (August 3), San Lorenzo (August 5), and La Virgen de la Paloma (August 15). In the *barrios castizos* (authentically typical neighborhoods, such as Lavapiés, Embajadores, Puerta de Toledo), *madrileños,* from toddlers to great-grandparents, dress in the traditional attire of *chulos* and *chulapas* reminiscent of 19th-century *zarzuelas.* They gather at lively street fairs to eat, drink, and dance the *chotis*

and *pasodoble,* enjoying musical groups, folk music performances, organ-grinders, processions, *limonada* (not lemonade, but a kind of white-wine sangria), and their own innate ebullience. The world-class *Madrid International Jazz Festival* is held in late October and/or early November. From October to the beginning of December, the *Fiesta de Otoño* (Autumn Festival), also organized by the city government, presents an abundance of concerts and performances by top international and Spanish companies at Madrid theaters and concert halls. November 9 celebrates the day of Madrid's patroness, La Virgen de la Almudena. During the *Christmas* season, the city is bedecked with festive lights, and the Plaza Mayor fills with countless stands selling decorations, figurines for Nativity scenes, candies, wreaths, and *Christmas* trees. On *New Year's Eve,* throngs gather at the Puerta del Sol to swallow one grape at each stroke of the clock at midnight, wishing for 12 months of good luck in the new year. The *Christmas* season lasts until *Epiphany,* January 6, on the eve of which children delight at the *Cabalgata de los Reyes,* the procession through the city streets by the gift-giving Three Wise Men. As if all of this weren't enough, each barrio expresses its individual personality with its own fiestas and *festivales* throughout the year.

 MUSEUMS: Many museums are described in *Special Places* (above). Included in the following list of additional museums are certain churches that, because of their high artistic quality, should not be overlooked. Note that the *Museo de América* (Americas Museum; 6 Avenida Reyes Católicos), housing Latin American crafts and folk art along with pre-Columbian artifacts, is closed for restoration, scheduled to reopen in 1992 (possibly in a new location). Also closed for restoration, but scheduled to reopen this year, is the *Casa Museo de Lope de Vega* (Lope de Vega House Museum, 11 Calle Cervantes; phone: 239-4605), consisting of the home and garden of Spain's great Golden Age dramatist; it ordinarily is open Tuesdays and Thursdays only, from 10AM to 2 PM, and closed in summer. Admission charge. Keep in mind that the hours of many museums may vary during the summer, and smaller museums may be closed during July and August. The Office of Museums will be able to supply the latest information (phone: 248-7404).

Basílica de San Miguel – An unusual 18th-century church with an air of Italian baroque in its convex façade and graceful interior. 4 Calle de San Justo.

Catedral de San Isidro – This imposing 17th-century church was *temporarily* designated the Cathedral of Madrid in 1885, pending the completion of the Catedral de la Almudena — which has been under construction for over a century. The entombed remains of St. Isidro, patron saint of Madrid, and those of his wife, Santa María de la Cabeza, sit on the altar. 37 Calle Toledo.

Círculo de Bellas Artes (Fine Arts Circle) – Several galleries of this art, design, and photography center display works by students and prominent teachers. Open daily; exhibits and events are scheduled at varying hours; pick up a monthly program at the tourist office. Admission charge to most exhibits. 42 Calle de Alcalá (phone: 531-8505).

Estudio y Museo Sorolla (Sorolla Studio and Museum) – The house in which Joaquín Sorolla, the Valencian Impressionist "Painter of Light," lived, worked, and died in 1923. Contents include a collection of his works; the studio and library remain intact. Open from 10 AM to 3 PM; closed Mondays. Admission charge. 37 Calle General Martínez Campos (phone: 410-1584).

Fundación Casa de Alba (House of Alba Foundation) – The magnificent 18th-century Palacio de Liria, former residence of the Duchess of Alba, containing the family's priceless private collection of art, tapestries, archives, and furnishings. Admission (free) must be requested well in advance by writing to: Fundación Casa de Alba, 20 Calle Princesa, 28008 Madrid (phone: 247-5302).

Iglesia y Convento de San Jerónimo el Real (Church and Convent of San

Jeronimo) – This giant Gothic temple overlooking the *Prado* was built by order of King Ferdinand and Queen Isabella in 1503. It is closed for massive renovation, and is not scheduled to reopen until the mid-1990s. 19 Calle Ruiz de Alarcón.

Museo Cerralbo – The palatial 19th-century mansion of the Marqués de Cerralbo houses an important collection of art, antiques, ceramics, tapestries, and ancient artifacts. Outstanding among the paintings are works by El Greco, Ribera, Velázquez, Zurbarán, and Van Dyck. Open from 10 AM to 2 PM and 4 to 6 PM; closed Mondays and in August. Admission charge. 17 Calle Ventura Rodríguez (phone: 247-3647).

Museo Español de Arte Contemporáneo (Spanish Contemporary Art Museum) – Art from the mid-19th century onward, including works by Eduardo Rosales, Eduardo Vicente, Picasso, Juan de Echevarría, José Gutiérrez Solana, and Antoni Tàpies. (At press time, there were plans to move the core of the permanent collection to the *Museo Nacional Centro de Arte Reina Sofía,* leaving this for changing exhibitions). Open Tuesdays through Saturdays, from 10 AM to 6 PM; Sundays and holidays, from 10 AM to 3 PM. Admission charge. 2 Avenida Juan de Herrera, Ciudad Universitaria (phone: 549-7150).

Museo de Escultura Abstracta al Aire Libre (Outdoor Museum of Abstract Sculpture) – Contemporary Spanish sculptures permanently placed in a pedestrian area on the Castellana, under the Calles Eduardo Dato–Juan Bravo overpass. Open continuously; no admission charge. Paseo de la Castellana.

Museo de Figuras de Cera (Wax Museum) – An international gallery of historic personages, including celebrity bullfighters and such fictional Spanish notables as Don Quixote and Sancho Panza. Open daily, from 10:30 AM to 1:30 PM and 4 to 8 PM. Admission charge. Centro Colón (phone: 308-0825).

Museo Lázaro Galdiano – Named for its founder, whose palatial mansion houses his extraordinary collection of art, jewelry, ivory, and enamel. Open from 10 AM to 2 PM; closed Mondays and in August. Admission charge. 122 Calle Serrano (phone: 261-6084).

Museo Nacional de Artes Decorativas (National Museum of Decorative Arts) – Four floors of furniture, porcelains, jewelry, Spanish tiles and fans, a full Valencian kitchen, and handicrafts from the 16th through 19th centuries. Open Tuesdays through Fridays, from 10 AM to 3 PM; Saturdays and Sundays, from 10 AM to 2 PM; closed in summer. Admission charge. 12 Calle Montálban (phone: 521-3440).

Museo Nacional Ferroviario (National Railroad Museum) – Madrid's first train station, Estación de las Delicias, now is a museum complete with intact antique trains, royal cars, and other predecessors of the modern railroad. From May through October, the restored 19th-century "Strawberry Train" (*Tren de la Fresa*) departs here on 1-day excursions to Aranjuez. Open Tuesdays through Saturdays, from 10 AM to 5 PM; Sundays and holidays, from 10 AM to 2 PM. Admission charge. 61 Paseo de las Delicias (phone: 227-3121).

Museo Naval (Maritime Museum) – Models of ships and ports, nautical instruments, and maps, including Juan de la Cosa's historic *mapa mundi,* the first map to include the New World, drawn in 1500. Open from 10:30 AM to 1:30 PM; closed Mondays and in August. Admission charge. 2 Calle Montálban (phone: 521-0419).

Museo Panteón de Goya (Pantheon of Goya, also called Ermita de San Antonio) – Goya painted the magnificent religious frescoes on the dome and walls of this small 18th-century church, which was to become his tomb. Open Tuesdays through Fridays, from 10 AM to 1:30 PM and 4 to 7 PM; weekends and holidays, from 10 AM to 1:30 PM. No admission charge. Glorieta de San Antonio de la Florida (phone: 542-0722).

Museo Romántico (Romantic Museum) – Paintings, furniture, and decor of 19th-century Madrid, housed in an 18th-century mansion. Open Tuesdays through

Saturdays, from 10 AM to 6 PM; Sundays, from 10 AM to 2 PM. Closed August. Admission charge. 13 Calle San Mateo (phone: 448-1071).

Museo Taurino (Bullfighting Museum) – An important collection of bullfighting memorabilia, including photographs, celebrity bullfighters' "suits of lights," and even taxidermic trophies of ears, tails, and entire bulls. Open Mondays through Fridays, from 9 AM to 3 PM; during bullfighting season (May through October), open Sundays, closed Mondays. Admission charge. Plaza de Toros Monumental de las Ventas, 237 Calle de Alcalá (phone: 255-1857).

Templo de Debod – A gift from the Egyptian government in the 1970s, this 2,500-year-old Egyptian temple was shipped to Madrid in 1,359 cases and reassembled, towering over a reflecting pool. Theater and music performances are held here in summer. Open daily, from 10 AM to 1 PM; holidays, from 10 AM to 3 PM. No admission charge. Parque del Oeste.

SHOPPING: Madrid's 54,000 stores and shops offer everything imaginable, from high fashion to flamenco guitars. Handicrafts, fine leather goods, embroidery, ceramics, Lladró porcelains, art, and antiques are among the enticing buys available throughout the city. Everything goes on sale twice a year — after *Christmas* (which in Spain means January 7, the day after *Epiphany*) and during the summer. The big summer sales (*rebajas*) begin in July, and prices are reduced even more during the first 3 weeks of August. Shops generally open at 9:30 AM, close from 1:30 to 4:30 PM for lunch and the siesta, and close for the night at 8 PM. The huge flagship stores of Spain's two major department store chains are next to each other in the pedestrian shopping area between the Gran Vía and Puerta del Sol: *El Corte Inglés* (3 Calle Preciados; phone: 532-8100) and *Galerías Preciados* (1 Plaza de Callao; phone: 522-4771). Unlike most retailers, they remain open during the lunch and siesta hours, and they provide special services for tourists, such as English-speaking escorts to accompany shoppers and coordination of shipping services to hotel or home. Branch stores of *El Corte Inglés* are at 56 Calle Princesa, 76 Calle Goya, and 79 Calle Raimundo Fernández Villaverde (the biggest of all, just off the Castellana). Branches of *Galerías Preciados* are at 10-11 Calle Arapiles, 87 Calle Goya, 47 Calle Serrano, and at the *Madrid 2 Shopping Center* (also known as *La Vaguada*) in northern Madrid.

Near the two department stores, four stores specializing in fine china, porcelain (especially Lladró), and Majórica pearls, line the Gran Vía: *Souvenirs* (11 Gran Vía, near Calle de Alcalá; phone: 521-5119); *Vinvinda* (44 Gran Vía, near Plaza de Callao; phone: 213-0514); *Regalos A.R.* (46 Gran Vía; phone: 522-6869); and *La Galette* (67 Gran Vía, near Plaza de España; phone: 248-8938). Window shopping is a favorite pastime along Calle Serrano, which is full of elegant boutiques and galleries; the Plaza Mayor area is another place to look for appealing shopping opportunities.

Other places to browse or buy include the rebuilt *Mercado Puerta de Toledo* (see *Special Places*), where over 150 shops, boutiques, and galleries are stuffed with the finest in Spanish handicrafts, art, fashion, antiques, jewelry, housewares, and food products. Easy-to-operate computer terminals reveal what and where everything is in this sparkling complex, which is all under one roof (1 Ronda de Toledo; phone: 266-7200). *La Galería del Prado* (phone: 429-7551), a recent addition to the *Palace* hotel (7 Plaza de las Cortes), is a glamorous assembly of 38 top fashion boutiques, art galleries, jewelers, and gift shops, as well as a fancy food shop, a beauty salon, bookstore, and a buffet-style restaurant. Still another new shopping mall, in modern Madrid, just off the Castellana, is *Moda Shopping* (40 Avenida General Perón), with over 60 establishments selling everything from high fashion to sporting goods, and with plenty of restaurants and bars to enjoy during shopping breaks.

El Rastro, Madrid's legendary outdoor flea market, (open Sundays and holiday mornings only) spreads for countless blocks in the old section of the city, beginning at Plaza de Cascorro and fanning south to Ronda de Toledo. Hundreds of stands are set up to sell everything from canaries to museum-piece antiques, and bargaining, preferably in Spanish, is customary. (Guard wallets and purses from pickpockets.) Open daily, year-round, is the *Cuesta de Moyano,* a stretch of Calle de Claudio Moyano (along the south side of the Botanical Gardens) with a string of bookstalls selling new, used, and out of print "finds" of everything imaginable that's been published.

Antigua Casa Talavera – Authentic regional handcrafted ceramics and dinnerware from all over Spain form an overwhelming display in this small, family-owned shop just off the Gran Vía, near Plaza de Santo Domingo. 2 Calle Isabel la Católica (phone: 247-3417).

Artespaña – Government run, with a wide range of handicrafts and home furnishings from all over Spain. 3 Plaza de las Cortes, 14 Calle Hermosilla, 33 Calle Don Ramón de la Cruz, and *Centro Comercial Madrid 2–La Vaguada* (phone for all locations: 413-6262).

Ascot – An excellent women's boutique selling haute couture and ready-to-wear fashions by María Teresa de Vega, who clothes some of Madrid's most beautiful people. 88 Calle Serrano (phone: 431-3712).

El Aventurero – A small bookstore specializing in guidebooks, maps, books on the art of bullfighting, and outstanding "coffee-table" tomes on Spanish subjects, with an ample selection in English, too. Just off Plaza Mayor at 15 Calle Toledo (phone: 266-4457).

Elena Benarroch – Stylish designs in women's furs. This well-known furrier also has a shop in New York. 24 Calle Monte Esquinza (phone: 308-2816).

Joaquín Berao – Fine jewelry by the young Spanish designer — earrings, bracelets, rings, and pendants in ultramodern designs. 13 Calle Conde de Xiquena (phone: 410-1620).

Boutique Granada – A small shop selling leather goods of the highest quality. 12 Calle de Vergara (phone: 241-0746).

Canalejas – Top-quality men's shirtmakers, specializing in the classic European formfitting cut. 20 Carrera de San Jerónimo (phone: 521-8075).

Casa de Diego – Founded in 1858, this old-time store makes hand-painted fans — and frames for displaying them — as well as canes and umbrellas. Two locations: 12 Puerta del Sol (phone: 522-6643), and 4 Calle Mesonero Romanos (phone: 531-0223).

Casa Jiménez – Another classic store specializing in fans and *mantones de manila,* fine lace shawls. 42 Calle Preciados (phone: 248-0526).

Casa del Libro – Madrid's biggest book store. 29 Gran Vía (phone: 521-1932). A brand-new branch, on 4 floors, is at 3 Calle Maestro Vitoria (phone: 521-4898).

Cortefiel – Leading men's and women's fashions and accessories are carried at 40 Calle Serrano (phone: 431-3342). Branches at 178 Paseo de la Castellana (phone: 259-5713) and 27 Gran Vía (phone: 247-1701) specialize in men's fashions only, while those at 146 Paseo de la Castellana (phone: 250-3638) and 13 Calle Preciados (phone: 522-6567) cater exclusively to women.

El Corte Inglés Record Department – The latest in Spanish classical, pop, and flamenco music on record, tape, and compact disc, as well as a complete selection of every other type of recorded music. They even carry *sevillanas* dance lessons on videocassette. Across the street from the main store at 3 Calle Preciados (phone: 532-8100).

Discos Sol – For the collector, this unique store carries a valuable inventory of Spanish classical, popular, *sevillanas,* and flamenco records spanning generations and available nowhere else. 1 Calle Espoz y Mina, 2nd floor (phone: 531-3828).

Adolfo Domínguez – The boutique of the innovative Spanish celebrity designer, whose daring women's fashions set the "wrinkles (in the fabric, that is) are beautiful" trend. 4 Calle Ortega y Gasset (phone: 276-0084).

Gil, Sucesor de Anatolín Quevedo – Spanish and international celebrities purchase work-of-art shawls, *mantillas,* and embroidery at this generations-old establishment. 2 Carrera de San Jerónimo (phone: 521-2549).

Gritos de Madrid – A fine ceramics shop owned by master craftsman Eduardo Fernández, and featuring his works. He is responsible for the restoration of Madrid's interesting hand-illustrated tile street signs, and his famous ceramic mural of 17th-century Madrid hangs in the City Hall's museum collection. 6 Plaza Mayor (phone: 265-9154).

Lepanto – Fashions, luggage, and accessories, in leather. 3 Plaza de Oriente (phone: 242-2357).

Loewe – Fine leather fashions for men and women, as well as accessories and luggage. At several locations: 8 Gran Vía, 26 Calle Serrano, and at the *Palace* hotel; a shop at 34 Calle Serrano carries men's fashions exclusively (phone for all locations: 435-3023).

Maty – For dance enthusiasts: authentic regional costumes for men, women, and children, and dance shoes and boots as well. 2 Calle Maestro Vitoria (phone: 479-8802).

Seseña – Always in style in Spain, capes are becoming the "in" thing for evening-wear everywhere, and this store, founded in 1901, manufactures a fine line for men and women. (It also instructs clients on the fine art of wearing a cape.) 23 Calle Cruz (phone: 531-6840).

 SPORTS AND FITNESS: Basketball – Madrid plays host to much of the finest basketball in Europe. The city is represented by such teams as *Real Madrid* and *Estudiantes* and also is the home of the Spanish National and Olympic squads. The most important games are played at the *Palacio de Deportes* (99 Calle Jorge Juan; phone: 401-9100), and at the *Polideportivo Magariños* (127 Calle Serrano; phone: 262-4022).

Bullfighting – Although not universally appreciated, bullfighting is the most renowned sport of Spain — Spaniards insist it is an art — and the largest bullfighting ring in Madrid is *Plaza de Toros Monumental de las Ventas,* which seats 22,300 people. There also is a smaller ring, *Plaza de Toros de Carabanchel,* near the Vista Alegre metro stop. The season runs from mid-May through October. Tickets may be purchased the day of the event at a counter at 3 Calle Vitoria (near the Puerta del Sol), at the bullring, or through a hotel concierge.

Fishing – There are fishing reserves along the Lozoya, Madarquillos, Jarama, and Cofio rivers not far from Madrid. They are populated mostly by trout, carp, black bass, pike, and barbel. The Santillana reservoir is particularly good for pike. For season and license information, contact the *Dirección General del Medio Rural,* 39 Calle Jorge Juan (phone: 435-5121).

Fitness Centers – Madrid has 27 municipal gymnasiums; for information on the one nearest your hotel, call 464-9050.

Golf – The Madrid area boasts several excellent private golf courses, such as the two 18-hole courses at the *Real Club de la Puerta de Hierro* (Avenida Miraflores; phone: 316-1745); the 18-hole and 9-hole courses at the *Club de Campo Villa de Madrid* (Carretera de Castilla; phone: 207-0395); the Jack Nicklaus–designed 18-hole course of the *Club de Golf La Moraleja* (7 miles/11 km north of town along the Burgos–Madrid highway; phone: 650-0700); and the 18 holes of the *Nuevo Club de Golf de Madrid* (at Las Matas, 16 miles/26 km west of town via the Carretera de La Coruña; phone: 630-0820). The *Federación Española de Golf* (9 Calle Capitán Haya; phone: 555-2682) has details on most of the area's facilities; hotels also can provide information regarding the use of the clubs by non-members.

Horse Racing – The *Hipódromo de la Zarzuela* (4 miles/7 km north of the center, along Carretera de La Coruña) features Sunday-afternoon races during spring and fall meetings. Buses for the track leave from the corner of Calles Princesa and Hilarión Eslava (phone: 207-0140).

Jogging – Parque del Retiro and Casa de Campo both have jogging tracks.

Skiing – *Puerto de Navacerrada,* a mountain resort (just 37 miles/60 km north of Madrid; phone: 852-1435) has 12 ski runs and 6 lifts.

Soccer – One of Spain's most popular teams, the capital's *Real Madrid,* plays its home games at the *Estadio Santiago Bernabéu* (1 Calle Concha Espina; phone: 250-0600), while its rival, *Atlético de Madrid,* takes the field at the *Estadio Vicente Calderón* (6 Paseo Virgen del Puerto; phone: 266-4707).

Swimming – Many hotels have pools, but Madrid also has 150 public swimming pools, including those indoors and outdoors at *Casa de Campo* (Avenida del Angel; phone: 463-0050). Another nice pool is at *La Elipa* (Avenida de la Paz; phone: 430-3358), which also has an area set aside for co-ed nude sunbathing. For information on other municipal pools, call 463-5498.

Tennis – Among the hundreds of public and private tennis courts in town are the 35 courts at the *Club de Campo Villa de Madrid,* Carretera de Castilla (phone: 207-0395), and the 28 courts of the *Club de Tenis Chamartín* (2 Calle Federico Salmón; phone: 250-5965).

 THEATER: Theater productions are in Spanish. Anyone fluent and interested in the Spanish classics should check the *Guía del Ocio* for what's on at the *Teatro Español* (25 Calle del Príncipe; phone: 429-0318), which stages the classics of the Golden Age; at the nearby *Teatro de la Comedia* (14 Calle del Príncipe; phone: 521-4931), where the *Compañía Nacional de Teatro Clásico* (National Classical Theater Company) also puts on a fine repertoire of classic Spanish plays, as well as modern ones and foreign adaptations; and at the *Teatro Nacional María Guerrero* (Calle Tamayo y Baus; phone: 319-4769), still another venue for both modern plays and classics of the Spanish and international repertoires. For the strictly modern and avant-garde, there's the *Centro Nacional de Nuevas Tendencias Escénicas* (National Center of New Theater Trends), housed at the *Sala Olimpia* (Plaza de Lavapiés; phone: 227-4622). Madrid is a city of film buffs, but if you feel like taking in a film and your Spanish is not good enough for the latest Almodóvar, note that foreign films usually are not dubbed into Spanish — look for "V.O.," meaning '*versión original*" in the ad. *Cine Doré,* known as the Filmoteca Española (3 Calle Santa Isabel; phone: 227-3866), has all the avant-garde foreign films; *Alphavilla* (14 Calle Martín de los Heros; phone: 248-4524) is another possibility. Ballets, operas, and *zarzuelas* (or operettas — some *zarzuelas* resemble musical comedy, others light opera), present fewer difficulties for nonspeakers of Spanish. Check listings for the restored *Nuevo Apolo Teatro Musical de Madrid* (1 Plaza Tirso de Molina; phone: 227-3816), home base for director José Tamayo's *Nueva Antología de la Zarzuela* company; *Teatro de la Zarzuela* (4 Calle Jovellanos; phone: 429-82225), which also hosts opera, ballet, and concerts, in addition to traditional *zarzuela;* and the *Centro Cultural de la Villa* (Plaza de Colón; phone: 275-6080), which does both theater and *zarzuela.*

MUSIC: Bolero and fandango are the typically Castilian dances and flamenco is Andalusian, but it is the latter most tourists want to see and hear, so there are numerous excellent flamenco *tablaos* (cabarets) in Madrid. Some of the best are *Corral de la Morería* (17 Calle Morería; phone: 265-1137); *Café de Chinitas* (7 Calle Torija; phone: 248-5135); *Torres Bermejas* (11 Calle Mesonero Romanos; phone: 532-3322); and, *Venta del Gato* (about 5 miles/8 km outside Madrid on the road to Burgos, 214 Avenida de Burgos; phone: 776-6060). *Café*

Central (10 Plaza del Angel; phone: 468-0844) offers live music nightly (jazz, classical, salsa, or folk) as well as late dinner. Madrid's main hall for classical concerts is the new *Auditorio Nacional de Música* (Calle Príncipe de Vergara; phone: 337-0100), the home of the *Orquestra Nacional de España* and the *Coro Nacional de España* — the *Spanish National Orchestra* and the *Spanish National Chorus.* At present, the *Teatro Real,* formerly the city's premier concert hall, at Plaza de Oriente, is being converted into the *Teatro de la Opera,* scheduled to open this year. Classical music also can be heard at several other locations, including the *Fundación Juan March* (77 Calle Castelló; phone: 435-4240). For a list of theaters presenting *zarzuela,* Spain's traditional form of operetta, see *Theater* above.

 NIGHTCLUBS AND NIGHTLIFE: Nightlife in Madrid can continue all night. Cover charges at cabarets and nightclubs include one drink, dancing, and floor shows that are becoming more risqué by the minute. Top choices include *Scala-Meliá Castilla* (43 Calle Capitán Haya; phone: 571-4411) and *Florida Park* (in the Parque del Retiro; phone: 273-7804). For a night of gambling, dining, dancing, and entertainment, the *Casino Gran Madrid* has it all (it's 20 minutes from downtown at Torrelodones, with free transportation from 6 Plaza de España; phone: 856-1100). The latest dance rage in Madrid is the *sevillanas. Madrileños* have adopted the delightful dance music of their Andalusian cousins as their own and, by popular demand, *sevillanas* music plays at many discos; dozens of *salas rocieras* — new nightclubs dedicated to dancing and watching *sevillanas* — attract teens, married couples, and diplomats alike. Among the best are *El Portón* (25 Calle Lopez de Hoyos; phone: 262-4956), *Al Andalus* (19 Calle Capitán Haya; phone: 556-1439), *La Caseta* (13 Calle General Castaños; phone: 419-0343), and *Almonte* (35 Calle de Juan Bravo; phone: 411-6880). *La Maestranza* (16 Calle Mauricio Legendre, near Plaza de Castilla; phone: 315-9059) features star *sevillanas* performers in its floor shows and also serves outstanding Andalusian cuisine. Some discotheques and *boîtes* run two sessions a night, at 7 and 11 PM until the wee hours. Among the more popular are *Pachá* (11 Calle Barceló; phone: 446-0137); *Boccaccio* (16 Calle Marqués de la Ensenada; phone: 319-1008); and *Joy Eslava* (11 Calle Arenal; phone: 266-3733). Striptease shows are the attraction at *Alazán* (24 Paseo de la Castellana; phone: 435-8948). There's late dining and an energetic downstairs disco at *Archy* (11 Calle Marqués de Riscal; phone: 308-2736), while the latest gathering spot for the glitterati is *Teatriz* (15 Calle Hermosilla; phone: 577-5379). The *Cervecería Alemana* (6 Plaza Santa Ana; phone: 429-7033), a tavern that's an old Hemingway hangout, remains a favorite nightspot. *Cock* (16 Calle Reina; no phone) draws an avant-garde set. *Madrileños* love to *pasear,* or stroll along the streets, and from April through October thousands of *terrazas* — outdoor cafés lining plazas, parks, and avenues — are jumping with nocturnal activity. Late revelers usually cap the evening with thick hot chocolate and *churros* at *Chocolatería de San Ginés* (in the alley behind San Ginés church), open all night.

BEST IN TOWN

CHECKING IN: Modern Madrid boasts over 50,000 hotel rooms, with accommodations ranging from "grand luxe" to countless *hostales* and *pensiones.* Reservations are nonetheless recommended, especially between May and September and during such special events as national and local festivals, expositions, and conventions. Expect to pay $550 or more a night for a double room in a hotel listed as very expensive, from $170 to $300 in an establishment listed as expensive, from $65 to $160 in a moderately priced hotel, and $50 or less in an inexpensive one. All telephone numbers are in the 1 city code unless otherwise indicated.

Ritz – The epitome of elegance, luxury, and Belle Epoque grace, this impeccably maintained classic opened in 1910. It was built at the behest of King Alfonso XIII, and its construction and decoration were overseen by César Ritz himself. No two of the 156 air conditioned rooms and suites are alike, but all are adorned with paintings, antiques, and tailored handwoven carpeting from the Royal Tapestry Factory. Jacket-and-tie attire is appropriate for men in the bar and the exquisite *Ritz* restaurant, one of Madrid's finest (see *Eating Out*). The casual *Ritz Garden Terrace* also offers delightful dining, cocktails, and *tapas.* 5 Plaza de la Lealtad (phone: 521-2857). Very expensive.

Villa Magna – Taken over by Hyatt hotels in 1990, this 194-room property has had a sterling reputation since its construction in the early 1970s. The modern, yet stately, building of glass and marble is set amid landscaped gardens in the heart of aristocratic Madrid. A recent multimillion-dollar remodeling project added unequaled luster — and technology — to the spacious, air conditioned rooms; high quality personal service enhances the hotel's casual elegance. The *Champagne Bar* boasts one of Europe's finest selection of bubbly beverages, and the, *Villa Magna* restaurant is celebrated for its imaginative specialties (see *Eating Out*). Richly decorated private salons accommodate meetings and banquets. 22 Paseo de la Castellana (phone: 261-4900). Very expensive.

Villa Real – Among Madrid's newest establishments, its design and atmosphere embody Old World grace; marble, bronze, and handcrafted wood, works of fine art and antique furnishings create a seignorial interior decor. All 115 luxurious rooms and suites are air conditioned and feature satellite television sets, mini-bars, and 3 or more high-tech telephones. Elegantly furnished top-floor duplexes have 2 bathrooms — 1 with a sauna, the other with a Jacuzzi — and large private balconies overlooking the Spanish Parliament Palace, the Neptune Fountain, and the *Prado Museum's* Villahermosa Palace. There is 24-hour room service and a friendly, competent staff. The hotel's choice setting — between Paseo del Prado and Puerta del Sol — couldn't be better. 10-11 Plaza de la Cortes (phone: 420-3767). Very expensive to expensive.

Barajas – The raison d'être of this 230-room hotel is its proximity to Madrid's Barajas International Airport. All rooms are air conditioned and have color television sets. Guests can enjoy the garden swimming pool, bar, restaurant, and health club. Half-day rates are available for meetings or jet-lag therapy. Free transportation is provided to and from the airport terminals. 305 Avenida Logroño (phone: 747-7700). Expensive.

Castellana Inter-Continental – Opened in the early 1950s as the *Castellana Hilton,* this has been a traditional favorite of Americans traveling to Madrid for business or pleasure. Its 310 air conditioned rooms, all containing modern accoutrements, are large and nicely decorated in pleasant pastels. Adjacent to the stately, marble-pillared lobby are car rental, airline, and tour desks, boutiques, a health club, and a business services department. *Los Continentes* restaurant and *La Ronda* piano bar are pleasant for meeting and eating. 49 Paseo de la Castellana (phone: 410-0200). Expensive.

Eurobuilding – An extremely well designed modern complex off the northern section of the Castellana near the *Convention Center* and *Estadio Santiago Bernabéu.* Within the complex, in addition to the 421-room hotel building, the *Eurobuilding* 2 tower comprises 154 apartment-style units. All rooms and apartments are air conditioned. There also are 2 swimming pools, a health club, a hair salon, stores, and 4 restaurants. 23 Calle Padre Damián (phone: 457-1700). Expensive.

Holiday Inn Madrid – Typical of the US Holiday Inn chain, this modern and busy establishment with 344 air conditioned rooms, has a swimming pool, health club, gymnasium, shopping arcade, and restaurants. A perfect place for anyone who wants to be near the Azca shopping and commercial complex, the *Convention Center, Estadio Santiago Bernabéu,* and the Castellana. 4 Plaza Carlos Trías Bertrán (phone: 597-0102). Expensive.

Meliá Castilla – Nearly 1,000 air conditioned rooms in a modern high-rise just off the Castellana in northern Madrid's business section. Facilities and meeting rooms cater primarily to executive travelers. There also is a swimming pool, gymnasium, sauna, shopping arcade, several restaurants and bars, and the *Scala Meliá Castilla,* a Las Vegas–style nightclub. 43 Calle Capitán Haya (phone: 571-2211). Expensive.

Meliá Madrid – Ideally located near the Plaza de España and very well run. The 266 air conditioned rooms in this gleaming white, modern building are tastefully decorated in various styles, and have color television sets. The dining room, grill, bar, and *Bong Bing* discotheque are popular meeting places. There also is a gymnasium, sauna, and conference facilities complete with state-of-the-art audio-visual equipment. 27 Calle Princesa (phone: 541-8200). Expensive.

Miguel Angel – Conveniently located on Paseo de la Castellana, this 304-room property combines modern luxuries with classic decor; 17th-, 18th-, and 19th-century paintings, tapestries, and furniture decorate the lobby and suites. Most rooms have balconies, and all offer color television sets. Facilities include a health club, with sauna, Jacuzzi, gymnasium, and heated, indoor swimming pool. Guests can enjoy fine food at the *Florencia* restaurant, afternoon tea and cocktails at the *Bar Farnesio,* and dinner, dancing, and live entertainment at the *Boite Zacarías* restaurant. 31 Calle Miguel Angel (phone: 442-8199). Expensive.

Monte Real – Located in a tranquil residential district about 20 minutes from the city center, this luxurious establishment is near the *Puerta de Hierro Golf Club.* All 77 rooms are air conditioned and have color television sets. Facilities include a swimming pool, sauna, lovely gardens, a restaurant, and a bar. 17 Calle Arroyo del Fresno, Puerta de Hierro (phone: 316-2140). Expensive.

Palace – Inaugurated in 1920, this aristocratic Madrid landmark was, like the *Ritz,* built by personal order of King Alfonso XIII. Its Old World Belle Epoque elegance and decor are faithfully maintained, while the utmost of modern facilities makes for true luxury in the spacious 518 air conditioned rooms and suites. Located in the heart of the city, the hotel overlooks the Neptune Fountain and Paseo del Prado. The lobby, embellished with trompe l'oeil painting, leads to the elegant, cozy lounge, which is topped by an immense painted-glass rotunda — an inviting setting for cocktails or informal dining at *El Ambiqú,* with a musical backdrop of piano and violin until 2 AM.. A recent addition, on the ground floor, is the *Galería del Prado,* a collection of 38 fine boutiques, galleries, and shops, as well as *La Plaza,* a self-service restaurant. 7 Plaza de las Cortes (phone: 429-7551). Expensive.

Wellington – Classic and nicely located in the Salamanca district, with fine boutiques, galleries, and the Parque del Retiro practically at the doorstep. The owner raised brave bulls; a stuffed triumphant one, named Cucharito, resides in the lounge amid the antique tapestries. Bullfighters, breeders, and aficionados stay and congregate here. All of the spacious 258 rooms are air conditioned, with color television sets. In summer, the outdoor swimming pool and the garden, with its restaurant, bar, and health club, are lively gathering spots. 8 Calle Velázquez (phone: 575-4400). Expensive.

Tryp Fénix – This Madrid aristocrat has been refurbished and reborn and once again is considered among the city's finest. Ideally situated on the tree-lined Castellana at Plaza de Colón, it has 216 air conditioned rooms and up-to-the-minute amenities enhanced by an air of sparkling elegance. 2 Calle Hermosilla (phone: 431-6700). Expensive to moderate.

Alcalá – Right on the north edge of Parque del Retiro and Plaza de la Independencia, in the genteel Salamanca district, it is within easy walking distance of fine shops and restaurants on Calle Serrano, as well as the *Prado* and other museums. All 153 air conditioned rooms have color television sets. The restaurant serves enticing Basque specialties. 66 Calle de Alcalá (phone: 435-1060). Moderate.

Arosa – Although it's on the bustling Gran Vía, it has the charm, peaceful mood, and personalized service of a small luxury establishment. The 126 air conditioned rooms, no two exactly alike, are tastefully decorated; luxurious bathrooms feature built-in hair dryers, fabulous showers in the bathtubs, and other treats, such as soothing bath salts. The atmosphere is delightful in the bar, lounge, and restaurant. Doormen at the small, elegant side-street entrance know guests by name. 21 Calle de la Salud (phone: 532-1600). Moderate.

Carlton – A complete renovation has raised the comfort level here. In a unique location — the southern part of central Madrid — it is near the Atocha train station complex, as well as within easy walking distance of the *National Museum Queen Sofia Art Center* and, a little farther north, the Botanical Gardens and the *Prado*. All of the 133 air conditioned rooms have color television sets. 26 Paseo de las Delicias (phone: 239-7100). Moderate.

Chamartín – The single advantage of this 378-room property is the fact that it is located within the modern Chamartín train station complex at the north end of the city. All rooms are air conditioned, have color television sets, and offer excellent views. Estación de Chamartín (phone: 733-7011). Moderate.

Emperador – Centrally located right on the Gran Vía. All 232 rooms are air conditioned and have color television sets. Unusual among the many hotels in the immediate area, it boasts a rooftop garden with a swimming pool and excellent views of the city. 53 Gran Vía (phone: 413-6511). Moderate.

Escultor – Conveniently located near the Castellana in a quiet residential area, its 82 air conditioned, apartment-style units offer separate sitting rooms with color television sets, complete kitchens, and mini-bars. 5 Calle Miguel Angel (phone: 410-4203). Moderate.

Mayorazgo – Excellent service and 200 well-appointed, comfortable, air conditioned rooms just a step from the central Gran Vía. The decor provides a retreat to a pleasant Castilian past. 3 Calle Flor Baja (phone: 247-2600). Moderate.

Plaza – Located within the gigantic Edificio España landmark building of the early 1950s, this hotel with 306 rooms (all air conditioned) is usually swarming with tour groups. The 26th-floor swimming pool and terrace restaurant offer marvelous panoramic views of the city. 2 Plaza de España (phone: 247-1200). Moderate.

Pullman Calatrava – Contemporary couches and antique desks in the lobby are set off by scenes of English fox hunting and horse racing. The 99 rooms, brightly decorated and air conditioned, have color TV sets and mini-bars. There is also a full-service restaurant and bar. On a quiet street just off the Plaza de España. 1 Calle Tutor (phone: 541-9880). Moderate.

Reina Victoria – After acquisition by the Tryp hotel chain and a total remodeling of its interior in 1990, this Madrid classic is once again worthy of its royal namesake (wife of King Alfonso XIII and grandmother of the present King Juan Carlos). Built in 1923 and designated a building of National Historic Interest, its unaltered 6-story façade, elaborate with pilasters, turrets, wrought-iron balconies, and bay windows, dominates the entire west side of the picturesque Plaza Santa Ana, a prime Old Madrid location. The 201 rooms and suites all have modern amenities (at less than regal prices). The new *Bar Taurino* revives the hotel's decades-old tradition as a rendezvous for bullfighters, breeders, and aficionados. 14 Plaza Santa Ana (phone: 531-4500). Moderate.

Serrano – Small and tasteful, refined and immaculate, on a quiet street between the Castellana and the boutique-lined Calle Serrano. Its marble-floored lobby is comfortably furnished and richly decorated with antiques (including a large 17th-century tapestry) and huge arrangements of fresh flowers. All 34 rooms are air conditioned and have color television sets. No restaurant, but snacks and sandwiches are available at the bar. 8 Calle Marqués de Villamejor (phone: 435-5200). Moderate.

Suecia – Recent expansion of this Swedish-managed (hence its name) hotel has added modern rooms and suites within the same building, but the original ones are still well maintained and very comfortable. All 67 rooms, old and new, are air conditioned, with color television sets, mini-bars, and safes. Hemingway lived here, enjoying the great advantage of the location — on a quiet street just west of Paseo del Prado, around the corner from Calle de Alcalá. Smoked salmon and smorgasbord are main attractions in the *Bellman* restaurant. 4 Calle Marqués de Casa Riera (phone: 531-6900). Moderate.

Tryp Ambassador – This restored 6-story noble mansion was converted into a fine 181-room hotel only recently. It has all the latest conveniences, and its unique location, close to the *Teatro Real* opera house, and also to Plaza de Oriente and the Royal Palace, makes it especially appealing. The restaurant serves Spanish and international fare. 5 Cuesta Santo Domingo (phone: 541-6700) Moderate.

Carlos V – Conveniently located, with 67 air conditioned rooms, right in the lively pedestrian area between the Gran Vía and Puerta del Sol, near the Convento de las Descalzas Reales and *El Corte Inglés* department store. 5 Calle Maestro Vitoria (phone: 531-4100). Moderate to inexpensive.

Don Diego – A well-kept *pensión* near the Parque del Retiro in Madrid's lovely Salamanca district. The 58 rooms are nicely furnished, and several have ample balconies. There is a television lounge and a bar that serves sandwiches and breakfast. 45 Calle Velázquez (phone: 435-0760). Moderate to inexpensive.

Galiano – A converted mansion, complete with marble floors, antique paintings, tapestries, and carved-wood furniture in the lobby and lounge. On a tranquil side street just off the Castellana and Plaza de Colón, it has 29 comfortable singles, doubles, and suites. Breakfast and color television sets are optional. 6 Calle Alcalá Galiano (phone: 319-2000). Moderate to inexpensive.

Puerta Toledo – Away from major hotel clusters, it is located on the fringe of picturesque Old Madrid, facing the Triumphal Arch of the Puerta de Toledo and near the new Mercado Puerta de Toledo. Its 160 rooms are air conditioned, comfortable, and well maintained. 4 Glorieta Puerta de Toledo (phone: 474-7100). Moderate to inexpensive.

Jamic – A small pension centrally located across the street from the *Palace* hotel and near the *Prado*. 4 Plaza de las Cortes (phone: 429-0068). Inexpensive.

Lisboa – This well run residential *hostal* has 23 rooms, all with private baths and telephones, plus maid service, a television lounge, and an elevator. The location is terrific: just off the Plaza Santa Ana in charming Old Madrid, yet a short walk to the *Palace,* the *Ritz,* and the *Prado.* English is spoken and credit cards are accepted. Fine restaurants of all price ranges line the street. 17 Calle Ventura de la Vega (phone: 429-9894). Inexpensive.

 EATING OUT: *Madrileños* eat the main meal of their day during the work break from 2 to 4 PM. An early-evening snack (*merienda*), such as wine and those typically Spanish tidbits called *tapas, chocolate con churros,* or coffee and sweets takes the edge off appetites until a light supper is eaten after 10

PM. For those who can't adjust to the Spanish schedule, there are always *cafeterías* and snack bars, and many restaurants start serving dinner at about 8:30 PM to accommodate non-Spaniards. Restaurants listed below as very expensive will charge $150 or more for a dinner for two with wine; similar fare will cost $75 to $130 at restaurants listed as expensive, between $30 and $70 at moderate eateries, and $25 or less at inexpensive ones. Most restaurants offer a set menu (*menú del día*), a complete meal for an economical price. Some restaurants include the 6% Value Added Tax in their menu prices. Check beforehand whether the menu says *IVA incluido* or *IVA no incluido*. All telephone numbers are in the 1 city code unless otherwise indicated.

Horcher – Operated for generations by the Horcher family, this remains one of Madrid's most elegant dining places, serving continental fare with an Austro-Hungarian flavor. Dining here is an indulgence that should include such delicacies as *chuletas de ternasco a la castellana* (baby lamb chops), endive salad (with truffles), and crêpes Sir Holten for dessert. Diners might even try the classic goulash. Closed Sundays. Reservations are necessary for lunch and dinner. 6 Calle Alfonso XII (phone: 522-0731). Very expensive.

Jockey – A Madrid classic, intimate and elegant, and a recipient of the National Gastronomy Award. The continental cuisine is superb, as are traditional dishes such as *cocido madrileño*, a multi-faceted savory stew, the broth of which is served as a side dish. Other specialties include *perdiz española* (partridge), *lomo de lubina* (filet of sea bass), and *mousse de anguila* (eel mousse). Closed Sundays and August. Reservations necessary. 6 Calle Amador de los Ríos (phone: 319-1003). Very expensive.

Ritz – The sumptuous restaurant of the luxurious *Ritz* hotel, serving French cuisine befitting the Limoges dinnerware and Louis XV silver service. Chamber music adds to the regal rapture. Open daily for breakfast, lunch, and dinner. Reservations necessary. (The separate *Ritz Garden-Terrace* offers more casual dining, or simply afternoon tea or *tapas*.) 5 Plaza de la Lealtad (phone: 521-2857). Very expensive.

Villa Magna – The recent remodeling of Madrid's *Villa Magna* hotel has placed its restaurant among the city's finest. Cristóbal Blanco, the prize-winning chef, designs such nouvelle delicacies as grilled scallops with caviar in basil sauce, while the china on which they are served was designed by Paloma Picasso. The *Champagne Bar* dispenses 252 French and Spanish vintages. (By the way, those precious place settings — plates plus silverware — cost $600 each, so be careful!) Open for breakfast, lunch, and dinner. Reservations necessary. 22 Paseo de la Castellana (phone: 261-4900). Very expensive.

Zalacaín – Probably the finest restaurant in all of Spain, it was the first in the country to win three Michelin stars and still shares that honor only with *Arzak*, in San Sebastián. It serves highly imaginative Basque and French haute cuisines, particularly seafood, and the service — by loyal employees who adore owner Jesús Oyarbide — is perfection. Luxurious decor, gleaming silverware and glasses, fresh flowers, and an irresistible dessert cart all contribute to the dining experience. Closed Saturdays for lunch, Sundays, August, *Easter Week*, and holidays. Reservations necessary (call at least 2 days in advance). 4 Calle Alvarez de Baena (phone: 261-4840). Very expensive.

La Basílica – Once an old baroque church, this is now a baroque and elegant restaurant. Sophisticates enjoy international, nouvelle, and Spanish cuisines in the see-and-be-seen main dining room or in secluded alcoves. It's located on a narrow street in Old Madrid, near Plaza Mayor. Closed Saturdays at lunch and all day Sundays. Reservations essential. 12 Calle de la Bolsa (phone: 521-8623). Expensive.

Cabo Mayor – The owner and chef both have won the National Gastronomy Award, and for good reason: Their fresh seafood from the province of Santander is imaginatively prepared, and the vegetable dishes are superlative. If it's on the menu, try the *cigalas y langostinos con verduras al jerez sibarita* (crayfish and prawns with green vegetables in sherry sauce). Closed Sundays, the last 2 weeks of August, *Christmas Week, New Year's Week,* and *Easter Week.* Reservations advised. 37 Calle Juan Ramón Jiménez (phone: 250-8776). Expensive.

El Cenador del Prado – Favored by aficionados of nouvelle cuisine and artistically decorated in a style reminiscent of an elegant conservatory, allowing indoor dining under the stars. Try *patatas a la importancia con almejas* (potatoes with clams) or the *pato al vinagre de frambuesas* (duck with raspberry vinegar). Politicians from the nearby Spanish Parliament may be at the next table. Closed for lunch on Saturdays and all day Sundays. Reservations necessary. 4 Calle del Prado (phone: 429-1561). Expensive.

La Dorada – Fresh seafood of every imaginable variety is flown in daily from the Mediterranean to this mammoth establishment, which serves Andalusian fare. (There also are two *Doradas* in Seville, another in Barcelona.) Particularly noteworthy is the fish baked in a crust of salt, an Andalusian practice that results, surprisingly, in a dish that's not salty. Closed Sundays and August. Reservations are essential, as this place is always crowded — and you'll enjoy the food even more if you reserve one of the private dining rooms. 64-66 Calle Orense (phone: 270-2002). Expensive.

Fortuny – Relatively new on Madrid's restaurant scene, it soon established its place among the preferred, with outstanding international haute cuisine. Housed in an aristocratic 19th-century mansion, it offers private dining rooms for banquets or intimacy. There also is a terrace with a waterfall, for outdoor summer dining. Closed Sundays and holidays. Reservations necessary. 34 Calle Fortuny (phone: 308-3268). Expensive.

La Gamella – The owner-chef-host is Richard Stephens, an American who also is an instructor at Madrid's Alambique School of Gastronomy. His intimate restaurant here, in the building in which philosopher José Ortega y Gasset was born, is dedicated to new Spanish cuisine — and it's one of Madrid's best. The creative appetizers and main dishes, the irresistible desserts, and the fine wine list add up to an adventure in taste, and the *colorista* design and art of the decor enhance the experience. A private dining room downstairs seats 10. Closed Saturdays for lunch. Reservations advised. 4 Calle Alfonso XII (phone: 532-4509). Expensive.

Gure-Etxea – One of the best for Basque dishes in Madrid, serving specialties such as *porrusalda* (leek and potato soup with cod) and a variety of fish dishes. Both the atmosphere and the service are pleasant. Closed Sundays and August. Reservations advised. 12 Plaza de la Paja (phone: 265-6149). Expensive.

Lhardy – A *madrileño* institution since 1839, and the decor, atmosphere, and table settings haven't changed much since then. One specialty in the upstairs dining rooms and private salons is *cocido madrileño,* the typical stew. At *merienda* time in the late afternoon, the street-entrance restaurant and stand-up bar fill with regulars who serve themselves the *caldo* (broth) of the *cocido* from a silver tureen, and also enjoy finger sandwiches, canapés, cold cuts, pastries, cocktails, or coffee. Closed Sunday and holiday evenings and the month of August. Reservations essential for the private dining rooms. Carrera de San Jerónimo (phone: 521-3385). Expensive.

O'Pazo – The morning catch from the Cantabrian Sea — lobster, hake, turbot, endemic sea bass, and varieties of shellfish — is flown in wiggling fresh and prepared with loving care to delight the clientele, who fill the place for both lunch and dinner. Closed Sundays and August. Reservations advised. 20 Calle Reina Mercedes (phone: 253-2333). Expensive.

Platerías – Its intimate low-key elegance in the heart of Old Madrid creates a pleasant atmosphere for enjoying authentic Spanish dishes, such as *callos madrileños* (succulent tripe, Madrid style), *chipirones* (cuttlefish in its own ink), and remarkable vegetable plates. Closed Sundays. Reservations advised. 11 Plaza Santa Ana (phone: 429-7048). Expensive.

Príncipe de Viana – Fine seasonal Basque-Navarrese specialties are served in a relaxed, elegant atmosphere. Closed Saturdays for lunch, Sundays, and from mid-August through the first week of September. Reservations advised. 5 Calle Manuel de Falla (phone: 259-1448). Expensive.

La Trainera – Another favorite of seafood lovers. The owner prizes his flown-in catch and serves fish and shellfish as nature intended. No fishing village in the world can compete with the grilled sole served here. Reservations advised. Closed Sundays and August. Reservations advised. 60 Calle Lagasca (phone: 276-8035). Expensive.

Café de Oriente – Anything from *tapas* to French haute cuisine can be enjoyed here in a delightful *madrileño* atmosphere. It is an ideal place for afternoon tea or cocktails at a sidewalk table overlooking the square and the Royal Palace or inside the café (reservations unnecessary); for fine Castilian dining downstairs in the vaulted 17th-century Sala Capitular de San Gil (reservations advised); or for superb French-Basque cuisine in the adjacent restaurant (reservations advised) or one of the private dining rooms frequented by royalty and diplomats (reservations essential). Closed Mondays for lunch, Sundays, and August. 2 Plaza de Oriente (phone: 247-1564). Expensive to moderate.

El Abanico Gastronómico – The "Gastronomic Fan" is a combination restaurant and food shop located within the *Mercado de Puerta Toledo* (see *Special Places*). Regional cuisines, wines, and delicacies from all over Spain are the stock in trade. Open from 11:30 AM to midnight; closed Mondays. Reservations unnecessary. 1 Ronda de Toledo (phone: 276-0009). Moderate.

Antigua Casa Sobrino de Botín – Also known as *Casa Botín*, this is one of Madrid's oldest restaurants — founded in 1725. It is famous for its Castilian-style roast suckling pig and baby lamb, one of which is usually featured on the *menú del día*. Lunch and dinner each seem to fall into two "shifts," with the early-eating tourists first, followed by *madrileños*, whose normal dining hours are after 2 and 9 PM, respectively. Open daily. Reservations unnecessary. 17 Calle Cuchilleros (phone: 266-4217). Moderate.

Café Gijón – This 100-year-old Madrid institution is a traditional meeting and greeting place for intellectuals and artists, who gather here to enjoy good food and conversation. During the summer, the sidewalk café is one of the city's liveliest. Open daily. No reservations. 21 Paseo de Recoletos (phone: 532-5425). Moderate.

El Callejón – A bust of Hemingway and walls chockablock with celebrity photos attest to those who have enjoyed the friendly atmosphere and home-cooked food here in the past. An informal Old Madrid place, it serves a different regional specialty each day of the week, but *callos madrileños* is always on the menu, and *tapas* abound. Open daily. Reservations unnecessary. 6 Calle Ternera (phone: 531-9195). Moderate.

Casa Lucio – This casual restaurant has become an institution among the elite (and that includes members of the royal family), who enjoy fine Spanish food — especially seafood. Its location in Old Madrid adds to the flavor. Closed Saturdays for lunch and during August. Reservations essential. 35 Calle Cava Baja (phone: 265-3252). Moderate.

Casa Paco – The steaks served in this old tavern are excellent. Other specialties include typical *madrileño* dishes. Closed Sundays and August. No reservations. 11 Calle Puerta Cerrada (phone: 266-3166). Moderate.

La Chata – This totally typical *mesón* bears the nickname of Madrid's adored Infanta Isabel (the only child of Queen Isabel II), who is depicted on the wonderful hand-painted tile façade by artist Eduardo Fernández. Delicious morsels are served at the *tapas* bar, and the small restaurant specializes in roast suckling pig and lamb dishes. Closed Sunday evenings and Wednesdays. No reservations. 25 Calle Cava Baja (phone: 266-1458). Moderate.

El Cuchi – The Spanish link of Mexico's famous *Carlos 'n' Charlie's* chain, with specialties of both worlds served by a gregarious staff. It's casual, and jammed with humorous paraphernalia. One of its claims to fame: "Hemingway never ate here." Open daily. Reservations unnecessary. 3 Calle Cuchilleros (phone: 255-4424). Moderate.

El Estragón Tropical – Imaginative French-Caribbean cooking and exotic fresh fruit drinks are served at this casual and congenial place on one of Madrid's oldest and most characteristic squares. Pleasant decor combines old Spanish tilework with parrot and other tropical motifs. Closed Mondays and for dinner on Sundays and holidays. Reservations unnecessary. 12 Plaza de la Paja (phone: 266-0634). Moderate.

Los Galayos – A typical tavern serving fine Castilian roast suckling pig and lamb, with a *tapas* bar and an outdoor café right alongside the Plaza Mayor. Open daily. Reservations unnecessary. 1 Plaza Mayor (phone: 265-6222). Moderate.

La Galette – Outstanding vegetarian and non-vegetarian dishes and Viennese pastries are served in a delightful atmosphere at a good location in the elegant Salamanca district. Its popularity makes reservations essential. Closed Sundays. 11 Calle Conde de Aranda (phone: 276-0641). Moderate.

El Ingenio – This unpretentious, family-run restaurant is decorated with Don Quixote and Sancho Panza memorabilia, and its menu delights diners who fall into either category of physique. The seafood is impeccably fresh since it is flown in from the Bay of Biscay, and the pork, lamb, and beef are all locally farm-grown. Closed Sundays and holidays. Reservations unnecessary. Just off the Plaza de España at 10 Calle Leganitos (phone: 541-9133). Moderate.

La Maestranza – Andalusian in its cooking, atmosphere, and decor, with great *sevillanas* music groups playing for professional dancers and the customers who know this Andalusian folk dance, which has become Madrid's latest rage. Closed Sundays. Reservations advised. 16 Calle Mauricio Legendre (phone: 315-9059). Moderate.

El Mentidero de la Villa – Inventive French cuisine by Japanese chef Ken Sato, in a delightful modern-art decor. Specialties include *rollo de primavera con puerros y gambas* (spring rolls with leeks and shrimp). Closed Sundays. Reservations advised. 6 Calle Santo Tomé (phone: 308-1285). Moderate.

La Mesa Redonda – A small eatery on one of Old Madrid's most charming little streets. Its American owners serve the best *Thanksgiving* dinner in town. Other specialties include beef bourguignon and stews. Dinner only; closed Sundays. Reservations unnecessary (except for *Thanksgiving*). 17 Calle Nuncio (phone: 265-0289). Moderate.

La Plaza – Within the sparkling new *Galería del Prado* at the *Palace* hotel, amid the exquisite boutiques and galleries, this combination buffet-style and self-service restaurant dispenses enticing salads, entrées, and pastries. Serve yourself a multi-course meal or just a snack, to eat in a choice of surrounding settings. The adjacent bar serves cocktails and coffee. Closed Sundays. No reservations. 7 Plaza de las Cortes (phone: 429-7551). Moderate.

Posada de la Villa – Although the 3-story building is relatively new, this authentic eatery dates back to 1642, when it was originally a posada (inn) for out-of-towners.

It has retained its tradition of hospitality and still offers fine typical dishes such as *cocido madrileño* and roast pig and lamb. Closed Sunday evenings. Reservations unnecessary. 9 Calle Cava Baja (phone: 266-1860). Moderate.

La Quinta del Sordo – The façade of this award-winning restaurant is adorned with fine hand-painted tile mosaics. Its name means "house of the deaf man," referring to the place where Goya lived in Madrid. Reproductions of Goya art and memorabilia add to the decor. An array of fine Castilian dishes offers memorable dining in a pleasant atmosphere. Closed Sunday evenings. Reservations unnecessary. 10 Calle Sacramento (phone: 248-1852). Moderate.

Riazor – An unpretentious turn-of-the-century establishment with a cordial atmosphere, fine traditional fare, and a cornucopia of hot and cold *tapas* served with verve at the bar. The upstairs dining room has panels adjustable to fit a size range of banquet parties. Open daily. Reservations unnecessary, except for groups. Located 1 short block south of Plaza Mayor at 19 Calle Toledo (phone: 266-5466). Moderate.

Taberna del Alabardero – A Madrid classic, this was the tavern of the Royal Palace guards (*alabardero* means "halberdier," or a soldier armed with a halberd — a 15th- and 16th-century weapon combining a pike and an ax). There is a wonderful *tapas* bar, and succulent Spanish and Basque dishes are served in cozy dining rooms reminiscent of 19th-century Madrid. Open for lunch and dinner daily. Reservations unnecessary. (Father Lezama, the famous and popular Basque priest-restaurateur-owner, also has a version of this restaurant in Washington, DC.) 6 Calle Felipe V (phone: 541-5192). Moderate.

Foster's Hollywood – It's a *restaurante americano*, complete with a variety of hamburgers and barbecued spare ribs. But far from being a *yanqui* fast-food joint, this small chain of pleasant restaurants offers good service and atmosphere. No reservations. Several locations: 1 Calle Magallanes (phone: 488-9165); 3 Calle Apolonio Morales (phone: 457-7911); 1 Calle Tamayo y Baus (phone: 231-5115); 16 Calle del Cristo (phone: 638-6791); 14-16 Avenida de Brasil (phone: 455-1688); 80 Calle Velázquez (phone: 435-6128); and 100 Calle Guzmán el Bueno (phone: 234-4923). Inexpensive.

El Granero de Lavapiés – Good vegetarian food in one of Old Madrid's most typical neighborhoods. No reservations. 10 Calle Argumosa (phone: 467-7611). Inexpensive.

Mesón Museo del Jamón – Any restaurant with 4,000 hams dangling from its ceiling and draping its walls deserves the name "Ham Museum," and there are four such pork paradises in central Madrid. Fine hams from the regions of Jabugo, Murcia, Salamanca, and Extremadura are served in various ways, including sandwiches, at the stand-up bars and at dining tables. Also featured are an array of cheeses, a great deli, and roast chicken. Any dish can also be prepared to take out. No reservations. 6 Carrera San Jerónimo (phone: 521-0340); 72 Gran Vía (phone: 541-2023); 44 Paseo del Prado (phone: 230-4385); and 54 Calle Atocha (phone: 227-0716). Inexpensive.

La Salsería – Befitting its name, this small bar with an outdoor café specializes in sauces — 15 kinds, served in the holes of a conveniently held artist's palette, in the center of which are ruffled fried potatoes for dipping. Try *spaghetti a la siciliana* as well. Closed Mondays. No reservations. Across the traffic circle from the Mercado Puerta de Toledo. 2 Calle Ronda de Toledo (phone: 266-0890). Inexpensive.

Taberna de Antonio Sánchez – Genuinely typical of Old Madrid, it has been a venerated favorite ever since it was founded by a legendary bullfighter more than 150 years ago. The small, unpretentious dining rooms are charming, the realm of wonderful food — seafood, Spanish cuisine, salads, and desserts — served with care. Closed Sunday evenings. No reservations. 13 Calle Mesón de Paredes (phone: 239-7826). Inexpensive.

 TAPAS BARS: The uniquely Spanish snacks known as *tapas* probably originated in Seville, when a slice of ham or a piece of bread was discovered to be a convenient *tapa* (lid) to keep flies out of a glass of wine. Today, the drink departs little from the time-tested standard, but the inventiveness of the Spanish chef knows no bounds when it comes to *tapas*. The definition embraces everything from a little plate of green olives through an array of cheeses, sausages, hams, seafood, eggs, and vegetables that have been sliced, diced, wrapped, filled, marinated, sauced, sautéed, or otherwise cooked for hot or cold consumption, to a variety of tidbits swallowed raw and naked as nature made them. *El tapeo* (enjoying *tapas*) is a way of life in Spain, especially in Madrid, where there are literally thousands of places to do so. Practically every bar (not to be confused with pubs or *bares americanos,* which are for drinks only) serves *tapas,* as do *tabernas, mesones, tascas, cervecerías,* and even *cafeterías.* And most establishments specializing in *tapas* also have a few tables or even dining rooms in addition to their stand-up bar. Toothpicks and fingers are the most common utensils; shrimp, langostine, mussel, and clam shells, olive pits, napkins, and almost everything else are dropped on the floor, which is swept and scoured after each surge (from 1 to 3 PM and 7 to 9 PM, more or less — usually more).

A *chato* (glass of wine) or *caña* (draft beer) customarily is served with a free *tapita.* If you want more and if the vast array of *tapas* on display is overwhelming, just point to what you want. If you prefer a larger portion, ask for a *ración,* which can be a small meal in itself. Don't pay until you've completely finished; the bartender probably will remember everything you consumed, even if you don't. He'll deliver your change on a saucer; leave a few *duros* (5-peseta coins) as a tip, and always say *gracias* and *adios* when you depart.

Tapas bar hopping is at its best in the central and old sections of Madrid. One of the city's best is *La Trucha* (with two locations, both just off Plaza Santa Ana: 3 Calle Manuel Fernández y González; phone: 259-1448; and 6 Calle Nuñez de Arce; phone: 532-0882). They're jammed at *tapa* time, and with good reason: Everything from bull tails to succulent red pimentos, as well as *trucha* (trout), is served with gusto (closed Sunday nights, and they take turns for July and August vacations). Nearby, the *Cervecería Alemana* (6 Plaza Santa Ana; phone: 429-7033) is, despite its name ("German Beer Parlor"), thoroughly *madrileño,* which is why the ubiquitous Hemingway frequented it and artists, intellectuals, and students continue to flock here. Among the *tapas* are good hams, sausages, and cheeses (closed Tuesdays and August). Around Puerta del Sol are *Casa Labra* (12 Calle Tetuán; phone: 532-1405), which was founded in 1860 and has been jam-packed ever since — among the specialties is fluff-fried *bacalao* (cod) that melts in the mouth, and *Mejillonería El Pasaje* (3 Pasaje de Matheu; phone: 521-5155), which deals in mussels exclusively, fresh from Galicia, served in any quantity, and prepared in various delicious ways. *La Torre del Oro* (26 Plaza Mayor; phone: 266-5016) is a lively Andalusian bar appropriately decorated with stunning bullfight photos and memorabilia (including a mounted earless bull's head), with recorded *sevillanas* music adding to the ambience; the *tapas* include such delicacies as baby eels and fresh anchovies, fried or marinated. In the same vicinity, *Valle del Tietar* (5 Calle Ciudad Rodrigo; phone: 248-0511), in the northwest arcade entrance to the plaza, offers *tapas,* Avila style, with suckling pig and kid specialties, while *El Oso y el Madroño* (4 Calle de la Bolsa; phone: 532-1377) is as *madrileño* as its name, which refers to the "bear and the madrona tree" on the city's coat of arms; the nonstop hand-cranked hurdy-gurdy and jovial local clientele make for authentic atmosphere. *El Shotis* (11 Calle Cava Baja; phone: 265-3230) is south of Plaza Mayor. Named after Madrid's traditional 19th-century couple dance (which you'll hear playing on the jukebox, this unpretentious tavern is as typical as can be (closed Mondays and August). Elsewhere, there's *Monje Cervecería* (21 Calle del Arenal; phone: 248-3598), a showcase of fresh seafood, and lamb sweetbreads as well, and *La Mi Venta* (7 Plaza Marina Española; phone: 248-5091), where a friendly neighborhood atmosphere prevails and fine hot and cold *tapas* and *raciones* are served, with select hams as the specialty. At *Bocaito* (6 Calle Libertad; phone: 532-1219), north of the Gran Vía and Calle de Alcalá, animated *tapas* makers behind the bar prepare a limitless selection of outstanding treats, and giant Talavera ceramic plates on the walls are painted with fine reproductions of Goya's "Wine Harvest." Adjacent is a deli and small dining room with communal tables.

PAMPLONA

The ultimate expression of Pamplona's gusto is the renowned *Fiesta de San Fermín,* held annually from July 6 through 14 in honor of the city's native-born patron saint, who was martyred in 287. Without any doubt it is Spain's wildest and wackiest event, highlighted by the famous *encierros,* or "running of the bulls" through the town streets, and by attendant nonstop revelry. The fiesta, also known as the *Festival de los Sanfermines,* originated in the 17th century and was immortalized by Ernest Hemingway in his first novel, *The Sun also Rises* (known as *Fiesta* in Spain), a story of 1920s expatriates who come to Pamplona from Paris for the party. The book's vivid descriptions have drawn millions to the city over the years, and in deference to his place in the fortunes of the city, there is a statue of the writer on Paseo Hemingway, next to the *Plaza de Toros.*

Pamplona, capital of the ancient Pyrenean kingdom of Navarre, got its name from the Roman general Pompey, who camped here with his troops on a hillside above the Arga River in the winter of 75–74 BC. Long known as the Gateway to Spain, because it lies at the junction of two mountain passes through the Pyrenees from France, the city now serves as the capital of the region of Navarre, one of Spain's 17 autonomous communities, and has grown beyond the core of the Old Town and its massive fortress walls.

The city was occupied by the Visigoths in the 5th century, by the Franks in the 6th century, and by the Moors in the 8th century. The Basques, with the help of Charlemagne, drove the Moors out in 750. Charlemagne remained, however, and soon after he sacked the city and tore down its defensive walls. In an act of patriotic revenge, Basque forces annihilated the rear guard of Charlemagne's army, led by the legendary Roland, in the Roncesvalles Pass in 778, an event later romanticized in the epic poem *Song of Roland.* Sancho III of Navarre made the city the capital of his kingdom in the year 1000, and so it remained until 1512, when the forces of King Ferdinand and Queen Isabella destroyed a second set of walls and occupied the city in the process of annexing Navarre to Castile. In the same century, during a battle to recapture the city, a young army captain named Iñigo López de Loyola (who ultimately became known to the world as St. Ignatius of Loyola) was seriously wounded and endured a lengthy convalescence here. He began to study religion, and in the 1530s founded the Society of Jesus, the Catholic religious order whose members are called Jesuits. Still later in the century, Philip II began a third set of walls, turning Pamplona into the most heavily fortified city in northern Spain.

Today, visitors put on their walking shoes and meander through the cobblestone streets of the old section of the city — "the palpitating heart of Pamplona" — as they call it, still partly surrounded by the historic fortress walls and filled with old noble mansions, convents, and churches. The central point of the town is the Plaza del Castillo, which offers a suggestion of Pamplona's somewhat confusing diversity of architectural styles. Fascist classic, Art Nouveau, and chrome and glass mix; arcades only make it partway around the plaza, and streets enter at odd, irregular angles. The lack of architectural consistency carries over to the city's churches. The mostly Gothic cathedral bears an unusual classical Greco-Roman façade of the baroque era; the church of San Saturnino, a former fortress, is a composite of Gothic and Romanesque; while the exterior of the Church of San Nicolás is that of a medieval castle with Gothic embellishments.

What is consistent, however, is the strong bond among the people of Pamplona, and their independent spirit. When Charlemagne came down from the north to drive out the Moors, the *pamplonicos* welcomed him with open arms as a liberator, but when his desire to be a conqueror revealed itself, they quickly changed their attitude toward him. It also was in Pamplona that the Fueros, a bill of rights similar to the Magna Carta, was signed in the 13th century, guaranteeing the people of Navarre independence from Castilian monarchs, and imposing a system of justice that is still practiced today.

Neighbors of the strongly separatist Basque Country, the *pamplonicos* nonetheless maintain a tolerance for political and cultural differences. They also balance hard work with hard play. Economically, Navarre is one of the most industrious and affluent of Spanish regions, yet most business-oriented residents of the city participate in entertainment, dance, and other elements of the typical Spanish lifestyle. Culturally, Pamplona is the home of the University of Navarre, as well as various other professional and private institutes and schools. *Pamplonicos* are generally warm, friendly people who, like their city, are cordial and hospitable to visitors.

PAMPLONA AT-A-GLANCE

SEEING THE CITY: The most spectacular view of Pamplona is from the roads descending the Pyrenees over the Roncesvalles and Puerto de Velate passes from France. As you approach the city limits, the fortress walls rise powerfully over the hilltop city and are topped by the spires of the cathedral and the clustered Old Town. The wide green belt of parks, gardens, and tree-lined avenues that surrounds the Old Town adds contrast, making the immense walls appear even more spectacular.

SPECIAL PLACES: Pamplona is composed of an Old Town surrounded by modern suburbs. Just about everything a visitor will want to see is located in the old section, which is a compact area of extremely narrow, picturesque streets that can be traversed on foot in less than 15 minutes. It's best to park your car on one of the streets surrounding it, preferably around the shaded bullring, near the Plaza del Castillo, and walk. Pamplona's modern suburbs, more than mere residential areas, are centers of life complete with bars, restaurants, shops, nightclubs, and discotheques. The suburb of San Juan, west of the Old Town, is considered the most desirable place to live.

Plaza del Castillo – An elegant, arcaded square, shaded by the intertwining boughs of carefully pruned trees. At the southwest corner of the plaza is the Palacio de la Diputación Foral. Built in 1847 and enlarged in 1932, it is the seat of the regional government (open to the public, but because it is a working building, the timetable for visits is variable; no admission charge). The tree-lined Paseo de Sarasate, Pamplona's main promenade, begins at the south end of the plaza and runs past the Monumento de los Fueros, commemorating the region's 13th-century bill of rights.

Cathedral – Pamplona's cathedral stands at the northern tip of the Old Town, hard against the ramparts. Built on the foundations of a 12th-century Romanesque church, it is basically 14th- and 15th-century Gothic, but it has a west façade that is a baroque, Greco-Roman fantasy. The work of architect Ventura Rodríguez, this was constructed over the original Gothic portals in the late 18th century. The effect of stepping through a baroque façade to find a soaring Gothic church on the inside is strange, to say the least. The major work in the otherwise bare cathedral is the alabaster tomb of King Carlos III, the founder of the cathedral, and his wife, Queen Leonor of Castile — a 15th-century Flemish work carved with figures of the couple and a relief of hooded men and lamenting women. Besides various chapels and altarpieces (the 15th-century altarpiece in the ambulatory chapel is notable), there is a beautiful Gothic cloister, with lacelike stonework over the arches and delicately carved doorways. The 14th-century Puerta Preciosa (Precious Doorway), on the cloister's south side, has a tympanum carved with scenes of the life of the Virgin. The *Diocesan Museum,* housed in the former monks' kitchen and refectory, contains polychrome sculptures of sacred figures and other religious relics. The cathedral is open daily from 10:30 AM to 1:30 PM and from 4 to 7 PM; the museum is open daily, May through September only, from 10:30 AM to 1:30 PM; admission charge to the museum. Plaza de la Catedral.

Ayuntamiento (Town Hall) – This stunningly ornate baroque building is noted for its 18th-century façade topped with allegorical statues. Not open to the public. Plaza Consistorial.

San Saturnino – A block away from the Town Hall, this 12th-century Romanesque church, extended by 13th-century Gothic additions, was constructed within former city fortifications, two defensive towers of which were converted into bell towers. The beautiful main portal is decorated with Gothic arches supported by columns whose capitals are embellished with scenes from the childhood of Christ and the Passion. Inside, notice the dark stained glass windows, as well as the dome, more becoming to an American state capitol, which provides the only light. Open daily, from 8 AM to 1 PM and from 4:30 to 7 PM. Calle Mayor.

San Nicolás – At the edge of the Old Town, this 13th-century, partly Romanesque church looks more like a fortified castle, complete with tower and fortress walls. The tower now has a spire on one of its corners, and the fortress walls have Gothic flourishes. The interior resembles a castle throne room, with wooden floors and starkly bare walls, but a few altars are worthy of closer inspection. Open daily, from 8 AM to 1 PM and from 4:30 to 7 PM. 10 Paseo de Sarasate.

San Lorenzo – Beside the Parque de la Taconera (Taconera Park), this church is home to the heart and soul of Pamplona — the baroque chapel of San Fermín, the town's patron saint. Unfortunately, the quarters for this soul are relatively soulless, and the chapel is, indeed, the only reason to visit. The statue of the saint that is paraded through town on the first day of the renowned *Fiesta de San Fermín* is positioned in the chapel under a marble pavilion. Open daily, from 8 AM to 1 PM and from 4 to 8 PM. Corner of Calle Mayor and Calle Taconera.

Museo de Navarra – The 16th-century Hospital de la Misericórdia once occupied this site and its Plateresque portal remains. Among the region's artistic treasures housed here, in recently renovated quarters, are Roman mosaics, capitals from Pamplona's long-gone 12th-century Romanesque cathedral, paintings from the Gothic through the Renaissance periods, murals, a Goya portrait of the *Marqués de San Adrián* that is considered one of the painter's finest works, and luxurious 19th-century furniture. An 11th-century Moorish ivory casket consisting of 19 ivory plaques adorned with scenes from the lives of the caliphs is among the more interesting pieces. Open Tuesdays through Sundays, from 10 AM to 2 PM. Admission charge. Calle Santo Domingo.

SOURCES AND RESOURCES

TOURIST INFORMATION: The tourist information office (3 Calle Duque de Ahumada; phone: 220741) is just off Plaza del Castillo. English-speaking personnel can supply maps of the city, booklets, and brochures, including one with some interesting regional history and folklore. The office can also help with hotel reservations; local train and bus schedules are posted. Open daily from April through September, 9 AM to 9 PM. The rest of the year, open Mondays through Fridays from 9 AM to 2 PM and from 4 to 7 PM, Saturdays from 9 AM to 2 PM; closed Sundays.

Local Coverage – The *Diario de Navarra* discusses local and regional events.

TELEPHONE: The city code for Pamplona is 48. If calling from within Spain, dial 948 before the local number.

GETTING AROUND: Airport – The Noaín airport is 3 miles (5 km) south of town via the N121 highway toward Zaragoza. A taxi from the airport to virtually anywhere in Pamplona costs from about $5 to $7. There is daily direct air service to Madrid and Barcelona. The airport (phone: 317202) will provide information.

Bus – An excellent city bus system crosses the town and all areas of interest, including the out-of-the-way train station (take bus No. 9). Buses to Roncesvalles, Burguete, and Estella depart daily before 7 AM from the main station for long-distance buses, Estación de Autobuses de Pamplona, 2 Calle Conde Oliveto (phone: 111531).

Car Rental – *Hertz* (in the *Tres Reyes* hotel, Calle Jardines de la Taconera; phone: 223569; and at the airport; phone: 318255); *Avis* (5 Calle Iturralde; phone: 243896).

Train – Pamplona is on the main line connecting San Sebastián, Zaragoza, and Barcelona, with service twice daily in both directions. The train station (phone: 250246) is on Calle Rochapea, 1½ miles (2 km) from the center of town. To reach it, take the No. 9 bus, which runs every 15 minutes from Paseo de Sarasate. A taxi will cost about $3. There is a *RENFE* ticket office (8 Calle Estella; phone: 222429).

SPECIAL EVENTS: The *Fiesta de San Fermín* takes place annually from July 6 through 14 and is Pamplona's claim to fame. Popularized by Ernest Hemingway in *The Sun Also Rises,* the festival (aka the *Festival de los Sanfermines*) was also extensively described in *The Drifters* by James Michener. This 24-hour-a-day party reaches the intensity levels of a mystical experience, or a Keystone Cops movie, depending on one's orientation. The fun begins at noon on the 6th, when a bottle of champagne is uncorked at the Town Hall — the opening shot of a day full of ceremony, pageantry, and parades including one to the Chapel of San Fermín in San Lorenzo. The first running of the bulls (*encierro*) from the bull corral by the river to the bullring takes place at 8 AM the next morning (July 7), and the bulls are then run every morning through July 14; every evening at 6:30 PM bullfights take place in the *Plaza de Toros* bullring. Hundreds of brave and/or crazy men run in front of the bulls each morning in the traditional costume of white shirt and pants, red beret, bandanna, sash, and a rolled-up newspaper. Women are prohibited from participation, and those who attempt it are physically rebuffed. Still, a couple of determined women were among those injured during the 1990 runnings.

The route from the bull corral to the bullring is 1.8 miles. At 8 AM, a *chupinazo,* or signal rocket, is launched as a warning to the participants, most of whom immediately start to run. Seconds later, another rocket is launched, signaling the release of the bulls and the start of the *encierro.* If the bulls are not in a tight herd, a third rocket is fired to warn the runners of a separated or stray bull, more dangerous because it is overly excited, disoriented, or on the rampage. The six bulls that are run each morning are outstanding specimens, the same that appear — once they've caught their breath — in the ring at the afternoon bullfights. For the running, they are accompanied by a small herd of calves and steers to help keep them bunched up and, therefore, a bit less dangerous.

The side streets along the course over which this mad, run-for-your-life dash takes place are planked up, funneling both runners and bulls from the corral to the ring. The smarter runners plot out every step of the route so that when the bulls catch up, they know where to find shelter. Some just make a mad dash for the bullring in a desperate attempt to outrun the bulls. Santo Domingo, the street leading from the corral, is filled with such seasoned veterans; some bait the bulls and even run toward them! Santo Domingo leads toward Plaza Consistorial and into Doña Blanca de Navarra, a treacherous *S* curve with few places to hide. Estafeta (Suicide Alley), a long and narrow canyon, follows (fraught with peril because of the squeeze), leading to the Paseo Hemingway and the ramp into the bullring. Vantage points for spectators are hard to obtain after about 7 AM, by which time the route is thoroughly jammed.

The *encierro* lasts only a few minutes. Once the bulls reach the ring, they are quickly penned, although the festivities continue inside the ring as the runners and other amateur matadors (equipped with blankets, sheets, newspapers, and other homemade capes) do "battle" with the assorted escort calves and steers. Despite all the fun, the element of risk is always present; serious injuries and even fatalities are not uncommon.

At 6:30 PM, the bullfights begin, with the bravest bulls (possibly even angrier than usual because of the morning's trauma), some of Spain's best matadors, and high-level enthusiasm from one of the rowdiest crowds in the country. For many spectators, the real show is not the bullfights but the antics of the *peñas* in the stands, who spend the entire time spraying each other with champagne, flour, powdered sugar, and *sangría.* Tickets for the bullfights are sold almost a year in advance, but 10% are held back and sold at the bullring each evening for the next day's fights. Get in line at about 5 PM if you hope to get one of these tickets; otherwise, deal with the dozens of scalpers who ring the arena each afternoon.

Hotel space is a virtual impossibility for foreigners during *San Fermín.* The tourist office will arrange accommodations with local families; many of these are excellent bargains. For those interested in participating in the bull run, it's a good idea to get friendly with someone who has been through the routine previously. Take a few minutes to discuss the run with a seasoned veteran and decide upon a strategy. Americans tend to congregate at the *Bar Txoco* in Plaza del Castillo (on the corner nearest the bullring) and at the *Windsor Pub* in front of *La Perla* hotel (see *Checking In*). Local officials are inclined to discourage foreigners from participating in the *encierro,* because (they say) they can't run fast enough and usually get run over by the bulls or the other runners. Postcards and photos posted throughout the town showing gory scenes of bull's horns sticking through runners are usually enough to dissuade foreigners with only a casual interest in participating. Many who simply wish to watch the festivities are encouraged to make arrangements to see it from the balcony of a pension or a private house, or to watch it on television (the runs are broadcast daily throughout Spain).

Additional *San Fermín* festivities are focused in the Old Town, including parades of papier-mâché giants and bands from Pamplona and neighboring towns. Bars remain packed throughout the day and night. The only lull takes place between noon and 5 PM, when the hot sun makes wandering through the streets uncomfortable. This afternoon respite also serves as a time to recharge for the late-night partying that awaits.

SHOPPING: With the exception of leather wineskins, which are sold in every shop in town, Pamplona is not noted for any particular locally made products. There is, however, a Pamplona food specialty — coffee-, vanilla-, and milk-flavored toffees called *pastillas.* There also is an anise-flavored Basque liqueur, *pacharán,* that is worth a try. A top brand is Exteko, which comes in a black bottle. Pamplona has only one department store, *Unzu,* located in the center of town (7 Calle Mercaderes). The store is well stocked, and prices are somewhat lower than those of the boutiques surrounding it. The most fashionable, newest, and most spacious shops are in Pamplona's New Town, off Avenida Carlos III. The Old Town area just to the west of the Plaza del Castillo, on Calles San Nicolás, San Miguel, Comedias, and Zapatería, is another shopping district, but the shops — selling everything from perfume, shoes, dresses, shirts, and watches to cosmetics, candy, linen, yarn, and yard goods — are smaller and more pedestrian. General shopping hours are from 9:30 AM to 1:30 PM and from 4:30 to 7 PM, but may vary from shop to shop.

Casa Azagra – The choice for pure saffron. 56 Calle Zapatería (phone: 222355).

Cristal – Trendy fashions in bright colors and at reasonable prices. 37 Calle Castillo de Maya (phone: 240542).

María Alonzo – Women's European designer fashions. 22 Calle Gorriti (phone: 238871).

SPORTS AND FITNESS: Among the most popular sports is jai alai, a form of *pelota,* played in *frontóns,* or courts, throughout the region. Mountaineering and cycling also are widely practiced in the area.

Fishing – The rivers around Pamplona and the outlying areas boast an abundance of salmon, trout, barbel, tench, carp, eels, and freshwater crabs. Be sure to check on any local or seasonal regulations before casting.

Golf – The 9-hole *Club de Golf Ulzama* course is located in the town of Guerendian, in the Ulzama Valley, 13 miles (21 km) south of Pamplona. Call for information on tee times and greens fees (phone: 313162).

Jogging – The best area for jogging in Pamplona is around the city walls in the vicinity of the cathedral.

Swimming – Pamplona's most popular public swimming spot is the municipal pool at *Aranzadi,* just north of the city walls (open daily, June through September, from 10:30 AM to 9 PM; admission charge). The *Tres Reyes* hotel (see *Checking In*) has a heated pool for the use of guests.

THEATER: There is no major resident theater company in Pamplona. The Escuela Navarra de Teatro (5 Calle San Agustín; phone: 229239) is a theater school that stages various performances and occasionally hosts visits by theater companies from Barcelona and Madrid. Almost all performances are in Spanish.

NIGHTCLUBS AND NIGHTLIFE: Pamplona has some of the most active nightlife in Spain, centered around the city's many bars. At about 7 PM, the citizenry empties into the streets for the evening *paseo* (stroll). Soon after, everyone converges on the bars for *tapas,* and children joyfully play around sidewalk café tables. This camaraderie continues until approximately 10 PM, when many head off for dinner, and then picks up again around midnight. Weeknights are naturally much quieter than weekends; on Saturday nights, bars, cafés, and discotheques stay packed until the wee hours.

The most popular discos are in the San Juan district, just outside the Old Town walls. Try *Reverendos* (5 Calle Monasterio de Velate), a private club that will admit anyone dressed in the latest trend, or *Más y Más* (Avenida Bayona), another favorite. *O.N.B.* (outside San Juan on Calle Abejeras) is a dual disco with rooms for both trendy young people and single professionals. Two top San Juan district pubs are the *Opera* and *Baby* (the latter is an abbreviation of its longer name — *Conocerte es Amarte Baby* — "To Know You Is to Love You, Baby"). For live music, try the *Boulevard Jazz Bar* (6 Plaza Reyes de Navarra), around the corner from the *Ciudad de Pamplona* hotel.

BEST IN TOWN

CHECKING IN: For a thriving industrial town, Pamplona has very few hotels. Note that during the *Fiesta de San Fermín,* hotels are allowed to double their normal high-season rates, which can make a stay a very expensive proposition. Many families rent space in their homes at this time — ask at the tourist office about such accommodations. Normally, expect to pay $90 or more for a double room in a hotel listed as expensive, $55 to $85 for a room in a hotel listed as moderate, and $50 or less in an inexpensive one. All telephone numbers are in the 48 city code unless otherwise indicated.

Tres Reyes – The best Pamplona has to offer, set in a park between the Old Town and the San Juan district. All 168 rooms are air conditioned and comfortable. There is also a heated swimming pool and a good restaurant, and the service is excellent. Perfect for shelter from the storm of *San Fermín,* but be prepared to pay for it. Jardines de la Taconera (phone: 226600). Expensive.

Ciudad de Pamplona – One of Pamplona's newer hotels, this modern establishment with 117 rooms has all the amenities, but its distance — a 25-minute walk from the center of town — is too far out of the way for easy exploring. 21 Calle Iturrama (phone: 266011). Moderate.

Nuevo Maisonnave – A traditional favorite, offering 152 comfortable rooms, centrally located in the Old Town on a quiet street (one that remains relatively quiet even during *San Fermín*). This place is similar to the *Tres Reyes* but lacks its pool and some of its amenities. Air conditioning is limited to the public rooms. 20 Calle Nueva (phone: 222600). Moderate.

Orhi – Located across from the Plaza de Toros, this smaller, 55-room hotel is a 5-minute walk from the Plaza del Castillo. 7 Calle Leyre (phone: 228500). Moderate.

La Perla – On the Plaza del Castillo, this 67-room hostelry is a favorite during *San Fermín* as it overlooks Calle Estafeta, the longest straightaway of the *encierro.* Unfortunately, it offers little else. 1 Plaza del Castillo (phone: 227704). Moderate.

Yoldi – The 48 rooms here are modern and comfortable. For years, this establishment has been the choice of visiting matadors, and it is the place where all the aficionados gather to discuss the bullfights during *San Fermín.* Located on a quiet street, a short walk from the bullring and the Plaza del Castillo. 11 Avenida San Ignacio (phone: 224800). Moderate.

Eslava – A small, old, 28-room hotel in the Old Town. The rustic wood-beamed rooms all have private baths. Some offer beautiful views over the city walls and into the valley beyond. 7 Plaza Virgen de la O (phone: 222270). Inexpensive.

EATING OUT: Pamplona is not a diner's paradise, but it does offer some interesting dishes that combine the heartiness of the mountains with the traditional fare of northern Spain. The local cuisine is Basque, which means plenty of grilled meats, stews, and fresh fish from nearby mountain streams and the Atlantic. Favorites include local *trucha* (trout), cooked and served whole with a slice of salty smoked ham slotted into it; and *merluza* (hake). Lamb might be baked in a wood-fired oven, chopped up and soaked in a sauce, or served simply as chops. During *San Fermín,* the bulls killed in the previous day's fights are served up in a wonderful stew. Dinner for two, including wine, will cost $60 or more in restaurants listed as expensive, $30 to $60 at restaurants listed as moderate, and $25 or less at inexpensive ones. All phone numbers are in the 48 city code unless otherwise indicated.

Europa – An opulent dining room, considered the home of nouvelle cuisine in Pamplona, as well as of excellent roquefort filet steaks. Closed Sundays. Reservations necessary, especially during *San Fermín.* 11 Calle Espoz y Mina (phone: 221800). Expensive.

Hartza – One of two restaurants in Pamplona boasting a Michelin star. It offers traditional regional food, including fish, game, wild mushrooms, and fresh seasonal produce. Try the *merluza de la casa* or *besugo a la bermeana* (sea bream). Closed Mondays, mid-July to mid-August, and *Christmas* week. Reservations advised. 19 Calle Juan de Labrit (phone: 224568). Expensive.

Josetxo – Famous for 30 years for its Basque dishes, this is another local leader with a Michelin star. Specialties include *sopa crema de cangrejos* (cream of crab soup), highly praised trout and rabbit dishes, hake with salmon sauce, and *lubina* (sea bass), grilled or in a white wine sauce. Closed Sundays and August. Reservations advised. 1 Plaza Príncipe de Viana (phone: 222097). Expensive.

Las Pocholas – Among the best Pamplona has to offer, a place for dishes such as vegetable stew, bull's tail stew, lobster with garlic sauce, and other traditional fare. The restaurant's official name is *Hostal del Rey Noble,* but everyone in town knows it as *Las Pocholas.* Closed Sundays and August. Reservations necessary. 6 Paseo de Sarasate (phone: 222214). Expensive.

Casa Angel – A favorite for lunches, the grill here is renowned for its excellent meat dishes, such as *solomillo a la prusina* (broiled filet of beef) and *salchicha* (small sausages). Other specialties include fried peppers and traditional Basque fare. Open daily. Reservations advised. 43 Calle Abejeras (phone: 243962). Expensive to moderate.

Casa Otano – On the second floor over the bar of the same name, it serves one of the best all-purpose menus in town, featuring traditional local dishes. Closed Sunday afternoons. Reservations advised. 5 Calle San Nicolás (phone: 225095). Expensive to moderate.

Don Pablo – Across from the *Tres Reyes* hotel, with a menu of both French and Spanish dishes and a modern atmosphere of smoked glass and chrome. Try the *berenjena* (eggplant) specials (in season), *merluza* (hake), and *lenguado a la romana* (filet of sole). Closed Sunday evenings. Reservations necessary. 19 Calle Navas de Tolosa (phone: 225299). Expensive to moderate.

Arala – Baby lamb cooked in an open, wood-fired oven is the specialty here, accompanied by a bottle from the excellent wine list. Closed Wednesday afternoons. Reservations advised. 12 Calle San Nicolás (phone: 221116). Moderate.

Casa Mauleon – The main dining room resembles a wine cellar with giant barrels lining the walls, and if you're lucky, you may have a serenade by locals singing up a storm here during *San Fermín.* Excellent meals are served at lunch and dinner — try the stuffed peppers. Closed Sunday evenings. Reservations advised. 4 Calle Amaya (phone: 228474). Moderate.

Erburu – Tucked in one of the back streets of the Old Town, it's hard to find but worth the search. Try the *liebre con ajo* (rabbit with garlic) or any of the other local specialties. This is a crowded but friendly place. Closed Mondays. No reservations. 19 Calle San Lorenzo (phone: 225169). Moderate.

Marceliano – A favorite with foreigners during *San Fermín,* since Hemingway was rumored to have stayed and dined here. Join the pilgrimage and order a plate of the best bull stew in Pamplona. Closed Mondays. Reservations advised. 7 Calle Mercado (phone: 221426). Moderate.

Café Iruña – The food is good and plentiful, the atmosphere is unhurried and unharried, and the fixed-price menu is reasonable. What's more, the Art Nouveau touches to the bar and the rest of the rooms — carved wood, ornate lamps, mirrored glass, statues, silver beer taps — make this 1880s-vintage place an experience in itself. Open daily. Reservations advised. 44 Plaza del Castillo (phone: 222064). Inexpensive.

Estafeta – A self-service, cafeteria-style restaurant — a welcome sight for a low-budget meal. The food is acceptably prepared and the surroundings are clean and pleasant. Closed Sunday evenings. No reservations. 57 Calle Estafeta (phone: 222605). Inexpensive.

 TAPAS BARS: It seems that *tapas* bars in Pamplona are spaced every 50 feet throughout the Old Town. *Codovilla* (Calle Navarraría) is well known for its *pimientos fritos, calamares fritos,* and *tortillas,* while *Bar Noé* (9 Calle de las Comedias) has excellent *tapas* ranging from peppers and pâtés to fish salads. The bars around Plaza del Castillo also serve great *tapas.* One popular spot is the *Windsor Pub* (at the *La Perla* hotel), which features seafood *tapas* including small crabs, langoustines, and shrimp.

PORTO

Few cities can boast of having a wine, a language, and a country named after them. And many would rest on these laurels alone. But not Porto (Oporto in English). The city is simply too busy doing business. Merchants rule here. The solid gray buildings of Porto's financial district reflect their practical nature, while the sprawl of the city and the industrial belt surrounding it attest to their commercial savvy. But don't let first appearances turn you away. Deep inside the modern jungle is an old city, where Gothic elegance harmonizes with baroque flair, houses cling precariously to terraced slopes like the vines that produce the region's celebrated wine, and the soft pastels of crumbling riverside houses shimmer in the misty morning waters of the golden Douro River.

Portugal's second-largest city, with 450,000 inhabitants, Porto may currently play second fiddle to Lisbon, but it hasn't always. Proud *portuenses* claim their city is the country's hereditary capital, more quintessentially Portuguese than their southern rival. After all, it was the serious, hardworking, and fiercely independent people of Porto who helped give the nation its start, who played a key role in freeing Lisbon from the Moors, and who financed and built the bulk of the Portuguese armadas. In return, the city became known as the *capital do trabalho,* the work capital, and its burghers became the unofficial guardians of the nation's values and traditions. Porto, solid, prosperous, and conservative, makes sure that Lisbon does not step too far out of line. It even allows the flashy and temperamental capital occasional flights of fancy — as long as it doesn't interfere with the important business of making money.

The city's prime location at the estuary of the Douro has always made it attractive to traders and settlers. The Phoenicians, drawn by the region's metal deposits, came to the mouth of the river to trade. By the time the Romans arrived in the 3rd century BC, a city already existed on the north bank of the Douro. The Romans fortified it and called it Portus (port or harbor), and built an urban metropolis on the south bank, which they named Cale. The twin cities became the major military and commercial center of Portus Cale, from which the name, language, and nation of Portugal were later derived.

Porto proved its mettle in the 9th century by being one of the first urban centers in Iberia to shake off the Moorish yoke. At the end of the 11th century, when the daughter of the King of León and Castile married Henry of Burgundy, the city, along with the rest of the county of Portucale, was part of her dowry. She, in turn, handed over the town charter to its powerful bishops. For centuries thereafter, the bishops, aristocrats, and merchants of Porto struggled for control of the city, and in the 14th century, the merchants claimed a major victory: The crown, in return for the merchants' support against powerful rivals, issued a decree in their favor barring the nobility from taking residence in the city's commercial district.

In the 15th century, Porto's most famous son, Prince Henry the Navigator, put the merchants' wealth and shipyards to use: The city built the bulk of the ships used in Portugal's voyages of discovery and reaped many of the profits that came with them. The 16th century was bleak, however. Porto was hit hard by the loss of the country's spice monopoly and the general economic and military decline, which culminated in Portugal's humiliating annexation by Spain in 1580. When the country reclaimed its independence in 1640, João of Bragança was crowned in Porto as King João IV.

By the 18th century, the resilient city was back on top, buoyed by wealth from Portugal's Brazilian colony and a phenomenal increase in port wine exports following the signing of the Treaty of Methuen with England. Under its terms, English cloth received favored status in Portugal, and Portuguese wine was accorded similar treatment in Britain. British wine merchants set up shop in Porto and went on to play a major role in the success of port wine and the city's subsequent history. Soon, English words such as ruby and tawny were being used to describe the wine, and others, such as the bastard-ized *chumeco,* for shoemaker, appeared in the popular vocabulary.

But not all went well for the British. In the mid-18th century, to curb their growing influence in the port wine trade (and their practice of adulterating the wine with elderberries), the powerful Marquis of Pombal set up the Alto Douro Company, giving it monopolistic control of wines from the Upper Douro region. But the company's strict rules and pricing policies annoyed producers and British shippers alike and led to violence when a supposedly drunken mob set fire to the company offices in what came to be known as the *revolta dos borrachos,* or "drunkards' revolt." Pombal's reprisal was vicious — public hanging of 25 participants. Eventually, however, the British merchants found ways to work with the Portuguese company, and to this day their descendants flourish in Porto. The British have their own club (where cricket is played), a school, and a church with a cemetery. Today, both the club and school are very international.

In the early 19th century, Porto was occupied twice by Napoleonic armies. The first invasion, in 1808, ended when the British, who were not amused at the prospect of having their coveted supplies of port cut off, sent troops under the command of Sir Arthur Wellesley, later named the Duke of Wellington. Wellesley expelled the French but had to return a year later to repel a second French force, after which Porto's grateful British merchants made him and his officers honorary members of their posh club and opened their wine lodges to the troops. Porto's citizens talk about the raucous behavior of the drunken British soldiers to this day.

Soon after, Porto played a major role in the social struggles of the 19th century. In 1820, liberal army officers with merchant connections formed an alliance in Porto to curb the powers of the crown. The movement spread to Lisbon, where, 2 years later, a representative *cortes* drafted a liberal constitu-tion putting an end to feudal rights. King João VI accepted the constitution, but when Miguel I, his son, dismissed it in 1828 and went on to rule like an absolute monarch, Porto rebelled. This caused Miguel's brother, Pedro of

Brazil, to abdicate his own throne and return to Portugal to restore the liberal order. Pedro's forces landed north of Porto in 1832 and marched on the city, forcing Miguel to abandon it. Before the War of the Two Brothers, as it came to be known, was over, however, the Miguelites laid siege to Porto for a year — a year in which the populace was reduced to eating cats and dogs. The siege was finally lifted with Miguel's definitive defeat south of Lisbon, and Pedro returned to Porto to thank its citizens for their support. When he died 4 months later, leaving his daughter, Maria da Glória, on the Portuguese throne, he bequeathed his heart (encased in gold) to the city.

With the 20th century and the downfall of the monarchy came the triumph of the republicanism for which Porto's merchants had worked so hard, along with a new era of economic development and public works. Already in the late 19th century, two metal bridges had been built across the Douro gorge, linking Porto with Vila Nova de Gaia (formerly Cale) and the rest of the country. Recently, a solution to the age-old problem of devastating floods was attempted (unsuccessfully) with the damming of the Douro. Another headache, a treacherous sandbar at the river's mouth, was bypassed by building the new artificial port of Leixões north of the city, between the town of Leça da Palmeira and the onetime fishing village of Matosinhos, now a suburb of Porto. Today, the city's economic emphasis has shifted from the river to the Leixões area, where fish canning, oil refining, wood processing, and shipping thrive, and the new Exponor exhibition center regularly hosts trade fairs.

The Old City, for better or worse, has been left to age in peace. It is weathered, somewhat tattered, and no stranger to poverty, but it's also teeming with life. Venture into the picturesque Barredo quarter, with its narrow alleyways and stone stairways that meander down to the river, and you will encounter a rich and vibrant world of tiny houses stacked against each other, fanned by the colorful morning wash, and of old women in black leaning over wrought-iron balconies and listening to the laughter of young children echoing off ancient walls. Stroll along the Ribeira, where the sweet smell of flowers emanates from quayside stalls and fish mongers exhibit their wares. Dine at a riverside tavern and gaze out at the south bank, where the city's wine treasure is stored and its handsome *rabelo* boats are docked. This is vintage Porto. Like the venerated wine, it should be savored slowly for its charm to work. And if it doesn't, there are other options: Porto is also the gateway to Portugal's northern lake country and the verdant Minho.

PORTO AT-A-GLANCE

SEEING THE CITY: Porto is built on several hills, so the city offers more than one panoramic vantage point. The best view is from the former Convent of Nossa Senhora da Serra do Pilar, on the south bank of the river in Vila Nova de Gaia, just across one of the city's two 19th-century bridges, the Ponte de Dom Luís I. Here, a tree-lined terrace looks down at the 2-tiered metal bridge and across to the Old City, the remains of the 14th-century Fernandina wall (which at one time encircled Porto but was torn down during 18th-century expansion), and the towers of the cathedral and the Clérigos church. On the north bank, the latter tower, the Torre dos Clérigos, provides an alternative view: Climb its 225 steps and be rewarded with a sweeping panorama that includes the sea to the west and the south bank's wine lodges. (For admission information, see the Igreja dos Clérigos below.)

SPECIAL PLACES: Porto is vast, but monumental Porto — extending roughly from the 20th-century Câmara Municipal (Town Hall) at the northern end of the wide Avenida dos Aliados to the riverfront Praça da Ribeira — is fairly concentrated and can be visited on foot. Within this area is the old, or medieval, city. It begins at the southern end of the Avenida dos Aliados, at Praça da Liberdade, where the old Fernandina wall and an entrance to the city once stood, but which is now the heart of the Baixa, Porto's commercial and shopping district. South of the square is the cathedral — the nucleus of the medieval town — sitting at the crest of the Pena Ventosa, a steep hill or cliff overlooking the Douro and Vila Nova de Gaia on its south bank. The terrain suddenly drops sharply south of the cathedral, forcing houses in the Barredo quarter right below it to cling precariously to the slopes, as narrow cobbled streets and granite stairways make their way down to the quayside Ribeira quarter. Thus, there are two levels to Porto, the upper level stretching northward from the edge of the cliff and the lower level along the river. Be sure to wear comfortable walking shoes.

Three bridges join Porto proper to its Vila Nova de Gaia suburb. The Ponte Dona Maria Pia, the easternmost bridge, is a railway bridge designed by Alexandre-Gustave Eiffel and built in 1877 (a new railway bridge is under construction next to it). Not too far to the west is the Ponte de Dom Luís I, built in 1886, a 2-tiered structure that ingeniously joins both the upper and lower parts of the city on both sides, and was the brainchild of an Eiffel disciple. Still farther west is the Ponte da Arrábida, dating from 1963 and also an example of ingenuity in that it stretches 885 feet across the Douro in a single reinforced-concrete span.

DOWNTOWN

Sé (Cathedral) – The twin-towered, fortress-like 12th-century cathedral, with its 17th- and 18th-century modifications, is perched on a hill overlooking the Old Town. Outside, a 13th-century Romanesque rose window stands above the highly stylized baroque doorway. Inside, in the Chapel of the Holy Sacrament, is the church's famous 17th-century silver altar, which was painted over for a period during the French occupation to save it from marauding troops. Also of note are three marble stoups in the nave and a bronze relief of the baptism of Christ in the baptistery to the left of the entrance. The sacristy off the south transept contains a gold-carved retable dating from 1610, as well as the crypt of the Bishops of Porto. A door on the south side of the south transept leads to a 14th-century Gothic cloister decorated with *azulejos* depicting the life of the Virgin and Ovid's *Metamorphoses*. The parents of Prince Henry the Navigator were married at the cathedral in 1387. Open daily from 9 AM to noon and from 3 to 5 PM. Admission charge to the cloister. Terreiro da Sé (phone: 314837).

Terreiro da Sé (Cathedral Square) – Bordering the cathedral is an imposing 14th-century tower; beside it is the former Bishop's Palace (now a municipal office), an 18th-century building with a flamboyant baroque façade. From the square, you can gaze upon the Douro — or thread your way down to it via a maze of alleys leading to the *cais,* or quay.

Igreja dos Grilos (Grilos Church) – The first building owned by the Jesuits in Porto. The 17th-century structure, laid out in the form of a cross with a vaulted dome, has a handsome baroque wooden altar representing the Presentation of Jesus in the temple. More formally known as São Lourenço, the church is open only for services, weekdays from 7 to 9 AM, Saturdays from 3 to 5 PM, and Sundays from 9:30 to 11 AM. Largo do Colégio (phone: 200-8056).

Casa Museu Guerra Junqueiro (Guerra Junqueiro House Museum) – The house of the 19th-century Portuguese poet Guerra Junqueiro, on a street behind the cathedral, contains the art objects he collected, including 15th-century Hispano-Arabic pottery and a large assortment of 16th-century Portuguese furniture and Flemish tapestries. Open Tuesdays through Fridays from 10 AM to noon and from 2 to 5 PM (Saturdays to 5:30 PM); open Sundays from 2 to 5:30 PM. Admission charge (Tuesdays through Fridays). 32 Rua de Dom Hugo (phone: 313644).

Igreja de Santa Clara (St. Clara Church) – East of the cathedral, this basically Romanesque church was founded in the early 15th century but underwent later transformation. The door is a mix of Gothic, Manueline, and Renaissance stonework, while the interior is covered from top to bottom with gilded woodwork. The ceiling is Mudéjar in style. Open Mondays through Fridays from 9:30 to 11:30 AM and 2 to 6 PM, Saturdays and Sundays from 9 AM to 1 PM. Admission charge. Largo Primeiro de Dezembro (phone: 314837).

Estação de São Bento (St. Benedict Station) – The interior walls of Porto's commuter train station are covered with *azulejos* done in 1930 by Jorge Colaço. They depict scenes of the development of the train and other historic events such as the capture of Ceuta by João I in the 15th century. Praça de Almeida Garrett.

Igreja dos Congregados (Congregados Church) – The showy *azulejos* decorating its exterior are the most notable feature of this 17th-century church. Beside the São Bento Station, at the corner of Avenida Dom Afonso Henriques.

Igreja dos Clérigos (Church of the Clerics) – This 18th-century baroque church with the unusual, oval shape was designed by the Italian architect Niccolò Nasoni. It is flanked by the Torre dos Clérigos, a 250-foot-high bell tower that dominates the Porto skyline. The 225-step climb to the top of the tower provides a panoramic view of Porto, the Atlantic Ocean, the Douro, and the wine lodges at Vila Nova de Gaia. The church is open daily from 7:30 to 9 AM, 10 AM to noon, 3 to 5 PM, and 6 to 8 PM; the tower is open daily from 10 AM to noon and from 3 to 5 PM. Admission charge for the tower. Rua dos Clérigos (phone: 200-1729).

Igreja do Carmo (Carmo Church) – Another 18th-century church, this one designed in an elaborate rococo style and dedicated to Our Lady. The outer eastern wall, covered with 20th-century glazed tiles depicting important events of the age of discovery and expansion, faces the lovely Fountain of the Lions. Open Mondays through Fridays from 7:30 AM to noon and from 2 to 5 PM; Saturdays and Sundays, open mornings only. Rua do Carmo (phone: 200-8113).

Museu Nacional Soares dos Reis – The most interesting museum by far in Porto is housed in an 18th-century palace (the Palácio dos Carrancas, a former residence of the Portuguese royal family) and contains art from the 16th century onward. There are paintings by such 16th-century Portuguese masters as Vasco Fernandes, who was known as Grão Vasco (Great Vasco), and Gaspar Vaz; also represented are 19th-century painters Silva Porto, a naturalist, and Henrique Pousão, an Impressionist, as well as Columbano Pinheiro, the 19th- and 20th-century portraitist and still life painter. On display besides paintings are sculptures by António Soares dos Reis, the 19th-century Porto native for whom the museum is named, local pottery, gold and silver liturgical objects, a set of 16th-century Limoges enamels representing the life of Christ, and a sword that belonged to the first King of Portugal, Dom Afonso Henriques. Open from 10 AM to 1 PM and from 2 to 5 PM; closed Mondays. Admission charge. 56 Rua Dom Manuel II (phone: 200-7110).

Museu Romântico (Romantic Museum) – Art objects and furniture from the 19th century make up the contents of this museum lodged in a 19th-century house overlooking the river on the far side of Porto's Palácio de Cristal exhibition center. See the museum and then go down to the basement to the *Solar do Vinho do Porto,* a comfortable wine bar run by the Port Wine Institute, the body that has supervised and certified the quality of port wine since 1935. Museum (phone: 691131) open Tuesdays through Saturdays from 10 AM to 12:30 PM and from 2 to 5 PM, Sundays from 2 to 5:30 PM. Admission charge. The bar (phone: 694749) keeps later hours, opening at 10 AM weekdays (at 11 PM on Saturdays) and closing at 11:30 PM (10:30 PM on Saturdays); closed Sundays. 220 Rua de Entre Quintas.

Museu de Etnografia e História do Douro Litoral (Museum of Ethnography and History of the Douro Littoral) – Typical costumes, farm implements, pottery, and other objects illustrate the daily life and customs of the people of the Douro region. There are also reconstructions of an old wine cellar and a weaver's workshop. Open Tuesdays through Saturdays from 10 AM to noon and from 2 to 5 PM. Admission charge. 11 Largo de São João Novo (phone: 200-2010).

Palácio da Bolsa (Stock Exchange) – The 19th-century granite building is known for its impressive marble staircase and its dazzling oval Arab Room, whose arabesques and stained glass windows imitate the highly decorative style of the Moorish Alhambra in Granada. Open for guided tours Mondays through Fridays from 9 AM to noon and from 2 to 5:30 PM. Admission charge. A statue of Prince Henry the Navigator stands in the square in front of the building. Rua Ferreira Borges (phone: 200-4497).

Igreja de São Francisco (St. Francis Church) – This was originally a Gothic church — and it has a fine rose window at its entrance. Step inside, however, and see the most dramatic and lavish church interior in all of Porto, the result of remodeling in the 17th and 18th centuries. Walls, vaulting, and pillars are generously covered with carved and gilded wood vines, grapes, birds, angels, cherubs; a forest of carved, gilded wood covers the high altar. About the only object not dressed in sumptuous gold is the polychrome granite statue of St. Francis in a 13th-century chapel. Open Tuesdays through Saturdays from 10 AM to 12:30 PM and from 2:30 to 5 PM. Admission charge. Praça Infante Dom Henrique (phone: 200-6493).

Casa do Infante – Prince Henry the Navigator was born in this 14th-century house, or so it is traditionally — and dubiously — thought. The building was a customs house up to the 19th century. Recently restored, it now serves as Porto's *Museu Histórico* (Historical Museum), containing artifacts and documents pertinent to the city's history. Open Mondays through Fridays from 9 AM to noon and from 2 to 5:30 PM. No admission charge. Rua da Alfândega (phone: 316025).

Igreja da Cedofeita (Cedofeita Church) – Porto's oldest church dates from the 12th century. A 5-minute cab ride northwest of the city center, it has a simple and elegant Romanesque exterior; inside, a single-vaulted nave rests on three arches. Open daily from 7:30 AM to noon PM and from 4 to 8 PM. 193 Rua Anibal Cunha (phone: 200-5620).

Museu de Arte Moderna (Museum of Modern Art) – Porto's newest museum, in the Casa Serralves, a former private mansion of the 1930s, is notable for its changing exhibitions of modern art, as well as for its fine, traditional Portuguese garden. Open Tuesdays through Sundays from 2 to 8 PM (gardens open until sunset). Admission charge (except Thursdays). 977 Rua de Serralves (phone: 680057).

PORT WINE CELLARS

No visit to Porto would be complete or entirely satisfying without a tour of one of the wine "lodges," or cellars, where wine from the Douro Valley matures and turns into port — now officially called Porto, to distinguish it from wines of the port type made elsewhere. There are some 80 or so wine lodges in the area, located at Vila Nova de Gaia, on the south bank of the Douro. Some say they're kept at this safe distance from the city in order not to interfere with the sober requirements of business. But experts cite more practical reasons: The lodges are on the south side of the river, facing north, to take advantage of the greater humidity and cooler temperatures, which reduce the wine's evaporation in the cellars. Some of the better known names to be found here include Cálem, Cockburn, Dow/Graham/Warre, Ferreira, Kopke/Barros, Real Vinícola, Sandeman, and Taylor/Fonseca.

Most of the houses offer free guided tours, in English, which can be arranged through the tourist office or hotels or by calling the lodges directly. In general, visiting hours are weekdays, except holidays, from 9:30 AM to noon or 1 PM and from 2 to 5:30 PM; Sandeman and Real Vinícola also are open on Saturdays and Sundays during the summer. Tours generally include a courtesy tasting; bottles can also be purchased. To reach the wine lodges at Vila Nova de Gaia, walk or drive across the lower level of Ponte de Dom Luís I and turn right. A stop at one of the several outdoor cafés on an esplanade by the quay would be in order — from here you can admire Porto proper across the river, as well as the old wine barges docked at the river's edge. These elegant, Egyptian-looking boats, Porto's characteristic *rabelos,* are the last of their kind, remnants of a pre-dam era when wine from the Upper Douro production area traveled downstream to the lodges by boat, rather than by truck and train. The following are some of the most accessible lodges.

Ferreira – One of the largest Portuguese port wine companies, it has a long and colorful history. In the early 19th century, its founder, Dona Antonia Adelaide Ferreira, expanded the family holdings from 3 vineyards to 30 large estates stretching all the way up the Douro to the Spanish border. She became the richest woman in Portugal and endeared herself to the local population — who affectionately nicknamed her "Ferreirinha" (little Ferreira) — by building roads, school nurseries, and hospitals. Ferreirinha almost drowned in the Douro in 1861 when the boat on which she and Baron de Forrester, an Englishman, were traveling capsized. He perished, but she managed to survive, apparently buoyed by her voluminous petticoat. 19 Rua da Carvalhosa, Vila Nova de Gaia (phone: 300866).

Real Companhia Vinícola do Norte de Portugal – The company, founded by royal decree in 1756, is housed in a large estate on the eastern side of Vila Nova de Gaia, a distance away from most of the other lodges. It produces not only vintage port but also Portuguese champagne, or *espumante,* which is stored and aged in a long tunnel on the premises. To reach the estate, drive across the upper level of the Dom Luís bridge and follow the signs for Lisbon, turning left at the second intersection. 314 Rua Azevedo Magalhães, Vila Nova de Gaia (phone: 303013).

Sandeman – The lodge is housed, in part, in a former 16th-century convent. It holds about 20 million liters of port in bottles and oak barrels, as well as a small museum of tools and other implements used in the wine industry as early as the 18th century. The oldest section has an interesting floor of soft wood "stilts," placed upright as a cushion to prevent damage to the wine barrels as they are rolled over it. Sandeman was established in 1790 by the Scotsman George Sandeman, and the founder's family continues to supervise the company, although it now is owned by Seagrams of Canada. 2 Largo Miguel Bombarda, Vila Nova de Gaia (phone: 304081).

ENVIRONS

Igreja do Bom Jesus (Good Jesus Church) – This church in a secluded, cozy garden alongside a viaduct about 7 miles (12 km) north of the center of Porto is the object of a large pilgrimage every June, because it contains an ancient wooden statue of Christ that was found on a beach several hundred years ago and was, according to legend, carved in biblical times by Nicodemus. The church has a lively, bold 18th-century façade by Niccolò Nasoni; inside, the nave and chancel are covered with a sumptuous coffered ceiling. To reach Bom Jesus, take Avenida da Boavista west out of town and proceed north in the direction of the suburb of Matosinhos. Continue past Matosinhos beach and the docks at Leixões. Open daily from 7:30 AM to 7 PM, but during the week it may be closed between noon and 2:30 PM. Visitors generally have lunch at the beachside fish restaurants at Matosinhos. Avenida Dom Afonso Henriques, Matosinhos (phone: 930734).

■**EXTRA SPECIAL:** For centuries before the arrival of the railroad, roads, and dams, the Douro was the lifeline of the people of Porto and the other towns lining the river. Its quicksilver waters carried the handsome, square-sailed *rabelo* boats with their precious cargos downriver from major wine producing and storage centers such as Régua. It is now possible to cruise up the river and admire the terraced slopes that rise like pyramids from the river's edge and surround the stately *quintas* — farms — of the wine families. The most popular of several options is a 15-mile cruise as far as Crestuma, but longer trips, to Entre-os-Rios, Régua, and Pinhão, can also be booked. The Crestuma cruise (about $40 per person) leaves Tuesdays at 11 AM and returns at 2:45 PM, with lunch served on the boat. Weekend cruises are another possibility; the port wine itinerary (about $150 per person), for example, runs from Porto to Pinhão in the heart of the port wine valley, with lunch and dinner aboard the boat on the first day and an overnight at Régua. The next day, passengers continue to Pinhão and have lunch at a wine estate before returning to Porto on the scenic Douro train line. Contact *Endouro Turismo* (49 Rua da Reboleira; phone: 324236). Advance booking is necessary; no cruises in the months of January and February. The boats leave from the quay at Praça da Ribeira. Another possibility, for visitors on a tight schedule, is the short cruise under the city's three bridges, which leaves every hour from the quay in front of the Ferreira wine lodge at Vila Nova de Gaia. It runs from 10 AM to 6 PM Mondays through Fridays and to 1 PM on Saturdays, from April through September.

SOURCES AND RESOURCES

TOURIST INFORMATION: The Porto Tourist Board (25 Rua Clube Fenianos; phone: 312740), open Mondays through Fridays from 9 AM to 12:30 PM and 2 to 5:30 PM, Saturdays from 9 AM to 4 PM (closed Sundays), provides information on the city and the region. Copies of the English-language *What's on in Porto,* a monthly publication with a calendar of activities, facts and phone numbers, and lists of hotels and restaurants, are available. The tourist office also publishes a handy red pamphlet called *Oporto/Portugal,* an English-language mini-guide of facts about the city, and a blue map of town showing bus routes. A third brochure contains pictures of the city's sights as well as a simple guide to port wine and its history. A 20-minute slide show with voice-over can be seen on the premises. The office will make hotel reservations within Porto for those who arrive with no place to stay; lists of manor houses in the area that take in guests are also available. A branch of the national tourist office (Praça Dom João I; phone: 317514) also has information on the city and the region; it is open Mondays through Fridays from 9 AM to 7 PM (Saturdays until 4 PM) and on Sundays from 10 AM to 2 PM.)

The US Consulate is at 826 Rua Júlio Dinis (phone: 63094).

Local Coverage – The *Jornal de Notícias* is one of Portugal's oldest dailies. The *International Herald Tribune* can be purchased the day after publication at the airport, at major hotels, and at the larger newsstands around Praça da Liberdade.

TELEPHONE: The city code for Porto is 2. If calling from within Portugal, dial 02 before the local number.

GETTING AROUND: Central Porto can and should be seen on foot, but a car or public transportation is necessary for suburban areas and the environs.

Airport – Porto's Aeroporto de Pedras Rubras (phone: 948-2141; for flight information: 948-2144), 9½ miles (15 km) northwest of the city along N107, handles both domestic and international traffic. A taxi ride into town can cost up to $15; the No. 56 bus provides regular service to Praça da Liberdade in the center of town and to the Campanhã train station. *TAP Air Portugal* has a local office (105 Praça Mousinho de Albuquerque; phone: 696041). The regional shuttle airline, *Linhas Aéreas Regionais (LAR),* flies over the Douro Valley and connects Porto to northern tourist spots such as Bragança and Vila Real (phone: 200-4656).

Bus – Buses, trams, and trolleys cover the city. Booklets of discount tickets or unlimited-travel tourist passes (good for 4 or 7 days) can be purchased from the *Serviço de Transportes Coletivos do Porto (STCP,* Praça de Almeida Garrett; phone: 668226), between 8 AM and 7:30 PM Mondays through Fridays. An interesting trip can be taken aboard the No. 1 tram — from Praça do Infante Dom Henrique (opposite the St. Francis Church) along the river past suburban Foz do Douro and right through to Matosinhos. (On Sundays, the route is covered by bus.) *Rodoviária Nacional (RN),* the national bus company (629 Rua Sá da Bandeira; phone: 200-1109), provides sightseeing tours aboard special buses with English-speaking hostesses.

Car Rental – The major international firms represented include *Hertz* (899 Rua de Santa Catarina; phone: 312387; and at the airport; phone: 948-1400); *Avis* (125 Rua Guedes de Azevedo; phone: 315947; and at the airport; phone: 948-1525); and *Europcar* (1158-1164 Rua de Santa Catarina; phone: 318398; and at the airport; phone: 948-2452).

Taxi – Taxis can be hailed on the street or picked up at a cabstand — there is a large stand at Avenida dos Aliados (phone: 200-2046). Or call *Radio Taxi* (phone: 489898). Meters are not used beyond the city limits, so if you are going a long distance, be sure to ask the hotel concierge for an estimate and discuss the amount with the cab driver before setting off.

Train – There are three train stations. The main one, Estação de Campanhã (Rua da Estação; phone: 564141), on the eastern outskirts of the city, serves most of the country and foreign destinations. (A cab from the center costs under $7.) Estação de São Bento (phone: 200-2722), on Praça de Almeida Garrett in the city center, is a commuter station. The third station, Estação de Trindade (at the end of Rua António Sardinha; phone: 200-5224), near the tourist office, serves the northern part of the country.

SPECIAL EVENTS: The enterprising side of the city can be seen throughout the year at a host of industrial fairs, conventions, and congresses, the largest of which is the *International Industrial Machines Exhibition* in November. But there are also more colorful events, such as the *International Folk Dance Festival,* sponsored by City Hall in August, and the popular festivals of *São João* (St. John) and *São Bartolomeu* (St. Bartholomew). *São João,* which takes place on June 23 and 24, is a mix of pagan and Catholic rituals celebrating the summer solstice and involves curious customs such as passing around leeks and buying small earthenware pots of basil. The population stays up all night drinking *vinho verde* and eating roast kid, and lovers leap over huge bonfires. The feast of *São Bartolomeu,* held on the third Sunday in August, has evolved into a *cortejo de papal,* or "paper parade," in which people dress in paper costumes to satirize public personages and politicians. They follow a float carrying Neptune and sirens to the beach, where they battle "pirates" from the sea; the battle ends with all the participants and some of the onlookers rushing into the water for a holy bath, a practice no doubt related to the old superstition that a dip in the sea can cast out the devil.

MUSEUMS: Besides those mentioned in *Special Places,* several other museums in Porto may be of interest:

Museu de Arqueologia e Pré-História (Archaeology and Prehistory Museum) – Local artifacts dating as far back as 4,000 years. Open Mondays through Fridays from 9 AM to noon and from 2 to 5 PM. No admission charge. Praça de Gomes Teixeira (phone: 310290).

Museu de Arte Sacra (Museum of Sacred Art) – Religious art, liturgical vestments, old coins, and glass objects. Open Tuesdays through Fridays from 2:30 to 4 PM. No admission charge. 2 Largo de Pedro Vitorino (phone: 200-8056).

Depósito de Eléctricos (Tram Depot) – Old trams, destined for a future museum. Visits by appointment. No admission charge. 51 Alameda de Basílio Teles (phone: 64054).

SHOPPING: Porto and its environs are known for their elaborate gold and silver filigree work, embroidery, lace, leather goods (shoes, purses, wallets, belts), ceramics, tapestry, glass, and crystal. The Baixa, on either side of Praça da Liberdade, is the main shopping district — among the best shopping streets here are Rua de Santa Catarina (gift shops and clothing stores), Rua 31 de Janeiro (leather goods and glassware), Rua das Flores (jewelry), Rua das Carmelitas (ceramics and clothing), and Rua dos Clérigos. There are also several popular markets carrying regional handicrafts such as wooden model boats and ox carts, wicker articles, and pottery at bargain prices, as well as clothing and shoes at below store prices. The *Bolhão* market, Rua de Sá da Bandeira, is in the Baixa district, while the more popular *Bom Sucesso* market is in the square of the same name on the western side of town. Both function Mondays through Fridays from 7 AM to 5 PM, and on Saturdays from 7 AM to 1 PM. The outdoor *Vandoma* fair, a small flea market near the cathedral, specializes in antiques and knickknacks and is in operation on Saturdays from 7 AM to 1 PM. Regular shops are open from 9 AM to noon and from 2:30 to 7 PM on weekdays, 9 AM to 1 PM on Saturdays, but some shopping centers stay open on Saturday afternoons. *Galerias Palladium,* in the heart of the Baixa (61-73 Rua de Santa Catarina), is an extensive complex of small boutiques selling jewelry, clothing, leather goods, luggage, and perfume; the *Centro Comercial Brasilia* (113 Praça Mousinho de Albuquerque) is a mini-mall with everything from gift and clothing shops to pastry shops and hairdressers. Individual shops of note include the following:

Casa dos Linhos – A family-run firm that has specialized in the sale of linen and embroidery for over a century. 660 Rua de Fernandes Tomás (phone: 200-0044).

Galerias de Vandoma – An antiques shop and auction house. 181 Rua Mouzinho da Silveira (phone: 200-1286).

José Rosas – Antique and secondhand jewelry. 282 Rua Eugénio Castro (phone: 695785).

Rosior – Manufacturers of traditional and modern jewelry. 38 Rua da Cunha (phone: 401519).

Vista Alegre – Fine handmade porcelain and glass from the town of Vista Alegre; the shop can handle shipping. 18 Rua Cândido dos Reis (phone: 200-4554.)

SPORTS AND FITNESS: Golf – Two golf clubs within easy reach of Porto are the *Clube de Golfe de Miramar* (phone: 762-2067), which has a 9-hole course on the beach at Praia Miramar, 7½ miles (12 km) south of town off N109 (the road to Espinho), and the *Oporto Golf Club* (phone: 722008), with an 18-hole course beside the beach about 3 miles (5 km) south of Espinho and 14 miles (22 km) south of Porto. The latter was opened in 1890 by British wine shippers, and the atmosphere of a British club continues to prevail in its wood-paneled clubhouse. Equipment rental, caddies, and classes are available throughout the year at both clubs; guests of the *Praia do Golfe* hotel in Espinho may use the greens free of charge.

Jogging – Try the gardens (admission charge) of the Palácio de Cristal, the old exhibition center on Rua Dom Manuel II, or take the No. 18 bus 3 miles (5 km) west to suburban Foz do Douro, at the mouth of the river, and jog along the long esplanade by the beach.

Soccer – The season runs from September through May. One of Porto's two major clubs, the *Futebol Clube do Porto* (Avenida de Fernão de Magalhães; phone: 481738), based at the *Estadio das Antas,* was European champion in 1987; the other club is the *Boavista Futebol Clube* (Rua 1 de Janeiro; phone: 690975).

Squash – The *Clube de Squash do Porto* (164 Rua João Branco; phone: 666771) is one possibility; the *Porto Sheraton* (1269 Avenida da Boavista; phone: 668822) also has a squash court.

Swimming – For a tan, go to the Foz do Douro or Matosinhos beaches, but swim farther from the city at Espinho, 10½ miles (17 km) south. An Olympic-size municipal swimming pool, the *Piscina de Campanhã* (Rua Dr. Sousa Avides; phone: 572041), is near the Campanhã train station.

Tennis – The *Clube Tênis do Porto,* Rua Damiao Gois (phone: 488506), offers courts and classes.

 THEATER: Classic Portuguese plays and *revistas,* lighthearted political and social satires, can be seen at the *Teatro Sá da Bandeira* (Rua de Sá da Bandeira; phone: 200-3595). The *Teatro Experimental do Porto* (134 Rua Duque de Palmela; phone: 569567) offers more modern experimental theater.

 MUSIC: The symphony orchestras of both Porto and Lisbon play at the elegant *Auditório Nacional Carlos Alberto,* Rua das Oliveiras (phone: 200-4540).

 NIGHTCLUBS AND NIGHTLIFE: Porto has a varied nightlife. *Swing* (766 Praçeta Engenheiro Amaro de Costa; phone: 690019) attracts the well-heeled, who like its pub (upstairs) and disco (downstairs) combination. *Twins* (1000 Rua do Passeio Alegre; phone: 685740), in the affluent suburb of Foz, 3 miles (5 km) west of the center, has a similar setup, but it also provides intimate, continental dining. (It's also a members-only club, but this rule is not strictly enforced.) The *Olympia* in the *Meridien* hotel (1466 Avenida da Boavista; phone: 600-1913) is a discotheque frequented by the business community, while the younger set flocks to *Griffon's* (Centro Comercial Brasilia; phone: 666091), which is somewhat smaller and noisier. New-wave types congregate at *Indústria* (Centro Comercial de Foz); the decor is spartan (no tables, no chairs), the music loud, and the air filled with smoke. *Amnésia* (Praia Francelos; phone: 762-2668), 6 miles (10 km) south of Porto, indulges in the latest craze in local discos: There is a weekly theme, and waiters double as *animadores,* who not only serve guests but also entertain and dance with them.

It is possible to avoid the glitz and fast pace of the disco crowd, however. Although the *fado* tradition did not take hold north of the Douro, the *Restaurante Tipico O Fado* (16 Largo São João Novo; phone: 200-9135) is a *fado* house where this style of singing, so popular in the south, is given a fair hearing from 10 PM to 4 AM (closed Sundays). Guests can enjoy dinner and listen to the show for about $40 for two (reservations are necessary). There's also *fado* at the *Taberna São Jorge* (35 Passeio das Virtudes; phone: 318230), from 9 PM to 3 AM daily except Sundays (about $60 for two; reservations advised), and at the *Mal Cozinhado* (13 Rua do Outeirinho; phone: 381319), near the Campanhã train station, from 8:30 PM daily except Sundays (reservations necessary; see *Eating Out*). Several pubs in the Ribeira district have live music: *Postigo do Carvão* (26-34 Rua da Fonte Taurina; phone: 200-4539), in a refurbished warehouse by the river, is an animated restaurant and piano bar, and *Aniki-Bobo,* next door, offers a jazz and folk repertoire popular with the college crowd. Downtown, businesspeople frequent the bar at the *Infante de Sagres* hotel (62 Praça Dona Filipa de Lencastre; phone: 200-8101). *Bela Cruz* (5458 Avenida da Boavista; phone: 680891) is a pub in an old fort, the Castelo do Queijo, by the sea at Foz.

A final option: At Espinho, there's the *Casino Solverde* (phone: 724045), open from 3 PM to 3 AM, with roulette, slot machines, and bingo, as well as dining, dancing, and a floor show. Portuguese law requires foreigners to show their passports at the door; there's a small entrance fee to the gambling room.

BEST IN TOWN

CHECKING IN: Until recently, Porto suffered from a lack of topnotch accommodations. The situation was remedied somewhat with the addition of several new deluxe hotels and the refurbishing of some older establishments, but because the new establishments are in the suburbs (en route to the airport), the supply of recommendable accommodations in the historic part of the city is still limited — and many of them are overrated. It is essential to choose carefully and make reservations well in advance, particularly for the summer months. Expect to pay $95 and up for a double room in the top hotels, listed as expensive; from $40 to $70 in those listed as moderate. All telephone numbers are in the 2 city code unless otherwise indicated.

Dom Henrique – A modern, 112-room hotel beside the Trindade train station, up the street from the tourist office. Panoramic views are its best asset. There's a new coffee shop on the ground floor and the *Navegador* restaurant on the 18th floor, overlooking the city. 179 Rua Guedes de Azevedo (phone: 200-5755). Expensive.

Infante de Sagres – Porto's most luxurious hotel — whose guest list has included the British royal family — is tucked away in a small, quiet square near the center of town. It certainly doesn't look its age: It was built during the early 1950s, but has an Old World appearance, a product of decoration in the grand style encompassing several centuries of antiques and a rich assortment of carved wood paneling, stained glass, and wrought iron. (The magnificent fireplace at the entrance is the work of a former night porter who carved it during his spare time.) The 84 rooms are spacious and plush, the service is efficient and friendly, the bar is a favorite haunt of local and visiting businesspeople, and the restaurant (see *Eating Out*) is the most elegant eating place in the city. A Best Western affiliate. 62 Praça Dona Filipa de Lencastre (phone: 200-8101). Expensive.

Ipanema – This medium-size property (150 rooms), to the west of the city center near the Palácio de Cristal, would be a second choice when downtown hotels are full. It has a restaurant, a piano bar, and its own private parking facility. 156-174 Rua do Campo Alegre (phone: 668061). Expensive.

Meridien – A modern, luxury, 232-room hotel located in a residential part of town en route to the airport, about a 10-minute bus or cab ride to the center. A favorite of young executives, who like the spacious conference facilities and the efficient communications system, it has most of the facilities of a chain hotel, including *Les Terrasses* (see *Eating Out*), a fine French restaurant, as well as a piano bar, health club (there is a charge), and a discotheque. 1466 Avenida da Boavista (phone: 600-1913). Expensive.

Porto Sheraton – Even newer than the nearby *Meridien,* this 253-room establishment provides all the familiar comforts of the chain, including a heated indoor swimming pool, a squash court, and a health club that guests may use for an extra charge. The *Madruga* restaurant offers both regional and continental food. Free parking. 1269 Avenida da Boavista (phone: 668822). Expensive.

Tivoli Porto Atlântico – This medium-size place (58 rooms) in the modern hotel row not far from the *Meridien* and the *Porto Sheraton* has both outdoor and indoor swimming pools, a sauna, a mini-gym, and the *Foco* restaurant (phone: 667248) next door. 66 Rua Afonso Lopes Vieira (phone: 694941). Expensive.

Batalha – Simple and clean and ideally located in the commercial hub of the city. Affiliated with Best Western, it has a bar, restaurant, and 143 rooms. 116 Praça da Batalha (phone: 200-0571). Moderate.

Boavista – Small and cozy, and about 3 miles (5 km) west of the center of town in the affluent suburb of Foz do Douro. The building seems a cross between a French château and an English country inn, and most of the 39 rooms, furnished with pine furniture, command views of the Douro estuary and Foz fortress. There's a notable dining room (see *Eating Out*), a small patio with a fountain, and terraces for sunning. For an extra payment, guests may use the *Oslo Club* in the basement, which has a small indoor swimming pool, a Jacuzzi, a Turkish bath, sauna, and a massage room. Parking in front. 58 Esplanada do Castelo, Foz do Douro (phone: 680083). Moderate.

Novotel Porto – One of the city's newer hotels, this is a modern place on the south bank of the river by the Arrábida Bridge, convenient for visiting the port wine lodges. There are 93 rooms (about half with a view of the Douro estuary), a restaurant (*Le Grill*), a small outdoor pool, and parking facilities. Lugar das Chas, Afurada (phone: 781-4242). Moderate.

Peninsular – A family-run place with 57 rooms, conveniently located in the middle of the Baixa district. It offers simple, no-frills lodging for short stays. The restaurant serves a set menu of home cooking. No parking. 21 Rua de Sá da Bandeira (phone: 200-3012). Moderate.

Porto – A classic old hotel in a pedestrian island in the heart of the shopping district. It has a charming *fin de siècle* look to it, and the management and staff are gracious and deferential. The furniture in the 100 bedrooms has known better days, but the splendor and details of the salons and dining room (see *Eating Out*) make up for this, recalling past glory. Another Best Western affiliate; adjacent parking. 197 Rua de Santa Catarina (phone: 200-8176). Moderate.

 EATING OUT: Porto's native dish is tripe. The preference began of necessity in the 15th century, when the city's residents slaughtered all their animals to feed the armada of Prince Henry the Navigator on its way to North Africa and were left with only the offal for themselves. They invented various ways to cook it and earned themselves the nickname *tripeiros* (tripe eaters). Ingredients for the most typical dish — *tripas à moda do Porto* (tripe, Porto-style) — include tripe, chopped bits of pig's ear and pig's snout, bacon, sausages, white beans, onions, carrots, parsley, bay leaves, cumin seed, salt, and pepper. Served with rice, its advocates swear, it is quite tasty. Before trying the tripe, however, sample the *caldo verde,* or green soup, a northern Portuguese dish made with green cabbage, puréed potatoes, and spicy sausage. Other popular dishes are *bacalhau à Gomes de Sá,* a casserole of salt cod, onions, and potatoes attributed to a Porto restaurant owner, and the local version of *caldeirada,* a steamy stew of many different kinds of fish cooked in a tomato, onion, and herb sauce. Desserts are rich in eggs, almonds, and sugar, and have religious names, such as *barrigas de freira* (nuns' bellies), because they originally were made in convents. A word of caution for shellfish eaters: Lobster and shrimp are prohibitively expensive (up to $50 for a lobster). A delicious, more reasonably priced alternative is *arroz de marisco,* which contains several kinds of shellfish and is Portugal's juicier answer to Spanish paella.

Accompany the meal with the region's *vinho verde* (green wine — but young rather than actually green) or with mature red and white Douro wines. But begin with an extra-dry white port accompanied by a small plate of cheese and cured ham, and finish with a vintage port or an *aguardente velha,* an aged cognac-style brandy that goes well with coffee. Expect to pay anywhere from $50 to $70 for a meal for two at a restaurant listed as expensive, from $30 to $50 in a moderate one, and about $20 to $25 in an inexpensive place. It's a good idea to make reservations at the top restaurants, particularly at lunchtime. All telephone numbers are in the 2 city code unless otherwise indicated.

Infante de Sagres – The poshest place in town, in the posh hotel of the same name. The game dishes are excellent, the wine cellar large, the service ultra-professional, and the decor is the height of 19th-century elegance: crystal chandeliers, mirrors, and wood-paneled walls. Open daily. Reservations advised. 62 Praça Dona Filipa de Lencastre (phone: 200-8101). Expensive.

Portucale – Probably the best restaurant in town, it's favored by executives for its varied menu of Portuguese and continental dishes, attentive service, and sweeping view of the city and countryside. Wood paneling, leather chairs, and colorful modern tapestries make up the simple, lively decor that serves as the background for such house specialties as artichokes au gratin, lobster and rice stew, pheasant stuffed with almonds, chateaubriand with mushroom sauce, and wild boar, as well as tripe, Porto-style. Open daily. Reservations necessary. 598 Rua da Alegria, 13th Floor (phone: 570717). Expensive.

Les Terrasses – Another hotel dining room, it offers a choice of traditional French cooking or nouvelle cuisine. Large plants, wicker, and a decor of light greens and browns provide a lively garden-like atmosphere. Open daily. Reservations advised. *Meridien Hotel,* 1466 Avenida da Boavista (phone: 600-1913). Expensive.

Dom Manuel – Housed in a pleasant seaside villa overlooking the Atlantic Ocean. The food is traditionally Portuguese and consistently topnotch, particularly the fish dishes and the multi-fish *caldeirada* stew. Closed Sundays. Reservations advised. To reach the restaurant, turn left at the end of Avenida da Boavista. 384 Avenida de Montevideu (phone: 670179). Expensive to moderate.

Escondidinho – This popular place serves the best regional food in the city. Tiles, marble, and local crafts decorate it inside, while outside it has been designed to look like a typical country house — which makes it stand out in the otherwise modern urban street. Closed Sundays. Reservations advised. 144 Rua Passos Manuel (phone: 200-1079). Expensive to moderate.

Green's – Elegant dining in a restaurant with the atmosphere of a private club. It's a favorite of Porto's socialites, who also frequent the disco and pub at the same suburban Foz address. Closed Saturdays at lunch and Sundays. Reservations advised. 1086 Rua Padre Luis Cabral (phone: 685704). Expensive to moderate.

Orfeu – A modern steak-and-fish establishment with paneled wood and soft piped-in music. It's favored by fish lovers, particularly cod enthusiasts. Open daily. Reservations advised. 928 Rua Júlio Dinis (phone: 64322). Expensive to moderate.

Boavista – The greenhouse look of it, the views of the Foz fortress and the Douro estuary, and dinner served by candlelight make this glass-enclosed verandah, the main dining room of the *Boavista* hotel, a good choice for a romantic evening.

Fondue and chateaubriand, steak tartare, pepper steaks, and grilled sole are among the specialties. Open daily. Reservations advised. 58 Esplanada do Castelo, Foz do Douro (phone: 680083). Moderate.

Cervejaria Galiza – Beer on tap and fast, efficient service are the trademarks of this modern, lively fish-and-steak spot. Try the spicy clams *bulhão pato* style (with garlic and parsley), the *arroz de marisco,* or shellfish stew, or the *bife a frigideira,* a butter-fried beefsteak with a fried egg on top, done in an earthenware pot. Open until 2 AM daily. No reservations. 55 Rua do Campo Alegre (phone: 690059). Moderate.

Downing Street – A pleasant family-run place located in a former warehouse in the Ribeira district. On the street level, there's a bar; for dining, there's an intimate, candlelit, tiled cellar or an upstairs room that's decorated with old photos of Porto and looks out onto a picturesque square of colorful houses. Try the *arroz de tamboril,* or monkfish and rice stew. Open daily. Reservations advised. 10 Praça da Ribeira (phone: 380-6777). Moderate.

Mal Cozinhado – A fairly large and busy restaurant near the Campanhã train station, it's also known for *fado* singing. Try the codfish stuffed with ham; if *fado* is of interest, call to make sure it's scheduled — it usually begins at 8:30 PM. Closed Sundays. Reservations necessary. 13 Rua do Outeirinho (phone: 381319). Moderate.

Porto – Elaborate stucco ceilings, crystal chandeliers, warm red walls, velour curtains, and flowers contribute to the turn-of-the-century elegance that endears this hotel dining room to an older, sedate crowd. Grilled ox steaks and the grilled turbot are good menu choices. Open daily. Reservations unnecessary. *Grande Hotel do Porto,* 197 Rua de Santa Catarina (phone: 200-8176). Moderate.

Porto Fino – Fairly small, upstairs in a Foz do Douro house. The pleasant atmosphere and the range of fish specialties — try the *arroz de marisco* or the *lulas* (squid) — have made it popular with the city's social set. Closed at lunch on Saturdays. Reservations advised. 103 Rua do Padrão, Foz do Douro (phone: 677339). Moderate.

Tripeiro – This popular, no-frills eatery serves fine regional cooking and fish specialties. Try the *linguado grelhado* (grilled sole), *truta recheada com fiambre* (trout stuffed with cured ham), or *filetes de pescada* (hake). Closed Sundays. Reservations unnecessary. 191-195 Rua Passos Manuel (phone: 200-5886). Moderate.

Chez Lapin – A pleasant, typical Ribeira restaurant lodged in a centuries-old arcade by the river. Walls and ceilings of this tiny but cozy tavern are filled with hunting and kitchen utensils, its busy kitchen is open, and there are two floors for dining. The house specialty is *coelho* (rabbit) in white wine sauce, but for fish lovers, there is tender, black swordfish. Open daily. Reservations advised. 40 Rua dos Canastreiros (phone: 200-6418). Inexpensive.

Taverna Bebodos – The most authentic of several waterfront taverns serving typical regional dishes. Closed Sundays. Reservations advised. 24 Cais da Ribeira (phone: 313565). Inexpensive.

SALAMANCA

The golden glow of Salamanca lingers long after you have left this city of amber sandstone. The splendid Plateresque, Renaissance, and baroque façades of the buildings in the historic section of town — made of soft, fine, easy-to-work *piedra arenisca* — have, with age, acquired a warm distinctive patina that grows ever richer with the passing centuries. No wonder the city long has been nicknamed "Little Rome."

Unlike many another town in Spain, including nearby Madrid, Salamanca has remained reasonably free of the deleterious effects of modern architecture and mass tourism. As the home of one of the world's most ancient universities, it has conducted itself through the ages with dignity — so much so that its magnificent monuments and academic structures can seem somewhat imposing to visitors. But Salamanca is really an intimate, lively place, with an army of students to nip any nascent pompousness in the bud.

From 217 BC, when the Romans constructed a bridge of 26 arches across the Tormes River, and throughout the Middle Ages, Salamanca enjoyed an enviable position along important trade routes. Later, after the foundation of the famed university in the 13th century, the steady influx of merchants bent on business was matched by a steady stream of students. Today, although the Roman Bridge is open to pedestrian traffic only, it still seems to echo with the sounds of its commercial heyday, while the tradespeople of old have been largely replaced by a global society of culture seekers drawn to the city's numerous architectural and intellectual legacies. The university, true to its long-standing tradition, continues to attract a sizable foreign student body that lends a cosmopolitan air to this otherwise staunchly Castilian town.

While the Phoenicians were busy establishing Cádiz in the south, the area of Salamanca was inhabited by Iberian tribes who left their mark with the enormous carved stone bulls, or *verracos,* that are seen throughout the province (there is one in the middle of the Roman Bridge). Beginning about 900 BC, the Celts from the north, mingling with the Iberians of the central plateau, created two Celt-Iberian tribes known as Vettons (primarily herdsmen) and Vacceos (primarily farmers).

The next great shift in Salamanca's fortunes came at the hands of Hannibal, who conquered the city in 220 BC during the Second Punic War. Soon after, under the Romans, it became an important communications center. A long, peaceful, and prosperous Roman reign was brought to a contentious halt with the arrival of Germanic tribes in the 5th century. Under the Vandals and Visigoths, and then the Islamic Moors, Salamanca fell into relative obscurity. After its reconquest from the latter in 1085, the area was resettled by an ethnic mix of Franks, Castilians, Portuguese, Jews, Galicians, and some English.

The University of Salamanca was established in 1218, making it —

with Paris, Bologna, and Oxford — one of Europe's oldest universities. It achieved great renown and garnered tremendous intellectual respect for its role in reintroducing the world to the works of the ancient Greek and Muslim philosophers, translated into Latin and Old Spanish by the university's Muslim, Jewish, and Christian scholars. Favored by kings and popes, the university reached its peak of prestige during Spain's Golden Age; John, the son of the Catholic Monarchs, was one of its students. Early in the 16th century, 8,000 of Salamanca's 20,000 residents were university students. Cervantes, St. John of the Cross, and other famed historic personages studied, taught, or spent time in Salamanca, the prime intellectual breeding ground of the period. Delicate and elaborately detailed, the Plateresque façade of the university in the Patio de Escuelas is a symbol of the spirit and wealth of those times.

With the waning of Spain's Golden Age during the 17th century, Salamanca shared in the decline of Castilian cities, a condition that lasted throughout the 18th century. At the turn of this century, when Miguel de Unamuno was university rector, the city had only 25,000 inhabitants; but despite the tremendous political upheavals of 20th-century Spain, Salamanca has regained some of its earlier momentum and today boasts a population of over 150,000, as well as burgeoning hordes of annual visitors. Present-day Salamanca society is clearly divided into students and non-students, who, for the most part, studiously avoid each other. The university — which is not what it used to be — has its classrooms and facilities spread throughout the city, and most after-class socializing takes place in the city's numerous bars. Meanwhile, the *salamanqueses* go about their business largely indifferent to the cultural legacy handed down to them through the centuries. It is left to visitors, then, to "Ooh!" and "Aah!" at the city's golden splendor.

SALAMANCA AT-A-GLANCE

SEEING THE CITY: The best view of the city is from the *Parador de Salamanca* (see *Checking In*), located on a hill south of the city and across the Tormes River. On Saturdays, Sundays, and holidays, many of the monuments are illuminated for several hours after nightfall. The spires of the city's side-by-side cathedrals and the dome and towers of La Clerecía dominate the scene.

SPECIAL PLACES: Salamanca's streets are often narrow and winding, with many one-way throughfares, but the Centro Ciudad (City Center) signs leading into the core of town are excellent, and for those arriving by car, there's no trouble driving right to the heart of the city. Once there, it is best to proceed on foot, as all the main sights are concentrated compactly in the *zona monumental* (monument zone), largely between the Plaza Mayor and the river. Visiting hours for the city's sights are erratic, to say the least, and subject to change without notice. No standard hours are set, so each monument sets its own, which vary with the season and other unpredictable factors. It is best to check with the tourist information office (39 Gran Vía; phone: 243730) for current hours, though even those may not turn out to be completely accurate.

CITY CENTER

Plaza Mayor – Deemed by many to be the most beautiful plaza in all of Spain, this harmonious construction, in a muted baroque style, measures roughly 63,500 square feet and, despite all appearances, is trapezoidal, not rectangular. Arcades housing boutiques, souvenir stores, pastry shops, and assorted bars and eateries surround it at ground level; above the arches all around rise 3 stories of balconies, interrupted only by the façade of the Town Hall, which juts out and up to break the uniformity. Begun in 1729 and completed 34 years later, the plaza was originally built as an enclosed market area and arena for public fiestas. Once used for bullfights, it is still the heart of town and the focal point of the festivities of the *Feria de Salamanca,* celebrated every year during the second 2 weeks in September. It's hard to imagine that at one time in the 1960s, cars were allowed into the square. Fortunately, it belongs to pedestrians again.

Catedral Vieja (Old Cathedral) and Catedral Nueva (New Cathedral) – These stand adjacent to one another, though they are 4 centuries apart in age. Visitors ordinarily enter the old structure through the new one. The Catedral Nueva was begun in 1513 and was in use by 1560, although it wasn't consecrated until 1733. Conceived in a Gothic vein — one of the last Gothic churches in Spain, in fact — in actual construction it also drew from the Renaissance and baroque vernaculars. Outside, the church bristles with more than 400 Gothic spikes, and the main doorway, facing Calle Cardenal Playdeniel, is a prime example of the Plateresque stone carvers' art, with biblical scenes in high relief and ornamental borders so richly detailed they tax the eye. Inside, the New Cathedral is notable for the ornate wooden choir stalls, 18th-century baroque works by the Churriguera brothers, and for the two organs; for the Cristo de las Batallas, which is a famous 11th-century Romanesque crucifix said to have been carried into battle by El Cid (this comparatively tiny statue is in the center of an ornate Churrigueresque golden altarpiece in the central chapel behind the Capilla Mayor); and for the Capilla Dorada, located near the entrance to the old cathedral, its walls plastered with small statues of saints, angels, prophets.

The Catedral Vieja, down a flight of stairs off the south aisle of the new one, dates from the 12th century, its plan, columns, capitals, and external arches in Romanesque style, its internal arches and vaults in Gothic. Simpler and more fortress-like than its replacement, the church's monochromatic interior is enlivened by an extraordinary 15th-century main altarpiece made up of 53 panels, painted by Nicolás Florentino, narrating the lives of Christ and the Virgin Mary. Above it, against a dark background, is a Last Judgment by the same painter, and in the center of the altarpiece is the 12th-century image of Nuestra Señora de la Vega, the city's patron. Among the rooms around the adjoining cloister, be sure to note the 12th-century Talavera Chapel, used at one time for Mozarabic rite masses and topped with a distinctive Romanesque-Mudéjar dome; the 14th-century Santa Barbara Chapel, where university examinations once were held and where candidates for the degree customarily spent the night before finals praying; and the Santa Catalina Chapel and Salas Capitulares (Chapter Rooms), set up as a museum. Most of the exterior of the Old Cathedral is obscured by the new one, but before leaving the complex entirely, walk around back to the Patio Chico (Small Courtyard), from where the older church's strange-looking Torre del Gallo (Rooster Tower), covered with scale-like stones, is visible. Open daily from 9:30 AM to 1:15 PM and from 3:30 to 5:45 PM; closed Sunday afternoons in winter. There is an admission charge to the Old Cathedral (which includes the cloister chapels and museum off the Old Cathedral). Plaza de Anaya (phone: 217476).

Universidad (University) – The university's facilities are dispersed through the city, but the core of its "campus" is just around the block from the cathedrals. Here, at one end of the Patio de Escuelas, is the university building, erected during the reign of the Catholic Monarchs, that bears the most famed Plateresque façade in Spain. It's a real beauty, considered the apogee of this ornamental genre, and one of Salamanca's enduring landmarks. Immediately inside is a courtyard ringed by classrooms — compare a modern one with the Aula Fray Luis de León, where rough benches have been left as they were in the 16th century. A couple of doors beyond it is the interesting Paraninfo Room, featuring Belgian tapestries and a portrait of King Carlos IV by Goya. Note the beautiful painted ceilings all around the courtyard, and especially the ceiling of the university foyer (opposite the visitors' entrance), a lacy Moorish one of star shapes in dark wood. A beautiful staircase with carved balustrade leads to the upper level of the courtyard, topped by another fine coffered Mozarabic ceiling. (The university's old library, a repository of over 40,000 volumes and 3,000 manuscripts, is located up here, but it is no longer open to visitors.)

At the opposite end of the Patio de Escuelas is the Escuelas Menores (Minor Schools), marked by another Plateresque façade and a beautiful interior courtyard, on the far side of which is a room containing a fresco of the zodiac by Fernando Gallego known as *Cielo de Salamanca* (Salamancan Sky — it is currently undergoing restoration, however, and should be completed by the middle of this year). Both the main university building and the Escuelas Menores are open from 9 AM to 2 PM and from 4 to 8 PM Mondays through Saturdays (closed Sunday afternoons) in summer; winter hours are Mondays through Fridays from 9:30 AM to 1:30 PM and from 4 to 6 PM, Saturdays from 9:30 AM to 1:30 PM, and Sundays from 11 AM to 1 PM. One admission charge for both buildings. Patio de Escuelas (phone: 219708).

Museo de Bellas Artes/Museo de Salamanca (Fine Arts Museum/Salamanca Museum) – Through the door adjacent to the Escuelas Menores and under the 15th-century roof of the former house of Dr. Alvarez Abarca, Queen Isabella's physician, the museum has an eclectic display of paintings and sculptures, both Spanish and foreign, old and modern. Open weekdays from 8 AM to 3 PM and weekends from 10 AM to 2 PM, except when there are temporary exhibitions, which are open from 7 to 9 PM weekdays and from 10 AM to 2 PM weekends. Admission charge. Patio de Escuelas (phone: 212235).

Convento de San Esteban (Convent of St. Stephen) – This 16th-century church, part of a Dominican convent, is just down Calle Tostado from Plaza de Anaya. It sports another of Salamanca's stunning Plateresque façades, this one described by some as a tapestry in stone because of its elaborate depictions of the martyrdom of San Esteban and the crucifixion of Christ. Inside is a sumptuous, late-17th-century golden altarpiece by José Benito de Churriguera, in the upper reaches of which is a *Martirio de San Esteban* (Martydom of St. Stephen) painted by Claudio Coello. To the side of the church is the beautiful 2-story Claustro de los Reyes (Kings' Cloister), the only one of the convent's three cloisters that is open to the public. From its second story, a door opens into the church's *coro alto,* from which the view of the altarpiece is breathtaking. Open daily, from 9 AM to 1:30 PM and from 4 to 6 PM. Admission charge. Plaza Santo Domingo (phone: 215000).

Convento de las Dueñas – Nearly next door to San Esteban, the 15th-century Moorish-style structure here was a private home before it was donated to a group of *dueñas* (nuns, or pious women of high social standing living in community). Only the five-sided, 16th-century Renaissance cloister is open to visitors, but it's a real treat. Whereas most of the rich stone carving in Salamanca is too distant or too much in the dark to be easily seen, the elaborate capitals of the cloister's upper tier are only slightly above eye level, so their charming, amusing, and grotesque human and animal figures can be brought into sharp focus. The nuns who run the convent also make sweets, which they sell at the *Despacho* (shop) in a corner of the entry courtyard. Open daily from 10 AM to 1:30 PM and from 4 to 6 PM from April through September; from 10:30 AM to 1 PM and from 4 to 5:30 PM from October through March. Admission charge. The *Despacho* is open from 10 AM to 1 PM and from 4 to 7 PM. Plaza del Concilio de Trento (phone: 215442).

Casa de las Conchas (House of Shells) – One of the more famous buildings in Salamanca, it dates from the 15th century and incorporates Moorish, Gothic, and Renaissance elements. Unfortunately, it's not open to the public, but the façade, covered with the carved seashells that give the building its name, is noteworthy. They were the symbol of the Pimental family, one of whose members was the bride of the building's owner, a member of the Maldonado family, whose symbol, the fleur de lys, is on the coat of arms above the door. Note, too, the Gothic window grilles. Corner of Rua Antigua and Calle de la Compañía.

In addition to the Casa de las Conchas, there are a number of other monuments in Salamanca that are pure façade with interiors that are either off-limits or merely mundane. Be sure to give a passing glance to the Clerecía (or Real Clerecía de San Marcos), a huge 17th-century collegiate church on the corner opposite the Casa de las Conchas, and to the Palacio de Monterrey, a characteristic Spanish Renaissance palace of the early 16th century at the Plaza de Monterrey end of Calle de la Compañía.

ENVIRONS

Alba de Tormes – About 11 miles (18 km) southeast of Salamanca is the village of Alba de Tormes, just over a medieval bridge with 22 arches crossing the Tormes River. Turn left at the end of the bridge and park beside the unfinished Basílica de Santa Teresa. Then walk up between the basilica and the Iglesia de San Pedro (with the red brick bell tower) to the Plaza de Santa Teresa, where the Convento de Madres Carmelitas Descalzas and the Iglesia de Santa Teresa are the goals of a steady influx of faithful pilgrims. The church is primarily Renaissance, with Gothic and baroque flourishes. The marble vault above the altar bears the mortal remains of St. Teresa of Avila, who founded the convent, and died here in 1582. On either side of the altar is a reliquary, one containing an arm and the other the heart of the beloved saint. At the back of the church, opposite the entrance door, is a grating that affords a glimpse of the cell where she died. To see the relics and the cell illuminated, apply at the Centro Teresiano Información across the plaza, open Mondays through Fridays, from 10 AM to 1 PM and 4 to 8 PM. The center also houses a small museum exhibiting mementos of St. Teresa's life, and photos of Pope John Paul II's visit to Alba de Tormes in 1982, the 400th anniversary of the saint's death.

■ **EXTRA SPECIAL:** The *Casa-Museo Unamuno* (Unamuno House-Museum), the 18th-century house where the renowned scholar, poet, and philosopher Miguel de Unamuno lived from 1900 to 1914 (while he was rector of the University of Salamanca), is now an intimate museum containing his notebooks, library, and many of his most prized personal possessions, including drawings, paper birds, a large crucifix, a small deck of cards (he enjoyed playing solitaire), and his brass bed. Open weekdays from 4 to 6 PM, weekends from 11 AM to 1 PM. Admission charge. (Note — the museum is not to be confused with the house Unamuno moved into when he was no longer university rector, which is at 6 Calle Bordadores and not open to the public.) 25 Calle de los Libreros (phone: 214817).

SOURCES AND RESOURCES

TOURIST INFORMATION: The main tourist information office (39-41 Gran Vía; phone: 268571) is open weekdays, from 9:30 AM to 2 PM and from 4:30 to 7 PM; Saturdays, from 9:30 AM to 2 PM. Information is also available at the Oficina de Información kiosk (in the eastern wall of the Plaza Mayor; phone: 218342). It's open Mondays through Saturdays, from 10 AM to 1:30 PM and from 5 to 7 PM; Sundays and holidays, from 11 AM to 2 PM. Both outlets can provide current information regarding hours and admission fees, as well as maps, brochures, and detailed information on local accommodations in all price ranges. For a detailed city map, go to *Librería Cervantes* (11-13 Calle Azafranal; phone: 218602), one of Salamanca's top bookshops, and ask for a *callejero*.

Local Coverage – *El Adelanto* and *La Gaceta Regional* are local dailies in Spanish, covering local, provincial, national, and international news and events. The monthly *Lugares,* distributed free of charge, is the best source for information on nightlife and entertainment in Salamanca.

TELEPHONE: The city code for Salamanca is 23. If calling from within Spain, dial 923 before the local number.

GETTING AROUND: Salamanca is a small, compact city, and all the sights are within walking distance of one another, so getting around is a simple matter. Sites are easy to find, too, at least in the *zona monumental,* which is a good thing, because the buildings of Salamanca were renumbered in 1989. For some time to come, brochures and other published materials probably will be full of wrong street numbers. In this chapter, every effort has been made to supply the correct number — but even when the visitor is armed with the correct address, it can be difficult to determine which number beside any given doorway is the correct one.

Bus – The bus station (33 Calle Filiberto Villalobos; phone: 236717) is a short distance from the center of town. Schedules are printed in *El Adelanto* and *Lugares.* There is frequent daily service to Zamora, Madrid, Avila, Seville, Barcelona, and León, as well as to nearby Alba de Tormes.

Car Rental – Major rental companies include *Hertz* (131 Avenida de Portugal; phone: 243134; and 23 Calle General Sanjurjo; phone: 232554) and *Avis* (49 Paseo de Canalejas; phone: 257430; and 3 Plaza Madrid; phone: 251632). Local car rental firms include *Castilla* (49 Paseo de Canalejas; phone: 257430); *Prado Martín* (5 Plaza de Santo; phone: 242549); and *Sánchez González* (163 Avenida de Portugal; phone: 220396).

Taxi – There are two taxi stands by the Plaza Mayor, one on Calle del Corrillo, and the other on Plaza del Poeta Iglesias, in front of the *Gran* hotel. Taxis can be hailed throughout the city, or by radio service (phone: 254444 or 250000).

Train – The Salamanca train station (Paseo de la Estación; phone: 220395) is a short cab ride from the city center. There is a *RENFE* office (10 Plaza de la Libertad; phone: 212454). Frequent daily service goes to Madrid, Avila, Valladolid, Barcelona, and Porto, Portugal.

SPECIAL EVENTS: In mid-July, the city sponsors the *Verano Cultural de Salamanca,* a week-long series of silent movies, contemporary Spanish cinema, singers, and theater groups from Spain and abroad. The *Feria de Salamanca,* held annually during the second 2 weeks in September, features music, costumes, parades, various theatrical events, and almost daily bullfights.

MUSEUMS: In addition to those described in *Special Places,* Salamanca's museums include the following:

Convento y Museo de las Ursulas – The small museum — a room adjoining the Ursulas church — contains painting, sculpture, and *artesonado* ceilings; the church is Gothic and contains the alabaster tomb of the convent's founder. Open daily from 9:30 AM to 1 PM and from 4 to 6 PM. Admission charge. Calle las Ursulas (phone: 219877).

Museo de Historia de la Ciudad y Museo Diocesano (Museum of City History and Diocesan Museum) – Various stones of archaeological and architectural interest, plus items associated with local composer Tomás Bretón (1850–1923), in the former; the latter, upstairs, has several late-15th-century paintings by Fernando and Francisco Gallego, and a triptych of St. Michael by Juan de Flandes. Open Tuesdays through Saturdays, from 10 AM to 1:30 PM and from 5 to 8 PM. Plaza de Juan XXIII (phone: 213067).

SHOPPING: Most of the more interesting shops are in the Plaza Mayor and the surrounding streets to the north, although there is almost nothing sold in Salamanca that isn't also available almost anywhere else in Old Castile. Stores are generally open from 10 AM to 1:30 PM and from 5 to 7 or 8 PM.

Escarlata – The most avant-garde clothes shop in town. 9 Calle Padilleros.

Feres – Lladró porcelain and Majórica pearls. 27 Plaza Mayor (phone: 215913).

Handy-Craft – Belts, ceramics, baskets, and assorted international handicrafts. 53 Rua Mayor (phone: 263395).

Oscar – Mantillas, fans, flamenco paraphernalia, and other Spanish souvenirs. 15 Plaza Mayor (phone: 213636).

Segurado – Traditional Spanish souvenirs and novelty items. 10 Plaza Mayor (phone: 212362).

SPORTS AND FITNESS: Salamanca's modern sports complex, *Pabellón Deportivo* (Parque de la Alamedilla; phone: 234069), has a swimming pool, ice skating rink, and basketball and handball courts. Call for availability information and costs. The city also has a variety of gymnasiums and fitness clubs that are open to the public for a fee. Contact the tourist office for further information.

Fishing – Trout fishing in the Tormes, Francia, Mayas, and Frio rivers requires a license and the payment of a fee, with the season usually running from March through October. There are no special restrictions or requirements for non-residents. For more information, contact the *Consejeria de Agricultura,* Ganadería y Montes, (Sección de Montes), 28-30 Calle Alfonso de Castro (phone: 232600).

Hunting – Some hunting areas are restricted to Spaniards only, while others have very strict rules and regulations for all would-be hunters. Small game includes hare, rabbit, partridge, and turtledove; bigger game consists of wild boar, mountain goats, and deer. For more information, contact the *Consejeria de Agricultura,* listed above.

Squash – The *Kata Squash Club* (79 Avenida de Alemania; phone: 259689) rents courts and also has a well-equipped gymnasium.

Swimming – Besides the *Pabellón Deportivo* (see above), both the *Complejo Torres*

(Carretera de Madrid; phone: 215754) and the Parque Sindical (Carretera de Fuentesanco) have swimming pools open to the public for an admission charge.

 THEATER AND MUSIC: During the academic year, theatrical performances take place under the auspices of the university, and concerts also are presented by the university, by the *Sociedad de Conciertos,* and by other organizations. The stage at the university's *Teatro Juan del Enzina* (phone: 214274) hosts many of the theatrical events, while the *Paraninfo Room* and the university chapel are used for concerts. The *Teatro Bretón* (Plaza Bretón; phone: 269844), one of several movie theaters in town, is also used for concerts. During the July and September festivals, events proliferate.

 NIGHTCLUBS AND NIGHTLIFE: Although there is a disco scene, nightlife in Salamanca usually involves more traditional pursuits, such as hanging out at a bar with friends or, in good weather, people watching at an outdoor café in Plaza Mayor. At the northeast corner of the plaza, the *Café Novelty,* Unamuno's former haunt, has been going strong since 1905; the Art Nouveau details of its doors and mirrors, its black wrought-iron and brass railings, still give it plenty of character. Two bars offer live jazz performances during the university year (October through May) — *Corrillo* (1 Cerrada del Corrillo, at the edge of Plaza Mayor; phone: 269111) and *Mezcal* (9 Cuesta del Carmen; phone: 213077). Discos come and go, but among those with staying power are *María* (36 Avenida Mirat), *Limón y Menta* (18 Calle Bermejoros), and *Hindagala* (Plaza de la Reina).

BEST IN TOWN

 CHECKING IN: Considering its rather modest size, Salamanca has an impressive array of lodgings, ranging from student pensions and *hostales* to large, full-service hotels. The tourist information office offers a listing of hotels it has inspected and graded, complete with prices and details on facilities with private bath. Expect to pay $75 to $105 for a double room with private bath in hotels classified as expensive, $35 to $75 for a moderate room, and less than $35 for an inexpensive one. All telephone numbers are in the 23 city code unless otherwise indicated.

Gran – Just off the Plaza Mayor's southeastern corner, its lobby is a spacious local gathering place and its 100 rooms just have been redone in a traditional style, with dark wood furnishings — all in all, the feeling is one of substance and comfort. Rooms have private baths (large, marble ones), soundproofed windows, TV sets, and air conditioning; the hostelry has 2 bars and the *Feudal* restaurant, featuring regional dishes. 6-9 Plaza del Poeta Iglesias (phone: 213500). Expensive.

Monterrey – Sister to the *Gran* hotel, it's not far from the Plaza Mayor, although it's located beyond the *zona monumental.* The lobby, with upholstery in pale green velvet contrasting nicely with reddish wood, is attractive; the 85 rooms and 4 suites are not quite as nicely furnished as those of its sister, but are air conditioned. A pleasant café, spacious public rooms, and the fine *El Fogón* restaurant. 21 Calle Azafranal (phone: 214400). Expensive.

Parador de Salamanca – The local *parador,* just across the Tormes River from the city, offers modern facilities and conscientious service that are the best in town. The 94 double rooms, 10 singles, and 4 suites are all centrally heated and air conditioned, with private bath and direct-dial telephones. There is also a coffee shop, a dining room, an outdoor swimming pool, a garden, and ample parking. 2 Calle Teso de la Feria (phone: 268700). Expensive.

Regio – Located 2½ miles (4 km) south of town, on the N501 highway heading toward Avila, its 121 rooms are centrally heated and air conditioned, with private bath. Facilities include a cafeteria, the *Lazarillo de Tormes* restaurant, an Olympic-size pool and a children's pool, 2 bars, and gardens. Carretera de Salamanca, Santa Marta (phone: 200250). Expensive to moderate.

Emperatriz – Housed in one of Salamanca's medieval buildings in the heart of town, its 24 newer rooms have full, private baths, whereas some of the original 38 rooms have showers only. The halls are rather dark and forbidding, but the rooms are comfortable and clean, if somewhat spartan. 44 Calle de la Compañía (phone: 219200). Moderate.

El Zaguan – This clean and pleasant 15-room hotel is located just off the Plaza Mayor. All doubles have full, private baths; singles have showers, no bathtubs. 7-9 Calle Ventura Ruiz Aguilera (phone: 214705). Moderate.

Estefania – Located in a narrow, central street (a cross street of the Rua Mayor), this pension offers 20 beds. Some doubles have complete baths, and a number of rooms have only sinks. 3 Calle Jesús (phone: 217372). Inexpensive.

 EATING OUT: The traditional roast suckling pig and lamb of Castile are also the staples of Salamanca's finest restaurants. Sausages such as *farinato* and *morcilla* are local specialties, more typically served in *tapas* bars than in full-fledged eateries. While regional wines appear on most menus, they are generally considered inferior to the better riojas. Dinner for two with wine will cost $60 to $85 in expensive restaurants, $30 to $55 in those listed as moderate, $25 or less in inexpensive ones. All telephone numbers are in the 23 city code unless otherwise indicated.

Chez Victor – The napkins here are beautifully embroidered and the bread is served warm and crisp. Owner-chef Victoriano spent 13 years perfecting his craft in France; thus, his innovative cuisine has a decidedly French accent — as well as Salamanca's only Michelin star. The fare changes with the seasons, but year-round standards include *raviolis rellenos de marisco* (ravioli stuffed with seafood), *ragú de salmón y alcachofas* (salmon and artichoke stew), and *tarta de cebolla* (savory onion tart). The ice cream and sorbets in unusual flavors are homemade and served on attractive wafers. Closed Sunday evenings, Mondays, and August. Reservations advised in June and July. 26 Calle Espoz y Mina (phone: 213123). Expensive.

Nuevo Candil – The decor and menu are typically Castilian, with such dishes as *tostón* and *lechazo pierna asado* (two variations of suckling pig), *truchas del Tormes* (Tormes trout), and *sopa de rabo de buey* (oxtail soup). The restaurant is the offspring of *El Candil* (see *Tapas Bars*), a quarter of a century old and located 100 yards or so away. Closed Mondays. Reservations unnecessary. 1 Plaza de la Reina (phone: 219027). Expensive.

El Botón Charro – Tucked away in a narrow alley off the Plaza del Mercado, the attraction is a nouvelle twist to traditional Castilian cuisine. Closed Sundays. Reservations unnecessary. 6-8 Calle Hovohambre (phone: 216462). Expensive to moderate.

La Posada – Located next to the Torre del Aire, its regional specialties include *alubias con codornices o con almejas* (beans with quail or clams) and assorted game in season; or try the chef's suggestions of the day. Open daily; closed for 3 weeks in August. Reservations unnecessary. 1 Calle Aire y Azucena (phone: 217251). Moderate.

Rio de la Plata – Small, charming, and usually very crowded, this eatery is a block from the Plaza Mayor. In addition to Castilian dishes, the kitchen excels at seafood. Good homemade desserts and fine wines. Closed Mondays and July. Reservations unnecessary. 1 Plaza del Peso (phone: 219005). Moderate.

El Bardo – The clientele here consists mainly of students. The menu could best be termed "national" rather than regional, and the set meals are particularly economical. Closed Mondays and October. Reservations unnecessary. 8 Calle de la Compañía (phone: 219089). Inexpensive.

El Dorado – Near the Plaza del Mercado, with a reputation for marvelous service and solid home-style cooking. Closed Tuesdays. Reservations unnecessary. 3 Calle del Clavel (phone: 217212). Inexpensive.

 TAPAS BARS: A standard feature of Salamanca's social scene. Visit a few and call it a meal. Calle Prado has a string of them, including *Gran Tasca* (3 Calle Prado), *Marín* (5 Calle Prado), and *Bar Mi Vaca y Yo* (11 Calle Prado). So does Calle Ventura Ruiz Aguilera (better known to locals as *la calleja* — the alley). Outstanding here is *El Candil* (10 Calle Ventura Ruiz Aguilera). Also try *Plus-Ultra* (Calle del Concejo, off Plaza Mayor). There is often someone playing guitar in these and other *tapas* bars, and sometimes even a group of musicians from the university.

SAN SEBASTIÁN

Its cafés serve the best croissants south of the Pyrenees, it is the only city in Spain without a bullring, and it has no naughty red-light district — not even a business area. Its avenues are broad and tree-lined, its shops luxurious and chic, and its climate is more Atlantic than Mediterranean. No, this is not the Spain of the Costa del Sol, nor of clamorous cities such as Madrid, Barcelona, or even its Basque neighbor, Bilbao. And yet if you ask any traveler to name his two favorite cities in Spain, one of them is bound to be San Sebastián (probably with Seville), in the same way that most Europeans cite San Francisco and New York as the two cities they'd most like to visit in the United States.

Set around one of Europe's finest natural bays, the Bahía de la Concha (Bay of the Shell), this most elegant turn-of-the-century Belle Epoque beach resort is protected from northerly winds by two mountains that rise up on either side of the town — Mt. Urgull and Mt. Igueldo — while Santa Clara Island in the middle of the shell-shaped bay takes strength out of the breakers that crash in from the vast Bay of Biscay. The wide, curved Playa de la Concha, one of the most beautiful beaches in Spain, is topped by an exquisite promenade of ornate railings and impressive buildings, and the walkways on either side of the Urumea River are another taste of 19th-century elegance in this otherwise modern, tidy, and pretty city that has the calming effect of a small town. San Sebastián is surprisingly small (pop. 175,000) and unrushed, even in midsummer, when there isn't a spare hotel room to be had.

The first recorded mention of San Sebastián was in 1014, when a donation was made by King Sancho el Mayor to a monastery here. In 1200, the new castle on Urgull fell to King Alfonso VIII of Castile. San Sebastián joined the Sea Brotherhood with other coastal towns in 1294 and established trade relations with England and Brittany. Harbor construction began in 1450; in the Middle Ages, the city's inhabitants were well known for the whaling and cod fishing that took them as far as the Newfoundland banks. San Sebastián became a port for a much larger area than the surrounding province of Guipúzcoa, and from its wharves, oil and wine were shipped to the rest of Europe. Indeed, by the 18th century, the city had a special cacao trading deal with Caracas, Venezuela. With the growth of Bilbao along the coast, however, the city's importance as a port declined, and today its seafaring activities are limited to a little anchovy, sardine, and tuna fishing.

Just 12 miles (19 km) from the French border, San Sebastián has a definite Francophile air about it. Its affinity to the French caused it to be burned to the ground for the 12th — and so far, last — time on August 31, 1813. On that date the Duke of Wellington's combined British and Portuguese forces looted and destroyed the town as Napoleon's troops, after 5 years of occupation, fled to the border toward the end of the Peninsular

War. The local residents decided to rebuild the town, and in 1814 the four cornerstones of the Plaza de la Constitución in the center of the Parte Vieja (Old Town) were laid. The Old Town, a cramped warren of narrow streets packed with bars and restaurants adjacent to the old fishing port on the city's eastern promontory, was the first part of San Sebastián to be rebuilt. Its bustling streets, bordered by the Alameda del Boulevard, the estuary of the Urumea River, Mt. Urgull, and the port, are where locals and visitors today gather every evening for the pre-dinner *poteo,* a wine or two with *tapas.*

By the 1840s, the Old Town had been rebuilt and San Sebastián was quietly reestablishing itself as the major town on the Spanish coast between France and Bilbao. But it wasn't until 1845 that the place began to take off as a vacation spot. That year, Queen Isabella II spent the summer in San Sebastián, heralding the city's role as a high class holiday resort. It soon became the summer residence of the royal court, the government, and much of the aristocracy. In 1863, a decision was made to demilitarize the town by demolishing the city walls. This allowed urban expansion to boom in the 1860s, and the first buildings in the residential and shopping districts were raised as the glorious line of promenade buildings above La Concha began taking shape. By the 1870s, San Sebastián was the summer home for many European aristocrats, in 1887 La Concha was awarded the title of royal beach, and in 1902 a municipal company was established to promote the city and build a grand hotel. By this time, San Sebastián had been a Spanish pioneer in installing a tram system, electric street lighting, and telephone service.

On July 8, 1912, Queen María Cristina opened the grand hotel named after her. The hotel became King Alfonso XIII's winter residence, and members of many European royal families spent long periods there. Completely restored during the 1980s — and at an astronomical cost — it is still reputed by many to be the best hotel in northern Spain, and with the majestic *Victoria Eugenia Theater* standing alongside it on the Paseo República Argentina, overlooking the Urumea and the sea, it forms a marvelous monument to the Belle Epoque for which San Sebastián is still renowned. This lavish period reached its zenith just after World War I as money poured into the city from some of Europe's richest families, refugees of a war-ravaged continent. By the 1950s, tourist tastes had changed. The nobility joined mere mortals farther south, where sunshine is a much surer commodity. Today, San Sebastián is packed in July and August with visitors from France, Italy, and the rest of Spain, and is especially busy during the international jazz and film festivals in July and September.

Visitors should not be surprised to find the walls of the Old Town daubed with graffiti, because San Sebastián is in the midst of Basque Country — known as the Pais Vasco to the Spanish, as Euskadi to the Basques themselves. The graffiti extols the justice of the Basque fight for self-determination and the violence of the armed separatist organization ETA, and are a clear sign of the Basque political upheaval. Over 600 people have died since democracy was restored in 1977, putting San Sebastián — known to its inhabitants by its Basque name, Donostia — on the front pages of Spanish newspapers for all the wrong reasons. The Old Town and the Alameda del Boulevard are the scenes of occasional clashes between radical separatists and riot police. The City Council is dominated by anti-Spanish Basque nationalist parties, which on paper at least makes this one of the most revolutionary cities in Europe. This blend of the elegant and the radical adds to San Sebastián's charm, and locals are keen to tell visitors that they are different from "the Spanish." ETA terrorism, when it takes place, is directed against the security forces, and tourists have nothing to fear from the political situation — unless they are caught in a police charge! In any case, street fighting is rare away from the Old Town.

The province of Guipúzcoa, one of the three provinces making up the Basque Country, is the smallest province in Spain and the Basque province that has best preserved its historic customs. The extremely complex Euskera language is spoken by at least 50% of the *donostiarras,* as the city folk are known, and by up to 90% in neighboring towns. This is crucial to the local sense of "national identity," or Basqueness, which is evident during the many fiestas held throughout the year. Traditional Basque music is played on three-holed tin whistles known as *txistus,* and on small drums. Basque folkloric dancing is animated and ceremonial. Rural sports, whose aim is to demonstrate speed and strength rather than skill, are an integral part of Basque culture; pelota, or jai alai, is well known outside the Basque region.

Less well known internationally, except to those who pay more than the usual amount of attention to gastronomy, is San Sebastián's reputation for excellent food. The city is acknowledged as the birthplace of the new Basque cooking, a culinary culture that emerged in earnest about 15 years ago. But the city's reputation as a culinary center goes back more than 100 years, when the first gastronomic societies were founded. Developed in the days when local fishermen cooked and ate on the quayside as soon as they landed with their catch, the societies then founded places with kitchens, where they could enjoy their food and company in comfort. Over the years, the societies and their style of cooking became more sophisticated, and many classic Basque dishes were born in men-only kitchens of San Sebastián where, the men say, they have more time than the housewife to pamper the food and cultivate the sauces. Most of the 1,000 societies in the Basque Country, and the best-known ones in San Sebastián's Old Town, now allow women in to dine at certain hours, but they are still *never* allowed in the kitchens.

The societies' dining rooms are for members and guests only (inquire at the tourist office about the chances of being invited), but San Sebastíian's restaurants offer some of the best food in Spain, second only to the restaurants of Madrid in terms of the total number of Michelin stars they have won. And to build up an appetite, it's hard to do better than an early evening stroll along the Paseo de la Concha above the beach and an hour of *poteo* (happy hour) in the Old Town. Even if the city's streets and avenues were not so charming, San Sebastián's natural setting, around the deep, still bay and enclosed by low undulating hills, would ensure its reputation for unusual beauty.

SAN SEBASTIÁN AT-A-GLANCE

 SEEING THE CITY: San Sebastián is so small and compact that the entire city can be seen within 20 minutes of walking up Mt. Igueldo or Mt. Urgull. Contemplated from above, San Sebastián is a soothing experience. The bay and beaches could hardly be shaped more perfectly, and the relative newness of the city is evident in the way the avenues and streets are laid out in straight lines. Urgull is the lower vantage point and, therefore, the more accessible. The hill is crisscrossed by wooded and winding paths that can be joined where the Old Town meets the fishing port, or from the Paseo Nuevo, the promenade that begins beyond the aquarium and skirts the hill. Below is the tiny fishing port, brightly colored and more touristic than industrial, with its fish restaurants. Then there's the splendid La Concha, backed by 2 miles of elegant hotels and apartment blocks; no building is higher than 7 stories, giving the promenade a special aesthetic cohesion. A rocky promontory separates the Playa de la Concha from the next beach, Playa de Ondarreta, and beyond it is the higher Mt. Igueldo.

Mt. Igueldo is best ascended by car, by the bus that leaves every few minutes from the Boulevard (marked Igueldo), or by the funicular that leaves from the end of Ondarreta beach. The hill dominates the western end of the city, and it offers wonderful views of the Basque coast toward Zarauz and Guetaria. There is an amusement park and an extremely good camping site at the top of the hill, with excellent views inland. And the view of the city is superb: the bay, Ondarreta beach and La Concha's semicircle of fine golden sand, the fishing port, the Old Town, and the central shopping and residential area, which is dominated by the Buen Pastor (Good Shepherd) Cathedral.

SPECIAL PLACES: La Concha beach is the pearl in the San Sebastián oyster, and together with its promenade dominates the city — except at night, when the Old Town and the fishing port at La Concha's eastern end take over. South of the Old Town and La Concha is the charming shopping and residential area, bordered to the east by the Urumea River. This area (from the Alameda del Boulevard to Plaza de Guipúzcoa, on past Avenida de la Libertad to Plaza de Bilbao and the cathedral) is placid and pleasant, not much more than 100 years old. Indeed, because most of the city was built within the past 130 years — even the "Old Town" is 19th century — San Sebastián is short on historical monuments. Every single sight, monument, and museum can easily be exhausted in a day — even more reason for a calm and unhurried visit.

IN THE CITY

Playa de la Concha – This superb beach is the symbol of San Sebastián and undoubtedly the most famous stretch of sand in Spain. When the tide is out, several acres of fine sand are exposed. In the winter, soccer tournaments are held here, with several games being played simultaneously. In the summer, it is a family beach, thankfully free of hordes of radio-blasting rowdies. Meet the tide as it comes in and watch the fish swim around your legs. The promenade above the beach — Paseo de la Concha — is equally delightful, with ornate balustrades and richly ornamental lampposts reflecting the refined tastes of the Belle Epoque. It's an ideal place for leisurely strolls, with periodic pauses to gaze at the crowds on the beach below. Extending westward beyond a small rocky outlet is Ondarreta beach, also clean and excellent, but smaller than La Concha and without its peerless shell shape. At the end of Ondarreta is *El Peine* *del Viento* (The Comb of the Wind), a work of modern art, by the local sculptor Eduardo Chillida, formed by three large, pincer-shaped metal objects protruding from lumps of rock.

La Parte Vieja – The Old Town is not architecturally significant, apart from a handful of buildings that survived the burning of the city in 1813, but it is the market-place and social center of San Sebastián. Its narrow, straight streets are packed with bars, taverns, specialty shops, restaurants, and gastronomic societies. Popular among locals as well as visitors, it is virtually a "tourist trap"-free area. The arcaded Plaza de la Constitución, with the former City Hall at one end, stands in the center. Bullfights used to be held in the square, but the only remaining evidence of that are the numbered balconies where spectators once gathered. The city's two most important churches are survivors of the 1813 fire. The Gothic Church of San Vicente (Calle Narrica) is San Sebastián's oldest building, dating from 1570. Its interior is somber but impressive, with three naves, an octagonal apse, and large buttresses, all crowned with a tall presbytery that covers the altarpiece. At the other end of the Old Town is the graffiti-covered baroque Church of Santa María (Calle 31 de Agosto; phone: 423124). Completed in 1764, it has a richly ornate porch and central pillars supporting its lofty vaults. The statue of the Virgen del Coro (Virgin of the Choir), the city's patroness, is venerated at the main altar.

Museo de San Telmo – The early-16th-century building opposite the Church of San Vicente began as a Dominican monastery (1530–1830), became an artillery barracks in 1836, and was finally converted into a beautiful museum in 1932. Of greatest interest is the section dedicated to Basque ethnography, with paintings, statues, farming uten-sils, fossilized skeletons, and spinning tools to make flax, linen, and canvas. Artist José María Sert painted a series of works on the subject of Basque mythology especially for the museum; there also are three paintings by El Greco. The building's cloister is Renaissance with columns, semicircular arches, and ribbed vaults. Open in summer, Mondays through Saturdays from 9 AM to 9 PM, Sundays from 9 AM to 1 PM; in winter, Mondays through Saturdays from 9:45 AM to 1 PM and 3:30 to 7 PM, Sundays from 10 AM to 1 PM. Admission charge. Plaza de Zuluaga (phone: 424970).

City Hall – One of the most impressive Ayuntamientos (City Halls) in Spain, brim-ming with exquisite decor and marble staircases, this twin-towered building was erected as the *Gran Casino* worthy of San Sebastián's growing European status after the Second Carlist War (1876). The City Council donated 22,960 square feet of land where La Concha and the Boulevard met, facing the Old Town. The casino opened in 1887 and instantly became the center of business activity and progress in the city. Among other things, the casino financed the Alderdi-Eder Gardens, which brighten the area around City Hall with their characteristic squat tamarind trees with umbrella-shaped branches, offering protection from the frequent showers. A ban on gambling in 1924 closed the building until 1947, when the City Council moved in. City Hall is open to the public during office hours; no admission charge. Calle Ijentea.

Aquarium – Officially known as the *Oceanographical Museum* or the Palace of the Sea, the aquarium is a 3-story building that opened in 1928 where the harbor meets the foot of Mt. Urgull, near the beginning of the Paseo Nuevo. The ground floor is an aquarium with many types of marine fauna on view; the first-floor *Oceanographical Museum* boasts collections of shells, fish, seabirds, seaweed, crustacea, and coral, as well as the skeleton of the last whale to be caught in local waters, in 1878; the second floor houses the *Naval Museum,* with documents and models pertaining to the Basque Country's seafaring tradition. Open daily, from 10 AM to 1:30 PM and 3:30 to 7:30 PM (summers until 8 PM); closed Mondays from mid-September through mid-May. Admis-sion charge. Paseo Nuevo (phone: 421905).

Castle of Santa Cruz de la Mota – The ruins of the castle on top of Mt. Urgull house a *Military Museum* of little interest. But the castle grounds are dotted with several rusting cannon left by Napoleon's troops when the Duke of Wellington stormed the town in 1813. It's hard to believe that they have been lying in their original locations for nearly 180 years, and haven't been carted off to some museum in London or Madrid. Within the castle is a modern chapel topped by a nearly 100-foot statue of Christ, visible from anywhere in the city. The museum, containing displays of artillery, swords, and pistols dating from the 15th to the 18th century, is open Mondays through Saturdays from 10 AM to 1 PM and 3:30 to 5:30 PM, Sundays from 10 AM to 1 PM. Admission charge. Mt. Urgull.

Urumea River – The real delight here consists of the walks along either side of the river as it flows into the Bay of Biscay. The Urumea is spanned by three Parisian-style bridges of great charm for lovers of the Belle Epoque ornate. The 1905 Puente María Cristina, which leads from the residential area at Plaza de Bilbao to the main France–Madrid railway station, is especially flamboyant, with tiered turrets at either end. The Puente Santa Catalina, nearer to the sea, takes traffic over to the uninteresting Gros district, where there is a third San Sebastián beach (not recommended). The Puente Zurriola de Kursaal is just yards from the sea, near the *Victoria Eugenia Theater* and the *María Cristina* hotel. These buildings, erected early in this century, have both undergone lavish refurbishing in the past decade and form a stunning unity beside the bridge with its huge lampposts, especially when floodlit at night. On either side of the river, along the Paseo República Argentina or the Paseo de Francia, the 10-minute stroll offers a pleasant alternative to La Concha. The large modern sculpture dominating the outcrop between the Zurriola de Kursaal Bridge and the Gros beach is the work of local sculptor Néstor Basterretxea; called the *Dove of Peace,* it is 23 feet high and weighs 4 tons.

Catedral Buen Pastor – San Sebastián's largest church, the 250-foot-high ogival-style Good Shepherd Cathedral was inaugurated in 1897. A neo-Gothic structure with striking exterior flying buttresses and a belfry that opens to a central nave, it stands in a large square in the modern quarter. Open daily, from 7:30 AM to 12:30 PM and from 5 to 8:30 PM. Płaza del Buen Pastor (phone: 464516).

Palacio Miramar – The English-style Miramar Palace stands on a low hill overlooking La Concha and Ondarreta, with the residential district of Antiguo behind it. Funded by Queen María Cristina and opened in 1893, the palace fell into decline and was closed during the 1931–36 Republic and the 1936–39 Civil War. Purchased by the City Council in 1971, it is currently under renovation, but the expansive lawns are open to the public from 9 AM to 9 PM in summer and from 10 AM to 5 PM in winter. No admission charge.

Palacio de Ayete – Built by the Duke of Bailen in 1878, the Ayete Palace was the summer residence of King Alfonso XII and Queen María Cristina until the Miramar Palace was constructed. Set back from the bay on the Ayete estate, amid 243,000 square feet of beautiful parkland, the palace was also the summer residence of Generalísimo Francisco Franco from 1940 until his death in 1975, and the site of his cabinet meetings every summer. The palace is closed to the public, but the lush forest trails are worth a stroll. Open summers, from 10 AM to 8:30 PM; winters, from 10 AM to 5 PM. No admission charge.

ENVIRONS

Monte Igueldo – A trip to the heart of Mt. Igueldo affords some idyllic panoramas of the dramatic coastline of the Bay of Biscay and the Guipúzcoan countryside, not to mention a chance to sample some traditional local cider, second in fame and quality only to that from Asturias. Take the steep road to the Igueldo campsite and turn right, down a narrow lane opposite the *Bar Gure-etxea.* After a mile, there is the *Bar Asador*

Nícolas, a simple *sidrería* (cider house) that has stupendous views over the haystack-dotted countryside, with the sea visible beyond. A liter of the excellent local cider costs just $1.50, and the best brewing months are February through April.

Fuenterrabía – Known as Hondarribia in Euskera (the Basque language), this beautiful town lies 14½ miles (23 km) east of San Sebastián, and overlooks the French town of Hendaye, from which it is divided by the Bidasoa River. Not surprisingly, Fuenterrabía was a fortress town for centuries, and historians have lost count of the number of sieges it suffered. So many Castilian kings honored it for fighting off French attacks that the town bears an official title meaning "very noble, very loyal, very courageous, and always very faithful." (Most medieval towns were lucky to have a simple "loyal" or "noble" conferred on them.) The town's Nagusi Kalea (Main Street) is straight out of the Middle Ages, and the nearby narrow streets are flanked by Renaissance and baroque mansions with huge carved eaves and wrought-iron balconies. The town is dominated by an 11th-century fortress that was restored by the Holy Roman Emperor Charles V in the 16th century and now serves as the *Parador El Emperador* (Plaza de Armas del Castillo; phone: 642140). The only *parador* in Guipúzcoa, it has 16 rooms overlooking the French border, and is in itself an excellent reason for visiting Fuenterrabía.

■**EXTRA SPECIAL:** Stand anywhere on or near the beach from Mt. Urgull to Mt. Igueldo at 11 PM on any night during the *Aste Nagusia* (Great Week) fiestas, around August 15, for San Sebastián's renowned fireworks displays. The fiestas coincide with the *International Fireworks Competition,* when manufacturers from many countries compete for the coveted first prize. San Sebastián's fireworks week is regarded by Spaniards as the best in Europe — although Monaco and Cannes might have a different opinion. What makes San Sebastián's celebration so wonderful is the unique setting: A 40-minute display might take in Mt. Igueldo to the left, Santa Clara Island in the middle, and Mt. Urgull to the right, all marvelously floodlit. Find a spot early — after 10:30 it's usually impossible to get a good vantage point.

SOURCES AND RESOURCES

TOURIST INFORMATION: There are two very helpful tourist offices, a short walk from one another. The Centro de Atracción y Turismo (CAT), run by the City Council (on Calle Reina Regente, next door to the *Victoria Eugenia Theater;* phone: 481166). The office is open Mondays through Fridays from 9 AM to 2 PM and 3:30 to 7:30 PM, Saturdays from 9 AM to 2 PM. This office is responsible for the promotion of San Sebastián and Guipúzcoa only, and has excellent information on local fiestas, rural sports, and so on. At the eastern end of La Concha is the Oficina de Turismo del Gobierno Vasco (13 Calle Andia; phone: 426282), run by the Basque Autonomous Government. It is open Mondays through Fridays from 9 AM to 1:30 PM and 3:30 to 6:30 PM, Saturdays from 9 AM to 1:30 PM. Many of the English-language tourist brochures available at both locations are poorly translated, but this should not present any major problem in understanding them.

Local Coverage – The best newspapers for local news in San Sebastián are the moderate *Diario Vasco,* the radical nationalist *Egin,* and the moderate nationalist *Deia.* The best place to buy international newspapers is the kiosk in front of the Banco de Bilbao, near the La Concha end of Avenida de la Libertad.

TELEPHONE: The city code for San Sebastián is 43. If calling from within Spain, dial 943 before the local number.

GETTING AROUND: Any point in San Sebastián is easily reached on foot, except for the top of Mt. Igueldo, which can be reached by taxi or the bus marked Igueldo from the Boulevard.

Airport – San Sebastián Airport is in nearby Fuenterrabía, but it handles only domestic flights (phone: 642144). The nearest international airport is Bilbao's Sondika Airport.

Bicycle – Bicycles can be rented from *Mini* (10 Calle Escolta Real; phone: 211758), for between $5 and $10 per day.

Bus – City buses stop running at around midnight. It's best to buy a *bonobus,* a card allowing 10 trips for about $4); a single journey costs 60 pesetas (about 50¢). Several different bus companies offer service within the Basque Country and beyond. Their offices are on or around the Plaza de Pio XII. Ask for details at either of the tourist offices.

Car Rental – The major car rental companies with offices in San Sebastián are *Atesa* (2 Plaza Zaragoza; phone: 425976); *Avis* (2 Calle Triunfo; phone: 461556); *Diago* (9 Calle Aguirre Miramón; phone: 283701); *Europcar* (60 Calle San Martín; phone: 461717); and *Hertz* (2 Calle Marina; phone: 461084).

Taxi – Taxis are not plentiful. The main stands are located on the Alameda del Boulevard by Calle Mayor and at 31 Avenida de la Libertad, or call 420340.

Train – All trains from the French border crossing of Hendaye-Irún, 12 miles (19 km) away, stop at San Sebastián's Estación Norte, just over the María Cristina Bridge by the Paseo de Francia (phone: 283599), on their way to Madrid. A second station, the Estación Amara, of the narrow-gauge *FEVE* line linking San Sebastián with Bilbao, is by the Paseo de Errondo (phone: 450131).

SPECIAL EVENTS: Beyond any doubt, San Sebastián enjoys more than its fair share of riotous carnivals and fiestas, beginning with one of Spain's great undiscovered festivals, the January 19 and 20 *Tamborrada* (Festival of Drums). January 20 is *St. Sebastián's Day,* and for 24 hours beginning at midnight on the 19th, the Old Town is filled with young and old dressed as 19th-century soldiers, bakers, and chefs, all banging *tambores* (drums) to mark the annual recurrence of a tradition that began in the early 19th century — although nobody knows exactly how or why. The festivities start on the 19th, with a hearty feast in one of the gastronomic societies or restaurants, and go on to include over 40 *tamborrada* processions, but the two most important are the adults' procession at midnight on the 19th in the Plaza de la Constitución, and the children's procession — with 4,000 children — at midday on the 20th outside City Hall.

The next important event is the *International Jazz Festival,* or *Jazzaldia,* during the second half of July, conveniently following the *Fiesta de San Fermín* and the running of the bulls in nearby Pamplona. The *Aste Nagusia* (Great Week) of carnivals around August 15 involves much more than incredible nightly fireworks displays: Basque sports, processions, folkloric displays, gastronomic competitions, and even pro-independence alternative events are included. The last 2 weeks of August offer the *Classical Music Fortnight,* after which the *Basque Fiestas,* with the emphasis on the promotion of Euskera, the Basque language, begin on the first Sunday in September. Also in September, the first two Sundays, are the famous *Regatas de Traineras* (fishing-boat rowing races), which have been held on La Concha bay since 1879. Tens of thousands gather to watch and wager money on teams from every town and village along the

Basque coast, and in the week between the races, to participate in Basque sports — tree chopping, rock lifting, pelota, oxen dragging rocks — as well as folkloric dancing, improvised poetry and theater performances in Euskera, basket making, and so on. The most prestigious annual event is San Sebastián's *International Film Festival,* during the second half of September, now one of the premier events of its type in Europe.

SHOPPING: San Sebastián is one of the wealthiest cities in Spain, and perhaps more important, its proximity to France gives it a certain snobbery when it comes to taste and style — not to mention price. Probably the most distinctive local feature is the Basque beret, or *txapela,* but these are going out of fashion and, in many cases, have a "country yokel" air about them. Note that San Sebastián does not have any department stores and has few supermarkets. Its two central food markets, very colorful and interesting, are *Mercado La Brecha* (at the river end of the Boulevard) and *Mercado San Martín* (on Calle Urbieta, 2 blocks from La Concha). The best shopping streets are Avenida de la Libertad, Calle San Marcial, Calle Loyola, and the square surrounding the Buen Pastor Cathedral. Shopping hours are generally from 9:30 AM to 1:30 PM and 3:30 to 8 PM. Most stores and shops are closed Sundays; some close Monday mornings as well.

Auzmendi – Very trendy clothes for men and women by the best known-local designer. 28 Avenida de la Libertad (phone: 420204).

Ayestarán – Excellent handmade shoes and leather bags, at reasonable prices. 29 Avenida de la Libertad (phone: 424060).

Bárbara – Exquisite and very expensive gold jewelry sold behind an unimposing wood exterior. 23 Calle Guetaria (phone: 422680).

Casa Basarte – The best selection of genuine *txapelas* (Basque berets) in town. Also a good range of leather goods. 18 Calle San Jerónimo (phone: 426096).

Delgado – The oldest and one of the best clothing shops in San Sebastián, a family-run affair dating from 1899. Much of the material is now imported from Italy, but the conservatively styled menswear is still made on the premises. 43 Avenida de la Libertad (phone: 426625).

Elizondo – Sports shop with the latest equipment for windsurfing, surfing, sailing, skating, and basketball (including NBA badges and coaching manuals). Calle Arrasate, corner of Paseo de los Fueros (phone: 424097).

Ramón Hernández – Exclusive gentlemen's and ladies' outfitters, with expensive imported and local styles. 23 Avenida de la Libertad (phone: 426849).

Juguetería Antón – Basically a toy shop, but with an amazing collection of Spanish jigsaw puzzles. Designs range from Goya paintings to Moorish tiles, containing up to 8,000 pieces. 21 Calle San Jerónimo (phone: 425017).

Sanfor – The best leather and fur store, featuring beautiful coats, bags, and accessories. 21 Calle Hernani (phone: 421657).

SPORTS AND FITNESS: Boating – Rowing is a Basque passion, especially when the vessel is a large *trainera,* or fishing boat. The tradition dates from the days when fishermen used to row back into harbor, usually against a fierce cross wind. There are many events throughout the year, but don't miss the *Regatas de Traineras* at La Concha (see *Special Events*) on the first two Sundays in September.

Fishing – Fishing from the rocks and even surf casting are popular. The tourist offices can provide exact information.

Golf – The 18-hole course at the *Real Club de Golf de San Sebastián* is 14½ miles (23 km) east of the city in Fuenterrabía (phone: 616845). The 9-hole *Real Club de Golf de Zarauz* is 16 miles (26 km) to the west in Barrio de Mendilauta (phone: 830145).

Horse Racing – San Sebastián's racetrack (in the town of Lasarte, about 4 miles/6 km south of the city) is the only one in Spain to hold summer races. Indeed, there is only one other racetrack still in use in Spain: Madrid's winter-and-spring-only track. For more information, contact the *Sociedad Hipódromo de San Sebastián,* 2 Plaza de Zaragoza (phone: 421002).

Pelota – A pelota court is called a frontón, and there are many in the city. The most popular is the *Frontón de Anoeta,* in the excellent indoor sports complex of the same name (phone: 455917). From a spectator's point of view, the most exciting form of pelota is the very fast *cesta punta,* played with a curved wicker basket used to whip the ball off the wall at lightning speeds.

Soccer – San Sebastián's *Real Sociedad* was one of the shock teams of the 1980s in the Spanish League. After winning nothing since its formation in 1909, it won the coveted league title in 1981 and 1982, the *Spanish Cup* in 1987, and was league runner-up on two other occasions. The club plays its home games in the 28,000-seat *Atotxa Stadium,* located behind the Estación Norte.

Swimming – La Concha is obviously the first choice, for its beauty, fine sand, and safe waters. Even on rough days, Santa Clara Island tames the mightier waves, although they are often big enough for reasonable surfing. Ondarreta beach is also very good, and popular among locals. Gros Beach, the smallest, is dirty and unattractive. There are indoor pools in the La Perla building (Paseo de la Concha; phone: 461258), and at the *Piscina de Tenis Ondarreta* (Plaza de Ondarreta; phone: 218136); the *Anoeta Sports Complex* (phone: 273113) has an open-air pool. All indoor facilities have an admission charge.

Tennis – Courts are available for rent at the *Real Club de Tenis* (Paseo de Ondarreta; phone: 212702) just behind the beach.

 THEATER AND MUSIC: The grand *Teatro Victoria Eugenia,* with its richly decorated ceiling, dome, and spacious foyer, opened just 11 days after the neighboring *María Cristina* hotel in 1912. Home of theater, classical music, ballet, and opera in San Sebastián, as well as the *International Film Festival,* which has been held here every September since 1953, the theater (Calle Reina Regente; phone: 421874) is also the home of the *Classical Music Fortnight* in late August. July's *International Jazz Festival* is held in the pavilion at the *Anoeta Sports Complex* and the open-air Plaza de Trinidad in the Old Town. *Anoeta* is also the venue for major rock concerts, since San Sebastián, together with Madrid and Barcelona, is a "must" on the European tours of many US and British groups.

 NIGHTCLUBS AND NIGHTLIFE: A good night out in San Sebastián involves a hearty Basque meal followed by drinks in one of the numerous late-night bars in the Old Town or in one of the classier pubs in the streets close to La Concha. There are no nightclubs or shows as such, but the discotheques vary from wild and teenage to somewhat more sedate. The best known is *Discoteca Ku* (in Barrio de Igueldo, halfway toward the campsite; phone: 212051), open from midnight to dawn for the super-cool. There are three very lively discotheques along the Paseo de la Concha, virtually on the beach: *La Perla* (phone: 460439), *Bataplán* (phone: 460436), and *La Rotonda* (phone: 428095). The *Be Bop Bar* (3 Paseo de Salamanca) is a piano bar with occasional live jazz performances, not far from the *Victoria Eugenia Theater.* The city's hippest music bars are grouped on Calle San Bartolomé — the best are *Bañeros* (17 San Bartolomé); *Boomerang* (No. 21); *Bowie* (No. 34); *Porsche* (No. 40); *Twickenham* (No. 36); and *Trocadero* (No. 23). The *Casino Gran Kursaal* (in the *Londres y de Inglaterra* hotel, but not affiliated with the hotel) is open Mondays through Fridays, from 6 PM to 2 AM; Saturdays and Sundays, from 6 PM to 3 AM. The entrance fee is about $7.

presence had a tremendous influence on Spanish history. With the discovery of the tomb, Christian Spain found its patron saint.

The famous Way of St. James (Camino de Santiago), the pilgrims' route to Santiago, is one of the world's oldest tour routes, marked by the churches, monasteries, hospitals, and hospices (the latter the hotels of the day) set up to accommodate them as they moved toward their destination. (For further details of the history of St. James and the pilgrimages, see *Pilgrims' Route,* DIRECTIONS.) The route remained heavily traveled until the 16th century, when, in 1589, Sir Francis Drake attacked La Coruña, and the Bishop of Santiago de Compostela removed the relics from the church for safekeeping, as a result of which they disappeared for 3 centuries. This effectively put an end to pilgrimages until the relics were found again in 1879 and the pilgrimages resumed. Today, pilgrims and the city still do the saint honor, and in *Jubilee* years — years when his holy day (July 25) falls on a Sunday (the next one is in 1993) — the celebrations are especially intense.

Santiago's center of attraction is its cathedral, begun in the 11th century, but not finished until the 13th century. It can be seen from plazas on all sides, the largest of which is the Plaza del Obradoiro, or the Plaza de España. The magnificent Obradoiro façade, an 18th-century creation of Fernando Casas y Novoa, is richly ornate, sculpted in a blend of straight and curved lines characteristic of the baroque style. Also wonderful to behold are the 12th-century Romanesque Gate of Glory, the Romanesque Goldsmith's Door, and the 17th-century Puerta Santa, or Holy Door, which is open only in *Jubilee* years. Beyond the cathedral, the city's narrow streets and dozens of other, smaller churches, monasteries, and convents, as well as bars, shops, and old merchant houses, are appealing. There is a mystical feel to the place, church bells constantly chiming.

But Santiago also is the site of one of Spain's earliest and most important universities, which means that it has something of the flavor of a modern, earthy university town, with tiny pubs, Celtic music, and nonstop conversations on the affairs of the world. Most of the 30,000-odd students live in the new districts of Santiago, however, districts that surround the Old Town but are well separated from it by broad avenues. Thus, in many ways, it seems that life in the Galician capital (pop. 93,000) hasn't changed at all. The feeling of a lived-in museum is heightened when its inhabitants empty into the streets to discuss the ramifications of life, using Gallego, the local dialect, which closely resembles Portuguese and is spoken interchangeably with Spanish. Though still remote, Santiago is as much a focus of tourism as ever, even if today's pilgrims come as much to see the sights as to see their souls.

SANTIAGO AT-A-GLANCE

SEEING THE CITY: There are two favorite vantage points from which to view Santiago. The walkway along the Coto de Santa Susana, a hill that rises across from the cathedral, offers a wonderful panoramic view. For an evocative look at the city from the midst of its clustered buildings, the choice is the balcony off the cathedral cloister, which looks out over the roofs of the town and down the bustling Calle del Franco.

SPECIAL PLACES: The main commercial streets — Calle del Franco, Rúa del Villar, and Rúa Nueva — radiate from the right front of the cathedral and are exquisite examples of medieval thoroughfares, lined with opulent houses with elegantly sculpted façades and intricate ironwork. Behind the cathedral are the historic streets that for centuries led pilgrims — many of them on their knees — into Santiago at the completion of their long journey. Also behind the cathedral is the bustling town marketplace, packed with fish, meat, fruit, and vegetable stands, open every morning except Sundays.

Cathedral – The goal of one of the world's primary pilgrimages, the cathedral was built on the site of a Roman graveyard and the foundations of Alfonso II's 9th-century basilica housing the remains of St. James. All but St. James's tomb were destroyed by Al-Mansur, the Moorish leader, in 997. The present structure was begun around 1075, and was largely completed in the 13th century. The relics of St. James, the object of devotion of centuries of pilgrims, are buried under the high altar.

The cathedral is basically a baroque shell around a Romanesque interior. The Obradoiro façade, the cathedral's western front, faces the Plaza del Obradoiro (Square of Goldwork; also called the Plaza de España) and is considered among the most beautiful cathedral façades in Christendom. Towering above a broad flight of steps (completed in 1606), the Obradoiro façade was designed by Fernando Casas y Novoa and completed in 1750; it is a baroque masterpiece of decorative flourishes and merging curves and lines. The two bell towers, Torre de la Carraca and Torre de las Campanas, were completed in the 17th and 18th centuries, respectively.

The Puerta de las Platerías, facing south onto Plaza de las Platerías, is the cathedral's famous Goldsmith's Door, 12th-century Romanesque. The Puerta Santa, or Holy Door (also known as the Puerta del Perdón, or Pardon Door), because it is open only in *Jubilee* years, faces east onto Plaza de la Quintana, and dates from 1611; the 17th-century Torre del Reloj flanks it. The north façade, facing Plaza de la Azabachería (or Plaza Inmaculada), contains the Puerta de la Azabachería, rebuilt by Ventura Rodríguez in 1765–70.

Illuminated only by candles and occasional shafts of sunlight, the cathedral's interior is a magnificent world of Romanesque opulence and hushed reverence. Just inside the Obradoiro entrance is the Pórtico de la Gloria (Gate of Glory), essentially an older, Romanesque façade within the baroque one, carved by the renowned sculptor Master Mateo between 1168 and 1188. An unsurpassed sculptural masterpiece of the original Romanesque cathedral, the Gate of Glory has three arched doorways, one each for the main nave and side aisles, and more than 200 carved figures. Its overall harmony is magical, yet it also demands careful examination. The central column of the main doorway, carved as a Tree of Jesse, rises to a figure of the seated St. James. It is customary for pilgrims to touch the marble pillar upon their safe arrival, and after centuries, smooth holes in the form of the hand's five fingers have been worn into the marble. At the base of the pillar, kneeling and facing the high altar, is a sculpted self-portrait of Master Mateo. Many pilgrims tap their head against his, hoping to receive some of his genius. Above, on the central arch, are the 24 old men of the Apocalypse surrounding Christ; they hold instruments, one of which (the central one) is a Galician *zanfona,* found only in Celtic regions of the world. The left arch bears a grouping of statues depicting the imprisoned ten tribes of Israel, and Adam and Eve on either side of Christ. On the right arch is the Last Judgment. Angels protect the "blessed" on the left side of the arch, while the "damned" are devoured by devils to the right. Note the local flavor — one of the "damned" is eating an *empanada* (Galician flat pie with meat or fish filling), while another squeezes a drink from a wineskin, symbolizing gluttony.

The remaining focus of the interior is the high altar, a dazzling creation in silver and gold backed by another statue of St. James. The altar is built atop the crypt of St. James, and the faithful can climb down the stairs to pay their respects. Many pilgrims also climb up behind the altar to embrace the statue and kiss the saint's mantle. The cathedral museum, divided into three sections, contains the usual ecclesiastic paraphernalia, in addition to a collection of tapestries showing everyday life in the Middle Ages, archaeological artifacts, and the *botafumeiro* (giant incense burner), which is swung like a bell through the transept during the most important services and celebrations. The portico off the museum offers excellent views of the town and of the Plaza del Obradoiro. The cathedral is open daily from 8 AM to 8 PM; museum hours are 10 AM to 1:30 PM and 3:30 to 7:30 PM. Admission charge to the museum. Plaza del Obradoiro.

Hostal de los Reyes Católicos – This magnificently decorated 15th-century former royal hospital and pilgrims' *hostal,* located in the Plaza del Obradoiro next to the cathedral, is now one of Spain's most memorable hotels (see *Checking In*). Designed by Enrique de Egas, a favorite architect of King Ferdinand and Queen Isabella, the building so captured the interest of the Catholic Monarchs that they personally made decisions about its interior details, such as where to install fireplaces and what wood to select for the floors. Completed in the 17th century, its highlights include an exquisite Plateresque entrance and four 16th- and 18th-century cloistered courtyards with lovely fountains. Also notice the central chapel's wrought-iron designs and beamed ceilings. The complex can be toured with a personal guide; it's also normally included as part of wider group tours of Santiago. Plaza del Obradoiro (phone: 582200).

Monasterio de San Pelayo de Ante-Altares – A colossal monastery located directly behind (east of) the cathedral. Originally founded by Alfonso II, the present structure dates back to the late 17th century and contains a small church with a baroque altarpiece flanked by altars bearing the story of the life of the Virgin Mary. There is also a small museum. Open from 10 AM to 1 PM and 4 to 6:30 PM. Admission charge to the museum. Vía Sacra.

Casa de la Parra – Next to San Pelayo and named for a bunch of grapes, this 17th-century baroque mansion is now an art gallery, featuring exhibitions of contemporary works in revolving 25-day displays. Exhibits include paintings, ceramics, sculpture, and videos, sometimes in combination. Open from noon to 2 PM and 7 to 9:30 PM; closed Sundays. No admission charge. Vía Sacra.

Monasterio de San Martín Pinario – Originally dating from 912, this multi-styled monastery features three majestic 17th- and 18th-century cloisters and a church with a wide central nave and an ornate baroque altarpiece by Casas y Novoa. The supporting altarpieces are as ornate as the main altar, behind which are some of the most beautiful choir stalls imaginable, carved with scenes from the birth, life, and death of Christ, as well as the death of the Virgin Mary and her assumption into heaven. Open daily, from 10 AM to 1 PM and 4 to 7 PM. Plaza Inmaculada, with the church opening onto Plaza San Martín.

Santa María la Real del Sar – This 12th-century Romanesque collegiate church appears odd in that it is not large, yet has giant 18th-century flying buttresses supporting its walls. The need for them becomes apparent inside. It seems the church was built on soft, sandy soil, and the columns began to slip as the weight of the ceiling bore down over the years. From an interior perspective, they appear to be falling outward — thus the buttresses to keep the church stable. About half a mile (1 km) south of the Old Town. Open from 10 AM to 1 PM and 4 to 6 PM. Admission charge. Calle de Castrón d'Ouro.

SOURCES AND RESOURCES

TOURIST INFORMATION: Santiago's *Oficina de Turismo* (43 Rúa del Villar; phone: 584081) can provide general information and an excellent glossy brochure on the city that includes a detailed map. During the annual *Feast of St. James,* the tourist office also distributes a guide to events. Open weekdays, from 10 AM to 2 PM and 4 to 7 PM; Saturdays, from 9 AM to 2 PM.

Local Coverage – The local newspaper is *El Correo Gallego,* a daily publication written in Spanish with the occasional article in the Galician dialect.

TELEPHONE: The city code for Santiago is 81 If calling from within Spain, dial 981 before the local number.

GETTING AROUND: Santiago is very concentrated. Most pubs, restaurants, and shops are within a relatively small, walkable area.

Airport – The Santiago airport is in Labacolla, 7 miles (11 km) east of the city via the C547 highway. Buses to Santiago leave the airport eight times a day, coinciding with flight schedules. Buses to the airport leave from the entrance of the *Iberia* office (24 Calle General Pardiñas) in the new part of town. To reserve bus tickets, call *Iberia*'s airport office (phone: 597554), or stop in at the ticket office at the above address. (For additional airport information call 597400 or 597550; for *Iberia* reservations, call 594100).

Bus – Santiago's city bus routes connect various points of the Old Town, but there is little cause to use them, as the town is so compact. The fare is about 50¢. The central bus station is located on Calle San Cayetano (phone: 587700). There is frequent daily service to Madrid, Barcelona, La Coruña, Vigo, Pontevedra, and San Sebastián.

Car Rental – Rental companies include *Hertz* (145 Avenida de Lugo; phone: 585362; and at the airport), *Avis* (10 Calle República de El Salvador; phone: 561122), and *Budget/Autotour* (in *Los Reyes Católicos* hotel; phone: 586496).

Taxi – Call one of the city cabstands for a taxi (your hotel will know the nearest one). There are two main, midtown taxi stands (Avenida de Figueroa; phone: 585973; and Avenida General Franco; phone: 561020). Late-night service is available from the Plaza Galicia stand (phone: 561028).

Train – The Santiago train station (phone: 596050) is about a 10-minute walk down Avenida General Franco from the Old Town — or take the No. 14 bus. There is frequent, daily train service to Madrid, La Coruña, San Sebastián, Irún, Pontevedra, Vigo, and Porto, Portugal.

SPECIAL EVENTS: Santiago's major annual celebration is the *Fiesta del Apóstol* (Feast of the Apostle, or Feast of St. James), which takes place on July 25. The actual festivities are played out between July 15 and month's end, with the main events occurring from July 23 through July 26. Galician folkloric shows, competitions, special theater presentations, daily concerts, and a jazz festival consisting of performances by major international groups in the Plaza de Tournal are among the attractions. A spectacular fireworks display is held in front of the cathedral on the eve of the feast day (July 24), and the day itself is marked by a high mass in the morning, street bands, special theater, and an orchestral presentation in the Plaza del Obradoiro. The swinging of the *botafumeiro* (giant incense burner) across the cathedral transepts during the mass on July 25 is televised live throughout Spain. During *Jubilee* years, established by papal bull in the 12th century, the St. James celebrations are particularly intense, the cathedral's Puerta Santa is open, and pilgrims who visit the shrine receive special grace. These days occur when July 25 falls on a Sunday, which happens in a sequence of every 6, 5, 6, and 11 years. The next *Jubilee* year will be 1993.

MUSEUMS: Besides the attractions listed in *Special Places,* Santiago boasts a number of other churches, monasteries, and religious buildings, some housing small museums. Two worth visiting are the *Museo de Pobo Galego* and the *Museo Municipal,* both set up in the Convento de Santo Domingo and containing various ethnographic illustrations of rural Galician life. Open Mondays through Saturdays, from 10 AM to 1 PM and 4 to 7 PM. Admission charge. Calle de las Casas Reals (phone: 583620).

SHOPPING: Santiago's main shopping district is located in the New Town on Calles General Pardiñas, República de El Salvador, Alfredo Brañas, and Montero Rios. The Old Town's most popular street for shopping is Calle Calderería, which runs parallel to Rúa Nueva. A wide variety of street vendors operate along Rúa Nueva, and there is a weekly Sunday market at Plaza Abestos, next to the Convent of San Agustín. Many shops are worth browsing. General shopping hours are Mondays through Fridays from 9:30 AM to 1:30 PM and 4:30 to 7 PM, Saturdays from 9:30 AM to 2 PM, but may vary from shop to shop.

Antiquedades Sanonia – Featuring antiques, glassware, jewelry, and fine furniture. 22 Calle Gelmírez (phone: 582830).

Confitería Mora – One of the best-known pastry shops in town, a good place to buy a *tarta de Santiago.* Rúa del Villar (phone: 581014).

Fernando Meyer – Very good old European prints and paintings. 6 Plaza de las Platerías (phone: 582536).

Retablo – Fine antiques and artworks. 1 Plaza de la Quintana (phone: 582526).

Sargadelos – One of the best places for Galicia's unique Sargadelos ceramics. Rúa Nueva (phone: 581905).

Tenda – Another shop specializing in fine antiques, ceramics, and jewelry. 23 Calle Gelmírez (phone: 582520).

Xanela – Creative local souvenirs, including tiny, hand-carved cathedrals, ceramic dolls, and religious medallions. 14 Rúa Nueva (phone: 584171)

SPORTS AND FITNESS: Golf – The private, 9-hole *Real Aero Club* golf course is located near the airport. Non-members and visitors are permitted to play on a space-available basis. Call in advance for information (phone: 592092).

Swimming – A public pool is available in the *Santa Isabela Sports Complex* (just south of the Old Town; phone: 581209). There is also a public swimming pool at the university (phone: 584216). Both facilities charge a small admission fee.

Tennis – The university has tennis courts (phone: 584795). Call well in advance for information on availability and to book court time.

THEATER AND MUSIC: There are no regularly scheduled theater or musical seasons in Santiago, but like most Spanish university towns, there is a student *tuna* group, which performs in Plaza del Obradoiro and surrounding squares. Members of the *tuna* wear student capes, and when they are not serenading a woman, their songs tend to be indelicate.

NIGHTCLUBS AND NIGHTLIFE: Santiago is packed with pubs, bars, and discotheques. A night on the town might consist of *tapas* (see *Eating Out* and *Tapas Bars*) from 6 PM to 8 PM, dinner from 9 PM to midnight, and a combination of pubs and discos from 11 PM to 3 AM. Among the popular pubs in the Old Town, mostly found around the walls of the San Pelayo monastery, are *O'Galo d'Ouro* (14 Calle de Conga), which provides a cozy atmosphere in a series of small rooms built into medieval horse stables, and *Modus Vivendi* (1 Plaza Feixou), small and also occupying old stables; in the far back room an ancient watering trough is used as a table and the ribbed horse ramp still leads customers down to lower levels. A small pub with no advertised name at 22 Calle de San Pelayo de Antes-Altares is also worth testing. Farther around the monastery, at *Paradiso Perdito* (3 Plaza de los Gattos), customers walk down a stairway where thousands of students have carved their names. *The Casa dos Crechas* (3 Vía Sacra) is a Celtic music pub where the bartenders and waitresses speak only Gallego — at any moment both the upstairs and downstairs rooms may be filled with the sound of impromptu musicians playing a reel or two on fiddle, tin whistle, and guitar. Popular discotheques include *Discoteca Araguaney* (at the *Araguaney Hotel,* 5 Calle Alfredo Brañas; phone: 595900); *Disco Kilaté* (Calle Santiago de Guayaquil); and *Discoteca Negro* (in the *Peregrino Hotel,* Avenida Rosalía de Castro; phone: 591850).

BEST IN TOWN

CHECKING IN: As the destination of Christianity's third most important pilgrimage and a major university town, Santiago boasts hundreds of places to stay, ranging from luxurious hotels to tiny pilgrim's *hostals,* although the options shrink when only those with private bathrooms and locations within walking distance of the monumental area of town are considered. A double room will cost $100 or more in a hotel listed as expensive, from $55 to $90 in a moderate one, and $45 or less in an inexpensive one. Since the summer weather is generally mild, air conditioned rooms are relatively nonexistent. All telephone numbers are in the 81 city code unless otherwise indicated.

Araguaney – A modern, luxurious, 62-room hotel in the heart of the New Town. It's a popular choice of visiting businesspeople, with a heated swimming pool and a discotheque, but its plain structure doesn't make any particular architectural statement. 5 Calle Alfredo Brañas (phone: 595900). Expensive.

Parador Los Reyes Católicos – One of Spain's great *paradores,* its architecture alone helps to place it among Europe's finest properties. The building itself is a tourist attraction (see *Special Places*), with 136 elegant rooms surrounding four splendid Renaissance courtyards. The *Peregrinos* restaurant is magnificent, although the international cuisine doesn't match the splendid setting. The location is excellent, with the front door opening right onto Plaza del Obradoiro, adjacent to the cathedral. 1 Plaza del Obradoiro (phone: 582200). Expensive.

Compostela – Another old establishment in a great location, just across the street from one of the main entrances into the Old Town. The 99 rooms have all the amenities (telephones, color TV sets, room service), although the hotel could use some sprucing up and a bit of brightness. 1 Avenida General Franco (phone: 585700). Moderate.

Gelmírez – Located between the railway station and the Old Town, it's a clean, modern, soulless creation, the second-largest (138 rooms) in town after the *Pere-*

grino. Service must be extracted from the staff. 92 Avenida General Franco (phone: 561100). Moderate.

Peregrino – A rather nondescript modern hotel, some distance from the center of town, it has 148 plain rooms and a restaurant. But it does have two major advantages: good, quick service and an excellent, large pool. Avenida Rosalía de Castro (phone: 591850). Moderate.

Rey Fernando – A pleasant, modern place close to the train station, with a charming staff and a comfortable TV lounge. The 24 rooms are bright and functional, and the surrounding streets are lively during the school year, without being noisy. 30 Calle Fernando III El Santo (phone: 593550). Moderate.

Windsor – Santiago's most popular *hostal,* this pleasant establishment remains full almost year-round, so book well in advance. The 50 rooms are spotless, the lobby glistening, and service is always rendered with a smile. 16 Calle República de El Salvador (phone: 592939). Moderate.

Mapoula – Another *hostal* in the Old Town, a few steps from the Plaza Galicia. The 10 rooms are all nicely furnished and have private baths; the proprietor takes a personal interest in her guests. 10 Calle Entremurallas (phone: 580124). Inexpensive.

Universal – At the top of Santiago's inexpensive list, in an excellent location across the street from the Old Town, and across the square from the *Compostela* hotel, it has direct-dial phones, beds, showers, breakfasts, and low-priced laundry service. There are 54 rooms. 2 Plaza Galicia (phone: 585800). Inexpensive.

 EATING OUT: Galician cooking manifests the region's Celtic influences and its proximity to the sea. One specialty is the *empanada,* a flat potpie filled with anything from salami and mushrooms to squid and octopus or rabbit with hot peppers. Another favorite is *pulpo* (octopus), which might be served simply, with potatoes and onions, or chopped up, salted, and topped with a tangy pepper sauce to be enjoyed with beer or wine as a *tapa.* Still another specialty is *caldo gallego,* a hearty vegetable soup made with beef or ham broth. Shellfish is prepared in many styles with a variety of sauces. Fish is generally baked, broiled, or sautéed, and then combined with potatoes, onions, peppers, and asparagus. Dinner for two with wine will cost $60 or more in restaurants listed as expensive, $30 to $50 in moderate restaurants, and $25 or less in inexpensive ones. With its large student population, Santiago can be one of the least expensive places to eat in Spain. Many restaurants regularly offer inexpensive student lunch and dinner specials, consisting of an appetizer, entrée, fruit, bread, and wine, all in generous portions. Another inexpensive way to dine is to find a restaurant serving *platos combinados* — prearranged groupings of appetizers and entrées, such as salad, pork with peppers, and potato croquettes, or soup, veal, or steaks with potatoes — which cost $5 to $7 per plate. All telephone numbers are in the 81 city code unless otherwise indicated.

Anexo Vilas – Under the same management as *Vilas* (see below), serving similarly superb Galician dishes — the food here may even be a touch better. The menu is virtually identical to that of its sister restaurant, so expect to savor some of the best cooking northwestern Spain has to offer. Closed Mondays. Reservations necessary. 21 Avenida Villagarcía (phone: 598387). Expensive.

Don Gaiferos – There's a rivalry of sorts between *Vilas* and *Don Gaiferos* for the best cooking in town, and diners are the winners. This has a beautiful Old Town location in three stone-arched rooms, a wonderful regional atmosphere and excellent Galician food. Closed Sunday evenings and from *Christmas* through early January. Reservations advised. 23 Rúa Nueva (phone: 583894). Expensive.

Retablo – Relatively new on Santiago's restaurant scene, featuring local and continental cuisine, superbly prepared and served in an elegant, mauve-colored dining room by the light of brass chandeliers. Closed Sunday nights and Mondays. Reservations advised. 13 Rúa Nueva (phone: 565950). Expensive.

Vilas – One of the shrines of Galician cooking and certainly one of Santiago's best restaurants, it's an unassuming place, with simple decor, but it has been turning out excellent food since early in this century. A long bar with photographs of Spanish soccer heroes leads to dining rooms adorned with oil paintings, white tablecloths, barrels, and a bookshelf full of wine bottles. Try any of the fish dishes, including *sardinas "Mama Sueiro"* (sardines with sweet peppers and garlic). Closed Sundays. Reservations necessary. 88 Avenida Rosalía de Castro (phone: 591000). Expensive.

La Arzuana – One of Santiago's most popular restaurants, it is normally packed with locals. The dining room opens out to a vine-covered patio. Specialties include seafood creations made with clams, mussels, and shrimp. Open daily. No reservations. 40 Calle del Franco (phone: 581198). Moderate.

Mesón La Cigala – Very popular with the locals, who feast on filling and appetizing dishes including giant prawns, roast veal, and Santiago almond tart. Closed Mondays. No reservations. 10 Calle del Franco (phone: 582952). Moderate to inexpensive.

Casa Manolo – This small spot tucked into a small street near the town market is a local institution. Galician specialties are served up as fast as you can order; the fixed-price menu has over a dozen appetizer and entrée choices; portions are enormous. Closed Sundays. No reservations. 27 Rúa Traviesa (phone: 582950). Inexpensive.

 TAPAS BARS: The Old Town's *tapas* bars are primarily concentrated on Calle del Franco and Rúa del Villar. Here, bar after bar can be found serving seafood *tapas*, such as small clams, sardines, and octopus with spicy peppers and salt, along with beer and wine, including traditional country wine — something like a new wine, not fully fermented — served in small bowls called *tazas* (it can also be ordered in larger bowls called *cuncas*, the size of a soup bowl). The tiny *Bar Negreira* (75 Rúa del Villar; phone: 580740) is frequented by virtually everyone in town — stay long enough and you'll have a chance to meet journalists, lawyers, shop owners, students, and probably the mayor. At *Bar O'Buraquino* (Calle Entremuras) *tapas* and *tazas* are served out the windows into the narrow street (it seems that as much wine is spilled onto the marble windowsills as makes it into the cups).

SEGOVIA

Occupying a rocky perch high above two deep valleys, between the northern slopes of the Sierra de Guadarrama and the high, flat tableland of Castile, Segovia has a city center that reaches an altitude of 3,280 feet. Many compare its overall silhouette to that of a ship, with the Alcázar rising high in the west like a prow above the confluence of the Eresma and Clamores rivers. Its proximity to Madrid, only 57 miles (91 km) away, makes it a favorite retreat for both foreign travelers and Spaniards themselves, who often come out from the capital for the day to savor its scenic charm, historic sights, and outstanding food.

The Romans endowed the city with its greatest marvel: a 2,000-year-old aqueduct that rises almost 100 feet above the Plaza del Azoguejo, where the bulk of the city's traffic passes through the same slender arches that once watched Roman chariots trundle by. The aqueduct is incredibly well preserved, although it no longer performs its duty of delivering water to the upper reaches of the city. Two Roman roads also converged in Segovia, further attesting to its importance during that era when it was a strategic military town. With the incursion of the Visigoths in the 6th century, a gradual decline began, subsequently accelerated by 200 years of Muslim rule. Then, revitalized by the Reconquest, Segovia greatly enhanced its prestige in 1474 when Isabella la Católica (the Catholic) was proclaimed Queen of Castile in the Plaza Mayor. Decline set in again, however, after the Comuneros uprising of 1520–21, when the *comunidades* (autonomous cities) of Castile, led by Juan de Padilla of Toledo and Juan Bravo of Segovia, revolted unsuccessfully against the absolutism of the Holy Roman Emperor Charles V.

At the turn of the 20th century, two artists — one painter and one poet — focused their creative attentions upon Segovia and Castile. The painter, Ignacio Zuloaga, was a master at capturing Segovia's special light and the earthy quality of its inhabitants. The poet, Antonio Machado, an Andalusian who lived for more than a decade in a house on Calle de los Desamparados that is now a small museum, proclaimed his enchantment with the region in a book of poems entitled *Campos de Castilla*.

Today, resting largely on its historic laurels, Segovia's population of just over 50,000 depends greatly on a steady stream of visitors from the capital for its continuing prosperity. And many return again and again, if only for the roast suckling pig that is the city's greatest gastronomic lure. Most Sundays throughout the year, the Plaza Mayor bristles with exuberant throngs honing their appetites on aperitifs and *tapas* in anticipation of the succulent, sweet pork nestled beneath crisp, brown skin. Later, those who can, walk off their extravagance with a stroll through the narrow streets of the city center, making their way from the Alcázar to the cathedral to the Roman Aqueduct, past Romanesque churches, buildings covered with the *esgrafiado* designs that are characteristic of Segovia, and numerous spots from which to admire panoramic views.

SEGOVIA AT-A-GLANCE

 SEEING THE CITY: Approximately 1¼ miles (2 km) north of Segovia along the N601 highway leading to Valladolid, the *Parador de Segovia* offers a marvelous view of the entire city. On Saturday and Sunday nights, the aqueduct and cathedral are illuminated.

 SPECIAL PLACES: The major monuments of Segovia are within the confines of the old walled city. Although the walls, which date from the time of the Reconquest, are barely in evidence today, three of the original seven gates — San Cebrián, Santiago, and San Andrés — still stand, and it is the wall that gives the old part of Segovia its ship shape. If the Alcázar is considered to be the prow of the ship, then the Roman Aqueduct is the stern. The cathedral and Plaza Mayor are roughly amidships. Numerous other monuments are within the walls, but a number of remaining sights are beyond and below them, on the other side of the Eresma River. As with most medieval cities in Spain, driving in the old part of town is a tortuous affair. Come by car or a taxi to the Plaza Mayor, then explore the area within the walls on foot.

WITHIN THE WALLS

Alcázar – This Disneyesque castle-palace at the western end of town perches above the confluence of the Eresma and Clamores rivers. In fact, Walt Disney used it as a model for the castle in *Snow White and the Seven Dwarfs*. Built during the 12th and 13th centuries on top of an older fortress, it was enriched and enlarged in the 15th and 18th centuries with numerous magnificent chambers. In 1474, Princess Isabella set forth from the Alcázar to be crowned Queen of Castile in Segovia's Plaza Mayor; a painting commemorating that event today hangs in the castle's Sala de la Galera. The Alcázar also was the site of Philip II's fourth marriage — this one to Anne of Austria. Also in the 16th century, the Torre del Homenaje (Tower of Homage, also known as the Tower of Juan II), covered with the typically Segovian *esgrafiado* decoration suggestive of Moorish times, was used as a state prison. King Carlos III installed the Artillery Academy in the Alcázar in the 18th century, and in 1862, a fierce fire gutted the place. Rebuilt in a romantic vein, it has a simplistic charm that is still magical and elegant. Of special interest are the Mudéjar ceilings and tilework and the authentic period furnishings. The 360° view of the Castilian countryside from the top of the Tower of Juan II is worth the 152 steps up, but you can get a good view of sights outside the city walls from the garden in front of the Alcázar. Open daily from 10 AM to 7 PM (until 6 PM from October through March). Admission charge. Plaza del Alcázar (phone: 430176).

Cathedral – Deliberately built in the late Gothic style at a time when Renaissance structures were in vogue (1515 to 1558), the cathedral was, by order of the Holy Roman Emperor Charles V, constructed on a higher and more secure site than the cathedral it replaced, which had been destroyed in the revolt of the Comuneros. Though known as the "Lady of the Spanish cathedrals" because of its elegance, slender lines, and restrained austerity, its treasures are not comparable to those of the cathedrals of León or Salamanca. Among them are the Flamboyant-style choir stalls and cloister, both brought from the old cathedral; the 16th-century carving of *La Piedad* by Juan de Juni in the Capilla Santo Entierro (the first chapel to the right as you enter the church — a *Deposition* by Ambrosio Benson is in the same chapel); and the altarpiece in the Capilla Santiago (next to the museum entrance). Also note the chapels around the apse, which are quite different in feeling from the rest, painted in pale rococo colors. The museum contains an 18th-century gold carriage used in *Corpus Christi* processions, with the cathedral's silver monstrance on top. A collection of 17th-century Flemish tapestries in the Sala Capitular, which has a richly carved ceiling, completes the list of notable exhibits. Open daily from 9 AM to 7 PM in summer; from October through May, open from 9:30 AM to 1 PM and from 3 to 6 PM weekdays, and from 9:30 AM to 6 PM weekends and holidays. Admission charge to the cloister, museum, and Sala Capitular. Plaza Mayor (phone: 435325).

Plaza de San Martín – This square, at the heart of the walled city, is bordered by old mansions, including the Casa del Siglo XV (House of the 15th Century), often mistakenly identified as the house of Juan Bravo, a 16th-century Segovian who was one of the leaders of the Comuneros' Revolt and whose statue presides over the lower level of the square. The tower off to one end is the 14th-century Torreón de Lozoya, and the portico running along a side belongs to the 11th-century Iglesia de San Martín, the most centrally located of numerous Romanesque churches in Segovia.

Casa de los Picos – A late-15th-century Renaissance mansion, distinguished by the pyramidal stones adorning its façade, is now home to the Escuela de Artes Aplicadas y Oficios Artísticos (School of Applied Arts and Artistic Pursuits). As a result, the visitor often is rewarded with student displays and other somewhat unusual exhibitions. Calle Juan Bravo (phone: 430711 or 428198).

Roman Aqueduct – This landmark is one of Europe's finest examples of Roman architecture. Built some 2,000 years ago to carry water to the upper reaches of the city from the Acebeda River, the 166 double-tiered arches stretch some 21,500 feet in total length and reach a maximum height of 96 feet in the Plaza del Azoguejo. The aqueduct was constructed of granite blocks, without the use of mortar. Many of the original arches were destroyed during the 11th-century Arab conquest, but they were rebuilt in the 15th century. Today, the residents of Segovia consider the spaces beneath them ideal places to park. Climb the steps to the side of the square for the best longitudinal view of the arches stretching into the distance (the rear ends of the cars parked beneath them just visible). At the very top, go through the wall, under an arch, and around to the lookout point. Plaza del Azoguejo.

BEYOND THE WALLS

Iglesia de la Vera Cruz – Across the Eresma River just northwest of the city, this early-13th-century church was constructed by the Knights Templars in the late Romanesque style. Its shape, with 12 sides, is unusual in Spain, and was modeled after the Holy Sepulchre in Jerusalem. Inside is a 2-story circular room (a sort of church-within-a-church), a 13th-century carved wooden Christ above the central apse, and the Lignum Crucis chapel in the base of the tower. Open from 10:30 AM to 1:30 PM and from 3:30 to 7 PM in spring and summer (until 6 PM in fall and winter); closed Mondays. Admission charge. Carretera a Zamarramala (phone: 431475).

Monasterio de El Parral – Founded by Henry IV in the mid-15th century and given to the Spanish order of St. Hieronymus, the monastery is another monument located across the Eresma River, about one-half mile (1 km) north of the city. The church, a blend of Gothic, Renaissance, and Plateresque elements, was designed and begun by Juan Gallego at the end of the century, but its façade was left unfinished. The monastery was abandoned after the suppression of religious orders in 1835, but it has been restored and is once again occupied by the Jerónymos brothers. Notable are the polychrome altarpiece carved by Juan Rodríguez and the alabaster tombs of the Marqués de Villena and his wife, also carved by Rodríguez. Ordinarily, the monastery is open daily from 10 AM to 12:30 PM and from 4 to 6 PM (admission by donation), but at press time it was closed for repairs, with the date of its reopening uncertain. Calle del Marqués de Villena (phone: 431298).

Convento de San Antonio el Real – This also was founded by Henry IV during the mid-15th century, but as a country house; later it was given to the Franciscans and the Poor Clares, who inhabit it today. In the church is a wonderful original Mudéjar ceiling over a huge, lavishly gilt main altarpiece, plus three smaller altarpieces, including one with a remarkable 15th-century Flemish rendering of Calvary in three-dimensional carved wood. A nun takes visitors around the cloister and adjoining rooms, where there are more original *artesonado* ceilings and, set in the walls, several small Flemish Calvary scenes in painted terra cotta. Open weekdays from 10 AM to 1 PM and from 4 to 6 PM (Sundays and holidays from 11 AM). Admission charge to the cloister. To reach the convent, follow the Roman aqueduct from behind the *Mesón Cándido* side of Plaza del Azoguejo; when it ends, with arches about waist high, the convent is only a short distance away. Calle San Antonio el Real (phone: 420228).

Iglesia de San Millán – One of the most beautiful of Segovia's Romanesque churches, it stands in full view in an open square between the aqueduct and the bus station. It was built during the 12th century and has four apses, three doorways, two 13th-century porches, and a remodeled 11th-century Mozarabic tower that dates from a previous structure on the spot. Open during services. Avenida Fernández Ladreda.

ENVIRONS

Palacio Real de la Granja de San Ildefonso – Seven miles (11 km) along the N601 highway toward Madrid stands La Granja, a royal palace built by Philip V, the first Bourbon King of Spain, grandson of Louis XIV of France; it is surrounded by meticulously manicured gardens. Construction began in 1721, on land acquired from the Hieronymite monks of El Parral, who had operated a farm, or *granja,* here. The result was the most impressive example of 18th-century architecture in Spain, more European than Spanish in feeling, however, since the French-born king and his Italian wife, Isabella Farnese, employed architects schooled in the Hapsburg tradition. Unfortunately, a fire in 1918 destroyed the private quarters of the royal family and damaged much of the remaining structure. Extensive restoration has re-created the public and official areas, which remained in use through the days of Alfonso XIII (who reigned until 1931). Visitors see room after room with marble floors, painted ceilings, lace curtains, tapestries, and crystal chandeliers — most of the latter outstanding works produced by the nearby Fábrica de Cristal de La Granja. Included are the throne room, Philip and Isabella's mausoleum, and in the former private quarters, reconstructed rooms serving as a *Tapestry Museum* to accommodate a priceless collection of 16th-century tapestries. Visits to the palace are by guided tour only, usually conducted in Spanish (although an English- and French-speaking interpreter is available), but you can wander at will through the lovely French-style gardens behind the palace, a wonderland of fountains, pools, statues, tree-lined avenues, and water flowing from high ground to low ground through a series of stepped pools known as the Great Cascade. The gardens are open daily all year, from 10 AM to 8 PM in summer (until 6 PM in winter). The palace keeps the same hours year-round, open from 10 AM to 1:30 PM and from 3 to 5 PM; Sundays and holidays, from 10 AM to 2 PM; closed Mondays. The fountains, dependent on rainwater, normally are turned on only a couple of days a week (Thursdays and Sundays in 1990), from late March through early July. Admission charge to the palace. San Ildefonso (phone: 470019).

Palacio de Riofrio – Heading back to Segovia from La Granja on N601, look for the sign and turnoff marked Riofrio. Follow the road 4 miles (6 km) and pass through the intersection following the second sign marked Palacio y Bosque de Riofrio. Continue another 4 miles (6 km) and turn left at the intersection for SG724. A guard signals the entrance to a protected parkland where fallow deer are abundant along the road leading the last few miles to the palace. (Save your admission ticket to show to the guard on your way out.)

The rather plain exterior of this 18th-century peach-colored palace with lime-green shutters belies the elegance that awaits within. It was built by Isabella Farnese, who feared that she might be ousted from La Granja by the new king, her stepson, after Philip V's death, and it was originally conceived as a hunting palace for her own son. It later served as a residence for Alfonso XII, grandfather of Juan Carlos, the present king. Notice the striking series of draped doorways that create uniquely colorful, curtained corridors; the chandeliers (mostly of Spanish construction); several tapestries by Goya and Bayeu; and the furnishings and decorations from the days of Alfonso XII. Since the palace was never completely outfitted, the northern wing has been given over to a *Museo de la Caza* (Museum of the Hunt), complete with reproductions of hunting paraphernalia from the prehistoric to the modern era. There is also an elaborate array of dioramas depicting animals of Spain in their respective habitats — among them the chamois, ibex, capercaillie, golden eagle, wild boar, pheasant, and lynx. Several rooms are also dedicated to hunting trophies acquired by members of the local nobility. Open from 10 AM to 1:30 PM and from 3 to 5 PM (until 2 PM on Sundays and holidays); closed Tuesdays. All visits to the palace are by guided tour only (in Spanish usually, but an English- and French-speaking guide is available); admission charge (phone: 470019).

SOURCES AND RESOURCES

 TOURIST INFORMATION: The tourist information office (10 Plaza Mayor; phone: 430328) has a variety of helpful brochures, current information regarding hours and admission fees, and general information on accommodations in all price ranges. Open Mondays through Fridays from 9 AM to 2 PM, Saturdays from 10 AM to 2 PM.

Local Coverage – *El Adelantado de Segovia* is the city's daily Spanish-language newspaper. The *Guía Semanal de Segovia* and the related *Guía Provincial de Segovia,* available free in hotels and at the tourist office, provide up-to-the-minute information on what's happening around town. Though written in Spanish, most of the material is decipherable by non-Spanish-speaking readers. Also look for a copy of the English edition of *Segovia — Patrimonio de la Humanidad* (Segovia — Heritage of Mankind), complete with suggested itineraries and detailed historic, cultural, and artistic information.

 TELEPHONE: The city code for Segovia is 11. If calling from within Spain, dial 911 before the local number.

GETTING AROUND: Segovia is a small city, and most of its sights can be easily visited on foot. Seeing sights on the edge of town, however, will require a car or taxi.

Bus – City buses ply the streets daily from 7 AM to 11 PM, stopping at most of the major attractions. The Estación de Autobuses (phone: 427725), Segovia's main bus station for long-distance buses, is located on Paseo de Ezequiel González, corner of Avenida Fernández Ladreda (reachable from Plaza Mayor by the No. 3 bus marked Puente de Hierro). There is daily service to and from Madrid, Avila, Valladolid, and other towns and villages throughout the province of Segovia. Buses for La Granja, 20 minutes away, also depart from here. Bus schedules can be found in the *Guía Provincial de Segovia.*

Car Rental – *Avis* has an office at 123 Calle Zorilla (phone: 422584 or 422032).

Taxi – A taxi almost always can be found in the Plaza Mayor; another stand is in Plaza del Azoguejo. Radio-dispatched cabs also are available (phone: 436680 or 436681). If you are going to a site outside the city, be sure to arrange a pickup time with the driver.

Train – Segovia's train station, Estación de Ferrocarril *RENFE* (phone: 420774), is located on Plaza Obispo Quesada, reachable by bus #3 from Plaza Mayor. There is daily service to Madrid, Medina del Campo, and Valladolid. Schedules of service to Madrid are in the *Guía Provincial de Segovia.*

MUSEUMS: In addition to those described in *Special Places,* the museums below may be of interest. Note that the *Zuloaga Museum,* dedicated to the famous local ceramist Daniel Zuloaga (a relative of Ignacio Zuloaga) and set up in the former Iglesia de San Juan de los Caballeros, which he acquired in 1905 and used as a workshop, is closed for restoration.

Casa-Museo Antonio Machado (Antonio Machado House-Museum) – The simple old house that was the home of the poet from 1919 to 1932, with his kitchen, dining room, and bedroom complete with washstand, chamber pots, and wrought-iron bed. Open Tuesdays through Sundays from 4 to 7 PM (to 6 PM in winter). No admission charge. 5 Calle de los Desamparados (phone: 436649).

Museo Provincial de Bellas Artes (Provincial Fine Arts Museum) – A collection of local paintings from the 15th, 16th, and 17th centuries, including the *Conversion of St. Paul* by Francisco Camilo, displayed in a reconstructed 16th-century house. Open from 10 AM to 2 PM and from 4 to 6 PM (Sundays, mornings only); closed Mondays. Admission charge. 12 Calle de San Agustín (phone: 431585).

SHOPPING: Because Segovia is popular with day-trippers from Madrid, its shopping opportunities tend to consist mostly of souvenirs and mementos. The usual assortment of wineskins, castanets, T-shirts, fans, and mantillas blossoms around all the major sights, and along Calle Marqués del Arco near the cathedral.

El Alfar – Ceramics and souvenir items. 22 Calle del Roble (phone: 424215).

Artesanía Monjas Dominicas – Reproductions of antique figures, such as those found in Renaissance altarpieces, made (of resin) and sold by nuns; prices range from $20 to $150 for an angel with wings, up to $2,000 for a large Nativity scene. Convento de Santo Domingo, Calle Capuchinos Alta (phone: 433876).

La Casa del Siglo XV – Glassware, porcelain, leather goods, jewelry, records and tapes, and toys. 32 Calle Juan Bravo (phone: 434531).

Mi Piel – High-quality leather goods — belts, handbags, suitcases. Centro Comercial Almuzara, 6 Calle Juan Bravo (phone: 426141).

La Suiza – Lladró porcelain, crystal, silver, and other souvenirs. 14 Plaza Mayor (phone: 430334).

SPORTS AND FITNESS: There are two popular ski areas in the Guadarramas near Segovia. Both La Pinilla (35 miles/56 km to the northeast) and Navacerrada (17 miles/27 km south) offer a wide range of skiing opportunities and various accommodations. Consult the tourist information office for details.

THEATER AND MUSIC: Madrid is too close for Segovia to have become a theater- or concertgoer's dream. Nevertheless, the *Teatro Juan Bravo* (Plaza Mayor; phone: 431228) manages to maintain a fairly full schedule of drama, ballet, and orchestral, chamber, and popular music concerts.

 NIGHTCLUBS AND NIGHTLIFE: Segovia has no nightclubs of note, so most nightlife activity consists of socializing over *tapas* and *copas* in the bars and cafés of the Plaza Mayor or along Calle Infanta Isabel.

BEST IN TOWN

 CHECKING IN: Expect to pay $60 to $90 for a double room with private bath in hotels classified as expensive, $30 to $60 for a moderate one, and less than $30 for an inexpensive one. All telephone numbers are in the 11 city code unless otherwise indicated.

Los Arcos – Modern and cheerful, it's located outside the walls near the Church of San Millán and the Roman aqueduct, within walking distance of the rest of the prime sights. There are 59 rooms with bath or shower and air conditioning (some facing the city's steepled skyline); the *Cocina de Segovia* restaurant and 2 bars. Parking is available. Affiliated with Best Western. 24 Paseo de Ezequiel González (phone: 437462). Expensive.

Los Linajes – Within the walls of the Old City, this hotel retains an 11th-century façade that was part of a palace belonging to the Falconi family, and it has charming public rooms arranged around a minuscule inner courtyard. The 55 rooms offer panoramic views, have complete bath, color television sets, and central heating. 9 Calle Dr. Velasco (phone: 431712). Expensive.

Parador de Segovia – In a modern building, opened in 1978, this cathedral-like, hilltop *parador* lies 3,280 feet above sea level in a panoramic spot and offers 80 centrally heated, air conditioned rooms. Facilities include a bar, spacious public areas, lush gardens, a sauna, indoor and outdoor swimming pools, and a restaurant (see *Eating Out*). Ask for a room with a view of the city and the Sierra de Guadarrama. About 1½ miles (2 km) along the road to Valladolid. Carretera de Valladolid (phone: 430462). Expensive.

Las Sirenas – Located in the center of the city, on the main shopping street, right in front of the San Martín church, this pleasant, older hostelry has beautiful wood furnishings throughout its 39 rooms, all of which have private baths. Ask for an exterior room, the best of which overlook the church. 30 Calle Juan Bravo (phone: 434011). Moderate.

Plaza – A fine, affordable *hostal,* with 28 rooms. All the doubles have complete private baths and telephones; some singles have a sink or a sink and shower only. The *José María* restaurant (see *Eating Out*) is located next door. 11 Calle Cronista Lecea (phone: 431228). Moderate to inexpensive.

 EATING OUT: Segovia is a favorite spot for *madrileños* (residents of Madrid) to spend a Sunday and indulge in what is reported by many to be some of the finest *cochinillo* — roast suckling pig — in Castile. A *horno de asar* (roasting oven) sign outside announces a "roast" restaurant serving this specialty; so does the poor naked piglet on a platter that is usually displayed in the window. Expect such places to be crowded on weekends, even in low season, when business might otherwise be slow. *Cochifrito,* a local variation of the pervasive suckling pig, is fried with garlic and parsley. The hearty, flavorful *sopa castellana,* a soup of ham, paprika, bread, and poached eggs, is another local specialty, well worth sampling. Dinner for two with wine will cost $60 to $85 in an expensive restaurant, $30 to $55 in a moderate one. All phone numbers are in the 11 city code unless otherwise indicated.

Mesón de Cándido – Located at the foot of the aqueduct and equally a beacon for visitors, as evidenced by the photos of famous people who have dined here and the guestbooks with their autographs. But unlike many other high-profile restaurants, this one offers good food as well as good PR. The traditional dishes of Segovia, including *cochinillo,* are here, accompanied by a fine ribera del duero house wine. The building, with parts dating from the 15th century, has been classified as an official historic monument, and the restaurant, in operation since the 1860s, has walls adorned with hand-painted plates, copper pots, and other memorabilia. The economical fixed-price menu is famed throughout Spain. Open daily. Reservations advised on weekends. 5 Plaza del Azoguejo (phone: 428103). Expensive.

Mesón Duque – The sign outside still boasts of the Maestro Asador de Segovia (Segovia's Master Roaster) title won in 1895. Situated on a street running between the aqueduct and the Plaza Mayor, this is *Cándido*'s main competitor. Its ambience is classic Castilian, and it is noted for its *cochinillo, judiones de la Granja* (white bean stew), and various beef and veal dishes. Open daily. Reservations advised on weekends. 12 Calle Cervantes (phone: 430537). Expensive.

Parador de Segovia – A cut above the quality of conventional *parador* cooking, this restaurant offers a fine view of Segovia to go along with the *sopa castellana,* sweetbreads, salmon, *merluza* (hake), *perdiz* (partridge), roast lamb, *cochinillo,* and fresh crayfish and trout from the Eresma River. Outside of town, 1¼ miles (2 km) along the road to Valladolid. Open daily. Reservations advised on weekends. Carretera de Valladolid (phone: 430462). Expensive.

El Bernardino – Another traditionally decorated place for sampling the Castilian mainstays, it has plates and paintings on the walls, a beamed ceiling, and a rough-hewn look that extends to the stuffed head of a boar on a pillar. There are set menus in several reasonable price ranges. Open daily; closed in January. Reservations advised on weekends. 2 Calle Cervantes (phone: 433225). Moderate.

Casa Amado – The decor is less elaborate than that of some of Segovia's other establishments, but the food surpasses the lackluster ambience. Besides the Castilian standards, specialties include many fine fish dishes and a memorable *cordero leachal al ajillo* (suckling lamb with garlic sauce). Good bread, fine flan (custard), and attentive service complete the offering. Closed Wednesdays and October. Reservations advised on weekends. 9 Avenida Fernández Ladreda (phone: 432077). Moderate.

José María – Segovia's most popular place for Sunday lunch and *tapas* throughout the week — with good reason: The food is extremely good, the service friendly, and the house wine a fine ribera del duero red. Besides *cochinillo* and *cochifrito,* specialties include *ancas de rana rebozadas* (breaded frog's legs), homemade *morcilla* (blood sausage), and, for dessert, *pastel de frambuesa con nueces* (raspberry cream with walnuts). Closed November. Reservations advised for Sunday lunch, or go early. 11 Calle Cronista Lecea (phone: 434484). Moderate.

SEVILLE

For a city without an opera house, Seville has been the stage for more than its share of operatic heroes and heroines. The temptress Carmen, the famous barber of Seville, and Don Giovanni, the musical equivalent of the legendary Don Juan, all played out their high drama and romantic nonsense in its winding alleys, secluded patios, jasmine-scented gardens, and fountain-filled plazas. And no one has ever taken down the set. Carmen's cigarette factory, Escamillo's bullring, the wrought-iron balconies where Don Juan trysted — even, some claim, the barbershop — are all still in place, waiting for the curtain to go up each morning on the friendly, fun-loving southern city that epitomizes all we envision when we think of sunny Spain.

After Madrid, Barcelona, and Valencia, Seville, a university center with a population of 650,000, is Spain's fourth-largest city. It is also Spain's loveliest, and it works at preserving the fascinating Roman-Arabic-Judaic-Christian past that made it so. A downtown subway project was abandoned — with 3 miles of tunnel already completed — partly because the digging was discovered to be endangering historic foundations. Traditional Andalusian colors are faithfully maintained on traditional Andalusian buildings — white walls to deflect the southern heat, gold trim to echo the ocher earth. Golden sand (*alvero*) is trucked in 20 miles from the hills of Carmona to be used ornamentally in local gardens, and the famous Seville orange trees, loaded with bitter fruit that the city contracts with marmalade-makers to harvest, shade the town's tiled sidewalks. Restaurants, hotels, and shops lean to fanciful Moorish arabesque details, colored tiles, and white-walled beam-ceilinged interiors, while computerized 20th-century businesses hide behind the Plateresque façades and wrought-iron gates of Renaissance palaces. Splashing fountains, tiled benches, leafy plazas, and patios with canvas awnings are, as for centuries past, the everyday amenities of a city on the doorstep of Africa, with summer temperatures reaching up to 112F.

Beginning in spring, Seville (Sevilla in Spanish) lives in its streets. *Semana Santa* (Holy Week) fills them with 7 nights of religious pageantry. On its heels, the *Feria* (April Fair) is a week of nonstop revelry, and even after it's over, the fun goes on: Teenagers strum their guitars at café tables, the rattle of castanets sounds from around a corner, a group at the *tapas* bar breaks out in steady, wordless, syncopated flamenco clapping, and 10-year-old *señoritas* in brilliant polka-dot dresses practice dancing the *sevillanas* in the plaza. All the while, horses and carriages clip-clop through city traffic.

It takes a somewhat selective focus to isolate a view this romantic of any modern city. But it's not easy to ignore the posters announcing *Expo '92*, the world's fair that will be held from mid-April to mid-October, 1992, in honor of the 500th anniversary of Christopher Columbus's big discovery. Until then, visitors are likely to find some museums and monuments closed for restoration and classic city views crisscrossed by construction cranes. Much of the activity centers around the city's Guadalquivir River and the Island of Cartuja, formed by two of its branches, which will serve as the fairgrounds. The *Expo* pavilions will be grouped around the Carthusian Monastery of Santa María de las Cuevas, where Columbus's body lay for 27 years before it was moved to its final resting place in the cathedral, and where a sapote tree he brought back from the New World still grows in one of the courtyards. New bridges will span the Guadalquivir, and the river itself is being rechanneled (it was diverted in the 1940s) to match the course Columbus followed on his triumphant return to the port of Seville on *Palm Sunday,* 1493.

Seville has successfully survived some far more traumatic renovations in its time. Since earliest days, conquerors — Phoenicians, Greeks, Carthaginians — prized it for its river, a 70-mile-long highway to the sea. Spain's only inland port city was taken by the Romans in 205 BC and made the capital of the province of Baetica, their name for what we now call Andalusia. They called the river the Baetis, a name that survives as Calle Betis, the riverfront street of clubs and cafés in the Triana district, across the Guadalquivir from the bullring. (The name Guadalquivir comes from the Moors, who arrived centuries later.)

With the waning of the Roman Empire in the 5th century, Seville was ruled by the Vandals and then by the Visigoths, but the character of the city that is seen today dates largely from the 8th century, when the Moors crossed the Strait of Gibraltar to begin a fruitful 500-year reign. After takeovers by several successive Moorish contingents, the city enjoyed a flourishing 100 years under the Almohads, Moorish conquerors who arrived in the mid-12th century and fostered an unprecedented climate of intellectual, artistic, and commercial cooperation among the resident communities of Christians, Arabs, and Jews. Skilled engineers, they built up the port and repaired the city's fortifications, silent testimony of which remains in the outer walls of the Alcázar, the clean-lined Torre del Oro, and the lower portion of the Giralda tower, survivors of the Almohad reign.

Though Seville fell to Ferdinand III (the Christian king who later became a saint) in 1248, the Moorish influence continued for at least 2 centuries. It can be seen inside the Alcázar walls, in the ornate 14th-century palace of King Pedro el Cruel (Peter the Cruel), which was built by Mudéjar workmen (Moors who continued to live and work in Spain after the Christian conquest) using traditional Arab design.

Columbus's voyage to the New World was the beginning of Seville's most glorious period. The Catholic Monarchs, Ferdinand and Isabella, established their headquarters for New World exploration and trade in the Alcázar, and Columbus's return up the Guadalquivir inspired successful trips by Ferdinand Magellan and Amerigo Vespucci, who sailed out from the Torre del Oro. The golden age of Seville was under way — though not for the city's ill-fated Jews, who were forcibly converted, slain, or driven from their homes in the Judería (the present Barrio de Santa Cruz) by the Royal Inquisition.

During the 16th and 17th centuries, Seville was the richest and most powerful city in Spain, filled with Renaissance palaces, churches, and monasteries decorated with frescoes and paintings of native sons Bartolomé Esteban

Murillo and Juan de Valdés Leal and of adopted son Francisco de Zurbarán, who was born in a village nearby. (Seville-born Diego Velázquez left early for the court in Madrid, and his hometown is seriously deficient in his works.) Ironically, the river that earned the city its earlier acclaim was the same conduit that would turn its economic tides. With the gradual silting up of the Guadalquivir, which once had been navigable all the way to Córdoba, the city's fortunes turned down sharply, and Cádiz, perched on the Atlantic, took over Seville's lucrative trade.

Today, with the river long since restored, Seville is once again a major port, shipping minerals, manufactured goods, and agricultural products. But like the rest of the south, which considers itself Madrid's economic stepchild, the city has gone through hard times. Now, as prospects of a smash-hit *Expo* escalate from day to day, city fathers expect that besides attracting more international commerce, the world's fair will build tourism for Andalusia's chain of Moorish masterpiece cities: Córdoba and Granada, as well as Seville. It's better to visit now, before the hordes descend! If there's time to see just one of these treasures, Seville, the largest, is the best choice. Once you've been here, you'll agree, *"Quien ha visto Sevilla ha visto maravilla"* — to see Seville is to see a wonder.

SEVILLE AT-A-GLANCE

SEEING THE CITY: Seville sprawls along both banks of the Guadalquivir in a lowland rich with olive groves and farms. The nearest hill is a bus ride from town, so the best view of the city is from the top of the Giralda tower in the cathedral square (see below).

SPECIAL PLACES: Spain's fourth-largest city does look big from the top of the Giralda tower, but remember that the visitor's time is spent mainly on the east bank of the river in the compact area of an Old Town that once huddled inside city walls. Most touristic highlights are concentrated around or between two of the city's bridges, the Triana Bridge to the north (some maps call it Puente Isabel II) and the San Telmo Bridge to the south. Near the former are the *Maestranza* bullring, downtown shopping streets, and the *Museo de Bellas Artes* (Museum of Fine Arts). Near the San Telmo Bridge are María Luisa Park, the University, and the Torre del Oro. Clustered in the middle are Seville's three greatest treasures: the cathedral, with its Giralda tower; the Alcázar; and the winding streets of the Barrio de Santa Cruz. Visitors usually cross the river only after dark, for dinner in the modern, high-rise Los Remedios district or for dancing and *tapas* in Triana, once a Gypsy haven but now a working class suburb.

Public attractions are open from 9:30 or 10 AM to 1:30 or 2 PM and from around 4 or 5 PM to 7 or 8 PM; some hours change with the seasons. Museums tend to be open mornings only; closing days tend to be Sundays or Mondays. Check with the tourist office (phone: 422-1404) for the most up-to-date hours.

■ **Warning:** For all its present upward mobility, Seville still has a bad record when it comes to theft. Most *sevillanos* pride themselves on their friendliness and hospitality, and one way they show it is with constant warnings about the wave of pickpocketing and purse snatching, usually by gangs of young thugs from the suburbs. Women should keep money in a pocket, not a purse. Men should keep track of their wallets. Never put purses down in a café or on the seat of the car beside you, and nothing you wouldn't want to lose should ever be left in a parked car. As for the Gypsies from Granada who have taken up residence outside the cathedral, enjoy their shenanigans, but be cautious. Many simply want to charge outrageous sums to tell your fortune, but others will distract you with chatter and jostling while an accomplice goes to work on your wallet. Crimes against foreigners here are usually for profit, not bodily harm. Be prudent, not fearful.

CITY CENTER

Reales Alcázares (Alcázar, or Royal Palace) – Although surrounded by rough Almohad walls that would lead anyone to expect a military compound within, King Pedro's delicate Mudéjar palace, built by Moorish craftsmen at a time when this had been a Christian city for over a century, is the most wondrous and beguiling building in Seville. Work on the palace began in 1350, on the site of the previous Moorish fortress, and ended abruptly in 1369, when the king, known as Pedro el Cruel — Peter the Cruel to the English-speaking world — was done in by a brother. (Pedro himself had earned his reputation by murdering his half brothers as well as a Granadan potentate he had invited to the palace for dinner — the ruby he stole from his guest, after spearing him, is now the center stone in the British crown.) Unlike the Alhambra in Granada, which deteriorated during years of abandonment and has required massive restoration, the Alcázar compound was kept pretty much in shape by Spanish royalty, who used it as a residence into our own century, adding upper stories and new wings. There's even one remnant of the earlier Almohad palace, the fragile Patio del Yeso, which is closed to the public.

Pass through the narrow Puerta del León (Lion's Gate), the entrance to the Alcázar, and Pedro's palace is directly across the Patio de la Montería (Hunter's Court). Once inside the palace, bear in mind that the intricately pierced and curlicued decorations clinging to the upper walls like lacy veils are merely plaster, molded and sculpted to look like marble, as are the dizzying carved stalactite clusters. The Mudéjars were masters at disguising mundane materials, piecing dazzlingly painted ceramic tiles, or *azulejos,* into mosaics of star forms and zigzag ribbons, and using wood for gorgeous *artesonado* ceilings that are carved, gilded, coffered, and inlaid in an infinite variety of geometric patterns. They also displayed their inner feelings in disguise: The graceful Arabic script worked into their decorations for the walls of the Christian king are prayers from the Koran.

The best way to see the palace is to wander at random through the clusters of courtyards and chambers, so typical of Moorish palaces, although the visit begins at the colonnaded Patio de las Doncellas (Court of the Maidens), with its multi-lobed arches resting on sets of twin marble columns. This was the center of official palace life and it leads to the great, square Salón de Embajadores (Ambassadors' Hall), where Pedro betrayed his guest and where the Holy Roman Emperor Charles V (King Carlos I of Spain) was wed to Isabella of Portugal. The salon's complex, colored and faceted cedarwood cupola, resting on vaults of gilded plasterwork, is the palace masterpiece. Not to be missed is the graceful Puerta de los Pavones (Peacock Arch), a surprising note, since Moorish designs usually derive from botanical and geometric forms, rarely from animal life. Among the dozens of other splendid royal rooms, a universal favorite is the Patio de las Muñecas (Dolls' Court), which was the hub of the palace's living quarters; to ensure privacy, only blind musicians played here. Look for the two little dolls' faces carved into a marble column. Notice, too, the marble capitals, each different, brought from the ruins of the Medina Azahara near Córdoba.

For a trip back to the Age of Discovery, return to the Patio de la Montería and enter

Queen Isabella's 15th-century addition. Here, in the Cuarto del Almirante (Admiral's Apartment), she established the Casa de Contratación, headquarters for New World exploration and commerce. The austere rooms hold such New World mementos as a model of the *Santa María,* 15th-century navigators' maps, and an altarpiece, Virgen de los Navegantes, in which Columbus is among the figures beneath the Virgin's cloak. Stairs at the rear lead to royal apartments, including Isabella's Gothic chapel, the Oratorio de los Reyes Católicos, which has a famous tiled altar by Niculoso Pisano finished in 1504, the year of Isabella's death. Another wing, added by Charles V, is entered through Pedro's palace. Filled with an exceptional series of Flemish tapestries woven with silk, gold, and wool, chronicling the Holy Roman Emperor's triumphs in his Tunisian campaign of 1535 (a 16th-century equivalent of a war photographer, Jan Vermayan, had gone along to sketch it), it's also the wing that leads to the overgrown palace gardens, a sight straight out of the Arabian Nights (see below). The Alcázar is open Mondays through Saturdays from 10:30 AM to 6 PM, Sundays and holidays from 10 AM to 2 PM. Admission charge includes the gardens. Plaza del Triunfo (phone: 422-7163).

Jardines del Alcázar (Alcázar Gardens) – Moorish, Renaissance, and modern gardens are all part of the Alcázar complex. Charles V erected the monumental pink stone wall with recessed frescoes that backstops the terrace and the outsize lily pond (the statue in the center of the pond is of Mercury). Steps lead down to the baths of María de Padilla, King Pedro's mistress (whose apartment can be seen in the palace). There's a choice of paths through flower-filled gardens past the Charles V Pavilion (geraniums sprout from the roof), past an orange tree supposed to have been in existence in Pedro's day, to a myrtlewood maze, palm groves, rose gardens, and a fountain where ducklings bathe. In an upper garden, a narrow, tiled trough carries a stream of water downhill from terrace to terrace. Engineers for *Expo '92,* borrowing from this old Arab "air conditioning" system, plan to lower temperatures on the fairgrounds at least 10 degrees by circulating cold water under the plazas. Opening hours are the same as for the Alcázar, above, and the admission charge to the Alcázar includes the gardens.

Cathedral – Seville's Gothic cathedral, the third-largest Christian church in Europe after St. Peter's Basilica in Rome and St. Paul's Cathedral in London, hunkers down along Avenida de la Constitución, displaying three carved, arched portals — but not the soaring façade that might be expected. Go around to the Plaza del Triunfo visitors' entrance. There, at the south transept, the 19th-century tomb of Christopher Columbus, his coffin borne by figures representing the Kings of Aragon, Navarre, Castile, and León, stands just inside the door. The cathedral was begun in 1402 as a grandiose symbol of Christian Seville at a time when Granada was still to be in Muslim hands for another 90 years. The Great Mosque of the Almohads, on the same site, had already been serving as a Christian church (many of Seville's churches are former mosques) when the church fathers decided to demolish it. And at record speed — only 104 years — this 380-foot-long, 250-foot-wide, and 184-foot-high vaulted and buttressed behemoth rose in its place. Only the mosque's most exquisite minaret (the present Giralda tower) was saved to become the cathedral's spire.

The enormous sweep of the cathedral is hard to appreciate because bulky choir stalls and a soaring Capilla Mayor (Main Chapel), or chancel, block the center aisle, and the Flemish stained glass windows are set so high that their light barely penetrates the shadows. A magnificent three-sided gold *reja* (grille) encloses the chancel and its 70-foot-high carved wooden *retablo* (altarpiece), the largest in Spain. The 45 niches, with over 1,000 figures in scenes from the lives of Christ and the Virgin, took Flemish sculptor Pieter Dancart 10 years to finish. It's here that ten young boys in red-and-white tunics and cocked hats click their castanets in the ritual dance of the *seises* (sixes, even though there are ten dancers) on church holidays. Behind the choir there's a stone marking the tomb of Columbus's son, Hernando, rewarded by burial here because he donated the 3,000-volume family book collection, some with his father's margin notes, to the cathedral library. At the apse stands the domed 16th-century Capilla Royal (Royal Chapel) with a *reja* showing Ferdinand III, conqueror of Seville and later sainted, receiving the keys to the city. His well-preserved body, displayed to the public on the *Feast of San Fernando* (May 30) and on the anniversary of the day he reconquered the city from the Moors (November 23), lies in a silver tomb at the feet of the city's patron saint, the Virgen de los Reyes, or Virgin of the Kings. (Both she and the Virgen de la Macarena, in the Basílica de la Macarena across town, are so popular here that when Spaniards anywhere meet a woman named Reyes or Macarena, they assume she's from Seville.) King Pedro and his mistress, María de Padilla, are in a crypt below the chapel.

Masterpieces by Murillo, Valdés Leal, Zurbarán, and Jacob Jordaens are in the ill-lit St. Anthony Chapel, although they may be moved to a brighter location by next year. Look closely at Murillo's *Vision of St. Anthony,* to make out the fine line where restorers pieced it back together after thieves, in 1874, cut out the figure of the saint. (It was recovered in New York City 3 months later.) Two more Murillos are in the Sacristía Mayor (Treasury) along with the crown, studded with more than 1,000 colored stones, that is worn by the Virgen de los Reyes for her processon on August 15. Also in the treasury are a 650-pound silver monstrance by Juan de Arfe, which is carried in the *Corpus Christi Day* procession, and a cross said to have been made from the first gold Columbus brought back from the New World. Murillo's *Holy Family,* and works by Leal, Zurbarán, Titian, and Goya are in the Sacristía de los Calices (Chalice Treasury), and Murillo's *Immaculate Conception* is in the oval Sala Capitular (Chapter House). On the north side of the cathedral is the Patio de los Naranjos (Orange Tree Court) with remnants of the original fountain of ablutions and the bronze-sheathed Puerta del Perdón (Door of Forgiveness) from the Great Mosque. Open Mondays through Fridays from 11 AM to 6 PM, Saturdays from 11 AM to 5 PM, and Sundays from 2 to 5 PM. Admission charge. Plaza del Triunfo.

La Giralda (Giralda Tower) – On a clear day, it's possible to see the olive groves around Seville in a 360-degree view from this 20-story bell tower, the same one from which the muezzin called the faithful to prayer when it was the minaret of the Great Mosque. Its ingenious *sebka* rhomboid brick patterning so pleased the Christians that they spared the tower and used it for their new cathedral. The four huge golden spheres, called the Apples of Yanmur, with which the Almohads had topped their tower in the 12th century (and which reflected beams of sunlight across the countryside), are no longer extant. Instead, the tower is topped with a belfry, lantern, and 13-foot revolving statue representing the Faith, all additions of the 16th century. The statue, known locally as the *Giraldillo,* serves as a weather vane (*giralda* in Spanish, hence the name of the tower). There's no elevator, but the climb is easy, via a wide, Moorish-style ramp so gentle that Ferdinand III rode up on horseback. Windows along the way present gargoyle-framed previews of the full panorama. Hours are the same as for the cathedral, above, and the admission charge to the cathedral includes La Giralda.

Barrio de Santa Cruz (Santa Cruz Quarter) – Hugging the walls of the Alcázar is the old Jewish quarter, or Judería, a medieval neighborhood of winding streets, handkerchief-size plazas dotted with café tables, whitewashed houses where geraniums spill from wrought-iron balconies, and flower-filled patios glimpsed from beyond fanciful gates. Seville's Jewish community flourished here for generations under the Moors but vanished in the 15th century after the Inquisition. Later the area became the playground of the aristocracy, and today it still attracts the Spanish well-to-do. One convenient way to begin a tour is by turning right upon leaving the Patio de Banderas at the exit of the Alcázar. Turn right again at the Plaza de la Alianza and head down Calle Rodrigo Caro to the lovely pebble-paved Plaza de Doña Elvira, where there are inviting benches under the orange trees. From here, any street will lead to one or another of the barrio's loveliest places.

Plaza de Santa Cruz – Though it is on the outer edge of the barrio, near an entrance to the quarter at the Jardines de Murillo (Murillo Gardens), this tiny square is its heart. The 17th-century filigreed, wrought-iron Cruz de Cerrajería (Cross of the Locksmith), which once stood downtown on Calle Sierpes, has been its centerpiece since the 1920s. Murillo's ashes are buried in an unmarked place in the square. (One of his famous paintings, *The Last Supper,* is in the nearby 17th-century baroque church of Santa María la Blanca.)

Casa de Murillo (Murillo's House) – Seville's favorite son lived his last years in this typical old barrio house, now furnished with period pieces (not Murillo's own) and five of his lesser paintings. The visit is especially interesting if the caretaker has time to take you around. Open Tuesdays through Sundays, from 10 AM to 2 PM. Admission charge. Calle de Santa Teresa (phone: 421-7535).

Hospital de la Caridad (Charity Hospital) – The name may not be appealing, but this 17th-century baroque masterpiece shouldn't be missed, if only because the man-about-town who founded it was the model for Don Juan. Saddened by the death of his wife or repentant over past peccadilloes (both stories circulate), the aristocratic Miguel de Mañara became a monk and used his wealth to build this hospital for the indigent, where the elderly can still be seen taking their ease among the tropical plants in the ocher- and rose-walled patios. He also financed the adjoining church, San Jorge, worthy of a visit for its rich ornamentation, with great golden twisted columns before the altar, beneath which Mañara is buried, and for its trove of Murillos and Valdés Leals. Good lighting here lets the viewer closely examine Murillo's massive canvases of *Moses Striking Water from the Rock* and the *Miracle of the Loaves and Fishes.* The most talked about paintings, though, are two by Valdés Leal over the entrance door and on the wall just opposite. His macabre *Finis Gloria Mundi* and *In Ictu Oculi* don't spare the corpses, maggots, and skulls in delivering their message about man's mortality. Open Mondays through Saturdays from 10 AM to 1 PM and from 3:30 to 6 PM,, Sundays and holidays from 10 AM to 12:30 PM. Admission charge. Near the Torre del Oro. 3 Calle Temprado (phone: 422-3232).

Torre del Oro (Tower of Gold) – Seville's most romantic symbol, on the banks of the Guadalquivir, was once one of 64 defensive towers built along the city wall (remnants of the wall can be seen near the Basílica de la Macarena, in the northeast section of town). Dating from 1220, its clean lines are typical of the simple but forceful Almohad style that produced the Alcázar walls and the Giralda. The tower is 12-sided and was originally faced with ceramic tiles finished in gold, an Andalusian specialty. The tiles have disappeared, but when it's illuminated at night, the Torre del Oro still glows. It has served as a prison and a storehouse for New World gold, and it once secured a chain that stretched to a twin tower (no longer in existence) on the opposite shore, enabling toll collectors to stop ships entering the port. Now the tower contains a small maritime museum and provides a nice view. Open Tuesdays through Fridays from 10 AM to 2 PM, Saturdays and Sundays from 10 AM to 1 PM. Admission charge. Paseo de Colón (phone: 422-2419).

Archivo General de Indias (Archive of the Indies) – Juan de Herrera, the same architect who planned the 16th-century Escorial monastery near Madrid for Philip II, designed this building to house the old Lonja (Stock Exchange). In the 1660s, the building housed the Seville Academy, the art academy founded largely by Murillo. Today it's the repository of documents on Spain's role in New World exploration, conquest, and commerce. A majestic red marble stairway leads to a great L-shaped gallery where carved shelves of mahogany brought from Cuba hold matching cardboard files filled with original documents. More of the 400,000 priceless papers, which include correspondence between Columbus and Queen Isabella, are locked away in air conditioned storage. Only scholars may examine the documents (successful hunts for sunken treasure in the New World have begun here), but anyone will get the idea from the displays of drawings, charts, letters, account books, and royal decrees in the many glass cases along the center. Open from 9 AM to 1 PM; closed Sundays. Next to the cathedral. Avenida de la Constitución (phone: 421-1234).

Plaza Nueva – A short walk north from the cathedral along Avenida de la Constitución leads to Seville's central city square, with the block-long Renaissance Ayuntamiento (City Hall) fronting it and a bronze horseman (Ferdinand III) in the middle. Another entrance to the Ayuntamiento is around the back, on Plaza de San Francisco, the scene of Inquisition *autos-da-fé,* as well as tournaments, bullfights, and political rallies.

Museo de Bellas Artes (Fine Arts Museum) – Still farther north, near the Córdoba train station, this is a superb museum whose collection of international art from the 16th through the 20th centuries — with an especially fine selection of paintings by Murillo, Zurbarán, Valdés Leal, and other Spanish artists — is second only to that of the *Prado* in Madrid. Unfortunately, it has been closed for renovation, and although a few rooms reopened in 1990 (putting some of the more prized Spanish Old Masters back on view), the full museum is not expected to be open again until 1992. It is housed in the 17th-century baroque Convent of La Merced, whose patios, cloisters, and chapel — and façade the color of the oranges on the trees outside — are works of art in themselves. Open Tuesdays through Sundays from 9:30 AM to 3 PM. Admission charge. 9 Plaza del Museo (phone: 422-0790).

Universidad de Sevilla (University of Seville) – The monumental Royal Tobacco Factory that Bizet used as the setting for the first act of his opera *Carmen* has been part of the University of Seville since the 1950s. It still hints of its past at its main entrances, carved with bas reliefs of tobacco plants, Indians, galleons, and the faces of Columbus and Cortés. The largest building in Spain after the Escorial, it is worth walking through at least some of it for a look at student life in the vast graffiti-covered halls and courtyards. Just south of the *Alfonso XIII* hotel. Calle San Fernando.

Parque María Luisa (María Luisa Park) – The San Telmo Palace, whose colorful baroque façade can be seen behind the *Alfonso XIII* hotel, was built as a naval college and now is used as a seminary. During the 19th century, however, it belonged to María Luisa, sister of Queen Isabella II, and the present María Luisa Park, the Bois de Boulogne of Seville, was the palace grounds. The park was given to the city in the early 1900s, and the extravagant period buildings in it were built for the *1929 Ibero-American Exposition.* Cars have been banned from the park for the past decade, leaving room for jogging, bicycling, and sightseeing by horse and carriage. In summer, all Seville strolls its long, forested allées. In winter, sun worshipers crowd into the open Plaza de España, at its eastern edge.

Plaza de España – Practically at the entrance to María Luisa Park, along Avenida Isabel la Católica, is a grandiose, semicircular plaza surrounded by a Renaissance-style government office complex, originally built for the 1929 exposition. The canal that follows the semicircle of the plaza is so long that rowboats can be rented for mini-excursions. Take time to walk over the canal's beautiful all-tile bridges and to browse the alcoves — each highlights one of Spain's 50 provinces with a lively tiled mural — set into the curving plaza wall.

Plaza de América – At the far end of the park, in a beautifully laid-out area of palm-shaded terraces, rose gardens, lily ponds, and splashing fountains, stand three more stunning buildings left from the exposition. The one in the center houses Andalusia's government headquarters; the other two are the *Museo Arqueológico* (see below) and the *Museo de Arte y Costumbres Populares* (phone: 423-2576), a folk museum with exhibits of regional life (open Tuesdays through Sundays from 10 AM to 2 PM). Parque María Luisa.

Museo Arqueológico (Archaeological Museum) – This museum, in a Plateresque-style exposition building, contains a definitive collection of artifacts from excavations in western Andalusia. Don't miss the Roman section, which has statues, jewelry, and coins found in the ruins of the ancient city of Itálica (see below), just outside Seville. Open Tuesdays through Sundays, from 10 AM to 2 PM. Admission charge. Plaza de América (phone: 423-2401).

Casa de Pilatos (House of Pilate) – A trip to this 16th-century mansion, the last of the great private houses in Seville open to visitors, is an entrée to the splendid lifestyle of an Andalusian nobleman of days long past. The Marqués de Tarifa, who finished it in 1540, is supposed to have been inspired by the house of the Roman emperor in Jerusalem, but his architects didn't spare Mudéjar, Plateresque, and Gothic glories. The ceiling of the grand staircase has been compared to the Alcázar and the tiled walls and patios are sensational. There's also a collection of Roman sculpture. Open daily, from 9 AM to 6 PM. Admission charge. In the ancient San Esteban eastern part of town. 1 Plaza de Pilatos (phone: 422-5298).

ENVIRONS

Itálica – The impressive ruins of this Roman city, founded at the end of the 3rd century BC by the Roman general Scipio Africanus, are about 5 miles (8 km) northwest of Seville, just outside the town of Santiponce. The birthplace of Hadrian and Trajan, its main attraction is the colossal amphitheater, said to have held 25,000 spectators. Digging, begun in 1971, was recently completed down to the last pit for wild animals. There are also largely intact mosaic floors, baths, temple remains, and a museum (although major finds are in the *Museo Arqueológico* in Seville). From April through September, open Tuesdays through Saturdays from 9 AM to 6:30 PM, Sundays from 9 AM to 3 PM; the rest of the year, open Tuesdays through Saturdays from 9 AM to 5:30 PM, Sundays from 10 AM to 4 PM. Admission charge. Buses leave every 30 minutes from Calle Marqués de Paradas in Seville, near the Córdoba train station (phone: 439-4900 or 439-2784).

■**EXTRA SPECIAL:** The giant crimson door of the *Plaza de Toros de la Real Maestranza* — Seville's bullring — swings open on *Easter Sunday* to begin the bullfight season, which runs until October. The quintessentially Spanish spectacle of the *corrida,* or bullfight, is quintessentially Andalusian — modern bullfighting began in the Andalusian town of Ronda, near Seville, in the 18th century — and while the bullring in Madrid may be larger, Seville's *Maestranza,* built in the 1760s, is more beautiful. An appearance here is a must for all of the world's greatest matadors. The *corridas,* with sparkling pageantry and the inevitable moment of truth, are held Sunday and holiday afternoons at 6:30 PM (daily during the *Feria*). Buy tickets, ranging from about $25 in the sun to $75 in full shade (remember, the summer sun is still blazing at 7 PM in the south of Spain), at the ring on Paseo de Colón or in bars along Calle Sierpes.

SOURCES AND RESOURCES

TOURIST INFORMATION: The regional Oficina de Información de Turismo (Tourist Information Office; 21B Avenida de la Constitución; phone: 422-1404), conveniently located near the cathedral and endowed with an enthusiastic, English-speaking staff, is open Mondays through Fridays from 9:30 AM to 7:30 PM, and until 2 PM on Saturdays. Ask for a copy of *El Giraldillo,* a free monthly guide to upcoming events distributed in several languages, including English. Unfortunately, most free city maps and pamphlets (sometimes available only in Spanish) are appallingly sketchy. Plan on shopping in several bookstores for supplemental materials. (Worth having is the easy-to-follow city map available free at *El Corte Inglés,* the big department store on Plaza del Duque.) A get-acquainted bus tour of the city isn't a bad idea; a combination of the morning and afternoon trips will hit all the highlights. Hotels can book visitors on those offered by *Sevilla Tours* at about $22 each trip. For a licensed private guide, call *Guidetour de Sevilla* (phone: 422-2374) or ask at the tourist office.

The US Consulate is at 7 Paseo de las Delicias (phone: 423-1885).

Local Coverage – Two daily newspapers widely read in Seville are *El Correo de Andalucía* and *ABC.* Visitors rely on the monthly *El Giraldillo,* available free in shops and hotels, as well as at the tourist office.

TELEPHONE: The city code for Seville is 5. If calling from within Spain, dial 95 before the local number. Note that all Seville phone numbers now have seven digits and begin with a 4. Many brochures and other printed materials still give old numbers with fewer than seven digits. To convert these to the new system, simply preface them with a 4.

GETTING AROUND: It's possible to walk almost anywhere in the city, but the summer heat and the duration of most tourist visits, too short for a leisurely pace, may make a bit of help desirable.

Airport – Seville's Aeropuerto San Pablo (phone: 451-0677) is 8 miles (13 km) from town. Airport bus service is erratic. Cab fare for the 20-minute ride should be around $12.

Bus – Bright orange buses go everywhere in the city. Pick up a route map at the tourist office or in front of the *Inglaterra* hotel in Plaza Nueva, where city routes begin. Fare is 70 pesetas (about 65¢ — exact change not required); discounted 10-trip tickets are available in Plaza Nueva and at kiosks elsewhere. The tourist office also has schedules of intercity buses, which leave from the Estación de Autobuses (Central Bus Station), 1 Prado de San Sebastián (phone: 441-7111).

Car Rental – International rental companies represented include *Hertz* (3 Avenida República Argentina; phone: 427-8887; and at the airport); *Avis* (15 Avenida de la Constitución; phone: 421-6549; and at the airport); and *Europcar* (32 Calle Recaredo; phone: 441-9506; and at the airport).

Horse and Carriage – The way to go. During the *Feria,* even the locals do it. Rates, regulated by the city, run about $20 per hour. Choose your *coche de caballo* from the lineup around the cathedral square or at María Luisa Park.

Taxi – Since distances are short, fares in town average under $3. Drivers legitimately charge extra for bigger pieces of luggage and for travel after 10 PM and on holidays. Hail cabs on the street or call *Radio-Taxi* (phone: 458-0000) or *Tele-Taxi* (phone: 462-2222).

Train – Trains leave from two stations, each with two names. Most destinations in Spain are served by trains from Estación Plaza de Armas (56 Plaza de Armas; phone: 422-8817), also known as Estación de Córdoba. The other station, Estación de San Bernardo (13 Calle San Bernardo; phone: 422-8817), is also known as Estación de Cádiz and serves points southwest of Seville. Schedules and tickets can be obtained from the *RENFE* office (29 Calle Zaragoza; phone: 441-4111), near Plaza Nueva.

SPECIAL EVENTS: Two world famous festivals make springtime prime time. The city is mobbed for both events, with hotels booked a year in advance, restaurant tables at a premium, and rates for horse and carriage doubled. But you get a lot of Seville for the money. During the emotion-packed *Semana Santa* (Holy Week), which begins on *Palm Sunday,* members of the city's more than 50 *cofradías* (brotherhoods) — religious organizations with origins in 16th-century guilds — take to the streets each evening in candlelit processions. Robed and hooded in traditional penitential garb, they are followed by *costaleros* (porters) staggering under the weight of elaborate gilt and bejeweled *pasos* (floats) bearing statues of Christ or the Virgin Mary that are carried to the cathedral and back to their own parish churches. The most popular images, such as the beloved Virgen de la Macarena, crying crystal tears, bring out a mixture of mourning and revelry in the crowd as spectators fall into step behind the penitents, break into flamenco laments called *saetas,* and root for their favorite floats.

By the time *Semana Santa* ends on *Easter Sunday,* Seville is ready to begin dressing for the riotous *Feria* (April Fair), which usually opens on April 18. Across the river, near Los Remedios, workers already are putting up rows of green- and white-striped *casetas* (little tents) where families, companies, and clubs hold open house around the clock during the 6 days of celebration. The fair began in the 19th century as a rural livestock market, but it has gussied itself up considerably since then: Andalusia's high-stepping horses, in tassels and bells, go through their paces, and brightly costumed groups parade around town in flower-decked coaches. There are nightly *corridas,* fireworks, amusements, and dancing in the streets.

Expo '92, the city's big bash in honor of the 500th anniversary of Columbus's discovery of America, is scheduled to open April 20, 1992, and close 6 months later on October 12, 1992. More than 100 countries, as well as numerous international organizations and corporations, will be participating, in pavilions illustrating *Expo's* Age of Discovery theme and their own contributions to human progress, the sciences, technology, and art. Besides the pavilions themselves (architecturally varied and sure to be interesting), the 538-acre fairgrounds will hold scores of restaurants and shops, theaters, and a panoramic railway — in short, enough distractions to keep the antici- pated 250,000 daily visitors entertained. For those visiting Seville before the fair, a sneak preview is possible, in the form of maps and models on view at the fairgrounds, along with some construction. Call the *Expo '92* information office (10 Plaza de Cuba; phone: 427-7271) to find out on which days visitors are permitted and to reserve a place on the tour. Transportation is provided from the office to the fairgrounds.

MUSEUMS: Most of the museums of interest to visitors are discussed in *Special Places.* In addition, Seville has the *Museo de Arte Contemporaneo* (5 Calle Santo Tomás; phone: 421-5830). A repository of Spanish art of the 20th century in an 18th-century building, it's open Tuesdays through Fri- days from 10 PM to 7 PM, and Saturdays and Sundays from 10 AM to 2 PM. Admission charge.

SHOPPING: Anyone looking for the across-the-board bargains of a few years back will do better shopping at home, but anyone coveting a gorgeous hand-embroidered, silk-fringed shawl that would be hard to find elsewhere has come to the right place. Seville has Andalusia's largest selection of mantillas, fans, hand-embroidered linen and shawls (if prices sound too low, make sure it's not machine embroidery), flamenco dresses, castanets, and guitars. Plenty of the above can be found in colorful shops around the cathedral and in the Barrio de Santa Cruz. For more, plus shoes and handbags, go downtown, and don't miss Calle Sierpes. Seville's favorite pedestrian street, tiled in rose and blue, winds downtown for about 5 blocks between Plaza de San Francisco, behind the Ayuntamiento, and the Campana, an intersection of several streets near Plaza del Duque (some maps give its full name, Plaza del Duque de la Victoria). Nearby are tiny Calle Rosario and Calle Muñoz Olive, lined with boutiques selling Italian and French fashions. Seville's two big downtown department stores, *El Corte Inglés* (Plaza del Duque) and *Galerías Preciados* (Plaza de la Magdalena) are good fallback stops because they don't close for siesta — and they're good bets for a quick, inexpensive lunch. The latter has an upstairs coffee shop (about the only nonsmoking section in Seville) serving burgers and malts as well as Spanish snacks and luncheon specials, wines, and cocktails; the cafeteria in the former store offers similar values but is much more crowded. (*El Corte Inglés* is also strong on guidebooks and maps.)

Other possibilities include a leather crafts and jewelry fair that takes place daily except Sundays on Plaza del Duque opposite *El Corte Inglés,* a Sunday morning crafts fair downtown at Alameda de Hércules, and a Sunday morning stamp and coin market at Plaza del Cabildo. The picturesque Triana food market occupies tumbledown stalls under the Triana Bridge across the river, and the indoor *El Arenal* food market is near the bullring at Calle Pastor y Landero (both markets are open mornings and closed Sundays).

La Alcazaba – Delicate hand-painted ceramic tiles and platters from Seville and other regions, including the lovely florals from Valencia. Near the Alcázar exit. 1A Calle Joaquin Romero Murube (phone: 421-8088).

Artesanía Textil – Mantillas, silk shawls, embroidered linens, fans, and everyday leather coats and jackets for men and women, sold in a factory-to-customer atmosphere near Plaza del Cabildo. 33 Calle García de Vinuesa (phone: 422-1606). Also in the Barrio de Santa Cruz at 4 Plaza de Doña Elvira (phone: 421-4748).

Artespaña – Part of the Spain-wide, government-sponsored chain, selling arts and crafts from all over the country — and they pack and ship. Near *El Corte Inglés.* 2 Plaza de la Gavidia (phone: 422-1865).

Bolsos Casal – Medium-priced handbags and luggage. There are several branches downtown; a helpful sales staff can be found at 73 Calles Sierpes (phone: 422-6055).

El Caballo – Andalusian horsemen come to this shop near the bullring for the finest leather boots, saddles, hunting gear, traditional riding suits, and flat, wide-brimmed hats. 14 Calle Adriano (phone: 422-2047).

Casa Rubio – Exquisite lacy, hand-painted fans. 56 Calle Sierpes (phone: 422-6872).

Cerámica Santa Ana – A large selection of ceramics at good prices. In Triana. 31 Calle San Jorge (phone: 433-3990).

Convento de San Leandro – It's impossible to buy more authentic *yemas* (dainty sweets of egg yolk and sugar) than the ones made by the nuns here. Near the Casa de Pilatos. 1 Plaza de San Ildefonso (phone: 422-4195).

Juan Feronda – Mantillas, shawls, flamenco dresses, linen; several stores, but the best selection is at the one near La Giralda. 18 Calle Argote de Molina (phone: 422-8467).

Loewe – The ultimate in luxury leather purses (women's handbags begin at around $350), wallets, attaché cases, luggage, and couture by a fifth-generation Madrid firm, with some items up to 30% less than at US branches. 12 Plaza Nueva (phone: 422-5253) and at the *Alfonso XIII* hotel (phone: 422-1371).

Martian – Hand-painted ceramics of the highest quality. 74 Calle Sierpes (phone: 421-3413).

El Postigo Artesanía – Not a single shop but a group of boutiques in a 3-story arcade; made-to-measure flamenco dresses, religious art, antiques, contemporary jewelry, ceramics, paintings, and leather goods. Calle Arfe at Plaza del Cabildo (phone: 421-3976).

Sevillarte – A beautiful selection of hand-painted ceramics. 66 Calle Sierpes (phone: 421-2836).

Vértice – Guidebooks and maps in Spanish and English, as well as books on Spanish art and history. In the Barrio de Santa Cruz. 24 Calle Mateos Gago (phone: 421-1654).

 SPORTS AND FITNESS: Seville is not set up with sports facilities for tourists; most visitors don't stay long enough to have time for much beyond swimming in the hotel pool or jogging.

Boating – Paddleboats are for rent by the hour (about $3 for two people,

$5 for four). Look for the *Barcos* sign along the river in the vicinity of Plaza de Cuba.

Horse Racing – Seville's racetrack is the *Hipódromo del Club Pineda* (Avenida de Jerez). Races take place on Sundays from October through February or March.

Jogging – María Luisa Park in the cool of the morning is the place to run.

Soccer – The city's two first division teams are *Real Betis,* based at the *Benito Villamarín* stadium, and *Sevilla,* which plays at the *Sánchez Pizjuán* stadium. The season runs from September to the beginning of May.

Swimming – The *Alfonso XIII, Meliá Sevilla, Doña María,* and other hotels have pools; if yours doesn't, try the *Municipales Chapina* (Avenida Cristo de la Expiración; phone: 433-3654), one of several municipal pools in town.

Tennis – Hotel concierges sometimes can arrange guest sessions at private tennis facilities such as the *Betis Tenis Club,* Calle San Salvador (phone: 423-1028).

THEATER AND MUSIC: Theatrical and musical events are listed in the free monthly *El Giraldillo,* but it's better to buy the weekly magazine *Ocio,* a combination city, sports, TV, arts, and entertainment guide. Watch for drama, dance, and concerts at the *Teatro Nacional Lope de Vega* (at the edge of María Luisa Park; phone: 423-1835); popular revues at *Teatro Maravillas* (downtown on Calle San Vicente; phone: 438-8609); drama at *Teatro Imperial* (Calle Sierpes; phone: 422-6878); classical music at conservatories, colleges, and churches; and open-air rock and pop concerts in the Prado de San Sebastián near María Luisa Park. *Cita en Sevilla,* a festival of contemporary popular music, Spanish and foreign, held from mid-May to mid-June, also usually takes place in the Prado de San Sebastián. Theater in English is limited to the occasional event sponsored by the university, but American and British motion pictures often play here in English with Spanish subtitles.

NIGHTCLUBS AND NIGHTLIFE: Seville keeps the flamenco flame burning nightly in rousing song and dance performances called *tablaos,* the most authentic and best performed outside Madrid. The *tablao*'s handful of dancers, guitarists, and singers, some young and sleek, some mature and dumpy (looks matter less than ability and *duende* — raw emotion), run through a repertoire of stylized songs and dances that express Gypsy sorrows, loves, and joys. The show begins with an innocent tune from two guitarists seated on a bare wooden stage the size of a postage stamp and ends in a whirlwind of ruffles and the thunder of guitar strings, handclaps, and heels. Tickets, which can usually be reserved through hotels, cost around $20, one glass of wine included; depending on the season, there are two or three shows a night. *Los Gallos* (11 Plaza de Santa Cruz; phone: 421-6981), a romantic little theater in the Barrio de Santa Cruz, has a well-known troupe. *El Arenal* (7 Calle Rodo; phone: 421-6492), in a cobbled alley near the river, puts on a stirring, authentic *tablao* and also offers a dinner show for about $40. *El Patio Sevillano* (11 Paseo de Cristóbal Colón; phone: 421-4120) offers a program that includes flamenco, folk dance, and classical guitar. Do-it-yourself flamenco can be sampled by joining the locals on the floor of a flamenco-disco on Triana's notorious Calle Salado. But go at your own risk, because it's purse snatching heaven (don't ask what else) — or why would they need a guard at every other door? Go after 1 AM, when the young crowd begins warming up to the *sevillanas* (the local flamenco) at *Canela Pura,* a modest storefront pub (9 Calle Salado), or drop in at nearby *Tres Faroles* (8A Calle Salado) or at *La Garrocha* (11 Calle Salado).

For a safe and sane change of pace, save an evening for the little Euro-style bars, pubs, and outdoor cafés between Calle Virgen de Africa and Calle Virgen de las Montañas near *La Dorada* restaurant in Los Remedios. For international disco, the action is at *Holiday* (downtown at 73 Calle Jesús del Gran Poder, in the former red-light district); *El Coto* (in the *Lebreros Hotel,* 118 Calle Luis Montoto); or *Río* (Calle Betis), where you can cruise a whole gaggle of riverside clubs. Go late.

BEST IN TOWN

CHECKING IN: As the capital of Andalusia, Seville attracts business and government travelers as well as tourists, so there's a wide selection of hotels. With a few exceptions, our choices are confined to those most suitable for leisure travelers; unless otherwise noted, all are within reasonable walking distance of the central area including the cathedral, Alcázar, and the Barrio de Santa Cruz. All have some English-speaking personnel, and their concierges or desk clerks are generous with advice to help guests get around the city. Rates are lowest in the hot summer months, when Spaniards are taking their own vacations at the beach. Prices are slightly higher the rest of the year and steeply higher during *Semana Santa* and the *Feria.* Price ranges here are for summer, when most Americans take their vacations. Hotels have air conditioning unless otherwise noted, and breakfast is available even when there is no restaurant. Expect to pay from $125 to $250 for a double room in hotels listed as expensive, from $75 to $125 for those listed as moderate, and from $30 to $75 for the inexpensive ones. All telephone numbers are in the 5 city code unless otherwise indicated.

Alfonso XIII – It makes no difference that this handsome Spanish palace is a reproduction, built in 1929 for the *Ibero-American Exposition.* Even a caliph could be fooled by its *azulejo*-lined hallways, spacious guestrooms (149), regal lobby, white marble courtyard, and Moroccan garden with a big swimming pool. Unsurpassed for location, Seville's grande dame (now part of the CIGA chain) not only is a hop, skip, and jump from the Alcázar, but also central enough to let a visitor walk downtown in one direction and to María Luisa Park in the other. Its restaurant is the elegant continental *Itálica.* 2 Calle San Fernando (phone: 422-2850). Expensive.

Casas de la Judería – Just the thing for anyone who wants to go native, in a very upscale sort of way. In the Barrio de Santa Cruz, near Plaza Santa Maria la Blanca, these furnished luxury apartments occupy a group of refurbished 3-story buildings that once belonged to the Duke of Bejár, patron and benefactor of Cervantes. Each of the 35 units — 1 to 3 bedrooms — has a fully equipped kitchen, direct dial telephones, and satellite television; some have terraces, and some even have Andalusian-style patios with a fountain. No restaurant, but breakfast is served. Callejon de Dos Hermanas (phone: 441-5150). Expensive.

Colón – A luxurious rival to the *Alfonso XIII,* this is an old hotel that's been completely redone, right down to the new white sofas and the restored antique glass dome in the upstairs lobby. Because the property — with its 204 rooms and 14 suites — is handy to the bullring, it is the traditional headquarters for touring toreros, and a bullfighting theme prevails in the fine *El Burladero* restaurant (see *Eating Out*). 1 Calle Canalejas (phone: 422-2900). Expensive.

Inglaterra – Its very central location makes this sleek, remodeled old-timer a convenient headquarters for an in-depth visit to the city. (All buses stop at its front door.) The big, comfortable, contemporary salon is an after-work gathering spot for downtown bankers and businessmen. Rooms (116 of them, some with terraces on the square) have modern furnishings; service is efficient, the concierge desk is helpful, and there is a sunny second-floor restaurant. 7 Plaza Nueva (phone: 422-4970). Expensive.

Meliá Sevilla – The jazziest of the newer hotels in town is in an L-shaped high-rise apartment and shopping complex near María Luisa Park. The bright white marble atrium lobby, decidedly trendy café scene, choice of restaurants, disco, and swimming pool, and the adjoining boutiques could hold up any sightseeing. Decor in the 366 rooms is ultramodern. 3 Avenida de la Borbolla (phone: 442-2611). Expensive.

Husa Sevilla – Facing a small square in the Triana district, this place is brand new and in a new building, but one that is true to traditional Sevillian style — pastel stucco façade, wood-beamed ceilings, potted plants, hand-painted tiles, and marble accents. It has 116 rooms and 16 suites (all soundproof), a bar, café, and a restaurant, and it's only a few blocks back from the river, a 15-minute walk across the Triana Bridge to the core of the city. 90 Pagés del Corro (phone: 434-2414). Expensive to moderate.

Macarena – Casablanca kitsch describes the mirror-trimmed Andalusian façade and rattan-furnished lobby court, but this 327-room hotel is a good bet when those closer to the center are booked. Ask for a room in back, off the noisy avenue. It's a cab ride to the cathedral area and most other attractions, although it's across from the old Roman and Moorish walls and the Basílica de la Macarena. There is a restaurant. 2 Calle San Juan de Ribera (phone: 437-5700). Expensive to moderate.

Pasarela – Near the *Meliá Sevilla* but closer to the park, this one is small (82 rooms), modern, efficient, and a current favorite with Spanish business travelers. No restaurant. 11 Avenida de la Borbolla (phone: 441-5511). Expensive to moderate.

América – An affordable, efficient, modern businessman's hotel in the heart of the downtown shopping district, across from the *El Corte Inglés* department store. It has 100 rooms, motel decor, a cafeteria, and no atmosphere, but the service is good and it's close to Calle Sierpes, the *Museo de Bellas Artes,* and the Triana Bridge. 2 Calle Jesús del Gran Poder (phone: 422-0951). Moderate.

Bécquer – On a lovely café-lined street 2 blocks from the Triana Bridge and only a short walk to the *Maestranza* bullring, shopping, and the *Museo de Bellas Artes.* It offers a wood-paneled lobby, big-hotel service, and 126 average rooms. No restaurant. 4 Calle Reyes Católicos (phone: 422-2172). Moderate.

Doña María – Every morning this intimate, luxurious little place gets calls from people hoping for cancellations. The location (one door up from the cathedral square), the combination of period charm and up-to-date convenience, the romantic decor in the 61 rooms (all one-of-a-kind), and the little rooftop swimming pool in the shadow of La Giralda make it the number one small hotel choice. No restaurant. 19 Calle Don Remondo (phone: 422-4990). Moderate.

Puerta de Triana – New ownership, new name (it used to be the *Niza*), but little else has changed. It shares the same attractive, convenient location as the *Bécquer* across the street, but it costs even less, and many of the 56 rooms have balconies on the avenue. Despite the postage-stamp lobby with the soft-drink machine and blaring TV set, it's an outstanding buy. 5 Calle Reyes Católicos (phone: 421-5401). Moderate to inexpensive.

Goya – This *hostal* (inn) is one of those too-good-to-be true bargains: a narrow house with gaily striped awnings in the Barrio de Santa Cruz, 20 shipshape rooms, a charming upstairs garden — and budget-minded guests congratulating one another on finding it. No air conditioning; no restaurant. Write early for reservations. 31 Calle Mateos Gago (phone: 421-1170). Inexpensive.

 EATING OUT: Seville is not known for restaurants, but it sets a fine table, although all of the city's dazzling *tapas* bars (see below) may keep you from sitting down to it. The star of restaurant menus haute or lowly is sweet Atlantic seafood from Huelva. Try baby fish and eels, batter-dipped and deep-fried to airy crispness, as in *fritura;* bass baked in a tomato casserole as in *urta*

a la roteña; shrimp sautéed in olive oil and hot red peppers as in *gambas al pil pil;* or hake simply pan-fried in a bit of olive oil as in *merluza a la plancha.* Delicious cured country ham is found everywhere in Spain, but the local mahogany-colored *jamón de Jabugo,* found in better *tapas* bars, is the best. Other dishes to try are Seville's favorite, *huevos a la flamenca* (baked eggs with asparagus and peas), and, in cold weather, *rabo de toro* (oxtail stew), or, in warm weather, gazpacho, the cold tomato and cucumber soup. No wine is made in Seville, so the "local" wine comes from Jerez. When a dry sherry aperitif is in order, ask for a *fino* or for the very special dry, amber-colored *manzanilla* from Sanlúcar de Barrameda. Or try a big pitcher of cooling sangria laden with orange and lemon halves.

Seville's restaurants observe the traditional long lunches, closing in late afternoon and opening again around 8 PM for early-bird diners. (If you crave a sandwich in between, drop by an American-style cafeteria or ask for a *bocadillo* — a sandwich on a hard roll — anywhere you see *tapas.*) Menus with English translations are the rule, and many economy restaurants compete for tourists by displaying photographs of their popular dishes. Expect to pay from $60 to $100 for an average three-course meal for two with house wine in a restaurant listed below as expensive (the *menu de la casa* could run less), from $20 to $60 in a moderate restaurant, and under $20 in an inexpensive one. Opening days and hours change from time to time and some places close for at least a month's vacation. Call before you go. All telephone numbers are in the 5 city code unless otherwise indicated.

La Albahaca – Gracious dining prevails in this stately old mansion that a famed Spanish architect built for himself in the Barrio de Santa Cruz. Dine late on such delicacies as *perdíz del coto en cazerola* (partridge casserole) or *lubina al hinojo* (a type of sea bass with fennel) and attend the midnight *tablao* at *Los Gallos* right next door. Closed Sundays. Reservations necessary. 12 Plaza de Santa Cruz (phone: 422-0714). Expensive.

Egaña-Oriza – A chic, Basque-owned bastion of nouvelle cuisine, it's *the* place to be seen in Seville. It enjoys a glamorous greenhouse setting against a wall of the Alcázar Gardens (a small section of the wall, a national monument, is actually inside the entrance). Out front, café tables have a good view of the adjoining Murillo Gardens, the flashy fountain in Plaza San Juan de Austria, and promenading *sevillanos.* The menu runs to elegant innovations such as *gazpacho con langostinos de Sanlúcar* (gazpacho with Sanlúcar prawns) or *solomillo con mousse de foie a las uvas de Corintio* (steak with foie gras in a grape sauce). Closed Sundays and August. Reservations essential for lunch or dinner. 41 Calle San Fernando (phone: 422-7211). Expensive.

Enrique Becerra – Most visitors never take the trouble to find this elite little gem hidden away on a narrow street off the Plaza Nueva. Besides the cozy dining room on the main floor, there are private dining salons upstairs (two people can reserve the smallest one for themselves). Friendly waiters offer advice about the chef's highly personalized menu. Closed Sundays at lunch. Reservations advised. 2 Calle Gamazo (phone: 421-3049). Expensive.

La Isla – Though regulars are put off by its new formality, the restaurant's high-backed, black-lacquer chairs and salmon tablecloths make a relaxing setting in which to enjoy extraordinarily fresh seafood flown in from Galicia. Select a personal favorite from the refrigerated window display on the street. This is a comfortable place to spend the afternoon after a hard day in the Alcázar across Avenida de la Constitución. Closed August. Reservations advised. 25 Calle Arfe (phone: 421-5376). Expensive.

Ox's – A typical Basque *asador* (barbecue restaurant) specializing in the finest quality charcoal-grilled meats, fish, and some Sevillian specialties. It's a local favorite, on a par in its way, with *Egaña-Oriza,* which used to share the building.

Closed Sundays and August. Reservations advised. 61 Calle Betis (phone: 427-9585). Expensive.

El Burladero – The name refers to the bullfighter's protective barrier at the entrances to the arena, and the taurine theme here is carried all the way from photographs of past heroes such as Juan Belmonte and Rafael El Gallo on the walls to cattle-brand designs woven into the damask tablecloths. And, since it's in the elegant *Colón* hotel, tuxedoed waiters serve with a style that attracts a top-drawer clientele — stop in at the bar and watch the city's yuppies networking. The menu, largely continental, includes regional specialties from all over Spain, among them the Andalusian *bacalao al horno con patatas* (baked salt cod with saffron and potatoes) and *pochas con almejas* (white kidney beans with clams). Open daily. Reservations necessary. 1 Calle Canalejas (phone: 422-2900). Expensive to moderate.

La Dorada – This big, bright, seafood restaurant — with waiters and waitresses in snappy nautical uniforms, and a doorman in captain's garb — was the model for *La Doradas* in Barcelona and Madrid. Order the specialty, *dorada a la sal,* sea bream baked in a crust of rock salt, which is cracked open at tableside to release the tender, sweet, steaming fish, or the *fritura malagueña* (tiny baby eels, baby squid, and red mullet, none longer than a little finger, dipped in batter and fried to a crunch). Closed Sundays and August. Reservations advised. 6 Calle Virgen de Aguas Santas (phone: 445-5100). Expensive to moderate.

Figón del Cabildo – The decor of heavy plaster, brick, and wood beams is the perfect setting for Sevillian specialties in this popular spot across Avenida de la Constitución from the cathedral. Try *berenjenas gratinadas con jamón y langostinos* (eggplant with ham and crayfish) or *sopa de picadillo* (consommé with egg yolk and ham). Closed Sunday evenings. Reservations advised. Plaza del Cabildo (phone: 422-0117). Expensive to moderate.

El Rincón de Curro – Anyone will tell you that this comfortable restaurant (another place where white plaster and dark wood beams predominate) in Los Remedios is the best place in town for meat dishes, although there's a good seafood menu, too. Food critics have singled out the *cochinillo asado a la segoviana* (roast suckling pig) and the *chuletón de buey al plato caliente* (steak sizzling on a hot clay plate). Closed Sunday evenings and August. Reservations necessary. 45 Calle Virgen de Luján (phone: 445-0238). Expensive to moderate.

Hostería del Laurel – This place has a come-on that's better than its food — Don Juan supped here (or at least the man who inspired the legend did). Nevertheless, an acceptable menu of Andalusian standards, served in country dining rooms hung with bunches of garlic and dried laurel, makes it a pleasant lunch stop in the Barrio de Santa Cruz. (The large ruined wall across the way belongs to the Hospital de los Venerables Sacerdotes, a 17th-century home for old priests that is noted for its patio and church, but closed for renovation at present.) Open daily. Reservations advised. 5 Plaza de los Venerables (phone: 422-0295). Moderate.

Mesón Don Raimundo – If there's time for only one meal in Seville, have it in this restaurant, in a convent ruin in the Barrio de Santa Cruz. A long, dark alley overgrown with vines leads to capacious dining rooms decorated with massive Arab cooking vessels and farm utensils; a cozy barroom is patterned in tiles clear to the ceiling. Ask owner Raimundo Fernández for advice on the dishes he's adapted from old Arab-Spanish cookbooks: The baby lamb roasted over grape vines is especially good in the fall. Also try his *sopa de almejas con piñones* (clam soup with pine nuts) and the *pato mozárabe (*duck stuffed with apples, honey, nuts, and sultanas). Closed Sunday evenings. Reservations advised. 26 Calle Argote de Molina (phone: 422-3355). Moderate.

La Raza – This pretty terrace-restaurant in a park setting serves typical Andalusian food and drink and is most festive on a Friday or Saturday when there's music. Open daily. Reservations unnecessary. It's just inside the entrance to María Luisa Park (phone: 423-2024). Moderate.

Río Grande – The best time here is evening, when the Torre del Oro across the river is bathed in lights. Dine indoors in the formal peach-walled Salon Reina Sofía or catch the river breeze on the broad terrace. There's a paella that's rich with goodies, perfect gazpacho, and *salteado de ternera a la sevillana* (diced veal with local green olives, carrots, and potatoes). Everyone should eat here once, or at least come for *tapas* at the long bar in the building across the patio. Open daily. Reservations necessary. 70 Calle Betis (phone: 427-3956). Moderate.

Taberna Dorada – Newer and snappier than most Seville seafood spots, this place attracts the young set. Closed Sundays and August. Reservations advised. 18 Calle José Luis de Casso (phone: 465-2720). Moderate.

Bodega El Diamante – A chain of *buffets libres* (all you can eat, self-service), not only a great buy, but also a way to eat quickly and without language problems. There's more than one, but this location generates so much traffic that the food is fresher and hotter. Load up on paella, *ensalada russa* (vegetable salad in mayonnaise), fried fishsticks, fish salads, hard-boiled eggs in mayonnaise, sliced tomatoes, fried eggplant, green and red peppers, and fresh fruit, but leave the *salchichas* (rubbery hot dogs) alone. Closed Sundays. No reservations. 10 Avenida de la Constitución (no phone). Inexpensive.

Las Escobas – It claims to be Seville's oldest restaurant, having fed the likes of Lope de Vega, Miguel de Cervantes, and Lord Byron, and the elaborately carved bar and oak-paneled ceiling are convincing, despite the remodeling it has undergone. Of all the competing little eateries lined up on the streets north of the cathedral, this is the most pleasant place for *platos combinados* (economy specials), paper tablecloths notwithstanding. Open daily. Reservations unnecessary. 62 Calle Alvarez Quintero (phone: 421-4479). Inexpensive.

 TAPAS BARS: *Tapas* originated in Andalusia. In fact, it is said that they were invented in Seville when young men took to ordering a slice of ham as a *tapa* (lid) for their glasses of sherry. Whatever the truth, the selection of *tascas* (*tapas* bars) in Seville is bountiful and the camaraderie of *tasca* hopping, chowing down enough tidbits of seafood, hams, sausages, cheeses, and marinated vegetables to hold you until breakfast, is irresistible. Follow the crowd and you'll find it beating a path to the door of *Modesto* (5 Calle Cano y Queto, next to the Murillo Gardens), where the *acedías* (deep-fried baby sole) and *pimientos aliñados* (red and green peppers in a spicy marinade) are the talk of the town. Upstairs, there's a moderately priced restaurant. At *Sanlúcar-Mar* (in a tower at the far end of the Triana Bridge), a cozy basement restaurant and small upper dining terraces are among the choices, but the selection of *tapas* at the inviting U-shaped glass-and-brass bar on the main floor is so spectacular that you'll want to make a meal right there — or take *tapas* on a terrace that looks straight down the river with the city gleaming on both sides. (Dining is expensive to moderate here, but for the *tapas,* as elsewhere, figure about $1 for each little dish.) Also at the end of the bridge, just down the steps from *Sanlúcar-Mar,* is a little sailors' bar, *Kiosko de las Flores,* where the young crowd chugs beer along with plates of big green olives into the night. Not far away are *El Puerto* (on Calle Betis, next door to the *Río Grande* restaurant), with a multilevel terrace right on the river — you serve yourself from a cafeteria bar — and a sit-down restaurant indoors; and *La Albariza Bodega* (6 Calle Betis), where upended black wine barrels serve as tables. Order plates of dry *serrano* ham, aged *manchego* cheese, olives, and sausages from the counter in back and stand around a barrel with a *copa* (glass of wine). Back across the river, in the Barrio de Santa Cruz (next to the *Hostéria del Laurel* restaurant in Plaza de los Venerables), is the venerable *Casa Roman,* a *tasca* that looks like a shabby country store (there's a deli counter up front). It serves the finest Jabugo ham in town — at around $11.50 per 100-gram portion (just short of a quarter pound). People who can — and can't — afford it meet here for a *fino* and *jamón* — it's the great leveler.

TOLEDO

The very first glimpse of Toledo, whether its spires are piercing a winter mist or pointing heavenward toward a vibrant blue sky, confirms that it was not some newfangled city in Ohio that gave rise to the hackneyed exclamation "Holy Toledo!" This *is* the place — the original.

Even today, the Catholic Primate of Spain is based here, and within the old Arab ramparts that El Cid reclaimed, dozens of churches and convents stand atop older places of worship, holy archaeological heaps hidden beneath their foundations. History and legend glower from their very stones. The local Carpetani tribe of the Celt-Iberians lived here before the Romans founded the city of Toletum in 193 BC. Imperial coins were minted here, and a since-vanished aqueduct tapped the Tagus River. There are still traces of the Roman Circus on the north side of town, and the looming Alcázar, riddled by Civil War machine-gun fire, is built over the site of a 3rd-century Roman encampment. Later, Toledo became the seat of power for the Visigothic kingdom, which ultimately stretched into France during the 6th and 7th centuries. Leovigild, the Visigothic king, held council with his advisers near where the Cristo de la Luz hermitage now stands. The few relics from this era are displayed in the *Visigothic Museum* in the Church of San Román.

Known to the Moors as Tulaytulah, Toledo was required to pay tribute to the caliphs in Córdoba, but considerable autonomy was granted because it had put up so little resistance against the initial Arab invaders in 712. Toledo flourished, far removed from the intrigues and infighting of Al-Andalus to the south, and over the next 3 centuries grew into a city of silk and steel where clergy, merchants, and the military peacefully coexisted. Toledo's intimate courtyards, its characteristic covered passages bridging upper stories across alleyways, and its crooked streets, like narrow streams cutting through a mountain ravine, are all of obvious Moorish legacy. Its population of 200,000 was almost four times what it is today, and a prominent Jewish community — which was well established back in Visigothic times — throve alongside the Moors and Mozarabic Christians.

Even when King Alfonso VI and El Cid recaptured the city for Christendom in 1085, a cosmopolitan tolerance endured. During its first century as Spain's Christian capital, Toledo constantly fortified its walls and towers in readiness for war, but workaday life within the ramparts went largely uninterrupted. Before the full weight of the Catholic church pressed down to obliterate or banish the competition during the Spanish Inquisition, three religions enriched the lives of Toledo's citizenry. Christians, Muslims, and Jews cooperated in intellectual exchange and trade, and for nearly 5 centuries, Toledo enjoyed a reputation throughout the Mediterranean as a center of learning. Alfonso the Wise, King of Castile, grew up in this heady cultural mix and founded the influential School of Translators here during the 13th century.

Under his rule, Castilian Spanish became the official language, replacing Latin. His court of Jewish scholars made esoteric Greek and Arabic science (as well as the Islamic and Jewish religions) accessible to the people of northern Europe. Alchemists studied and worked alongside mathematicians and philosophers. Prosperity brought commissions for exquisite Mudéjar buildings; plaster ceilings as intricately carved as filigree complement sumptuously patterned tile and brick walls. Much of this craftsmanship still can be seen in Toledo's chapels, synagogues, hospitals, and palaces. High taxes, especially aimed at the wealthy Jewish merchants who worshiped at 12 different temples in the city, helped fund civic projects in the kingdom's capital. However, an abrupt pogrom in 1355 and the 1391 massacre at the Santa María la Blanca Synagogue were early warnings that Toledo's tolerance would not last, regardless of local traditions.

While the clergy in Toledo grew extremely potent, they were not always too pious to be expedient. Despite the persecutory efforts of Torquemada, the grand inquisitor, it was clear that Arab craftsmen were a mainstay of the city's livelihood. So on December 18, 1499, 4,000 Moors were baptized in Toledo by Cardinal Jiménez de Cisneros. Any Jew who refused the rite had already been killed or banished from Spain. The new Moorish converts kept up their swordsmithery and tile work, but concentrated on embellishing the interiors of the churches and monasteries. The convent Church of San Juan de los Reyes received special attention, intended as the eventual mausoleum for the Catholic Monarchs, King Ferdinand and Queen Isabella. Later events overtook this advance planning, and lavish tombs at Granada's cathedral now hold the pair. Isabella, who died in 1504, ultimately chose Granada as her burial site in order to commemorate the proudest moment of her reign: not the discovery of the New World, but the transformation of her present one, by the final act of the Reconquest — ousting the Moors from their last stronghold on the Iberian Peninsula, the Alhambra in Granada.

After Isabella's death, aging King Ferdinand ruled from Toledo; well-married daughter Juana was branded La Loca (the mad), unfit to reign. Cardinal Cisneros, the undisputed power behind the throne, took over the kingdom openly for a brief period after Ferdinand died in 1516, but the arrival of Juana's son, the Hapsburg heir to the throne, greatly diminished the cardinal's personal authority. Toledo became an imperial city when the new king, Carlos I of Spain, inherited the mantle of Holy Roman Emperor in 1519 and became Charles V. His double-headed eagle was unfurled, and from Toledo he also commanded Naples, Sicily, Sardinia, Germany, Franche-Comté, and the Low Countries, as well as the American lands newly plundered by the conquistadores. Great resentment quickly grew against the king and his court of foreigners. What rankled was his insistence on absolute rule, thwarting aspiring local nobles and church officials who were politically sophisticated. Tax hikes, which now would finance the European empire rather than go through the accustomed channels, were the final straw. Toledo's Juan de Padilla joined with Juan Bravo of Segovia in a local citizens' revolt, known as the Comuneros uprising. Both leaders were executed in 1521 when their rebellion was crushed, but they set the tone for Charles V's reign. Far-flung wars and revolts would continually strain his patience and his treasury, even with its unprecedented influx of Aztec gold and Inca silver.

Cervantes hailed Toledo as that "rocky gravity, glory of Spain and light of her cities," and it became the focus of Spain's golden age of literature. But that didn't stop Philip II, son of Charles V, from snubbing the arrogant clergy and moving the capital up the road to Madrid just 5 years after he assumed the throne in 1556, as his father prepared to retire to a monastery. Nevertheless, with the political distractions removed, Toledo remained the spiritual center of Spain, perched on a granite spire in the midst of the country. Traditionally, retiring Spanish cardinals can choose wherever they wish to hang up their official hats for the last time, and the number of odd tasseled scraps that are even now suspended like red velvet bats from unlikely spots in the vaulting of Toledo's cathedral attest that the city is still the cardinals' prize pick.

Distancing himself from the established church, King Philip II aimed to build from scratch a somber state retreat that might override the centuries of pious greed in Toledo. His palace-cum-mausoleum north of Madrid was meant to be a grand statement, a counter-reformation in stone. Eager artists from all over Europe competed for commissions at El Escorial, but one Cretan painter, Doménikos Theotokópoulos, soon fell from Philip's favor and was dismissed. He set up his studio in Toledo, where he became known simply as El Greco.

It is El Greco's skewed vision of Toledo, with its roiling clouds over elongated figures and startling clashes of color in almost geometric composition, that most visitors come to see. Indeed, the skyline has not changed measurably since he completed his *View over Toledo*. There are paintings galore: the *Burial of the Count of Orgaz* in the Church of San Tomé is held as a masterpiece, as is *El Expolio*. The artist's adopted hometown has no shortage of his work. In fact, El Greco has become such a significant local money-maker that the relentless promotion is off-putting. One might be tempted to take Philip's side and dismiss El Greco as a minor talent whose draftsmanship cannot compare with such masters as Titian or Rubens. For those inclined to adopt this line of thought, canvases are there for side-by-side comparison. Certainly, though, El Greco shattered the painterly conventions of his time, and the best of his work is breathtaking. Some art historians claim his use of color influenced a much later genius, Paul Cézanne.

Toledo's new status as a mere provincial capital and the fact that far more politically significant prizes were within striking distance spared this city from the worst of the battles that ravaged Spain in succeeding generations. But the Spanish Civil War was fought here with full fury. The huge restored Alcázar, which dominates the highest ground in Toledo and was once rebuilt by Charles V as a royal residence, was besieged for a grim 2 months in the summer of 1936. Franco's Nationalist forces held out against the Republicans despite blasts of dynamite that collapsed much of the fortress, formerly the most prestigious military academy in the nation.

The residents of contemporary Toledo are as long-suffering as any earlier forces inside the Alcázar. Hordes of visitors come daily to gawk at the city's treasures, inevitably getting lost in the tangle of narrow alleyways. The citizens resolutely provide directions, in response to queries in countless languages, and rarely lose their courtesy. When the last tour bus pulls away at dusk and the onslaught subsides, Toledo comes into its own. This is the best time to explore, finding the way back by remembering the coats of arms carved in stone on the buildings. The tackiest souvenir windows appear almost as comic relief, a balance to the weight of history.

TOLEDO AT-A-GLANCE

 SEEING THE CITY: For an overall perspective, drive along Carretera de Circunvalación, which follows the banks of the Tagus River which surrounds Toledo like a moat. As the road climbs the hillsides, it passes close to a little hermitage called Virgen del Valle, and provides a sweeping view of the city. Close by is an outcropping called Cabeza del Moro (Moor's Head). Anywhere on the hillside offers a good view. Just to the left is the *Parador Conde de Orgaz* (see *Checking In*), the best place to watch the sunset, a drink in hand on the patio, with all of Toledo stretched out below. Just above the Alcántara Bridge is the Castillo de San Servando, a monastery revamped as a school, which offers a panorama from a different angle. For a more intimate view over Toledo's tiled rooftops and spires, climb the cathedral's belfry. A door on Calle Hombre de Palo (Straw Man Street) opens onto stairs in the cloisters that ascend the tower. *Miradero* literally means "lookout," and from this area, not far above the Puerta del Sol on the Cuesta de las Armas, informal cafés offer a fine vantage point out over the river and beyond. From nearly any strategic spot along the old walls, there is a sentry's view of the surrounding countryside.

 SPECIAL PLACES: Toledo has so many points of interest that tourists would be hard-pressed to view even the exteriors of all historically important monuments on a single visit. If time is especially limited, pick up the free brochure from the tourist office at the Puerto de la Bisagra and follow its "essential itinerary," which is arranged in a very convenient sequence. Even though Toledo is quite small, its steep streets and dead ends can make monuments seem very far indeed. Be aware that Spanish visiting hours are erratic. To make the most of a visit, try to take the time to experience each place fully, rather than rush around checking off sites on a list and remembering nothing more than a blur.

Alcázar – Reconstruction atop reconstruction, this foursquare fortress has always been one of Toledo's key landmarks. Despite numerous sackings, torchings, and even bombings, this strategic building has been regirded, patched up, and continually put back into service. The Moors refashioned the Visigothic citadel built over an old Roman fort on the site, and El Cid reputedly served as the city's first governor here. The present structure dates from the time of Charles V, who converted it into a palace, though most of it is now a product of reconstruction. The north façade, with its Plateresque portal, was designed by Alonso de Covarrubias, as was the east façade, which is by far the oldest. Since the Imperial Court left the building almost 500 years ago, it has been wracked by misfortune. The palace became a state prison in 1643, and German, British, and Portuguese troops burned it in 1710, during the War of the Spanish Succession. After restoration by Cardinal Lorenzana, it stood only 35 years before French troops gutted it during the Peninsular War. It later reemerged as the national military academy, though it suffered another blaze at the hands of careless cadets and again had to be overhauled. Its worst days were during a Civil War siege in 1936, when a band of Nationalists, together with over 600 women and children, holed up inside for 2 months.

Republican bombs again reduced it to ruins. The dungeons are worth a visit, to see items like the motorcycle rigged to grind meal for the besieged. The emphasis on the ultimate Falangist victory brings out raw emotion in visiting Spaniards, and most who come to the *Museo de Asedio* (Siege Museum) are uncompromisingly rightist. There also is a reconstruction of Queen Blanca's medieval prison cell (Peter I locked her up here while he consorted with his mistress; no wonder he was nicknamed "the Cruel"). Open from 9:30 AM to 1:30 PM and from 4 to 6:30 PM; closed Mondays. Admission charge. Calle Capuchinos (phone: 223038).

Cathedral – For such an enormous building, the cathedral can be surprisingly difficult to locate. On approach, it seems to disappear. The site, like so many in Spain, was formerly occupied by a mosque, but it is not elevated, and in the time elapsed since construction began in the early 13th century, other buildings have boxed it in. In the main (or west) façade, between the tower and the dome, are three lovely Gothic portals: Most of the parish would choose the middle Puerta del Perdón (Gate of Pardon) over the Puerta del Juicio (Gate of Justice) to the right and the Puerta del Infierno (Gate of Hell) to the left. The Puerta del Perdón has a tympanum showing one of Toledo's favorite miracles, said to have occurred on the very spot. The Virgin Mary descends to San Ildefonso, who wrote in ardent defense of her virginity, and presents him with the robes for his next mass. The 14th-century Puerta de Reloj (also called de la Chapinería, or Clock Gate), in the north wall, is the cathedral's oldest, and is lavishly adorned with Gothic pointed arches and ornaments. The Puerta de los Leones (Lions' Gate), on the south, is the most flamboyant, with its great bronze doors. The modern entrance is a plain doorway to the left of the Puerta de Mollete, just off Calle Hombre de Palo.

Inside, the architectural styles run the gamut from Gothic to Mudéjar to flagrant rococo. The wrought-iron screens are magnificent, and 800 stained glass windows from the 15th and 16th centuries help light the vast space. Yet even the glorious rose window looks ordinary next to a bizarre skylight that directs a single celestial beam onto the altar. Known as the Transparente, the altar was created in 1732 by hacking through the ambulatory's vaulting and the wall of the Capilla Mayor (Main Chapel). Narciso Tomé then embellished it all and created a bit of baroque heaven by confecting a swirl of saints and chubby angels that peer from the cathedral stones. Some are paintings with three-dimensional appendages, innovations that have remained controversial throughout the centuries. The polychrome retable is exquisitely carved, and the walnut choir stalls are also exceptional. Panels above them show deep relief carvings of the battles fought in 1492 at Granada, made just 3 years after the event. In contrast to this fervent depiction of the infidels' defeat, one Muslim has a place of honor on the right pier of the main altar. This pacifist Moorish leader, Abu Walid, dissuaded the enraged King Alfonso X from taking retribution against an upstart bishop who, against the king's wishes, had desecrated the mosque that used to stand here. The sacristy contains a wealth of paintings, including 27 by El Greco, as well as works by Velázquez, Titian, Van Dyck, and Goya. The Capilla Mozárabe, beneath a dome designed by El Greco's son, is the only place on earth that still follows the ancient rituals of the Visigoths; it is kept locked between masses. The treasury (*tesoro*) displays the gold and silver Arfe monstrance, which is always hefted through the streets during *Corpus Christi.* Standing 10 feet high and weighing 450 pounds, this elaborate reliquary incorporates gold from Columbus's first shipload back from the New World. The cathedral is still very much an active church, and visitors often encounter a mass or a lavish wedding party in progress. Open daily, from 10:30 AM to 1 PM and from 3:30 to 6 PM (7 PM in summer). Admission charge to the sacristy, treasury, choir, chapterhouse, and King's Chapel. Plaza Mayor (phone: 222241).

Iglesia de Santo Tomé – This unremarkable 14th-century Mudéjar church is crowded with visitors because of one painting, El Greco's *El Entierro del Conde de*

Orgaz (Burial of the Count of Orgaz). The famous canvas was painted some 250 years after the funeral of the count, who had funded the church's first major reconstruction. The scene is split into heaven and earth, with a row of mourners marking the divide. Their faces are portraits of prominent citizens, all in 16th-century dress. El Greco's own face is supposedly just above that of the young St. Stephen, and the boy in the foreground is the painter's son, Jorge. The monogram on his pocket handkerchief is El Greco's signature. The count's ascent to heaven is conveyed by the strong use of color, but any sense of joy or release in death is oddly absent. Each brushstroke is laden with the austere yet fervent faith of 16th-century Castile. Open Tuesdays through Saturdays, from 10 AM to 1:45 PM and from 3:30 to 6 PM; Sundays, from 10 AM to 1:45 PM. Admission charge. 1 Plaza Conde (phone: 210209).

Taller del Moro (Moor's Workshop) – This almost palatial 14th-century building was once used as a workshop by Moorish masons completing cathedral commissions. Displays are mostly of carpentry and tiles, and the Mudéjar style of the building is exemplary in itself with its *artesonado* ceilings and plasterwork. Open Tuesdays through Saturdays, from 10 AM to 2 PM and from 4 to 7 PM; Sundays, from 10 AM to 2 PM. Admission charge. Calle Taller del Moro (phone: 227115).

Casa y Museo del Greco (El Greco House and Museum) – The name is a misnomer, for El Greco never lived precisely here, but this was certainly his old neighborhood and this house indeed belonged to his landlord. Admirably restored to its 16th-century state, the house is charming due to the small scale of the furnishings, especially the tiny kitchen. The courtyard and garden are very pleasant, and a fine collection of the painter's later works, particularly bold portraits of the apostles, is worth a look. An early version of *St. Peter Repentant* is considered of the highest artistic merit, and *St. John,* with a dragon inside his cup, looks peculiarly sinister. Two works by Zurbarán are also noteworthy. Open Tuesdays through Saturdays, from 10 AM to 2 PM and from 4 to 6 PM (7 PM in summer); Sundays, from 10 AM to 2 PM. Admission charge. 3 Calle Samuel Ha-Levi (phone: 224046).

Sinagoga del Tránsito (El Tránsito Synagogue) – This major synagogue was founded in 1366 by Samuel Ha-Levi, Peter the Cruel's Jewish treasurer. Rich cedar carvings on the 12-foot-high *artesonado* ceiling and lacy Mudéjar plasterwork incised with Hebrew inscriptions and stars of David show that he spared no expense. Long after he was put to death, the warrior Knights of Calatrava revamped part of the synagogue as a monastery, but preserved many of the original trappings. The *Sephardic Museum* installed here opened in 1971; its exhibits include a marble pillar from the 1st or 2nd century, with carved Hebrew inscriptions, alongside silver manuscript cases, robes and wedding costumes, amulets, and elaborate objects used in Jewish festivals. Detailed explanations are included for Spaniards understandably ignorant of Jewish customs after a 500-year absence. Open Tuesdays through Saturdays, from 10 AM to 2 PM and from 4 to 6 PM (7 PM in summer); Sundays, from 10 AM to 2 PM. Admission charge. Calle Samuel Ha-Levi (phone: 223655).

Sinagoga de Santa María la Blanca – This architectural gem, built in 1180, was the primary Jewish synagogue in Toledo, and was later converted into a church by the Knights of Calatrava. The façade is rather drab, but inside, horseshoe arches and delicately carved columns shimmer with diaphanous whiteness. The polychrome altarpiece was added in the 16th century. Demoted to a mere barracks until 1791 until a general commanded its make-over into a quartermaster's store and saved it from further abuse, the synagogue has been remarkably restored to its original Almohad-period splendor. Open daily, from 10 AM to 2 PM and from 3:30 to 6 PM (7 PM in summer). Admission charge. Cuesta de los Reyes Católicos (phone: 228429).

Monasterio de San Juan de los Reyes – The outside walls of this grandiose monastery are hung with chains once worn by Christian slaves in Moorish Granada and brought here, after they gained their freedom, in testament to a faith that fueled the final Christian victory of the Reconquest. Inside, the great church is done in soaring Isabeline style, and incorporates Mudéjar and Gothic touches with Renaissance art. Construction, undertaken in 1476, continued through the 16th century, when Covarrubias designed the northern portal, and was not completed until the early 17th century. Although originally planned as the mausoleum of King Ferdinand and Queen Isabella, the monastery became an important center for the Franciscan order. Heraldry is heavy-handed, even on the stained glass windows. The initials F&Y (for Fernando and Ysabel) are repeated constantly between the shields of Castile, León, and Aragon, the pomegranate of Granada, and the royal yoke and arrows motif. The Flemish architect Juan Guas designed most of the interior, with its massive round columns and the great shields supported by haloed eagles, each eyeing the altar. The cloister has graceful arches and decorated tracery on the gallery, under a Mudéjar ceiling celebrating the Catholic Monarchs. A pine and an orange tree are the focal points for the simple courtyard. On the second floor, beneath the arches, 18th-century restorers added whimsically irreverent gargoyles and waterspouts. Open daily, from 10 AM to 1:45 PM and from 3:30 to 6 PM (7 PM in summer); closed *Christmas* and *New Year's Day.* Admission charge. Cuesta de los Reyes Católicos (phone: 223802).

Hospital de Santa Cruz – Cardinal Pedro González de Mendoza initiated plans for this elaborate orphanage and hospital just off Plaza de Zocodover in the early 16th century, and the project was completed by Queen Isabel after this death. Designed by Enrique Egas, with a façade and patio by Covarrubias, the building now houses the *Museum of Fine Arts,* the *Museum of Applied Arts,* and the *Provincial Museum of Archaeology,* showcasing swords and scimitars, ceramics, vestments, bits of furniture, tapestries, and paintings, including 22 by El Greco. Off the lovely Plateresque patio is an archaeology exhibit of mostly Roman finds. A display of prehistoric items is in the basement. The intricate ceiling, lavish stairways, and spacious rooms are typical of 16th-century hospitals where pleasant surroundings were vital to the cure. Open Tuesdays through Saturdays, from 10 AM to 6 PM; Sundays from 10 AM to 2 PM. Admission charge includes entrance to the San Román Visigothic museum (see below). 3 Calle Cervantes (phone: 221402).

Museo de los Concilios y de la Cultura Visigótica (Museum of the Councils and Visigothic Art) – It was here in the heights of the city that the Visigothic kings held several councils of the Western church. A 13th-century Mudéjar church, the Iglesia de San Román, now occupies the site, and it has been turned into a museum — the sole museum of Visigothic art and artifacts in Spain. The collection of votive crowns, bronze brooches, Maltese crosses, and funerary inscriptions from the period seems rather paltry, however, but the church merits a close look for its architecture alone. Mudéjar horseshoe arches are balanced on Arabic columns, with carved capitals from Visigothic, Byzantine, and Mozarabic artisans. Late Romanesque frescoes, preserved on the walls, show strong Moorish influence. Open Tuesdays through Saturdays, from 10 AM to 2 PM and from 4 to 7 PM; Sundays, from 10 AM to 2 PM. Admission charge includes entrance to the Santa Cruz Hospital. Calle San Clemente.

Posada de la Hermandad (Inn of the Brotherhood) – The entrance of this former prison is marked by two archers with crossbows, supporting a wooden coat of arms. The Holy Brotherhood based here was a paramilitary order founded during the Reconquest to police lines of access between Andalusia and central Spain. It was an early precursor to today's Civil Guard — with its odd black patent leather hats — which was formed in 1844. After the brotherhood was disbanded in the 19th century for abuse of its privileges, the building became an inn. Despite an intricate ceiling in the immense Sala de Juntas, the overriding atmosphere is unsettling. The dank basement resembles a quintessential medieval torture chamber. Temporary exhibits are held here frequently. Open Mondays through Fridays, from 10 AM to 2 PM and from 4 to 8 PM (9

PM in summer); Saturdays and Sundays, from 10 AM to 8 PM (9 PM in summer). Admission charge. 6 Calle de la Hermandad (phone: 214150).

Cristo de la Luz (Christ of the Light) – Also known as the Mezquita, this minuscule "mosque," perhaps intended originally as a sepulchral chamber, is one of the most venerable Moorish buildings on the Iberian Peninsula. Near the Puerta del Sol, it was erected on top of Visigothic ruins and later became a Mudéjar church. Kufic characters in the brickwork spell out the name of Muza Ibn Ali, the architect, and give the dedication date as 980. Nine domes rise from the bays, each different, as though the designer were flaunting his versatility. Delicate horseshoe arches inside are supported by more ancient Visigothic capitals, and paintings in the Mudéjar annex, though worn, are rare surviving examples of Toledan Romanesque art. (The few others are displayed in the San Román Visigothic museum.) Cristo de la Luz is shrouded in legend; according to one, El Cid's charger fell to its knees here during a post-Reconquest victory parade and refused to rise until a Visigothic crucifix, with a votive candle still flickering, was miraculously uncovered in a bricked-up niche. Opening hours are erratic, depending on the doorkeeper's whim. No admission charge. Calle Cristo de la Luz.

Hospital de Tavera – This large 16th-century hospital located outside the city gates contains Cardinal Juan Pardo de Tavera's extensive collection of paintings and also features apartments furnished by the Duchess of Lerma in a lavish 17th-century style. The cardinal's magnificent tomb and the family crypt for the Dukes of Medinaceli are in the chapel off the double patio. Impressive portraits by Titian, including the huge *Portrait of Charles V,* hang in the vast dining hall, but Ribera's odd *Bearded Woman* is stashed in a side room, camouflaged by bland cityscapes on either side. Upstairs are works by Tintoretto, Zurbarán, and, of course, El Greco. His last canvas, the *Baptism of Christ by St. John,* is enormous and serves as a sampler of all his trademarks: Vivid clothing stakes out geometric zones on the picture, but the lines of the angel hailing a dove pull the composition together. Drapery on another angel is lighted like a thunderbolt, which points down to a most omnipotent-looking God robed in bright white. Open daily, from 10:30 AM to 1:30 PM and from 3:30 to 6 PM. Admission charge. Calle Baja (phone: 220529).

Circo Romano (Roman Circus) – Not much remains of the Roman arena, only a few mosaics and a reconstructed building outside the gates north of town. Still, this is a pleasant place to stroll after the cramped and twisting streets of the city, and it size (original capacity 20,000) hints at the strength of the Roman settlement, Toletum. Off Avenida de la Reconquista.

ENVIRONS

Montes de Toledo – South and west of Toledo, along either the C401 road or the N401 highway and the local routes branching off of them, rise the harsh uplands that were long celebrated in troubadors' couplets. These were trysting spots for Moorish princesses and caballeros locked in doomed romances, and later they became the haunts of bandits. There are villages and dusty hamlets here, but they are unobtrusive. Streams interlace the scrubby bush cover of rock roses, heather, and cork oaks. The area is best explored by car. Picnickers should be aware of the wild variety of game, mostly in the heights: deer, wild boar, lynx, foxes, and even wolves. Much of the land is private hunting ground, particularly in the southern stretches near Los Yébenes, but there are prehistoric sites scattered throughout the area. Calancho, Los Navalucillos, and Hontanar all boast curious megalithic relics. Ciudad de Vascos, near Navalmoralejo, is an ancient Hispano-Moorish ghost town protected by a fortress. Odd stone boars or bulls — *verracos* — that have grazed in the rubble of forgotten fields since early Celtic tribes lived in Castile can be seen at the Castillo de Bayuela and Torecilla de la Jara. Driving over these rough roads past crumbling castles feels like time travel. Guadalerzas is spanned by an impressive late Roman aqueduct with 24 arches. One of the prettiest valleys, heading west toward the higher sierra behind Guadalupe, is Robledo del Mazo, where the locals still wear traditional straw hats decorated with baubles and tiny mirrors.

Illescas – Though this town looks forgotten in the highway dust, with only a slender Mudéjar tower lifting it off the flats, it was an influential midway point in the 16th century between the old court in Toledo and the new one in Madrid. As the chief town of the region of La Sagra, located 21 miles (34 km) north of Toledo, Illescas figures in the golden age of Spanish literature, but its main claim to fame is five splendid El Greco canvases displayed in the Hospital de la Caridad, which was built by Cardinal Cisneros. Open Mondays through Saturdays, from 9 AM to 2 PM and from 4 to 7 PM. Admission charge.

■**EXTRA SPECIAL:** Talavera de la Reina and Puente de Arzobispo are traditional ceramic centers for the whole of Spain and are an easy day's excursion from Toledo via C502. Talavera is the largest city in the province, so don't expect a quaint potter's village. This is not a heritage city like Toledo, for modern industries have penetrated the thick ramparts, and biweekly livestock fairs are the major social events. On the fringes of the city, just past the main park, is the Hermitage de la Virgen del Prado. This is a showcase for the famous *azulejos,* distinctive blue and yellow glazed picture tiles, which date back to the 14th century and were the preferred decor for the finest palaces and monasteries. Browse along the main street, where vendors sell shelf after shelf of platters, vases, and bowls inspired by these classic designs.

Continuing west on the N-V highway, just past Oropesa, is a turnoff to Lagartera, the village where the best La Mancha embroidery originates. Every cottage has its own display of the free-form floral stitching, which decorates silk hangings, tablecloths, peasant bonnets, and full skirts. Advertising is understated, inscribed on shiny tile plaques. In summer, the women working outdoors in the clear light provide an excellent photo opportunity. With luck, a wedding party may be in progress, allowing a glimpse of heirloom finery in full flower.

To reach Puente de Arzobispo, popular for its green-toned pottery, double back through Oropresa and drive south for 9 miles (14 km) to a fortified bridge across the Tagus River. A 14th-century archbishop had the bridge built to protect pilgrims trekking to the shrine at Guadalupe, hence the name: Puente de Arzobispo. Shops and vendors in the village sell ceramics for less than the equivalent items would cost in Toledo, but since quality here is consistently high, there are no astonishingly inexpensive wares. Valdeverdeja, a smaller and prettier village, lies just 4½ miles (7 km) to the west and sells distinctive unglazed red earthenware. Return to Toledo through Talavera (the quickest route), or loop down on local roads through the Montes de Toledo for a leisurely drive back.

SOURCES AND RESOURCES

TOURIST INFORMATION: The Oficina de Turismo (just outside the Puerta de la Bisagra; phone: 220843) provides brochures and an excellent foldout map — indispensable for negotiating the winding streets. The Provincial Tourist Office (11 Plaza de Zocodover; phone: 221400) has detailed information about touring the surrounding villages. Both are open Mondays through Fridays, from 9 AM to 2 PM and from 4 to 6 PM; Saturdays, from 9 AM to 1:30 PM.

Local Coverage – Understanding Spanish is a must for gleaning information from the local press. The local daily newspaper, *La Voz del Tajo,* has good entertainment and dining listings. Regional editions of the formidably right-wing *El Alcázar* and the Catholic national daily, *Ya,* also cover local events. More esoteric topics are explored in *Toletum,* published sporadically by Toledo's Academy of Fine Arts and Historical Sciences. *Castilla–La Mancha* is the provincial monthly magazine.

 TELEPHONE: The city code for Toledo is 25. If calling from within Spain, dial 925 before the local number.

 GETTING AROUND: The visitor's own two feet are the best bet in a town full of dead ends, blind corners, twisting cobbled alleys, and very steep hills. If a car is available, it's a good idea to park in one of the eight covered garages within the walled precinct, as far uphill as possible, and then wander.

Bus – There is a bus station, Nueva Estación de Autobuses, on the ring road around Toledo (Carretera de Circunvalación; phone: 226307). Two companies — *Continental* (4 Calle Geraldo Lobo; phone: 227360) and *Galiano* (Paseo de Miradero; phone: 223641) — offer frequent daily service to Madrid and other towns in La Mancha.

Car Rental – Like most medieval towns, Toledo is meant for pedestrians; car rental is not advisable. With the exception of *Avis* (Paseo de Miradero; phone: 214535), the international firms do not have offices in Toledo, but operate out of Madrid, an hour's drive away. Local agencies include *López Salazar* (Avenida Plaza de Toros; phone: 220615) and *Maroto Iglesia* (4 Calle Don Diego; phone: 224347).

Taxi – Toledo's two taxi stands are located on Cuesta de Alcázar and Cuesta de la Vega. Roving taxis with an illuminated green light can be hailed as they pass or called (phone: 221968).

Train – Frequent train service to Madrid takes slightly longer than the bus journey. The train station is located across the Puente de Safont (on Paseo de la Rosa; phone: 223099). There is a *RENFE* office (7 Calle Sillería; phone: 221272).

 SPECIAL EVENTS: *Semana Santa,* or *Holy Week,* has subdued beauty in Toledo when the Procession of Silence winds through the streets on *Good Friday.* A more boisterous procession, the carrying of the Virgen del Valle around the hillsides near her hermitage on the far side of the river, occurs during the local *Romería,* on *May Day* afternoon. Enormous excitement is unleashed each May or June when the town dresses up in folk costume for *Corpus Christi* and the precious gold Arfe monstrance from the cathedral treasury is unlocked and carried through the city streets. Wild thyme and rosemary underfoot scent the parade. For 8 centuries, this has been Toledo's ultimate celebration (and one of the most important in Spain), always scheduled for the Thursday of the 9th week after *Holy Week.* Check with the tourist office for full details and the traditional parade route. Fireworks light the August skies during the *Fiesta de la Virgen del Sagrario,* held annually from August 14 through 20. This fiesta solicits the Virgin's protection for the coming year, and part of the festivities are set inside the cathedral cloisters.

 MUSEUMS: Besides those mentioned in *Special Places,* Toledo has other museums, listed below. In addition, there are over 40 churches and convents in the city, along with seven palaces, containing collections of sculpture and precious paintings that would demand special mention anywhere else. Amid such a surfeit of art and historic relics, a visitor often can stumble onto treasures merely by investigating what is behind a promising-looking doorway.

Museo de Armas Blancas de la Real Fábrica de Armas (Royal Arms Factory Museum of Hand Weaponry) – The Royal Arms Factory itself, dating from 1783, is on the outskirts of town. It is now a military installation manufacturing modern weaponry and is closed to the public, but its comprehensive collection of traditional swords, shields, and lances, including the weapons of such personages as El Cid and Boabdil, is on display on the patio of the Alcázar. Open from 9:30 AM to 1:30 PM and from 4 to 6:30 PM; closed Mondays; admission charge to the Alcázar includes entrance to the museum. Calle Capuchinos (phone: 221673).

Museo de Arte Contemporáneo – Installed in the distinguished Casa de las Cadenas, the museum contains works by contemporary Spanish artists, including Alberto Sanchez, who lived and worked in exile in Moscow until his death in 1962. Prohibited throughout Generalísimo Francisco Franco's regime, his paintings now fill two rooms of their own. Open Tuesdays through Saturdays, from 10 AM to 2 PM and from 4:30 to 6:45 PM; Sundays, from 10 AM to 2 PM. Admission charge. Calle de los Bulos (phone: 220615).

SHOPPING: The swordsmiths of Toledo were renowned in more swash-buckling days, and it was no idle fear to dwell on the consequences of being run through with sharp Toledo steel. Knives of all sorts and even suits of armor on sale today continue this tradition. Damascene, the Moorish art of inlaying gold, copper, or silver threads on a matte black steel background, is also a thriving craft. Souvenir shops throughout the city offer an amazing range of items, some quite mysterious in their function, all decorated in the distinctive black-and-yellow inlaid patterns. Most traditional are the small sewing scissors that snap threads in the sharp beak of a gilded stork, but there is a vast choice of earrings, bangles, cuff links, tie tacks, letter openers, picture frames, and decorative platters. Good, handcrafted damascene is expensive; machine-made items cost less than half the handmade price. Also available is pottery, sold in shops and along the roadside, and generally of high quality, although it's not strictly local. Still, unless a specific trip is planned to the neighboring ceramic centers of Puente de Arzobispo or Talavera de la Reina (see *Extra Special*), Toledo's shops offer a wide selection. Highly caloric marzipan, some of it prepared by nuns, is definitely a local specialty, another one celebrated throughout Spain. The small forms of sweet almond paste, a Moorish legacy, are a traditional Christmas treat, though available year-round.

Bargaining is not unheard of in Toledo, but it is best to haggle only if seeking a discount for buying a number of items. If this is the case, be sure to pay in cash. Bargaining ruthlessly and then pulling out a credit card is an invitation to ridicule. With the waves of day-trippers from Madrid, many merchants have little time for dickering over prices, whereas others in quieter shops view it as entertainment. Of the many stores and shops in Toledo, the following are of particular interest:

Casa Bermejo – A source of top-quality Toledo damascene, including that made by Santiago Sanchez Martin (see below). 5 Calle Airosos (phone: 220346).

Casa Telesforo – Some of the best marzipan in town. 17 Plaza de Zocodover (phone: 223379).

Confitería Santo Tomé – More marzipan — marginally less expensive than that of *Casa Telesforo* and a close match for quality. 5 Calle Santo Tomé (phone: 223763), with a branch at 11 Plaza de Zocodover (phone: 221168).

Santiago Sanchez Martín – A damascene artisan who has been inlaying 24-carat gold by hand on the most special pieces for 40-plus years. This is his workshop, featuring 40 different models of mirror frames, jewelry, decorative pitchers, and other items. 18 Calle Río Llano (phone: 227757).

Suárez – A wide range of damascene items; personalized shields with your own family crest can be made up, if you supply the design. 19 Paseo de los Canónigos (phone: 225615).

SPORTS AND FITNESS: Fishing – The best fishing in the Tagus River, which forms a natural moat around Toledo, is in the river basin, far from the city. Near Finisterre Dam, about 28 miles (45 km) southeast of the city, black bass have been introduced. In other reservoirs where fishing is encouraged, carp and large pike abound. Fishing permits are available from the Valencia office of *ICONA* (*Instituto Nacional para la Conservación de la Naturaleza;* 6 Plaza San Vicente; phone: 222158); or call *Caza y Pesca* (phone: 213124). The standard permits are issued for a year, so ask for the special visitor's license, valid for 2 weeks.

Flying – Anything from a hang glider to a propeller plane is a possibility in the skies over Toledo, where unseen assets beckon pleasure pilots from all over Europe. Steady updrafts and less-predictable waves and slopes in the air occur when La Mancha's miles of broad plateau suddenly rear up as a range of mountains, producing almost a washboard effect. The *Royal Aero Club of Toledo* (20 miles/32 km from the city in Mora de Toledo; phone: 300194) specializes in gliding. The *Ocaña/Toledo Aerodrome,* regional headquarters for the Civil Aviation Authority, offers instruction in gliding, ultra-lights, ballooning, skydiving, and powered flight. Some courses include lodging (for more information, call 130700 or 130769). Pilots must have foreign licenses validated before taking off.

Hunting – The season for small game (partridge, rabbit, hare, quail, dove, and so on) runs from the third Sunday in October through the first Sunday in February. Stalking of larger game starts in September, and the waterfowl season continues through March. The most plentiful hunting grounds are on the highest slopes of the Montes de Toledo. Any area signposted *coto* is a hunting reserve in one of four categories: common use, local, private, or national. Hunters must have a license from their own country, as well as a seasonal permit and insurance. Obtain a customs permit for shotguns and rifles before entering Spain. A separate permit is also required for leaving the country. For more information, contact *Caza y Pesca* (phone: 213124) or visit *ICONA*'s office (6 Plaza San Vicente; phone: 222158).

Swimming – Swimmers can use several public pools in town, but the biggest and cleanest (aside from the guests-only facility at the *Parador Conde de Orgaz*) is at the Circo Romano campground (21 Calle Circo Romano; phone: 220442), just north of the old walls. There is an admission charge, plus a weekend surcharge.

Tennis – Arrangements can be made to use courts at the private *Club de Tenis de Toledo* (Calle Navalpino, Km 49; phone: 224278). Admission charge.

Windsurfing – The sport is forbidden in many of the manmade lakes, but when the Cazalegas Reservoir is full, sailing and windsurfing are popular. Contact the tourist office for further details.

THEATER: The *Teatro de Rojas* (4 Plaza Mayor; phone: 223970) has been carefully restored to its 19th-century grandeur. Details regarding any classical Spanish production to be staged here are available from the box office or through the tourist office. Usually, however, this lovely venue is used as a cinema for dubbed foreign movies.

MUSIC: Sacred music is the norm in Holy Toledo, and can be heard at vespers services at most of the 40-odd churches throughout the city.

NIGHTCLUBS AND NIGHTLIFE: The clue to nightlife in Toledo is to be part of *la movida,* the movement, or the action, and not to stay in any one place too long. Most people stop for a drink or two, then move on to another café or pub. In summer, the open-air terraces near the ramparts come alive. The youngest crowd gravitates to the sundry establishments along Calle Chapinería, Calle Sillería, and Callejón Barrio Rey, while a more sophisticated scene takes place beneath the arcades of the Plaza de Zocodover and the adjoining streets. *La Sal que Esta* (Calle de la Sal) attracts young professionals who scrutinize each other without mercy. Discos tend to be quite provincial and young. The brashest one in town is *Sithon's* (4 Calle Lucio). *Mascara* (in the *Galería del Miradero*) is the trendiest, while *Gris Disco* (Carretera Toledo–Avila, Km 2.5) is the most self-conscious.

BEST IN TOWN

CHECKING IN: Considering the number of tourists who traipse through town, Toledo seems a bit short on lodgings. This is because the vast majority of visitors are here just for the day. But quite a few are enticed to stay the night, so good hotel rooms can be at a premium. Expect to pay $80 and up for a double room in a hotel listed as expensive and $40 to $75 at a moderate one. All telephone numbers are in the 25 city code unless otherwise indicated.

Parador Conde de Orgaz – The stunning view of Toledo is the focal point here, and though inconveniently distant from the center of town, the 77 well-equipped, air conditioned rooms feature color television sets and private baths, and provide guests with their own skyscapes just outside the picture window. Modern design incorporates traditional architectural styles of the region, and decorations include lovely provincial ceramics. The restaurant serves regional specialties, at a price, and there is an outdoor swimming pool. Advance reservations are recommended. Paseo de los Cigarrales (phone: 221850). Expensive.

María Cristina – Situated within the walls of the former Hospital de San Lázaro near the bullring, it offers 65 air conditioned rooms with private baths and all modern conveniences. A popular spot for business meetings and banquets, the place has a lively Spanish atmosphere, yet remains comfortable and peaceful nonetheless. Honeymooners can book a special suite under the dome of the ancient chapel. The vast dining room of the restaurant *El Abside* resembles a Moorish tent (see *Eating Out*). 1 Calle Marqués de Mendigorría (phone: 213202). Expensive to moderate.

Alfonso VI – Comfortable lodgings directly in front of the Alcázar. All 88 air conditioned rooms have color television sets and private baths, and the public areas are done up in austere Castilian style, which contrasts with the bright commercial gallery near the lobby. 2 Calle General Moscardó (phone: 222600). Moderate.

Almazara – A particularly tranquil spot, with splendid views and friendly service. All 21 rooms have color television sets and private baths. Well worth the 2-mile (3-km) detour outside town, though it is only open from mid-March through October. 47 Carretera Piedrabuena (phone: 223866). Moderate.

Cardenal – This 18th-century cardinal's palace in the shade of the city ramparts is now a *hostal,* evocative of a grand age. All 27 rooms are air conditioned, with private baths. The overall atmosphere is elegant and distinguished, but the service can be a bit desultory. The place is best known for the meals served in its 2-tiered garden (see *Eating Out*). 24 Paseo de Recaredo (phone: 224900). Moderate.

Carlos V – A very proper, modern establishment, offering views over the cathedral from many of its 55 rooms. The quiet plaza is deceptive, however, for music often blares from the noisy bar next door. 1 Calle Trastamara (phone: 222100 or 222104). Moderate.

Los Cigarrales – This pleasant 29-room country house on the far side of the Tagus River has excellent views of Toledo. Each room is air conditioned and decorated with wooden beams and glazed tiles. The management is friendly. 12 Carretera de Circunvalación (phone: 220053). Moderate.

Los Guerreros – The 13 clean and comfortable rooms are air conditioned and have private baths, and the extremely friendly management and staff makes this *hostal* a favorite with students. Quite a distance from the city's principal sites. 8 Avenida de la Reconquista (phone: 211807). Moderate.

Imperio – Modern efficiency in the medieval midst of Toledo. Despite the somewhat charmless, simple rooms (21, all with private baths), this place is a good value. 7 Calle Cadenas (phone: 227650). Moderate.

Sol – A central location and pretty terrace distinguish this 14-room hostelry, not to mention its resident hairdresser and doctor. 15 Calle Azacanes (phone: 213650). Moderate.

EATING OUT: La Manchan cuisine is not particularly distinguished, other than the basics: a good sharp cheese and a hearty red wine. It is based on ingredients from a harsh land of shepherds and hunters. Be prepared to eat *perdiz estofada* (marinated partridge) at room temperature; it won't be served piping hot. Toledan-style partridge, stewed in red wine, is less tart. Roast lamb is usually a good bet, and crisp grilled *chuletas* (lamb chops) can be exquisite. In season, venison, hare, and game birds are served with originality and pride. Low-cost meals are scarce in this city, where restaurants raise prices for tourists too tired to look for something else. An à la carte, three-course dinner for two with wine will cost $70 or more in a restaurant listed as expensive, $40 to $65 in a moderate restaurant, and $35 or less in an inexpensive one. The *menú del día*, or daily special, is almost always the most reasonably priced option and usually includes wine and bread along with at least two courses. All telephone numbers are in the 25 city code unless otherwise indicated.

Asador Adolfo – The chef has a light touch with some of the heavy Manchegan classics such as *perdiz en paté*, served with white beans. The seafood and roast meats are also excellent, and the wine made from the brujidero grape, *Priorato de Ucles*, is a very special treat. Closed Sunday evenings. Reservations advised. Situated near the cathedral, this 14th-century building can be hard to find, hidden away on a corner shared by 7 Calle Hombre de Palo and 6 Calle La Granada (phone: 227321). Expensive.

Aurelio – The flagship of Toledo's sole "chain" establishment has traditional ambience with antique pottery on the wall, and presents the most time-honored Castilian recipes. Aurelio Montero is one of Toledo's classic chefs. Like his father, he keeps a watchful eye on the authentic Castilian cuisine. Partridge and sea bream are the house specialties, but save room for the *arroz con leche* (rice with milk), a far cry from ordinary rice pudding. Closed Tuesdays. Reservations advised. 8 Plaza del Ayuntamiento (phone: 227716). Expensive.

Cardenal – In an elegant 18th-century palace tucked up against the city walls, this is worth seeking out even if you are bedding down somewhere less grand. It is linked with the celebrated Madrid restaurant *Botín*, and clients are eager eaters. In fine weather, dine alfresco in the split-level garden. Roast lamb and suckling pig, Castilian specialties, rival the partridge *a la toledana*. Fresh asparagus and strawberries are a must in the spring. Open daily. Reservations advised. 24 Paseo de Recaredo (phone: 220862). Expensive.

El Abside – Quite offbeat, by Toledan standards, with an adventurous crowd. The ancient Moorish tower adjacent to the *María Cristina* hotel has been revamped as a spacious and bright dining room; the bright blue decor and painted Moorish patterns are as festive as a nomad's party tent. The cuisine is imaginative, but the nouvelle touch can be a bit shaky. Try the almond soup and duck with honey-orange sauce. Various Arab-Sephardic dishes provide a choice for vegetarians, not always easy in Castilian restaurants, which cater to carnivores. Open daily. Reservations advised. 1 Calle Marqués de Mendigorría (phone: 213202). Expensive to moderate.

La Botica – Located in the heart of the city, this stylish place has a more formal dining room upstairs, along with a cafeteria and outdoor terrace for those who want to people watch. Cosmopolitan variations of Castilian standards and innovative dishes like eggplant and shrimp gratin are served with flair. Fresh fruit sherbets provide a light finish. Open daily. Reservations unnecessary. 13 Plaza de Zocodover (phone: 225557). Expensive to moderate.

Casa Aurelio – Sister to *Restaurante Aurelio,* serving excellent cream of crab soup, partridge, quail, sirloin, and other traditional Castilian dishes in a somewhat less formal atmosphere. Closed Wednesdays. Reservations advised. 6 Calle Sinagoga (phone: 222097). Moderate.

Chirón – A comfortably air conditioned dining place that serves the Toledo standards: partridge, thick slabs of potato omelette, homemade crusty bread, and *manchego* cheese. Open daily. Reservations advised. Paseo de Recaredo (phone: 220150). Moderate.

La Cubana – Cross the Tagus River at the Puente de Alcántara for filling dishes that taste just that much better when eaten on the open-air terrace. There also is a wood-paneled indoor dining room. Open daily, except the first 2 weeks in September. Reservations unnecessary. 2 Paseo de la Rosa (phone: 220088). Moderate.

Hierbabuena – A romantic spot where diners eat by candlelight beneath an intricate Mudéjar ceiling. Latecomers may be seated in a slightly musty side chamber, which is plainly a whitewashed cave. Service is elegant yet friendly. Game (when in season) and duck in plum sauce are the house specialties. Closed Sunday evenings and all day Mondays. Reservations advised. 9 Calle Cristo de la Luz (phone: 223463). Moderate.

Mesón Aurelio – A sister to the formal *Restaurante Aurelio* and the less formal *Casa Aurelio,* this casual place serves traditional Castilian dishes plus partridge, quail, and steaks. Closed Mondays. Reservations advised. 1 Calle Sinagoga (phone: 221392). Moderate.

Venta de Aires – An old and famous Toledo establishment. As many locals as tourists eat here for the typical Toledo fare: marinated partridge, tortilla (potato omelette), garlic soup, and the regional *manchego* cheese. The marzipan is made on the premises. A large tree-shaded terrace is wonderful for summer dining. Closed Mondays. Reservations unnecessary. 25 Calle Circo Romano (phone: 220545). Moderate.

Sinaí – Although this street in the Judería (old Jewish quarter) is solemnly named for the Catholic Monarchs, who drove both Jews and Moors from Spain, kosher and Moroccan dishes are the wave of the present here. Couscous or tangerine steaks makes an unusual and pleasant change of pace from tepid partridge. The restaurant plays host to an annual *Passover* feast. Open daily, but closes at 6 PM. Reservations unnecessary. 7 Cuesta de los Reyes Católicos (phone: 225623). Moderate to inexpensive.

El Nido – Bustling with students and hungry tourists. The fixed-price *menú del día* here makes this lively place the best deal in town. But be forewarned: The house wine is ghastly. Closed Mondays. Reservations unnecessary. 5 Plaza de la Magdalena. Inexpensive.

TAPAS BARS: Several *tapas* bars line the narrow streets just off the Plaza de Zocodover, particular Callejón Barrio Rey. *Bar Ludeña* (in Plaza de la Magdalena, just below Barrio Rey) is a colorful place offering a wide variety of *tapas,* snacks, and inexpensive meals. *Los Cuatro Tiempos* (5-7 Calle Sixto Ramón Parro) has a downstairs *tapas* bar featuring a splendid ceramic decor. *La Tarasca* (6 Calle Hombre de Palo) is an overpriced restaurant that nevertheless serves good *tapas,* which are less expensive when eaten standing at the bar.

VALENCIA

Valencia is known the world over as the home of paella, possibly the most international of all Spanish dishes, and rightly so. But this city, an agricultural capital that is Spain's third-largest, offers far more than fish, sausage, and rice. A character in Ernest Hemingway's *For Whom the Bell Tolls,* describing the town during a bullfight fiesta more than a half a century ago, put it like this: "Never have I seen so many people. Never have I seen cafés so crowded. For hours it would be impossible to get a seat and it was impossible to board the tram cars. In Valencia, there was movement all day and all night."

And so there is today. Like nowhere else in Spain, the residents of Valencia took to the Arabs' love for flame and fireworks, still evidenced in the city's *fallas,* riotous celebrations that draw tens of thousands of visitors every March. The cafés of the old city bustle with people year round, and the economy thrives. The city has, as its local cheerleaders say, *mucha marcha* — lots of life.

But Valencia is a pearl that must be sought out among the swine. The Old City is surrounded by a depressing sprawl of working class housing blocks, and most prospective visitors pass it by in favor of the better known sites to the north and south. Only once you enter the Old City, clustered along an elbow of the Turia River, will you find the architecture, museums, and unusually rich historical heritage of what once was one of Spain's most powerful kingdoms.

Valencia lies at the heart of the *huerta,* a fertile crescent of alluvial plain that is irrigated according to a complex system begun some 2,100 years ago. Water has transformed the area into an agricultural paradise: a flat, rich plain covered with millions of orange trees, ubiquitous market gardens, flower nurseries, and nut tree orchards. "The soil never rests in these *huertas,* crops succeed each other without interruption," a Spanish naturalist enthused almost 200 years ago, and farmers today are still harvesting as many as four crops a year from their fields. Everything depends on the precious water of the Turia River, and the elected judges of Valencia's Water Tribunal have been meeting every Thursday since the Middle Ages outside the cathedral to settle disputes. The proceedings are open to the public and are held in Valencian, a dialect of the Catalan language; decisions are recorded only in the local farmers' memories.

The Romans founded Valentia in 137 BC, although Greeks, Phoenicians, and Carthaginians coasted this area and traded with the native Iberians long before. The city eventually fell into the hands of the Visigoths and, in the 8th century, the Arabs, who invaded the peninsula from northern Africa. It was the Arabs who gave the region some of its most lasting features — its orange groves, the palm trees that line its avenues, the glazing techniques that made its ceramics famous, tremendous improvements to the irrigation system still in use today, fireworks, silk, and rice, which is grown in paddies to the south. But the favor was not to be repaid: In succeeding centuries, Catholics would raze all Moorish landmarks, leaving only an Arab bathhouse that cannot be visited today. The first of the Catholic "liberators" was El Cid, the legendary hero who took the town in 1094 and died here 5 years later. Following his death, his brave wife, Doña Jimena, was unable to hold the city, and it slipped back under Arab control for another 150 years.

Valencians regard King Jaime I of Aragon, known as the Conqueror, as their true liberator. Following a 5-month siege, the warrior-king marched into the city in triumph one September day in 1238, granting its Christian inhabitants special rights, or *costums,* in return for their allegiance to the crown of Aragon. But toward the end of the Middle Ages, the kingdom of Valencia entered a dark period. The Black Death ravaged the city twice. A violent pogrom in Valencia's old Jewish quarter, around the Plaza Virgen, set off further popular attacks on Jews and converted Moors. Vicente Ferrer, a brilliant but bigoted Valencian cleric who was later sainted and made patron of his native city, delivered virulent anti-Semitic diatribes and helped frame discriminatory laws aimed at religious minorities. When the Spanish Inquisition came to the city in 1482, at least 100 Valencians were burned at the stake for refusing to convert. This sad story of religious intolerance and narrow-mindedness would be completed about 130 years later, when the expulsion from Spain of converted Moors deprived the kingdom of 170,000 of its most skilled artists, craftsmen, and traders.

The Bourbons came to rule Spain in the early 18th century via the War of the Spanish Succession — a war in which Valencia, along with Aragon and Catalonia, made a fatefully bad choice, backing the Hapsburg favorite. The city paid for its mistake with the Nueva Planta decree of 1707, stripping it of its ancient rights and generating resentment that still exists today. The kingdom became a province; its viceroy, a captain general sent from Madrid.

For better or for worse, Valencia has since been involved in just about every war and rebellion in Spain, winning a gritty reputation for independence and liberal-mindedness. In 1808, led by one Father Rico, the populace stormed the city arsenal and rose bloodily against Napoleon's occupying troops; Marshal Louis Gabriel Suchet managed to restore French rule only 4 years later. Over the following decades, Valencia was a hothouse of conspiracies, plots, and failed uprisings, notably the Republican-inspired insurrections of 1856 and 1864. A rebellion during the Revolution of 1868 was settled only with an artillery bombardment of the city.

True to its liberal past, Valencia fought on the losing side during the Spanish Civil War, wringing crops from the overworked *huerta* to feed the starving population of besieged Madrid. For most of 1937, with the war going badly in Madrid, Valencia became the Republican capital. It was shelled and bombed until, as the war came to a close in March 1939, it finally fell to Generalísimo Francisco Franco's troops. In the decades of repression that followed, the local language was almost stamped out; but after Franco died, it made a strong comeback and is now widely spoken.

All this bad luck in war and rebellion appears to have done little to dampen the spirits of the typical Valencian. He seems a hardy fellow, a citified dirt farmer who has seen all manner of catastrophes come and go. Kick the pavement in Valencia, the saying goes, and an artichoke springs up. The city today does have the feel of an overgrown agricultural capital of 750,000, despite its heavy industry and sprawling development. Valencia had its age of glory, but in the last few centuries it certainly has not produced many of Spain's leading artists or intellectuals.

Still, exceptions make the rule, and Valencia boasts one exceptional and famous 20th-century writer: Vicente Blasco Ibáñez, an intellectual and Republican politician who died before the Civil War. To English speakers, he is probably best known for *Blood and Sand,* possibly the finest novel ever written on bullfighting (from an opponent's point of view); it was later made into movies starring Rudolph Valentino (1922) and Tyrone Power (1941). He also wrote the novel *The Four Horsemen of the Apocalypse.* Some of the city's best-known artists include Joaquín Sorolla y Bastida (1863–1923), a Spanish Impressionist who loved to paint sunlight, and the sculptor Mariano Benlliure y Gil (1862–1947), the best known of a family of prolific artists.

One of the great attractions of Valencia is precisely that it is not a major tourist attraction. With its furniture, ceramics, and many other industries, and the industrial port of El Grao that serves it, it can be off-putting to the casual passerby. But once its many charms are discovered, it is seen as a particularly Spanish place. Valencians are less affected than most by the onslaught of coastal tourism in recent decades, so they are more apt to be generous in that most valuable of foreign-exchange earners — a genuine desire to show the visitor why their city deserves a second look.

VALENCIA AT-A-GLANCE

 SEEING THE CITY: For those who don't mind a grueling, 207-step climb, a perfect view of the city can be had from El Miguelete, Valencia's most popular monument, the 14th-century octagonal bell tower of the cathedral, on the Plaza de la Reina. Clustered around the tower are all the principal buildings of the Old City, and the visitor sees a vista of bridges over the Turia River bed, blue-domed churches, and the fertile *huerta* stretching beyond the ends of the city's streets. Although they are now seldom used in chorus, El Micalet (as the tower is fondly known to Valencians in their native language) used to ring all 12 of its named bells a half hour before the city's gates were locked for the night (they were also sounded to regulate the irrigation of the *huerta*). Under no circumstances was anyone allowed in after the doors swung shut, giving rise to the Spanish expression *quedarse a la luna de Valencia,* literally, to be left in the moonlight of Valencia — out in the cold. The tower is open daily, from 10:30 AM to 12:30 PM and from 5 to 6 PM. Admission charge. Enter through the cathedral.

 SPECIAL PLACES: Valencia's last set of city walls was torn down in 1865, but almost all of the city's main monuments and museums are within the relatively small area it once enclosed. The area is defined to the north by the bed of the Turia River, which has been rerouted farther away from the city to solve the chronic flooding that had long plagued the old section, and on the west, south, and east by Avenida de Guillem de Castro, Calle de Xàtiva, and Calle Colón, respectively. A major shopping, restaurant, and hotel district, however, lies southeast of the old section, in the blocks just beyond Calle Colón. In the city's port of El Grao, 2½ miles (4 km) to the east, and especially on the Levante beach just north of it, there are dozens of popular seafood restaurants, as well as some interesting turn-of-the-century Spanish Modern buildings, reminiscent of Art Deco.

Cathedral – Angled oddly into a corner of the Plaza de la Reina, the Old City's main square, the Seo Metropolitan Cathedral is a mixture of styles, as reflected in its three portals, which are Romanesque, Gothic, and baroque (it is outside the Gothic Apostle's Door that the Water Tribunal meets on Thursdays). Begun in 1262 on the site of a mosque razed by the Catholic conquerors, the cathedral also is rather eclectic inside. The architectural highlights are the Gothic dome and the chapter house. The main altarpiece depicts the life of Christ in six sections, including birth and crucifixion panels. The main chapel contains the pulpit used by San Vicente Ferrer to give some of his apocalyptic orations, and one of the leading Spanish candidates for the "true" Holy Grail — a much-revered agate cup, set with emeralds and pearls on a base of pure gold. The church also boasts some fine paintings, including the *Baptism of Christ* by Juan de Juanes, but the real art treasures are housed in the *Museo de la Catedral,* which contains works by Zurbarán, Juan de Juanes, and others. Notice also the Goya murals, one of which depicts San Francisco de Borja surrounded by devilish creatures as he exorcises a dying man. The cathedral and its museum are open Mondays through Saturdays, from 10 AM to 1 PM and from 4:30 to 6 PM; Sundays for mass only. Admission charges for the museum and tower. Plaza de la Reina (phone: 331-8127).

Basílica de la Virgen de los Desamparados (Basilica of the Virgin of the Forsaken) – An arcade connects the cathedral to this elliptical building, which was completed in 1667 and is said to have been the first mental asylum in the world. The basilica was founded by a priest who called for donations in a sermon after seeing a madman beaten in the streets; the institution later became responsible for burying dead travelers found on roads outside the city. Today, the structure contains fine frescoes by Antonio Palomino on the interior of the dome, and a sculpted image of the Virgin of the Forsaken, the patroness of Valencia, that was supposedly sculpted by angels. On the second Sunday in May (*Virgin's Day*), and on *Corpus Christi,* the Virgin is carried throught nearby streets in processions marked by showers of rose petals and other flowers. Plaza de la Virgen.

Museo Provincial de Bellas Artes (Provincial Fine Arts Museum) – Many people come to this first-rate art museum, one of Spain's best (but least-visited), simply to see the small, brooding self-portrait painted by Velázquez in 1640. While this is the museum's single unquestioned gem, its most interesting display is the collection of Valencian religious "primitives" of the 14th, 15th, and 16th centuries. It is remarkable just how graphic much of this work was before centuries of further "refinement" drained altarpieces and other types of painting of much of their naive vigor. Blood gushes from Christ's sword wound into a goblet in one painting; the Lactating Virgin spouts milk from her swollen breasts into the mouth of the infant Christ in another. Downstairs, there are early Iberian and Hispano-Roman artifacts, including an altar to a pagan Roman emperor, Claudius Gothicus, on which some rebellious Christian chiseled the words "Christus Magis" — Christ is More. There is also a small treasure of works upstairs by Francisco Ribalta (who died in Valencia in 1628), Ribera, Murillo, El Greco (*St. John the Baptist*), Van Dyck, Hieronymus Bosch, and Goya, who once taught at the Fine Arts Academy that runs the museum. There are several rooms dedicated to 19th- and 20th-century Valencian artists, the most interesting of which display works by Ignacio Pinazo and Sorolla. Open Tuesdays through Saturdays, from 10 AM to 2 PM and from 4 to 6 PM; Sundays, from 10 AM to 2 PM. Admission charge. Located just across the Real Bridge. 9 Calle de San Pío V (phone: 360-5793).

Jardínes del Real (Royal Gardens) – Also just across the Real Bridge and next door to the fine arts museum, this small paradise of rose gardens, bougainvillea, palms, mimosas, jacarandas, cypress, and myrtle trees also has a diminutive but pleasant zoo. The gardens are open daily, from 8 AM to sundown; the zoo is open daily, from 10 AM to sundown. Admission charge for the zoo. Calle de San Pío V (phone: 362-3512).

La Lonja de la Seda (Silk Exchange) – In a city known for its Gothic architecture, this structure in the heart of the Old City is the undoubted highlight of the genre. The Valencian Père Compte completed La Lonja in 1498, leaving a nearly hidden plaque boasting that construction took just 15 years and exhorting merchants to honesty. In addition to an array of gargoyles, the façade also features a series of fantastic and often erotic small figures: centaurs playing flutes, orgies, a monkey and a hare, naked men clasping great clubs, a miser trapped by the devil — even a squatting man defecating. The first room is the main Silk Exchange, a great vaulted hall supported by 24 twisting columns reminiscent of massive hanks of silk; on Fridays from 1 to 3 PM, fruit wholesalers hold auctions reminiscent of 16th-century silk fairs here. Next to this hall is the tower of La Lonja, said to have once served as a prison for bankrupt silk merchants. A remarkable circular stairway, with no central support, leads from a courtyard of orange trees to an upstairs hall famous for the elaborately gilded and carved wooden ceiling that looks down on otherwise sober surroundings. Open Tuesdays through Fridays, from 10 AM to 2 PM and from 4 to 6 PM; Saturdays and Sundays, from 10 AM to 1 PM. No admission charge. Plaza del Mercado (phone: 331-6158).

Mercado Central (Main Market) – One of the finest — and largest — market buildings in Spain is made additionally delightful by the colors and smells of the products of the *huerta,* along with the glazed *azulejo* tiles showing Valencian citrus fruits and vegetables. Built in 1928, the market is a fine example of Valencian modernism, and is visually similar to a turn-of-the-century railroad station, with glass skylights supported by an elaborate framework of iron girders. Open Mondays through Saturdays, the market offers a quick taste of modern Valencian life. Plaza del Mercado.

Palacio del Marqués de Dos Aquas – The amazing façade of this 18th-century rococo palace was designed by the painter Hypólito Rovira, who died in a Valencian mental asylum in 1740. Its main entrance is a riotous alabaster fantasy of crocodiles, Cupids, a Virgin with Child, and two men spilling jugs of water — the "two waters" of the Marqués de Dos Aguas. The building, which was once even wilder, with paintings on the plasterwork that have since been destroyed, now houses the *Museo Nacional de Cerámica,* Spain's leading ceramics museum. The gilded and tiled interior of the building, a kind of Hollywood version of a European palace, is a showcase of centuries of excellent pottery from the outlying towns of Paterna, Alcora, and Manises, beautifully glazed work that was widely sought across Europe in the late Middle Ages. In other rooms, there are works by Picasso, a Valencian tiled kitchen, and pottery from other regions of Spain and abroad. Finally, downstairs, is the marquis's fairy-tale carriage. Open Tuesdays through Saturdays, from 10 AM to 2 PM and from 4 to 6 PM; Sundays, from 10 AM to 2 PM. Admission charge. 2 Calle Poeta Querol (phone: 351-6392).

Real Colegio del Patriarca – This Renaissance collegiate church, founded in 1610 by San Juan de Ribera, the Archbishop of Valencia, is memorable for the severity of its lines and its lack of exterior embellishment. The first thing seen upon entering is a huge alligator nailed to the wall — the so-called Dragon of the Patriarch. Legend has it that the beast devoured dozens of Valencians before being slain by a brave Jew who, in order to escape a death sentence for previous crimes, devised an ingenious suit of armor to do the deed; historians claim that the beast was sent as a gift by the Viceroy of Peru in 1606, and hung by the patriarch as a symbol of silence. Besides the church and a lovely arcaded courtyard, the complex houses the *Museo del Patriarca,* a rich little museum containing paintings by El Greco, Rogier van der Weyden, Juan de Juanes, Ribalta, and others. Open daily, from 11 AM to 1:30 PM. Admission charge to the museum. 1 Calle de la Nave (phone: 351-4176).

Museo Fallero – Located southeast of the Old City in a drab, temporary building, this small museum is crammed with *ninots* — the satirical papier-mâché figures that ordinarily are burned in effigy at midnight on *St. Joseph's Day* (March 19) as part of the *falla* celebrations for which Valencia is famous. Each year a selection committee votes to save the best one from the flames, and this museum is a repository of such *ninots indultas,* or figures "pardoned" at the last minute. Big-busted women, "typical" Valencians, politicians, and a girl on a swing representing Spain's young democracy are just a few of the cartoon-like, lampooning figures preserved here since 1935, along with exceptionally colorful and historic *falla* posters. Open Tuesdays through Sundays, from 10 AM to 2 PM and from 4 to 7 PM (closed afternoons in August and September). Admission charge. Note that at press time this museum was scheduled for a future move; it has no telephone, so check with the tourist office before setting out. 4 Plaza de Monteolivete.

Museo Taurino – Almost hidden away in a covered concourse next to the bullring, one of Spain's leading taurine museums is filled with bullfighting memorabilia. The exhibit contains examples of 19th-century bullfighting garb, a savage-looking collection of swords and pics, lances, suits of lights worn by some leading toreros when they were gored, and the stuffed heads of some of the offending beasts. Valencia was for many centuries a leading city for bullfighting, though its reputation has fallen off in recent decades. Open Mondays through Fridays, from 10:30 AM to 1:30 PM. No admission charge. Pasaje Doctor Serra (phone: 351-1850).

Estación del Norte – Many visitors, whether arriving by train or not, take the time to visit this charming railroad station, one of the most beautiful in Europe. Both the interior and exterior are decorated with *azulejo* tiles bearing such Valencian motifs as oranges, the *huerta,* and *barracas,* the region's traditional thatch-roofed houses. The ticket counters and the cafeteria are especially delightful. 24 Calle de Xàtiva (phone: 351-3612).

Torres de Serranos (Serranos Towers) – The 14th-century gate next to the northern Puente Serranos (Serranos Bridge) was fully restored in 1930 and remains an imposing fortified arch. From 10 AM to 2 PM Tuesdays through Saturdays, the towers can be climbed for an excellent view of Valencia and the old Turia River bed, which is slowly being converted into a lengthy concourse of gardens. A second gate remaining from the medieval walls is the 15th-century Torres de Quart, nearby on Avenida de Guillem de Castro. Like a proud old warrior, it still bears the scars of French cannonballs from the War of Independence, known as the Peninsular War.

Instituto Valenciano de Arte Moderno/IVAM (Valencian Institute of Modern Art) – Hard by what remains of the Old City walls (in fact, a vestige of the medieval ramparts protrudes into one of the galleries), not far from the Torres de Quart, this is one of a crop of new museums in Spain devoted exclusively to modern art. Opened in 1989 with much fanfare, the collection is housed in two locations — an ultramodern stone-and-glass building called the Centre Julio González and, nearby (and in complete contrast), a restored 13th- to 16th-century Carmelite convent called the Centre del Carme. Besides the permanent collection of some 1,400 pieces (paintings, drawings, and sculpture by Julio González, a lifelong friend of Picasso form the nucleus), the Centre Julio González has an auditorium, restaurant-bar, and a bookshop, and is host to a year-round schedule of changing exhibitions and special cultural events that are international in scope. Both buildings are open Tuesdays through Sundays from 11 AM to 8 PM; admission charge, except on Sundays. Centre Julio González, 118 Avenida de Guillem de Castro; Centre del Carme, 2 Calle Museu (phone for both: 386-3000).

Palau de la Musica – Across the Aragón Bridge from the Old City, Valencia's concert hall, built in the now-dry bed of the Turia River in 1987, is a rather bizarre mix of reflecting pools, palm trees, small temple-like structures, and a main building that resembles an exceptionally swank greenhouse. It is known to locals as the "microwave" because of its initial lack of air conditioning, and its designers also failed to include a system to clean its vast glass surfaces — leading the city to hire mountaineers to do the job. 1 Plaza del Rey (phone: 360-3356, for information; 361-5212, for tickets).

ENVIRONS

Manises – The town of Manises has been a major pottery center since the Middle Ages, when its fame reached far and wide and emissaries from the richest courts of Europe vied to buy its fine wares. Although it suffered centuries of eclipse as Spanish tastes turned to the Toledan city of Talavera de la Reina, Manises today, while otherwise unattractive, is packed with ceramics factories and retail shops, many of which sell good reproductions of pieces in Valencia's *Museo Nacional de Cerámica* at bargain prices. Manises is about 4½ miles (7 km) from Valencia, and is well served by city buses.

Sagunto – In 219 BC, the first inhabitants of this fortified rocky ridge, the Iberians, set their possessions and themselves afire in a gigantic holocaust rather than surrender to the Carthaginian general Hannibal. The Romans eventually rebuilt the town, and it was successively held by the Visigoths, the Arabs, and, in the 19th century, the French. Today, Sagunto has an impressive 8,000-seat amphitheater, which is, unfortunately, in relatively poor shape, as well as an ancient acropolis, and nearly half a mile of mostly Moorish medieval walls and ramparts. An old Roman forum is marked by a huge broken stone marked with the letters "FORV." The long ridge occupied by the fortifications provides a dramatic, 360-degree view of orange groves, the surrounding mountains, and the Mediterranean. The castle and amphitheater complex is open Mondays through Saturdays, from 10 AM to 2 PM and from 4 to 6 PM (7 PM in summer); Sundays and holidays, from 10 AM to 2 PM. Admission charge. The complex also includes a *Museo Arqueológico* (phone: 266-2213), which contains Roman mosaics and other artifacts. Though closed for renovations at press time, the museum is expected to reopen by mid-year.

Modern Sagunto has a population of nearly 60,000, and boasts an old Jewish quarter, a supposed Temple of Diana, and other sites. For more information on Sagunto, contact the tourist office (Plaza de Cronista Chabret; phone: 266-2213). Theater performances are frequently staged in the ancient amphitheater, against a panoramic backdrop (phone: 246-1230). Sagunto is 16 miles (26 km) north of Valencia, is easily reached by car, and has frequent bus and train service.

■**EXTRA SPECIAL:** Just 9½ miles (15 km) south of Valencia lies one of Spain's largest and most beautiful lakes, La Albufera, in the center of the new Albufera national park. This peaceful, lagoon-like lake, surrounded by rice paddies, is home to more than 250 species of fowl, including European flamingos and other unusual birds, as well as the baby eels and fish that have long attracted local fishermen. The lake is separated from the sea by a thin strand of sand and pine trees between the towns of El Saler and El Palmar. In either of these places, or along the highway connecting them, visitors can easily rent flat-bottom boats from local fishermen. The sunsets from this side of the lake are stupendous, marked by golden yellows and reddish tints and the calls of the waterfowl. In El Palmar, the farther away of the two towns, try the *alli al pebre* (baby eels from the lake fried in a garlic sauce) at the *Racó de l'Olla* (Carretera de El Saler; phone: 161-0072) near the lake, before heading back to the city.

SOURCES AND RESOURCES

 TOURIST INFORMATION: There is no shortage of tourist information offices in Valencia, with four run by the city and a large fifth one under the aegis of the regional government. This regional office, the Conselleria d'Industria Comerc y Turisme (48 Calle de la Paz; phone: 352-4000), near the Plaza Alfonso el Magnánimo, can provide information on both the city and the surrounding areas, and also has some good publications. The office is open Mondays through Fridays, from 9 AM to 2 PM and from 5 to 7 PM; Saturdays, from 9:30 AM to 2 PM. The main Municipal Tourism Office is located in Valencia's City Hall (1 Plaza del Ayuntamiento; phone: 351-0417), and is open Mondays through Fridays, from 9:30 AM to 1:30 PM and from 4:30 to 7 PM; Saturdays, from 9:30 AM to 2 PM. The other offices are located in the Estación del Norte (phone: 352-2882); at the airport in Manises (phone: 153-0325); and near the city's northern limits (at 1 Avenida de Cataluña; phone: 369-7932). These offices are open Mondays through Fridays, from 9 AM to 2 PM and from 5 to 7 PM.

Local Coverage – Two small, locally oriented newspapers serve Valencia: *Las Provincias* and *Levante*. *Turia* is a weekly guide to local entertainment, including theater, music, and dining. *Geográfica Valenciana,* a paperback collection of excellent photographs of the region, is sold at the regional tourist office and in local shops. English-language newspapers are easily found in the Plaza del Ayuntamiento and other central squares in the Old City.

 TELEPHONE: The city code for Valencia is 6. If calling from within Spain, dial 96 before the local number.

 GETTING AROUND: Downtown Valencia is perpetually packed with cars, and on-street parking is nearly impossible, so it's advisable to walk through the Old City, which is relatively small and easily seen on foot. Trips to outlying areas, including the port, can be made by train or bus; but taxis are quick and quite inexpensive.

Airport – The surprisingly busy Valencia Manises Airport (phone: 370-9500), 4½ miles (7 km) northwest of Valencia, near the pottery center of Manises, has flights to most Spanish cities, as well as most major European capitals. Take bus No. 15, which departs the main bus station hourly.

Boat – From Valencia, it's a quick trip to the Balearic Islands of Mallorca, Minorca, and Ibiza. *Trasmediterránea* (15 Calle Manuel Soto; phone: 367-6512/0704; and at the port; phone: 323-7580) offers year-round, daily ferry service Mondays through Saturdays, from the port of El Grao to Mallorca (less often to the other islands).

Bus – Most of the city bus lines a visitor will want to use depart from the Plaza del Ayuntamiento. Ask for help at the Municipal Tourism Office in the same square or get a schedule at *EMT* (1 Calle Nuestra Señora de Gracia; phone: 352-8399). The long-distance bus station (13 Avenida Menéndez Pidal; phone: 349-7222), which also serves the airport, is a 10-minute walk north of the Old City, across the Glorias Valencianas Bridge. There is frequent daily service to Madrid, Barcelona, Málaga, and other cities and towns.

Car Rental – The leading international and Spanish firms have offices at the airport and downtown. Agencies in the city include *Avis* (17 Calle Isabel la Católica; phone:

351-0734); *Hertz* (7 Calle Segorbe; phone: 341-5036); *Europcar* (7 Avenida de Antic Regne de Valencia; phone: 374-1512); *Ital* (19 Calle Isabel la Católica; phone: 351-6818); *Flycar* (3 Calle San José de Calasanz; phone: 326-7155); and *Furgocar* (12 Calle Linares; phone: 326-5500).

Subway – A new metro, or subway, serves the city's west side, but virtually no tourist sites. Fare depends on the distance traveled.

Taxi – Taxis can be hailed on the street or called by telephone (phone: 370-3333 or 357-1313).

Train – Valencia's main railway station for long-distance trains is the Estación del Norte (Calle de Xàtiva; phone: 351-3612), a colorful iron-and-glass building at the foot of the Old City. Tickets also can be bought at the *RENFE* office (2 Plaza Alfonso el Magnánimo; phone: 352-0202). The creaky old narrow-gauge train that goes to the port of El Grao and northwest through the outlying *huerta* to Liria leaves from the Estación Puente de Madera (1 Calle Cronista Rivelles; phone: 347-3750), just across the Turia River bed from the Serranos Towers.

SPECIAL EVENTS: If there's one thing for which Valencia is famous, it's the *Fallas de San José* — those annual eruptions of flame and popular mirth each *St. Joseph's Day,* March 19. A week of flower-bedecked processions, fireworks, bullfights, and all-out partying ends at midnight on the saint's day, when a fantastic array of satirical effigies is set afire in huge towers, as fire trucks prudently stand by. Some of the *ninots,* lovingly crafted over the entire proceeding year, reach 40 feet high. The fiesta dates back to the Middle Ages, when the carpenters' guild used to burn a year's worth of accumulated wood shavings on the feast day of its patron saint. Today, no one is immune to the papier-mâché lampooning — politicians, the church, the rich, and the poor are all fair game. The *fallas* draw huge crowds from Spain and abroad, so hotel reservations are essential. Around the same time of year, *Holy Week* is marked by boats parading in maritime processions. The patroness of the city, the Virgin of the Unprotected, has her day on the first Sunday of May, followed by *Corpus Christi,* when Valencian *rocas,* baroque holy images of great beauty, are rolled through the streets. The city fills up with tourists again during its *Feria de Julio,* a week-long fair in early July that includes topnotch bullfights, music, fireworks, and even a paella contest. And in early October, Valencians — a strange breed in love with all manner of pop, fizzle, and flare — host the *International Pyrotechnic Festival,* a tournament of the world's finest makers of fireworks.

MUSEUMS: Noteworthy museums not mentioned in *Special Places* include the following:

Museo Histórico Municipal – A small but interesting museum containing a collection of paintings and mementos pertaining to the history of Valencia, ensconced in the Ayuntamiento (City Hall). Open Mondays through Fridays, from 9 AM to 1:30 PM. No admission charge. Plaza del Ayuntamiento (phone: 352-5478).

Museo José Benlliure – The former home of one of the city's most famous painters now houses a museum of his work. Benlliure spent most of his life in Italy, but returned to Valencia in his later years and died here in 1937. Open Mondays through Fridays, from 10 AM to 2 PM. No admission charge. 23 Calle Blanquerías, near Portal Nuevo (phone: 331-1662).

Museo Paleontológico – Skeletal remains and other artifacts in the Almudín, a 14th-to-16th-century granary decorated with *azulejos* and curious frescoes. Open Tuesdays through Fridays, from 10 AM to 1 PM and from 4 to 6:30 PM; Saturdays and Sundays, from 10 AM to 1 PM. No admission charge. Note that winter flooding in 1990 caused damage to the museum and reopening is not scheduled until later this year; check with the tourist office. Calle Almudín (phone: 331-8562).

Museo de la Prehistoria – In the former Bailía Palace, with exhibits of cave paintings, Roman pots, Stone Age and Iberian ceramics, and other archaeological remains of the Valencian region. Open Tuesdays through Sundays, from 10 AM to 2 PM. No admission charge. 36 Calle Corona (phone: 331-7164).

SHOPPING: Valencia thinks of itself as a design center, and this is reflected in the scores of attractive and very upscale boutiques and designer shops found here. Some of the finer shopping streets — Calle de la Paz, Calle Poeta Querol, Calle de Colón, and Calle Sorni — compare favorably with anything found in Madrid or Barcelona. Valencia is also home to some of Spain's best pottery, Manises stoneware (see *Environs* above), and Lladró porcelain; and *azulejos,* the brightly colored ceramic tiles so gloriously developed by the Arabs in Spain, are a local pride and joy. Glassware is also blown and sold in the region. Another indigenous specialty is seen in the painstakingly hand-sewn silk garments that make up traditional Valencian women's costumes — and sell at huge prices. Business hours are generally 9:30 AM to 1:30 PM and 4:30 to 8 PM. The best stores are generally found around the southeastern portions of the Old City.

Altarriba – A remarkable toy store with a wide selection of model trains from around the world, as well as a collection of peculiarly Spanish miniatures. 22 Calle Mar (phone: 332-3024).

Artespaña – A state-run crafts shop featuring fine handmade ceramics, furniture, hand-blown glass, and leather goods at reasonable prices. 7 Calle de la Paz (phone: 331-6404 or 331-6403).

Carla – Specializing in fine silk, including garments for women. 4 Calle Bordadores (phone: 331-2986).

El Corte Inglés – Valencia has two branches of the popular national department store chain, offering just about everything; they remain open during the lunch hour and on Saturday afternoons. 26 Calle Pintor Sorolla (phone: 351-2444) and in the *Nuevo Centro* shopping mall, 15 Avenida Menéndez Pidal (phone: 347-4142).

Lladró – The internationally known porcelain maker — the place for those whose tastes run to figurines of forest dryads, small children, and animals. Also, its own line of leather goods. Three locations: Calle Marqués de Sotelo (phone: 351-0937), Calle Poeta Querol (phone: 351-1625), and in the *Nuevo Centro* shopping mall (phone: 347-0086).

Loewe – One of Spain's most elegant — and expensive — purveyors of men's and women's clothing, leather goods, luggage, and accessories. Men's store at 7 Calle Poeta Querol (phone: 352-7372); women's store at 7 Calle Marqués de Dos Aguas (phone: 352-4301).

Francis Montesinos – Trendy men's and women's fashions by Valencia's best-known designer. 40 Calle Caballeros (phone: 331-2844).

Neri – An exclusive ceramics and kitchenware store, offering some of the finest traditional pottery in the city. 1 Calle Poeta Querol (phone: 351-8961).

J. Sugrañes – When this atmospheric little shop opened in 1885, its silk dresses, shawls, mantillas, and other items were still worn regularly by Valencia's moneyed damsels; today, the finely crafted, very expensive women's wear made by the Sugrañes family counts as "traditional" finery for fiestas only. 18 Calle de la Paz (phone: 352-6432).

SPORTS AND FITNESS: Boating – The *Real Club Náutico* (Royal Nautical Club) offers boat rentals, a sailing school, fishing, scuba diving and snorkeling, and full yacht service. Camino Canal (phone: 367-9011).

Bullfighting – One of the largest rings in Spain is located next to the train station (28 Calle de Xàtiva; phone: 351-9315). *Corridas,* or bullfights, are held for a week during the *fallas* and the July festival, otherwise irregularly.

Golf – There are four golf courses near Valencia. The 18-hole, par 72 *Campo de Golf El Saler* is at the *Parador Luis Vives,* sandwiched between the Mediterranean and the Albufera lagoon 11 miles (18 km) south of Valencia on a strand of pine trees and sand dunes (phone: 161-1186). Also try the 18-hole *Club de Campo del Bosque* (Calle Chiva, phone: 251-1011), 2½ miles (4 km) from town; or the 18-hole *Club de Golf Escorpión* at Bétera, 12 miles (19 km) northwest along the road to Liria (phone: 160-1211). There is also a 9-hole course 7½ miles (12 km) west of town in Manises (phone: 379-0850).

Soccer – Valencia's first-division team is a cause célebre in the area, with victory liable to provoke flag waving, horn honking parades downtown. Valencia plays at the *Estadio Luis Casanova,* Avenida de Suecia (phone: 360-0550).

Swimming – The beaches just north and south of the port, Playa de Levante and Playa de la Punta, are too polluted to make swimming advisable. There are miles of popular beaches to the south, however, toward El Saler, that are cleaner.

Trinquete – This is a peculiarly Valencian form of that great Spanish sport, pelota (best known to Americans in one of its many forms, jai alai). The crowd sits along one side of the frontón while players bat a calfskin ball over a net with their hands. Afternoon games are played daily except Tuesdays and Sundays at the *Trinquete Pelayo,* 6 Calle Pelayo (phone: 352-6845).

 THEATER: There are several theaters in Valencia, but only one has consistently interesting Spanish and European productions: the *Teatro Principal* (15 Calle Barcas; phone: 351-0051). North of the city, in Sagunto, productions are at times staged in the old Roman amphitheater against a spectacular backdrop of the town, the plain, the sea, and the mountains (see *Environs*).

 MUSIC: Valencia's futuristic *Palau de la Música* (see *Special Places;* 1 Plaza del Rey; phone: 360-3356 for information, 361-5212 for tickets), east of the Old City across the Aragón Bridge, hosts world class concerts of classical and other music during much of the year. The 19th-century *Teatro Principal* (see *Theater*) holds an opera season, usually in the fall and winter, and hosts occasional jazz, dance, and other festivals.

 NIGHTCLUBS AND NIGHTLIFE: As does every large Spanish town, Valencia has a thriving bar scene, although in this city it is unusually scattered. Younger and hipper bars tend to be concentrated around the Plaza del Carmen and Calle Caballeros in the Old City — *Café Lisboa* (35 Calle Caballeros; phone: 332-1764) doubles as a photo gallery. Quite a trek northeast of the Old City, around the Plaza Xuquer, the bars and fast-food joints are popular with students from the nearby university. A truly charming Old City bar, the *Cervecería Madrid* (10 Calle Abadía de San Martín; phone: 352-9671), is owned by Constante Gil, who painted the hundreds of naive canvases that decorate the place's 2 floors. Nearby, in the Plaza del Ayuntamiento, walk through the front door of the old *Cine Rialto* (phone: 351-5603), a theater that shows foreign films in their original language, into the *Cafetería Rialto* (phone: 351-5603), a perfect spot for a drink. Less chic but more "elegant" bars, aimed at an older crowd, are on Gran Vía Marqués del Turia, east of the Estación del Norte, the main train station. Large, all-night discotheques are found on the highway to El Saler — the *Spook Factory* (Carretera del Saler, Pinedo) is one of the most popular. For those with a taste for the tables, there's the very classic — and expensive — *Hotel-Casino Monte Picayo* (phone: 142-0100), a luxury complex featuring every gaming, lodging, and sporting service imaginable. Casino hours are 7 PM to 5 AM nightly. Monte Picayo is 9½ miles (15 km) north of Valencia, on the N-340 highway to Barcelona.

BEST IN TOWN

CHECKING IN: Valencia generally has no shortage of hotel space — but this rule of thumb does not apply during the March 12–19 *fallas* (see *Special Events*), when reservations are an absolute must. The city also hosts a number of business conventions throughout the year that can suddenly fill several hotels. Parking is a year-round nightmare anywhere close to the Old City, a fact that should be considered when choosing accommodations. The city is among the more economical ones in Spain to visit — its hotel rooms cost less on the whole than those in other large cities that are more firmly established on the tourist track. Expect to pay $75 and up for a double room listed as expensive, $45 to $75 for a moderate room, and $30 or less for an inexpensive one. All phone numbers are in the 6 city code unless otherwise indicated.

Astoria Palace – When Spanish politicians, entertainers, and other celebrities visit Valencia, this is where they stay. Manuel Benítez, "El Cordobés," rode the shoulders of a crowd direct from the bullring into the lobby here; opera diva Montserrat Caballé is a more contemporary visitor. Sumptuously decorated and ideally located on a small square in the heart of the Old City, the hotel manages to retain an atmosphere of personal attention. All of its 207 rooms and 20 suites are air conditioned and have color television sets, radios, and, on request, mini-bars. Other facilities include a restaurant, a convention center, private dining rooms, parking, and a discotheque. 5 Plaza Rodrigo Botet (phone: 352-6737). Expensive.

Dimar – Functional is the operative word at this 95-room modern establishment, just far enough from the central city to make it a long walk. A pleasant lobby leads to clean and carpeted air conditioned rooms that offer color television sets, mini-bars, and rambling bathrooms. The hotel is only a few steps from a district well known for its upscale boutiques and fine restaurants. As you walk out the front door, listen for the occasional cacophony of thousands of birds gathering in the trees of the Gran Vía. 80 Gran Vía Marqués del Turia (phone: 334-1807). Expensive.

Reina Victoria – Luis Ferreres Soler, the designer of this centrally located 1910-vintage building, was clearly influenced by 19th-century French architecture, but threw in a splash of modernism. Glass encloses corner balconies, the dining room, and the lobby, giving the interior a light and airy feel. Many of the 92 air conditioned rooms offer striking views of the Old City. The bar is dark, woody, and very English; the restaurant and its marble-floored dining room are local favorites. All around, the service here is excellent. Convention facilities are also available. 4-6 Calle Barcas (phone: 352-0487). Expensive.

Rey Don Jaime – A short taxi ride from the city center, near the *Palau de la Música,* stands this luxurious, spacious, and somewhat impersonal establishment. The lower lobby contains a concourse of shops, a hairdresser, and a sweeping marble staircase that leads up to a sitting room, an English-style bar, and convention and meeting rooms. The restaurant offers both international dishes and reasonable examples of Valencian specialties. Upstairs, the 314 air conditioned rooms are very large and well serviced, the bathrooms, huge. The hotel is primarily a businessperson's place, however, in a somewhat gloomy location outside the life of the Old City. 2 Avenida Baleares (phone: 360-7300). Expensive.

Bristol – Behind a turn-of-the-century brick, stone, and glassed-in façade are 40 pleasant rooms in the center of the Old City. It's a short walk from the *Ceramics Museum* and other downtown monuments — not to mention the *Cervecería Ma-*

drid (see *Nightclubs and Nightlife*). The service is pleasant and helpful. 3 Calle Abadía de San Martín (phone: 352-1176). Moderate.

Excelsior – Comfortable and pleasant, with a wood-paneled lobby, it's just a few steps from the *Astoria Palace* and costs only half as much. Downstairs, a white brick cafeteria-bar and an elegant little dining room are both enjoyable spots, and the service is good. All 65 rooms have color television sets and clean, comfortable appointments and facilities. 5 Calle Barcelonina (phone: 351-4612). Moderate.

Inglés – The elegant Old World charm here fades rather quickly beyond the lobby and the connected restaurant. The building, which overlooks the *Ceramics Museum* in the heart of the Old City, is the former palace of the Duke and Duchess of Cardona, and is a historical landmark. Its sunlit restaurant is elegant, with classy if slightly stuffy service — an especially pleasant place for a lingering breakfast. All 62 rooms have color television sets. 6 Calle Marqués de Dos Aguas (phone: 351-6426). Moderate.

Llar – Cheerful, helpful service, an ideal location for those who aren't set on staying smack-dab in the Old City, and unusually homey wood-and-plaster rooms. This 50-room establishment is located on the artery of a bustling and upscale shopping district, where designer boutiques and quality department stores compete for the milling crowds, but it is neither noisy nor unpleasantly busy. No more than a 10-minute walk to almost anywhere in the city, less to most places. 46 Calle Colón (phone: 352-8460). Moderate.

Alcázar – Offering 18 quiet rooms just off the Plaza del Ayuntamiento, easily located by a huge and somewhat garish 4-story sign hanging out over the street. The rooms are small and a bit depressing, but it's hard to beat the price. The larger part of the establishment is a 2-story restaurant specializing in popular Valencian and Spanish dishes; the tavern downstairs, hung with hams, is particularly charming. Try the *tapas* and shellfish on display under glass at the bar. 11 Calle Mosén Femades (phone: 351-5551). Inexpensive.

Castelar – At the foot of the Plaza del Ayuntamiento, this family-run property offers 17 clean, comfortable rooms for less than half the price of similar digs across the street at the much larger *Europa*. Each room has running water; the shared bathrooms are well maintained and clean. 1 Calle Ribera (phone: 351-3199). Inexpensive.

 EATING OUT: Valencia is home to Spain's most internationally famous dish of all — paella — and the city's restaurants compete vigorously with one another to concoct the most delightful examples of this rice plate. Paella was originally a peasant's dish, rice with whatever happened to be at hand; but today, it can come with shellfish, rabbit, chicken, lobster, snails, eels, and more. Other delicious rice dishes, based like paella on the paddies of the wetlands around the Albufera National Park south of Valencia, include *arroz a banda* (rice with fish, garlic, onion, tomato, and saffron); *arroz en bledes* (rice with stewed cabbage, tomato, red peppers, white beans, and garlic); and *arroz al forn* (rice cooked in an oven casserole with chickpeas, potatoes, garlic, paprika, and sometimes pork ribs). *Fideuà,* a paella in which vermicelli is used in place of saffron rice, is the rage among Valencia's contemporary master chefs, and should be sampled. All vegetables in the region — not to mention the ubiquitous citrus fruits, which are best from December through March — are likely to be excellent, as they come straight from the fertile *huerta* that surrounds the city. Another local delight is *horchata,* a cold, refreshing summer drink made with *chufas* (earth almonds), water, and sugar; the best way to sample it is in the cafeterias and orchards of Alboraya, the village — about 4 miles (6 km) north of Valencia — where it's made. A local pastry is *mona de pascua,* a spongy *Easter* cake. The region's wines are many, with a tendency to the slightly sweet, but none has so far received much recognition elsewhere. Note that good restaurants in Valencia are not concentrated in the Old City, and several are in the port of El Grao. Expect to pay $75 or more for a meal for two with wine in restaurants listed as expensive, $44 to $75 in moderate restaurants, and $40 or less at inexpensive ones. All telephone numbers are in the 6 city code unless otherwise indicated.

Eladio – Eladio, the Swiss-trained owner, is a master of fish — hake, sea bass, angler, turbot, and sole, which he brings south from the stormy Atlantic waters off his native Galicia. The menu occasionally verges on nouvelle cuisine but generally sticks to European and Galician dishes. Try the *pulpo a la gallega* (Galician octopus), and don't miss the pastries prepared by Eladio's wife, Violette Fontaine. Closed Sundays and August. Reservations necessary. 40 Calle Chiva (phone: 326-2244). Expensive.

La Hacienda – A few steps outside the city's old east gate, serving Spanish dishes and other selections in an atmosphere of mirrored walls and elegant old furniture. The *rabo de toro a la cordobesa* (oxtail stew, Cordoban style) is renowned, and game, in general, is very good. Closed Saturday afternoons, Sundays, and *Holy Week*. Reservations advised. 12 Avenida Navarro Reverter (phone: 373-1859). Expensive.

Ma Cuina – Valencians still flock here, but it's no longer considered the best place in town. The Basque and Valencian cooking remains delightful, however, and private dining rooms are still available. Very much worth a visit. Closed Sundays. Reservations advised. 49 Gran Vía Germanias (phone: 341-7799). Expensive.

Marisquería Civera – Without a doubt, the best shellfish in the city — and that probably goes for the fish, too. There's a galaxy of seafood and vegetable *tapas* laid out on the counters, all absolutely fresh. Closed Mondays. This *marisquería*, or shellfishery, is always busy, so go early or make reservations. Across the Serranos Bridge, at 11 Calle Lérida (phone: 347-5917). Expensive.

El Gourmet – Consistently fine Spanish and continental food, coupled with excellent service, have made this place one of Valencia's most popular. Try some of chef Jaime Capilla's specialties: *revueltos de berenjenas con gambas* (scrambled eggs with eggplant and shrimp), *merluza con almejas* (hake with clams), and *perdiz moscovita al hojaldre* (Muscovy partridge in pastry), among others. Closed Sundays and mid-August through mid-September. Reservations advised. 3 Calle Taquígrafo Martí (phone: 374-5071). Moderate.

Lionel – A dining room that is meant to reflect elegant French turn-of-the-century style, it is pleasant but perhaps a bit grandmotherly. Usually good are the home-made soup, croquettes, partridge, and rabbit. The kitchen specializes in duck and turkey dishes, but tends to overcook both. Service is adequate. Closed Saturdays at lunch and Sunday evenings. Reservations advised on weekends. 9 Calle Pizarro (phone: 351-6566). Moderate.

La Marcelina – In a row of several dozen restaurants lining the beach near the port of El Grao, this is one of the more famous of Valencia's old beach establishments, having made a remarkable comeback recently after years of decline. For more than a century, it has been offering great paellas and, in summer, music on an outdoor terrace. Closed Sundays in summer. Reservations unnecessary except Saturday evenings in summer. 10 Avenida del Neptuno (phone: 371-2025). Moderate.

Nevada – In 1979, this hidden treasure won the international prize for *fideuà*, and, if anything since then, its offering has improved. An excellent — and exceedingly fairly priced — place to sample Valencian rice dishes. Try *arroz al horno, arroz negro con chipirones* (black rice with squid), or *arroz al marisco* (shellfish and rice). Closed Tuesdays and Sunday evenings (all day Sunday during summer). In a nondescript residential neighborhood. No reservations. 53 Avenida Fernando el Católico (phone: 325-5152). Moderate.

La Pepica – This grand old eatery is on the beach next to *La Marcelina* and is known as *the* lunchtime spot for paella and other Valencian rice dishes. Walk past the great open kitchen, hung with hundreds of black paella pans, and into a spacious dining room overlooking a white sand beach (there are outdoor tables in summer). Open daily; closed November. No reservations. 6-8 Avenida del Neptuno (phone: 371-0366). Moderate.

La Riuà – *Arroz a banda* (rice with seafood) is Pilar Lozano's specialty, and although only men are supposed to be Valencia's greatest rice chefs, she is an exception. Two different rice dishes are served daily, 12 a week, in a three-level dining room lavishly decorated with glazed tiles and handicrafts and located in the heart of the Old City. Seafood dishes also are very good, and the *menú del día* (menu of the day) is a bargain. Closed Sunday evenings (all day Sunday during summer), *Holy Week,* and August 15 through the first week in September. Reservations advised on weekends. 27 Calle Mar (phone: 331-7172). Moderate.

L'Estimat – Also in the port of El Grao, specializing in Valencian rice dishes, with its own circle of fans who swear it's the best. Closed Tuesdays and September. Reservations advised. 18 Avenida del Neptuno (phone: 371-1018). Inexpensive.

Los Madriles – Pablo Martínez opened this small Castilian restaurant in 1964, and it has since become a favorite of Valencia's bullfighting aficionados, serving such Madrid regional specialties as *cocido* (chickpea stew), *cordero al horno* (oven-baked lamb), and *ternera en su jugo* (veal in its own juices). Good rioja wines are served in a humble but charming atmosphere under walls of bullfight posters. Closed Sunday evenings (all day Sunday during summer), August, and *Holy Week.* Reservations unnecessary. 50 Avenida de Antic Regne de Valencia (phone: 374-2335). Inexpensive.

La Montaraza – Spanish cooking with good roast meats and sausages at a fair price. Closed for dinner on Sundays and holidays; in summer, closed all day Sunday. No reservations. 47 Calle Olta (phone: 373-1653). Inexpensive.

Rue de la Paix – Decent, reasonably priced French cooking that's even less expensive if ordered from the *menú del día.* Closed Saturdays at lunch and all day Sundays. Reservations unnecessary. 18 Calle de la Paz (phone: 351-2610). Inexpensive.

 TAPAS BARS: The best way to sample *tapas* is to go on a *tapeo* — a round-robin tour of *tapas* bars. Valencia's leading *tapas* streets are Calle Mosén Femades, just off the Plaza del Ayuntamiento, and Calles Ribera and Convento Jerusalén. *Taberna Alcázar* (9 Calle Mosén Femades; phone: 352-9575) is a rustic and charming bar in the hotel and restaurant of the same name (the dining room is upstairs and the hotel is next door); its old wooden bar practically groans under the weight of the colorful offering of *tapas.* At *Trocadero* (3 Plaza del Ayuntamiento; phone: 351-7582), another of the city's busier *tapas* spots, try a *ración* (larger than a *tapa*) of one of the rice specialties or the wonderful anchovies in vinegar. Mushroom *tapas* are especially good at *Amorós* (3 Calle Llop; phone: 351-7057), centrally located and sometimes thronged; while *Casa Mario* (3 Calle Roteros; phone: 331-7006). in the offbeat and increasingly interesting Barrio del Carmen near the Serranos Towers, does a terrific job serving shellfish *tapas* and *raciones. Glorieta* (1 Calle General Tovar; phone: 321-2687) is centrally located at the east end of Calle de la Paz. On October 14, 1957, the worst floods in Valencian memory reached a level about 9 feet up the wall in this charming corner bar, lit beautifully by a full-length window. Look up above the bar to the left for the commemorative plaque.

DIVERSIONS

For the Experience

Quintessential Spain and Portugal

 The Iberian Peninsula is like a hypothetical aisle marked "Experience" in a choice-laden supermarket — full of good things that come in a variety of enticing packages. So just as sherry comes in *fino, amontillado, manzanilla,* and *dulce,* flamenco can be either raucous side-street strumming, a tourist sideshow in Granada's Sacromonte Caves, or a whirl-perfect spectacle on a limelighted Madrid stage. Gazpacho can be eaten with a spoon or drunk with a straw, and there are endless varieties of seafood, from the hearty cod stews of the Basque Country to fresh, grilled tuna (with just a squirt of lemon juice) in the Algarve to the elaborate mussel-and-shrimp paella of Valencia. Nor do all Spaniards speak Castilian. There is the "s"-less Andalusian sing-song, a different form of Catalan on each Balearic Island, and the exotic language of the Basques, called Euskera, that isn't related to anything else on this planet.

Iberia's range of flavors comes from its capacity for absorption. One of Spain's most characteristic painters was a Greek (El Greco), the Bourbon dynasty was French, and an American popularized Pamplona's *Fiesta de San Fermín* (in recognition of which the city named a square for him — Plaza Hemingway). The New World sent the old one tomatoes, potatoes, coffee, and the gold that decorated Toledan swords, and made Lisbon and Madrid the most powerful cities in Europe. Africa gave Spain and Portugal an architectural heritage, the microtonal wail of both Spanish flamenco and Portuguese *fado,* and an often crushing heat that spawned such relaxing institutions as the afternoon siesta, the evening *paseo,* the strategically placed café, and the evening gathering around the motor scooter in a small town square.

Still, there are several things that capture the special spirit of this singular peninsula, and provide a visitor with an insight into its irresistible personality.

OPENING NIGHT AT THE LICEU AND DINNER AT SET PORTES, Barcelona, Spain: Behind a façade made drab by a layer of 20th-century soot, the interior of the *Gran Teatre del Liceu,* one of Europe's great opera houses, gleams with the polish, plushness, and crystal sparkle that was the hallmark of the 19th century. Almost every Spaniard sings, but see if the concierge at your hotel can wheedle tickets to hear homespun pro Placido Domingo do a slow burn at the Royal Tobacco Factory in *Carmen,* that quintessentially Spanish story of smoldering sex, jealousy, and clicking castanets. The warbles and guitar twangs that float down the alleyways of the Barri Gòtic are reminders that a Spain filled with melody is not just a figment of Bizet's fantasy. When you emerge, it still may be a little early to eat, so join the rest of the city for a languid amble along La Rambla. On a cool, clear night, the pedestrian traffic on this thoroughfare lined with bookstands and birdstalls may be at a standstill, as bench-sitters, browsers, and boulevardiers jostle through the midnight ritual of strolling and stopping and doffing of caps. Wend your way to the waterfront and to *Set Portes* (see *Best Restaurants of Spain and Portugal,* in this section), where a jovial roar and a tinkling piano fill the huge dining rooms, and the clientele seems to have been sitting at the same leisurely Catalan dinner since the restaurant's opening in 1836. Try the braised partridge, the *zarzuela* (a local, family-size version of bouillabaisse), or the *escalivada* (a cold, roast vegetable platter).

BULLFIGHT IN PAMPLONA, Navarre, Spain: This Sunday ritual, heralded by fanfare and pomp, is an assault on all the senses: the ocher turf glaring in the late afternoon sun; the band's tinny blare; the gaudy, spangled costumes of the procession; the *bandilleros'* ballet; the coarse, feverish crowd watering its passion with warm wine squirted from bulging skins; the black bull's thundering fury; the arrogant grace of the matador; the swirl of the red *muleta,* the flash and plunge of the sword blade. This celebration of blood and manhood, idly watched on television in living rooms and bars all over Spain, is a reminder of the time when Christians dueled lions in a Colosseum full of Romans. Like an emperor decreeing mercy or death for a gladiator with a flick of his thumb, the president of the *corrida* rewards the matador by tossing him one or two ears of the vanquished bull or, for extremely glorious displays of virtuosity, the tail. The animals receive a measure of revenge during the *Fiesta de San Fermín,* in July (see "The Best Festivals" in *For the Mind*), when they manage to gore a handful of the hundreds of brave (or crazy) men who, dressed in white with red sashes around their waists, race before the bulls through the streets of the city to the *Plaza de Toros.*

LONELY ARAB CASTLES OF ANDALUSIA, Spain: It takes a car, a sharp eye, a love of detours, and a well-stocked picnic hamper to find the romantic, weed-strewn ruins of castles that once guarded every hill and port in Arab Al-Andalus. Perched on crag-tops that look stormable only by eagles, these worn, but still stern, battlements formed a Maginot Line along the tense border between the Muslim and Christian worlds of long ago, where the names of towns still bear the epithet *de la frontera* ("on the border"). But this martial past acquires a latter-day peaceful haze if the scant remains are contemplated with the benefit of a bottle of wine, a hunk of *manchego* cheese, some smoky slices of *jamón serrano,* and a handful of Spanish olives. Because the road to the top can be nearly vertical, it's probably best to leave the car in the olive grove or by the cluster of whitewashed houses that invariably cower in the castle's shadow. Count on being alone at the top, except perhaps for a state employee who is likely to be as lonely as the ruins he guards and will be more than happy to point out the storerooms, the water drains, the narrow, L-shaped passageways meant to thwart a battering ram, the direction from which the Christians finally came, the best angle for a snapshot, and the precise plot in the distant cemetery where his grandfather is buried.

TAPAS AND PATIOS, Córdoba, Andalusia, Spain: The glare of the southern sun and the heady odor of orange blossoms are everywhere in Córdoba, settling on the city, seeping from the cobblestones, sliding through the painted shutters, making everyone sleepy and sultry and hot. A *tapas* (Spanish smorgasbord) bar is the perfect refuge for sodden sightseers and lounging locals, who gather in the grudging breeze from a creaking electric fan, nursing chilled sangría and gazpacho. Beneath the glass counter are countless accompaniments to a glass of beer — marinated mushrooms, shrimp in garlic sauce, olives seasoned with thyme, fried squid, bits of sausage, roasted sweet peppers with olive oil, smoked ham, spicy meatballs — all available in the mouthful-size portions that make them *tapas* and not a meal. Throughout the day, the floor becomes littered with shrimp tails, toothpicks, and crumpled paper napkins, and when, periodically, the counterman sweeps up this traditional litter, the customers do a distracted dance around the broom that is as much a part of Spanish culinary culture as the *seguidilla* (flamenco song and dance). For those who can bring themselves to step out into the sticky Andalusian summer, occasional cool gusts of comfort come from the patios not quite hidden behind wrought-iron grilles or wooden doors left ajar just enough for one to peer in and breathe deeply. Geraniums, jasmine, and lemon trees lovingly arranged against patterned, tiled walls offer sun-stroked visitors a fresh, perfumed caress. The lushest and most colorful patios win prizes in the city's 2-week *Fiesta de los Patios* in May (see "The Best Festivals" in *For the Mind*).

FLAMENCO IN THE BARRIO TRIANA, Seville, Spain: The impromptu stomp, strum, snap, clap, and growl gets going around 1 or 2 AM in the working-class district of Triana, with all the spark and ancient pathos of those Gypsy blues. The patrons of the slightly seedy bars along the Calle Salado bring their own guitars and tambourines — the dancing is unrefined and improvised, and the singing is soulful and throaty. Flamenco grew out of a mixture of Jewish liturgical chants, the call of the Moorish muezzin, and plaintive Gypsy folk tunes, catalyzed by the Inquisition into a music of guttural sounds lamenting the fate of the heathen in brutally Catholic Spain. Now that the Word is no longer spread by the pyre, singers moan more about music and lust, and syncopated clapping and flashy fingerwork have replaced campfire thrumming. But while the high artistry of the song and dance performances — *tablaos* — in the more gentrified Barrio de Santa Cruz, for which foreigners pay a pricey cover charge, can also be heard at *Carnegie Hall,* this, with its rough edges and drinking and picking of pockets, is the real thing.

ON HORSEBACK THROUGH EXTREMADURA, Spain: Alhough the name just means "beyond the Duero River," it seems apt for this remote and *duro* (tough) region, where the local specialties are black-bull steaks and cured hams made from snake-fed pigs. Ride here in the spring, before the heat has burned away the tapestry of flowers and turned the rich, red soil a cracked and sunbaked brown. At a leisurely canter, you can't help but savor the cork woods and chestnut groves that motorists mostly miss on their way to the hilltop monasteries of Guadalupe and Yuste. And in some parts, you and your mounts will be the only visitors — few cars ever make it up the stomach-tightening curves through the rugged forests of Las Hurdes, the northernmost part of Extremadura, populated by the Spanish equivalent of hillbillies. There is some poetic justice in the stares you will attract as you ride into a dusty shepherd town, for it was Extremaduran peasants-turned-conquerors who rode the first horses off Spanish galleons and into the New World — and were taken for half-equine gods.

THE ROYALTY TRAIL, Castile-León, Spain: Like children romping in a playroom shin-deep in toys, the Kings and Queens of Spain scattered palaces, gardens, and summer retreats all over Castile. They all can be visited, but take it slow, because if you try to retrace the dainty steps of royalty in one whirlwind day, your tour will meld into a sumptuous haze of polished wood and tarnished mirrors and the very chair where Carlos the Somethingth sat. Start at the *Prado,* once the storehouse for the king's art collection, to see court life through Diego Velázquez's keen, cruel eye for the pomposity, frills, and formalities of the 17th century. His portraits of the royal family and paintings such as *Las Meninas* (The Maids of Honor) seem like virtual anthropological studies of how the other half a handful live. The itinerary then spirals out from King Juan Carlos's current throne room in Madrid's Palacio Real, swooping through extremes of opulence: the once suburban, still idyllic Parque del Retiro; the tapestried walls of El Pardo; the passionate austerity of the royal monastery of El Escorial, glowing fervently in its halo of mountains; the fussy weave of graveled walks and marble stairways at Aranjuez; the bursting geyser fountain at La Granja de San Ildefonso, outside Segovia.

MID-ATLANTIC HONEYMOON, Flores, Azores, Portugal: Somewhere between Lisbon and New York, the Azores roll like a cluster of billiard balls in the pool-table green waves of the Atlantic. The island of Flores is the spot to get stranded for a week or two in another century, to kick up your heels or kick off your shoes and wade through the wildflowers that give this remote fleck of land its name. It is the westernmost island of this westernmost outpost of Europe, but still close enough to the New World to have been the site of a battle between Confederate and Union gunboats during the Civil War. Yet this velvet archipelago, brilliantly embroidered with azaleas, hydrangeas, and lemon-yellow 16th-century churches, may be more Portuguese than mainland Portugal itself. Here, where windmills and bell towers still define the skyline, devotion is even stronger, the waterfalls even clearer, the hairpin curves even hairier. While the quaintness of mainland towns may now be somewhat packaged for the benefit of foreigners, the economy of Azorean villages is still tied to the land and sea.

CLIMBING THE BEANSTALK TO SINTRA, Portugal: After a day spent among the gritty realities of Lisbon, it's just a whoosh up the beanstalk to the mist-shrouded fairyland of Sintra. This town that floats above the mortal world sports a glorious mishmash of extravagant styles, from the time-torn towers of an ancient Moorish castle, to the lacy Mudéjar and frilly baroque of the Palácio Nacional de Sintra and the eccentric turrets and domes of the Bavarian-kitsch Palácio Nacional da Pena. You can sleep, dine, or just have a drink in the *Palácio dos Seteais,* once the country retreat of the Dutch consul; its marbled floors and muraled halls are a fine example of 18th-century Dutch Diplomatic–deco. The eclectic architecture of this medieval town narrates the passing of peoples through Portugal and, as if the country had also been colonized by a series of foreign plant kingdoms, the Parque da Pena is the meeting place for an international crowd of shrubs, trees, and flowers, all kept moist and luxuriant by the fine spray from the obliging Atlantic down below.

EXPLORING THE END OF THE WORLD, Sagres, Algarve, Portugal: Here, where navigators once thought land ended and the ocean dropped into nothingness, it is worth trying to catch both ends of the day. So get up early, while the lighthouse at the tip of Cabo de São Vicente still beams its comforting nightlight out to exotic pleasure boats and local trawlers. Go sit on the sharp, pointy rocks beneath Henry the Navigator's clifftop fortress at Sagres, where fishermen cast their lines into the surging froth, and watch the sun's first beams light up the ancient trade routes to the Orient. And when the cool air begins to vibrate with the summer heat, head a few miles north to stretch out on the beach at Carrapateira, wide enough so that there is no need to stake out shoreline turf in meager deck-chair widths even in the highest season. On this wind-cooled coast, your skin may burn before you feel it, so stuff your towels in the trunk, roll back the sunroof, and drive into the wooded hills of Monchique and up to the 3,000-foot peaklet of Fóia, from which, if you squint a little, you can convince yourself your eyes are good enough to see the Moroccan coast. Spend the hottest part of the day napping under a cypress tree, or sipping a glass of *vinho verde* in the shaded main square of Caldas de Monchique. But make it back to the coast in time to curl your toes in the sand and watch the blood-orange sun slip off the edge of the Earth. Then end the day with a platter of grilled sardines or tuna in one of the small, smoky restaurants in which the owner is also both waiter and chef.

Paradores and Pousadas

 No visit to the Iberian Peninsula is complete without a visit or an overnight stay in a Spanish *parador,* a Portuguese *pousada,* or even a manor house. Imagine sleeping where kings and queens slept, walking corridors and chambers where Franciscan monks walked, and dining in elegant rooms where nobles and aristocrats sat down to countless formal meals over the centuries. The Spanish and Portuguese people pride themselves on their rich sense of such traditions, and have impeccably restored and converted ancient landmark castles and monasteries into magnificent hotel accommodations, offering travelers a historic return to the past, complete with modern — and often luxurious — facilities.

Spain's first *parador* (an inn that offers food and shelter to travelers) was introduced west of Madrid in the Sierra de Gredos in 1928, when King Alfonso XIII opened a lodge to be used primarily as a base for hunting excursions. This concept of low-cost accommodation became so popular that it eventually expanded into the world's most successful transformation of long-abandoned national treasures. Of the 86 *paradores* in the countrywide network today, many are restored convents, palaces, and castles, filled with original decorations and antiques. It's not unusual to be escorted past standing figures in coats of armor, or up winding stone staircases past hanging wrought-iron lanterns. Other *paradores* are constructed of gleaming marble and boast the latest modern touches — including indoor and outdoor swimming pools, golf courses, and other sports facilities. All have fine restaurants serving breakfast, lunch, and dinner; most serve regional specialties and carry wine bottled under their own labels. The restaurants are of simple design and usually match the *parador*'s overall decor.

Not all *paradores* are for everyone. About 90% of the rooms are doubles furnished with twin beds. Travelers who want a double bed should request a room with a *cama de matrimonio*, but be advised that normally there are only a few per *parador*. Some *paradores* are low-key, and may be considered too remote (or too dull for a traveler seeking continuous activity). Not every room in every *parador* has a television set or a radio, and many are located on the outskirts of town (requiring a car to get to most sightseeing stops). Travelers unable to climb stairs should inquire about elevators, since some *paradores* do not have easy access to all rooms and public areas.

Reservations for *paradores* in or near major cities such as Toledo, Segovia, and Granada should be made well in advance. Although it is possible to travel through Spain from *parador* to *parador* without reservations, this practice is not recommended. Ask the *parador* concierge to phone ahead to determine availability and to make reservations. Rates are seasonal in the majority of the *paradores*, but also can be one price year-round in the more popular ones. Low season runs from November through March, mid-season is from April through June, and high season is from July through October. Expect to pay between $75 and $150 for a double room. This rate includes breakfast, taxes, and service charges. For more information about the *paradores* of Spain, contact *Paradores del Estado* (18 Calle Velázquez, Madrid 28001, Spain; phone: 1-435-9700), or the network's US representative, *Marketing Ahead* (433 Fifth Ave., New York, NY 10016; phone: 212-686-9213).

In Portugal, the choices are similar. The country began its *pousada* program in 1940, and today there are 32 government *pousadas,* including 2 on the island of Madeira. Nine *pousadas* are restored castles, 16 are modern hotels, and the remainder are small country inns. Their sizes range from 6 to 54 rooms. All are meticulously clean and decorated with attractive furnishings from various centuries. As with Spain's *paradores, pousada* restaurants emphasize regional foods and wines. Rates for a double room, including continental breakfast, range from $42 to $126 per night, depending on category and season. Low season runs from November through March, shoulder seasons are from April through June and all of October, and high season is from July through September. There is a 3-night maximum-stay policy (exceptions are permitted in some cases) throughout the *pousada* network. For more information, contact *Enatur* (10-A Avenida Santa Joana a Princesa, Lisbon 1100, Portugal; phone: 1-881221); the *Portuguese National Tourist Office* (590 Fifth Ave., New York, NY 10036; phone: 212-354-4403); or the network's US representative, *Marketing Ahead* (433 Fifth Ave., New York, NY 10016; phone: 212-686-9213).

Another option, in Portugal, is to sleep in a manor house, perhaps the *casa, solar,* or *quinta* of one of the country's oldest families. Such aristocratic accommodations are the province of Portugal's *Tourism in the Country* program, a network of privately owned rural properties that take in paying guests. Begun in the 1980s, the program includes three types of properties. Travelers bent on lodgings with recognized architectural merit or a historic past should investigate the manor houses and country estates gathered under the heading of *Turismo de Habitação*. Billing as *Turismo Rural* or

Agroturismo means less imposing — although equally traditional — houses or rustic farmhouses. Happily, it is the top-of-the-line manor house that is in greatest supply, particularly in northern Portugal. In most cases, the owner lives in the house with his family, but can no longer keep up with the large expense of running such an estate. (Some simply enjoy the company of foreign travelers.) Guest quarters are almost always separate and private, sometimes in apartments and adjoining cottages. Some properties have a swimming pool and tennis courts, while others have stables for horseback riding. Many owners help with sightseeing arrangements. The majority of the owners speak English, as well as other languages.

A complete listing of houses is available from the Portuguese National Tourist Office. A 2-month advance notice for booking is usually required. When booking, provide as much information about the intended visit as possible. Prices range from approximately $35 to $65 for two people per night, breakfast included, depending on the type of lodging. The availability of other meals varies from house to house, at the discretion of the owner. A 2- or 3-day minimum stay is usually required. For more information, contact *Direcção-Geral do Turismo* (86 Avenida António Augusto de Aguiar, Lisbon 1000, Portugal; phone: 1-575015). Bookings can be made directly with the houses or through owners' associations. Many houses in the north are represented by the *Associação de Turismo de Habitação* (Praça da República, Ponte de Lima 4990, Portugal; phone: 58-942335 or 58-942729). Others throughout the country are represented by the *Promoções e Ideias Turísticas* (Alto da Pampilheira, Torre D-2 8-A, Cascais 2750, Portugal; phone: 1-284-4464 or 1-286-7958), or by the *Associação Portuguesa de Turismo de Habitação (Privetur)* (209 Rua Castilho, Lisbon 1000, Portugal; for reservations call 1-654953).

PARADOR DE ALMAGRO, Almagro, Castile–La Mancha, Spain: Don Quixote loved the region of La Mancha, and so will any guest staying in this former 15th-century Franciscan convent. The elegant touches of this 55-room *parador* recall the building's original functions, and it also features 16 courtyards and patios, gardens, a wine cellar, a swimming pool, and a convention hall. Note, however, that the beds are of hammock configuration. From May through October, Almagro's main square becomes an open-air theater for classical works performed by topnotch national and international companies. The town is also famous for its lace. Information: *Parador de Almagro,* Calle Ronda de San Francisco, Almagro 13270, Spain (phone: 26-860100).

PARADOR ALCÁZAR DEL REY DON PEDRO, Carmona, near Seville, Andalusia, Spain: This majestic *parador,* the former 14th-century retreat of King Pedro the Cruel, overlooks the lush green countryside below, where cows graze and farmers plow. The high-ceilinged dining room, with its coats of arms and huge paintings, is fit for a king. There is also a lovely Moorish garden full of colorful tiles and bright yellow seats, an excellent spot to sit and sip a drink of sherry, special to the region. The 59 rooms are immaculate but otherwise routine. Information: *Parador Alcázar del Rey Don Pedro,* Carmona 41410, Spain (phone: 5-414-1010).

PARADOR DE CHINCHÓN, Chinchón, near Madrid, Spain: This lovely village, only a half-hour's drive south of Madrid, is primarily known for its anisette liqueur, its *Holy Week* re-creation of the Crucifixion and the Resurrection, and its summer amateur bullfights in the main square. In 1982, the town's 17th-century convent was transformed into a 38-room *parador,* complete with settees, murals, wall tapestries, and other ornate furnishings. There's a wonderful glass-walled circular hallway overlooking a beautiful courtyard — a perfect spot for afternoon tea. The *parador* also boasts a chapel and garden with winding paths, plus a swimming pool and a convention hall. Information: *Parador de Chinchón,* 1 Avenida de Generalísimo, Chinchón 28370, Spain (phone: 1-894-0836).

PARADOR SAN FRANCISCO, Granada, Andalusia, Spain: Because Granada's Alhambra Palace is one of the most visited sites in Spain, it's no wonder that this *parador,* located within its sprawling complex, is booked months in advance. The building is a former Franciscan monastery, founded by Queen Isabella (she was even temporarily buried here) when she was in Granada with her husband, King Ferdinand, sending troops against the Moors. The 39-room *parador* has meandering corridors, carved bedroom doorways reminiscent of 18th-century monks' cells, and religious statues. Rich Moorish purples and golds decorate the public rooms. Other features include gardens, a convention hall, and an outdoor café overlooking the Alhambra. The wait for rooms is from 6 months to a year, depending on the season, but cancellations do come up; ask for a room in the old wing. Information: *Parador San Francisco,* Recinto de la Alhambra, Granada 18009, Spain (phone: 58-221440).

PARADOR ZURBARÁN, Guadalupe, Extremadura, Spain: Adventurous travelers should take a ride south from Oropesa to the town of Guadalupe to visit the Monasterio de Nuestra Señora de Guadalupe. A reported appearance of the Virgin Mary in 1300 on this site was the reason for the construction of the monastery. A statue of the Virgin (it had been buried in a nearby hillside for nearly 700 years) is enshrined on the altar. Pilgrims and tourists travel hundreds of miles to view the statue, and to examine the extensive collection of art by Francisco de Zurbarán, as well as embroideries, frontals, and precious stones. The 40-room *parador,* once a 15th-century hospice, is next door. The rooms look out over a central courtyard with Moorish-style gardens. Information: *Parador Zurbarán,* 10 Calle Marqués de la Romana, Guadalupe 10140, Spain (phone: 27-367075).

PARADOR DE SAN MARCOS, León, Castile-León, Spain: For centuries, Christians making their yearly pilgrimage to Santiago de Compostela used this majestic former hospice as a resting point. Travelers making the trek from Madrid to northern Spain today find this *parador,* with its 16th-century coffered ceiling, Plateresque exterior, and grand staircases, a perfect stop. The 253 rooms make it the largest property in the *parador* network. Facilities include gardens, a nightclub, hairdresser's salon, children's day-care center, and a convention hall. Information: *Parador de San Marcos,* 7 Plaza de San Marcos, León 24001, Spain (phone: 87-237300).

PARADOR VIRREY TOLEDO, Oropesa, near Toledo, Castile–La Mancha, Spain: According to legend, this massive medieval stone castle was built by Hercules' army, and later housed powerful Spanish and Moorish lords and kings. Today, it looms over a valley of squat olive trees and small farms. After a rain shower, the sweet smell of hay often wafts upward and into the 44 rooms. A short walk from Oropesa's Plaza Mayor, this *parador* is just 2 miles (3 km) away from the small town of Lagartera, famous for its lacework, where local women still sit outside their homes practicing this centuries-old craft. Information: *Parador Virrey Toledo,* 1 Plaza del Palacio, Oropesa 45560, Spain (phone: 25-430000).

PARADOR DE SALAMANCA, Salamanca, Castile-León, Spain: Opened a decade ago in response to the general mediocrity of this university city's hotels, this modern, multilevel, 108-room *parador* overlooks golden brick Salamanca and offers truly glorious views. Located on the outskirts of town, it features an outdoor swimming pool, a garden, and a convention hall. All rooms have glass-enclosed terraces with cushioned bamboo chairs — an excellent vantage point to watch the sunset, when Salamanca's buildings turn rich shades ranging from golden yellow to crimson. Information: *Parador de Salamanca,* 2 Calle Teso de la Feria, Salamanca 37008, Spain (phone: 23-268700).

PARADOR LOS REYES CATÓLICOS, Santiago de Compostela, Galicia, Spain: This magnificently decorated 15th-century former royal hospital and pilgrims' *hostal,* located in the Plaza del Obradoiro next to the cathedral, is now one of Spain's most memorable *paradores.* King Ferdinand and Queen Isabella personally made decisions about its interior details. The 157 elegant rooms, which feature canopied beds, antique desks, and individual safes, surround four splendid Renaissance courtyards and a chapel with a beamed ceiling and wrought-iron grill. There are also shops, a garden, a nightclub, and concert, conference, and exhibition halls. Information: *Parador Los Reyes Católicos,* Plaza de Obradoiro, Santiago de Compostela 15705, Spain (phone: 81-582200).

PARADOR DE SANTILLANA DEL MAR, Santillana del Mar, Cantabria, Spain: A graceful manor house and former home of the local Barreda-Bracho family, this *parador* affords visitors the experience of typical life in this region centuries ago. The building is made of heavy stone walls and arches, and the 56 rooms feature wood-beamed ceilings, tile floors, gracious rustic furnishings, and spacious patios. Information: *Parador de Santillana del Mar,* 8 Plaza Ramón Pelayo, Santillana del Mar 39330, Spain (phone: 42-818000).

PARADOR DEL GOLF, Torremolinos, Andalusia, Spain: This 60-room *parador* is a golfer's paradise. The 18-hole course was designed by Robert Trent Jones, Sr., and it has a resident professional and a well-stocked pro shop. The *parador* is also a favorite of traveling and vacationing families, who enjoy its oceanfront location and its circular swimming pool. There are also tennis courts, a children's playground, a library, and gardens. Information: *Parador del Golf,* Apartado 324, Torremolinos, Málaga 29620, Spain (phone: 52-381255).

POUSADA SANTA MARINHA DA COSTA, Guimarães, Costa Verde, Portugal: The largest of all the *pousadas.* Once a 14th-century monastery, it changed owners continuously through the centuries until finally it was sold to a private family. They kept it until the 1940s and, as a game, often rode horses throughout the long hallways. At the end of one hallway was a fountain and a terrace, which still overlooks the entire town. A chapel is next door. Abandoned in the 1940s, and almost destroyed by fire, it was eventually taken over by the government and restored into a 55-room *pousada.* Information: *Pousada Santa Marinha da Costa,* Estrada da Penha, Guimarães 4800, Portugal (phone: 53-418453).

POUSADA DO CASTELO, Obidos, Costa de Prata, Portugal: If Portugal ever had fair maidens scanning the horizons for their returning heroes, surely they sat in the towers of this former castle, located in the picture-perfect village of Obidos. About 60 miles (96 km) north of Lisbon, the town was a traditional wedding gift of the King of Portugal to his bride. An ideal transformation of one wing of the castle has created a 9-room *pousada,* including 3 tower suites. The cobblestone courtyard and thick granite stairways are tasteful reminders of its storybook history. The antique furnishings also tell a tale of age, honor, and strong Portuguese heritage. Outside, the views of the surrounding farmlands are breathtaking. Information: *Pousada do Castelo,* Obidos 2510, Portugal (phone: 62-959105).

POUSADA SÃO FILIPE, Setúbal, near Lisbon, Portugal: This former 16th-century castle sits atop a hill and overlooks a busy, picturesque waterfront. Inside, the chapel walls boast hand-painted blue tiles depicting scenes from the life of São Filipe and the Virgin Mary. Just a 1-hour drive from Lisbon, this 14-room *pousada* is popular with weekend travelers. The town of Setúbal is itself an attraction worth seeing; it was once an important center of Catholicism, having as many as 13 convents and monasteries. Information: *Pousada São Filipe,* Setúbal 2900, Portugal (phone: 65-23844).

POUSADA DOS LÓIOS, Evora, Alto Alentejo, Portugal: The Portuguese call Evora their "museum city" because of its ancient origins and numerous monuments. The university here dates to the 16th century, and the individual wall tiles depict the subject taught in each room. This 32-room *pousada* in the center of town was once the 15th-century monastery of the Lóios Order. Today's weary and pensive traveler will feel refreshed in the cloisters within the walls. Information: *Pousada dos Lóios,* Evora 7000, Portugal (phone: 66-24051).

POUSADA DE SÃO BENTO, Caniçada, Costa Verde, Portugal: The feel of a

Swiss chalet and rustic mountain wilderness are what make this *pousada* an excellent diversion. In the Peneda-Gêres National Park, on a hilltop overlooking the Caniçada dam, this modern building has balconies with spectacular views. Bringing its guests close to the nature of Portugal, the 18-room *pousada* offers outdoor sports activities with local campers, hunters, riders, and mountain climbers; daily trips to the surrounding villages and the city of Braga also are available. Information: *Pousada de São Bento,* Caniçada, Vieira do Minho 4850, Portugal (phone: 53-647190).

POUSADA DO PICO DO ARIEIRO, Arieiro, Madeira, Portugal: Prepare for an ear-popping ride up the mountainside. All 18 rooms here have balconies commanding a view below that combines the pines and woodland on this hilly island and the beautiful expanse of the open sea stretching to the horizon. Comfortable rattan chairs and floral upholstery brighten the rather austere appearance of most of the rooms; the full-service restaurant features regional foods, with a heavy emphasis on fish. Definitely a place for the sports enthusiast, it offers nature hikes with English-speaking guides to Madeira's highest mountains, the nearby Pico do Arieiro and the Pico Ruivo. Information: *Pousada do Pico do Arieiro,* Funchal 9000, Madeira, Portugal (phone: 91-48188).

POUSADA DO INFANTE, Sagres, Algarve, Portugal: At the western end of the sunny, sandy Algarve coast is this small, 23-room *pousada* — so popular that rooms must be booked months in advance — named for Prince Henry the Navigator. Balconies overlook a grassy terrace and the sea, often dotted with small fishing boats. On cool winter nights, guests gather in front of the fireplace in the circular lounge, which extends from one end of the bar and into the dining room. The restaurant offers a variety of well-prepared fish dishes, and features an extensive Portuguese and international wine list. Information: *Pousada do Infante,* Sagres 8650, Portugal (phone: 82-64222).

QUINTA DE SÃO THIAGO, Sintra, near Lisbon, Portugal: An Englishman and his Spanish wife now own this centuries-old manor house, set in one of Portugal's beauty spots, the verdant Serra de Sintra. The house has 7 luxuriously furnished double rooms and 2 singles, all with private bath. There are also several quaint sitting rooms, a bar, a music room, a swimming pool, and 2 tennis courts. Information: *Maria Teresa Bradell, Quinta de São Thiago,* Sintra 2710, Portugal (phone: 1-923-2923).

QUINTA DE SANTO ANDRÉ, near Lisbon, Portugal: Just up the Tagus, outside Vila Franca de Xira, about 20 miles (32 km) from Lisbon, this lovely estate is in the midst of horse and cattle country, where Portugal's fighting bulls are raised. It's the perfect spot for travelers interested in horseback riding, because the *quinta* has its own stable and riding ring, with plenty of countryside to explore, both on the grounds and beyond. There are 4 double and 3 single rooms, numerous sitting rooms, and a swimming pool. Information: *Karl Gerhard Brumm, Quinta de Santo André,* Estrada de Monte Gordo, Vila Franca de Xira 2600, Portugal (phone: 63-22776 or 63-22143).

QUINTA DA PRAIA, near Lisbon, Portugal: This old country mansion overlooks the Tagus River and boasts 4 double rooms, 1 single room, huge sitting areas, beautiful gardens, and a swimming pool. Information: *José Gonçalves Gomes, Quinta da Praia,* Alcochete 2890, Portugal (phone: 1-603864 or 1-661648).

CASA DE CORTEGAÇA, Viana do Castelo, Costa Verde, Portugal: A historic 16th-century manor house on the left bank of the Lima River, it offers the ultimate in modern comforts, in a setting steeped in tradition. There are 4 double rooms, several sitting and dining rooms, a lovely garden, a farmhouse, and plenty of rippling streams to explore. Information: *Maria Filomena de Abreu Coutinho, Casa de Cortegaça,* Subportela, Viana do Castelo 4900, Portugal (phone: 58-971639).

CASA DO ANTEPAÇO, near Ponte de Lima, Costa Verde, Portugal: This restored stone house combines the qualities of the past with the comforts of the present and provides a peaceful atmosphere in rural surroundings. There are 4 large double rooms, a living room with a fireplace, a library, a garden, and a terrace offering superb views of the Lima River. Information: *Dr. Francisco de Abreu Lima, Casa do Antepaço,* Ponte de Lima 4990, Portugal (phone: 52-941702; bookings through 58-942729).

CASA DO AMEAL, Viana do Castelo, Costa Verde, Portugal: A manor house whose long aristocratic pedigree explains the almost museum-like display of antiques and memorabilia that it contains, it has 4 double rooms and 2 apartments (each for 4 people) with private baths, sitting rooms, and pleasant gardens and grounds. Information: *Maria Elisa Araújo, Casa do Ameal,* Meadela, Viana do Castelo 4900, Portugal (phone: 58-22403).

CASA DO SABUGUEIRO, Sabugueiro, Beira Alta, Portugal: Situated in a lofty village in the Serra da Estrela, this typical village house still maintains and operates a *queijaria* (cheese dairy), as well as a traditional oven used to bake corn and rye bread. There is a special "tasting" room, where guests can sample the breads as well as the local serra cheese. The house offers 2 double rooms, a bathroom (shared), and a quaint living room with a fireplace. Information: *Teresa da Graça Trindade, Casa do Sabugueiro,* Sabugueiro, Seia 6270, Portugal (phone: 38-22825).

QUINTA DA PONTE, Faia, Beira Alta, Portugal: This imposing manor house with 3 double rooms and a deluxe suite, all with private baths, is a good base from which to explore the Serra da Estrela. Information: *Mary Alvim, Quinta da Ponte, Faia,* Celorico da Beira 6360, Portugal (phone: 71-685597).

CASA DA PALMEIRA, near Evora, Alto Alentejo, Portugal: This turn-of-the-century mansion has 8 double rooms, a sitting room, and a dining room, all characteristic of its original architecture. There is also a lovely garden. Information: *Fernando Nunes Gonçalves, Casa da Palmeira,* Praça de Santo António, Reguengos de Monsaraz 7200, Portugal (phone: 66-52362).

The Best Restaurants of Spain and Portugal

When it comes to dining, Spaniards seem to have it all: Thousands of restaurants throughout the country's 52 provinces feature a vast repertoire of their own delicious specialties — from seafood, meats, and fowl to fruit, vegetables, and fine wines — with all the flavor (and often only a fraction of the calories) found in the dishes of many other European countries. But don't confuse "Spanish food" with hot and spicy Mexican-style dishes: The Spanish are strangers to piquant seasonings. They also insist on *materia prima,* or wholesome, chemical-free ingredients — most dishes are olive oil and garlic based.

Though many regional specialties have become countrywide — even worldwide — favorites, nothing can replace the mystique of eating regional food on its home ground. Castile's local cooking is king, even in cosmopolitan Madrid, but the word *vasco* (Basque) crops up in restaurant names everywhere. Many of Spain's best chefs come from the Basque Country, renowned for its hundreds of all-male, members-only cooking clubs. And then there is paella, the communal pan of creamy, short-grained, saffron-flavored rice, crusty from a wood-burning fire, which is served all over Spain in varying delectable combinations of seafood, sausage, poultry, and vegetables.

Portuguese food also offers a surprising variety of tastes. Over the centuries, this seagoing nation's cuisine has come under the influence of far-flung countries in Asia, Africa, and the Americas, as well as neighboring Spain and nearby France. The Portuguese love affair with the sea and its bounty is intense. Of all fish, *bacalhau* (codfish) is dearest to the Portuguese palate. *Caldeirada* (fish stew) is another popular seafood dish; its content varies from region to region and with the day's catch, but a good *caldeirada* should include about nine varieties of fish and shellfish, including clams, mussels, squid, and octopus. Carnivores need not despair, as meat dishes and stews, such as *cozido à portuguesa* (made of meats, sausages, and vegetables), are equally abundant.

ELDORADO PETIT, Barcelona, Spain: A proud recipient of the National Gastronomy Award, owner Luis Cruañas made a big hit with his first restaurant of the same name, in Sant Feliu de Guíxols on the Costa Brava, before opening this culinary shrine in the Catalan capital. Situated in one of Barcelona's elite neighborhoods, the restaurant combines local and French dishes in a "new Catalan" style. For starters, try the shrimp salad vinaigrette, or the cold cod salad with cilantro and thyme. Entrées include *bacalao* wrapped in bell peppers, scallops with leeks julienne, salmon lasagna, and goose liver and duck liver pâtés. Dessert specialties include exquisite homemade ice creams and sherbets. There is also a walk-through wine cellar. Closed Sundays and the first 2 weeks in August. Information: *Eldorado Petit,* 51 Carrer de Dolors Monserdá, Barcelona 08017, Spain (phone: 3-204-5153).

NEICHEL, Barcelona, Spain: Owner Jean Luis Neichel serves Catalan specialties with a French flair, among them rare slices of duck breast lavished with juniper and wild raspberries, lobster salad garnished with quail eggs and truffle strips, a wonderful seafood platter of *merluza,* mollusks, and freshwater crab in two tasty sauces, filet of sea bass in cream of sea urchin, fish pot-au-feu with wine, and the best pastry cart in all of Spain. When the taste buds crave something French, this luxurious and elegant restaurant is the place to visit. Closed August, Sundays, holidays, *Christmas week,* and *Holy Week.* Information: *Neichel,* 16 bis Avinguda de Pedralbes, Barcelona 08034, Spain (phone: 3-203-8408).

SET PORTES, Barcelona, Spain: Situated on the waterfront, this Barcelona favorite still retains much of its original decor (including 150-year-old furnishings) and all of the charm of its 1836 debut. Catalan cuisine, including great seafood and homemade desserts, is served in abundant portions, and the large dining rooms are packed on weekends. Try the rice with sardines, among other delicacies. Open daily. Information: *Set Portes,* 14 Passeig Isabel II, Barcelona 08024, Spain (phone: 3-319-3033).

LA GAMELLA, Madrid, Spain: American owner-chef-host Richard Stephens, also an instructor at Madrid's famed Alambique School of Gastronomy, dedicates his creative flair to new Spanish cuisine. Using choice ingredients, he offers adventures in taste with such dishes as slices of cured duck breast in Belgian endives with walnut oil, for starters, followed by turbot in wild mushroom sauce with a fresh tomato *coulis* and irresistible desserts, all complemented with a fine wine list. Facing Parque del Retiro, in the aristocratic building in which philosopher José Ortega y Gasset was born in 1883, this intimate restaurant is decorated with *colorista* design and art. A private dining room downstairs seats 10. Closed Saturdays for lunch. Information: *La Gamella,* 4 Calle Alfonso XII, Madrid 28014, Spain (phone: 1-532-4509).

EL MENTIDERO DE LA VILLA, Madrid, Spain: This delightfully intimate restaurant, situated near the famous Convento de las Salesas Reales, just off the bustling Castellana, boasts a charming combination of classic and modern decor, inventive food, and efficient and friendly service. Co-owners Mario Martínez and award-winning Japanese chef Ken Sato provide a creative French menu with a Spanish and Japanese flair. The salads are superb, as are *pato con manzana* (duck with apple) and *rollo de primavera con puerros y gambas* (spring rolls with leeks and shrimp). For dessert, try the homemade chocolate mousse. Closed Sundays. Information: *El Mentidero de la Villa,* 6 Calle Santo Tomé, Madrid 28004, Spain (phone: 1-308-1285).

PRÍNCIPE DE VIANA, Madrid, Spain: Owner Iñaki Oyarbide, another of Madrid's top restaurateurs, and the son of *Zalacaín's* famous proprietor, offers fine seasonal Basque-Navarran specialties (the menu changes from season to season) in a relaxed, elegant atmosphere. Loyal clientele includes the crème de la crème of Madrid's financial community, as well as some of his father's longtime clientele. Reservations should be made at least a day in advance. Closed Saturdays for lunch, Sundays, and August 15 through September 1. Information: *Príncipe de Viana,* 5 Calle Manuel de Falla, Madrid 28036, Spain (phone: 1-259-1448).

ZALACAÍN, Madrid, Spain: Considered by many to be the finest restaurant in all of Spain, winner of three Michelin stars (only one other establishment in the country has been so honored — see *Arzak* below), it celebrates Basque, French, and highly imaginative haute cuisines, with an emphasis on seafood. Owner Jesús Oyarbide is often on the road to the Rioja, Navarre, and Aragon regions, in search of new products and additions to his wine cellar. Luxuriously decorated, the restaurant shimmers with gleaming glasses, polished silverware, and fresh floral arrangements. Try the fish and shellfish soup, and pigs' feet stuffed with lamb. Daily specials are also served, and private dining rooms are available. Reservations are necessary. Closed Saturdays for lunch, Sundays, August, *Easter Week, Holy Week,* and holidays. Information: *Zalacaín,* 4 Calle Alvarez de Baena, Madrid 28006, Spain (phone: 1-261-4840).

LA HACIENDA, Marbella, Spain: Belgian-born owner-chef Paul Schiff fell in love with Marbella, became a Spanish national, opened this lovely Costa del Sol restaurant, and won a National Gastronomy Award. Situated just outside the city in the Urbanización Las Chapas, with an excellent view of the African coast, this serious dining establishment has developed an excellent reputation, based on Paul's interpretations of favorite French dishes. The menu requires close study, but pay extra attention to the lemon swordfish, duck liver with figs, fish mousse, guinea fowl, and red mullet. Closed Mondays, and Tuesdays except in August. Information: *La Hacienda,* Carretera Cádiz–Málaga, Km 192, Marbella 29600, Spain (phone: 52-821267).

AKELARRE, San Sebastián, Spain: Venerated champion of new Basque cooking, picturesquely situated on the slopes of Mt. Igueldo overlooking the city. National Gastronomy Award–winning owner-chef Pedro Subijana, a legend of culinary creation, blends the traditional with the new in an always-changing menu; regular patrons customarily consult him for his suggestions of the day. Always outstanding, however, are his herb salads, leg of lamb with mushrooms, *rodaballo* (trout) with nettle sauce, and a fine array of homemade desserts and pastries. Other specialties, from time to time, include *morcilla envuelta en hoja de berza sobre puré de alubias rojas* (blood pudding wrapped in a cabbage leaf on a purée of red beans), and *lubina a la pimienta verde* (sea bass with green pepper). Salmon is also served in many excellent combinations. Make reservations well in advance. Closed Sunday nights, Mondays, and October. Information: *Akelarre,* Barrio de Igueldo, San Sebastián 20008, Spain (phone: 43-212052).

ARZAK, San Sebastián, Spain: Truly an institution in the Basque Country, this restaurant is, with *Zalacaín* in Madrid, one of only two restaurants in Spain to have earned three Michelin stars. It won the National Gastronomy Award in 1974 and has been on the crest of the wave ever since. New Basque cuisine is the featured specialty, as well as *nueva cocina* (nouvelle cuisine), which owner-chef Juan Mari Arzak says "is geared for the year 2000." Seafood is the highlight; try *krabarroka* (scorpion fish pâté), *merluza* (hake) in green sauce, *chipirones en su tinta* (squid in its own ink), oyster soup with green asparagus, *consumé de buey con cigalas y caviar a los aromas a perifollo y estragón* (ox consumé with Norway lobster and caviar in a chervil and tarragon sauce), or smoked salmon tartar with caviar. Non-seafood choices include salted baby lambs' brains seasoned with mint and lime. Make reservations well in advance. Closed Sunday nights, Mondays, 2 weeks in June, and November. Information: *Arzak,* 21 Calle Alto de Miracruz, San Sebastián 20015, Spain (phone: 43-278465).

T CLUB, Almansil, Portugal: The latest, most luxurious culinary spot in the Algarve, set on the grounds of the exclusive, posh Quinta do Lago resort. Owner José Manuel Trigo learned his trade from Regine, the queen of clubs, managing her establishments in Brazil. Marbled wood, velour curtains, impeccably set tables, and soft lighting set the tone in this elegant place, where international nouvelle cuisine and traditional dishes from Portugal and Europe share the menu. A central European flavor is imported in the summer season with the arrival of a Belgian cook. Dinner is served until 1 AM. Guests can dance their calories away in the adjoining *boîte,* or adjourn to the plush bar for a glass of port. Information: *T Club,* Quinta do Lago, Almansil, Loulé 8100, Portugal (phone: 89-96755).

ALBATROZ, Cascais, Portugal: Perched on the rocks overlooking the blue waters of Cascais Bay, on the grounds of a manorial home, this luxury hotel harbors one of the most enchanting restaurants on Portugal's mini-Riviera. The impeccable, classical elegance of the wood-paneled piano bar and romantic, candlelit atmosphere of the glass-enclosed dining room with unobstructed sea view, make it a favorite haunt of the Estoril coast jet set. Manager Avellos runs the facility with discreet efficiency. White linen and freshly cut flowers add to the decor, enhancing the varied international and Portuguese menu, which includes mouth-watering *arroz de marisco* (rice with shellfish), pheasant, partridge, and the house veal stuffed with cured ham. Highlights among the desserts are flaming crêpes Suzette, sweet *tamaras* (dates) with hot chocolate sauce, and crusty apple pie topped with warm cream. A select wine list of 12 special vintages, such as rare colares '31 and mouchão '63, is available for appreciative connoisseurs. Dinner reservations are advised, ties recommended. Information: *Albatroz,* 100 Rua Federico Arouca, Cascais 2750, Portugal (phone: 1-282821).

FOUR SEASONS, Estoril, Portugal: True to its name, this fancy restaurant on the grounds of Estoril's grand *Palácio* hotel, where many of Europe's exiled royalty and other personages waited out World War II, changes its decor and the uniforms of its staff to suit the season. Its large central table blooms with flowers in the spring and is laden with fruit in the summer. Creative dishes such as *linguado à Four Seasons* (sole stuffed with shrimp and mushrooms and flambéed with whiskey) abound. But the main attraction is its grill. Guests on the ground floor and upper mezzanine can watch the chef at work on a huge, open grill, tending to such savory delectables as *espetada mista* (diced veal and monkfish kebabs bathed in butter sauce). Not to be outdone by the grill captain, the maître d' lights up the room with his flambéed creations or *crêpes de metre* stuffed with almonds and bananas and doused with lemon ice cream. Though the decor is sharp and metallic — copper place mats and bronze columns — the wooden tables, leather-lined chairs and glowing coals in the fireplace help soften the ambience. The restaurant is open for dinner daily, from 7:30 PM to 1 AM. Information: *Four Seasons, Palácio Hotel,* Ruo do Parque, Estoril 2675, Portugal (phone: 1-268-0400).

FIALHO, Evora, Portugal: The three Fialho brothers have built their temple to Alentejo food in the center of one of Portugal's most beautiful towns. The restaurant's bar and two dining rooms are tastefully decorated with regional copper, pottery, handwoven Arrailos rugs, and paintings; stuffed game mounted on the walls reflect the hunting fervor of the people of the region. Guests can nibble from a cornucopia of *petiscos* (starters), which range from spicy sweet meats to more exotic dishes, such as *cabeça de xara* (pork head). The award-winning restaurant, which is popular among wealthy ranchers of the region, university professors, and politicians, boasts the best and most authentic *carne de porco com amêijoas* (pork and clam stew) in Evora, and *sopa de cação,* a rich, aromatic soup made with shark, bread, garlic, vinegar, and coriander. During the fall hunting season, partridge, wild rabbit, and boar are featured. Egg, almond, and pumpkin desserts provide the sweet touch to the meal, while the region's soft sheep cheeses, the creamy *serpas,* are an equally rewarding finale. Meals can be accompanied by Evora's estate-bottled cartuxa white wine, or other Alentejo greats such as the light, dry white herdade de esporrão and the heavy red reguengos de monsaraz. Closed Mondays and September 1–15. Information: *Fialho,* 16 Travessa das Mascarenhas, Evora 7000, Portugal (phone: 66-23079).

AVIZ, Lisbon, Portugal: When the elegant, turn-of-the-century *Aviz* hotel closed its doors during the early 1960s, its chef and maître d' joined forces and started a new restaurant — same name, same furnishings — in a former tailor's shop. Legend has it that the Armenian oil millionaire Calouste Sarkis Gulbenkian, a frequent client of the hotel, may have contributed to the venture. Today, the restaurant's clients continue to be captains of industry, who like its subdued intimacy and refined, Old World look. Guests have a choice of dining rooms: the cozy silk-lined *salão verde* (green room), or the lighter *salão amarelo* (yellow room), decorated with old musical instruments. Parties of 14 to 18 persons can retire to the intimacy of a private salon under the watchful eye of a 19th-century wooden statue of Pocahontas. Other attractions are its wooden pub-like bar and its tile-lined marble staircase. The chef's enticing culinary creations — smoked swordfish, gratinéed cod *Conde de Guarda* style, rack of lamb with ground herbs, and chilled *bolo de ananas* (pineapple cake) — help make the restaurant one of Portugal's dining landmarks. Closed Saturdays for lunch and Sundays. Information: *Aviz,* 12-B Rua Serpa Pinto, Lisbon 1200, Portugal (phone: 1-328391).

TÁGIDE, Lisbon, Portugal: Its closeness to Lisbon's financial district makes this restaurant atop one of the city's seven hills a favorite with businesspeople and government officials, including the president. Other attractions are its large wine list of over 70 vintages, spanning Portugal's eight main wine regions, and its fish delicacies. The house salmon pâté and its *cherne no forno com coentros* (oven-baked stone bass with coriander) reflect the Portuguese penchant for fish. Meat lovers can savor the succulent *churrasco de cabrito* (grilled kid) or *carne de porco à alentejana* (pork Alentejo-style), an ingenious dish of pork and clams prepared with wine, garlic, red pepper, coriander, and oil. The fruit and almond crêpes, topped with vanilla sauce, have been known to seduce the most ardent dieters. Though white walls, leather chairs, and 18th-century tiles depicting mythological characters give the dining room a classical elegance and order, they do not detract from the panoramic view of Lisbon. Closed Saturday nights and Sundays. Information: *Tágide,* 18 Largo da Biblioteca Pública, Lisbon 1200, Portugal (phone: 1-320720).

TAVARES, Lisbon, Portugal: The grande dame of Lisbon restaurants, opened as a café in 1784, celebrated its 200th birthday with a face-lift. The splendor of the Belle Epoque was restored and Lisbon's old guard flocked to see the doyenne's newly resplendent, gold-painted and paneled walls, large, imperial gilded mirrors, polished silver, and china. Patrons were delighted to find that the old menu was maintained. Maître d' Rodrigo Paia has drilled his black-tied waiters to perform their duties with such finesse that diners are scarcely aware of their presence. House specialties include *santola recheada* (stuffed crab) in Madeira sauce and *cherne à portuguesa* (stone bass Portuguese-style) with a smooth tomato, onion, garlic, and clam sauce. Guests with a predilection for sweets can treat themselves to the *soufflé à Tavares,* with both vanilla and chocolate sauces, or the baked Alaska. Closed Saturday evenings and Sundays for lunch. Information: *Tavares,* 35 Rua da Misericórdia, Lisbon 1200, Portugal (phone: 1-321112).

PORTUCALE, Porto, Portugal: This Porto landmark is favored by executives for its varied menu of Portuguese and continental dishes, attentive service, and sweeping view of the city and countryside. Wood paneling, leather chairs, and colorful modern tapestries make up the simple, lively decor that serves as the background for such house specialties as artichokes au gratin, lobster and rice stew, pheasant stuffed with almonds, chateaubriand with mushroom sauce, and wild boar, as well as tripe, Porto-style. Open daily. Information: *Portucale,* 598 Rua da Alegria, 14th Floor, Porto 4000, Portugal (phone: 2-570717).

COZINHA VELHA, Queluz, Portugal: Guests get the royal treatment at this restaurant housed in the kitchen of the 18th-century palace of the Kings of Portugal, a 15-minute drive west of Lisbon. Remnants of its royal past can be seen in the large copper kitchen utensils bearing the royal seal and displayed on the walls, and in the huge chimney supported by six marble pillars, where whole oxen were once roasted on the spit. Banquets are still held in the antique-tiled *sala dourada* (gold room) for foreign dignitaries who are lodged in the adjoining pink palace. Maître d' José Marinho Carreira has served such distinguished guests as Queen Elizabeth and Ronald and Nancy Reagan, and accompanies Portugal's head of state on his tours. The decor and the food are as refined as the service: Wood-vaulted ceilings, red tile floors, iron lamps, and soft, piped-in music provide an elegant backdrop for such delectables as *terrina de casa* (veal pâté), *linguado suado* (steamed sole) served in a delicate onion, carrot, mushroom, and sour cream sauce, and souffléed, oven-baked *bacalhau espiritual* (codfish). The latter takes 40 minutes to prepare and should be ordered in advance. Guests have a choice of wines from all over the country and neighboring Colares, which produces the light-bodied tavares rodrigues. The restaurant's *pièces de résistance* are its desserts, fashioned from ancient convent recipes. Very apropos is the *doce real* (royal sweet), which comes stamped with the Portuguese royal seal in confectionery sugar and is made of squash, eggs, and nuts. Information: *Cozinha Velha,* Palácio Nacional de Queluz, Queluz 2745, Portugal (phone: 1-435-0232).

Shopping Spree

No matter where the dollar stands relative to the peseta or the escudo, the temptation of shopping in Spain and Portugal is irresistible. Colorful hand-painted tiles and lovingly sewn handicrafts are eye-catching, easily luring the visitor into one of Madrid's 54,000 shops and stores, or through the bric-a-brac in its famous flea market, *El Rastro.* In Portugal, small roadside stalls along the Algarve coast offer a dazzling array of ceramics, and small boutiques in Lisbon are like mini-museums, with a fine assortment of antiques dating back to the 15th century. And what's best of all is that these items are almost all affordable. In both countries, visitors will be surprised at how much US dollars can buy. Once they begin, there's an almost irrepressible urge to keep shopping right across the Iberian Peninsula, where there's also a predominance of leather goods, embroideries, jewelry, fine porcelain, and fashion ranging from very basic handicraft sweaters and clothing to haute couture.

The shopping day often begins around 9:30 AM, when shopkeepers are still hosing down the sidewalk in front of their stores. Most owners take pride in their shops; their business is a very personal affair, and they'll no doubt strike up a conversation with curious browsers. It isn't uncommon, either, for those who opt to ship their purchases back to the US to get a handwritten note from shopkeepers. (More stores in Spain practice this than in Portugal; visitors will also notice that more stores in Spain take credit cards than their Portuguese counterparts.)

Spaniards are traditional strollers. They take to the streets as a pastime, particularly for browsing in the plethora of small specialty shops found in most cities. But the relaxed ambience and 3-hour lunchtime shop closings (except for major department stores) mean careful shopping plans should be made. Shopkeepers are helpful, warm people who take extra time to satisfy customers. Most, however, do not speak English.

While Madrid is charming and a pleasure to shop in, Barcelona is closer to northern European fashion capitals, and has adopted a more cosmopolitan style. Seville is the land of castanets, flamenco, and vivid colors. Spain's designers have a flair for fashion, experiment with styling and color, and have emerged as strong rivals to French and Italian creators. Spanish fashion has become provocatively alluring, yet it keeps a classical line. Spanish porcelain, particularly the Lladró figurines, are collectors' items. Ceramic and porcelain tableware and giftware are well made and exported worldwide.

Leather goods are subtle, soft, and a good value. Majórica pearls, made in Spain, carry a worldwide 10-year guarantee. Fine gold jewelry, by law, is 18 karat.

General shopping hours in Spain are Mondays through Fridays, from 9:30 AM to 1:30 PM and from 4:30 to 8 PM; Saturdays, from 9:30 AM to 3 PM. Department stores are open Mondays through Saturdays, from 10 AM to 8 PM. Most shops are closed in August, but department stores remain open year-round.

The Portuguese approach life and shopping with less passion than the neighboring Spaniards. This is not to say, however, that Portuguese shopping should be considered second class. Many of the products do not have the flair of Spanish counterparts. Lisbon is a logical choice, and Porto is worth a visit, particularly for silver. Madeira is known for its embroidery. Portuguese artisans mold earthenware and ceramics into works of art, as do modern Portuguese manufacturing plants, producing whimsical pottery, elegant porcelain, and gleaming crystal befitting any table. Tiles are everywhere: on churches, restaurants, palaces, storefronts, homes, and shops. They capture the bright colors and sunny vistas that are so much a part of Portugal's landscape and heritage. Handwoven rugs, both designer-quality and functional, as well as hand-knit sweaters and intricate embroidery symbolizing a national pride lovingly worked at for centuries, can be found throughout the country.

Portuguese shops are generally open Mondays through Fridays, from 9:30 AM to 1 PM and from 3 to 7 PM; Saturdays, from 9:30 AM to 1 PM (except in December, when they remain open until 7 PM). Shopping malls are open daily, from 10 AM to midnight. In Porto, shops close at 12:30 PM for the afternoon break and reopen at 2:30 PM. Many shops throughout the country are closed in August. Although store hours are generally observed, shops sometimes close unexpectedly or, when open, leave shoppers waiting for service. Many shopkeepers speak English.

WHERE TO SHOP

Travelers can find good buys all over Spain and Portugal, provided they know where to look.

POST-CHRISTMAS AND SUMMER SALES: In Spain, they're called *rebajas* and unlike in the US, they're held only twice a year. Here's the good part: They're universal; practically *all* stores and shops have them. Winter *rebajas* start January 6, which in Spain marks the *Day of the Three Wise Men,* the traditional *Christmastime* gift-giving day. Summer sales start in mid-July and last through the month of August (prices drop even more toward the end of August). Portugal's *saldos* are held around the same time but last a little longer; they begin in January and February and are repeated in September and October. In general, almost everything in Portugal is reasonably priced; in fact, Lisbon is one of the most reasonably priced of Europe's shopping capitals.

OPEN MARKETS: Never pass up a chance to wander through some of Spain's and Portugal's bustling open markets. It is here that visitors have the opportunity to see the *real* Madrid and the *real* Lisbon come alive — people selling their crafts, friends meeting for a meal or a drink, and curious onlookers taking in the vast array of goods and daily bargains. These open markets are a smorgasbord of vibrant colors, overflowing with the song of the people.

Madrid, Spain – *El Rastro* (The Thieves Market) is one of Europe's largest and most famous flea markets. It is open year-round on Sundays and holidays from 9 AM to 2 PM. Beginning near Glorieta de Embajadores square, *El Rastro* meanders down to the Ronda de Toledo and spills over into small side streets. Antiques buyers should visit the area's permanent stores, which are open throughout the week, to avoid the massive Sunday crowds. Also on Sunday mornings, at the nearby Plaza Mayor, arcades overflow with stamp and coin dealers.

Barcelona, Spain – Spain's most cosmopolitan city has a variety of outdoor offerings throughout the week. From dawn to dusk on Mondays, Wednesdays, Fridays, and Saturdays, *Els Encants,* just off the Plaça de les Glòries Catalanes, hosts a huge flea market with everything from clothes to antiques on display. The Plaça Nova has a weekly antiques market every Thursday. The Plaça Sant Josep Oriol transforms itself into one of Spain's largest open-air painting exhibitions and marketplaces every weekend, and the Plaça Reial features coin and stamp markets on Sunday mornings.

Seville, Spain – The city's biggest market sets up its stalls from 10 AM to 3 PM every Sunday along Alameda de Hércules. This is the place for crafts, costume jewelry, antiques, and novelty items. The Plaza del Cabildo (opposite the cathedral) hosts a coin and stamp mart every Sunday morning as well.

Lisbon, Portugal – Portuguese Gypsies buy closeout items, discontinued, second-hand, overrun, and leftover stock from many top Portuguese clothing manufacturers and boutiques, then peddle them from stands on street corners throughout the week, especially during lunchtime. Also look for the Gypsies every Tuesday and Saturday at the large flea market in the Alfama district, at Largo de Santa Clara.

Evora, Portugal – The *Mercado Municipal* on Praça Primeiro de Maio, open every morning except Mondays, is not only the best place for fresh food and delicacies such as the excellent local cheeses and cured sausages, but also a colorful place to visit. Handicrafts, including good, brown-glazed oven pots, are sold from stalls outside, along with the omnipresent plastic goods.

DEPARTMENT STORES: Expect to find anything and everything at the department stores in Spain and Portugal. Spain's *El Corte Inglés* ranks at the top of Europe's best department store list. It's desirable for travelers to have an idea about what they wish to purchase before shopping in one of the store's branches (there are 18 throughout the country); otherwise the visitor is almost guaranteed to get lost, as this store is literally a city within a city. Free translators, shoppers' cards (for purchases to be sent to a central depot for pickup), food (take-out and eat-in), a travel agency, currency exchange, hairdresser, ample parking, and, in some stores, international communications centers are among the many special services provided. *El Corte Inglés* even manufactures some of its own designs, and sells them exclusively at prices up to one-third less than fashions of similar quality found in other European capitals. Many of Spain's top designers also sell here. There are four locations in Madrid: 3 Calle Preciados (phone: 1-532-8100); 76 Calle Goya (phone: 1-448-0111); 79 Calle Raimundo Fernández Villaverde, just off upper Paseo de la Castellana (phone: 1-556-2300); and 56 Calle Princesa (phone: 1-542-4800). Barcelona boasts the chain's largest store (in Plaça de Catalunya; 3-301-3256). All *El Corte Inglés* branches remain open during normal afternoon siesta hours.

Spain's other major department store chain, *Galerías Preciados,* offers many of the same services as *El Corte Inglés,* though its offerings are a bit more downscale and less comprehensive. Its "passport service" offers discounts to foreign visitors, in addition to IVA (value added tax) rebates. Specialty items include Spanish ceramics, rugs, glassware, handicrafts, and souvenirs. Branches can be found throughout Madrid, as well as other major cities. The main store is at 1 Plaza de Callao (phone: 1-522-4771) in Madrid. Barcelona has a branch (19 Avinguda Portal de l'Angel).

SPECIAL SHOPPING STREETS AND DISTRICTS: The mixture of old and new, the lively sounds of families and couples linked arm in arm, make strolling through the streets an inviting experience. Stop and savor both the street scenes and the shops that line them.

Madrid, Spain – With over 54,000 specialty shops to choose from, shopping in Madrid is varied and fun, and can occupy seemingly endless hours. Start at the maze of streets surrounding Plaza Mayor, the heart of Old Madrid. Most of the small shops here have thrived for hundreds of years. Gran Vía is the city's Fifth Avenue, its busiest and most commercial thoroughfare. Explore its side streets and check out some of the lesser known but more charming shops. Other popular areas include the Salamanca district, located near the Plaza de Colón. This 12-block grid is bordered by Calles Serrano, Goya, Velázquez, and José Ortega y Gasset, and features some of Madrid's pricier offerings.

More affordable stores are located in the city center around the Puerta del Sol, the adjoining Calle Preciados pedestrian mall, and around Calles Arenal and Mayor in Old Madrid.

Barcelona, Spain – The rest of Spain admires the Catalans and their capital city, Barcelona, for their long-standing business and commercial attributes. Most of Spain's textiles are woven in the Catalan region surrounding Barcelona, and because of the strong influence of Spanish designers in the fashion world now, the city is considered to be in the same ranks as Milan and New York. For concentrated shopping, the major streets are the Passeig de Gràcia, Avinguda Diagonal, the Rambla de Catalunya, and Gran Via de les Corts Catalanes.

Córdoba, Spain – The busiest area is in the upper part of the city, in the vicinity of Calle Gondomar, Plaza de las Tendillas, and Ronda de los Tejares. The shops surrounding the mosque and in the old Jewish Quarter sell mostly souvenirs and other touristy items.

Granada, Spain – The city's old Arab silk market, next to the cathedral, has been reconstructed and now houses mainly souvenir shops. There are numerous small crafts shops in the Albaicín quarter, particularly along the Cuesta de Gomérez, the Plaza Nueva, and the adjoining side streets.

Lisbon, Portugal – The major shopping area, the Baixa section, consists of about 20 blocks, some for pedestrians only. Up and down the city's hills, small shops are the norm, and they are great places for peeking and poking. The area is anchored by the Praça do Comércio at the water's edge, leading up to the Praça da Figueira. The bordering side streets are Rua do Ouro and Rua da Prata. For pricier shopping, head to the Chiado district, particularly Rua do Carmo and Rua Garrett. Rua Dom Pedro V houses a variety of antiques shops. Gypsies also set up shop on many sidewalks for several hours a day.

Porto, Portugal – Porto's commercial centers are in the newer part of the city. Rua de Santa Catarina is the main commercial street, with one portion set aside as an open-air pedestrian mall. There are some good boutiques and shops along Avenida da Boavista, near the *Meridien* hotel. Rua das Flores, near the train station, is the street for those interested in buying silver. Rua 31 de Janeiro has a fine assortment of clothing boutiques and shoe stores.

COMMERCIAL CENTERS (SHOPPING MALLS): Visitors will feel right at home in the bright lights, chain stores, and fast-food restaurants of a Spanish or Portuguese shopping mall. Most stay open from 9 AM to midnight, 7 days a week, including holidays.

Madrid, Spain – *Madrid 2,* just north of central Madrid, is an enormous 350-shop complex, complete with restaurants, movie theaters, discos, amusement arcades, and parking for 4,000 cars. The *Mercado Puerta de Toledo* (at the Puerta de Toledo, on the western edge of the city) is a former fish market, now transformed into a 150-shop showcase for Spain's finest designers in fashion, jewelry, interior design, and antiques.

Barcelona, Spain – If there's time for only one shopping excursion, head straight for the elegant *Bulevard Rosa* (55 Passeig de Gràcia). Here, several hundred shops display an elegant flair in items ranging from trendy young fashions to sophisticated jet setter designs. *Diagonal Center* (584 Avinguda Diagonal) is small but brims with good shops.

Lisbon, Portugal – There are 30 *centros comerciais* (shopping centers) in Lisbon, of all sizes and quality. The most famous, with sophisticated shops of all kinds — more than 300 of them — is the *Centro Comercial das Amoreiras* (Avenida Engenheiro

Duarte Pacheco; phone: 1-692558), a post-Modernist complex with huge towers in pinks and greens and glass, designed by architect Tomás Taveira. *Centro Comercial Fonte Nova* (497 Estrada de Benfica; phone: 1-714-4654), just outside the city, has 80 shops including excellent leather goods and home-decoration stores. *Centro Comercial Alvalade*'s 45 shops offer a classy assortment of giftware, clothing, shoes, and general shopping-mall merchandise.

Porto, Portugal – *Dallas* (1588 Avenida da Boavista) is a huge center with 500 stores on 5 levels, and is the best place to buy handicrafts and jewelry in Porto.

BEST BUYS

ANTIQUES: Both Spain and Portugal are excellent hunting grounds for antiques, with a wide range of dealers, auction houses, and non-commercial institutions that offer many items at bargain prices.

Madrid, Spain – In addition to the antiques shops in and around the Plaza Mayor area, Calle del Prado, and Carrera de Jerónimo, where religious antiques shops abound, the magnificent 5-story *Serrano Cinco Central de Arte Antiquedades* (Calle Serrano) houses 50 antiques shops, each with an honored reputation. There are also antiques in *El Rastro,* Madrid's famous flea market (see *Open Markets*).

Barcelona, Spain – Most of Barcelona's 150 antiques shops are found in the Barri Gòtic, the old medieval heart of the city. Wonderful pieces from a host of major periods, such as the 12th and 15th centuries and Queen Anne, as well as pieces showing French, Catalan, and English influences, are readily available here. Spain protects its treasures carefully, and reputable dealers will assist visitors with Spanish customs and regulations. Generally speaking, a work of art is considered of cultural and artistic importance if the artist is not living or, if living, his or her prominence is widely accepted. The second floor of the *Bulevard Rosa Mall* (Passeig de Gràcia) is dedicated entirely to antiques shops and auction houses.

Seville, Spain – Seville's antiques shops are among Spain's best. Some of the more popular shops include *Andrés Moro* (8 Calle Placentines; phone: 5-422-4633); *Lola Ortega* (Plaza del Cabildo; phone: 5-421-8771); *María Dolores Mellado Valencia* (5 Avenida de la Constitución; phone: 5-422-3345); and *Pedro Montelongo* (17 Calle Santa Teresa; phone: 5-421-6353). Seville hosts a special antiques fair every year in April. Contact the *Associación de Anticuarios* (7 Calle Rodrigo Caro; phone: 5-421-6558) for complete details.

Lisbon, Portugal – The city has a fine antiques shop tradition that is broadening into the areas of prints and rare books. Hundreds of shops await the treasure hunter; most are spread along a 1-mile area beginning at Rua da Escola Politécnica, which changes into Rua Dom Pedro V, Rua de São Pedro de Alcântara, Rua da Misericórdia, and, when approaching the Tagus River, Rua do Alecrim. Always be sure to inquire about an item's age, and always request the proper documentation to back it up. *Solar* (68-70 Rua Dom Pedro V; phone: 1-365522) has the largest selection of antique Portuguese glazed tiles, arranged by century, beginning with the 15th, as well as a fine collection of pewter and furniture. *Xairel* (3 Rua Dom Pedro V) is another excellent choice. *Sotheby's* and *Christie's* are represented in Lisbon by *Teixeira Victor* (103 Rua Dom Pedro V; phone: 1-321973), well known for its 17th-, 18th-, and 19th-century pieces. *António Campos Trindade* (18 Rua do Alecrim; phone: 1-324660) specializes in Portuguese, English, and French furniture, as well as Chinese porcelain and paintings.

BOOKS AND MAPS: Most visitors may not be able to read many of Spain's and Portugal's treasured old books, but it's still fun to browse. Many bookstores have dozens of booths and stalls filled with books from around the world, both old and new; some stores specialize in reduced-rate and secondhand books, old editions, and rare titles. Much of Spanish literature is printed in both Spanish and English; for those interested in learning the language, why not learn while reading one of the classics? Addicted browsers will have to be dragged out of the following bookworm haunts.

Madrid, Spain – *Mexico II* (20 Calle Huertas; phone: 1-228-2896) has over 200,000 books from the 16th century to the 18th, as well as drawers full of historical prints and maps. *Casa del Libro* is Madrid's largest bookstore, with 5 floors for browsing at its old location (29 Gran Vía), and another 4 floors at its new location (3 Calle Maestro Victoria). *Turner English Bookshop* (3 Calle Genova, on Plaza de Santa Barbara; phone: 1-410-4359) stocks an impressive collection of English, French, and Spanish titles. Also visit *La Tienda Verde* (38 Calle Maudes; phone: 1-533-0791), for the best in adventure travel. *El Corte Inglés* department stores also have *librerías,* with fine selections of Spanish- and English-language books. Browsers should walk along the stretch of pavement known as the Cuesta de Moyano, near Calle Claudio Moyano, between Calle Alfonso XII and the corner of Paseo del Prado and Calle Glorieta de Atocha. This virtually permanent book fair is stocked with dozens of stalls of reduced-rate and secondhand books.

Barcelona, Spain – It is no coincidence that Catalonia has the highest literacy rate in Spain and can claim to be the only city in the country where the patron saint's day (*St. George's Day,* April 23) is celebrated with gifts of books to friends. In Barcelona, there's a bookshop on every block, and residents are often buried in books that on closer inspection turn out to be French, German, or English classics, rather than Spanish mystery novels. The bookstalls on La Rambla, which bustle each afternoon, are a good place to find an interesting title. *Librería Francesa* (91 Passeig de Gràcia), Barcelona's largest bookstore, also has a nice selection.

Seville, Spain – *Cervantes* (5 Calle Azafranal) is one of Spain's largest general bookstores. There is sure to be a title on one of its 7 floors for any who wish to spend an afternoon browsing.

Lisbon, Portugal – Original maps and lithographs from the 16th through the 18th centuries can be found at *O Mundo Do Livro* (11 Largo da Trindade; phone: 1-369951), one of Lisbon's oldest and most famous bookstores. *Livraria Bertrand* (73 Rua Garrett; phone: 1-320081) also has an enormous selection, as well as many English titles.

CERAMICS AND TILES: The diversity of Spain's regions is highly evident in the country's wide range of ceramics. The 700-year Arab domination prevails in ceramic designs of the southern regions; wall plates are enameled and trimmed in 24-karat gold. Later, when the English settled in the area around Cádiz, florals and busy scenic designs became the preferred style. The story is much the same in Portugal. Tiles are called *azulejos* in Portuguese, and most of them are the color of the sky. Uniquely Portuguese, the tiles can be found throughout the country, and many visitors are tempted to purchase enough to decorate their homes — but are soon discouraged by the shipping costs. Remember, shipping sand is heavy; about 14 fragile tiles packed in sand weigh 10 pounds. The best reminder of any visit could be the many hand-decorated, easily portable tiles, either in blue and white or depicting scenes.

Madrid, Spain – *Cerámica El Alfar* (112 Calle Claudio Coello; phone: 1-411-3587) has a large assortment of regional ceramics and earthenware. Glazed-tile reproductions of famous Spanish paintings are a specialty. *La Cerámica Talavera* (44 Calle Lagasca) offers a fine selection of wall plates, dinner sets, planters, cups, and other larger items.

Seville, Spain – *La Alcazaba* (1-A Calle Joaquín Romero Murube) carries delicate hand-painted ceramic tiles and platters from Seville and other regions, including the lovely florals from Valencia. *Cerámica Santa Ana* (31 Calle San Jorge) also stocks a large selection of ceramics at good prices.

Lisbon, Portugal – *Fábrica de Cerâmica Viúva Lamego* (25 Largo do Intendente Pina Manique; phone: 1-521401) makes and sells hand-painted reproductions of tiles from the 15th to the 18th century; its bird and animal motifs are famous. It also makes high-quality modern designs, as well as a variety of planters, dishes, lamp bases, and pottery. The outside of the store is completely covered with brightly colored tile scenes.

Founded in 1741, *Faianças e Azulejos Sant'Anna* (95 Rua do Alecrim; phone: 1-322537) carries fabulous reproductions of 17th- and 18th-century tiles, made in the shop's own factory, as well as individual wall tiles, chandeliers, tables with tile inserts, flowerpots, and small kitchen-tile trivets. It will also create tiles for special orders. Even a browse around the store is a shopper's delight. The factory (96 Calçada da Boa Hora; phone: 1-638292) also can be visited, but call for an appointment first. *Vista Alegre* (52 Rua Ivens; phone: 1-328612; and 18 Largo do Chiado; phone: 1-361401) is recognized as the maker of Portugal's finest porcelain.

Coimbra, Portugal – *Jorge Mendes* (9 Praça do Comercio; phone: 39-25646) sells some of the finest copies of 15th- to 17th-century porcelain and ceramics in town; artisans can be seen making them in the workshop. *Sociedade de Cerâmica Antiga de Coimbra* (2 Quintal do Prior; phone: 39-23829) makes and sells reproductions of old Portuguese ceramics, and is the only factory currently producing the special, pale flora and fauna designs typical of the 18th century. Open to visitors on weekdays.

CURIOSITY SHOPS: A peek into the numerous boutiques and specialty shops should provide ample insight into the Spanish and Portuguese ways of life, of both the past and the present.

Madrid, Spain – *Musgo* (36 Calle Hermosilla; phone: 1-431-5510) comprises five row houses joined together as one huge store and filled with contemporary clothing and furnishings. *Capas Seseña* (23 Calle Cruz; phone: 1-531-6840) makes a fine line of capes for men and women, from the finest available wool, and has been selling them at this store for almost a century. Porcelain dolls and restorations are the specialty at *La Boutique de las Muñecas* (2 Calle Sevilla; phone: 1-429-4499). *Casa Jiménez* (42 Calle Preciados; phone: 1-248-0526) is one of Madrid's oldest shops for custom-made shawls and fans. *Maty* (5 Plaza Comandante las Morenas; phone: 1-541-2016) specializes in flamenco dresses and accessories.

San Sebastián, Spain – *Casa Basarte* (18 Calle San Jerónimo) has the best selection of genuine *txapelas* (Basque berets) in town. *Juguetería Antón* (21 Calle San Jerónimo) features an amazing collection of Spanish jigsaw puzzles. Designs range from Goya paintings to Moorish tiles, containing up to 8,000 pieces.

Braga, Portugal – *Casa Fânzeres* (132-134 Rua do Souto; phone: 53-22704) is the oldest religious-artifacts shop in town, both selling and restoring religious objects.

DESIGNER CLOTHING: While Portugal may not be a center for haute couture, neighboring Spain demonstrates a more cosmopolitan flair, especially in and around the cities and towns close to the French border. Whatever the latest trend, visitors can rest assured that both country's designers are up-to-date.

Madrid, Spain – *Molinero Costura* (3 Calle Ayala; phone: 1-275-1157) is the exclusive Valentino representative, featuring his ready-to-wear, haute couture, and evening clothes — all the latest. This sleek and very expensive shop with a marble interior boasts Queen Sofia as a regular client. *Pedro Muñoz* (72 Calle Serrano; phone: 1-431-1661), a shirtmaker and tailor, designs fashions for men only. *Don Algodón* is Spain's answer to *Benetton*. This 30-year-old designer has taken cotton and color to create smashing mix-and-match sportswear. This chain store has nationwide outlets, with its headquarters at 58 Calle Claudio Coello. *Adolfo Domínguez* (4 Calle Ortega y Gasset; phone: 1-276-0084) is the boutique of the innovative Spanish celebrity designer whose daring women's fashions illustrate his "wrinkles (in the fabric, that is) are beautiful" philosophy. *Ascot* (88 Calle Serrano; phone: 1-431-3712) is an excellent women's boutique selling haute couture and ready-to-wear garments by María Teresa de Vega, a favorite designer among Madrid's beautiful people.

San Sebastián, Spain – *Delgado* (43 Avenida de la Libertad; phone: 43-426625) is one of the oldest and best clothing shops in town. Founded in 1899, it's still a family-run affair. Much of the material is imported from Italy, but the conservatively styled men's suits, shirts, and ready-to-wear outfits are still made on the premises.

Lisbon, Portugal – *Ana Salazar* (87 Rua do Carmo; phone: 1-372289) is the forerunner in the capital. She draws artistic inspirations from the turn of the century and the 1940s. Also considered among the best by locals is *Harriet Hubbard Ayer* (12 Rua Manuel de Jesus Coelho; phone: 1-542323), where trendy Portuguese designer José Carlos sells his clothes exclusively. *New York* (206 Rua do Ouro; phone: 1-321764) is a classy shop featuring the latest in women's clothes. *Porfirios* (63 Rua da Vitória; phone: 1-368274) is popular with young and with-it dressers. *Rosa & Teixeira* (204 Avenida da Liberdade; phone: 1-542063) is a highly ranked tailor selling his own lines for men and women.

Porto, Portugal – *Helena Kendall* (1471 Avenida da Boavista; phone: 2-694673) is recognized as one of Portugal's better designers of women's clothes. Her shop carries her latest designs and accessories. *Nanni Strada* (1533 Avenida da Boavista; phone: 2-692745) is a Milan designer currently designing and manufacturing a hot line of clothes in Porto for men and women. *Pereira da Silva & Araújo* (114 Rua 31 de Janeiro; phone: 2-21009) is also a well-respected designer of menswear.

EMBROIDERY AND LACE: In Spain and Portugal, embroidery prices are determined by the intricacy of the stitch, not by the size of the item. Look carefully: Stitches made by a human hand cannot duplicate themselves over and over, and will therefore lack consistency; the more perfect the stitch, the more likely that an item was machine made. In Portugal, lace and embroidery come from Madeira; crocheted items come from the Azores. Regions such as Viana do Castelo produce a coarse, embroidered linen. In order to protect their handicraft industry, the government of Madeira attaches a small lead tag to each piece of Madeira embroidery sold either on the island, on mainland Portugal, or anywhere else in the world. Madeira embroidery is slightly higher in price, but is a timeless heirloom.

Madrid, Spain – *Casa Bonet* (76 Calle Núñez de Balboa; phone: 1-275-0912) stocks a variety of handmade embroidery, including the beautiful ones from Palma de Mallorca on the island of Majorca. The prices here are very reasonable, whether it's a handkerchief or linens. Also try *Gil, Sucesor de Anatolín Quevedo* (2 Carrera de San Jerónimo; phone: 1-521-2549), a generations-old establishment that has supplied Spanish and international celebrities with high-quality embroidery for many years.

Toledo, Spain – Toledo and the nearby village of Lagartera are famous for their embroidery, lace, and needlework. In Lagartera, the village where the best La Mancha embroidery originates, every cottage has its own display of the free-form floral stitching, which decorates silk hangings, tablecloths, peasant bonnets, and full skirts. Damascene, the Moorish art of inlaying gold, copper, or silver threads on a matte black steel background, is also a thriving craft in Toledo, used on boxes, plates, and swords, as well as in jewelry. *Santiago Sanchez Martín* (18 Calle Río Llano; phone: 25-227757) is named for its owner, a damascene artisan who, after 40 years in the business, still inlays 24-carat gold by hand on the most special pieces. *Casa Bermejo* (5 Calle Airosos) also carries top-quality Toledo damascene.

Lisbon, Portugal – *Príncipe Real Enxoval* (12 Rua da Escola Politécnica; phone: 1-365945) specializes in handmade embroidery shipped in from one of the best factories in Madeira. *Madeira Superbia* (75-A Avenida Duque de Loulé; phone: 1-531837) carries a fine selection of high-quality linen. *Madeira House* (131 Rua Augusta; phone: 1-320557), Lisbon's oldest shop dealing in genuine Madeira embroidery and lace, sells less-expensive embroidered linens. *Madeira Gobelins* (40 Rua Castilho; phone: 1-563708) also carries fine embroidery, woven tapestries, and carpets from Madeira, as does *Casa dos Bordados da Madeira* (135 Rua Primeiro de Dezembro; phone: 1-321447), along with an excellent selection of lace and a wide variety of other Portuguese handicrafts.

Madeira, Portugal – This tiny island overflows with embroidery shops, located principally in the capital city of Funchal. The British are credited with creating a market for Madeira embroidery and building a reputation for quality that continues to this day, with thousands of Madeiran women carrying on the craft. There is an abundance of embroidered tablecloths, napkins, nightgowns, and other clothing, as Funchal's well-stocked shops reveal. *Oliveiras,* at two adjoining downtown locations (22 Rua dos Murças; phone: 91-29340; and 11 Rua da Alfândega; phone: 91-20245), has one of the widest selections in town. The workroom housed on the floors above is one of 25 such factories in Funchal. Ask to visit, and see what it takes to create a finished tablecloth or negligee (and ask for the 25% factory discount). *Texeiras* (13 Rua do Aljube; phone: 91-22049) is the place to go for something special; the prices are a bit higher, but the quality is a bit better, too. *Jabara* (59 Rua Dr. Fernão de Ornelas; phone: 91-29500) is another place to shop for embroidery. Opened in 1908, the store is a downtown landmark. *Mima* (298 Estrada Monumental; phone: 91-62267) is an excellent place for smaller items at good prices. Be sure to take the factory tour at *Bazar Anadia* (33 Rua do Visconde de Anadia; phone: 91-22928), which demonstrates how items are finished after being embroidered by the women in the island's small villages. Its downstairs shop is well stocked. Also try *Arte Ricamo* (34 Rua dos Murças; phone: 91-20705), specializing in large tablecloths, sheets, and pillowcases. *Agulha d'Ouro* (30 Rua dos Murças; phone: 91-24885) also has a fine selection of hand-embroidered linens at good prices.

Porto, Portugal – *Casa dos Linhos* (660 Rua de Fernandes Tomás; phone: 2-20044) is a 100-year-old family-run firm specializing in the sale of linen and embroidery. *O Sonho* (320 Rua das Flores; phone: 2-27827), another family-run store, has a limited selection of fine embroidered baptismal dresses with lace and lace-trimmed bibs, plus hand-knit sweaters.

FOOD AND WINE: Food shopping in Spain and Portugal is a pleasure, probably because local customers are so demanding. Everything is fresh — sometimes so fresh that food stores hang unskinned rabbits in their windows. And of course, both countries are famous for their wines — the sherries and anisettes of Spain and the *vinhos verdes* and ports of Portugal.

Madrid, Spain – *El Corte Inglés* (see *Department Stores*) has everything, including a well-stocked supermarket with an excellent meat and fish section, its own brand of olive oil, and delicious breads and cakes, most of which are baked on the premises. Also visit *Horno del Pozo* (9 Calle del Pozo), a small shop established in 1830 with a reputation for the best *hojaldres* (puff pastries) in town. Others include *Cebada* (Plaza de la Cebada); *Chamberi* (61 Calle Alonso Cano); and *Maravilla* (134 Calle Bravo Murillo). *Santa Cecilia* (74 Calle Blasco de Garay) has a fine selection of wines, spirits, liqueurs, beers, and *cavas* (sparkling wines) at reasonable prices. Another good choice for Spanish and foreign wines is *Bolsa de Licores* (13 Calle Infantas).

Granada, Spain – *Casa Hita* (7 Carrera del Genil; phone: 58-221322) is the best place in town for local hams and traditional confectioneries.

Toledo, Spain – A trip to Toledo is incomplete without a sampling of its famous marzipan. Popular shops include *Barosso* (11 Calle Real del Arrabel); *Casa Telesforo* (17 Plaza de Zocodover); and *Santo Tomé* (5 Calle Santo Tomé and 11 Plaza de Zocodover).

Lisbon, Portugal – Some of the country's best pastries are made by *Pasteis de Belém* (84 Rua de Belém; phone: 1-637423), an Old World coffeehouse famous for its delicious offerings sprinkled with cinnamon. *Martins & Costa* (41 Rua do Carmo) has the largest selection of fine foods, delicious regional cheeses, and Portuguese and foreign wines.

GIFTWARE: In Spain, nothing is as famous as fine Lladró porcelain. The Lladró factory is located in Valencia, along the Mediterranean coastline. There is also a factory store that sells hard-to-distinguish seconds for one-third to one-half off retail (cash-and-carry only). Travelers can go crazy buying giftware in Portugal. The country is famous for its Atlantis brand crystal, which ranks in quality and design with Waterford and Baccarat. Vista Alegre for porcelain giftware and dinnerware is another safe bet. It is exported worldwide to better stores; New York's *Metropolitan Museum of Art* sells famous reproductions. Portuguese silver products are also well known and range from place settings to elaborately hammered-out soup tureens.

Madrid, Spain – *Fernando Durán* (8 Calle Serrano) is one of the city's most prestigious shops for antique furniture, sculptures, china, and a wide variety of silver products ranging from miniature frames to decorative pieces. *Paulino* (68 Gran Vía) imports giftware from all over Europe and has exclusive, limited editions of Lladró porcelain figures. *Plata Meneses* (4 Plaza de Canalejas; phone: 1-429-6545) is Spain's leading silver manufacturer, featuring a huge line of giftware and place settings, which fill two showrooms. *Grife & Escoda* (30 Calle Alcalá; phone: 1-232-0505) also has a large selection of crystal, porcelain, silver-plate giftware, and small furnishings, all of excellent quality.

Lisbon, Portugal – *Vista Alegre* (18 Largo do Chiado; phone: 1-361401) offers a complete line of porcelain, from dinnerware to figurines. Some of the samples and discontinued designs sold downstairs are great values. This is a very sophisticated operation; it will even ship purchases to the US. *A. Chave de Prata* (174 Rua da Prata; phone: 1-877915) features well-stocked shelves of porcelain and glass giftware and some interesting bronze objects. *Vidraria da Marina Grande* (38 Rua de São Nicolau; phone: 1-321840; and 62 Rua dos Fanqueiros; phone: 1-873039) is a unique store selling glass and crystal exclusively, with one of the largest selections in the country.

GUNS: The King of Spain and other aristocrats shop at *Diana Turba* (68 Calle Serrano, Madrid; phone: 1-401-6250), where everything from guns and fishing tackle to clothing is spread out on 2 huge floors. The store will also take care of all the necessary paperwork involved in shipping guns back to the US.

HANDICRAFTS: Handicrafts are ubiquitous in Spain and Portugal.

Madrid, Spain – The Spanish government formed the *Artespaña* group to preserve the country's handicraft traditions and to promote the sale of goods from the finest artisans. These shops sell a wide range of handicrafts and home furnishings from all over Spain. Among several locations is one at 3 Plaza de las Cortes (phone: 1-429-1251).

Barcelona, Spain – The *Poble Espanyol* (Spanish Village), on Montjuïc, is a 5-acre exhibition of Spanish art and architecture in the form of a traditional village. Built for the *1929 World's Fair*, it was later transformed into a miniature artisans' community representing the entire country. Plan a full day visiting traditional artisans at work; their carvings, pottery, glass, leather, and metalworks are sold in the village's 35 shops.

Lisbon, Portugal – *Centro de Artesanato* is one of the finest handicrafts centers in Europe, operated by the government to promote regional crafts and their creators. Shops sell copper, lace, wicker, pottery, jewelry, hand-knit fisherman's sweaters, ceramic and copper cooking dishes, embroidered tablecloths, crystal, Arraiolos rugs, and much more. Feira Internacional de Lisboa (Praça das Industrias; phone: 1-644952). Also visit *Artesanato Arameiro* (62 Praça dos Restauradores; phone: 1-320238), which offers a wide variety of regional handicrafts including lace, rugs, ceramics, copperware, and filigree.

Coimbra, Portugal – Coimbra has beautiful handicrafts, examples of which are exhibited and sold in the *Casa de Artesanato da Região de Coimbra*, in the historic Torre de Anto (45 Rua de Sobre-Ripas; phone: 39-23886).

JEWELRY: There are excellent jewelry bargains in both Spain and Portugal. In Spain, look for the famous Majórica pearls, but watch out for imitations. There is only one authentic brand — *Perlas Majórica* — and "Majorca" or "Mallorca" pearls should not be confused with the real thing. Look for the official agency seal and for the unique, 10-year International Certificate of Guarantee that comes with each piece. Sizes run from 4 to 14 millimeters in diameter, in hundreds of combinations. The pearls can be found throughout Spain, but the factory is in Manacor, on the island of Majorca. In Palma, the shop is at 11 Avenida Rey Jaime III. In Portugal, the thing to buy is silver or gold. Filigree is delicate silver threads made into earrings, necklaces, and bracelets. All Portuguese gold jewelry, by law, must contain at least 19.2 karats. Rua da Prata and Rua Augusta are two of the better streets for jewelry in Lisbon, Rua das Flores in Porto.

Madrid, Spain – Spanish sculptor and jeweler *Veiga* (22 Gran Vía; phone: 1-221-5506) has created his own distinctive designs, all in bronze. *Aldao* (15 Gran Vía and 43 Calle Velázquez) is a long-established jeweler that makes unique and limited-edition pieces in its own workshop. *Joaquín Berao* (13 Calle Conde de Xiquena) is an imaginative young Spanish designer selling limited-edition earrings, bracelets, and rings in gold, silver, bronze, and titanium in ultramodern designs. *Suárez* (63 Calle Serrano) is one of Madrid's great jewelers. Stones and jewels are mounted in settings of its own design. The store also carries a huge line of international big-name watches.

Córdoba, Spain – Cordoban silver filigree pieces are favorite souvenir items. Travelers will find a good selection at the *Zoco Municipal de Artesanía* (Calle de los Judíos; phone: 57-204033) and *José Villar Jiménez* (3 Calle Muro de la Misericórdia; phone: 57-481034).

Lisbon, Portugal – *The King of Filigree* (58 Rua da Prata; phone: 1-877441) sells silver filigree items made in Porto. Some are dipped in gold. Also try *W.A. Sarmento* (251 Rua do Ouro) for gold pieces. *Ouriversaria Diadema* (166 Rua Aurea; phone: 1-321362) sells gold, filigree, and souvenirs. Two other shops worth a try are *Ourivesaria Pimenta* (257 Rua Augusta; phone: 1-324564), offering fine jewelry, watches, and silver, and *Joalharia Mergulhão* (162 Rua de São Paulo; phone: 1-346-0013), one of the oldest jewelers in the city.

Coimbra, Portugal – *Patrão Joalheiros* (104 Rua Visconde da Luz; phone: 39-23096) is one of the oldest and most respected jewelers in Coimbra, selling lovely Portuguese filigree, silver salvers, and silver tea and coffee services. *Agata Joalharia* (2 Escadas de São Tiago; phone: 39-22361) sells fine jewelry, beautifully mounted at reasonable prices.

Porto, Portugal – *Luiz Ferreira & Filhos* (9 Rua Trindade Coelho; phone: 2-316146) is a small shop featuring chic and expensive jewelry and giftware. Its own designs mix sterling silver with quartz, marble, and other interesting stones. *M. Eugenia da Silveira Rodrigues* (275 Rua das Flores; phone: 2-21840) has many antique jewelry pieces, as well as the shop's own creations, including some interesting silver animal figurines, all of superior quality. *David Rosas* (1471 Avenida da Boavista; phone: 2-668464) is a sleek shop carrying expensive pieces. It is Portugal's largest manufacturer of silver animals, many life-size! It also specializes in custom silver frames. *Rosior* (38 Rua da Cunha; phone: 2-401519) also carries a fine line of traditional and modern jewelry.

LEATHER GOODS: Most leather on the Iberian Peninsula comes from sheep and lambs; cows produce a heavier quality skin that's made into jackets associated with motorcycle riding. Antelope skin is not available in Spain. There are literally thousands of stores selling leather jackets, coats, gloves, pocketbooks, wallets, and other items. Generally speaking, shoppers can tell the quality of the leather by the feel. The softer it is, the more expensive. Spain is the better place to buy leather fashions; Portugal's selection is smaller and concentrates on leather accessories and shoes.

Madrid, Spain – *Loewe* specializes in fine leather fashions for men and women, as well as accessories and luggage. The several locations include 8 Gran Vía, 26 Calle Serrano, a shop at the *Palace* hotel (7 Plaza de las Cortes), and a shop at 34 Calle Serrano that carries men's fashions exclusively. There are also branches in Seville, Granada, Valencia, Bilbao, and Palma. *Manuel Herrero* (7 and 23 Calle Preciados) is also a popular leather outlet, offering a wide selection and good prices. *Lepanto* (3 Plaza de Oriente) overflows with leather jackets, gloves, handbags, belts, briefcases, and accessories. Drawers of leather gloves and handbags line the walls at *Zurro* (16 Calle Preciados and 4 Calle Carmen). Classically styled items made of reptile skins are available at *Vivar* (11 Calle Preciados and 64 Gran Vía). *La Casa de las Maletas* (45 Calle Claudio Coello; phone: 1-431-7765) offers beautifully displayed luggage, shoes, briefcases, pocketbooks, and accessories, all at attractive prices.

Barcelona, Spain – *Loewe* (35 Passeig de Gràcia) is the place for handbags and traditional Spanish leather goods. Also check the merchandise at *Yanko* (100 Passeig de Gràcia).

Córdoba, Spain – Shopping at *Meryan* (2 Calleja de las Flores; phone: 57-475902) is more like visiting a museum, unless the customer is prepared for a serious purchase. The artistic hand-embossed and tinted leather (*guadamecil*) goods are done in the Renaissance style (with some designs derived from classical paintings), the handwork is painstaking and magnificent, and prices on the larger pieces run into the thousands of dollars. Wander up and down the stairs in this centuries-old mansion, whose gardens once extended down to the mosque, to inspect leather chairs, chests, wall hangings, maps, picture frames, and even some wooden pieces, and ask to see the workshops surrounding the serene white marble patio. The more affordable leather bags and wallets that many visitors end up buying here are of excellent quality but not made by *Meryan.*

Seville, Spain – Andalusian horsemen come to *El Caballo* (14 Calle Adriano), near the bullring, for the finest leather boots, saddles, hunting gear, traditional riding suits, and flat, wide-brimmed hats.

Lisbon, Portugal – *Luvaria Ulisses* (87 Rua do Carmo; phone: 1-32095) specializes in leather gloves. *Escondipel* (9 Rua Romalho Ortigão; phone: 1-542275) has fine leather goods and is well known for its fur creations.

Braga, Portugal – *Herdeiros de Francisco José Ferreira* (124 Rua do Souto; phone: 53-25155) is the place for high-quality leather goods including suitcases, briefcases, and ladies' handbags. Try *Sapataria Teresinha* (84-86 Rua do Souto; phone: 53-22943) for top-quality leather shoes made in the region.

Porto, Portugal – *Vincent* (174 Rua 31 de Janeiro) has a wonderful antique interior and sells top-quality leather jackets, pants, and coats.

MUSICAL INSTRUMENTS: Who can resist listening to the beautiful sounds of Spanish guitars? Those in Spain are primarily classical.

Madrid, Spain – *Manuel Contreras* (80 Calle Mayor; phone: 1-248-5926) has one of the city's largest collections of guitars and other musical instruments. *Real Musical* (111 Calle Carlos) also carries guitars, other musical instruments, and records.

Braga, Portugal – *Vadeca* (Largo do Barão São Martinho; phone: 53-71045) sells the typical handmade *viola braguesa,* or *cavaquinho* guitar, from which the ukelele was developed.

RUGS AND TAPESTRIES: Rugs from Arraiolos, a small town near Evora, are reminders of the Moorish occupation of the Iberian Peninsula centuries ago. Today, local women still do needlepoint on these rugs in small workshops. They use 100% wool in the small petit point and the larger *ponto largo* stitch to create animals, birds, or more elaborate scenes. Depending upon the design and its intricacy, prices vary per square foot. Most establishments welcome special orders. The rugs can be found in stores all over the country, even tourist souvenir shops. Prices in the US, in some cases, are three to four times higher.

Lisbon, Portugal – *Casa Quintão* (30 Rua Ivens; phone: 1-365847) is one of Lisbon's finest Arraiolos rug stores. Several other shops selling Arraiolos rugs are *Casa dos Tapetes de Arraiolos* (116 Rua da Imprensa Nacional; phone: 1-668246); *Tapetes Trevo* (33 Avenida Oscar Monteiro Torres; phone: 1-778415); and *Casa Regional da Ilha Verde* (4 Rua Paiva de Andrade). *Galerias Sesimbra* (77 Rua Castilho; phone: 1-560291), Lisbon's second-oldest gallery, commissions well-known Portuguese artists to create designs that are transferred onto needlepoint canvases. The gallery stocks a huge supply of Agulha tapestries, which are 100% wool, hand-stitched, limited editions in three-dimensional motifs.

SHOES: Portuguese styles are fashionable, but not as sleek as Spanish designs. The leathers used are soft and durable. Women's shoes rarely come in half sizes, but men's do. The Charles Jourdan brand is in many shops and is more reasonably priced than in French stores. Many shoe stores also carry leather accessories. When buying a pair of Spanish shoes, use the size only as a reference; the last of a Spanish shoe sold in Spain is different from the last of a Spanish shoe made for the American market.

Madrid, Spain – *Yanko* (40 Gran Vía; phone: 1-232-5328) is famous for its hand-made shoes for men and women. *Bravo* (42 Calle Serrano, 31 Gran Vía, and 68 Gran Vía) carries the finest in European shoes, particularly good buys on Charles Jourdan styles. *La Inesperada* (11 Calle Cruz; phone: 1-221-0770) is a specialist in wide widths for men and women. Pierre Cardin, Elio Berhanyer, Pertegaz, and many more designer shoes are available at *Los Pequeños Suizos* (68 Calle Serrano), which also carries half sizes, a rarity in Spain.

Barcelona, Spain – *Francesc Tasies i Ginesta* (7 Carrer d'Avinyó; phone: 3-301-0172) is noted for handmade, rope-soled espadrilles, the sort of footwear used for dancing the *sardana*.

Lisbon, Portugal – *Charles* (275 Rua Augusta; phone: 1-320700; and 105 Rua do Carmo; phone: 1-325500) is a national chain store that has its own factory. It's the only store in Portugal that makes women's half sizes. It also specializes in Italian designer brands.

SPORTING GOODS: Department stores are usually the best bet, carrying everything including equipment and clothing for hunting, camping, surfing, tennis, golf, skiing, fishing, and aerobic workouts.

Most Visitable Vineyards

 Both Spain and Portugal have long-standing wine making traditions, but the practice of opening wineries to the visiting public is still relatively new. Because of this, and the vast profusion of small vineyards, it is advisable to make arrangements in advance. Since the days of the Phoenicians and Greeks, sweet wine has been made in southern Spain. Under the Romans, wine production spread throughout the country and was eventually brought to the Americas along with the Spanish conquistadores. In Roman times, when Portugal was known as Lusitania, its wines were being shipped to Italy. During the middle of the 13th century, the Portuguese monarchy ordained that all wine growing be submitted to royal protection and regulation, and that vineyards be planted on all arable lands not suited to growing grain.

Today, Spain is the world's third-largest wine producer, with more acreage devoted to vines than in any other European country. Much like Italy, production is fragmented and spread over a wide area, with half of it organized into 850 cooperatives comprising some 200,000 members. Except for the highest elevations, there is virtually no corner of the country that does not produce wine. Similarly, wine grapes are grown almost everywhere today in Portugal; approximately 8% percent of its arable land is devoted to vineyards. Production, however, is concentrated in the central and northern parts of the country.

Running the full range from the aperitif and dessert wines of Andalusia to the brut *cavas* of the Penedés and a fine assortment of brandies, Spain's viniculture is a vast and varied adventure in good drinking. In addition to the famous rioja reds, Spain produces a large assortment of red wines, the best hailing from the temperate northern climes. East of the Rioja region, Navarre makes full-bodied, fruity red wines from the same Rioja grape varieties; south of the Rioja along the Duero Valley, the Ribera del Duero demarcation is gaining increasing cachet; and Catalonia's Penedés and Lleida areas produce some of the country's best red wines from the native monastrell, ull de llebre, and garnacha grapes, as well as from such acclimatized varieties as the cabernet sauvignon, merlot, and pinot noir. Less sophisticated, but still eminently drinkable, are the reds of the central plateau and the regions around Valencia and Alicante.

Though white wines are produced throughout Spain, those of Rioja and Catalonia have earned international renown. Made from the native viura, malvasi, and garnacha blanca grapes, the rioja whites were formerly matured in oak, but are now mostly cold-fermented in stainless steel to retain the crisp freshness of the fruit. La Mancha now produces a flowery white from the airén grape, and Jerez produces table wines from the palomino sherry grape. In Galicia, the whites have a light, natural effervescence.

For free educational maps, brochures, and other information on all Spanish wines, contact *Wines of Spain* (Commercial Office of Spain, 405 Lexington Ave., New York, NY 10174; phone: 212-661-4814). There is no admission fee at any Spanish winery, and all of those mentioned below are accustomed to receiving visitors.

RIOJA, Spain: Best known among the Spanish table wines, riojas — emanating from a hilly region on the western side of the Ebro Valley in northern Spain — have been around since Roman times. At the end of the 19th century, when French vineyards were devasted by disease, wine makers from Bordeaux moved here, giving an immense boost to the regional production, which leans toward reds over whites. No wonder, then, that these wines are similar to a bordeaux or burgundy, but with a higher alcoholic content (between 10 and 12.5%) — which is generally true of most Spanish wines in comparison with those of other European countries. The rioja reds, made from a blend of the native tempranillo, garnacha, mazuelo, and graciano grapes, have a characteristic oaken taste and vanilla aroma. Within the Rioja region are three sub-regions: Rioja Alta, Rioja Alavesa, and Rioja Baja. The wines of the first two, in the hilly west, are the best.

The younger wines are labeled either *crianza* or *sin crianza,* meaning with or without aging. The *crianza* wines are aged for no less than 2 years, of which at least a year must be spent in a 225-liter oak cask. *Reservas* and *gran reservas* are the mellow old wines that have spent long years in cask and bottle. Red *reservas* are aged for at least a year in oak casks and 2 years in the bottle, leaving the winery no earlier than the 4th year after vintage. Red *gran reservas* spend no less than 2 years in casks and a minimum of 3 in the bottle, leaving the winery no sooner than the 6th year after vintage. The same production regulations apply throughout Spain, but in the Rioja, the hoary old bodegas steeped in tradition still age their reds considerably longer in oak to cultivate the vanilla bouquet and the velvety texture that are their trademarks. Rioja also produces saucy *claretes* (light reds or rosés) and dry whites. There are dozens of vineyards in the Rioja, with the most important ones found in Logroño (the region's capital), Haro, Cenicero, and Fuenmayor.

Bodegas Montecillo – Located in Fuenmayor, 10 miles (16 km) from Logroño, this winery dates from 1874. Visits must be arranged in advance, and a full selection of whites, reds, and rosés is for sale at the bodega. The whites are young and fruity; the rosés, slightly matured; and the reds, rounded and pleasant, with good color and aroma. Information: *34 Calle San Cristóbal,* Fuenmayor, La Rioja 26360, Spain (phone: 41-440125).

Bodegas Campo Viejo – Visitors to the regional capital will enjoy sampling the wines of this bodega, produced from its own vines and nourished in its vast store of wooden casks. The whites and rosés are young and fruity; the reds, mature, aromatic, and light on the palate. The *reserva* reds are full-bodied and velvety. Visits must be arranged in advance. Information: *3 Calle Gostavo Adolfo Bécquer,* Logroño, La Rioja 26000, Spain (phone: 41-238100).

Bodegas Berceo – Established in 1872, this winery in Haro, some 30 miles (48 km) from Logroño, makes fresh, fruity whites and rosés, fruity young reds with good color, and well-rounded *reserva* reds with body and acidity. Visits must be arranged in advance. Information: *32 Calle Cuevas,* Haro, La Rioja 26200, Spain (phone: 41-310744).

Unión Vitivinicola (Bodegas Marqués de Cáceres) – A mere 20 years old, this Cenicero winery, located 14 miles (22 km) from Logroño, has made quite an international name for itself in a very short time. Its whites and rosés are fresh and fruity, and its reds are full-bodied, smooth, and long. Visiting hours are weekdays from 8:30 AM to 6:15 PM. Closed August. Information: *Carretera Logroño,* Cenicero, La Rioja 26000, Spain (phone: 41-454000).

For further information on the region and its wineries, contact either of the following associations: *ARBOR-Agrupación de Artesanos Bodegueros de Rioja* (43 Gran Vía Juan Carlos I, Logroño 26002, Spain; phone: 41-225304), or *Grupo de Exportadores de Vinos de Rioja* (6-7 Gran Vía, Logroño 26002, Spain; phone: 41-257555).

CATALONIA, Spain: This region in the northeast corner of Spain borders the Mediterranean and produces a great variety of wines, the best known among them those of Ampordá (reds and rosés), Alella (dry or sweet whites), and the Penedès (whites and reds). But the *pièce de résistance* of the region are the champagne-like sparkling wines known as *cavas,* produced in brut, sec, and demi-sec varieties. Since 1872, when Spain produced its first bottle of *cava,* the country has become the largest producer of sparkling wines in the world. Although *cava* is made by the *méthode champenoise,* or champagne method, it is not a budget substitute for champagne, since the native parellada, macabeo, and xarello grapes give it its own distinctive regional characteristics. About 95% of Spanish *cava* comes from the Penedès, with the majority of producers grouped around the town of Sant Sadurní d'Anoia. Information: *Consejo Regulador Vinos Espumoso,* 24-26 Calle Tarragona, Vilafranca del Penedès, Barcelona 08000, Spain.

In the Penedès, which spreads across the south of Barcelona province and the northeast of Tarragona province, table wines are also produced. The careful harvesting and elaboration of base wines to create sparkling wines have given rise to high-quality whites that are fruity and fresh and have an alcoholic strength of between 9 and 13%. The rosés are similar to the whites, and the area also produces light, smooth reds.

Codorníu – Since 1551, the Codorníu family has been producing still wines. In 1872, it produced Spain's first *cava.* Now a national monument welcoming over 250,000 visitors a year, the winery produces more than 45 million bottles of *cava* annually in the world's largest underground wine cellar network — extending 11 miles on 5 levels. These pale yellow sparkling wines have a hint of green, with a smooth, flowery aroma and lovely flavor. The winery is open Mondays through Thursdays, from 8 AM to noon and from 3 to 6 PM; Fridays, from 8 AM to noon. Closed August. Information: *Calle Afueras,* Sant Sadurní d'Anoia, Barcelona 08770, Spain (phone: 3-891-0125).

Freixenet – This winery has been producing light, fresh, and aromatic *cavas* for just over 100 years. Open Mondays through Fridays, from 9:30 AM to noon and from 3:30 to 5:30 PM. Closed holidays and August. Information: *c/o Mercedes Argany,* Plaza Estación, Sant Sadurní d'Anoia, Barcelona 08770, Spain (phone: 3-891-0700).

JEREZ DE LA FRONTERA, Spain: Among the world's most popular aperitif wines, genuine sherry comes only from the region of Jerez de la Frontera at the southern tip of Spain. Produced in great cathedral-like bodegas, these wines are continuously blended, the younger and older wines mixing in a series of casks that constitute the *solera.* The result — no vintage sherries and a quality that is absolutely consistent from year to year.

The predominant grape varieties are palomino *fino,* palomino jerez, pedro ximénez, and muscatel. The four standard styles of sherries are *finos* (pale, dry, and light, often with a hint of bitter almonds), *manzanillas finas* (driest of all, with the tang of the sea air of their native Sanlúcar de Barrameda), *amontillados* (amber sherries with more depth and body, and a nutty flavor), and *olorosos* (dark and fragrant, dry in their natural state, but often sweetened with pedro ximénez wine to achieve the rich, raisiny creams that elegantly top off a meal). In addition, pale cream is a new style — a light, medium sherry with a touch of sweetness.

Before heading down to Jerez, contact the *Sherry Exporters Association,* which coordinates visits and has its own educational installations, c/o Bartolomé Vergara, Director of Public Relations, A.C.E.S. (Asociación de Criadores y Exportadores de Sherry), 2 Calle Eguiluz, Jerez de la Frontera, Cádiz 11400, Spain (phone: 56-341046).

Pedro Domecq – A maker of wines since 1730, Domecq produces the full range of sherries in its vast facilities. All visits must be arranged through the public relations department, and the winery is closed on Saturdays and August 1 through 20. Information: *Pedro Domecq,* S.A. 1 Calle Colón, Jerez de la Frontera, Cádiz 11400, Spain (phone: 56-330950).

González Byass – Established in 1835, this winery produces *finos, olorosos,* and sweet sherries. It also offers a unique ritual, featuring a mouse that climbs a miniature ladder to sip a daily dram of sherry from a glass set out expressly for it. All visits are by appointment, made through the public relations department. Closed Saturdays and August. Information: *González Byass,* S.A. 12 Calle Manuel María González, Jerez de la Frontera, Cádiz 11400, Spain (phone: 56-340000).

PORTUGAL: Portugal's northern Minho district is famed for its *vinho verde,* or "green wine," so named not for its color (there is also a red *vinho verde*), but for the fact that the grapes are gathered before they are quite ripe and are then allowed to ferment for a very brief period, to produce a light, dry wine that is often slightly effervescent and has a low alcohol content. The special grapes used are such unfamiliar varieties as louzão, docar, maurisco, azal, espadeiro, vendelho, and borracal. A few of the better *vinhos verdes* come from just north of the Douro in the Amarante region, but the finest hail from the area between the Lima and the Minho in the far north of the country. *Vinhos verdes* account for one-quarter of Portugal's total wine production.

From the granite hills and sandy soil along the northern Dão, Alva, and Mondego rivers come the white and red dão wines. The former can be a bit astringent; the latter, when aged, fruity, clean, and smooth.

Although most of the greater vineyards of the Douro Valley produce the famous fortified port wines, there is also a notable production of excellent red and white table wines, which are mostly consumed locally. Among them are the evel and grandjo wines. Lancers and Mateus have made the Portuguese rosés famous; they tend to be pink, fruity, and refreshing. Some are still wines, while others display varying degrees of effervescence reminiscent of the *vinho verde.*

But Portugal's particular vinicultural strength is in the fortified vintage port and madeira wines. The former stem from the hillside vines of the upper Douro Valley and take their name from the city of Porto, where the wine is bottled and marketed. Made from partly fermented red wine mixed with brandy, port is a wine of considerable strength and high sugar content. The maturation process ranges from 2 to 5 years. When the wine of a particular year is considered of especially high quality, it is declared a vintage year. In non-vintage years, the wines are blended to produce standard-quality ports, which are usually drier than vintage ports. Madeira wine is produced on the island of the same name and is similar to port.

Though the wine dealers in the Porto suburb of Vila Nova de Gaia offer winery visits and tastings at their lodges (where the port is stored before shipment), this most often includes just a brief explanation — with mock-ups — of the port wine making process and a meager sampling of the more mediocre wares. This is an opportunity, however, to taste the sherry-like white port, which is not exported. Beyond this, winery visits are by no means a touristic event in Portugal. Those interested in learning more about the wines of the country can write ahead to the port wine and Dão wine associations, whose experts will provide literature and opportunities to observe the wine making process. The port wine organization is the *Instituto do Vinho do Porto* (Rua Ferreira Borges, Porto 4000, Portugal). The Dão wine producers are at *Federação dos Vinicultores do Dão* (102 Rua Dr. Duarte, Viseu 3500, Portugal). For more information about Portuguese wine dealers that conduct public tours and wine tasting visits, see *Porto*, THE CITIES, and *Madeira*, DIRECTIONS.

Spas

 The spas of Spain and Portugal are a slightly different breed from those of the US. Unlike their American counterparts, which are predominantly exercise- and fitness-oriented, Spanish and Portuguese spas take more of a therapeutic approach. They are health resorts in a purer sense, and are monitored by each country's National Health Association. In Spain, *balnearios* (spas) tend to focus on three specific approaches: thalassotherapy, in which ocean water, seaweed, and algae are used for therapeutic purposes; hydrotherapy, using mineral water drawn from natural springs; and mud therapy, which relies on rich volcanic or natural spring sources. Spain has over 90 spa resorts spread throughout its various regions. Some are simple, concentrating solely on relaxation and cures, while others are more elaborate, offering the best in resort, spa, and sports facilities. The *Spanish National Health Association* (23 Calle Martin de los Heros, 4-D, Madrid; phone: 1-542-9775) provides detailed information about the country's *balnearios*.

In Portugal, spas are generally more primitive and don't offer much in the way of facilities. Most have been built around the many mineral and thermal springs of the northern and central regions of the country. Their charm lies in the fact that they aren't overcommercialized commodities, but places where one can bathe in soothing waters and find peace with nature. Further details are available from the *Associação Nacional dos Industrias de Aguas Minero-Medicinais e de Mesa* (93 Rua de São José, Lisbon 1100; phone: 1-324523). Additionally, many US travel agencies specialize in spa vacations. Two of the best are *Spa-Finders Travel Arrangements* (784 Broadway, New York, NY 10003; phone: 212-475-1000; 800-255-7727 outside New York), and *Spa Trek International* (470 Park Ave. S., New York, NY 10016; phone: 212-779-3480).

BALNEARIO DEL GRAN HOTEL DE LA TOJA, Isla de la Toja, Pontevedra, Spain: Built in 1903 and recently renovated, this is one of Spain's finest spa resorts, offering the perfect recipe for stress reduction. Tucked away on a small, secluded island in the Atlantic Ocean off the coast of the northwestern Galician province of Pontevedra, it rises in grand majesty from a lush forest. Surrounded by tranquil waters, romantic beaches, and ample vegetation, the spa specializes in cures for skin diseases, rheumatism, and respiratory disorders, reduction of stress and tension, and physical rehabilitation. Facilities include thermal baths, vapor inhalation rooms, a thermal swimming pool, mud and bubble baths, a gymnasium, and a sauna. Physiotherapy and massages are also administered. In addition, the 200-room *Toja* hotel offers a wide range of leisure activities and facilities, including tennis, golf, swimming, elegant restaurants, entertainment, and a casino. A 10-day stay is recommended for best results. Information: *Gran Hotel de la Toja,* Isla de la Toja, Pontevedra 36991, Spain (phone: 86-730025).

BALNEARIO VICHY CATALÁN, Caldes de Malavella, Girona, Spain: This small, comfortable, and relatively undiscovered traditional spa resort north of Barcelona may be short on elegance, but it makes up for that with its commitment to health. Facilities include pressure baths with controlled jets, bubble baths, massage and pressure jet showers, paraffin mud baths, Finnish and steam saunas, vapor inhalation treatments, a gymnasium, tennis courts, a swimming pool, and a children's playground. Information: *Hotel Balneario Vichy Catalán,* 32 Avenida Dr. Furest, Caldes de Malavella, Girona 17455, Spain (phone: 72-470000).

INCOSOL SPA AND RESORT, Marbella, Costa del Sol, Spain: This 9-story, 200-room modern hotel, set along Spain's famous Costa de Sol, has everything. The spa facilities are so wide-ranging that guests could spend a week just sorting through the choices. Treatments include medical checkups and thorough case histories by a resident doctor, obesity treatments, massage, toning, laser therapy, acupunture, mud baths, a variety of facial treatments, physiotherapy, hydrotherapy, electrotherapy, and more. The spa specializes in helping patients with weight problems, geriatric problems, and beauty care. There is also tennis, golf, squash, and water sports at the nearby beach. Information: *Incosol Spa & Resort Hotel,* Golf Rio Real, Marbella, Costa del Sol 29600, Spain (phone: 52-773700; in the US, 800-R-WARNER; in Canada, 800-344-6535).

LOUISON BOBET'S THALASSOTHERAPY, Mijas, Costa del Sol, Spain: Built in 1986, the *Byblos Andaluz* hotel is one of Spain's most modern and most efficient spa resorts. The Institute of Thalassotherapy's philosophy is based on the medicinal properties of warm sea water; there are up to 18 different treatments using water heated to 99F to penetrate the skin and tone up the body. Other treatments include the application of seaweed to relax muscles and the treatment of circulatory problems, varicose veins, and cramps. The institute also specializes in treating rheumatic illness, body pampering, and overall physical fitness. Accommodations consist of deluxe suites and mini-suites overlooking rolling greens, mountains, and the whitewashed town of Mijas. The hotel was designed to resemble a Moorish palace, complete with patios and long white porticoes; rooms open onto small courtyards filled with fountains, flowers, and orange trees. Many guests come here to play golf on the 2 courses, or to bask in the pleasures of *salud y sol* — health and sun. The 135-room hotel also features 3 restaurants, 5 tennis courts, sightseeing, and entertainment. Information: *Hotel Byblos Andaluz,* Mijas Golf, Apt. 138, Fuengirola, Málaga 29650, Spain (phone: 52-473050 or 52-460250); in the US, *Crown International,* 11 W. Passaic St., Rochelle Park, NJ 07662 (phone: 800-628-8929 or 800-323-7500).

VITATOP, Loja, Granada, Spain: This modern resort, built in 1986, is a sparkling Moorish wonder, neatly tucked amid a lush Mediterranean forest high up in the Sierra Nevada. Each of the 35 elegantly appointed rooms in *La Bobadilla* hotel offers maximum comfort — all have private terraces and gardens, and huge bathtubs. The spa here is similar to a fitness club, featuring a modern gymnasium with full Nautilus equipment, a heated indoor swimming pool, a Jacuzzi, 2 Finnish saunas, 2 Turkish steambaths, and a solarium. Professional fitness counseling, personal programs, and massages are also available. There is also a beauty salon, 3 restaurants, an outdoor swimming pool, 2 tennis courts, horseback riding, and nearby skiing. Information: *Hotel La Bobadilla,* Finca La Bobadilla, 52 Apartado, Loja, Granada 18006, Spain (phone: 58-321861); in the US, *Marketing Ahead,* 433 Fifth Ave., New York, NY 10016 (phone: 212-686-9213).

TERMAS, Archena, Murcia, Spain: The hotel is simple: 69 rooms and 6 suites. Its claim to fame is its mineral water, which features chlorinated, iodized, brominated, and sulfurous properties with regenerative power. The spa specializes in treating rheumatism, respiratory ailments, and obesity. Thermal pools, a fitness center, massage, mud applications, and beauty treatments are also available. Information: *Hotel Termas,* Carretera del Balneario, Balneario de Archena, Archena, Murcia 30600, Spain (phone: 68-670100).

BALNEARIO PRATS, Caldes de Malavella, Girona, Spain: This casual spa is situated in a 100-room Catalan-style hotel. The spa specializes in treating rheumatism, arthritis, and other circulatory and respiratory ailments, through the use of hydrotherapy, bubble baths, Scottish showers, underwater massages, sauna, infrared lamp therapy, and paraffin, wax, and clay treatments. Information: *Hotel Balneario Prats,* Caldes de Malavella, Girona 17455, Spain (phone: 72-470051).

CALDAS DO GERÊS, near Braga, Costa Verde, Portugal: One of Portugal's most picturesque spas, it's situated in an unspoiled valley on the left bank of the Gerês River and inside the Peneda-Gerês National Park. The spa features immersion baths, bubble baths, and underwater massages, to aid in curing liver and kidney ailments and hypertension. The water here supposedly has the highest fluoride content in Europe. In addition to the natural springs, guests can enjoy swimming, tennis, roller skating, fishing, boating, and hiking. Information: *Empresa das Aguas do Gerês,* SARL, 114 Praça da Liberdade, Sala E, Porto 4000, Portugal (phone: 2-313584 or 2-313587).

CALDAS DE VIZELA, near Guimarães, Costa Verde, Portugal: A typical Portuguese retreat built along the Vizela River. The spa here dates back to Roman times; its waters are believed to cure rheumatism, respiratory problems, and traumatic disturbances. Treatments include immersion baths, steambaths, medicinal mud, and electrotherapy. Leisure activities include swimming, tennis, rowing, fishing, and sightseeing. Information: *Companhia dos Banhos de Vizela,* SARL, Rua Dr. Abilio Torres, Caldas de Vizela, Guimarães 4800, Portugal (phone: 53-481234).

CURIA, near Coimbra, Costa de Prata, Portugal: Portugal's most famous and most recommended spa. Located in the Bairrada region amid the freshness, peace, and shade of the forest of Buçaco, this spa is well known for its medicinal waters and its treatments for rheumatism, hypertension, gout, kidney ailments, gastric disturbances, and stress, including immersion baths and massages. There is also a gymnasium, a sauna, a swimming pool, tennis courts, fishing, boating, and a beach. Accommodations are available at the nearby *Curia Palace, Hotel das Termas,* or the *Estalagem Sangalhos.* For a truly memorable experience, stay at the *Buçaco* hotel, a former 19th-century palace. The old-fashioned spa town of Luso and the glittering nightlife of Figueira da Foz are nearby. Information: *Sociedade das Aguas da Curia,* Anadia 3780, Portugal (phone: 31-521856 or 31-521857).

LUSO, near Buçaco, Costa de Prata, Portugal: Like Curia, the Luso spa is set in the secular purity of the Buçaco woods and is one of the most renowned spas in Portugal. The mild climate and natural conditions of the region make for excellent physical and mental recuperation. The famous Luso waters rise in the São João spring in the center of town. Treatments include immersion baths, mud applications, and underwater massages. There is also a swimming pool, tennis courts, sauna, gymnasium, and hiking. Accommodations are available at the nearby *Eden* hotel, *Grande Hotel das Termas do Luso,* and the ultra-deluxe *Buçaco Palace* hotel. Information: *Sociedade das Aguas do Luso,* SARL, Rua Alvaro de Castelões, Mealhada 3050, Portugal (phone: 31-93211).

MONTE REAL, near Leiria, Costa de Prata, Portugal: Near the coast, halfway between Lisbon and Porto, Monte Real features some of Portugal's most famous ruins, as well as some of its most varied activities. There are nearby beaches at São Pedro de Muel, Pedrogão, and Vieira. There is also a swimming pool, tennis courts, and fishing on the premises. The spa features Old World charm and a wonderful view of the poetic green fields of the Lis and Lena valleys. Information: *Termas de Monte Real,* Monte Real 2425, Portugal (phone: 44-62151).

VIDAGO, near Chaves, northern Portugal: A cosmopolitan resort that produces most of the fresh water consumed in the country. Treatments include intramuscular injections of mineral water and medicinal baths. Located in a peaceful forest, the resort also has a swimming pool, sauna, horseback riding, tennis courts, golf, hunting, fishing, and a nightclub. Information: *SOVIPE, Vidago, Melgaço, and Pedras Salgadas, SARL,* 463 Rua de Santo António do Telheiro, São Mamaede de Infesta 4465, Portugal (phone: 76-902503 or 76-902626).

VIMEIRO, Torres Vedras, Costa de Prata, Portugal: The Vimeiro village, which dates back to the first French invasion in 1808, is today a much-frequented spa, known for its perfect climate. Activities include horseback riding, golf, fishing, swimming, and tennis. Vimeiro's famous waters are recommended for liver, kidney, and skin ailments. Information: *1876 Empresa das Aguas do Vimeiro,* Avenida Conselheiro Fernando de Sousa, Lisbon 1000, Portugal (phone: 1-680568 or 1-651445).

For the Body

Great Golf

The British brought golf to the Iberian Peninsula around the turn of the century, but it was another 50 years before the game acquired any degree of popularity — and then it remained an activity of only the very social or the very rich. Today, an increasing number of foreign golfers have discovered that Spain and Portugal's 100 or so courses offer the perfect formula for a golfing vacation: a beautiful natural setting, ideal climate almost year-round, and some rather challenging layouts. In Spain alone, the number of golf clubs has quadrupled over the last 2 decades. American visitors will find little problem adjusting to Spanish and Portuguese course configurations; both tend to be designed in the American mold — target golf, with fairly narrow fairways leading to greens surrounded by bunkers and trees.

Most trips to Spain and Portugal begin in their respective capitals, and championship courses surround both Madrid and Lisbon. The most popular courses, however, are found in the south — in both countries. There are over a dozen courses along the 85-mile stretch of highway between Málaga and Sotogrande on Spain's Costa del Sol, among them the oldest and best known in the land. But some courses have become so overrun that increasing numbers of golfers are turning to the less-crowded courses of northern Spain, where spectacular scenery is often an added attraction. In Portugal, there are some 20 courses scattered across the mainland and the islands of Madeira and the Azores. Among them are the championship courses in the southern Algarve, where perfect climate and increasing numbers of courses have made the region a magnet for golfers. The Lisbon/Estoril area also contains some of the finest playing places on the Continent. Some of the best are listed below.

Golf fees vary at most resorts. For guests staying at a golf hotel, greens fees usually are included. In Spain, the cost for 18 holes generally runs about $20; in Portugal, expect to pay $25 and up. Club rentals start at $6, handcarts at $2, gas or electric carts at $20. Lesson costs in both countries vary according to the reputation of the pro and the price level of the resort. Some courses require a valid US handicap certificate. Information: *Royal Spanish Golf Federation,* 9 Calle Capitán Haya, Madrid 28020, Spain (phone: 1-555-2682 or 1-555-2757), and the *Direcção-Geral do Turismo,* 86 Avenida António Augusto de Aguiar, Lisbon 1000, Portugal (phone: 1-575091).

LA MANGA CAMPO DE GOLF, Los Belones, Spain: The two 18-hole championship layouts offer tantalizing views of the Mediterranean from nearly every tee, and the sights and scenery provide a sort of ancillary hazard. Gary Player has called it the "most superbly maintained course in the world." Information: *La Manga Campo de Golf,* Los Belones, Cartagena, Murcia 30385, Spain (phone: 68-564511).

GOLF LA TOJA, Isla de La Toja, Spain: This 9-hole course lies on an island in the Ría de Arosa, 50 miles (80 km) south of Santiago de Compostela; a bridge links the island to the mainland. At first sight, the course seems rather easy. But looming pines, the adjacent sea, and a constant wind add unexpected pressure. *La Toja's* club membership totals 250, but some 5,000 golfers tackle its narrow fairways and doglegs every summer. Since it is open year-round, it is possible to avoid the summertime crowds. Information: *Golf La Toja,* Isla de La Toja, Pontevedra 36991, Spain (phone: 86-730726 or 86-730818).

REAL SOCIEDAD HÍPICA ESPAÑOLA CLUB DE CAMPO, Madrid, Spain: This 18-hole course, founded in 1932, is 2½ miles (4 km) from Madrid on the right bank of the Manzanares River. One of Madrid's best, it hosted the *World Cup* in 1975 and the *Spanish Open* in 1957, 1960, and 1982. The course is characterized by very narrow fairways, flanked by oak trees, which lead to elevated greens protected by bunkers. There also is a 9-hole course. Information: *Real Sociedad Hípica Española Club de Campo,* 6 Calle Fernanflor, Madrid 2801, Spain (phone: 1-429-8889).

REAL CLUB DE PUERTA DE HIERRO, Madrid, Spain: Founded at the turn of the 20th century, this prestigious club occupies a slope studded with pines and oaks. There are 2 18-hole courses (known as Course I and Course II), and several holes are crossed by bridle paths. Information: *Real Club de Puerta de Hierro,* Avenida de Miraflores, Madrid 28035, Spain (phone: 1-316-1745).

CLUB DE GOLF LOMAS-BOSQUE, Madrid, Spain: Built in the early 1970s, this pleasantly rambling 18-hole, par 72 course offers some deceptive challenges. Eleven of its fairways and greens lie against, or very close to, a manmade lake and stream. Information: *Club de Golf Lomas-Bosque,* Villaviciosa de Odón, Apartado 51, Madrid 28003, Spain (phone: 1-616-2170 or 1-616-2382).

CLUB DE CAMPO DE GOLF DE MÁLAGA, Málaga, Spain: Just 6 miles (10 km) from Málaga and 4 miles (6 km) from Torremolinos, this 18-hole Costa del Sol seaside course is over half a century old. Studded with eucalyptus trees, it is completely flat; its greens are well defined by bunkers. Information: *Club de Campo de Golf de Málaga,* Apartado 324, Málaga, 2900 Spain (phone: 52-381120 or 52-381121).

GOLF TORREQUEBRADA, Málaga, Spain: A stunning 18-hole, par 72 mountain-side course, 6,446 yards long. Numerous elevated tees offer fine views of the countryside and the sea. One especially challenging hole requires players to clear the tops of a grove of trees. Alternative (though still tricky) routes are provided where the more obvious challenges may prove too much for less talented players. There is plenty of other activity for non-golfers who have tagged along: The *Torrequebrada* hotel offers tennis, swimming, and a casino. Numerous villas and condominiums built in whitewashed elegance surround the course, giving it a Mediterranean charm unlike other such sites on the Costa del Sol. Information: *Golf Torrequebrada,* Apartado 67, Benalmádena Costa, Málaga 29630, Spain (phone: 52-442742).

GOLF NUEVA ANDALUCÍA, Marbella, Spain: Just 5 miles (8 km) from Marbella; two 18-hole courses designed by Robert Trent Jones, Sr. undulate along a river valley below the Sierra Blanca. One course is called *Los Naranjos,* for the orange groves that dot the back 9; the other, *Las Brisas,* was the site of the *1983 Spanish Open.* Both courses are often tormented by wind, and they contain a full complement of water hazards and bunkers. Information: *Golf Nueva Andalucía,* Apartado 64, Marbella, Málaga 29660, Spain (phone: 52-815206 or 52-811428).

GOLF GUADALMINA, Marbella, Spain: Part of a resort complex offering 2 courses, tennis, horseback riding, water skiing, a private beach, and 3 swimming pools, this is an ideal destination for golfers with non-golfing family members or friends along. The southern course, along the sea, is largely flat with only an occasional dogleg. The northern course is hilly, with elevated greens, varied bunkers, and water hazards, making it the more challenging of the two. There is a golf pro, pro shop, club and gas cart rental, a driving range, and putting green. The complex offers superb views of the Rock of Gibraltar on the horizon, and the hotel-restaurant offers first-rate Spanish and international fare. Information: *Golf Hotel Guadalmina,* San Pedro de Alcántara, Marbella, Málaga 29670, Spain (phone: 52-780008 or 52-781377).

HOTEL BYBLOS ANDALUZ, Mijas, Spain: This Moorish hideaway is situated in the heart of two 18-hole Robert Trent Jones, Sr. courses. The first course, *Mijas,* a par 72, spreads out before the hotel, offering postcard views of whitewashed Andalusian villages and azure skies. The second course, *Los Olivos,* a par 71, is to the west of the hotel. This gently rolling track requires long shots and considerable technical skill to deal with the numerous water hazards and closely sheltered greens. The hotel organizes its own annual *Challenge Competition* during the first weeks of November. Facilities include 3 swimming pools, horseback riding, 5 tennis courts, a world class spa (see *Spas,* in this section), and shopping excursions. Information: *Hotel Byblos Andaluz,* Urbanización Mijas Golf, Apartado 138, Fuengirola, Málaga 29650, Spain (phone: 52-460250).

CLUB DE GOLF DE PALS, Playa de Pals, Spain: Twenty minutes up the coast from the Costa Brava course (see below), this club by the sea is studded with Mediterranean pines. It hosted the *Spanish Open* in 1972. Now and then, between the dunes, the Mediterranean is visible. Less alluring is the wind, which proves a year-round hazard and blows most defiantly during the *tramuntana,* Catalonia's version of the French mistral — a cold, dry wind that knows no particular season. The small club membership welcomes visitors year-round. Closed Tuesdays from mid-September through June. Information: *Club de Golf de Pals,* Playa de Pals, Girona 17256, Spain (phone: 72-636006).

REAL CLUB DE GOLF DE CERDAÑA, Puigcerdá, Spain: This 60-year-old club in the Pyrenees is often touted as Europe's finest mountain course. Located 19 miles (30 km) east of the principality of Andorra, the club is a 4-hour drive from Barcelona. Its 18 holes dot a valley, 4,000 feet above sea level, that extends into nearby France. Open year-round, it's primarily a summer and autumn course, but mild weather from January through March often makes for comfortable play during these months as well. The *Chalet de Golf* clubhouse offers simple, comfortable rooms and suites. Accommodations are also available at the nearby *Del Prado* and *Park* hotels. Information: *Real Club de Golf de Cerdaña,* Apartado de Correos 63, Puigcerdá, Girona 17520, Spain (phone: 72-881338 or 72-880950).

CLUB DE GOLF COSTA BRAVA, Santa Cristina de Aro, Catalonia, Spain: The nearest golf course to Barcelona, it is set in a wooded valley a few miles from the Mediterranean and 19 miles (30 km) southeast of Girona. Pines and cork oaks line the fairways of the par 70 course; some holes are quite narrow and sharply doglegged. The clubhouse is a distinctive, well-preserved, 18th-century Catalan country manor. The front 9 has its ups and downs, and snakes through a forest of oaks; the back 9, down in the valley, is relatively flat. The 4th and 18th holes are among Catalonia's best. The Ridaura River, dry for much of the year, cuts across the former; a long par 4 uphill bedevils the latter. Closed Wednesdays. Nearby hotels include the *Costa Brava, Murla Park,* and the *Park San Jordi.* Information: *Club de Golf Costa Brava,* Santa Cristina de Aro, Girona 17246, Spain (phone: 72-837150 or 72-837152).

REAL GOLF DE PEDREÑA, Santander, Spain: This course lies on a peninsula in the middle of a bay, some 15 miles (24 km) east of Santander. Pine, cypress, and eucalyptus trees adorn the challenging 6,277 yards, which require the use of virtually every club in the bag. Severiano Ballesteros, Spain's most famous golfer and international superstar, lives adjacent to the 7th hole. All guests must be accompanied by a member. Information: *Real Golf de Pedreña,* Apartado 233, Santander 39000, Spain (phone: 42-500001 or 42-500266).

PARADOR DEL GOLF, Torremolinos, Spain: This 60-room *parador* near Málaga is a golfer's paradise. The 18-hole course — the oldest on the Costa del Sol — was designed in 1925 by English architect Tom Simpson and has a resident pro on the premises. It is popular with vacationing families, thanks in part to its non-golf facilities, which include the ocean, a swimming pool, tennis courts, and a children's playground.

Information: *Parador del Golf,* Apartado 324, Torremolinos, Málaga 29620, Spain (phone: 52-381255).

REAL SOCIEDAD DE GOLF DE NEGURI, Vizcaya, Spain: Dating from 1911, this par 72 course is one of Spain's oldest. Its front 9 abuts the sea, amid dwindling pines reminiscent of English links. The back 9 features narrow fairways and an occasional dogleg. There are various accommodations nearby. Information: *Real Sociedad de Golf de Neguri,* Apartado de Correos 9, Algorta, Vizcaya 48990, Spain (phone: 44-690200 or 44-690208).

QUINTA DO LAGO, Almansil, Algarve, Portugal: Three different 18-hole combinations are possible on these 27 holes, featuring several doglegs and lakeside tees. The holes are spread over some 300 acres, and were designed by the late American golf course architect William Mitchell. The three 9-hole layouts (A, B, and C) are considered among the best courses in Europe by *Golf Digest* and are most popular with British golfers, which makes English the prevalent language. The surrounding resort is a city within a city, featuring a shopping complex, a nightclub, and various restaurants, as well as other non-golf activities including horseback riding, swimming, and tennis. Some of the finest hotels in Portugal are nearby, including the deluxe *Four Seasons.* Information: *Quinta do Lago,* Almansil 8100, Algarve, Portugal (phone: 89-94529 or 89-94782).

QUINTA DA MARINHA GOLF, Cascais, Portugal: Carved out of a thick umbrella pine forest, this 18-hole, par 72 course designed by Robert Trent Jones, Sr. is the centerpiece of a deluxe 330-acre residential resort complex. Sea-washed rock outcroppings and windblown dunes are visible along its 6,684 yards. The 14th hole features both the sea and a deep rocky gorge, which separates the tee and the plateau including the green. The 10th hole presents two large lakes joined in a figure eight by a narrow isthmus of land. Information: *Quinta da Marinha Golf,* Cascais 2750, Portugal (phone: 1-289881).

ESTORIL GOLF CLUB, Estoril, Portugal: Opened in 1928 and expanded in 1945, the club now features 27 holes in a compact layout that winds through pines, eucalyptus, and mimosa, and offers wonderful views of the sea, the rolling countryside, and the Sintra Mountains. To score low on this course, players must drive the ball well. The accent here is on accuracy rather than distance. The well-trapped greens offer plenty of birdie opportunities. For unusual play, take note of the 9th hole, which has to be seen to be believed — a highway runs between the tee and the green. The course is administered by the elegant *Estoril Palácio* hotel, which includes a swimming pool, tennis courts, and a casino among its facilities. Information: *Estoril Golf Club,* Estoril 2765, Portugal (phone: 1-268-0176 or 1-268-1376).

PALMARES GOLF COURSE, Lagos, Algarve, Portugal: Not only is this 18-hole course, designed by Frank Pennink, an Algarve attraction, but it is also the only championship course in southern Europe offering anything remotely similar to links golf. The first 5 holes are strategically placed on dunes along an immense Atlantic beach of white sand. Then the course takes on a different stance, namely high hills and deep valleys. Palmares is also the site of the Portuguese championship, *Amendoeiras em Flor,* and hosted the European Zone qualifying competition for the *1985 World Cup.* Facilities include a clubhouse with a restaurant and bar, pro shop, beach, and water sports. Accommodations are available at the nearby *Hotel de Lagos.* Information: *Palmares Golf Course,* Lagos 8600, Algarve, Portugal (phone: 82-62953 or 82-62961).

LISBOA COUNTRY CLUB, Monte de Caparica, Portugal: Located 11 miles (18 km) from Lisbon on the Setúbal Peninsula, this 18-hole course, designed by Frank Pennink, stretches across rolling hills. Highlights are the 11th and 14th greens, both surrounded by seemingly unavoidable lakes and bunkers. Information: *Lisboa Country Club,* Monte de Caparica 2825, Portugal (phone: 1-226-3244 or 1-226-1358).

PENINA GOLF CLUB, Penina, Algarve, Portugal: In the heart of the Algarve,

3 courses surround the large *Penina Golf* hotel. Designed by three-time *British Open* champion Henry Cotton, the courses have managed to overcome the disadvantage of being set on very flat terrain. Literally hundreds of thousands of trees and shrubs were planted to provide a frame for the golf holes, and this former rice field is now a fine test of golfing skill. The south course has been a frequent venue for championships and tournaments, with 18 holes ranging from easy to difficult. The 13th hole, a 190-yard par 3 that doglegs to the right around a lake to a tightly guarded green, requires a tee shot of 190 yards in order to avoid the aquatic wildlife. There also are two 9-hole courses, which are said to "separate the men from the boys." Information: *Penina Golf Club,* PO Box 146, Penina, Portimão 8500, Algarve, Portugal (phone: 82-22051).

   LISBON SPORTS CLUB, Queluz, Portugal: This relaxing 18-hole, par 72 course is set amid green hills, 15 miles (24 km) from Lisbon on the Belas–Sabugo road. Other facilities include a clubhouse, swimming pool, tennis courts, and a restaurant. Information: *Lisbon Sports Club,* Queluz, Lisbon 2745, Portugal (phone: 1-960077 or 1-960358).

   PARQUE DA FLORESTA, Salema, Algarve, Portugal: This new development, just inland from the little coastal fishing village of Salema (15 minutes from Lagos), provides the ideal environment for golfers yearning to get away from it all. The unspoiled 318-acre estate features an 18-hole course designed by Pepe Gancedo, the Spanish architect responsible for the *Torrequebrada* course on the Costa del Sol. The 564-yard-long 1st hole curves gracefully into the horizon, while the short 5th hole is a mere 120 yards, with no place to go except on or over the green. The 17th hole, surrounded by lakes, gives way to the 18th, which climbs past a magnificent pine to the green set in an amphitheater below the clubhouse terrace. Information: *Parque da Floresta,* Vale do Poço, Budens, Vila do Bispo 8650, Algarve, Portugal (phone: 82-65333, 82-65334, or 82-65335).

   TRÓIA GOLF CLUB, Setúbal, Portugal: This club is on the Tróia Peninsula, about 20 minutes from Setúbal by ferry, and a 30-mile (48-km) drive from Lisbon. Another challenging Robert Trent Jones, Sr. creation, it offers fine views of the sea, sand dunes, and pines. Be careful of the 13th hole, where a sharp dogleg demands a good drive. Other facilities include a private beach, swimming pool, tennis courts, and a variety of water sports. Accommodations are available nearby. Information: *Tróia Golf Club,* Setúbal 2900, Portugal (phone: 65-44151 or 65-44236).

   ESTORIL-SOL GOLF CLUB, Sintra, Portugal: In the Sintra Mountains 20 miles (32 km) from Lisbon, this course moves through pines, eucalyptus, and acacias, with the fairy-tale Pena Palace perched above. Although it is a short course (4,644 yards), offering 9 holes with 18 tees, it presents numerous challenges — among them, the second green, which lies 33 feet above a sheer drop. Information: *Estoril-Sol Golf Club,* Sintra 2710, Portugal (phone: 1-923-2461).

   CLUBE DE GOLF, Vale do Lobo, Algarve, Portugal: Rugged and beautiful, this is perhaps Portugal's most scenic course. Located 20 minutes from Faro, the 27 holes here were designed by three-time *British Open* champion Henry Cotton. The famous 7th hole, perched atop sandstone cliffs at the edge of the ocean, is among the most photographed in Europe. There is also a driving range. This self-contained resort also offers the *Roger Taylor Tennis Clinic* (see *Tennis,* in this section), and a full range of water sports. Information: *Clube de Golfe,* Vale do Lobo, Loulé 8100, Algarve, Portugal (phone: 89-94444).

   VILAMOURA GOLF CLUB, Vilamoura, Algarve, Portugal: Two courses set among umbrella pines and gentle slopes in sight of the sea. *Vilamoura I,* designed by Frank Pennink, plays to par 73, and its 6,923 yards add up to one of the best courses in the Algarve. The 6th hole is by far the most spectacular: an excellent par 3 with a narrow fairway cut through wild pine trees. Another feature favored by golfers is that the 5th,

9th, and 15th greens are close to the clubhouse, making for frequent stops at the "19th hole." *Vilamoura II* is the newer course, designed by Robert Trent Jones, Sr. In addition, the resort features tennis, horseback riding, shopping, water sports, and excellent restaurants. The resort complex has began an ambitious expansion to include new villas, hotels, restaurants, and sports facilities, and expects to be *the* center for golf and tennis enthusiasts by 1992. Numerous international tournaments are already held here, and it is one of the most popular resorts in the Algarve. In the meantime, accommodations are available at the nearby *Dom Pedro Vilamoura* hotel and the *Vilamoura Marinotel;* both offer special packages, reduced greens fees, and other golf specials. Information: *Vilamoura Golf Club,* Vilamoura, Loulé 8100, Algarve, Portugal (phone: 89-35562 or 89-35552).

Tennis

In both Spain and Portugal, tennis usually takes a back seat to golf. But many hotels and resorts in both countries have tennis facilities, and beginners and experts alike will find an abundance of places to play. Racquets, balls, and courts are easily rented, and a single player can find a partner easily. The actual tennis-oriented resorts and clubs, however, are concentrated in two main areas. In Spain, the majority of tennis facilities are located along the Costa del Sol; in Portugal, the Algarve is foremost. Both regions are in the midst of rapid expansion, with more and more emphasis being placed on residential developments — small communities of villas and townhouses clustered around sports facilities and the sea. So far, only the British have truly "discovered" these areas, and thanks in part to their inroads, almost everyone speaks English. The Costa del Sol is considerably more developed than the Algarve; many have labeled it the Miami of the Mediterranean. There are a number of exclusive areas where the tennis enthusiast can enjoy a vacation amid golden beaches, turquoise waters, and the uniquely Spanish atmosphere of Andalusia.

Most Spanish and Portuguese tennis courts have either an asphalt or clay surface, and traditional tennis whites are preferred — often required. Expect to pay about $5 per hour for court time in Spain, $7 per hour in Portugal. In most cases, court time must be reserved in advance. There is also an emphasis on the social aspects of tennis, and visitors will find that many hotels sponsor weekly tournaments and "get acquainted" parties where tennis enthusiasts can meet and mingle. In addition, there are a variety of members-only tennis clubs spread throughout the major cities and resort areas of both countries where, for a small additional fee, guests are permitted to play. Also keep in mind that tennis can be fun to watch, and despite its slow start, tennis as a spectator sport is catching on in both countries. Portugal hosted its first tournament sponsored by the ATP (Association of Tennis Professionals) in April 1989, in Estoril, and Spain plays host to a continual series of championship events each year. For details on Spanish tennis tournaments, contact the *Royal Spanish Tennis Federation* (186 Diagonal, Barcelona 08028; phone: 3-201-0844, 3-200-5355, or 3-201-5586); for more information on tennis tournaments in both Spain and Portugal, contact the *ATP* (4 Sawgrass Village, Suite 240, Ponte Vedra Beach, FL 32082; phone: 904-285-5776).

CAMPO DE TENIS DE LEW HOAD, Mijas, Costa del Sol, Spain: Australian Lewis Hoad, the 1956 and 1957 *Wimbledon* champion, first spotted this hilly enclave in 1966, and decided it was the perfect spot to build a tennis ranch. Twenty-five years later, the "ranch" is a favorite spot for both serious players and beginners serious about learning the game. This facility is not a resort, but a full-service tennis center and club, where guests sharpen their skills and socialize with other tennis enthusiasts. The tennis school is run by Manrique Floreal, a professional who teaches the Aussie style, a gentle technique that emphasizes the reception of opponents' serves. Facilities include 8 hard courts (the Spanish refer to this surface as "quick"), which are surrounded by exotic and carefully landscaped gardens, and a well-stocked pro shop. There are weekly singles and doubles tournaments for advanced players. There is also a bar overlooking the courts, a restaurant, changing rooms, sauna, swimming pool, massage facilities, beauty salon, aerobics classes, art exhibits, and occasional concerts. Guests can rent one of the exclusive villas that surround the club, or find accommodations in nearby Fuengirola and Mijas. Information: *Campo de Tenis de Lew Hoad,* Apartado 111, Fuengirola, Málaga 29640, Spain (phone: 52-474858).

DON CARLOS, Marbella, Costa del Sol, Spain: The privacy and excellent facilities here have helped this 212-room resort, located in the heart of a 130-acre private estate of pine woods, exotic flowers, and subtropical gardens, achieve its standing as the official home of the European Women's Tennis Association. Martina Navratilova and Chris Evert are just two of the many top-ranked professionals who have practiced and competed here. Throughout the year, visitors usually can catch a glimpse of a superstar or two either playing or relaxing at the restaurant overlooking the courts. Don't be overwhelmed by the abundance of talent; the mood here is casual and relaxed, and a beginner will feel as comfortable as a pro. There are 11 courts (6 clay, 5 hard; 4 courts are floodlit), between the swimming pool and the sea. In addition, the hotel offers windsurfing, sailing, water skiing, a driving range, horseback riding, a gymnasium, a sauna, and a Jacuzzi — all free to hotel guests. Information: *Don Carlos Hotel,* Jardínes de las Golondrinas, Marbella, Málaga 29600, Spain (phone: 52-831140 or 52-831940); in the US, *Utell International,* 119 W. 57th St., New York, NY 10019 (phone: 212-245-7130).

LOS MONTEROS, Marbella, Costa del Sol, Spain: One of the most prestigious hotels and sporting resorts on the coast. Set among pine woods and tropical gardens, it makes for an ideal vacation getaway that will keep guests as busy or as relaxed as they wish. There are 10 hard courts, 2 of which are floodlit for night play, as well as 5 squash courts, a paddle tennis court, 2 swimming pools, a terrace bar, pro shop, gymnasium, sauna, massage facilities, beautician, nursery, nightclub, and nearby golf. Guests are automatically considered tennis club members and may use the courts free of charge, subject to availability and club regulations. Information: *Los Monteros Hotel,* Marbella, Málaga 29600, Spain (phone: 52-771700); in the US, *Distinguished Hotels,* c/o Robert F. Warner, Inc., 307 Fifth Ave., New York, NY 10016 (phone: 800-792-7637; 800-344-6535 in Canada).

PUENTE ROMANO, Marbella, Costa del Sol, Spain: This self-contained Moorish residence is a city in itself. For the tennis enthusiast, there are 11 courts — 4 hard, 5 clay, and 2 artificial surface (Astroturf) — on which to practice, as well as a large stadium that plays host to many national and international tournaments. Björn Borg was once the pro at the tennis center here; today, former *Wimbledon* champion Manolo Santana sets the tone. In addition to tennis, the resort offers surfing, water skiing, a fitness center, swimming pool, horseback riding, polo, and nearby golf. The 200 rooms and suites are built in pueblo-style Andalusian *casitas,* which overlook tropical gardens and waterfalls. Information: *Puente Romano Hotel,* PO Box 204, Marbella, Málaga 29600, Spain (phone: 52-770100); in the US, *Utell International,* 500 Plaza Dr., Secaucus, NJ 07096 (phone: 201-902-7800 or 800-223-9868).

MARBELLA CLUB, Marbella, Costa del Sol, Spain: One of the most famous hotels on the coast, and the cornerstone of Marbella. Set in a subtropical garden by the sea, this resort is a fine place to mix tennis and beach life. There are 11 tennis courts, and

Manolo Santana serves as the coach. Information: *Marbella Club Hotel,* Carretera de Cádiz, Km 178, Marbella, Málaga 29600, Spain (phone: 52-771300).

SOTOGRANDE, Estepona, Costa del Sol, Spain: Set in the enormous Sotogrande complex, where guests have access to some of the best and most varied sports facilities on the coast. The tennis center offers first-rate instruction, and the secluded hotel is peaceful and well looked after by a helpful and attentive staff. All rooms have separate sleeping and living areas, as well as private patios and fountains. Information: *Hotel Sotogrande,* Sotogrande, Cádiz 11310, Spain (phone: 52-792100).

CARVOEIRO CLUBE DE TÊNIS, Praia do Carvoeiro, Algarve, Portugal: Perched atop a mountain development overlooking the small fishing village of Carvoeiro, this private resort community and racquet club commands one of the most breathtaking views of the Atlantic and the whitewashed town below. Five of the 10 hard courts are floodlit for night play, and there is a half-size children's court — all adjacent to the racket-shaped swimming pool. The tennis center can provide as much (or as little) tennis activity as is desired. There is also a pro shop, various social activities, and occasional tournaments. Guest accommodations range from small apartments and townhouses to villas, complete with fireplaces, terraces, and gardens. Information: *Carvoeiro Clube de Tênis,* Apartado 231, Lagoa Codex 8400, Algarve, Portugal (phone: 82-357847).

ROGER TAYLOR TENNIS CLINIC, Vale do Lobo, Algarve, Portugal: Roger Taylor is to the Algarve what Lew Hoad is to the Costa del Sol. Built amid the very planned, very developed, and very neatly organized Vale do Lobo complex, this 12-court (6 floodlit) facility has earned a reputation as one of Europe's top tennis centers. The club hosts special amateur tennis weeks twice a year, in June and November. Facilities include a pro shop, swimming pool, restaurant, and 6 squash courts. Accommodations surrounding the club range from standard and deluxe rooms at the *Dona Filipa* hotel to exclusive villas. Information: *Roger Taylor Tennis Holidays, Ltd.,* 85 High St., Wimbledon, SW19 5EG, England (phone: 81-947-9727).

VILAMOURATÊNIS, Vilamoura, Algarve, Portugal: Although it does not have the name of a *Wimbledon* champion behind it, this tennis resort has the push of a young up-and-comer, Victor Gonçalves, who is determined to put Vilamoura on the map as a premier tennis resort and host to international events. Currently, guests stay at the nearby *Dom Pedro Vilamoura* hotel or the *Vilamoura Marinotel,* both of which offer plenty of opportunity for windsurfing, fishing, sailing, scuba diving, and golf. Scheduled for completion this September are 108 luxurious villas with private pools, terraces, fireplaces, and landscaped gardens, and the 150-room *Vilamouratênis* hotel, which will offer satellite television, elegant restaurants, a health club, swimming pools, shops, and a conference center. The resort also plans to add to its existing 13 courts (11 hard, 2 clay; 3 courts floodlit), eventually bringing its total to 30; 4 will be in competition stadiums — one seating 3,000, another seating 10,000. Information: *Vilamouratênis,* Vilamoura 8125, Algarve, Portugal (phone: 89-32125).

ESTORIL PALÁCIO, Estoril, Portugal: Each of the 200 rooms and suites of this luxurious resort is neatly appointed and overlooks the landscape of the Estoril coast. Three of the 7 hard courts are floodlit for night play, and a casino and a golf course are nearby (free to hotel guests). Other facilities include a heated swimming pool and lovely gardens. Information: *Estoril Palácio Hotel,* Parque Estoril, Estoril 2765, Portugal (phone: 1-268-0400).

QUINTA DA MARINHA, Cascais, Portugal: Also within view of the Atlantic on the aristocratic Estoril coast west of Lisbon, this golf and country club development offers privacy amid splendid, pine-studded surroundings. Villas and townhouses blend in with the landscape. Three of the 6 tennis courts are floodlit, and the estate also has a swimming pool and horseback riding, as well as golf. Information: *Quinta da Marinha,* Cascais 2750, Portugal (phone: 1-289881).

Sensational Spanish Skiing

 Skiing is one of the most memorable activities any winter sports enthusiast can enjoy during a European vacation, and when most unsophisticated skiers think "snow," they immediately think "Switzerland and France." For although the sport continues to gain eager enthusiasts in large numbers, skiing remains one of Spain's best-kept secrets. Yet to the north, the Pyrenees guard the border with France, and to the south, the Sierra Nevada rise over 10,000 feet. In addition, there is the Cantabrian range on the Galician massif, the Iberian Range, and the Gúdar Range, with skiable areas in the provinces of Burgos, Soria, Logroño, and Teruel.

One of the most mountainous countries in Europe, with skiing available from January through May, Spain offers novice through advanced skiers the thrills of a lifetime — and once experienced, these hills will not soon be forgotten. Spain is also one of European skiing's bargain capitals; hotels, meals, drinks, equipment, and lift passes are available at prices far below those found in the Alps. Other benefits include an abundance of snow, relatively mild weather conditions, and regular sunshine. Some large international resorts like Tuca-Betrén, Baqueria-Beret, Cerler, and Pal in Andorra have it all — a vast array of runs and lifts, troops of multilingual instructors, a selection of winter sporting opportunities such as ice skating and tobogganing, a horde of shops, shimmering hotels, high-speed nightlife, and the glossy aura of Europe's leisure classes. But there also are numerous cozier, family-oriented villages, many of them linked to a constellation of neighbors by far-reaching networks of chair lifts and cable cars.

Throughout most of the resort regions, those who like their luxury rugged can hire a helicopter for a quick trip up a slope heavy with glittery virgin powder, and the subsequent opportunity to carve a solitary trail back down through miles of untracked mountainside. For those whose special pleasure is cross-country skiing, be aware that the sport is beginning to boom here; a wide choice of trails and excursions (and a good supply of the necessary equipment) is readily available. And no matter where you go, there's a very high standard of cooking in the restaurant dining rooms adjacent to the slopes.

Words of caution: If you need an English-speaking instructor from the area's ski school, say so when signing up, or risk having to learn to recognize "Bend your knees" enunciated in all-too-faultless Spanish. Know the local trail markings — green for novice, blue for intermediate, and red for expert. Be prepared for sometimes hair-raising traffic — both on the mountain roads and on the slopes. Since skiing as a mass activity is a Juan-come-lately in Spain, the average level of expertise is lower than is routinely found in Switzerland, France, or Austria, and the traditions of slope safety and etiquette are not readily apparent. For those familiar with European skiing, be aware that the high and low skiing seasons in Spain are significantly different from those of the better-known Alpine regions. All weekends are designated as high season, with premium prices on hotels, lessons, and lifts. High season also applies to the period from *Christmas* through *New Year's,* and the first week of January. Prices rise again during February and the first 2 weeks of March.

Skiing in Portugal is virtually nonexistent, mostly due to its mild winter temperatures and lack of sizable mountain peaks.

VAL D'ARAN, Lleida (Lérida), Catalonia, Spain: Past the orchards and vineyards of Catalonia and up into the Pyrenees Mountains bordering France lies one of the most beautiful alpine valleys in the world — and the ski resorts of Tuca-Betrén and Baqueria-

Beret. Tuca-Betrén, the lesser known of the two, offers a wide variety of slopes and trails that will challenge even the most experienced skier. In fact, all of the resort's 18 slopes and trails are marked either advanced or expert. The first trail starts at the 5,000-foot level; the highest peaks overhead top off at 9,000 feet. Eight miles (13 km) away is Baqueria-Beret, one of the most extensive ski resorts in Europe outside the Alps. It is the favorite ski resort of King Juan Carlos and also attracts a predominantly French clientele from north of the border. The facilities and restaurants are more modern and sophisticated here than in Tuca-Betrén. The skiing on the Baqueria side is down tight trails with a dense lift network of T-bars and double chair lifts. The skiing above Beret is in a wide-open bowl served by three strategically placed triple chair lifts. Together, Baqueria-Beret offers 43 slopes and trails, 22 lifts, 2 slalom courses, and helicopter service to the peaks for the thrills of fresh powder. Due to the terrain — steep slopes and wide courses — there is great skiing variety. Of special note is the descent from the peak of Cap de Baqueira, the highest point. Val d'Aran's two distinct segments are separated by a row of natural stone and mortar villages, scenery for which the word "charm" was coined. Much of this area looks the way it did in the 13th, 14th, 15th, and 16th centuries — give or take a few power lines and Seats (Spanish-built Fiats). This area alone has a total of almost 5,000 rooms spread throughout hotels, inns, and quaint *pensiones.* Information: *Oficina d'Informació Turística de Baqueira-Beret,* Apartado 60, Viella, Val d'Aran, Lleida 25530, Spain (phone: 73-645050 or 73-645025), or *Oficina d'Informació Turística,* Arc del Pont, Lleida 25000, Spain (phone: 73-248120).

EL FORMIGAL, Huesca, Aragonese Pyrenees, Spain: Another favorite stomping ground of the current King of Spain and his family, this is just one of five resorts in the area (Astún, Cerler, Panticosa, and Candanchú are the others). Together they constitute one of the most attractive and unspoiled regions in Spain, guaranteed to motivate even the most sedentary to hit the hills. As the westernmost resort in the Pyrenees, El Formigal lacks woodland, but instead boasts great open spaces — perfect for beginners and intermediates. Only 2 of the 24 runs are designated for experts, but most are rated as difficult. The wide-open off-piste possibilities, however, compensate for those strong enough to handle heavy snow. A double chair lift rises out of the town, reaching the mid-station and the main mountain restaurant. From here, beginners can enjoy gentle slopes, intermediates can drop down to the lower gondola station, and experts can take a chair lift or T-bar to the summit and enjoy a 3,000-foot drop back into the village. There is also a slalom course, 6 hotels, and a wide variety of activities, including very lively nightlife. Information: *Oficina de Turismo,* Estación de Formigal, Sallent de Gallego, El Formigal, Huesca 22000, Spain (phone: 74-488125), or *Oficina de Turismo de Huesca,* 23 Calle Coso Alto, Huesca 22000, Spain (phone: 74-225778).

CERLER, Huesca, Aragonese Pyrenees, Spain: Larger than El Formigal and closer to the French border, Cerler boasts 5,875 acres of spectacular skiable terrain for skiers of all abilities. The 23 trails, the highest slopes the Pyrenees have to offer, provide plenty of challenges; the majority of the trails are over 3 miles long and are served by 11 chair lifts, and there is also an ice skating rink and a wide variety of other activities, including sledding and swimming. Information: *Oficina de Turismo de Huesca,* 23 Calle Coso Alto, Huesca 22000, Spain (phone: 74-225778).

LA MOLINA, Girona, Catalan Pyrenees, Spain: This is one of the oldest ski resorts in Spain, as well as the closest to Barcelona. For this reason, the resort attracts a weekend crowd that usually overwhelms the 17 chair lifts. During the week, however, there are rarely any lines. Only 3 of the 22 trails are listed as difficult, making the resort a favorite for skiers of all abilities. There is also a 3-mile cross-country course, and 3 ramps for ski jumping. The resort was created with skiers specifically in mind, and features modern, self-contained hotels, good restaurants, a smattering of shops, and a group of lively discos and bars. There are also 9 *hostales* located nearby. Information: *Oficina de Turismo,* La Molina, Girona 17537, Spain (phone: 72-892031), or *Oficina de Turismo,* 1 Plaça del Vi, Girona 17000, Spain (phone: 72-202679).

SOLYNIEVE, Sierra Nevada, near Granada, Spain: This resort is a cluster of concrete buildings huddled above the tree line in the far south of Spain, only 20 miles (32 km) from Granada and 60 miles (96 km) from the coast at Motril. Here, the perpetually snow-covered mountains rise to 11,420 feet. The scenery is inspiring and the snowfields are seemingly endless. Its status as a ski resort, however, is not all that high. The skiing here, though extensive, is tame and not particularly demanding; it will, however, keep advanced beginners and intermediates busy. With its wide, treeless slopes and patient Spanish instructors, Solynieve is perfect for beginning skiers. The resort boasts 19 lifts, which serve some 30 miles of trails. The village itself is rather soulless; even the southern Spanish personality can't seem to help fire up the nightlife. But in the spring, Solynieve does offer dependable snow and the opportunity to ski in the morning and then drive down to the Costa del Sol for an afternoon of sun on the beach or a round of golf — so be sure to pack sunscreen and sunglasses. Information: *Federación Andaluza de Esquí,* 78 Paseo de Ronda, Veleta, Granada 18000, Spain (phone: 58-250706), or *Patronato Provincial de Turismo de Granada,* 10 Plaza Mariana Pineda, Granada 18000, Spain (phone: 58-223527).

ALTO CAMPO, Santander, Cantabria, Spain: This is one of those resorts where the skiing season lasts until late May. The resort lies in the Brana Vieja Valley, sheltered from harsh winds. On a clear day, the distant peak of Tres Mares, the Polaciones Valley, and the heights of the Picos de Europa are visible. The slopes here vary from easy to extremely difficult, making skiing available for enthusiasts of all levels. Information: *Oficina de Turismo,* 1 Plaza Porticada, Santander 39001, Spain (phone: 42-310708 or 42-310756).

ANDORRA: One of Europe's last feudal protectorates, this tiny co-principality, governed nominally by Spain and France, has abundant snow from November through April. Combined with an excellent climate of dry air and sunny skies, this is truly a skiers' paradise. Some of Europe's best inexpensive skiing can be found at the resorts of Pas de la Casa–Grau Roig, Soldeu–El Tarter, Pals, Arinsal, and Ordino Arcalis. Pas de la Casa–Grau Roig, just within the French border, is the oldest resort, and has 18 trails for advanced skiers, a slalom course, and several tame slopes for beginners, as well as 25 lifts and 33 hotels. Soldeu–El Tarter is the largest complex, with 28 slopes (including 5 designed especially for children), a 7½-mile cross-country course, 22 lifts, 20 hotels, and 3 self-contained apartment blocks. Pals features 20 trails, a forest slalom course, 2 children's slopes, and 14 lifts. Arinsal, next to the village of the same name, has 23 slopes ranging from beginner to expert, all served by 15 lifts. Ordino Arcalis is the most dramatically beautiful of Andorra's resorts, offering 16 slopes, 11 lifts, and 4 modern hotels in nearby El Serrat. Information: *Sindicat d'Iniciativa de les Valls d'Andorra,* Carrer Dr. Vilanova, Andorra la Vella, Andorra (phone: 738-20214).

Horsing Around

 It almost goes without saying that Spain is the land of the horse. It was here that the Moorish invaders crossed the Bab steeds of their homeland with the native Iberian stock that had provided mounts for conquerors from Julius Caesar to Richard the Lion-Hearted. They came up with a noble breed renowned for its sturdy legs, strong back, and agility — the Andalusian.

Raising Andalusian thoroughbreds is still a tradition carried on at over 100 ranches in southwestern Spain. Visits can be arranged through the breeders' association, the

Real Sociedad Española de Fomento del Cría Caballar, located at the *Hipódromo de la Zarzuela* in Madrid (phone: 1-207-0140). The association also provides a free brochure listing the names and addresses of its members. In addition, there are some 50 other ranches dedicated to preserving the pure Arabian bloodline, reintroduced at the turn of the century. Information: *Asociación de Criadores de Caballos Arabes,* 20 Calle Hermosila, Madrid 28009, Spain (phone: 1-275-9068).

To witness with what grace Andalusian horses lend themselves to classical European and Spanish dressage, a visit to Jerez de la Frontera's *Real Escuela Andaluza del Arte Ecuestre* (on the Recreo de las Cadenas; phone: 56-311111) is a must. This school was founded in 1972 by Alvaro Domecq, of the local sherry dynasty, who has since retired after years as Spain's top-ranked *rejoneador,* a bullfighter on horseback. The 35 Spanish mounts are trotted out in their fancy dress gear every Thursday for a 2-hour show entitled "How the Andalusian Horses Dance." During the second week of May, the people of Jerez de la Frontera emerge blinking from their sherry vaults to welcome riding enthusiasts from all over the world for their annual week-long *Horse Fair.* Spanish equestrian specialties on display, along with much dancing, hand-clapping, and *fino*-drinking, include the *acoso y deribo,* in which riders use long blunt poles to isolate one bull from a stampeding herd and overturn it. The colorfully dressed riders then try their hand at *doma vaquera,* or Spanish rustic dressage, performing a series of showy maneuvers that climax when the horses approach at full gallop, then come to a dead halt before the judges' stand. Some extremely flashy carriage driving rounds out the city's tribute to the animal that was originally bred with patient perfectionism by the Carthusian monks, who were based here until the last century.

Horseback riding is not organized in Portugal. Equestrians will find the most accessible facilities among the various resorts spread throughout the Algarve. The *Portuguese National Tourist Office* (590 Fifth Ave., New York, NY 10036; phone: 212-354-4400) can provide further details.

HORSE TREKKING

"The remembrance of those wild and weary rides through tawny Spain where hardship was forgotten ere undergone," sighed Richard Ford, the grand old man of wandering Hispanophiles, reflecting back on the various ambles from Santiago de Compostela to Seville that he made during the 1830s. "Then and there will be learnt golden rules of patience, perseverance, good temper, and good fellowship."

Horse trekking involves day-long trips on the back of a sturdy native horse or pony, and has participants traveling mainly at a walk — partly because most are inexperienced riders, partly because the riding is through dense forests and steep mountain terrain, along narrow trails and roads that don't lend themselves to a faster pace. Absolute novices may be provided with some instruction, but ordinarily it will be at a relatively elementary level. In recent years, a number of agencies specializing in horseback treks have rediscovered the old cattle trails and royal bridle paths of the Middle Ages — all to prove their point that Spain looks very different when observed up close from the back of a congenial quadruped. The following include some of the best Spanish horse trekking centers, which offer trips lasting anywhere from a day to a month. Backup vehicle, insurance, meals, and lodging are usually included.

> *Rutas a Caballo,* Madrid, Spain. Fifteen years' experience and numerous repeat clients from the US, Germany, and Switzerland make this a best bet for everyone from serious riders to the merely determined. Popular routes include trails through Segovia, Andalusia, and Coto Doñana. Information: *Rutas a Caballo,* 21 Calle Juan Bravo Madrid 28006, Spain (phone: 1-577-0297).
>
> *Equestrian Tours Almansur,* Madrid, Spain. One of Spain's most popular trekking centers, catering to the American market. Most of the clientele come back for

a second look at Extremadura and the Sierra de Gredos. Information: *Equestrian Tours Almansur,* 3 Glorieta Puente de Segovia, Madrid 28011, Spain (phone: 1-402-1187); in the US, *FITS Equestrian,* 2011 Alamo Pintado Rd., Solvang, CA 93463 (phone: 805-688-9494).

Viajes Geosud, Madrid, Spain. Organizes outings to order for groups of 3 to 15 in Almería, the Sierra de Alpujarra of Granada, and northern Navarre. Information: *Viajes Geosud,* 9 Calle Juan de Dios, Madrid 28015, Spain (phone: 1-542-6194).

Viajes Nobel, Madrid, Spain. This agency pioneered the practice of bringing riders from abroad to accompany the *Transhumancia* cattle drive (see *Extra Special*). Popular routes include the Sierra de Gredos, Málaga, Avila, and Andalusia. Information: *Viajes Nobel,* 3 Calle Duque de Liria, Madrid 28015, Spain (phone: 1-542-3125).

POST TREKKING/TRAIL RIDING

There's nothing quite as delightful as seeing the Spanish countryside from the back of a horse or sure-footed native pony, heading from ranch to ranch through narrow trails, along abandoned train beds, and down wide sandy beaches — and staying away from the trekking center for up to a week at a time. Post trekking, or trail riding, as this activity is called, is not generally recommended for riders without experience, as it usually involves good horses and a fast enough pace to cover about 25 miles (40 km) a day. Usually a warm camaraderie develops among riders en route, as they traverse the rural miles. Post trekking is also a practically worry-free holiday: There are guides to keep riders going at a reasonable pace, to make sure the group doesn't get lost, and to arrange for the rider's luggage to be transported from one hostelry to the next.

ALMERÍA, Spain: Those who think they know the desert probably haven't seen or even imagined anything quite like the arid wastelands of Tabernas, a stretch of mind-boggling barrenness between the Sierra Nevada and Almería's still undeveloped Mediterranean beach resorts. After 3 days riding through a scallop-edged sea of surreal sandstone, where the sun has bleached every color out of the landscape, it's a relief to return to the *cortijo,* or workday ranch, located on the Cabo de Gata Peninsula, and the greenery of its adjacent national park. People can also visit Yuka City, which has kept the corner saloon doors swinging even after the paella-western boom of the 1970s went bust. Groups require a minimum of three riders; there are no fixed departure dates, and accommodations (an ad hoc combination of inland ranches alternating with hotels on the coast) and itineraries are available by specific arrangement only. Information: *Viajes Geosud,* 9 Calle Juan de Dios, Madrid 28015, Spain (phone: 1-542-6194).

ASTURIAS, Spain: Misty, mountainous, gorgeous, and green, Spain's northern coast serves as a gateway to secluded inland valleys settled by a hard-boiled race of cider-swigging mountain men who spend their days tending their cattle and flocks of merino sheep. All this is within a few hours' riding time from Gijón, where excursions of 1 to 3 days lead up into the sierra to the sprawling Valle del Peón, the seven lakes of Saliencia, the Somiedo Wildlife Reserve (full of brown bears, wolves, wild boar, and imperial eagles), and other no-frills natural wonders. Information: *Compañia Asturiana de Rutas y Excursiones,* 8 Plaza Romualde Alvargonzález, Gijón 33202, Spain (phone: 85-341968).

In adjacent Oviedo Province, *Trastur,* a cooperative of youthful trekking enthusiasts, has a setup aimed at a young, casual, and outdoorsy clientele: riding by day and partying determinedly through the night in the log cabin shelters of the *vaquieros,* the Asturian livestock drovers. Their trails lead from the crossroad towns of Tineo and Navelgas, where this rough-and-ready culture is best preserved, then north to the pretty fishing village of Luarca. Arrangements must be made by telephone from the enthusiasts' base in Tineo (phone: 85-806036), and they will pick guests up in Oviedo. In Madrid, call 1-477-9236 to find out when the next outing is scheduled.

AVILA, Spain: The Sierra de Gredos is where Madrid's horsey set heads for a taste of real wilderness. The mountains have a certain preeminence for trail riders and boast 7,500-foot peaks, as well as deep ravines clawed out of the landmass by glaciers. Many of the routes also overlap the adjoining Tietar Valley. *Viajes Nobel* (see above) buses clients from Madrid to Navaredonda de Gredos, the starting point for an 8-day trek that leads into the lush Barco de Avila, following roads laid down by Roman legionnaires. One night is spent at a log cabin shelter run by the *Spanish Mountaineering Federation,* so a sleeping bag is necessary. All guides speak English, and departures are scheduled once a month from March through November. Weekend excursions for 1 or 2 days, departing from the *Parador de Gredos,* Navarredonda de Gredos 05635 (phone: 18-348048), are also available throughout the year, except in December.

Another week-long trek is offered by *Gredos — Rutas a Caballo* (13 Calle Guijuelos, Hoya de Espina, Avila 05001, Spain; phone: 18-384110). This trek and other short half-day outings can also be booked in Madrid (phone: 1-467-3105).

In August, when the plains of Extremadura are broiling, *Equestrian Tours Almansur* (3 Glorieta Puente de Segovia, Madrid 28011, Spain; phone: 1-402-1187) moves its horses to the northern side of the Gredos range to keep cool. Twice a month, week-long sallies take riders down to visit the walled city of Avila, as well as along the Piedrahita River for a look at the palace of the Dukes of Alba. Another group, *Turismo Ecuestre La Isla,* has 3-day rides from its ranch in Navaluenga to Avila, and week-long trips through the Gredos central highlands and to the remote Lagoons of Gredos. Departures are from May through September (phone: 1-633-3692).

CÁDIZ, Spain: Dusty cattle trails head down the heartland of Andalusia's wild west, where the whitewashed towns all bear the tag *de la frontera* as a reminder that this was where Muslim and Christian Spain fought most furiously for control. The 260-mile (416-km) route starts in Arcos de la Frontera, with 5- to 7-hour stretches in the saddle, then breaks for an unhurried picnic lunch. The trail leads through bull breeding ranches and fields of cultivated sunflowers drooping on their 5-foot stalks, and it ends with a gallop through the Atlantic surf. Stopover specials include a day in Jerez de la Frontera, with a visit to that city's celebrated School of Equestrian Arts, and a canter along the beachside Roman ruins of Bolonia. Provision is made for an occasional afternoon on two legs for a peek at the pueblo or to bask on the beach. Accommodations at the *Arco* ranch, as well as the *hostales* along the way, are clean and comfortable, but not luxurious. Private baths are included — and will be needed. Bring a 10-gallon hat and a canteen of equivalent capacity, as the summer temperatures can hover around 100F.

Rutas a Caballo (21 Calle Juan Bravo, Madrid 28006, Spain; phone: 1-577-0297), which pioneered this trek, offers departures every third weekend from March through October, including accommodations and all meals — which are simple and good. A shorter 8-day version that heads to the sea, forsaking the return trek, is also available. *Viajes Nobel* (3 Calle Duque de Liria, Madrid 28015, Spain; phone: 1-542-3125) offers essentially the same 8-day route from Arcos to the coast, with similar overnight stops, but offers different weekend departure dates. In May, June, October, and November, *Rutas a Caballo* offers an inland tour of the *pueblos blancos,* the celebrated whitewashed towns of Andalusia, including Arcos de la Frontera, Grazalema, Zahara de la Sierra, and Ronda. It also offers a 1-week variant, the 140-mile(224-km) "Atlantic Sea Tour," allowing for 3 days inland riding and 4 days splashing along the beach as the breakers come rolling in from the Strait of Gibraltar, with Morocco's Atlas Mountains visible on the other side.

COTO CONANA NATIONAL PARK, Huelva, Spain: A unique chance to spend a week trotting through the salt marsh and scrub of one of Europe's largest and most ecologically vital wildlife sanctuaries. After picking up riders in Seville, the organizers get one and all saddled up in Arcos de la Frontera. From there, it's a 2-day ride via Jerez de la Frontera to where the land turns swampy and some of more than 150 different species of birds — including flamingos, imperial eagles, and many more birds of prey — can be observed roosting above the deer, lynx, and wild boar that inhabit the 50,000 acres of restricted parkland. Riders and mounts are ferried across the marshes in shallow-draft skiffs. A visit to the shrine of the Virgen del Rocío, which is inundated by pilgrims each May during one of Spain's most colorful outbursts of religious fervor, is also included. Contact *Rutas a Caballo* (21 Calle Juan Bravo, Madrid 28006, Spain; phone: 1-577-0297) for details. It offers departures in May, July, September, and November.

EXTREMADURA, Spain: The rugged and still-backward land that toughened up Spanish conquistadores such as Cortés and Pizarro opens itself up for reciprocal exploration from the New World on treks ranging from 1 to 3 weeks. The wide-ranging Route of the Conquistadores leaves very little of the region unseen. Riders explore the Monfragüe National Park, a unique sanctuary for migratory birds, the poor but pretty pueblos of the Jerte Valley and La Vera, the Roman city of Mérida, the monasteries of Guadalupe and Yuste, and the historic towns of Cáceres, Trujillo, and Plasencia. Departures are scheduled in early September only, and include 22 days on the trail.

The Monastery of Guadalupe, where Columbus pleaded for cash before King Ferdinand and Queen Isabella, is a 14th-century sanctuary visited by pilgrims from all over the Spanish-speaking world. But its larger mountain setting is a treat seldom seen by anyone, although its deep valleys and dense oak forests make it well worth the 8-day outing, covering 105 miles (168 km). Departures are scheduled for April, May, September, and October.

All of the Extremadura excursions can be booked through *Equestrian Tours Almansur* (3 Glorieta Puente de Segovia, Madrid 28011, Spain; phone: 1-402-1187), which offers an excellent selection of Hispano-Arab mounts and provides first class accommodations and meals at the various *paradores* in the region. It also offers a week-long close look at the Tietar River Valley, on the fertile southern flanks of the Gredos mountain range. This route is also trekked by *Viajes Nobel* (3 Calle Duque de Liria, Madrid 28015, Spain; phone: 1-542-3125), which shares mounts and facilities at the Dehesa del Roble ranch estate. Departures are scheduled from May through November, except in August, when it's simply too hot to trot.

GALICIA, Spain: The *Club Equitación de la Espuela* (at Noalla, La Lanzada, outside Pontevedra; phone: 86-731092) can arrange tours around the fjord-like Rías Bajas of Galicia, as well as trips to stately inland manor estates for groups with a minimum of 6 riders. Accommodations include farmhouses, fishermen's cottages, or hotels. Outings are scheduled irregularly, most often around public holidays. Otherwise, group prices can be negotiated by arrangement.

GRANADA, Spain: No visit to the Andalusian hinterland would be complete without a side trip to the rugged and impressive Alpujarras Range, where experienced mounts negotiate the sharp precipices through chestnut woods, lavender scrubland, and steep pueblos. Tours of 1 to 10 days on the trail are available year-round; each includes approximately 5 hours of daily saddle time and lodging at village inns along the way. Non-riders can accompany the caravan in a covered jeep-type support vehicle. Information: *Viajes Geosud,* 9 Calle Juan de Dios, Madrid 28015, Spain (phone: 1-542-6194), or *Viajes Granatur,* Granada 18412, Spain (phone: 58-223580), or *Rutas Alternativas,* Bubion 18412, Granada, Spain (phone: 58-766146).

Each year, during the first week in August, arrangements can be made through any of the above agencies to take part in a week-long excursion that heads from the outskirts of Granada, through the Sierra Nevada (the second highest mountain range in Europe, after the Alps), and into the High Alpujarras, coming down onto the beaches of the Mediterranean around Almuñecar. Most of the riders taking part bring their own horses, but steeds supplied by the organizers are also available.

LEÓN, Spain: Seldom visited — except by hunters out for pheasant or skiers on their way to the nearby ski resorts — the extensive facilities offered by this modern campsite complex 25 miles (40 km) north of the provincial capital include access to up to ten horses and guides for 1- to 3-day sallies into the high sierra, visiting an island saltwater lake, the Valdecortero caverns, the hermitage of Valdorria, and more. This is the place to go for those who wish to do some trout fishing. Information: *Campament-Finca* "La Granja," La Vecilla, León 24001, Spain (phone: 87-741222).

NAVARRE, Spain: Riders (a minimum of three) can tour one of the farthest-off-the-beaten-track regions in all the Iberian Peninsula, the northern part of the province of Navarre. The route travels along hidden, willow-shrouded rivers, forests of oak and beechnut, hilly pastureland, and up into the foothills of the Pyrenees, where the Cima de San Martín, the world's second-deepest canyon, is located. One- and 2-week routes are offered. Accommodations consist of simple village inns, with the odd night spent in a hotel. Horses are 7- to 11-year-old mixed Spanish-English veterans. Information: *Viajes Geosud,* 9 Calle Juan de Dios, Madrid 28015, Spain (phone: 1-542-6194).

SEGOVIA, Spain: The royal bridle paths laid down by the 14th-century Castilian sovereigns to tie their precarious kingdom together, along the trails of the *mesta* (medieval sheepherders guild), are the arteries leading straight into the heart of ancient Spain. *Rutas a Caballo* brings the highlands of Old Castile, with its castles, churches, hermitages, rivers, and forests, within easy reach of its home base, a ranch set around a centuries-old water mill, Molino de Rio Viejo, 12 miles (19 km) northwest of the provincial capital.

A 2-week excursion leads through the Sierra de Guadarrama, along the Duratón River canyon, and past the royal summer palace of La Granja, stopping in Sepúlveda, Pedraza, Turegano, and other towns with emblazoned palaces gone to ruin after their medieval glory. Departures are scheduled twice monthly, May through August, and once each during March, April, September, and October. A shorter 8-day version of the same route can be booked any month of the year. One-day and weekend outings from the mill are also offered, in which clients not only get to ride a horse, but also get to eat like one! Information: *Rutas a Caballo,* 21 Calle Juan Bravo, Madrid 28006, Spain (phone: 1-577-0297).

ALGARVE, Portugal: Southern Portugal's cork forests and beaches are within easy access of the Quinto do Lago estate, where Englishwoman Beverly Gibbons takes groups of riders out on elegant Lusitano steeds to tour the dunes and lagoons of the Algarve. Information: *Centro Hipico,* Quinto do Lago, Almansil 8100, Algarve, Portugal (phone: 89-94529 or 89-94782).

ESTORIL AND CASCAIS, Portugal: There is year-round riding along the sandy paths and beaches of Estoril and through the Marinha pine woods in Cascais. *Quinta da Marinha* has its own stable, which offers lessons and an English-style pub. Information: *Quinta da Marinha,* Quinta da Marinha, Lisbon 2750, Portugal (phone: 1-289282). Senhor Nuno Veloso, in Cascais, organizes riding circuits and can provide details on watching horse jumping competitions. Call him at 1-289282 or 1-289233.

EXTRA SPECIAL

EL TRANSHUMANCIA: This is the big chance for closet cowboys. Every year, Spanish cowpunchers round up their stock from the winter pastures of Extremadura and move 'em on up to the cooler grasslands of the Gredos range in a week-long cattle drive that is one of Europe's largest. Visitors can accompany them as they go off branding them dogies and fording the Tagus River, while sampling a lifestyle that did not end when Clint Eastwood left the rawhide range. But in between the long stretches of prairie, visitors will bed down at the luxury *paradores* of Trujillo and Oropesa, and at other stylish hotels. The roundup takes place around the second week of June, but the number of participants is limited. Bring along a pouch of Bull Durham. Information: *Rutas a Caballo, Viajes Nobel,* and *Equestrian Tours Almansur* (see above).

SPAIN FROM THE SADDLE: A solid month in the stirrups, from Segovia down the royal bridle paths running southeast to the Atlantic coast of Andalusia. The route also passes the foothills of the Sierra de Guadarrama into the barren 4,000-foot-high tableland of Avila province, followed by the evergreen oak forests of Extremadura to Guadalupe, Trujillo, Cáceres, and Mérida, up into the Sierra Morena and through the Guadalquivir River Valley to Seville and Arcos de la Frontera. Information: *Rutas a Caballo* (see above), which offers this tour in June and October.

Best Beaches

 Welded to Europe by a thin strip of land reinforced by the Pyrenees Mountains, the Iberian Peninsula seems to have been made to maximize its shoreline. The fantastically varied blends of sea, sand, and civilization range from the bathtub-like waters of the Mediterranean to the shivering shocks of the Atlantic surf, from the lonely and lush, mist-soaked greenery of northwest Spain to the teeming glitz of the Costa del Sol.

One way to choose a beach is by its lack of recognition. Since many of Spain's and Portugal's most popular beach resorts are now being reduced to functional blots encased in concrete, visiting them is as much of a return to nature as going to lunch at a salad bar. Many visitors, therefore, carefully take the time to seek out remote and undiscovered ocean paradises, far removed from the sands of mass tourism. Many others, however, head straight for the crowds. For those unable to avoid the large resorts, but wishing to escape the masses, try a visit in late August or September. Portugal's less-than-torrid Costa Verde is rather quiet during May — the tradeoff is paler tans and cooler waters for the luxury of a private beach.

BALEARIC ISLANDS, Spain: In an archipelago whose recent history is a catalogue of famous visitors, ranging from the Spanish royal family on Majorca to a generation's worth of hippies on Ibiza, the number of people who share these beaches is in inverse proportion to the time one invests in reaching them. Palma de Mallorca, seemingly everyone's first stop, is a busy port city complete with condos, a cathedral, and convention-size hotels. Miles of sandy beaches stretch to the east; those from Ca'n Pastilla to El Arenal are lined with high-rise hotels, restaurants, and discos, known collectively as the Playa de Palma. To the west lie a cluster of smaller beaches — Cala Major, Palma Nova, Magaluf, and, beyond the Bay of Palma, Paguera. The smaller island of Minorca has miles of solitary pine-ringed beaches, sloping countrysides, and historic ruins, making it a worthwhile trek from even the tiniest town. Its capital is Mahón, whose serried whitewashed houses were given distinguished Georgian make-overs during the island's British colonial days. Just outside town is the Stone Age village of Trepuco, one of the prehistoric mini-Stonehenges that dot the island (another reason 17th-century colonists thought that Minorca should belong to England). Information: *Oficina de Turismo,* 13 Plaza de la Constitución, Mahón, Minorca 07701, Spain (phone: 71-363790).

EL CABO DE GATA, near Almería, Andalusia, Spain: At the southeastern tip of Spain, on the edge of the Costa del Sol and squarely in the middle of nowhere, El Cabo de Gata ("the Cape of the Cat") is the place to go to get away from it all — including hotels, paved roads, and vegetation. The dusty, brush-covered desert that turns imperceptibly into beach looks as if it should be accompanied by the twang and whistled tune of a spaghetti (or paella) western. This is indeed where many a parched cowboy squinted into the pretend Texas sun before whipping out his Colt .45. San José is the cape's only (barely) burgeoning resort, but the city of Almería is only a short drive away, and the town of Mojácar (just up the coast, though a long way around by road) clambers quaintly up a hillside a mile or two back from the shore and has a *parador*. Accommodations here are scarce and by no means luxurious, but the food is good and there are some bargain prices to be enjoyed. Information: *Oficina de Turismo,* Calle Hermanos Machado, Edificios Servicios Multiples, Almería 04071, Spain (phone: 51-230607).

CANARY ISLANDS, Spain: An hour's water skiing from the coast of the Western Sahara, the volcanic archipelago of the Canaries belongs technically to Spain, geographically to Africa, and physically to the moon. Join a camel caravan through the gray-brown, crater-marked interior of the island of Lanzarote to the Cueva de los Verdes, a 4-mile tube tunneled by flowing lava. Pause for a dinner of suckling pig roasted over jets of heat escaping through the earth's thin crust, and wash it down with wine made from grapes nurtured in the warm, moist ash that covers the ground. Then descend to the coast through cinder-black fields, between towers of hardened lava, to vast stretches of sand, which make this all seem like a desert island. Those seeking less-tortured landscapes and manicured lawns should head for the larger islands of Tenerife or Grand Canary. Information: on Lanzarote, *Oficina de Turismo,* Parque Municipal, Arrecife 35500 (phone: 28-811860); other islands, *Oficina de Turismo,* Parque de Santa Catalina, Las Palmas 35007, Grand Canary, Spain (phone: 28-264623).

COSTA BRAVA, Tossa del Mar, Catalonia, Spain: The Costa Brava looks like a landscape painted by Cézanne — straight brushstrokes of ocher cliffs rising from the flat blue base to a daub of pine-tree green, the clean horizontals of Tossa's old port, and the vertical slice of a fishing boat's mast. The town lies in one of this weatherbeaten coast's many snug, sandy inlets; these once gave shelter to Phoenician sailors, but now provide exposure to Nordic bathers. Choose from Tossa's three beaches: La Playa Grande, Mar Menuda, and Es Codolar, each as spectacular as the next. If Tossa seems too tame after dark, or its medieval Villa Vella too old, head for Lloret de Mar, a casino-powered resort where young people sizzle till dawn. If even Tossa seems rowdy, the cliff-top *Parador de Aiguablava* in Bagur offers contemplative views of the see-through water 400 feet below and the sea-floor rocks 40 feet below that. Information: *Oficina d'Informació Turística,* 12 Carrer Ciutadans, Girona 17004, Spain (phone: 72-201694), or at the bus terminal on Carretera de Lloret in Tossa (phone: 72-340108).

COSTA CANTÁBRICA, Santander, Cantabria, Spain: This elegant city, almost as close to the powdery snow as it is to the powdery sand, is proud of the quality of its double life — its measured off-season pace and its summer pulsation of students, orchestras, and tourists, all drawn by Santander's spectacular beaches, its festivals of music and dance, and its university. Dense crowds and a rather rough Atlantic are the trademarks of the Playa del Sardinero, while the beaches on the bay are graced by ladies and gentlemen who prefer gentler surf. When visiting the nearby Altamira Caves, it may take a while for the medieval town of Santillana del Mar to stop seeming garishly modern and harshly sunlit after emerging from the prehistoric underground dwellings. Only small groups (up to 10 people per day in summer and 35 per day in winter) may take the 20-minute guided tour of the caves. Tour reservations must be made at least 3 months in advance by letter. Specify the number of people in the group and a range of possible dates for a visit. Reservations: *Director, Centro de Investigación y Museo de Altamira* (Santillana del Mar, Cantabria 39330, Spain; phone: 42-818102 or 42-818005). Comillas, some 40 miles (64 km) from Santander, is a quiet, still-aristocratic resort, where visitors are more likely to run across a marquis than a marquee. The wide

Playa Comillas, where the titled sunbathe until they achieve the color of expensive leather, ends in a small pleasure port. The nearby Oyambre beach is twice as long, with half the tourists. Information: *Oficina de Turismo,* 1 Plaza Porticada, Santander 39001, Spain (phone: 42-310708 or 42-310756).

COSTA DEL SOL, Marbella, Andalusia, Spain: The Costa del Sol is a glittering avenue of low-slung bathing suits and high-rise prices, and Marbella is the center of Europe's wealthy worshipers of sun and self. The tennis courts and golf courses are world class, but the primary sport here is people watching. The world's wet set finds shelter in the nearby yacht harbor at Puerto Banus, and the smoothness of Estepona's silky water is guarded from the rough and tumble of the Atlantic by the Rock of Gibraltar, visible from the town's wide beachfront. In the other direction, past Málaga (pass it quickly; it is the tourists' Ellis Island), is the town of Nerja, with a *parador,* a cliff-top boardwalk, and a set of spectacular caves scooped out by water flowing through the soft limestone. Information: in Marbella, *Oficina de Turismo,* 1 Avenida Miguel Cano, Marbella 29600, Spain (phone: 52-771442); the rest of the Costa del Sol, *Oficina de Turismo,* 5 Calle Marqués de Larios, Málaga 29015, Spain (phone: 52-213445).

RÍAS BAJAS, La Toja, Galicia, Spain: The Celts once came to green Galicia and gave it their bagpipes, heaths, and a wet Gallic fog. But when the mist slides off the fjords of the Rías Bajas, it reveals some of the peninsula's most voluptuous coastline, where meadow lanes link small stone churches to shingle-roofed villages, and the people speak a language of their own. Reachable by bridge from the town of O Grove, La Toja is a dressed-up island off a sensibly shod shore, complete with large, expensive hotels, swimming pools, golf courses, a spa, and a casino. In a region where the specialty is squid cooked in its own ink, O Grove is religious about its seafood. On the second Sunday in October, the town celebrates the *Feast of the Exaltation of Shellfish.* Information: *Oficina de Turismo,* 2 Calle General Mola, Pontevedra 36001, Spain (phone: 86-850814).

SAN SEBASTIÁN, Spain: This pearl of a city in an oyster shell–shaped bay situated between two emerald mountains is one of the most popular resorts in Spain — and the Basques are fighting it all the way. They are fiercely jealous of their difference; they play jai alai, not tennis, call their region Euskadi, and occasionally clear the deck chairs on the city's beach with their separatist stirrings. Most summers, though, this slice of coast is thickly spread with oiled bodies, and when the crowds begin to ebb for no reason more violent than sunset, they flow into the streets of San Sebastián's Old Quarter, drifting between *tapas* bars and dining at stand-up counters on mini-courses of dried cod in tomato sauce and cuttlefish in ink. Information: *Oficina de Turismo,* 13 Calle Andía, San Sebastián 20004, Spain (phone: 43-426282).

ALGARVE, Tavira, Portugal: It was in the Algarve, this nether corner of Europe a ferry ride and a time zone away from Spain, that the end of the world was thought to begin. The lighthouse at Cabo de São Vicente still beams out over the horizon to keep ships from falling off the disk of the earth. The white stucco town of Tavira is still untouched by tourism. Fishing boats depart daily and return loaded with tuna and sardines for the evening's grill. The spacious beach is on the long, sandy island of Tavira, where shoreline turf is abundant, so much so that on Sundays in July, there's even room for an oceanside game of touch football. The pallid be warned — the water is warm and the waves gentle, but the Algarvian sun is deceptively wind-cooled and burningly fierce. Information: *Região de Turismo do Algarve,* 100 Rua Ataide de Oliveira, Faro 8000, Portugal (phone: 89-24067 or 89-26049); in Tavira, at the tourist office on Praça da República (phone: 89-22511).

ESTORIL AND CASCAIS, Lisbon, Portugal: As the countries of Europe found democracy, their exiled monarchs came here, turning this slice of coast into a retirement community for kings and queens, with even a tiny, turreted castle on the beach at Estoril. The villas have faded some, but the sand, the casino, and the nightlife still gleam. And if this isn't temptation enough, outside Cascais awaits the Boca do Inferno (Mouth of Hell), a large hole bitten out of rock by the angry Atlantic. A little farther out, the ocean spits white spray and hammers at the chiseled cliffs of the Cabo da Roca, the westernmost point of the mass of land that stretches from here east to the Bering Straits. Ideal for windsurfing, the beach at Guincho at sunset has a perfect view of the Cabo, as well as the last drops of daylight in Europe. Information: *Junta de Turismo da Costa do Estoril,* Arcadas do Parque, Estoril 2765, Portugal (phone: 1-268-0113).

NAZARÉ, Costa de Prata, Portugal: Unlike any other village in Portugal, this one sticks to its ancient customs and traditional garb. Men typically wear plaid pants rolled up to their knees and stock their tobacco, matches, and lighters in their black caps. Women often wear seven petticoats and help their men clean and salt the fish. There isn't much to do here except take in the scenery and spend time in the Praia quarter, the area near the beach. At night, when the fishing boats return, head over to the port to watch the local restaurateurs bid for the best-looking catches of the day. Information: *Posto de Turismo,* 23 Rua Mouzinho de Albuquerque, Nazaré 2450, Portugal (phone: 62-46120 or 62-52194).

Gone Fishing

 With countless miles of sun-soaked Atlantic and Mediterranean coastline, unpolluted waters, and over 200 varieties of fish, Spain and Portugal are truly an angler's paradise. Deep-sea enthusiasts can wrestle year-round with swordfish, ray, tuna, shark, trout, and snapper, while freshwater anglers can cast for tench, salmon, carp, trout, pike, bass, barbel, and chub. Although there are numerous lakes and rivers for fishing, it is not a wide-open free-for-all. In order to protect and maintain their fish populations, both Spain and Portugal have instituted numerous restrictions for visiting fishermen, as well as for locals. Each country has limits on where and when fishing is permitted, as well as various catch limits. These laws are often so dizzying that the effort to obtain permits and satisfy restrictions may not be worth the day spent at sea. In Spain, a lottery-style drawing is held each fishing season and permits are issued to the winners. If the maximum number of seasonal permits has been distributed before a visitor's arrival, he or she may be out of luck. In Portugal, the restrictions are a bit more relaxed. There are none for deep-sea fishing, but freshwater fishing has its share. Consequently, many of the best — and most convenient — outings are organized through marinas and the various resorts along the water.

Nearly all game-fishing waters in Spain and Portugal are tightly controlled by each country's various local and regional governments. Some regions do not allow foreigners to fish in their waters, period! Those that do require the appropriate licenses and permits, but bear in mind that these documents do not grant fishermen the right to clean out the ocean, lakes, rivers, or streams. Both countries have strongly enforced catch limits, as well as strict rules regulating minimum sizes, bait and tackle, and Sunday fishing. Sea angling is discouraged in Spain, and is considered illegal in some regions; the seas along the Costa del Sol and the Costa Brava are rare exceptions. In Portugal, however, it is very common, and no license is required.

In Spain, three types of fishing are available: deep-sea, river and lake, and underwater. Permits are available from the *Instituto Nacional para la Conservación de la Naturaleza (ICONA)* through each of its offices in the various autonomous communities. In Madrid, *ICONA* is located at 35-41 Avenida Gran Vía de San Francisco (phone: 1-266-8200). The permits vary according to the type of fishing to be practiced. Be warned: Most federations have strange hours; some don't open until after 6 PM, and some are open only from 9 AM to noon. Also, many *ICONA* staff members throughout Spain do not speak English. Permits cost about $10 per day, and a passport is required. Salmon and trout permits cost about $2; a license, which is separate, costs about $10. It is advisable to check with a travel agent or the National Tourist Office of Spain in the US before going. The tourist office provides a fishing map called *Pesca* (fishing), which outlines the best available areas. For the particulars once there, check with the *Spanish Fishing Federation* (3 Calle Navas de Tolosa, Madrid 28013, Spain; phone: 1-532-8353). Other good sources include the *Promocion de Caza y Pesca* (41 Duque de Sexto, Madrid, 28010 Spain; phone: 1-276-3661); and the *Consejeria de Agricultura y Cooperación de la Comunidad Autónoma de Madrid* (60 Calle Orense, Madrid 28020, Spain; phone: 1-455-7703). The most rewarding months for angling in Spain are March through August.

Because of the mild climate in Portugal, fishing tends to be good year-round. There is an awesome variety of over 200 species; some such as the scabbard fish, which averages 6 feet in length, are unique to Portuguese waters. There are three species of trout native to Portuguese waters: rainbow trout, *fareo* trout, and sea trout. The rainbow can be found only in lagoons and dams in the northern and central regions of the country, the *fareo* is common in almost every river and stream, and the sea trout is found in the Minho and Lima Rivers. Black bass is best found in lagoons and dams throughout the country, especially in the Algarve, as well as the natural lagoon in Pateia de Fermentelos, near Agueda, about 25 miles (40 km) north of Coimbra. Salmon appears only in the Minho and Lima Rivers. The best spot to catch it is in the north end of the Gadanha, a Minho tributary, near Monção. Portugal also boasts a variety of shellfish, namely dog whelks, rock and giant lobsters, crabs, and spider crabs. Sports fishermen divide the Portuguese coastline into two distinct zones, with the frontier between the two lying more or less at Peniche (regarded as the center of Portuguese big-game fishing), in the center of the coastal area. The northern zone tends to be richer in cold-water fish, such as skate, grouper, tope, shark, and bass. The coast between Moledo and Porto, encompassing Vila Praca de Ancora, Esposende, Ofir, Póvoa de Varzim, Viana do Castelo, Vila do Conde, and Espinho, Figueira da Foz, plus the towns of Nazaré, and São Martinho do Porto, are among the best areas, and are especially good for visitors because of the abundance of fishing boats.

ANDALUSIA, Spain: Outside the cities of Granada and Jaén are some of the country's best spots for catching trout, crab, pike, and cyprinids. Maximum catches allowed range from 10 to 80. The season is best from March 1 through August 15, except along the Guadalquivir, Jándula, Rumblar, and Guadalén rivers in the fishing reserves of Estación, Andújar, San Juan, San Julian, and Rumblar, where people can fish (mostly for cyprinids) year-round. Surrounded by the ranges of the Sierra Morena and the Segura, this is one of the most scenic and enjoyable fishing sites around. Information: *Oficina de Turismo,* Calle Arquitecto Bergés, Jaén 23007, Spain (phone: 53-222737).

CANTABRIAN COAST, Spain: Wedged between the Basque Country to the east and Galicia to the west, this area is one of Spain's most unspoiled. Choose a base in Santander, Oviedo, Pontevedra, or Lugo, and experience the pleasures of medieval living. This natural paradise remains virtually untouched, and visitors will relish in its history, artistry, modesty, and gorgeous beaches. On top of all that, fresh fish is never far away. This is the place for catching salmon and enjoying a meal while overlooking the twinkling waters. Information: *Oficina de Turismo,* 1 Plaza Porticada, Santander 39001, Spain (phone: 42-310708 or 42-310756), or *Consejeria de Ganaderia, Agricultura y Pesca de la Diputación Regional de Cantabria,* 1 Pasaje de la Puntida, Santander 39071, Spain (phone: 42-312969).

CASTILE-LEÓN, Spain: Head to Avila, Burgos, or Seville for some of the best angling central Spain has to offer. Restrictions apply a bit more heavily here, to the point where people have to check their days for fishing. Usually, Fridays and Saturdays are all right. Catches are restricted as well; the take-home limit ranges from 6 to 10. Best bets are trout and cyprinids. Information: *Oficina de Turismo,* 4 Plaza de la Catedral, Avila 05001, Spain (phone: 18-211387), or *Oficina de Turismo,* 7 Plaza de Alonso Martinez, Burgos 09003, Spain (phone: 47-203125).

CATALONIA, Spain: Most avid fishermen know the areas around Barcelona, Girona, and Lleida as some of the most prolific year-round spots for catching trout, black bass, and cyprinids. Like other areas, strict restrictions apply. Also check out the areas along the Costa Brava. These rough waters are perfect for underwater fishing. Check with *ICONA* or the local tourist office for details. The Catalan Pyrenees are also good for trout and salmon. About half of the 250 lakes in the Pyrenees National Park are stocked with various kinds of trout, and there is at least one good fishing stream in each valley. Information: *Patronat Municipal de Turisme de Barcelona,* 658 Gran Via de les Corts Catalanes, Barcelona 08010, Spain (phone: 3-301-7443 or 3-317-2246), or *Consejeria de Agricultura, Ganaderia y Pesca de la Generalidad de Catalunya,* 329 Carrer Còrsega, Barcelona 08037, Spain (phone: 3-237-7862).

ALGARVE, Portugal: It is truly an experience of a lifetime to hook and finally bring in a mako or a hammerhead shark. The warm southeastern currents provide this area with a prolific and varied marine life. For many years, only fishing villages existed along Portugal's southern coast. Today, the extreme ends of the Algarve remain much as they were. The sun-roughed skin of fishermen, their hands tough and calloused, their character lines smooth and telling, will greet visitors who decide to venture out on their own. In between, near the resort areas of Faro, Vilamoura, Lagos, and Portimão, visitors are better off taking an organized tour out to sea. Big-game fishing is the sport here. Spectators are invited as well, and there are sun decks and bar service to keep them occupied. Information: *Surfpesca,* 35 Rua Santa Isabel, Portimão 8500, Portugal (phone: 82-25450). Other big-game fishing is available through the Algarve's *Big-Game Fishing Center,* Cepemar, 24-A Praça da República, Portimão 8500, Portugal (phone: 82-25866).

AZORES, Portugal: The nine-island Azorean archipelago, called the stepping-stones between the Old and New Worlds, offers astounding results for big game fishermen. Much of the sea surrounding the islands, especially the islands of São Miguel, Faial, and Terceira, are truly virgin waters, virtually untouched and undiscovered. From May through July, millions of large fish such as Allison tuna roam the surface, feeding on smaller fish. White and blue marlin, broadbill swordfish, and bluefin tuna have also been spotted here on a regular basis. For the light caster, the Azores present a fascinating array of amberjack, bluefish, barracuda, tuna, mackerel, and jack crevalle. Information: *Pescatour,* 49 Rua João Francisco Cabral, Ponta Delgada, São Miguel, Azores 9500, Portugal, or *World Wide Sportsman, Inc.,* PO Drawer 787, Islamorada, FL 33036 (phone: 305-664-4615 or 305-238-9252; 800-327-2880 outside Florida).

COSTA VERDE, Portugal: The Minho River and its tributaries, particularly the area between Valença and Melgaço, are ideal for game fishing. The Lima and Homen rivers near Gerês, and the rivers near Trás-os-Montes, are excellent spots for trout and bass. A good base for a Costa Verde fishing trip is Viana do Castelo. Once a Roman outpost, this small, pleasant town offers easy access to the lakes and streams of the upper Minho River. Information: *Posto de Turismo,* Rua Cândido dos Reis, Viana do Castelo 4900, Portugal (phone: 58-22620).

NAZARÉ, Costa de Prata, Portugal: This little village lives for the sea. Its people spend the day either on the water, cleaning and salting fish, or preparing bait. Once known only to diehard fishermen, Nazaré has lately become a very popular, rather touristy beach resort, but its fishing tradition remains intact. Information: *Posto de Turismo,* 23 Rua Mouzinho de Albuquerque, Nazaré 2450, Portugal (phone: 62-46120 or 62-52194).

PENICHE AND THE BERLENGA ISLANDS, Costa de Prata, Portugal: Long dependent on the fishing industry, the city of Peniche, some 30 miles (48 km) from Obidos, is a working town often ignored by tourists on their way to the Ilhas Berlengas (Berlenga Islands). This is a bustling fishing port whose colorful fleet can be seen unloading the daily catch by the tons and where seafood restaurants are plentiful (the local version of *caldeirada* is famous). Information: *Posto de Turismo,* Rua Alexandre Herculano, Peniche, Leiria 2520, Portugal (phone: 62-72271).

TOMAR, Ribatejo, Portugal: Mix with the locals at Tomar's *Clube dos Amadores de Pesca* and hook up with a fisherman familiar with the ways of the famous Nabão River, which crosses through the town. The Alva River and the Ribeira de Alge, north of Tomar, are also good spots for catching trout and bass, among other fish. Information: *Posto de Turismo,* Avenida Dr. Cândido Madureira, 2300 Tomar, Portugal (phone: 49-313237).

Freewheeling by Two-Wheeler

 Because of the mild climate in Spain and Portugal, touring by bicycle is easy and the itinerary possibilities are nearly inexhaustible. Visitors who pedal through the Spanish and Portuguese countrysides will get to know parts of the countries that most people never see. These are the real sights, the hidden enclaves still untouched by tourism. Leisurely bicycle rides pass through tiny fishing villages and medieval towns dotted with Moorish ruins. In Spain, a bike ride can cover a variety of terrain, from the hilly land of olive groves to flat vineyards and lush countryside overflowing with orange and lemon trees. There's an unleashed sense of freedom out on the open road; days are spent exploring, always wondering what lies ahead when climbing over the next hill. A variety of terrain exists in Portugal, too, although there is much flat land and the roads tend to be narrower, and cyclists almost always share them with farmers riding their mules, a sack of feed draped over each side. It is not uncommon for riders to have to stop to let shepherds, with crooked walking sticks in their hands and toothy grins on their faces, cross the road with their flocks.

Those who have traveled around Europe by bicycle before will find that a cycling vacation in Spain and Portugal is slightly more primitive than in most other western European countries. There is hardly an abundance of sophisticated repair shops, nor even the guarantee of well-surfaced secondary roads (though Spain is getting there). Bicycle rentals are available in both countries, but not omnipresent. Intermediate and diehard cyclists will want to bring their own bicycles and gear. Airlines will generally transport bikes as part of passengers' personal baggage, but they may insist that the entire bike be crated; check with the airline before departure. Also be sure to confirm insurance coverage. And note that when traveling by train in Spain, a bike (like luggage) must be placed in the last car, so make sure that it is properly labeled with name, address, and the stations of origin and destination. A sturdy lock is another sensible precaution.

Some cyclists choose to travel alone through Spain and Portugal. Others, however, team up with fellow cyclists and soon become fast friends. The natives are so friendly, they will practically apologize if they cannot accompany a rider to his or her destination (many riders often wind up staying in one place longer than they had planned). It does help, however, to have a rudimentary understanding of Spanish, especially when touring the rural routes, as most people in the countryside do not speak English. Knowing Spanish helps in Portugal as well, as written Portuguese is very similar to Spanish. A pocket dictionary is heartily recommended. As usual, taking along a basic set of tools and spares, including a tire pump, puncture repair kit, tire levers, spoke key, oil can, batteries and bulbs, rag, extra spokes, inner tubes and tires, pliers, and odd nuts and bolts is also a good idea. Traveling with a minimal amount of cash and a credit card is also advised. In addition, take along a good map; Michelin generally has the best. In Madrid, check out the maps and books at *La Tienda Verde* (The Green Bookshop; 38 Calle Maudes; phone: 1-533-0791), which stocks the best assortment on naturalist tours; books are available in both Spanish and English. In Barcelona, try *Liberia Quera* (2 Carrer Petritxol; phone: 3-318-0743) for good maps and guides of Catalonia.

If the thought of biking alone is less than a satisfactory vacation idea, there are numerous organized bicycle tours in both countries. For information on bicycle tours, see *Camping and Caravanning, Hiking and Biking,* GETTING READY TO GO.

When cycling in Spain and Portugal, always remember that it is more relaxing and enjoyable to take it slowly and enjoy the country's sights and sounds. After choosing a region, consult the local tourist literature. Then plot out the tour on a large-scale highway map of the country. Base daily mileage on what usually iscovered on the road at home, but be sure to allot time for en route dawdling — chats with the natives, walks through ruined castles, wine and *tapas* at the local bar.

ANDALUSIA, Spain: This region's warm year-round climate, well-marked and well-paved roads, and scenery rank it as one of the best places to go biking in Spain. Home to feisty flamenco dancers and sun-splashed villages, Andalusia also boasts three of the country's most fascinating cities: Granada, Córdoba, and Seville. Begin the tour in Granada, with a steep ride up to the Alhambra, a complex of palaces, fortresses, and gardens built during the 13th and 14th centuries. Then meander in Columbus's historic footsteps to Sante Fe, the city where King Ferdinand and Queen Isabella signed the famous agreement sponsoring the explorer's famous voyage. Next, head to Córdoba, one of Spain's oldest cities. Along the way, the route skirts past two rivers, the Marbella and the Guadajoz. The terrain along the route is fairly easy, consisting mostly of gentle downhill slopes and flat land. The road begins to climb just beyond the small village of Torres Cabrera. At the top of the next stretch, the slope of Lobaton (best climbed with a 20–24 gear ratio), awaits a picture-postcard view of Córdoba, which is reached by an easy descent. The main attraction here is the Mezquita, the Arab palace famous for its red-and-white arches. Other Córdoba attractions include its synagogue and its European-style cafés; at the latter, local women casually dance the flamenco. The city's roads are narrow and cobbled, but soon after leaving the city limits, following the Avenida de Medina Azahara, they get better. Heading south toward Seville, the route passes through alternating views of extensive fields and barren wastelands. Occasionally, a fortress pokes its revered head in the distance. Seville is one of the most romantic cities in Spain and one of its most touristic. The roads are well marked, the scenes full of history and intrigue. Visit the old Jewish Quarter and the Santa Cruz barrio, as well as the cathedral and the Alcázar. Always be careful to lock up the bike and take off one of its wheels; unfortunately, caution is necessary here (as in most major Spanish cities), as crime has become an all-too-frequent problem. After Seville, it's a 1-hour ride northeast to Carmona, once a thriving Arab stronghold, to view its famous 14th-century mansions. Stop for lunch at Carmona's *Parador del Rey Don Pedro* (phone: 54-141010), the former palace of the king called Pedro el Cruel (Peter the Cruel). Information: *Oficina de Turismo,* 2 Calle de los Libreros, Granada 18001, Spain (phone: 58-221022 or 58-225990); *Oficina de Turismo,* 10 Calle Torrijos, Córdoba 14003, Spain (phone: 57-471235 or 57-483112); and *Oficina de Turismo,* 21-B Avenida de la Constitución, Seville 41004, Spain (phone: 5-422-1404).

BASQUE COUNTRY, Spain: The hilly Basque Country is best known for the town of Guernica, made famous by Pablo Picasso's painting of the Spanish Civil War. It is an interesting area to explore because its culture and its people — even its language — are quite different from the rest of Spain. The area will appeal to cyclists who enjoy diverse geography. The tour rolls past rugged mountains and stony undulations to soft, sloping, wide sandy shores and steep, pine-covered hillsides. In San Sebastián, the road along the *puerto*'s edge travels past some of the best seafood restaurants serving fresh food caught that day. Cycle along the Bilbao coast for some of the finest and most surprising scenery along the North Atlantic Coast. Information: *Oficina de Turismo,* 13 Calle Andía, San Sebastián 20004, Spain (phone: 43-426282).

CASTILE-LEÓN, Spain: This is a land of fairy-tale images, including that of El Escorial, King Philip II's somber yet lavish palace-monastery near Madrid; the near-perfect 11th-century walled city of Avila, framed by the snow-capped ridge of the Sierra de Gredos; and Segovia, home to an ancient Roman aqueduct and the Alcázar, a medieval castle that looks as if it came straight out of a Hollywood movie. This trip pedals past the royal palace and gardens of La Granja de San Ildefonso, often referred to as the Versailles of Spain, and the romantic spiraling cathedrals of Valladolid. Start either in Madrid or at El Escorial, and plan enough time for a visit to the *Valle de los Caídos* (Valley of the Fallen), a spectacular memorial to those who died in the Spanish Civil War. A huge basilica containing the tombs of soldiers from both sides has been hollowed into a mountain. Generalísimo Francisco Franco, who ordered the monument's construction, is also buried here. Information: *Oficina de Turismo,* 10 Calle Floridablanca, San Lorenzo de El Escorial, Madrid 28036, Spain (phone: 1-890-1554); *Oficina de Turismo,* 4 Plaza de la Catedral, Avila 05001, Spain (phone: 18-211387); and *Oficina de Turismo,* 10 Plaza Mayor, Segovia 34001, Spain (phone: 11-430328).

CATALAN PYRENEES, Spain: Intermediate pedalers will enjoy the challenge of this region, as it is filled with a number of ups and downs, but the views here are so spectacular that even beginners should give it a try. The area is the home of many of Spain's better ski resorts, including Baqueira-Beret and Tuca-Betrén, and during spring and summer, rich green and yellow fields crisscross the wide valleys and small undiscovered villages. Because of the proximity to France, the French influence on the food and the people here is very obvious. Ask the staff at the tourist office for the map *Valles Superiores del Segre/Ariege,* which covers the High Urgell, Cerdanya, and the Ribes Valley. A favorite tour is through the Aigües Tortes National Park, with the Sant Maurici Lake, just south of Val d'Aran. This national park is a wonderland of crashing waterfalls and serene lakes, which makes for very pleasant bicycling. Information: *Oficina d'Informació Turística,* Passeis Brodieur, La Seu d'Urgell, Lleida 25700, Spain (phone: 73-350991).

COSTA DEL SOL, Spain: Although this area along Spain's southern coast falls under the jurisdiction of the region of Andalusia, it warrants a special mention. This tour passes through hills that drop off into the pounding surf of the Mediterranean and along roads that coil around the crashing waves. The Costa del Sol officially extends from Tarifa, west of Gibraltar, in the Spanish southwest, to the town of Cabo de Gata, just east of Almería. Those seeking the action and international flavor of some of Europe's most popular and lively beach resorts should pedal into the crowded resorts of Málaga, Marbella, and Torremolinos. Those seeking the scenic but quiet Spanish coast, without the trappings of mass tourism, may prefer the more forgotten towns of Vejar de la Frontera, Salobreña, and Ronda. Throughout the coast, the beaches are great, the weather is perfect, and the resort atmosphere instills that "get away from it all" vacation feeling. One of the best places to enjoy a fiery Andalusian sunset is from the Puente Nuevo in Ronda, where the cliffs glow a soothing orange and red, reflecting the strong Spanish sun. In general, the roads along the Costa del Sol are in fairly good condition and easy to follow. Cyclists traveling in the off-season should prepare to ride west to east, thus avoiding the strong easterly winds. Also not to be missed is the great Rock of Gibraltar. The view is breathtaking along the Straits of Gibraltar all the way to the Moroccan coast. Although the area itself is more British than Spanish (Gibraltar is a British Crown Colony), a visit here offers a chance to view one of the Iberian Peninsula's most famous sights. Information: *Oficina de Turismo,* 5 Calle Marqués de Larios, Málaga 29015, Spain (phone: 52-213445).

COSTA BLANCA, Spain: The "White Coast," which extends from Denia down to

Torrevieja, is another resort rich in natural beauty that is perfectly conditioned for the cyclist. Like the Costa del Sol, it has its share of unspoiled spots. Venture to Alicante, inlaid with festive red tiles and graced with the famous Castillo de Santa Bárbara, full of secret passageways and tunnels. Nearby, Elche is known for its half-million palm trees, which supply all of Spain with fronds for *Palm Sunday.* Information: *Oficina de Turismo,* 2 Esplanada de España, Alicante 03002, Spain (phone: 65-212285).

COSTA BRAVA, Spain: This coast is rougher and rockier than its sister resort areas, but just as magnificent. Most people flock here during the summer, so try to visit during the off-season, when it is more tranquil and easier to explore. Be careful, though, as many hotels and restaurants close at the end of the high season. The roads here are well paved, but the terrain is often steep, physically challenging, and, in some spots, even dangerous. This tour is not recommended for novice cyclists. Information: *Oficina de Turismo,* 4 Calle Iglesia, Tossa de Mar, Girona 17320, Spain (phone: 72-340108).

NAVARRESE PYRENEES, Spain: There is probably no area in Spain quite as suited for quiet pedaling than this region along the valleys of the Arga and Aragón rivers, where mountain valleys swoop down to the dusty red desert. Begin this itinerary in Sangüesa, an ancient town on the Aragon River, and travel northeast, past the large and austere Cistercian monastery of Leyre, whose ancient church with its 12th-century crypt was the final resting place of the Kings of Navarre. Continue west into the sleepy town of Roncal, with its cobbled streets and stone houses, and the more upbeat town of Isaba, just to the north. Ahead lies Roncesvalles, historically known for the *Song of Roland,* an epic poem that romanticized the defeat of Charlemagne's rear guard during its retreat from Spain. The monastery here marked the beginning of the famous Pilgrims' Route as it entered Spain from France en route to Santiago de Compostela in the northwestern corner of the country. Don't be surprised by the sign warning of cattle on the loose in the valley of Valcarlos, a few miles from the French border, which marks the end of this tour. Information: *Oficina de Turismo,* 2 Calle Mercado, Sangüesa, Navarre 31400, Spain (phone: 48-870329).

ALGARVE, Portugal: Portugal's coastal resort area provides some of the country's best cycling. The roads are fairly flat, the temperatures remain moderate year-round, the towns are very attractive and well spaced, and the landscape is a lyrical mixture of blue sky, fine golden sand, and crystalline water. This circuit begins in Vale do Lobo or Quinta do Lago area, the center of activity in the Algarve and the point from which cyclists can choose to ride either east or west. Ride out to Sagres, the southwesternmost point of Europe, and watch the sun set like a ball falling off the edge of the earth. The region between Faro and the Spanish border is the least developed and most undiscovered, and makes for a very tranquil and leisurely ride. Information: *Posto de Turismo,* 8-12 Rua da Misericórdia, Faro 8000, Portugal (phone: 89-25404).

ALTO ALENTEJO, Portugal: This is the northern part of Portugal's plains region, flat and largely unpopulated. For cyclists looking to escape the city, this is a perfect route. Begin in the walled town of Elvas, conveniently situated some 20 miles (32 km) west of the Spanish border, and known throughout Portugal for its sugarplums. The tour passes through large farms and whitewashed hamlets, where olive and cork trees dot the countryside, to Evora, a medieval university town filled with reminders of the 15th and 16th centuries. The entire city is practically a living museum. Information: *Posto de Turismo,* 73-74 Praça do Giraldo, Evora 7000, Portugal (phone: 66-22671).

COSTA VERDE, Portugal: This very green region in the northwestern corner of the country extends from the Douro River to Porto and up to the Minho River near the Spanish frontier. The route offers a close look at Porto, home of Portugal's famous port wines, and continues into the rolling hills and elegant parks of Braga, as well as the wine region of Viseu. The terrain here is challenging, but the roads are in good condition and very quiet. Information: *Posto de Turismo,* 25 Rua Clube Fenianos, Porto 4000, Portugal (phone: 2-312740).

SINTRA, Portugal: When setting out from Lisbon, the fairy-tale land of Sintra — once dubbed "glorious Eden" by Lord Byron in his autobiographical poem *Childe Harold* — is a tour full of meandering roads and strenuous hills. Though challenging, the route can be covered by cyclists of all levels, and is certainly worth the effort. Nowhere else in Portugal is there such an abundance of assorted architectural fantasies surrounded by thick magical forests. For those wishing to pedal only one way, there is frequent train service between Sintra and Lisbon. Information: *Posto de Turismo,* Praça da República, Sintra 2710, Portugal (phone: 1-923-1157).

Great Walks and Mountain Rambles

Almost any walker will say that it is the footpaths of a country — not its roadways — that show off the local landscape to best advantage. Closer to earth than when driving or even biking, those on foot notice details that might not otherwise come to their attention: hills perfumed with edelweiss, for instance, or valleys dotted with medieval villages; sheep gambol in the shade of fig and cork oak trees, and the friendly company of the sun makes the leaves shine and the mountaintops glisten.

The geographic diversity of the Iberian Peninsula makes walking here a wonderful journey full of surprises. Many paths were literally walked into existence by generations of people traveling to work, market, or church, or were carved by medieval pilgrims and advancing or retreating soldiers. Today, there is terrain for walkers and hikers of all abilities — from picnic stroller to fearless alpinist. The high mountain ranges of Spain's Picos de Europa and the Pyrenees, the green valleys of the Basque Country, and the sandy beaches of Portugal's Algarve all make for peaceful, pleasant strolls or climbs. Both countries also boast a number of national parks to explore, while visitors less attracted to wilderness will find villages perched on high, with cobblestone streets, mansions, churches, ruins, and shops that are guaranteed to hold their interest and challenge their feet. Add to this a climate that is generally benign (Portugal is often referred to as the California of Europe, and Spain's southern coast is a Mediterranean paradise year-round), friendly natives, and good food — all the ingredients of a perfect expedition.

Before choosing a specific area of the country for hiking, look at a general road map of Spain or Portugal that shows physical characteristics, so as not to opt for terrain that is too demanding for one's level of fitness. For those who are sedentary, the choice of a mountainous region would be foolhardy. To make the outing safe and pleasant, it is imperative for hikers to know their own limits. Unless they are very experienced, hikers always should stick to the defined areas — and *always* let someone know the planned destination and time of expected return (leave a note on the car if hiking alone). Those who prefer going as part of an organized tour should contact a local hiking club, a travel agent, or one of the many tour packagers specializing in hiking tours. For information on Iberian hikes, see *Camping and Caravanning, Hiking and Biking,* GETTING READY TO GO.

Since hot weather is not necessarily a welcome companion on a walk, it's best to avoid the southern regions in midsummer. And since it can get warm almost anywhere in Spain and Portugal between May and September, the wise walker will get most of a day's journey done before midday. Basic hiking essentials should include a sturdy pair of shoes and socks, long pants if headed into heavily wooded areas, a canteen, a hat, sunblock, rainwear, and something warm, just in case. It is always best to dress in layers. Also make sure to wear clothes with pockets, or bring along a pack so that both hands can remain free. Some useful but often overlooked tools include a jackknife, waterproof matches, a map, a compass, and snacks. In the more remote areas, a backpack, sleeping bag and pad, cookstove, food, and other gear are required.

Spain is consistent only in its diversity. There are the extreme peaks of the highlands, the Pyrenees, and the Picos de Europa, and the lowlands of the Basque Country — where, incidentally, the rain does not fall mainly on the plain. The most advisable times of year to hike these areas are late spring and early autumn, when the flora and fauna are at their most vibrant and the temperatures are at their most delightful. Always check the weather in advance. Like the topography, the temperature varies enormously from region to region; the high plains of the center suffer from fierce extremes — stiflingly hot in summer and bitterly cold in winter. The Atlantic Coast, in contrast, has a permanent tendency to dampness and a relatively brief summer. The Mediterranean is warm virtually the entire year.

Portugal's best treks are not quite as varied as those in its Iberian neighbor. The country is generally flat, with its highest peak, Malhão da Estrela (or Torre), rising only 6,530 feet. Still, there are numerous enjoyable walks to be had — rambles through countrysides laden with natural beauty and the occasional Moorish ruin. Best bets include the Algarve, the Costa Verde, and the Costa de Prata.

BASQUE COUNTRY, San Sebastián, Spain: The Basque Country is a land of contrasts. Just steps away from its industrial centers sit isolated hamlets, submerged in the silent surroundings of valleys and forests. The most spectacular sight here is the city of San Sebastián, and the green mountains and thundering ocean that surround it. Climb to the top of Mt. Igueldo, at the far side of the bay, for the best view of the countryside and the Atlantic. Information: *Club Vasco de Acampado,* 19 Calle San Marcial Bajo, San Sebastián 20008, Spain (phone: 43-428479), or *Club de Montana Kresala,* 9 Calle Euskal Erria, San Sebastián 20003, Spain (phone: 43-420905).

CATALAN PYRENEES, Spain: Good, fairly gentle trails, coupled with plenty of historic sights and a hospitable nature, make this northeast corner of Spain a sensible choice for the less ambitious walker in need of wayside distractions. By virtue of its location (just across from the border with France), hikers can experience a variety of cultures, languages, and foods. In La Seu d'Urgell, nature buffs will have a field day roaming quiet peaks, scouting for wild mushrooms. Other expeditions lie in the valley of Nuria, where wildflowers and waterfalls dot the landscape. Also popular is the majestic Puigmal peak, rising over 9,500 feet, and the nearby Queranca Lakes. Information: *Oficina d'Informació Turística,* Passeis Brodieur, La Seu d'Urgell, Lleida 25700, Spain (phone: 73-350991).

AIGÜES TORTES NATIONAL PARK AND SANT MAURICI LAKE, Catalan Pyrenees, Spain: This is for the hiker who rejoices in waterfalls and serene lakes. Some 20,000 years ago, a glacier blasted its way through what is now northern Lleida province, leaving behind a panoramic wonderland. The park is reached either from the town of Bo Hi to the west or from Espot, on its eastern edge. The park's tourist office provides numerous hiking suggestions. Of special interest is a 16-mile (26-km) walk that passes the mountain lakes surrounding Estany de la Llosa and enters the valley of Estany de Sant Maurici. Wild goats roaming the area are a frequent sight. Less traveled but equally rewarding is the path leading up to Aigües Tortes. Along the way, the trail passes through the Vall d'Bo Hi, reputedly one of the best places to view Romanesque architecture in the world. The land is predominantly rural and dotted with churches dating from the 12th and 13th centuries. The park is best viewed in late spring, summer, and autumn. Information: *Oficina d'Informació Turística,* 3 Avinguda Blondel, Lleida 25002, Spain (phone: 73-248120).

COVADONGA MOUNTAIN NATIONAL PARK, near Oviedo, Spain: This national park, separating the provinces of Asturias and Castile-León, lays claim to the western region of the Picos de Europa and boasts some of the most beautiful scenery, as well as the largest number of annual visitors. It was here, according to legend, that the Virgin Mary interceded with God on behalf of the king, Don Pelayo, and created an invisible shield, ensuring his warriors of victory against the Moors. Today, the park caters to both naturists and religious entourages. The Santa Cueva (Sacred Cave) is where Don Pelayo supposedly prayed to the Virgin. For those seeking solitude, it's best to avoid the park on and around September 8, when the area celebrates the *Day of the Virgin* with numerous festivities. During this period, head instead for the hills and enjoy the real master of the park: the wildlife that inhabits it. The higher you hike, the more likely you are to encounter a fleeting glimpse of a bear, wolf, wildcat, or fox. At the mountain's base are two lakes of glacial origin: El Enol and La Ercina. Both swimming and camping are permitted here. The best times to visit are summer and autumn. The area gets a lot of rain, so be sure to bring the appropriate clothing. Information: *Federación Asturiana de Montañismo,* 16 Calle Melquiades Alvarez, Oviedo 33007, Spain (phone: 85-211099).

NAVARRESE PYRENEES, east of Pamplona, Spain: It takes a dedicated hiker to navigate his or her way through this rugged profile of the mountains and the valleys along the Arga and Aragon rivers. In return for the effort, however, the intrepid will get a close glimpse of some vital bits of history. The 24-mile (40-km) route from the Pyrenees through Navarre's mountain passes bisects the river valleys and is the same route used by thousands of 11th- and 12th-century pilgrims on their journey from France to Santiago de Compostela and the shrine of St. James. In Yesa, the route leads past a weathered stone monastery, once a center of power and wealth and the favorite charity and residence of the Kings of Navarre during the Middle Ages. Other remnants of medieval life worth exploring include nearby Tierman, an abandoned town on the shore of Yesa Lake, and Javier Castle, once a fortress and now a Jesuit College. Upon moving west through the mountains, each valley becomes a bit more green and moist. Noteworthy towns along the way include Roncal, Isaba, and Ochagava. Of special note is the town of Roncesvalles, historically known for the *Song of Roland,* the epic poem about Charlemagne's retreat from Spain, and the starting point for many medieval pilgrims. Information: *Oficina de Turismo,* 2 Calle Duque de Ahumada, Pamplona 31002, Spain (phone: 48-220741).

ORDESA AND MONTE PERDIDO NATIONAL PARK, near Jaca, Aragonese Pyrenees, Spain: Here, in Spain's northeast, is terrain that will please hikers of all abilities. This is one of the country's most beautiful areas. Its jewel-like gorges and waterfalls, steep mountains flowered with edelweiss, and dazzling forests of pine and beech are enough to encourage even the most sedentary of hikers. The park's finest scenic assets lie near the magnificent Escuain Gorge and the Yago River. There are also four distinct valleys to explore; the visitors' center provides a guided itinerary with recommended routes. The Ordesa area is a walker's paradise, with many routes available. One way to learn more about the park is to buy the red *Cartographic Guide to Ordesa, Vignemale, and Monte Perdido,* about $2 in local bookstores. Although written in Spanish, its maps are easy to understand.

Recommended itineraries include Torla–Ordesa, an easy 8-mile (13-km) hike that winds through beautiful valleys and forests. Cross the bridge below Torla (Puente de la Glera) and follow the trail marked Camino de Turieto. More ambitious hikers may want to undertake the Torla–Gavarnie tour, a 24-mile (38-km) walk to the French town of Gavarnie. Following the valley, turn left at the river fork and continue along the Ara River for about 6 miles (10 km) before reaching the hamlet of San Nicolas de Bujaruelo. The trail goes directly into the mountains, crosses through the 828-foot-high Puerto de Bujaruelo, and descends straight into Gavarnie. For an even more scenic view of the Pyrenees, experienced hikers should take the Valle de Ordesa–Sierra Custodia–Valle de Vio triangle, which winds past thundering waterfalls, pine forests, and alpine valleys. Another challenging adventure is the 44-mile (71-km) Ordesa–Gavarnie trail, which starts near the Ordesa information hut and shoots straight up the steep gorge of the Circo de Salarons.

The Soasa Circle is a more realistic and relatively easy walk through the natural wonders of the Aragonese Pyrenees. Take a hearty lunch, as this walk covers a good 28 miles (45 km). Begin by following the gently sloping Arazas River eastward to the surging Cascada del Abanico. Here, the river roars over the rocks at lightning speeds. For a close view, cross the bridge a few minutes upstream and come back down to the observation point, situated on a huge rock. Continue toward Soasa, past more thundering falls, until the path leaves the forest. Once beyond the Gradas de Soasa (stepped waterfalls), the valley broadens and flattens. The fan-shaped Cascada de Soasa at the far end of the valley jets forth from between two cliffs, and is a welcome resting point. This marks the approximate halfway point of the climb; it is also a perfect vantage point for surveying the sweeping panorama of snow-capped peaks: Monte Arruebo, Monte Perdido, and Pico de Anisclo. Cross the river and follow the semi-hidden path that hems the tree line into mountain goat territory. The mountaintops and meadows blanketed with woolly-leafed edelweiss and multicolored butterflies are inspiring. But don't get too light-footed. The last leg of the excursion is a challenging climb, as the path clambers near jutting rocks and abrupt edges. It tumbles down, down, down, with views of the parking lot below teasing the mind until it is reached in about an hour.

The best areas of the park can usually be covered in 2 to 4 days. Accommodations can be found in the nearby towns of Huesca and Jaca. There is also the *Parador Monte Perdido* (inside the park, at the head of the Pineta Valley; phone: 74-501011). The best time of year to visit the park is from mid-July through late August. Information: *Oficina de Turismo,* 2 Avenida Regimiento de Galicia, Jaca 22700, Spain (phone: 74-360098), or *Oficina de Turismo,* 23 Calle Coso Alto, Huesca 22002, Spain (phone: 74-225778).

PICOS DE EUROPA, near Potes, Spain: This stretch of remote territory is especially popular with backpackers and experienced hikers, who take advantage of its numerous trails that transcend the range's jagged profile, valleys, and lower slopes. Always be sure to check weather forecasts before setting off on a hike in this region, as the area is partial to sudden drops in temperature and surprise rainstorms. Note that only well-equipped and very advanced alpinists should attempt to scale the peaks themselves. Accommodations are few and far between here, and most hikers use the nearby town of Potes, along the Deva River, as a base. Quiet and snowbound in winter, Potes becomes a cosmopolitan climber's town in summer. Information: *Federación Asturiana de Montañismo,* 16 Calle Melquiades Alvarez, Oviedo 33007, Spain (phone: 85-211099). Detailed maps, including those published by the Instituto Geográfico Nacional and the Federación Española de Montañismo, are available at *Bustamante,* a photo shop in Potes's main square; each costs about $3.

SIERRA DE GUADARRAMA, near Madrid: This pine-covered mountain range, halfway between Madrid and Segovia, is one of the most beautiful in central Spain. Particularly noteworthy are the alpine village of Cercedilla and the breathtaking mountain pass of Puerto de Navacerrada, the geographic border between Old and New Castile. Cercedilla is a town of picturesque alpine chalets and cow pastures. Its *piscinas* (ponds), set below cascading waterfalls, are a popular summer attraction. The peaks of Puerto de Navacerrada reach 6,102 feet and offer excellent views of the surrounding Castilian plains. Nearby, in the town of Rascafría, take a swim in La Laguna de Peñalara, a beautiful lagoon situated in a valley below the commanding mountain peak. Use either Madrid or Segovia as a base, but be forewarned: The weather here is wild, so dress warmly, even in summer. Information: *Oficina de Turismo,* 1 Calle Princesa, Madrid 28008, Spain (phone: 1-241-2325), or *Oficina de Turismo,* 10 Plaza Mayor, Segovia 34001, Spain (phone: 11-430328).

SIERRA MORENA, near Córdoba, Spain: Few travelers know of the Sierra Morena, and even most Andalusians have trouble placing it. Though not one of Spain's more dramatic mountain ranges (its highest peak rises to just over 4,300 feet), it is nonetheless an enjoyable and very mellowing climb. The best time to visit is in March and April, when the flowers are in full bloom. Expect to be given a private performance by armies of frogs and turtles that live along the stream. Most often, they are a hiker's only companions. The Moorish towns of Córdoba and Jaén make the best bases and starting points. Information: *Oficina de Turismo,* 10 Calle Torrijos, Córdoba 14003, Spain (phone: 57-471235), or *Oficina de Turismo,* 1 Calle Arquitecto Bergés, Jaén 23007, Spain (phone: 53-222737).

SIERRA NEVADA, near Granada, Spain: The tallest range in all of Spain is also the most challenging. Even in summer, the weather is severe, with whipping winds and temperatures that drop considerably at night. The peaks of these mountains, Mulhacén (11,407 feet) and Veleta (11,128 feet), are best tackled as a day trip, using Granada as a base. Particularly rewarding is the 25-mile (40-km) route surrounding Las Alpujarras, the small white villages that line the range's base. Capilera is the closest thing to a tourist center in the area, offering good accommodations and a few other adventurous activities. Those who decide to climb farther than Las Alpujarras should be no less than intermediate climbers, able to handle sudden wind changes and a fair ammount of rough terrain. The region is best tackled in the summer, long after all the snow has melted. Spain's highest peak and ultimate vantage point is Mulhacén, often most accessible after May. The area is noticeably secluded; wild goats and birds are often the only company. Nearby are the town of Trevelez, Spain's highest community, renowned for its ham, and the cozy hamlet of Pitres. An alternative route is a hike up Mt. Veleta. Buses run year-round and climb as high as they can; from mid-June on, they can usually make it clear up the road to a point from where it's a treacherous 3-hour hike to the peak. Under clear skies, the view extends all the way to the Rif Mountains of Morocco. The most detailed map of the region is published by the *Federación Española de Montañismo* ($3), available in both English and Spanish in most of Granada's bookstores. Information: *Oficina de Turismo,* 2 Calle de los Libreros, Granada 18001, Spain (phone: 58-225990).

TORCAL MOUNTAINS, near Antequera, Spain: Some 30 miles (48 km) north of Málaga, and just south of the tidy agricultural-industrial town of Antequera, await two circular trails that will enthrall adventurous hikers who delight in exploring desolate rock gardens. The path marked with yellow arrows is about 8 miles (13 km); the red-arrowed tour covers about 12 miles (19 km). Both feature spectacular vistas of curious rock formations and begin and end in Antequera, at the *refugio* (refuge hut) at the base of the mountain. Information: *Oficina de Turismo,* Palacio de Nájera, Antequera 29200, Spain (phone: 52-841827).

ALGARVE, Portugal: This is one of the most ideal places for hiking because the temperature is always just right — visitors are practically guaranteed clear skies all summer and steady breezes that keep the temperatures bearable. One of the most interesting places to walk along Portugal's southern coast is in the vicinity of Sagres, at the extreme southwestern corner of the country, and once considered the end of the world. The sunsets here alone are worthy of a visit. Some 40 miles (64 km) inland to the east is Porto de Lagos, on the road to Monchique. The town of Silves is 6 miles (10 km) east of Porto de Lagos, and between the two is a circular hiking route that skirts groves of orange trees and an irrigation ditch as it follows the course of the Arade River and Ribeira de Odelouca. Where the two meet, the Arade estuary, islands, and rice fields are visible. The village of Monchique and the hills surrounding it are also worthy hiking country. After perusing the village streets, follow a track of stone pavement that leads through the woods to an old convent, from where there is a wonderful view over the valley. The route begins at Monchique's main square, then rises up the slope along Rua do Porto Fundo, located at the top of the square. Upon reaching Rua Dr. Bernardino Moreira, turn right and continue to follow the road up, along Rua da Igreja, through Praça Alexandre Herculano, and along Rua Costa Gerdo, until finally reaching the Largo de São Gonçalo de Lagos, a small square. The street becomes steep here, but the reward is the scenic old convent in the distance. There are many walking tours of this region, and most can be found with the help of each individual area's tourist office. Ask for the book called *The Algarve Guide to Walks* (in English), which provides complete instructions on transportation, levels of difficulty, cafés along the way, length of tours, and more. Information: *Posto de Turismo,* 8-12 Rua da Misericórdia, Faro 8000, Portugal (phone: 89-25404).

ALTO ALENTEJO, Portugal: Lonely little villages set between olive and cork trees are the treasures that await hikers in Portugal's plains region. The city of Portalegre, in the northern part of the region, lies in the foothills of the Serra de São Mamede, a mere 30 miles (48 km) from the Spanish border. This is a charming area, full of history. Sights include homes emblazoned with ageless family crests, as well as Moorish ruins, remnants of another era that ironically fit right in today. There are numerous footpaths between the villages surrounding Portalegre, and this is an idyllic place to escape the tourist traps of the coastal areas and truly savor the traditions of the Portuguese. Information: *Posto de Turismo,* 40 Rua 19 de Junho, Portalegre 7300, Portugal (phone: 45-21815).

COSTA VERDE, near Porto, Portugal: This region has been called the cradle of the Portuguese nation throughout its vast history. Originally inhabited by the Celts some 3,000 years ago, it remains rich in tradition, natural beauty, and wonder. This is one of Portugal's least inhabited and developed areas — perfect terrain for the hiker willing to tackle the unknown. Along with the historical monuments dotting the countryside, the tour passes vineyards where the famous port and *vinho verde* wines are produced. Begin in Braga, one of Portugal's oldest Christian towns, surrounded by rolling green hills and elegant parks. Nearby is the Peneda-Gerês National Park, a splendidly unspoiled expanse of mountains, lakes, vegetation, and wildlife. Hiking routes between the main village of Gerês and Pedro Bela pass crashing waterfalls and natural pools. Information: *Posto de Turismo,* Avenida Manuel Francisco da Costa, Gerês 4845, Portugal (phone: 53-65133).

COSTA DE PRATA, near Coimbra, Portugal: The Silver Coast of Portugal offers hikers some of the country's most diverse terrain. Among the region's many scenic towns is a wide variety of magnificent mountain ranges, poetic green valleys, and high dunes. Among the must-sees is the Buçaco Forest, situated just outside the university town of Coimbra. Rocky paths shaded by luxurious foliage have drawn solitary hikers to this enchanted forest for centuries. The forest contains over 700 varieties of flora, including exotic plants from Asia and the Far East, brought by the first Portuguese explorers. What makes the area even more endearing is the lovely *Buçaco Palace* hotel, a former palace and hunting lodge. Wandering freely among the forest's many paths can be confusing, so pick up a map at the refreshment stand, located next to the palace. Information: *Posto de Turismo,* Largo da Portagem, Coimbra 3000, Portugal (phone: 39-23886 and 39-25576).

TRÁS-OS-MONTES, Portugal: The Marão and Alvão ranges are among the mountains separating Portugal's northern coastal area from the more remote reaches of the Trás-os-Montes region. While difficult to reach, the fertile fields and rocky slopes of this zone are both challenging and rewarding to the dedicated and experienced hiker. Start off in Vila Real. Information: *Região de Turismo da Serra do Marão,* 70 Avenida 1 de Maio, Vila Real 5000, Portugal (phone: 59-22819).

For the Mind

Museums, Monuments, and Ruins

From paleolithic bison to Picasso's bulls, Spanish painting has always been wildly intense: El Greco's emaciated, longing saints, Goya's *Disasters of War,* Picasso's *Guernica,* Velázquez's portraits of monarchs in armor, rearing their horses against threatening skies. All depict a passion released in religious fury or desperate wars, against a backdrop of deserts, mountains, and gorgetop towns.

A series of conquests, losses, and clever marriages left Roman ruins, Moorish castles, medieval turrets, and sinuous spires sculpted out of the land all over the Iberian Peninsula. Preserved and renovated, or ruined and crumbling, they stand as reminders of a turbulent and fascinating past. The Alhambra stands starkly against the Sierra Nevada, while Cuenca's *Museum of Spanish Abstract Art* hangs 200 feet above the rushing Huécar River. Prince Henry the Navigator's fortress at Sagres looks out over "the end of the world," and Segovia's Alcázar is raised on its natural, jagged pedestal above the stark Castilian plain.

Both Spain and Portugal have fostered the development of some of the most original artists in Europe. While some of the works of Velázquez, Goya, Picasso, and others have made their way to various museums and art galleries in the US, the bulk of the masters' works remain where they originated; for example, canvases by Murillo and Zurbarán hang in Seville's *Museo de Bellas Artes* (unfortunately, large parts of this Fine Arts Museum are closed for renovation until 1992, although a few rooms, displaying the most prized paintings, are open), El Greco's treasures grace museum walls in Toledo, and the paintings of Jorge Afonso are displayed in Lisbon's *Convento da Madre de Deus.*

A museum can be all the more pleasurable if a few simple guidelines are kept in mind. Rather than one long visit to a large museum, plan several short ones, staying for an hour and taking in no more than a dozen fine works each time. There's no fatigue quite like aching, yawning museum fatigue — which has been described as the dread "museum foot" — and when it has set in, merely sitting in front of a Picasso for 3 minutes will not effect a cure.

WALLS OF AVILA, Castile-León, Spain: Avila's ramparts look like a row of sharpened teeth amid the dry stubble of the battlefield-brown plain. The 11th-century walls seem unweathered and brand-new, and the stocky, somewhat rectilinear, 12th-century stone cathedral looms over and leans on them, glaring out at the forbidding mass of the Sierra de Gredos. Construction of the wall began in 1090; it took 10 years and more than 2,000 workers to complete 90 semicircular towers, 9 gates, several posterns, and innumerable battlements along an 8,200-foot perimeter. It may feel as if the only way to get into the city is with a battering ram, but only a walk through a gate in the walls is necessary to see banks and cafés and hear the televised sounds of soccer games blaring through open windows. From the gardens of the *Parador Raimundo de Borgoña,* it's an easy climb up to the battlements for a squint into the distance for an approaching army of Moors. Also patrol the town's perimeter from the outside — though you may find yourself glancing nervously up at the battlements, checking for boiling oil. Information: *Oficina de Turismo,* 4 Plaza de la Catedral, Avila 05001, Spain (phone: 1-821-1387).

FUNDACIÓ JOAN MIRÓ, Barcelona, Catalonia, Spain: This museum is a light, airy tribute to Catalonia's Surrealist master and native son, Joan Miró, who was also an outstanding sculptor and weaver — as his 35-foot-long *Tapis de la Fundació* demonstrates. The permanent exhibit spans Miró's life, and a stroll through the galleries illuminates the artist's various styles and mediums — most evident in his *Self-Portrait,* which is, in effect, two pictures on one canvas. Miró's images are surreal, and emphasize his commitment to make even the most ordinary object complex. The museum hosts frequent special exhibitions, and also features a library and a bookstore. Information: *Fundació Joan Miró,* Plaça Neptú, Parc de Montjuïc, Barcelona 08004, Spain (phone: 3-329-1908).

MUSEU D'ART DE CATALUNYA, Barcelona, Catalonia, Spain: Perched in a park above Barcelona's busy port, this luminous collection of medieval religious panels, carvings, and walls teems with the tumultuous detail of births, benedictions, and agonized deaths. Dragons are slain, saints martyred, and sinners stirred into infernal cauldrons — all beautifully hung, labeled, and lighted. The collection includes 11th-century frescoes peeled off the walls of small Catalonian mountain churches and reassembled on brand-new apses, making this one of the world's great collections of Romanesque and Gothic art — featuring not just frescoes, but also woodcarvings, ceramics, and everyday utensils of medieval life. Of special note is the Gothic altarpiece by Luis Dalmau (active 1428–60), the *Madonna of the Aldermen of Barcelona,* and the excellent 12th-century wall paintings from San Clemente at Tahull. The museum building itself is a sight to be seen: A huge palace built for the *1929 World's Fair,* it covers nearly 8 acres atop Montjuïc, and offers a spectacular view of the city. Information: *Museu d'Art de Catalunya,* Mirador del Palau, Parc de Montjuïc, Barcelona 08004, Spain (phone: 3-423-1824).

MUSEU PICASSO, Barcelona, Catalonia, Spain: Although Pablo Picasso lived in France for 69 years, Barcelona was his childhood home, and it occupied a warm spot in his heart throughout his life. The museum was founded in 1963 when Jaime Sabartés, a native of Barcelona and friend of Picasso's, presented his collection of the master's work to the city. Picasso himself donated 58 paintings, including 44 bizarre variations of *Las Meninas,* the famous Velázquez painting in Madrid's *Prado.* Later, he donated more than 800 of his lithographs and early works from his years in Málaga and Barcelona (1889–1905), which constitute most of the collection. Information: *Museu Picasso,* 15 Carrer de Montcada, Barcelona 08010, Spain (phone: 3-319-6310).

TEATRE-MUSEU DALÍ, Figueres, Catalonia, Spain: This small town, equidistant from the mountains, the sea, and the French border, was the birthplace in 1904 of the late Surrealist artist Salvador Dalí, one of the most eccentric in a profession famous for eccentrics. His sculptures feature a lobster basking on the receiver of a telephone, and a giant woman standing on the hood of a Cadillac. His paintings offer much of the same: A dog collar doubles as a viaduct, locks of hair curl into fruit, and a chest of drawers with huge, bare human feet ascends into heaven. Dalí worked here until 1982, and lived bedridden in the building's Galatea Tower until his death in 1989. The artist is buried in the museum's inner court, beneath the building's great glass dome. Over 300,000 annual visitors make the museum Spain's second most popular (Madrid's *Prado* ranks number one). Information: *Oficina d'Informació Turística,* Plaça del Sol, Figueres 17600, Spain (phone: 72-503155).

ALHAMBRA, Granada, Andalusia, Spain: The mountain snow of the Sierra Nevada and the gleaming whitewash of the Albaicín's medieval houses, reflected in Granada's clear sky, illuminate the Alhambra's frosty plaster filigree with a dazzling ray of white. The green shade of the courtyards and gardens, decked with oranges swaying lusciously within reach, and the cool gurgle of the fountains and pools offer refuge from Andalusia's rugged glare. In the darkening years of their rule, the Moorish sultans retreated behind the fortress's forbidding walls to this maze of lavish rooms, decorated with delicate mosaics of minute colored tiles. This was the palace and harem of the Arab conquerors (its name is a corruption of the Arabic for "red castle"), begun during the 14th century. After the Catholic Monarchs conquered it in 1492, it was left to decay. Restoration began during the late 19th century, and today it retains much of its former splendor. The main complex is made up of four areas: the Alcázar, or royal palace; the 16th-century Palace of Carlos V; the Alcazaba, the oldest portion of the fortress; and the Generalife, the summer palace. There are no guided tours in English, but many of the locals who loiter around the main entrance conduct informal English-speaking tours for a small fee. Don't worry; they are legitimate guides, and though the English-language guidebook is adequate, the Alhambra is so colorful and rich with history that it is a good idea to give these locals a try. The admission charge also includes the treasury and the cathedral museum. Also worthwhile is an illuminated nighttime visit. Information: *Oficina de Turismo,* 2 Calle de los Libreros, Granada 18001, Spain (phone: 58-225990).

MUSEO NACIONAL DEL PRADO, Madrid, Spain: One of the world's supreme art museums, the *Prado* is a treasure house of over 4,000 universal masterpieces, a polychrome smorgasbord of Spanish painting, with a rich dessert of Rembrandts and Raphaels. Try a bit of everything, and come back for seconds: Bosch's grotesque and electrifying *Garden of Earthly Delights,* Goya's frothy scenes from Spanish country life and his creamy *Maja Desnuda,* Rubens's portraits with their cherry-red noses and cheeks, El Greco's wild, wine-tinted skies and religious scenes suffused with a pale, lemon-yellow light. And leave some room for *Las Meninas,* Diego Rodríguez de Silva Velázquez's famous *Maids of Honor,* a portrayal of the court during the 17th century. There is also an impressive collection of the works of the Italian masters Fra Angelico, Botticelli, Raphael, Correggio, Caravaggio, Titian, Tintoretto, and Veronese. The neoclassical *Prado* building originally was a natural science museum, later converted into a museum to house the royal art collection. In addition to the main *Prado,* or Villanueva building, the museum also comprises two annexes, the Casón del Buen Retiro and the Villahermosa Palace. The Casón del Buen Retiro is home to the *Museum of 19th-Century Spanish Painting,* as well as *Guernica,* Picasso's epic painting of the Spanish Civil War, which, following the artist's instructions, remained in New York's *Museum of Modern Art* until democracy was restored to Spain after Generalísimo Francisco Franco's death. The Villahermosa Palace is currently being redesigned to house the Thyssen-Bornemisza Collection, on long-term loan to the museum and considered the most important private art collection in the world. The *Prado* collection is so vast that it is impossible to savor its wonders in a single visit. If time is limited, it is best to select a few galleries of special interest, or enlist the services of the extremely knowledgeable, government-licensed free-lance guides at the main entrance. Reproductions from the *Prado*'s collection, postcards, and fine-arts books are sold at the shop inside the museum. Information: *Museo Nacional del Prado,* Paseo del Prado, Madrid 28014, Spain (phone: 1-202836).

REAL MONASTERIO DE EL ESCORIAL, San Lorenzo de El Escorial, Madrid, Spain: Sixteenth-century Spain was fervently, often brutally, Catholic. Its fire-eyed monarchs had defeated the Moors, hunted down heretics, and banished or killed all the Jews who didn't convert. Their wars were fought with God on their side, and their trips to the New World were equal parts of conquest and conversion. King Philip II built the Real Monasterio de San Lorenzo de El Escorial — El Escorial for short — in thanksgiving for his victory over the French at Saint-Quentin in Flanders in 1557. The lean architecture of this royal and religious complex in the mountains outside

Madrid bears the mark of Philip's asceticism, but the collection of works by the likes of Ribera, El Greco, Velázquez, Titian, Veronese, and Bosch in the *Nuevos Museos* (New Museums) is sinfully opulent. The combination of truly royal grandeur with monastic austerity here is unique in the world. The small, monastic chambers in the Palacios (Royal Apartments), from which Philip governed the Spanish Empire for 14 years (1584–98), are in stark contrast to the splendor of the rest of the structure. The monastery also houses the Panteón de los Reyes (Royal Pantheon), which contains the remains of 26 Spanish monarchs. Information: *Oficina de Turismo,* 10 Calle Floridablanca, San Lorenzo de El Escorial 28036, Spain (phone: 1-890-1554).

VALLE DE LOS CAÍDOS (Valley of the Fallen), San Lorenzo de El Escorial, Madrid, Spain: North of the Monasterio de San Lorenzo de El Escorial, the *Valley of the Fallen* is a spectacular memorial to those who died in the Spanish Civil War. A huge basilica containing the tombs of soldiers from both sides has been hollowed into a mountain. Generalísimo Francisco Franco, who ordered the monument's construction, is also buried here. A granite cross stands 500 feet in the air atop the mountain peak. Information: *Oficina de Turismo,* 10 Calle Floridablanca, San Lorenzo de El Escorial 28036, Spain (phone: 1-890-1554).

UNIVERSIDAD, Salamanca, Castile-León, Spain: Formed from golden stone during the Middle Ages, and now well into its golden years, Salamanca's university is pushing a perky 800 years of age. Accumulated centuries of wisdom have given the buildings a soft, restful glow. On the Patio de Escuelas is the university's original main building, erected during the reign of the Catholic Monarchs and bearing a famed Plateresque façade. The leafy curlicues, twisted gargoyles, imaginary birds, and heraldic animals, seem to have been the work of an army of jewelers. The classrooms are pampered and polished, and the only signs of decrepitude are the eroded pews etched with 16th-century graffiti in the Aula de Fray Luis de León. The lecture hall has been kept as it was when the legendary professor, returning to work after 4 years in the Inquisition's jails, started his first class by saying, "*Decíamos ayer* . . ." ("As we were saying yesterday . . ."). At the opposite end of the Patio de Escuelas is the Escuelas Menores (Minor Schools), which has another Plateresque façade and a beautiful courtyard. Information: *Oficina de Turismo,* 41 Gran Vía, Salamanca 37001, Spain (phone: 23-243730).

CUEVAS DE ALTAMIRA, Santillana del Mar, Cantabria, Spain: Tucked beneath the soft green cow pastures that roll down to the cloudy Cantabrian beaches, the caves seem chilly and dank today. But to the Stone Age Spaniard, it must have felt like a cozy place to come home to after a hard day chasing bison through the ice and snow. Drawings of running, hunted, wounded animals, painted with blood and mineral pigments and incredibly preserved after 16,000 years, cover the walls and ceilings, earning Altamira the title of the "Sistine Chapel of Primitive Art." No more than 10 people a day may take the 20-minute guided tour of the caves in the summer, no more than 35 in winter, and all tour requests must be made in writing 3 months in advance, specifying group size and a range of possible dates for a visit. Send requests to: *Director, Centro de Investigación y Museo de Altamira,* Santillana del Mar, Santander 39001, Spain (phone: 42-818102 or 42-818005).

ROMAN AQUEDUCT, Segovia, Castile-León, Spain: A majestic row of double arches, made only of oiled granite blocks, stretches from the dusty-orange hills above the dry Castilian plain to the hilltop city of Segovia. The aqueduct was built some 2,000 years ago without the use of cranes, pumps, or even mortar, but with that sense of elegance that the Romans brought to even their most functional creations. They cut the granite to a perfect, jigsaw fit, then stacked the blocks into a remarkable feat of engineering to siphon spring water to the city from the Acebeda River. On the eastern side of Segovia, the aqueduct is formed by 166 arches in 2 tiers (the lower level forming prized parking spaces), and is 21,500 feet long and 96 feet high. The most impressive frontal view is from Plaza del Azoguejo, where the aqueduct reaches its highest point. Climb up the stairs on the left side of the plaza for an internal view, and a good look at the fairy-tale city below. Information: *Oficina de Turismo,* 10 Plaza Mayor, Segovia 34001, Spain (phone: 11-430328).

REALES ALCÁZARES, Seville, Andalusia, Spain: The mosaics, patios, and wrought-stucco windows, the finely tooled ceilings, and the dizzying, interlocking patterns will make the visitor dream of turbaned sultans reclining on oversize cushions and puffing on elaborate pipes. But it was mainly Spanish royalty that took its ease (or was otherwise engaged) in Seville's Alcázar, which was begun in the 14th century by King Peter the Cruel (he was not always a perfect host) and later expanded by Ferdinand and Isabella and by the Holy Roman Emperor Charles V. For all their furor against the Moors, the Spanish monarchs recognized the Moorish talent for palaces. Thus, this lovely Mudéjar creation, the work of Moorish craftsmen left unexpelled after Seville was reconquered in the 13th century. The lavish interior is similar to Granada's Alhambra, but on a smaller scale. Of special note here are the gardens surrounding the Hall of the Ambassadors, full of cheerful Moorish fountains and colorful tiles. Also not to be missed in Seville (and there really is no way to miss it) is the Catedral de Sevilla across the street, the third-largest church in Europe (after St. Peter's in Rome and St. Paul's in London). Begun in 1402, it took nearly a century to complete. Inside lie hidden treasures, among them the Tumba de Cristobal Colón (Tomb of Christopher Columbus). Information: *Oficina de Turismo,* 21-B Avenida de la Constitución, Seville 41004, Spain (phone: 5-422-1404).

EL GRECO'S TOLEDO, Castile–La Mancha, Spain: Doménikos Theotokópoulos, alias El Greco, was born in Crete, studied in Venice, and painted in Toledo, where he was dubbed "the Greek." Ancient, stylized figures, their bodies twisting in supple Venetian curves and shining with the mystic fervor of Castile, are the painter's trademarks. From a hillside just outside the city, the pile of tangled streets, often threatened by purplish clouds, looks much the same as it did in El Greco's *View of Toledo* in the *Casa y Museo del Greco.* This bite-size museum is an imaginative re-creation of the painter's house, and its collection includes a breathtaking series of portraits of Christ and the Apostles. A single painting with a cast of thousands, *The Burial of the Count of Orgaz,* is in the nearby Church of Santo Tomé. The cathedral sacristy and the *Museo de Santa Cruz* contain another 50 or so El Grecos between them. Toledo's cathedral, the second-largest in Spain (after Seville's), is a storehouse of artwork. Start in the Capilla Mayor, with its glittering altarpiece. Behind the high altar is the *Transparente,* an 18th-century baroque work by Narciso Tomé. Next, behold the *coro* (choir) with its set of stalls carved by Spain's finest sculptor, Alonso Berruguete. Down the winding and narrow Toledo streets are two synagogues, which attest to the fact that this city once was a thriving Jewish community. The 14th-century Sinagoga del Tránsito is a simple building with wonderful Mudéjar decorations. Its *Museo Sefardí* houses a fine collection of Sephardic Jewish manuscripts, inscriptions, and personal ornaments. Nearby, on Cuesta de los Reyes Católicos, is the Sinagoga de Santa María la Blanca, a 12th-century synagogue; it resembles a mosque, and for most of its life has served as a Catholic church. Information: *Oficina de Turismo,* Puerta de la Bisagra, Toledo 45003, Spain (phone: 25-220843).

MUSEU CALOUSTE GULBENKIAN Y CENTRO DE ARTE MODERNA, Lisbon, Portugal: Calouste Gulbenkian was an Armenian who lived in France and later in Portugal, invested in Iraqi oil, and bought Dutch paintings, Egyptian sculptures, Persian tapestries, and Oriental ivories, which now form the core of Portugal's artistic patrimony. The addition of the *Center of Modern Art* in the elegant, sprawling complex of the Gulbenkian Foundation brings this collection of 4,000 years of ancient art and exquisite bric-a-brac up to the minute with the latest in Op and Pop Art. A sinuous sculpture by Henry Moore and the oversize tapestries of the Portuguese Modernist

Almada Negreiros are among the permanent fixtures, while thousands of other works play an ongoing game of musical walls. Information: *Museu Calouste Gulbenkian,* 45 Avenida de Berna, Lisbon 1000, Portugal (phone: 1-734309).

MUSEU NACIONAL DE ARTE ANTIGA, Lisbon, Portugal: Established in 1833 in the former palace of the Counts of Alvor, this is the best place to see Portuguese painting, dating back to its 15th-century origins. Since there is not much Portuguese painting abroad, the museum is worth a special visit, especially to see the works of Nuno Gonçalves and Domingos António Sequeira. The most prized possession is the six-panel polyptych of the *Adoration of St. Vincent* (Lisbon's patron saint), which launched Gonçalves to fame. Information: *Museu Nacional de Arte Antiga,* 95 Rua das Janelas Verdes, Lisbon 1100, Portugal (phone: 1-672725).

MUSEU NACIONAL DOS COCHES, Belém, Lisbon, Portugal: Whether by curricle, chaise, litter, or tilbury, royalty travels in style. And of the stylish coaches that came from other courts, some of the most ornate, gilded, garnished, and tooled now sit in Lisbon's western suburb of Belém. Decorated with painted myths and sculpted cherubs, they carried princess brides from Paris or Vienna, paraded monarchs through Portugal, and simply wheeled nobles around gardens. Opened in 1905, the museum is housed in what was originally an 18th-century riding academy. Connected to the Belém Royal Palace, it also houses an important collection of livery, harnesses, and bullfighting costumes. Information: *Museu Nacional dos Coches,* Praça Afonso de Albuquerque, Belém, Lisbon 1100, Portugal (phone: 1-638022).

TORRE DE BELÉM, Belém, Lisbon, Portugal: Built between 1515 and 1520 to protect the seaward entrance of the Portuguese capital, this majestic, quadrangular, 5-story tower stands along the banks of the Tagus River, defying anyone to enter. The Portuguese consider it a symbol of their brave past, and its image is often used on official papers. Built during the 16th century to protect the river from pirates (because land has been reclaimed from the river since then, the tower was at one time farther out, surrounded by water), it later functioned as a prison. An excellent example of typically Portuguese Manueline architecture, it is richly decorated with sea motifs, statues, stone tracery, and Moorish balconies. Inside is a permanent exhibition of 15th- and 16th-century armaments and navigational instruments. Information: *Torre de Belém,* Avenida Marginal, Belém, Lisbon 1100, Portugal (phone: 1-616892).

PALÁCIO NACIONAL DA PENA, Sintra, Portugal: High atop one of the highest peaks in the Sintra range sits the Pena Palace, a fairy-tale castle that inspired Lord Byron to dub Sintra "glorious Eden" in his autobiographical poem *Childe Harold.* Built in 1840 by Ferdinand of Saxe-Coburg-Gotha, Queen Maria II's consort, who had bought a 16th-century monastery on the spot, this was the royal summer residence through 1910, when a republic was proclaimed in Portugal. The rooms inside are a delightful mixture of Indo-Portuguese and Sino-Portuguese furnishings, a fantasy in which only the eccentric would choose to live. The original cloister and chapel of the monastery were preserved; the latter has a black alabaster and marble altarpiece executed during the 16th century by Nicolas Chanterene, although its stained glass windows are 19th-century German. A short distance away sits the Moorish-style, 14th- to 16th-century Sintra Palace, erected over the remains of an 8th-century Arab structure. Most noticeable is the Hall of Swans, featuring paintings of swans with crown-shaped collars of gold. Information: *Palácio Nacional da Pena,* Parque da Pena, Sintra 2710, Portugal (phone: 1-923-0227), or *Posto de Turismo,* Praça da República, Sintra 2710, Portugal (phone: 1-31157).

TOMAR, Ribatejo, Portugal: The striking monuments of the medieval town of Tomar attest to its former status as the headquarters of the Knights Templars. These warrior-monks first set up residence here during the 12th century, but their fierce determination was passed down over generations to the villagers. The town's imposing fortress-palace, the Convento de Cristo, was built by the templars and their successors, the Knights of Christ, from the 12th to the 17th century. It is richly designed and decorated to express a triumphant Christianity during a time of exploration and conquest when Portuguese explorers set their sails and opened up the East for commerce and adventure. The exotic oceanic iconography associated with that era is displayed here. Tomar also was the home of a thriving Jewish community during the 15th century; its remains can be seen at the *Luso-Hebraic Museum of Abraham Zacuto* (73 Rua da Judiaria). This small museum, set up in the old Synagogue of Tomar, contains an assortment of tombstones with Hebrew inscriptions, collected from various sites. Information: *Posto de Turismo,* Avenida Dr. Cândido Madureira, Tomar 2300, Portugal (phone: 49-313237).

The Performing Arts

 Spain overflows with cultural activities, from the colorful flamenco shows to the poignant strains of a classical guitar concert. This is where the famous Don Juan and the barber of Seville were born, as were the works of Cervantes and Calderón de la Barca. But the stage in Spain is not simply a showcase for the traditional and the classical. Since the death of Generalísimo Francisco Franco in 1975, the country has been undergoing a cultural renaissance. The current Minister of Culture, Jorge Semprún, is preparing Spain for its role as host of the *1992 Summer Olympic Games* in Barcelona, as well as for Seville's *Expo '92,* the largest of the celebrations scheduled for the 500th anniversary of Columbus's discovery of the Americas. Madrid, in fact, has been declared the Cultural Capital of Europe for 1992 by the Council of Ministers of the European Economic Commission. During any summer, Madrid is *the* city for free cultural events, including international film festivals, theater performances, and concerts. *Guía del Ocio* and *Vila de Madrid,* both available throughout the city, offer the most comprehensive listings of all events, and the information in them is readily understood even by non-speakers of Spanish. Nowhere is the stage grander than at a live concert in the Plaza Mayor. The Plaza de Lavapiés and the Plaza Vila de Paris also host summer shows.

In Portugal, cultural activity centers around the *fado* (literally meaning "fate"), a style of singing and the country's unofficial national ballad. Its nostalgic strains pour out of numerous city and village nightspots through the early-morning hours. In addition, Portuguese culture offers a variety of opera, ballet, and theater possibilities. A complete listing of concerts, movies, plays, and exhibits is available in the Portuguese newspaper *Sete.* The *Gulkenkian Foundation* in Lisbon sponsors classical and jazz concerts throughout the year. During the summer, there are regularly scheduled folk concerts and dance performances in the *Congress Palace* in Estoril. The Portuguese opera season begins in late September and lasts through mid-June.

AUDITORIO NACIONAL DE MÚSICA, Madrid, Spain: Spain's newest center for the performing arts, this "temple of symphonic music" opened in late 1988. Its two soundproof theaters — with 707 and 2,280 seats, respectively — are home to the *Orquestra Nacional de España* (Spanish National Orchestra) and the *Coro Nacional de España* (Spanish National Chorus). Symphonic, choral, chamber, and solo works are presented during a season that stretches from May through October. The hall has a unique layout that brings the audience closer to the orchestra; 20% of the audience is distributed on each side of and directly behind the performers, and the main section is tiered. The separate chamber music hall is semicircular, providing an intimate proximity between the performers and the audience. In addition to its 23 rehearsal halls, private suites, and dressing rooms, the *Auditorio* is equipped with state-of-the-art television broadcast and recording facilities. Information: *Auditorio Nacional de Música,* 136 Calle Principe de Vergara, Madrid 28002, Spain (phone: 1-337-0100).

TEATRO LIRICO NACIONAL DE LA ZARZUELA, Madrid, Spain: The *zarzuela* is a Spanish form of light opera, and this is its citadel. The stage also hosts some of the world's greatest operas and performances by the *National Ballet Company.* Information: *Teatro de la Zarzuela,* 4 Calle Jovellanos, Madrid 28014, Spain (phone: 1-429-8225).

TEATRO REAL, Madrid, Spain: Long a home for classical music, this performance house was opened in 1850, and following a massive restoration, it is scheduled to reopen this May as the *Teatro de la Opera,* one of Europe's finest "modern" opera houses, as well as the largest in the world. Outdoor classical music concerts are held on weekends during the summer. Information: *Teatro Real,* Plaza de Oriente, Madrid 28003, Spain (phone: 1-247-1405).

TEATRO NACIONAL MARÍA GUERRERO, Madrid, Spain: Full-scale revivals of Spain's great dramas, by the likes of Lope de Vega or Calderón de la Barca, are staged here, as well as examples of the international repertoire. Opened in 1885, this richly decorated, state-subsidized theater presents classic and modern performances from October through June. Information: *Teatro Nacional María Guerrero,* Calle Tamayo y Baus, Madrid 28010, Spain (phone: 1-319-4769).

SALA OLIMPIA, Madrid, Spain: This is the place for those whose taste runs to the avant-garde or the experimental. It is the home of the *Centro Nacional de Nuevas Tendencias Escénicas* (National Center of New Theater Trends). Information: *Sala Olimpia,* Plaza de Lavapiés, Madrid 28008, Spain (phone: 1-227-4622).

ARCO DE CUCHILLEROS, Madrid, Spain: The place to go to watch stamping by flamenco dancers in beautiful costumes. The seating area here is smaller than most other venues, making the room all the more intimate. There are two dance performances daily, at 10:30 PM and 12:30 AM. Information: *Arco de Cuchilleros,* 7 Calle Cuchilleros, Madrid 28010, Spain (phone: 1-266-5867).

TORRES BERMEJAS, Madrid, Spain: This dinner-theater (dinners are somewhat overpriced) stages what many consider to be the most authentic flamenco show in town. Information: *Torres Bermejas,* 11 Calle Mesonero Romanos, Madrid 28013, Spain (phone: 1-532-3322).

CORRAL DE LA MORERÍA, Madrid, Spain: Authentic flamenco dancing is featured in this *tablao* (nightclub), located in a simply furnished cellar in the Caba Baja district of the Old City. Information: *Corral de la Morería,* 17 Calle Morería, Madrid 28005, Spain (phone: 1-265-1137).

GRAN TEATRE DEL LICEU, Barcelona, Catalonia, Spain: The city's principal opera house presents about 15 productions a year from the international repertoire. One of Barcelona's proudest structures, it opened in 1847 and is one of the world's leading stages — and the only facility in Spain that is currently devoted almost solely to opera (with a very small concession made to ballet). The building itself is an attraction. The stage, one of Europe's largest, is especially suited to grand opera. The original gas lamps still line the auditorium's halls, and the foyer is richly decorated with mirrors and columns, which support arches with medallions representing a history of famous composers, singers, and actors. The opera season opens in November. Information: *Gran Teatre del Liceu,* 1 Carrer de Sant Pau, Barcelona 08001, Spain (phone: 3-318-9122).

PALAU DE LA MÚSICA CATALANA, Barcelona, Catalonia, Spain: Just off Via Laietana, near the Barri Gòtic, this dazzling 1908 landmark by the Catalan architect Lluís Domènech i Montaner hosts concerts of all varieties of symphonic and choral music. Worth a look for its grandeur alone, it's a jewel of a concert hall, combining a symphony of artistic notes from Art Nouveau to Moorish revival, executed in a colorful chorus of stained glass, mosaics, and ceramics, into a bewitching stylistic whole known to turn-of-the-century Barcelonans as *Modernisme.* The *Palau* was conceived amid the cultural euphoria that filled Barcelona in 1888, the year of the city's *Universal Exposition* (world's fair). The fair was meant to be a Spanish cultural event, but it actually turned into a display of regional pride as Catalans went out of their way to prove their inherent superiority over their Castilian brothers. One of the primary focuses of the fair was music, so the Catalans raised the idea of a permanent center for secular choral music in their capital city. The *Municipal Orchestra* and visiting orchestras perform here, and every October the *Palau* hosts Barcelona's *International Festival of Music,* featuring classical concerts. Information: *Palau de la Música Catalana,* Carrer d'Amadeu Vives, Barcelona 08005, Spain (phone: 3-301-1104).

BARRIO DE SANTA CRUZ, Seville, Andalusia, Spain: This area of the city where flamenco originated is rich with local talent dancing to the traditional music of the region. Try *Bodega Santa Cruz,* at the entrance to the barrio, as well as *La Gitanilla; La Hosteria del Laurel* and *Casa Romana* are other favorites. Information: *Oficina de Turismo,* 21-B Avenida de la Constitución, Seville 41004, Spain (phone: 5-422-1404).

BARRIO DE LA JUDERÍA, Córdoba, Andalusia, Spain: The fast footwork of flamenco is featured here; just follow the music. Numerous performances are staged nightly at the restaurants in front of the Mezquita. The entertainment is impromptu, and the experience is delightful. Popular spots include *Mesón de la Luna, Restaurante Rafael,* and *Mesón La Muralla.* Information: *Oficina de Turismo,* 10 Calle Torrijos, Córdoba 14003, Spain (phone: 57-483112).

GRANDE AUDITORIUM DE FUNDAÇÃO CALOUSTE GULBENKIAN, Lisbon, Portugal: This performing arts center presents orchestral, choral, and solo works next to the museum that houses the formidable art collection of the late Armenian financier Calouste Gulbenkian. The foundation also supports its own ballet, orchestra, and choir. Information: *Grande Auditorium de Fundação Calouste Gulbenkian,* 45 Avenida de Berna, Lisbon 1200, Portugal (phone: 1-774167).

TEATRO NACIONAL DE MARIA II, Lisbon, Portugal: Some of the most important classical and contemporary plays are staged here year-round (except during July). All performances are in Portuguese. The theater stands on the site of a onetime royal palace that, during the 16th century, became the seat of the Inquisition. The square is much cheerier now, graced with many flower stalls, fountains, and open-air cafés. Information: *Teatro Nacional de Maria II,* Praça Dom Pedro IV, Lisbon 1200, Portugal (phone: 1-371078).

PARQUE MAYER, Lisbon, Portugal: Located in the center of the city off Avenida da Liberdade, Lisbon's theater district hosts plays and *revistas* (revues) that combine satirical sketches, music, and dancing. They're performed in Portuguese, but that shouldn't stop anyone from enjoying the spectacle. Two Parque Mayer theaters are *Teatro ABC* (phone: 1-366745) and *Teatro Maria Vitoria* (phone: 1-361740).

TEATRO TRINDADE, Lisbon, Portugal: Musicals and ballet are the fare in this theater. Information: *Teatro Trindade,* 9 Rua Nova da Trindade, Lisbon 1200, Portugal (phone: 1-320000).

FADO MENOR, Lisbon, Portugal: This is one of Lisbon's newest spots for *fado.* In a small room on a back street, it's somewhat hidden, but well worth the search. All performances include dinner. Information: *Fado Menor,* 18 Rua das Praças, Lisbon 1200, Portugal (phone: 1-672681).

TEATRO MUNICIPAL DE SÃO LUÍS, Lisbon, Portugal: Located in the Chiado district, this is where the *National Ballet Company* performs with the *Portuguese National Broadcasting Station Orchestra.* Plays are also staged here. Information: *Teatro Municipal de São Luís,* 54 Rua António Maria Cardoso, Lisbon 1000, Portugal (phone: 1-327172).

TEATRO NACIONAL SÃO CARLOS, Lisbon, Portugal: Also in the Chiado district, this is the city's principal concert hall and opera house, an 18th-century jewel adorned in apricot, green, and gold. Performances include operas by such greats as Verdi, Rossini, and Mozart. The *National Ballet Company* also performs here, along with the theater's own symphony orchestra and choir. Information: *Teatro Nacional São Carlos,* Rua Serpa Pinto, Lisbon 1000, Portugal (phone: 1-368664).

Best Festivals

 Festivals, direct descendants of the Greek drama marathons and the first *Olympic* games, are annual celebrations of the pleasures of creating, competing, or just plain existing. They let a visitor cram the best and most of any given experience into the shortest possible time — whether it's auto racing or chamber music, wine tasting or bullfighting.

In Spain and Portugal, the calendar year is a kaleidoscope of celebration, a constant whirl of dancing, drinking, and devotion. There are festivals to honor saints, bulls, horses, flowers, grapes, and shellfish. There are symphony orchestras and blaring local bands, dancers in ballet slippers and on stilts, and evenings lit by chandeliers or fireworks. The festivals provide a chance for young Spanish men to show off their skills — and the original *machismo* — in climbing poles, wrestling bulls, or standing on each other's shoulders to form Catalonia's six-story *castellers,* or human towers. Each festival bears the trademark of its town, like the stomp, strum, clap, and yodel of Granada's summer flamenco festival, or the flowers and frills of Seville's *Feria de Abril.* Most festivals fall on Catholic holidays — *Carnaval, Corpus Christi,* and *Holy Week* before *Easter* are celebrated everywhere — but many still show traces of their pagan roots. The *Bonfires of San Juan* mark the summer solstice, and on the Portuguese *Feast of St. Bartholomew* (April 21–23) in Esposende, women dressed in white bathe in the ocean, then sacrifice a black chicken to exorcise the devil. For a complete listing of events, contact the *National Tourist Office of Spain,* 665 Fifth Ave., New York, NY 10022 (phone: 212-759-8822), or the *Portuguese National Tourist Office,* 590 Fifth Ave., New York, NY 10036 (phone: 212-354-4403).

A word of sober caution to those planning to hurl themselves into the merriment at one of Spain's or Portugal's frothiest celebrations: Crowds are very much a part of most festivals, so be prepared for crowded hotels, crowded restaurants, crowded streets, and crowded auditoriums. Advance planning will mitigate much of the discomfort — so reserve rooms ahead of time — but it's still recommended to be prepared mentally for being jostled, for waiting in line, and for paying $2 or more for a can of warm cola — all part and parcel of festival-going.

WORTH A LONG DETOUR

MOORS AND CHRISTIANS, Alcoy, Valencia, Spain: The 7-century war of the Reconquest is shrunk every April into a tightly scripted, 2-day game of capture-the-flag. This town near Alicante is first duly conquered by Moors in blackface, wielding scimitars and wearing feathered turbans, embroidered cloaks, and shoes with 6-inch, turned-up points. On the second day, the Christians, firing harquebuses, storm the "castle" erected in the town square for the occasion. The routed infidels flee through the smoke and embers, still carrying their vicious-looking pikes but, in their baubled headgear, fringes, and feather boas, looking more like primitive witch doctors than Moorish warriors. The victors parade triumphantly with their protecting statue of the Virgin, amid the beating of drums and the dull thuds and crackling of fireworks. Not far away, in the coastal town of Villajoyosa, the *Feast of St. Martha* in July features a naval battle at dawn and a Saracen landing on the beach. Information: *Oficina de Turismo,* 2 Esplanada de España, Alicante 03002, Spain (phone 65-212285).

LAS FALLAS DE SAN JOSÉ, Valencia, Spain: The *cremá,* or bonfire, is a popular means of celebration in the region of Valencia, and the one for St. Joseph is the *crème de la cremá.* Originally planned as a way for local carpenters to get rid of a year's worth of wood chips and sawdust, as well as to honor their patron saint, this tradition spawned an art for the sake of destruction. The city's neighborhoods compete in building hundreds of elaborate *fallas* — giant, satirical floats made of colored papier-mâché and wood. Six-foot cherubs, overweight athletes, and paunchy politicians dance on a fallen *Olympic* torch, and a grimacing globe staggers under the weight of nuclear arms. The week-long rush of bullfights, concerts, and parades begins on March 19 to a thundering chant of *"Fuego"* — "Fire!" — and a burst of fireworks, as the *falleros* light their own constructions and the flames leap into the sky. The fire consumes the sins of the winter and the woes of the world, reducing stock-market crashes to ashes and lust to dust. The next morning, it's back to the drawing board for next year's floats. Information: *Oficina de Turismo,* 48 Calle de la Paz, Valencia 46003, Spain (phone: 6-352-4000).

THE BONFIRES OF SAN JUAN, Alicante, Valencia, Spain: After the longest day of the year, the light keeps burning through the short *nit de foc,* or "night of fire." From June 21 through 29, scavenged boards, blocks of wood, shoeboxes, and old upholstery are feverishly assembled into a gigantic tower resembling an oversize, highly flammable Erector Set. Then, in the name of St. John the Baptist, it is burned: a sort of latter-day bonfire of vanities or auto-da-fé. The pyre symbolizes the sins of the town, and the cardboard human figures writhing in the flames look like heretics and witches sacrificed by the Spanish Inquisition. By dawn, the wind has dispersed the cinders and the sunshine has dissolved the lurid lights, but the festival continues with 5 more days of parades and nightly fireworks shows that make the thought of sleep a purely theological quibble. Information: *Oficina de Turismo,* 2 Esplanada de España, Alicante 03002, Spain (phone: 65-212285).

ROMERIA DEL ROCÍO, Almonte, Andalusia, Spain: As in the grand finale of a Broadway musical, the white covered wagons and little surreys with a fringe on top trundle westward, flanked by extras in wide-brimmed hats and brightly colored, flouncy skirts, dancing to the music of flutes and tambourines. Fifty days after *Easter,* pilgrims pour through the fields and olive groves of Andalusia in a slow stream of flower-festooned horses and beribboned oxen, converging on the rural sanctuary of El Rocío, 40 miles (64 km) from Seville. The festival mixes equal parts of fervor and fun. Pilgrims march silently at night over the candlelit marshes, then break out into foot-stomping, finger-snapping *seguidillas.* The climax comes with the parading of the statue of the *Virgen del Rocío,* hoisted on the shoulders of the faithful in a brilliant scene painted in sun, sweat, and tears. There are no accommodations in El Rocío or in Almonte, so stay in Seville, Cádiz, or Huelva, and try to hitch a ride on a wagon. Information: *Oficina de Turismo,* 5 Calle Vázquez López, Huelva 21001, Spain (phone: 55-257403).

SEMANA SANTA AND FERIA DE ABRIL, Seville, Andalusia: Perhaps one of the most popular fiestas is *Holy Week,* a 7-day celebration in Seville that begins on *Palm Sunday* and lasts through *Easter.* The week is highlighted by some of the most colorful floats around (guaranteed to dazzle even the most weary paradegoer), as well as rows and rows of masked paraders prancing through the streets. When the curtain falls on *Holy Week,* Sevillians disappear into the wings of the city for a brief intermission, to switch from pointed hoods to black felt hats. The plot thins, and *Passion Plays* give way to passionate playing, sober robes are exchanged for ruffled Gypsy dresses, and solemn hymns segue into throaty flamenco warbles. Across the river from the pious Old Town that cleaves to its cathedral lies a fairy-tale city of striped tents and avenues of colored lights. Transportation is by horse and buggy, and traffic noises are the tinkling of harness bells and the clicking of castanets. What began in the 19th century as a local market where peasants bartered grain for plowshares has become a showy convention of Andalusian merrymakers. Be sure to book well in advance; rooms get very crowded during this time of year. Information: *Oficina de Turismo,* 21-B Avenida de la Constitución, Seville 41004, Spain (phone: 5-422-1404).

FERIA DEL CABALLO, Jerez de la Frontera, Andalusia, Spain: Jerez is famous for sherry and horses, and even has a museum devoted to both, but for 5 days at the end of April, the horses steal the show. Straight-backed riders in felt hats and embroidered uniforms canter through the streets, and carriage drivers guide harnessed teams through the myriad maneuvers of dressage. All around the city, horses jump, trot, whinny, rear, gallop, spar with bulls, or simply stand still to be admired. The preening white Cartujanos with cottony manes are the graceful stars, descended from the horses the Moors rode during their conquest of Spain, and bred through the centuries at Jerez de la Frontera's Royal School for Equestrian Art. The fair is still faithful to its 13th-century origins as a livestock market; you may have come for the costumes, parades, and bullfights that are part of any Spanish festival, but if in a Walter Mitty life you ever cast yourself as a cowboy, or if you have a weakness for gambling, you just might ride away on a horse. Information: *Oficina de Turismo,* 7 Alameda Cristina, Jerez de la Frontera 11400, Spain (phone: 56-342037), or *Oficina de Turismo,* 1 Calle Calderón de la Barca, Cádiz 11003, Spain (phone: 56-211313).

CARNAVAL, Santa Cruz de Tenerife, Canary Islands, Spain: Rooted in an ancient pagan rite, and mixed with the apocalyptic Catholic bingeing before the severity of *Lent,* this *Carnaval* has the flavor of a Spanish *Halloween.* It is celebrated for 12 days in February throughout Spain, but nowhere more extravagantly than on the island of Tenerife, where tradition melds with a Greenwich Village sense of fashion to produce wild parades and costumes that would have made Liberace look staid. It is an orgy of purple makeup, leopard-skin leotards, sequined hats, masks, feathers, capes, and wigs. Ornate carts function as mobile bandstands, stages, and puppet theaters, and the air is filled with strums and songs and wheezing clarinets. Information: *Oficina de Turismo,* 57 Calle de la Marina, Santa Cruz de Tenerife 38001, Spain (phone: 22-287254).

HOLY WEEK AND THE FESTIVAL OF RELIGIOUS MUSIC, Cuenca, Castile–La Mancha, Spain: Cuenca froths over the sides of its cliff, leaving a frozen dribble of houses hanging in the gorge above the Huecar River. During *Holy Week,* trumpets echo between the sheer, rock walls — eerie calls from the Middle Ages to the modern world below. Above, austere processions, silent except for the solemn fanfares, wind slowly through the narrow alleys. Penitents carry sculpted and painted scenes from the Passion story, and members of religious brotherhoods march together in the forbidding robes and pointed hoods of the Spanish Inquisition. Each evening, in the church of San Miguel, orchestras and choirs from all over Europe perform recitals of religious music ranging from somber motets to Wagner's mystical *Tannhäuser.* Every year, a new work commissioned for the festival is played here for the first time. Information: *Oficina de Turismo,* 9 Calle Dalmacio García Izcarra, Cuenca 16004, Spain (phone: 66-222231).

FIESTA DE SAN FERMÍN, Pamplona, Navarre, Spain: The crowd crackles nervously at dawn around a group of young men dressed in white with scarlet sashes around their waists, who wait with clammy hands and a slightly drunk, defiant swagger. At 8 AM, a rocket is fired from the Town Hall balcony, speeding bulls shoot through the streets, and the young men run, knowing that to stop or to tire is to die. Nobody has sentenced them to this — running with the bulls is a test of *machismo,* like climbing Mt. Everest or wrestling a bear. A couple of minutes and maybe a couple of gorings later, the bulls burst into the ring at the end of the run, and another rocket is fired to signal that the streets are safe again. But in the bullring, young bulls with sawed-off but still dangerous horns charge the second rank of heroes. Then the day's casualties are counted, and the survivors go off to prepare for the next morning's rocket with a sleepless party in which blood turns to wine and Basque flutes and bagpipes whistle through the fluttering bunting. This celebration of stamina, held for 9 days at the beginning of July, and immortalized by Ernest Hemingway in *The Sun Also Rises,* actually honors San Fermín, who was martyred by being dragged through the streets by bulls. Information: *Oficina de Turismo,* 3 Calle Duque de Ahumada, 31002 Pamplona, Spain (phone: 48-220741).

FEAST OF ST. JAMES, Santiago de Compostela, Galicia, Spain: Santiago de Compostela grew famous as a result of the great medieval pilgrimages to the tomb of St. James the Apostle. The *Fiesta del Apóstol* (Feast of St. James), which takes place on July 25, highlights 10 days of festivities; Galician folkloric shows, competitions, special theater presentations, and daily concerts are among the attractions. There is also a jazz festival, consisting of performances by major international groups, in the Plaza de Tournal during the days immediately preceding the feast day. A spectacular fireworks display is held in front of the cathedral on the eve of the feast (July 24), and the day itself is marked by high mass, street bands, special theater, and an orchestral presentation in the Plaza del Obradoiro. Another main event is the swinging of the *botafumeiro* (giant incense burner) across the cathedral transepts. Check with the church for the date — it's well worth the experience. Information: *Oficina de Turismo,* 43 Rua del Villar, Santiago de Compostela 15705, Spain (phone: 81-584081).

A RAPA DAS BESTAS, San Lorenzo de Sabuceno, near Pontevedra, Galicia, Spain: For most of the year, horses roam over Galicia's green hills, but on the first weekend of July, an age-old chore becomes a spectacle, as hundreds of horses are rounded up, pounded down the mountainside, and careened into *curros* (corrals). They spend 2 days of imprisonment, eating bales of hay and thinking of the greener grass on the wild side of the fence. The town's young men then wrestle them to the ground and crop their manes or mark their hides with a symbol to identify their owners, afterward releasing them as branded animals. Information: *Oficina de Turismo,* 3 Calle General Mola, Pontevedra 36001, Spain (phone: 86-850841).

FATIMA, near Tomar, Ribatejo, Portugal: Twice a year, the desolate land around Fatima teems with pilgrims who ride, walk, and drag themselves to where three children said they saw the Virgin Mary in 1917. Unlike most *romerías,* worshipers come in modern clothes, without pomp or pageants or flowered carts, unorganized by any festival committee. This pilgrimage is not swanky but sincere, not a folksy celebration of a shrouded local myth but a mass veneration of a 20th-century front-page story. Up to 1 million people converge on this tiny town on the eves of May 13 and October 13 to commemorate the reported appearances of the Virgin; the first witnessed only by the three young shepherds, the last by a crowd of 70,000 people. Information: *Direcção-Geral do Turismo,* 86 Avenida António Augusto de Aguiar, Lisbon 1000, Portugal (phone: 1-575015), or *Posto de Turismo,* Avenida Dr. Cândido Madureira, 2300 Tomar, Portugal (phone 49-313237).

NOSSA SENHORA DA AGONIA, Viana do Castelo, Costa Verde, Portugal: A dawn serenade of bursting rockets and pounding drums awakens this seaside town for the joyous *Feast of Our Lady of Sorrow.* For 2 days in August, there's a bustle of pilgrims and a burble of pouring wine. The holy statue of the Virgin is followed along a carpet of flowers by reverent revelers wearing giant heads with shiny red noses and toothy grins. The women deck themselves in golden heirlooms and the men strut in waistcoats, vests, and colored cummerbunds worn once a year for generations. The festival may be named for the agony of indecision visitors will go through to select from the pottery and porcelain for sale at the outdoor market. Information: *Posto de Turismo,* Rua Cândido dos Reis, Viana do Castelo 4900, Portugal (phone: 58-22620).

IF TRAVELING NEARBY

CARNAVAL, Madrid, Spain: Prohibited during Generalísimo Francisco Franco's 40-year reign, this nonstop street fiesta is filled with lively parades and dancing from noon until night. The activity takes place from late February to early April and climaxes with the "Encierro de la Sardina" — the "Burial of the Sardine." Information: *Oficina de Turismo,* 1 Calle Princesa, Madrid 28008, Spain (phone: 1-541-2325).

CORPUS CHRISTI, Granada, Andalusia, Spain: This is Granada's most famous festival, complete with parades and bullfights. The party begins on the Thursday following the 8th Sunday after *Easter.* Information: *Oficina de Turismo,* 2 Calle de los Libreros, Granada 18001, Spain (phone: 58-225990).

FEAST OF ST. ANTHONY, Lisbon, Portugal: Although most people associate St. Anthony (of Padua) with Italy, he was actually born in the Alfama in Lisbon, and people here make much ado about it. The *Feast of St. Anthony,* held June 13 and the night before, is a bit like *New Year's Eve* and *New Year's Day.* Lisbon's Old Quarter comes alive on the eve: Dances are held in streets festooned with colored lanterns, and throughout the night gallons of good, rough wine are drunk to wash down mountains of sardines roasted on open barbecues. The saint is a powerful matchmaker, so this is the night when the city's young girls hope to meet their future husbands. Street stalls sell little pots of a spicy-smelling green herb called *manjerico,* each pot holding a message of advice or consolation for lovers. Information: *Direcção-Geral do Turismo,* 86 Avenida António Augusto de Aguiar, Lisbon 1000, Portugal (phone: 1-575015).

HOLY WEEK, Braga, Costa Verde, Portugal: Braga is a town famous for its processions, and though the crowds may be smaller than those that gather for *Holy Week* in Seville, the enthusiasm is no less fervent. Held annually a week before *Easter Sunday,* a day that also marks the start of Portugal's bullfighting season. Information: *Posto de Turismo,* 1 Avenida da Liberdade, Braga 4700, Portugal (phone: 53-22550).

Antiques and Auctions

 Antiques bargains abound in Spain and Portugal for the careful, tireless shopper. Spain is particularly notable for its antique jewelry, old books, and ceramics, especially the boldly designed 17th-century Talavera polychrome plates, modeled after the Italian works of Faenza and Urbino. There's not as much of a variety in Portugal, where much that is antique has already been sold. Although Portugal is now one of the least expensive European destinations, antiques prices have skyrocketed as their supply has dwindled. Nevertheless, the ardent antiques hunter will still find a variety of pleasures in Lisbon and, to a lesser extent, in other cities. Portugal is famous for its needlepoint rugs, glazed ceramic tiles, and pottery.

The Fundação Ricardo Espírito Santo Silva in Lisbon is dedicated to Portugal's decorative arts. It features a museum full of antique furniture, silver, tapestries, paintings, rugs, and ceramics, as well as a school complete with a workshop, where artisans are trained to restore antiques and make accurate reproductions. The foundation is also a good source of information on Portuguese auctions. 2 Largo das Portas do Sol (phone: 1-862183).

A REPERTOIRE OF ANTIQUES SOURCES

SHOPS AND ANTIQUES CENTERS: There are basically three different types of places in Spain and Portugal to hunt for antiques. At the low end of the scale are the flea markets, where those willing to sift through piles of miscellanea may uncover a true gem, or at least a good bargain. Auction houses are another option that can often yield a good find or two. Antiques shops, however, are usually the best bet. They are convenient; the dealer already has made the rounds through the markets and has purchased the cream of the crop. These shops do tend to be on the expensive side, but the quality is excellent and the selection can't be beat. Antiques hunters are practically guaranteed to find something of interest in one of these shops.

Madrid, Spain – As in other European capitals, Madrid's antiques shops are often found clustered in certain areas. Antiques row is the Calle del Prado, near the *Prado* museum. Worth a look is *Luis Rodríguez-Morueco* (16 Calle del Prado; phone: 1-429-5757), which features treasures from the 16th, 17th, and 18th centuries; objects of interest include fans, boxes, and canes. For more concentrated antiques browsing and buying, try *Centro de Anticuarios Lagasca* (36 Calle Lagasca). It has 11 antiques shops under one roof, including *Carabe* (phone: 1-431-5872), which has an interesting collection of crystal. Also browse along Calle Serrano, where many antiques shops are located; the 5-story *Serrano Cinco Central de Arte Antiguedades* houses 50 shops with honored reputations. For fine ceramics, try *Abelardo Linares* (11 Plaza de la Cortes; phone: 1-432-4962; and 48 Carrera de San Jerónimo; phone: 1-429-5551). *Alcocer* (5 Calle Santa Catalina, 68 Calle Pelayo, and 104 Calle Hortaleza) is a fourth-generation antiques dealer specializing in furniture, paintings, and other objects, including antique Spanish silver. The bibliophile also can savor the experience of *Luis Bardon Mesa* (3 Plaza San Martín; phone: 1-221-5514), which counts among its 50,000 volumes masterpieces by authors such as Cervantes, Lope de Vega, and Calderón de la Barca. Also try *Ramón Montero* (4 Callejón de Preciados; phone: 1-221-7167) and *Antolín Palomino Olalla* (11 Calle del Conde Duque).

Madrid's old *Central Fish Market* was rebuilt in 1988 and opened as the *Mercado Puerta de Toledo,* a sparkling cultural and shopping showcase of fine handicrafts, art, jewelry, fashion, interior design, and gastronomy, as well as antiques.

Barcelona, Spain – More than 150 antiques shops are spread along the narrow streets of the Barri Gòtic in Barcelona. Major periods as far back as the 12th century are represented. One of the best shops is *Alberto Grasas* (10 Carrer Banys Nous de la Palla, or Carrer Palla for short; phone: 3-317-8838), which sells antique paintings and decorative objects, principally porcelain. For ceramics, one of the city's top showrooms is *Arturo Ramón* (25 Carrer Palla; phone: 3-302-5974). Its prize possessions include 18th-century furniture, as well as the highly prized ceramics from Manises. Also visit *Bulevard Rosa* (Passeig de Gràcia), with 70 shops, including *Sotheby's,* representing the finest collections.

Pontevedra, Spain – *Platería Antiguedades* (Plaza de la Liena) sells antique wooden religious figures such as baroque angels.

Seville, Spain – Seville's antiques shops are among Spain's best. Try *Lola Ortega* (Plaza del Cabildo; phone: 5-421-8771); *Segundo Antiguedades* (89 Calle Sierpes; phone: 5-422-5652); and the shops along Calle Placentines. A 4-story shopping complex at Plaza del Cabildo houses antiques shops such as *Antiguedades Lola Ortega*.

Toledo, Spain – Toledo is a major supplier of furniture to the Spanish market, and has been for many years. Most of the antiques shops are on the Toledo–Madrid highway, within the area just outside the city. Try *Balaguer* (Pasadizo del Ayuntamiento and Calle Puerta Llana); *Linares* (Calle de los Reyes Católicos in front of the San Juan de los Reyes monastery); and the *Olrey* shopping complex (in Olías, about 10 miles/16 km from Toledo on the Toledo–Madrid highway).

Lisbon, Portugal – Portuguese antiques dealers, like those of Spain, tend to congregate in certain areas. Most of the best Lisbon shops are spread along a 1-mile stretch, including Rua Dom Pedro V and Rua do Alecrim, that winds its way from the Bairro Alto to the Tagus River. Most are open Mondays through Fridays, from 9 AM to 1 PM and from 3 to 7 PM; Saturdays from 9 AM to 1 PM. For *azulejos* (antique tiles), go to *Solar* (68-70 Rua Dom Pedro V; phone: 1-365522), where stacks of glazed tiles from monasteries and palaces date back to the 15th century. Visitors also can find old pewter plates and oversize candlesticks. *Xairel* (3 Rua Dom Pedro V) is another winner.

Sotheby's and *Christie's* are represented by *Teixeira Victor* (103 Rua Dom Pedro V; phone: 1-321-1973), well known for its 17th-, 18th-, and 19th-century pieces. Portugal is also noted for its beautiful hand-stitched wool Arraiolos rugs. Antique rugs can be found at *Jalco* (44 Rua Ivens; phone: 1-32895). *Ourivesaria Alianca* (50 Rua Garrett; phone: 1-323419) has a selection of silver trays and tea service sets. At *Ana,* the tiny shop at the *Ritz Intercontinental* hotel (88 Rua Rodrigo da Fonesca; phone: 1-658767), visitors can find tiles and small 18th-century plaques. For antique as well as modern jewelry, the place to shop is *W.A. Sarmento* (251 Rua do Ouro; phone: 1-326744). A family business begun in 1870, it has a collection of antique gold jewelry in its back room.

Anyone heading for Lisbon's antiques row should prepare for possible disappointment. One day there may be a stunning assortment; the next day, not much at all. Note that current regulations make it hard for foreigners to ship antique furniture home from Portugal, so make the proper inquiries before buying. To send purchases by air mail, parcel post, or freight, go to the American Visitors Bureau at 61 Rua Castilho (phone: 1-534879).

Outside Lisbon, there are some interesting buys in small villages around Porto, or in the Alentejo area east of Lisbon. The towns of Borba, Estremoz, and Evora are also good for antiques hunting.

FLEA MARKETS AND OTHER SPECTACLES: The heady mixture of rubbish and relic affords collectors the chance to find that special, unrecognized rarity. Try to arrive early, as markets quickly get crowded with other people who have the same idea.

Madrid, Spain – The city's biggest flea market, *El Rastro,* is held every Sunday from 9 AM to 2 PM. Behind the stalls of clothing, accessories, and household furnishings are permanent — and elegant — antiques shops, which generally offer high-quality merchandise. (It's better to shop at these places during the week, when things are not so hectic.) Try *Galerías Piquer* (29 Calle Ribera de Curtidores) and *Nuevas Galerías* (12 Calle Ribera de Curtidores) for antique glass.

Barcelona, Spain – Spain's most cosmopolitan city has a variety of outdoor offerings throughout the week. From dawn to dusk on Mondays, Wednesdays, Fridays, and Saturdays, *Els Encants* (just off the Plaça de les Glòries Catalanes hosts a huge flea market with everything from clothes to antiques on display. The Plaça Nova has a weekly antiques market every Thursday. The Plaça de Sant Josep Oriol transforms itself into one of Spain's largest open-air painting exhibitions and marketplaces every weekend, and the Plaça Reial features coin and stamp markets on Sunday mornings.

Seville, Spain – One of Spain's best antiques fairs is held every April in Seville. Information: *Associación de Anticuarios,* 7 Calle Rodrigo Caro (phone: 5-421-6558).

Lisbon, Portugal – The best bazaar is in the Alfama, the old Moorish part of town, Saturdays and Tuesdays on Largo de Santa Clara. Bargaining begins at sunrise. Though the market is open until noon, the best buys are gone long before that, so come early. Outside Lisbon, in São Pedro, near Sintra, antiques shops are open all day at the market on Largo Primeiro de Dezembro.

AUCTIONS: As any auction addict knows, this is a sport that combines the fanaticism of the stock market, gambling casino, and living theater. *Subastas* (the Spanish word for auctions) are held mainly in the two largest cities, Madrid and Barcelona, although antiques dealers may be able to tell visitors about some in other parts of the country. Unlike auctions in New York, which usually are quite specialized, Spanish *subastas* offer an assortment of many kinds of objects. There are none held on any regular basis in Lisbon, although *Sotheby's* and *Christie's* are represented in Lisbon by *Teixeira Victor* (103 Rua Dom Pedro V; phone: 1-321973); to find auctions in other areas of Portugal, inquire among antiques dealers and hotel concierges. Also check newspapers. The Portuguese word for auction is *leilão.* Auctions are the perfect answer to rainy day blues, provided newcomers pay attention to these notes:

Don't expect to make a killing. Even Chinese peasant children are hip to the art market today, it seems. But chances of unearthing a real find are better for those who shop at smaller auctions.

Buy the catalogue before bidding. Catalogues often include a list of estimated prices. Those prices are not a contractual commitment, but they do act as a guide for prospective buyers. An elaborate stylistic code hints at the conviction the house may have about the age or authenticity of an item. The use of capital letters, of artists' full names, and of words like "fine," "rare," and "important" all carry positive connotations. The use of a last name only and of words like "style" and "attributed" should serve as warnings.

Visit the pre-sale exhibition carefully, thoroughly, and even repeatedly. There is the pleasure of browsing in a store without a hovering clerk. Even more important is the prospective buyer's chance to examine the offerings. *Caveat emptor* is the prevailing rule at any auction. Serious buyers should have paintings taken down from the wall and ask to handle objects under lock and key. Those who can't be at the sale can leave a commission bid with the auctioneer, or even place a bid by telephone, but if they can't be at the exhibition they should be wary of buying.

Decide on a top bid before the auction begins, and don't go beyond it. Bidding has its own rhythm and tension. The auctioneer becomes a Pied Piper, with buyers winking, blinking, and nodding in time to his or her music. This situation arouses unusual behavior in some people. Suddenly their self-worth is at stake, and they'll bid far beyond what the item is worth — or even what they can afford. A bid may be canceled by promptly calling out "Withdrawn." *Note:* In determining their top price, bidders should remember to add the house commission, which is generally 10%, but can be more, and any value added tax. The following spots warrant prime attention:

Madrid, Spain – In Madrid, the international auction house *Sotheby's* has a branch at 8 Plaza de la Independencia (phone: 1-522-2902). Auctions are conducted at the *Ritz* hotel about five times a year, alternating between paintings and decorative objects. Works by such famous artists as Goya and El Greco may be sold at astronomical prices. Other places in Madrid for *subastas* include *Ansorena* (52 Calle Alcalá; phone: 1-531-6353), where jewelry and *platería* (silver) are auctioned off monthly; *Durán Subastas* (12 Calle Serrano; phone: 1-401-3400), which has about five sessions monthly, divided according to the type of selections; *Fernando Durán* (11 Calle Conde de Aranda; phone: 1-431-3806), which conducts between six and ten events a year at the *Wellington* hotel; and *Siena* (8 Calle General Ramírez de Madrid; phone: 1-270-1205), which is more modest than the others in both price and selection of objects. Commissions usually range from 12% to 15% above *el precio de adjudicación* (the sale price).

Barcelona, Spain – A wide assortment of antiques is auctioned periodically at *Balcli* (227 Carrer del Roselló; phone: 3-217-5607). Best known for quality of goods are the monthly *subastas* held at *Brok* (167 Carrer de Pau Claris; phone: 3-215-5028) and at *Prestige* (277 Carrer de València; phone: 3-215-6857). Jewelry auctions are held periodically at *Subarna* (257 Carrer de Provença; phone: 3-215-6518).

RULES OF THE ROAD FOR AN ODYSSEY OF THE OLD

Buy for sheer pleasure and not for investment. Treasure seekers should forget about the supposed resale value that dealers habitually dangle in front of amateur clients. If you love an object, you'll never part with it. If you don't love it, let someone else adopt it.

Don't be timid about haggling. That's as true at a posh Madrid shop on Calle Serrano as at *El Rastro* flea market. You'll be surprised at how much is negotiable — and the higher the price the more it has to fall.

Buy the finest example you can afford of any item, in as close to mint condition as possible. Chipped or tarnished "bargains" will haunt you later with their shabbiness.

Train your eye in museums. Museums that specialize in items you collect are the best of all. Take a close look at the furniture and clocks in Lisbon's *Gulbenkian Museum,* and the famous paintings and sculptures in Madrid's *Prado* museum.

Peruse art books and periodicals — preferably before you go auction hunting. Unfortunately, however, there is a lack of English-language reading material available.

Get advice from a specialist when contemplating a major acquisition. Major auction houses like *Sotheby's* have fleets of resident specialists available for consultation. The Spanish and Portuguese tourist offices may also be able to offer some assistance.

Sacred Spain and Portugal

All over Spain and Portugal, every invasion, migration, and wave of conversion left its signature in stone, much of which has been all but erased by time and the furor of the Reconquest. As generations of Catholics poked at the hegemony of the Moors, finally pushing them back into North Africa in 1492, they destroyed mosques and erected huge cathedrals in their place. And despite the recently named *calles de la Judería* that crop up in medieval quarters, the statues of Maimonides, and the Star of David pendants for sale in trinket stores, not many traces remain of the thousands of Jews who, until their expulsion or forcible conversion in 1492, lived in Spain for centuries alongside Phoenicians, Romans, Visigoths, Arabs, and Christians.

The ritual drawings of bulls in the caves of Altamira, the Roman Temple of Diana at Evora in Portugal, the small Visigothic Church of Santa María del Naranco in the countryside near Oviedo, the Jewish Cabala school tucked away in an alley in Girona, the grand mosque in Córdoba, the somber palace-monastery of El Escorial — each is an entry in the guestbook of religions come and gone. Here is a sampling of the Church's catholic tastes in architecture, ranging from the severity of Guadalupe to the niceties of Seville, as well as a few reminders of "infidel" times.

LA SAGRADA FAMILIA, Barcelona, Catalonia, Spain: The knobby towers reaching twistingly for the sky look like an enormous set of melting candles or the wavy walls of a sandcastle made by some oversize child. La Sagrada Familia is in the great Gothic tradition of Flamboyant swirls, jutting gargoyles, allegorical façades — and lifetimes of construction. The architect Antoni Gaudí's estimate that the completion of his final project would take 200 years may prove to be overly optimistic. Begun over a century ago, this gingerbread church in the middle of the residential neighborhood of the Eixample still doesn't have four complete walls or a roof. In the basement museum, there is a scale model of the structure as it will be one day, although we may never be able to compare it to the real thing. Information: *Patronat Municipal de Turisme de Barcelona,* 658 Gran Via de les Corts Catalanes, Barcelona 08010, Spain (phone: 3-301-7443 or 3-317-2246).

CATHEDRAL, Burgos, Castile-León, Spain: Burgos is a reminder that the center of the world can move. The quiet town that nestles in its cathedral's colossal shadow was once the capital of a kingdom and the stamping ground of the Spanish Superman

— El Cid Campeador, whose epic feats of war won him a tomb of honor in the transept. This elegant cathedral's spikes, steeples, and spires stand in memory of Burgos's Gothic glory. From the interior, the windows, the screens, and the light shining through the star-shaped skylight and glinting on the grillwork inside all make the building appear as if it were made mostly of air. Information: *Oficina de Turismo,* 7 Plaza de Alonso Martinez, Burgos 09003, Spain (phone 47-203125 or 47-201846).

MEZQUITA, Córdoba, Andalusia, Spain: Inside the plain brown wrapper of its walls is a fantasy assortment of fruit-colored columns and candy-cane arches stacked in twos and threes. The biggest treat of all is the *mihrab,* a holy niche iced with colored stucco and stones and topped with a golden cupola. For centuries (from the middle of the 8th to the middle of the 11th), Córdoba was the center of Al-Andalus, the Moorish Western world, and the mosque was spun lovingly out in stages, each addition fulfilling the grandest dreams of a different ruler. But with the Reconquest came the Christian kingdom, which dropped a cathedral in the middle of the mosque and clothed the minaret in a 17th-century bell tower. The new church did not impress the Holy Roman Emperor, who commented: "You have replaced something unique with something ordinary." Information: *Oficina de Turismo,* Plaza de Juda Levi, Córdoba 14003, Spain (phone: 57-290740 or 57-200505).

CABALA SCHOOL, Girona, Catalonia, Spain: The steep, narrow streets of the Call, climbing away from Girona's ocher reflection in the Onyar River, was home to a medieval Jewish community teeming with merchants and mystics. The Centre Isaac el Cec is named for a blind sage of the *cabala,* a sort of 12th-century teacher of the Jewish brand of mysticism that promised its disciples control over the universe through the mastery of a special force. Few buildings in Spain are unmistakably Jewish, but here a Star of David is laid in the floor of the patio, under the tables of the café that now shares the building with a center for Sephardic studies and an exhibition hall. Information: *Oficina d'Informació Turística,* 12 Carrer Ciutadans, Girona 17004, Spain (phone: 72-201694).

CAPILLA REAL, Granada, Andalusia, Spain: For King Ferdinand and Queen Isabella, to die in Granada was a triumph, and the Capilla Real (Royal Chapel) was their eternal gilded trophy. For 7 centuries, Spain had belonged to the Moors, and Granada was their last stand. So when the Catholic Monarchs finally conquered the city, they built a small chapel and filled it with themselves: their swords and crowns, their royal jewels, and priceless gems of Christian art — Italian sculptures, Flemish paintings, and Spanish grillwork. The chapel is a monument to their achievements, faith, and wealth, and their righteous challenge to the Alhambra's decadent dazzle. Information: *Oficina de Turismo,* 2 Calle de los Libreros, Granada 18001, Spain (phone: 58-225990).

REAL MONASTERIO DE SANTA MARÍA DE GUADALUPE, Guadalupe, near Cáceres, Extremadura, Spain: Within the grim fortress walls, standing guard over the rocky dry landscape, is a womb of luxury. In the center, on a golden throne, sits the *Virgen Negra de Guadalupe,* made of carved and painted wood. With her black face and silver hand, she rules over the Catholic Hispanic world. From here, and in her name, tough sons of Extremadura left with stony faces and iron hands to ensure that America became part of that world. It was here that Christopher Columbus signed the contract entitling him to the *Niña,* the *Pinta,* and the *Santa María,* and where he returned with his first cargo of Indians to be baptized in her faith. The Italian painter Luca Giordano, whose stunning paintings of the life of the Virgin cover the walls, must also have been rebaptized — as the paintings are attributed to Lucas Jordan. Information: *Oficina de Turismo,* Plaza General Mola, Cáceres 10003, Spain (phone: 27-246347).

CATHEDRAL, León, Castile-León, Spain: With sparer lines and fewer frills than those of Burgos or Seville, León's cathedral looks more French, softened by a Spanish, orangish hue. Step out of the León sun and into its cool interior, where the heavy walls seem like slender frames for the panoramic movie-screen-size windows, whose stained glass saints throw a bejeweled glimmer on the gray, stone floor. The windows are an illustrated catalogue of vices, virtues, and the wages of both, which taught, warned, and admonished illiterate medieval Spaniards — but modern visitors may need a catalogue and a pair of binoculars to understand them. Information: *Oficina de Turismo,* 3 Plaza de la Regla, León 24003, Spain (phone: 87-237082).

SANTIAGO DE COMPOSTELA, Galicia, Spain: Gliding west through Galicia on the sleek black highway, remember the pilgrims who trudged through the Pyrenees from all corners of medieval Europe, just as they walked from Ostend to·Rome or from Vienna to Jerusalem. The road to Santiago, lined with *hostales*, churches, and shrines, wound through Burgos, León, and Astorga. Today, airlines and air conditioned buses deliver millions of Catholics to the soaring granite cathedral that houses the tomb of St. James the Apostle, quaintly dubbed "the Moor-killer" for the pious feats of his ghost during the Reconquest. The cathedral's pride, the Gate of Glory, is the original façade — neither outside nor in, but slipped between the church's baroque envelope and the Romanesque interior. Almost as spectacular are the façade, patios, and Gothic chapel of the *Parador de los Reyes Católicos* (who might be among the few who could afford to stay here). Information: *Oficina de Turismo,* 43 Rua del Villar, Santiago de Compostela 15705, Spain (phone: 81-584081).

CATHEDRAL, Seville, Andalusia, Spain: It is somehow symbolic of Spain's religious history that her largest cathedral should be squeezed between a Moorish Alcázar and a once-Arab neighborhood renamed for the Holy Cross, and that its bell tower should be a dressed-up minaret. After the city was reconquered from the Moors, the mosque was razed and its minaret raised by half a dozen stories of bells and columns crowned by a revolving bronze statue of Faith. From the top of the tower, the horizon is filled by the gargoyles, turrets, spires, and buttresses of this cathedral, built to be so large that "those who come after us will take us for madmen." Information: *Oficina de Turismo,* 21-B Avenida de la Constitución, Seville 41004, Spain (phone: 5-422-1404).

JEWISH TOLEDO, Castile–La Mancha, Spain: Of the dozen or so synagogues in medieval Toledo's sprawling Jewish quarter, only two still exist, but neither is functioning. Look carefully around the city to find — wedged beneath a sagging windowsill or propping up a crumbling wall — bits of Hebrew writing on a stone from a pillaged synagogue. But when the banker who built the sumptuous Sinagoga del Tránsito was arrested and his house sacked by order of his client, King Pedro I of Castile, the synagogue itself, with praises of the king sculpted into its ornate walls, went miraculously unscathed. Information: *Oficina de Turismo,* Puerta de la Bisagra, Toledo 45003, Spain (phone: 25-220843).

TEMPLO DE DIANA, Evora, Alto Alentejo, Portugal: Just the sight of the sleek Corinthian columns stretching toward the sky here is in itself inspiring. When gazing at the heavens, it is easy to envision the generations of people who have stood at this spot in prayer and meditation for hundreds of years. The temple dates back to the 2nd century, when the city of Evora, then called Liberalitas Julia, was one of the most important Roman towns on the Iberian Peninsula. Information: *Posto de Turismo,* Praça do Giraldo, Evora 7000, Portugal (phone: 66-22671).

FATIMA, near Tomar, Ribatejo, Portugal: Even in this skeptical century, we have become used to the idea that miracles take place in desolate or remote spots like the sweaty flatness of Cape Canaveral, the laboratories of Silicon Valley — or this arid Portuguese plateau. But while we know the sites of manmade miracles mostly as newspaper headlines, every year millions of pilgrims, riding everything from hired buses to tired donkeys, converge on this land of shrubs and goats and sheep. On May 13, 1917, the Virgin Mary, it is said, appeared before three shepherd children, preaching peace and anti-communism, and telling them to wait at the same spot, on the same day, each month for a new manifestation. The news quickly spread, and more and more people came for each new vigil until, 6 months later, many in a crowd of 70,000 believers, journalists, and curious skeptics saw the sun "spinning out of its axis," descending toward earth, and filling the sky with a sensational light. Soon after, a modern church was erected, as was a square bigger than St. Peter's, along with flocks of souvenir stands and hotels. The site received the official approval of a papal visit in 1967. Information: *Direcção-Geral do Turismo,* 86 Avenida António Augusto de Aguiar, Lisbon 1000, Portugal (phone: 1-575015).

Parks, Plazas, and Paseos

Regardless of a visitor's touristic fervor, fatigue will eventually slow the maddest rush from site to sight, forcing a periodic stop for a stretch, a drink, or a snack. Fortunately, the Spanish have made the snack an institution and the stroll a national pastime. They have turned musty quays and dusty castles into sleek spaces specifically for lazing, lounging, and loafing. So when planning a trip, be sure to include a dollop of idleness on the list of musts, and *tapas* (snacks) and the *paseo* (stroll) at the top of the vocabulary list. Here are some of the lushest parks, the most languid plazas, and the most luxurious *paseos* in Spain and Portugal.

LA RAMBLA, Barcelona, Catalonia, Spain: Even at 2 AM, it seems as if it's always Sunday afternoon here. While the rest of the world sleeps, Barcelona is just finishing a meal and funneling from the alleyways of the medieval Barri Gòtic into this quintessential *paseo.* Running from the harbor to Plaça de Catalunya (with several name changes en route), La Rambla was originally designed as a drainage channel. Now, young mothers take their babies for an after-dinner stroller ride along this tree-lined promenade, their husbands riffle through the bookstalls' offerings of everything from porn to Proust, children paint beards of ice cream on their faces, and grandfathers sit on benches reading tomorrow's newspaper. Phalanxes of foreign sailors moving up from the port meet lines of teenage girls coming arm in arm from the Plaça de Catalunya. The two groups cross and pass each other with giggles and ogles, like a well-rehearsed dance. The birds in their cages tune their chirps to the horns of cars in the narrow traffic lanes squeezed to the sides of this pedestrian highway. Note the sidewalk mosaic by Joan Miró at the Plaça de Boquería; stroll to the nearby *Mercat de Sant Josep* (St. Joseph's Market, better known as the Boquería); or visit the *Gran Teatre del Liceu* (at the corner of La Rambla and Carrer de Sant Pau), one of the world's great opera houses. Information: *Patronat Municipal de Turisme de Barcelona,* 658 Gran Via de les Corts Catalanes, Barcelona 08010, Spain (phone: 3-301-7443 or 3-317-2246).

PARC GÜELL AND PASSEIG DE GRÀCIA, Barcelona, Catalonia, Spain: The works of the architect Antoni Gaudí are scattered through Barcelona like candies on a deep-pile rug. Some are brightly colored clumps; others line the city's fringes. Originally planned as a real estate development by Gaudí and his friend Count Eusebio Güell, a noted Barcelona industrialist and civic leader, Parc Güell is a confectioner's pastoral fantasy. At its core, resting on 86 pillars and edged with an undulating stone bench "upholstered" with a mosaic quilt of broken glass and tiles, is a plaza that was meant to be the garden city's marketplace. Only two of the development's houses — the gingerbread cottages flanking the park entrance — were ever built; a third, not designed by Gaudí but his home for the last 2 decades of his life, has been turned into the *Casa-Museu Gaudí,* containing drawings, models, furniture, and other items that belonged to him. South of the park, the Passeig de Gràcia ambles past some impish turn-of-the-century houses that — with their technicolored tiles and curved facades — seem to be laughing at their neighbors' stodgy grayness. Gaudí designed the liquid Casa Batlló, with mask-shaped balconies, swelling wooden doors, delicate tiles, and sensuous curves in stone and iron, and the wavy Casa Milá (popularly known as La Pedrera), with its almost sculptural attempt to distance itself from the harsh, square lines of the adjoining apartment blocks. But he was not the only member of what might be called the Dramamine School: Josep Puig i Cadafalch was responsible for the Casa Amatller, which also contrasts greatly with its neighbors. Parc Güell is open daily from 10 AM to dusk. Information: *Patronat Municipal de Turisme de Barcelona*, 658 Gran Via de les Corts Catalanes, Barcelona 08010, Spain (phone: 3-301-7443 or 3-317-2246).

PLAZA DE SANTA MARÍA, Cáceres, Extremadura, Spain: The Arco de la Estrella is like a sound barrier between the contemporary noises of the new city and the antique quiet of the old. Step through it from the honking of traffic in the Plaza Mayor to the cooing of pigeons in the Plaza de Santa María. Here, in this many-sided square, this cobblestone patch of sunlight in a city of dark alleys, Cáceres looks like a classic tweed town. Its brown, textured stones are cut in strong, simple lines suitable to the Middle Ages. But for all its ancient sternness and looming towers, there is an occasional touch of frivolous grillwork or a patterned frame of tiles around a window. Information: *Oficina de Turismo*, Plaza General Mola, Cáceres 10003, Spain (phone: 27-246347).

PATIOS OF CÓRDOBA, Andalusia, Spain: In the narrow streets of the Judería, a quarter that hasn't been Jewish for over 500 years, front doors are left ajar with a purposeful carelessness and a studied pretense of privacy. So lean through the head-wide crack or peer through the convenient gaps in the vines that veil the iron gate, into the preening patios inside. They are tiled oases, green-filled refuges from the Andalusian sun, which bounces glaringly off the whitewashed walls of Córdoba's North African–style houses. They are lovingly tended — water burbles from hoses and laps lavishly onto plants, flowers, and white-and-blue patterned ceramic floors. In a yearly pageant in May, Córdobans shed their coyness, open their doors wide, and bare their patios to the judges who award a city prize to the best. Information: *Oficina de Turismo*, 10 Calle Torrijos, Córdoba 14003, Spain (phone: 57-471235 or 57-483112).

LA GRANJA DE SAN ILDEFONSO, Castile-León, Spain: There is a little of Versailles in the purple mountains between Segovia and Madrid. King Philip V began this 18th-century palace as a simple country grange, but foreign architects and landscapers fussed over it until it became a Frenchified weave of fountains, frescoes, and façades. The formal gardens, with a high geyser rising from a pool, flow into less-manicured grounds, where sculpted gods, frogs, and cherubs cavort among the leaves. Open daily, from 10 AM to 8 PM in summer, until 6 PM in winter. (The palace itself keeps shorter hours and is closed on Mondays.) Information: *Oficina de Turismo*, 10 Plaza Mayor, Segovia 34001, Spain (phone: 11-430328).

PARQUE DEL RETIRO, Madrid, Spain: If a morning in the *Prado* museum has left you with artache, this civilized swath of nature is a perfect place to soothe a sizzling brain amid the blended smells of cedar and suede. On a sunny Sunday afternoon, all of Madrid comes to jog, hug, gossip, or walk the dog around the lakeside colonnade. The splashing of oars and the rustle of gravel provide a gentle counterpoint to the beating and blaring of the concert bands. The range of shades of the lovingly tended flowers in the Rosaleda, from saffron to cream to vermilion, will create doubt about whether a rose is necessarily a rose. The park has a style to which anyone easily can become accustomed, so indulge in a *coupe royale* — a deluxe ice cream — among statues of kings, a cocktail on the satin-white terrace of the *Ritz* hotel, and dinner at the discreet, patrician *Horcher*'s just outside the gates on Calle Alfonso XII. Information: *Oficina de Turismo*, 1 Calle Princesa, Madrid 28008, Spain (phone: 1-541-2325).

FROM THE BRIDGE TO THE BULLRING, Ronda, Andalusia, Spain: The old and new parts of Ronda tilt away from each other like neighborhoods split by a cleaver, tenuously tied by a bridge over a stomach-tightening gorge. Stand on the bridge and lean over into a mighty crack in the earth. At sunset, the red rays of sunlight seem to flow under the city, along the bottom of El Tajo. Catch your breath and step back into the newer part of town, toward the oldest bullring in Spain. In early September, Ronda celebrates itself as the birthplace of the modern *corrida* by holding costumed bullfights in the 18th-century Plaza de Toros. On quiet days, wander through the *Bullfighting Museum* (open daily, from 9 AM to 7 PM), and wonder why a people on a precipice should invent such a dangerous game. Information: *Oficina de Turismo,* 1 Plaza de España, Ronda 29400, Spain (phone: 52-871272).

PLAZA MAYOR, Salamanca, Castile-León, Spain: A golden, ingot-shaped, perfect square. It is a happy place, sunny and carefree, and there can be no better place to sit down and enjoy a cup of coffee. Foreign students sit on the cobblestones and practice their Spanish, while mothers sit on benches and try to keep children, clad in brightly colored overalls, from rolling on the ground. In the evening, bands of students uniformed in black and red breeches, leotards, and puffy sleeves wander through the plaza armed with violins, guitars, and mandolins. They are *la tuna,* occasionally coming to rest around a café table, singing local songs, attracting crowds, and drinking on the house. Like most places in Spain, this 18th-century square wasn't always quite so peaceful; it used to double as the city's bullring. Information: *Oficina de Turismo,* 41 Gran Vía, Salamanca 37001, Spain (phone: 23-268571).

BARRIO DE SANTA CRUZ, Seville, Andalusia, Spain: The streets stop simmering in the summer twilight, and start to boil with people by night. In the maze of whitewashed alleys, little girls in calico, scruffy students, and burly men in undershirts squeeze past lounging armies of the dapper unemployed. Laundry, brightly flowered vines, and old women hang out of windows. People lean against Moorish arches, stand and chat at the top of their lungs, emerge through the fly screens of crowded *tapas* bars with a beer and a plate of shrimp in garlic sauce or olives seasoned with thyme. Flamenco wails through every set of painted shutters and mingles with the jukebox jingles in a steady crescendo until, after 20-course meals, bedtime finally comes at 2 AM. Information: *Oficina de Turismo,* 21-B Avenida de la Constitución, Seville 41004, Spain (phone: 5-422-1404).

PARQUE MARÍA LUISA AND PLAZA DE ESPAÑA, Seville, Andalusia, Spain: This swanky park and elegant plaza out of some fairy-tale colonial city were all that remained when the *1929 Iberian-American Fair* collapsed with the economy. Now communion parties row in canals dug for visitors who never came. Pavilions built for exhibits that never took place stand ready for the *1992 World's Fair.* Stroll down the park's graveled avenues in June and you may become part of some local family's history, caught in the background of a wedding photograph, or simply recover from Seville's drenching heat on a bench protected by a high hedge. Through the leaves, the sunlight spatters on the brick floor and miniature ornamental tiles. Twin baroque towers, ornate lampposts, and bridges with blue and white terra cotta balustrades make the Plaza de España look like a Mexican fantasy of Venice. Information: *Oficina de Turismo,* 21-B Avenida de la Constitución, Seville 41004, Spain (phone: 5-422-1404).

SLIDING INTO TOWN, Funchal, Madeira, Portugal: The most dramatic way to reach Funchal is to toboggan into town in a wicker chair. Entrust your life to two men in white who run alongside and brake and steer the open, wheelless carriage of straw. Relax while clattering down a cobblestone hill from the village of Monte, perhaps holding a cocktail in one hand and crossing two fingers of the other. As you whiz by, remember to admire the islandful of orchids and fuschia, of passion fruit and papaw. Information: *Direcção-Geral do Turismo,* 86 Avenida António Augusto de Aguiar, Lisbon 1000, Portugal (phone: 1-575015).

ESTUFA FRIA AND ESTUFA QUENTE, Lisbon, Portugal: In these botanical gardens, as in a state dinner in the plant kingdom, a Mexican cactus is seated near a

Balinese banana tree, and a Korean date palm swaps yarns with an African flower. In these circles, the common language is still Latin, and the placecards read *Australis alsophila* and *Brunfelsia hopeana.* Thorny shrubs, lanky ferns, filigreed buds, and wide, flopping leaves mill among the pathways, tunnels, and bridges over goldfish ponds. Come sit in the year-round gentle warmth and read, woo, or mull in the nooks colored a million shades of green, with exotic splashes of scarlet, turquoise, and magenta. If a visitor gets some heavenly idea, it may be thanks to the tree called "Muse of Paradise." Open daily from 9 AM to 6 PM (5 PM in winter). Information: *Direcção-Geral do Turismo,* 86 Avenida António Augusto de Aguiar, Lisbon 1000, Portugal (phone: 1-575015).

DIRECTIONS

DIRECTIONS

Galicia

Despite Eliza Doolittle's assertion, the rain in Spain does *not* fall mainly on the plain: It falls on Galicia. In fact, Spain's northwestern corner wages a constant battle against the moisture-laden winds that roll in from across the Atlantic, making the region the country's wettest.

Cut off both geographically and culturally from mainstream Spain, Galicia contradicts the country's arid image. Instead of the familiar parched plains of central and southern Spain, its annual 64 inches of rain produce green mountain slopes, a network of blue-green rivers, pine and eucalyptus forests, palm trees, and lush terraces of vines. *Gallegos* rarely go out without umbrellas — even if a natural immunity to a few splashes means they often forget to use them. And in the fishing villages scattered along the coast and beside the *rías* (estuaries, or inlets), where the riverbeds are regularly raked for mussels and clams, the local costume includes an oilskin, over-the-knee galoshes, a pair of rubber gloves, and a resigned grin.

Galicia is also one of Spain's poorest regions. There are no Porsches here, only small domestic vehicles and shaky mopeds. There are also relatively few tractors, compared with the number of bullocks to be seen pulling carts of corn and other produce. And since there are also relatively few foreign visitors, the sight of a tourist car is often enough to stop a peasant in his or her tracks.

Historically, rather than farm in the traditional cooperative manner, the Galicians carved their land into hundreds of small holdings, each consisting of little more than a terra cotta–roofed shack, a few vines, a field of corn, and a donkey. By the turn of this century, as transatlantic travel became more accessible, those who could scrape together the pesetas emigrated to Central and South America. Argentina, in particular, was such a popular destination that, today, there are more *gallegos* in Buenos Aires than in Galicia.

The region was not always so undeveloped and far from the mainstream. During the Middle Ages, this distant corner of Europe was transformed, in the course of only a century or two, from a sleepy backwater into the world's first mass "tourist destination," with one of Christendom's three holiest cities. The metamorphosis began in 813, when a peasant, led to a field by shining starlight, discovered what was thought to be the long-forgotten tomb of St. James, one of the 12 Christian apostles. Over the years, the saint's remains became the object of a pilgrimage ranking second in importance only to one to Jerusalem or Rome, and the chapel built to house the bones grew to be the magnificent Cathedral of Santiago de Compostela, the final jewel in a chain of churches, monasteries, and hospices strung across northern Spain along the Camino de Santiago — the famous Way of St. James. (For further details, see *Pilgrims' Route,* DIRECTIONS.)

At the end of their journey, medieval pilgrims hobbled across the Plaza del

Obradoiro from the cathedral to have their blisters treated in the Hostal de los Reyes Católicos, a hospital and inn built in 1499 by King Ferdinand and Queen Isabella. Pilgrims knocking on the doors today find themselves ushered into cloistered comfort, their luggage whisked away by maroon-coated porters, because the former hospice is now the *Parador Los Reyes Católicos* (phone: 81-582200). Converted into a hotel in 1954, it is not only the flagship of Spanish *paradores,* but also one of the finest hotels in Europe. Seen from the outside, the only concession to modernity appears to be a pair of glass doors slotted into the magnificent Plateresque granite façade that stretches across the entire northern side of the plaza. Within, thick stone walls, heavy wooden furniture, fountains, and patios provide a luxurious retreat for weary travelers.

Buildings in Galicia, it must be said, are either monumental or monumentally ugly. To be sure, the historic centers of towns such as Santiago, La Coruña, Lugo, Pontevedra, and Bayona are archetypical Spain — the Spain of one's imagination. A cathedral, usually modeled on that of Santiago, overlooks a peaceful square shaded by plane trees. Children kick a soccer ball around, old men huddle and talk, black-veiled widows remember times long gone, and the cobbled streets are so quiet that passersby can hear the clatter of coffee cups coming from a bar long before they reach it.

But beyond these oases of aestheticism, grim and granite ugliness prevails. Suburbs in the larger towns consist of characterless and often unfinished apartment blocks; the smaller, one-street towns are strung out in shades of gray; and even vast stretches of otherwise stunning coastline have been marred by tasteless, prefabricated holiday bungalows. There are exceptions, of course, including the *pazos* — the former homes of noble Spanish families, standing aloof in the countryside — and, attached to most small holdings, the *horreos* — distinctive wooden and granite huts, perched on stilts, traditionally used for storing grain.

Many parts of Galicia, however, are free from modern encroachment. In summer, as foreign hordes descend on Spain's southern and eastern coasts and the inland plains suffocate in soaring temperatures, many Spaniards seek refuge along the cool, deserted Galician coastline. From the Eo River, which borders Asturias, around to the Miño River on the Portuguese frontier, the shoreline is rugged and beautiful, as yet uncluttered by vacation homes and attendant businesses.

Galicia consists of four provinces — La Coruña and Lugo to the north, Pontevedra and land-locked Orense to the south — and its deeply indented coastline is divided into two sections. The wild, more exposed Rías Altas (Upper Estuaries) run westward along the coast of the provinces of Lugo and La Coruña, from Ribadeo roughly to the city of La Coruña; and the gentler coves, wooded hills, and fishing villages of the Rías Bajas (Lower Estuaries) run south along the coast of the provinces of La Coruña and Pontevedra, from Muros down to Bayona.

The still and quiet estuaries closely resemble Norwegian fjords or Scottish lochs, while long stretches of palm-fringed sand have yet to experience the commercialization that has altered the shore along much of the Mediterranean. But between the Rías Altas and the Rías Bajas is a stretch of coast called the Costa de la Muerte (Coast of Death), treacherous to sailors through the ages (the roads are none too good, either). It begins at Malpica and comes to an abrupt end at Cabo Finisterre, literally the "end of the land" for medieval man.

Galician cuisine revolves around seafood. Along the coast, entire communities are engaged in milking the sea and rushing the day's (or night's) catch to restaurant tables. Even the smallest restaurant has at least one fish tank full of crabs and lobsters: Window decor is often no more than a huge, refrigerated display packed with regimental lineups of hake, bass, shrimp, crayfish, squid, and octopus. *Gallegos* tired of the sight of fish will probably opt for a plate of *lacón con grelos.* A potage of salted pork and turnip tops, this is Galicia's traditional soul food, and it's usually accompanied by local wine drunk from a white porcelain cup.

Galicia is a wonderful region in which to drive. A well-planned network of freeways, fast and scenic, delves into the remotest corners, backed up by numerous and fairly well maintained country roads. Traffic is light beyond the pinpricks of urbanization, and distances that may look lengthy on a map are covered in a relatively short time. Road signs are excellent, even though several Castilian place-names have been altered by Galician separatists, who demand (thankfully, in a less violent manner than in other areas) that the region be accorded the rights and status of an independent nation.

The route outlined below is a circular one, encompassing significant stretches of both coastline and countryside. It begins in Santiago de Compostela and hugs the coastline from the vicinity of Padrón, southwest of Santiago, to Pontevedra, before continuing due south through Vigo to Bayona. From here it follows the seashore again, at times only yards from the water, before turning east along the Miño River, which forms the border with Portugal (and is known as the Minho in Portuguese), to the frontier town of Túy (where it is possible to walk or drive to Portugal across the bridge spanning the river.) The itinerary then cuts inland from Túy, following the Miño to Orense, keeping to the north bank of the river at first, then to the southern bank, and passing through the Ribeiro vineyard country around Ribadavia. From Orense, the route heads north via the old walled town of Lugo to Ribadeo on Galicia's north coast. Except for an excursion inland to Mondoñedo, the route now stays on the coast, exploring the Rías Altas around the northwest corner of Galicia (and of Spain) to El Ferrol and La Coruña.

Because Galicia is not, relatively speaking, a hotbed of tourism, the choice of accommodations is rather grim. The region's nine *paradores,* particularly the two in Santiago and Bayona, however, are among the notable exceptions. For their price, the *paradores* represent the best value for the money, and their reliably high standards are not only rewarding but almost essential at the end of a long day's drive.

Expect to pay $75 or more for a double room in a hotel or *parador* described as expensive, $50 to $75 in one listed as moderate, and under $50 in one listed as inexpensive. Prices do not include breakfast, but eating out in Galicia is rarely a costly experience. Restaurants listed as expensive charge around $70 for a dinner for two, including wine; a moderate establishment, $40 to $70; and an inexpensive one, under $40.

■ **Note:** When two spellings are given (usually in the first reference to a place), the first one is in Spanish, and the second is in Galician, the local, Portuguese-like language.

SANTIAGO DE COMPOSTELA: By some stroke of good fortune, Santiago has remained much as it was in its days as a religious mecca. All streets lead to the cobbled Plaza del Obradoiro (also known as Plaza de España). One of the world's most spacious, majestic squares, it has managed to escape the ubiquitous neon signs, bars, restaurants, and cafés, and instead is snugly protected by four splendid, historic buildings: the cathedral, the College of San Jerónimo, the Town Hall, and the *Parador Los Reyes Católicos,* all built in the same honey-colored granite. The paucity of action in the plaza (beyond the frantic clicking of camera shutters) is more than compensated for down the side streets, particularly Rúa Nueva, Rúa del Villar, and Calle del Franco. Pedestrians in a constant stream pass under the porticoes or sip coffee in the sidewalk cafés — university students clutching clipboards, couples gossiping arm in arm, puzzled visitors poring over maps, and police casually patrolling in blue. (For full details on sights, hotels, and restaurants, see *Santiago de Compostela,* THE CITIES.)

En Route from Santiago de Compostela – Leave the outskirts of Santiago and head 12½ miles (20 km) south to Padrón on N550, an easy, fast main road that cuts through green fields and passes several *pazos* camouflaged behind iron gateways. The majority of these stately manor houses were built along the rivers leading into the Rías Bajas by families who made their fortunes across the Atlantic and returned to invest their newfound wealth. Beyond Padrón, at Ponte Cesures, leave N550 and take the coast road off to the right, signposted Villagarcía de Arousa. As the road hugs the woody southern shores of the Ulla River, leading into the Ría de Arousa, there are fine views across the water — unless it's raining, in which case mist rolls up the valley and settles in a low, dense layer. Lucky travelers will arrive in Villagarcía, 15½ miles (25 km) from Padrón, in time to see the townspeople up to their knees in the estuary, plucking shellfish from the sand flats. The *ría,* like the land in Galicia, has been sectioned off into "plots," and the scene is one of organized chaos as gulls scream, dogs bark excitedly, men chug around in boats, and well-built women hunker down to scour the beds for fish.

Continue on the coast road south, curving around the peninsula to Pontevedra, 34½ miles (55 km) from Villagarcía. En route, a short detour to the right, following the signposts to El Grove (O Grove), leads across a bridge to the island of La Toja (A Toxa), one of the region's few tourist developments — site of large expensive hotels, swimming pools, a spa, and a casino. Out of season, the scene is one of closed shutters, gentle drizzle, and old ladies valiantly trying to sell armfuls of shell necklaces to anyone with a foreign-looking complexion. Signs to Praia da Lanzada lead to the most beautiful beach in Galicia, with long swathes of pale sands, palm trees, and shallow waters. Still on the island, Combarro, a few miles farther, is a lost-in-time fishing village. With its line of waterfront *horreos* (granaries), it has been declared an artistic monument by the locals.

PONTEVEDRA: The streets of this old, charming town are lined with characteristic Galician glazed balconies called *solanas,* built to catch all the available sun but keep out the rain and wind. The town sits above the Pontevedra River, which at its wider points resembles a peaceful lake. There was a time when Pontevedra was a thriving hub for fishermen, merchants, and traders; but by the 18th century the delta had silted up, and sea traffic was forced to use the port at nearby Marín. (Ironically, the closest good beach is also at Marín.)

Concentrate on the Old Quarter, sitting on the doorstep of the *parador.* It's a peaceful mishmash of streets that rarely plays host to visitors. Finding the town's main museum, the *Provincial Museum,* an unmarked, solid granite building on Plaza de la Leña, is a task in itself. The museum (open Mondays through Saturdays, 11 AM to 1:30 PM and 5 to 8 PM; Sundays and holidays, 11 AM to 1 PM) contains maritime exhibits, artifacts from Galician history through the 19th century, and a valuable collection of jewelry. Other sights include Plaza de la Herrería, an arcaded square presided over by the Convento de San Francisco, and the Church of La Peregrina.

CHECKING IN: *Parador Casa del Barón* – Believed to stand on the site of an old Roman villa, like many *paradores* it is a former *pazo;* but during its checkered past it has also been a school, a granary, a masonic lodge, and, lastly, an 18th-century residence owned by the Barons of Casa Goda, who restored it. It has 47 rooms and flower-filled gardens. Plaza de Maceda. Pontevedra (phone: 86-855800). Moderate.

En Route from Pontevedra – Take the A9 freeway southwest 17 miles (27 km) to Vigo. Apart from Santiago, it is here, in the Rías Bajas areas around Pontevedra, Vigo, and Bayona (Baiona), that Galicia welcomes most of its holiday visitors. With a milder and sunnier climate than their northern counterparts, the Rías Bajas are backed by thick pine forests, and the hidden coves and gently shelving beaches make this the only strip of coastline where swimming is a viable (though not very warm) option.

VIGO: On the southern shore of the Ría de Vigo, Spain's largest fishing port is a lively, modern city, as well as a good example of how the deepwater anchorages and shelter of Galicia's coastline have been commercially exploited. Sir Francis Drake sacked the city in 1585 and again in 1589, and in 1702, a combined English and Dutch force attacked a Spanish treasure fleet returning from the Americas, sending many gold-laden galleons to the bottom of the estuary; they have yet to be discovered.

Vigo is a remarkably clean and manicured place, perhaps because hulking transatlantic liners no longer berth at the city's harbor terminal. During the day, visitors can shop for the city's famous *angulas* (eels) at the morning fish auction down near the waterfront, or climb to the heights of Parque del Castro. This superb public park is built around the Castillo de San Sebastián, a 10th-century fortress. The views overlook the estuary and its narrow neck, where the galleons were sunk. For lively nighttime bars, head for the old fishermen's quarter.

The entrance to the Ría de Vigo is sheltered by the Islas Cíes, a cluster of steep, abrupt rock islands with magnificent beaches, rich flora and fauna, spectacular cliff paths, and turquoise water. Passenger boats cross regularly to the islands from the port. Other beaches line the southern shores of the estuary in a practically unbroken strip.

CHECKING IN: *Bahía de Vigo* – A comfortable, 110-room hotel, strategically placed opposite the old transatlantic terminal. Its nautical decor includes portholes in the bar and naval trappings throughout. 5 Avenida Cánovas del Castillo, Vigo (phone: 86-226700). Expensive to moderate.

Ciudad de Vigo – Functional and impersonal, this 101-room hotel, in a pretty part of town, primarily serves local businessmen. 5 Calle Concepción Arenal, Vigo (phone: 86-435233). Expensive to moderate.

BAYONA (BAIONA): A lively tourist town 13 miles (21 km) south of Vigo via C550, Bayona sweeps along the shore at the entrance to the Ría de Vigo. It's a pretty town, as well as a historic one — Bayona welcomed Columbus's return on the *Pinta* in 1493 after his discovery of the Americas — and it has retained many of its medieval features. Much of the long harbor road is lined with nautically themed clothing shops and restaurants; stores on the maze of streets behind the harbor (try *Nautic Mare* on Calle

Ramón y Cajals, a clothes shop with branches in Marbella and other chic points south) echo the maritime theme.

The town is dominated by Monte Real, a fortified peninsula across the bay; besides a defensive wall, the peninsula is the site of a 16th-century castle that pokes into the river and is now the the town's *parador* (see below). When the winds get up, and the rain sweeps across the bay (which it frequently does), the waters turn gray and choppy — and the reason for the shipwreck lying on a group of treacherous rocks suddenly becomes clear. A huge statue of the Virgin (known as the Virgen de la Roca), stands on the shoreline to the south of town, looking out to the Cíes Islands.

CHECKING IN: *Parador Conde de Gondomar* – Widely ranked as the most beautifully located *parador* in northern Spain, it commands a privileged position atop Monte Real. A turreted castle with its own fortress gate, the *parador*'s 124 rooms exude somber, monastic characteristics — even the staff moves silently along the corridors. Stay on a hot summer's day and make use of the outdoor swimming pool, sauna, tennis courts, or enjoy dining at the excellent seafood restaurant. Carretera de Bayona, Bayona (phone: 86-355000). Expensive.

Tres Carabelas – Tucked down the back streets where ancient buildings echo to the sounds of noisy, adolescent-filled bars. Homey and comfortable though basic, with television sets in all 10 rooms. 61 Calle Ventura Misa, Bayona (phone: 86-355133). Inexpensive.

EATING OUT: *O Moscón* – Don't let the name (The Fly) put you off. The lobster tank is on view from the promenade outside, and there is also a display of gigantic crabs, an indication of the extensive range of seafood served here. It is cozy and smart, and features good local dishes; the menu has English translations. Reservations advised. 2 Calle Alférez Barreiro, Bayona (phone: 86-355008). Moderate.

En Route from Bayona – The 19 miles (30 km) along C550 heading south to La Guardia (A Garda) are bleak, but this is where the route is at its most intimate with the white foaming seas, the waves breaking dramatically against giant rocks — sometimes spraying the car windshield. A sharp turn inland at La Guardia brings an equally sharp change in landscape — the gentle Miño River, which forms the frontier with Portugal, replacing the waves and the coastal stone walls and springy turf giving way to woods, scruffy villages, the occasional oxen, and fields of green maize and sinewy bamboo. Follow C550 as it twists eastward along the river 17 miles (28 km) to the frontier town of Túy (Tui). The town has an attractive historic center, including a 12th-to-13th-century fortress-like cathedral, but it's worth a stop primarily to stroll across the river to Valença do Minho, Portugal, on the Ponte Internacional, the 19th-century suspension bridge designed by Alexandre-Gustave Eiffel, of Paris tower fame.

From Túy, take the N550 9 miles (14 km) north to Porriño (signposted Redondela and Vigo), then turn east along N120 and continue 34 miles (55 km) to Ribadavia, proof that fast roads don't necessarily compromise dramatic, mountain scenery. Ribadavia is a scruffy but lively market town that heralds the entrance to Ribeiro vineyard country. Thick vines suddenly cover the slopes to the left and right as the road crosses the green waters of the Miño and connects to the rougher N202 which runs along the river's southern bank for 14 miles (22 km) to Orense (Ourense).

ORENSE (OURENSE): The approach to town, thick with dull apartment and office blocks, is suddenly relieved by a beautiful, seven-arched Roman bridge crossing the Miño into the town center. The bridge — the Puente Viejo — was reconstructed during the 13th century to ease the heavy traffic of pilgrims on their journey to Santiago.

Orense is primarily an industrial town today, but it has been famous since ancient times for Las Burgas — springs of medicinal drinking water, which rise at around 149F in the center of the Old Town. The 12th-century cathedral is the last of the great western Romanesque churches; the grandiose scale of its nave, aisles, and east end and the sculptures of the Pórtico del Paraíso (Paradise Doorway) have been excelled only by the work of Master Mateo on the Gate of Glory in the cathedral in Santiago de Compostela.

 CHECKING IN: *San Martín* – Smack in the Old Town; its 90 rooms are modern and functional. 1 Calle Curros Enríquez, Orense (phone: 88-235690). Moderate.

Padre Fejióo – Close to the Old Town, this 71-room establishment is surrounded by a variety of fine restaurants. 1 Plaza Eugenio Montes, Orense (phone: 88-223100). Inexpensive.

EATING OUT: *San Miguel* – Sample excellent shellfish and Galician dishes on the summer terrace or in the tastefully decorated dining room. Closed Tuesdays. Reservations necessary. 12 Calle San Miguel, Orense (phone: 88-221245). Expensive.

En Route from Orense – Leaving town, cross the Miño River and head north on N525 to the N540 intersection, 7 miles (11 km) from Orense. Take N540 north 16 miles (26 km) to Chantada, a charming little town known for its Monastery of San Salvador de Asma, an 11th-century Romanesque creation just outside town to the east; recently restored, the monastery's highlight is a collection of old Galician frescoes. Continue north on N540 another 24½ miles (39 km) to Guntín de Pallares, where N540 becomes N640 and continues another 11 miles (18 km) north to Lugo.

LUGO: The center of this provincial capital, one of Galicia's quintessentially Spanish towns, is wholly surrounded by a thick Roman wall, the best-preserved example of its kind in Spain. Join the handful of citizens walking their dogs along the ramparts, and you'll have a bird's-eye view of Lugo's terra cotta roofs and its street life, not to mention of the wall itself — about a mile in length, 30 to 45 feet high, about 15 feet thick, and interrupted at regular intervals by 85 semicircular towers. There are some 10 gates, but the most interesting one is the Santiago Gate, which opens before the Romanesque-Gothic Cathedral de Santa María overlooking Plaza Mayor. Arrive on a sunny Sunday morning and the entire town will be out taking a slow *paseo* (walk) in this tree-lined plaza: little girls in their best dresses and ribbons, old men in somber suits, and smart ladies whispering together, carrying freshly bought cakes oozing cream and dusted with powdered sugar. The outdoor tables of the cafés down one side of the square are packed, and toward lunchtime, as further crowds emerge from morning mass, the Lugo band begins to play on the turn-of-the-century bandstand at the center of the square. The town's gracious 18th-century Town Hall is also located here.

 CHECKING IN: *Méndez Núñez* – An upscale but friendly establishment with 96 comfortable rooms, just around the corner from the main plaza. 1 Calle Reina, Lugo (phone: 86-230711). Moderate.

En Route from Lugo – There's not much sign of civilization along N640 as it heads 56 miles (90 km) north to Ribadeo. It rides high, at first, over the green open plain, an occasional cattle farm camouflaged behind huge granite walls. As the road begins to follow the contours of the Eo River, it narrows to a single lane, its regular bends cutting through towering, pine-forested gorges. During the last few miles, watch the picturesque river — which here forms the boundary between the regions of Asturias and Galicia — unfold toward the coast at Ribadeo.

RIBADEO: The sights of this palm-fringed resort town on the Ría de Ribadeo, where the Eo River meets the sea, include the Art Nouveau buildings of the Plaza de España in the town center, as well as a pretty beach. There is a pleasant walk out to the lighthouse on the Eo estuary, to see fishermen taking in their catch and children clambering down the cliffs, as the waves crash against the rocks in the stiff Atlantic breeze. The town is dominated by the Torre de los Moreno, a tower built in 1905, whose copper dome is supported by four draped female figures. The Santa Cruz hill and hermitage, 1¼ miles (2 km) out of town, offers a marvelous view of the coastline. This is the site of the *Xira a Santa Cruz* pilgrimage, held annually on the first Sunday in August, with much traditional dancing and bagpipe music. Notice the bagpiper monument on the hill. Ribadeo's fishermen's quarter is full of *pulperías,* bars dedicated to the eating of octopus and the drinking of fine Galician wine from cups that resemble Chinese tea bowls.

From Ribadeo, a worthwhile excursion can be made inland to the old Galician town of Mondoñedo, 24 miles (39 km) southwest on N634. Mondoñedo's twin-towered 12th-century cathedral is a treasure, and the entire straggling, sleepy farming town is delightfully nestled in a broad-bottomed valley. The cathedral has a carved and painted 15th-century wooden statue, La Virgen Inglesa (English Virgin), rescued from St. Paul's Cathedral in London during the Reformation and brought to Spain, where it was acquired by a Mondoñedo aristocrat. The church also contains a superb, though cluttered and unkempt, museum filled with 12th- and 13th-century objects such as Arab boards, candle holders, sand clocks, and marble images of Christ. Mondoñedo is famous for its sweet, sticky baked goods made from sponge cakes, vermicelli, and almonds.

CHECKING IN: *Parador de Ribadeo* – The local link in the government-run chain, a modern, 47-room hostelry, inspires mixed reviews. Critics note that it's a could-be-anywhere *parador* of endless, shabbily carpeted corridors, bearable in summer but depressing under gray skies. Fans point out its wonderful views across the broad Eo estuary into Asturias. The breakfast display is impressive, but it's worth finding a more atmospheric restaurant in town in the evening. Popular despite the difference of opinion, so reserve rooms well in advance. Calle Amador Fernández, Ribadeo (phone: 82-110825). Moderate.

EATING OUT: *O Xardin* – A 5-minute walk into town from the *parador,* it's the nearest Galicia comes to a bistro-style restaurant-bar. It has a comprehensive menu of fish and meat dishes, a large selection of wines, and one very overworked waitress. Closed February. Reservations advised. 20 Calle Reinante, Ribadeo (phone: 82-110222). Moderate to inexpensive.

En Route from Ribadeo – West of town, the route explores the Rías Altas portion of the Galician coastline, hopping from one long, indented inlet to the next as far as La Coruña (A Coruña). Take N634 out of Ribadeo and follow it 15 miles (24 km) west to Foz, a fishing village and beach resort on the far side of the Ría de Foz. From Foz, C642 continues westward 12 miles (19 km) to Cervo, where a left turn and subsequent signs lead visitors the extra mile or so to the Royal Ceramics factory at Sargadelos. It's a large, futuristic-looking building; the factory makes and sells distinctive plates, jewelry, pots, and figurines (closed during early afternoon siesta).

Return to C642 and head west for 12 miles (19 km) to Vivero (Viveiro), where the scenery improves dramatically. Here, steep cliffs drop down to spectacular panoramas of flat sands and shallow seas, unmarred by hotels, restaurants, boats, or even people. The province of Lugo ends at the Sor River and the Ría de Barqueiro, just beyond Vivero, but C642 continues west to Ortigueira, a fishing town on the Ría de Santa Marta de Ortigueira 22 miles (35 km) west of Vivero, and then to Campo de Hospital. At this point, C642 bends south, while C646 continues west to the most beautiful of the Rías Altas, the Ría de Cedeira. Cedeira itself, 17 miles (27 km) from Ortigueira, is a sleepy, pretty little sardine fishing town built along the banks of the Condeminas River.

El Ferrol (O Ferrol) is a pleasant 24-mile (38-km) drive south of Cedeira on C646. It's set directly across the water from La Coruña — the *gallegos* say that "If you can't see El Ferrol from La Coruña, it must be raining, and if you can, rain is on the way!" It's notable mainly as the birthplace of Generalísimo Francisco Franco (1892–1975). It certainly doesn't score on looks but thrives today as Spain's principal naval base and dockyard. The main shopping area, lined with clothing, footwear, and pastry shops, leads down to a square in front of the Town Hall, and makes for lively *paseos* in the early evening. Also of interest is the 18th-century church of El Socorro, which houses a famous statue of Christ walking on water.

 CHECKING IN: Parador El Ferrol – A 39-room *parador* in an unlikely position overlooking the docks. Visitors are quite likely to be awakened at 8 AM to the sounds of a pre-recorded trumpet fanfare as sailors perform their ritual flag hoisting ceremony in the mini-square outside the hotel. Calle Almirante Vierna, El Ferrol (phone: 81-356720). Moderate.

LA CORUÑA (A CORUÑA): A 38-mile (61-km) drive around three of the Rías Altas from El Ferrol leads to Galicia's largest city and business center. An important trading post on the ancient tin route, La Coruña is today one of Galicia's largest coastal developments and an active commercial port, its main trade the curing, salting, and tinning of fish. Philip II's Invincible Armada was launched from here in 1588; its defeat resulted in 15,000 deaths and the loss of half the fleet.

The town, which sits on a peninsula jutting out into the Ría de la Coruña, is divided roughly into three sectors: the Old Quarter (around the neck of the peninsula), with its two 12th-century, Romanesque-Gothic churches, Iglesia de Santiago and Santa María del Campo; the modern shopping quarter; and the busy port, bordering the beaches of Orzan and Riazor. The town is noted for its typically Galician 19th-century balconied buildings on the waterfront, but the most important single monument is the 2nd-century Tower of Hercules, the last remaining Roman lighthouse in operation (although in 1791 its original crumbling masonry was encased in modern brickwork).

 CHECKING IN: Finisterre – On La Coruña's seafront, it has 3 swimming pools, tennis courts, and 127 small but comfortable rooms, the best of which overlook the harbor. Paseo del Parrote, La Coruña (phone: 81-205400). Expensive to moderate.

EATING OUT: El Rápido – Serving excellent grilled shellfish and other seafood specialties for over 40 years. Closed Monday evenings. Reservations necessary. 7 Calle Estrella, La Coruña (phone: 81-224221). Expensive.

Castile-León (Old Castile)

Rather formidable and stern, the Castilian *meseta* (plateau) is the historical and spiritual heartland that eventually gathered a united Spain around it. After the impetus for the country's protracted Reconquest was born in the early 8th century in Asturias — a remnant of the old Visigothic, and therefore Christian, Spain, and the only part the Moors had failed to conquer — the movement spread southward across León and into the vast, elevated plateau of Castile, where it gained its greatest foothold. A shared commitment to driving the Moors out of Spain forged a firm bond between the kingdoms of Castile and León, one that was politically sealed early in the 13th century when León was united with Castile. Then, in 1469, the region began a rapid rise to prominence when Isabella of Castile wedded her personal and political fortunes to those of Ferdinand of Aragon. By 1479, the couple had become the embryo of the present Spanish monarchy, ruling over a joint kingdom of Aragon and Castile that was the basis of modern Spain. Their union also set in motion the centuries-long and notoriously cruel quest for religious uniformity known as the Spanish Inquisition, first instituted by Isabella in Castile in 1478 and not abolished until the early 19th century.

The singlemindedness of purpose, raw courage of conviction, and unflinching historic vision characteristic of Isabella (called Isabel la Católica — a title she was granted by Alexander VI, a Spanish pope, in 1496) were undoubtedly attributes she absorbed from the hard-edged reality of her native Castile. Virtually ringed by high mountain ranges, the immense Castilian plateau occupies the central part of Spain at an average altitude of 2,600 feet. Here, vast fields stretch long, flat, and often uninterrupted to a dusty horizon. Exposed to everything from scorching hot summers to blustery, bone-chilling winters, this is not a region that pampers its populace. Here, too, religion, ritual, and tradition of the ages keep a firm rein on the imagination.

Castilians are a hearty, no-nonsense lot who, when their security is threatened, often act first and ask questions afterward. Recently, the leader of an extreme right-wing Catholic organization came to visit the Iglesia de Santa Teresa in the small village of Alba de Tormes, not far from Salamanca. Enshrined in the church are two important relics of St. Teresa of Avila — her heart and a portion of bone from her arm. A fray soon broke out between members of the organization and other visitors to the church, and the church deacon, mistakenly believing that the extremist leader was trying to steal St. Teresa's arm bone, rang the church bell to summon the townspeople to the rescue. As rumor of the alleged theft attempt spread, villagers prepared to lynch the man on the spot. When he sought refuge in his car, they pushed it into the Tormes River. Eventually the Guardia Civil of Salamanca was summoned to fish him out. Such is the character of Castile.

Today's autonomous community of Castile-León, the result of the reorganization of the map of Spain following the death of Generalísimo Francisco Franco, encompasses the former kingdom of León and the northern half of the former kingdom of Castile. In all, it comprises 9 provinces: Zamora, León, and Salamanca, which correspond to the former kingdom of León, plus Palencia, Valladolid, Avila, Burgos, Segovia, and Soria, which correspond to the northern half of the former kingdom of Castile. The latter also conforms roughly to the historic region known as Old Castile, or Castilla la Vieja. (The autonomous community of Castile–La Mancha is the latter-day version of the historic region of New Castile, or Castilla la Nueva.)

Before León and Castile joined forces against the Moors early in the 13th century, they had already enjoyed an on-again, off-again arrangement as far as their autonomy was concerned, since the kingdom of León had once before been united with Castile, from 1037 to 1157, and then become independent again until the final reunion in 1230. But after the Reconquest, jockeying for position in the larger entity of a newly unified Spanish kingdom created regional rifts that linger today. There is token resistance, for instance, to the tandem nature of the recently constituted autonomous community of Castile-León. Sporadic graffiti spied in the provinces of León at times crosses out the Spanish name "Castilla" in expressing a desire for independent status, or suggests León get top billing by transposing the names. Throughout the provinces of Castile, on the other hand, the name "León" occasionally is deleted with equally chauvinistic zeal.

At the dawn of the 16th century, with Spain at the height of its power, Castile composed more than half of the Iberian Peninsula, extending from the Pyrenees to Gibraltar. But with the decline of Spain that took place after the defeat of its "Invincible Armada" came the decline of Castile, and the 18th century saw a steady emigration deplete the populations of its most prosperous cities and towns by as much as one-half. Today's autonomous community of Castile-León makes up about one-fifth of modern-day Spain, yet its population barely tops 2,500,000. It remains largely a region of wheat and corn fields, vegetable patches, and dairy and sheep farms, although it is not immune to changes mandated by Common Market membership and the subsequent progress that is sweeping through the peninsula. Still, habits die hard, and customs of vocation, craft, and sentimental allegiance are slow to change. Donkeys are still a common beast of burden, daily masses still draw appreciable numbers of parishioners to local churches, and in scattered villages pottery is still made as it has been for centuries — by women sitting at potter's wheels in the backs of family barns.

A certain cultural and culinary unity binds the nine provinces of Castile-León. This is *la tierra de asados,* the land of roasts — especially lamb and pork. And although the region is at a significant remove from the sea, its rivers provide fine tench, trout, and *ancas de rana* (frogs' legs). Chickpeas, lentils, and assorted varieties of broad beans are the prime ingredients of some tasty, rib-sticking regional stews. A prime hunting ground, this region is also noted for its *liebre* (hare), *codorniz* (quail), *pichón* (pigeon), and *perdiz* (partridge).

Among the favored desserts are *leche frita* (fried milk), *almendrados* (almond paste), and *yemas de Santa Teresa* (candied egg yolks).

Castile-León also produces one of the widest ranges of wines in all of Spain — from the robust reds of Toro to the delicate whites of Rueda. With over 50,000 acres devoted to the grape, the region is third within Spain in terms of area planted in vines, and seventh in terms of production. Among the 13 noteworthy wine growing areas in the region, Ribera del Duero, Rueda, and Toro have achieved "Denomination of Origin" status (the equivalent of the French *appelation*). The remaining vinicultural areas are Benavente, Cebreros, Cigales, El Bierzo, Fermoselle, La Ribera del Arlanza, La Ribera del Cea, La Ribera de Salamanca, La Sierra de Salamanca, and Valdevimbre–Los Oteros.

Hunting of both big and small game is a popular sport in this landscape of vast cultivated plains interspersed with occasional mountains and forests. Perhaps most prized among small game is the red partridge, abundant in the provinces of Zamora, Salamanca, Valladolid, Avila, Segovia, Burgos, and Soria. The cereal growing areas of León and Zamora, and the provinces of Palencia, Valladolid, Burgos, Soria, Avila, and Segovia, are prime quail turf, and hare and rabbit abound throughout the region. Among big game, roe deer and boar are readily found in the provinces of Burgos and Soria. The *capra hispánica* (mountain goat), a unique national treasure and prized hunting trophy, is also indigenous to the region; and organized expeditions led by experienced guides provide the greatest assurance of success.

Architecturally, Castile-León is primarily fluent in the Romanesque, Gothic, and Mudéjar vernaculars, which achieve their finest expressions in a profusion of cathedrals, castles, and palaces. Castile derives its name from the abundance of castles that guarded its numerous feudal interests during the Middle Ages. Given the ravages of time and man, however, these structures are notably scarce along the 500-mile (800-km) route described below. The itinerary stays mainly along the plain of what was Castilla la Vieja (Old Castile), before the recent division of Spanish territory into autonomous communities. A stern and sober land, Castile-León demands of visitors a certain immunity to scenic monotony and to a lack of scenic definition. For here the earth is often the color of golden sand — as are the houses and churches that loom infrequently against the blur of a horizon smudged with a golden dust. But that is after the harvest, when the land is spent. In the spring, when the wheat and corn are green, and the fields rich with the promise of succulent vegetables, the scenery becomes less lunar and more lush.

Throughout Castile-León, hotels charging $65 and above for a double room with private bath are classified as expensive, $40 to $65 as moderate, and less than $30, inexpensive. Dinner for two with wine will cost $65 and up in an expensive restaurant, $40 to $65 in a moderate restaurant, and under $35 in an inexpensive one.

The following journey into the Spanish heartland begins in Madrid, which is geographically separated from Castile-León by the Sierra de Guadarrama. For a full report on Madrid, its sights, hotels, and restaurants, see *Madrid,* THE CITIES.

En Route from Madrid – As a point of reference, begin at the Plaza de Cibeles in the heart of Madrid and follow the Gran Vía and its extension, Calle Princesa, out past Moncloa until it becomes the N-VI highway at the edge of the city. Eager suburban development in recent years has blurred the former sharp demarcation between city and country, and nowadays the transition is marked by gradually decreasing numbers of billboards and housing developments as the distant mountains approach.

From Madrid to Avila, via N-VI and C505, is a distance of 69 miles (110 km). Take C505, which branches off from N-VI about 10 miles (16 km) northwest of Plaza de Cibeles. At this point, the city has been left behind, and after crossing a big bridge over the very small Río Guadarrama, the road becomes more rurally curvaceous. After another 11 miles (18 km), just before the bridge crossing the Embalse de Valmayor (Valmayor Reservoir), there is a glimpse of Philip II's palace-monastery of El Escorial straight ahead. The massive yellow walls and crowning cupolas of this eminently conspicuous construction are the architectural manifestation of Philip's own proud, pious, and tormented soul. For the next few miles, his imposing monument ducks in and out of sight, looming ever larger and more insistent until the traveler makes the turn to explore its austere, lugubrious charms. The turnoff occurs 4½ miles (7 km) beyond the reservoir, when the road splits, veering right for San Lorenzo de El Escorial, the village that abuts the palace-monastery, and left for Avila and El Escorial itself (follow signs for "Monasterio de El Escorial," not just for "El Escorial"). About half a mile (1 km) farther on, C505 turns left to Avila, while C600 goes straight for a little over a mile (2 km) to the El Escorial parking lot.

Philip built the monastery-palace in thanksgiving for his victory over the French in Flanders in 1557. Construction went on for 21 years, from 1563 to 1584 — record time for such an extensive edifice — and from 1584 to his death in 1598, this was the isolated residence from which the ascetic king ruled the vast Spanish Empire. The monastery-palace stands in eloquent testimony to the acute religious mania that clouded Philip's mind during his later years, and the combination of truly royal grandeur with austerity evident here is unique. His small, monastic chambers in the Palacios (Royal Apartments) are in stark contrast to the splendor of the rest of the structure. It was here that Philip learned of the defeat of the Armada; and in the adjoining bedroom, where a window overlooks the high altar of the monastery's grandiose, cross-shaped church, that he died. The monastery also houses the Panteón de los Reyes (Royal Pantheon), which contains the remains of 26 Spanish monarchs (all but Philip V and Ferdinand VI), and the *Nuevos Museos* (New Museums), complete with works by Ribera, Velázquez, and El Greco. The Escorial complex (phone: 1-890-5903) is open Tuesdays through Sundays, from 10 AM to 1:30 PM and 3:15 to 6 PM; admission charge. For further details, see *Madrid Region*, DIRECTIONS.

Head with care back to C505, en route to Avila. (Although well marked approaching El Escorial, the way out of town is not clearly signposted.) The road offers a good view of the towering monastery to the right, then continues to Avila amid mountains that were only a hazy mirage from Madrid, bald mountains with sporadic tufts of trees and assorted evergreens. Ahead, a large sign marks the border of Castile-León, and in particular, the province of Avila; then the road gradually ascends the Castilian plateau to Spain's highest provincial capital (3,600 feet), which appears after the crest of a hill. Follow the Centro Urbano or Centro Ciudad signs into the city.

AVILA: Built on the banks of the Adaja River, Avila is a city whose historical center is surrounded by remarkably well preserved rectangular walls that are most dramatic when viewed in silhouette against the surrounding Castilian plain. To the southwest, the wall divides Avila from an expanse of undeveloped land, but to the northeast, it has failed to contain the city, which has grown beyond its medieval boundaries to a current population of just over 43,000. Construction of the wall began in 1090; it took 10 years and more than 2,000 workers to complete 90 semicircular towers, 9 gates, several posterns, and innumerable battlements along an 8,200-foot perimeter. The result still looks astonishingly new, and many sections of the city that are built up against the wall have an unfinished feel about them. In fact, much of the city seems unfinished — even the modern areas that have leap-frogged the wall, possibly because of the unadorned bluntness of the architecture combined with Avila's elevated vantage point upon a rather bleak, barren *meseta*.

As the birthplace and religious training ground of the famous Santa Teresa de Jesús de Avila, commonly known as St. Teresa, a Carmelite nun who founded a reformed order of Carmelites, the Barefoot (or Discalced) Carmelites, Avila has played a strong spiritual role in the evolution of both Castile and Spain. Born in 1515 in what is now the Convento de Santa Teresa (Plaza de la Santa; open daily, 8 AM to 1 PM and 3:30 to 9 PM; no admission charge), St. Teresa took her vows and had the spiritual experiences that paved the way for her canonization in the Monasterio de la Encarnación (Plaza de la Encarnación; open daily, 9:30 AM to 1 PM and 4 to 6 PM; admission charge). Nearby, in the Convento de San José, or Convento de las Madres (Calle del Duque; open daily, from 10 AM to 1 PM and 4 to 7 PM; admission charge) — the first Convent of the Barefoot Carmelite order — St. Teresa first put her religious principles into practice in a place of her own.

Though St. Teresa is not the only reason to visit the town, Avila's other noted sights are also religious in nature. Just inside the Puerta de los Leales is the starkly rectilinear, 12th-century stone cathedral, a structure that is building-block plain, except for an incongruous inset of ornately carved excess above the multi-arched Gothic entrance. Forming part of the old wall, the cathedral had a military raison d'être, and it shows. Comic relief is at hand, however, in the sets of carved lions surrounding the plaza, their haunches protruding prominently beyond their supporting pedestals. Inside the cathedral are three aisles and a central choir. The museum, housed in the 15th-century Capilla del Cardenal, contains hymnal tomes from the 15th century; silk-embroidered, gold- and lace-adorned garments of the 18th century; a 5-foot tall, 16th-century silver Custodia del Corpus that is paraded through the streets every *Corpus Christi Day* and looks very much like an overgrown, 6-tiered wedding cake ornament; a carved wooden coffin containing the remains of San Segundo, Avila's first archbishop; and a 16th-century Ecce Homo. Just inside the cathedral entrance, the bronze statue of San Pedro is kept shiny at the knees, nose, and hands by the faithful hoping that good fortune will rub off on them. The cathedral is open daily, May through September, 8 AM to 1 PM and 3 to 7 PM; October through April, 10 AM to 1:30 PM and 3 to 7 PM. The museum is open daily, May through September, 10 AM to 1:30 PM and 3 to 7 PM; October through April, 10 AM to 1:30 PM and 3 to 5 PM. Admission charge to the museum. Across the square from the cathedral is the town's tourist office, 4 Plaza de la Catedral (phone: 18-211387).

Avila's Romanesque Iglesia de San Vicente (open daily, 10 AM to 1 PM and 4 to 6 PM; admission charge) is just outside the walls on the northeast, through the Puerta de San Vicente. Built between the 12th and 14th centuries, it has an arched loggia of gray stone that clashes in tone and tenor with the amber blocks of the main structure. The main attraction inside is the Sepulcro de los Niños Mártires, recalling the church's founding legend, which holds that three young siblings were martyred on this spot. Of a more welcoming nature is the Iglesia de San Pedro (open daily, 10 AM to 1 PM and 4 to 6 PM), begun in 1100 as a Romanesque structure and later fitted with Gothic flourishes. Situated outside the walls opposite the Puerta del Alcázar at the far end of the Plaza de Santa Teresa, it contains — since Pope John Paul II's 1983 visit — a mounted "chapel" honoring the "Virgin of Czestochowa, Queen of Poland." The Monasterio de Santo Tomás, on Plaza de Granada, once isolated from the city proper, now stands at the very edge of Avila's urban expansion. Its checkered past includes use as the headquarters of the Inquisition (Tomás de Torquemada, the inquisitor general, lived here), a turn as the summer palace of Ferdinand and Isabella, and an interlude as the seat of a university. The final resting place of Ferdinand and Isabella's son, Prince Juan, today it continues as a Dominican monastery complete with church, cloisters, and choir, as well as an Oriental art gallery in the former royal apartments. The complex is open daily, from 10:30 AM to 1 PM and 4 to 7 PM. Admission charge to the cloister, through which the complex is entered; additional charge for the art gallery.

CHECKING IN: *Palacio de Valderrábanos* – Built as a palatial home by the family of the same name late in the 14th century. Diagonally across from the cathedral, it offers 73 rooms, all with private baths, and 3 suites, one of which is romantically situated in the tower. Lamps with cloth shades and skirted chairs impart a cozy, country feeling. The restaurant, *El Fogón de Santa Teresa,* serves traditional Castilian dishes. 9 Plaza de la Catedral, Avila (phone: 18-211023). Expensive.

Parador Raimundo de Borgoña – One of the state-run *paradores,* it incorporates the Palacio de Benavides, also known as the Palacio de Piedras Albas, built during the late 15th century. Abutting the northern walls, its 62 rooms (12 of which are of palace vintage) all have private baths. The hostelry's gardens are next to walkways on top of the city walls that offer choice views of Avila and the *meseta* beyond. Local delicacies such as roast suckling pig, as well as more generic Spanish dishes (gazpacho, *truchas fritas con jamón serrano,* or fried trout with smoked ham), are served in the dining room. 16 Calle Marqués de Canales y Chozas, Avila (phone: 18-211340). Expensive.

Rey Niño – Built in 1840 as a hotel, it is near the cathedral and has has 24 rooms that are structurally romantic but spare of furnishings. All is clean, and the plumbing is modern. 1 Plaza de José Tomé, Avila (phone: 18-211404). Moderate.

EATING OUT: *Mesón del Rastro* – Castilian cuisine featuring *truchas del Tormes* (trout from the Tormes River) and *mollejas de ternera* (veal sweetbreads), served in a rustic decor. Reservations unnecessary. 1 Plaza del Rastro, Avila (phone: 18-211219). Moderate.

En Route from Avila – Leaving town by the western gate, cross over the Adaja River and follow the signs for N501 and Salamanca. One-half mile (1 km) on, there is a fine panoramic view of Avila at Cuatro Postes, a spot marked by four concrete posts with a cross in the center. The N501 highway covers the entire 61-mile (98-km) distance to Salamanca, passing a scenic potpourri of broad fields marked by rock walls, sporadic outcroppings, occasional outbursts of trees and scrub, wheat fields, grazing sheep, and stands of sunflowers. Here and there, the *meseta* slopes down on either side of the road, giving the impression that the world drops off beyond the dust-hazy horizon. Suddenly, without fanfare, Salamanca materializes in spired splendor to the right.

SALAMANCA: For a complete report on the city and its sights, hotels, and restaurants, see *Salamanca,* THE CITIES.

En Route from Salamanca – The N630 highway from Salamanca to Zamora stretches north for 39 rather unscenic miles (62 km), crossing the border into the province of Zamora about halfway along the route. On the outskirts of town, avoid following the signposts to Zamora Este; continue straight on N630, bear right, and follow the signs for Centro Ciudad.

ZAMORA: A 13th-century Romanesque bridge over the Duero River marks the historic center of Zamora, which rises 2,000 feet on the river's right bank. This is the city where El Cid spent part of his youth and was reportedly knighted. Its most outstanding feature is the cathedral (Plaza del Castillo); built during the 12th century with a few later additions, it has a great dome decorated in a curious Byzantine scalloped pattern. The cathedral museum contains an unsurpassed collection of tapestries, yet another example of the numerous hidden treasures Spain offers to those willing to stray off the beaten track. The ten tapestries on the upper floor are the most splendid, the largest measuring 30 feet in length. Exquisite for their vibrant colors, scrupulous detail, and expert three-dimensional illusion, these 15th-century Flemish masterpieces depict Greek mythological scenes. The remaining, 17th-century tapestries of Hannibal are smaller and would be more impressive than they appear here, if displayed separately. The museum is open daily, 11 AM to 2 PM and 4 to 8 PM, though times are unpredictable. (Out of season, the museum door is closed while the cashier-guide shows small groups around, so wait for the tour to end.) Admission charge. A fine view of the Duero River and the Romanesque bridge that spans it can be appreciated from the Puerta del Obispo, an arched gateway in the city wall behind the cathedral.

A favorite excursion from Zamora is to Pereruela, a small village with a few hundred inhabitants 10 miles (16 km) southwest of town via C527. A handful of families here still make fine ceramic cookware by hand; visitors can see the clay being sculpted and ovens being fired out back by the family barns. Although there are no shops, the goods can be purchased from the source, or from family members displaying their wares along the road.

CHECKING IN: *Parador Condes de Alba y Aliste* – Installed in the former 15th-century palace of the Count of Alba y Aliste in the city's historic core, this beautiful *parador* offers 27 double rooms with private bath on the second floor of a Renaissance cloister. The property is endowed with a bar, a restaurant, gardens, and a swimming pool. Plaza de Cánovas, Zamora (phone: 88-514497). Expensive.

***Dos Infantas* –** Very pleasant, comfortable, and central, with 68 rooms, 5 of which are a tub shy of a complete bath. 3 Cortinas de San Miguel, Zamora (phone: 88-532875). Moderate.

EATING OUT: *París* – An elegant and intimate continental atmosphere accompanies a menu featuring the traditional Castilian *ancas de rana* (frogs' legs) and roast lamb, along with offbeat entries such as fresh vegetable pie and *rodaballo* (turbot) with spinach sauce. Open daily. Reservations advised. 14 Avenida Portugal, Zamora (phone: 88-514325). Expensive.

***Serafín* –** Seafood is the specialty here, along with traditional Castilian and Zamoran fare. Open daily. Reservations advised. 10 Plaza Maestro Haedo, Zamora (phone: 88-531422). Expensive.

***La Posada* –** Quiet and refined, with local specialties including *mollejas a la zamorana* (sweetbreads in a spicy red sauce) and *lentejas* (lentil soup with garlic-spiced sausage and potato). Closed July 1–15. Reservations advised. 2 Calle Benavente, Zamora (phone: 88-516474). Moderate.

En Route from Zamora – There are two ways to reach Benavente. If time is short, take N630 about 37 miles (60 km) north, then follow the Benavente signs to the N-VI highway, which leads to the turnoff for the center of town, another 5 miles (8 km) away from N630.

If time permits, however, take the longer route (a total of 69 miles/110 km), via the town of Toro, which is 20½ miles (33 km) due east of Zamora. Leave Zamora on N122, a road that parallels the Duero River. About halfway to Toro, the *meseta* stretches expansively into the distance on the right, with the Duero marking the boundary between the Tierra del Pan (Land of Bread) to the north and the Tierra del Vino (Land of Wine) to the south. Besides recently having its wine accorded *denominación* (appellation) status, Toro enjoys some historic and artistic distinctions. During the Second Punic War, Hannibal passed through the town; and during the early centuries of the Reconquest, Toro was a frequent battleground between Christian and Muslim forces. The peripatetic St. Teresa also established a convent here; and the Inquisition, one of its cruel tribunals. Follow the signs for Centro Ciudad, and the service road into town. The center is reached through either of two arched gateways. The first is the Puerta de Corredera (Sliding Gate), which leads straight beneath the arch of the 18th-century Torre del Reloj (Clock Tower), past the Plaza de España, and on to the town's main sight, the Church of Santa María la Mayor. The second gateway, Puerta Santa Catalina, is near the tourist information kiosk and a stone statue of an Iberian pig in the center of a small traffic circle. Passing through this gate, follow the street into the Plaza de España and turn left to the church.

The Colegiata de Santa María la Mayor, Toro's highlight, is a 12th-century Romanesque collegiate church (open daily, May through August, 10:30 AM to 1:30 PM and 5 to 7 PM; September through April, noon to 1 PM and 7 to 8 PM — but hours are erratic, and if a guide is not on duty, ask for the priest in charge, who will gladly open the church). The western door, the Puerta de la Majestad, where guided tours begin, is crowned by seven pointed arches and compares favorably with the famed Pórtico de Gloria in Santiago de Compostela's cathedral. The sacristy contains several treasures, among them the well-known Virgen de la Mosca (Virgin of the Fly) — so named because of the fly on her knee — painted by Fernando Gallego. Also notice, in the church itself, the unusual 14th-century statue of a pregnant Virgin, one of a very few in Spain.

The 12th-to-13th-century Romanesque-Mudéjar Church of San Lorenzo is another church worth visiting. Sweet and simple, it has a wonderful altar by Fernando Gallego, Plateresque tombs, and a beautiful polychrome mezzanine sagging with the weight of centuries. If the church is locked, ask someone at the tourist information kiosk to open it, but bear in mind that the presence of the tourist board staff is unpredictable.

Leaving Toro through the Puerta Santa Catalina, take N122 west, back toward Zamora, but turn right almost immediately at the sign indicating the road to Pozoantiguo and Castronuevo. After crossing the Valderaduey River and exiting Castronuevo, turn left onto ZA702 toward Villarrín de Campos, some 7½ miles (12 km) away. This entire route crosses the flat wheat fields that earned the area the epithet Tierra del Pan (Land of Bread). Pass Villarrín de Campos and head toward Estación de la Tabla, a mere scattering of warehouses and a granary, then continue on ZA701 toward Granja de Moreruela. This will lead to the right turn back onto N630 toward Benavente.

 EATING OUT: *Catayo* – A typical village tavern just off the Plaza de España, serving home-style meals at home-style prices and offering a selection of regional wines from the newly established *denominación* Toro. Open daily. No reservations. 7 Calle José María Cid, Toro (phone: 88-690060). Inexpensive.

BENAVENTE: Situated on a promontory near the confluence of the Orbigo and Esla rivers, this town of 13,000 inhabitants offers a stunning view of the Castilian plain to the south and west. Santa María del Azoque, a 12th-century church of very irregular construction, is one of two special sights in town — be sure to walk around it to appreciate the kaleidoscopic effect of its diverse architectural elements. Most striking in its interior are three slender Gothic naves with precisely pointed arches. Open for mass at 9 AM and 7 PM daily, and more frequently on Sundays, the church is best visited just before or after the service.

The town's other special sight is the *Parador Fernando II de León,* on Paseo Ramón y Cajal (see below). Built on the elevated site of the former 12th-century castle-palace of the Counts and Dukes of Benavente, it incorporates a well-preserved, 16th-century Gothic-Renaissance tower that was part of that noble complex. Inside, two engravings of the castle in its heyday and an 1880 photo of it in ruins are on display. Installed in the vestigial tower are a lovely salon and, below that, an impressive bar (open 5 to 11:30 PM) with a new wooden ceiling and rusty chandelier that are remarkable imitations of antiques. Watching the sun set though the bar's oversized windows is a rare treat.

CHECKING IN/EATING OUT: *Parador Fernando II de León* – This lovely *parador* offers 28 double rooms and 2 singles, all with private bath, and many with terraces offering splendid views. The dining room menu features such provincial dishes as *arroz a la zamorana* (rice Zamora-style — a kind of peasant paella with tripe, pig's ear, pig's knuckles, and *chorizo* sausage in a red sauce), as well as sweetbreads with prawns, and more of the town's fine panorama. Paseo Ramón y Cajal, Benavente (phone: 88-630300). Expensive.

En Route from Benavente – León lies 44½ miles (71 km) north of Benavente via N630. Coming into town, follow the Centro Ciudad signs, cross over the Bernesga River, then turn left and follow the tree-lined boulevard that parallels the river all the way to the *Parador San Marcos.*

LEÓN: This provincial capital traces its origins back to the mid-1st century, when the Romans built a fortification at the confluence of the Bernesga and Torió rivers. Its most remarkable structure is the cathedral, built during the 13th and 14th centuries. One of the most beautiful ever built, it was modeled after the cathedrals at Reims and Amiens in France, and is an exquisite example of Spanish Gothic architecture. Its crowning glory lies not in its stonework, but in its over 16,000 square feet of stained glass,the most dazzling display in Spain. Almost hallucinatory in their effect, the windows, which date from every century since the cathedral's birth, depict religious scenes from the lives of Christ, the Virgin Mary, and the saints, as well as purely ornamental motifs. In a country brimming with stunning cathedrals, the colored shafts of light that slice through the stone-gray gloom here make León's among the most memorable in the land. Its museum, too, stands out for its commendable collections of Roman bronze figures and weapons, neolithic artifacts, and Romanesque statues; also of interest is the exhibit of vintage sketches referred to in the restoration of many of the cathedral's stained glass treasures. The cathedral is open daily, from 8:30 AM to 1:30 PM and 4 to 7 PM. The museum is open daily, May through August, from 10 AM to 1:30 PM and 4 to 6:30 PM; September through April, from 10 AM to 1:30 PM and 4 to 7:30 PM. Admission charge to the museum.

About a 10-minute walk from the cathedral is another important León sight, the Romanesque basilica of San Isidoro, a hybrid house of God born during the 11th century, adorned and cloistered during the 12th, and partially reconstructed and enlarged during the 16th. Regrettably, the later remodeling obliterated much of the original Romanesque, but the basilica's pantheon remains one of the earliest examples of the Romanesque architectural genre in Spain. Here, 22 kings and queens of the old kingdom of León are buried beneath 12th-century frescoes that have prompted many to refer to this as the "Sistine Chapel" of Romanesque art; the pantheon can also boast capitals and a portal carved with scenes from the gospel, the earliest in Spain to be so decorated. A separate room houses the treasury, complete with illuminated Bibles and other fine relics. The church is open daily, 7 AM to midnight. The pantheon is open daily, May through August, 9 AM to 2 PM and 3:30 to 8 PM; September through April, 10 AM to 1:30 PM and 4 to 6:30 PM. There is an admission charge to the pantheon and treasury, which are seen on tours conducted by multilingual guides.

A third important monument in León, the *Parador San Marcos* (see *Checking In*), is located along the river and built in the Renaissance style. One of León's liveliest and loveliest landmarks, this was formerly the Monasterio de San Marcos, which was donated to the Order of Santiago by the Catholic Monarchs in appreciation of services rendered during the Reconquest. The monastery then became a hospital for pilgrims en route to Santiago de Compostela. During the Renaissance, it blossomed to its present sumptuousness; the *parador* now shares the grounds of the original monastery with the *Provincial Archaeological Museum,* which contains items from the Stone Age to the Renaissance. The adjacent Gothic church with its ornately carved choir stalls was a 16th-century addition. The museum is open daily, from 10 AM to noon and 4 to 6 PM; admission charge.

All of the above sights of León are in the Old Town, which is surrounded by a modern city of high-rises, and which has itself been substantially rebuilt, although its streets still follow the old twists and turns. The tourist office (4 Plaza de Regla; phone: 87-237082) is just across from the cathedral. Not far away is the Plaza Mayor, surrounded by porticoes and, on most days, alive with a market selling fruits and vegetables.

CHECKING IN: *Parador San Marcos* – One of the most impressive hostelries in the country, in a converted 16th-century monastery that also hosted pilgrims on their way to Santiago, it has 245 majestic double rooms and 7 suites. Most are in a newly built section, but 30 ample rooms in the old structure have vintage decorations. The rooms in the modern addition, as well as the lobby, open onto the monastery's original cloister. The hotel has a fine restaurant. 7 Plaza San Marcos, León (phone: 87-237300). Expensive.

Quindós – This very comfortable hotel has 96 rooms, each with private bath, direct-dial telephone, and a color television set. Centrally located, only 2 blocks from the *parador,* with a public video salon and a restaurant. 24 Avenida José Antonio, León (phone: 87-236200). Moderate.

Riosol – Functional and comfortable following recent renovations, it has 139 rooms with private baths, direct-dial telephones, and color television sets. This place is across the river from the other hotels. 3 Avenida de Palencia, León (phone: 87-216850). Moderate.

Don Suero – On the street that runs from San Isidoro to the *parador,* it has over 100 rooms with varying in-room bath facilities; all very clean. 15 Calle Suero de Quiñones, León (phone: 87-230600). Inexpensive.

EATING OUT: *Adonías* – The decor features a distinguished collection of Spanish ceramics, and the same emphasis on quality is present in both the food and the service. Run by the brother of the owner of *Casa Pozo* (below). Closed Sundays and 3 weeks in July. Reservations advised. 16 Calle Santa Nonia, León (phone: 87-252665 or 87-206768). Moderate.

Casa Pozo – From the coarse peasant bread (delicious!) to the homemade desserts, this is a fine restaurant with service to match; it also boasts an extensive selection of rioja wines. Closed Sundays, the first half of July, and December 23 through January 7. Reservations unnecessary. 15 Plaza San Marcelo, León (phone: 87-237103). Moderate.

El Racim de Oro – Just off the Plaza San Martín in a 17th-century mansion, this restaurant serves dishes made from good local produce. Walk past the bar and upstairs to the beautiful rustic dining room. Closed Sunday evenings and Tuesdays. No reservations. 2 Calle Caño Vadillo, León (phone: 87-257575). Moderate.

En Route from León – It is 80 miles (128 km) from León southeast to Palencia via N601 and N610, the latter of which veers off to the left about 42 miles (67 km) into the route at Becilla de Valderaduey.

PALENCIA: Located on the left bank of the Carrión River, Palencia was once a capital of the *vacceos,* a Celtic tribe. Construction of its cathedral spanned 2 centuries (14th to 16th) and took place on the site of a 7th-century Visigothic basilica dedicated to San Antolín, the city's patron saint. This earlier basilica, marked by three arches and a single rectangular Romanesque nave, has become the crypt of the present church and is accessible via a Plateresque stairway. The cathedral museum (admission charge) contains a painting of *San Sebastián* by El Greco, a small sampling of Romanesque statues, and some 15th-century tapestries. Stop in at the Palencia Tourist Office (105 Calle Mayor; phone: 88-720068) for information on other sights in town, which include the Iglesia de San Miguel, where, according to legend, El Cid married Doña Jimena. Its crenelated tower makes it look more like a fortress than a church.

CHECKING IN: *Castilla la Vieja* – Not far from the Plaza Mayor, this place offers all the usual facilities in its 87 rooms, plus a restaurant. 26 Avenida Casado del Alisal, Palencia (phone: 88-749044). Moderate.

Monclus – Smaller (40 rooms) and less endowed than the *Castilla la Vieja,* but still clean and comfortable; near the Plaza Mayor. 3 Calle Menéndez Pelayo, Palencia (phone: 88-744300). Moderate.

EATING OUT: *Casa Damián* – Featuring Castilian classics and fine duero wines. Closed Mondays and July 25 through August 25. Reservations necessary. 9 Calle Martínez de Azcoitia, Palencia (phone: 88-744628). Expensive.

Mesón del Concejo – Traditional Castilian fare is served; *chuleta de cervera* (veal cutlet from free-range calves) is a specialty. Open daily. Reservations unnecessary. 5 Calle Martínez de Azcoitia, Palencia (phone: 88-743239). Moderate.

En Route from Palencia – Valladolid is 29½ miles (47 km) south via N611 and N620. Here the Castilian *meseta* is at its harshest and most alienating. An ambitious irrigation project may soon alleviate some of the dry, dusty monotony, however. Along the way, 9 miles (14 km) south of Palencia, at Baños de Cerrato — near the railway junction of Venta de Baños — is what is reputed to be the oldest church in Spain, the Basílica de San Juan Bautista, built in 661 by the Visigoths.

VALLADOLID: A former capital of Spain, this is where the Catholic Monarchs were married in 1469, where Columbus died in 1506, and where Philip II was born in 1527. For those willing to fight the traffic and battle the lack of coherent signs in this rather unattractive and fairly large (330,000 inhabitants) city, there are several sights worthy of attention. The 15th-century Colegio de San Gregorio (Cadenas de San Gregorio) is noted for its façade, a masterpiece of the Isabeline style, and for its courtyard, wonderfully Plateresque, but above all as the home of one of Spain's most important museums, the *Museo Nacional de Escultura Policromada* (phone: 83-250375). A repository of the types of polychrome wooden sculptures seen in churches all over the country, the museum includes works from the 13th through the 17th centuries. But it is particularly strong in sculptures by Castilian masters of the Renaissance, including Alonso Berruguete, Diego de Siloé, and Juan de Juni, as well as by the later sculptor Gregorio

Fernández (open Tuesdays through Saturdays, from 9 AM to 2 PM and 4 to 6 PM; admission charge). The adjacent 15th-century Iglesia de San Pablo (Plaza de San Pablo, open daily, from 9 AM to 1 PM and 4 to 6 PM) is also worthy of note, above all for the ornate façade, its lower level a Gothic design carved by Simon of Cologne, its upper reaches Plateresque. Valladolid's cathedral was designed in the late 16th century by Juan de Herrera, of El Escorial fame, but it was finished much later, according to plans by Alberto Churriguera — note that the upper part of the façade is baroque. The *Museo Oriental,* located in the basement of the Real Colegio Padres Agustinos Filipinos (7 Paseo Filipinos), houses the best collection of Asian art in Spain, consisting, not surprisingly, mainly of works from the Philippines and China (open Mondays through Saturdays, from 4 to 7 PM; Sundays, 10 AM to 2 PM; admission charge). Valladolid's Tourist Office is at 3 Plaza de Zorrilla (phone: 83-351801).

En Route from Valladolid – The itinerary continues southeast on N601 via Cuellár, to Segovia and back to Madrid. For those not in a hurry, however, a detour of 37½ miles (60 km) round-trip southwest from Valladolid will lead to the small town of Tordesillas, perched some 7,000 feet above the Duero River. A typical Castilian *pueblo* and the place where Juana la Loca, mother of Philip II, was imprisoned until her death, Tordesillas was also the spot where the Spanish and Portuguese met in 1494 to sign the Treaty of Tordesillas, which divided the New World in two, giving all lands west of a line to Spain and all lands east to Portugal, a decision that ultimately resulted in Spanish-speaking Latin America and Portuguese-speaking Brazil. Of less import beyond the confines of Iberia, Tordesillas was also the headquarters of the 16th-century Comuneros revolt. Besides a somewhat austerely attractive Plaza Mayor, the Church of San Antolín is worth a visit if only for the vista of the Duero and the medieval bridge that leads into town. The church museum houses the *Inmaculada* by Pedro de Mena, and an almost life-size representation of the Holy Family attributed to Gregorio Fernández. The palace-cum-monastery known as Santa Clara is a fine example of Mudéjar architecture, with a beautiful Arabic patio — a rarity in these parts. Both are closed Mondays.

Return to Valladolid and pick up the N601 highway south to Segovia. Along the 31-mile (50-km) stretch from Valladolid to the town of Cuellár, the terrain begins to roll a bit, and welcome hills appear near Santiago del Arroyo. Here and there, too, mesas jut into the horizon, providing scenic pegs upon which to fix one's gaze. Just before Cuellár, the route passes into the province of Segovia.

CHECKING IN/EATING OUT: *Parador de Tordesillas* – A modern structure barely half a mile from the center of town, this hostelry has 73 rooms, a bar, garden, and swimming pool. Like other *paradores,* its restaurant is of dependable quality and offers a mixture of regional and national dishes and wines. Carretera Salamanca, Km 152, Tordesillas (phone: 83-770051). Expensive.

CUELLÁR: From the crown of a hill, Cuellár commands an ample panorama, especially from just outside the walls of its 15th-century castle; now home to a school, the castle courtyard can be visited only if it happens to be open (there is no posted schedule).

EATING OUT: *El Rincón Castellano* – Tucked away in a corner of the Plaza Mayor, this cozy restaurant has lots of Castilian charm to complement its fine home-style cooking, featuring the typical Castilian roast baby lamb, tasty *mollejas lechazo* (lamb sweetbreads sautéed with garlic and oil), and an ample *ensalada mesonero* (mixed salad with tuna, eggs, and olives). Open daily. No reservations. 13 Plaza Mayor, Cuellár (phone: 11-141031). Moderate.

En Route from Cuellár – Stands of trees become more frequent along N601 south toward Segovia, 37½ miles (60 km) away. A little more than halfway there, the vague silhouette of the Sierra de Guadarrama appears in the distance. The entrance into Segovia is dramatic — the cathedral dominates the crest of a hill and the fairy-tale Alcázar perches at the extreme right (western) edge of town.

SEGOVIA: For a detailed report on Segovia and its sights, hotels, and restaurants, see *Segovia,* THE CITIES.

En Route from Segovia – The 55-mile (88-km) stretch of road between Segovia and Madrid via N601 (sometimes posted as CL601) winds through the pines of the scenic Sierra de Guadarrama, where many *madrileños* spend their weekends and the better part of the summer school holidays. Here, too, in the winter they come to ski the slopes around Navacerrada. Puerto de Navacerrada, the mountain pass 17½ miles (28 km) beyond Segovia, is 6,000 feet above sea level and marks the border between the province of Segovia and the Comunidad de Madrid. Several miles beyond the mountain-ringed Embalse de Navacerrada at Villalba, the A6 highway veers off to the left for Madrid, becoming the N-VI highway about 5 miles (8 km) before reaching the capital.

North Atlantic Coast

The Romans could never fully conquer the area, the Visigoths were plagued by perpetual uprisings, the Moors suffered their first setback here as they tried to sweep across the Iberian Peninsula in the 8th century — and the most fearsome plunderers of them all, 20th-century tourists, have so far managed to establish only a handful of beachheads. While the rest of Spain fell under the influence of one marauder after another, the country's northern coast, along the Atlantic Ocean, remained determinedly independent. And for that very reason, it remains truly fascinating.

A Spanish saying has it that "In summer, the rich go south and the wise go north." For south, read constant and often blistering sun, packed beaches, and nonstop flamenco-flavored discotheques. The northern coast, on the other hand, offers thickly forested mountainsides, intensely green hills, and lush valleys and meadows to offset the stormy sea and the wave-battered cliffs. The entire coast from San Sebastián, just 12 miles (19 km) from the French border, to Ribadeo, 272 miles (435 km) to the west, is prone to dampness — from mist and fog, from a fine drizzle called *sirimiri* by the Basques, and from good old-fashioned rain. A filtered light — not the brilliant Castilian sky-blue sunlight seen farther south — glows on this coast. But when the sun shines there are numerous beaches to equal the best of "package-tour Spain" to the south. Many of these beaches are isolated and remote, protected by rugged cliffs, just as this area and its peoples have been throughout history.

Spain's Atlantic coastline edges four traditional regions that have become, in the post-Franco era, four *comunidades autónomas,* or "autonomous communities," and are actually four distinct "countries." Our route covers three of them, ending just inside the fourth. It starts out at San Sebastián, the queen of northern Spain's beach resorts, in the thick of Basque Country, a region known to the Basques themselves as Euskadi, to the rest of Spain as the País Vasco, and to the outside world as the site of 2 decades of political violence in the fight for Basque self-determination. Westward beyond the bustling industrial port of Bilbao, the route leaves the Costa Vasca (Basque Coast) behind and enters Cantabria, the most Spanish of the northern regions, with its attractive coastal capital of Santander. Still farther west, it reaches Asturias, a beautiful, little-visited, emerald-colored region with a coast known, appropriately, as the Costa Verde (Green Coast). It then ends just inside Galicia, another region steeped in history and rich in folklore, which looks and sings like the Irish but speaks like the Portuguese who live to the south. Four languages — Basque (or Euskera), Spanish, Bable (the old Asturian tongue, but barely spoken nowadays), and Gallego, a kind of Spanish-Portuguese — and four peoples.

If the Basques are a mystery to most Spaniards today, they completely stump anthropologists and philologists trying to ascertain the origin of Euskera. It has no apparent linguistic connection with any other language, and nobody knows where the extremely complex tongue came from, but it certainly predates the arrival in Europe of the Indo-European languages some 3,000 years ago. Recent research has tried, with little success, to link Euskera to pre-Indo-European languages such as those still spoken in the Caucasus and among the Berbers of North Africa.

Indeed, there is considerable evidence that the Basques are the last surviving representatives of Europe's aboriginal population. Although the Romans did occupy parts of the Basque region, they had a difficult time of it. Plutarch and others described a poor, warlike people with strong tribal features — which is perhaps why many males from the area were sent to man the Roman garrisons in equally warlike Britain. The Basque Country was the last area of southern and western Europe to be converted to Christianity, and the last region of Europe to construct towns — away from the big cities, many Basques still live in isolated homesteads of fewer than 30 people. In other words, this wild place was one of the last corners of Europe to be civilized.

The Basque homesteads are characteristic flat-roofed, Alpine-style farmhouses known as *caseríos,* where occupants sleep upstairs but share the downstairs with their animals. The Basques' highly individual lifestyle — they were renowned as North Sea whalers until the 18th century, and many of the small fishing ports feature whales on their coats of arms — meant that, much as today, they were little given to central control, especially from outside the region. Not only did this cause potential invaders to give up and leave them alone, but it also meant that they enjoyed a long tradition of great personal liberties at a time when most of Europe lived in serfdom. By the 15th century, these liberties were enshrined in the *fueros,* a body of ancient laws and privileges that the Basques in Spain did not lose until well into the 19th century. A bizarre mystery language, immunity from invasion, life in remote settlements with little or no central government, and the freedoms of the *fueros* all help to explain the current political turmoil, which the visitor cannot fail to recognize when touring the Basque Country, if only because of the abundant street graffiti.

The Basques are the most indomitable of all the Spanish peoples as well as the most fun-loving of those in the north. They enjoy a reputation for being the biggest drinkers and the heartiest eaters in Spain, and for having the best cuisine, whether it's traditional fare or the new Basque cuisine that is all the rage. Basque specialties include such distinctive dishes as *cogote de merluza* (baked hake's head), *kokotxas y almejas* (hake gills and clams in a lemon, oil, and parsley sauce), *angulas* (tiny silvery elvers, or young eels), *bacalao al pil pil* (cod in a Bilbao-style green sauce), *porrusalda* (leek, cod, and potato stew), *marmitako* (fresh tuna, tomato, and potato stew), and *alubias* (beans).

Equally distinctive is the folklore of the region. Rural sports, whose aim is to demonstrate speed and strength rather than skill, are an integral part of the Basque culture. The only Basque sport widely known outside the region is *pelota* (related to jai alai), but others include wood chopping, grass scything, rock dragging by bulls, and ram butting. Any fiesta will include traditional dances such as the *aurreska* — which honors the Basque flag, or *ikurriña* — and the *espatadanza,* or sword dance. They are accompanied by the simple music of the *txistu,* or three-holed tin whistle, and a small drum.

Cantabria is often referred to as the piece of Spain that separates the Basque Country from Asturias. The mountainous green region has taken advantage of this slight slur to push its own identity, an alloy of fiery Castile tempered by the damp influence of the Cantabrian mountains. The earliest evidence of human settlement in Spain, about 25,000 to 30,000 years ago, has been found around Santander, the capital of Cantabria. The culture of these early settlers, who crossed the Pyrenees from southern France, peaked around 15,000 BC, which is approximately the date of the most treasured of several caves with prehistoric paintings in northern Spain — those at Altamira, near Santander.

The Romans found life easier in Cantabria than in the Basque Country, and this is the part of the coast with the most Roman remains, including bridges. Documents show that Santander was a busy port in 1068, and the city received a boost early in the 20th century when King Alfonso XIII made it his summer residence. However, Santander never had sufficient charm to rival San Sebastián, and a devastating fire in 1941 destroyed most of the lower Old Town, leaving a legacy of pedestrian new buildings.

Westward, and only 25 miles (40 km) inland, are some of Spain's most remarkable mountains, the Picos de Europa. They are just that, peaks — mighty, craggy peaks that rise giddily from the Bay of Biscay to form a buttress that divides Cantabria from Asturias. On the western fringe of the Picos is the National Park of Covadonga, a haunt of bears and wolves that takes its name from the hamlet of Covadonga, site of the battle in AD 718 at which the Christian forces of Pelayo, a Visigothic aristocrat, defeated the powerful Moors. Pelayo became the first monarch of the tiny kingdom of Asturias, which at first covered just 1,200 square miles, and which was, for about 200 years, Christianity's only stronghold in Spain.

From the time they crossed into Spain at what is now Gibraltar with 7,000 men in AD 711, it had taken the Moors only 2 years to sweep across the whole of Spain and Portugal and conquer all of it except this outpost in the heart of the Asturian mountains. The significance of the battle of Covadonga in AD 722 is that it marked the beginning of what the Spanish called the "Reconquest" — even though the Moors wouldn't be completely driven out of Spain until 1492! The tough Asturians, who had fiercely resisted the Romans and were subdued only after a 10-year war (29–19 BC) that ended with the presence of Augustus himself, now turned their attention to building churches and hermitages, while the rest of Spain skirmished with the Moorish armies. Many of these early Asturian or pre-Romanesque buildings still stand today, constituting the best and most complete series of 9th-century edifices in Europe.

The Reconquest pushed the Moors southward, and by 914 Asturias had gained control of León, most of Galicia, and the north of Portugal. This power was ceded only when the Asturian kings moved their court south from Oviedo and made León the capital of a combined Asturias-Léon. In 1388, Asturias became a principality, much as Wales is in Great Britain; to extend the analogy, the present heir to the Spanish throne currently occupied by King Juan Carlos, his son Felipe, is the Prince of Asturias.

Much of Asturias today consists of red-roofed villages with their characteristic *hórreos,* or granaries built on stone supports several feet high, scattered over the green carpets of the valleys and meadows. But the storm-ridden sea is the real spectacle, and the uneven coastline exposes increasingly dramatic wave-battered cliffs as the route moves toward Galicia. Local food matches the local character: strong blue cabrales cheese, and a hearty stew of broad beans, pork, and sausages called *fabada,* are downed with cider, *the* drink of Asturias — a popular image of the place is of an apple orchard. Accompanying this is the sound of the region's best-known instrument, the *gaita,* a small bagpipe.

Anyone driving the entire route, including the two or three inland excursions, should allow several weeks to do justice to it. Most of it is sea, fishing village, beach, and mountain, but there is also the bustle and shopping of Bilbao, Santander, Oviedo, or Gijón to add variety. (Bilbao and Avilés, west of Gijón, add a sample of old-fashioned European smokestack industry, too.) From Bilbao westward into Galicia, the route is seconded by a narrow-gauge railway line — *FEVE* — that is a travelers' dream. The *FEVE* line is slow and cumbersome (the state-owned *RENFE* rail network has long since taken over as the region's primary means of ground transportation) but it skirts beaches, runs across estuaries and through limestone gorges, and is often surrounded by forest and hills. The main road joining San Sebastián and Galicia, N634, is generally poor, and in summer traffic snarls are common. The only stretches of motorway on the route are A8, from San Sebastián to Bilbao, and A66 and A8, which link Gijón, Oviedo, and Avilés.

The disadvantage of getting away from it all is the generally poor tourist infrastructure. There are few top class hotels or restaurants outside the main cities, and even in town, accommodations are very hard to find in July and August. A double room with bath will cost $130 or more in a hotel listed as expensive, $70 to $120 in a moderate one, and below $60 in an inexpensive one. Dinner for two with wine costs $70 or more at restaurants listed as expensive, $50 to $65 at moderate restaurants, and $45 or less at inexpensive places. But be aware that it is not difficult to find superb cooking at moderately priced restaurants, sometimes right next door to an expensive eating house that charges three times the price. Quality, but not necessarily price, is generally higher in the Basque Country than elsewhere.

■ **Note:** Most place-names in the Basque Country have two spellings. In this chapter, when two spellings are given (usually at the first reference to a place), the first one is Spanish, and the second — often vital for following signs along the route — is Basque.

SAN SEBASTIÁN (DONOSTIA): This most elegant turn-of-the-century Belle Epoque beach resort is set on a fine shell-shaped bay. It is edged by a wide curving beach, which is, in turn, topped by an exquisite promenade of ornate railings and impressive buildings. Mountains on either side of town protect it from northerly winds, and a small island in the bay softens the surf. Home to a famous annual *International Film Festival,* San Sebastián is small (pop. 175,000), and in midsummer there isn't a spare hotel room to be had. For full details on this charming city just 12 miles (19 km) from the French border, see *San Sebastián,* THE CITIES.

En Route from San Sebastián – The chief Basque city and port of Bilbao, just 62½ miles (100 km) to the west, can be reached in an hour on the excellent A8 highway, which skirts undulating deep green Basque hills. But it would be an enormous shame to miss some of the pretty Basque fishing villages, not to mention a chance to sample some fine cuisine. Take A8 out of San Sebastián to reach the first stop, Zarauz (Zarautz), 14 miles (22 km) away. The turnoff, 2 miles (3 km) past the tiny fishing port of Orio, leads right into the town. Zarauz is a booming resort that hugs a magnificent 1½-mile beach. A vacation home for thousands of Basques from inland industrial towns, it has a population of approximately 16,000 year-round — quadruple that in summer. During the Middle Ages, Zarauz was the site of much factional warring, and defensive structures typical of the period sprang up. One of the few surviving is the 15th-century, 3-story Luzea Tower, in the central Kale Nagusia (*kale,* or *kalea,* means street in Basque), with an exterior staircase and 16th-century paintings. The tower's ground floor is now a bank, though the thick stone façade has not been altered. The 16th-century Palacio de Narros stands at the western end of town — the "wrong way around," with its back facing the sea. The 9-hole *Real Club de Golf de Zarauz* (Barrio de Mendilauta; phone: 43-830145), at the eastern end of town by the beach, is one of the Basque Country's best.

The beautiful fishing village of Guetaria (Getaria), 2 miles (3 km) from Zarauz, had Roman origins but was subsequently founded as a country estate by Alfonso VIII in 1209. Guetaria was the birthplace of Juan Sebastián de Elcano, the first man to sail around the world. Regardless of inaccurate schoolbook history, the fact is that Ferdinand Magellan was killed en route in 1521, and Elcano's ship was the only one in the fleet to make it back. The mighty San Salvador church in which he was christened still stands amid a remarkable group of medieval houses. Today, with a population of 2,000, the village is nationally famous for seafood — dishes such as the local *cogote de merluza a la Getaria* (hake head grilled over charcoal in wire holders) and *txangurro al horno* (baked spider crab prepared in its own shell) — and as the home of *txakoli* wine, white and slightly sour, a perfect accompaniment to the seafood. Often compared to a good moselle, the Rolls-Royce of the *txakolis* is the locally produced Txomin Etxániz. Guetaria is also famous for El Ratón (The Mouse), the rodent-shaped islet of San Antón that juts out from the harbor and can be seen for miles from either side of the village.

Zarauz and Guetaria used to be whaling ports, and in 1878 the towns virtually declared war on each other over the disputed catch of a monster whale. The dispute, which still causes heated words today, lasted so long that the whale's meat rotted and its skeleton was donated to San Sebastián's aquarium, where it is still exhibited.

Six miles (10 km) along N634 is Zumaya (Zumaia), a less-attractive version of Zarauz that nonetheless enjoys the best surfing waves in the region. Take the C6317 turnoff southward, 1¼ miles (2 km) beyond Zumaya, for a worthwhile excursion to the Belle Epoque spa resort of Cestona (Zestoa), 6 miles (10 km) inland, and to the Sanctuary of Loyola, between Azkoitia and Azpeitia, another 6 miles (10 km) farther on. The imposing shrine here was built on the site of the home of St. Ignatius of Loyola, the 16th-century founder of the Society of Jesus — the religious order of the Jesuits.

Return through Cestona and join the A8 highway for the 3 miles (5 km) to the turnoff for Deva (Deba). Then, instead of taking N634, which turns inland at Deva, exit at the coastal C6212, a truly scenic road atop a cliff. Past the unattractive port of Motrico (Mutriku), the road leaves the province of Guipúzcoa (Gipuzkoa), one of three provinces making up the Basque Country, and enters Vizcaya (Biskaia), another Basque province (landlocked Alava, or Araba, is the third). The Vizcaya coast is a world of rocks and cliffs, small ports and coves, sheltered beaches, and small industries merging with the sea. The squawking of seagulls and the smell of grilled sardines await at any stop, but nowhere more so than at

Ondárroa, the largest Basque fishing port. Nevertheless, the real treasure of Vizcayan fishing villages is Lequeitio (Lekeitio), 8 miles (13 km) farther along a winding road with breathtaking views.

Lequeitio has a beautiful bay and two beaches, and is a typical Basque fishing port. Its vessels are a riot of color, mainly the red, green, and white of the Basque flag, and the wooden balconies and tall, narrow façades of its houses rest on the harbor itself. The 16th-century Santa María church is an impressive example of Vizcaya Gothic. The town is notorious for its September 1 fiesta, which includes a boat race during which competitors pull off the heads of live geese tied to a rope across the bay!

Continue 15 miles (24 km) inland along C6212 to Guernica (Gernika), immortalized by Pablo Picasso's *Guernica,* a nightmarish painting of the world's first major aerial bombing of civilians. German bombers, assisting Generalísimo Francisco Franco in the 1936–39 Civil War, flattened the town in 1937, because of its symbolic value to the Basques, who were fighting on the Republican side. Thousands died, and the town has suffered from unimaginative postwar rebuilding, but it remains the traditional heart of Basque nationalism. It was here, under the Tree of Guernica, that the Basque parliament met throughout the Middle Ages. From the 15th century through most of the 19th century, successive Spanish monarchs were obliged to visit the same oak tree, which still stands outside the Casa de Juntas parliament building, to acknowledge their acceptance of the *fueros* system of privilege. Three miles (5 km) away, just off C6212 at Kortezubi, are the Santimamiñe caves, containing 13,000-year-old paintings.

Take C6315 south from Guernica to the junction with the A8 highway at Amorebieta, then follow the signs for Bilbao, 22½ miles (36 km) from Guernica.

CHECKING IN: *Gran Hotel Balneario de Cestona* – A grand Belle Epoque spa, with 110 rooms, built in 1900. Facilities include hot thermal baths, meeting rooms, a period conference hall, 4 restaurants, tennis courts, a chapel, and gardens. Closed mid-December through February. Paseo de San Juan, Cestona (phone: 43-147140). Moderate.

Zarauz – The largest hotel along the Basque coast outside San Sebastián, offering 82 rooms, 100 yards from the beach. Facilities include a television lounge, lovely gardens, and a restaurant. 26 Avenida de Nafarroa, Zarauz (phone: 43-830200). Moderate.

EATING OUT: *Elkano* – Locals say it serves the best grilled fish in Guipúzcoa province, and the most succulent *rodaballo* (turbot) in the Basque Country. Also renowned for its *salpicón de bogavante* (lobster cocktail), *rape entero a la brasa* (whole braised angler), and any northern fish in season. Closed Tuesdays and for the month of November. Reservations advised. 2 Calle Herrerieta, Guetaria (phone: 43-831614). Expensive.

Kaia y Kaipe – Guetaria is where the chefs prepare fish in wire holders over charcoal grills, and this is a seafood house par excellence. Its name means Upstairs and Downstairs in Basque, so there is dining with a view. Try *txangurro al horno* (spider crab prepared in its shell) and the regional favorite, *cogote de merluza a la Getaria* (charcoal-grilled hake head). Wash it all down with the local *txakoli* white wine. Closed October. Reservations necessary. 10 Calle General Arnao, Guetaria (phone: 43-832414). Expensive.

Karlos Arguiñano – One of the bright lights of the new Basque cuisine. The food here is vigorously Basque yet surprisingly original, combining recent "discoveries" with traditional fare. Specialties include *liebre con rabo de ternera* (hare with calf's tail) and *sesos de ternera con hongos* (veal brains with mushrooms). Closed Sunday nights, Wednesdays, and the last 3 weeks of October. Reservations advised. 13 Calle Mendilauta, Zarauz (phone: 43-830178). Expensive.

Masoparri – Another good fish house, in an old country manor with a terrace facing the sea high above the harbor. Try *bonito a la parrilla* (grilled tuna) or *kokotxas en su gelatina* (hake's gill muscles in gelatin). Closed mid-December through mid-January. Reservations advised. 1 Calle Sagartzaga, Guetaria (phone: 43-835707). Moderate.

BILBAO (BILBO): It's hard to believe sometimes, as you look up from any part of the city and see green hills beyond the drab apartment blocks, that this is Spain's sixth-largest city and the country's main port, with approximately 530,000 inhabitants (1.2 million in Greater Bilbao). Standing on the central Arenal Bridge that spans the Nervión River and looking at the glorious City Hall and its utterly rural backdrop, you'd think you were in some middling river town. But look again. The Gran Vía, Bilbao's chief avenue, boasts gleaming skyscrapers, huge department stores, and elegant clothing shops. And a train ride along the banks of the Nervión estuary to the Bay of Biscay passes scores of dockyard cranes, shipyards, warehouses, factories, wharves, and iron and steel foundries. Bilbao's smokestack industries are in decline, and the air of industrial decay, political tension, and frequent rain make the city less than a touristic glamour spot. But Bilbao does have a great feel to it, the locals are renowned for their friendliness, and the city is packed with good places to eat and drink.

The city was founded in 1300, although it didn't really take off until the Industrial Revolution arrived in the mid-19th century. Then, from the 1860s until World War I, Britain became Bilbao's main trading partner. Even today the city betrays a strong British influence, seen in the way people dress, the architecture, and even in the long list of English managers in charge of the local soccer team, *Athletic Bilbao,* traditionally one of Spain's top three. Touristic interest centers on the Casco Viejo, or Old Quarter, which combines numerous fine clothing outfitters, specialty stores, traditional Basque restaurants, and bars. It is here that locals indulge in two Bilbao customs. One is the *chiquiteo,* the drinking in rapid succession of small wines or beers — no more than a mouthful each — at several bars in double-quick time. The custom has an important social dimension, as does the *copa y puro,* the sipping of a liqueur, usually brandy or an anise-based brew called *patxarán,* and the smoking of a cigar after a hearty lunch. These customs are no longer sexist — Bilbao women take part, too.

The grandiose Santiago Cathedral, in the heart of the Old Quarter, has a cloister built in 1404, although the church was largely rebuilt in the 16th century, after a fire. Nearby is the Plaza Nueva; built in 1830 and enclosed by 64 arches, it houses a flea market on Sunday mornings. *Gorostiaga* (9 Calle Victor; phone: 4-416-1276) is a curious Old Quarter shop where seven generations of the same family have been making hats since 1857; the specialty is the famous Basque beret, or *txapela,* although trilbys and panama hats are also made. The *Teatro Arriaga* (in the Plaza Arriaga next to the Arenal Bridge just before the Old Quarter; phone: 4-416-3244) was exactly a century old last year, and freshly renovated. A delightful building amid the industrial grime, its jolly imitation French architecture is in contrast with Bilbao's neo-classical style. (Like the magnificent City Hall, 2 years younger, it is floodlit at night and reflected in the waters of the Nervión.) Two museums are worth a visit. The *Museum of Basque Archaeology, Ethnology, and History* (4 Calle Cruz Conde; phone: 4-415-5423; open Tuesdays through Saturdays, from 10:30 AM to 1:30 PM and from 4 to 7 PM; Sundays, from 10:30 AM to 1:30 PM; admission charge) has a special room devoted to the commercial life of Bilbao since 1500. The ivy-covered *Museum of Fine Arts* (in the English-style Doña Casilda Iturrízar Park; phone: 4-441-9536; open Tuesdays through Saturdays, from 10 AM to 1:30 PM and from 4:30 to 7:30 PM; Sundays, from 11 AM to 2 PM; admission charge) features an extensive collection of Spanish and foreign paintings and sculpture from the Romanesque period to the early 20th century. El Greco, Velázquez, Ribera, Ribalta, Zurbarán, and Goya are represented, as are modern artists, from Gauguin to Sorolla.

Two city center coffeehouses are worthy haunts for an early evening break. The *Café*

Iruña (13 Calle Colón de Larreátegui; phone: 4-423-7021), built in 1903, has tiled arabesque decor and imitation carved-wood ceilings; the *Café La Granja* (Plaza Circular; phone: 4-423-0813), opposite the statue to Bilbao's founder, Don Diego López de Haro, has peach-red decor that imparts a genteel feel. (If in doubt, order the *Copa Feliz* — burned rum, banana, cream, and ice cream.) The *Heladería Nossi-Be* (1 Calle Navarra) serves 34 different flavors of ice cream, as well as milkshakes, and is open daily from March through October. *Semana Grande* (Aste Nagusia in Basque, Big Week in English), Bilbao's week-long fiesta, runs from August 15 to 22, and is among the best in Spain. Ask at the tourist office (Alameda de Mazarredo; phone: 4-424-4819) for information — bullfights, rural sports, male-only open-air gastronomy contests, and folk dancing are all part of it.

CHECKING IN: *Ercilla* – Nearly always full, it is the choice of politicians, journalists, bullfighters, and businessmen, as well as conventions of all types, so book well in advance. All 350 rooms have air conditioning and private baths. The *Bermeo* restaurant (see *Eating Out*) is one of the city's best. 37 Calle Ercilla, Bilbao (phone: 4-443-8800). Expensive.

López de Haro – A new, luxury establishment in town, needed more because of the city's growing role as a convention center than for touristic purposes. In the city center, 6 stories high, it's built in the quasi-English classic style of Bilbao, and the 53 rooms have a full range of amenities. The *Club Naútico* restaurant is highly acclaimed. 2 Calle Obispo Orueta, Bilbao (phone: 4-423-5500). Expensive.

Villa de Bilbao – Modern and luxurious, with 142 large air conditioned rooms, tennis courts, a heated swimming pool, a discotheque, hair salons, and a restaurant. Pets are welcome. 87 Gran Vía, Bilbao (phone: 4-441-6000). Expensive.

Roquefer – A delightful, family-run establishment in the Old Quarter. The 18 rooms are simple, but clean. 2 Calle Lotería, Bilbao (phone: 4-415-0755). Inexpensive.

EATING OUT: *Bermeo* – At the *Ercilla* hotel, and rated as one of Spain's best hotel-restaurants, it is the culinary gathering spot for all social, political, sporting, and cultural events. A Basque-Navarrese menu suggests mushrooms, woodcock and partridge with turnip, steamed hake, and oxtail (the latter during the August bullfight week). Closed Sunday nights. Reservations necessary. 37 Calle Ercilla, Bilbao (phone: 4-443-8800). Expensive.

Guria – Codfish is *the* Bilbao specialty, and they say it is never better than when prepared by Chef Génaro Pildain in his own restaurant. *Bacalao al pil pil* (cod baked in green sauce with peppers) is just one of the succulent dishes served. The menu is traditionally Basque, but the best around. Closed Sundays, the last week of July, and the first week of August. Reservations advised. 66 Gran Vía, Bilbao (phone: 4-441-0543). Expensive.

Zortziko – The choice for new Basque cuisine in Bilbao, run by Chef Daniel García and his six brothers and sisters, with great attention to detail. The menu is pure poetry: *tartar de salmon en flor al aroma de eneldo* (salmon tartar in a flower shape with dilled mint sauce), *rodaballo asado a la vinagreta tibia y al aroma de genjibre natural* (baked turbot in a vinaigrette sauce with a hint of ginger), and *mousse de polen a la miel de encina* (honey mousse). Closed Sundays and September 1–15. Reservations advised. 17 Calle Alameda de Mazarredo, Bilbao (phone: 4-423-9743). Expensive.

Aitxiar – Modest but atmospheric, in the Old Quarter, with a charming dining room beyond the bar. Basque favorites include *chipirones en su tinta* (squid in its own ink) and *porrusalda* (leek, onion, and cod stew). Closed Mondays and September. No reservations. 8 Calle María Muñoz, Bilbao (phone: 4-415-0917). Inexpensive.

En Route from Bilbao – The newly improved N634 leads through 8 miles (13 km) of heavily industrial Greater Bilbao towns — Barakaldo, Sestao, Portugalete, and Santurce (Santurtzi) — on the left bank of the Nervión before it hits the countryside and, suddenly, Cantabria. For a last glimpse of the Basque Country and a view of the amazing Puente Colgante (Hanging Bridge), turn into the steep roads leading down to Portugalete.

Just a mile (1.6 km) farther on, Santurtzi is famous for its sardines, grilled in the open air by fisherwomen. Beyond it, the stretch of N634 to Castro-Urdiales, a surprisingly unspoiled fishing town, is particularly bad, but there is no alternative route. Trucks, buses, and cars creep along steep and narrow bends, so the arrival in Castro-Urdiales is a relief. Its harbor is dominated by the dauntingly buttressed 13th-century Gothic church of Santa María and the nearby Knights Templars Castle, complete with lighthouse; in 1814, locals escaped from Napoleon's troops through secret castle passages to waiting British ships. Cave paintings in the vicinity show human presence 12,000 years ago. The town was called Flaviógriga by the Romans, Alfonso VIII granted it special favors in 1163, and it was the regional capital until French troops sacked it during the 18th century and Santander took over. From the broad promenade and gardens on the seafront, the scene often includes the brightly colored sails of windsurfers and little boys fishing for crabs from the harbor steps.

Another 16 miles (26 km) along N634, past the lush green valley of Guriezo and after a spectacular descent into the town of Liendo, is Laredo. Doubtless it once had all the charm of Castro-Urdiales, but a 1960s building boom, and a parallel influx of European tourism, has disfigured the promenade facing the otherwise wonderful La Salvé beach. There is also a marvelous 13th-century Gothic church, Santa María; its exterior is not imposing, but its Bethlehem altarpiece is reckoned to be one of the finest jewels of Flemish sculpture in Spain. The church stands atop the Old Town, whose narrow cobbled streets wind down to the harbor. Laredo's *Battle of the Flowers,* when flower-bedecked carnival floats parade through town, takes place annually on the last Friday in August.

Toward Santander, the road passes through unattractive Colindres and over a steel bridge that spans the Asón estuary, to Solares. Here, just after the pink house with a Sala de Fiestas neon sign, the road divides. Take the N635 turnoff to Santander and follow the signs to the city center.

■ **EATING OUT:** *Risco* – Famed for its traditional Cantabrian cooking and splendid sea views. Zacarías and Inés Puente have perfected *pimientos rellenos de cangrejo* (peppers stuffed with crab), and offer a great selection of Cantabrian cheeses. Reservations advised. 2 Calle La Arenosa, Laredo (phone: 42-605030). Moderate.

SANTANDER: A kind of staid San Sebastián, Santander has tried without real success since the early 1900s to rival the Basque resort. The city even paid for the construction of the English-style Magdalena Palace as a gift to Alfonso XIII and Victoria Eugenia in 1912, in an attempt to give Santander the "royal residence" status that San Sebastián had earlier gained. Although it *was* the royal summer residence from 1913 to 1930, the town (pop. 185,000) never quite knocked San Sebastián off the throne as the queen of northern Spanish resorts, perhaps due to its greater distance from France or to its not having a beach and a bay quite as stunning as La Concha. Or to the terrible fire that destroyed much of it in 1941, leaving it essentially modern and dull — albeit leafy, with a large number of gardens (by Spanish city standards), as well as some very pleasant beaches.

The first surprise, for those entering the city from the east, is the bronze statue of Franco on horseback in the aptly named Plaza del Generalísimo, opposite City Hall. It is the first statue of the autocratic ruler along the entire coast from the French border. Activity in the city center revolves around the porticoed Plaza Porticada, or Plaza de

Velarde, where the tourist office (phone: 42-310708) is found. Until 1990, when it moved to a new auditorium on the Palace of Festivals site, this was also the home of the annual *International Festival of Dance and Music,* one of Spain's most prestigious, held in August. One block toward the bay from the plaza is the very unattractive cathedral, largely rebuilt after the 1941 fire. It does, however, contain a beautiful high altar and the tiny 13th-century Crypt of Christ, the city's oldest monument, dating back to days — from the 12th to the 16th centuries — when Santander was a booming port. For a while, it was the busiest port in northern Spain, with a near monopoly on the export of Castilian wool to Flanders.

Santander's beauty lies in its beaches, gardens, and promenades. The Paseo de Pereda, which begins at the seaward end of the Plaza Porticada, is a broad, elegant promenade with palm trees and the huge, red arum flowers that dot the city. Notice the *Palacete del Embarcadero,* a small art gallery (admission charge), and the dock from which the only ferry between Spain and Great Britain sails (twice a week, Santander to Plymouth, *Brittany Ferries;* phone: 42-214500). Farther along, past lines of 5-story glass-balconied houses that escaped the 1941 fire, is Puerto Chico, where dockland Santander ends and pleasure Santander begins. The first building here is the *Royal Maritime Club,* which rises out of the sea on concrete columns in the shape of a ship's upper decks. Beyond it, the road turns away from the sea for a while, then steps lead down to the first great local beach, the Magdalena. Clean and placid, it has a 100-foot backdrop of cliffs and trees (the ivy-covered structure up above belongs to the Royal Tennis Society). At the end of the beach and up the hill is the Magdalena Palace, which was turned into the International Menéndez Pelayo University after the abdication of Alfonso XIII in 1931, and is now famous for summer seminars and language courses for foreign students.

On the other side of the Magdalena promontory is the mile-long El Sardinero beach, dominated by the lavish 1914 Belle Epoque *Gran Casino* at Plaza Italia. One of only two casinos on the coast (the other is at San Sebastián), it is open from 7 PM to 4 AM (5 AM on weekends). Across the bay are the villages of Pedreña and Somo, both with huge, sand-duned beaches. Pedreña is the birthplace of golf pro Severiano Ballesteros and home to the golf course where he developed his skills, the *Royal Pedreña Golf Club* (phone: 42-500266). Also to be seen in Santander are the *Fine Arts Museum* (4 Calle Rubio), which can claim a Goya, and the *Museum of Prehistory* (4 Casimiro Sainz), which has important collections from the Upper Paleolithic period. The best restaurants are located along Calle Hernán Cortés, in the vicinity of Puerto Chico, but for an inexpensive meal and an authentic experience, go to the Barrio Pesquero (Fishing Quarter) — where the Santander working class eats — and choose any one of several fish restaurants with their huge dining rooms, simple decor, and unfussy, yet friendly, service.

CHECKING IN: *Real* – Opened in 1917 during Santander's heyday, when Alfonso XIII spent his summers in the city. Luxurious, set amid terraces and gardens, it retains its early-20th-century architecture and atmosphere. The 124-room hostelry only recently reversed its decades-old policy of closing in winter, and is now open year-round. 28 Paseo de Pérez Galdós, Santander (phone: 42-272550). Expensive.

***Bahia* –** In the city center, facing the bay and close to the ferry quay. This 181-room hotel is spacious if plain, with a good restaurant and several convention rooms. 6 Avenida Alfonso XIII, Santander (phone: 42-221700). Expensive to moderate.

EATING OUT: *Bar El Puerto* – Not just a bar, nor a fishermen's tavern as it once was, but a restaurant of great renown, especially for its seafood. Upstairs dining overlooks Puerto Chico, with shrubs and hanging plants decorating the façade. Reservations necessary. 63 Calle Hernán Cortés, Santander (phone: 42-213001). Expensive.

Zacarías – Featuring such specialties as *jibiones de huerta* (small peppers stuffed with shellfish) and *maganos encebollados* (squid fried in onions). Reservations advised. 38 Calle Hernán Cortés, Santander (phone: 42-210688). Moderate.

Los Peñucos – One of many excellent homespun fish restaurants in the Barrio Pesquero. Noisy, friendly, and full of locals. Try the *marmita* (tuna stew) and *besugo al horno* (baked sea bream). No reservations. 2 Calle Mocejon, Santander (phone: 42-222091). Inexpensive.

En Route from Santander – Santillana del Mar and the Altamira Caves are 19 miles (31 km) to the west. Take N611 out of Santander, through the village of Igollo and into the gently undulating countryside. Eight miles (13 km) down the road is Puente Arce, where a Roman bridge spans the creek-size Pas River. It's another 8 miles (13 km) to the C6316 turnoff for Santillana del Mar.

EATING OUT: *El Molino* – Delightfully situated in gardens beside a creek, with an ancient coat of arms above the entrance, and two low wood-beamed dining rooms. The restaurant, set in a converted 17th-century farmhouse, was made famous by the late, award-winning chef Victor Merino, and is now in the capable hands of his son, Antonio. Try the Cantabrian fish and clam salad or the sea bream stew with thyme. Closed Mondays. Reservations advised. Carretera N611, Km 12, Puente Arce (phone: 42-574000). Moderate.

SANTILLANA DEL MAR/ALTAMIRA CAVES: These two treasures — one practically forbidden to all but the chosen few — are unrelated, but less than 2 miles (3 km) apart. Santillana del Mar, which despite its name is nearly 3 miles (5 km) from the sea, is a unique collection of perfectly preserved medieval mansions and palaces strung out along two streets. Jean-Paul Sartre described it as "the prettiest village in Spain." Legend has it that during the 3rd century St. Juliana was murdered by her husband for refusing to renounce her Christian faith and her virginity. Her remains were said to have been brought here during the 8th century by monks who built a small monastery. The village's first name — Sancta Iuliana, after its martyred saint — was in time transformed to Santillana.

The spirit of Cantabria laces the town. The imposing Romanesque houses and mansions lining the dark, ironstone streets are a chunk of the Middle Ages lifted into the 20th century. Happily, the village, with a population just short of 4,000, is a living rural community that does not rely solely on tourism to survive. The locals sell cheese, sponge cake, and fresh milk from their stable doors, and despite the dozens of tourist buses that pour in every day, a medieval air pervades. The original monastery is now the 12th-century Collegiate Church of St. Juliana, with a wonderful façade and high altar complemented by sculptures and carvings added through the centuries. At the other end of the main street is the *Diocesan Museum*, formerly the 16th-century Convent of Regina Coeli, which houses an exceptional collection of painted wooden saints and other religious figures. There are several 16th- to 18th-century mansions to admire, each boasting an impressive coat of arms. Even the relatively humble rural homes, with their solid walls, eaves, balconies, and elegant doorways, are a joy to wander past. One-half mile south of the village is a zoo, which is open year-round. Among the usual animals are some European bison, descendants of those depicted in the Altamira Cave paintings.

Often described as the Sistine Chapel of Prehistoric Art, the Altamira Caves — Cuevas de Altamira — contain the best Upper Paleolithic cave paintings in Europe. They are only a short walk southwest of Santillana, along a well-marked road. Unfortunately, it is now extremely difficult to enter; only those with legitimate academic interests are permitted, and entrance applications must be submitted at least 6 months in advance. Discovered by a hunter in 1879, the paintings, which cover a time span from

15,000 to 9500 BC, consist of bison, bulls, boars, and horses etched in red or yellow ocher and delineated in black. They range from 4 to 8 feet high and were in perfect condition when discovered, but they have suffered serious deterioration recently — caused mainly by moisture from the breath of thousands of visitors during recent decades! Now there is a limit to the number of daily visitors (usually 20 are permitted, and these include research students and other non-tourists). There is a museum next to the cave, open Tuesdays through Saturdays, from 10 AM to 1 PM and from 4 to 8 PM; Sundays from 10 AM to 1 PM. Admission charge. A replica cave, using local rock and imitation paintings, is scheduled to open next door this year, but to apply for entrance permission to the real thing, write to Centro de Investigación de Altamira (Santillana del Mar, Cantabria 39330, Spain). For information on the other sights of Santillana, visit the tourist office in the town's main square (Plaza de Ramón Pelayo; phone: 42-818251).

CHECKING IN: *Parador Gil Blas* – One of Spain's most exciting *paradores,* this 17th-century converted mansion used to belong to the noble Barreda-Bracho family. In the heart of the complex of medieval stone buildings, it retains all of its original charm and has a fine restaurant. A visit to Santillana del Mar is incomplete without staying in one of its lovely 56 rooms, but make reservations well in advance. 11 Plaza de Ramón Pelayo, Santillana de Mar (phone: 42-818000). Expensive to moderate.

En Route from Santillana del Mar/Altamira Caves – Continue west on C6316 to Comillas, 11 miles (18 km) away. The drive is a beautiful one past unspoiled villages, green meadows, the occasional Romanesque church, and the first sight of the massed backdrop of hills that roll away toward the Picos de Europa. Comillas is a curious town, fascinatingly gloomy and leafy, dominated by three buildings designed by Barcelona architects in the late 19th century. The huge neo-Gothic Pontifical University, the work of Lluís Domènech i Montaner (who designed Barcelona's Palau de la Música Catalana), can be seen high up on a hill from any spot in the village. The private modernist-style palace of the Marqués de Comillas, designed by Juan Martorell, is on another hill nearer the village's two fine beaches. But the jewel of the ensemble is El Capricho (The Whim), on a still lower slope, the only building in Cantabria designed by the inimitable Antoni Gaudí. El Capricho is actually a Moorish-style optical illusion, a bizarre villa whose huge cylindrical tower, topped by a dome half-suspended in the air and supported by squat columns, makes the building look smaller than it is. Closed for some 20 years, it has now been restored and converted into a luxury restaurant (see *Eating Out* below).

Leaving Comillas, follow the signposts 5 miles (8 km) to La Revilla, where C6316 rejoins N634. Two miles (3 km) on, across the La Maza Bridge, which has been modernized since it first spanned the broad estuary during the 15th century, is San Vicente de la Barquera, and its national monument, the 13th-century Church of Santa María. Six miles (10 km) farther is Unquera, marking the end of Cantabria and the beginning of the Principality of Asturias. Unquera is a good place to stop and sample *corbatas,* a local puff pastry and almond sweet, and a good starting point for a drive into the Picos de Europa — N621 leads through spectacular scenery alongside the Deva River to the town of Potes, 24 miles (39 km) inland. Alternatively, stay on N634 through Unquera and drive 12 miles (19 km) to La Arquera and the AS263 turnoff to the beach resort of Llanes, the first sizable town in Asturias.

EATING OUT: *El Capricho de Gaudí* – This modernist folly, a landmark building designed by Antoni Gaudí, has been restored to its onetime glory and put into service as a deluxe restaurant specializing in Basque and international cooking. There is a bar lounge on the top floor. Closed Mondays and the month of February. Reservations advised. Barrio de Sobrellano, Comillas (phone: 42-720365). Expensive to moderate.

Fonda Colasa – A favorite, humble eating house of the old style, with down-home, hearty fare in abundant portions — it's been in the same family since 1890. The meat stews and fish are excellent, and all the desserts are made on the premises. Closed October through April. No reservations. 9 Calle Antonio López, Comillas (phone: 42-720001). Inexpensive.

LLANES: The capital of eastern Asturias, Llanes is often written off as dull. In fact, the town has a delightful Old Quarter, the gentle feel of a typical Asturian fishing port, and about 30 remote and very clean beaches, including La Franca, Poo, Celorio, and Barros within a few miles to either side — ask at the tourist office (1 Calle Nemesio Sobrino; phone: 85-400164). Llanes is also famous for its August 16 *Fiesta de San Roque,* a day-long binge of folkloric dancing in traditional costumes. The town spreads upward from the tiny sheltered harbor at the foot of picturesque green hills and still retains chunks of its 13th-century ramparts. One segment girds the beer garden of the *El Antiguo* restaurant in Posada Herrera — a wonderful setting in which to enjoy a cold drink on a warm afternoon. Llanes is yet another coastal town with a magnificent church dedicated to Santa María, this one part 14th- and part 15th-century, part Romanesque and part Gothic. It also has a selection of interesting 15th- to 17th-century mansions, boasting their heraldic coats of arms.

CHECKING IN: *Don Paco* – Fairly atmospheric, it has 42 rooms within the walls of a 17th-century palace adjacent to the old ramparts, with a lovely view of the harbor. Closed October through May. Parque de Posada Herrera, Llanes (phone: 85-400150). Moderate to inexpensive.

EATING OUT: *La Bolera* – This small upstairs dining room overlooks the quayside; the food is simple but of the highest quality. Seafood predominates — try *colas de langosta* (lobster tails) or *salmón a la ribereña* (local riverside salmon). Closed Wednesdays in winter. Reservations advised. El Muella, Llanes (phone: 85-401336). Moderate.

En Route from Llanes – Take AS263 signposted to Celorio 3 miles (5 km) away, where it rejoins N634 for a good drive to Ribadesella; the latter is on N632, just after the turnoff at Llovio and some dramatic mist-shrouded mountains that creep to the very edge of the road.

RIBADESELLA: A good base for Picos de Europa excursions, Ribadesella offers a magnificent beach, great hotels, rustic eating houses, a fabulous cave with prehistoric paintings, and *sidrerías* (Asturian cider bars). It is also home to the world's premier canoe festival, the *International Descent of the Sella River,* held annually since 1930 on the first Saturday of August. It attracts 800 participants from many countries and over 200,000 festive spectators, who join in all-night revelry after following the canoeists 11 miles down the river from Arriondas.

The town straddles the broad Sella estuary, crossed by a long, narrow bridge that is actually the N632 highway, from which the locals can be seen fishing for bass, sargo, and red mullet. The "port" side of town brims with bars, restaurants, and shops. The other side is residential, but includes the beach, flanked by two headlands, and the best promenade hotels and mansions, glorious with their creeping purple bougainvillea. At the beach end of the bridge is an odd-looking tourist office (phone: 85-860038; closed in winter), occupying what is, in fact, a converted *hórreo,* one of the ancient granaries that dot the Asturian countryside. Wooden huts erected on 10-foot concrete stilts, they are designed to protect grain from dampness and rodents.

A few hundred yards from the tourist office is the Cave of Tito Bustillo, named for the man who discovered it in 1968. Inside are 15,000- to 20,000-year-old cave paintings that have been pronounced the equal of those at Altamira and France's Lascaux. Three galleries make up the cavern. A vaulted niche in the first has shield-shaped red marks, identified as representing female vulva in an invocation to fertility. In another gallery are a large red horse, deer, reindeer, and a purple and black horse, many over 6 feet tall. A maximum of 400 visitors per day is permitted, so it's best to go in the morning. Open from 10 AM to 1 PM and from 3:30 to 6:30 PM, April 1 through September 30 (closed Mondays in April, May, June, and September; Sundays in July and August). Admission charge.

Ribadesella is also a good place from which to take a ride on the *FEVE* railway. Take this classic rural train, which offers good glimpses of the sea, four stops east to the hamlet of Villahormes, and walk a mile to the deserted beach past cornfields and a tiny chapel. A half-hour stroll along AS263 and you'll find the station, at Nueva, from which to catch the train back to Ribadesella. Another pleasant excursion is to drive west of Ribadesella along N632 about 14 miles (22 km) to Colunga. Turn 2 miles (3 km) down AS257 to the delightful fishing village of Lastres, whose steep, cobbled streets rise dizzily above the old harbor. A final treat before leaving Ribadesella is a taste of the local cider. In any of the quayside *sidrerías,* the waiter will pour the first glass from a bottle raised as high as the right arm can reach, while the left hand holds the glass low at an acute angle so the fine spray splashes on the inside of the glass — "aerating" the drink. No Asturian would pour cider any other way, but even the experts wear rubber boots because of the amount of liquid that splashes to the floor!

CHECKING IN: *Gran Hotel del Sella* – The view from this hotel is an open panorama of the town's beautiful surroundings. The old part was formerly the palace of the Argüelles family. All 82 rooms have private baths. Facilities include a swimming pool and tennis court. Closed October through March. Calle La Playa, Ribadesella (phone: 85-860150). Expensive.

***Ribadesella Playa* –** A simple but very comfortable 17-room mansion overlooking the beach. The murmur of breakers lulls guests to sleep. Closed November through February. 34 Calle La Playa, Ribadesella (phone: 85-860715). Moderate.

EATING OUT: *El Repollu* – Small, basic, and family-run, with the finest fish in town. The house cabrales cheese is a powerful experience. No reservations. 2 Calle Santa Marina, Ribadesella (phone: 85-860734). Inexpensive.

***Mesón Tinín* –** This old-style cider-tavern restaurant is down to earth and lively. Try the Asturian *fabada* (bean, sausage, and bacon stew). No reservations. 20 Calle Caso de la Villa, Ribadesella (phone: 85-860839). Inexpensive.

En Route from Ribadesella – Western Europe's wildest mountains, the Picos de Europa, are only 16 miles (26 km) inland, and for anyone traveling westward along the coast, Ribadesella is the last logical point from which to detour for a visit. To kill two birds with one stone, now is also the time to visit the national shrine of Covadonga, marking the spot where Pelayo defeated the Moors in 722, thus beginning the Reconquest. The shrine is set at the edge of the National Park of Covadonga, which occupies the western part of the Picos de Europa, and while it may not be of interest to everyone, it is set in magnificent scenery, with 8,000-foot-high mountains soaring into the sky behind a lush valley. Leave Ribadesella along Oviedo-bound N634 for Arriondas, 11 miles (18 km) away, and from there take the C637 turnoff for Cangas de Onis, which was the first Christian capital of Spain and Pelayo's home after he founded the kingdom of Asturias. Cangas is beautifully positioned: Its famous ivy-covered Roman bridge over the Sella River offers some of the best salmon fishing in Spain. Covadonga, consisting of a small cave, with the image of the Virgin Mary and the tombs of Pelayo and King Alfonso

I, as well as a large, late-19th-century pink stone basilica, and a museum, is 5 miles (8 km) ahead, and another 12 miles (19 km) beyond are the two lakes at the center of the national park. The basilica and cave are open daily year-round from 9 AM to 7 PM; the museum is open from 11 AM to 2 PM and from 4 to 7 PM; admission charge to the museum.

Drive back to Arriondas, and turn west onto N634 toward Oviedo. A mile (1.6 km) after Infiesto, take AS255 to Villaviciosa, near the coast. The cider capital of Spain, Villaviciosa has a beautiful Old Quarter and is famous for its jet stone handicrafts. Then, for a different route back to N234, take AS113 out of town and, after about 6 miles (10 km), the turnoff signposted to San Salvador de Valdediós, down a steep lane. The monastery here, better known as El Conventín (Little Convent), is one of a remarkable series of 8th- and 9th-century buildings the Asturian pre-Romanesque style. The site includes a separate stone chapel deep inside a verdant valley, built during the reign of King Alfonso III (866–911), at the time when Mozarabic influences had been introduced. Note the Cross of Victory, a symbol of Pelayo's feat (the original of which is in Oviedo Cathedral), in the small twin windows of the main façade. Afterward, return up the steep, unpaved climb to AS113, rejoin N634 at Pola, and drive the remaining 5 undistinguished miles (8 km) to Oviedo.

EATING OUT: *Pelayo* – Not surprisingly, there's a Catholic air to the place. Nestled in a wild setting, a step from the National Park of Covadonga, the menu offers typical Asturian cuisine. Reservations advised. Covadonga (phone: 85-846000). Moderate.

OVIEDO: The capital of Asturias, 17½ miles (28 km) from the coast, Oviedo forms a geographic triangle with Gijón and Avilés. It is the least grim and industrial of the three, has the most interesting Old Quarter, and can claim genuine historical significance. Early in the 9th century, the city became the capital of the tiny kingdom of Asturias, the Christian outpost of otherwise Muslim Spain. A millennium of history, from the 8th to the 18th centuries, is represented by dozens of buildings in the Old Town, including a handful of remarkable pre-Romanesque structures whose styles were 200 years before their time. Otherwise, Oviedo (pop. 190,000), is fairly nondescript.

The Old Town spreads around the 15th-to-16th-century cathedral, which has a marvelous Gothic tower and one of Spain's best altarpieces. But the real treasure is the tiny Cámara Santa (Holy Chamber), built by Alfonso II (who reigned from 792 to 842) to house relics rescued from Toledo when it fell to the Moors. The chamber, which was incorporated into the later cathedral (and which was damaged by an explosion in 1934 and was actually rebuilt after the Civil War), contains a startling array of priceless objects, including the gold-covered oak cross carried by Pelayo in the battle of Covadonga. Also on display is a cedar wood chest of relics donated in 901 and covered with silver bas-reliefs in 1075. Spain was stunned in 1977 when thieves stayed in the chamber overnight and filled their sacks with the treasure. Luckily, the booty was later recovered and the thieves jailed. Open Mondays through Saturdays, from 10:15 AM to 1 PM and from 4 to 7 PM; Sundays from 4 AM to 7 PM; admission charge. Behind the cathedral is the *Provincial Archaeological Museum* (3 Calle San Vicente), one of the most important in Spain, with collections from the paleolithic period onward (open Tuesdays through Saturdays from 10 AM to 1:30 PM and from 4 to 6 PM, Sundays from 11 AM to 1 PM; closed Mondays; admission charge). There are many palaces and mansions in the surrounding streets, but most are closed to the public. The tourist office is in front of the cathedral at 6 Plaza de la Catedral (phone: 85-213385).

Two miles (3 km) from the city, within 250 yards of each other on Naranco Hill, are two churches that are probably the finest examples of Asturian pre-Romanesque art. Santa María del Naranco and San Miguel de Lillo were both built by Ramiro I during his short 9th-century reign, and the former in particular is regarded as exemplary. Originally built as a palace, it included baths and attached living quarters until it was converted to a church during the 12th century. A rectangular, 2-floor building, it has a complex structure using barrel vaulting with reinforced arches resting on a system of blind arches. From the upper floor, huge open windows offer wide views. Other interesting features include the intricately chiseled stonework depicting hunting scenes, and the Byzantine-style capitals and the open porticoes at both ends, a revolutionary concept at the time. Open Mondays through Saturdays, May to October 15, from 9:30 AM to 1 PM and from 3 to 7 PM; October 15 through April, from 10 AM to 1 PM and from 3 to 5 PM; admission charge. San Miguel de Lillo, built as a church, is a narrow, elevated building — its height is three times the width of its central nave.

Two minutes from Oviedo's Old Town is San Francisco Park, a huge square of gardens, trees, and fountains — a pleasant refuge from the urban sprawl, right in the city center. Nearby is an excellent gift shop, *Escanda* (5 Calle Jovellanos), where Felipe Prieto makes beautiful leather objects. The third week of September is fiesta time in Oviedo, with celebrations for San Mateo, the local patron saint, on the 21st, and processions, folkloric dancing, and music in honor of Latin America on the 19th.

CHECKING IN: *La Reconquista* – A converted 17th-century hospital, sumptuously decorated and boasting a baroque façade. All 139 rooms are air conditioned and have private baths. The bar is a former cloister; there is a good restaurant and a concert hall. 16 Calle Gil de Jaz, Oviedo (phone: 85-241100). Expensive.

Gran Hotel España – Stylish yet modern, with impeccable service, this place is geared especially to the business traveler. There are 89 rooms. 2 Calle Jovellanos, Oviedo (phone: 85-220596). Expensive to moderate.

EATING OUT: *Casa Fermín* – Chef Luis Gil has developed a super-Asturian cuisine over the past 22 years, using cider, apples, and local *fabes* beans. Try the *sopa de puerros y almejas* (leek and clam soup) and *merluza a la sidra* (hake in cider). Closed Sunday evenings. Reservations advised. 8 Calle San Francisco, Oviedo (phone: 85-216452). Expensive.

Trascorrales – A beautiful wooden building set in a delightful medieval square in the heart of the Old Town, with main, back, and private dining rooms. Try the *perdiz con lombarda y castañas* (partridge with red cabbage and chestnuts) and *crema de manzanas gratinados* (grated apple cream). Closed Sundays and August 15–30. Reservations necessary. Plaza Trascorrales, Oviedo (phone: 85-222441). Expensive.

En Route from Oviedo – Follow the A66 highway 11 miles (18 km) due north, then join A8 for the remaining 7 miles (11 km) into Gijón.

GIJÓN: Asturias's largest city, Gijón (pronounced Hee-*hon*) has a population of 256,000 and manages to be an active industrial center, a busy port, and a booming summer beach resort all at once. The city dates back to the 13th century, but few historical traces remain. Of chief interest to visitors is the sea-faring Cimadevilla district on the Santa Catalina hill, which forms a headland at the western end of the 1½-mile-long San Lorenzo beach. The 15th-century Palacio de Revillagigedo, the *Jovellanos Museum,* the City Hall, and the remains of some Roman baths are the noteworthy structures, found at the entrance to Cimadevilla. Also here is the tourist office (1 Calle Marqués de San Esteban; phone: 85-346046), and an impressive statue of Pelayo, brandishing his victory cross aloft. On the right bank of the River Piles is the interesting *Museo de las Gaitas* (Bagpipe Museum; in the Pueblo de Asturias; phone: 85-373335), with a collection of bagpipes from all over the world and a workshop (open weekdays, from 10 AM to 7 PM; admission charge). Unlike Oviedo, Gijón *feels* like a city, vital and bustling, whether in the fishermen's cider bars in the Cimadevilla or in the commercial center a short walk away. August is the big month: The *Day of Asturias* is celebrated on the first Sunday with a procession and music, and the *Semana Grande* carnival begins on August 15. The annual *International Trade Fair,* a 2-week exposition of the latest technology, also is held in August.

CHECKING IN: *Hernán Cortés* – Dignified and graceful, in the city center, its 109 rooms feature all the usual comforts. 5 Calle Fernández Vallín, Gijón (phone: 85-346000). Expensive to moderate.

Parador Molino Viejo – The only *parador* in Asturias (and the only *parador* in Spain with a cider bar), this is a delightful old mill, with 40 rooms, located in a large park close to San Lorenzo beach. Parque de Isabel la Católica, Gijón (phone: 85-370511). Expensive to moderate.

EATING OUT: *Casa Victor* – Regarded as the town's best restaurant for fish, served in tavern-style ambience. Closed Thursdays, Sunday evenings, and November. Reservations advised. 11 Calle Carmen, Gijón (phone: 85-350093). Moderate.

El Pasaje – A modest establishment facing the harbor, next door to the tourist office. The *merluza a la cazuela* (hake casserole) is excellent. No reservations. 3 Calle Marqués de San Esteban, Gijón (phone: 85-345923). Inexpensive.

En Route from Gijón – Avilés is 15 miles (24 km) to the west. To avoid miles of soulless industrial suburbs and housing estates on the way, and drive through some rolling green Asturian hills, take the A8 highway rather than N362.

AVILÉS: Dominated by heavy industry, Avilés is a major iron and steel producing center that has trebled in size in the past few years. The few historical landmarks it possesses are swamped by new housing estates or smokestack scenarios, and the sea, only 2½ miles (4 km) away, is one of Spain's pollution blackspots. But the city does have an Old Quarter (around Galiana, La Ferrería, and Rivero Streets) with a few 12th-century churches and several medieval mansions. The Church of San Nicolás has three 14th- and 15th-century chapels attached to it, and in front of the church of San Francisco there is an ornate 17th-century fountain. On *Easter Sunday* and *Monday,* the city celebrates the *Fiesta del Bollu,* when everybody dons folk costume to eat iced *Easter* buns, drink white wine, and dance to traditional music.

En Route from Avilés – The western Asturian coast is thankfully undeveloped, so there are picturesque villages en route; but good hotels and restaurants are hard to find. Less than 3 miles (5 km) west of Avilés, at the small town of Salinas, which has a splendid, long, horseshoe-shaped beach with a pinewood backdrop, industrial pollution is already left behind. Then the N632 road runs through rolling countryside toward Soto de Barco, after which it crosses the Ría de Pravia estuary. Two miles (3 km) ahead is the CU2 turnoff to Cudillero, a typical Asturian fishing village whose steep cliffside is wedged around the harbor. Return to N632 via CU1 and proceed to Soto de Luiña, a tiny village from which a narrow lane leads to the Cabo Vidio headland, with magnificent coastal views. Then N632 continues past arable farmland, away from the sea, through numerous pretty villages, and into Cadavedo, where a large creaking road sign boasts "Voted prettiest town in Asturias — 1954." Cadavedo hasn't changed much since then, and its large sandy beach appears as clean and fine as ever. Soon after Cadavedo, the N632 rejoins the N634 on the way to Luarca, 45 miles (72 km) from Avilés.

LUARCA: Tucked into an S-shaped cove with a delightful bay and fishing port, unrushed and unpretentious Luarca is a maze of cobbled streets, stone stairways, and beautiful walks. The simple, colorful flowerpots that decorate the whitewashed harbor walls are as near as the place gets to ostentation, except for the stupendously ornate cemetery, with marble burial niches and grand family tombs, which is worth some attention. It's located just before the lighthouse and Atalaya chapel, 20 minutes' walk above the town. Another excellent stroll begins up a stone stairway by the bridge that crosses the town's small river, leading up to the Ermita (Hermitage). Walk 10 minutes beyond the hermitage and you'll come to an old village crammed with ancient *hórreos* (granaries).

Luarca has a fine beach, and is one of the last chances before Ribadeo to enjoy an evening of cider with the locals in a traditional Asturian tavern. Three local celebrations are worth noting. On the last Sunday in July, representatives of a nomadic tribe of Asturian shepherds, the Vaqueiros, participate in the *Vaqueirada,* wearing traditional costumes and playing strange instruments such as the *paye tsa,* a pan with a long handle struck with an iron key. A colorful sea processon takes place on August 15, and August 22 is the *Day of San Timoteo,* Luarca's patron saint. The tourist office (Plaza Alfonso X El Sabio; phone: 85-640083) is open from June through September.

CHECKING IN: *Gayoso* – Old and atmospheric, with wooden balconies; its restaurant a few doors away is very good. Closed November through April. 4 Paseo de Gómez, Luarca (phone: 85-640054). Moderate.

EATING OUT: *Leonés* – Three huge metal chandeliers and rural antiques and cowbells lining the walls evoke medieval images. Try *revuelto de gambas, ajo y espinaca* (scrambled eggs with shrimp, garlic, and spinach) and *sorbete de manzana* (apple sherbet). Reservations advised. El Parque, Luarca (phone: 85-640995). Moderate.

En Route from Luarca – To reach N634, follow the signposts for La Coruña. Ribadeo is 30 miles (48 km) away, past undistinguished Navia and Tapia de Casariago, which has a spacious bay, a picturesque beach, and good surfing. A new bridge over the Eo River leads out of Asturias and into Galicia and, a mile away, Ribadeo. (For a complete description of Ribadeo, see *Galicia,* DIRECTIONS.)

Pilgrims' Route

According to legend, a Spanish peasant was led to a distant field by a single shining star on an otherwise uneventful night in 813. Upon reaching the field, the peasant discovered what he believed to be the tomb of St. James the Apostle. The remains of the saint, martyred in Jerusalem in AD 44, had reportedly been returned by his followers to northern Spain, where he was said to have traveled and proselytized. Over time, the tomb had been forgotten and presumed lost — until 813. Although historians doubt that St. James actually ever entered the region — alive or dead — their down-to-earth testimony has failed to detract from the devotions accorded the site. St. James died centuries before Islam was even conceived, but the repossession of his sacred remains served as an inspirational presence in the war against the Moors, a spiritual device to rival the influence of the prophet Muhammad in the enemy ranks. As a result, the disciple of Jesus was subsequently acclaimed as Matamoros, "Slayer of the Moors." After receiving papal recognition, the town of Santiago de Compostela, where the remains of St. James (Santiago in Spanish) were discovered, became the third most important pilgrimage site in Christendom, after Jerusalem and Rome.

During the first half of the 12th century, Amerique Picaud, a French priest, wrote five volumes of stories connected with St. James, including a detailed guide for pilgrims on the journey to Santiago. This *Pilgrims' Guide* is considered to be the first travel guidebook ever written. It provided information on hospices, churches, difficult portions of the journey, meals and lodging, local customs, where good water could be found and bad water avoided, and the character of the people in each area. Though the Picaud itinerary was not the only one followed, it became known over the centuries as the primary Camino de Santiago (Way of St. James), or the Pilgrims' Route.

The pilgrims, easily identified by the scallop shell (the emblem of St. James) pinned to their cloaks and by their floppy felt hats, believed that completion of the long and arduous journey excused them from half of their allotted time in purgatory. Historically, they proved to have been a melting pot of European cultures, languages and dialects, and architectural tastes. The Pilgrims' Route, as it developed over the centuries, provides one of the most concentrated collections of Romanesque churches and Gothic cathedrals in the world, and the art decorating these religious monuments is a brilliant merging of Moorish, French, Italian, and Spanish influences.

The main Pilgrims' Route runs some 506 miles (810 km) through Spain, crossing the French border near Roncesvalles, in the region of Navarre, and passing through Pamplona, Logroño in La Rioja, and Burgos and León, in the region of Castile-León, on its way to the Galician capital, Santiago. Marked by crucifixes during medieval days, it is designated today by modern signs showing the scallop shell of St. James — the international symbol for pilgrims — stylized in the form of a star. It crosses the extremes of Spanish geography and climate, beginning high in the Pyrenees, then dropping into the fertile foothills and crossing the wide open, dry plains, before rising again over the mountains separating León and Galicia and winding through the hilly, lush green landscape of the Spanish northwest.

Today's pilgrims arrive in Santiago under vastly different circumstances from those of their medieval counterparts. Although 3,000 to 4,000 still arrive on foot each year as genuine pilgrims (who fulfill certain requirements, including mode of travel — on foot, horseback, or by bicycle — and in return receive 3 days' free food and lodging in Santiago), for most visitors the journey is more comfortable (usually in an air conditioned car or bus), and they come primarily to view the massive cathedral and its shrine as sightseers. Judging by the awe-inspired sighs that echo around the Plaza del Obradoiro, they are not disappointed. To round the last corner and come face-to-face with the cathedral's golden granite baroque face, tinged with green lichen, and its magnificently sculpted grand portal and two soaring towers, is to be as inspired as any pilgrim of the Middle Ages. It is, as travel author Jan Morris maintains, "one of the great moments of travel."

A room for two in a hotel listed below as expensive will cost $80 and up; a room in a hotel listed as moderate, between $50 and $80; and in an inexpensive one, $45 or less. A meal for two will run $70 or more in an expensive restaurant, $35 to $65 in the moderate range (the majority of the restaurants), and under $30 in an inexpensive place (also plentiful).

RONCESVALLES: The valley and pass through the Pyrenees here enjoy a certain historical renown because of the *Song of Roland,* an epic poem that romanticized the defeat of Charlemagne's rear guard during its retreat from Spain in 778. Later, the pass became the prime conduit for travelers along the Pilgrims' Route as it entered Spain from France, and in the 12th century King Sancho VII of Navarre (Sancho el Fuerte, the Strong) added an Augustinian monastery to the hospital that had already grown up to serve pilgrims on the Spanish side of the pass. Legend has it that a monk constantly rang a bell to guide pilgrims through the pass. Still in use, the monastery buildings are open to the public. A cloister leads to the entrance of the Colegiata Real (Royal Collegiate Church), one of the first Gothic churches built in Spain, consecrated in 1219, with a nave and two aisles that are beautiful examples of the Romanesque-to-Gothic transition. The church houses the famous *Madonna de Roncesvalles,* a 13th-century cedar figure of the Virgin Mary, clad in silver and adorned with jewels. According to legend, the figure appeared miraculously, pointed out by a red stag with a star shining in its antlers. Also off the cloister is the chapter house, containing the tombs of the monastery's founder, King Sancho, and his wife, Doña Clemencia, and a massive stained glass window depicting the king's victories. The monastery is open daily, from 8:30 AM to 7 PM, depending on when masses are scheduled. An adjoining monastery building houses the small *Roncesvalles Museum,* with artifacts from the Camino de Santiago or related to it: desks, tapestries, illuminated manuscripts, books on plants, herbs, and philosophy, coins, and letters pilgrims wrote to people back home — a picture of life on the road in the Middle Ages. The museum is open daily, June through September, from 11 AM to 1:30 PM and from 4 to 6 PM (in winter it opens for groups only); admission charge.

Down a road from the monastery is the Chapel of Sancti Spiritus, the oldest building in Roncesvalles, dating from the early 12th century.

CHECKING IN/EATING OUT: *La Posada* – A small, quaint, 11-room hotel. Beautiful and quiet, it is just steps away from the monastery. The restaurant offers high-quality fare. Roncesvalles (phone: 48-760225). Moderate.

En Route from Roncesvalles – Take C135 south about 2 miles (3 km) to Burguete, a picturesque Basque town, where Ernest Hemingway is known to have gone trout fishing. The town has the small Romanesque Church of San Nicolás, and a number of charming hotels and restaurants. Continuing southwest, stay on C135 as it winds along the Arga River to Pamplona. The sights from the road, as it passes over hills and around sharp bends, are spectacular. Ahead are the walls of Pamplona, 29½ miles (47 km) from Roncesvalles; its cathedral and massive fortifications resemble a glowing postcard photo when approached at sunset.

CHECKING IN: *Burguete* – A *hostal* of 22 rooms with bath, across from the ancient church. The owner is an avid fisherman and if you arrive on a day when he was lucky at the stream, you're in for a treat in the dining room — trout so pink you'll swear you're dreaming. Closed December through February. 51 Calle Unica, Burguete (phone: 48-760005). Inexpensive.

Loizu – This 27-room *hostal* with private baths is kept spotless by the owner, who rules over the establishment with an iron hand. It has a restaurant, a long dining room with a rustic, beamed ceiling in which local specialties, including a variety of lamb and trout dishes, are served. Closed December through mid-March. 3 Calle Unica, Burguete (phone: 48-760008). Inexpensive.

EATING OUT: *Marichu* – A grill restaurant serving meat dishes only. No reservations. 2 Calle Roncesvalles, Burguete (phone: 48-760086). Inexpensive.

Txiki Polit – The area's most picturesque eatery. Dine in either the small, elegant, wood-paneled room with the giant wooden chandelier, in front, or in the long, traditional Basque dining room in the rear. Specialties include mountain trout with smoked ham, and *cordero al chilindrón* (Basque-style lamb). Reservations advised. 42 Calle Unica, Burguete (phone: 48-760019). Inexpensive.

PAMPLONA: For a detailed report on the city, its sights, hotels, and restaurants, see *Pamplona,* THE CITIES.

En Route from Pamplona – Follow N111 southwest for 27 miles (43 km) to Estella. Along the way, the topography changes from relatively mountainous terrain north of Pamplona to rolling plateau land that gradually declines in altitude as it nears the central Spanish plains. For the most part, the road runs parallel to the original Camino de Santiago, passing through wide open fields that erupt into brilliant carpets of sunflowers in the summer. Ruins of old pilgrim hospitals can be found in the town of Cizur Menor, just outside Pamplona, and a stretch of the original route has been preserved in the small village of Zarquiegui. Both are obscure and hard to find, however, even with residents' directions. The first monument of note concerning the pilgrims' progress is the bronze statue of a pilgrim just outside the town of Puente la Reina, 15 miles (24 km) from Pamplona. The statue depicts the traditional pilgrim in flowing cape and wide-brimmed hat, carrying a staff and a gourd for water — an image that is seen repeatedly along the route, particularly in statues of St. James dressed as a pilgrim.

It was in Puente la Reina that a less-traveled pilgrims' road, one that came from Arles (in the Provence region of France) and crossed the Pyrenees via the Somfort Pass, joined the main route (which originated in Paris and descended via Vezelay and Le Puy to the Pyrenees and crossed into Spain via the Roncesvalles Pass). The two trails most likely joined here to take advantage of the bridge that gave the town its name, built across the Arga River in the 11th century. The bridge, with its six arches and peaked central span, stands as strong as ever, one of the best examples of medieval engineering still in existence. The Iglesia del Crucifijo (Church of the Crucifix), a 12th-century Romanesque church that was part of a pilgrims' hospice, was rebuilt in the 15th century and is famous for a Y-shaped crucifix carved with an expressionistic Christ, which is believed to have been brought from Germany by a 14th-century pilgrim.

Continue along N111 to the next significant town, Cirauqui, which clings to the top of a hill overlooking the Salado River and is noted for the San Román church, with an excellent portal. Because the roads leading to town and the streets in town are very steep, drivers should make sure that they are handy with the clutch or have an automatic transmission. In medieval days, the outskirts of Cirauqui were considered a danger spot for pilgrims; the *Pilgrims' Guide* warned of "evil doers" who would encourage pilgrims to water their horses in a nearby stream with bad water. When the horses became ill, the schemers drove off the pilgrims and skinned their steeds.

Back on N111, Estella, 12 miles (19 km) from Puente la Reina, becomes visible after a few more bends in the road.

CHECKING IN: *Mesón del Peregrino* – At the junction of the two pilgrims' routes. The 15 rooms all have private baths, there is a swimming pool, and the restaurant receives rave reviews for its substantial meals. Carretera Pamplona–Logroño (N111), Km 23, Puente la Reina (phone: 48-340075). Inexpensive.

EATING OUT: *Fonda Restaurante Lorca* – This small, family-run eatery is in the center of Cirauqui, where its upstairs dining room overlooks the town square. The menu is a simple one, featuring chicken and veal entrées. There are some small rooms, but they are recommended only in an emergency. No reservations. 54 Calle Mayor, Cirauqui (no phone). Inexpensive.

ESTELLA: Once the seat of the Kings of Navarre, this major stopping point on the Pilgrims' Route is packed with churches. The church of San Pedro de la Rúa (St. Peter of the Way) dominates the entire town. Built during the 12th century, it is Estella's oldest church. A massive portal graces it, and its interior features a mixture of Romanesque and Gothic influences. But its real gem is the small cloister tucked between the church and the towering cliff; its two remaining rows of columns are topped by some of the most intricately carved capitals in Europe, some depicting the life of Christ, but others, in contrast, portraying mythological subjects, with scenes of couples kissing — virtually unheard of in Catholic settings.

The exter:ors of Estella's other churches are generally more impressive than their interiors. The Iglesia del Santo Sepulcro (Holy Sepulcher), also in a transitional Romanesque-Gothic style, boasts a Gothic portal with carvings of the Last Supper, the Virgin Mary, and the Crucifixion. The church of San Miguel has a magnificent portal with carvings of the Guardian Angels, the Old Men of the Apocalypse, the childhood of Christ, and the Apostles. The Estella Tourist Office (phone: 48-554011) is in the 12th-century Palacio de los Reyes de Navarra (Palace of the Kings of Navarre), one of the oldest secular buildings in Spain, located directly across from the monumental staircase that rises up to San Pedro.

CHECKING IN: *Irache* – Estella's best *hostal,* modern with 74 clean rooms and private baths. The restaurant is uninspiring, but there are plenty of good dining spots nearby. Carretera Pamplona–Logroño (N111), Km 43, Estella (phone: 48-551150). Moderate.

EATING OUT: *La Cepa* – An elegant establishment with a classic wood-carved bar overlooking the main square. The wine list offers extensive selections from the Rioja and Navarre regions. Reservations advised. 19 Plaza de los Fueros, Estella (phone: 48-550032). Expensive to moderate.

Maracaibo – Across the square from *La Cepa,* it serves excellent regional specialties. Reservations advised. 22 Plaza de los Fueros, Estella (phone: 48-550483). Expensive to moderate.

En Route from Estella – The Monasterio de Irache, just 2 miles (3 km) south of Estella along N111, was built in the 12th and 13th centuries and is considered by many to be a particularly beautiful example of the transitional Romanesque-to-Gothic style. It now can be visited once again, after having been closed several years for renovations (open Tuesdays through Fridays from 10 AM to 2 PM and from 5 to 7 PM, Saturdays and Sundays from 9 AM to 2 PM and from 4 to 7 PM; admission charge). Continue southwest on N111 to the town of Los Arcos, 13 miles (21 km) from Estella, where the Iglesia Parroquial de la Asunción (Church of the Assumption) in Plaza Mayor offers a perfect example of baroque excesses. Virtually every inch of the interior walls and domes is covered with gilted decoration, that of the domes in a swirling shell design. The high altar has a 15th-century altarpiece and a fine Gothic statue of the Madonna, while the magnificent choir stalls are also Gothic. Continuing another 4½ miles (7 km), N111 leads to Torres del Río, a town that is beautifully perched on a hillside dropping down to the river. Founded by the Knights of the Holy Sepulcher, it has an interesting octagonal church complete with Moorish decor, including Mudéjar art in the vaulting of the main dome. The route continues another 13 miles (21 km) to Logroño, the only major town in the region of La Rioja.

LOGROÑO: This is the capital of one of the most prosperous regions in Spain, and one of its main wine producing regions. Rioja wines have long been considered among the best in Europe (they are now enjoying increasing popularity in the US), and anyone who has noticed the popularity of asparagus in Spanish salads can get an idea of the income generated by the other local crop — the Rioja region grows over 90% of Spain's asparagus. The modern town of Logroño is uninteresting, but the small Old Town at its core holds several religious treasures associated with the Pilgrims' Route. Everything is within easy walking distance of the massive main square. The Rua Vieja and Calle Mayor, the two main arteries of the Old Town, have been trod by countless pilgrims over the centuries. The 15th-century Catedral de Santa María la Redonda is austerely Gothic, set off by twin baroque towers and a baroque façade added in 1742. The Church of Santa María del Palacio, built on the site of the palace of the Kings of Castile, is famous for its eight-sided, pyramid-shaped steeple, originally constructed during the 13th century (the rest of the church is mostly from the 16th to 18th centuries). The portal of the smaller church of St. Bartholomew, seemingly designed for a grand cathedral, is a fine example of Gothic sculpture, depicting the life of the saint.

CHECKING IN: *Murrieta* – There are more modern and more luxurious hotels elsewhere, but this 113-room hostelry is a good choice for older elegance. Located in the center of town, the *tapas* bars and monuments of the Old Town are only steps away. 1 Calle Marqués de Murrieta, Logroño (phone: 41-224150). Moderate.

La Numantina – Near the main square in the Old Town, this *hostal* offers 17 clean rooms, plus wonderful breakfast pastries imported from across the street. 4 Calle Sagasta, Logroño (phone: 41-251411). Moderate to inexpensive.

EATING OUT: *Asador González* – Also known as *La Chata,* this place serves Logroño's best roast baby goat and baby lamb. Closed Sundays. Reservations advised. 3 Calle Carnicerías, Logroño (phone: 41-251296). Moderate.

Mesón Charro – The best *chuletas de cordero* (lamb chops) in town are found here, in an informal, picnic-table setting. Reservations advised. 12 Calle Laurel, Logroño (phone: 41-224663). Moderate.

En Route from Logroño – Take N232 out of Logroño to N120. From here, the road is very well marked as the Camino de Santiago; the landscape becomes drier, the fertile green of Navarre changing to a dusty brown. Follow N120 west toward Burgos, 70½ miles (113 km) from Logroño. Along the way, three small towns of the Rioja region offer important pilgrim sights. The first is Navarrete, a small town with a large 16th-century church. The next is Nájera, which was at one time the capital of the kingdom of Navarre and which became a main stop on the route when a large bridge was built over the Najerilla River, along with a monastery. The Monastery of Santa María la Real was founded by García, a Navarrese king, in the 11th century, on the site where a statue of the Virgin had been found. Its 15th-century church is notable as a pantheon of 11th- and 12th-century royalty (the 12th-century tomb of Blanca de Navarra is outstanding), and for the particulary intricate Flamboyant Gothic carving of the choir stalls, completed around 1500; the cloister, too, is a fine example of Flamboyant Gothic design. The monastery and church are open daily, from 10 AM to noon and 4 to 6 PM. No admission charge.

Continue to Santo Domingo de la Calzada, the third significant town between Logroño and Burgos, and one of the most important stops on the Pilgrims' Route. The town was named for an 11th-century monk who spent his life helping pilgrims, constructing a bridge across the Oca River for their use, and building a road (his name translates as St. Dominic of the Causeway). Some 300 years later, the same monk reentered church lore when a young man, falsely accused of theft, was sentenced to be hanged. As the sentence was carried out, the young man's parents prayed fervently before the monk's tomb. Passing the gallows, they found their son alive and well, while still hanging by the neck. They immediately raced to the governor and implored him to cut their son down and allow him to live. The governor, understandably, found all of this hard to believe and murmured that if the boy were still alive, then the well-cooked cock could probably crow — which it proceeded to do. The startled governor freed the young man, and to this day, a white cock and hen are kept in the cathedral as a reminder of the miracle. (This miracle, by the way, closely resembles one that occurred in Barcelos, Portugal, and gave rise to the rooster as the Portuguese symbol of good luck; in that story, it was a Galician on his way to Santiago who was falsely accused of stealing.) After this stop, continue west on N120 into the region of Castile-León, driving the remaining 42½ miles (68 km) to Burgos, capital of the province of the same name.

CHECKING IN: *Parador Santo Domingo de la Calzada* – A beautiful *parador* situated in an old pilgrims' hostel that dates back to the 11th century. All 27 rooms have private baths. There are often concerts at the small church next door. 3 Plaza del Santo, Santo Domingo de la Calzada (phone: 41-340300). Moderate.

BURGOS: A onetime capital of the kingdom of Castile, Burgos is associated with the legendary warrior El Cid, who was born nearby. An equestrian statue of the 11th-century hero stands by the Arlanzón River. The city has a lovely riverside promenade, the Paseo del Espolón, supremely conducive to strolling, which begins just outside the city's 14th-century Arco de Santa María gate. A short way inside the gate is the massive 13th-century cathedral, built by King Ferdinand III (the Saint). The city also has two monasteries beyond its Old Town — the Cartuja de Miraflores and the Monasterio de las Huelgas — that are well worth a visit. (For a detailed report on the city, its sights, hotels, and restaurants, see *Burgos,* THE CITIES.)

En Route from Burgos – Follow N120 westward for 19 miles (30 km) to the town of Olmillos de Sasamón, recognizable by the massive castle along the highway, then turn left down the road toward Castellanos de Castro and Castrojeriz. At this point, the Pilgrims' Route temporarily stops running parallel to the national highways and becomes quite convoluted, but the signs for the Camino de Santiago are excellent and easy to follow. About a mile (1.6 km) after the left turn, make a right turn at the sign for Castellanos de Castro. The road winds through fields and between densely planted trees, and actually passes through the ruins of the Convent of San Antonio, under the Gothic arches and past the ornate portal. Soon after, the Castle of Castrojeriz appears in the distance, 11 miles (18 km) from Olmillos.

CASTROJERIZ: A poor pueblo of a place, Castrojeriz has three massive churches. Santa María del Manzano, a 13th-century collegiate church, is just to the left as the Pilgrims' Route enters the village. Now a veritable art museum, it was one of the most important churches along the route until the cathedral in Burgos was completed. The church features a 16th-century stained glass window, four ornate wooden altarpieces carved by Italian craftsmen, and a polychromatic sculpture of the Virgin of the Apple Tree. The town's three other churches, San Juan, Santa Clara, and Santo Domingo, are impressive from the outside (the parish priest or one of his assistants will open them for visitors between *Easter* and October; phone: 47-377036). Castrojeriz's portico-lined main square is surprisingly well maintained for what is otherwise a dusty and forgotten town.

En Route from Castrojeriz – Heading west out of town, be prepared to share the road with herds of sheep that, at times, graze in the area. Follow the local road (marked Melgar) for 16 miles (26 km) to Frómista, an agricultural center boasting perhaps the most beautifully constructed Romanesque church along the route. Built early in the 11th century, San Martín has three perfectly formed naves, ribbed arches, and sculpted capitals on the columns. The exterior has two round towers, small arched windows, and an octagonal cupola, all fashioned to breathtaking excellence. Open daily, from 10 AM to 2 PM and 4 to 8 PM.

The narrow country roads, still well marked as the Camino de Santiago, continue for about 12 miles (20 km) to Carrión de los Condes, another important stop on the Pilgrims' Route. Its two churches feature excellent exterior carvings. The Church of Santa María has crumbling carvings of the Old Men of the Apocalypse and the Three Kings. The Church of St. James, tucked just off the main town square, has a beautiful façade with statues of the Apostles and an even more impressive portal with carvings depicting men at everyday work — an architect with a compass, a sheep shearer with scissors, and a farmer.

At Carrión de los Condes, the Pilgrims' Route returns to N120; follow it about 27 miles (43 km) west to Sahagún. Here, the churches of San Tirso and San Lorenzo are fine examples of early Romanesque brick construction, with interiors bearing extensive Mudéjar decorations. Continue along to the next stop of importance, León, a 42-mile (67-km) drive from Sahagún, reached by heading west along N120 to the N601 intersection, and then taking N601 north into the provincial capital.

LEÓN: For centuries a center of Spanish culture, León, like most of Spain's larger cities, is composed of an Old Town surrounded by a spreading new city of high-rises. The old medieval section has been substantially rebuilt, but still follows the maze-like twists and turns of the original streets. León's crowning jewel is its cathedral. The beauty of this 14th- and 15th-century structure is not apparent outside, but once inside the visitor is overwhelmed by the most dazzling display of stained glass in all of Spain. The Romanesque Basilica of San Isidro, containing a pantheon of kings and queens of the old kingdom of León, is another important building, as is the *Parador de San Marcos* (7 Plaza de San Marcos; phone: 987-237300), a 15-minute walk from the Old Town, at one time a monastery that saw service as a way station for pilgrims. The main square of the Old Town (Plaza Mayor) fills daily with a vast fruit and vegetable market. The surrounding neighborhood is the place where the city's evening *paseo* takes place, and is also the quarter where most of the best restaurants and nightlife are found. For further details on León, see *Castile-León (Old Castile),* DIRECTIONS.

En Route from León – Take N120 heading west from León 18 miles (29 km) to the town of Hospital de Orbigo, where a famous bridge crosses the Orbigo River. The bridge was the site of a celebrated series of jousts by the love-struck knight Suero de Quiñones, who, to prove his valor to his love, challenged anyone who tried to cross the bridge for 30 days. Together with nine companions whose names are inscribed on the bridge, he took on all comers, breaking over 300 lances in all. His fame spread throughout medieval Europe, and the bridge crossing became known as the Passage of Honor. Eventually Quiñones made the pilgrimage to Santiago de Compostela and placed a gold-plated silver collar around the bust of St. James, which remains in Santiago's Chapel of Relics. Another 10 miles (16 km) west of Hospital de Orbigo along N120 is the town of Astorga, with its medieval city walls, an impressive cathedral, and a palace designed by Gaudí.

EATING OUT: *Il Suero de Quiñones* – Enjoy a drink and the view on the deck overlooking the Passage of Honor Bridge, then try one of the dining room's massive mixed salads or highly recommended lamb chops. Located directly at the end of the bridge. No reservations. Hospital de Orbigo (phone: 87-374938). Inexpensive.

ASTORGA: Beautifully situated on a mountain spur 2,850 feet above sea level, Astorga served as a staging point for the final third of the Pilgrims' Route to Santiago. The Romans knew the city as Asturica Augusta, and Pliny the Elder described it as "magnificent." The Cathedral de Santa María, built during the 13th century on the site of an 11th-century church, has bell towers similar to those of León's cathedral, as well as similar massive stained glass windows. Its museum houses noteworthy works of medieval religious art, including an ivory crucifix with small rubies inlaid to represent trickling blood. The cannonballs on the staircase are remnants of the Peninsular War against Napoleon. Take a close look at the four-panel painting of the life of San Antonio Abab. The museum is open daily, from 10 AM to 2 PM and from 4 to 8 PM; no admission charge.

Another sightseeing stop, the Episcopal Palace (Plaza de la Catedral), is a fanciful 19th-to-20th-century mock medieval creation of soaring towers, circular staircases, and an interior where light dances through the rooms. The work of Antoni Gaudí — his most imaginative, spectacular creation outside Barcelona — it was commissioned by the bishop, a fellow Catalan, after a fire destroyed its predecessor in 1886, but wasn't finished until 1909. The first two floors now house a museum dedicated to the subject of the Pilgrims' Route, the *Museo de los Caminos,* with an extensive collection of statues, paintings, notebooks, and journals from the heyday of the pilgrimage (open from 10 AM to 2 PM and from 4 to 8 PM; admission charge). The third floor houses a permanent exhibition of regional art from the last 2 decades.

CHECKING IN/EATING OUT: *Gaudí* – Astorga's top choice, with a traditional Spanish decor of light walls and dark furnishings. Most of the 35 rooms overlook the fanciful Episcopal Palace, and the restaurant downstairs is one of the best within miles, serving excellent fare in tremendous portions. 6 Plaza Eduardo de Castro, Astorga (phone: 87-615654). Moderate.

En Route from Astorga – Continue westward on N-VI, an excellent four-lane highway. As the road begins to climb, the views on both sides clearly show how arduous this part of the pilgrimage must have been. Though the highway here doesn't exactly follow the Pilgrims' Route, the smaller C120 does, winding through the Valley of El Silencio, bordered by rugged mountains, and passing the Cross of Iron. The cross is set into a pile of stones, created as a result of a tradition that each passing pilgrim add his own stone. The mountains that line the N-VI highway are marked by giant coal deposits, evidence of the importance of mining in this region of Spain.

After 38 miles (61 km), N-VI drops to the town of Ponferrada, where an 11th-century iron bridge carried pilgrims over the Sil River. The massive Templar castle, overlooking the river, appears spectacular from a distance, but it is little more than a standing outer wall (open from 9 AM to 1 PM and from 3 to 6 PM. Ponferrada does have an excellent example of Mozarabic architecture in the tiny 10th-century Church of Santo Tomás de las Ollas, in which a ring of horseshoe-shaped arches surrounds the altar. The church is up a side road — there's a sign just as the main road enters the town (knock on the door of the adjacent house, where the caretaker lives). Ponferrada marks the beginning of the last stretch of the Pilgrims' Route before it enters the region of Galicia. Follow N-VI 12½ miles (20 km) to the town of Villafranca del Bierzo, with its outstanding *parador.*

VILLAFRANCA DEL BIERZO: The town owes its foundation to French pilgrims, who used the area as a stopover during the 11th century. The medieval buildings here include manor houses that line the famous Calle del Agua, which was known to pilgrims as one of the route's most beautiful streets. The Church of St. James, a typical example of 12th-century Romanesque architecture, boasts an excellent Portal of Forgiveness opening onto the route. Exhausted pilgrims, unable to complete the trek as far as Santiago, could pass through it into the church and receive the same indulgences as those given in Santiago. The town's other churches — all worth a visit — include San Juan en San Fiz, a well-preserved Romanesque building; Santa María de Cluniaco, its floor plan in the form of a Latin cross; and San Nicolás, a 17th-century church that was part of a Jesuit college.

CHECKING IN: *Parador Villafranca del Bierzo* – A modern, 40-room hostelry, at the edge of town, a short walk from most of the ancient buildings. Avenida Calvo Sotelo, Villafranca del Bierzo (phone: 87-540175). Moderate.

EATING OUT: *La Charola* – A real dining experience. For centuries, pilgrims have stopped here to fill up and drink before beginning the most difficult part of the pilgrimage. Today, it's also the sort of place to which truck drivers make a beeline the minute their jobs bring them into the area. Order the *cocido,* the typical stewed meat platter, and a huge tureen of noodle soup will appear, followed by a platter of vegetables, one of garbanzo beans, and one of stewed meats and sausages — guests take what they want, because no one could possibly eat it all. Wash it down with a bottle of wine or *gaseosa* (soda water), and finish with some of the local firewater — *orujo* — in your coffee. Reservations advised. 19 Calle Doctor Aren, Villafranca del Bierzo (phone: 87-540200). Inexpensive.

En Route from Villafranca del Bierzo – Leave town via N-VI, and the valley immediately narrows. The road zigs and zags as it climbs to enter the region of Galicia through the Puerto de Pedrafita do Cebreiro, 18 miles (29 km) from Villafranca. This is the last major pass to be negotiated before Santiago, and it is at this point that the main highway and the Pilgrims' Route once again part company, as the N-VI takes a more northwesterly course for

Lugo and the Pilgrims' Route turns into tiny mountain roads on a more southwesterly course to Santiago. As the road skirts the ridge rising to the summit, almost as a reward for the pilgrims' tenacity, the views to the north are breathtaking, with bright yellow flowers punctuating the green mountains that stretch as far as the eye can see.

O CEBREIRO: The village of O Cebreiro (in Galician — its Castilian spelling is El Cebreiro), not far from the Pedrafita do Cebreiro pass, is an ancient one, with a church and a pilgrims' hospice that were constructed as early as the 9th century, as well as some old reconstructed dry stone huts of Celtic origin. The church became famous following a miracle that was reported around 1300. A priest of little faith was saying mass in the presence of a peasant who had climbed through deep snow and wind to get there. Suddenly, as the priest was musing that it was silly for anyone to brave such weather for only a bit of wine and bread, the Host turned into flesh and the wine into blood. Word of this miracle of the Holy Eucharist spread throughout Europe, and the chalice in which it is said to have occurred is still kept in the church.

CHECKING IN/EATING OUT: *San Giraldo de Aurillac* – Simple accommodations in one of Europe's most mystical locations. The 6 rooms of this *hostal* were built into the original, centuries-old hospice. The restaurant features simple but filling fare. Try the *caldo gallego* (Galician soup), *cocido* (stew), and locally produced cebreiro cheese. O Cebreiro (phone: 82-369025). Inexpensive.

En Route from O Cebreiro – The narrow road continues westward. After Linares, there is a wonderful view to the left of mountain after mountain, all of differing shades of green against a pale sky, eventually fading into the mist. Low stone walls (similar to those in Scotland and Ireland) appear, the sun glistens off shiny slate roofs, and lush ferns line the road. As cattle graze in small roadside pastures, hay wagons, tractors, oxen carts, and cows share the road with cars. In the winter, the vista is of stark, windswept snow punctuated by the forms of naked trees. The tiny towns encountered along these winding roads all have pilgrims in their past, and they have inherited an architecture that is more reminiscent of Ireland than Spain. The village of Triacastela has a pilgrims' jail with interesting graffiti on its walls; farther along, after passing through narrow gorges, the road turns around the massive Monastery of Samos, which goes back to the Middle Ages, although little of its early times remains. The monastery has a small Gothic cloister and a larger neo-classical one, the latter with modern frescoes on its upper level depicting the life of Saint Benedict. The church, built in the 18th century, is purely classical in design. Tours of the monastery take place daily, beginning every half hour from 10:30 AM to 1 PM and from 4 to 6:30 PM. No admission charge.

Sarria is 32 miles (51 km) beyond O Cebreiro. After Sarria, the road, C535, continues westward and about 15 miles (24 km) past Sarria, it crosses the Miño River (Portugal's Minho), which has been turned into a massive lake by a dam. The old village of Portomarín has been lost forever, covered in water, but before that metamorphosis happened, the tower-like church of the Knights of St. John of Jerusalem had been dismantled and rebuilt on a hill behind the new town of Portomarín. It still has a beautiful rose window, and the decoration of its portal, resembling the *Gate of Glory* in Santiago de Compostela, is believed to be the work of Master Mateo.

About 7½ miles (12 km) west of Portomarín, C535 joins N540/N640, the main Orense–Lugo highway. Turn north toward Lugo, but drive only 5 miles (8 km) to the turnoff for C547, which leads to Santiago. Continue about 6 miles (10 km) to the sign marking Vilar de Doñas (just off the main road), a final church of significance along the Pilgrims' Route. The church was a chapter house of the Knights of St. James and a burial place for Galician knights killed fighting the Moors. Its name derives from the frescoes in the apse depicting women with sultry smiles dressed in bonnets and finery. After seeing the church, return to C547 and continue to Santiago de Compostela, which is another 59 miles (94 km) west. (For a detailed report on the city, its sights, hotels, and restaurants, see *Santiago de Compostela,* THE CITIES.)

Catalonia and Andorra

Every year, the beaches of the Costa Brava attract millions of tourists lured by the promise of inexpensive, fun-filled vacations. Most fly to Barcelona or Gerona and head straight for the coast, unaware of the traditional Catalan life that continues in villages, on farms, and in small towns throughout the region, just waiting to be discovered. Barcelona itself is a sophisticated city rich in history, with a lively cultural scene. Tarragona has its Roman heritage. And a few miles away from the high-rise hotels of the best-known resorts there are glorious rocky coves with beautiful beaches and little fishing villages. Inland, the countryside ranges from snow-capped mountains to plains baked red by a fierce sun. The rewards for the visitor include grandiose castles and cathedrals, creepy medieval passages, a 900-year-old nunnery, and a surrealistic art museum.

Not long ago, most tourists had no idea that this region considered itself separate from the rest of Spain. Under Generalísimo Francisco Franco, Catalonia was a province to be subjugated; expressions of nationalism — such as the teaching of the staccato native language — were suppressed. Following Franco's death in 1975, however, things began to change, and Catalonia became one of Spain's 17 autonomous communities, enjoying the equivalent of US statehood. At long last, Catalans had their own *generalitat* (government). With the revival of their language, street signs were changed from Spanish to Catalan, and the red-and-yellow Catalan flag was raised above public and private buildings alike. Throughout the area, roads and public utilities were improved and ancient buildings were restored as Catalan pride manifested itself — a pride that is reflected today in the welcoming of foreigners.

As early as 500 BC, the Greeks were trading along the coast of northeastern Spain, establishing colonies at Empúries and Roses. As elsewhere in the Mediterranean, the Romans soon followed, and by 200 BC Tarragona was the fortress city of an extensive imperial province that stretched across the northern Iberian Peninsula. About 1,000 years later, in 801, Barcelona became the focal point when it was conquered by Charlemagne and turned into the front line of an offensive against the Moors, who controlled the rest of Spain. The demise of the Carolingian Empire at the end of the 9th century led to the founding of the House of Barcelona, which united the counties of what is basically today's Catalonia (plus territory on the French side of the Pyrenees.) This unification was the work of Guifré el Pilós (Wilfred the Shaggy), who had proclaimed himself Count of Barcelona and, legend has it, also was responsible for creating the Catalan flag. While supporting Charles the Bald, Charlemagne's grandson, in battle, Wilfred fought fiercely despite being seriously wounded. Acknowledging this bravery, Charles dipped his fingers in the blood pouring from Wilfred's wounds and drew four gory lines across the count's yellow shield. It's a good story, as legends go, but the first recorded use of the Catalan colors actually came some 200 years later, in 1082. Even that date, however, enables Catalans to boast that their flag is Europe's oldest.

The first usages of "Catalunya" and "Catalan" can also be traced back to the 11th century, when Barcelona was a center of shipbuilding and trade. Later, thanks to the exploits of James the Conqueror, Catalonia became a major Mediterranean force. James reigned from 1213 to 1276 and led the capture of Majorca, Ibiza, and Valencia; his family later continued the expansion, roping in Sicily, Minorca, Athens, Sardinia, and Naples. Catalan power did not last, however. Less than 50 years after its peak, the conquest of Naples in 1423, the marriage of Queen Isabella of Castile and King Ferdinand of Aragon began the unification of Spain, and by the end of the 15th century, Catalonia had lost control of its own affairs and was excluded from the lucrative trade with the newly discovered Americas.

By 1640, the suppression had become so intense that the peasants revolted. But like so many other valiant struggles, the War of the Reapers (1640–52) was in vain; lost was the idea of an independent Catalan republic, along with territories east and north of the Pyrenees, which were ceded to France. All that remained was "Els Segadors" (The Reapers), a marching song that became the Catalan anthem.

The next great upheaval was the War of the Spanish Succession early in the 18th century, with all of Europe embroiled in a battle for the Spanish throne between Archduke Charles of Austria and Philip V of the House of Bourbon. Having allied itself with the archduke, who promised Catalonia her independence, the region again suffered when the victorious Philip stringently repressed the would-be nation. Castilian law ruled; the use of Catalan was forbidden in the courts, and the universities in Barcelona and Lérida were closed. Catalonia was again reduced to a mere province.

It takes more than a defeat or two to keep a Catalan down, however, and by the end of the 19th century, the region was thriving, thanks to the burgeoning Industrial Revolution, centered in Barcelona, which saw the first steam trains chug the 20 miles (32 km) north to Mataró in 1848. Forty years later, the city symbolized the resurgence of a strong and confident Catalonia when it hosted an international *Universal Exhibition*. As the arts flourished anew, so did interest in Catalan as a written language, and poems and novels wound the web of solidarity ever more tightly. At the turn of the century, Barcelona, like Paris, was a hotbed of revolutionary creativity. Pablo Picasso was here, having arrived from his native Málaga at the age of 14; he would spend almost 10 years in the Catalan capital. Architects such as Antoni Gaudí were in the vanguard, adorning new city quarters with buildings of astonishing design — the local version of Art Nouveau, called Modernisme. Later, Joan Miró, Salvador Dalí, Antoni Tàpies, and other artists came to the fore. Barcelona was even the capital of a short-lived Catalan government, set up in 1932.

Unfortunately, the potential of Catalan power posed a threat to centralist forces in Madrid, and during the Spanish Civil War Catalonia made the mistake of backing the "wrong" side. When Franco took power, the Catalan language was once again banned in businesses, churches, the press, and, most wounding of all, in schools. The only place that Catalans could gather in great numbers was at the local soccer club, *F.C. Barcelona.* Boys were (and still are) signed up at birth to become members of the club that epitomizes the Catalan spirit, regularly attracting more than 125,000 aficionados to its games. Famous coaches and superstar players boost fans to a fever pitch, and the *Camp Nou Stadium* rings with wild chants of "Barça, Barça," particularly when the opposition is *Real Madrid.* No wonder the Catalans are proud that they will host the *1992 Summer Olympic Games* and that their language is one of the "official" languages of the games — a fitting highlight of the quincentennial celebrations marking the famous voyage of Christopher Columbus, who set sail from the Catalan capital in 1492.

Catalonia today spans some 12,370 square miles and is divided into four provinces — Tarragona, Barcelona, Lérida (Lleida in Catalan), and Gerona (Girona in Catalan) — although the significance of these boundaries is purely administrative. What little rivalry exists takes on a good-natured tone, even down to the 38 *comarques* (counties, or districts), each of which produces its own tourist pamphlet extolling local traditions such as the *festa major* (town fair). Every village and town has its own, and there are thousands in all. Around Tarragona, the highlight is the building of *castells dels xiquets* (human towers), with as many as six "stories" of men and boys standing on one another's shoulders. The festival of *Corpus Christi* brings out masked *gegants* (giants) and *capgrossos* (clowns with giant heads) to entertain the crowds, who dance the traditional *sardana* to the sounds of *las coblas* (traditional bands) playing old-fashioned wind instruments. Music plays an important part in Catalan life: not the Moorish wailing of flamenco as in the south, but more "European" folk songs, and there is a strong choral tradition that is unique in Spain. Catalonia's most famous musical son was Pau (Pablo) Casals (1876–1973), who refused to live in Spain while Franco was in power, and made his home in Prades, just over the border in the French foothills of the Pyrenees.

As for customs, warm evenings bring people out into the street for a promenade just as they do elsewhere in the country, but despite the two large bullrings in Barcelona, bullfighting is not popular and the newspapers devote little space to the subject. Catalans have the reputation of being hardworking businesspeople, and are the butt and punchline of numerous jokes and stories that caricature their thriftiness as stinginess. Visitors should not be put off by this image of a fiercely proud and independent people. Since the 1950s, Catalans have used their business acumen to promote tourism, so hospitality is second nature throughout the region. Nor should visitors who speak Spanish be put off by the Catalan language, which is not totally removed from Spanish, although there are words, such as *tancat,* that have no relation to their Castilian counterparts (*cerrado,* or closed, in this case). In fact, at times Catalan is more understandable; the road sign *perill* needs no translation.

Catalan cooking is part of the resurgence of Catalan culture. Traditional recipes are being revived: rabbit with almonds, partridge with grapes, chicken with lobster, and sea bass with thyme and baked squash. Not surprisingly, the cuisine features fish, fresh from the Mediterranean. The catch may be cooked *a la planxa* (grilled) or simmered with peas, tomatoes, and peppers in a *sarsuela;* trout from Pyrenean lakes and rivers is delicious *a l'agredolç,* with vinegar and honey. Confusingly, *truita* means both trout and omelette, so look under the heading *peix* (fish) on the menu, if you want to order seafood. The most famous Catalan specialty, however, is also the simplest: *Pà amb tomàquet* is a slice of bread rubbed with raw tomato and enlivened with olive oil, salt, and pepper. When abroad, homesick Catalans drool at the thought of this snack, washed down with a glass of wine — not rioja, but penedès, a regional wine that nowadays impresses experts around the world. Miguel Torres is perhaps the best-known name, and the family headquarters at Vilafranca del Penedès welcomes visitors for a tour and tasting. For special occasions, Catalans open a bottle of *cava*, their own champagne-style sparkling wine.

The 703-mile (1,125-km) route outlined below begins in Barcelona and heads north for some 41 flat miles (65 km) past the Costa Brava (Wild Coast) shoreline that is the playground of Europe, with some 15 million visitors per year. High-rises and crowded beaches have thoroughly domesticated the wilderness here, ads push British-style pubs, fish-and-chips, and even cups of tea. At Lloret de Mar, the real Costa Brava begins, and the farther north the route goes, the more nature defeats the developers. Pinkish-red rock tumbles down to lime-green water, sandy inlets and bays are shaded by dense umbrella pines and cork oaks, fishing boats can still be found among the yachts. It is an area that has attracted artists to picture-postcard villages, such as Cadaqués, still charming despite being "discovered."

The northern limits of Catalonia today are the Pyrenees, ancient green-gray mountains that provided little to sustain villages in the past, but now offer the golden rewards of skiing. Here, the route crosses the border into the tiny principality of Andorra, with its dramatic mountains, picturesque villages, scenic landscapes, and duty-free shopping. Beyond, the agricultural hinterland beckons, locked between mountain and sea and dotted by walled towns and villages, each more mysterious than the last. Dark with shadows from turrets and towers, arches and cloisters, they conjure up an illusion of medieval life that is broken only by the sputtering cough of a motorbike or the sight of rooftop television antennas.

Roads vary from four-lane highways to small but well-paved country roads. Local truck drivers are surprisingly polite and encourage the passing of their lumbering vehicles. Along the route, a double room can cost $100 or more at a hotel listed as expensive; $55 to $95 at a hotel listed as moderate; and $50 or less at an inexpensive one. Expect to pay $50 or more for a meal for two with wine at restaurants categorized as expensive, $20 to $45 at a moderate restaurant, and $20 or less at an inexpensive one.

■ **Note:** Many place-names in Catalonia have both a Catalan and a Castilian spelling. In this chapter, where two forms exist, the first one given (usually at the first, or most conspicuous, mention of a town) is the Catalan version and the version in parentheses that follows it is Castilian.

En Route from Barcelona – Take the A7 highway north for 60½ miles (97 km) to Girona. After the industrial suburbs of Barcelona, it's a relief to see open countryside; across the fields, small villages sit on hilltops, always with a solid ocher church, sometimes a castle as well. The Tordera River marks the boundary between the province of Barcelona and the province of Girona, and soon the provincial capital looms up on the right. Take the Girona Sur exit and follow signs through the suburbs to the Centre Ciutat (City Center).

GIRONA (GERONA): The ancient part of the city has always been attractive, and recent renovations have enhanced its appeal. The Romans called it Gerunda; the Moors considered it a stronghold, and Christian folklore holds that this was the first spot where St. James and St. Paul rested on their visit to Spain — although they never really visited the Iberian Peninsula. Another legend, this one based on fact, tells of the defense of the city against invading Napoleonic troops in 1809. The governor held out for 7 months before capitulating, earning the city its sobriquet, *Ciudad de los Sitios* (City of a Thousand Sieges).

The best views of Girona are from the ancient stone footbridges across the Onyar River, but the city's main attraction, the cathedral, is located amid the steep, narrow alleys of the Old Town and is reached by an impressive 17th-century flight of 90 steps. Dating from 1316, the cathedral is of Gothic design, with a baroque façade, and it reflects the Catalan love of honest, simple lines. Awesomely vast inside, it has the world's widest Gothic nave (75 feet wide, as well as 200 feet long and 110 feet high), plus splendid 14th-century stained glass windows high in the gray stone walls. The museum contains invaluable illuminated manuscripts, including a *Commentary on the Apocalypse* dated 975, a bible that belonged to King Charles V of France, and the unusual 12th-century *Tapestry of the Creation.* The cathedral and museum are open daily, March through June, from 10 AM to 1 PM and from 3:30 to 7 PM; July through September, from 10 AM to 7 PM; October through November 3, from 10 AM to 1 PM and 3 to 6 PM; and from November 4 through February, from 10 AM to 1 PM; admission charge to the museum (phone: 72-214426).

Another fine example of local architecture is the nearby Sant Pere de Galligants (Plaça Sant Pere), a Romanesque monastery with a 12th-century octagonal tower; the monastery houses Girona's *Archaeological Museum* (open Mondays through Saturdays from 10 AM to 1 PM and from 4:30 to 7 PM; open mornings only on Sundays and holidays; admission charge; phone: 72-202632). Close by, the 12th-century Banys Arabs (Arab Baths) are an unexpected reminder that Girona was a Moorish stronghold for some 300 years; the eight slender columns in the *sala freda,* or cold room, are straight out of the Arabian Nights, although the capitals are Romanesque. The Jewish Quarter, Call Jueu, is a haunting maze of alleys and medieval buildings, and the synagogue in the *Museu d'Isaac el Cec* hosts Sephardic song recitals on Friday evenings in summer (ordinarily daily, from 10 AM to 1 PM, but closed for repairs at press time, scheduled to reopen this year; admission charge; phone: 72-216761). The nearby *Museu d'Art,* in the former bishop's palace, houses an art gallery with an exemplary selection of medieval and 19th- and 20th-century Catalan paintings, and a 15th-century Catalogue of Martyrs. Open Mondays through Saturdays, from 10 AM to 1 PM and 4:30 to 7 PM, mornings only on Sundays and holidays; admission charge; phone: 72-209536).

 CHECKING IN: *Novotel Girona* – Modern, air conditioned, and comfortable, with 81 rooms, a swimming pool and tennis courts, located near the airport, 7½ miles (12 km) from town, just off A17 at exit 8. Riudellots de la Selva (phone: 72-477100). Moderate.

 EATING OUT: *La Pequeña* – A family-run country eatery near the airport, featuring local Catalan specialties and *canalones* stuffed with foie gras. Closed Tuesdays. Reservations unnecessary. Riudellots de la Selva, Girona (phone: 72-477132). Inexpensive.

En Route from Girona – Follow C255 and the signs for Palamós. Pass Flaça and Corça, where signs advertising ceramics hint of the local industry. Continue another 2½ miles (4 km) to La Bisbal, a town well known for its pottery, where shops and factories line the main street, piled high with platters, umbrella stands, garden ornaments, hand-painted murals, and tiles. From La Bisbal, continue on C255 about 5 miles (8 km), following signs for Begur (Bagur), Palafrugell, and Palamós. Beyond the rise in the road, the Mediterranean appears to the left, dotted by islands — the Islas Medes. Turn left at the sign for Torrent, Pals, and Begur. Pals, a lovely old medieval town, is straight ahead, but follow the signs to Begur.

BEGUR (BAGUR): A small inland town surrounded by beautiful beaches and coves, Begur is at the heart of the Costa Brava — a term, meaning wild or rugged coast, that was coined in the vicinity in a speech by a turn-of-the-century local dignitary. Begur has narrow streets, whitewashed houses, and at the top, an imposing castle dating back to the 11th century and commanding wonderful views of the countryside. South of town, Aiguablava, or Blue Water, is an appropriately named *cala* (cove) and beach; neighboring Fornells rivals it; just north of town are Sa Tuna, Aiguafreda, and Sa Riera. The area is a good base for local excursions and diversions, which include taking a boat to explore the little coves, circumnavigating the Medes islands' nature reserves by glass-bottom boat, or strolling the spectacular Cap Roig botanical gardens. Many of the medieval villages inland, such as Peratallada and Ullastret, are worth a visit. The former, 900 years old, has only 500 inhabitants now, but hides behind impressive sandstone walls (its name means "cut rock"). Ullastret features an 11th-century church and a double wall, much of which has been restored.

CHECKING IN/EATING OUT: *Aiguablava* – Xiquet Sabater, one of the Costa Brava's great characters, has been running this charming seaside place since the late 1940s. All 85 rooms are air conditioned, with private baths, and many have a wonderful view of the sea. Facilities include a swimming pool, tennis courts, nightclub, and 2 bars. The main dining room offers an international menu with Spanish overtones, but there is also a more intimate room serving à la carte Spanish selections. English is spoken. Located a bit over 2 miles (3 km) southeast of Begur. Playa de Fornells (phone: 72-622058). Expensive.

Parador Costa Brava – A low, white building, shaded by pine trees, overlooking a beautiful beach; this modern *parador* (the only *parador* on the Costa Brava) has 87 air conditioned rooms, a bar, restaurant, gymnasium, sauna, swimming pool, and convention hall. It's located across the bay from the *Aiguablava* hotel, about 3 miles (5 km) southeast of Begur. Playa de Aiguablava (phone: 72-622162). Expensive.

En Route from Begur – Backtrack westward in the direction of Girona and Figueres. Turn off to Pals, go through Regenços, follow signs for Pals and Figueres, then for Pals itself, 4½ miles (7 km) from Begur. Follow signs to the Recinte Gòtic.

PALS: What was once a farming community is now a tourist attraction, thanks in part to restoration that has brought this 14th-century village back to life and earned it two national awards for its efforts. The village church, originally Romanesque but with some Gothic features as a result of later rebuilding, has an 18th-century façade. Climb the Torre de les Hores (Tower of the Hours) — so named because it once had a clock — in the 9th-century castle of Monteáspero, for lovely views of the coast. The Casa Pruna contains some important archaeological finds from the nearby beach, where there is also an 18-hole championship golf course at the *Club de Golf de Pals* (Playa de Pals; phone: 72-633006), and a worthy restaurant (see *Eating Out* below).

EATING OUT: *Sa Punta* – Well known for its simple treatment of fresh seafood, an excellent wine list, and interesting desserts, it enjoys the distinction of a Michelin star. Closed Mondays in winter and from mid-January to mid-February. Reservations advised. Playa de Pals, Pals (phone: 72-636410). Expensive.

En Route from Pals – Continue north along the main road for 6 miles (9 km) to Toroella de Montgrí, where the square block of the 13th-century castle of Montgrí sits on a bare bump of a hill. Head 9 miles (14 km) for the coastal village of L'Escala, passing through Bellcaire d'Emporda and miles of flat fields where old men still scythe the grass by hand, and on to Empúries. A sign to the Ruines d'Empúries is off to the right.

EMPÚRIES (AMPURIAS): The archaeological site here consists of 8 acres of Greek and Roman ruins undergoing constant excavation (which yielded a notable statue of Aesculapius among other treasures) and reconstruction. The Greeks built the lower town during the 6th century BC, and Julius Caesar later constructed a "new" town for retired soldiers higher on the hill. It's worth the effort to climb up to the former Roman town to inspect the forum and the two houses, with courtyards and rooms paved with black-and-white mosaics (open Tuesdays through Sundays, from 10 AM to 1 PM and 3 to 5 PM; admission charge).

 CHECKING IN/EATING OUT: *Nieves-Mar* – An old but comfortable family-run establishment of 80 rooms just south of Empúries. The beachfront location offers ideal views across the Golf de Roses (Bay of Roses); there is also a swimming pool and tennis courts. The restaurant offers a variety of fresh fish, simply prepared, as well as homemade fish soup. 8 Passeig Marítim, L'Escala (phone: 72-770300). Moderate.

En Route from Empúries – Take the main road north toward Roses (Rosas), skirting the old fishing village of Sant Pere Pescador and then Castelló d'Empúries, a small town with a magnificent 13th- to 15th-century Gothic church. Continue northeast toward Roses, a popular resort town clustered on low hills 6 miles (10 km) around the bay from Castelló, but after the angular, modern development of Ampuriabrava rears up into view and the turnoff for Roses appears, go straight, following signs inland toward Cadaqués and turning left at the Campsa gas station. For the next 10 miles (16 km), the road crosses an open, rock-strewn Wuthering Heights–like moor flecked with rosemary and thyme.

CADAQUÉS: This picture-postcard fishing village, made famous by Salvador Dalí and once the haunt of artists and intellectuals, has remained peacefully quaint, with a harbor, whitewashed houses, narrow lanes, and, in summer, art exhibitions and a music festival. The 18th-century parish church houses a valuable baroque high altar, carved by Pau Costa. A mile away, the cove of Port Lligat boasts Dalí's split-level house — surmounted by what appears to be a giant boiled egg.

 CHECKING IN: *Playa Sol* – Standard and modern, offering 50 rooms overlooking the sea. There is also a swimming pool, tennis courts, and a cafeteria. 3 Carrer Platja Planch, Cadaqués (phone: 72-258100). Moderate.

 EATING OUT: *La Galiota* – By far the best in town, boasting a Michelin star. This small place caters to an "artsy" clientele, and serves local seafood dishes and outstanding soufflés. It's very crowded in summer. Closed weekdays from September through May. Reservations advised. 9 Carrer Narciso Monturiol, Cadaqués (phone: 72-258187). Moderate.

En Route from Cadaqués – Backtrack across the moor and make a right turn onto the local road north toward the village of Vilajuiga. At the entrance to the village, make a sharp right turn at the sign for Monestir de Sant Pere de Rodes. A new road swoops up alongside olives and vines to open, rugged countryside, and after approximately 6 miles (10 km), there's a small parking lot. Park here and walk along the path to the majestic, brooding castle-cum-monastery, built by the Benedictines 1,000 years ago. On an overcast day, the two 90-foot-high towers loom out of the mist, while on a clear day the attractive former fishing village of El Port de la Selva and the entire peninsula are visible some 2,000 feet below — not to mention the town of Cerbère across the French border, the snow-capped Mt. Canigou inland, and the Golf de Roses to the south. The monastery buildings have been restored to reflect the wealth and power of Catalonia in the 10th and 11th centuries. Open daily, from 9 AM to 1:45 PM and from 3 to 6:45 PM. Admission charge.

Return to the main road at Vilajuiga and follow it for 8 miles (13 km) to Figueres, passing the old town of Perelada, which lends its name to the popular, often sparkling, local wines and has a luxury casino, the *Casino Castillo de Perelada,* housed in the old castle.

FIGUERES (FIGUERAS): Serious Spanish guides point out that this was the heart of Catalonia at the time the Moors were expelled, and that Philip V wed Maria Luisa of Savoy here in the Church of Sant Pere in 1701, a marriage that led to the War of the Spanish Succession. But Figueres, in the heart of the Ampurdan plain, is best known as the birthplace of Salvador Dalí (in 1904) and as the home of the *Dalí Museum.* Identified by a beehive logo in the center of town, the museum is housed in a converted movie theater that has been painted pink and decorated with replica boiled eggs and bubble gum. From the piles of old tractor tires in the square outside to the plastic store mannequins inside, the entire display is best described as weird. Dalí worked here until 1982, and lived, bedridden, in one of the building's towers until his death in 1989. He is now buried in the museum's inner court, beneath the building's great glass dome. More than 300,000 visitors annually make the museum Spain's second most popular (Madrid's *Prado* ranks number one), and contribute to the zoo-like atmosphere. It's difficult to take any of it seriously, though a few good paintings can be seen. There is also a complete orchestra (made of plaster of Paris), plenty of interesting murals, dolls hiding in niches, a Cadillac, and an assortment of plastic and metal kitsch of the 20th century. Unfortunately, cameras are not permitted. To avoid the crowds, visit the museum during lunchtime hours. Open daily, October through June, from 11:30 AM to 5:30 PM; July through September, from 9 AM to 8:30 PM; admission charge (phone: 72-505697). The Figueres Tourist Office is at Plaça del Sol (phone: 72-503155).

CHECKING IN/EATING OUT: *Ampurdán* – Adequate and comfortable, it offers 42 rooms in motel-style simplicity on the outskirts of town. The restaurant is the real prize here, rated one of Spain's best (it has a Michelin star). The Mercader family specializes in real Catalan dishes, often pairing meat with fruit. Try the rabbit and prune terrine, or braised venison with quince sauce. Fish is also a good choice, and the local wines are excellent. Reservations essential for the restaurant. Antigua Carretera de Francia, Km 763, Figueres (phone: 72-500562). Moderate.

Durán – In the heart of the Old Town, this is a real family-style establishment dating from 1870, with 67 modernized rooms. Like the *Ampurdán,* it is famous for food — whether the delicate fresh salmon in lemon-butter sauce or the hearty stuffed squash, the local ingredients and flavors are outstanding and honest. Try the *sarsuela* (fish stew) or eggplant mousse with fresh tuna. Reservations essential for the restaurant. 5 Carrer Lasauca, Figueres (phone: 72-501250). Moderate.

Mas Pau – A pretty, old, beamed farmhouse has been converted, and now offers 7 guestrooms. Set in a quiet garden 3 miles (5 km) southwest of Figueres, it also has a swimming pool and an award-winning (including a Michelin star) restaurant to tempt the traveler. Delicious saffron-flavored chicken and lobster, hearty venison, and subtle lambs' brains ravioli are a few of the menu favorites. Reservations advised for the restaurant. Carretera de Olot (phone: 72-546154). Moderate.

En Route from Figueres – Aiming west along C260 toward Olot and Ripoll, the Pyrenees rear to the north as the road curves through pine forests and, in spring, acres of wildflowers — scarlet poppies, golden buttercups, and snowy daisies. The village of Besalú, 15 miles (24 km) from Figueres, is worth a stroll-through. Follow signs to the Centre Vila and park in the large square, El Prat de Sant Pere. Careful renovation has beautified this mostly forgotten village. The church, Curia Reial (Law Courts), Town Hall, and covered marketplace are still in use; the Casa dels Cornellà must have been a merchant's house, judging by its courtyard, arches, and cloistered second floor. Cross the irregular arches of the fortified medieval bridge and observe, on the far side of the Fluvià River, the old Jewish quarter, complete with a *mikvah* (ritual bath), one of only a handful still existing in Europe. As a souvenir, purchase a floppy red Catalan cap, made in the town.

Proceed on C150 into a district known as La Gárrotxa, which means "torn earth," a reminder that the newly improved road to Olot, 13 miles (21 km) away, goes through volcanic countryside, though the 40 extinct cones are now overgrown. On the left, a sheer basalt cliff supports the dusty old village of Castellfollit de la Roca (Mad Castle on the Rock), some 200 feet above the abyss.

OLOT: Although this town has succumbed to dreary industrial development and local workshops churn out seemingly endless religious souvenirs, Olot has managed to keep its folkloric traditions alive. Annually, on the second Sunday of July, some 5,000 dancers arrive to weave magical *sardanas,* traditional Catalan folk dances. On September 8, *gegants, nans, i cavallets* (papier-mâché giants, dwarves, and horses) perform dances, and on October 18, the *cena de duro,* "2-cent dinner," instituted in honor of Sant Lluc (St. Luke) in 1314, still includes wine, bread, and rice for a few pesetas. The *Museum of Modern Art,* housed in a 19th-century palace (Carrer Hospici), displays a collection of Catalan art from the Olot School of Art, which was founded in the 19th century and became the workplace of many Catalan who were inspired by the surrounding countryside (open Mondays through Saturdays from 10 AM to 1 PM and from 4 to 7 PM, Sundays and holidays from 10 AM to 2 PM; admission charge). Also admire the elegant modernist façade of the Sola Morales house (38 Carrer Mulleres). The tourist office (Edifici Plaça del Mercat, Carrer Mulleres; phone: 72-260141) is nearby on the same street.

En Route from Olot – Continue west along C150; after about 7½ miles (12 km), the road forks, with a right turn leading to Sant Joan de les Abadesses. The road sign says it's only 8 miles (11 km) to this remote village where a monastery of Benedictine nuns was founded in the 9th century (what is visible today is no earlier than the 11th century, however); Wilfred the Shaggy, the first Count of Barcelona, made his daughter Emma the first abbess. But the drive is a tortuous one, recommended for enthusiasts only, although the peace of the pretty cloisters and convent may be worth the stress and strain. Otherwise, bear left at the fork and head on to Ripoll, 12 miles (19 km) away.

RIPOLL: This town deserves greater recognition of its past role as a torchbearer for civilization. Wilfred the Shaggy, founder of more than one monastery in Catalonia, founded the Benedictine monastery of Santa María here in the 9th century (there had been an earlier establishment that was destroyed by the Moors), and his influence ensured that it would become a center of learning. By the 11th century, under the stewardship of Abbot Oliba, the library was one of the richest in Christendom, housing 246 books, and it was famed throughout Europe as an intellectual meeting place for Christian and Arab philosophers. The town is pretty dreary now, except for the wonderful (but worn) 12th-century carved stone portal that decorates the entrance to the monastery church, considered one of the finest examples of Catalan Romanesque sculpture. In the days when few could read, the seven horizontal bands of biblical and allegorical scenes here constituted a classic comic book: From the monsters fighting at the bottom, past King David and the musicians, the Books of Kings and Exodus, up to the vision of the Apocalypse, the main stories are all shown. A booklet that includes a tracing-paper guide to the 87 pictures is available. During the summer, classical music recitals often take place in the cloisters. The monastery is open in summer, Mondays through Fridays from 10 AM to 2 PM and from 4 to 7 PM; Saturdays, Sundays, and holidays from 10 AM to 7 PM (winter hours are 11 AM to 2:30 PM weekdays, 11 AM to 2 PM and 4 to 6 PM Saturdays and Sundays; admission charge; phone: 72-720013). For further information, contact the tourist office in Ripoll (3 Plaça de l'Abat Oliba; phone: 72-702351).

En Route from Ripoll – Take N152 due north into the Pyrenees, following the twisting, rocky bed of the Freser River. High cliffs are typical, and tiny, seemingly inaccessible dark-stone villages blend into the hillsides above. Beyond Ribes de Freser, 9 miles (14 km) from Ripoll, the road climbs endlessly (15½ miles/25 km) up to Tosas, a village 6,000 feet up, where snow-capped peaks are visible even in summer. A sleepy gas station provides welcome refueling for car, body, and soul, after which, instead of taking the main road to Puigcerdà, make a sharp left turn down to La Molina, a popular ski resort, and follow the new valley road to Puigcerdà. Compared with other towns along the route, Puigcerdà is visually unremarkable, but it does have a dozen ski resorts within 30 miles to keep it busy. Hard by the border with France, it is only 4 miles (6 km) away from Llívia, which is also visually unremarkable, but worthy of note. In 1659, a border dispute in the region was settled when Spain ceded 33 villages high in the Pyrenees to France. Llívia, however, considered itself a *town,* and thus remained a Spanish enclave, totally surrounded by French soil, a few miles from the Spanish border.

Rather than enter Puigcerdà, turn left at the outskirts, taking C1313 southwest in the direction of Bellver de Cerdanya and La Seu d'Urgell. The road leads past the delightful mountain golf course of the *Real Club de Golf de Cerdaña* (phone: 72-881338), goes on through a wide valley dotted with little hill villages, and crosses into the province of Lleida (Lérida). After Bellver, it runs alongside the Segre River, where fishermen stand waist-deep casting for trout, and goes through Martinet, a trout-fishing and hiking center; 20 miles (32 km) beyond Bellver is La Seu d'Urgell.

CHECKING IN/EATING OUT: *Boix* – A comfortable, 34-room hotel by the Segre River, known for its breakfasts — a rarity in Spain — of homemade bread, jam, and local honey and butter. The restaurant is a splendid one (with a Michelin star), serving a French/Catalan menu: crayfish with mushrooms, trout with thyme, chicken in pastry, and duck with truffles, plus an excellent selection of Spanish and French wines. Reservations essential for the restaurant, which is closed Tuesdays off season and for 3 weeks in January. Carretera Lleida–Puigcerdà, Km 154, Martinet de Cerdanya (phone: 73-515050). Moderate.

Can Borell – Originally meant to be the retirement home of Lola Pijoan and Jaume Guillén, whose friends persuaded the couple to open a restaurant in the old farmhouse in 1977. In a small village up a mountain road between Puigcerdà and

Bellver de Cerdanya, with 8 comfortable, rustic rooms available, it has magnificent mountain views. The establishment also serves as a cooking school, where Lola teaches the simple but richly flavored dishes of the Cerdanya. *Conill amb peras i naps* (rabbit with pears and turnips), pigs' trotters with apple sauce, leek tart, and pears poached in the thick black wines of Tarragona are among the specialties. Reservations essential for the restaurant (and for the rooms), which is closed Sunday nights and Mondays (except in July, August, and September); both hotel and restaurant are closed from January 7 to mid-March. 3 Carrer Regreso, Meranges (phone: 72-880033). Moderate.

Chalet del Golf – The timber clubhouse of the *Real Club de Golf de Cerdaña* has 16 rooms, plus a swimming pool, tennis courts, and a restaurant. Located 3 miles (5 km) southwest of Puigcerdà. Devesa del Golf, Puigcerdà (phone: 72-880962). Moderate.

LA SEU D'URGELL (SEO DE URGEL): This is another ancient town that flourished at the conjunction of two river valleys, in this case the Valira from the north and the Segre from the east. All around are rolling orchards and farmlands — the foothills of the Pyrenees. Boasting a bishop since 527, a cathedral since 839, and two saints (Just and Ermengol), La Seu is both historically rich and more conventionally affluent, but its main claim to fame is the status of its bishop, who, since 1278, has been the joint ruler — or co-prince — of the co-principality of Andorra. The other holder of the title is the President of France. The Catedral de Santa María, rebuilt during the 12th century and again during the 18th century, features the uncluttered openness that appeals to Catalans, and is noted for its façade and its 13th-century cloister. The church museum, *Museu Diocesà d'Urgell,* in a chapel of the cloister, possesses a prized 11th-century illuminated manuscript of the *Apocalypse of St. John the Divine,* written during the 8th century by the priest Beatus of Liébana. Open Mondays through Saturdays from 10 AM to 1 PM and from 3 to 6 PM (to 5 PM from October through March); Sundays and holidays from 10 AM to 2 PM; admission charge (phone: 73-351177). Across from the church is the Carrer Major, with its medieval equivalent of a shopping mall, the great *porxos,* or arcades, that have sheltered vendors from sun and rain for centuries. The market on Tuesdays and Fridays is worth a visit.

CHECKING IN/EATING OUT: *El Castell* – A discreet, delightful, modern crescent of wood and slate, built into the hillside underneath the ruins of a 13th-century fortress about half a mile (1 km) southwest of town, offering lovely views over the town and the valley and across to the Sierra del Cadí. A luxury hotel, member of Relais & Châteaux group, it has 42 rooms and suites with (rare in Spain) king-size beds, as well as a swimming pool. Eat on the terrace or dine magnificently in the *Celler Grill,* which serves regional and national dishes; the wine cellar has a priceless collection of French and Spanish vintages dating back to the 19th century. Reservations essential for the restaurant, which is closed Mondays; both hotel and restaurant closed from mid-January to mid-February. Carretera Lleida, Km 129, La Seu d'Urgell (phone: 73-350704). Expensive.

Parador de Seo de Urgel – This modern, comfortable *parador* in town offers 84 spacious, air conditioned rooms, a swimming pool, and a restaurant serving French and Catalan specialties. Tapestries are part of the decor, and a 12th-century cloister from a former nearby church has been incorporated into the lobby and reception lounge. Reservations advised for the restaurant. Carrer Santo Domingo, La Seu d'Urgell (phone: 73-352000). Moderate.

En Route from La Seu d'Urgell – Driving north on C145, it's a quick 6 miles (10 km) to the border of one of the world's smallest countries, the autonomous principality of Andorra.

ANDORRA: A co-principality governed nominally by Spain and France through the Bishop of Urgell and the President of France, Andorra is an independent country of approximately 50,000 inhabitants and a duty-free haven set high in the Pyrenees. Its mere 175 square miles contain a dramatic landscape of scenic lakes, racing rivers, verdant meadows, quaint mountain villages, good ski slopes, and the nation's capital city, Andorra la Vella, the highest in Europe (3,000 feet), where modern, high-rise buildings almost block out the view of the surrounding peaks. According to tradition, the founding of Andorra dates back to the 9th century, when Louis I, the son of Charlemagne, granted a tract of land to the Bishop of Urgell; dual allegiance dates to the 13th century, when later bishops, feeling their rule challenged by French noblemen, agreed to joint control. The country's blue, red, and yellow flag first waved in 1298, at which time Andorrans also accepted an agreement whereby, in even-numbered years, the Spanish bishop would receive the equivalent of $12 as tribute, in addition to six hams, six chickens, and six cheeses. In odd-numbered years, the French prince (originally the Count of Foix) would be presented with a cash tribute of 960 pesetas.

Because the same rules pertain today, Andorra is Europe's last feudal protectorate. French and Spanish authorities oversee the justice and postal systems (all mail is delivered free within Andorra, and peseta or franc denominations of stamps are issued for mail outside the country). But since 1419, the Andorrans also have elected a 24-member Council General and are, therefore, proud to have one of the oldest parliaments in Europe. The semi-independent state suits most Andorrans just fine, and as is evident in the words of the national anthem — "Faithful and free I wish to live, with my Princes as my protectors" — further autonomy is not on the agenda. One reason is that the unique joint political arrangement and the country's related status as a tax-free enclave benefit Andorra economically. Not too long ago, a visit was an adventure back in time. But the past 2 decades have seen the country jump from medieval feudalism to 20th-century prosperity, from a strictly agricultural country to a model of modernization and growth.

One main, winding road cuts diagonally through Andorra, southwest to northeast, and along it traffic creeps in both directions, especially on weekends and during Spanish and French national holidays. At the borders, traffic jams of cars lined up to return to Spain and France can be monumental, caused by conscientious Spanish and French customs agents assessing the value of the duty-free purchases filling every nook and cranny of the departing convoy — cars, luggage, pockets, and purses of sated bargain hunters. One visit to this "supermarket in the sky" is usually enough for most foreign travelers, but the country has positive appeal beyond the shopping. The Pyrenees may not be as dramatic or even as high as the Alps, but they are wider and far more rugged (which explains why Andorra remained a mostly medieval community until this century). Since the country is perched atop the mountains facing south, it has an excellent climate of dry air, brisk in winter and fresh in summer. Most of its villages are deep in the low valley, but in winter, some of Europe's best inexpensive skiing can be found at the resorts of Pas de la Casa, Grau Roig, Soldeu, Tarter, Pals, Arinsal, and Arcalis. In June, the high valleys, as yet untainted by developers, unveil some of the rarest, yet most abundant wildflowers in Europe; carpets of narcissi, orchids, and iris stretching for hundreds of yards are common sights.

Stamp collectors have long appreciated the variety and abundance of Andorra's impressions, though few realize that they are unnecessary for internal mailings. The police force here can be counted on the fingers of a single hand, and as the folksinger Pete Seeger once noted, "The annual defense budget is spent on fireworks!" As a banking center, Andorra's private, numbered accounts are taken a bit more seriously by those with an embarrassment of riches.

As for historic sights, there are some attractive bridges arching across rushing streams, as well as a few tall, square bell towers on Romanesque churches. In Andorra .

la Vella, the 16th-century Casa de la Vall, which houses the governing Council General, is worth a visit (open Mondays through Fridays, from 9 AM to 1 PM and from 3:30 to 7 PM; Saturdays, from 9 AM to 1 PM; no admission charge). Outside of the capital, in Encamp, is the *Museu Nacional de l'Automòbil d'Andorra* (64 Avinguda Príncep Episcopal; phone: 628-32266), displaying a rich collection of antique cars, motorcycles, and bicycles from 1898 through 1950 (open from 10 AM to 8 PM, with a lunchtime closing; closed Mondays; no admission charge).

Still, shopping is the main attraction, although in many cases the prices are only attractive to the French and the Spanish, thousands of whom cross the border daily to stock up on cigarettes, liquor, electronic equipment, leather goods, and fashions. The best stores are found in Andorra la Vella, whose main streets bustle like the aisles of *Macy's*. To recommend one store over another is futile, since most shops have standard prices and stock only the most marketable merchandise. This may prove less fun for the kind of shopper who loves to compare and haggle over the price, but it is a pleasure for those who know the cost of the item at home and recognize a bargain.

Spanish currency is accepted throughout the tiny principality. While there are no customs or passport formalities for entering Andorra (visitors will have to beg the officials to mark passports with their flowery stamp), remember that lines for re-entering Spain are often very long, especially in late afternoon (a lunchtime escape is probably best). So are the lines at the service stations just within the Andorran border — a mandatory last stop for motorists, since gasoline prices are often one-third less than those of Spain or France. The country's tourist office, Sindicat d'Iniciativa, is located in Andorra la Vella (Carrer Dr. Vilanova; phone: 628-20214).

Note: to call Andorra from Spain, the area code is 9738; from the US, dial 33 (country code), 628 (area code), and the local number.

CHECKING IN: *Andorra Palace* – The principality's best, offering 140 rooms with excellent mountain views. Modern and comfortable, it has a swimming pool, tennis courts, and a garage (parking in Andorra is a nightmare). Prat de la Creu, Andorra la Vella (phone: 628-21072). Expensive.

Mercure Andorra – Part of the popular French chain; modern, efficient and comfortable, with 70 rooms, an indoor swimming pool, sauna, and garage. 58 Avinguda Meritxell, Andorra la Vella (phone: 628-20773). Moderate.

EATING OUT: *1900* – The French fare here has made many of Iberia's "top 30" listings, thanks to nouvelle dishes such as scallops with wild mushrooms, *magret de canard* (sliced breast of duck) with raspberry vinegar and beans, woodcock with wild garlic, and chocolate *millefeuilles* (pastry with whipped cream). Located in a spa about half a mile (1 km) east of the capital. Reservations essential. 11 Unió, Les Escaldes (phone: 628-26716). Expensive.

En Route from Andorra – Leaving behind the glamour of the coast, the history of the old cities, and the romance of the mountains, the route now enters territory not often visited by tourists. Backtrack south on C145 to La Seu d'Urgell and continue south on C1313, following the Segre River and snaking through the gray, rugged gorge of Organyà), past Organyà itself (the proud possessor of the oldest document written in Catalan), and past the dammed valley at Oliana, with its reservoir, beehives, and orchards of almonds and apricots. The river, lined with poplars, broadens, streaked with shoals of boulders that have tumbled for miles from the heights of the Pyrenees.

Just beyond Oliana, at Bassella, 32 miles (51 km) south of La Seu d'Urgell, is the intersection with C1410. For those wishing to return to Barcelona, about 90 miles (144 km) from Bassella, this road (via Solsona, Cardona, and Manresa) is a shortcut. Along the way, the *Parador Duques de Cardona* (in an old castle in Cardona; phone: 3-869-1275), has 60 moderately priced rooms for guests. Otherwise, to continue the itinerary, continue south along C1313 for about 11 miles (18 km) to Ponts, a logging town, and turn left onto the local road to Calaf. After a few minutes, turn right onto the road to Cervera, 21 miles (34 km) from Ponts, driving through rolling wheat fields and past hilltop hamlets, and crossing the main Barcelona-to-Zaragoza railroad tracks.

CERVERA: The town was originally built around a 13th-century castle. Aim for the ancient main street, Carrer Major, which runs along the top of the ridge, with old houses on both sides. Halfway down, a sign points to the Carreró de les Bruixes Segle XIII (Passage of the 13th-Century Witches). The passage, which runs some 400 yards parallel to Carrer Major and underneath the old houses, has been decorated (quite recently) with black cats, moons, witches' brooms, owls, and cobwebs, but is a spooky-enough experience even without these embellishments. Back into the daylight of the Plaça Major, which is a small square with a row of gargoyle-like faces holding up the balconies of the 18th-century Town Hall, wander to the Carrer Major to see the house where the Generalitat de Catalunya was established in 1359, and where, about a century later, King Ferdinand and Queen Isabella's marriage contract was signed. Cervera has literally been bypassed by the 20th century, as the main road between Barcelona and Zaragoza tunnels under the old town, but it was still in the mainstream in the 18th and 19th centuries. When Philip V suppressed all Catalan universities in 1718, he opened a new Castilian/Bourbon university in Cervera. Not surprisingly, it lasted little more than a century, closing down in 1841. The town is also known for its annual *Crist Misteri de Passió* (Passion Play), some 500 years old. A special theater was built for the crowds that flock to Cervera to witness the play, enacted by over 500 local citizens in March and April. The town's tourist office is at 4 Passeig Balmes (phone: 73-531350).

En Route from Cervera – The main road (N11) to Tàrrega, 7½ miles (12 km) away, is fast and straight, but Tàrrega itself can be a bottleneck. In the center of town, take the turn for C240 south toward Montblanch (Montblanc) and Tarragona and follow it through fields and vineyards, with intriguing villages off to either side, some with castles, some with churches. Just beyond Belltall, there is a sharp rise and the land drops away with a lovely panoramic view across the plains of Conça de Barberà. Look for the sign down the hill, off to the right, for Vallbona de les Monges.

VALLBONA DE LES MONGES: Catalonia boasts three great Cistercian abbeys: Vallbona de les Monges (nuns), and Poblet and Santes Creus (monks). Vallbona de les Monges is the least known, yet nuns have lived here without interruption since 1157. Fairly cut off from the rest of the world until a new road was pushed through in 1988, the convent is wedged into the middle of a village (pop. 275) and held up by tons of cement that are being poured into the foundations to keep it from falling down. Nuns in gray tunics and dark blue cardigans answer a bell at the main gate and conduct guided tours that include the church, whose soaring nave and belfry in a transitional Gothic style (12th to 13th century) are worthy of admiration. Only 26 nuns remain, working in the fields, praying, and making souvenirs, which include pottery, dolls for wedding cakes, bookmarks, and bags of herbs. The convent abbess is a simple soul compared to her mighty antecedents, who once had the power to appoint local mayors and raise taxes to fight the king's crusades. Plans for a museum overlooking the cloisters, the wings of which were built successively during the 12th through 15th centuries, are in the works. Open for guided tours daily from 10 AM to 2 PM and 4:30 to 7:30 PM; admission by donation (phone: 73-330266).

En Route from Vallbona de les Monges – Return to the main road (C240) and continue through Solivella to Montblanch (Montblanc), an attractive town with 34 towers along its castellated walls, medieval streets, and handsome squares

— worth a stop for a photo. Another 4 miles (6 km) west is the uninspiring town of L'Espluga de Francolí, 3 miles (5 km) above which is the thoroughly inspiring Monastery of Poblet.

POBLET: The celebrated Monasterio de Santa María de Poblet — a combined monastery, castle, and palace — was founded in 1151 by Ramón Berenguer IV, Count of Barcelona, as thanks to God for the recapture of Catalonia from the Moors. Originally, it housed only 12 Cistercian monks, who arrived from France. The number grew to 200 when the monastery was at its peak, when the Kings of Aragon and Catalonia used it as the halfway resting point on their journeys between the capitals of Barcelona and Zaragoza, and more importantly, honored it as as their royal burial place.

The buildings were abandoned when religious orders were suppressed in 1835, but a group of monks reestablished the monastery in 1940. Following 50 years of careful restoration and rebuilding, which finished on schedule in 1990, Poblet is now perhaps the finest monastic complex in Europe. Surrounded by over a mile of walls, guarded by a dozen turrets, it looks more like a castle than an ecclesiastical establishment, but the monks (35 or so) in their white habits and surplices belie the fortified aspect. Visits can include guided tours (conducted in Spanish, Catalan, and French only), which progress through a series of courtyards and gatehouses to the church, the huge, elegant cloister with its beautifully carved capitals, the Royal Pantheon with its alabastar tombs of kings, and the luxurious, pure Gothic palace built by King Martin the Humane in 1392. Although the treasures that were amassed over the centuries were confiscated during the 19th-century suppression, the church's 16th-century alabaster altarpiece remains, almost too rich in contrast with the pure lines of the rest of the structure. In total, some half-dozen kings and queens are buried at the monastery, along with some 40 princes. The complex is open daily, from 10 AM to 12:30 PM and from 3 to 6 PM; admission charge (phone: 77-870030).

En Route from Poblet – Return to Montblanch and take the main Tarragona road (N240) as far, as Valls, famous for the strange art of building *castells dels xiquets* (human towers); teams of men and boys from the town compete on June 23, 24, and 25, and on the Sunday following October 21, to see who can build the highest tower. After Valls, follow signs to the left turn for C246 and Vendrell. Beyond Alío, follow the signs for the third great Cistercian institution, Santes Creus, which appears suddenly over the brow of a hill, about 21 miles (34 km) from Montblanch.

EATING OUT: *Masía Bou* – Huge pottery wine jars mark this eatery, where the waiters and waitresses wear traditional outfits with vests and cummerbunds, which adds to the rustic atmosphere. Specialties include grilled meat dishes and *calçotada,* a local dish consisting of chops, sausages, broiled onions, and gravy that the restaurant has made famous. Weekends are especially busy: reservations advised. Carretera de Lleida, Km 21, Valls (phone: 77-600427). Moderate.

SANTES CREUS: Like the Poblet Monastery, the Monasterio de Santes Creus was founded for the Cistercians by the Berenguer dynasty in the 12th century, in 1157 to be exact. The Kings of Aragon and Catalonia were among its patrons, and the monastery's abbot served as the royal chaplain. Monks no longer live here, so the buildings, situated out in the country with a few houses lining the approach to the main gate, are now used for exhibitions, conferences, and concerts. Inside, the large forecourt is walled in by medieval apartment blocks — onetime servants' quarters. In the middle, a mitred bishop peers down into a coin-filled fountain in front of the church, begun in 1174 and endowed with a beautiful rose window. The cloister was added during the 14th century, followed by the houses for the dependents a century later. There appear to be much earlier influences, however, even Byzantine and Oriental ones, especially on the tomb of King Pere el Gran (1285), which is in the church and resembles an Egyptian bathtub, complete with a drain! The wine-colored porphyry could well have been captured during the Crusades and delivered to the king by his faithful pirate Roger de Llúria, who is buried by his side. In contrast to the chunky pavilion in the cloister garden, the flame-shaped tracery in the cloister itself shows the more elegant English influence brought to this part of Catalonia by the 14th-century architect Reinard Fonoll. Open daily from 10 AM to 1 PM and from 3:30 to 7 PM (to 6 PM from April through September); admission charge (phone: 77-638329).

En Route from Santes Creus – Backtrack south to C246, then west toward Valls to pick up N240, which leads south 12½ miles (20 km) to Tarragona.

TARRAGONA: There are very few "undiscovered" cities in Europe, but Tarragona may well be one of them. A combination of excavation and restoration has revealed just how important the ancient city of Tarraco was to the Roman Empire for over 600 years. Julius Caesar, Augustus, and Hadrian lived here for a time; legend has it that Pontius Pilate was born here. The streets of the Old Town still run where the Roman streets once lay; yet on top of all this, there is a pleasant, large hill city with medieval areas, long avenues, and views out over the ocean. The Passeig Arqueològic (Archaeological Promenade) is literally a walk of about half a mile through the history of Tarragona, around the ancient walls enclosing the highest part of the town. At the base of the walls are the huge Cyclopean boulders laid down by Iberian tribes in the 6th century BC; above these 25-ton megalithic rocks are the Roman walls built by the Scipio brothers in the 3rd century BC, topped by a later Roman dressed stone layer, then a medieval layer, and added during the War of the Spanish Succession, extra English-built ramparts. To interpret all this, a personal multilingual guide is a good investment, as pieces of Roman history crop up in the shadows of medieval houses and modern apartment blocks. The *Museu Arqueològic* (Archaeological Museum), Plaça del Rei, exhibits mosaics, capitals, statues, ancient household utensils, and other local finds. Most famous is the Head of Medusa mosaic, with a stare fit to turn onlookers to stone. Also not to be missed is the jointed ivory doll, which was found alongside its young owner in a 4th-century grave. Open Mondays through Saturdays, from 10 AM to 1:30 PM and from 4:30 to 8 PM (4 to 7 PM in winter); Sundays and holidays, from 10 AM to 2 PM; admission charge (phone: 77-236211 or 77-236206).

Next to the museum is the Pretori Romà (Roman Pretorium), a 2,000-year-old fortress, presumed to have been Pilate's birthplace. Just below, built into the hillside by the beach, is the Roman Amphitheater, where excavations have unearthed the remains of what is believed to be a 2nd- or 3rd-century Christian church. Just above the ruins is the Balcon del Mediterráneo (Balcony of the Mediterranean), a cliffside promenade offering excellent views of the sea. A flight of Roman steps leads up to the fortress-like cathedral in the heart of the Old City, built on the site of the former Temple of Jupiter, which subsequently became a mosque under Moorish rule. The construction lasted from the 1150s to 1331; thus, the interior is an intriguing mixture of Romanesque and Gothic, with Plateresque and Churrigueresque additions from the 16th and 18th centuries. The cathedral is noted for its 15th-century Santa Tecla altarpiece at the main altar; the cloister, similar to those at Poblet and Vallbona, has beautifully carved capitals. Open daily, from 10 AM to 1 PM and from 4 to 7 PM.

There are two splendid Roman remains on the outskirts of town. Pont de les Ferreres aqueduct (or Pont del Diable — the "Devil's Bridge"), some 200 feet long and located 2½ miles (4 km) from the center via N240, is a 2-tiered example of Roman engineering from Emperor Trajan's day. The Roda de Barà (Bara's Arch), a 2nd-century triumphal arch, is located 12½ miles (20 km) north of Tarragona via A7. For more information, consult the tourist office in Tarragona (4 Calle Fortuny; phone: 77-201859), just off the Rambla Nova.

CHECKING IN: *Imperial Tarraco* – Tarragona's best, with 170 spacious, modern rooms. Set high atop a cliff, it has spectacular views of the ocean and the ancient Roman amphitheater below. 2 Rambla Vella, Tarragona (phone: 77-233040). Moderate.

EATING OUT: *Sol Ric* – About half a mile (1 km) from town, it has a country feel, with a terrace under the trees. The fish dishes are outstanding, and the house wines from Priorato are excellent. (They're served in a *porrón,* a Catalan pitcher with a long spout that aims a stream of liquid into the mouth.) Closed Sunday evenings, Mondays, and mid-December to mid-January. Reservations essential. 227 Via Augusta, Tarragona (phone: 77-232032). Moderate.

En Route from Tarragona – A seaside break from sightseeing is in order, so follow N340, then C246, north along the coast 33 miles (53 km) to Sitges, the prettiest resort on the Costa Dorada (Gold Coast). An alternative route to the same destination would be the faster A7, turning east at Vilafranca del Penedès.

SITGES: A typical Mediterranean seaside resort town, which means that it is both popular and classy, lively and cultured, tacky here and pretty there. The 1½-mile-long sandy beach of La Ribera is backed by a promenade lined with flowers and palm trees, cafés and restaurants, with a church at the north end. The Old Town is made up of little lanes and some magnificent old villas, homes of "Americanos" — Spaniards who made their fortune a century ago in Central and South America and retired here to enjoy the mild climate. Although the town has expanded over the years, there are few apartment blocks and no towering hotels. To the north, beyond La Punta, a 450-berth yacht harbor at Aiguadolç attracts the nautical fraternity. Summer weekends are very crowded, especially in late July and August, but a stay is very pleasant during the week and out of season.

Sitges has three surprisingly good museums. *Museu Cau-Ferrat* (Carrer Fonollar; phone: 3-894-0364) has one of Europe's finest collections of artistic ironwork along with tiled walls and paintings by El Greco, Utrillo, and Santiago Rusiñol, the 19th-century romantic writer-artist (the museum is housed in his former studio). Next door, and functioning as an annex, is the *Museu Maricel de Mar* (phone: 3-894-0364), with sculptures, glass, mosaics, and drawings from the Middle Ages through the baroque period. The *Museu Romàntic* (Carrer Sant Gaudenci; phone: 3-894-2669), also known as *Casa Llopis,* is an 18th-century mansion sumptuously furnished with neo-classical antiques and paintings, as well as a doll collection on the upper floor. Opening hours for all three museums are Mondays through Saturdays, from 10 AM to 1 PM and from 5 to 7 PM (4 to 6 PM from October through May); Sundays and holidays from 10 AM to 2 PM. There are admission charges to all three museums.

Always staging some sort of festival, Sitges has a *Corpus Christi* celebration in early June that features floral carpets made of over 600,000 carnations, which cover the cobbled streets in intricate, sweet-smelling designs. Lawn cuttings from the local golf course form the base; carnation heads mixed with other flowers produce rich patterns from butterflies to soldiers. Since 1950, the *National Carnation Show,* which runs concurrently, has been enlivened with a competition among the streets for the best *catifa de flors* (carpet of flowers), and visitors file along the narrow pavements to admire the highly proficient handiwork. For almost as many years, the first weekend of March has been highlighted by a splendid car rally, featuring vintage automobiles. De Dion-Boutons and Daimlers, Panhards and Bugattis, Fords, Hispanos, and Rolls-Royces put-put from Barcelona to Sitges, carrying ladies and gentlemen dressed in the style of the respective eras.

CHECKING IN: *Calipolis* – Facing the waterfront, this modern establishment bears the brunt of conventions and international visitors year-round. Though somewhat frayed at the edges, the 160 rooms are air conditioned and have private baths; most have terraces overlooking the beach. The *La Brasa* restaurant serves international and regional fare. Passeig Marítim, Sitges (phone: 3-894-1500). Expensive.

Terramar – Isolated at the southern end of town, offering 209 comfortable rooms and plenty of sports facilities, including tennis courts, a golf course, and riding stables. Passeig Marítim, Sitges (phone: 3-894-0050). Moderate.

EATING OUT: *Fregata* – A typically bustling Spanish restaurant, with fabulous views over the water from a clifftop site. Various fish dishes (served in large portions) and a thick fish soup are on the menu. Closed Thursdays. Reservations advised. 1 Passeig de la Ribera, Sitges (phone: 3-894-1086). Moderate.

La Masía – Traditional Catalan cooking, with an emphasis on grilled meats, served in an old, rustic *masía,* or farmhouse. Reservations advised. 164 Passeig Vilanova, Sitges (phone: 3-894-1076). Moderate.

El Velero César – Specializing in excellent local fish dishes. Try the *rape con alcachofas* (angler or monkfish with artichokes) or shrimp and cabbage gratin. Closed Sunday evenings in winter, and Mondays. Reservations advised. 38 Passeig de la Ribera, Sitges (phone: 3-894-2051). Moderate.

En Route from Sitges – For a final side trip before returning to Barcelona, head north through Sant Pere de Ribes into the Penedès wine region. After crossing the main Tarragona–Barcelona freeway, on the very edge of Vilafranca del Penedès, 14 miles (22 km) from Sitges, turn right for the Bodega Torres (22 Carrer Commerç; phone: 3-890-0100). This family wine business (Spain's largest independent one) dates back to 1870, but it is only in the last decade that Torres wines have had an impact on international palates. Miguel Torres studied in France and returned to revolutionize his father's wine making methods, using stainless steel vats, cold fermentation, and small oak barrels. The combination proved to be a winning one when his 1970 Gran Coronas Black Label won a gold medal in the cabernet class at the *1979 Gault-Millau Wine Olympics* in France, besting a 1970 Château Latour! Guided tours are available by appointment, Mondays through Fridays, from 9 AM to noon and from 3 to 5 PM; ask for Alberto Fornós. The *Museu del Ví* (Plaça Jaume I; phone: 3-890-0582), in the center of town, is dedicated to the history of wine making in the region (open daily, from 10 AM to 2 PM and from 4 to 6 PM; admission charge). Another wine-related excursion is to Sant Sadurní d'Anoia, 7½ miles (12 km) north of Vilafranca, the center of the sparkling wine — *cava* — industry in Spain. Here Cavas Codorníu, on the edge of town, has been making sparkling wine by the champagne method since the 1870s, and the estate buildings, designed by the 19th-century modernist architect Josep Puig i Catafalch (who designed one of the landmark buildings on Barcelona's Passeig de Gràcia), are open for tours (English-language tours are possible) Mondays through Thursdays from 8 AM to noon and from 3 to 6 PM, Fridays from 8 AM to noon; closed August (phone: 3-891-0125).

CHECKING IN/EATING OUT: *Sumidors* – This rustic, mountain *hostal* just outside of Sant Pere de Ribes has 11 traditionally furnished, stone-walled suites with beamed ceilings, tiled floors, and wooden doors. Facilities include a television salon, swimming pool, sauna, and solarium. The *Carnivor* restaurant, as its name suggests, specializes in grilled meats in large portions. Reservations advised. Sant Pere de Ribes (phone: 3-896-0125 or 3-896-0302). Moderate.

Aragon

Aragon makes up a significant slice of east-central Spain, taking in the central Pyrenees at their rugged best, with deep glacial valleys scoured between the highest peaks. A knot of rivers unravels through rich Aragonese orchards, vineyards, and farms, but especially through high pastures and bleak badlands. The fighting bull has long held the locals in thrall, with taurine strength and power almost magically evoked in petroglyphs daubed by prehistoric cave dwellers.

Thousands of years later, Roman legions came marching through the region on a wide road from Mérida, in the southwest, and built a sizable settlement at Zaragoza. Still later, in far-flung outposts on unassailable ridges, Christian knights clashed with the Moors for almost the entire centuries-long duration of the Reconquest. Yet Moorish customs never were obliterated; instead, they were revitalized and became part of a distinctive regional style. Geometric Mudéjar brickwork persists in tall towers that dominate the skyline like monochrome mosaics. Some are scarred now by Spanish Civil War bullets, but that only adds to the fierce pride of the region.

Since there is no coast in Aragon, many visitors — Spaniards included — dismiss this region as a place to be passed through quickly, a place where they can bear down on the accelerator and make good time in the dark, cruising up to the mountains or over to the seaside in great haste. This lack of recognition may have roots in the region's avaricious past, dating back to its beginnings as a kingdom in 1035. An advantageous alliance that would result in new territory was never spurned. The kingdom of Navarre was an early ally (1076–1134), and a royal wedding in 1137 tied the knot with the powerful Berenguer family, bringing in the potent House of Barcelona and the region of Catalonia. Aragon quietly began to grow with Catalonia, eventually to encompass a swath of land from the southern stretches of Murcia up to Roussillon in France, as well as the Balearic Islands, Naples, and Sicily. Commerce was a driving force, and further alliances were forged through astute matchmaking rather than through military might. Aragonese daughters usually wed well, but the biggest matchmaking coup was the marriage of King Ferdinand II of Aragon, who could claim Castile and León along with his clever bride, the Catholic Queen Isabella. Under their rule, a united Spain extended its reach to the New World. Yet even they reverted to the Aragonese tradition: Daughter Catherine of Aragon was dispatched to England in hopes of gaining a strong ally against France through wedlock. But their son-in-law — who became the notorious King Henry VIII — had a few surprises up his own sleeve.

Aragon enjoys the dubious distinction of having Spain's worst climate. Heating or air conditioning, depending on the season, is absolutely necessary for those heading to the southern part of the region, where summers are unbearably hot and winters can be extremely bitter. Visitors in late spring or early autumn will have few complaints, for the countryside will be at its best. Southeast of Zaragoza there are vineyards and wineries that welcome curious visitors and encourage wine tasting. With few outsiders interfering in village life, many of the local fiestas are still completely traditional. The odd, jig-like *jota* is about as different as could be from the sinuous arching of flamenco, but it is every bit as Spanish; the embroidered aprons and the pretty ankle-laced slippers are instantly recognizable as the peasant dress of Aragon. In September, especially in the southernmost stretches, bull fever hits. *Encierros*, or the running of bulls through the streets into an enclosure, are certainly not unique to Pamplona. Small local variations, minus the Hemingway hype and the hordes of drunken foreigners, occur near harvest time during celebrations of patron saints in the villages close to Teruel.

The route outlined below begins in Pamplona and enters the old kingdom of Aragon at the base of the Pyrenees, then goes south through a dreamscape of strange mounds and past a strategic castle on its way to Huesca. As it continues south, fields give way to wide flats near Zaragoza, the only sizable city in this sparsely populated region. Still farther to the southwest, past Calatayud, stark badlands hold such surprises as the Piedra Monastery, which is blessed with cascades and iris grottoes and looks like some colorful mirage in these raw, red hills. Once past a valley of orchards and vineyards, brick towers in geometric Mudéjar patterns rise above the arid scrub near Daroca and Teruel, at Aragon's southern extreme. From here, the traveler can opt to head for Valencia, on the coast, or turn inland, toward Cuenca and Madrid. Either way, a detour to the medieval town of Albarracín, guarding the heights to the west, is recommended.

Accommodations in Aragon range from expensive, in Zaragoza, where the priciest doubles go for over $80 a night, to many moderate hotels that charge between $40 and $75, down to the unprepossessing inexpensive inns where a room for two costs $35 or less. Weekend rates are almost always higher, even during low season. Dinner for two with wine will cost $80 or more in restaurants listed as expensive, $40 to $75 in moderate restaurants, and under $40 in inexpensive ones.

PAMPLONA: For a detailed report on the city and its sights, hotels, and restaurants, see *Pamplona,* THE CITIES.

En Route from Pamplona – Take the N240 highway southeast. If there's plenty of daylight and more than a couple of hours to spare for the initial leg of the trip, turn right onto C127 after about 25 miles (40 km) and detour through Sangüesa to the historic town of Sos del Rey Católico, the birthplace of King Ferdinand in 1452. This solemn medieval town is the largest of the Cinco Villas de Aragón (Five Towns of Aragon), which were singled out for honor because of their loyalty to King Philip V during the 18th-century War of the Spanish Succession. King Ferdinand spent his childhood in the Palacio de Sada here, and the building, which contains his nursery, is open to visitors, although ongoing restoration work may temporarily put some rooms off-limits (open from 9 AM to 1 PM and from 4 to 6 PM; no admission charge). San Esteban, a 14th-century Romanesque church with fine 13th-century frescoes, carved capitals and columns, and a wooden Virgin, the Virgen del Perdón, is also worth a visit. But it is the overall atmosphere of the town that is most interesting; it's small and beautiful, and a stroll through its narrow cobbled streets leads past intricate grillwork and carved coats of arms on the mansions of aristocratic families.

From Sos del Rey Católico, loop back to N240, and turn right onto the highway. (Those coming directly from Pamplona will already be on N240 and will have just passed a huge reservoir.) At Puente la Reina de Jaca, a signpost indicates the turnoff to Jaca, another 12½ miles (20 km) east along C134.

CHECKING IN/EATING OUT: *Parador Fernando de Aragón* – Perched on a hill near some remains of the town's ramparts, this *parador* somehow blends in well with the older parts of town, despite a 400-year architectural gap. Built of local wood and stone, it has 65 rooms, all air conditioned. The outdoor terrace off the dining room is a pleasant spot for a long lunch. If they're in season, order the plump white asparagus served with two sauces, the quintessential appetizer of north Aragon (at other times they will be canned). Other typical regional fare, such as *conejo con caracoles* (rabbit with snails) or *pochas con oreja de cerdo* (white beans garnished with pig's ear), may not appeal to squeamish types, but the blend of unusual flavors is quite delicious. Simpler dishes are also available. Room reservations should be made well in advance. Closed December and January. Sáinz de Vicuña, Sos del Rey Católico (phone: 48-888011). Expensive to moderate.

JACA: This ancient garrison town, on a hill above the left bank of the Aragon River, still has many young soldiers mixed in with visiting mountaineers and tourists. Medieval pilgrims en route to Santiago de Compostela recuperated from their arduous trek over the Pyrenees here, but today this is a principal base for exploring the Aragonese Pyrenees, so most visitors head *toward* the mountains. During the summer, the University of Zaragoza holds courses for foreign students; during the winter, the town bustles with skiers. The tourist office (Paseo Calvo Sotelo; phone: 74-360098) has detailed maps for exploring the distant peaks and high valleys, such as Hecho and Anso. In town, Jaca's primary sight is its Romanesque cathedral, completed in 1076. The first important Romanesque building in Spain, the cathedral influenced every artist, architect, and craftsman who entered the country to work on churches during the 11th century. Though partially restored in Gothic and later decorated in Plateresque styles, much of the original Romanesque remains, including the square bell tower, the exterior walls, the main and south portals, and the pillars of the nave. The cathedral and its museum are open daily, from 11:30 AM to 1:30 PM and from 4 to 6 PM. Admission charge. Buy some local cream cakes in the heavenly scented *Pastelería Echeta* (Plaza Catedrales; phone: 74-360343), or try the local candies made from pine nuts, known as *besitos* — or "little kisses." The *Palacio del Hielo* ice-skating rink (Avenida Perimetral; phone: 74-361032), Spain's largest, stays open year-round and is the hub of the young social scene. If visiting here in the summer, join in the *Festival Folklorico de los Pirineos* (Folklore Festival of the Pyrenees), held in odd-numbered years in late July or early August; it's a week-long celebration starring traditional dance groups and bands from around the world.

CHECKING IN: *Conde de Aznar* – This small, cozy, family-run establishment has 23 rooms, pleasant gardens, an eccentric staff, and an especially good restaurant, *La Cocina Aragonesa* (see below). 3 Paseo del General Franco, Jaca (phone: 74-361050). Moderate.

***Gran* –** The prestige hotel in town, with 166 rooms, and a swimming pool open in summer, a bright garden, and tennis courts. Advance booking is recommended during the winter. 1 Paseo del General Franco, Jaca (phone: 74-360900). Moderate.

EATING OUT: *La Cocina Aragonesa* – Regional cooking is done with panache here — the distinguished restaurant of the *Conde de Aznar*. During the fall, order exquisite game dishes such as *rollitos de jabali* (wild boar in puff pastry). Closed Tuesdays, except during high season. Reservations advised. 5 Calle Cervantes, Jaca (phone: 74-361050). Moderate.

La Fragua – This converted blacksmith's shop now fires up the flames beneath appetizing pork chops, lamb, and beef. Open daily during high season (closed mid-April to mid-June). Reservations unnecessary. 4 Calle Gil Berges, Jaca (phone: 74-360618). Moderate to inexpensive.

Gaston – A charmingly intimate family place, with a small upstairs terrace. The hearty fare includes stuffed peppers and pigs' trotters. Closed Wednesdays, except in high season, and September 20–30. Reservations unnecessary. 14 Avenida Primo de Rivera, Jaca (phone: 74-362909). Inexpensive.

En Route from Jaca – Proceed south on C125, following the twisting road past the green Lake Peña. The ruddy formations that loom like sculptures are called Los Mallos (The Evil Ones). Take the N240 turnoff to Ayerbe, then follow the rough local road to the village of Loarre and its Castillo de Loarre. Regarded as one of Spain's most important Romanesque fortresses, this 11th-century castle, built by Sancho Ramírez as a stronghold against the Moors, commands a sweeping view over a broad plain. Perched on its rocky precipice, it is most striking, even in a country famed for its castles. Pay particular attention to its three magnificently restored towers and its Romanesque chapel (open Tuesdays through Sundays, from 9 AM to 1 PM and from 4 to 7 PM; no admission charge). Backtrack to N240 and drive east toward Huesca.

EATING OUT: *Venta del Sotón* – One of Aragon's best restaurants, this is 9 miles (14 km) west of Huesca. A huge fireplace sets the atmosphere, and guests are urged to warm themselves further with a vast choice of *aguardientes,* powerful liqueurs. Grilled *chorizo* (sausage) is a good starter, and the menu offers a fine selection of Spanish nouvelle cuisine, which is somewhat experimental but not too gimmicky. There is also a good wine cellar. Closed Tuesdays. Reservations advised. Carretera N240, Km 227, Esquedas (phone: 74-270241). Expensive to moderate.

HUESCA: A venerable town, marking the start of the rich Ebro plain, Huesca was, in the first century BC, an independent state founded by the Roman Quintus Sertorius, who even founded a school of Latin and Greek here, Spain's first university. The town was swept up in ensuing invasions by the Romans and the Moors, until Peter I of Aragon liberated it from the Moors in 1096 and made it the residence of the Aragonese kings until 1118. During the Spanish Civil War, it was a Franco stronghold and as such, suffered considerable damage. Subsequent restoration and recent prosperity have made the town sprawl, but there is a medieval core to explore. The Gothic cathedral, built from the 13th to the 16th centuries, has a lovely, famous 16th-century alabaster altarpiece by Damián Forment, a sculptor who worked extensively in Aragon in both the Renaissance and Gothic styles.

More than anything, however, Huesca's renown has to do with the bloody Legenda de la Campana (Legend of the Bell), a 12th-century atrocity that is depicted across the street from the cathedral in a painting at the Town Hall. On the pretext of wanting advice from rebellious nobles about how to cast a bell big enough to be heard through the entire kingdom, King Ramiro II lured his rivals into his council room and beheaded them as they filed in one by one. The actual chamber can be visited in the *Museo Provincial,* Plaza de la Universidad, which is set up in a building incorporating part of the 12th-century palace of the Aragonese kings and which also housed a portion of the university during the 17th century. Displays include Gothic frescoes, 13th- through 16th-century Aragonese paintings, architectural exhibits, sculptures, and archaeological finds (open Tuesdays through Saturdays, from 10 AM to 2 PM and from 4 to 6 PM; Sundays, from 10 AM to 2 PM; admission charge). Also visit San Pedro el Viejo, the 12th-century Romanesque church (Calle Cuarto Reyes); King Ramiro spent the last years of his life as a monk here and is now buried in the church's San Bartolomé chapel (open Mondays through Saturdays, from 9 AM to 1:30 PM and from 4 to 6 PM; Sundays, from 10 AM to 1:30 PM; admission charge).

CHECKING IN: *Montearagón* – The place to stay for those who are loath to leave the mountains. It's unpretentious, with views back to the Pyrenees, and it's worth the 2-mile (3-km) drive to the outskirts of squat Huesca to enjoy it. Swimming pool and 27 rooms. Carretera San Sebastián (N240), Km 208, Huesca (phone: 74-222350). Moderate.

***Sancho Abarca* –** Near the center of town, close to the principal sites, in a very pretty setting. Management is friendly and the 32 rooms are comfortable. 15 Plaza Lizana, Huesca (phone: 74-220650). Moderate.

EATING OUT: *Navas* – A comfortable, clubby kind of place, offering shellfish and beef specialties. After coffee and liqueur, they pass out Havana cigars. Reservations advised. 15 Calle San Lorenzo, Huesca (phone: 74-224738). Moderate.

En Route from Huesca – It's a quick, flat, 45-mile (72-km) run south along N123/N330 to Zaragoza, Aragon's regional capital, with over 750,000 inhabitants.

ZARAGOZA: Seen from the road, the slender towers and imposing domes of Zaragoza's two cathedrals are the only grace notes in a huddle of ugly warehouses, factories, and high-rise apartments. The Ebro River shines through the dusty heart of the city like a great ribbon, and there are some elegant fountains and tree-lined avenues. Don Quixote supposedly balked at entering this city because it had unwittingly welcomed an impostor in his stead, but most other travelers — raiders and traders — have rolled right on through. The tongue twister name (try lisping it the way true Castilians do!) has ancient roots, in that the Roman colony founded on the Iberian site of Salduba in 25 BC was called Caesaraugusta. When the Moors conquered the city in 716, they dubbed it Sarakusta. Despite 400 years of Moorish rule, only the Palacio Aljafaría, constructed in 1030, remains as a testament to their presence. This was built as a pleasure palace for Moorish kings, but its original Arabian Nights architecture has been tampered with, first by the Aragonese kings and then by Ferdinand and Isabella, who claimed it as their throne room, and afterward by the Christian zealots of the Inquisition, who used it as a headquarters. Though it also endured an ignoble stint in the 19th century as an army barracks and most of its interior fixtures have been removed, it has noteworthy *artesonado* ceilings and other Moorish and Gothic ornamentation, as well as a splendid tiny mosque (open Tuesdays through Saturdays, from 10 AM to 2 PM and from 4:30 to 6:30 PM; Sundays, from 10 AM to 2 PM; admission charge).

By the time the Reconquest proclaimed the city as the capital of Aragon, Zaragoza was already a rich agricultural center. The local nobility, wary of any sovereign, managed to secure guarantees of autonomy known as *fueros,* and under these conditions, commerce in this crossroads city boomed. The impressive 16th-century Lonja, or commercial exchange building, has a lovely Gothic vaulted ceiling, with cherubs dancing around the tops of the supporting columns; the building today houses temporary exhibits of local artists (Plaza Catedrales; open only during exhibitions, from 9 AM to 2 PM).

On either side of La Lonja are Zaragoza's two cathedrals. The Básilica de Nuestra Señora del Pilar, a striking 16th- to 18th-century structure that incorporates elements of previous churches on the same site, has nearly a dozen *azulejo*-covered domes and four towers surrounding a larger, central dome. On the interior of the domes are frescoes, some by Goya. Also inside is a famous 16th-century alabaster altarpiece by Damián Forment and the Capilla de Nuestra Señor del Pilar. The latter is a small church-within-the-church housing a Gothic statue of the Virgin and the sacred jasper pillar that, according to legend, once stood in a Roman temple here, and atop which the Virgin Mary is said to have miraculously appeared before St. James the Apostle in AD 40. The Virgen del Pilar attracts devout pilgrims and is claimed by the Civil Guard as their patroness. During the Spanish Civil War, she was officially appointed Captain General of Zaragoza, and two Republican bombs that clattered off the roof of the cathedral without exploding now hang in the chapel as a reminder of her divine intervention. The cathedral's *Museo del Pilar* contains some Goya sketches for the ceiling frescoes, as well as the *joyero de la Virgen* — the jewelry and vestments that constitute her wardrobe. Open daily, from 9:30 AM to 2 PM and from 4 to 7 PM. Admission charge. Zaragoza'a older cathedral, the 14th-century Gothic Catedral de la Seo, closed for major renovations at press time, is expected to be open to the public once again by the middle of this year.

Zaragozans are a pragmatic lot. They have enraged purists by installing the first roof and lighting system on a bullring, a concession to unpredictable weather. Yet tradition runs strong in the city, and every October 13, the *Fiesta de la Virgen del Pilar,* fervent followers parade the bejeweled statue through the city streets by the light of 350 carriage-borne lamps. American servicemen from the huge air base outside the city are frequent visitors, and consequently a smattering of English is common in many of the local bars.

CHECKING IN: *Gran* – This stately old hotel, with 138 air conditioned rooms, is considered to be Zaragoza's best. 5 Calle Joaquín Costa, Zaragoza (phone: 76-221901). Very expensive.

***Don Yo* –** Complete luxury without a stuffy staff, and with 180 beautifully appointed rooms — there is usually space on short notice. The *Doña Taberna* restaurant next door is associated with the hotel, but is not exceptional. 4 Calle Bruil, Zaragoza (phone: 76-226741). Expensive.

***Conde Blanco* –** Reasonable rates in an efficient 83-room hostelry, in one of the prettier sections of the city. No dining room, but a cafeteria provides quick snacks. 84 Calle Predicadores, Zaragoza (phone: 76-441411). Moderate.

EATING OUT: *Los Borrachos* – The name translates as "drunkards," but it merely celebrates a favorite Velázquez canvas. Despite its ostentatious decor, this is a Zaragoza institution. Fresh game is the specialty, with boar, venison, and game birds on the menu in season. The asparagus soufflé is outstanding; only the homemade ice creams and sherbets surpass it. Service is attentive and the wine cellar is well stocked. Try the deep red cariñena from the local vineyards. Closed Sundays and August. Reservations advised. 64 Calle Sagasta, Zaragoza (phone: 76-275036). Expensive to moderate.

***Costa Vasca* –** Zaragoza's only Michelin star is the glory of this restaurant, where the host is also the chef. Enjoy a customary *tapa* and champagne appetizer before sampling one of the various Basque fish specialties that are served in the very proper dining room. Closed Sundays and *Christmas.* Reservations advised. 13 Calle Teniente Coronel Valenzuela, Zaragoza (phone: 76-227339). Expensive to moderate.

La Matilde – Run by a single family — a couple, their three sons, plus the sons' wives — this place is informal and trendy. The cooking is adventurous: deep-fried camembert with homemade tomato chutney, exquisite monkfish steamed with clams, and for the brave, a celebrated *mollejas con trufas,* a delicacy made from young bird gizzards and black truffles. The wine cellar is extensive. Closed Sundays and holidays, *Holy Week,* August, and *Christmas.* Reservations advised. 10 Calle Casta Alvarez, Zaragoza (phone: 76-441008). Expensive to moderate.

En Route from Zaragoza – Leave Zaragoza heading southwest on the N-II highway, a woeful two-lane link to Madrid shared with enormous trucks and impatient long-distance drivers who break their boredom by passing on blind curves. Often a lane will suddenly narrow around construction and other road "improvements." The distant mountains edge in and soon after, the scenery becomes stark. After 54½ miles (87 km), the highway enters the heart of Calatayud, the second largest city in the province of Zaragoza. At first, the city seems to be a dismal cluster of traffic jams and neon signs. Its name is usually said to be an Arabic rendering of "Castle of Job" (Kalat Ayub), but some insist it derives from Kalat-al-Yeud, a Jew who is said to have founded the city. Either way, local pride centers on the town's tawny brick Mudéjar towers. The striking octagonal belfry on the collegiate Church of Santa María la Mayor (Calle de Obispo Arrué), which also has a notable Plateresque façade, is the best example — it once was the minaret of a mosque and it soars above the rooftops of the houses. There is another notable tower on the 12th-century Church of San Andrés (Calle Dato).

Don't linger in Calatayud if it can be helped, but proceed 9 miles (14 km) west along N-II and, just past Ateca, turn off at the sign for Nuévalos and the Monasterio de Piedra. The road goes through folds of scrubby plateau until it twists along the mountainside above the Tranquera reservoir, startlingly blue-green in the arid landscape.

NUÉVALOS: The town itself is extremely small, with just one main street and few facilities. Its main attraction is the *Monasterio de Piedra* south of town, and the public park that surrounds it. The overriding sounds on the approach are the trickles of cascades and a 174-foot waterfall thundering into the green stillness of old woods. This handsome monastery was founded by Cistercian monks from the all-powerful Poblet Abbey in Tarragona in 1194, as a retreat from the court intrigues that royal visitors inflicted on Poblet. By the early 13th century, its construction was well under way, and substantial additions in a range of architectural styles were made over the years. Abandoned in 1835, the monastery itself is now a hotel (see *Checking In*), but the grounds — a true water garden — are open to the public. They are extremely crowded in the summer, when the mists from the cascades are the only antidote to the blazing heat of southern Aragon. Paths weave through mossy rocks and lush gardens, descending slick steps into a damp grotto behind a falling curtain of water. One path leads up to an ancient hermitage perched high on the hillside. Tunnels and stairways date from the 19th century, when Juan Federico Muntadas tamed the overgrown thickets of the deserted monastery to create a remarkable waterscape with an offshoot of the Piedra River. At the end of the park is a trout hatchery, near a natural reflecting pool poised between two steep cliffs. The park is open weekdays from dawn till dusk and weekends from 9 AM to 6 PM. Admission charge.

CHECKING IN/EATING OUT: *Monasterio de Piedra* – In its present incarnation, complete with a swimming pool and tennis courts, this former monastery would sorely tempt medieval monks to break their vows and indulge themselves in the comforts of one of the 61 modern, air conditioned rooms that have replaced their former cells. Rooms overlooking the inner courtyard are smaller, but more private; others, on the other side, have balconies looking down on the main public pathway, although privacy prevails in the early morning and after dusk. The restaurant is formal and serves tastier meals than the place next door, which dishes up chow for hungry hikers. Make reservations well in advance. Monasterio de Piedra, Nuévalos (phone: 76-849011). Moderate.

Las Truchas – Don't despair if the great monastery is booked solid, because this friendly *hostal*, with a busy restaurant and outdoor terrace, has 30 comfortable (though unstylish) rooms. There's also a playground, a miniature golf course, a swimming pool, tennis courts, and a convention room. The owners cater to bus-loads of tourists, so the restaurant's menu is in three languages and features non-regional dishes such as a particularly oily and bland paella. The service, however, is quite friendly and efficient. Carretera de Cillas a Alhama (C202), Km 37, Nuévalos (phone: 76-849040). Inexpensive.

   En Route from Nuévalos – Because the direct road to Daroca is so narrow that drivers are likely to get stuck behind frustratingly slow tractors with no place to pass, take the valley road (C202) 16 miles (26 km) *back* to Calatayud. With the rugged hills sheltering vineyards and orchards of peaches, cherries, pears, al-monds, and walnuts, the drive can be a sheer joy during spring blossoming. At Calatayud, turn right onto N234 for the final 22 miles (35 km) to Daroca. Pines stipple the hills here, and the town is hidden in a hollow, surrounded by 2 miles of crumbling walls that once boasted 114 fortified towers, many of which still stand. On the banks of the Jiloca River, Daroca was once a Roman military settlement, then saw heavy fighting under the Moors — mainly for control of the province by rival Moorish factions. King Alfonso I of Aragon liberated the town in 1122. Today, Daroca has few visitors, and not much sightseeing to offer aside from the impressive city gates and a few Mudéjar churches, which are currently undergoing restoration. Not much is left of the craft tradition that distinguished the medieval town; what remains is on display in the *Museo del Santísmo Misterio,* which has distinguished woodcarvings, as well as an interesting alabaster altar-piece showing Flemish influence. Most of the pottery on sale in town comes from Teruel and Zaragoza, but the best comes from Muel. The 16th-century, barrel-vaulted tunnel, dug half a mile through the mountains to divert floodwaters from the town, is a remarkable example of canny Aragonese engineering, but it's not much of a sight; the 20 spouts on the fountain just outside the town gates are much more impressive.

   Drive south along N234 to Teruel, 62 miles (100 km) away, past cultivated fields that stretch to either side, with stark mountains on the distant horizon.

   EATING OUT: *El Ruejo* – In the heart of town, this pension is a favorite of young couples and young bullfight fans. Don't be put off by the dingy bar; the place is clean, comfortable, and heated and air conditioned. A spacious dining room up the tiled stairway is very pleasant. The waiter will dissuade diners from any odd, non-regional offerings; listen to him and stick to the most popular foods, which will be the freshest. Pork or lamb is the best bet, accompanied by a glass of the heavy and potent *vino de la tierra.* Reservations unnecessary. 112 Calle Mayor, Daroca (phone: 76-800335). Inexpensive.

TERUEL: The barren, flat-topped hills that surround this old-fashioned town, capital of the province of Teruel, are echoed in the ocher brick of its five Mudéjar towers. In fact, Teruel is considered to have the best examples of Mudéjar architecture in Spain. The city was recaptured from the Moors in 1171, but the Muslim population that remained was soon granted special privileges, allowing it to live in harmony with the Christian amd Jewish inhabitants. The last mosque was still operating in 1502, which shows that the Inquisition got a late start in this arid backwater, and in the meantime, the Moorish artisans who built and decorated the towers had the opportunity to develop their style in peace. The most distinguished are the Torre de San Martín, at the San Martín church (Plaza de Pérez Prado), and the Torre del Salvador, at the church of the same name (on Calle Salvador); both date from the 13th century and both are adorned with porcelain plaques and tiles worked in decorative patterns into already fancy brickwork. A third tower is that of the cathedral, originally 13th century, but rebuilt in the 16th and 17th centuries and in this one, following Civil War damage (inside, there's a notable Mudéjar ceiling). A particularly grim winter during the Civil War in 1937 saw Teruel devastated as the Republicans gained control, only to lose it a fortnight later to the Nationalists. Los Arcos, the 16th-century aqueduct north of town, managed to remain intact despite the heavy shelling and machine gun fire.

Teruel's main square is the Plaza de Torico, which is marked by an unusual fountain. In its center is a statue of a baby bull with a star between his horns, which has become the town's official symbol. Throughout Spain, however, Teruel is best known as the scene of the tragic love affair between Diego de Marcilla and Isabella de Segura, the star-crossed, 13th-century "Lovers of Teruel" — a story reminiscent of *Romeo and Juliet*. Diego, dismissed as an unsuitable suitor by Isabella's father, left town heartsick. Determined to make his fortune in 5 years' time and return to Teruel and marry his love, he came back 1 day late, to a wedding feast: Isabella had been forced to marry a rich local rival. In despair, Diego expired at her feet, and she died of a broken heart at his funeral. A double grave, unearthed in the 16th century, was presumed to be theirs, and they now lie buried in the funerary chapel by another of the city's Mudéjar towers (San Pedro; open daily, from 10 AM to 1 PM and from 5 to 7 PM). Sculpted figures of the two, atop alabaster sarcophogi, reach out to hold hands, and a macabre transparent crypt displays their embracing skeletons. Over the centuries, many Spanish poets, dramatists, and artists have been inspired by the story, which has also made Teruel a favorite destination for honeymoon couples.

CHECKING IN: *Parador de Teruel* – Outside the city limits, a bit over 1¼ miles (2 km) north of town on N234 and in a disappointingly modern building (in regional style, however), it has 60 spacious rooms, surrounded by attractive gardens. Carretera Teruel–Zaragoza, Teruel (phone: 74-601800). Expensive.

Reina Cristina – The only comfortable establishment in town, it's near the Salvador church and tower and has 62 rooms equipped with the most modern conveniences. The dining room serves regional specialties, along with the standard "international" fare, but demonstrates no particular flair. 1 Paseo del Ovalo, Teruel (phone: 74-606860). Expensive.

EATING OUT: *El Milagro* – Good home cooking that makes the most of local products is the attraction here. Roasts and mountain-cured ham, or *jamón serrano*, go well with the hearty cariñena wine. Reservations unnecessary. Located just past the *Parador de Teruel*, it also has some modest rooms with showers available. Carretera Teruel–Zaragoza (N234), Km 3, Teruel (phone: 74-603095). Moderate.

En Route from Teruel – To the southeast, N234 leads to Valencia; to the southwest, N420 leads to Cuenca and ultimately back to Madrid. But Albarracín, a village practically plastered against a steep slope 24 miles (38 km) west of Teruel, is worth a detour even for those planning to backtrack to Valencia rather than continue over the mountains to Cuenca. Leave Teruel heading north on N234, following the signs to the airport, and after about 6 miles (10 km), turn off where signposted to Albarracín. The road climbs steadily until it reaches the Guadalaviar River, which threads past a handful of modern apartments on the outskirts of the town.

ALBARRACÍN: This small medieval village rises in a breathtaking vertical sweep to the snaggletoothed battlements that guard its rear, circled by the Guadalaviar River like a natural moat. The town has been independent on two occasions, once in the 11th century as an autonomous Muslim *taifa,* and once in the mid-12th-century as a Christian holdout from the expanding Aragonese kingdom. Its fortifications date from the late 10th century and the 11th century, and exemplify the caliphs' military style. The village has retained its medieval character to such an extent that it has been declared a national monument. Tall, half-timbered houses are daubed in rosy plaster, with balconies made of wrought iron or carved wood. Escutcheons mark the nobler houses, and around each corner is a view on a new level. The museum in the chapterhouse of the 13th-century Catedral de El Salvador contains a collection of rather worn 16th-century Flemish tapestries, but the life-size trout carved from rock crystal is more treasured by the villagers. Despite its isolation, Albarracín has been discovered by intrepid summer crowds.

 CHECKING IN: *Albarracín* – This old house stands out from the rest of the village — because it's the only building with a satellite dish. With 30 rooms, it is the most comfortable — if not the most authentic — place to stay, and it also has a passable restaurant. 9 Calle Azagra, Albarracín (phone: 74-710011). Expensive.

 EATING OUT: *El Portal* – A welcoming bar serving hot snacks and hearty meals, right in the middle of the village. The impressive doorway has a knocker and handle fashioned as iron lizards. The set menu is filling, and the owner even accepts credit cards. Reservations unnecessary. 14 Portal de Molina, Albarracín (phone: 74-710290). Moderate to inexpensive.

En Route from Albarracín – If the pass over the Montes Universales is open, take the spectacular winding drive through Tragacete and on to the strange formations of the Ciudad Encantada outside Cuenca (see *Castile–La Mancha (New Castile),* DIRECTIONS). Otherwise, return to Teruel via the southern loop, past the three protected caves containing prehistoric petroglyphs of bulls stenciled on the rocks near Abrigos del Callejon. The caves are well marked and can't easily be missed (huge arrows posted on trees and painted on cliffs mark the trails). From Teruel, head toward Valencia on the N234 and E26 highways, both clearly marked. The road passes through a wild area of the southeast corner of Teruel province called the Maestrazgo and soon flattens into the fertile Valencian *huerta.*

Madrid Region

It's not necessary to go as far as Toledo or Segovia to escape the bustle of Madrid or see a bit of Castile. Within an hour's drive of the capital, traffic chaos permitting, it's possible to sample huge fresh strawberries at a green oasis in the dusty plains to the south, to visit the house where Miguel de Cervantes was born in an ancient university town to the east, to view one of the world's great monuments just to the west, or to take in the cool peaks of the Sierra de Guadarrama to the northwest.

At 2,119 feet, Madrid is the highest capital in Europe, but the Sierra de Guadarrama range to the northwest (the setting for much of Ernest Hemingway's *For Whom the Bell Tolls*) is considerably higher. Madrid is often blisteringly hot in summer, and *madrileños* who don't go to the coast head for the hills. This is very important to a city in the geographic heart of Spain, far from any sea. It matters little that the mountain towns are not especially beautiful. Their chief function is as weekend retreats, bases for hiking, and in the case of the higher villages, settings for winter sports. There are also some beautiful scenic views, especially where the mountains overlook a river or a reservoir.

The picture is quite different to the south, where the dusty plains of Castile–La Mancha begin. The countryside is far from exciting, but there are at least two spots in this area worth visiting. One is the delightful little medieval village of Chinchón, today famous for its widely consumed *anís de Chinchón* liqueur. The other is Aranjuez, a onetime royal residence, and still an oasis of luxuriant gardens and abundant vegetation, thanks to the confluence of two rivers here.

Alcalá de Henares to the east has seen better days, but that is not to say it isn't a busy commercial center today. The birthplace of the man who wrote *Don Quixote* conserves many important medieval buildings in the center of town, but the downtown area in general has lost its charm to traffic and industry. Visitors won't have come to Spain to tour a US air base, presumably, but there is one nearby, and it's closing down in 1992, so now would be the time to see it. In any case, many of the stores in Torrejón de Ardoz, near the base, cater to American tastes.

Without doubt, the greatest cultural treat in the immediate Madrid region is the monumental monastery and palace of El Escorial. Many people have mixed feelings about this bleak place, erected when Spain was the world's most powerful country, while dominated by a Catholic faith that was ruthless and often fanatic. El Escorial was designed to reflect much of this. It is only logical while visiting it to continue a few miles to an even more controversial monument — the Valley of the Fallen, the burial site of Generalísimo Francisco Franco. Like El Escorial, it is hard to deny the fascination of the place, even if it is not the visitor's own cup of tea.

This chapter has been designed so that, with one exception, these locations can be enjoyed in easily managed day trips. In the case of the Sierra de Guadarrama, a 2-day excursion seems more appropriate and leisurely, and a wonderful modern hotel set in a 14th-century monastery (*Santa María de El Paular*) has been selected as a place to spend the night. Apart from this establishment and the *Parador de Chinchón,* no hotels have been recommended in this chapter, as it is assumed that the traveler will be based in Madrid. Both hostelries are categorized as expensive, although in this peripheral area that means much less than it would in the capital — a double room at the *parador* costs about $150 a night, while at the monastery-hotel a double room ranges from about $125 to $150. Along the way, lunch or dinner for two with wine will cost $65 and above in an expensive restaurant, $45 to $60 in a moderate restaurant, and below $40 in an inexpensive one. Note that the Province of Madrid Tourist Office (2 Calle Duque de Medinaceli; phone: 1-429-4951) can be very helpful in furnishing information regarding the sightseeing attractions in the Madrid region.

Day Trip 1: Chinchón and Aranjuez

These two towns are the most beautiful in the southern Madrid region, but in contrasting ways. Chinchón, little more than a village, has hardly changed since the Middle Ages, and it has a splendid medieval Plaza Mayor, one of the most prized in Spain. Aranjuez is a green, spacious oasis in the dusty La Mancha plain, overflowing with luxurious gardens surrounding royal palaces and other mainly 18th-century regal retreats.

En Route from Madrid – Leave town at the main Atocha railway station in southern Madrid, following the A3 (which becomes the N-III) signs to Valencia. Fourteen miles (22 km) along a freshly improved highway, the Arganda Bridge crosses the Jarama River; immediately afterward is the C300 turnoff to Chinchón, 28 miles (45 km) from Madrid.

CHINCHÓN: To say there is nothing much to Chinchón (pop. 4,100) would be an understatement, but it is nonetheless worth a stop on the way to Aranjuez. The village was founded in 1085, when Alfonso VI reconquered nearby Toledo from the Moors. The village's centerpiece today is the 16th-century Plaza Mayor, an oddly shaped "square" of rickety 3-story arcaded buildings topped with 224 wooden balconies. The village was immortalized in the film *Around the World in 80 Days,* and has been drawing as many as 15,000 visitors per weekend in recent years, many of whom arrive in cars and park in and around the square. That situation, along with the general neglect of the shaky-looking balconies, led to a long-awaited renovation in 1990 and the building of an underground car park, leaving the square traffic-free and even more attractive. Since 1502, the square has been the site of bullfights, and it is still occasionally cordoned off for them. The best time is fiesta week, August 13 through 18, but be warned — it is usually scorching hot at that time of the year.

Try to visit Chinchón during spring or early summer. Sit at one of the many open-air cafés in the Plaza Mayor and enjoy a small glass of the drink for which the village is nationally famous. The *anís* of Chinchón is made with the oily aniseed produced from locally grown anise, a member of the parsley family, and alcohol. Those who haven't eaten yet should ask for *dulce,* or sweet — the *seco,* or dry, is potent stuff! Speaking of drinks, it was the Marquesa de Chinchón, wife of a 17th-century Viceroy of Peru, who first introduced quinine — a key ingredient of tonic water — to Europe from South America after she had been cured of malaria by the drug, obtained by local Indians from a tree that she named "cinchona" after her hometown. A statue of the marquise is to be placed in the Plaza Mayor in 1992, in time for the 500th anniversary of the discovery of the Americas.

Chinchón is also famous for its garlic and decorative bread, loaves baked in the shapes of fish, horses, owls, eagles, and other animals. The bread can be bought varnished for decoration or unvarnished to eat. There are several bakeries on the Plaza Mayor — perhaps the widest assortment of strange breads is found at *Luis Ontalva* (25 Plaza Mayor). Most of the other buildings sell garlic or *anís,* or are restaurants. Looming over one side of the square is the parish church, the Iglesia de la Asunción, built between 1534 and 1626, with an *Assumption of the Virgin* by Goya, who often stayed in Chinchón. Just behind the opposite corner is the *Parador de Chinchón* (see below), from which there is a good view of the well-preserved 15th-century castle, with its circular fortified towers; it was sacked along with the rest of the town by Napoleon's troops in 1808.

CHECKING IN: *Parador de Chinchón* – A former 17th-century Augustinian convent that was restored in the 1970s but still preserves its chapel, this *parador* is extremely tranquil. The 38 air conditioned rooms are the height of comfort, and behind the building there are fine terraced gardens with quince trees and goldfish ponds, an open-air swimming pool, and a view of the castle. There is also a bar and a good restaurant. 1 Avenida Generalísimo, Chinchón (phone: 1-894-0836). Expensive.

EATING OUT: *Mesón Cuevas del Vino* – An informal eating place located in converted wine and oil stores. In the basement, notice the 400-year-old caves between huge, centuries-old wine vats. The upstairs dining room is decorated with large, autographed wine jars. Try *alubias de Chinchón* (local haricot beans laced with meaty stock) and *cochinillo asado* (roast suckling pig). Reservations advised. 13 Calle Benito Hortelano, Chinchón (phone: 1-894-0206). Moderate.

Plaza Mayor – Long a favorite of Madrid's weekend tourists as well as the non-Spanish, this delightful narrow building has 3 floors of small dining rooms, with a lovely balcony on the third. Fresh fish arrives daily and is well prepared; the roast lamb is succulent. Reservations unnecessary, except for lunch on Sundays. 10 Plaza Mayor, Chinchón (phone: 1-894-0929). Moderate.

En Route from Chinchón – The pleasant country road to Aranjuez, 14 miles (22 km) away, passing through the village of Villaconejos, is clearly marked. Apart from the odd gravel quarry and olive grove, there is little to see. As Aranjuez nears, the vegetation thickens and the landscape becomes greener.

ARANJUEZ: Despite a Roman and later an Arab presence, Aranjuez (pronounced Ah-rahn-*hwayth*) is largely a whimsical creation of Spanish monarchs from the 15th to the 18th centuries. However, the lush foliage and respite from the blistering summer heat is a natural phenomenon. Aranjuez (pop. 36,000) lies in the valley formed by the Tagus and Jarama rivers, and the area is fertile and humid. Ferdinand and Isabella, the Catholic Monarchs, first noted its pleasant climate during the 15th century, and late in the 16th century, Philip II ordered buildings to be constructed. But it was the first Spanish Bourbon, Philip V, whose rule spanned the first half of the 18th century, who chose Aranjuez as a royal residence, especially in the spring. His successors, Ferdinand VI and Carlos III, embellished the Royal Palace — the present building dates from 1744, after a fire destroyed much of the palace in 1712 — and built a huge square in front of it and the large, French-modeled Parterre gardens around it. From 1792 to 1803, Carlos IV built a second "palace," the Casa del Labrador, in some ways as beautiful as the first though much smaller, and added the vast landscaped park — Jardín del Príncipe (Prince's Garden) — that surrounds it. The informal Jardín de la Isla, on an island in the river next to the Royal Palace, dates from Philip II's time in the 16th century.

The spacious leafy gardens and long, tree-shaded avenues of Aranjuez are the perfect place for an unhurried stroll. The monarchs wanted to create a Spanish Versailles, and their efforts still attract many visitors. The Royal Palace and the Casa del Labrador are both richly decorated with ornamental fantasies, including priceless gifts from royalty around the world and over the centuries. The palace has hundreds of rooms, the best known being the Porcelain Salon, the former reception hall, whose walls and ceilings are covered with white porcelain by the Italian artist Gricci. The Casa del Labrador (or Peasant's House, so named because a farmworker's home used to stand on the site), in the nearby Jardín del Príncipe, contains an abundance of marble, gold, semi-precious stone, crystal, silk hangings, Roman mosaics, huge chandeliers, and 27 elaborate clocks. The gardens are open daily, from 10 AM to dusk. The Royal Palace and the Casa del Labrador are open Wednesdays through Mondays, from 10 AM to 1:30 PM and from 3:30 to 6:30 PM. A combined ticket allows entry to the palace (the visit here is by guided tour) and the Casa del Labrador; no admission charge to the gardens.

Aranjuez played an important role at the outset of the Peninsular War in 1808, when Carlos IV and Napoleon signed a treaty against Britain. A popular insurrection in the town led to the downfall of the hated minister Godoy, the abdication of Carlos IV in favor of hs son, Ferdinand VII, and the Peninsular War itself. The *Motín,* or Uprising, is celebrated every September during a 5-day annual fair, when thousands of exuberant residents reenact the rebellion in festive style. Napoleon's troops did in fact cause much damage to Aranjuez before the tide turned against them, when the future Duke of Wellington entered the war.

The town is nationally famous for its delicious crops, asparagus and strawberries in particular, and especially during spring and early summer, the roadsides are crammed with stalls selling produce. A meal isn't complete here without a first course of green asparagus and a dessert of strawberries and cream. A popular excursion for *madrileños* is the wonderful *Tren de la Fresa* (Strawberry Train), a 19th-century–style steam train that runs to Aranjuez from Delicias Station in Madrid every Saturday, Sunday, and public holiday from May through mid-October. The ticket (currently about $14) includes visits to the palace and the gardens — and free strawberries on the train. A popular compliment to a girl in Spain is "Your lips are like the strawberries of Aranjuez," but the train's hostesses probably hear it 100 times a day.

 EATING OUT: ***Casa Pablo*** – Pablo Guzmán has turned his restaurant into a popular haunt over the years, with an extensive menu of Castilian specialties, including fresh fish and game. The walls of the bar and the 2 dining rooms — the larger one is upstairs — are covered with bullfighting posters and photos. Closed August. Reservations unnecessary. 42 Calle Almíbar, Aranjuez (phone: 1-891-1451). Expensive.

La Rana Verde – The *Green Frog* is indeed green, like the town, down to the waiters' jackets, the menu covers, the decor — and even the Tagus River, which flows gently by outside the plentiful windows. Get here early for a riverside table. The place is touristy and large, but with good food — try *espárragos verdes naturales* (fresh green asparagus), *pavo en salsa de almendra* (turkey in almond sauce), and the inevitable *fresones con nata* (strawberries and cream). Reservations advised. 1 Calle Reina, Aranjuez (phone: 1-891-1325). Moderate.

En Route to Madrid – For a quick drive 30 miles (48 km) back to Madrid, take the N-IV Madrid–Andalusia highway heading north.

En Route to Toledo – Just south of Aranjuez on N-IV is the N400 turnoff to Toledo, 27 miles (43 km) away along a straight road that follows the Tagus River.

Day Trip 2: Alcalá de Henares and Nuevo Baztán

A person needs a strong interest in history to profit from a journey to Alcalá de Henares, formerly an ancient university center but now little more than a bustling dormitory town for Madrid, 19 miles (31 km) away, with medieval buildings that are choked by permanent traffic jams. The only other place in this region east of Madrid worth visiting is the village of Nuevo Baztán, which has some curiosity value.

En Route from Madrid – Take the A2 highway (it later becomes the N-II) out of northeast Madrid, easily found because it is the route to the well-marked Barajas Airport. This means the traffic is often brutal — especially as this is also the main highway to Barcelona. A few miles before Alcalá de Henares, the highway passes the controversial US air base of Torrejón de Ardoz. After much wrangling with the Spanish government, the Reagan administration agreed to transfer the locally unpopular 401st Tactical Wing of 72 F-16 fighter-bombers to Italy by 1992. At Torrejón, travelers might want to take a 7½-mile (12-km) detour south along N206 to the sleepy village of Loeches (pop. 2,100), which was a Moorish fortress and still has a 16th-century church and two convents.

ALCALÁ DE HENARES: The greatest writer in the Spanish language, Miguel de Cervantes, author of *Don Quixote,* was born here in 1547, but the town's history goes back much further. The area around Alcalá de Henares (pop. 145,000) includes several prehistoric, Roman, and Visigothic sites, but unfortunately none is open to the public. A 3,600-square-foot Roman site from the 4th century was discovered in 1988, and it includes an important multicolored mosaic from a villa in the Roman settlement of Complutum, in the Henares River valley. The nearest anyone can get to the remains is the *Museo Tear* (Paseo Juncal; phone: 1-881-3250), an archaeological museum and workshop where students piece together the remains (open Fridays, from 4 to 8 PM, and Saturdays, from 10 AM to 2 PM). The name of the town, incidentally, comes from the Arabic Al-Qalat, or "fortress" — which fell to the Catholic forces in 1088.

Alcalá's golden age began at the end of the 15th century, when Cardinal Cisneros founded the famous Complutensian University in 1498. For many years the most important in Spain, it published Europe's first polyglot Bible, a six-volume work printed from 1514 to 1517, with side-by-side texts in Hebrew, Greek, and Latin, Chaldee, and Syriac. Many colleges and convents were built in the next 2 centuries, but the university was moved to Madrid in 1836, and the city has declined in importance and attraction ever since, although there is a new Alcalá University that is an important center of North American studies. The original university complex, the Colegio de San Ildefonso, in the Plaza San Diego (near the main Plaza Cervantes), is now the new university. Its 16th-century Plateresque façade is interesting; the doorway leads into the arcaded Patio de Santo Tomás and the Paraninfo, or auditorium, and on to the adjacent Patio Trilingüe (Courtyard of Three Languages), so named because Greek, Latin, and

Hebrew were taught here. (The old university was a renowned language center, and the author of the first Spanish grammar was among its professors.) The university can be visited weekends and holidays, from 11 AM to 1 PM and from 4 to 6 PM; no admission charge. Other monuments of note include the Iglesia Magistral de San Justo, an imposing 17th-century building with a Gothic portal; the 13th- through 16th-century Archbishop's Palace, of several different styles though badly damaged by fire in 1939 (most of the town's churches suffered damage during the 1931–39 Second Republic and Spanish Civil War); and the Capilla de San Ildefonso (2 Calle Pedro Gumiel), where Cardinal Cisneros's 16th-century marble tomb is on display. The *Salon Cervantes* (Calle Santiago), the town's only theater, was built in 1888 and is now open after many years of restoration.

The *Casa de Cervantes* (48 Calle Mayor) is the author's purported birthplace, but is, in fact, a well-reproduced period house and museum. Built in 1956, the house contains original furniture, an arcaded interior patio with eight granite columns holding up wooden balconies, and many old manuscripts and copies of *Don Quixote*. Local authorities are "75% certain" that Cervantes was born in the house that was on this site — what is 100% certain is that the literary genius was born in Alcalá de Henares in 1547 and moved with most of his family to Valladolid when he was 6. The house is open Mondays through Fridays, from 10 AM to 2 PM and from 4 to 7 PM; weekends, from 10 AM to noon; admission charge. The tourist office nearby (Callejón de Santa María; phone: 1-889-2694) is open mornings only (10 AM to 2 PM) daily.

EATING OUT: *Hostería del Estudiante* – This early-16th-century eating house is part of the original university complex, adjacent to the Patio Trilingüe. A large hall decorated in period style, it has thick beams, whitewashed walls, a tiled floor, and a large chimney contributing to a welcoming atmosphere. The food is typically Castilian. Try *sopa castellana* (bread and garlic soup) and, in mid-afternoon, *chocolate con migas* (hot chocolate with fried bread crumbs). Reservations advised during class terms (from October through June approximately). 3 Calle Los Colegios, Alcalá de Henares (phone: 1-888-0330). Expensive.

***San Diego* –** A pleasant upstairs dining room facing the 16th-century university façade. Try the *churrasco de ternera* (thick steaks served on a grill over hot coals in a metal bowl, so that it slowly cooks on the table while diners are finishing the first course). Reservations unnecessary. 5 Plaza San Diego, Alcalá de Henares (phone: 1-888-3097). Inexpensive.

En Route from Alcalá de Henares – Take N230 south to Nuevo Baztán, 12½ miles (20 km) away, past the villages of El Gurugu and Valverde de Alcalá.

NUEVO BAZTÁN: This semi-derelict village of barely 500 people is undergoing much-needed repairs. Its interest lies in the fact that it was designed during the early 18th century by the leading baroque architect, José de Churriguera, and is the only example of his work in the Madrid region. He was commissioned by Marqués Juan de Goyeneche, a wealthy banker, who wanted to undertake an experiment in town planning, as well as create a local ceramics and decorative glass industry. Churriguera was from the Basque valley of Baztán in the Navarrese Pyrenees near the French border — hence the name. The parish Church of San Francisco Javier and the palace here are noteworthy, but are not expected to regain their full Churrigueresque charm until restoration is completed this year.

En Route to Madrid – Madrid is 32 miles (51 km) from Nuevo Baztán, via Alcalá de Henares.

En Route to Guadalajara – Another 15½ miles (25 km) along the N-II highway from Alcalá de Henares toward Barcelona is Guadalajara, a historic town; see *Castile–La Mancha (New Castile)*, DIRECTIONS.

Day Trip 3: El Pardo, El Escorial, and the Valley of the Fallen

This trip takes in the foothills of the Sierra de Guadarrama and includes some of the prettier villages — as well as the most popular weekend and summer resorts — in the Madrid region. But for first-time visitors, at least, there is only one real attraction: the Real Monasterio de El Escorial, one of the most famous monasteries in the world. It's both a fascinating and a grim experience, as is the *Valley of the Fallen*, so perhaps a quick side trip to El Pardo will lighten the mood.

En Route from Madrid – Take the A6 Madrid–La Coruña highway out of northwest Madrid; while still in the city's outskirts at Puerto de Hierro, take the C601 turnoff to El Pardo, a few miles ahead through some lovely woods.

EL PARDO: The highlight of the quiet village, 9 miles (14 km) from Madrid, is the delightful El Pardo Palace, a royal residence built in the 16th century on the foundations of a former hunting lodge, partly destroyed by fire in 1604 and enlarged in 1772. Generalísimo Francisco Franco lived here until his death in 1975, and the palace now serves as home to visiting heads of state; when not occupied, it is open to the public. Inside are paintings, frescoes (including some showing the palace's original furnishings), period furniture, and an extensive, fine collection of wall tapestries. Other charming buildings nearby include the Casita del Príncipe (Prince's Cottage), also built in 1772, and the Quinta del Pardo, with a collection of 19th-century wallpapers. These two and the palace (when not pressed into service as guest quarters for VIPs) are open Mondays through Saturdays from 10:30 AM to 1 PM and from 4 to 7 PM; mornings only on Sundays; a single admission charge covers all three (phone: 1-216-4845). The Convento de los Capuchinos, on the outskirts of town, contains a magnificent early-17th-century wooden carving of the *Recumbent Christ* by Gregorio Fernández. The royal park preceding El Pardo houses the smaller Palacio de la Zarzuela, also a former hunting lodge, dating from the 17th century and rebuilt during the 18th century. Badly damaged during the Spanish Civil War, it was rebuilt in the 1960s and is now the principal residence of King Juan Carlos and thus closed to the public.

En Route from El Pardo – Back on A6, the turnoff to El Escorial — C505 — is clearly marked at Las Rozas, which is 10 miles (16 km) from Madrid. The road leads to the small town of San Lorenzo de El Escorial, 29 miles (46 km) from Madrid, but way before reaching it, travelers see the enormous rectangular monastery looming in the distance.

EL ESCORIAL: Philip II, the man who sent the "invincible" Spanish Armada to conquer Queen Elizabeth I's England and transferred the Spanish capital from Toledo to Madrid, was a deeply religious ruler of Spain's Catholic Empire at its zenith. The monastery that he built, the Real Monasterio de San Lorenzo de El Escorial, with its patios, palaces, and Pantheon, or Royal Mausoleum, reflects not only that grandeur, but also Philip's Catholic obsession, his grim, austere nature, and his sense of order. In 1557, Philip had four reasons to order the monastery's construction. First, in that year, his Spanish army defeated the French at the Battle of San Quintín on August 10, the *Day of San Lorenzo* (St. Lawrence). The saint had been martyred on a grill, and the building, the masterpiece of architect Juan de Herrera, is shaped like a gridiron, with the church as its handle. Second, Philip wanted to build a mausoleum for his father, the Holy Roman Emperor Charles V, and his mother, Queen Isabel. Third, he wanted to construct a center of solid religious education. Fourth, he wanted a magnificent summer residence where he could escape from the Madrid heat and go hunting.

El Escorial, however, is more than just a homage to a martyred saint, a mausoleum, a monastery, and a royal residence. It's a church, two palaces, a school, and one of the most important libraries in Spain. But the overall attraction of the place is its ambiguity. It is at the same time a home of splendor and riches, treasures and art, and also a monument of grim, monastic austerity, a place that chills rather than thrills. It was built over 21 years by 3,000 people who worked daily from 1563 to 1584, a feat of great speed for its time. Philip used to like to sit on a slab of sculpted rock above the village, today called Philip's Chair, and watch the work in progress. The main entrance is part of the grand western façade, and just above the doorway are two sculpted grills. There is also a statue of St. Lawrence — the granite is from the local mountains, while his face and hands are made from marble brought from Portugal and southern Spain. Special carts drawn by 40 pair of oxen were built to bring huge granite blocks from the mountains to construct the entrance, which leads into the Kings' Patio, one of El Escorial's 16 courtyards. Granite statues of six Kings of Israel stare down. The left side of the patio is a school, still in use. The monastery is to the right, and in front is the church. A bowl underneath the cross above the church contains a solid gold rock, the only gold in the whole of El Escorial.

Inside the church, the exterior's austerity gives way somewhat to the rich decoration of the high altar, the painted ceilings, and the side chapels. All the paintings are by Italian artists and show events in the life of Christ — except for one that portrays St. Lawrence being grilled! A gilded bronze, marble, and jasper model tabernacle, which took 7 years to make, is outstanding. There are statues here of Philip and three of his four wives; England's Mary Tudor is missing simply because she never visited Spain. One of the chapels contains a beautiful statue of *Christ on the Cross,* made by Benvenuto Cellini in 1562 from one piece of marble. Visitors can even see the "veins" in Christ's legs. Unfortunately, they can also see a chip where the statue was damaged by Napoleon's troops in 1808. Directly below the main altar is the Panteón de los Reyes, or Royal Pantheon, reached by a marble and jasper stairway into the crypt. Here, in black and brown gilded marble tombs, lies every Spanish monarch since the Holy Roman Emperor Charles V (King Charles I of Spain), except Philip V and Ferdinand VI. Also entombed are some of the country's queens, but only those who gave birth to a future king. Next door is the Panteón de los Infantes, where several princes and princesses are buried.

Many sections of El Escorial were added by later monarchs, which explains the varied styles in the Palacios (Royal Apartments). The centerpiece of the earlier, 16th-century Hapsburg Palace is a long room with a single 180-foot fresco depicting a glorious Catholic victory over the Moors. Philip's cell-like bedroom, where he died at age 71 from gout, says everything about the man. It is virtually undecorated, simple and austere, and in it hangs a single portrait of his pallid face, painted when he was already 70. Also in the Hapsburg section of the Palacios are five beautiful inlaid-ebony doors, gifts from Maximilian of Austria, and in one room there is a mighty wooden chair, made especially for Philip's last agonizing trip from Madrid to El Escorial, during which his gout-ridden body was carried for a whole week. When Philip V came from France in 1700, the Bourbon dynasty began, and the 18th century Bourbon Palace is considerably less somber. There are dozens of fine tapestries made at the Royal

Factory in Madrid, many showing scenes designed by Goya and Francisco Bayeu, his snootier brother-in-law. Elsewhere, the Biblioteca (Library), above the monastery entrance, has a marvelous Renaissance vaulted ceiling; among its treasures are the personal collection of Philip II, unique Arab and Hebrew manuscripts, the 10th-century Codex Albedensis, St. Teresa of Avila's personal diary, and a Bible lettered entirely in gold. The *Nuevos Museos* (New Museums) contains many works of art by Bosch, Zurburán, Titian, and many others. The Escorial complex (phone: 1-890-5903) is open Tuesdays through Sundays, from 10 AM to 1:30 PM (to 2 PM September through April) and from 3:30 to 6:30 PM (4 to 6 PM from September through April); admission charge. The tourist office in San Lorenzo de El Escorial is at 10 Calle Floridablanca (phone: 1-890-1554).

EATING OUT: Charolés – Traditional Castilian food in traditionally the best place in "monastery town." The menu features some international fare as well. Try *cocido madrileño* (a mixture of chickpeas, boiled vegetables, and boiled meats) and *berenjenas rellenas con langostinos frescos* (eggplants stuffed with fresh prawns). In summer, dine on the charming open-air terrace. Closed Mondays. Reservations advised. 24 Calle Floridablanca, San Lorenzo de El Escorial (phone: 1-890-5975). Expensive.

Mesón La Cueva – Situated in a former 18th-century inn, The Cave (in English — and that's what it feels like) is full of atmosphere and charm. The usual Castilian specialties and roast meats prevail. Reservations advised. 4 Calle San Antón, San Lorenzo de El Escorial (phone: 1-890-1516). Moderate.

En Route from El Escorial – Take C600 north for 6 miles (10 km) to the turnoff for *El Valle de los Caídos* (Valley of the Fallen). The huge cross is visible a few miles in the distance.

VALLEY OF THE FALLEN: While in a gloomy frame of mind, why not visit a stark place that not only pays homage to the estimated 1 million dead of Spain's 1936–39 Civil War, but also is where thousands of men on the losing side died while building the monument. The *Valle de los Caídos* is a huge basilica carved deep into the granite of a mountain in the forbidding Cuelgamuros valley. It is topped by an enormous granite cross that stands 495 feet high — as tall as a 33-floor building — on the hill above it.

Everything here is even more austere than El Escorial. The place was ordered built by Generalísimo Francisco Franco as a final resting place for himself and for José Antonio Primo de Rivera, founder of the Spanish Falange, and in honor of the war dead. The crypt contains the coffins of 40,000 soldiers of both sides who were killed in the Civil War, but only prisoners of war from the losing Republican side worked on the monument. The basilica took 10 years, from 1940 to 1950, to construct, and the cross another 9 years — 19 years and thousands of lives in all. Everything was designed to have religious significance — the sculpture of Pity over the entrance is of the Virgin Mary holding Christ. Franco himself chose the tree from which a wooden cross inside the basilica was cut. The dome of the altar under the cross is a mosaic with 5 million pieces, one of the rare examples of gaiety in this dank underground tunnel (open Tuesdays through Sundays from dawn to dusk; no admission charge).

En Route to Madrid – Drive back to San Lorenzo de El Escorial and then proceed along C505 to Las Rozas for the final stretch along A6 to Madrid.

En Route to Avila – Thirty-six miles (58 km) west of El Escorial along C505 is the walled city of Avila, the highest provincial capital in Spain. For details on Avila, see *Castile-León (Old Castile)*, DIRECTIONS.

Day Trip 4: Sierra de Guadarrama

This is actually a 2-day trip, with an overnight stop at the converted 14th-century monastery high up in the Sierra de Guadarrama range. The range, which runs along a line about 55 miles (88 km) northwest of Madrid, includes several small towns, peaks at close to 6,560 feet, and limited skiing facilities in the winter. It must be said that none of the towns has much to commend it, and the views are easily surpassed in northern Spain, but the mountains offer an easy and pleasant escape from Madrid's summer heat.

En Route from Madrid – Leave Madrid through the Arch of Triumph at Moncloa in the west of the city and drive past university buildings onto the A6 highway. Twenty-four miles (38 km) away, straddling A6, is Collado-Villalba (at an altitude of 3,000 feet). There is little to see here besides the 16th-to-17th-century Church of Our Lady of Enebral; cross the bridge spanning A6 and get on the old N-VI highway. Six miles (10 km) along is the village of Guadarrama (pop. 6,000), mentioned in Cervantes's classic, *Don Quixote*. It's a busy little place, founded by Alfonso X in 1268 and surrounded by pine, oak, and poplar trees. A handful of 18th-century buildings and an ornate fountain are all that there is to show of its history.

The M710 turnoff for Cercedilla is 200 yards beyond the village, and the old road climbs as it follows the Guadarrama River. Although its population is only 4,000, Cercedilla sprawls over several hills with its weekend chalets, whose development boosted by the construction of a railway line from Madrid. At 3,900 feet, it is a very popular hiking center. *Madrileños* drive out the 37 miles (59 km) on weekends, go for a 6-hour trek in the hills, and return in the evening. In winter, it is also an important base for skiing at Puerto de Navacerrada, just 8 miles (13 km) away.

Take C607 east out of town to N601, which leads to the village of Navacerrada, 3,945 feet above sea level. Apart from one 17th-century church, the village has nothing noteworthy to offer, except for its surrounding countryside. From Navacerrada, the 2-day trip can be continued along two possible routes. Five miles (8 km) north on C601 is the ski resort of Puerto de Navacerrada, which stands at 6,100 feet at the beginning of the most rugged part of the Sierra de Guadarrama. For those not skiing, there's little point in stopping here for more than a quick look to admire the view at the highest point in the region accessible by road. (The hotels and restaurants are standard fare for a middling ski resort.) But Puerto de Navacerrada is also the point where C604 starts and leads northeast into the mountains, toward El Paular, while N601 begins to descend as it continues northwest.

En Route to Segovia – The N601 highway from Puerto de Navacerrada continues directly northwest to Segovia. For complete details on the city and its sights, hotels, and restaurants, see *Segovia*, THE CITIES.

En Route to El Paular – Take C604 north from Puerto de Navacerrada, signposted to Rascafría. The road is very twisting and the mountains on either side are thickly wooded, with some very pretty sights. The hotel-monastery of *Santa María de El Paular* is 14 miles (22 km) away, over the 6,000-foot-high Puerto de los Cotos pass.

A gentler alternative to El Paular is the long way around from Navacerrada, taking C607 eastward toward Cerceda, 5½ miles (9 km) away, then M611 another 4½ miles (7 km) to Manzanares el Real (pop. 1,550; altitude 2,980 feet). Manzanares el Real is famous for the charming and well-restored 15th-century castle of the Dukes of Infantado, one of Spain's best examples of Castilian military architecture. The castle, with its three cyclindrical towers, is a mixture of Mudéjar and Renaissance-Gothic styles, and it houses a small museum displaying models and documents relating to various Spanish castles. The presence of the adjacent Santillana reservoir enhances the castle's beauty (open Tuesdays through Saturdays, from 10 AM to 1:30 PM and from 5 to 7 PM; Sundays, from 10 AM to 1 PM; admission charge).

From Manzanares, take M612 for 5 miles (8 km) to Soto del Real, and then M614 another 5 miles (8 km) northward to the pretty town of Miraflores de la Sierra (pop. 2,400). Despite recent expansion as a holiday center, the oldest part around the Plaza España retains a mountain village charm. The 16th-century parish church is of several different styles.

EATING OUT: *Asador La Fuente* – Opened in 1987 in the style of a traditional roast house, it has a 2-story dining room tastefully decorated with tiles, wood, and rustic bricks. There is also a terrace for summer dining. Try *morcilla de Burgos* (Burgos blood pudding) and *buey gallego en parrilla de carbón* (Galician beefsteak grilled over hot coals). Closed Mondays. Reservations necessary on weekends. 12 Calle Mayor, Miraflores de la Sierra (phone: 1-844-4216). Expensive.

Maito – A comfortable and solid mountain house with a genuine log fire and thick wooden beams. Down-home cooking is featured, with many of the fruits and vegetables coming from the restaurant's own garden. Try *sopa pastora* (garlic and bread soup) and *cochinillo asado* (roast suckling pig). Reservations advised. 5 Calle Calvo Sotelo, Miraflores de la Sierra (phone: 1-844-3567). Moderate.

En Route from Miraflores de la Sierra – Take M6141 16 miles (26 km) away over the twisting, 5,890-foot-high Puerto de la Morcuera pass to the village of Rascafría (pop. 1,130). Less than a mile (1.6 km) away is El Paular, or rather, the hotel-monastery of *Santa María de El Paular* (see below), which is really all there is in El Paular. Both villages lie on C604.

CHECKING IN/EATING OUT: *Santa María de El Paular* – A converted 14th-century monastery, with 58 luxurious air conditioned rooms overlooking an arcaded patio, a fountain, and the surrounding pine forests. It would be hard to find quieter quarters in the Madrid region. There is a heated swimming pool, tennis courts, gardens, and bicycles for rent. The *Don Lope* restaurant is extremely good — try *sopa de cebolla gratinada* (onion soup with grated cheese topping) and *chuletón de Lozoya* (grilled local steaks). El Paular (phone: 1-869-1011). Expensive.

En Route from El Paular and Rascafría – Continue northward on C604 past the village of Lozoya, where the road skirts the beautiful La Pinilla reservoir, to the main N-I highway. Before taking the highway south to Madrid, drive 4 miles (6 km) north to the walled village of Buitrago del Lozoya (pop. 1,300; altitude 3,200 feet), which is actually on a jut of land surrounded on three sides by the Lozoya River. There are some remains of the 10th-century Arab wall, and ruins of a 14th-century castle. The village had been a Roman settlement and later a fortress.

En Route to Madrid – Madrid is 48 miles (77 km) directly south on N-I, which is now in excellent condition, thanks to recent improvements.

Castile–La Mancha (New Castile)

Until fairly recently, it would not have been overstating the case by much to lament that the region extending south and east of Madrid was the one region of Spain that tended to be seen — if it was seen at all — by people on their way to somewhere else. The southeastern quadrant of the central Castilian tableland saw travelers, goods, and, to a large extent, the currents of progress flow along the radial arteries linking Madrid to the bustling, cosmopolitan northeast and to the agricultural heartland of Andalusia. And as they all sliced heedlessly through its 50,000 square miles of territory, the region did very little to draw attention to itself.

No visitor to Spain expects to find the equivalent of a neat series of theme parks laid out one after another, even in regions where culture and landscape make for a fair degree of uniformity. Castile–La Mancha, one of Spain's 17 autonomous communities, consisting of the provinces of Guadalajara, Cuenca, Albacete, Ciudad Real, and Toledo, is nothing more or less than the sum of its parts: topographical remnants administratively lumped together because they did not fit in anywhere else. Take away Albacete and add Madrid itself, and it corresponds to the historic region of New Castile, which was the southern half of the old kingdom of Castile. Nevertheless, southeastern Castile is a place that defies easy categorization, and for that reason, perhaps, it has often struck travelers as the most quintessentially Spanish region of all.

Part of what makes this so are the region's brutal winters and torrid summers. Its 3-tiered landscape — arid mountains, thick-forested river valleys, and endless flat, stultifying plains — is another factor, a compendium of the geographic facts of life that have dominated Spanish history. So is the regions's ample inventory of castles, convents, and palaces left behind from the clash between two cultures evoked by the region's hyphenated name (La Mancha means "the dry lands" in Arabic).

The common thread that unites the area — and recalls the Spain that so fascinated and exasperated 19th-century travelers — is Castile–La Mancha's contemporary socio-economic backwardness. Tilled grain fields, vineyards, and shepherds who brave traffic to maneuver their flocks across the highway are all a reminder that hardscrabble agriculture provides over a third of this vast region's million and a half inhabitants with their only livelihood. Towns and villages of striking charm seemingly cloaked in a sense of doom, little jewels of Renaissance religious architecture boarded up and abandoned, John Deere service signs along the main drag of dusty prairie crossroad towns, woodland streams and glens with strong overtones of the better side of the

Appalachians — all these are part of the picture. Even omitting Toledo from the itinerary, the region's claim on the visitor's attention span is justified by three first-rate towns — Sigüenza, Cuenca, and Almagro — plus some unique swaths of landscape that stand out amid all the empty space that in some curious way manages to bind a vast, diverse region together.

Castile–La Mancha's identity problem is nothing new. The region known to history as New Castile had as its nucleus the southern lands that fell under Christian domination just after the reconquest of Toledo by King Alfonso VI of Castile and León in 1085. These were enlarged by the domains of the harsh-contoured eastern plateau that came under the sway of his successors following the battle of Las Navas de Tolosa in 1212. After the Moors had been duly removed or assimilated, the first to put their stamp on the newly won territories were the Knights of Santiago, the Knights Templars, and the Knights of Calatrava — fighting religious brotherhoods who received land and feudal privileges in payment for services rendered during the Reconquest. The monumental legacy they left behind attests to their might, but their heyday was brief, because the Kings of Castile realized the potential for havoc, should these freewheeling warrior castes become too powerful. So the monarchs whittled away at their potential rivals or suppressed the orders altogether, the fate that befell the Templars in 1310. The last great order of crusading monks to succumb were the Almagro-based Knights of Calatrava, who became victims of medieval Spanish realpolitik in 1495, when Queen Isabella finagled the post of grand master for her husband, King Ferdinand. The Catholic church, whose immense power radiated from Toledo, moved in to fill the vacuum, building lavish cathedrals and grandiose parish churches that have survived even in the most run-down, depopulated towns. Secular control passed to a later generation of noble dynasties that emerged during Spain's 16th-century burst of imperial glory, which is why so much of what is to be seen here is of a late Gothic or Renaissance character.

For years afterward, New Castile remained the breadbasket of central Spain. Agriculture was always the key to the way of life that evolved here, as settlers moved in and set about making a livelihood as best they could. But aside from providing acceptable grazing in the rugged east, and vast plains to the south for the cultivation of grain and, from the 18th century on, wine grapes, New Castile land was never able to sustain a booming economy, especially after new and agriculturally more productive lands had been incorporated into the greater nation unified by King Ferdinand and Queen Isabella. Even during the 16th century, the writer Miguel de Cervantes knew what he was doing when he had his fictitious Don Quixote seek out knightly adventures in the tiny, dreary farm towns of the flatlands, and he succeeded in putting La Mancha on the cultural map of the literary world.

By the time Philip II designated Madrid his capital in the mid-16th century, New Castile had come to rely ever more heavily on a traditional cluster of small-scale skilled industries such as ceramics, ironware, and textiles. But after a short-lived 17th-century boom period, the aftershocks of the Industrial Revolution put these artisans out of business, increasing their sense of economic impotence and social isolation from the rest of Spain. The situation was finally put right in 1977, when the Spanish map was drastically overhauled

2 years after the death of Generalísimo Francisco Franco. Madrid was scooped out to stand on its lofty own, and what was left of New Castile was joined to the adjacent province of Albacete, with which it shared many geographic and demographic characteristics, to form the autonomous community of Castile–La Mancha. New regional authorities began to take inventory of what had come under their administrative purview, following centuries of neglect by a national government that had put its money into resort complexes meant to lure package tourists from northern Europe to the Mediterranean coast. They happily found a region that had a lot more going for it than almost anyone would have given it credit for: a varied and almost entirely untouched landscape, complete with winding rivers and inland lakes, stretching from the arid, rust-colored foothills of Guadalajara to the lush green pine forests, towering granite cliffs, and deep-cut canyons of Cuenca. Even the vast, flat stretches of pokey old La Mancha — the southern part of this region, made up of the province of Ciudad Real, southern Toledo, northwest Albacete, and southwest Cuenca — turned out to possess towns of considerable charm, with extraordinary architectural flourishes in no way inferior to the castles, churches, and convents of the rest of the area. Roman, Visigothic, and Moorish remains are far scarcer than those of the post-Reconquest and Renaissance periods, but they are well worth the trouble of seeking out.

One important point needs to be made. Unlike other parts of Spain, where visitors must pick their way through ugly industrial zones and shabby high-rise apartment blocks to locate the "Old Quarter," this region not only has its monumental jewels fairly intact, but their settings as well. The market towns and villages that form the backbone of this route have not changed much from former times, although they've paid a heavy social and economic price. Many villages have been abandoned altogether, and nearly all the towns along the way seem to be given over to elderly, beret-clad men. Women, strangely enough, remain unseen, and such adolescents as there are still hang around listlessly on the street corners or in the rock 'n' roll bars, waiting for their chance to escape to a factory job in up-to-date, pseudo-Europeanized, un-Spanish Spain.

As might be expected in what formerly was a no-man's-land between two warring cultures, variety is the keynote in the culinary department. In northern Guadalajara, the Castilian taste for tender roast meat — suckling pig, lamb, and baby kid — predominates. Once into Cuenca, the visitor will come across a few dishes unheard-of elsewhere, slow-to-spoil and portable fare created by mule teams and nomadic herdsmen. One such specialty is *ajo arriero,* a creamy paste of mashed codfish and garlic, delicious when spread on Cuenca's excellent bread, which is second only to that of Soria as Spain's best. In both areas, however, pride of place goes to small-game dishes — the ubiquitous partridge, stewed and marinated a dozen different ways, rabbit, and wild boar — and the trout, now mostly fattened in fish farms, but nevertheless inexpensive and not too inferior to its riverbed cousin, and available year-round. La Mancha, where wine and cheese are first and foremost, is an altogether different story. But it, too, has a very tasty and unique menu, which shows its Moorish origins in unusual combinations of flavors: for instance, *migas del pastor* — croutons fried in olive oil, with garlic, ham, fatback, sausage, and grapes — or stewed lamb seasoned with nutmeg, saffron, and white wine. In addition to the millions of gallons of blended table wines produced in Valdepeñas, Daimiel, and Manzanares, a few really choice, fruity young wines have been developed and aged with care. Also, the ubiquitous cheese, *queso manchego,* from ewe's milk, can be fresh from the farm or aged to bring out its strong flavor.

In laying out the following week-long drive through Castile–La Mancha, the entire province of Albacete has been omitted. Although it does have its share of nice touches — the Lagoons of Riudera and Villanueva de los Infantes are beautiful — its features are too similar to what will already have been covered elsewhere. Similarly, the provincial capital of Ciudad Real is simply not worth going that far out of the way to see. (It, and the city of Albacete, rate as two of the dullest towns in Spain.) Autumn is by far the best time to visit, so as to catch the birch trees as their leaves change color. At night, at these altitudes of 800 to 1,200 feet, the temperature can drop drastically — even in summer — so be prepared. And don't come in the winter; even the people who live here aren't too happy about it.

Expect to pay $65 and above for a double room with private bath in hotels classified as expensive, $45 to $65 in moderate hotels, and less than $40 in inexpensive ones. Dinner for two with wine will cost $50 and above in an expensive restaurant, $30 to $55 in a moderate restaurant, and below $30 in an inexpensive one.

En Route from Madrid – Leave the city on the N-II highway heading northeast in the direction of the airport and Zaragoza. Be prepared for hideous traffic and a view of endless factories and warehouses and the automobile plants of Alacalá de Henares. Continue following the Zaragoza signs, giving Guadalajara a wide berth some 35 miles (56 km) along. Then, after about 11 miles (18 km) of what begins to look like real country, and after the 13th-century Templar Castle of Torija is visible on the right, take the turnoff for Brihuega (C201) immediately before the next overpass. Brihuega is a lovely, run-down old town, perched above a dried-up river gorge. It's worth a stop for a cup of coffee, some leg-stretching, and a look at the much-restored 13th-century Romanesque and Gothic Church of Santa María de la Peña and the ruins of the Old City walls, of which two city gates remain. Up the hill, the structure resembling a gigantic bandstand pavilion once served as the Royal Cloth Factory, established by the enlightened King Carlos III during the 18th century. It later became a marvelous French garden, but it has been left unattended for years, growing surrealistically wild. On the way out of Brihuega, a signpost indicates the old road to Sigüenza, forking to the right; take this, to avoid backtracking to the N-II, and follow it through fields that, in season, are a mass of sunflowers. After 11 miles (18 km), turn briefly north onto C204 to rejoin N-II heading for Zaragoza. Almost immediately afterward, exit N-II via the ramp for Sigüenza, and again join C204 north for 16 miles (26 km) into town.

SIGÜENZA: By themselves, a castle and a cathedral do not a medieval town make, but when both dominate the skyline from surrounding hills, they seem equal to the task. The fairly prosperous farmers and artisans who live here, in what once was a major medieval archdiocese (in its heyday before the rest of the region was even properly reconquered by the Christians), confer a pleasant rural bustle. The town is set at an altitude of 3,360 feet, overlooking the Henares River, and inevitably all of the climbing streets lead to the 12th-century cathedral (open Mondays through Saturdays, from 10 AM to 1 PM and from 5 to 7 PM). Unlike many of its more famous counterparts, where interiors don't live up to exteriors or vice versa, this cathedral is a true beauty, the result of centuries of changing architectural and decorative styles, from the Mudéjar — the star-studded chapter house ceiling — to the Plateresque, all blending together with unusual harmony. Seek out and pay one of the ushers a *duro* (5-peseta coin) or two to unlock and illuminate the side chapel for a look at the town's main attraction, the tomb of the Doncel (Page Boy), who is represented in alabaster as a young man in knightly battle dress, with a sweetly innocent, melancholy expression, reclining on his side and reading from what might as well be a book of love sonnets. Beneath this captivating but mislabeled anonymous sepulchral statue are the remains of Don Martín Vázquez de Arce, who was, in fact, not a page boy but a 25-year-old married man and a full knight in Queen Isabella's service when he died in battle in 1486 during the Granada campaigns.

Other sites in town include an Ursuline convent, a baroque seminary, and the Romanesque Church of San Vicente. The *Diocesan Museum* (opposite the cathedral; open daily, from 11 AM to 2 PM; admission charge) has a vigorous late El Greco *Annunciation,* as well as Zurbarán's extraordinary *Immaculate Conception,* showing a pre-teen Virgin Mary floating over the city of Seville. (The ineffable sweetness of her expression would have come out as pure saccharine kitsch from the brush of anyone other than such a genius.) A pleasant short walk, through the medieval arch between the cathedral and the Renaissance Plaza Mayor, keeping to the right where the modern bungalows begin, and on up the hill to the cemetery, leads to a great view of the cathedral and Sigüenza's castle, which has been turned into a *parador* (see *Checking In*); both are kept well lit after dark. The streets leading up to the *parador* also reveal crafts shops where hooked rugs, wrought ironware, and decorative mirrors in hammered-copper and hardwood frames are sold. The latter are a particularly good buy, though a bit awkward to carry home. Jesús Blasco's workshop (Calle Cruz Dorada) is the place for hand-sewn goatskin fishermen's boots and wineskins.

CHECKING IN/EATING OUT: *Parador Castillo de Sigüenza* – Commanding the crest of the town, it offers 77 rooms within its admirably reconstructed medieval battlements, some with canopied beds. Ask for one of the rooms with a balcony overlooking the Patio de Armas, available at a slight surcharge. In addition to air conditioning, this old Moorish fortress, later occupied and neglected by Sigüenza's bishops, has central heating, which will be much appreciated because temperatures can plummet after dark, even in summer. Its huge interior halls make it a favorite place for business conventions. The restaurant offers a fine selection of regional specialties — game in season, fresh river crayfish, and roasts — in a pleasant atmosphere, though it's a bit overpriced. Plaza del Castillo, Sigüenza (phone: 11-390100). Expensive.

El Doncel – A comfortable, clean, 16-room *hostal* facing the town's elm-lined promenade. The restaurant specializes in roast kid. 1 Calle General Mola, Sigüenza (phone: 11-391090). Inexpensive.

El Motor – This *hostal* on the town's farthest outskirts has 8 rooms and a restaurant that does a reliable if unexciting job with its mostly international menu, especially steaks. A few concessions to regional cooking occasionally appear. The restaurant is closed Mondays, the last 2 weeks in April, and the first 2 weeks in November. 11 Calle Calvo Sotelo, Sigüenza (phone: 11-390343 or 11-390827). Inexpensive.

En Route from Sigüenza – It's well worth an extra night in Sigüenza to allow for an excursion into the surrounding mountain towns. All told, the suggested loop that follows entails a detour of 172 miles (275 km), but it can be cut short at more than one point for the return to Sigüenza. From Paseo de la Alameda, head northwest on C114, following signs for Atienza, 19½ miles (31 km) away. Atienza's lordly 12th-century castle will be visible long before the rest of the town comes into view; a closer look reveals four Romanesque churches, red-tiled and half-timbered townhouses, lovely stone columns supporting the Plaza del Trigo, and the 11th-to-13th-century arches of the town walls. At the fork in the road outside of town, make a left onto C101 going south toward Guadalajara. Jadraque lies 20½ miles (33 km) ahead, with its castle on a conical hill towering over lavender-studded fields that feed the bees that make the honey that is the province's main cash crop. Another 12 miles (19 km) ahead on C101 lies the walled town of Hita, famous for the Archpriest of Hita, a renowned 14th-century poet. Early in July, this seemingly abandoned town comes to life for a somewhat overblown but enthusiastic medieval festival, complete with jousting tourneys, colorful folk dancing, and open-air theater performances. Continue south along C101 for 14 miles (22 km) until it rejoins N-II 4 miles (6 km) north of Guadalajara, the provincial capital. Leveled during the Spanish Civil War, Guadalajara does not pretend to be anything other than a high-rise dormitory suburb of Madrid, not worth the bother except to see the 15th-century Palacio de las Infantadas on the Plaza de los Caídos (open daily, from 9 AM to 2 PM and 4 to 9 PM; admission charge) and its diamond-studded façade, and as a possible meal stop. Afterward, if not returning to Sigüenza directly, take N320 east toward Sacedón and Cuenca, but turn onto C200 about 14 miles (22 km) down the road. Soon after, the town of Pastrana rises up on a geologic hump over the surrounding patchwork plains. A pleasant place for a stroll is the steep quarter that once housed Moors from Granada who worked on silk tapestries commissioned by the Dukes of Pastrana. Some of the tapestries are on display at the *Museo Parroquial* in the collegiate church. At lunchtime on weekends and holidays, the nuns who live in the Convento de las Monjas de Abajo serve inexpensive home-cooked meals in the annex ot their 16th-century convent on Calle de las Monjas. Return to Sigüenza by backtracking (the easiest route) on C200 to N320 west and around the Guadalajara bypass to N-II, then heading north.

To continue the route from Sigüenza, proceed south on C204 to N-II, taking it a short 1½ miles (2 km) in the direction of Guadalajara until it meets C204 going south again. Pass Cifuentes and the nuclear power plant at Trillo, to the left. The reactor is cooled by the waters of the Tajo River, which the road does not cross until it is well up into the bluffs overlooking the Embalse de Entrepeñas (Entrepeñas Reservoir). Just outside the town of Sacedón, C204 intersects with N320, which forks sharply left toward Cuenca. For a coffee break, however, bear right for cottage-lined Sacedón, strategically placed on the so-called Sea of Castile, a manmade lake formed by the Entrepeñas Reservoir and the Buendia Reservoir just south of it. (The turnoff to a well-groomed garden and picnic area overlooking the dam is just before the first tunnel.) Then double back along N320, cross over the Guadiela River into Cuenca province, and drive the remaining straight, fast, level road to the intersection with N400 and, a little farther on, the provincial capital, some 59 miles (94 km) from Sacedón and 119 miles (191 km) from Sigüenza.

EATING OUT: El Castillo – The reputation of this roadside *hostal* just outside Jadraque is based on the roast kid that comes sizzling from the wood-fired brick oven located around back. Castilian cooking. Open daily. Reservations necessary. Carretera Guadalajara-Soria, km 46, Jadraque (phone: 11-890254). Moderate.

El Ventorrero – This *mesón* boasts rustic Castilian decor and has been run by the same family since the 1880s. The menu is traditional Castilian, which means excellent roast meats and game. Open daily. No reservations. 4 Calle López de Haro, Guadalajara (phone: 11-272296). Moderate.

CUENCA: A spectacular setting, picturesquely and precariously located "hanging houses," natural wonders, elegant monuments, modern art, and good local food — it's almost impossible to be disappointed by Cuenca. Imagine all the best elements of inland Spain brought together, shuffled, and stacked vertically by a master set designer to produce a showpiece citadel rising from the heart of an otherwise fairly dull provincial capital. The city's medieval Old Town is perched atop a steep escarpment where the Huécar River, a narrow trickle of a stream, intersects with the meandering Júcar River, graced by a bower of birch trees angled like crossed swords over its banks. The town's medieval streets cascade down the escarpment, so exploring it entails just two directions, up or down, and is best done on foot. (For those short of wind, there is a bus that runs every 20 minutes from the new quarter up to the Old Town's main square, the Plaza Mayor de Pio XII, or simply Plaza Mayor.) A preliminary, excellent view of the city as a sculptural ensemble, seen from an outside vantage point, is recommended first, however. Walk behind the cathedral, which edges the Plaza Mayor, past the Casas Colgadas (Hanging Houses), and over the steel footbridge that leads to the opposite side of the Huécar gorge, and the most photogenic side of the Old Town will be directly in front.

The Casas Colgadas are 14th-century houses that, for want of space, were built several stories high and right at the edge of the escarpment, they and their wooden balconies cantilevered out over the gorge itself. Dizzyingly vertical, they are staggered artfully over the cliffside, a masterful feat of 14th-century engineering. Two have been hollowed out, their lath-and-timber innards wonderfully restored to form the *Museum of Spanish Abstract Art,* displaying works by modern masters of the non-figurative who settled in Cuenca in the 1950s and 1960s; featured are works by Fernando Zóbel, Luis Feito, Antoni Tàpies, Eduardo Chillida, Antonio Saura, and others (open Tuesdays through Saturdays, from 11 AM to 2 PM and from 4 to 6 PM; Sundays, from 11 AM to 2 PM; admission charge). Across the street, the *Museum of Archaeology* displays imperial busts and artifacts from the Roman settlements of Segóbriga and Valeria, as well as remains from the province's Bronze Age (open Tuesdays through Saturdays, from 10 AM to 2 PM and from 4 to 7 PM; Sundays, from 10 AM to 2 PM; admission charge).

Cuenca's cathedral, built in the 12th and 13th centuries with a later façade, is notable for its design, an amalgam of French Gothic and Anglo-Norman styles unique to Spain, and for the mix of baroque and neo-classical elegance lavished on the 18th-century altarpiece and side chapels, as well as a profusion of iron grillwork. Part of the west front was damaged in 1902 when the north tower collapsed, but it has been reconstructed in strict accordance with the original plans (whereas the damaged structure it replaced had not been completed until several hundred years later). The cathedral's *Diocesan Museum* (open daily, from 9 AM to 1:30 PM and from 4:30 to 7:30 PM; admission charge) contains two El Greco canvases, the 12th-century statue of the Virgen del Sagrario, and some interesting Flemish tapestries.

For more spectacular views, over both river gorges and the granite cliffs opposite, take any of the streets going left — uphill — from the Plaza Mayor to the highest part of the rock plinth on which old Cuenca sits. A town map identifying the profusion of ruined convents, churches, and noble palaces along the way is available from the tourist office down in the New City (8 Calle Dalmacio García Izcara; phone: 66-222231). There are three ceramic shops on the Plaza Mayor, but these are stocked with far too much bargain merchandise imported from Andalusia. Since master ceramist Pedro Mercedes retired a few years ago, the laurels have been passed to Alejandro Fernández Cruz, whose workshop on the Carretera de Madrid almost a mile (1.6 km) outside town is a good place to pick up decorated plates, water jugs, pitchers, and other ceramic knickknacks for reasonable prices. Segundo Santos's small shop (in town on the Plaza Mayor; phone: 66-214038), open only on weekends, is the place to buy lampshades, desk organizers, and notebooks made from his delicate hand-laid paper, a decorative-textured white fashioned from wool scraps and *esparto* grass and stippled with colored threads.

Cuenca is known for its annual *Semana de Música Religiosa,* held the week before *Easter,* with performances packing the Church of San Pablo and other venues, although a new auditorium being built into the Huécar cliffside is expected to become its new home this year. Orchestral and polyphonic choral groups from all of Europe take part in the festival, notable for airing the works of lesser-known Renaissance composers.

CHECKING IN: *Torremangana* – Conveniently located in the humdrum modern town that sprawls at the foot of the Old City. All 155 modern rooms are air conditioned. Comfortable and efficient, it has parking facilities — always at a premium in Cuenca — and its excellent service also argue strongly in its favor. 9 Calle San Ignacio de Loyola, Cuenca (phone: 66-223351). Expensive.

La Cueva del Fraile – A 16th-century manor house 5 miles (8 km) northwest of town. Built in the corral-style common to La Mancha, it has been so expertly reconstructed it looks completely fake. The combination of thin walls, barking dogs, and noisy Spanish families on bus tours is somewhat of a drawback, but the 54 rooms are generally quiet and always comfortable. The restaurant offers a tasting menu of regional specialties. Closed January and February. Carretera de Buenache, Cuenca (phone: 66-211571). Expensive to moderate.

Posada de San José – This 17th-century house, projecting ever so slightly over the Huécar gorge in the Old Town, was built by a son-in-law of the painter Velázquez and was later put to use as a convent. Subjected to a major restoration in the 1950s, which respected even the uncomfortably low ceiling beams, this is now a 24-room *hostal* (not all with private baths), expertly managed by Jennifer Morter, a transplanted Canadian. As unique as a *parador* without the mini-bars (there is central heating, but no air conditioning), the place is invariably full on weekends, so make reservations well in advance. 4 Calle Julián Romero, Cuenca (phone: 66-211300). Inexpensive.

EATING OUT: *Figón de Pedro* – Owner Pedro Torres put Cuenca on the culinary map with this atmospheric place, located in the heart of the new city. The extensive menu highlights trout, for which Cuenca is deservedly famous, as well as stewed lamb, partridge, and other regional specialties. Closed Sunday evenings. Reservations necessary. 13 Calle Cervantes, Cuenca (phone: 66-226821). Expensive.

Mesón Casas Colgadas – In a hanging house next door to the *Museum of Spanish Abstract Art,* with a balcony out over the gorge. Under the ownership of Pedro Torres of *Figón de Pedro* fame, the restaurant features a menu very similar to its famous sister, and also boasts a good selection of reasonably priced rioja wines. Closed Monday evenings. Reservations advised. Calle Canónigos, Cuenca (phone: 66-223509). Expensive.

El Espolon – Devoid of decorative charm and on an unattractive street, it nevertheless serves excellent food. Try fixed-price menu standards such as garlic and egg soup, followed by trout or chicken in garlic sauce; wine and dessert are included. Open daily. No reservations. 10 Calle 18 de Julio, Cuenca (phone: 66-211872). Inexpensive.

San Nicolás – Another place to sample the fixed-price menu of regional specialties. Try *morturelo,* a lumpy, purple-gray concoction of seasoned partridge, rabbit, and lamb's liver — traditional shepherd's food. Open daily; closed mid-November through mid-December. No reservations. 15 Calle San Pedro, Cuenca (phone: 66-212205 or 66-214539). Inexpensive.

En Route from Cuenca – The itinerary continues southwest from Cuenca, but those with the time to spend an extra day in the area and a desire for a change of scenery — trout streams, spectacular birch and pine trees, Appalachia-like mountains glens, and a variety of out-of-the-ordinary natural sights — may wish to pack a picnic lunch and make a detour to the northeast, into the surrounding Serranía de Cuenca mountain range. To make the 94-mile (150-km) detour, take CU920/921, which begins at the small bridge where the Huécar and Júcar rivers converge, and head north along the Júcar for 13 miles (21 km) to the village of Villalba de la Sierra. Bear sharply left there at the sign for Tragacete–Ciudad Encantada. Approximately 200 yards ahead, bear left again, remaining on CU921. Climb up the mountain for 2½ miles (4 km), park at the souvenir stand, and walk up to the Ventano del Diablo, a natural balcony carved by wind and water erosion, which commands a striking view down the 10-mile-long canyon that the Júcar River has gouged out of its limestone bed. Return to the car, continue upward, and take the well-marked road to the right (CU913) to the Ciudad Encantada (Enchanted City). Here the sights are almost as Disneyesque as the name suggests. Centuries of erosion have sculpted the rock into fanciful shapes that resemble everything from balancing seals to gigantic mushrooms. It takes about 40 minutes to walk from end to end (admission charge).

Continuing along CU921 over the Júcar gorge toward Tragacete, the road is narrow but well graded (there are guard rails only on the sharpest curves, but two-way traffic, thankfully, is almost nonexistent). Pass the reservoir and the trout hatcheries of Uña, and follow the road inland, now some 4,600 feet above sea level. At Tragacete, a popular hunting village, turn left at the sign for Nacimiento del Rio Cuervo and continue another 8 miles (13 km) on the rough road to the rest area and picnic grounds. At the Cuervo's source, streams come trickling in a crystal curtain out of the rock face and down a mossy, juniper-framed cliffside. Hiking paths abound.

After viewing the valley at Vega del Coronado, continue along the same road, which now curves back on itself and leads down the other side of the sierra, even more thickly forested with Scotch pine and holm oak. Follow the signs to Las Majadas. Along the way, the El Hosquillo Game Reserve allows 30 visitors per weekend from mid-October through June. Reservations must be made at least 1 week in advance through the National Conservation Agency (ICONA) office in Cuenca (phone: 66-228020, ext. 409). Tours, consisting of a guided excursion in a Land Rover, turn up wild mountain sheep, ibex, wild boar, mouflon, roe deer, fallow deer, and some of the last brown bears in Europe — a must for those with the time and the interest. Returning to the main road, proceed down the mountain about 6 miles (10 km) to the entrance to Las Majadas, a few acres of parkland where erosion has once again produced natural sculptures that rival those of the Ciudad Encantada. From here, the road emerges from the shadows of the pine and holm oaks and circles back to Villalba de la Sierra, then onto CU921 back to Cuenca.

To resume the itinerary, begin at the intersection in front of the tourist office in Cuenca and follow the signs to N400 for Tarancón and Madrid. After 32 miles (51 km), get off the N400 at the Carracosa del Campo exit, and take the poorly paved road to the monastery of Uclés, which becomes visible after 8 miles (13 km). From the outside, this rectangular, 16th-to-18th-century monastery-fortress, once the headquarters of the Order of Santiago, doesn't quite live up to its billing as the "junior Escorial," though it was in fact designed in part by the same architect who designed Philip II's gloomy retreat. Today, the Uclés monastery serves as a church-run boarding school for boys. While class is in session, the women who cook and clean for their charges permit visitors to look at the interesting baroque fountain in the courtyard (incongruously converted into a basketball court) and at the breathtaking Mudéjar refectory ceiling.

Continue along C720/C700 to the N-III Madrid–Valencia highway heading southeast; get off at the Saelices exit, but stay clear of the town and remain on the same road (CU304) for about 4 more miles (6 km). At this point, a turnoff leads to the low-lying mounds that are the remains of the Roman colony of Segóbriga, which flourished briefly but handsomely under the Claudian emperors. The inhabitants did well enough raising cattle and working the extensive selenite deposits nearby to build a considerable amphitheater and a theater for their leisure-time pursuits. Both are substantially intact and still bear ocher traces of Latin graffiti. A small museum (closed Mondays) displays archaeological finds, but the best pieces excavated here have long since been removed to Cuenca. Still, the Roman thermal baths and the Visigothic cemetery are worth a look.

Return to Saelices and the N-III highway, heading southeast in the direction of Valencia for 30½ miles (49 km) to the town of La Almarcha and the turnoff for N420 south. Here, the hills begin to flatten out and give way to the plains of La Mancha. Just ahead (22½ miles/36 km) is Belmonte, and the must-see castle of the Marqués de Villena, attached to the remnants of the Old City walls. This late-15th-century structure, complete with a drawbridge and dungeon, is of a variety uncommon in Spain, built with Renaissance flair as a fortified palace rather than a simply functional military outpost. The caretaker escorts visitors through the curious triangular precincts of this national monument. Though much has sadly decayed, and the inside patio has been done over with 19th-century brickwork, the Mudéjar ceilings and the extraordinary carved-walnut and inlaid-glass cupola suspended over the main bedroom — it once revolved over the room by means of a clockworks' mechanism — are worthy of inspection. The contemporary collegiate Church of San Bartolomé in the center of town is a fine example of noble Renaissance architectural severity combined with the ornamental lavishness of the Gothic interior, well attested by the alabaster funerary sculptures and grillwork.

Back on N420, the landscape is now flat — fields of grapevines, grain, and melons, or vast horizons of empty plains under endless blue skies. The town of Mota del Cuervo, 10 miles (16 km) beyond Belmonte and aptly called "the balcony of La Mancha," provides a handy base from which to sally forth into Don Quixote's old stomping grounds. At the town's crossroads, take N301 north toward Quintanar de la Orden and proceed 10 miles (16 km) to the tile-encrusted *Venta de Don Quijote,* purported to be the inn where the earnest daydreamer was jocularly dubbed a knight by the locals. Make a left at the intersection here, and proceed 3 miles (5 km) to El Toboso, which has cashed in on its fame as the home of Don Quixote's slatternly sweetheart.

CHECKING IN/EATING OUT: *Mesón El Quijote* – A modern, comfortable Best Western affiliate, 10 miles (16 km) from Belmonte, with 36 air conditioned rooms, a swimming pool, beautiful gardens, and 2 restaurants where regional cuisine is in its glory. Specialties include the famous *pisto manchego,* a sort of ratatouille; *chuletas con salsa diabla* (lamb chops with hot sauce); and partridge and quail in spicy casseroles. 2 Calle Francisco Costi, Mota del Cuervo (phone: 67-180200). Expensive.

EL TOBOSO: This neat little town has been embellished with plaques citing phrases from the Miguel de Cervantes classic to help visitors retrace the steps of Don Quixote, the fictional knight, and his squire, and remind all of his praise of its civic virtues. The House of Dulcinea (Calle José Antonio; phone: 25-197288), once the home of a local lady of loose morals who supposedly was the inspiration for the Cervantes character (she was known to her customers as *la dulce Ana,* or sweet Annie), has been converted into the so-called *Museo de Amor.* On display are an assortment of regional ethnological relics that could have been associated with the region's most famous personage — that is, if he had ever really existed (open Tuesdays through Sundays, from 10 AM to 2 PM and from 4 to 6:30 PM; admission charge). The scallop shell over the entrance to the town's disproportionately large 15th-century late Gothic church, which Don Quixote himself commended, indicates that El Toboso once was under the control of the Knights of Santiago.

En Route from El Toboso – Take the local road south to N420 and head west (if setting out after an overnight in Mota del Cuervo, get on N420 directly). Just ahead are the windmills that in the novel unseated the loony Knight of La Mancha, beginning with the eight stalwart structures standing on the ridge above Campo de Criptana. Follow the pictographic signs pointing the way up through the one-way streets for a closer look. On three of the windmills, the gears and milling mechanisms have been maintained, though there is no schedule to indicate when the sailcloth sails will be revolving. Leaflets available at a tiny tourist office around the corner explain the history and function of these devices — which were, in fact, high-tech innovations imported from the Low Countries at the time Cervantes was writing.

Alcázar de San Juan, 7 miles (11 km) from Campo de Criptana, is a crossroads town totally dependent on an enormous oil refinery, and of more interest to the stomach than to the eye (see *Eating Out*). Turn south on C400 to Tomelloso, 19½ miles (31 km) away, a town floating on a sea of wine — it's said to be the world's number one alcohol-producing municipality — and at Tomelloso, turn sharp right onto the local road to Argamasilla del Alba. Stop here at the church, and if you're lucky enough to find someone to open it up, he or she will point out the portrait of Rodrigo Pacheco, a gentleman of the vicinity whose loss of wits and subsequent odd behavior are said to have set Cervantes to musing, "Now, what if . . ." Ring the bell at 8 Calle Cervantes, the unmarked street at the rear left corner of the church, and a caretaker will come out to unlock the Cueva del Medrano, where Cervantes was tossed in jail in 1597, accused of embezzlement during a disastrous stint as a government tax collector. It was apparently from this subterranean small-town hoosegow — "where every discomfort has a seat and every dismal noise its habitation" — that Cervantes passed the time by letting his imagination beget what he called the child of his "sterile and ill-cultivated genius," the literary masterpiece of Spain's Golden Age.

Continue along the local road to Manzanares, 24½ miles (39 km) from Tomelloso. Trucks carrying sugar beets and poultry feed make the going very slow, but the situation improves after the road skirts the silos and melon sheds of Manzanares. Follow the signs for Ciudad Real to reach N430 west, which intersects with N420. Follow the latter for for 2 miles (3 km), passing through the center of the wine-producing town of Daimiel, then take the turnoff for C417, which leads to Almagro, some 15½ miles (25 km) to the south.

EATING OUT: *Caso Paco* – A lunch stop favored by truckers making the all-day haul between Andalusia and central Spain. In addition to regional dishes that will be new to most travelers, there are a few properly prepared fish choices on the menu. Closed Mondays. No reservations. 5 Avenida Alvarez Guerra, Alcázar de San Juan (phone: 26-540606). Moderate to inexpensive.

ALMAGRO: The landscape is pure Kansas, but visitors will not find a Renaissance jewel of a town like this one anywhere within wishing distance of Wichita. The Order of Calatrava, the oldest and most important Spanish knightly order, established its headquarters here after winning the battle of Las Navas de Tolosa in 1212; the order's squiggly cross emblem can be seen on nearly every one of the historic buildings in town. The 16th-century Monastery of the Assumption of Calatrava, now commonly called the Convento de los Padres Dominicanos, located on the main street, Campo de Calatrava, should not be missed. The friars in residence happily escort visitors around the extraordinary Renaissance cloister, which surrounds pillars of solid Carrara marble, and the attached Gothic church.

If there appears something distinctly odd about the green, glassed-in balconies propped up by the stone pillars of the elongated 14th-century Plaza Mayor, it's the southern German influence of the Fugger dynasty of banker-princes, who made Almagro their Iberian branch office during the 16th-century New World gold boom that helped keep Holy Roman Emperor Charles V solvent. Their palace, the Palacio de los Fúcares (now the Town Hall), is on Calle Feria Madre de Dios, just opposite the Plaza Mayor. The stone staircase and assembly hall here are worth seeing.

Midway along the Plaza Mayor's south portico is the entrance to Almagro's unique *Corral de Comedias,* a theater dating back to the 16th century's Golden Age of Spanish drama. That it has survived at all is thanks to the fact that it was bricked up and forgotten until 1954. If there's nobody on duty to show off the 2-tiered, half-timbered stage, surrounded by linteled galleries and the pit for the groundlings, the tourist office (11 Calle Gran Maestre; phone: 26-860717) will provide an escort. During the annual *Festival de Teatro Clásico,* held during the first 2 weeks of September, theater companies from all over the Spanish-speaking world muster forces on its creaky stage and perform classics by Calderón de la Barca, Lope de Vega, and their foreign contemporaries such as Shakespeare and Molière. Tickets go on sale in mid-August and sell out quickly. (They also can be reserved through the tourist office.)

A stroll around the heraldic mansions and palaces of the town's oldest quarter offers strong indication that the women of Almagro continue to honor the local tradition of lace making. It's not uncommon to find practitioners sitting in doorways, wooden bobbins flying and clacking in their hands. There are also a few lace shops in the Plaza Mayor, where the markup is negligible. For fine table linen, handkerchiefs, and towels at bargain prices, call on the home/shop of María Carmen Manzano (24 Calle Dominicas; phone: 26-860908). Families from all over Spain also travel to Almagro to stock up on pickled baby eggplants, a regional delicacy packed in the earthenware jugs that are laid out on display in front of every shop in town.

CHECKING IN: *Parador de Almagro* – Formerly a 16th-century convent, this is one of the most charming restoration efforts in the entire *parador* network. The 56 air conditioned rooms are built around no fewer than 16 galleried inner patios. The building abounds in decorative touches that recall its original functions, and its popularity often exceeds its room capacity, so make reservations well in advance. The restaurant is especially good, featuring imaginative variations worked up from regional raw materials, fabulous desserts, and an excellent selection of *reservas* — the *parador* takes top pick from the 25 million liters produced annually at the wine cooperative of nearby Daimiel. Ronda de San Francisco, Almagro (phone: 26-860100). Expensive to moderate.

EATING OUT: *Restaurante Calatrava* – A dining alternative to the *parador,* featuring good, home-cooked Castilian dishes, and specializing in the traditional roast lamb and kid. Closed Monday evenings. Reservations unnecessary. 7 Calle Bolaños, Almagro (phone: 26-860185). Moderate.

En Route from Almagro – Backtrack north on C417. Upon reaching Daimiel, take the turnoff on the left for the Tablas de Daimiel Nature Reserve. This road crosses the 4-lane N420, then follows a bumpy 7-mile (11-km) path out into the marshlands. After seeing so much of flat and dry old La Mancha, the vast shallow lagoons formed by the confluence of the Guadiana and Gigüela rivers here come as a surprise. Equally surprising is the abundance of migratory waterfowl, notably herons, kingfishers, mallards, terns, cranes, and gulls. Unrestricted hunting and clandestine drainage to irrigate the surrounding farmland almost destroyed the lagoons and their nesting nomads until the area was declared a protected reserve in 1973. Four hiking trails with wooden bridges spanning the bulrushes, reeds, and tiny islands that emerge from the fluvial floodlands have been laid out, allowing for walks that range from 1 to 3 hours. Camouflaged observation posts along the way serve as resting points and allow for close inspection of the winged residents. A free map and helpful English-language brochure are available at the reserve's entrance lodge.

Head back toward Daimiel on the old bumpy road and pick up N420 north to Madrid on the outskirts of town. (Those wanting to stock up on Castillo de Daimiel wine at giveaway prices, however, should stop in at the co-op outlet in town, on Paseo del Carmen.) Puerto Lápice, another crossroads town, lies 21 miles (34 km) ahead; it has possibly made a bit too much of its mention in *Don Quixote* — as the countless signs and statues attest. Follow the N-IV highway, from here on into Madrid, making brief detours from it as required. Ten and a half miles (17 km) north of Puerto Lápice, the highway slices through Madridejos, where a sharp left onto C400 toward Toledo leads to Consuegra, another 4½ miles (7 km) down the road.

EATING OUT: *Venta del Quijote* – Situated in a former farmhouse complete with wooden beams, cartwheels, and huge earthenware wine tuns, this restaurant offers an extensive menu of exceptionally prepared Manchegan dishes and choice wines. A nice patio makes outdoor dining a possibility, weather permitting. The English translations on the menu will probably prove more baffling than enlightening, however. Open daily. Reservations unnecessary. Carretera Madrid–Cádiz (N-IV), Puerto Lápice (phone: 26-576110). Moderate.

CONSUEGRA: The seven windmills lined up here are hollow shells of their former selves, unlike those in Campo de Criptana, but they are placed in a far more dramatic — and photogenic — setting, high on a cliffside overlooking the entire town and next to the ruins of a windswept 14th-century castle (Don Quixote did not, however, sleep here!). Consuegra is famous for its production of those expensive and irreplaceable reddish threads that make a good paella worth wolfing down. To get just 1 pound of saffron together, it is necessary to pull the stigmas from over 100,000 crocuses. This shortcut to eyestrain is what sustains the economy of Consuegra, evident by the haystack-size heaps of purple petals discarded after an autumn harvest. The *Saffron Festival* falls on the last Sunday in October, complete with folk dancing, wine tasting, and bullfighting, and provides the locals with a chance to whoop it up a bit after the pickers — almost all of whom are women — have finished their laborious task. Unfortunately, visitors can't buy saffron here — it's all sold to out-of-town dealers who toast and package the finished product elsewhere.

En Route from Consuegra – Head back to Madridejos and, once again, take the N-IV highway going north. Make a quick stop in Tembleque, 16 miles (26 km) north of Madridejos, for a glance at the remarkable Plaza Mayor, a graceful, 2-tiered arcade of old beams and plaster, its one entrance crowned by the most un-Spanish-looking 3-story, peaked, gable-like structure. In a town with little else going for it nowadays, if ever, the stunning plaza leaves a most unforgettable impression. The N-IV highway leads next to Ocaña, 19½ miles (31 km) from Tembleque, and then to Aranjuez, another 10 miles (16 km) along (see *Madrid*

Region, DIRECTIONS, for more on this town, a favored residence of the Catholic Monarchs and later Spanish royalty). Then traffic jams become a common reminder that Madrid is only 29½ miles (47 km) away. But long before entering the Puerta del Sol, the gruesome industrial suburbs of the capital's southern outskirts might well make the traveler pause — and think about turning around and going back to do it all over again.

Levante: Valencia to Murcia

Almond blossoms and white beaches, verdant orchards and stern mountain ranges, palm trees and sparkling blue water, and at least 300 days of sunshine a year — is it any wonder that the Mediterranean coast south of Valencia has become one of Europe's most popular vacation areas? Or that thousands of expatriates of all nationalities have made it their home?

Roughly speaking, Spain's Levante is the coastal fringe bridging the gap between Catalonia and Andalusia. It includes the three provinces that make up the autonomous community of Valencia (Castellón, Valencia, and Alicante) and the single-province autonomous community of Murcia. From end to end, it is highlighted by striking scenery, lively fiestas, unusual historical sights, and — given the fact that this is the market garden of Spain — distinctive food.

It is the middle section, the Costa Blanca (White Coast), which lies in the province of Alicante, that is the most popular. Every summer, hundreds of thousands of Spaniards and other Europeans flock here to bask in the sunshine and enjoy a wide range of sporting and entertainment activities. Resorts have mushroomed where there were only fishing villages and deserted beaches barely 25 years ago. Those with an aversion to mass tourism need not worry, however, as the region caters to all tastes — from the sophisticated to the mundane. But although it is easy to escape the crowds, it's not advisable to plan a vacation here during July and August, simply because that's when everyone else in the world does — or at least it seems that way. Spring and autumn are fine times to visit; and rainy winter days are usually followed by weeks of dazzling sunshine.

To the people of the Levante, the flood of tourists hardly causes a raised eyebrow, for the region has been a target of invaders throughout its long history. Paleolithic people lived in caves here. Three thousand years ago, the Phoenicians arrived to trade and settle. Later, the Greeks established the colony of Akra Leuka (White Headland) near Alicante. The Carthaginians established a naval base on the site of present-day Cartagena, and after them, the Romans stayed in the region for several centuries. But it was the Moors, who arrived during the 8th century and ruled the region as part of Al-Andalus, who had the most lasting influence, converting the arid but fertile plain between the treeless mountains and the sea into lush *huertas* (orchards and vegetable farms) by introducing an ingenious irrigation system. Remains of *norias,* the giant Moorish water-raising wheels, can still be found on the *huertas* where today, citrus fruits flourish, and thousands of tons of oranges and lemons are exported annually — not to mention dates, tomatoes, and a wealth of other fruits of the earth.

When the Córdoba caliphate collapsed in 1031, warring local leaders struggled for supremacy, and several *taifas,* or kingdoms, were formed. From the early 11th century, the independent Moorish kingdom of Valencia dominated a vast slice of the coast, from Almería to the Ebro River, but the region was racked by war. Toward the end of the century, Spain's legendary warrior El Cid fought long campaigns and wrested it from the Moors, albeit only briefly (1094–99). Only in 1238 was James I of Aragon able to add it to his Christian domain, although it was administered as a separate kingdom until it was added, with the rest of the Aragonese lands, to the kingdom of Castile in the late 15th century. The kingdom of Murcia had a checkered history, at one time acting as intermediary between the Moors and the Christians. Murcia finally came under the rule of the kingdom of Castile in 1243, 5 years after Valencia was conquered by Aragon, but it continued for 2 more centuries as a separately administered kingdom. Today, although the one-province region of Murcia and the much larger region of Valencia are both considered part of the Levante, part of one agricultural land of plenty and both noted for fine beaches (Murcia is attempting to attract more people to its Costa Cálida — Warm Coast), the regions have distinct characteristics, including different languages.

Although Castilian Spanish is the language of Murcia, the language commonly spoken in the region of Valencia is a local version of Catalan, known variously as *valenciano* in Valencia and as *alicantino* in Alicante. Anyone speaking Castilian, French, or any other Latin language will not find this too difficult to read, and anyone attempting to master a few spoken phrases will certainly please the native residents. "Good morning" is *bon dia* and "please" is *per favor.* Place-names often appear in both languages — for example, Alicante is Alacant in the local language; Elche is Elx. But everybody speaks Castilian, too, and since the Costa Blanca is such a popular vacation spot for British tourists, it is easier in some areas to find a speaker of English than of any other tongue.

Gastronomically speaking, this is paella paradise. Because rice is grown here, it forms the basis for scores of dishes. *Paella valenciana* contains both meat and fish, including octopus and mussels, whereas *paella marinera* contains only fish. *Arroz con costra* is prepared with pork and sausage, topped off with a half-dozen eggs. Squid and octopus are also popular local delicacies. Moorish influence is evident when it comes to desserts, with such sticky sweet treats as *turrón* (nougat) and glazed walnuts. *Horchata de chufa,* a chilled mixture of *chufas* (earth almonds), cinnamon, sugar, and water, is a favorite drink. Some good wines are also produced in the region, particularly the hearty jumilla and yecla reds in Murcia.

Many who travel to the region time their journeys to coincide with one of the many reenactments of the epic struggles between Moors and Christians, some of which are the most colorful, exuberant fiestas to be found anywhere in the world. All along the coast, towns and villages spend the entire year preparing for their annual *Moros y Cristianos* battles. Sumptuous Oriental and medieval costumes are worn by the participants as they parade through the streets, each group trying to outdo the other. Lasting several days, these fiestas usually feature the "Moors" capturing a "Christian" stronghold, only to be ousted amid a deafening fusillade of "gunfire." Altogether, more than 70,000 people take part in these historic fiestas and, amid the general revelry, some don't sleep for an entire week. The towns of Alcoy (April 22), Elda (first week in June), and Villajoyosa (July 25), all in the province of Alicante, stage particularly spectacular make-believe battles.

The route outlined below begins in Valencia (for a complete report on this city and its sights, hotels, and restaurants, see *Valencia,* THE CITIES), and heads south to the gracious seaport city of Alicante and on to the inland city of Murcia, with a spur to Cartagena back on the coast before veering southwest toward Granada. From Valencia to Murcia (158 miles/ 255 km), it's a fast trip if the four-lane A-7 *autopista,* which runs much of the way, is followed. From Murcia, it's 179 miles (286 km) to Granada, over mountainous terrain, most of which is spanned by the much-improved N301 and N342 highways. Those who can't wait to see the glories of the Alhambra can do the Valencia–Granada run in 1 day, but there are abundant reasons to spend at least 4 to 5 days on the journey. By taking the A-7, which runs from Valencia to Alicante, and exiting at appropriate points along the coast, a good deal of time can be saved. For a more leisurely drive, take the N332 from Valencia to Alicante (it follows largely the same coastal route as the A-7). From Alicante to Murcia, the road is the N340.

Along the way, expect to pay $100 or more for a double room in a hotel listed as expensive, $60 to $100 in those marked moderate, and under $50 in an inexpensive one. Restaurants listed as expensive charge around $65 or more for a dinner for two, including wine; a moderate establishment, $40 to $55; and an inexpensive one, under $40.

En Route from Valencia – The most interesting route out of Valencia follows the coast, past long sandy beaches, orange groves, and large rice fields (harvesting, now mechanized, takes place in October). Head south on the A-V15 highway, and follow the signs to El Saler, 6 miles (10 km) south of Valencia. Just past it is La Albufera, Spain's largest lake, renowned for its wildlife and freshwater fish. A pine-fringed sandbar holds back the sea on the left. Follow the local road on the right for 2 miles (3 km) to El Palmar, a village of thatch-roofed cottages on the lake edge, where rustic eateries serve *all i pebre,* a local specialty of eels fried in garlic. Return to A-V15 and proceed to Cullera, 25 miles (40 km) from Valencia; the town is hard to miss, since giant manmade white letters spell out its name on the rocky hill rising above it. A small port town on the Júcar River, Cullera has been dwarfed by dozens of modern apartment blocks on the beaches toward the lighthouse, but it offers magnificent views from its castle ruins. Continue south, via N332 or A-7, some 18 miles (29 km) to Gandía.

EATING OUT:
Les Mouettes – Enjoy French delicacies such as oyster ragout with leeks and truffles, as well as wines from Bordeaux and the Loire, on a pleasant terrace overlooking the beach (and high-rises). This place is famous among *valencianos* and has earned a Michelin star. Closed Mondays and December 15 through February 15. Reservations advised. Subida al Santuario del Castillo, Cullera (phone: 6-152-0010). Expensive to moderate.

GANDÍA: A modern town with some fine buildings, Gandía is set inland, surrounded by rice fields and groves of oranges — which are shipped from the harbor formed by the mouth of the Serpis River. It once was the capital of a duchy, which was given by King Ferdinand to the Borgia family (known in Spain as the Borjas) in 1485. Alexander VI, the infamous Borgia pope, father of the equally infamous Cesare and Lucrezia Borgia, was born in Játiva, 25 miles inland, but a later member of the family, the fourth duke, who restored the family's good name by becoming a Jesuit, founding Jesuit missions in the New World and eventually being named a saint — St. Francis Borgia — was born in the family mansion. This, the 16th-century Palacio Ducal (Calle Santo Duque; phone: 6-287-1203), offers an impressive mix of Gothic and Renaissance styles, with a fine patio and staircase, as well as beautifully decorated apartments. Now the property of the Jesuit Order, the building can be visited only on guided tours (conducted in Spanish only), which begin daily at 11 AM and noon and at 6 and 7 PM (May through October; in winter they begin at 4:30 and 5:30 PM); admission charge. Gandía's tourist office is at 1 Plaza de la Constitución (phone: 6-287-4544). Three miles (5 km) from the town lies its port, El Grau, and a vast sandy beach that has succumbed to extensive tourist development. It comes to life at *Easter* and in summer, and most of the hotels are located here.

CHECKING IN: *Bayren I* – Like most others in the area, this comfortable beachfront establishment caters primarily to Spanish vacationers. All 164 rooms are air conditioned, and there is a swimming pool, tennis courts, and in summer, live music and dancing in the gardens. Closed for a month in late November and early December. Paseo de Neptuno, Playa de Gandía (phone: 6-284-0300). Expensive.

Bayren II – This equally comfortable but less-expensive sister of *Bayren I* is just behind its namesake, and offers 125 air conditioned rooms and tennis courts. Closed from November through February. 19 Calle Majorca, Playa de Gandía (phone: 6-284-0700). Moderate.

EATING OUT: *As de Oros* – On the lengthy Gandía beachfront, this eatery is a shrine to the great national obsession for fresh seafood. Sit back and enjoy everything from juicy prawns to succulent squid and grilled mullet, washed down by some of the country's best wines. Fast service is provided by an army of waiters. Closed Mondays and 2 weeks in January. Reservations unnecessary. Edificio Bonaire, Paseo de Neptuno, Playa de Gandía (phone: 6-284-0239). Expensive.

En Route from Gandía – It's a run of about 20 minutes down the A-7 into the province of Alicante and the pleasant old port town of Denia (take exit 62 at Ondara). Travelers in the mood for an excursion or seeking an entertaining diversion for young children should detour to the *Vergel Safari Park* by taking N332 north at Ondara and proceeding 4 miles (6 km) before turning left (west) onto C3311 toward Pego for the park. Elephants, tigers, zebras, and lions, as well as "singing" dolphins and roller-skating parrots, are on hand (open daily, from 10 AM to 5:30 PM; admission charge). To reach Denia from Ondara, take C3311 east.

DENIA: Thanks to its mild climate and excellent beach, Denia has prospered from tourism, yet it has retained its old charm. Founded by the Phoenicians, the town takes its name from a Roman Temple of Diana. The Visigoths made it an episcopal seat, and it later served as the capital of a Moorish kingdom. The 18th-century castle or citadel perched above the town was the scene of a bitter siege during the Napoleonic Wars, when French troops held it for 5 months. Within lies the *Museo Arqueológico,* which contains some noteworthy Roman and Arabic relics unearthed in the area (open daily, from 10 AM to 1 PM and from 3 to 6 PM; admission charge). There are also some interesting 18th-century buildings in the Plaza de los Caídos, including the Church of Santa María and the Town Hall.

Denia is a good base for excursions. There is year-round service to the island of Ibiza via a passenger and vehicle ferry, which departs every evening at 10 o'clock and takes 5 hours; from *Easter* through summer, a passengers-only ferry departs at 7:30 AM and takes 3½ hours. For those in a rush, afternoon hydrofoils make the journey in 90 minutes. Contact *Flebasa* (at the port; phone: 6-578-4011) for details. Another pleasant way to see the Costa Blanca is on the narrow-gauge railroad that runs from Denia to Alicante. The trip takes 2 hours and 20 minutes and the first train leaves at 6:45 AM from Denia; the train departs daily from the station on Calle Calderón (phone: 6-578-0445), about a block from Denia's Tourist Office (Calle Patricio Ferrándiz; phone: 6-578-0957).

CHECKING IN: *Los Angeles* – Located in a tranquil setting on an excellent sandy beach, 3 miles (5 km) north of town. All 60 rooms are air conditioned, and facilities include tennis courts. Closed November through mid-March. 649 Playa de las Marinas, Denia (phone: 6-578-0458). Moderate.

EATING OUT: *El Pegolí* – A favorite with seafood lovers. Gaze out from the spick-and-span dining room or the outdoor terrace at the blue Mediterranean and the rocky coastline below while enjoying one of two set menus, which usually include a salad, a plate full of shellfish, a well-grilled fish, wine, bread, and dessert. Closed Sunday evenings and from mid-December to mid-January. Reservations advised. Playa de Les Rotes, Denia (phone: 6-578-1035). Moderate.

En Route from Denia – Head south, following the coast road, which offers magnificent views. As it corkscrews up from Denia over the San Antonio headland and winds down through almond trees to Jávea (Xabia in *valenciano*), look for the old windmills that once ground wheat.

JÁVEA: Situated on one of the Costa Blanca's finer bays, between two capes — Cabo de San Antonio and the Cabo San Martín (the latter just around the coast from Cabo de la Nao), this resort town consists of an Old Quarter with narrow streets and stone houses that stands on a rise inland from the fishing and pleasure port. Watchtowers, surviving city walls and gateways, and an old castle contribute to its medieval look. Worth a visit is the *Municipal Museum* (1 Calle Primicias; phone: 6-579-1098), built by King Philip III during the early 17th century. It contains Roman and Punic remains, ceramics, and traditional crafts (open Tuesdays through Sundays, from 10 AM to 1 PM; also open from 5 to 8 PM from June through September; admission charge). The great bulk of Montgó, rising 2,465 feet, shelters Jávea from winter blasts, and the surrounding area has experienced a development boom; thousands of villas have joined the vines and almond trees along the attractive coast of rocky headlands and bays. Jávea's Tourist Office is in the port area (24 Plaza Almirante Bastarreche; phone: 6-579-0736; open in summer only).

CHECKING IN: *Bahía Vista* – A secluded setting on a pine-covered headland 5 miles (8 km) southeast of Jávea proper, with beautiful views over the sea. British run, so there are no language problems, it has 17 rooms, a swimming pool, and a bowling green, plus a restaurant serving international food. Portichol, Cabo la Nao, Jávea (phone: 6-577-0461). Moderate.

Parador Costa Blanca – On Jávea's beautiful bay, 2½ miles (4 km) southeast of the town proper, this is an ideal base from which to explore the area. All 65 rooms are air conditioned; each has a mini-bar and a balcony overlooking the beach. Other facilities include a swimming pool, gardens, and a nearby boat dock. The restaurant features regional food. 2 Playa del Arenal, Jávea (phone: 6-579-0200). Moderate.

EATING OUT: *Chez Angel* – The emphasis here is on French cooking, served in a friendly atmosphere, although it is located in a rather drab shopping center (just under 2 miles/3 km southeast of the Old Quarter.) Try the onion soup and *tournedos calvados,* or Provençal-style lamb. Closed Tuesdays and December 20 through January 20. Reservations unnecessary. Carretera Cabo la Nao, Centro Comercial Jávea Park, Jávea (phone: 6-579-2723). Moderate.

Turpins – Just opposite the *parador* and, therefore, handy for anyone staying there. Stuffed peppers and Dijon chicken are especially recommended dishes on a menu that features international cooking. Closed Sundays and from December 20 through January. Reservations unnecessary. 4 Playa del Arenal, Jávea (phone: 6-579-0713). Inexpensive.

En Route from Jávea – The A134 runs inland to join N332 near Gata de Gorgos, which bills itself as the "Bazaar of the Costa Blanca." The shops along its main street offer baskets, mats, and bags of bamboo, willow, palm leaf, and esparto, some of them made locally. In the nearby hills are the picturesque vineyards of the *Maserof Wine Club* (11 La Mar, Denia), whose members own individual vines and each year receive the wine made from their own grapes. Peter Pateman, the bearded, Falstaffian Englishman who founded the club, loves to talk wine and welcomes visitors to his bodega on Sundays. To reach it from Gata, turn off N332 onto the road to Lliber and Jalón. In Jalón, turn left onto the road signposted Bernia; Maserof is 3 miles (5 km) along on the left. It's best to call the club's Denia office (phone: 6-578-1887) first or write to them at the address above.

Back on N332, the route continues south past eroded ocher hills, the azure sea, and countless almond trees, a breathtaking sight when they are in bloom in February. Just ahead, huge apartment blocks have blossomed on the beaches in the vicinity of Calpe. Fortunately, however, developers have been pushed back from the foot of Peñón de Ifach, now a natural park. Resembling the Rock of Gibraltar, the Peñón soars to a height of over 1,000 feet; a hike up to the top takes about an hour, but no one suffering from vertigo should try it — somebody topples off every year. Take a sweater, as it can be breezy up there.

Continue on N332 to Altea, a charming hillside town perched below the rugged Sierra de Bernia, 20 miles (32 km) from Gata.

ALTEA: The name comes from the Moorish "Altaya," meaning "health for all," and many visitors proclaim this the Costa Blanca's prettiest town. A fortress under the Hapsburgs, it now has modern buildings lining the waterfront, but fortunately, the Old Quarter remains. Narrow streets climb steeply up to the parish church with its blue tile dome, characteristic of churches in the Levante region. In recent years, a number of artists of various nationalities have made their homes here, no doubt seeking inspiration from the surrounding beauty. One of the more pleasant ways to spend a summer evening is to sit in the church square, (Plaza de Calvo Sotelo), high above the Mediterranean, sipping a cool drink and watching the passersby and the stallholders selling their crafts. If you're here on a Sunday afternoon, watch out for *pilota de carrer,* a fiercely competitive game played in the nearby streets by men who whack a small hard ball at one another with their bare hands. Altea's Tourist Office is on the seafront, Paseo Marítimo (phone: 6-584-2301).

 EATING OUT: *La Costera* – Swiss specialties are served with a unique flair in this bizarre Old Quarter eatery. Rodolfo, the owner, puts on a hilarious, uninhibited musical show nightly, featuring everything from cossack dancing to flamenco. Open for dinner only. Closed Wednesdays. Reservations advised. 8 Costera del Mestre de Música, Altea (phone: 6-584-0230). Moderate.

Bahía – Functional decor and friendly service highlight this family-run establishment, a popular lunchtime favorite, situated between the highway and the sea. Specialties include a variety of tasty rice dishes and excellent *zarzuela* (fish stew). Closed January, *Christmas,* and winter Saturdays and evenings. Reservations advised on weekends. Carretera Alicante, Altea (phone: 6-584-0011). Moderate to inexpensive.

En Route from Altea – Follow N332 south toward Benidorm, 7 miles (11 km) away. If there's time for a pleasant, half-day excursion before entering the city limits, however, make a right turn onto C3318 and drive 7 miles (11 km) to the village of Polop. Once there, turn left onto the small local road that swoops 9 miles (14 km) over the mountains to Guadalest, a medieval village that is one of Spain's most spectacular — and impregnable — fortresses. Built by the Moors, it perches on a crag, accessible only through a 50-foot tunnel cut through the rock. Inside are old women who sit knitting, souvenir shops, and magnificent views of the surrounding countryside. Returning toward the coast, stop in Callosa, locally renowned for its production of honey. Just off C3318, to the north, are the spectacular Algar waterfalls, a good place to cool off on a hot day. Sit in one of the rock pools under a cascade of refreshing water, spilling down some 50 feet from the rocks above. Several of the nearby restaurants have pools, too.

BENIDORM: This is the place for anyone who wants to take a day off from Spain. Formerly a simple fishing village, it has become an international resort town (almost everyone speaks English), cluttered with high-rise buildings and catering mainly to those on inexpensive package tours. Pensioners from all over Europe flock here in winter, and teenagers of all ages take over the place during the summer. Despite its image, Benidorm can still be fun, provided visitors are willing to enter into its easygoing spirit. There are two fine beaches (topless), and the town is immaculately maintained. Jousting tournaments, dog races, discotheques, and bars (the nightlife tends to get a bit wild) are some of the more active attractions. The huge *Benidorm Palace* nightclub (Calle Diputación; phone: 6-585-1661) is the Costa Blanca's answer to the *Folies-Bergères,* complete with bare-breasted dancers and flamenco, while the *Casino Costa Blanca* (Carretera Benidorm–Villajoyosa, N332, Km 115, Villajoyosa; phone: 6-589-0700) packs in gamblers by the busload. This low, off-white building on the main highway between Benidorm and Villajoyosa offers every gambling adventure from roulette to blackjack (admission charge; a passport also is required), and also boasts a small but impressive art gallery. Benidorm's Tourist Office is at 16 Avenida Martínez Alejos (phone: 6-585-6986).

CHECKING IN: *Gran Delfín* – A first-rate establishment on the quieter, southern beach, often busy, but far from the crowded mayhem found at some of Benidorm's other hotels. The 87 spacious and comfortable rooms are air conditioned; there also is a swimming pool, tennis courts, lovely tropical gardens, and a good restaurant. Closed October to *Easter.* Playa de Poniente, La Cala, Benidorm (phone: 6-585-3400). Expensive.

Don Pancho – Right in town, the 251 rooms in this popular high-rise are air conditioned, comfortably furnished, and have individual balconies. There also is a swimming pool, lighted tennis courts, and gardens. 39 Avenida del Mediterráneo, Benidorm (phone: 6-585-2950). Moderate.

EATING OUT: *I Fratelli* – Elegant candlelit dining, intimate alcoves, an outdoor patio, and an Italian atmosphere — this is an unexpected find in Benidorm. The pasta is homemade; try the veal marsala with *tagliatelle,* or the duck *à l'orange.* Closed November. Reservations necessary. 21 Calle Orts Llorca, Benidorm (phone: 6-585-3979). Expensive.

La Pérgola – Masses of greenery give a refreshing air to this restaurant slotted into a cliff. But the dazzling view of Benidorm Bay from the terrace is its most outstanding feature. The international menu includes Basque and French dishes and delicious desserts. Closed December through February. Reservations advised. Edificio Coblanca, Calle 25, Barrio Rincón de Loix, Benidorm (phone: 6-583-3800). Expensive.

En Route from Benidorm – Once again, pick up N332 and continue 6 miles (10 km) south to Villajoyosa, a fishing town surrounded by fruit trees and olive groves. The narrow streets of the Old Town lead down to a pleasant palm-lined promenade and houses with colorful, sun-bleached façades. Continue toward Alicante, which is 27½ miles (44 km) from Benidorm; 5 miles (8 km) short of the city, at the small village of San Juan, an opportunity presents itself for a half-day excursion to the Canalobre Caves: Turn right onto N340, and follow the signs for A183, which leads to the village of Busot. The caves are 4½ miles (7 km) beyond, in the stark Cabeco d'Or mountains. Well-lit walkways lead through vast caverns filled with giant stalagmites and stalactites. The caves are open daily, April through September, from 10:30 AM to 8:30 PM; October through March, from 11 AM to 6:30 PM. Afterward, return toward Busot, but take the first right on the local road to Jijona, noted for its production of *turrón* (nougat), eaten by the ton throughout Spain during the *Christmas* season. *El Lobo* factory (62 Calle Alcoy; phone: 6-561-0225) has a visitors' area, where the tooth-wrenching but delicious product can be sampled (open Mondays through Fridays, from 9:30 AM to 1 PM and 4 to 8 PM). From Jijona, proceed back to San Juan on N340 south and pick up N332 for the remaining drive to Alicante.

CHECKING IN:
El Montíboli – Located about 2 miles (3 km) south of Villajoyosa, this is an ideal rest stop, safely away from the hubbub found farther north along the coast. It sits on a headland, with magnificent views over the sea, a swimming pool, a private beach, tennis courts, and a well-regarded restaurant. All of the 52 spacious rooms are air conditioned and have mini-bars. Reservations advised. Carretera Benidorm–Alicante (N332), Km 108, Villajoyosa (phone: 6-589-0250).

ALICANTE: This provincial capital (pop. 300,000), capital of the Costa Blanca resort area, is a gracious Mediterranean city dominated by the Castillo Santa Bárbara, which glowers down from a hilltop. Long before the present tourist boom, Alicante was a fashionable wintering place, thanks to its mild climate. Around 200 BC, the Romans had a settlement here known as Lucentum. The same settlement, during 500 years of Moorish rule, was known as Al-Akant. In more recent times, Alicante has been an important port, exporting wine, raisins, and other agricultural products. Palm trees and arid surrounding hills give a hint of Africa to the city, an impression that is strengthened around the port area by the sight of Algerian women in caftans and Senegalese peddlers offering their wares. One of the greatest pleasures is to stroll along the Explanada de España, the promenade that fronts the harbor — an ideal place to relax, sip a drink, and listen to the city band on Sunday mornings. (Don't gaze too intently at the seafront paving, however. The beautiful wavy pattern in marble mosaic may disturb your balance.)

Alicante is a modern city of wide boulevards and numerous shops, but it does have an Old Quarter, a labyrinth of narrow streets lying on the lower slope of the Santa Bárbara hill. And despite the hordes of tourists who alight here to soak up the sun along the local beaches, Alicante remains surprisingly Spanish in character.

The Castillo Santa Bárbara, whose foundations date back 2,200 years, is Alicante's main attraction and should be a sightseer's first stop. The Carthaginians, the Romans, and the Moors each had a base here, before the Spanish kings took over and expanded the structure. What survives is primarily from the 13th to 16th centuries. To reach the castle, walk along Paseo de Gómiz, which continues northeast along the beach from the Explanada, to the 660-foot tunnel penetrating the rock; an elevator takes visitors up to see the dungeons, moats, and battlements which offer splendid views over the city and coast. The castle is open mid-June through September, Mondays through Fridays from 9 AM to 9 PM, Saturdays from 9 AM to 2 PM; October through mid-June, Mondays through Fridays from 9 AM to 7:30 PM, Saturdays from 9 AM to 2 PM. Admission charge.

In the Old Quarter, the *Museo de Arte Siglo XX* (Museum of 20th-Century Art), also known as the *Museo de la Asegurada,* in a fine stone building (3 Plaza de Santa María; phone: 6-521-4578), contains some impressive modern art, with sculptures, paintings, and etchings by the likes of Picasso, Dalí, and Tápies (open Tuesdays through Saturdays from 10 AM to 1 PM and from 5 to 8 PM, Sundays from 10 AM to 1 PM; admission charge). The Iglesia de Santa María, almost opposite the museum, has a wonderful 18th-century baroque façade, although the church, remodeled more than once, dates back to a much earlier period and was built on the site of a mosque.

Head toward the center of town along Calle Jorge Juan to the Ayuntamiento (City Hall), a 17th-to-18th-century palace with a magnificently ornate façade. The rococo chapel and some of the baroque rooms are open to visitors in the mornings (ask the caretaker to open them). Note the brass plaque on the pillar of the main stairway; it's the sea level benchmark from which all of Spain's altitude measurements are calculated. Between the Ayuntamiento and the modern Rambla de Méndez Núñez — which is at the edge of the Old Quarter and is the city's main throughfare — is Alicante's cathedral, San Nicolás, built during the 17th century on the site of a mosque and dedicated to the city's patron saint, Nicholas of Bari. A national monument open during services, it has a severe Renaissance style, with beautifully carved gilded altars. The pedestrians-only Calle Mayor, which runs behind the Ayuntamiento to the Rambla, and the side streets off it, are full of fascinating small shops selling typically Spanish gifts, leatherwear, pottery, and antiques. *Turrones 1880* (9 Calle Mayor; phone: 6-521-9281), which has its own factory and museum at nearby Jijona, proudly boasts that its nougat is the most expensive of all — "because we use only the best almonds and honey. Up a sidestreet from the seafront, *Estudio Rita* (Calle Capitán Meca; phone: 6-520-3404) sells original designs in stoneware, made on the premises.

On Tuesday and Saturday mornings, the *Mercadillo,* a lively open-air market, is held along the Paseo de Campoamor, beyond the Old Quarter to the north of the Plaza de España and the bullring. The *Teatro Principal* (Calle Teatro, 2 blocks west of the Rambla) has concerts and musicals during the winter season. In summer, nightlife centers on the disco-pubs of the Playa de San Juan, the long beach north of town. Alicante's own local beach, El Postiguet, is even more crowded, but the tiny island of Tabarca, a former haunt of pirates, lies a pleasant boat ride away. It is a good spot for snorkeling, with outdoor restaurants but no accommodations. Trips leave from the harbor along the Explanada, or from Santa Pola (a much shorter sea trip), a fishing port 12½ miles (20 km) to the south. Alicante's Tourist Office (2 Explanada de España; phone: 6-521-2285) can provide schedules.

During the week of June 24, the city goes wild with the unforgettable *Hogueres de San Juan* (Bonfires of St. John). The fiesta includes processions, bullfights, and fireworks, but the climax comes with an arsonist's orgy, the burning of colossal images, sometimes at considerable risk to life and limb, a legacy of pagan midsummer rites.

 CHECKING IN: *Sidi San Juan Sol* – Modern and luxurious with a private beach, located 4½ miles (7 km) from the center of town, but close to the area with all the summer action. The 176 air conditioned rooms offer every comfort.

Facilities include 2 swimming pools (1 heated), a gymnasium, a sauna, a disco-theque, and a shopping arcade. Playa de San Juan, Alicante (phone: 6-516-1300). Expensive.

Gran Sol – A modern skyscraper on the main street in the city center, offering panoramic views from its 26th-floor bar and restaurant. It has 150 straightforward, functional rooms, all with air conditioning and TV sets. 3 Rambla de Méndez Núñez, Alicante (phone: 6-520-3000). Expensive to moderate.

Palas – This pleasant establishment offers old-style charm on the seafront, near the Ayuntamiento (City Hall). Chandeliers and antiques highlight the gracious decor, which caters to a more mature clientele. All 48 rooms are air conditioned and quite comfortable. 5 Calle Cervantes, Alicante (phone: 6-520-9211). Moderate.

EATING OUT: El Delfín – Look for the green canopy over the terrace on the Explanada — it marks a spot known for elegant snacking and dining in Alicante, a one-Michelin-star establishment. Downstairs is for simple dishes (and gossip); upstairs, it's mirrors, crystal, and efficient service. There is a broad range of traditional regional and French dishes to choose from (at moderate prices if you stick to the *menú alicantino*). Try the seafood pancake and the *salteado de foie gras, mollejas y pato* (sauté of foie gras, sweetbreads, and duck). Desserts are created from such local fruits as dates and oranges. Open daily. Reservations necessary. 12 Explanada de España, Alicante (phone: 6-521-4911). Expensive.

Dársena – An ideal lunch spot overlooking the harbor. More than 20 rice dishes, typical of the region, are served with style. Begin with *bisque de cangrejos al Armagnac* (crab soup), and move on to *pastel de atún y espinacas* (tuna and spinach tart). Closed Sunday evenings and Mondays. Reservations advised. Muelle del Puerto, Alicante (phone: 6-520-7399). Moderate.

Nou Manolín – At the justly renowned downstairs bar, order anything from oysters to "grandmother's stew," while sampling some of the fine wines smartly racked above the counter. Upstairs, amid beams and tiles, sample a variety of regional and national dishes, including some of the region's most superb paellas. Closed *Christmas Eve*. Reservations advised. 4 Calle Villegas, Alicante (phone: 6-520-0368). Moderate.

Quo Vadis – The large bar leads to a cozy, wood-paneled restaurant where diners feast on such local delicacies as *arroz a banda con pescado* (a rice and fish dish). The service is good, the atmosphere agreeable, and the wine cellar well stocked. Closed Mondays and Tuesdays. Reservations unnecessary. 3 Plaza Santísima Faz, Alicante (phone: 6-521-6660). Moderate.

En Route from Alicante – Take N340 and proceed 15 miles (24 km) inland (southwest) to Elche, city of palms, the Lady of Elche, and the Mystery of Elche.

ELCHE: Some 600,000 date palms, originally planted by the Phoenicians, grow around Elche (Elx in the local dialect), which is also important for shoe manufacturing. The irrigation system that waters them was created by the Moors 1,000 years ago. The dates, which grow only on female trees, are harvested from December to March. It's possible to stroll around the Huerto del Cura (Priest's Grove), a palm garden that also features an impressive collection of cacti and tropical flowers (open daily, from 9 AM to 8 PM mid-June to mid-September, to 6 PM the rest of the year; admission charge). The remarkable 150-year-old *palmera del cura,* or priest's palm, has seven branches sprouting from the same trunk. Look also for the palms dedicated to King Juan Carlos and Queen Sophia — dates from these trees are supplied to the royal palace. Also within the grove is a replica of the *Dama de Elche* (Lady of Elche), a remarkable bust dating back to 500 BC, the original of which is on display in the *National Archaeological Museum* in Madrid. It was discovered in 1897 about a mile (1.6 km) south of Elche in the ruins at La Alcudia, where there now is a museum of Iberian and Roman relics (open daylight hours; closed Mondays; admission charge).

For a spectacular emotional experience, visit Elche in August, when the world's longest-running play is staged in the blue-domed, 17th-century Church of Santa María. The *Misteri d'Elx* (Mystery of Elche), celebrating the Assumption of the Virgin Mary, has been performed by local townspeople for 6 centuries. Although the songs are performed in an ancient form of Catalan, the action is not hard to grasp, and the special effects, including the descent of angels from the lofty dome, are breathtaking. Entry is free (but competition for seats is keen) for the play's first (August 14, 6 PM) and second (August 15, 6 PM) acts. Alternatively, seats can be booked for condensed 1-day performances, staged on August 11, 12, and 13, by writing before July 15 to the Oficina de Turismo (Parque Municipal, Elche, Alicante; phone: 6-545-2747). Telephone after that date to confirm the reservation. A special performance is staged on November 1 in even-numbered years.

CHECKING IN/EATING OUT: *Huerto del Cura* – It would be worth a detour to stay in this tranquil hostelry, which is set amid beautiful gardens in its own palm grove and, in an unusual arrangement, is linked to the *parador* network, although not actually a *parador*. There's a swimming pool and tennis courts; the 70 rooms have TV sets, mini-bars, and air conditioning (important in August). The restaurant, *Els Capellans*, offers regional food and international dishes, and is especially pleasant in summer when tables are set out on the swimming pool terrace. Avenida Federico García Sánchiz, Elche (phone: 6-545-8040). Hotel, moderate; restaurant, expensive to moderate.

En Route from Elche – Continue along N340, passing more palm groves, through the town of Crevillente to Orihuela, 21 miles (34 km) southwest of Elche in the Segura River Valley. The center of a rich agricultural area, Orihuela has a 14th-to-16th-century Gothic cathedral in which a famous Velázquez canvas, the *Temptation of St. Thomas Aquinas,* is kept under lock and key in the *Diocesan Museum* (open Mondays through Fridays, from 10:30 AM to 1:30 PM and from 4 to 6 PM). Velázquez painted the work at the request of Dominican friars, whose 17th-century Monastery of Santo Domingo, later a university and currently a high school, has fine baroque cloisters. Orihuela is the birthplace of Miguel Hernández, a goatherd who became one of Spain's finest poets before dying tragically in Alicante's jail in 1942. His house (Calle Cantos) can be visited on Calle Cantos, but it's best to call the tourist office first (25 Calle Francisco Diez; phone: 6-530-2747).

Still on N340, the road crosses into the province and autonomous community of Murcia; at Monteagudo, it passes a white statue of Christ atop a rocky pinnacle commanding the *huerta,* a jigsaw of tomato, pepper, citrus fruit, and cereal fields. From here, it's only a few miles to the capital.

MURCIA: This pleasant and unhurried city of nearly 300,000 inhabitants on the Segura River was founded by the Emir of Córdoba in 825 on the remains of a Roman settlement. It enjoyed brief moments of independence under the Moors, but was conquered by King Ferdinand the Holy in 1243 and incorporated into Castile. Fire and pillage destroyed many of its finest buildings at the start of the Spanish Civil War, but Murcia later regained its pride when it was made the capital of the autonomous region of the same name. Most tourists who pass through are on their way to Cartagena or the coast, so this is a good place for a short respite from summer crowds. The most important sights are in the older part of town on the north bank of the river. There, on Plaza Cardenal Belluga, is the mainly Gothic cathedral, begun in the 14th century, but with a magnificent baroque façade that was not added until the 18th century. Inside, the Virgen de la Fuensanta, Murcia's patroness, presides over the altar dressed in rich vestments. The church's Renaissance–baroque bell tower can be climbed for a stirring view of the city and the surrounding *huerta*. The *Diocesan Museum* (phone: 68-216344) contains La Fuensanta's gold crown, as well as one of Spain's finest polychrome woodcarvings, depicting in amazingly lifelike detail the penitent St. Hieronymus, by the local sculptor Francisco Salzillo (1707–83). The museum is open daily, from 10 AM to 1 PM and from 5 to 8 PM; admission charge. More examples of the sculptor's work can be seen some distance away in the *Salzillo Museum* (1 Calle San Andrés; phone: 68-291893), which houses some of the woodcarvings that are carried in Murcia's *Holy Week* processions (see below), as well as a large number of terra cotta figurines depicting episodes from the Gospels and the daily life of Murcian peasants (open Mondays through Saturdays from 9:30 AM to 1 PM and from 3 to 6 PM, Sundays from 10 AM to 1 PM; admission charge).

Just north of the cathedral, on traffic-free Calle de la Trapería, stands the Casino (phone: 68-212255), a 19th-century building that is another of the city's landmarks. Once a sumptuous private club for wealthier citizens (it never was a gambling den), it is now a cultural center hosting a changing program of lectures, meetings, and other events. Marble, molded plaster, carved wood, and crystal chandeliers lend it an august air — visitors are welcome to look inside (open daily from 9 AM to 11 PM; no admission charge). North again, the street broadens into Avenida Alfonso X el Sabio, a boulevard with many sidewalk cafés and a favorite spot for people watching. Many small shops can be found in the network of narrow pedestrian streets between Calle de la Trapería and its parallel to the west, the Gran Vía. The local tourist office is on a parallel to the east, however, at 4 Calle Alejandro Séiquer (phone: 68-213716).

At Alcantarilla, 6 miles (10 km) outside of town on the road to Granada, is the *Museo de la Huerta* (Carretera de Andalucía; phone: 68-800340), which contains traditional crafts, costumes, and implements of the region. A huge *noria* (waterwheel), an iron replica of the wooden one used by the Moors to raise water, stands outside (open from 10:30 AM to 2 PM and 4 to 8 PM; closed Mondays; admission charge).

Murcia celebrates *Holy Week* with great solemnity and pomp in processions of stunning scope. Over 3,000 people take in a *Holy Wednesday* procession, which stretches for nearly a mile. Participants include musicians blowing horns so big that they must be trundled along on wheels. Several of Salzillo's sculptures are borne through the streets on *Good Friday*. On *Easter Sunday*, a burst of gaiety sweeps the city with the start of the *Spring Fiesta*. Folk dancing, a jazz festival, and street festivals fill a week that ends with fireworks and a bizarre pageant known as the *Entierro de la Sardina* (Burial of the Sardine).

 CHECKING IN: *Siete Coronas Meliá* – This large, modern establishment is situated opposite the gardens bordering the Segura River. It has an elegant black-and-white-marble circular lobby, and 108 well-appointed rooms with air conditioning and color television sets. There is also a garage — important in Murcia, where parking is a problem. 5 Paseo de Garay, Murcia (phone: 68-217771). Expensive.

Hispano II – Close to the cathedral, this modern, family-run establishment has 35 air conditioned rooms with color television sets. The restaurant serves good *tapas* and excellent regional food. Parking available. 3-5 Calle Lucas, Murcia (phone: 68-216152). Expensive to moderate.

Rincón de Pepe – Comfortable, tastefully decorated and located in the city center, with 117 air conditioned rooms featuring private baths and mini-bars, as well as a justifiably renowned restaurant (see below). 34 Calle Apóstoles, Murcia (phone: 68-212239). Expensive to moderate.

 EATING OUT: *Rincón de Pepe* – Its imaginative offerings of typical Murcian dishes have won it a Michelin star. It's possible to dine here in rustic style (beams and barrels) or in modern elegance, and there are several set menus

— one with a mighty seven courses. Try the succulent *cordero lechal asado al estilo de Murcia* (roast lamb Murcia style, cooked with apples, pine nuts, and wine), wild partridge in jumilla wine, or the shellfish and truffle salad. Closed Sunday evenings and July 15 through August 15. Reservations necessary. 34 Calle Apóstoles, Murcia (phone: 68-212239). Expensive.

CARTAGENA: Just 30½ miles (49 km) down the highway (N301) from Murcia is this ancient port city, which encapsulates the Mediterranean coast's turbulent past. Founded by the Carthaginians during the 3rd century BC, called Carthago Nova in its flourishing Roman epoch, pillaged by the Visigoths, independent under the Moors, and sacked by Sir Francis Drake in 1588, Cartagena was the port from which King Alfonso XIII sailed into exile after his 1931 abdication. Because of its deep sheltered harbor, Cartagena is Spain's most important naval base. Ancient ramparts lend a fortress-like air to the city, which is dominated by four hills. The best overall view is from the Castillo de la Concepción, which is now more a park or garden than a fortress, where an Arab-built lighthouse stands. To the west lie the ruins of the 13th-century cathedral, destroyed in the 1936–39 Spanish Civil War. At the port, opposite a monument to sailors who died in the Spanish-American War, is one of the world's first submarines. The 72-foot-long, 85-ton brown-and-gray cigar-shaped craft was built by a local inventor, Issac Peral, in 1888. The impressive City Hall lies close by and at one corner is the tourist office (Plaza del Ayuntamiento; phone: 68-506483). Calle Mayor, the pedestrian mall leading from the plaza, lined with cafés, is an ideal spot for a cup of coffee.

Don't miss the *Museo Nacional de Arqueología Marítima* (2 miles/3 km) from the center of town, at Dique de Navidad, Puerto de Cartagena; phone: 68-508415); take the Mazarrón road and look for the sign. It is a treasure house of exhibits related to Mediterranean shipping, including ancient amphoras, anchors, jewelry, and a full-size model of a Roman galley (open Tuesdays through Saturdays, from 10 AM to 3 PM; admission charge).

Easter Week attracts many visitors to Cartagena. Particularly impressive are the early-morning processions on *Good Friday.* During the procession from the fishing quarter of Santa Lucía, singers compete to show their mastery of the *saeta,* a spine-tingling flamenco lament. Around dawn, three processions blend together in an emotional encounter and continue as one.

CHECKING IN: *La Manga Club* – A luxurious, British-run, sports-oriented resort located 15 miles (24 km) east of Cartagena on N332. The 47 air conditioned rooms overlook a verdant, carefully landscaped complex, which includes 2 championship golf courses, 13 tennis courts, 2 swimming pools, and a cricket field. There is also horseback riding, scuba diving, and windsurfing. Apartments and bungalows are available. Los Belones, Cartagena (phone: 68-564511). Expensive.

***Cartagonova* –** On a quiet street near the center of town. All 127 rooms are air conditioned and have color television sets. Other facilities include a garage and a restaurant specializing in regional and international dishes. 3 Calle Marcos Redondo, Cartagena (phone: 68-504200). Moderate.

EATING OUT: *Los Habaneros* – Probably Cartagena's best restaurant, with an extensive wine cellar. Service is attentive, the atmosphere relaxing in rooms with wood-paneled pillars. Try the *paletilla de cabrita al horno* (roast kid) or *pollo con langosta* (chicken with prawns). Reservations unnecessary. 60 Calle San Diego, Cartagena (phone: 68-505250). Expensive to moderate.

En Route from Cartagena – If returning to Madrid (277 miles/444 km from Cartagena and 247 miles/395 km from Murcia), it's N301 nearly all the way (backtrack through Murcia). If proceeding to Granada, take N332, which weaves southwest over irrigated fields and barren ocher hills for 20½ miles (33 km) to

Puerto de Mazarrón, on Murcia's Costa Cálida (Warm Coast), where adjacent beaches have attracted considerable tourist development. From Puerto de Mazarrón, it's a quick 4½ miles (7 km) inland to the town of Mazarrón, from where N332 continues south toward Aguilas, through scenery that becomes increasingly desert-like on approaching the Andalusian province of Almería. Aguilas, an unhurried fishing port dominated by a 16th-century castle, has good beaches but limited accommodations and restaurant facilities. In the surrounding fields, large areas are covered with plastic sheeting designed to retain moisture and allow intensive year-round crop production.

From Aguilas, return inland on the Lorca road, but turn left after 5 miles (8 km) toward Puerto Lumbreras, where an overnight stop can be made. The next morning, head west on N342 to Granada, 127 miles (203 km) from Puerto Lumbreras.

CHECKING IN/EATING OUT: *Parador de Puerto Lumbreras* – A quiet, comfortable, modern *parador* with 60 air conditioned rooms, a swimming pool, and a garage. The restaurant, overlooking a pretty garden, serves local specialties, such as *costillos de cabrito en ajo cabañil* (kid cutlets cooked with garlic, paprika, and wine vinegar) and *berenjenas a la crema con gambas y jamón* (eggplants in a white sauce with prawns and ham). Carretera N340, Km 77, Puerto Lumbreras (phone: 68-402025). Moderate.

Andalusia and Gibraltar

Andalusia is a name that conjures up images long after the journey has ended. Hooded penitents and the ominous thud of drums during *Holy Week,* a glass of sherry thrust into the visitor's hands by a stranger during *feria,* dark-eyed descendants of Carmen decked out in mantillas and frilly dresses, dusk quietly embracing the Alhambra, a white village clutching a hillside like a determined mountaineer — such memories are the stuff of southern Spain.

Indeed, Andalusia has come to symbolize Spain itself for much of the world. Flamenco can be heard elsewhere, but the staccato hand-clapping and heart-wrenching refrains take on almost mystical qualities when reverberating through the dark alleys of Córdoba and Seville.

Spain's sunshine-swathed southern region — eight provinces in an area about the size of Indiana — is a wild, rugged landscape sprinkled with chalk-white villages, vineyards, and oceans of olive and citrus trees. The shadowy peaks of the Sierra Morena cut it off from the rest of the country to the north, and other ranges, such as the Sierra Nevada, crowned by 11,407-foot-high Mulhacén peak, cross it. Running through the heartland is the broad valley of the Guadalquivir River, carpeted with towns and rich farms since antiquity.

Andalusia is home to the fairy tale Alhambra palace in Granada, Córdoba's Great Mosque, and the massive Gothic cathedral and evocative Santa Cruz quarter of Seville. Beyond these three "queen cities" are provincial capitals such as wind-whipped Cádiz, where every street leads to the sea, and Jaén, spreading like a white fan at the foot of an awesome fortress. With coastlines on both the Mediterranean Sea and the Atlantic Ocean, this fabled land claims some of Europe's most popular beach resorts. Overbuilding in these areas has become a real problem, but devotees maintain that the coast is still a little piece of earthly paradise, its miles of golden sands covered with acres of golden bodies from every nation.

The invasion of foreigners is nothing new for Andalusia; throughout history it has been a magnet for wandering races. First on the scene were indigenous prehistoric peoples, who left primitive paintings in caves such as La Pileta near Ronda. Waves of settlers called Iberians began arriving from North Africa about 2000 BC, followed by Celts from the north. These Celt-Iberians created the nucleus of the peninsula's permanent population.

Phoenician traders from the eastern Mediterranean planted colonies along the southern shore, including Malaca (Málaga) and Gadir (Cádiz). Founded about 1100 BC, Cádiz is the oldest continuously inhabited city in Europe. The Romans then colonized the region, calling it Baetica, and made it the linchpin of their Iberian empire. Major cities sprouted throughout the Guadalquivir valley and along the coast.

With the decline of Rome came Vikings, Visigoths, and Vandals, the last a Germanic tribe usually credited with naming the region Vandalusia. When the North African Muslims, called the Moors, began their centuries-long occupation in 711, they called their kingdom Al-Andalus, and the name stuck. Omnipotent caliphs ruled from Córdoba; then, as the Moors were slowly pushed back by the Christian Reconquest, Granada became the last stronghold of medieval greatness. The fall of Granada in 1492 brought all of Andalusia into the newly united nation of Castile and Aragon, later to become modern Spain. It was from Andalusia that Castile ruled its vast colonial empire, and for several centuries treasure-laden galleons unloaded on the banks of the Guadalquivir. All this history left its mark, turning Andalusian cities and towns into vast museums of golden age art and architecture.

But Andalusia is much more than monuments and museums. If Castilians (with the exception of *madrileños*) can be called dignified and sedate, Andalusians are open, gregarious, and dedicated to the art of living life to the fullest. Nowhere is this philosophy more evident than at the seemingly endless Andalusian fiestas, kaleidoscopes of uninhibited singing and dancing, colorful costumes, horse shows, impressive religious rituals, and marathon drinking binges — all rolled into one helluva party!

One warning: Don't be taken in by all the purple prose about Andalusia. There are plenty of dull towns and villages, dirty beaches, barren and ugly stretches of countryside, urban purse snatchers, and awful excuses for roads. But anyone who is selective will discover a seemingly endless variety of travel delights to whet the appetite. And as with those succulent *tapas,* the tasty Spanish hors d'oeuvres that originated here, visitors will invariably find themselves craving one more round.

The driving route outlined below begins at Córdoba, gateway to Andalusia, and continues southwest through the Guadalquivir River valley — farmland for the most part and brutally hot in summer — to Seville, the capital of the region and one of Spain's greatest cities. It then traverses horse-and-sherry country around Jerez de la Frontera and makes its way to Cádiz, on the Atlantic coast, from which it heads southeast, skirting white villages and the Mediterranean coast before arriving at the Rock of Gibraltar, one of the world's great natural landmarks. After turning inland to visit another highlight, the gorge-split town of Ronda, it drops down to the coast again to pass through the touristic Costa del Sol. The route leaves the coast for good near the fairy-tale village of Salobreña, climbing rugged mountains en route to magical Granada, and finally heads north to the lesser-known towns of Jaén and Ubeda, almost untouched by tourism and well worth a visit.

Total highway driving for the route is approximately 612 miles (980 km). Including 2 nights each at the three major cities (Córdoba, Seville, and Granada), the minimum time to allow for the full tour is 15 days.

Accommodations include a few sinfully sumptuous abodes, starting at $90 a night for a double room in the expensive category (very expensive is more than $150). However, there is a wealth of perfectly acceptable, even exceptional, hotels (mostly government *paradores*) in the moderate range, from $60 to $90, and even the occasional inexpensive choice for under $60. Most Andalusian hotels with fewer than three stars (by the government's official classification system) tend to be of the semi-fleabag variety suitable for determined budgeteers only. Expect to pay $65 or more for a meal for two at restaurants rated as expensive; moderate means $40 to $65, and inexpensive less than $40. Prices include a bottle of house wine, dessert, and coffee.

CÓRDOBA: The first stop is time-scarred Córdoba, with its haunting silhouette and sad memories of a millennium ago when it was Europe's greatest city, surpassing such upstarts as Paris and London. The name seems to conjure up foreboding images of taciturn residents, cramped and gloomy streets, and the sad strains of flamenco sung in dramatic overtones. But there's another Córdoba: bright patios brimming with flowers, filigree silver and soft leather, evocative alleys twisting through the old Jewish Quarter, and the Great Mosque, or Mezquita, an incredible forest of jasper and marble columns. For full details on the city's sights, hotels, and restaurants, see *Córdoba*, THE CITIES.

En Route from Córdoba – Take N-IV toward Seville to Carmona, 65½ miles (105 km) southwest across gently rolling countryside known as "the frying pan of Andalusia" because of scorching summer temperatures. Suddenly in the distance loom a series of bluffs, where Carmona has sat perched like a potentate since antiquity, commanding the river plain of the Guadalquivir.

CARMONA: Still partially surrounded by ancient Roman walls, this town has one of the richest histories in Andalusia. Known as Carmo to the Romans, the town straddled the famous Via Augusta, the Roman road that stretched from Cádiz to the north of Spain. In 206 BC, the Roman general Scipio crushed a Carthaginian army nearby. The road into town passes beneath the remnants of a 14th-century fortress — the Alcázar — cleverly transformed into an excellent *parador* (see *Checking In*), and through the 17th-century Puerta de Córdoba (Córdoba Gate), built into the Old Town walls. Once inside, go left up the hill to the *parador* (follow the signs) or follow Calle Santa María de Grácia to the center.

With about 25,000 residents, Carmona is just the right size for strolling — alone through its quiet, white-walled streets or together with everyone else out for the evening *paseo* in the circular Plaza de San Fernando, the town's nucleus. The plaza is lined with wrought-iron lampposts and centuries-old buildings, including the present and former town halls. Within walking distance is the double-arched Puerta de Sevilla from Moorish times; outside stands the Church of San Pedro, with a 17th-century bell tower modeled after the famous Giralda in Seville. The Gothic Church of Santa María (on Calle Martín Lopez) contains the oldest calendar in Spain (6th century), carved on an arch in the Pátio de los Naranjos.

The Roman necropolis about half a mile (1 km) outside town (off the Seville road) shelters several hundred tombs from 2,000 years ago. The Elephant Tomb, named for a statue at its entrance, features dining rooms and a kitchen that once had running water; historians believe that priests must have held some kind of banquet in honor of the deceased. The Servilia Tomb is the size of a villa and has its own pool. The necropolis, which also contains a museum filled with Roman pottery, mosaics, busts, and glass vials, is open from 9 AM to 1 PM and from 4 to 6 PM, except Sunday afternoons and Mondays. Admission charge. For further details, contact Carmona's Tourist Information Office (2 Calle El Salvador; phone: 5-414-0011, and ask for the Oficina de Turismo).

CHECKING IN/EATING OUT: *Parador Alcázar del Rey Don Pedro* – A Moorish fortress that King Peter the Cruel turned into a luxurious palace in the 14th century, and which later housed Ferdinand and Isabella while they directed the siege of Granada, is the foundation of Carmona's *parador*. Little remains of the original except some walls along the cliff, but architects have brilliantly combined these remnants with modern conveniences. High on a ridge, its 59 air conditioned rooms offer spectacular views, and there is a huge outdoor pool, as well as an impressive vaulted dining hall serving classic Andalusian food. Carmona (phone: 5-414-1010). Expensive.

En Route from Carmona – Continue on N-IV and drive 24 miles (38 km) into Seville, the "queen" of Andalusia.

SEVILLE: When Madrid became the capital of Spain in the 16th century, it was hardly the richest, the most powerful, or even the best known of Spanish cities. All those superlatives belonged to Seville. For 2 centuries following Columbus's discovery of America, Seville was the chief trading port of an empire. Every ship from Spanish America docked at Seville, and armies of satin-clad bankers and merchants, roguish sailors, and assorted charlatans gave it the raffishness of a frontier boomtown. Much of the grandeur and ambience of those days still survives. Visit Europe's third-largest Christian cathedral, where the bones of Columbus lie in a marble crypt; climb the stone ramp of the Giralda Tower, built so that a king could ride his horse to the top; and wander by moonlight in the Barrio de Santa Cruz. For a detailed report on its sights, hotels, and restaurants, see *Seville,* THE CITIES.

En Route from Seville – From the center, take N-IV south in the direction of Jerez de la Frontera and Cádiz. Drive 34 miles (54 km) to the junction with C343 near Venta Nueva, turning off toward Espera and Arcos de la Frontera, 22 miles (35 km) away. Rather than go directly into Arcos, take the turnoff to Embalse de Arcos, a lake northeast of town along the road to El Bosque (C344). From this vantage point, Arcos looks like a white pyramid rising from the surrounding plain, with gravity-defying houses welded to a rocky hillside that falls sheer to the river valley below.

ARCOS DE LA FRONTERA: Arcos (*de la frontera* is tacked onto the names of many towns that once stood along the Christian-Moorish boundary) sits on a lofty hill hemmed in on three sides by the Guadalete River. One of its attractions for visitors is its spectacularly situated government *parador,* perched along the edge of a cliff (see *Checking In*). Arcos is also among the most picturesque of a dozen or so whitewashed Andalusian hill towns known as the *pueblos blancos* (white villages) and is included on the Ruta de los Pueblos Blancos (Route of the White Villages), a popular driving route in the region. (A brochure with maps is available from Spanish tourist authorities in the US or in Spain.) Impressive *Easter Week* processions, including the singing of piercing melodies called *saetas* — a kind of *Easter* flamenco — and the running of a lone bull on *Easter Sunday,* are another source of interest.

Legend has it that the town was founded by King Brigo, a grandson of Noah. Known as Medina Arkosh in Moorish times, this seemingly impregnable site was captured by Alfonso X in 1250. Today the sounds of clanging sabers have been replaced by the groans of tourists struggling to reach the Plaza de Cabildo (also known as Plaza de España), the town's main square and the site of both the *parador* and a hair-raising terrace overlooking a valley of neat green fields and orchards. Also on the square is the old Town Hall and the Iglesia de Santa María, a hodgepodge of styles slapped one on another over centuries. (The road up the hill passes right under the church's flying buttresses on the extemely narrow Callejón de las Monjas.) Inside, the supporting columns form a palm vault, and there is an altar of gilt and carved wood. Climb the 386 feet to the top of the bell tower, but try not to arrive at the stroke of 12. (On the way up, a parchment-faced old woman in black, who lives there, asks for a tip.) The views from on high are spectacular: Look for the 18th-century tower of the Iglesia de San Pedro at the other side of the hilltop and for the former castle of the Dukes of Arcos, below and to the right, now occupied by an English aristocrat.

 CHECKING IN/EATING OUT: *Parador Casa del Corregidor* – General de Gaulle stayed in this hostelry, formerly a vicar's home. Today it's a pleasing medley of tiles and antiques with 24 air conditioned rooms and a good restaurant that serves local specialties. Plaza de España, Arcos de la Frontera (phone: 56-700460). Expensive.

En Route from Arcos de la Frontera – Take N342 west 19 miles (30 km) to Jerez, a town steeped in all things Andalusian: bulls, horses, fiestas, and, of course, fine sherry.

JEREZ DE LA FRONTERA: Jerez is the home of Spain's distinctive fortified wine — "sherry," in fact, is an English corruption of the name of the town, from which English, Scottish, and Irish shippers began buying wine as early as the 16th century. The term can legally be given only to wine produced on about 60,000 acres of vineyards lying in a triangle bordered by Seville and Puerto de Santa María (southwest of Jerez) and Sanlúcar de Barrameda (northwest), where the essential white palomino grapes grow. Although Jerez, the main production center and a fairly large town of nearly 200,000 people, does have other points of interest, most visitors get into the spirit of things by touring one of the sherry wineries, or bodegas, that are the prime local attraction.

Jerez has some 100 bodegas (holding some 125 million gallons of wine), but not all of them are open to the public. The tourist office (7 Alameda Cristina; phone: 56-331150) has details of those that welcome visitors. Among them are the Harvey, González Byass, and Sandeman bodegas, but the best of the bunch quite possibly belongs to the Domecq family (3 Calle San Idelfonso; phone: 56-331900), open 10 AM to 1 PM; closed Sundays; no admission charge. Here visitors see the fermentation rooms, mixing tanks, warehouses for aging, and bottling lines, then sample one of the four main sherry varieties — *fino* (extra dry), *amontillado* (dry with fuller body), *oloroso* (medium dry with golden color), and *dulce* (sweet).

Horses run a close second to sherry in the hearts of Jerez residents, so it's not surprising that the outstanding Escuela Andaluza del Arte Ecuestre (Andalusian School of Equestrian Art), a rival to Vienna's renowned Spanish Riding School, is a second major attraction. Although the Jerez school has been open only since 1973, horse breeding and training has been an Andalusian enterprise since Moorish times, and it was the ancestors of these very Hispano-Arab stallions strutting their stuff in Jerez that sired the famous Lippizaners. The "Dancing Horses of Andalusia" perform every Thursday at noon at the school's 1,450-seat arena (Avenida Duque de Abrantes; phone: 56-311111). Admission charge. Among the show's highlights are the matched team of black horses pulling an old barouche, and the dressage exhibition performed exactingly to baroque music by 12 riders in blue velvet period costumes astride 12 perfectly white horses. If visiting Jerez any other day of the week (except Sundays), go to the school anyway; between 11 AM and 1 PM, visitors may watch a practice session free of charge.

Each year, in early September, Jerez hosts the *Fiesta de la Vendimia,* an annual wine harvest festival. An even better time of the year to be in town, however, is during the week-long *Feria del Caballo* (Horse Fair) in May, when aloof aristocrats, the *señoritos,* gather to show off their steeds and horsemanship, and the full impact of the Andalusian twist on the old adage — "wine, women, song, and horses" — can be felt. Each day begins with a promenade of riders, followed by a procession of ornate carriages. There are dressage and jumping competitions, a horse auction, and special *rejoneo* bullfights, when a man on horseback faces the bull. Visitors can test their stamina at scores of *casetas* — open booths overflowing with wine and the seductive rhythms of improvised flamenco.

Jerez has its fair share of historical monuments and churches. Among the best are the 11th-century Alcázar, with Arab baths, located off a large square called the Alameda Vieja (open daily from 10:30 AM to 1 PM; admission charge). Nearby, on the Plaza de Arroyo, is the 18th-century baroque Catedral de San Salvador (La Colegiata), built above an old mosque. Other notable churches include the late Gothic San Miguel and the Santiago, each with finely carved portals. Better known are the city's secular monuments: the Domecq mansion on Alameda Cristina (across from the tourist office); the home of the Ponce de León family, built by the explorer in 1557; and the Casa del Cabildo, the old Town Hall on the Plaza de la Asunción — today this Renaissance masterwork houses a library and an archaeological museum (closed Sundays; admission charge).

CHECKING IN: *Sherry Park* – An ultramodern establishment on an elegant, tree-lined avenue — the town's main drag — near the riding school. It has 300 air conditioned rooms, a restaurant, and a swimming pool to help beat the summer heat. 11 Avenida Alvaro Domecq, Jerez de la Frontera (phone: 56-303011). Expensive.

Avenida Jerez – Less sumptuous than its neighbor across the street, this modern high-rise offers comfort and a good location, if not a lot of atmosphere. There are 95 air conditioned rooms. 10 Avenida Alvaro Domecq, Jerez de la Frontera (phone: 56-347411). Moderate.

EATING OUT: *El Bosque* – On the main avenue near the hotel selections, it's said to cater to the local sherry aristocracy. Exotic Andalusian dishes on the menu include such unusual items as a shellfish-and-salmon salad. Closed Mondays. Reservations advised. 28 Avenida Alvaro Domecq, Jerez de la Frontera (phone: 56-303333). Moderate.

Gaitán – The Domecq family's former cook owns this small place, which is very conveniently located near the tourist office. It features rustic decor, with photos of famous guests on the walls, and a menu of Basque and traditional Spanish specialties. Closed Sunday nights and Mondays. Reservations unnecessary. 3 Calle Gaitán, Jerez de la Frontera (phone: 56-345859). Moderate.

En Route from Jerez de la Frontera – Leave town on N-IV bound for Cádiz, 22 miles (35 km) away. After 14 miles (22 km), the road to Cádiz veers to the right, while the main highway continues toward Algeciras as N340. Continue through prosaic, resort-style suburbs to the 18th-century Puerta de la Tierra, gateway to the Old Town of Cádiz.

CÁDIZ: From time immemorial, the sea has shaped Cádiz (pronounced *Cah*-dee). For the travel-weary coming from the sunbaked interior, the salty breeze is a soothing tonic; briny port smells and lively sounds jolt heat-deadened senses back to life. It's said to be impossible to get lost here, because every street leads to water: Old Cádiz occupies a club-shaped peninsula that juts out into the Atlantic like the prow of an ocean liner, with the Bay of Cádiz to its back. A narrow isthmus connects it to the mainland. The setting is dramatic, but Cádiz is a bit rough around the edges, with the kind of seedy charm found in such places as Marseilles and Naples — exhilarating or depressing, depending on the visitor's point of view.

A deep, sheltered harbor inspired the Phoenicians to found Gadir around 1100 BC, and every subsequent Mediterranean power made it an important port. The Greeks, for example, arrived about 600 BC, despite Homer's warning that the "Rivers of Hell" lay nearby. After a stint under the Carthaginians, it passed to the Romans, as Gades, and waxed and waned along with the Roman Empire. Much later, the city's role in the discovery and colonization of the New World — and above all as a conduit for trade with the new Spanish possessions — made it wealthy, and it became a favorite of raiding Barbary pirates and English sea dogs such as Sir Francis Drake. When the Guadalquivir River silted up, effectively removing Seville as a competitor, Cádiz became the headquarters of Spain's American fleet, only to slide into obscurity when the country lost its overseas colonies. Today, the port is booming once again.

The best way to get an overview of the town is to drive the loop road that circles the perimeter, skirting a lovely seaside promenade. In fact, travelers will probably want to limit driving to this route alone, because while Cádiz is only a bit smaller than Jerez in terms of population, it has none of that city's sprawl, and negotiating the cramped and confusing streets is extremely difficult. Directly in front of the port on the peninsula's east side is the bustling Plaza San Juan de Dios, site of the imposing City Hall and a dozen or so seafood restaurants with outdoor tables for people watching. (*Gaditanos* — the locals — appear to live on fish, shellfish, and wine, and the number of standup eateries in town, especially in the dank streets around this plaza, is astounding.) Not far away, but on the west side of town, sits the ultra-ornate, golden-domed Catedral Nueva (New Cathedral), an architectural peacock begun in the early 18th century and finished 116 years later, but still wholly baroque. Outstanding features inside include the choir stalls and, in the museum, the Custodia del Millón, a 17th-century silver monstrance studded with thousands of jewels; in the crypt is the tomb of the Spanish composer Manuel de Falla. The old cathedral, the Iglesia de Santa Cruz, a 17th-century rebuilding of a church with 13th-century origins, is near the new one.

The city's tourist office (1 Calle Calderon de la Barca, on a corner of the Plaza de Mina; phone: 56-211313) can direct you to the remaining sights in the city. The *Cádiz Museum,* also known as the *Museo de Bellas Artes y Arqueológico,* on the same square, has respectable collections of art, including paintings by Zurbarán and Murillo, and archaeology, especially Phoenician and Carthaginian artifacts. The museum is open from 10 AM to 2 PM; closed Sundays. Admission charge. Another stop might be the 17th-century Oratorio de San Felipe Neri, several blocks away on Calle Santa Inés; the small church is famous as the place where Spain's first liberal constitution was hammered out in 1812; a painting by Murillo hangs above the altar. Next door is the *Museo Histórico Municipal,* which has a fascinating ivory-and-mahogany scale model of Cádiz as it looked in the 18th century (open from 9 AM to 1 PM and from 4 to 7 PM; closed Mondays; no admission charge). The Oratorio de Santa Cueva (Calle Rosario) contains religious frescoes by Goya.

Strolling through Cádiz is a delight, especially along the seaside promenade with its enormous banyan trees and verdant oases such as the Parque de Genovés, which offers summer concerts and a palm garden. Within the loop of the promenade, the streets and alleys of the Old Town twist and turn like tunnels in a rabbit warren. Just when they become too claustrophobic, however, or a bit too grimy, a sunny, palm-lined square appears. The same streets witness the town's uproarious *Carnavales,* well known throughout Spain. The week before *Lent,* residents go for days without a wink of sleep — singing, dancing madly through the streets, playing odd musical instruments, and rattling nerve-racking noisemakers. A fireworks display signals the end of the carnival celebrations, and the next morning all that remains — besides a citywide hangover — are several tons of confetti and empty wine bottles.

CHECKING IN: Atlántico – A completely refurbished, modern, 6-story hotel that is now a member of the government *parador* chain, albeit an atypical one, without the traditional character of the others. It enjoys an ideal location, overlooking the ocean, and a beautiful pool. Its 173 rooms are air conditioned and have balconies; the dining room serves Andalusian food. 9 Parque de Genovés, Cádiz (phone: 56-226905). Moderate.

EATING OUT: *El Anteojo* – An excellent location and solid seafood dishes make this place a winner. Closed Mondays. Reservations advised. 22 Alameda de Apodaca, Cádiz (phone: 56-213639). Moderate.

El Sardinero – This simple spot is the best of the many seafood restaurants on a square known for good fish. It offers a Basque kitchen — with specialties such as *merluza a la vasca* (hake, Basque-style) — and outstanding *tapas* at the bar. Closed Mondays. No reservations. Plaza San Juan de Dios, Cádiz (phone: 56-282505). Inexpensive.

En Route from Cádiz – Head south toward Algeciras. The road, flanked by the Bay of Cádiz and the Atlantic, follows a narrow isthmus dotted with saltworks. After 10 miles (16 km), turn off to the main highway (N340), which travels along — a few miles inland, however — the southern half of the Costa de la Luz. This lesser-known Spanish *costa* stretches along the Atlantic all the way from Huelva near the Portuguese border to wind-pummeled Tarifa, where it meets the Mediterranean. The coastline is relatively unscathed by resort developments, and because of the extra effort necessary to reach it from the main highway, it's still possible to find isolated beaches of golden sand and mobs of seagulls.

VEJER DE LA FRONTERA: This picturesque village is another of Andalusia's "white villages" (and a stop on the Ruta de los Pueblos Blancos). It lords over the landscape 32½ miles (52 km) from Cádiz, just a mile (1.6 km) off the main road. The site is another exceptional one, used as a defensive bastion ever since the days when Romans were fighting Iberians. The Moors, naturally, couldn't pass up a chance to plunk down a hilltop castle, and some of its old walls have been restored. Nearby, the Church of San Salvador is a blending of Gothic and Mudéjar styles, built on the foundations of a mosque. Moorish influence is also evident in the unusually labyrinthine streets weaving up the hill. Trying to drive up to the castle would be a mistake; fortunately, there is a parking lot near the entrance to the village.

 CHECKING IN/EATING OUT: *Convento de San Francisco* – A hostelry occupying a former monastery that has been impeccably restored. It's family owned and operated, with one son managing the hotel restaurant, Vejer's best. None of the 25 rooms is air conditioned, but summers are moderate here. Vejer de la Frontera (phone: 56-451001). Moderate.

En Route from Vejer de la Frontera – The N340 highway south to Tarifa passes a wild and windy landscape, with huge limestone outcroppings and a smattering of whitewashed farmhouses. One of the largest hunks of rock marks Punta Paloma, where the highway turns seaward. The E-5 turnoff for Tarifa comes 28 miles (45 km) from Vejer, and it's another mile into town.

TARIFA: The town sits at Spain's southernmost point, looking out on the Strait of Gibraltar and, on a clear day, as far as Morocco. Head for the Old Quarter through an ancient portal. Within are the 16th-century Gothic Iglesia de San Mateo and the 13th-century (reconstructed) Castillo de Guzmán el Bueno, still used as an army barracks. The fortress was the scene of a celebrated incident in Spanish history. When the Moors were trying to retake it from the Christians in 1292, they captured the son of the Spanish commander, Alonso Pérez de Guzmán. The lad was brought forward and threatened with death unless the castle's defenders surrendered, but the elder Guzmán threw the Moors his weapon and shouted, "If you need help to murder my son, here is my knife, but we will not surrender." The attack was rebuffed and Guzmán became known as El Bueno (the Good); the son's fate is not clear. The castle is open from 11 AM to 2 PM and from 4 to 10 PM daily during the summer months, on weekends only the rest of the year. Admission charge. Most visitors who come to Tarifa do not come for the sightseeing, however. They come to take the hydrofoil that makes a daily run across the water to Tangier in Morocco. Windsurfing is another big draw — this is considered one of the best spots in Europe for the sport — as are beaches such as Playa Lances. Nordic types now roam the cobbled streets where Moors used to walk.

En Route from Tarifa – Return to N340 and head east toward Algeciras. This part of Andalusia, known as the Campo de Gibraltar, is mainly an industrial and shipping center, of little interest to tourists. Several miles east of Tarifa, however, the famous Rock of Gibraltar — a little piece of the British Empire isolated in the Mediterranean — comes into view. It thrusts up from across the Bay of Algeciras just as mighty and defiant as expected, a point not lost on neighboring Spaniards, who have claimed it for almost 3 centuries.

ALGECIRAS: The Moors arrived in 711 and named their settlement Al-Djezirah. They endured until the mid-14th century; a few scattered remnants of their presence survive west of the present town. A thousand years after the arrival of the Moors, Spanish refugees from Gibraltar arrived to settle the site. Today, this growing port city has little to offer visitors except wonderful views of the Rock. A great many visitors do get the picture, however, since each year more than 3 million passengers use the ferries and hydrofoils that ply the Strait of Gibraltar between Algeciras and both Tangier and the Spanish enclave of Ceuta in North Africa. The city also has a grand old landmark hotel, the *Reina Cristina* (see below), the brainchild of a turn-of-the-century English lord who constructed a railroad across Andalusia. During World War II, the harborside hotel's guests were joined by a number of German spies, who watched ship traffic through the strait from their second-story rooms.

CHECKING IN/EATING OUT: *Reina Cristina* – The pink lady with green shutters, turrets, and a tiled roof manages to blend Victorian and arabesque into a nostalgic hideaway. Built almost 100 years ago and named for Spain's queen regent, the hotel sits aloof from the rest of Algeciras, with its own terraced gardens, English library, and aging British clientele, who come for the service and the inspiring views of "Gib." It has 135 air conditioned rooms and a traditional, moderately priced restaurant. Paseo de la Conferencia, Algeciras (phone: 56-650061). Expensive.

En Route from Algeciras – If headed for Gibraltar, take N340 northeast 8 miles (13 km) to San Roque, then turn off to La Línea de la Concepción, from which the border lies 5 miles (8 km) away. If not visiting Gibraltar, turn off N340 onto C3331 just before San Roque and proceed directly to Ronda.

GIBRALTAR: The self-governing British colony of Gibraltar is only 3 miles long and three-quarters of a mile wide, with approximately 29,000 inhabitants settled mainly in Gibraltar Town, on the Rock's west side. Tiny as it is, the colony is an immense source of bitterness among the Spanish, who consider themselves its rightful owners; their attempts to reclaim it led to the closing of the frontier between Spain and Gibraltar in 1969. For years, the Rock was accessible only by air or sea from the United Kingdom or North Africa. But the steel mesh gates swung open again in February 1985, and the border is now open round the clock. Visitors need only a passport, not a visa, to cross.

Gibraltar's dramatic silhouette owes itself to a geologic cataclysm in some distant era that sent huge chunks of its north and east sides crashing into the sea. This left a sheer 1,400-foot-high face that was famous long before an American insurance ad made it familiar — for the ancients, the Rock was one of the Pillars of Hercules marking the limits of the Mediterranean. When the Moors launched their invasion of Spain from here in 711, they called it Gebel-Tarik (Tarik's Rock), in honor of their leader. The Moorish occupation left its legacy not only in the modern name of this piece of real estate, but also in an old castle and defensive walls and in the arabesque flourishes found in both Catholic and Protestant churches here; the tiled courtyard of St. Mary the Crowned, in fact, once belonged to a mosque.

Spaniards regained this colossal toehold from the Moors, but lost it again to Britain in 1713, after first losing the War of the Spanish Succession. Then came the Great Siege (1779–83), one of innumerable Spanish attempts to retake the mesmerizing hunk of limestone. So many cannonballs have been fired at the Rock that when more turn up during a new building project, residents no longer blink. Indeed, history itself turns up in every nook and cranny. In Trafalgar Cemetery, for example, heroes of the famous naval battle fought off Cape Trafalgar (about halfway between Cádiz and Tarifa) are buried near the spot where the body of the fallen Admiral Horatio Nelson was brought ashore. Two men lie in one grave here, both killed by the same cannonball. The *Gibraltar Museum* (off Main Street) tells the Rock's whole fascinating story and has a 30-foot scale model. It's open from 10 AM to 6 PM; closed Sundays. Admission charge.

Although Gibraltarians are really more Mediterranean than British, both in temperament and language (a strange variety of Spanish with an abundance of English expressions), the British presence is unmistakable, from fluttering Union Jacks and friendly bobbies to photos of the queen and gin-and-tonic urbanity at the yacht club. There's a changing-of-the-guard ceremony every Tuesday at 10 AM at the Governor's Residence on Main Street, as well as other displays of colonial pomp. Main Street itself, the Rock's backbone, is a throbbing half mile of discount shops (there's no VAT here), British retail institutions such as *Marks & Spencer,* and pubs like the *Angry Friar* and *Old Vic's.* Unfortunately, Gibraltar has taken on an increasingly seedy appearance, and traditional hospitality has suffered from the onslaught of visitors since 1985.

Willis's Road, to the east of Main Street, leads past the Moorish Castle, with its square Tower of Homage, built in 1333 (admission charge). From here, Queen's Road climbs to the Upper Galleries, huge tunnels for housing artillery that were carved out by hand during the Great Siege. They are open daily from 10 AM to 7 PM (to 5:30 in summer). Admission charge. Farther up lies the Apes' Den, home of perhaps the world's most famous simians. Gibraltar's official mascots, they are so revered that Churchill vowed to protect them when their numbers dwindled. (According to recent legend, the Rock will remain British as long as the monkeys stay.) Daily feedings take place at 8 AM and 4 PM. Another way to reach the den is via a spectacular cable car ride that goes to the top of the Rock from just below the *Rock* hotel. More information on the sights can be obtained at the Gibraltar Tourist Office in Cathedral Square.

Note: To call Gibraltar from Spain, dial the area code (9567) before the local number (except from La Línea de la Concepción, just across the border in Spain, where you dial only 7 before the local number in Gibraltar); from the US, dial only the country code (350) before the local number.

 CHECKING IN: *Rock* – Like *Raffles* in Singapore, this hotel is a classic of the British colonial genre, with 160 comfortable rooms, good service, and spectacular views. Other amenities are a restaurant with roast beef and Yorkshire pudding on the menu, a saltwater pool, miniature golf, and a nearby casino. 3 Europa Road, Gibraltar (phone: 350-73000). Expensive.

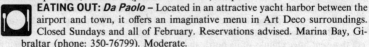 **EATING OUT: *Da Paolo*** – Located in an attractive yacht harbor between the airport and town, it offers an imaginative menu in Art Deco surroundings. Closed Sundays and all of February. Reservations advised. Marina Bay, Gibraltar (phone: 350-76799). Moderate.

Spinning Wheel – The convenient location and the recommendation of a loyal following make this a top traditional choice. Lamb dishes are the specialty. Closed

Sundays. Reservations unnecessary. 9 Horsebarrack Lane, Gibraltar (phone: 350-76091). Moderate.

En Route from Gibraltar – Return to San Roque and take C3331 to Ronda, spearing through farmland along the Guadarranque River and into the hills. Several of the towns passed before reaching the classic old Andalusian town of Ronda are included on the Ruta de los Pueblos Blancos, among them picturesque Jimena de la Frontera, draped like a sheepskin on the side of a hill 22 miles (35 km) from San Roque and crowned by a castle. From Jimena, take C341; the road passes golden hills dotted with olive trees, citrus orchards, and clusters of white houses. After a stretch that soars high above a spectacular valley, the village of Gaucín appears, then tiny Algatocín and Benadalíd. The final approach to Ronda, 37½ miles (60 km) from Jimena, provides inspiring scenery, with huge bare slabs of stone thrusting up from the landscape. This is the heart of the Serranía de Ronda range, a traditional retreat for bandits.

RONDA: Its fame rests chiefly on El Tajo, a 400-foot gorge cut by the Guadalevín River that literally splits the town in two. Incredible cliff-hanging houses perch right along the edge of the precipice and look as if they might slide into the abyss at any moment. The 5-foot-high iron grilles on the 18th-century Puente Nuevo, one of three bridges that span the gorge, are all that separate visitors from a horrifying drop. The bridge links two towns and two eras. To the north lies the "new" town, called El Mercadillo, begun around 1500, after Ronda fell to the Christians. Here, a pedestrian street, the Carrera de Espinel, is lined with scores of shops, becoming a vibrant sea of shoppers and strollers each afternoon. At the head of the street is the Plaza de Toros, Ronda's famous bullring. Although bullfights are held only about once a month from May through October, visitors may inspect Spain's most beautiful bullring and its second oldest (1785) daily from 10 AM to 1 PM and from 4 to 7 PM. Admission charge. Don't miss the opportunity, because Ronda is the cradle of modern bullfighting. The local Romero family developed most of the rules and techniques used today, including the introduction of the cape, the killing sword, and the group of assistants to the matador called the *cuadrilla.* Each September, at the *Corrida Goyesca,* aficionados pay homage to a 19th-century family member, Pedro Romero, who killed 5,000 bulls during his career and fought until the age of 90. (Goya immortalized the epoch in several sketches and engravings.) End a tour of the new town by strolling north from the bullring through the Alameda Gardens, supposedly paid for with fines levied on anyone using foul language in public.

The Old Town, called La Ciudad, is a symphony of cramped streets and wrought-iron balconies brimming with potted geraniums. Here are some of Andalusia's finest aristocratic mansions, such as the twin-turreted 16th-century Renaissance Casa de Mondragón, off the Plaza del Campillo (now a crafts school that is closed to the public). A short walk away is the circular Plaza de la Ciudad, the coolest spot in town on a summer day. Fronting it is a 15th-century church, Santa María la Mayor, with a baroque altar dripping with gilt and a former Muslim mihrab (a niche indicating the direction of Mecca); the church's tower was once a minaret. On the other side of the Old Town (near the bridge off Calle del Comandante Alejandro) are more mansions, including the Casa del Rey Moro, which is the restored home of King Badis, a Moorish ruler who drank wine from the jewel-encrusted skulls of his victims. (Today it's a private home that can't be visited.) Farther down the same street is the 18th-century Palacio del Marqués de Salvatierra, the home of a Spanish aristocrat complete with Plateresque portal, marble staircase, and Alhambra-style gardens. The house is open daily from 11 AM to 2 PM and from 4 to 6 PM. Admission charge. The Arab baths at the bottom of the same hill are among the finest in Spain. Check with the tourist office (1 Plaza de España; phone: 52-871272) for opening hours, which are variable. Admission charge.

CHECKING IN: *Reina Victoria* – The grand old dowager of Ronda in the Mercadillo section has a gabled roof, English gardens, chandeliers, and dark wood furniture. Its 89 air conditioned rooms are often crowded with tour groups, but it's still a treat in a town with few hotels. 25 Avenida Dr. Fleming, Ronda (phone: 52-871240). Moderate.

EATING OUT: *Don Miguel* – Clinging to one side of El Tajo next to the bridge, this spot offers a stunning outdoor terrace as well as good food. Rabbit in sherry sauce and devilfish with green peppers are on the inventive menu. Closed Mondays. Reservations unnecessary. 4 Calle Villanueva, Ronda (phone: 52-871090). Moderate.

Pedro Romero – Bullfighting memorabilia give it atmosphere, and the traditional Spanish food is good. Try the *rabo de toro* (oxtail stew). Closed Sunday evenings. Reservations unnecessary. 18 Calle Virgen de la Paz, Ronda (phone: 52-871110 or 52-874731). Moderate.

En Route from Ronda – The tour route of Andalusia proceeds from Ronda to the Costa del Sol. Those on a tight schedule, however (as well as those who eschew the ravages of mass tourism), may want to head directly to Granada. If done in 1 day, this trip involves a fairly strenuous drive of 120 miles (192 km) along routes C341 and N342 via Antequera, a pleasant, medium-size town with dozens of historic churches and a Moorish castle. If traveling at a leisurely pace, stop in Antequera or farther along for a meal or an overnight stay.

To continue the complete Andalusia route, proceed from Ronda south to the Costa del Sol via C339, which drops from about 2,300 feet to sea level in a distance of 30 miles. The landscape along the way is a harsh blending of volcanic rock and red clay, studded with rare *pinsapo* firs, black cork oaks, wild olives, and mauve rock roses.

CHECKING IN/EATING OUT: *La Bobadilla* – This extraordinary, sumptuous resort near Loja, about 20 miles (32 km) east of Antequera, is on the way from Ronda to Granada and is reason enough for anyone to break up this trip. The creation of a German hotelier and designed by a Granadan architect, it's set in the middle of isolated countryside looking much like a typical Andalusian "white village," with everything in authentic Andalusian style: tiled roofs, arches, wrought-iron grilles, a plaza, and as a central gathering place, a chapel with a 30-foot-high, 1,595-pipe organ. Most of the 35 rooms have their own patio or garden, and there is a gymnasium, a sauna, 2 pools, tennis courts, and a stable of horses for riding. Two highly rated restaurants serve meals for the likes of King Juan Carlos, who has been known to pop in. Finca La Bobadilla, Loja (phone: 58-321861). Very expensive.

Parador de Antequera – Another option for those en route to Granada. It features a pool and 55 air conditioned rooms, plus a popular restaurant serving regional specialties. Paseo García del Olmo, Antequera (phone: 52-840261). Moderate.

PUERTO BANÚS AND MARBELLA: The first town on the coast for those who arrive from Ronda is an insignificant resort, San Pedro de Alcántara. Only 2 miles (3 km) east of it, however, is the crown jewel of local tourism, Puerto José Banús, a yacht harbor filled with dozens of pleasant places to stop for a drink or a meal and, quite possibly, to rub elbows with a movie star or an Arab sheik. The Port, as it's known to residents, is home to hundreds of craft of all sizes and pedigrees; Rolls-Royces and Mercedes wait quayside, as their impeccably groomed owners join the evening parade of strollers who come to see and be seen on the promenade. Behind is a modern, quasi-Andalusian fishing village filled with luxury apartments and looking like a giant cardboard cutout.

Puerto Banús is technically part of San Pedro, but in spirit it belongs to Marbella, 5 miles (8 km) east, the fabled resort where the "beautiful people" play — or at least used to play, before package tourism began to drive them away. The golf is great at several local courses; so is the tennis, and the windsurfing and other water sports. Even sunbathing is better here than at other spots on the coast, thanks to a superb climate created by a backdrop of coastal mountains. Dining and nightlife aren't shabby either, although Marbella is not just limousines and popping champagne corks. Having cut its teeth as a Phoenician village called Salduba, it has a rich history. An ancient Arab wall still partially surrounds its Old Town, a traffic-free oasis of cool, cobbled alleys and half-hidden squares brimming with aromatic flowers and fruit trees. Among them, the Plaza de los Naranjos, a truly idyllic spot with orange trees, gurgling fountains, and outdoor cafés, is probably the best of the lot. Also on the square are a statue of King Juan Carlos (where one of Franco once loomed), the 16th-century Town Hall, and the *Museo Arqueológico*, recently closed for renovation but expected to reopen this year.

Other sights in the Old Town are the parish Church of La Encarnación and its clock tower on the Plaza Caridad, and the adjacent Calle Gloria, a tiny street that has become a floral showcase. Nearby Calle Alamo leads to a nice upstairs bar called *The Townhouse*. Just across Avenida Ricardo Soriano from the Old Town lies the Alameda del Parque, a park and promenade with an abundance of vegetation and beautifully tiled benches. Two blocks away is the Mediterranean in all its glory, framed nicely with a promenade, the Paseo Marítimo, and a much smaller, humbler version of Puerto Banús, the Puerto Deportivo. The tourist office (1 Avenida Miguel Cano; phone: 52-771442) can supply further information.

CHECKING IN: *Los Monteros* – One of Spain's most elegant hotels, set in a complete resort complex with few rivals. It caters to the affluent and famous, with prices to match, but it offers superb golf, tennis, horseback riding, 5 swimming pools plus the beachfront, water sports, a health clinic, and the acclaimed *El Corzo* restaurant, boasting one of Andalusia's few Michelin stars. The location, however, a few miles east of Marbella, is a drawback. Urbanización Los Monteros, Marbella (phone: 52-771700). Very expensive.

El Fuerte – Back down on earth, this older hotel, completely renovated, enjoys a wonderful location amid manicured gardens between Marbella's beach and the Old Town. There are 262 rooms, 2 swimming pools, an illuminated tennis court, and 2 restaurants; ask for an air conditioned room in the new wing. Llano de San Luis, Marbella (phone: 52-771500). Expensive.

EATING OUT: *Don Leone* – For years the best dining spot at Puerto Banús. It offers solid Italian cooking and an ideal situation for people watching. Open daily; closed from November 20 through December 20. Reservations necessary. Muelle Ribera, Puerto Banús (phone: 52-811718). Expensive.

Hostería del Mar – At the western edge of town at the beginning of the "golden mile," where Marbella's most expensive real estate is to be found. The menu — Spanish cooking, done with international finesse — features such dishes as sole stuffed with shrimp mousse and squid in ink sauce. Closed Sundays. Reservations advised. 1A Avenida Cánovas del Castillo, Marbella (phone: 52-770218). Expensive.

Mesón de Pasaje – This impeccably managed little restaurant occupies a friendly old house just off the Plaza de los Naranjos. Continental cooking at reasonable prices means it is often crowded, so reservations are a must. Closed Thursdays and from mid-November through mid-December. 5 Calle Pasaje, Marbella (phone: 52-771261). Moderate.

En Route from Puerto Banús and Marbella – The 16-mile (27-km) stretch of coast between Marbella and Fuengirola, once among the nicest on the Costa del Sol, now bristles with new developments. Fuengirola itself is a place to avoid, which is easy enough to do. Take the bypass (left toward Málaga) just west of town; 2 miles (3 km) farther along, another road heads 4 miles (6 km) into the hills to the pretty little village of Mijas, probably Spain's most photographed white *pueblo*.

MIJAS: It's often mobbed by busloads of sightseers and armies of souvenir hawkers, yet despite all this, Mijas retains a good deal of its original charm. Much of the appeal derives from its spectacular site, welded to the side of a mountain and looking like a stack of sugar cubes against a pine-draped backdrop. From stunning lookout points, a gaze spans much of the coast and the luminous Mediterranean as far as Morocco's foreboding Rif mountains.

The road splits at the entrance to Mijas; take the left fork to a wide parking area, then walk up the hill to an early Christian shrine, the Santuario de la Virgen de la Pena (after passing the "burro taxi" service — corny but fun). Walk toward the center of town to the Plaza de la Constitución, a shady spot for watching village life. From here, a path leads up past the ultramodern bullring (where seats go for more than $40 a head) to a terraced lookout area called the *cuesta de la villa* (literally, "slope of the town"), where visitors can enjoy that famous view.

CHECKING IN: *Mijas* – The only real hotel in town offers 100 rooms, swimming, tennis, and a hairdresser (but no air conditioning), at slightly inflated prices. Guests pay for the view, which is spectacular. Urbanización Tamisa, Mijas (phone: 52-485800). Expensive.

EATING OUT: *Mirlo Blanco* – The excellent location and tasty Basque cuisine such as *txanqurro* (spider crab baked in the shell) make this an ideal choice. Closed Sundays. Reservations necessary. Plaza de la Constitución, Mijas (phone: 52-485700). Moderate.

En Route from Mijas – To avoid the congested coast, take the turnoff for Benalmádena just below Mijas (on the road to Fuengirola). After 7 miles (11 km), this narrow road cuts down to Arroyo de la Miel and the fringes of Torremolinos, a package-tour paradise that has seen better days. Another 2 miles (3 km) east of Arroyo, the road joins the Torremolinos bypass road (N340); from here, the destination is Málaga, 7 miles (11 km) away.

MÁLAGA: The center of the Costa del Sol offers more shopping, cultural events, museums — more of everything — than any other place along the coast, but it also has more crime, traffic, noise, and pollution. Because of its busy international airport, the city's name is stamped in millions of passports every year, but most of the visitors who land here go elsewhere to stay. Málaga has been around since the Phoenicians, who founded a settlement to trade in salted fish; the hill overlooking the sinewy harbor was later fortified by every power to rule the Mediterranean. The sweet Málaga wine has been famous since antiquity and is still served from 500-liter barrels at murky little bodegas. (One of the best is the *Antigua Casa Guardia* on the Alameda.)

The center of town is dominated by the refreshing Paseo del Parque that begins at the Plaza de la Marina (where there is underground parking) and extends eastward. This pedestrian promenade and park, lined with palms and banana trees, features fountains, ponds with geese and ducks, and 3,000 species of luxuriant plants bathed in Málaga's intense light. Fronting it are the lemon-colored Ayuntamiento (Town Hall) and other government buildings. Beyond, to the east, are the bullring; the Paseo Marítimo promenade along La Malagueta beach; and a nostalgia-tinged district of aging buildings known as El Limonar. Better beaches lie to the east at Baños de Carmen and El Palo.

The Alcazaba, an 11th-century Moorish fortress-palace, is perched directly above the park and reached via Calle Alcazabilla. Although nicely restored, this is something of a "poor man's Alhambra" in terms of historical and architectural interest. The winding approach passes ruins of a Roman amphitheater, horseshoe arches, and walls draped in bougainvillea and wisteria. Peer down the murky hole where Christian prisoners were kept and, in the *Archaeological Museum* in the main building, peruse the collection of artifacts (the statue with an iron peg leg is curious). The Alcazaba is open daily from 10 AM to 1 PM and from 4 to 7 PM. Admission charge. Rearing up to the east is another Moorish fortress, the 14th-century Castillo de Gibralfaro, built on the site of an ancient Greek lighthouse. (It can be reached by a strenuous walk up from the Alcazaba, or by driving a mile east from the Paseo del Parque and then another mile up the hill.) Wander at will around the extensive ramparts and towers, which held off many an attack before the city fell to Christian armies in 1487. Open from 9 AM until dusk; no admission charge.

Málaga's Renaissance cathedral (Calle de Molina Larios in the center of town) has only one of the two towers originally planned because, so the story goes, money was diverted to help the colonials fight the American Revolution. It's quite dark inside, but look for the Corinthian columns as big as giant redwoods and the 17th-century choir stalls, with 100 seats and dozens of saints carved by the famous artisan Pedro de Mena. A small museum with religious artifacts is open daily from 10 AM to 1 PM and from 4 to 5:30 PM. Admission charge. From the cathedral's north side, follow the signs to the *Museo de Bellas Artes* (8 Calle San Agustín; open from 10 AM to 1:30 PM and from 5 to 8 PM; closed Mondays; admission charge). The eclectic collection — 20 rooms full, much of it on permanent loan from the *Prado* — includes paintings by Murillo and Ribera, as well as a small room devoted to the boyhood works of Málaga's most famous son, Pablo Picasso. The house where Picasso was born, in 1881, is 2 blocks away (take a right on Calle Granada) in Plaza de la Merced, whose 19th-century buildings — with green shutters, tile roofs, and peeling yellow paint — retain some of the charm of the epoch. A plaque commemorates the event.

Another throwback to earlier times not far from the museum (take Calle Granada toward the Plaza de la Constitución) is the Pasaje de Chinitas, where the *malagueña* style of flamenco evolved in the mid-19th century. Stroll along this car-free stretch of wrought-iron lamps and cobblestones, then stop for a drink at the *Bodega la Campana,* where the tab is kept with chalk on the bar counter. Or stop for *tapas* — Málaga is known for its *tapas,* and some of the best bars for sampling them are a short hop from the Pasaje de Chinitas. Among them is *Bar Orellana* (3 Calle Moreno Monroy) famous for its *lomo mechado* (loin of pork, veal, or other meat, larded with hard-boiled egg, bacon, and other stuffings, then sliced). The tourist office (4 Pasaje de Chinitas; phone: 52-213445) can recommend many others.

CHECKING IN: *Málaga Palacio* – Although it has slipped from a once loftier position, this 228-room establishment still features baronial-style public rooms, a rooftop pool, and an outstanding location. Ask for an air conditioned room with a view over the Paseo del Parque. 1 Cortina del Muelle, Málaga (phone: 52-215185). Moderate.

***Parador de Gibralfaro* –** On the south side of the Gibralfaro hill, next to the castle, its location is a mixed blessing. It's a 2-mile (3-km) drive from the center, but the splendid views over the harbor, bullring, and modern lighthouse of Málaga are worth the inconvenience, as is the good restaurant. None of the 12 rooms is air conditioned. Monte de Gibralfaro, Málaga (phone: 52-221902). Moderate.

EATING OUT: *Antonio Martín* – A traditional favorite, it has a somewhat erratic reputation but a superb location, especially for lunch outside on the terrace. Closed Mondays. Reservations unnecessary. 4 Paseo Marítimo, Málaga (phone: 52-222113). Moderate.

La Cancela – A pleasant choice, often crowded with tour groups at lunch. Specialties include *fritura malagueña,* or fried seafood, and *ajo blanco,* a cold soup made with garlic. Closed Sundays. Reservations unnecessary. 3 Calle Denis Belgrano, Málaga (phone: 52-223125). Inexpensive.

En Route from Málaga – Continue 33 miles (53 km) east on N340 to Nerja, passing a nearly continuous wall of resort developments along the way. To reach the center of Nerja, follow the Balcón de Europa signs.

NERJA: This resort town lies at the mouth of the Chillar River, on a sloping site beneath a wall of jagged coastal mountains. Its name comes from the Arabic *narixa,* or "abundant spring." The nicest spot in town is the Balcón de Europa, a palm-shaded promenade jutting dramatically into the Mediterranean. Built in 1885 and named by King Alfonso XIII, it's lined with antique iron lamp posts and old cannon, with one side overlooking a pretty beach and some fishing boats. On another side are several cafés with loyal customers and outdoor tables, the place to stop for a cup of *café con leche.* (Locals say the *Alhambra* serves the best coffee and is popular with visiting film crews in town to take advantage of the nearly perfect climate.) Just around the corner sits the parish church, which celebrated its 500th anniversary in 1983. The tourist office (4 Puerta del Mar; phone: 52-521531) is at the entrance to the Balcón.

CHECKING IN: *Parador de Nerja* – A gem in a beautiful setting atop a bluff overlooking the sea, with one of the area's best beaches just a stroll away. It has 73 air conditioned rooms, a nice pool, and a restaurant serving international and Andalusian cuisine. Calle Rodriguez Acosta, Nerja (phone: 52-520050). Moderate.

EATING OUT: *Casa Luque* – On one of the town's loveliest squares and loaded with atmosphere. The food blends traditional (rabbit stew) and innovative (asparagus mousse). Open daily. Reservations advised. 2 Plaza Cavana, Nerja (phone: 52-521004). Moderate.

En Route from Nerja – Those who like Andalusian villages may want to detour 4½ miles (7 km) inland along a well-paved road to the *pueblo* of Frigiliana, a stack of white blocks that was once voted Andalusia's prettiest village. Ceramic plaques in the Old Quarter tell a fascinating history. Here, in 1569, about 10,000 Moors dug in for a last stand against the forces of King Philip II. With defeat imminent, hundreds hurled themselves off a cliff rather than be captured — local yarn spinners claim that whitened bones and rusty weapons still occasionally turn up in the hills. Go to the Plaza de la Iglesia, where the old timers hang out, and drink in the heady scents of orange blossoms, or have a drink and some *tapas* at the *Bar-Café Viritudes,* opposite the bus stop and Civil Guard barracks.

Return to Nerja and head east, stopping 3 miles (5 km) from town, near the village of Maro, to visit the Cuevas de Nerja. These colossal caves, discovered in 1959 by boys trying to trap bats, boast the world's longest stalactite — 295 feet — and prehistoric paintings dating from 20,000 BC. Over the ages, underground water has worn down rocks and built up limestone deposits into bizarre shapes — known as the Tower of Pisa, Pinocchio, and so on — that are tastefully lit for full effect. Other highlights include the Hall of the Elephant's Tusk and its giant fossil embedded in stone, and the Cataclysm Chamber, where an enormous column fell and shattered millennia ago. An outstanding festival of music and dance, with top classical ballet, unfolds every August in the Cascade Chamber. The caves are open daily from 9:30 AM to 9 PM in summer and from 10 AM to 1:30 PM and 4 to 7 PM in winter. Admission charge.

Continue east into the province of Granada. Once a driver's nightmare, the highway is now quite good and very scenic: goatherds leading their flocks over the scrub-covered hills, old watchtowers grasping at hilltops, cliffs plummeting down to the glittering sea, and slender fingers of intensely cultivated land painting swathes of green. Fewer beaches, golf courses, and high rises line this stretch of the Costa del Sol, and the first significant settlement, the fishing village of La Herradura, sitting on a horseshoe-shape bay, is fully 10 miles (16 km) from Nerja. All around are terraced hillsides and orchards of dark green *chimayo,* a tropical fruit. A few miles farther along, Almuñecar appears, its Old Town clinging to a lofty hill. Unfortunately, the ravages of modern development have begun to take their toll on what was once an idyllic spot. Proceed 10½ miles (17 km) farther to Salobreña.

SALOBREÑA: On sunny days, this stunning village is nearly blinding from the endless layers of whitewash slapped on by old women wielding buckets and brushes. In the moonlight it becomes a dream town, rising above a broad plain, peacefully suspended between the stars and the sea. Its Moorish castle, one of Andalusia's most impressive, occupies an impregnable site that must have seemed like a gift from Allah. From the castle, flat-roofed houses spill down the hillside to the plain. It's possible to drive partway up, but park and walk to the top. The final stretch climbs along Calle Andrés Segovia, named for the renowned guitarist who called Salobreña home. Inside the castle, wander the battlements and catch an eyeful of coastal scenery (admission charge).

CHECKING IN: *Salobreña* – This little hideaway, a 2-story, 80-room modern structure perched on a cliff overlooking the Mediterranean, lies 2 miles (3 km) west of the village. There's a nice pool, but no air conditioning. Carretera Cádiz, Km 341, Salobreña (phone: 58-610261). Inexpensive.

En Route from Salobreña – Continue on the coastal road for 2 miles (3 km) to pick up N323 to Granada. The road slices 42 miles (67 km) north through the rugged Sierra Nevada, following the course of the Guadalfeo (Ugly River) and leaving the sensuous world of palm trees and tropical fruit behind. To the east lies a wild region of primitive villages called Las Alpujarras.

Seven miles (11 km) south of Granada a sign is marked Suspiro del Moro. It was from this hill that Boabdil, the last Muslim king in Spain, wept as he took a final look back on his way to exile in Morocco. From here, it's smooth sailing across a fertile plain to the fabled city of the Moors.

GRANADA: At first sight, the city of a thousand and one legends is a disappointing jumble of gray façades and snarling traffic. But Granada's delights are slightly veiled, making discovery more exciting. Among them: the exquisite golden web of filigree work sheltering the tombs of Ferdinand and Isabella in the Royal Chapel and the chalk white Albaicín quarter, huddling beneath one of Spain's great sights, the Alhambra. Despite the incursions of modern life, Granada still evokes images of courtesans in silk gowns and silver slippers. For full details of sights, hotels, and restaurants, see *Granada,* THE CITIES.

En Route from Granada – Leave town on N323 for Jaén, 61 miles (98 km) north, and enter a rolling sea of olive trees ringed by dusty mountains. The road cuts through rough hills to a mountain pass, Puerto de Carretero (3,400 feet high); suddenly, the provincial capital — olive trees at its feet and flanked by gray granite hills and a Moorish castle — appears in the distance. About 6 miles (10 km) before Jaén, another road (N321) veers to the right toward Ubeda. However, if going into Jaén, continue straight ahead on N323.

JAÉN: The capital of the province of Jaén sits at the confluence of the Guadalquivir and Guadalbullon rivers. The site was called Auringis by the Romans and became famous for its silver mines and olives. The Moors called it Geen, "way of the caravans," because it lay on the main route between Andalusia and Castile. The Moors were defeated in 1246, but they left behind the chief reason for a visit to Jaén: a spectacular hilltop fortress — the 13th-century Castillo de Santa Catalina — whose crumbling ruins have been reconstructed and converted into a government *parador*. Located 2 miles (3 km) from the center of town, the castle sits at the end of a steep, winding road that provides magnificent views of the entire area. Besides the *parador* (see *Checking In/Eating Out*), visit the former castle parade ground, ringed by defensive towers, and peek into the keep and the Santa Catalina Chapel. Then walk to the far end of the hill to reach a thrilling lookout spot over the town. From this viewpoint, the 16th-century Renaissance Catedral de Jaén looks imposing but a bit odd, its massive façade out of proportion with the surrounding buildings. Begun about 1525 by Andrés de Vandelvira, the cathedral tempts the limits of architectural good taste with its ornate façade, topped with statues of saints. Inside are choir stalls with delicately carved biblical scenes, marble columns, and soaring cupolas. One chapel contains a veil said to have been the one used by St. Veronica to wipe Christ's face, while some Ribera paintings and a bronze candelabrum with 15 arms are on display in the *Museo de la Catedral* (open Fridays through Sundays from 11 AM to 1 PM; admission charge).

For further information on the sights of Jaén, which include the *Museo Provincial* (27 Paseo de la Estación; phone: 53-250320), currently closed for restoration but scheduled to reopen this year, and several churches (the Capilla de San Andrés in particular), contact the tourist office (1 Calle Arquitecto Berges; phone: 53-222737).

CHECKING IN/EATING OUT: *Parador de Santa Catalina* – It incorporates much of the original structure of Jaén's Moorish castle and looks like something out of a Hollywood epic, with beamed sitting rooms replete with massive chandeliers, tapestries, armor, and coats of arms. Have lunch in the vast dining room with vaulted ceiling or spend the night in a canopied bed. There are 43 air conditioned rooms. Castillo de Santa Catalina, Jaén (phone: 53-264411). Moderate.

En Route from Jaén – Double back on N323 about 6 miles (10 km) to the junction of N321, a two-lane road called the Ruta del Renacimiento (Renaissance Route). Indeed, some of Spain's finest Renaissance architecture lies ahead. Baeza is 30 miles (48 km) from Jaén, Ubeda 35½ miles (57 km).

BAEZA: This sleepy little town looks as though its residents had closed the gates centuries ago and let time pass them by. Forget about the stark white of most Andalusian towns; Baeza's buildings of golden stone look Italian. Because it lies near the border with Castile and was an important frontier town during the Reconquest, Baeza, in 1227, was the first Andalusian town to be retaken by Christian armies. Subsequently, it became a showplace of grand mansions and religious buildings.

A good map for a walking tour is available at the tourist office (Plaza del Pópulo; phone: 53-740444). The office is housed in the Casa del Pópulo, a former courthouse with decorative Plateresque windows and six doors that once opened onto as many notaries' offices; the square was named for the four carved lions that grace the fountain. The Roman figure of a woman is said to be that of Hannibal's wife — her modern head is a replacement for the original, which was cut off during the Spanish Civil War when an anti-clerical mob mistook her for the Virgin. Also on the square is a former slaughterhouse that would be called a mansion in most other towns.

The most interesting part of Baeza surrounds the 16th-century, late Gothic Catedral de Santa María and the square of the same name. The church (open from 10:30 AM to 1 PM and from 5 to 7 PM) has an outstanding main chapel with gilded relief work and a hexagonal pulpit. A silver monstrance that sits behind a painting is an unusual feature: Put in 25 pesetas and the art rolls up, music commences, and the monstrance revolves in dazzling light. Then, just as suddenly, the show ends — until another coin is inserted. Across from the cathedral is the 17th-century Seminario de San Felipe Neri, whose carved main façade is covered with inscriptions written with bull's blood (as was the tradition) by graduates. Nearby is the ornate Palacio de Jabalquinto, built in the early 16th century, with huge studded doors, a harmonious main façade, and an interior patio with marble columns. (Both buildings are open only sporadically.)

CHECKING IN/EATING OUT: *Juanito* – A modest, old-fashioned hostelry on the road to Ubeda, it's better known as a restaurant of classic Spanish cooking, patronized by noble and commoner alike, than as a hotel. (Restaurant reservations advised on weekends.) There's no air conditioning in the 21 rooms. Avenida Arca del Agua, Baeza (phone: 53-740040). Inexpensive.

UBEDA: Just 5½ miles (9 km) away from Baeza and even more impressive is historic Ubeda, known as the Florence of Andalusia — and with good reason. Its Plaza Vázquez de Molina is the most architecturally harmonious square in Andalusia, an oasis from another time lined with Renaissance monuments to all the glory that was 16th-century Spain. To reach the square, follow the Conjunto Monumental signs into the confusing town center. Along the way, you'll pass the bustling Plaza de Andalucía, with a graceful clock tower, outdoor tables for relaxing, and a bullet-ridden statue of a Francoist general — in short, everything a small Andalusian town square should have.

Several noteworthy buildings front the shaded Plaza Vázquez de Molina. The 16th-century Renaissance Casa de las Cadenas serves as the town hall; its interior patio of slender arches was an elegant touch by architect Andrés de Vandelvira, who designed most of old Ubeda. The square's architectural highlight is the Iglesia de San Salvador, whose massive golden façade and sumptuous interior make it one of the best examples of Spanish Renaissance architecture. Built in the early 16th century as the family chapel and mausoleum for Francisco de los Cobos, secretary of the Holy Roman Emperor Charles V, it is still privately owned, but a live-in guide shows visitors the ornate altarpiece crowned by a sculpture of the Transfiguration and an enormous wrought-iron grille (open from 10 AM to 1 PM and from 4 to 7 PM; admission charge). The little Iglesia de Santa María, also on the square, stands on the site of a mosque that was demolished after Christians took the Moorish town of Ubbadat in the early 13th century.

The Muslim legacy survives here in the traditional crafts of esparto weaving and pottery making, and the Exposición de Artesanía Ubetense, next to the Casa de las Cadenas, displays green Ubeda ceramics, esparto rugs, and other examples of the best of this timeless craftsmanship. (Later, visit the San Millán district — especially Calle Valencia — to see artisans at work.)

Before the Plaza Vázquez de Molina was completed, a nearby square, the Plaza Primero de Mayo, was the heart of Ubeda; an outdoor market, sports events, and, while the Inquisition reigned, burnings at the stake took place here. On one corner today is the old City Hall, featuring a double row of elegant Gothic arches. Similar touches are found in the Iglesia de San Pablo on the plaza's opposite side, parts of which date from around 1400. Another Ubeda sight, the (former) Hospital de Santiago, a Vandelvira masterpiece, sits on Carrera del Obispo Cobos, far from the historic center. This imposing 16th-century edifice has been called the "Escorial of Andalusia." Note the monumental staircase leading upstairs from the inner courtyard and the woodcarvings in the chapel. Open from 9 AM to 2 PM and from 5 to 8 PM; closed Sundays. No admission charge. Ubeda's tourist office is on Plaza del Ayuntamiento (phone: 53-750897).

CHECKING IN/EATING OUT: *Parador Condestable Dávalos* – This time, a 16th-century palace served as inspiration for government architects, who converted it into a comfortable, history-steeped hotel. Antiques and fresh flowers fill the 26 air conditioned rooms (ask for number 12 for the best view). The moderately priced restaurant offers excellent traditional cuisine. Reservations unnecessary. 1 Plaza Vázquez de Molina, Ubeda (phone: 53-750345). Moderate.

En Route from Ubeda – Our Andalusia tour officially ends in Ubeda. Travelers can return to Castile and Madrid via Bailén, 25½ miles (41 km) west on N322, or proceed northeast toward Valencia via Albacete, also on N322.

Extremadura

Far to the west of Madrid, close against the Portuguese border, lies a remote and often rugged region that played a leading role in one of the most important chapters of Spanish history. During the 15th and 16th centuries, this vast, landlocked area exported its sons to the farthest reaches of the earth to chart unfamiliar and hazardous oceans to discover the New World of the Americas. Extremadura was the cradle of the conquistadores, men like Francisco Pizarro, an uneducated swineherd who set off to conquer for the Spanish the land they called Peru and to plunder the gold of the Inca. Pizarro came from Trujillo, today one of the jewels of Extremadura, a small town rich in fine 16th-century palaces built with American gold. Also from Trujillo was Francisco de Orellana, the first European to explore the Amazon, while Vasco Núñez de Balboa, who made the first European discovery of the Pacific Ocean, and Hernando de Soto, who colonized Florida for the Spaniards, both hailed from the southern Extremaduran town of Jerez de los Caballeros. Pedro de Valdivia, who conquered present-day Chile, was born and brought up in Villanueva de la Serena.

Today, the names of Extremadura's towns and cities echo all over Latin America. There are Trujillos in Peru, Honduras, and Venezuela. Medellín, the small Extremaduran citadel that produced Hernán Cortés, the European discoverer of Mexico, can also be found in Mexico itself, as well as in Colombia and Argentina. Numerous other New World sites, including the Caribbean island of Guadeloupe, take their name from the mountain Monastery of Guadalupe, the very place in which Queen Isabella of Spain drew up a contract with Christopher Columbus for his voyage of discovery to America and in which the first American Indians brought back as prisoners were baptized by their conquerors.

The modern-day sons of Extremadura continue to travel far from home, although now they are more likely to go to the big cities of Spain or the more industrially advanced north of Europe than to cross the Atlantic. Life can still be harsh and primitive in this wild corner of the country, and emigration is an attractive option for young people not drawn by the prospect of a life of rustic peace and tranquillity.

For the visitor, however, it is precisely this remoteness that gives Extremadura its appeal. As a region, it does not have the obvious charm of Andalusia, directly to the south. Its towns are not as lively as Madrid or Barcelona. There is no coastline and, consequently, there are none of the sophisticated resorts that can be found on the Costa del Sol or the Costa Brava. It is still largely undiscovered and undeveloped as a tourist spot, and in the towns that do have tourist offices, very few of the staff speak anything but Spanish.

For those who can bear to do without such refinements, the rewards are great. Extremadura is an area of immense natural beauty, with vast expanses of rolling countryside broken only occasionally by little whitewashed *pueblos,* or villages, peopled by shepherds and their families. In the north, the fertile plains of wheat, cotton, and tobacco give way to soft hills and tumbling olive groves, then to the snow-capped peaks of the Gredos and Gata mountain ranges. Farther south, the rich red soil is thickly wooded with pungent eucalyptus trees and holm and cork oaks. In spring and early summer, before the heat has burned the landscape brown, carpets of wildflowers stretch for miles.

Three great rivers bathe the region. The Guadiana is in the south, forming the border with Portugal for part of its length. The calm, slow-flowing Tagus is in the center, its high cliffs dotted with castles. Farther north, where the hills turn into mountains, the tributaries of the Alagon become rushing streams and waterfalls that plunge from huge granite boulders into pools of ice-cold, crystal-clear water.

Eagles, vultures, and buzzards all can be spotted in the more remote corners of the countryside, given a little patience. Storks can be seen everywhere, even in the towns, where they make their giant nests atop the towers and belfries of castles and churches. On the ground there are deer, wild ponies, dozens of species of lizards, and the lynx, now extinct in many parts of Europe.

But all is not wildlife and wide-open spaces. The region is also rich in architecture and history. The towns, especially Cáceres, Trujillo, and Guadalupe, contain palaces and fine churches built by the Spanish nouveaux riches with gold brought back in galleons from their newly discovered territories — fantastic examples of 16th-century one-upmanship. Mérida has a museum housing the finest collection of Roman finds in the whole of Spain — fittingly, since Extremadura was one of the chief colonies of the Romans' vast province of Lusitania, and Mérida, founded during the 1st century BC, was Lusitania's capital. The Visigoths, who came later, also left an important heritage, particularly in finely tooled stonework and jewelry. Again, Mérida has some of the best examples of this early Christian civilization.

During the 8th century, the Arabs arrived from North Africa, and they stayed for 500 years. They left behind them magnificently constructed castle-fortresses, which still dominate many a skyline in the region, as well as countless examples of more decorative architecture using elaborately sculpted friezes and richly designed *azulejos,* the glazed pottery tiles that still face many houses and doorways throughout the region.

Several orders of knights established themselves in Extremadura, making it their role to chase out the Moors and to protect Christian pilgrims on the long and arduous journey north to the sacred shrine of Santiago de Compostela, in Galicia. They controlled vast areas of land, given to them by grateful Spanish nobles in payment for their services. Alcántara, Monfragüe, Mérida, and Cáceres are still steeped in the history of these crusading orders, which wielded immense political and financial power in the late Middle Ages.

During the 19th century, Napoleon's armies tried to turn the plains of Extremadura into a French province. The region was the scene of much fierce fighting before the future Duke of Wellington, allied with the Spanish, came from his fortress stronghold in Portugal to beat the French back over the Pyrenees. Badajoz, near the Portuguese border, was the scene of a particularly brutal battle in 1812, with 5,000 of Wellington's 15,000 troops killed as they tried to storm the French-held ramparts.

The route outlined below enters the northeast corner of Extremadura, turning off the main N-V highway from Madrid just short of the small town of Navalmoral de la Mata and running down through the foothills of the Sierra de Altamira Mountains to the famous sanctuary town of Guadalupe. From there, it continues west to Trujillo, birthplace of two of Spain's most famous conquistadores, southwest to Mérida, with its fine amphitheater and other Roman remains, and west again to Badajoz, a town dominated by the imposing Moorish castle where generations of Muslim kings made their base. The itinerary then proceeds north to Cáceres, richly evocative of Spain's golden age, and on up to Plasencia, a charming town and a good base for trips into the picturesque valleys of the far north of Extremadura. Among these, a visit to the lovely wooded Monastery of Yuste, where the Holy Roman Emperor Charles V spent his last days, is particularly recommended. The total length of the route is between 422 and 453 miles (675/725 km), depending on excursions.

A few words of warning are warranted. The roads in Extremadura are generally good (provided you stick to those recommended in the itinerary) — with one notable exception in the remote Las Hurdes area, which can be explored as an optional detour. Distances are often greater than they seem on a map, however, and gas stations can be few and far between, so allow plenty of time and keep the tank full. Don't rely on renting a car locally, because tourism is still very new here and as yet there are only a few car rental offices in operation.

The food of the region is good and hearty, with lots of game and meat dishes. Extremadura is one of Spain's main cattle raising areas — black bulls are visible everywhere along a drive through the countryside. The bravest ones will end up in the bullring; the others will be used to make big, thick steaks. Lamb and pork are both good, and the strong, deep pink ham is superb. (Extremaduran pigs are reportedly fed on snakes to make the flesh more tender.) Fish such as trout and tench feature widely on most menus. Another favorite meal is braised partridge. The region produces some good wines, including two particularly noteworthy ones: the strong rosé from Cañamero and the justly renowned, full-bodied red named for the Marqués de Cáceres.

Extremadura is particularly rich in *paradores,* the state-run inns usually converted from old monasteries or castles. Staying in them is the best way to get a real taste of the region, but be sure to book well in advance, as they tend to fill up quickly, even outside the high season. As a general guide, the north is likely to prove more captivating than the south, so it's a good idea to allow more time around Trujillo, Cáceres, and Guadalupe when planning. Expect to pay $70 or more for a double room in hotels listed as expensive, from $45 to $70 in moderate hotels, and under $45 in the inexpensive ones. Expensive meals are $40 and up for two; moderate, between $25 and $40; and inexpensive, under $25.

GUADALUPE: Entering Extremadura from the east along the main N-V highway from Madrid, take the well-marked turnoff for Guadalupe to the left, 2 miles (3 km) before Navalmoral de la Mata. The road is narrow and often winding, but the drive is spectacular, through olive groves and chestnut woods and, 2½ miles (4 km) outside Guadalupe, past the exquisite Humilladero Hermitage, a small chapel in a panoramic spot where pilgrims of more impressionable times would fall to their knees at the first sight of the Monasterio de Guadalupe below them. It's not hard to understand why. The crenelated, turreted extravaganza makes a dramatic sight, nestling in the lee of the Guadalupe mountains, the old village that grew up as an adjunct to it hugging its doorstep. The edifice, a mishmash of architectural styles, honors the Virgin of Guadalupe, a small wooden statue reputedly carved by St. Luke and found buried on the site in the 13th century. At first, only a chapel marked the spot; the monastery was founded in the mid-14th century by King Alfonso XI, after he successfully invoked the Virgin's aid in a battle against the Moors in 1340. The conquistadores adopted the shrine as their own and heaped treasures on it from the New World, making it one of the most elaborate and richly decorated monasteries in the whole of Spain. Conquered Inca leaders were brought here to be baptized. Freed Christian slaves left their chains here in votive thanks. Although the monastery was abandoned in the 19th century, then restored and taken over by Franciscan friars in 1908 (it was originally run by Hieronymite monks), it is still, for the Spanish, one of the most important places of pilgrimage in Christendom, as well as a symbol of *hispanidad,* the cultural and linguistic link between Spain and Spanish America.

A guided tour (Spanish language) takes visitors around the complex (open daily, from 9:30 AM to 1 PM and 3:30 to 7 PM; admission charge; phone: 27-367000), including the manuscript room, which houses giant illuminated books of hours, and the sacristy, which has eight paintings by Extremadura's most famous artist, the 17th-century painter Francisco de Zurbarán. The 14th-century church, which was added to in later centuries, has an altarpiece with works by Carducci, Giraldo de Merlo, and Jorge Manuel Theotocópuli, son of El Greco. One of the main features of the monastery is the 15th-century Mudéjar cloister, unmistakably Moorish in influence and faced with glazed colored tiles (there is a smaller, Gothic cloister in the monastery as well). The tour ends with the crowning glory, a visit to the Camarín de la Virgen, where the Virgin reposes on a richly worked altar, a casket to one side of her stuffed full of peseta notes, gifts from grateful or hopeful pilgrims.

CHECKING IN: *Parador Zurbarán* – This imposing 15th-century palace opposite the monastery was founded by one of its priors to take care of pilgrims who came to Guadalupe. Queen Isabella stayed here — in fact, this was the building used for the signing of contracts with explorers setting out for the New World. Today, it is one of the region's most comfortable hotels, with 40 rooms, a swimming pool, and an excellent restaurant serving typical dishes such as *cabrito asado al tomillo* (roast kid with thyme). 10 Calle Marqués de la Romana, Guadalupe (phone: 27-367075). Expensive.

***Hospedería Real Monasterio* –** Housed in the monastery itself and run by the enterprising Franciscan friars. A stay here is an experience — it's not deluxe, but you are in a monastery! The 46 rooms are arranged around the Gothic cloister and furnished with hand-carved monks' tables and chests. Both hotel and restaurant, which serves an excellent fixed-price menu, are extraordinarily reasonable. Plaza Juan Carlos I, Guadalupe (phone: 27-367000). Moderate.

EATING OUT: *El Cordero* – The best restaurant in town, apart from those in the hotels. It's run by the very capable Angelita, whose specialty is *cordero asado,* the roast lamb from which the restaurant takes its name. Open daily. Reservations unnecessary. 11 Calle Convento, Guadalupe (phone: 27-367131). Moderate.

En Route from Guadalupe – Take the road marked Mérida and follow it down through more olive groves, over a gurgling stream on the valley floor, and on to Cañamero, where a stop to taste the deservedly famous local wine would not be a bad idea. But be careful if driving: The pale red liquid is deceptively strong. At Zorita, 32 miles (51 km) from Guadalupe, continue toward Trujillo instead of turning left for Mérida.

TRUJILLO: This enchanting town occupies a special place in Spanish history as the home of some of the most celebrated conquistadores. Francisco Pizarro, who waged war on the Inca to win Peru for Spain, was born here, the illegitimate son of a nobleman. A bronze statue of him astride a fiery steed, ready for battle, dominates the pretty Plaza Mayor in the heart of the Old Town. The statue, an early-20th-century work by the American sculptors Charles Runse and Mary Harriman, has its exact double in Peru's capital city, Lima. Trujillo's two other famous sons were Diego García de Paredes, who founded another Trujillo in Venezuela, and Francisco de Orellana, the first European to explore the Amazon. The Old Town, perched on a granite hill above the modern one, is full of grand 16th-century mansions financed with wealth brought back from the new territories. Of particular interest is the Palacio del Marqués de la Conquista, built by Pizarro's legitimate half-brother Hernando; it still contains busts of the explorer's family. The 13th-century Santa María church holds the tombs of some of the town's most prominent nobles, including García de Paredes, and is also noted for its 15th- to 16th-century Gothic altar. Towering over everything is the impressive Arab-built Castillo — a walk up to its ramparts at sunset gives a spectacular view over the town's rooftops. In Trujillo's narrow back streets, its people still live as they always have, the men tending their sheep and goats, and the women doing their washing by hand. In the evening, the main square is an evocative place to sit and sip a glass of sherry before going on to dine at one of the town's several good restaurants.

CHECKING IN: *Parador de Trujillo* – Beautifully converted from the 16th-century Convent of Santa Clara and tastefully decorated with furniture from that time. Built around a central cloister, it has 46 air conditioned rooms, a small swimming pool, and an excellent restaurant, housed in the old refectory. Try the *morteruelo,* a pâté of chicken, partridge, and rabbit, and the *cochinillo asado,* roast suckling pig. Plaza de Santa Clara, Trujillo (phone: 27-321350). Expensive.

Las Cigüeñas – This modern, air conditioned, 78-room hotel doesn't have the charm of the *parador,* but it's a comfortable alternative if the latter is booked. It's situated on the main highway from Madrid, a mile before Trujillo. N-V, Km 253, Trujillo (phone: 27-321250). Moderate.

EATING OUT: *La Cadena* – A relatively new venture, it's housed in a fine 18th-century palace in the main square, has whitewashed walls decorated with local ceramics, and serves a very reasonable fixed-price menu. Open daily. No reservations. Plaza Mayor, Trujillo (phone: 27-321463). Moderate.

Hostal Pizarro – Also in the main square, this restaurant produces some fine local dishes, including *estofado de perdices,* a partridge casserole, and a good *cordero asado,* roast lamb. Open daily. Reservations unnecessary. Plaza Mayor, Trujillo (phone: 27-320255). Moderate.

Mesón La Troya – Concha Alvarez, the delightful old woman who runs this superb restaurant, has been in the business for 50 years and still personally oversees the cooking and the dining room, imaginatively converted from former stables. The food is among the best in Extremadura. Diners receive a complimentary Spanish *tortilla* and a salad as soon as they sit down; other dishes may include *carne con tomate,* beef cooked in a tomato sauce, or *prueba de cerdo,* a wonderfully garlicky pork casserole. Don't be surprised to see the village priest — he eats here every night and has his own table. Open daily. No reservations. Plaza Mayor, Trujillo (phone: 27-321364). Inexpensive.

En Route from Trujillo – Take the N-V highway south in the direction of Mérida. After 36 miles (58 km), turn left at the signpost for Santa Amalia, and after another 4½ miles (7 km), turn right at the signpost for Medellín. The road leads over a magnificent 17th-century bridge on the Guadiana River into Medellín, a little town crowned by a well-preserved medieval castle. Medellín, which gave its name to three other towns in Latin America, owes its fame to Hernán Cortés, born here in 1485. The man who conquered the Aztec empire and colonized Mexico for the Spanish died forgotten in Spain at the age of 62, but a statue of him now dominates his home town's Plaza Mayor. Go to Plaza de España early enough, and you can watch a woman frying *churros* (fritters) in a huge vat of fat — the whole town's breakfast, evidently, judging by the lines forming outside the entrance to her small take-out place next to the tobacco shop. The town has a small but bustling market on Thursday mornings. From Medellín, retrace the route to the main N-V and turn left for Mérida.

MÉRIDA: Founded by the Romans in 25 BC as Emerita Augusta, a colony for the *emeriti,* or veterans, of the fifth and tenth Roman legions, Mérida quickly grew to be the Spanish Rome, capital of the vast and powerful province of Lusitania. The Roman ruins are among the best in Spain, with pride of place going to the Roman theater, which was built by Agrippa, son-in-law of Emperor Augustus, shortly after the city's foundation and had seating for 6,000. In summer, classical plays and flamenco dances are performed here. Nearby is a Roman amphitheater which held 14,000 spectators. (Both theaters are open daily, from 8 AM to 9:30 PM; admission charge; there's ample parking near the entrance.) The *Museo Nacional de Arte Romano* (National Museum of Roman Art), in a new building forming part of the theater complex, not only is acknowledged to be the finest repository of Roman artifacts in Spain, but also has drawn kudos for its design. It incorporates a Roman road, discovered when the museum was being built in the early 1980s, and contains a superb collection of statues, glassware, pottery, coins, and mosaics (open Tuesdays through Saturdays, from 10 AM to 2 PM and 4 to 6 PM; Sundays from 10 AM to 2 PM; Mondays from 4 to 6 PM; admission charge). Two Roman houses near the theaters have been excavated, revealing an intricate water system and some fine mosaics (open from Tuesdays through Saturdays, from 8 AM to 1 PM and 4 to 7 PM; Sundays and holidays, from 9 AM to 2 PM; admission charge). Other Roman remains include an exquisite Temple of Diana, recently restored; the circus, used for chariot racing; the well-preserved Trajan's Arch; the Milagros Aqueduct, the better preserved of two that served the city; and the 60-arched Roman bridge across the Guadiana, the longest bridge ever built in Spain.

Mérida's past as an Arab fiefdom is best seen in the Alcazaba, a Moorish castle built during the 9th century (open Tuesdays through Saturdays, from 8 AM to 1 PM and 4 to 7 PM; Sundays and holidays, from 9 AM to 2 PM; admission charge). Inside this fortress, note the cistern, a fine example of sophisticated Arab engineering — its construction assured the Moors a constant supply of water from the Guadiana. One last sight not to be missed in Mérida is the Hornito de Santa Eulalia, a shrine dedicated to the little girl who, according to local legend, was baked in an oven (*horno*) in the 4th century, after she spat in the eye of a pagan official rather than renounce Christianity.

CHECKING IN: *Las Lomas* – A recently built 134-room hotel, complete with air conditioning and a large swimming pool, a mile (1.6 km) out of town on the road (N-V) to Madrid. Carretera Madrid, Km 338, Mérida (phone: 24-311011). Expensive.

Parador Vía de la Plata – The 16th-century building housing this air conditioned, 44-room *parador* was at first a convent and later a prison. In a quiet but still central part of town, it has a markedly Moorish feel about it, with richly tiled floors and a cool, cloistered courtyard. There's a good restaurant, serving Spanish and Extremaduran specialties. 3 Plaza de Queipo de Llano, Mérida (phone: 24-301540). Expensive.

Emperatriz – Right in the heart of town in the main square, this 16th-century palace claims to have offered hospitality to such illustrious guests as the Holy Roman Emperor Charles V, Queen Isabella of Portugal, and Kings Philip II and III of Spain. Now a 41-room hotel, its entrance is a wonderful Moorish galleried foyer faced with intricate tiles. Its restaurant, popular with local folks, serves specialties that include *tencas fritas con limón* (fried tench) and *gazpacho ajo blanco,* an Extremaduran version of the Andalusian iced soup. 19 Plaza de España, Mérida (phone: 24-313800). Moderate.

Nova Roma – A clean, comfortable, modern hotel near the Roman theater, amphitheater, and museum, with 28 rooms, but no restaurant. 42 Calle Suárez Somonte, Mérida (phone: 24-311201). Moderate.

EATING OUT: Nicolás – Starched linen tablecloths and lots of marble grace this restaurant, which serves a good fixed-price menu with regional specialties. Open daily. Reservations unnecessary. Calle Félix Valverde, Mérida (phone: 24-313206). Moderate.

Briz – Close to the *Nicolás,* but not as smart. It may not look like much from the outside, but it turns out some fine local dishes, including *perdiz en salsa,* a casserole of partridge, and an interesting appetizer of artichokes and chorizo sausage. It also serves an excellent red house wine. Open daily. Reservations unnecessary. Calle Félix Valverde, Mérida (phone: 24-319307). Moderate to inexpensive.

Mesón Benito – It would be easy to miss this one, since it's tucked away in a small square off Mérida's main street, but that would be a pity, because it's easily the best eatery in town, with good regional cooking, an excellent fixed-price lunch menu that changes every day, and extremely friendly service. The walls are covered with pictures of Extremadura's most famous bullfighters. Very reasonably priced, even in the evening, when the menu goes à la carte. Open daily. Reservations unnecessary. Calle Santa Eulalia, Mérida (phone: 24-315502). Moderate to inexpensive.

En Route from Mérida – Leaving Mérida, take the N-V highway west about 39 miles (62 km) to Badajoz.

BADAJOZ: The most populous city in Extremadura and capital of the province of Badajoz, one of the two provinces into which the region is divided (the other is Cáceres), Badajoz was once one of the most important Arab strongholds in western Spain, home to Muslim kings who left behind an impressive castle-fortress and massive ramparts. Today, it's hard not to get the impression that the town has seen better days, hardly surprising considering its troubled history. Its frontier position, just 3 miles (5 km) from the Portuguese border, has made it particularly vulnerable, and it has been torn by just about every war fought on the Iberian Peninsula in the past 500 years. One of the worst scenes of carnage occurred in 1812, during the Peninsular War, when 5,000 of the Duke of Wellington's 15,000 troops died here trying to drive Napoleon's occupying forces back toward France. More recently, in the early stages of the Spanish Civil War, Badajoz was the scene of a brutal massacre when Franco's Nationalist forces captured it and then rounded up scores of citizens and herded them into the bullring, where they were summarily executed by machine gun.

Badajoz is not the kind of place in which to spend a great deal of time, but it is fascinating to climb up to the top of the town to get an idea of what it once was. Visit the Alcazaba, the Arab fortress (open daily, from 9 AM to 1 PM and 3 to 6 PM), and take a closer look at the Torre del Apendiz, known locally as the Torre de Espantaperros, or "Dog Scarer Tower." This vantage point also gives a good view of the Puente de las Palmas, the fine 16th-century bridge that leads across the Guadiana and into town through the crenelated Puerta de las Palmas gate. The area around the Alcazaba is still very Moorish in feeling — a glimpse into the courtyards of some of the houses reveals typically Arabic tiles and ornate columns. Farther down, in the town's main square, Plaza de España, stands a monument to the 16th-century painter Luis de Morales, nicknamed "the Divine," a native of Badajoz. Several of his works can be seen in the *Museo de Bellas Artes* (open Mondays through Saturdays, from 10 PM to 2 PM; admission charge), as well as in the 13th-century Gothic cathedral of San Juan, which stands in the same square. Other works in the cathedral are by Zurbarán and Ribera. The Badajoz Tourist Office is on Avenida de Huelva (phone: 24-222763); note that the office is expected to move this year.

CHECKING IN: Zurbarán – Badajoz has no outstanding hostelries such as the *paradores* of Trujillo, Guadalupe, and Mérida, but this hotel in the city center is an acceptable place to spend a day or two. It has 215 rooms, air conditioning, a big garden, a swimming pool, and a good restaurant. Paseo de Castelar, Badajoz (phone: 24-223741). Moderate.

Lisboa – A comfortable, modern, 176-room, air conditioned hotel that, as its name suggests, is on the road to Portugal, just under a mile (1km) out of town. 13 Avenida de Elvas, Badajoz (phone: 24-238200). Moderate to inexpensive.

Río – Close to the *Lisboa* on the way to Portugal and similar in quality and style, with 90 air conditioned rooms. Avenida Adolfo Díaz Ambrona, Badajoz (phone: 24-237600). Moderate to inexpensive.

EATING OUT: Mesón El Tronco – The only real restaurant in town (although there are several bars and cafés that serve food), and very good it is, too. It offers fixed-price menus, named for the various towns and regions of Extremadura, as well as a lively bar with an excellent range of *tapas.* Closed Sundays. Reservations unnecessary. 16 Calle Muñoz Torrero, Badajoz (phone: 24-222076). Moderate.

El Sótano – A good place for a quick lunch. The bar has a tempting array of *tapas* — ham, chorizo (sausage), small fried fish — or order something more substantial, such as the *caldereta de cordero,* a typical Extremaduran lamb casserole. Open daily. No reservations. 6 Calle Virgen de la Soledad, Badajoz (phone: 24-223161 or 24-220019). Inexpensive.

La Panda – Right on the main square, this bar has an upstairs restaurant that serves a daily three-course set menu of exceptional value. No reservations. 11 Plaza de España, Badajoz (phone: 24-222152 or 24-220537). Very inexpensive.

CÁCERES: The capital of the province of the same name, Cáceres is 57 miles (91 km) northeast of Badajoz via N523. The city is really in three parts, one of which is an Old Town surrounded by Moorish walls and so superbly preserved that it has served as a backdrop for more than one film that is set in the Middle Ages. A stroll through the sandy-colored maze of narrow streets in this Old Quarter is like stepping back hundreds of years, to the 15th and 16th centuries, when noblemen vied with each other to build more beautiful mansions and palaces with the wealth acquired in their exploits across the Atlantic. Almost every house bears a coat of arms, proudly carved out of the tawny stonework. Until the late 15th century, most of them had battlemented defensive towers as well, but Queen Isabella ordered all but one — that of the Casa de las Cigüeñas (House of the Storks) — to be razed in an effort to put a halt to internecine fighting. All is quiet now, and storks nest everywhere in old Cáceres — atop the Church of San Mateo, site of a former mosque, and up on the spire of the Church of Santa María. Step inside this latter church, in the main square of the walled city, to see the tombs of some of Cáceres's most famous citizens, marked with their heraldic crests. Keep an eye out for the 15th-to-16th-century Palacio de Ovando in the same square, for the intricately carved façade on the 15th-century Palacio de los Golfines de Abajo nearby, and, in a corner of the walled city, for the 16th-century Casa de Toledo-Moctezuma, where Juan Caño, a henchman of Hernán Cortés, lived with his wife, a daughter of Montezuma, the last Aztec emperor. The 16th-century Palacio de Godoy is just outside the walls. Still in the Old Town, on Calle de los Condes, a quiet back street, a plaque bears witness to another era in Spanish history. Here, reads the inscription, Generalísimo Francisco Franco was declared the supreme ruler of Spain. The whole effect is made more dramatic by a huge splotch of brown paint that someone has thrown at the plaque.

Near Plaza de San Mateo, the 17th-century Casa de los Veletas (House of the Weather Vanes), site of the onetime Moorish Alcázar, today serves as the town's *Museo Arqueológico.* It incorporates an interesting Arab cistern and houses collections of Celtic, Roman, and Visigothic remains. The Roman colony at Cáceres, founded during the 1st century BC, was one of the five most important in the province of Lusitania. Destroyed by barbarians, it was rebuilt by the Arabs, who called it Cazris, the forerunner of its modern name. The Moors used it as a fortress town from which to embark on other incursions, and built the walls that still stand today, setting them atop Roman foundations.

Besides the walled Old Town at the top, Cáceres has a much more bustling area at the foot of the walls in the vicinity of the Plaza del General Mola; the main square and the location of the tourist office (phone: 27-246347). Much farther down is the sprawling New Town, which houses most of the shops, hotels, and offices. Two miles (3 km) east of town, on a road that climbs steeply up through olive trees to the peak of the Sierra de la Mosca, stands the sanctuary of Nuestra Señora de la Montaña (Our Lady of the Mountain). From here, there is a spectacular view over Cáceres itself, with the Gredos mountains to the north and the Sierra de San Pedro range to the south.

 CHECKING IN: *Alcántara* – In the new part of town, along with most of the hotels in Cáceres. This one is comfortable and modern, with 67 rooms and air conditioning. No restaurant. 14 Avenida Virgen de Guadalupe, Cáceres (phone: 27-228900). Moderate.

Extremadura – One of the nicest hotels in town, just opposite the *Alcántara,* with 69 air conditioned rooms, gardens, a swimming pool, and a restaurant. 5 Avenida Virgen de Guadalupe, Cáceres (phone: 27-221604). Moderate.

EATING OUT: *El Atrio* – A chic establishment in the new part of town. It offers haute cuisine and has built up a faithful following. Open daily. Reservations advised. 30 Avenida de España, Bloque 4, Cáceres (phone: 27-242928). Expensive.

La Malvasia – Also in the new part of town, but serving more regional cooking than *El Atrio.* For dessert, try the *higo chumbo,* as exotic as its name suggests: it's an ice cream made of prickly pear. Open daily. Reservations unnecessary. 5 Calle Antonio Silva, Cáceres (phone: 27-244609). Expensive.

El Figón – One of the most popular restaurants in Cáceres, it serves finely cooked local dishes. Open daily. Reservations advised. 14 Plaza San Juan, Cáceres (phone: 27-244362). Expensive to moderate.

La Bodega Medieval – This attractive eatery, hidden away in a quiet alley of the walled Old Town, has painted beamed ceilings and a bottle-lined bodega next door, where customers can drink an aperitif and eat *tapas* before dining. On the menu, watch for *perdiz al estilo Alcántara,* a casserole of partridge with mushrooms, red pepper, and juniper berries. Open daily. Reservations advised. 1 Calle Orellana, Cáceres (phone: 27-245458). Moderate.

En Route from Cáceres – Instead of taking the main road north to Plasencia, head west on N521 toward Valencia de Alcántara, and after 7½ miles (12 km), at Malpartida de Cáceres, turn right onto C523, following it through Brozas to Alcántara. This quiet, peaceful town takes its name from the Arab word for bridge, *al kantara,* specifically referring to the magnificent Roman construction that spans the ravine of the Tagus River just below the town. Alcántara's position close to the Portuguese border has made it an important strategic point throughout history. After the Romans and the Arabs, the military order of the Knights of Alcántara made it their headquarters during the early 13th century, using it as a base for incursions against other Moorish strongholds in the area. The knights' now-crumbling castle can still be seen at the top of the town. Queen Isabella of Spain and her aunt, Beatrice of Portugal, signed a treaty here in 1479, ending years of enmity between the two countries. Napoleon's army occupied the town during the 19th century, billeting troops in the 16th-century Convent of San Benito.

From Alcántara, follow the signs to Mata de Alcántara, and turn left there for Garrovillas. The road passes fields strewn with giant, strangely shaped boulders, clusters of conical stone cattle sheds, and then some wild countryside, relieved only by fig trees and prickly pears, before coming out onto the main N630 highway, where a left turn leads to Plasencia. Along the way, a half-ruined 2nd-century Roman bridge still stands just outside Cañaveral.

PLASENCIA: Its name — derived from the Latin for "may it be pleasing to God and man," which is what Alfonso VIII hoped it would be when he rebuilt it in the 12th century after its recapture from the Moors — suggests that Plasencia is a charming town. With its whitewashed houses, narrow streets, and flowers on almost every wrought-iron balcony, it is that, as well as an ideal base to explore the north of Extremadura, one of the most beautiful corners of Spain as far as natural scenery is concerned. The town is set in a bend of the Jerte River and is crowned by a splendid cathedral, part 13th-century Romanesque and part late 15th-century Gothic, especially dramatic at sunset. The choir stalls, carved by Rodrigo Alemán during the 16th century, depict episodes from the Bible and from daily life in Extremadura — look for the scenes from an old-style bullfight. The area around the cathedral, containing the 13th-century San Nicolás church and, in a quiet plaza dotted with orange trees nearby, the magnificent Church of San Vicente, is the most interesting from a historical point of view. The porticoed Plaza Mayor, the town's main square, is a pleasant place to have a drink and watch the green man on top of the town hall at the north end of the square spring into action to strike the hours. If visiting the town on a Tuesday, note the market, which has been held in Plasencia since the 13th century.

CHECKING IN: *Alfonso VIII* – The only really good hotel in town. Don't be put off by its slightly tatty exterior or by its position on one of Plasencia's busiest streets. Inside, it's comfortable and elegant, with 57 rooms and air conditioning. 32 Calle Alfonso VIII, Plasencia (phone: 27-410250). Moderate.

EATING OUT: *Nykol's* – A popular place with Plasencians, it serves refined versions of classic Extremaduran dishes. Try the gazpacho with melon and the *solomillo de cerdo crema,* a filet of pork cooked with ham and cheese. Open daily. Reservations advised. 8 Calle Pedro Isidio, Plasencia (phone: 27-415850). Expensive to moderate.

Florida – Well-cooked international dishes and a few local specialties are the fare at this restaurant, about a mile out of town on the road to Cáceres. Open daily. Reservations unnecessary. 22 Avenida de España, Plasencia (phone: 27-413858). Moderate.

En Route from Plasencia – Madrid is 160½ miles (257 km) to the east, Salamanca 82½ miles (132 km) to the north, but if there is time to spare, it's worth spending an extra couple of days in Plasencia and using it as a point from which to explore one or more of the stunningly beautiful valleys to the north of town. Each can be taken in as a day trip, with nights spent in Plasencia.

Those visiting in spring or early summer should be sure to drive up the valley of the Jerte River, taking N110 northeast out of Plasencia and passing through the small towns of Navaconcejo, Cabezuela del Valle, Jerte, and Tornavacas. The valley is one of Spain's main cherry growing areas, and in May and June the fields are a profusion of pink and white blossoms.

The Vera Valley, which also runs northeast of Plasencia, is an idyllic spot any time of the year. Here, hidden among chestnut and pine woods, is the Monasterio de Yuste, the Hieronymite monastery where the great Holy Roman Emperor Charles V retired in 1557, and where he died, riddled with gout, in September 1558. The powerful monarch's rooms can still be seen, along with the chapel where he heard mass (guided tours only; open daily from 9 AM to 1 PM and from 4 to 7 PM; admission charge). A restaurant in the monastery serves lunch, but not dinner. To reach Yuste, follow the signs out of Plasencia and drive 28 miles (45 km) along C501 to the turnoff at the village of Cuacos; the monastery is a mile (1.6 km) farther and is well signposted. Before returning to Plasencia, drive to nearby Garganta la Olla and Aldeanueva de la Vera, picturesque mountain villages with cobbled streets and ornately carved overhanging wooden balconies.

The object of the third worthwhile excursion from Plasencia is the rugged area known as Las Hurdes, where some of the most remote and most beautiful scenery of Extremadura is to be found. This region has long been branded as one of the wildest in Spain, a place whose inhabitants, it is rumored, drink bull's blood and practice devil worship. It is certainly one of Spain's more backward areas, with high levels of illiteracy, but it is also one of the most stunning to view. Rolling hills studded with olive trees give way to fir trees and rushing streams, and those traveling early in the morning will see villagers riding their basket-laden mules and donkeys out for a day's work in the fields and women washing clothes in the streams the way their great-grandmothers did.

To reach this area, take the Salamanca road (N630) north from Plasencia and, after 20 miles (32 km), turn left toward Guijo de Granadilla and follow signs for Cerezo and Caminomorisco. It's a good idea, before setting out, to pick up one of the special enlarged maps of the area from the tourist office just off the main square in Plasencia (17 Calle Trujillo; phone: 27-412766). It is almost inevitable for a first-time visitor to get lost at least once, although it hardly matters, as long as there is plenty of time — and gas in the tank. As a rule of thumb, the farther north you go, the more remote and fascinating the villages become. If there is time, the entire circuit can be made, ending in the small mountain town of Hervás — but be warned, it's a long drive and will take the better part of a day. There are *hostales* offering good but basic food and accommodations at Cerezo, Caminomorisco, Nuñomoral, and La Alberca. Better still, make a picnic of slices of local ham and cheese, with fresh bread bought from one of the village *panaderías,* and eat it near a Roman bridge, with your feet dangling in the cool waters of one of the many mountain streams. Hervás is a pretty town, with an interesting and well-preserved Jewish quarter, still much as it was when its original inhabitants, along with the rest of Spain's unconverted Jews, were expelled from the country during the late 15th century.

From Hervás, just a mile or so off N630, it's a 60-mile (96-km) drive north to Salamanca, or a 28-mile (45-km) drive south back to Plasencia.

CHECKING IN/EATING OUT: _Parador Carlos V_ – The imposing 15th-century fortified castle where Charles V stayed for several months, while his rooms were being prepared at the Monastery of Yuste, is today a hotel with 53 air conditioned rooms, a garden, a swimming pool, and a first-rate restaurant. It's 7½ miles (12 km) beyond the monastery in the direction of Jarandilla de la Vera. Carretera de Plasencia, Jarandilla de la Vera (phone: 27-560117). Expensive.

The Balearic Islands

The Balearic Islands, set in the Mediterranean Sea southeast of Barcelona and east of Valencia, have been invaded repeatedly over the centuries, as the Phoenicians, Greeks, Carthaginians, Romans, Byzantines, Vandals, Moors, French, English, and Spanish successively became the dominant Mediterranean power. Today, the invasion continues, sustained by more annual air power than that focused on London during the Blitz and more foreign troops than those that stormed Normandy in the D-Day landings. Today's invasion, however, is one of tourists. While the Balearics (Islas Baleares to the Spanish) are relatively undiscovered by Americans visiting the Continent, as far as the Europeans — and particularly the British and the Germans — are concerned, they are Europe's most popular tourist destination.

Four main islands, aligned in two pairs — Majorca (Mallorca in Spanish) and its smaller neighbor, Minorca (Menorca in Spanish), plus Ibiza and its little sidekick, Formentera — make up the Balearic Archipelago, which also includes several smaller islets. Together, they constitute Spain's Baleares province, with Palma de Mallorca, on Majorca, as provincial capital. Majorca is not only the largest of the islands but also the best known and the most developed in terms of the tourist trade. Minorca is the second-largest island, but its tourist industry lags behind that of the slightly smaller Ibiza. Only in the past few years has Minorca entered the competition in earnest, so it still has plenty of undisturbed countryside and isolated beaches appearing much today as they were decades ago. The smallest island, Formentera, is equally tranquil.

Togetherness notwithstanding, each island has had its own history, although there are some common threads. Evidence that the archipelago was the home of an advanced megalithic civilization abounds, on Majorca and above all on Minorca, in the form of monuments in stone — cylindrical *talayots,* T-shaped *taulas,* and ship-shaped *navetas* — whose exact origins and purpose remain a mystery to scholars. Later, the islanders became mercenaries in the armies of Rome and Carthage; indeed, so renowned were they among the ancients for their skill with a slingshot that the very name of the island group derives from the Greek word for sling. History records that the Romans who captured Majorca in 123 BC used leather skins to protect their ships from the islanders' lead and stone pellets.

Arab incursions began during the 8th century, and by 902 the Moors were securely installed. They remained so, under succeeding dynasties, until James I of Aragon conquered the islands for the Christians, beginning in 1229; about a half century later, an independent kingdom of Majorca was created (including Montpellier and Roussillon in France as well as the Balearics), which endured until the mid-14th century. Thanks to the islands' position along the main seagoing trading route between northern Italy and northern Europe, these were prosperous times, a virtual Balearic golden age — as Palma's imposing Gothic cathedral, begun in 1230, can testify. Prosperity continued even after the islands reverted to the kingdom of Aragon in 1343 — witness the Lonja, Palma's old stock exchange, which was booming during the 15th century. But early in the 16th century, because of a plague of pirates off their shores, the Balearics were prohibited by the newly united crown of Aragon and Castile from engaging in trade with the New World, a ban that effectively cut them off from Spain's golden age and consigned them to a backwater of history.

The islands are closely tied culturally to the region of Catalonia. Two languages are spoken: Castilian Spanish and the local language, the Balearic dialect of Catalan, which varies slightly from island to island (thus the confusion of many island place-names, spelled one way in Spanish and another in the local language).

Each island has a distinct personality. Majorca (its name, dating back to the Romans, means "the larger") is a microcosm of Spain. On this small island is the very Spanish city of Palma, complete with a massive cathedral and a medieval Old Town. On either side of the capital city are beaches endowed with blocks of high-rise hotels, tourist-oriented restaurants, and late-night discos that stretch for miles, much like areas of the Costa del Sol. Mountains rising ruggedly along the western coast provide roads as narrow and twisting as those found in the Pyrenees and views across the sea as spectacular as those found in Galicia. It is an island of contrasts. In the countryside, only a 10-minute drive from the center of Palma, almond and olive groves blanket the fields, peasants still plow the land with oxen, and black-clad women with weathered hands help with the harvest. Sundials still tell the time in some places; in others, Europe's largest discos seem to be keeping pace with the space-age future. In one port, the world's most luxurious yachts lie at anchor, while in the next, fishermen drag their boats onto the beach after working through the night.

Majorca has been a magnet for writers, painters, and musicians for more than a century. The trend may have begun in the 1830s when the consumptive composer Frédéric Chopin and his mistress, the author who used the pseudonym George Sand, shivered through an unusually cold winter here in the Valldemosa Carthusian Monastery. Despite the aggravation to his already ill health, Chopin was inspired to write some of his finest work. His lover wrote *A Winter in Majorca,* a not exactly flattering account of island life (Majorcan society had not taken kindly to this illicit couple) that was nevertheless enthusiastic about the landscape. It was later translated into English by a 20th-century visitor, the poet and novelist Robert Graves. The author of *I, Claudius* and *The White Goddess,* Graves settled in Deya and presided over a virtual artists' and writers' colony on Majorca. The steady stream of books they generated spread the word of the island's beauty, creating the mass tourism industry that boomed in the 1960s.

Minorca (whose name means "the smaller") is far less developed than either Ibiza or Majorca. It bears its own gentle charm. If the desire is to disappear for a honeymoon, this is the island to choose. For those who really want to get away from it all and enjoy beaches in solitude, quiet dinners beside cozy fishing harbors, and evenings under the stars, Minorca is the place. The island is easy to explore — no part of it is more than an hour's drive away from another. Yet it has a split personality. At the Mahón end, the unmistakable stamp of almost 8 decades of British occupation during the 18th century caters to predominantly English-speaking visitors. At the opposite end, anchored by the distinctly Spanish town of Ciudadela, Germans fill the bungalows of the tourist villages. Nightlife here is tame by Spanish standards, with only a handful of discos pulsating until dawn. Ancient megaliths and burial grounds — very much a part of the contemporary Minorcan landscape — provide the major distraction from a very lazy beach existence.

Ibiza's history doesn't jump at the visitor the way the castles and cathedrals of Majorca do, nor do cows graze around its ancient ruins as they do on Minorca. The Carthaginians established a colony here during the 7th century BC to exploit the island's salt beds, and the remains of 500 years of this Punic culture — the island's most significant remains of its past — are preserved in museum displays and carved in the hillsides as tombs. Ibiza came to the world's attention relatively recently, as a haven for writers and artists and a refuge for the counterculture in the 1950s and 1960s, and then, as this advance guard was absorbed into the mainstream, as the jet set playground that it is today. Bob Dylan, Bruce Springsteen, *U2,* and Julio Iglesias have all made regular appearances on this small island, and some of them even maintain sprawling hidden villas here. Tucked-away recording studios churn out top-ten albums, and prominent European fashion designers run shops in the narrow streets of the port. Ibiza buzzes with an international energy. Don't bother looking for Spain here. But for those who want to pull out all stops, keep themselves entertained throughout the night, sleep on the beach, and then start all over again, this is nirvana.

Ibiza (pronounced Ee-*bee*-tha) is something Disney might have created had he desired the perfect holiday island. The town of Ibiza tumbles down from a cathedral and rampart that overlook the protected harbor. Narrow streets and stairs wind between picture-perfect whitewashed houses, with views of the more modern city and the bay around every corner. Tiny boutiques hawk gaily colored scarves, T-shirts, and postcards, as well as trendy art. Outside of town, there are hundreds of private coves for swimming — some with fine white sand, others with tiny, water-smoothed pebbles — rather than mile-long beaches. High-rise hotels are limited, and the tourist enclaves blend with the island's natural lines. Nightspots are truly that — coming to life late, with live entertainment and dancing that slows down only with the dawn. Tourism is unabashedly the mainstay of the economy. During the winter months, fewer than a dozen of the island's scores of hotels remain open, and the discos pack up the speakers and lights.

Formentera, counted among the four major islands of the Balearics, is little more than a spit of sand that lies 4 miles across a strait from Ibiza. But those short miles separate two worlds. Undeveloped Formentera is a retreat from the crush of tourists packing Ibiza during the height of summer. Here, a handful of hotels cater to those seeking long sandy beaches and a quiet vacation. Visitors should take a good look as they arrive on the island — what they see is what they'll get. Don't expect any major changes in scenery, though the cliffs at the far end of the island are spectacular. Remember, the point is to relax and lie in the sun. In Formentera, there aren't many distractions from those pursuits.

SOURCES AND RESOURCES

TOURIST INFORMATION: The islands have more than one level of tourist information office (provincial, island, city), although in many cases they occupy the same premises. On Majorca, there's the Balearic Government Tourist Office (located in the arrivals area of the island's Son San Juan Airport; phone: 71-260803) and in downtown Palma (8 Avenida Rey Jaime III; phone: 71-712216). These offices provide excellent maps, listings of hotels, and information on a host of other subjects, including golf courses and deserted beaches. There are also 15 municipal tourism offices (Oficinas Municipales de Turismo) on Majorca, one in each major town. The most important are the two in Palma (11 Calle Santo Domingo; phone: 71-724090; and in a booth on Plaza de España, near the train station; phone: 71-711527). These tourist offices have schedules of events, buses, and trains, restaurant listings, and excellent local maps. The hours of all tourist offices in Palma are from 9:30 AM to 1:30 PM and from 4 to 6 PM; some of the smaller municipal tourist offices are open only in the morning.

On Minorca, the main tourist office (40 Plaza Explanada, Mahón; phone: 71-363790) is open from 9 AM to 2 PM; closed Saturdays. The office distributes maps of the island and brochures outlining the historical sights of interest in Ciudadela and Mahón, as well as the island's archaeological sites. On Ibiza, the main tourist office (13 Paseo Vara de Rey; phone: 71-301900) is open from 9:30 AM to 1 PM and from 4 to 6 PM. The office provides a map of the island and of the town of Ibiza that is helpful, although it leaves much to the imagination.

Local Coverage – Those who read a smattering of Spanish should pick up a copy of the *Diario de Mallorca,* which publishes an edition for each island, or of *Ultima Hora,* which provides a good list of activities on Majorca. There is no dearth of information in English, however. The English-language *Majorca Daily Bulletin,* published in Palma and sold at newsstands, is packed with timetables and news about happenings around the island. The *Balearic Times,* a glossy magazine published every 2 months with information on upcoming events, nightlife, and restaurant recommendations, is sold at most magazine stands; *Majorca Today,* also sold at newsstands, outlines activities and events on the islands but without the style of the *Times.* The *Reader,* published monthly and distributed free through hotels and tourist agencies, has comments on tourist activities and plenty of advertisements for upcoming events.

Telephone – The area code for the Balearic Islands is 71. If calling from within Spain, dial 971 before the local number.

CLIMATE: The weather is sparklingly clear, with average high temperatures in the low to mid-80s in July and August, the warmest months, and in the high 50s in January and February, the coldest ones. (Average lows for July and August are in the high 60s to low 70s, and in the mid- to high 40s in January and February.) The temperate climate makes the islands year-round resorts, and even February, when the almonds are in bloom, is beautiful. Note that the swimming season extends from April through October and that the average sea temperature, about 60F in April, rises to about 80F in August. Ibiza and Formentera are a bit warmer than the other two islands, and Minorca is the coolest, although the differences are minimal.

GETTING THERE: The main connection between the islands and the Continent is by air; over 7½ million visitors a year arrive by plane, another 750,000 by ferry boat. Scheduled flights arrive directly from every European capital, along with hundreds of charter flights from cities such as Manchester, England, and Hamburg, Germany. Arriving European flights land most frequently at Son San Juan Airport on Majorca, though there also are direct flights to Ibiza and Minorca. Most European airlines maintain a minimum of one flight a week during the winter; in summer, the frequency is increased.

Inbound flights from Spain are aboard *Iberia* or its subsidiary, *Aviaco*. The greatest number of daily nonstops to Majorca depart from Barcelona (35 minutes flying time) and Madrid (1 hour, 10 minutes); Alicante, Málaga, Valencia, and Vitoria also have nonstop service, in most cases on a daily basis. In addition, there are direct (not nonstop) flights from the Canary Islands. Nonstop service to Minorca is from Barcelona, Madrid, and Valencia, and there is direct sevice from Bilbao and Vigo. Nonstop service to Ibiza departs from Barcelona, Madrid, Valencia, and, in summer, Alicante. (Note that the Balearics are among the 30 Spanish destinations that may be visited by holders of the Visit Spain Airpass, which must be bought in conjunction with a round-trip air ticket between the US and Spain, at least one leg of which must be aboard *Iberia*. See *Traveling by Plane*, GETTING READY TO GO).

The airplane is also the most important form of inter-island hopping, with Palma serving as the hub. Aviaco flies several times a day between Palma and Minorca and between Palma and Ibiza, a 30-minute trip in each case. Interestingly, the flights are no more expensive than the same trip by sea.

Car and passenger ferries operated by *Trasmediterránea* link the islands with Barcelona and Valencia (and Sète, France) and, via hydrofoil, with Alicante. The company has offices in several cities (2 Via Laietana, Barcelona; phone: 3-319-8212; at 15 Avenida Manuel Soto Ingeniero, Valencia; phone: 6-367-6512 or 6-367-0704; and at 2 Explanada de España, Alicante; phone: 6-520-6011). For Majorca, there are ferries daily throughout the year from Barcelona, 6 days a week from Valencia, and twice a week from Sète, France. For Minorca, there are ferries from Barcelona daily between mid-June and mid-September and then twice a week during the winter; connections between Valencia and Mahón operate only once a week. For Ibiza, there are ferries from Barcelona daily from mid-June to mid-September and then 4 or 5 days a week, depending on the month; ferries from Valencia to Ibiza run once or twice a week. The same company operates a hydrofoil service from Alicante to Ibiza daily year-round. Inter-island service links Palma and Mahón, Minorca, on Sundays, and Palma and Ibiza twice a week year-round by normal steamer and daily in summer by hydrofoil. Travel times for these trips are as follows: Barcelona to Palma, 8 hours; Valencia to Palma, 9 hours; Barcelona to Mahón, 9 hours; Valencia to Mahón, 16 hours (via Palma); Barcelona to Ibiza, 9½ hours; Valencia to Ibiza, 7 hours; Alicante to Ibiza by hydrofoil, 2¾ hours; Palma to Mahón, 6½ hours; and Palma to Ibiza, 4½ hours, or 2 hours by hydrofoil.

Another ferry company, *Flebasa*, connects Denia on the mainland (between Valencia and Alicante) with Ibiza, docking at San Antonio Abad rather than at Ibiza town. Departures are daily year-round, and the trip takes 3 hours. The company has offices in Denia (phone: 65-784200 or 65-784011), Valencia, and Alicante.

Formentera is reached by ferry from Ibiza daily year-round (about 1 hour).

SPECIAL EVENTS: The Balearic Government Tourist Office distributes a booklet outlining the traditional festivals that take place throughout the year. For the most part, these are small local events and, except for those mentioned below, not of particular interest to visitors. On Majorca, the *Majorca Open Golf Tournament* is held annually in March at the *Santa Ponsa* course. The *Chopin Festival*, which takes place throughout the month of August, features concerts every Sunday night at the Valldemosa Carthusian Monastery, north of Palma. The *Pollensa Music Festival,* held in August and early September, features classical music on Saturdays in the Convent of Santo Domingo, Pollensa, near the northern tip of the island. (The *Fiesta de Nuestra Señora de los Angeles,* on August 2, during which the Pollensa townfolk reenact a 16th-century battle against invading pirates, is worthwhile for visitors already in the area.) The *Majorca Jazz Festival* brings jazz greats such as Oscar Peterson, Chick Corea, and *Spyro Gyra* to Palma for performances running from mid-November through mid-December.

On Minorca, two music festivals share the season: The *Ciudadela Music Festival* presents classical music in the town square every Monday or Tuesday during July and August, while the *Mahón Music Festival* makes use of the majestic organ of the Santa María church on weekends from late July through mid-September. The *Fiestas de San Juan,* June 23 and 24 in Ciudadela, are the most important of the traditional celebrations: Centuries old, they revolve around horses and include mock jousts and displays of equestrian bravura such as the *jaleo* of prancing horses. Ibiza has two traditional festivals that are small affairs but worthwhile for visitors already on the island: On March 19, the *Fiesta de San José* includes a procession through the streets of the town of Ibiza; during the first week of September, Santa Eulalia del Río celebrates a *Semana Cultural,* with locals dressed in traditional costumes. Formentera islanders in traditional costume parade through San Francisco Javier, the island capital, on July 25 — *Santiago Apóstol* (Feast of Saint James).

SPORTS AND FITNESS: The islands provide opportunities for water sports of all kinds, as well as other spectator and participatory sports.

Golf – There are nine courses — seven on Majorca, one on Minorca, and one on Ibiza. Three of those on Majorca are 18-hole courses: the *Son Vida Club de Golf* (phone: 71-237620), about 3 miles (5 km) northwest of Palma, and the *Club de Golf de Poniente* (phone: 71-680148) and *Golf Santa Ponsa* (phone: 71-690211), approximately 10 to 12 miles (16 to 19 km) southwest along the Bay of Palma in the Magaluf area. The 9-hole *Club de Golf de Son Parc* on Minorca (phone: 71-363840) is about 14 miles (22 km) north of Mahón. On Ibiza, the *Club de Golf Roca Llisa* (phone: 71-304060), at Santa Eulalia del Río, also has 9 holes.

Hang Gliding – Along with parachuting and flying, this sport is available to the public at the *Royal Flying Club* (at the Aeropuerto de Son Bonet, Marratxi, Majorca; phone: 71-600114). Equipment is available for rental.

Horse Racing – On Majorca, racing takes place regularly at the *Son Pardo Hippodrome* (Carretera de Sóller Km 3; phone: 71-254032), and at the *Manacor Hippodrome* (Calle Es Pla; phone: 71-550023). But racing holds an even greater fascination for the islanders of Minorca, where trotting races take place every summer on Sunday at tracks in Mahón and Ciudadela.

Sailing – Virtually every hotel on a beach has facilities where small sailboats can be rented and lessons can be arranged. The main sailing school on Majorca is the *Escola Espanyola de Vela Cala Nova* (National Sailing School of Cala Nova) at San Agustín (phone: 71-402412).

Scuba Diving – Information on scuba diving around Majorca can be picked up at the *Scuba Club* (13 Calle Pedro Alcántara Peña, Palma; phone: 71-463315), or at the *Scuba Club of Santa Ponsa* (84 Vía Rey Jaime; phone: 71-690266).

Tennis – Numerous hotels have their own courts or courts nearby that are open to guests. On Majorca, tennis clubs operating independently of hotels are the *Tenis Club Aeropuerto de Son Bonet* (Marratxi; phone: 71-600114); *Tenis Arenal Son Veri* (1 Calle Costa y Llobera, El Arenal, Palma; phone: 71-263834); and the *Mallorca Club de Tenis* (Calle Artillería de Montaña, also in Palma; phone: 71-238473).

Windsurfing – Windsurfers (also called board sailers) can be rented at most beachfront hotels.

MAJORCA

The largest of the Balearic Islands is roughly diamond-shaped, measuring approximately 62 miles from east to west and 47 miles from north to south, with about 250 miles of coastline. The northeastern and southwestern sides of the island curve in long beaches and harbors conducive to perfect vacations. The northwestern part of the island is a rugged mountain range — the Sierra de Tramuntana — that drops sharply to the sea, with only Puerto de Sóller offering a small sandy beach and yacht mooring. The southeastern part is rolling farmland strewn with rock walls and stone windmills, with a rocky shore interrupted by a series of sandy coves that have been developed into tourist villages.

The city of Palma de Mallorca — Ciutat de Mallorca in the local dialect — is set on the Bay of Palma on the island's southwest coast. With approximately 300,000 residents, it is home to almost half of the Majorcan population. The city itself is not a beach resort, but miles of sandy beaches stretch to the east of it, with those from Ca'n Pastilla to El Arenal, lined by high rise hotels, restaurants, and discos, known collectively as the Playa de Palma. To the west, newer tourist developments — their high-rise hotels clustered rather than strung along the sea — have been created on smaller beaches at Cala Mayor, Palma Nova, Magaluf, and, beyond the Bay of Palma, at Paguera.

At the northern tip of the island is the town of Pollensa, a few miles inland from Puerto de Pollensa, on Pollensa Bay, which offers excellent swimming and boating. The rugged Cabo de Formentor (Cape Formentor), at the end of the peninsula curving up around the bay, offers spectacular scenery, especially to those who make it to the lighthouse at the end of the road. Just south of Pollensa Bay is Alcudia, where a Roman city once stood (and a ruined Roman theater still stands), and, a mile or so south of the village, Alcudia Bay, lined by a 6-mile beach that is much less developed than the Playa de Palma outside the capital city.

Majorca's mountainous western coast is dotted with small villages that have become retreats for those seeking to leave the crowds behind. Sóller is the largest town in this part of the island, and it, along with Puerto de Sóller a few miles away on the coast, does receive its share of tourists via the train that connects the beach with Palma. A bit to the south is Deya, a medieval-looking town built on a small mound between the sea and towering mountains. Still farther south, the villages of Banyalbufar and Estellenchs hug mountainsides that drop steeply to the sea. Valldemosa, where Chopin and George Sand stayed, lies at one of the few passes through the spine of mountains that separate Palma from the coast.

The bulk of Majorca lies to the east of Palma. Most visitors make their way in this direction to visit the Drach Caves and the Hams Caves, in the vicinity of the village of Porto Cristo on the island's eastern coast. They also stop in the city of Manacor, in the interior, 30½ miles (49 km) due east of Palma, where the island's pearl industry is based. Compared to the coasts, the interior of Majorca is a step back in time. Here, the life of the islanders still revolves around farming, shopkeeping, and early-morning markets, rather than around the housing, feeding, and entertaining of tourists. Inca, 17½ miles (28 km) northeast of Palma on the way to Pollensa and Alcudia, is probably the most interesting interior town. A leatherworking center, it also has the island's largest flea market, in full bustle every Thursday morning.

The real beauty of Majorca's countryside is enjoyed by driving — across the fields, through the mountains, along the coastline. Limit excursions to trips easily completed in a day, since detours to visit unexpected sights constantly crop up. Loop from Palma to Valldemosa, then along the coast to Banyalbufar, Estellenchs, San Telmo, Puerto de Andraitx, Paguers, Magaluf, and back to the city. On another day, go north to Pollensa, then take the narrow road to the tip of Cape Formentor. A visit to a pearl factory in Manacor and to one of the massive caves farther east is another day trip. Or head away from the crowds down to Arenal de la Rapita, a totally undeveloped beach near the southeast corner of the island.

 GETTING AROUND: Airport – Flights from Europe, mainland Spain, and the other islands arrive at the Aeropuerto de Son San Juan, 7 miles (11 km) to the east of Palma, or a 10-minute ride from the center and hotels along the Playa de Palma. An airport bus links the terminal with Plaza de España, where the bus and train stations are located; taxis to any hotel in the city will cost less than $10. For airport information, call 71-264162. The *Iberia* office is at 10 Paseo del Borne, Palma (phone: 71-463400 for information and reservations).

Bus – Palma has a well-organized bus system, used primarily by the local population. Two tourist offices (11 Calle Santo Domingo and on Plaza de España) distribute a timetable and route map. (Once a visitor is in the inner city, however, everything is within walking distance.) Buses also link every town on the island, as well as most of the beaches; a schedule is available from a third tourist office (8 Avenida Rey Jaime III). The main bus station in Palma is located on Plaza de España (phone: 71-752224).

Car Rental – The most extensive rental operations are provided by *Avis* (airport; phone: 71-260910; and on the Palma waterfront at 16 Paseo Marítimo; phone: 71-230720; as well as many others throughout the island). Some *Avis* offices are seasonal, so check with them for opening dates and hours. *Hertz* has several offices (at the airport; phone: 71-260809; and on the Palma waterfront, at 13 Paseo Marítimo; phone: 71-234737). In addition, there are many small local car rental operations that, in some cases, are significantly less expensive than *Avis* or *Hertz.* Check with your hotel for the closest one or, perhaps, for one offering hotel guests special discounts.

Ferry – Ferries connect the island with Barcelona (8 hours), Valencia (9 hours), Mahón on Minorca (6½ hours), and Ibiza (4½ hours, 2 hours by hydrofoil). *Trasmediterránea* (5 Muelle Viejo, Palma; phone: 71-726740) is the main source, but the ferries dock farther southwest along the bay at the Muelle de Pelaires. In addition to these basic mainland and inter-island services, numerous smaller companies operate around the island, linking the ports of Andraitx and San Telmo at the southwest corner of Majorca with the small offshore island of Dragonera, Palma with Magaluf, and Alcudia with Formentor. The tourist office provides a complete listing of such sailings.

Taxi – Plentiful, inexpensive, and much more convenient than buses. Call *Aero-Taxi* (phone: 71-267312), *Radio-Taxi* (phone: 71-755440), *Tele-Taxi* (phone: 71-401414), or *Fono-Taxi* (phone: 71-710403).

Tours – Sightseeing tours by motorcoach regularly reach every corner of the island.

They can be booked through tour operators or hotels — tour buses call to pick up participants at their hotels every morning. There are some 20 fairly standard, full-day itineraries, such as the tour from Palma to Alcudia Bay, including stops at a local market, the house of Father Junípero Serra in Petra (the Spanish Franciscan, who founded missions in California, was a native Majorcan), and Picafort beach; and the tour to the Drach Caves, with stops at a pearl factory in Manacor.

Train – The island has two railroad lines. One connects Palma with Sóller, one of the most spectacular and picturesque train rides in Europe. Trains leave five times a day from the station on Calle Eusebio Estrada, off Plaza de España, and wind their way to Sóller and then down to the beach at Puerto de Sóller. Another train links Palma with Inca, departing at least every hour from another station next door on Plaza de España.

SPECIAL PLACES: Palma de Mallorca – The city features remains of the Moorish occupation, one of Spain's largest cathedrals, and stately 15th- and 16th-century mansions that attest to the island's onetime mercantile prosperity. The cathedral (La Seu), an immense golden stone Gothic construction with flying buttresses that looms on the seafront like a ship anchored at port, is the city's most important sight. Begun in 1230 and not finished until 1601, it underwent alterations during the early 20th century when Antoni Gaudí, the famed Catalan architect who was restoring it, removed the central choir that blocks the nave of most Spanish cathedrals. The result was a greater feeling of space and an uninterrupted view from the main entrance to the high altar, above which hangs Gaudí's wrought-iron baldachin. The cathedral chapter house contains a small museum, open Mondays through Fridays from 10AM to 12:30 PM and from 4 to 6:30 PM, Saturdays from 10 AM to 1:30 PM; closed Sundays. Admission charge. The cathedral has the same hours and is also open during services.

Palma's cathedral, in Plaza Almoina, stands on high ground at the western edge of the oldest part of the city, which is to the east of the wide, tree-shaded promenade known as El Borne (or Paseo del Borne). Across from the cathedral is the Palacio de la Almudaina, the palace-fortress of the island's Arab rulers, later converted into a royal palace for the Spanish Kings of Majorca (and now used, in part, to house the *Museo del Patrimonio Nacional* — closed Saturday afternoons, Sundays, and Mondays; admission charge). Only an arch of the Moorish construction is intact, but not too far away, on Calle Serra, are the Baños Arabes (Arab Baths), which — although small and perhaps requiring some imagination to picture veiled women scurrying through the courtyard — remain essentially as they were under the caliphs. (Open daily from 10 AM to 1:30 PM and from 4 to 6 PM; admission charge.) Still in the Old Town, in the Portella quarter behind the cathedral, is the *Museo de Mallorca,* housed in an old mansion at 5 Calle de la Portella; it illustrates island history through a collection of archaeological artifacts, documents, paintings, and sculpture (open from 10 AM to 2 PM and from 4 to 7 PM; closed Sunday afternoons and Mondays; admission charge). Working your way north, you'll also see the 17th-century Casa Oleza (33 Calle Morey) — known for its inner courtyard — and the 16th-century Gothic and Renaissance Casa Palmer (17 Calle del Sol), before reaching Palma's second most renowned church, San Francisco, on the plaza with the same name. Built during the 13th and 14th centuries and given a baroque facade during the 17th, the church contains the tomb of Ramón Lull, a 13th-century philosopher, poet, theologian, and religious mystic who was born in Palma and martyred in North Africa while trying to convert the Arabs; it has a beautiful cloister attached to it. (Open from 9:30 AM to 1 PM and from 3:30 to 7 PM; closed Sunday afternoons.)

Proceed west from St. Francis to reach the Santa Eulalia church, a fine example of Majorcan Gothic, built from the 13th to the 15th centuries; behind it (at 2 Calle Zavella) is the 18th-century Casa Vivot, another mansion with a notable courtyard. Still farther west, but still in the Old Town on the east side of El Borne, is Palma's 17th-century Ayuntamiento (Town Hall), standing in a beautiful old square, Plaza Cort.

The Lonja, on the seafront west of El Borne, is one of Palma's star attractions. Built during the 15th century as a stock exchange and commercial building for the city's busy trading merchants, it now serves as an exhibition space for art shows (and is thus open irregularly); its secular Gothic design, by Guillermo Sagrera, is open and light, with spiral columns holding up the soaring ceiling. Also on the west side of El Borne is the Casa de los Marqueses de Sollerich (10 Calle San Cayetano), an 18th-century mansion with perhaps the finest courtyard in town.

The attractions beyond the center, on the west side of Palma, should not be missed. One of them, the Castillo de Bellver, an unusual round castle built during the 14th century and beautifully preserved, boasts perhaps the best view of Palma and the surrounding area. The courtyard has 2 levels of arcades, with classical arches ringing the lower level and Gothic arches soaring on the upper level. The rooms are sparsely furnished, but the kitchen has a massive cooking area; the adjoining Tower of Homage, looking like a stone rocket ready for blast-off, housed the dungeons. (Open from 8 AM to 10 PM from April through September, to 6 PM the rest of the year; admission charge.) The other attraction, the Pueblo Español (Spanish Village), located across from the Palacio de Congresos, offers a chance to see all of Spain at a glance. Much like its counterpart in Barcelona, this model village contains reproductions of houses and famous buildings from all parts of Spain. It also offers a chance to see Spanish artisans at work and shops where their handiwork can be purchased. The village is open daily from 9 AM to 8 PM. Admission charge.

ELSEWHERE ON THE ISLAND

La Cartuja de Valldemosa (Valldemosa Carthusian Monastery) – Set in the mountains 11 miles (18 km) north of Palma, this monastery was founded during the 14th century, although the present buildings are from the 17th and 18th centuries. After the Carthusian monks left it during the 18th century, its cells were rented out to guests, including Frédéric Chopin and George Sand, who spent the winter of 1838–39 here. The Cloister of Saint Mary offers beautiful views, and the neo-classical church is decorated with frescoes, an intricately carved choir stall, and rich tapestries. Closed Sundays; admission charge.

Deya – This lovely old village (Deiá in the local language) enjoys an enchanting setting perched loft-like over the sea and backed by evergreen mountains 17 miles (27 km) northwest of Palma. Its natural beauty lured those who made it an artists' and writers' colony — the poet Robert Graves, who lived here until his death in 1985, was probably its most famous long-term resident. He is now buried in the local cemetery, which also has a splendid view of the area.

Sóller – Almond, lemon, and orange groves surround this town 19 miles (30 km) north of Palma, the largest town on the western side of the island. Like many a settlement on Majorca, the threat of attack from the sea caused it to grow up a few miles inland from its port, Puerto de Sóller, which sits 3 miles (5 km) from the valley on a round, sheltered, beach-lined bay and has become a thriving resort center. Sóller itself has little to see, beyond a cathedral that is among the most elaborate on the island. Most visitors arrive aboard the turn-of-the-century narrow-gauge railroad train from Palma — a wonderfully scenic ride that is well worth the trip — then continue via an extension down to the port for the beach or a bite to eat.

Pollensa – On the northeast coast, 32½ miles (52 km) from Palma, Pollensa (Pollença in the Majorcan dialect), too, is an inland town; Puerto de Pollensa, a fishing village turned resort town, is 4 miles (6 km) away on one of the three largest bays of Majorca, with a big, sweeping beach. On the outskirts of Pollensa is Monte Calvario, a hill crowned by a small chapel reached by car or a climb of 365 steps. In town are the 14th-century parish Church of Nuestra Señora de los Angeles and the 16th-century Santo Domingo convent. Visitors not staying in the area invariably pass through both Pollensa and Puerto de Pollensa en route to Cabo de Formentor, at the extreme tip of the peninsula that forms the northern arm of Pollensa Bay.

Cabo de Formentor – The road from Puerto de Pollensa to Cape Formentor follows the spine of the Sierra de Tramuntana out to sea and provides stunning vistas, particularly at the Mirador d'Es Colomer and at the Formentor lighthouse at the end of the peninsula.

Cuevas de Artá (Artá Caves) – These extensive caves are perhaps the most beautiful of the many on the island, yet they are the least visited. They were first explored thoroughly during the 19th century — and are said to have inspired Jules Verne to write *Journey to the Center of the Earth* — but were known as long ago as the 13th century, when they served as a hiding place for Moors after the Reconquest. Open daily; admission charge. On the east coast of the island at Cabo Vermell, 6 miles (10 km) east of Artá (phone: 71-563293).

Cuevas del Drach (Drach Caves) – The largest of Majorca's caves are just over a mile long and contain a subterranean lake in addition to four chambers full of fanciful formations in limestone. Visits are guided (English-language tours are possible) and include a concert by floating musicians at the end of the tour. Be warned: The crowds are ridiculous during the summer months. Open daily; admission charge. On the east coast of Majorca, just south of Porto Cristo (phone: 71-570002).

Cuevas de Els Hams (Hams Caves) – Virtually next door to the Drach Caves and less impressive, although they are known for the whiteness of their stalactites and stalagmites. Open daily; admission charge. Just west of Porto Cristo (phone: 71-570227).

SHOPPING: Shopping in Palma is concentrated in the city center. Upscale shops, with such names as *Rodier, Gucci,* and *Armani,* tend to be found along Avenida Rey Jaime III. The shopping area that is more likely to be packed with Majorcans and thus with many more bargains is one on the east side of the Paseo del Borne, in small pedestrian streets that climb to the Plaza Mayor and then along Calle Sindicato and Calle San Miguel, which branch out from the square. Leather goods, embroidery, ceramics, and manufactured pearls are all good buys. For general purchases, stop in at *Galerías Preciados* (15 Avenida Rey Jaime III), a branch of the Spain-wide department store chain. Majorca also has a well-organized series of open-air markets. The main vegetable and fish market in Plaza Oliver is in operation daily and is worth a visit if only to see the colorful catch — orange crustaceans, black octopus, fish and shellfish of every other hue. An interesting crafts market takes place on Plaza Mayor on Saturday mornings year-round, and more frequently in summer. Markets in the smaller towns take place once or twice a week; the schedule is printed in the *Balearic Times,* as well as in several tourist office publications. Among the larger markets are the ones in Alcudia on Tuesday and Sunday mornings, in Artá on Tuesday mornings, Inca on Thursday mornings, Manacor on Monday mornings, Pollensa on Sunday mornings, and Sóller on Saturday mornings. Among the more interesting shops are the following:

Bamuco – Moderately priced leather goods. 19 Palau Reial, Palma de Mallorca (phone: 71-722512).

Casa Bonet – One of the best embroidery shops on the island. 3 Calle Puigdorfila, Palma de Mallorca (phone: 71-722117).

L'Ofre – Better-quality purses and other articles in leather. 28 Paseo del Borne, Palma de Mallorca (phone: 71-223665).

Perlas Majórica – The island's well-known pearls, of the highest quality, organically manmade (of fish scales), at factory prices. 11 Avenida Rey Jaime III, Palma de

Mallorca (phone: 71-725268). Pearls can also be bought directly from the factory, open daily, except Sundays, just off the main road in Manacor (phone: 71-551221).

P'tit Percay – More moderately priced leather goods. 2 Avenida Antonio Maura, Palma de Mallorca (phone: 71-210370).

Scherezade – The best place to buy Lladró porcelain. 5 Calle Brossa, Palma de Mallorca (phone: 71-711974).

NIGHTCLUBS AND NIGHTLIFE: The Balearics have a justly deserved reputation for offering some of the wildest nightlife in the world. Not only does Palma dance all night long, but *BCM* in Magaluf, which has a capacity of over 5,000 revelers, is indisputably the world's largest discotheque. Any disco tour of Palma begins in the western part of the city around Plaza Gomila. Here, the stunning glass façade of *Tito's* (phone: 71-237642) faces the sea on the Paseo Marítimo, with another entrance on Plaza Gomila. Glass elevators move party animals between the four bars and five levels of this extravaganza, and revolving lights present a stunning light show to those on the waterfront. *Alexandra's,* nearby (Plaza Mediterráneo; phone: 71-237810), has the loud music and light shows without the wild setting of *Tito's.* Farther along the bay on the western side of the city, in Cala Mayor, *Pepe's Centre* (322 Avenida Joan Miró; phone: 71-403047) and *Disco Liberty,* just down the road (phone: 71-403644), offer excellent late-night dancing and are packed with tourists from every corner of Europe. Still farther along the bay, Magaluf, a created tourist city about a 30-minute drive to the west of Palma, is the area's main disco scene. Here the mega-disco *BCM* (phone: 71-683869) reigns, hosting some of rock's top stars in live performance; *Alexandra's 2 Disco* packs them in as a good, smaller alternative to *BCM*'s massive madness; and plenty of bars percolate with nonstop parties, complete with giant snake dances rolling from one pub into the next. Majorca's *Casino* (Urbanización Sol de Mallorca; phone: 71-680000), featuring American and French roulette, blackjack, and other games of chance, as well as a restaurant and discotheque, is also out this way (take the Cala Figuera turnoff from the Andraitx road).

The Playa de Palma area along the bay to the east of the city also has its complement of nightspots. Try *Riù Palace* (Calle Laud, El Arenal; phone: 71-265704), Majorca's largest disco until the creation of *BCM,* and *Zorba's* (4 Avenida Son Rigo; phone: 71-266664), which offers open-air disco along the beach.

Downtown Palma can indulge other tastes. For early-evening drinks, there are *tapas* bars lining Calle Apuntadores. Later, a visit to the *Bar Abaco* (1 Calle San Juan; phone: 71-714939), installed in a former Majorcan palace, is a memorable experience. Guests enter a giant room with wide arches over columns, a bar 30 feet long, Oriental carpets, classical statues, café tables, and baskets of fruit spilling across the floor; upstairs patrons chat on couches surrounding a fireplace while others wander through a reconstructed kitchen and gaze into the garden below, where a small pond shimmers in the light of dozens of giant candles. Classical music plays quietly in the background of this sophisticated establishment, where a mixed drink can cost anywhere from $8 to $16.

CHECKING IN: The majority of the hotels on the islands are dedicated to the group tour trade, but accept individual guests should space be available. The hotels listed below have been selected from more than 1,000 that the island has to offer. Room prices are for a double room during high season, from June through September and at *Christmas* and *Easter.* Low-season rates can be 25% less. Expect to pay $90 and up in a hotel listed as expensive, from $50 to $90 in a moderate one, and less than $50 in an inexpensive one.

PALMA AND ENVIRONS

Meliá Victoria – At the western side of the bay, it overlooks the entire city, with one of the best views of the harbor. The 167 rooms all have television sets, the buffet breakfast is sumptuous, all the services that could be desired are available, and the location, next to the Plaza Gomila nightclubs, makes it central to Palma nightlife. (The pulsating lights of *Tito's* are next door, so get a room facing the other way to avoid the noise). There are 2 pools and open-air dancing in summer. 21 Avenida Joan Miró (phone: 71-234342). Very expensive.

Bellver Sol – Half the price of the *Victoria* and not far away from it, on the road that rims Palma's harbor. The 393 rooms are simply and sparsely furnished — ask for one with a panoramic view of the yacht harbor. There is a good pool. 11 Paseo Marítimo (phone: 71-238008). Expensive.

Nixe Palace – In the Cala Mayor beach area to the west of Palma, yet still within a 10-minute cab ride of the center. (There's no need to go into Palma for the nightlife, since there's more than enough in Cala Mayor.) This place is right on the beach, as a resort hotel should be, and there is a great pool. The 130 rooms are big and well furnished, in a contemporary style. 269 Avenida Joan Miró, Cala Mayor (phone: 71-403811). Expensive.

Punta Negra – A 61-room hotel with bungalows as well, a pool, and virtually a private beach tucked between the rocks at Palma Nova. Carretera Andraitx, Km 12, Palma Nova (phone: 71-680762). Expensive to moderate.

Aquarium – In Palma Nova, just across the street from the beach and a short walk from the nightlife. A good basic tourist hotel with 109 rooms; closed from November through March. Paseo del Mar, Palma Nova (phone: 71-680308). Moderate.

Costa Azul – One of the bargains on the road along Palma's harbor. It has 126 simple rooms and an indoor-outdoor pool with sliding glass overhead. This is closer to downtown Palma than it is to the Gomila nightlife quarter. Closed in December. 7 Paseo Marítimo (phone: 71-231940). Moderate.

Santa Ana – On the Cala Mayor beach, it has 190 simply furnished rooms, most with terraces overlooking the sea, and a pool. 9 Calle Gaviota, Cala Mayor (phone: 71-401052). Moderate to inexpensive.

La Cala – Sitting side by side with its sister hotel, the *Santa Ana,* on the Cala Mayor beach, it is less than half the size (70 rooms) and a bit less expensive. It, too, has a pool. Closed November through March. 4 Calle Gaviota, Cala Mayor (phone: 71-401612). Inexpensive.

Horizonte Sol – Located at the far western end of Palma, near Porto Pí, this is a basic tourist hotel (200 rooms) but the price is right. It's within a short taxi ride of the Gomila nightlife section and has good views of the bay. 1 Calle Vista Alegre (phone: 71-400661). Inexpensive.

ELSEWHERE ON THE ISLAND

La Residencia – An old mansion turned into a wondrous, low-key hotel with spectacular views over the sea. It's tucked just off the road leading into Deya from Valldemosa, perched high above the Mediterranean, a 15-minute walk from town. Simple antiques, four-poster beds, and marble floors grace the 31 rooms. There is a swimming pool and tennis. Son Moragues, Deya (phone: 71-639011). Very expensive.

L'Hermitage – Virtually a self-contained resort in a mountain setting off the road from Palma to Sóller, far from the crowds and the beach. Rustic elegance is done as perfectly here as it can be. There are only 20 rooms, with furniture in heavy wood; dining is outside when possible; there are tennis courts, and the swimming pool is surrounded by pines. Carretera de Sollerich Km 8, Orient (phone: 71-613300). Expensive.

Vistamar – A former manor house, this hostelry has 7 double rooms and a suite about 1¾ miles (3 km) from Valldemosa, on the road to Andraitx. It overlooks the sea on one side and is surrounded by olive and almond groves on the other. The restaurant is set on the porticoed terrace, the beds are four-poster, the house full of Spanish art. All is magic when lit at night. Valldemosa (phone: 71-612300). Expensive to moderate.

Ses Rotges – In the northeast corner of the island, it has 24 rooms, beautiful gardens, a pool, and an outdoor restaurant with a rustic lounge. Closed November through March. Calle Alcedo, Cala Ratjada (phone: 71-563108). Moderate.

Miramar – It's as if time had stopped in the 1930s. The 69-room hotel is right on the beach at the far north of Majorca and couldn't be more pleasant. Reserve early. Closed November through March. 39 Paseo Anglada Camarasa, Puerto de Pollensa (phone: 71-531400). Moderate to inexpensive.

Costa D'Or – A small place (42 rooms) just up the road from Deya in Lluch Alcari, with views of the crashing sea below. It's very simple, but the beauty of the spot cannot be improved. Closed November through March. Lluch Alcari (phone: 71-639025). Inexpensive.

Mar y Vent – Set just off the main highway and about 500 feet above the sea, which lies at the end of a long terraced slope dropping steeply in front of the hotel. It has 19 good, simple rooms, a swimming pool, and great food. Closed December through February. 49 Calle José Antonio, Banyalbufar (phone: 71-610025). Inexpensive.

EATING OUT: As with any popular tourist destination, restaurants abound in the Balearic Islands. They are as varied as the tourists who frequent them, seemingly bringing their own cooking with them as they come. Though German, Scandinavian, and English dining places easily can be found, there are still scores of restaurants serving up local specialties — fish restaurants and others stressing the lamb, goat, rabbit, chicken, and snail dishes typical of Balearic food. Wines to try are binisalem and felanitx, both from Majorca. Expect to pay $65 and up for a meal for two including an appetizer, main course, dessert, and wine in any restaurant listed as expensive; moderate means between $35 and $65, and inexpensive normally ranges between $25 and $35. Because the island economy is extremely seasonal, be sure to call restaurants to make sure they are open, especially off season.

PALMA AND ENVIRONS

Honoris – An excellent French restaurant in the northeastern part of Palma, near the industrial section. Only a handful of well-heeled tourists manage to make the pilgrimage, but those who are serious about eating and have money to spare should try it for a change of pace. Closed Sundays, holidays, *Holy Week,* and the first 2 weeks of August. Reservations advised. 76 Carretera Vieja de Bunyola (phone: 71-203212). Expensive.

La Lubina – Long established and one of the best fish places in Palma. Right on the old pier, it is as upscale and pricey as any that can be found in the city proper, with classical music filling the air, white tablecloths, and a hushed atmosphere. Try the grilled swordfish or the grilled fresh fish of the day, but avoid the lobster, since it would probably cost less to fly to Maine to satisfy those cravings. Open daily. Reservations advised. Muelle Viejo (phone: 71-723350). Expensive.

Porto Pí – Where King Juan Carlos eats when he comes to Palma — which means almost the top prices in town. Honored with a Michelin star, it is located in one of Palma's oldest mansions, and the menu features French Basque cooking. The fresh fish here is said to be some of the best on the island — try it baked in pastry, and then try one of the fabulous desserts. Closed Saturdays at lunch, Sundays, and mid-November to mid-December. Reservations necessary. 174 Avenida Joan Miró (phone: 71-400087). Expensive.

Caballito de Mar – Hard to beat for moderately priced outdoor eating along the seafront. On sunny days, the setting couldn't be better, and the food is normally well prepared, even with crowds of tourists descending from time to time. Have the fish of the day, perhaps grilled. Closed Sundays. Reservations advised. 5 Paseo de Sagrera (phone: 71-721074). Moderate.

Casa Eduardo – Come here just for the fish soup. It's located on the pier opposite *La Lubina* and is a "real people's" fish place, priced accordingly. Closed Sundays and Mondays. Reservations unnecessary. 4 Industria Pesquera, on Mollet (phone: 71-721182). Moderate.

Don Peppone – The best Italian food in town. Great antipasti, linguine with shellfish, and osso buco. It's packed with Palma yuppies, who love it when the roof is rolled back to let the sun shine in. Closed Sundays. Reservations necessary. 14 Calle Bayarte (phone: 71-454242). Moderate.

Gina – This dining spot has a beautiful terrace with a view of the magnificent Lonja. The specialties include *zarzuela de pescado* (fish soup) and chicken Kiev. Closed Wednesdays. Reservations necessary. 1 Plaza de la Lonja (phone: 71-226484). Moderate.

Es Parlament – In an ornate classical setting in the Balearic Autonomous Parliament building, it's particularly famous for its paella. Closed Sundays. Reservations necessary. 11 Calle Conquistador (phone: 71-726026). Moderate.

La Pergola – In the French bistro tradition, this tiny eatery has rustic wood details over whitewashed walls. The owner and chef, a former head chef at the *Waldorf Astoria* in New York, works magic with thin steaks. Reservations necessary. 13 Plaza Atarazanas (phone: 71-714808). Moderate.

Ca'n Juanito – A basic Spanish restaurant with simple, uninspired decor, it serves excellent local dishes such as rabbit, goat, and lamb. Closed Wednesday evenings. Reservations unnecessary. 11 Avenida Aragon (phone: 71-461065). Inexpensive.

Celler Sa Premsa – For those who've dreamed of the perfect Spanish restaurant — bullfight posters on the walls, long wooden tables shared with strangers, and great budget food. This is Palma's largest such dining place (seating for 250), and it's usually full. The roast suckling pig is a reliable choice. Open daily. Reservations advised on weekends. 8 Plaza Obispo Berenguer de Palou (phone: 71-723529). Inexpensive.

ELSEWHERE ON THE ISLAND

Na Burguesa – Just outside Palma in the small town of Génova (from where it has a marvelous view of the capital). Loud and boisterous, it serves Majorcan dishes, but be prepared to wait for a table. Try the roast shoulder of lamb or the pork loin. Closed Monday evenings. Reservations essential on weekends. Mirador de Na Burguesa, Génova (phone: 71-402043). Moderate.

Celler Ca'n Amer – An immense room with wine casks surrounding the diners. This has gained fame as one of the best spots on the island for local cooking; unfortunately, the prices have increased as its popularity has soared. Closed Sundays in summer, Saturdays and Sundays at other times. Reservations are essential for those planning to have lunch here on a Thursday, when the market brings an overload of hungry folks into town; at other times, reservations are advised. 39 Calle Miguel Durán, Inca (phone: 71-501261). Moderate.

Mandilego – In a small town on the Bay of Alcudia, on the north coast of the island, it offers excellent fish dishes, from swordfish steaks to Mediterranean lobsters. Closed Mondays. Reservations advised. 49 Calle Isabel Garau, Ca'n Picafort (phone: 71-527003). Moderate.

Mesón Ca'n Pedro – One of the shrines of Majorcan cooking, this rustic restaurant is also just outside Palma in Génova. Try the *cabrito* (kid) if any is available. Closed Wednesdays. Reservations necessary. 4 Calle Rector Vives, Génova (phone: 71-402479). Moderate.

Puig de Sant Miguel – Majorcan specialties are featured at this rambling rustic place in the interior, on the road from Montuiri to Manacor. Try suckling pig or leg of lamb, served on wooden tables surrounded with wagon wheels and local pottery. Closed Tuesdays. Reservations advised. Carretera Manacor–Montuiri, Km 31 (phone: 71-646314). Moderate.

Ses Porxeres – This Catalan eatery is best known for its fantastic appetizers. Order the appetizer plate and a good bottle of wine, and have a feast. In fact, for a party of six, four portions will be plenty. Closed Sunday evenings and Mondays. Reservations advised. Carretera Palma–Sóller, Km 17, Bunyola (phone: 71-613762). Moderate.

Ca'n Jaime – A simple, tiny, typical restaurant serving excellent food, in the tiny town of Deya. Try the *sopas mallorquinas* (Majorcan soup) and the *arroz brut* ("ugly rice" or "rice in the rough"), and wolf it all down with wine and olives. Closed Mondays. Reservations unnecessary. 13 Calle Archiduque Luis Salvador, Deya (phone: 71-639029). Inexpensive.

Escorca – High in the mountain between Sóller and Pollensa, near the Lluch Monastery, this rustic place with a giant fireplace specializes in roast leg of lamb and goat and has wonderful baked apples. Closed Thursdays. Reservations advised. Carretera Pollensa–Sóller, Km 25 (phone: 71-517095). Inexpensive.

El Guía – A simple Spanish place in Sóller, and a nice place to have lunch after taking the train up from Palma. The food is basic, the seafood excellent. Closed Mondays. Reservations unnecessary. 3 Calle Castañer, Sóller (phone: 71-630227). Inexpensive.

Es Pouet Francisca – In the western mountains, this place is built against a cliff high above Alaro, on the winding unpaved road to the Castillo de Alaro. The roast lamb and the snails are worth every bit of the effort; the homemade *tinto* (red) wine is dark and heavy. Reservations unnecessary. Leave Alaro on the road to Orient and look for a small sign indicating Espouet, then turn left and begin the climb. The restaurant is the last building reachable by car (phone: 71-510277). Inexpensive.

MINORCA

The second-largest of the Balearic Islands is the easternmost of the group and also the island farthest from the Spanish mainland. The Romans referred to it as the "smaller one," compared to Majorca, which is about 25 miles to the southwest. Although Minorca is larger than either Ibiza or Formentera, it measures only about 30 miles from east to west and between 6 and 12 miles from north to south. The island is relatively flat — a hilly plateau with its highest point, Monte Toro, rising just over 1,000 feet in the island's center. The absence of a mountain range such as the one on Majorca means that Minorca is without some of the larger island's spectacular scenery. Yet its outline is rugged and irregular, resulting in roughly 125 miles of coastline blessed with countless small coves and beautiful beaches. More and more tourists are beginning to appreciate Minorca's pleasures, but without inundating the island yet, and agriculture, particularly dairy products, remains a major industry, along with the making of shoes and costume jewelry.

Traces of past cultures have all but been destroyed on the island, except for massive megalithic constructions remaining from prehistoric times. Although Majorca has its share, Minorca is dotted with hundreds of these stone monuments, which are of three main types: Called *talayots, taulas,* and *navetas,* they are remnants of a so-called *talayotic* Bronze Age culture that may have begun about 2000 BC and was at its height around 1000 BC. Scholars do not yet fully understand the origins of the civilization that raised these monuments (the nuraghic culture of the Italian island of Sardinia may have been its kin), nor have they been able to fathom the structures' exact function. *Talayots* — circular mounds of stone built on high ground — may have been watchtowers or the houses of chieftains (or the roofs or foundations of such structures). *Taulas,* the form most peculiar to Minorca, consist of one large flat stone set upon another in a T-shape (the name means "table" in the local dialect). Reminiscent of Stonehenge, they are usually found in the center of other vertical stones and may have served a religious purpose. *Navetas,* similar to the conical mounds of the *talayots* but oblong and containing chambers (like the upside-down hull of a ship, whence the name), are thought to have been communal graves. These monuments are found on both government and private land; although some of the sites are easily accessible from the road, others are not.

The largest city on Minorca is its capital, Mahón (population 23,000), a port at the eastern end of the island. Known in the Minorcan language as Maó, it gave the world a favorite local sauce — mayonnaise. The second-largest city and former capital, Ciudadela (Ciutadella in the local language), is at the island's western extreme. The two are starkly different. Mahón shows the influence of 8 decades of 18th-century British rule in its architecture, which sports details such as sash windows and Georgian doors, while the architecture of Ciudadela is classically Spanish. Other towns, such as Alayor, Mercadal, and Ferrerias, are in the interior, along the main road that crosses the island from east to west. Fornells, at one time a fishing village and now a resort town, is on the north coast on a deeply indented bay.

Minorca's beaches are what most visitors come to explore. All are posted with flags due to capricious currents — red signals danger, yellow means caution, and green signifies safety. Son Bou and Santo Tomás, in the center of the southern shore, are the two longest beaches on the island. Cala Santa Galdana, to the west of these, is a beach in a sheltered cove, with very safe and shallow waters, and Cala Blanca, a few miles south of Ciudadela, is a tiny beach surrounded by rocky cliffs. Cala del Pilar, a deserted beach on the north side of the island, is known mainly to locals. To reach it, turn off the main Mahón–Ciudadela road about 3 miles (5 km) past Ferrerias, near the Alputzer farm. Cala Pregonda, east of Cala del Pilar, is also deserted but easier to reach. From Mercadal, take the road northwest toward Ferragut Nou, then walk the last hundred yards to the sea. Es Grao, one of the beaches closest to Mahón, is very shallow, perfect for children. Drive due north from the city to the sea.

 GETTING AROUND: Airport – Charter flights arrive from most European countries, scheduled flights aboard *Aviaco* from mainland Spain and from Palma de Mallorca. Mahón Airport (phone: 71-360150) is 3 miles (5 km)

southwest of the city at San Clemente. Expect to pay about $6 for a ride between the airport and downtown Mahón. The *Aviaco* office is at Plaza Explanada, Mahón (phone: 71-361588 for information and reservations).

Bus – Buses depart from Plaza Explanada, Mahón, for Ciudadela a half dozen times a day. Schedules are available from the tourist office (40 Plaza Explanada) and are also posted on the square.

Car Rental – A rented car is the recommended means of transportation. The island's main road, between Mahón and Ciudadela, has recently been widened, and traffic is no problem on the other roads, though parking in the center of Mahón is virtually impossible. *Avis* (at the airport; phone: 71-361576; and at 53 Plaza Explanada; phone: 71-361588) offers the most convenient rentals. *Hertz* has one office (42 Carrer Gran, Villacarlos; phone: 71-364881). Scores of smaller car rental agencies exist, many associated with hotels. Check with them if a car is needed for only a day or two. (The tourist office has a complete list of all car rental offices on the island.) Note that the best map of the island is the *Archaeological Map of Minorca,* available in local bookstores. It shows not only the roads, including tiny one-lane streets, but also the names of farms in the countryside — invaluable for those who have lost their way, with no road signs for miles, because farm names are clearly marked across the island.

Ferry – Ferry service connects the island with Barcelona (9 hours), Valencia (16 hours, via Palma de Mallorca), and Palma (6½ hours). Ferries land at Mahón's Estación Marítima. For *Trasmediterránea* information, call 71-362950.

Motor Scooter Rental – Because Minorca is small, many visitors see it by rented motor scooter or motorcycle. Among the scores of agencies are *Motos Ramos* (21 Anden de Levante; phone: 71-366813), *Motos Gelabert* (12 Calle José A. Clavé; phone: 71-360614), and *Motos Kike* (69 Calle Ciudadela; phone: 71-364120), all in Mahón.

Taxi – Cabs do not scurry around the island. Call *Radio-Taxi* in Mahón (phone: 71-367111) or in Ciudadela (phone: 71-382335 or 71-381197).

SPECIAL PLACES: Mahón – Throughout most of its history, the capital of modern Minorca was second in importance to Ciudadela. That changed during the 18th century with the arrival of the British, who found Mahón's long, narrow, deep harbor and port facilities preferable to those at the other end of the island. Mahón, set on a high cliff at the end of the harbor, does not have the wide avenues, majestic buildings, and tree-lined streets of other Spanish capitals, resembling an overgrown fishing village instead. Among the sights is the 18th-century Santa María church, which houses an extraordinary early-19th-century organ that is one of the largest in the world and is considered to be one of the finest (it's the raison d'être of the city's annual summer music festival). Not far away, the marketplace built into the arcaded cloister of a former Carmelite convent is worth a morning visit; otherwise, the town is best enjoyed by wandering through its narrow streets. At night, the port, reached by a steep, winding road called Abundancia, becomes the focus of most nightlife, with dozens of bars and restaurants in the area of the Estación Marítima and several excellent restaurants lining the harbor toward Villacarlos. The British founded this village, southeast of Mahón near the entrance to the harbor, to house the garrison of a nearby fort. Once called Georgetown, it remains even more British in atmosphere than the capital itself.

Trepucó – A 13-foot taula, the highest on Minorca, and a *talayot* are located at this easily accessible archaeological site a little over a mile south of Mahón.

Ciudadela – Minorca's second-largest city, at the western end of the island, is blessed with a beautiful location and ornate Spanish architecture that attests to its onetime importance as the former capital. Although it was largely destroyed by the Turks during the mid-16th century and then rebuilt, it has a wonderful Old City center with narrow streets and tiny shops. The Catedral de Santa María, a Gothic church begun during the 14th century, has a crumbling façade, but the interior has been restored and is especially beautiful when the morning light streams through its stained glass window; it contains columns with geometric designs that appear to have come from an old Arab mosque, intricately carved choir stalls, and a delicate cupola over the main altar. Outside the church, Calle Quadrado, lined with arcades and shops, leads to Calle Mayor Borne and to Plaza d'es Borne, Ciudadela's main square. Be sure to walk into the Palacio Saura on Calle Santísimo (south of Calle Quadrado and west of the market-place) to get a sense of an old Minorcan palace with courtyard, staircase, and dome.

Naveta d'es Tudons – The restored *naveta* at this accessible site 3 miles (5 km) east of Ciudadela, just south of the road to Mahón, is the best preserved, the most important, and the most famous megalithic monument on the island. It is also the *naveta* that looks most like an upside-down ship.

Torre d'en Gaumés – A megalithic settlement covering several acres, it includes *taulas, talayots,* and ancient caves used for habitation; it's easily accessible 2 miles (3 km) south of Alayor, off the road to Son Bou.

SHOPPING: Minorca has a reputation for making excellent leather goods and shoes and is a European leader in the manufacture of costume jewelry. The products of both industries can be bought from factory outlets. Market days on Minorca are Tuesday and Saturday mornings in Plaza Explanada, Mahón, Friday and Saturday mornings in Ciudadela, and Monday and Wednesday mornings in Villacarlos.

Catisa – The island's largest costume jewelry factory. 26 Calle Bellavista, Mahón (phone: 71-364545).

Massa – Upscale silver handicrafts. 36 San Fernando, Mahón (phone: 71-364189).

Patrizia – A prime place for leather goods. 2 Calle Favaller, Ciudadela (phone: 71-380397).

Salord Jovel – A factory outlet that is a good source of leather items. Located in the industrial area along the main road into Ciudadela (phone: 71-382300).

NIGHTCLUBS AND NIGHTLIFE: Nightlife here pales in comparison to that found on Ibiza and Majorca. There are bars and restaurants packed with locals near the Estación Marítima in Mahón and along the harbor to and including the port area of Villacarlos — which is also lively in the evening with crowds enjoying the bars and dining on the wharf. A number of discos do exist. One that is unique is *Cova d'en Xoroi* (no phone), built into a cave on the coast south of Alayor at Cala'n Porter. The cave opens to the sea below a cliff dropping straight to the water. Guests reach the disco via a staircase clinging to the rocks, then strut their stuff on a dance floor 100 feet above the crashing waves. Everything begins slowly after midnight and really begins to cook between 2 and 3 AM.

CHECKING IN: *Biniali* – A small *hostal,* much like a country inn, each of its 9 rooms is furnished differently with antiques. The villa, which also has a pool, is about 3 miles (5 km) south of Mahón, beyond the town of San Luis. Reservations should be made as much in advance as possible. 50 Calle Suestra, San Luis (phone: 71-361724). Moderate.

Club Falco Sol – This is a village complex at the far southwest corner of the island. A self-contained resort, it offers accommodations in a series of bungalows, several restaurants and pools, and nightlife, all a short walk from the sea. Closed from November through April. Reservations by the week are preferred. Playa de Son Xoriguer, Cala'n Bosch (phone: 71-384623). Moderate.

Port Mahón – A grand old hotel overlooking the port, within a short walk of both the town center and the port area. The 74 rooms are simply furnished; there is a pool. Avenida Fort de l'Eau, Mahón (phone: 71-362600). Moderate.

Rey Carlos III – This modern, 87-room hotel with a swimming pool overlooks the harbor at Villacarlos, only a short walk to the port area that is one of the nightlife centers of Minorca. Closed November through March. Miranda de Cala Corp, Villacarlos (phone: 71-363100). Moderate.

San Jaime – An apartment hotel only about 300 yards from the longest beach on the island, Playa Son Bou. Each of the 53 apartments has at least one bedroom; there is also a restaurant, pool, and tennis court. The beach is very quiet — any nightlife entails a half-hour drive. Closed November through March. Urbanización San Jaime, Playa Son Bou, Alayor (phone: 71-368011). Moderate.

S'Algar – A sprawling low building in the middle of the S'Algar resort development on the coast southeast of Mahón and Villacarlos. The 106 rooms have a bungalow feel, with most opening onto a garden area, and there is a pool. Closed November through March. Urbanización S'Algar, San Luis (phone: 71-361700). Moderate to inexpensive.

Royal – The rooms in this 17-unit apartment hotel are all 1-bedroom with foldout couches. There are a restaurant and bar downstairs, as well as a swimming pool, and it is only a 5-minute walk to the center of Mahón. 131 Calle del Carmen, Mahón (phone: 71-369534). Inexpensive.

EATING OUT: Casa Manolo – The premier fish restaurant in Ciudadela, located at the far end of the port with a great view back to the town. The fish is as fresh and the prices are as high as can be found on the island. Open daily. Reservations necessary. Marina 117, Puerto, Ciudadela (phone: 71-381728). Expensive.

Jágaro – In the port area of Mahón, it is closed in by French doors, with lush green plants separating the tables. Definitely upscale, but not too overpriced; the chef is proudest of his fresh fish, either grilled or with sauces. Open daily. Reservations advised. 80 Calle Mártires de Atlante, Mahón (phone: 71-364660). Expensive.

Ca'n Aguedet – Perhaps Minorca's best restaurant for Minorcan cooking. In the center of the island, it's family run and quietly elegant, with whitewashed walls and wicker furniture. For appetizers, sample the eggplant stuffed with shrimp or the stuffed onions, then tuck into the peppers stuffed with fish or the rabbit with figs. Open daily. Reservations necessary on weekends. 23 Calle Lepanto, Mercadal (phone: 71-375391). Moderate.

Ca'n Delio – A favorite among the cluster of several similar restaurants set on the romantic Villacarlos harbor, which crawls with tourists during the summer and is locked tighter than a drum from November through March. Reservations advised. 39 Muelle Cala Fons, Villacarlos (phone: 71-369971). Moderate.

Ca's Quintu – In the center of Ciudadela, this is a good, simple place serving dishes ranging from fish to Minorcan specialties; try the grilled crayfish. Open daily. Reservations unnecessary. 4 Plaza Alfonso III, Ciudadela (phone: 71-381002). Moderate.

Marivent – A marvelous terrace overlooking the harbor recommends it. Upstairs, the dining room — used mainly in winter — is fairly new, with a marble-topped bar in the center. Try any fish specialty. Closed Mondays in summer, Sundays and at lunch on Mondays in winter. Reservations advised. 54 Calle Mártires de Atlante, Mahón (phone: 71-369067). Moderate.

Es Moli d'es Reco – Housed in a converted windmill in Mercadal, on the main road between Mahón and Ciudadela, the Minorcan cooking here is exceptionally popular with locals and plates are heaped with food. Try the lamb or the rabbit and the local wine. Open daily. Reservations necessary. Carretera General, Mercadal (phone: 71-375392). Moderate.

Pilar – Minorcan specialties in the center of Mahón. This is a tiny eatery, and on most nights its dozen tables are filled with islanders lingering over lamb with parsnips and snails with mayonnaise. Closed Mondays. Reservations unnecessary. 61 Calle Cardona y Orfila, Mahón (phone: 71-366817). Moderate.

with red currants and pepper sauce. Closed Mondays and from mid-December to mid-March. Reservations necessary. 31 Calle San José, Santa Eulalia del Río (phone: 71-330324). Moderate.

S'Oficina – In the heart of Ibiza town, serving excellent Basque cooking. The fish is good, but for a change of pace, try the beef. Closed Sundays and from mid-December to mid-January. Reservations advised. 6 Avenida de España, Ibiza (phone: 71-300016). Moderate.

Ca'n Pujol – Right on the beach, with great seafood and paella. Playa Port des Torrent, San Antonio Abad (no phone). Moderate to inexpensive.

FORMENTERA

The sea is visible from every point on Formentera, which is nearly flat as a pancake except for a lump — the 630-foot-high La Mola "mountain" — at its eastern extremity. Set 4 miles south of Ibiza and made up of two islets joined by an isthmus, the island measures only about 12 miles from end to end. Ferries arrive at La Sabina, the island harbor, which is on the north coast between two lagoons, Estang de Peix and Estang Pudent (which translate as "fish" and "stinky" lagoon, respectively). The cluster of sparkling white houses just short of 2 miles (3 km) down the road from the port is San Francisco Javier, the capital, home to less than half the island's population of 4,500. Of the other tiny villages scattered throughout the island, San Fernando, 1¼ miles (2 km) to the east, is the next largest. For the rest, the island consists of pine forests and salt flats, generously fringed with beaches — Playa de Mitjorn, on the southern coast and 3 miles long, is long enough to escape being crowded. Others include Playa d'Es Pujols, north of San Fernando, which attracts a certain amount of business from package tours; Playa de Ses Illetas and Playa de Llevant, on either side of the Trocadors peninsula, which stretches north from La Sabina; and Cala Sahona, on the western side of the island, still reasonably remote.

The Carthaginians are known to have worked the salt pans, but they left no trace of settlement on the island. The Romans left it its name, a corruption of the Latin Frumentaria — from *frumentum,* or "wheat" — since Formentera served as a granary for the Roman camp on Ibiza. The Arabs were here, too, but when they left after the Reconquest, the island was uninhabited for much of the Middle Ages, due to fear of the marauding pirates who regularly sought refuge from the rough seas on its defenseless shores. Only late in the 17th century did homesteaders from Ibiza settle in; today, their descendants fish, work the fields and the salt pans, and cater to tourists. But Formentera is more tranquil than the other three Balearic Islands and likely to remain so, since a shortage of fresh water limits development. There are numerous small *hostales* and a couple of large hotels, but they're heavily booked, so anyone planning to stay the night should be sure to have a reservation.

Ferry service from Ibiza town to the Estación Marítima in La Sabina (phone: 71-322703) is frequent, with two lines — *Marítima de Formentera* and *Transmapi* — providing up to 11 round trips daily, year-round. A great many visitors, therefore, come over only for the day. One proviso, however:

Although the ride across the Es Freus channel is short (about 1 hour), it's not necessarily sweet, as the sea can be rough and the currents strong. Because ferries are sometimes canceled, make allowance for possible lost time if there's a plane to catch. Taxis line the pier when ferries arrive; they are reasonable, with an entire island tour costing under $25. The island does have bus service, but renting a car or a moped is preferable. *Autos Ibiza,* located in both Ibiza town (phone: 71-314611) and in La Sabina on Formentera (phone: 71-322031), is one of many companies represented. Formentera's Tourist Office (phone: 71-322034), open mornings only, is located in San Francisco Javier.

CHECKING IN: *Iberotel Club la Mola* – This 328-room resort complex provides the best accommodations on the island, right on its longest beach. Built in Spanish village–style, it offers rooms as well as independent villas, and is equipped with 2 swimming pools, facilities for a variety of water sports, tennis courts, a restaurant, bar, and discotheque. Closed from November through April. Playa de Mitjorn (phone: 71-328069). Expensive.

Sa Volta – A small *hostal* (18 rooms) near the beach, in the midst of the hottest nightlife on this quiet island. It has no pool, but there's a restaurant. Playa de Es Pujols (phone: 71-328125). Moderate to inexpensive.

EATING OUT: *Es Muli des Sal* – A small eatery on the sand dunes in the northern part of the island; the fresh fish and lobsters are mouth-watering. Ses Illetas (no phone). Moderate.

The Canary Islands

A cluster of seven major and six minor islands in the Atlantic Ocean, the Canary Island archipelago lies about 65 miles off the northwest coast of Africa. Not for nothing do they call the Canaries the Fortunate Isles. Bathed by the Gulf Stream and ruffled by the trade winds, they are spread out in a line only about 4° north of the Tropic of Cancer, at roughly the same latitude as Florida, and enjoy a spring-like climate throughout the year — with temperatures mostly in the 70s F. Extremes of heat and cold are unknown in this Spanish archipelago, where European, African, and American influences mingle.

Yet physical contrasts are dramatic. Verdant tropical vegetation flourishes near barren fields of hardened lava, while the snow-capped volcano, the 12,200-foot Pico del Teide, Spain's highest peak, looks down on banana plantations. Morocco and the Sahara lie just across the water, but European capitals are only a brief flight away. The Canaries' blend of the exotic and the familiar, their spectacular scenery, and their long hours of sunshine attract ever-increasing numbers of tourists — most of whom never venture too far from the beaches.

There are 13 islands altogether, but only Grand Canary (Gran Canaria in Spanish), Tenerife, Fuerteventura, Lanzarote, La Gomera, El Hierro, and La Palma are of any significant size. Geologically speaking, the islands were born millions of years ago, when volcanic eruptions from the bed of the Atlantic thrust up a string of islands of striking abruptness, each with its own peculiar characteristics. Hundreds of volcanoes dot the Canaries, and one or two are still smouldering. Because of variations in altitude, and thus of climate, some islands have justly been described as miniature continents. On the heights, the vegetation is alpine, and includes Canary pine and broom. On the lower slopes, irrigation of the rich volcanic soils produces an astonishing abundance of tropical and semi-tropical fruits. Scorching African winds from the Sahara, sometimes bearing a dust haze, create desert conditions on the easternmost islands of Lanzarote and Fuerteventura, as well as along the eastern coasts of Grand Canary and Tenerife. But lofty volcanic peaks block clouds rolling in from the ocean and create damp, luxuriant conditions elsewhere.

The Canary Islands were known to the ancient Greeks; Ptolemy, the 2nd-century geographer, situated his first meridian — 0° longitude — at El Hierro, the most remote of the islands. Although legends suggest to some that the Canaries are the remains of the lost continent of Atlantis, history's first recorded visit occurred during the 1st century. According to Pliny the Elder, the Roman historian, it was explorers from Roman Mauritania who first visited the islands. They found them full of wild dogs, two of which they took back to their king, Juba II. Accordingly, Juba had the islands dubbed *insulae canariae* — islands of dogs. (The descendants of these original canine inhabitants, a type of mastiff known as *verdino,* still live in the Canaries.) Other sources maintain that the islands got their name from a variety of finch (*serinus canarius*) found living in the trees. And to make the confusion just a little greater, a Berber-speaking tribe known as the Canarii lived in nearby Morocco, and some scholars believe it was they who gave their name to the islands. Whatever the etymology, the mainland Spaniards who conquered the seven cone-shaped volcanic islands during the 15th century adapted the Latin name to Spanish as Islas Canarias.

Acquiring mastery over this domain was not easy. The Spaniards faced fierce resistance from the original inhabitants, the Guanche cave dwellers, who were not conquered until 1496, although the islands had been rediscovered in 1402. Little is known about the Guanches, who were eventually decimated by Spanish armies, bubonic plague, locust-induced famine, and volcanic eruptions. A tall, fair-skinned, light-haired people, they probably were of Phoenician and/or Berber stock. They had no boats, however; so how they reached the islands, and from where, is still a mystery. They were reputedly generous and courageous, qualities put to the test by Jean de Béthencourt, a Norman knight who launched an invasion in 1402 and captured Lanzarote, Fuerteventura, La Gomera, and El Hierro. Conquest of the other islands was completed only after arduous campaigns met by ferocious resistance, and those Guanches not killed off by disease, disaster, or slavery were absorbed into the Spanish culture. Some of their distinctive physical characteristics are still visible in the modern population, and traces of their crude existence remain all over the archipelago in the form of ceramics and leather artifacts, geometric cave paintings, mummies, and remnants of their language (such place-names as Timanfaya and Tenerife were inherited from the Guanches) and traditions, not to mention their food — *gofio* remains an island staple. Today's islanders have a newly awakened interest in their ancestors, in reaction to what they often feel is neglect from distant Madrid. From time to time, throughout the islands, slogans appear on posters and walls saying "*Godos* go home!" — *Godo,* meaning "Goth" (as in Visigoth), is the islanders' name for a mainland Spaniard.

During the 18th and 19th centuries, sugarcane, wine, and the cochineal insect brought wealth to the Canaries. The dye obtained from the insect, which lives off the islands' cacti, was exported in large quantities to Britain and France until the invention of artificial colorings. Later, the Canaries prospered with new products, namely bananas, potatoes, tomatoes, and tobacco. For a long time, trade was monopolized by British firms, which also made the towns of Las Palmas on Grand Canary and Santa Cruz de Tenerife on Tenerife important coaling stations for their ships. The Spanish-American War proved a nervous interlude, as Spain was convinced that the United States was about to seize the Canaries before launching an attack on the mainland. Fortifications were built, and fear of an invasion at times reached panic proportions.

Wealthy Europeans began spending winters in the Canaries during the late

19th century. In 1896, Tenerife had eight hotels, all foreign owned. Today, the tourism industry has grown to the point that 5 million people visit the islands annually. British vacationers arrive in the largest numbers, followed by Germans, Italians, Swedes, and Spaniards from "La Península," as mainland Spain is called. It can be extremely difficult to get a room in the better resorts during high season, from December through *Easter* — even though the Canaries have more than 300,000 hotel beds.

The Canary archipelago is one of Spain's Comunidades Autónomas, the 17 autonomous communities, or regions, that make up the country's administrative framework in the post-Franco era. But since 1927, the islands have been split into two provinces, and there is considerable and ongoing rivalry between the ports of Las Palmas and Santa Cruz de Tenerife. Las Palmas is the provincial capital of the eastern islands: Grand Canary (the most populated), Fuerteventura (a virtual desert), and Lanzarote (which has the most impressive volcanic scenery). Santa Cruz de Tenerife is the capital of the western group: Tenerife (the largest island), La Palma (the green island), La Gomera, and El Hierro. The archipelago has its own parliament, and each island has its own *cabildo* (council) to look after local affairs. The nomenclature of the Canaries appears designed to confuse. There are two places named Santa Cruz, for example: One is the capital of Tenerife, the other the capital of La Palma.

A mixture of cultures influences Canarian food. *Gofio,* a belly-filling paste made of flour, water, and milk, comes from the Guanches. *Sancocho canario* is fresh fish cooked with potatoes and served with *mojo,* an essential Canarian seasoning made with oil, vinegar, garlic, salt, and various spices. *Mojo picón,* however, is a hot seasoning made with peppers; watch out, because it's ubiquitous, and its seemingly benign aroma belies its true, incendiary nature. *Papas arrugadas* (literally, wrinkled potatoes), or boiled potatoes cooked in their skins and served with *mojo,* are a popular snack. Restaurants in the Canary Islands span the culinary spectrum, from sleek international dining spots to funky regional places serving local dishes.

Today's Canary Islanders are peaceful, friendly, artistic people, who make their living farming, fishing (some of the world's richest fishing grounds lie between the Canaries and the African coast), and producing handicrafts — as well as by working at various jobs in the modern resort developments. They speak Spanish with a musical accent reminiscent of Latin America, a region to which many Canarians have emigrated over the years. Their folk music also has a Latin American rhythm; folk groups play flutes, drums, guitars, and the *timple,* a small stringed instrument. The quaint villages of white cottages with red roofs sprinkled throughout the mountainous interior of the volcanic islands make the archipelago inviting to travelers who enjoy exploring unusual places and discovering the distinctive character of each island.

SOURCES AND RESOURCES

TOURIST INFORMATION: The regional Oficina de Turismo for the Canary Islands is headquartered on the island of Grand Canary (Plaza Ramón Franco in the Parque Santa Catalina, Las Palmas; phone: 28-264623) and is open Mondays through Fridays from 9 AM to 1:30 PM and 5 to 7 PM, Saturdays from 9 AM to 1 PM. Tenerife's tourist office in the Palacio Insular (Plaza de España, Santa Cruz de Tenerife; phone: 22-242227) is open Mondays through Fridays from 8 AM to 5:45 PM and Saturdays from 9 AM to 1 PM; and a second office (3 Plaza de la Iglesia, phone: 22-386000) is open Mondays through Fridays from 9 AM to 7 PM and Saturdays from 10 AM to 2 PM. The Patronato de Turismo on Fuerteventura (33 Calle Uno de Mayo, Puerto del Rosario; phone: 28-851400) is open Mondays through Fridays from 9 AM to 2 PM and 4 to 7 PM. The Lanzarote Tourist Office (in the Parque Municipal, Arrecife; phone: 28-811762) is open Mondays through Fridays from 8 AM to 2:30 PM and 5:30 to 7 PM. The La Palma Patronato de Turismo (3 Avenida Marítima, Santa Cruz de La Palma; phone: 22-411641) is open Mondays through Fridays from 8 AM to 3 PM and Saturdays from 9 AM to 1 PM. The El Hierro Patronato de Turismo (1 Calle Licenciado Bueno, Valverde; phone: 22-550302) is open Mondays through Fridays from 8 AM to 5 PM. La Gomera has no tourist office, but information can be obtained from the Cabildo Insular (phone: 22-870155), open weekdays from 9 AM to 5 PM.

Local Coverage – Three daily newspapers are published in Las Palmas: *Canarias 7, Diario,* and *La Provincia.* In Santa Cruz de Tenerife, *El Día, Diario de Avisos, La Gaceta de Canarias,* and *Jornada* are also published daily. Newsstands throughout the islands carry a wide range of foreign newspapers and magazines, many of which arrive on the day of publication. A number of English-language publications cater to the needs of tourists and expatriate residents. *Canarias Tourist,* a monthly periodical, is sold on the major islands; published in several languages, it offers information on sights and services. *Tenerife Today* provides similar information on Tenerife. The *Island Gazette,* a monthly magazine long published on Tenerife and aimed mainly at long-term visitors and residents, also includes information on Grand Canary. On Lanzarote, the monthly magazine *Lancelot* serves the English-speaking public.

Telephone – The area code for the islands of Grand Canary, Fuerteventura, and Lanzarote is 28. If calling from mainland Spain (or from the Santa Cruz de Tenerife province), dial 928 before the local number. The area code for the islands of Tenerife, La Palma, La Gomera, and El Hierro is 22. If calling from mainland Spain (or from the Las Palmas province), dial 922 before the local number. No area code is necessary when dialing between islands of the same province. Note that time in the Canaries is 1 hour earlier than on mainland Spain all year.

CLIMATE: The Canaries are tropical islands situated just above the Tropic of Cancer. Their unique geographic features result in an agreeable climate year-round with no dramatic variations in temperature, which average a very comfortable 67 to 83F from the coldest to the hottest months. Even in the winter, it is rarely necessary to wear more than a sweater in the evening. On Grand Canary and Tenerife, the northern and eastern ends of the islands receive more rain than the mostly arid western and southern regions. Clouds often cover the north, while at the same time the south is basking in sunshine. Las Palmas residents admit that the high humidity and heat can be trying in August. The more low-lying Lanzarote and Fuerteventura have a desert-like climate, while La Palma's greenness testifies to its higher amount of rainfall.

 GETTING THERE: The Canaries are linked to the Spanish mainland by frequent air service and regular ferry service. *Iberia Airlines* and its associated commuter lines fly direct to the Canaries from several mainland cities, including Barcelona, Madrid, Málaga, and Seville. Frequent daily inter-island flights are provided by Iberia and Binter, the Canaries' regional carrier.

Trasmediterránea (26-27 Avenida Ramón de Carranza, Cádiz; phone: 56-284311; and 2 Calle Pedro Muñoz Seca, Madrid; phone: 1-431-0700) operates passenger and vehicle ferries several times a week between Cádiz and Santa Cruz de Tenerife, Las Palmas on Grand Canary, and Arrecife on Lanzarote. The trip from Cádiz to Tenerife takes about 36 hours and costs a minumum of $130 per person, one way. *Trasmediterránea* also has frequent inter-island ferry and hydrofoil service.

SPECIAL EVENTS: Camels, bands, and lavishly dressed islanders participate in the *Cabalgata de los Tres Reyes* (Cavalcade of the Three Kings), which takes place on January 5 or 6 in several towns throughout the islands, most notably Las Palmas and Santa Cruz de Tenerife. Also celebrated on all the islands, and with astonishing exuberance, is February's *Carnaval*, but once again Santa Cruz de Tenerife and Las Palmas break the bank to outdo each other with dazzling and outrageous parades, costumes, and nonstop music and dancing; the fiesta builds to a climax on *Mardi Gras* when, with due solemnity, the image of a sardine (the symbol of *Carnaval*) is laid to rest. *Semana Santa* (Holy Week), from *Palm Sunday* through *Easter Sunday,* is another occasion that is celebrated with appropriate solemnity and processions throughout the islands. Numerous other annual events may be peculiar to a single island or even to a single community, since each town has a fiesta to honor its patron saint, although exact dates can vary from year to year. During the last 2 weeks of April, Tegueste, near La Laguna, Tenerife, combines its *romería* (flower-bedecked oxcart procession) with a show of 15,000 bottles of wine from 20 Spanish bodegas; on the same island, in June, for *Corpus Christi* processions, carpets of flowers are arranged on the streets of La Laguna and La Orotava. Early in May, the *Día de la Cruz* (Day of the Cross) is the occasion for one of the year's most lighthearted fiestas, particularly in communities of the island of El Hierro. During September, San Sebastián on La Gomera holds its *Semana de Colón* (Columbus Week) celebrations. September 8 is a big day on Grand Canary, when a colorful procession pays homage to Nuestra Señora del Pino (Our Lady of the Pine) in Teror. Once every 5 years, La Palma holds its *Fiestas Lustrales,* a 2-week festival in Santa Cruz de la Palma in which the highlight is the *Danza de los Enanos* (Dwarfs' Dance); the next celebration will be held in 1995. Finally, to supplement the various regularly occurring music seasons, such as the *Grand Canary Philharmonic Orchestra* series from October to mid-June, the January-to-June concerts by the *Las Palmas Philharmonic Society,* and other music and dance events, Las Palmas hosts the *Festival de Opera* in February and March; in recent years, artists such as Placido Domingo, Montserrat Caballé, and Luciano Pavarotti have appeared here. On Tenerife, there is the *International Festival of Theater and Dance,* from March to June in La Laguna, in addition to the regular *Tenerife Symphony Orchestra* seasons in La Laguna and Santa Cruz and the annual winter and spring concert season in Puerto de la Cruz.

 SPORTS AND FITNESS: The Canaries' ideal climate makes the islands an outdoors lovers' paradise. A wide range of sports and fitness facilities are available, and for those preferring to limit themselves to spectator sports, there are such local favorites as stick fighting, which is believed to have been inherited from the Guanches, and *lucha canaria* — a primitive and colorful form of wrestling in which a wrestler wins by forcing any part of his opponent's body, except his feet, to the floor (regular exhibitions and team matches are held). Cock fighting is legal and usually held on Sundays from December to May; the *López Socas Stadium* (Calle Ortiz de Sarate) is the venue in Las Palmas. The fight is accompanied by excited wagering, and blood flies, but fights usually are stopped before a bird is killed. Soccer is also popular, and anyone catching a clash between Santa Cruz de Tenerife and Las Palmas may wonder whether this isn't a blood sport, too.

Boating – The Canaries have a variety of well-equipped marinas that serve vacationers as well as the yachtsmen who use the islands as a starting point for their transatlantic crossings. Lateen sailing is a Canarian specialty, and regular regattas are held in the summer. Grand Canary's yachting clubs include the *Real Club Náutico de Gran Canaria,* in Las Palmas (phone: 28-266690 or 28-245202), one of Spain's oldest, with a wide range of sports facilities; *Puerto Deportivo de Puerto Rico* (phone: 28-745757), which offers sea excursions and yacht rentals; and *Club de Yates Pasito Blanco* (in Maspalomas; phone: 28-762259).

Fishing – Swordfish, stingray, tunny, grouper, conger eel, and giant ray are some of the 1,500 species that thrive in the waters surrounding the Canaries. Craft and equipment rentals are available at most harbors throughout the islands, and fine catches are also possible casting off the islands' many rock cliffs; good catches also often result from little more than an effortless cast into the surf from the beach. Fishing excursions are organized from Puerto Rico on Grand Canary. *Nautisport* (phone: 22-791459) runs shark fishing trips from Los Cristianos quay on Tenerife (about $35 per person, including lunch and drinks), and daily fishing excursions are organized from Los Gigantes harbor in southeast Tenerife (phone: 22-331988). For deep-sea fishing from Corralejo on Fuerteventura, contact *Escualo* in Jandía (phone: 28-852293) or *Pez Velero* (phone: 28-866173).

Golf – Canary Island golf courses offer challenging conditions amid spectacular and unusual scenery. On Grand Canary, the *Club de Golf Las Palmas* (Carretera de Bandama, Km 5; phone: 28-351290), Spain's oldest golf club, offers beautiful surroundings 9 miles (14 km) south of Las Palmas on the edge of a volcanic crater, while the greens at *Campo de Maspalomas* (near the *Maspalamos Oasis* hotel; phone: 28-762581) are carpeted with Bermuda turf. Tenerife's offerings include the 18-hole championship course (plus another 9 holes) at *Club del Sur* (San Miguel de Abona; phone: 22-704555), laid out around lava fields; the *Club de Golf de Tenerife* (El Peñon, Tacoronte; phone: 22-250240); and the *Amarilla Golf and Country Club* (Costa del Silencio, Arona; phone: 22-103422).

Horseback Riding – Horses can be rented from a number of hotels and stables throughout the islands. On Grand Canary, try *Picadero del Club de Golf de Bandama* (phone: 28-351290) or *Picadero del Oasis de Maspalomas* (phone: 28-762378), both in Las Palmas. On Tenerife, the *Amarilla Golf and Country Club* (Costa del Silencio, Arona; phone: 22-103422) has an equestrian center.

Jeep Safaris – *Unisafari,* on Grand Canary (21 Calle Dr. Grau Bassas, Las Palmas; phone: 28-277100), is one of several companies running off-road driving safaris through the wilder parts of the islands.

Scuba Diving – Clear, warm water and myriad exotic fish attract scuba divers and snorkelers. One of the best spots for diving lies between the northern tip of Fuerteventura and the southern tip of Lanzarote, around the Isla de los Lobos. The *Diving Center Miguel Abella Cerdá* (Apartado 8, Corralejo, Fuerteventura; phone: 28-866243) offers a variety of boat trips and scuba courses with English-speaking instructors and dive masters. On Grand Canary, Heinz Lange, a German expatriate dive master, runs a scuba school in Maspalomas (phone: 28-765244); the *Sun Sub Club* (at the *Buenaventura* hotel in Playa del Inglés; phone: 28-761650, ext. 925) offers a variety of courses and reef trips, as does the *Club Canario de Investigaciones y Actividades Subacuáticas* (67 Calle Pío XII, Las Palmas; phone: 28-246810). On Tenerife, try the *Las Palmeras* hotel (Playa de las Américas; phone: 22-790911).

Swimming and Sunning – Sunbathing is *the* "sport" of the Canaries, and many of the islands' beaches (those away from the huge resort areas) are virtually untouched — at least as yet — by mass tourism. Miles of uncrowded golden sands can be found on Fuerteventura (at the northeastern tip and parts of the southern coast) and Lanzarote (on the southern coast). The most crowded of the islands' beaches are on Grand Canary and Tenerife. Topless bathing is more the rule than the exception, and nude bathing is very common in many of the secluded areas. The waters surrounding the islands are a dazzling blue, and are warm enough (an average of 72F) for year-round swimming.

Tennis – Most of the islands' larger hotels and resorts have tennis courts, and many new sports-oriented complexes are springing up. Tennis clubs on Grand Canary include the *Sun Club* (Playa del Inglés; phone: 28-762870); *Club de Tenis Biarritz* (San Agustín; phone: 28-760356); and *Helga Masthoff Tenis* hotel (Carretera de los Palmitos, Maspalomas; 28-761436). Clubs on Tenerife include the *British Sports Club* (Carretera de Taoro, Puerto de la Cruz; phone: 22-384823) and *Oceánico Tenis Club* (Carretera de Fuerteventura, Puerto de la Cruz; phone: 22-380018).

Water Skiing – Water skiing schools operate from the more popular beaches on Grand Canary, Tenerife, and Lanzarote.

Windsurfing – Steady breezes make the Canaries an ideal spot for this ever-growing sport. Enthusiasts trek here from all over Europe, and the islands have hosted several world championships over the years. Instruction is available and boards can be rented, for about $30 a day, on many of the islands' beaches. Popular Grand Canary windsurfing schools and centers include the *Mistral Windsurfing Club* (at the *Bahía Feliz Hotel,* Playa de Tarajalillo; phone: 28-763332) and the *Luis Molina Windsurfing School* (Playa del Inglés; phone: 28-761524). El Médano beach, near Reina Sofia Airport on Tenerife, is a favorite windsurfing site; *Looping Windsurf School* (Costa Teguise; phone: 22-815796) is the place to learn how to windsurf on Lanzarote. The beaches at Corralejo, Cotillo, and Jandía are the best spots for riding the wind and the waves off Fuerteventura.

GRAND CANARY

Grand Canary, the most heavily populated of the Canary Islands, is circular in shape and covers only 592 square miles, but it encompasses a variety of landscapes and climates. When it is cool and cloudy along the northern slopes — where tomatoes, potatoes, sugarcane, and bananas flourish — sunbathers will be soaking up the rays on beaches in the cloudless south. At the same time, chill winds may be sweeping over the island's 6,400-foot central heights, ruffling the upland forests of laurel, pine, and eucalyptus. Sheer ravines cut into the volcanic mountains of the center, and agriculture flourishes because of intricate irrigation schemes. To anyone flying into Gando International Airport, about midway along the island's eastern coast, Grand Canary looks like Mt. Everest rising from the Sahara. The stark, rugged landscape becomes greener upon descent, and it soon becomes possible to distinguish the banana trees, sugarcane, and other cultivation that make each village an oasis. The island has 600,000 inhabitants, most of whom live in the north in the bustling capital of Las Palmas, while ever-increasing numbers of sun-hungry visitors flock to the fine beaches of the southern coast, inspiring ambitious development.

Las Palmas, extending along a strip of seafront at the island's northeastern tip, is the largest city in the archipelago, a major port, tourist resort, and shopping center. It has, besides its 350,000 inhabitants, a large transient population, from globetrotting yachtsmen to African peddlers, from French sailors to windsurfing freaks. An easygoing place, its rhythm of life is determined by the sun. Visitors often spend the day lying in the sun from 8 or 9 AM until 4 or 5 PM. Then, in the cool of the evening, they head for the outdoor cafés, shops, restaurants, and bars of the seafront promenade. Shops remain open until dusk; if clouds or mist interferes with the sun, people stroll or shop — but only until the sun reappears.

In the interior of the island, southwest of Las Palmas along narrow, mountain roads, is Tejeda, standing about 4,800 feet above sea level amid a bleak, volcanic landscape. The setting, described by the Spanish poet Miguel de Unamuno as a "petrified storm," is awesome, but it's not the aspect of nature that most visitors to the Canaries come to see. More soothing is the Maspalomas–Playa del Inglés–San Agustín resort area, sometimes called the Costa Canaria, along the island's southern coast, about 34½ miles (55 km) from Las Palmas and 15½ miles (25 km) from Gando Airport. The area stretches for miles, embracing three resort developments, excellent beaches, and a mini-Sahara of spectacular sand dunes.

GETTING AROUND: Airport – Scheduled flights connect Grand Canary with Alicante, Asturias (Oviedo), Barcelona, Bilbao, Granada, Jerez de la Frontera, Madrid, Málaga, Santiago de Compostela, Seville, and Valencia on the Spanish mainland, as well as with Palma de Mallorca in the Balearics. There are also daily flights to and from Fuerteventura, El Hierro, Lanzarote, La Palma, and Tenerife. Grand Canary's airport, Gando, is located about 14 miles (22 km) from Las Palmas and 15½ miles (25 km) from San Agustín. The No. 60 bus runs hourly to downtown Las Palmas; a taxi ride costs about $20. The *Iberia* office in Las Palmas is at 8 Calle Alcalde Ramírez Bethencourt (phone: 28-360111).

Bus – The central bus station is next to Parque San Telmo. *Salcai* (phone: 28-368631) covers the southern part of the island and *Utinsa* (phone: 28-360179) handles the northern part. The most useful line in the city is the No. 1, or Teatro–Puerto route, which runs runs day and night along Calle León y Castillo from the resort area to the historic quarter.

Car Rental – Major rental car companies are *Avis* (phone: 28-265572 in Las Palmas; 28-760963 at Playa del Inglés; 28-700157 at the airport); *Hertz* (phone: 28-226497 in Las Palmas; 28-762572 at Playa del Inglés; 28-264576 at the airport); and *Europcar* (phone: 28-275997 in Las Palmas; 28-765500 at Playa del Inglés; 28-700147 at the airport).

Ferry – *Trasmediterránea* (Muelle Ribera Oeste, Las Palmas; phone: 28-267766) operates car and passenger ferries between Las Palmas and Cádiz and between Las Palmas and the six other major Canaries, and jetfoils between Las Palmas and the other islands.

Mopeds and Motorcycles – Throughout the island, mopeds (top speed 35 mph) are available for about $10 a day, motorcycles for about $20. Try *Motos Rent-Puig* (4 Calle Montevideo, Las Palmas; phone: 28-274901) or *Sun-Ped* (Edificio Barbados, Avenida Tirajana, Playa del Inglés; phone: 28-764434).

Taxi – Taxis in Las Palmas use meters; elsewhere on the island, it is best to agree on a rate with the driver before the trip. Las Palmas has numerous cabstands, as well as radio cabs (phone: 28-762871). For a radio cab in the Maspalomas area, call 28-762871 or 28-760293.

SPECIAL PLACES: Las Palmas – The city stretches from La Isleta peninsula and the Puerto de la Luz area, where cruise liners and merchant vessels dock, south along a narrow isthmus. The Castillo de la Luz, on the Isleta on Calle Juan Rejón, was built in 1494 to protect the town from pirates and other invaders (which included the English fleet of Sir Francis Drake) and has been restored to serve as a cultural center. Just south of the Isleta, on the western side of the isthmus, begins a 2-mile beach, Playa de las Canteras, which gently curves around a sheltered bay caused by a natural depression in the coastline. A rocky reef offshore, shaped rather like an arm, extends almost around the bay, making it as calm as a lake. Running parallel to the beach is the Paseo de las Canteras, a promenade boasting numerous bars, cafés, and restaurants: not just Spanish but also Swedish, Italian, Chinese, Finnish, Mexican, Indian, and German, as well as a few of the sit-down or stand-up, fast-food variety. Most resort hotels are in the vicinity as well. A pleasant way to spend time in this modern area is to go for a walk in Parque Santa Catalina, where Canarian families often come for their evening strolls, to take a drink at one of the cafés and eye the passing scene. To reach the park from the Paseo de las Canteras, walk along Calle Padre Cueto 3 or 4 blocks, turn right, and walk another 2 blocks. Farther south, the public market is a good place for photographing people engaged in the everyday commerce of buying and selling food and other provisions. It occupies an entire block at the corner of Calle Néstor de la Torre and Calle Galicia.

Still farther south are the palm trees and fountains of Parque Doramas, containing a zoo, a swimming pool, the stately old *Santa Catalina* hotel, and the Pueblo Canario. The latter is an unusual replica of a Canarian village, designed by the local painter and sculptor Néstor de la Torre (1888–1938), with a pleasant open-air café, craft shops, and regular folk dancing and singing performances (Sundays from 11:45 AM to 1:15 PM and Thursdays from 5:30 to 7 PM. It also contains the artist's house, now the *Museo Néstor,* displaying paintings and memorabilia (open Mondays, Tuesdays, Thursdays, and Fridays from 10 AM to 1 PM and from 4 to 7 PM, Saturdays from 10 AM to 1 PM; closed Wednesdays and Sundays; admission charge; phone: 28-245135). Any bus traveling along Calle León y Castillo at Parque Santa Catalina also goes to Parque Doramas. Another park, Parque de San Telmo, is farther south, where the broad, bustling shopping street, Calle Mayor de Triana, begins and leads south to the Vegueta, the city's Old Quarter. Parallel to Triana is the *Casa-Museo Pérez-Galdós* (33 Calle Caño; phone: 28-366976), the former home of a 19th- and 20th-century writer and campaigner against social injustice (open Mondays through Saturdays from 9 AM to 1 PM.)

The Vegueta, the city's historic center, an area of peaceful cobbled streets, old balconied buildings, and pleasant squares, is a short way farther south (but if heading for it directly from the Isleta or Puerto de la Luz area, take a taxi or bus No. 1). Here, fronting the noble Plaza de Santa Ana, where bronze statues commemorate Canarian canines, is the 15th-century cathedral, Gothic in origin, with a later, neo-classical exterior. Among the treasures of this vast volcanic-rock structure are a gold and emerald chalice, donated by King Philip IV, and an 18th-century gold throne, while the cathedral's *Museo Diocesano de Arte Sacroepiscopal* boasts a collection of magnificent Flemish and Castilian paintings. (The museum is open weekdays, except Wednesdays, from 9 AM to 2 PM and 4 to 6 PM; weekends, from 10 AM to 1:30 PM; admission charge; phone: 28-310889.)

Directly across the street from the cathedral is the *Casa de Colón* (1 Calle Colón; phone: 28-311255), the former governors' residence. This dignified mansion housed Christopher Columbus for a short time in 1502 before he headed to the Americas on one of his later voyages. It now functions as a small museum, containing objects of the period of Columbus's explorations, including heavy cannon, faded maps, and models of the explorer's vessels, as well as sculptures and paintings. Open Mondays through Fridays, from 9:30 AM to 1 PM, Saturdays from 9:30 AM to 12:45 PM. Admission charge. Another museum, nearby, is the *Museo Canario* (2 Calle Dr. Verneau; phone: 28-315600), displaying ceramics and implements of the original island inhabitants. The first floor is riveting — full of glass cases containing hundreds of skulls of the Guanches, some showing evidence of trepannage techniques used in primitive medicine. Most striking are the mummified remains of entire bodies — one, believed to be a king's son, is wrapped in layers of ceremonial skins and rush weavings. Open Mondays through Saturdays, from 10 AM to 1 PM and 4 to 6 PM. Admission charge.

The North – Cenobio de Valerón, a remarkable archaeological site, is 15½ miles (25 km) west of Las Palmas via the C810 coastal highway. Here the rock is honeycombed with caves where once, it is believed, young daughters of the Guanche nobility were kept as vestal virgins. From nearby Guía, a road zigags inland and back eastward through fertile terraced farmland, verdant with bananas and sugarcane, to Moya and Arucas. The latter, 10½ miles (17 km) out of Las Palmas, has a somber Gothic-style church, built during this century, standing out against the town's white houses — of which there are spectacular views from the observation deck at the top of the nearby Montaña de Arucas. Continue south to Teror, 13 miles (21 km) from Las Palmas, a marvel of traditional, harmonious architecture with wooden-balconied mansions. At its heart, in an 18th-century basilica with magnificent stonework and a fine coffered ceiling, Nuestra Señora del Pino, is the much-venerated statue of Our Lady of the Pine, Grand Canary's patron saint, said to have been found in a pine tree in 1481. The statue is the object of the island's annual pilgrimage on September 8.

The Interior – Drive south on C811 to Tafira, a green residential area overlooking Las Palmas, and follow signs beyond to the *mirador* (belvedere) on Pico de Bandama, a 1,865-foot peak that looks down on a perfect volcanic crater, more than 3,000 feet across and 650 feet deep. Continuing toward Tejeda, at San Mateo, the *Casa-Museo Cho Zacarías* is a rustically charming old house with rooms full of old furniture and implements, and has a restaurant serving simple, moderately priced meals between 1 and 4 PM (closed Mondays; no phone). From San Mateo, a road winds up into pinewoods and stark mountains. At Cruz de Tejeda, 26 miles (42 km) from Las Palmas and more than 4,825 feet above sea level, there are impressive views of a tortured landscape, including a vast amphitheater and the isolated Roque Nublo, a rock said to have been worshiped by the Guanches. The *Hostería de Cruz de Tejeda* (phone: 28-658050), part of the *parador* chain, but serving meals only, is a good place to stop for lunch (open daily; moderate).

The South – The Maspalomas–Playa del Inglés–San Agustín resort area lures most of Grand Canary's visitors. At Maspalomas, the southernmost part of the area, are spectacular sand dunes, a 4-mile beach, a sprawl of elegant resort hotels, and a lighthouse. San Agustín, the northernmost part, with another beach, also has luxury hotels, but tends to be more residential, while between the two, the endless high-rise hotels and apartment blocks of Playa del Inglés (Englishmen's Beach) attract large numbers of visitors on inexpensive packages. Most of the island's sports facilities and a variety of nightlife and other attractions are in this area — there's even a Sioux City (Ciudad del Oueste), a Western show town, where cowboys and Indians fight it out twice daily, and the *Three Stars Saloon* (Calle Cañon del Aguila, San Agustín; phone: 28-762573) serves meals to the twang of country and western music. At Playa del Inglés is Palmitos Park, home of 230 species of exotic birds that roam an area dotted with lakes and palm trees, and home also of hundreds of varieties of tropical butterflies (open from 9 AM to 7 PM). About a mile (1.6 km) to the west of the Maspalomas lighthouse, Playa

Pasito Blanco has a deep-water harbor with a marina where deep-sea charters can be hired. Also west of Maspalomas, just 20 miles (32 km) away, is the Puerto Rico apartment-condominium development, great for families and couples who want to spend a month, a summer, or the entire year in a setting complete with marina, beach, swimming pools, restaurants, shopping, and playgrounds.

SHOPPING: Las Palmas is a well-known shopper's paradise, offering a dazzling variety of products minus the IVA, or value added tax, found on the mainland. Each island does, however, impose its own luxury tax on imports. This means that products at the lower end of the market are less expensive than elsewhere — tobacco and liquor are particularly low-priced — but costlier goods may be no less expensive than on the mainland or elsewhere in Europe. As the European Economic Community gradually removes duties on the internal movement of goods around the Continent, there will be less variation in prices among the Canaries, mainland Spain, and the rest of Europe.

Large stores and small boutiques stock everything from the latest designer clothing to top-quality leatherware, sold at nonnegotiable prices, while in hundreds of shops known as bazaars, it's possible to bargain over the cost of electronic goods, precious and semi-precious stones, jewelry, and local handicrafts. This "negotiation," as it is otherwise called, is highly appropriate, but the shopper has to be good at it to best the Indian, Pakistani, and Lebanese merchants who own most of the bazaars. It's a good idea to know the range of prices of items under consideration throughout the city before actually buying. It's also a good idea to know the price of luxury goods at home; although items such as cameras, computers, and video and sound equipment may be less expensive than in European capitals, they often sell for less in the US, with more possibility of redress if a purchase proves faulty. Be sure to know the exact model number: It can make a big difference in the price. As for crafts, open-worked embroidery is a Canarian specialty; intricately hand-embroidered blouses, table linen, and bedspreads are especially appealing. Make sure the product is authentic, not a mass-produced imitation. Other interesting buys include the *timple,* the small guitar-like instrument featured in island folk music, and pottery — particularly the simple designs made without the use of a potter's wheel. Plenty of shops also sell Chinese silk, Indian marble, liquor, shoes, and souvenir items.

In Las Palmas, the traditional shopping street is Calle Mayor de Triana (or just Triana), while the larger stores and newer boutiques are found on Avenida Mesa y López, near the port. The bazaars are found mostly around the Parque Santa Catalina district. Shops are generally open from 9 AM to 1 PM and from 4:15 to 7:30 PM. The rival Spanish department stores have branches opposite each other: *El Corte Inglés* (18 Avenida Mesa y López; phone: 28-272600 or 28-263000), and *Galerías Preciados* (15 Avenida Mesa y López; phone: 28-233055).

Fataga – The place for high-quality island handicrafts. Plaza Ramón Franco, Las Palmas (phone: 28-265622).

Maya – Stocks everything from jade and porcelain giftware to computers and stereo equipment. 105-107 Calle Triana, Las Palmas (phone: 28-367167).

Mikel – Ceramics and other gifts. In the Edificio Vera Cruz, just off the Plaza de España, Las Palmas (phone: 28-274606).

Voula Mitsakou – A well-known furrier with shops in half a dozen European cities, charging 30% to 50% less for sable, ermine, and other skins at its Canary Island branch. 28 Calle Luis Morote, Las Palmas (phone: 28-267636).

Peridis Brothers – Fine display of luxury furs in a modern showroom. 6 Paseo de las Canteras, Las Palmas (phone: 28-274376).

Las Perlas – Precious stones, cultured pearls, and gold and silver jewelry. 32 Calle Luis Morote, Las Palmas (phone: 28-269701).

Saphir – A wide selection of Swiss watches, precious stones, cultured pearls, and silver and porcelain gift items. 97 Calle Triana (phone: 28-362388) and 70 Calle Sagasta, Las Palmas (phone: 28-275964).

 CHECKING IN: Hotels are concentrated in Las Palmas and the resort area around Maspalomas, where there are also many apartments for rent at reasonable prices. From November through *Easter,* bookings are heavy and reservations are advisable; in summer, rooms generally do not sell out and advance reservations are not needed. After *Easter,* many establishments offer discounts of 20% to 30% off their high-season rates. Most hotels cater to large tour groups — from northern Europe during winter, from Spain in summer. Expect to pay $115 or more for a double room at hotels listed as expensive, between $60 and $100 at a hotel listed as moderate, and under $60 in those listed as inexpensive.

LAS PALMAS

Meliá Las Palmas – Formerly the *Cristina Sol,* this large and luxurious property overlooking Las Canteras beach is a favorite of businesspeople; its conference rooms can accommodate up to 500 people. The 316 air conditioned rooms feature glass-enclosed balconies, color television sets, videocassette players, and mini-bars. There are also 2 swimming pools and a bather's terrace, which overlooks the beach, as well as 2 fine restaurants, a discotheque, and lovely gardens. 6 Calle Gomera, Las Palmas (phone: 28-267600). Expensive.

Reina Isabel – Relatively modern in decor and furnishings, this is one of the most luxurious establishments on the island, located right on Las Canteras beach. It could stand some renovations, but all 234 rooms are air conditioned and have color television sets, private balconies, and 24-hour room service. There is also a fine restaurant, a popular terrace bar, a rooftop, heated swimming pool (with an adjoining disco), a solarium, and a beachfront nightclub. 40 Calle Alfredo L. Jones, Paseo de las Canteras, Las Palmas (phone: 28-260100). Expensive.

Santa Catalina – Most of the city's hotels are modern, but this Spanish colonial fantasy, with carved wood balconies, bucks the trend. Spacious and charmingly old-fashioned, it stands in the middle of the flowers of Parque Doramas. Chandeliers light the marble lobby; the terrace, shaded by green-and-white awnings, is an ideal place to relax and sip a cold drink. The 200 rooms are large, with balconies, traditional furnishings, air conditioning, mini-bars, and color television sets (the rooms appear slightly shabby, but ongoing renovations should bring them up to the same high standards as the public spaces). Other facilities include a new casino, a large swimming pool, tennis courts, a miniature golf course, a shopping arcade, and fireplaces in the public rooms. Parque Doramas, Las Palmas (phone: 28-243040). Expensive.

Los Bardinos Sol – This circular structure near the Parque Santa Catalina offers fine views of the city and the sea. All 215 rooms are air conditioned and have color television sets. Other facilities include a rooftop swimming pool and a disco on the 24th floor. 3 Calle Eduardo Benot, Las Palmas (phone: 28-266100). Moderate.

Gran Canaria – A 90-room hotel that overlooks the beach and has a pleasant and efficient staff. The simple yet cheerful rooms are air conditioned and have mini-bars. There is also a good restaurant. 38 Paseo de las Canteras, Las Palmas (phone: 28-275078). Moderate to inexpensive.

Villa Blanca – For those on a tight budget, this 45-room hotel is comfortable, clean, and functional. Located near Las Canteras beach, across the street from the *Reina Isabel.* 35 Calle Alfredo L. Jones, Las Palmas (phone: 28-260016). Inexpensive.

MASPALOMAS AREA

Gloria Palace – An ultramodern luxury behemoth situated between Playa del Inglés and Maspalomas, its 448 air conditioned rooms have mini-bars and sea views.

Facilities include 4 pools, a snack bar, a garden restaurant and a rooftop restaurant, 3 tennis courts, a health club, and a casino. Calle Las Margaritas, Maspalomas (phone: 28-768304). Expensive.

Iberotel Maspalomas Oasis – The center of the action, this busy, large, luxury resort in the vicinity of the lighthouse offers guests idyllic surroundings in an oasis on Maspalomas beach. A low-rise establishment amid flowers, palm trees, lawns, and fountains, it has 342 air conditioned, good-size, and stylishly designed rooms. Tennis, archery, a children's nursery, and nightly entertainment are among the facilities. Excellent international food is served in *Le Jardin* grill. This is a popular place with tour groups, and German visitors outnumber English-speaking guests. Plaza Palmeras, Playa de Maspalomas (phone: 28-760170). Expensive.

Meliá Tamarindos – Surrounded by beautiful gardens, this hotel rivals the best of them in decor, grounds, and facilities. Its 2 swimming pools and beach make it a good place for simple lounging in the sun, although tennis, mini-golf, archery, bowling, and casino gambling are all available. There are 318 air conditioned rooms, several bars, and a disco. The huge, white, cast-concrete object on the hill across the highway with a pole in its center is a sundial, a gift from Sweden — and people can set their watches by it. 3 Calle Retama, Playa de San Agustín (phone: 28-762600). Expensive.

EATING OUT: Given its cosmopolitan nature, diners on Grand Canary can enjoy a wide range of international dishes, as well as local specialties and various Spanish offerings. Expect to pay $65 or more for a meal for two at places listed as expensive, between $30 and $60 at restaurants in the moderate category, and under $30 at inexpensive ones. Prices do not include drinks, wine, or tips.

LAS PALMAS

Churchill – In an old colonial-style building that houses the *British Club* upstairs, this restaurant features a menu that makes good use of imaginative recipes from a variety of countries. Specialties include pâtés, roast baby lamb, and home-baked pies. Closed Saturday afternoons, Sundays, and holidays. Reservations necessary. 274 Calle León y Castillo, Las Palmas (phone: 28-249192). Expensive to moderate.

Bodegón – A longtime favorite for Canarian cooking, especially seafood. Try the *cazuela canaria* (fish casserole) or the *sancocho de pescado* (fish stew). Closed Mondays. Reservations unnecessary. Parque Doramas, Las Palmas (phone: 28-242985). Moderate.

El Cortijo – This wood-beamed replica of a Castilian inn serves mighty portions of roast suckling pig, lamb chops, and Segovia-sausage in a hearty and informal atmosphere. Reservations unnecessary. 3 Calle Diderot, Las Palmas (phone: 28-275955). Moderate.

Le Francais – A few yards from Las Canteras beach, this is a family-run place, tastefully done in simple French style, with colorful flowered tablecloths accenting the whitewashed walls of the dining room. Try the delicious salmon quiche or the sole almondine. Closed Sundays. Reservations unnecessary. Calle Sargento Llagas, Las Palmas (phone: 28-268762). Moderate.

House of Ming – One of the town's best Chinese restaurants (there are over 20 in all), offering friendly service and picturesque views of the blue Atlantic. Reservations unnecessary. 30 Paseo de las Canteras, Las Palmas (phone: 28-274563). Moderate.

Mesón La Paella – Authentic Catalan cooking and excellent Middle Eastern rice dishes are the specialties in this eatery, one of the few places in the Canaries offering good paella. Closed Saturday evenings, Sundays, and holidays. Reservations unnecessary. 47 Calle Juan Manuel Durán, Las Palmas (phone: 28-271640). Moderate.

Nanking – It's a long way from the China Sea to the Mediterranean, but the Cantonese culinary influence has nonetheless weathered the tide. Many people's first choice as the best Chinese restaurant in town, this is certainly one of the most popular. Its air conditioned interior is undoubtedly a factor, along with the food. Reservations unnecessary. 11 Calle José F. Roca, Las Palmas (phone: 28-269870). Moderate.

El Pote – A popular spot for cooking in the style of Galicia — the Galician pork chops and Santiago tart make tasty eating. Closed Sundays. Reservations unnecessary. 41 Calle José María Durán, Las Palmas (phone: 28-278058). Moderate.

Tenderete – This restaurant is noted for its careful preparation of typical Canarian dishes, such as *papas arrugadas con mojo* (wrinkled potatoes in a piquant sauce). Fresh flowers on the tables and numerous hanging plants lend a pleasing air to the white-walled dining room (photos testify to the visit here of the Spanish king and queen). Baked fish, pork, lamb, and suckling pig are all good. Reservations unnecessary. 91 Calle León y Castillo, Las Palmas (phone: 28-246350). Moderate.

El Gallo Feliz – Its Danish owner attracts Scandinavians with plates of herring and smoked eel on toast with scrambled eggs. Friendly, fast service in a cozy room. Open evenings only, November through April. Reservations unnecessary. 35 Paseo de las Canteras, Las Palmas (no phone). Inexpensive.

MASPALOMAS AREA

San Agustín Beach Club – This restaurant, with an African decor, enjoys a strikingly contemporary setting overlooking the beach. It's renowned for topnotch and imaginative international fare — and guests can alternate plunges into the pool with open-air dining. Closed during May and June. Reservations advised. Playa de los Cocoteros, San Agustín (phone: 28-760400). Expensive.

La Toja – On the ground floor of an undistinguished apartment building, but very comfortable and welcoming inside. Seafood is the specialty here. Try the prawn crêpes, dill-marinated salmon, hake, or angler. Closed Sundays for lunch. Reservations unnecessary. Avenida Tirajana, Playa del Inglés (phone: 28-761196). Expensive to moderate.

Tenderete II – An offshoot of the original Las Palmas establishment, and now under new ownership, it serves good Canarian and seafood specialties. Reservations unnecessary. Just opposite the *Rey Carlos* hotel in the Edificio Aloe, Avenida Tirajana, Playa del Inglés (phone: 28-761460). Moderate.

TENERIFE

At 793 square miles, the largest of the Canary Islands is only 20 minutes by air west of Las Palmas and is also accessible by flights from Madrid in a little over 2 hours. Legend has it that God put so much effort into creating the beaches of Grand Canary that night fell before he could finish the mountains. When he came to Tenerife, he began with the mountains, and this time darkness fell before he could get around to the beaches. Thus Tenerife has fewer beaches than its neighbor and the sand is black. Still, there is enough to attract the visitor. Towering above Tenerife's mixture of lush vegetation and arid desert is the massive dormant volcano, Pico del Teide, Spain's highest peak at 12,200 feet — the island's name is believed to have evolved from a Guanche word meaning snow-capped mountain.

A somewhat higher rate of rainfall falls on Tenerife than on its neighbors, which explains why it is is sometimes called the "island of eternal spring." Consequently, Tenerife is the archipelago's main agricultural center, producing most of its vegetables. The northern and northwestern corners receive the most rainfall, which encourages forests and colorful vegetation, while the south is arid and desolate. Also in the north are the settlements of long standing: Santa Cruz de Tenerife, the provincial capital; La Laguna, accommodating one of Spain's oldest seats of learning; and Puerto de la Cruz, once important as a fruit- and wine-exporting port and now a prestigious tourism resort. Around southern beaches at Los Cristianos and Playa de las Américas, the all-year sunshine has fostered a development boom, covering tracts of desert with apartments and hotels. These new resorts, and the nearby Reina Sofía Airport, are linked with Santa Cruz by a fast four-lane highway, while another autoroute speeds traffic up to Puerto de la Cruz. Interior roads, in contrast, are narrow, winding, and tiring to drive.

 GETTING AROUND: Airport – Tenerife has direct air service with Alicante, Asturias (Oviedo), Barcelona, Bilbao, Granada, Jerez de la Frontera, Madrid, Málaga, Santiago de Compostela, Seville, and Valencia, on the mainland, as well as with Palma de Mallorca in the Balearics. There are also regular connections with Fuerteventura, Grand Canary, El Hierro, Lanzarote, and La Palma. National and international flights arrive and depart from Reina Sofía Airport, on the island's southern coast, about 37½ miles (60 km) from Santa Cruz de Tenerife. Most inter-island flights use Los Rodeos Airport (Aeropuerto del Norte), 8 miles (13 km) from Santa Cruz. *Iberia* has several Tenerife offices (23 Avenida de Anaga, Santa Cruz; phone: 22-288000; Avenida de Venezuela, Puerto de la Cruz; phone: 22-380050; and at the airport; phone: 22-252340). Buses run between Reina Sofía Airport and Santa Cruz, and there are regular buses from between Los Rodeos Airport and Santa Cruz and Puerto de la Cruz. The taxi fare from Reina Sofía to Santa Cruz is about $50, from Los Rodeos, about $12.

Bus – There is frequent bus service to all of the island's major centers. The main bus station in Santa Cruz is on Avenida 3 de Mayo (phone: 22-218122 or 22-219399); in Puerto de la Cruz, on Calle del Pozo, just opposite the post office (phone: 22-382814). At Los Cristianos, buses stop at the main taxi stand opposite the Cepsa gas station (for information, call 22-770606).

Car Rental – Major rental car companies are *Avis* (phone: 22-241294 in Santa Cruz; 22-384552 in Puerto de la Cruz; 22-770656 at Reina Sofía Airport; and 22-259090 at Los Rodeos Airport); *Hertz* (phone: 22-274805 in Santa Cruz; 22-384719 in Puerto de la Cruz and at Reina Sofía Airport; and 22-790861 at Playa de las Américas); and *Europcar* (phone: 22-387390 in Puerto de la Cruz and 22-771150 at Reina Sofía Airport).

Ferry – *Trasmediterránea* (59 Calle Marina, Santa Cruz; phone: 22-277500) has regular sailings between Cádiz and Santa Cruz, as well as between Tenerife and many of the other islands. The company also runs a jet foil from Santa Cruz to Las Palmas, Grand Canary (operating 5 to 7 days a week, 3 to 4 times a day), and to Morro Jable, Fuerteventura (5 weekly departures once a day), as well as a new hydrofoil service between Los Cristianos and San Sebastián, on the neighboring island of La Gomera, stopping occasionally at Las Palmas. Regular ferry service between Los Cristianos and San Sebastián is operated by *Ferry Gomera* (Edificio Rascacielos, Avenida 3 de Mayo, Santa Cruz; phone: 22-219244; and Muelle de Los Cristianos; phone: 22-790556). The ferries run three times a day except Tuesdays, when they offer only once-a-day service.

Mopeds and Motorcycles – These can be rented from *Moped Santos* (Playa Azul, Playa de las Américas; phone: 22-791639) for about $80 to $250 per week, $20 to $35 per day; hourly rates are also available.

Taxi – Cabs can be requested by telephone in Santa Cruz (phone: 22-641459 or 22-615111), Puerto de la Cruz (phone: 22-384910 or 22-385818), Playa de las Américas (phone: 22-791407 or 22-791669), and Los Cristianos (phone: 22-790352, 22-795459, or 22-795509).

SPECIAL PLACES: Santa Cruz de Tenerife and the North – Backed by sawtooth mountains, this provincial capital is an important port, with over 200,000 inhabitants and many modern buildings. More Spanish in character and aesthetically more pleasing than Las Palmas, it has no beaches to speak of, and is primarily a city of shops, with boutique-lined Calle del Castillo closed to traffic but filled with hordes of shoppers. Plaza de España, where this pedestrian island begins, is next to the port and is noteworthy for its memorial to the men of Tenerife who died in the Spanish Civil War. Visible from quite a distance, the towering monument also serves as a directional marker for tourists making their way back to the center of town. Just off the Plaza de España, on the third floor of the Palacio Insular, is the *Museo Arqueológico y Antropológico* (5 Calle Bravo Murillo; phone: 22-242090), which has a collection of 100 Guanches mummies, more than 1,000 skulls, and 300,-000 bones, as well as a variety of other artifacts of the Canary Islands' original inhabitants. The museum is open Mondays through Fridays from 9 AM to 1 PM and from 4 to 7 PM, Saturdays from 9 AM to 1 PM. Admission charge. North of the port, along Avenida de Anaga, where flame trees and palms provide a pleasant tropical air, is the Castillo de Paso Alto, a 17th-century fortress that now houses a regional military museum. Among the cannon on display is the one known as "the Tiger," which fired the ball that tore off Admiral Horatio Nelson's right arm when he laid siege to the town in 1797. The museum is open Tuesdays through Sundays from 10 AM to 2 PM.

Five miles (8 km) north of town lies Playa de las Teresitas, which claims to be the world's largest artificial beach; the golden sand covering this mile-long stretch — a pleasant place for sunbathing or a quick snack at one of its many inexpensive restaurants — was imported from the Sahara. From here, the road turns inland and corkscrews steeply upward to the Anaga headland, a dramatic area of knife-edge ridges, ravines, and dense evergreen woods. At El Bailadero pass, the picturesquely situated village of Taganana can be seen down below, but the road continues west along the crest of the range to the Pico del Inglés Belvedere, a lookout point 3,300 feet above sea level, from where there is a spectacular view of Pico del Teide rising in the distance. Soon after, the road descends to La Laguna, the university town and former island capital, which has an interesting old section highlighted by the Plaza del Adelantado, the 16th-century Iglesia de la Concepción (recently declared a national monument), and a 20th-century cathedral with a neo-classical façade.

Puerto de la Cruz – West of Santa Cruz, on the rocky Atlantic coast where the lush Orotava valley meets the sea, Puerto de la Cruz is a major resort center (despite the fact that it has no beach worthy of the name), and has been a cosmopolitan place for centuries. The last eruption of El Teide destroyed the harbor at Garachico, 20½ miles (33 km) to the west, giving added importance to the port here. European traders of many nationalities settled in, and wealthy British tourists began arriving to enjoy the mild winter climate during the last century. Today the town has many foreign residents and almost 100 hotels catering to visitors. Banana plantations, tropical fruits, jasmine, and bougainvillea flourish along the steeply terraced coast, behind which El Teide towers, often girded by cloud and covered with snow in winter.

The town has pleasant squares, especially the Plaza de la Iglesia, with its gardens and old buildings. Straw-hatted women in traditional bright embroidered skirts sell flowers near the Ayuntamiento (Town Hall) on Calle de Santo Domingo. Next to this street, Calle de San Telmo, the elegant main thoroughfare, runs along the waterfront, with a bevy of fine shops and hotels to match. Follow San Telmo until it becomes Avenida de Colón. Here, the resort's lack of safe beaches has been made up for by the creation of the Lago de Martiánez leisure complex, a series of beautifully landscaped seawater pools, promenades, and lounging areas set in and around rocky volcanic outcroppings that extend offshore for hundreds of yards. Don't miss it: Besides being a perfect sunbathing spot, the complex, designed by Lanzarote artist César Manrique, includes a gynmasium, a restaurant, bars, and a nightclub. Just opposite, on Avenida de Colón, is the *Café de Paris,* a popular meeting place where patrons eat and drink amid palms, mirrors, and a piano tinkling in the background.

Also visit the Jardín Botánico (Botanical Gardens), located on Carretera del Botánico at the eastern entrance to town. Rated among the world's finest, the gardens were created by order of King Carlos III in 1788, and cover 5 acres with thousands of varieties of tropical plants, including a 200-year-old rubber tree. The gardens (phone: 22-383572) are open daily from 9 AM to 7 PM. Admission charge. Another attraction, at the opposite end of town and reached by a free bus from Playa de Martiánez, is Loro Parque, a tropical park with a dolphin show and 1,300 parrots — some of which ride bicycles and do other tricks in a parrot show (open from 9 AM to 6 PM; admission charge). On Sundays at 11 AM, typical Canaries folk dancing and singing, plus an exhibition of local wrestling, take place in another park, on the grounds of the *Tigaiga* hotel (16 Parque de Taoro; phone: 22-383500).

La Orotava – In a valley of the same name, overlooking Puerto de la Cruz, which is 6 miles (10 km) away and 1,000 feet below, La Orotava occupies a site that was once the capital of a Guanche chief and is among the most compelling settings on the island. One of the oldest towns on Tenerife, it has steep cobbled streets and handsome homes with exquisite balconies, red roofs, and interior patios. The 18th-century Church of the Conception, now a museum, is a highlight, as is *Artesanía* (on Calle San Francisco) an arts and crafts center in an old balconied house with a flower-filled patio. Here visitors will find the delicate *calado,* or drawn-thread embroidery, used for everything from handkerchiefs to tablecloths and manufactured by women working at wooden looms. (They speak English and are glad to answer questions.) The annual *Corpus Christi* festival in June is a celebration of the religious fervor, energy, and artistry of the town's residents. Although the feast day is celebrated throughout the Canaries, the festivities are at their most colorful here. Before the procession, the town's squares and streets are covered with carpets made of hundreds of thousands of flower petals — bougainvillea, dahlias, geraniums, carnations — as well as crushed leaves, pine needles, and colorful designs in sand. The largest and most intricate carpet is laid on the Plaza del Ayuntamiento.

Pico del Teide – This is one excursion not to be missed on any visit to the Canaries. Mt. Teide, which towers 12,200 feet above sea level and overlooks a literal sea of clouds, is situated in the Parque Nacional de las Cañadas del Teide, a beautiful forest of heather, evergreens, eucalyptus, and Canarian pine at an altitude of some 6,500 feet. The park is reached via the town and the valley of La Orotava, where corn, chestnuts, and bananas are raised in abundance. Beyond La Orotava, the road leads to a desolate, treeless amphitheater. This is Las Cañadas, an ancient volcanic crater some 47 miles in diameter, from the center of which surges the great bulk of El Teide, a newer volcano and the tallest mountain in Spain. Las Cañadas is scarred and strewn with boulders; the last eruption in 1798 destroyed a peak that was even larger than El Teide. A cable car takes 35 passengers on a 10-minute journey to the base of the cone. From there it is a 25-minute hike to the edge, from where most of the Canaries — even the coast of Africa — are visible on a clear day. At dawn, the sun touching the mountains creates splendid shadows that blend with the various shades of lava and ash. The stillness and barrenness, intensified by sulfurous fumes filtering out of the volcano's depths, are intensely moving. Those short of breath should take care, as the air is quite rarefied at this altitude. Dedicated climbers can spend the night near the peak at the *Cueva de Hielo,* a mountain shelter (literally, the "Ice Cave"); for less adventurous sorts, there is a lovely *parador* (see *Checking In*) near the cable car. Free guided tours depart the visitors' center at 9:30 AM, 11:30 AM, and 1:30 PM daily (phone: 22-259903). Avoid Sundays and holidays, when the park is crowded. The cable car (phone: 22-383711) runs from 9 AM to 4:30 PM daily and costs about $6 each way.

Icod de los Vinos – West of Puerto de la Cruz, a road winds above sea-whipped rocks and black sand coves to this small town, the center of the island's wine-producing area. The town's proudest possession is the *drago,* Tenerife's oldest dragon tree, said to be more than 1,000 years old. From Icod, a drive through banana plantations leads to the nearby beach resort of San Marcos, amid black cliffs.

SHOPPING: On Tenerife, visitors will find Puerto de la Cruz the area with the most varied goods. In Santa Cruz, the main shopping streets are found in a square zone formed by Calle del Castillo, Calle Valentín Sanz, Calle Emilio Calzadillo, and the ocean; as in Las Palmas, the Indian, Pakistani, Lebanese, and Spanish shopkeepers are willing to negotiate but are not about to give anything away. Clothing, toys, watches, crafts, and lots more, including junk, are sold every Sunday morning at *El Rastro,* the open-air market on Avenida de Anaga in Santa Cruz. A crafts fair is held on the first Sunday of the month along the Garachico promenade, 20 miles (32 km) along the coast from Puerto de la Cruz (in winter, it usually is held in the patio of the San Francisco convent). A shopping center with 50 shops selling a broad range of goods is located under the *Valle-Mar* hotel on Avenida de Colón, Puerto de la Cruz.

Casa Iriarte – Local handicrafts; this fine old galleried house has over 40,000 gift items, including beautiful embroidery and Toledo ware. 21 Calle San Juan, Puerto de la Cruz (phone: 22-383993).

Casa Romy – A typical bazaar, stocking everything from binoculars to semi-precious stones. 2 Calle San Juan, Puerto de la Cruz (phone: 22-380651).

B. Choitram – Carries Lladró porcelain, jewelry, and fine crystal. 3 Calle Sargento Cáceres, Puerto de la Cruz (phone: 22-380420).

Mari Petri – Authentic hand-embroidered items, including blouses, shawls, and skirts. Two locations: Calle Obispo Pérez Cáceres, Puerto de la Cruz (phone: 22-381711), and Calle San Juan, Puerto de la Cruz (phone: 22-387416).

Joyería Purriños – Fine watches, crystal, and leather goods. 16 Calle Quintana, Puerto de la Cruz (phone: 22-384432).

Regalos Eros – A range of gifts, including Lladró porcelain. 22 Calle Santo Domingo, Puerto de la Cruz (phone: 22-380299).

CHECKING IN: Most of Tenerife's best hotels are concentrated in Puerto de la Cruz, where there is a large selection in all price ranges. Phenomenal development has taken place in the southern beach area around Playa de las Américas, where there are numerous apartment blocks, as well as hotels providing accommodations for package tours. Expect to pay $115 or more for a double room listed as expensive, $60 to $100 for a room listed as moderate, and $60 or less for an inexpensive room.

PUERTO DE LA CRUZ

Meliá Botánico – Set amid lush tropical gardens, this 282-room top-of-the-line establishment, with an attentive, English-speaking staff, is just a step away from the Botanical Gardens, about a mile from downtown. Rooms are air conditioned and tastefully furnished, with color television sets, videocassette players, mini-bars, and hair dryers. Other facilities include fine shops, a discotheque, tennis courts, a swimming pool, and a poolside restaurant. Calle Richard J. Yeoward, Puerto de la Cruz (phone: 22-381400). Expensive.

Meliá San Felipe – A deluxe, seafront hotel with an elegant marble lobby, its 260 air conditioned rooms have wall-to-wall carpeting, modern decor, and views of the sea or mountains. Tennis courts, a large pool, a children's playground, and a lively entertainment program make it a fine resort choice. 13 Avenida de Colón, Puerto de la Cruz (phone: 22-383311). Expensive.

Parque San Antonio – Those who want to get away from the madding throngs of tourists in Puerto de la Cruz, but wish to be close enough to the center of town to make quick forays, should consider this. Tucked away in a veritable botanical garden all its own, it is merely 5 minutes by bus from the center. All 211 rooms are air conditioned. There is also a restaurant. Carretera de las Arenas, Puerto de la Cruz (phone: 22-384851). Expensive.

Semiramis – A 15-story property imaginatively built into the cliff edge. All 275 air conditioned rooms have terraces overlooking the ocean, color television sets, videocassette players, mini-bars, and refrigerators; some have complete kitchens. A good dining room, a tropical garden, 3 swimming pools (2 heated), a tennis court, and shops are among the attractions. 12 Calle Leopoldo Cologán, Puerto de la Cruz (phone: 22-385551). Expensive to moderate.

Marquesa – Historic charm and modern comforts are combined in this 88-room hotel in the old section of Puerto de la Cruz. A leafy patio, a swimming pool, and a popular terrace and restaurant are among the facilities. 11 Calle Quintana, Puerto de la Cruz (phone: 22-383151). Moderate.

Monopol – This family-run hotel (since 1888) is a world away from the modern and sometimes soulless establishments found on Tenerife. Part of this structure dates back to 1742, and is worth a visit even for those not staying here, to see the charming old patio with its palms and rubber trees and carved wooden balconies. The 92 rooms are well kept. 15 Calle Quintana, Puerto de la Cruz (phone: 22-384611). Moderate.

La Paz – Situated in an upscale residential area of Puerto de la Cruz, this 167-room hotel features a tasteful interior with an abundant use of woodwork. All of the rooms are air conditioned and boast an attractive Spanish decor. There is also a swimming pool and tennis courts. The staff speaks English and is most attentive and friendly. Urbanización La Paz, Puerto de la Cruz (phone: 22-385011). Moderate.

ELSEWHERE ON THE ISLAND

Mencey – This charming old yellow building in the heart of the capital is part of the elegant CIGA chain, and by far the finest hotel on Tenerife. Its former grandeur has survived modernization, and the 275 air conditioned rooms have been splendidly refurbished; a new wing with motel-type units also has been added. There are 2 swimming pools, tennis courts, a bar, a poolside buffet, and lovely gardens. 38 Avenida José Naveiras, Santa Cruz de Tenerife (phone: 22-276700). Expensive.

Bitácora – A relatively new, L-shaped block, a quarter of a mile from the beach but with an attractive pool area. The marble lobby and general spaciousness are pleasant; the 314 rooms all have mini-bars and air conditioning. Playa de las Américas (phone: 22-791540). Moderate.

Bouganville Playa – Large and modern, this 481-room property has 3 swimming pools (1 for children), 4 bars, squash and tennis courts, a fitness center, a large sauna, and conference facilities. All rooms are air conditioned and have terraces with sea views. Urbanización San Eugenio, Playa de las Américas (phone: 22-790200). Moderate.

Gran Tinerfe – Open terraces and spacious gardens give a pleasant air to this well-maintained establishment on a black sand beach. The 356 air conditioned rooms are attractively furnished; 52 one-bedroom garden bungalows are also available. There are 3 ocean-fed saltwater swimming pools, tennis courts, and a nightly cabaret show. Playa de las Américas (phone: 22-791200). Moderate.

Parador de las Cañadas del Teide – Ideal for those seeking tranquillity and fresh mountain air, this place is about an hour by car from Puerto de la Cruz, more than 7,000 feet above sea level. A state-owned *parador,* it sits in the crater of an extinct volcano and offers remarkable views of lava fields and of El Teide, Spain's highest peak. The 16 large, spotlessly clean rooms are furnished in simple rustic style, the beds are comfortable, and there is a swimming pool, a lounge with a fireplace, and a restaurant serving typical Canaries dishes. Reservations are required well in advance. Las Cañadas del Teide (phone: 22-332304). Moderate.

Los Hibiscos – This pleasant low-rise development of 138 studio apartments and 180 hotel rooms surrounds a series of gardens and a swimming pool. Guests use the facilities of the adjacent *Bouganville Playa.* Urbanización San Eugenio, Playa de las Américas (phone: 22-791462). Moderate to inexpensive.

EATING OUT: Restaurants on Tenerife feature Canarian and international dishes. The better places, with the most extensive menus, are found in Puerto de la Cruz. For typical Canarian fare at good prices, try the smaller eateries in the narrow streets near the Plaza del Charco. Expect to pay $65 or more for dinner for two in restaurants listed as expensive, between $30 and $60 in restaurants listed as moderate, and $30 or less in inexpensive ones. Prices do not include drinks, wine, or tips.

PUERTO DE LA CRUZ

Magnolia – A light and airy restaurant with garden, serving Catalan and international dishes. Specialties include a delicious *zarzuela* (fish stew) and stuffed partridge. Closed Mondays and May. Reservations advised. 5 Carretera del Botánico, Puerto de la Cruz (phone: 22-385614). Expensive.

Peruano – Enjoy authentic Peruvian dishes such as *ceviche* (raw fish marinated in lemon juice with onions and hot peppers), as well as traditional Spanish favorites, in an agreeable atmosphere complete with appropriate Latin American music. Reservations unnecessary. Calle del Pozo, Puerto de la Cruz (phone: 22-382253). Moderate.

El Pescado – The name means "the fish," and that's what guests will find on the menu, prepared in a variety of intriguing ways. Closed Wednesdays and May through September. Reservations unnecessary. 38 Avenida Venezuela, Puerto de la Cruz (phone: 22-382806). Moderate.

La Papaya – Each guest is greeted with a complimentary glass of sherry in this converted old Canarian house. Local dishes are the specialty here; be sure to top off the meal with a dish of homemade ice cream. Reservations unnecessary. 14 Calle Lomo, Puerto de la Cruz (phone: 22-382811). Moderate to inexpensive.

La Marina – International dishes are served in a nautical setting near the port, with a strong emphasis on fish. Closed Saturdays and from June through mid-July. No reservations. 2 Calle San Juan, Puerto de la Cruz (phone: 22-385401). Inexpensive.

Patio Canario – Enjoy local specialties in this rustic Canarian house with a timber and tiled roof, potted plants, and fresh flowers on the tables. Try *conejo en salmorejo* (rabbit in a tasty sauce) or a hearty *potaje canario de verduras* (vegetable soup). Closed Thursdays. Reservations unnecessary. 4 Calle Lomo, Puerto de la Cruz (phone: 22-380451). Inexpensive.

ELSEWHERE ON THE ISLAND

Las Folías – Situated in a traditionally designed shopping center by the sea, the emphasis here is on fresh raw ingredients. Try the crab salad, roast lamb, or chateaubriand. The dining room provides an intimate atmosphere, aided by soft lamplight. Reservations advised. *Centro Comercial Pueblo Canario,* Playa de las Américas (phone: 22-792269). Expensive.

La Riviera – Snazzy continental dishes are the hallmark of this chic, tastefully decorated restaurant. Closed Sundays and mid-August through mid-September. Reservations advised. 155 Rambla General Franco, Santa Cruz de Tenerife (phone: 22-275812). Expensive.

La Caseta de Madera – This popular eatery in an old wooden building specializes in Canarian cooking with a Tenerife twist. The emphasis is on seafood, but the daily specials are also worth a try. Closed Saturday evenings and Sundays. Reservations unnecessary. Calle Regla, Barrio Los Llanos, Santa Cruz de Tenerife (phone: 22-210023). Expensive to moderate.

L'Scala – Near Los Cristianos beach, with an outside terrace, this restaurant serves authentic Castilian dishes, such as roast suckling pig, in agreeable surroundings. Closed Tuesdays. Reservations unnecessary. 7 Calle La Paloma, Los Cristianos (phone: 22-791051). Moderate.

Mesón del Orgaz – Seafood and Segovia-style roast meats cooked in a wood-fired oven are the specialties of this place, in the same shopping center as *Las Folías.* The dining room boasts a beamed ceiling and plush red seats. Closed Wednesdays in summer. Reservations unnecessary. *Centro Comercial Pueblo Canario,* Playa de las Américas (phone: 22-793169). Moderate.

LANZAROTE

An eerie, burnt-out island punctuated by hundreds of extinct volcanoes, Lanzarote is the most physically astonishing of the Canaries. Its scenery is so unusual that people who fly in from Tenerife or Grand Canary invariably describe it as unforgettable. A 1- or 2-day visit is enough to see this awe-inspiring landscape, but many travelers are tempted to linger longer on some of the island's white sand beaches. Set 85 miles northeast of Las Palmas and only 65 miles from the coast of Morocco, Lanzarote has some 300 volcanoes, and petrified seas of lava — known as *malpaís* — writhe across parts of the island. Nevertheless, its farms produce sumptuous melons, figs, onions, and tomatoes, thanks to a remarkable system of cultivation. Local farmers spread *picón* (black volcanic ash) on their fields to absorb and retain moisture, and thus manage to coax an abundant harvest in a land that has no running water and sparse rainfall. They also produce a notable wine from the malvasía, or malmsey, grape, which is grown on vines planted in walled hollows to protect them from the hot, searing winds.

By such ingenuity and persistence, the native population (now 50,000) managed to survive from approximatly the time when the Genoese navigator Lancelotto Malocello landed here in the 14th century (and gave the island its name) until mass tourism hit in the 1980s. Some 700,000 visitors now set foot in this easternmost of the Canaries annually, and many new hotels and apartment blocks have been built, as well as desalinization plants to provide water. Fortunately, new development may be no higher than 3 stories, billboards are banned, and construction is confined to three main zones. Except for Arrecife, the undistinguished, traffic-clogged capital on the island's eastern coast, and these three "artificial" resort areas — Costa Teguise (north of Arrecife), Puerto del Carmen (south of both Arrecife and the airport), and Playa Blanca (still farther south, facing Fuerteventura, where some of the best beaches are) — the island largely retains its magical quality. For this, much credit is due to César Manrique, its native artist, architect, and ecological campaigner, responsible for the development of various island sites.

GETTING AROUND: Airport – The Aeropuerto de Lanzarote is 4 miles (6 km) from Arrecife. *Iberia* offers direct service between the island and Alicante, Barcelona, Bilbao, Madrid, Málaga, and Seville, as well as inter-island service with Grand Canary, Tenerife, and Fuerteventura. *Iberia*'s Arrecife office is at 2 Avenida Rafael González (phone: 28-810354).

Bus – Bus service throughout the island is provided by *Arrecife Bus* (phone: 28-811546) and *Lanzarote Bus* (phone: 28-812458).

Car Rental – Major rental car companies are *Avis* (phone: 28-512400 in Tías; 28-816438, ext. 377, in Costa Teguise; and 28-823356 at the airport); *Hertz* (phone: 28-813711 at the airport); and *Europcar* (phone: 28-814440 at the airport).

Ferry – *Trasmediterránea* ferries sail regularly between Arrecife and Cádiz, as well as to Las Palmas, Grand Canary, Santa Cruz de Tenerife, and Puerto del Rosario, Fuerteventura. In addition, the company operates a jet foil between Playa Blanca and Corralejo and Puerto del Rosario on Fuerteventura. *Alisur*, a *Trasmediterránea* subsidiary, runs a ferry between Playa Blanca, Lanzarote, and Corralejo, Fuerteventura, 4 times daily. In Arrecife, contact *Trasmediterránea* (90 Calle José Antonio; phone: 28-811188) and *Alisur* (1 Calle La Esperanza; phone: 28-814272).

Taxi – Taxis are available on call in Arrecife (phone: 28-811680 and 28-810283) and in Puerto del Carmen (phone: 28-825034). Hiring a car and driver for a tour of the volcanoes costs about $60, while an organized bus tour with guide runs about $40.

SPECIAL PLACES: Las Montañas del Fuego (Fire Mountains) – Between 1730 and 1736, a series of terrifying eruptions devastated the western part of Lanzarote, burying farmland and a number of villages under volcanic debris. This area now makes up the Parque Nacional de Timanfaya. Entering from Yaiza, a village in the south, 14½ miles (23 km) from Arrecife, visitors come to the Echadero de los Camellos, where dromedaries wait to carry visitors on short journeys over the lava (there is a charge for this, in addition to the park admission). The main road through the park winds up a hill known as Islote de Hilario, where subsurface temperatures reach upward of 800F. A simple way to check is by merely touching the ground. Twigs placed in a hollow catch fire within seconds, and when a park ranger pours water down a vent in the earth's surface, a steam geyser instantly erupts. A tour bus cruises "The Route of the Volcanoes" (with commentary in English) for a close view of this lunar-like landscape of total desolation, where virtually no living creature exists. Before departing, try a volcano-broiled steak at *El Diablo,* the park restaurant (see *Eating Out*), where the meat is actually cooked by the earth's natural heat. The park is open daily, from 9 AM to 5 PM. Admission charge. *Note:* Strong footwear is recommended to explore the lava fields, and those with a camera should remember to bring a blower brush to clean off the dust.

The North – An 18-mile (29-km) drive north of Arrecife leads to Jameos del Agua, a beautiful grotto carved out of the black volcanic rock, with a lagoon formed when molten lava met the sea. At one end is an open-air swimming pool, in surroundings beautifully landscaped by the outstanding Lanzarote artist and environmentalist César Manrique. Folk music shows, with dinner and dancing, are held here. The cave is open daily from 11 AM to 8 PM (later for the show); admission charge (phone: 28-835010). Some 300 yards away is the Cueva de los Verdes (Green Cave), the world's largest volcanic tunnel, a place where Guanches and later inhabitants took refuge from invaders. Extending nearly 5 miles to the sea, it was created by cooling lava. Open from 11 AM to 6 PM daily; tours depart on the hour, sometimes with an English-speaking guide; admission charge. At the northernmost tip of the island, 7 miles (11 km) farther along, is the Mirador del Río, a lookout point atop old fortifications where there is a breathtaking view of some of the smaller Canaries — Graciosa, Montaña Clara, and Alegranza.

Returning southward, the road passes Haría, a village of white houses in a green valley dotted with hundreds of palms, and Teguise, the former island capital. Set on top of an extinct volcano, Teguise has a castle, the Castillo de Guanapay, perched on top of the cone and provides another splendid view of some of the smaller Canaries. The island's current capital, Arrecife, is not particularly interesting, but it does have two castles, the 16th-century Castillo de San Gabriel (open from 9 AM to 1 PM and from 3 to 7 PM, closed Saturdays and holidays; admission charge) and the 18th-century Castillo de San José. The latter, renovated by César Manrique, is now the home of the *International Museum of Contemporary Art* (open daily from 11 AM to 9 PM; no admission charge; phone: 28-812321) and of the deluxe *Castillo de San José* restaurant (which stays open until 1 AM — see *Eating Out*).

CHECKING IN: Until very recently, there were only a few spartan pensions on the island, but modern hotels and apartments now offer a wide range of accommodations, primarily in Costa Teguise and Puerto del Carmen. Expect to pay $115 or more for a double room in hotels listed as expensive, between $60 and $100 in hotels listed as moderate, and $60 or less in those listed as inexpensive.

La Gería – An attractive establishment facing the sea, situated 2 miles (3 km) east of Puerto del Carmen. The black marble steps from the lobby lead to a large circular bar and a huge heated swimming pool. All 244 rooms are air conditioned and have color television sets, videocassette players, and terraces with ocean views. Playa de los Pocillos, Puerto del Carmen (phone: 28-511918). Expensive.

Las Salinas Meliá – Looking like a giant spacecraft newly touched down in a tropical paradise, this former Sheraton property, decorated by César Manrique, offers 310 modern air conditioned rooms, each with a private terrace facing the sea. Outdoor delights include a private beach, free-form pool, large gardens, tennis courts, and the necessary equipment for scuba diving and sailing, in addition to restaurants, bars, massage services, a sauna, a cinema, and a disco. Calle Sur Teguise, Costa Teguise (phone: 28-813040). Expensive.

Arrecife Gran – A contemporary resort overlooking Arrecife harbor, with a large pool and sun deck, tennis courts, gym, and sauna. Its most unusual feature is a restaurant on an island in the middle of a small lake that can be reached only by boat. The 148 rooms are air conditioned, pleasant, and comfortable, with large terraces. Avenida Mancomunidad, Arrecife (phone: 28-811250). Moderate.

Los Fariones – Surrounded by tropical gardens, this friendly 237-room hotel fronts a small beach and features a heated swimming pool and tennis courts. The rooms are air conditioned, comfortable, and functional. Urbanización Playa Blanca, Puerto del Carmen (phone: 28-825175). Moderate.

Teguise Playa – A large new establishment on its own beach, only a short distance from the *Costa Teguise Golf Club*, it boasts 324 air conditioned rooms, all with sea views, and has 2 pools, a bar, and a restaurant. Playa El Jablillo, Costa Teguise (phone: 28-816654). Moderate.

Aparthotel Don Paco and Apartamentos Castilla – This resort complex near the beach, a few minutes drive from Arrecife and the airport, offers 228 spacious rooms and apartments with attractive pinewood fittings, cheerful fabrics, color television sets, and fully equipped kitchens; all have ocean views. Facilities include 2 swimming pools, squash courts, a gymnasium, 2 restaurants, a bar, and a disco. Playa de los Pocillos, Puerto del Carmen (phone: 28-511034 for the hotel, or 28-511618 for the apartments). Inexpensive.

EATING OUT: The tourist influx has spurred the establishment of restaurants offering international dishes, but a few places continue to serve authentic Canaries cooking. Try the local wine, made from the malvasía, or malmsey, grape, grown in the lava fields. The El Grifo Bodega label has been a favorite since 1775. Expect to pay $65 or more for dinner for two in restaurants listed as expensive, between $40 and $60 in restaurants listed as moderate, and $35 or less in inexpensive ones.

Castillo de San José – In the cellar of an old castle that now houses the *International Museum of Contemporary Art,* this is one of the most beautiful restaurants on the island. (Well-known local architect César Manrique was responsible for the renovation.) Open daily. Reservations advised. A bit over a mile (2 km) northeast of Arrecife on the road to Las Caletas (phone: 28-812321). Expensive.

Malvasía Grill – Bright checkered tablecloths, a rustic atmosphere, and efficient and friendly service make for pleasant dining in this restaurant in the *Los Zocos* resort club. The menu offers a varied sampling of international dishes and a good selection of international wines. Open for dinner only; closed holidays. Reservations advised. *Los Zocos,* Playa de las Cucharas, Costa Teguise (phone: 28-816436). Expensive.

Acatife – This centuries-old house in the old town of Teguise is the place for international cooking at reasonable prices. Willy, the German owner, also offers island sightseeing flights in his private plane — for an additional charge. Open for dinner only; closed Sundays and Mondays. Reservations unnecessary. Plaza de la Iglesia, Teguise (phone: 28-845027). Moderate.

La Bohème – Two parrots guard the entrance to the dining room, which is colorfully decorated with plenty of greenery. International dishes are the specialty, served at tables illuminated by cozy lamplight, which adds to the already intimate atmosphere. Open daily. Reservations unnecessary. 51 Avenida de las Playas, Puerto del Carmen (phone: 28-825915). Moderate.

La Marina – Canarian and South American fare highlight the menu in this promenade restaurant with a nautical air. Don't pass up the grilled lamb chops. Closed Tuesdays. Reservations unnecessary. Avenida Marítimo de las Playas, Puerto del Carmen (phone: 28-826096). Moderate to inexpensive.

La Casa Roja – Good, simple seafood dishes are served at this popular place overlooking the little harbor in Puerto del Carmen. Reservations unnecessary. 22 Plaza Varadero, Puerto del Carmen (phone: 28-826515). Inexpensive.

El Diablo – A dramatically located eatery, it stands amid the Montañas del Fuego, the island's volcanic Fire Mountains, and offers the unique opportunity to feast on a volcano-broiled steak. Open daily for lunch only. No reservations. Parque Nacional de Timanfaya (phone: 28-840057). Inexpensive.

La Era – A palm-shaded patio adds to the charm of this popular eating spot, situated in a 17th-century house in the southern village of Yaiza. The dining room walls are made of 2-foot-thick lava blocks, and the typical Canarian fare is served by a friendly staff, most efficient when tour groups are not around. Reservations unnecessary. Yaiza (phone: 28-830016). Inexpensive.

Playa Blanca – There is no menu; excellent seafood dishes depend on the catch of the day. No reservations. Yaiza (no phone). Inexpensive.

FUERTEVENTURA

The second-largest of the Canary Islands, Fuerteventura, has the longest shoreline, with plenty of spacious, empty beaches, and an arid climate that guarantees year-round sunshine — just the spot for windsurfers, beach bums, sun lovers, fishermen, and those seeking total seclusion. It is the island closest to Africa — only 59 miles offshore — and the dramatic, howling winds and impressive sand dunes never let visitors forget it.

Bare hills formed by extinct volcanoes, flat-roofed houses, and endless beaches are features of this sparsely populated island. There are some 30,000 permanent residents, plus 60,000 goats, a third of which graze wild. Most of the island's population resides in Puerto del Rosario, the capital, located about midway along the eastern coast. Atlantic rollers break against the rocky western coast, while the best beaches extend along the southeast coast, around Jandía, for instance, and in the north near Corralejo, once a quiet fishing village and now a growing resort. Fishing, from the beaches or a boat, is excellent.

The island can be toured in a day, taking in the rugged interior including Betancuria, a secluded oasis chosen by Béthencourt as the island's original capital in 1404 (the town now has an interesting cathedral). An enjoyable excursion can be made from Corralejo over translucent waters to the offshore Isla de los Lobos.

 GETTING AROUND: Airport – Fuerteventura's airport is located 3 miles (5 km) from Puerto del Rosario. *Iberia* (11 Calle 23 de Mayo; phone: 28-850516) has direct service to and from Barcelona, Bilbao, Málaga, Madrid and Seville, as well as Grand Canary, Tenerife, and Lanzarote.

Bus – The main bus station is located at 25 Calle Alfonso XIII, Puerto del Rosario (phone: 28-850951).

Car Rental – Major rental car companies are *Avis* (phone: 28-850261 in Corralejo and Puerto del Rosario; 28-876017 in Jandía); *Hertz* (phone: 28-866259 in Corralejo and at the airport; 28-876126 in Morro Jable); and *Europcar* (phone: 28-852436 in Puerto del Rosario and at the airport; 28-866167 in Corralejo; and 28-877044 in Jandía).

Ferry – *Trasmediterránea* (46 Calle León y Castillo, Puerto del Rosario; phone: 28-850877) has regular sailings from Puerto del Rosario to Las Palmas, Grand Canary, and Arrecife, Lanzarote, and from Morro Jable (at the southern tip of Fuerteventura) to Santa Cruz de Tenerife. The company also operates a jet foil between Morro Jable and Las Palmas and between Puerto del Rosario and Correlejo and Playa Blanca, Lanzarote. *Ferry Betancuria,* a subsidiary of *Ferry Gomera* headquartered at Edificio Rascacielos (Avenida 3 de Mayo, Santa Cruz de Tenerife; phone: 22-221040), has three daily sailings between Corralejo and Playa Blanca, Lanzarote, while *Alisur* (1 Calle La Esperanza, Arrecife; phone: 28-814272) covers the same route four times daily.

Taxi – Taxis sometimes can be hailed on the streets in Puerto del Rosario, or they can be requested by calling 28-850059.

CHECKING IN: Frenzied construction in recent years has added hundreds of hotel and apartment rooms to previously meager accommodations. Large hotels around Jandía in the south attract mainly German clients; inexpensive apartments are available in Corralejo. Expect to pay $100 or more for a double room listed as expensive, and between $60 and $90 for a room listed as moderate.

Iberotel Tres Islas – This spiffy, recently renovated, luxury establishment on a remote golden sand beach is surrounded by tropical gardens. All 365 rooms are air conditioned, with television sets and mini-bars, and there are three restaurants, a large saltwater swimming pool, tennis courts, and a fitness center. Playas de Corralejo (phone: 28-866000). Expensive.

Los Gorriones – A member of the Sol chain, this 309-room hotel is situated on a secluded beach in a town in the south of the island. Totally air conditioned, it is functional and comfortable, and includes tennis courts and windsurfing facilities. Playa Barca, Gran Tarajal (phone: 28-870850). Moderate.

Parador de Fuerteventura – Standing on the edge of the ocean about 2 miles (3 km) south of the capital, this modern *parador,* 2 decades old, is the most splendid hotel on the island. A pleasant place, with polished wood floors and oil paintings, it has 50 air conditioned rooms, a swimming pool, and a good restaurant. Playa Blanca, Puerto del Rosario (phone: 28-851150). Moderate.

EATING OUT: A moderately priced meal for two on Fuerteventura will cost between $30 and $45. Prices do not include drinks, wine, or tips.

Casa Juan – A rowboat full of ice proudly supports the day's catch in a display at this seafood house, where fried and baked fish are the specialties. Reservations unnecessary. 5 Calle General Linares, Corralejo (phone: 28-866219). Moderate.

El Patio – Whitewashed arches, a timber roof, and a floor of old tiles provide a cozy air to this quaint eatery near the harbor. Try the fish stew, the baked kid, and the banana flambé. Closed Mondays. Reservations unnecessary. Calle Lepanto, Corralejo (phone: 28-866668). Moderate.

LA PALMA

One of the few islands to have escaped inundation by tourists, possibly because it is short on good beaches, La Palma has sufficient numbers of other attractions to justify a visit. Shaped like a leaf, it measures approximately 13 miles by 29 miles and is the greenest, and possibly the most beautiful, island of the archipelago. A massive crater, the Caldera de Taburiente, occupies the center of the island, with ravines running down to the rugged coastline. Below the pine-forested heights are intensely cultivated, terraced fields producing tropical and other fruits (as well as tobacco plants, originally imported from Cuba, from which the island's noted cigars are made). The capital, Santa Cruz de la Palma, was once the third most important port of the Spanish empire. Today, with 18,000 inhabitants, it is one of the most pleasant towns in the Canaries. Although facilities and services for tourists are not as well developed on La Palma as on Grand Canary or Tenerife, it does attract good numbers of Europeans who prefer quiet vacations.

GETTING AROUND: Airport – La Palma's small airport is located 5 miles (8 km) from Santa Cruz. *Iberia* (1 Calle Apurón; phone: 22-411345) has direct flights to Barcelona and Madrid, to Grand Canary and Tenerife, as well as to El Hierro in the summer.

Car Rental – Major rental car companies are *Avis* (phone: 22-411480 at the airport); *Hertz* (phone: 22-413676 at the airport and in Santa Cruz); and *Europcar* (phone: 22-411540, ext. 221, at the airport; 22-414338 in Santa Cruz).

Ferry – *Trasmediterránea* (2 Calle Pérez de Brito, Santa Cruz; phone: 22-412415) offers regular sailings to Grand Canary, Tenerife, El Hierro, and La Gomera.

SPECIAL PLACES: Santa Cruz de la Palma – Standing at the foot of a colossal cliff, which is part of an eroded crater, the island capital has an unhurried Old World atmosphere. Along its quiet streets are excellent examples of the architecture of the Canary Islands, with wooden balconies, the Ayuntamiento (City Hall), with a beautiful Renaissance façade, and El Salvador (a 16th-century church with a fine coffered ceiling). Other attractions include the *Museo Naval,* a maritime museum in a life-size replica of Christopher Columbus's *Santa María* (on Avenida de las Nieves; open Mondays through Fridays from 10 AM to 1 PM and from 4 to 7 PM; admission charge).

La Caldera de Taburiente – A half-hour's drive west of the capital is the Mirador de la Concepción, a wonderful spot from which to gaze down on the coast and Santa Cruz. The road then proceeds upward and through a tunnel, from where a road to the right winds up amid pinewoods to La Cumbrecita, a lookout point offering a breathtaking panorama of the 5-mile-wide crater, a world of tumbled rock, craggy heights, and forest. The crater bottom can be visited by driving along a dirt track from Llanos de Aridane, a town in the island's western interior, up the Barranco de las Angustias, a giant cleft. A rock sacred to the Guanches stands in the crater, and it was here that the last of the original inhabitants held out against the Spaniards. Not far from Llanos is El Time, a cliff whose top affords a tremendous view up the yawning Angustias chasm and down on banana plantations climbing in steps from the ocean. On the northern edge of the crater, at El Roque de los Muchachos, the island's highest point (7,950 feet), stands an astronomical station, built by several European nations. (Permission to visit must be obtained from the Observatorio Astrofísico de Canarias, Edificio Tynabana, Avenida El Puente, Santa Cruz; phone: 22-413510). To reach El Roque, take the Barlovento road out of Santa Cruz and turn left after 2 miles (3 km); it is another 22 miles (35 km) through impressive scenery.

Fuencaliente – In the southern part of the island, near the village of Fuencaliente, stand the San Antonio and Teneguía volcanoes. Teneguía last erupted in 1971, sending molten lava flowing down to the sea. Sulfurous vapors rise from the crater, and water that pours down the fissures shoots back up as steam. Imperturbably, the local people continue farming nearby.

CHECKING IN: A moderately priced double room in a La Palma hotel will cost between $50 and $100; rooms costing less than $50 are considered inexpensive.

Parador de Santa Cruz de la Palma – Occupying a building that is typically Canarian in style, down to the characteristic wooden balconies, in an ideal seafront location. The 32 rooms are very comfortable; the restaurant specializes in international and local dishes. 34 Avenida Marítimo, Santa Cruz de la Palma (phone: 22-412340). Moderate.

Marítimo – A relatively new, 4-story, seafront hotel, with 78 air conditioned rooms complete with color television sets, mini-bars, and terraces. 80 Avenida Marítimo,

Santa Cruz de la Palma (phone: 22-420222 or 22-416340). Moderate to inexpensive.

 EATING OUT: Expect to pay between $30 and $60 for a meal for two at moderately priced restaurants on La Palma, and under $30 at inexpensive ones. Prices do not include drinks, wine, or tips.

La Fontana – Situated in a modern apartment block just off the beach south of Santa Cruz, this eatery has a bar and terrace, where patrons enjoy such delights as sirloin steaks cooked in whiskey and prawns fried in garlic. Closed Mondays. Reservations unnecessary. Urbanización Adelfas, Los Cancajos, Breña Baja (phone: 22-434250). Moderate.

El Parral – With its red tablecloths and fresh flowers, this eating spot opposite the Santa Catalina castle is the perfect place to sample baked fresh salmon, followed by strawberries and cream. Reservations unnecessary. 7 Calle Castillete, Santa Cruz de la Palma (phone: 22-413915). Moderate.

San Petronio – As the name suggests, this restaurant on the island's west coast serves high-quality Italian dishes. Closed Mondays. Reservations unnecessary. Llanos de Aridane (phone: 22-462403). Moderate.

La Abuela – Canarian and international specialties are served in this agreeable old tiled house, which has a large fireplace and a worn wooden floor. It stands just below the Mirador de la Concepción, along a rutted road. Closed Mondays. Reservations. unnecessary. Buenavista de Abajo, Breña Alta (phone: 22-415106). Moderate to inexpensive.

LA GOMERA

Although it measures only 146 square miles, this round island rises steeply from a precipitous shoreline to nearly 5,000 feet at its central peak, Mount Garajonay. The craggy seacoast and mountainous terrain make transportation from one valley to the next so difficult that the islanders have developed a whistling language to commmunicate with one another over great distances. Situated about 20 miles across the water from Tenerife's southwestern coast, La Gomera is usually visited as a day trip by tourists vacationing on one of the larger Canary Islands. The only historical events that the island has witnessed were brief visits paid by Christopher Columbus during the early stages of his trips to the New World, though these momentous layovers were made merely to procure water and provisions. Columbus's presence, however, has nonetheless served as a source of great local pride. In San Sebastián, the island's picturesque capital, is Nuestra Señora de la Asunción, where Columbus and his crews heard mass before setting off for parts unknown. The house in which he is said to have slept, called the *Casa de Colón,* is now a museum, and the Torre del Conde (Count's Tower), an old fortress standing near the sea, has been declared a national historic monument. The island's Garajonay National Park, encompassing the peak and surrounding woodlands — some 10,000 acres — is a UNESCO Natural World Heritage Site, home to over 850 species of plants and flowers. A worthwhile excursion out of San Sebastián is to the Valle Gran Rey, a spectacular ravine on the opposite side of the island, reached by hair-raising roads. The island also has several banana plantations, orchards, a fishing village called Playa de Santiago, with a pebble beach, and the whistling Gomerans themselves. Trade winds keep the skies clear and relatively cloudless, making for a crystalline visibility. Beaches are not a luminous white, but consist of black and red volcanic sand.

GETTING AROUND: Car Rental – Major rental car companies are *Avis* (21 Caseta del Muelle, San Sebastián; phone: 22-870461) and *Hertz* (6 Avenida Fred Olsen, San Sebastián; phone: 22-870924).

Ferry – *Trasmediterránea* (35 General Franco, San Sebastián; phone: 22-870802) has regular sailings to Grand Canary, Tenerife, La Palma, and El Hierro, as well as hydrofoil service between San Sebastián and Los Cristianos, Tenerife. *Ferry Gomera* (Avenida Fred Olsen, San Sebastián; phone: 22-871007) has three daily departures between San Sebastián and Los Cristianos (except Tuesdays, when there are two departures).

CHECKING IN/EATING OUT: *Parador Conde de la Gomera* – Built in the unique Canarian manorial style, this 42-room inn is surrounded by tropical gardens and has fine sea views and a swimming pool — an ideal, tranquil spot for escapists. The dining room serves good food, too. Accommodations on the island are severely limited and the rooms here are much in demand, so make reservations early. San Sebastián de la Gomera (phone: 22-871100). Moderate.

EL HIERRO

The smallest and least inhabited of the archipelago's major islands, El Hierro is the harshest of all, with black volcanic soil, steep massifs, deep craters, and barren mountains. Its name means "the iron one," and for centuries, this rocky, 107 square miles was another one of those places that civilization regarded as the end of the world. Anyone who is not a connoisseur of solitude and nature in a dramatic mood may still think it is.

The farthest west of the islands, it appears grim and unfriendly from the sea, since its coasts are of black lava dotted with cactus. Clouds often shroud its central area, a plateau 4,900 feet above sea level. Although the lack of springs deterred the first Spaniards to arrive, the population has managed to survive on agriculture and fishing. So poor is El Hierro that the ownership of one tree was a communal affair in times past, with different branches belonging to different proprietors. Much of the population, as is the case with the other islands, emigrated to South America.

About 3,500 of the current 6,000 residents live in the capital, Valverde, the central town of an agricultural area where wine is the major product. Other local products are figs and cheese. The island's interior consists of emerald-green pastures with flocks of sheep that, but for the stone walls, volcanic rock, the rough Castilian tone of the shepherds, and the frequent sunshine, could pass for corners of Ireland.

The island's tiny airport handles *Iberia*'s flights to Grand Canary, Tenerife, Madrid, and Valencia. *Trasmediterránea* (Puerto de la Estaca, Valverde; phone: 22-550129) has regular ferry service to Grand Canary, Tenerife, La

Palma, and Gomera. Though El Hierro usually is visited as a day trip by tourists vacationing on one of the larger islands, accommodations are available at the modern, but traditionally styled, 47-room *Parador de El Hierro* (Las Playas; phone: 22-550101), located on a black sand beach 12 miles (20 km) south of Valverde. Moderate.

Lisbon to Porto

The road from Lisbon to Portugal's second-largest city — about a 197-mile (315-km) trip if approached in a direct, no-distractions-permitted fashion — proves that there is more to Portugal than the 500 miles of beaches that customarily take pride of place in the tourist brochures. Beaches are certainly not lacking here; in fact, the Costa de Prata (Silver Coast), which bridges the gap between the Lisbon and Estoril coasts and northern Portugal's Costa Verde (Green Coast), is one long succession of them. But the two Portuguese provinces that this coastline borders — Estremadura and Beira Litoral — contain much more than distractions for the aquatic sportsman and the person who merely wants to lie in the sun.

For the historian, there are the remains of *castros* — ancient, fortified hilltop towns — from the Bronze and Iron Ages, as well as old Roman roads, bridges, and a whole Roman city, Conímbriga, to be seen. There are fortresses — which have repelled attacks by everyone from the Moors to the troops of Napoleon — and Portugal's first capital, Coimbra, to be explored. Students will be fascinated by Coimbra's old university, a contemporary of those at Oxford and Cambridge, and probably more so by its students, who hurry to class wearing traditional black capes.

Lovers of art and architecture will be impressed by the profusion of fine Romanesque, Gothic, and baroque buildings, not to mention structures carved with the entwined ropes, seashells, nets, waves, and anchors characteristic of Portugal's own Manueline style. Three of Europe's greatest buildings — the monasteries at Mafra, Alcobaça, and Batalha — are here, and everywhere there are carvings in marble and golden Ança stone by sculptors of the Mafra and Coimbra schools. Intricate gilt carvings and beautiful 17th- and 18th-century tiles adorn churches, as do some fine paintings, such as those by the 17th-century artist Josefa de Obidos.

Numerous visitors are less interested in landmarks than they are in the features of Portugal's landscape. Nature lovers will feel in tune with their surroundings in the vast pine forest between Leiria and the sea and in the wildlife preserve in the sand dunes by the Ria lagoon at Aveiro. In fact, the entire misty, rather eerie Ria is a restful place outside the summer season — only the birds and high-prowed, painted fishing boats seem to disturb the peace. Nature lovers who also happen to be concerned about health may want to spend time in one or more of the spas of Vimeiro, Luso, and Curia, reputed to cure all manner of complaints.

And then there are the beaches. Those who would like to sun themselves on a deserted strand or in a secluded cove between high cliffs have only to follow one of the many little roads that lead off the main route down to just such private worlds by the sea. Those who prefer something more domesticated can head for one of the area's numerous popular beach resorts, such as Figueira da Foz, which has a casino in addition to a beach that is more than 1,500 feet wide — it feels as if you're crossing the Sahara just to get your toes wet. Scuba divers might be lucky enough to discover one of the old treasure ships said to be sunk here, and enthusiasts of other water sports will find plenty to keep them busy. But the less adventuresome who prefer pools to the sea will find them at most hotels and, because the surf can be rough along this Atlantic coast, in some of the beach towns themselves.

The giant lobsters and crabs that abound in the chilly coastal waters are a delight for food connoisseurs. (Such treats can be washed down with the fine wines of the Bairrada region around Coimbra and Aveiro or the not-quite-so-high-caste, but very good, wines of Torres Vedras.) Visual pleasures of the seashore with universal appeal include the brightly painted boats in the harbors and on the beaches at Ericeira, Peniche, Nazaré, and Aveiro; the sturdy white windmills twirling on the hilltops; and the scenery in the mountains that climb up from the coast.

Finally, a vast number of visitors who come this way are the devout, drawn by the miracle that is believed to have occurred at Fatima early in this century. The spot where three shepherd children in 1917 claimed to have seen the Virgin Mary several times and to have spoken with her is now a shrine attracting hundreds of thousands of worshipers from all over the world every year.

The history of this region is that of all of northern Portugal. Lusitanians, probably Celtic in origin, were the first inhabitants of whom there is historical evidence; they were succeeded by Romans, waves of barbarians, Moors, and, during the 11th century, by conquering Christian kings. In 1385, the famous battle of Aljubarrota, between a Portuguese and a Spanish pretender to the Portuguese throne, led to a Portuguese victory and to the building of the beautiful monastery at Batalha (Battle) — a monumental token of thanksgiving. From 1580 to 1640, however, the area — along with the rest of Portugal — *was* ruled by Spanish kings. Napoleon's armies invaded during the early 19th century; the two lines of fortifications built from the Tagus to the sea in the vicinity of Torres Vedras and Mafra were paramount in expelling the French — although before that happened, the invasion caused King João VI to flee to Brazil, taking most of the portable riches of the Palace of Mafra with him.

Political chaos characterized the rest of the 19th century and the beginning of this one. In 1910, 2 years after King Carlos and his heir were assassinated in Lisbon, the inhabitants of the Estremaduran fishing port of Ericeira saw Portugal's last king, Manuel II, leave for exile in England. Later, economics students at Coimbra University saw a former professor, António de Oliveira Salazar, become Prime Minister of Portugal and install a dictatorship that lasted until a coup by the armed forces in 1974 led to the present democratic regime.

Today, the people of Estremadura and the Beira Litoral live by a variety of means. There are increasing numbers of chemical, cellulose, textile, and shoe factories, but many of the old professions, such as fishing, seaweed gathering, wine making, and cattle raising, persist. Tourism is growing rapidly, although this coastal region can still be considered underexplored and its people remain hospitable. Almost every town has a well signposted tourist office with a multi-lingual staff.

The route outlined below begins in Lisbon and runs north, zigzagging between inland and coastal towns all the way to Porto. The first major monument, the monastery-palace in the inland town of Mafra, is encountered almost immediately, followed by the first of the Costa de Prata beach towns, Ericeira. The route then takes in Torres Vedras en route to the ancient fishing village of Peniche, from which an excursion to the island of Berlenga can be made. The lovely walled town of Obidos comes next, then Caldas da Rainha and its hot springs, the fishing port and beach resort of Nazaré, and Alcobaça and Batalha, each of which can claim a monastery ranking among the most impressive buildings in Europe. After visits to Fatima, to Leiria (which has an impressive hilltop castle), and to the popular beach resort of Figueira da Foz, the itinerary leads the traveler into the ancient university town of Coimbra, where those who won't be going all the way to Porto can break the trip if desired. (Our driving route through the mountains to the east begins and ends in Coimbra — see *The Beiras,* DIRECTIONS.) The final leg of the route detours to the Roman ruins of Conímbriga and then proceeds to explore Aveiro and its misty lagoon, before pulling into Portugal's northern capital, Porto.

Towns are very close together, so more than one can be visited in a day. However, some, such as Obidos, Nazaré, and Aveiro, are each worth an entire day or more, and Coimbra is so rich in history and monuments that 2 or 3 days are needed to see it all. The area's beach resorts and spas can be pleasant places for rest and relaxation or, since they are close to the historical sites, convenient headquarters for touring. But be warned that with the exception of one stretch of toll highway between Coimbra and Aveiro, the roads in this area are not very good — narrow, potholed, and full of trucks — and Portuguese drivers can be a menace.

Hotels are scarce in some places, so visitors should try to make reservations far in advance — sometimes as much as 6 months. Compared with Lisbon and the Algarve, however, hotel prices are reasonable. For a double room with bath and breakfast in a hotel listed as expensive, expect to pay $60 and up in summer (generally no higher than $80, although the *Pousada do Castelo* in Obidos costs as much as $110 for a double in summer); the cost is from $35 to $55 in a hotel listed as moderate, and less than $35 in an inexpensive one. Rates can drop by as much as 25% off-season. Given the proximity of the sea and many rivers, most of the restaurants encountered specialize in fish and seafood; happily, lobster and other such delicacies cost less on this rocky coast than they do in the Lisbon and Algarve areas. Expect to pay $30 and up for a meal for two with wine at a restaurant listed as expensive, from $15 to $30 at a moderate one, and less than $15 in an inexpensive one.

En Route from Lisbon – Leave the city on the A7 highway west toward Estoril, turning right onto N117 toward Sintra and Queluz. After 2½ miles (4 km), turn right again at the signposts for Sintra and Queluz (avoid continuing to Amadora, which is an ugly, sprawling dormitory town). In Queluz (see *Lisbon,* THE CITIES), turn right in front of the lovely pink palace, make another right at the end of the avenue, and then bear left to Belas. Continue north through Pero Pinheiro (where N117 becomes N9) to Mafra, 25 miles (40 km) from Lisbon. The road passes marble quarries and factories where stone and marble are turned into ornaments, tables, and fireplaces; some have showrooms and will arrange to ship purchases.

An alternative, more commonly used, route to Mafra is to continue to Sintra (see *Lisbon,* THE CITIES) from Queluz; Mafra is 14½ miles (23 km) from Sintra via N9.

MAFRA: The Palácio Nacional de Mafra, an enormous monastery-palace that is one of the largest historic monuments in Europe, rises up without preamble. Work on the imposing structure, often compared to the Escorial in Spain, began in 1717, after Franciscan monks convinced King João V that his wife would produce a long-awaited heir if he built them a monastery. The first of the royal brood was soon born, and with gold pouring in from Brazil, the king spared no expense in showing his appreciation. An Italian-trained German architect, Johann Friedrich Ludwig, was commissioned to build a monastery for 13 friars (a number that quickly grew to 300), as well as a palace for the entire royal family and the court. At one time, more than 50,000 workers were engaged in the construction, which was completed in 1735.

The resulting edifice, consisting of the palace, the monastery, and a church, or basilica, covers 10 acres, with a main façade 725 feet long and, all told, some 4,500 doors and windows. Rife with pink, white, and black marble from the nearby quarries of Pero Pinheiro and with exotic woods from Brazil, the embellishments caused so many foreign artists to gather here that the project became a training ground for an entire generation of Portuguese artists. It eventually gave rise to the famous Mafra school of sculpture, founded in mid-century under the Italian master Alessandro Giusti.

The basilica, predominantly Italian neo-classic and German baroque in design, occupies the middle of the façade, flanked by two majestic bell towers. Together, the towers contain 100 Flemish-made 'bells — the carillons of Mafra — which are considered among the finest in Europe. Inside, the church is noted for its elegant proportions and its breathtakingly high, richly carved dome, as well as for the side chapels, which contain beautiful Carrara marble altarpieces with bas-reliefs carved by artists of the Mafra school. Note also the six great early-19th-century organs and the plethora of brass chandeliers, candlesticks, crosses, and beautiful wrought-iron work.

The remainder of the building is an overwhelming maze of interminable corridors, vast staircases, and living quarters for the royal family and the monks. Most worthwhile are the Throne Room, with 19th-century paintings, and the marble-vaulted Benediction Room, with its beautifully patterned mosaic floor and, in the center, a bust of João V by Giusti. From the windows of this austere but impressive space, the royal family looked down into the church to hear mass. Other rooms have richly painted ceilings and murals, and there is an odd dining room with furniture made of the antlers and skins of deer from the palace's royal preserve. Game rooms, a pharmacy, the kitchen, monks' cells, and a rich collection of religious art and vestments are also worth seeing, as is the largest single library room in Europe — 290 feet long. Walls covered with shelves and intricately carved balconies of white-painted wood, a white, coffered wood ceiling, and tall windows fill it with light. In all, there are some 40,000 16th- to 18th-century volumes, covered in white leather and gold.

The monastery-palace (phone: 61-52332) is open from 10 AM to 1 PM and from 2 to 5 PM; closed Tuesdays and national holidays. Admission charge. (The basilica, visited separately at no charge, is open daily.) Given the probable absence of English-speaking guides, the vast size of the building, and the enormous amount of artwork (even though João VI stripped it of a good deal of its paintings, tapestries, furniture, and china when he fled the French invasion during the early 19th century), it is best to buy a map and guidebook at the entrance. The tourist office (Avenida 25 de Abril; phone: 61-52023) can supply information on other sights in Mafra, although the town — which was at one time a hilltop *castro* inhabited by Celts and Lusitanians and later occupied by Romans and Moors — is overwhelmed by its single monument and has little else to see except for a church or two. Pottery — off-white and trimmed in pale blue — is made in the region and is for sale in local shops.

 CHECKING IN: *Castelão* – A modern *albergaria* (inn) on the main street, not far from the monastery-palace; it has 27 rooms with bath and a glassed-in restaurant and bar. Avenida 25 de Abril, Mafra (phone: 61-52320). Moderate.

 EATING OUT: *Frederico* – Good Portuguese dishes are served in this modest restaurant, whose windows look out on the monastery. Open daily. No reservations. Avenida 25 de Abril, Mafra (phone: 61-52089). Inexpensive.

ERICEIRA: A simple fishing village that has become popular with the Portuguese as a summer resort, Ericeira sits on cliffs above the Atlantic 7 miles (11 km) northwest of Mafra via N116. There is a small beach in town, where colorful fishing boats are drawn ashore, and another larger beach outside town, where the water can be rough. Small restaurants, bars, and shops abound. Among the sights is the chapel of Santo António, which has tiles portraying the royal family's departure into exile from the port of Ericeira in 1910. North of town is the ruined São Isidro fort, built to protect the coast against pirates. The Ericeira Tourist Office is at 33 Rua Dr. Eduardo Burnay (phone: 61-63122).

 CHECKING IN: *Pedro o Pescador* – A pretty place with pointed dormer windows, on the main street. White marble floors and blue-and-white decorations everywhere make it seem light and airy. Besides its 25 rooms, it has a small garden patio off the bar, air conditioned lounges, and a dining room. 22 Rua Dr. Eduardo Burnay, Ericeira (phone: 61-62504). Expensive.

Turismo – A sprawling white building roofed in green tiles and set in gardens atop the cliff, it has 250 rooms with bath and telephone. What it lacks in decorative taste, it makes up for with views of the sea, as well as its 3 seaside swimming pools, private beach, restaurants, bar, and disco. Rua Porto de Rezés, Ericeira (phone: 61-63545). Expensive.

Morais – This blue-trimmed *estalagem* (another category of inn) on a quiet side street has a lovely inner garden graced with trees, flowers, and a swimming pool (around which lunch is served in summer). It also has 40 modern, clean rooms with bath. Reserve far in advance. 3 Rua Dr. Miguel Bombarda, Ericeira (phone: 61-62611). Moderate.

EATING OUT: *O Cantinho do Madeirense* – English-owned, it specializes in meats done on a spit, Madeira-style. The red tile floor, gold-and-blue tablecloths, and mats on the wall make up the decor, and there is a patio in front. Open daily. Reservations advised. Praça dos Navegantes, Ericeira (phone: 61-63669). Expensive.

César – An enormous panoramic restaurant on the cliffs north of town. Lobsters swim in an indoor fountain, and beneath the restaurant is a huge vivarium filled with baroque-decorated tanks of shellfish. There is a bar and music for dancing. Open daily. Reservations advised. On N247, Km 1 (phone: 61-62926). Expensive to moderate.

O Barco – A highly recommended dining place on a narrow, cobbled street, down the stone steps that lead to the fishing harbor. Try the *arroz de marisco* (rice with seafood), the *arroz de polvo* (rice with octopus), the *caldeirada de enguias* (eel stew), or the curried shellfish. Windows have views of the sea. Closed Thursdays in winter. Reservations advised. Rua Capitão João Lopes, Ericeira (phone: 61-62759). Moderate.

Parque dos Mariscos – In a big, white building on the main street, it has green tables and green lattices and plants decorating its red brick walls. As expected, *arroz de marisco* is a specialty; so is *linguado a Parque* (sole, house-style). Open daily. Reservations advised. 28 Rua Dr. Eduardo Burnay, Ericeira (phone: 61-62162). Moderate.

Pátio das Marialvas – A small seafood restaurant with a terrace on the main street. Try the *mariscadas* (a variety of fried seafood), the fricassee of octopus, or the *arroz de marisco*. Closed in November. No reservations. 29 Rua Dr. Eduardo Burnay, Ericeira (phone: 61-62549). Moderate to inexpensive.

En Route from Ericeira – A good road, N247, leads north into the Costa de Prata. It runs along the tops of cliffs, with spectacular views of rough seas smashing onto rocks below, and little roads lead down from it to inlets and indented beaches — Praia de São Sebastião, Praia de São Lourenço, Porto da Calada. A number of windmills — some billed as "working windmills" — can be visited. The road then meets N9 and turns eastward across a flat plain beside the Sizandro River to Torres Vedras, 16½ miles (27 km) from Ericeira. Before town, there's a turnoff to the right (over an unpaved road) for the ruins of an important fortified hilltop town of the Iron and Bronze Ages — Castro do Zambujal — which has walls and towers still standing from 2500 BC. The many artifacts discovered here are in the *Municipal Museum* in Torres Vedras.

CHECKING IN/EATING OUT: *Dom Fernando* – This *estalagem* sits dramatically on a cliff in solitary splendor above the Atlantic 7 miles (11 km) north of Ericeira on N247. Originally a private house, it has a lovely garden and terrace over the sea, access to the beach below as well as a pool, a restaurant, and 14 rooms and suites, all with lovely views and furnished with elegant reproductions of antiques. Quinta da Calada, Talefe (phone: 61-55204). Moderate.

TORRES VEDRAS: An old town that has been inhabited by Celts, Visigoths, Romans, and Moors, Torres Vedras is most famous as the headquarters for the defense of Lisbon from Napoleon's troops during the early 19th century. The Linhas de Torres Vedras were two lines of earthen battlements incorporating fortresses and castles that English and Portuguese troops under the command of Arthur Wellesley (later to become the Duke of Wellington) raised clear across the peninsula jutting from the coast to the Tagus River. The more northerly line began at the mouth of the Sizandro on the Atlantic and ended just south of Vila Franca de Xira, passing through Torres Vedras. The southern line crossed the peninsula at a point just north of Mafra. To see the remains of the lines, turn left at the entrance to town, where the sign points upward. The ruins of the São Vicente fort, built as part of the lines (many of its round towers were disguised as windmills to fool the French), stand at the top of a nearly perpendicular hill commanding a wide view of the countryside. Inside the courtyard there are reconstructions of the earthen battlements, but nothing of the original fort remains except the walls and an empty dome.

Torres Vedras today is a modern town with little of its ancient character, except for the Old Quarter, which has narrow, cobblestone streets winding steeply up to the old castle on the hill opposite the São Vicente fort. The castle was badly damaged when it was wrested from the Moors during the 12th century, and again in the earthquake of 1755, but it, too, became part of Wellington's lines. The church of Santa Maria do Castelo, within its walls, has two Romanesque portals, numerous paintings, and 17th-century *azulejos,* but São Pedro, with its Manueline portal, opulent gilt work, and baroque tiles, is the most important of the town's churches — of which there are many more, including the 16th-century Graça with lovely 18th-century tiles, the flood-damaged Santiago, and the Misericórdia. Also to be seen are a Gothic fountain (the

Chafariz dos Canos) and the *Museu Municipal* (7 Rua Serpa Pinto; phone: 61-2201), where, in addition to items dug up at the prehistoric Castro do Zambujal site, silver crowns, coins, paintings, and ceramics are on display (open from 10 AM to noon and from 2 to 6 PM; closed Mondays and, from October through June, national holidays; no admission charge). The tourist office is on Rua 9 de Abril (phone: 61-23094).

 CHECKING IN: *Império* – Built in post-modernist style, it is in the center of town and is charming, light, and cheerful. Some of the 26 rooms have balconies with views of the town and the Graça church; there is a restaurant, a bar, and a café. Praça 25 de Abril, Torres Vedras (phone: 61-25232). Inexpensive.

EATING OUT: *Barrete Preto* – The most elegant restaurant in town, with 3 dining rooms — one of them wood paneled and carpeted, another done up in regional style, with decorative tiles and antique lanterns. The menu is long, but codfish, eel stew, roast kid, and *cozido à portuguesa* (Portuguese boiled dinner — a one-dish meal containing a variety of meats and vegetables) are specialties. Closed Thursdays and the month of September. Reservations advised. 25 Rua Paiva de Andrade, Torres Vedras (phone: 61-22150). Moderate.

O Diamante – New and charming, it provides light music as an accompaniment to meals. Closed Mondays. Reservations advised. 32A Rua António Leal da Assunção, Torres Vedras (phone 61-25988). Moderate.

Pateo – An old house has been turned into a modern restaurant, and with its white walls and pale pink and green decor, it's very attractive. Mixed grills, *porco recheado* (loin of pork stuffed with cheese and ham), Portuguese boiled dinner, and other well-cooked dishes are on the menu. Closed Sundays. Reservations advised. 1B Rua José Eduardo César, Torres Vedras (phone: 61-31496). Moderate.

En Route from Torres Vedras – Take N8-2 north through high hills covered with vineyards and pine woods. Proceed directly to Lourinhã or, after about 4½ miles (7 km), turn left to the spa town of Vimeiro (another 4 miles/17 km along a not-so-good road) and the wide sandy beach of Praia do Porto Novo (still another 2½ miles — 4 km — west); then backtrack through Vimeiro to rejoin N8-2 north. Lourinhã, a flat and medieval-looking town beside the sea, is the gateway to many of the region's beaches, and it has several interesting monuments in its own right, such as the 14th-century Gothic Igreja Matriz (Parish Church); the church of Nossa Senhora da Annunciação, which is part of a Franciscan monastery founded in 1598; and the Misericórdia church, with a Manueline door. North of town about 2½ miles (4 km) is the shell-shaped beach of Praia da Areia Branca, with several hotels and restaurants, and still farther along is the fishing port of Peniche, at the tip of a peninsula jutting out to sea 12 miles (19 km) from Lourinhã.

CHECKING IN: *Golf Mar* – Its beautiful, dramatic, solitary setting amid landscaped gardens very high above the rocky coast at Praia do Porto Novo gives guests the feeling of being suspended between the sky and the sea. Half of the nearly 300 rooms have terraces overlooking the water, and the hotel has a 9-hole golf course, a heated indoor pool in addition to an outdoor pool, a panoramic restaurant and bar, shops, a discotheque, a gameroom, a hairdresser, and lounges. Praia do Porto Novo (phone: 61-98157). Expensive.

Areia Branca – This modern *estalagem* (inn) near the beach has 29 rooms and a good restaurant. Praia da Areia Branca (phone: 61-46491). Moderate.

Apartamentos Turísticos São João – This modern complex of 18 well-furnished tourist apartments has a swimming pool, bar, discotheque, and a mini-market. Praia da Areia Branca (phone: 61-42491). Inexpensive.

Do Rossio – A contemporary *pensão* with 15 rooms (with bath), and use of the swimming pool at the *São João* apartments (see above) at Praia da Areia Branca.

No restaurant. Rua dos Bombeiros Voluntarios, Lourinhã (phone: 61-43049). Inexpensive.

 EATING OUT: O Chalé – Seafood is the specialty. Open daily. No reservations. Largo Mestre Anacleto Marcos da Silva, Lourinhã (phone: 61-43003). Moderate.

Frutos do Mar – At Porto das Barcas, south of Lourinhã, this eatery specializes in lobster — in fact, it has the largest vivarium in Portugal. Closed Tuesdays. No reservations. Agua Doce, Porto das Barcas (phone: 61-42774). Moderate.

PENICHE: This is a bustling fishing port whose colorful fleet can be seen unloading the daily catch by the tons and whose seafood restaurants are plentiful. (The local version of *caldeirada,* fish stew, is famous.) On a mile-long peninsula jutting out to sea, Peniche was once an island — silt deposited over the centuries built up the sand isthmus that now joins it to the mainland. In earlier times, the island was the last refuge of Lusitanian warriors fleeing Roman invaders and a port of call for Phoenicians, Crusaders, and pirates.

The massive, sprawling fortress that dominates the harbor was built during the 16th century and later enlarged until its moats, walls, bastions, cisterns, and towers occupied 5 acres. Used as a political prison during the Salazar regime and later as a camp for refugees from Angola, it now houses the *Museu Municipal* (Campo da República; phone: 62-71848), a repository of prehistoric artifacts, articles pertaining to ships, fishing, and lace making (the ancient art of *bilros,* or bobbin lace, still flourishes in Peniche), as well as relics from its past as a prison (open from 10 AM to noon and from 2 to 7 PM, July through September; closes at 5 PM the rest of the year; closed Mondays; admission charge). Several of the town's churches are also worth a visit, among them the Misericórdia, where the walls are covered with beautiful 17th-century tiles and the ceiling is painted with New Testament scenes — in all there are about 100 paintings in the church, five of them by Josefa de Obidos. The church of Nossa Senhora do Socorro (Our Lady of Succor) has paintings attributed to Josefa's father, as well as interesting glazed tiles and gilt carving; São Pedro has an enormous baroque altarpiece and paintings of the life of the saint; and Nossa Senhora da Conceição is completely covered with 18th-century tiles. Peniche's Tourist Office is on Rua Alexandre Herculano (phone: 62-72271).

The coast of the Peniche peninsula is lined with giant rock formations in the sea, many in fantastic, unreal shapes, as well as with caves, grottoes, and wide sandy beaches. At the tip of the peninsula is Cabo Carvoeiro, with another church, the tiny sanctuary of Nossa Senhora dos Remédios, which is completely covered with tiles attributed to the 18th-century master António de Oliveira Bernardes; nearby is an 18th-century lighthouse. The church is the focal point of one of Peniche's traditional festivals, the *Romaria da Nossa Senhora dos Remédios,* held in October, when the image of the Virgin is carried from the church down to the sea. Another local festival, also sea-related, is the *Festas da Senhora da Boa Viagem* (Festival of Our Lady of the Good Voyage,) held the first week in August in Peniche and marked by a procession of boats. Cabo Carvoeiro provides smashing views of the surf-pounded coast and, in the distance, of Berlenga, the main island of an archipelago (the Ilhas Berlengas) whose rocks, caves, and coves are home to migratory birds and rare flora and fauna. From June through September, boats run from Peniche to Berlenga (for schedules, call 62-72153 or 62-72484), making the trip in about an hour. During the 16th century, the island was inhabited by monks, who abandoned it after constant attacks by pirates. Today, a few fishermen and lighthouse keepers live here. The lighthouse stands on the highest point of the island, above the 17th-century São João Baptista fort, which is set on an islet connected to Berlenga by a winding stone bridge. The fort has been turned into a lovely hostel, or guesthouse, one of the two places to stay on the island (see below).

CHECKING IN: *Praia Norte* – This modern place at the entrance to town has 103 rooms and suites, a swimming pool, a discotheque, and a restaurant and grillroom. On N114, Praia Norte, Peniche (phone: 62-71171). Expensive.

Felita – A small *pensão* with 9 rooms, near the town gardens. 12 Largo Professor Franco Freire, Peniche (phone: 62-72190). Inexpensive.

Casa Abrigo São João Baptista – In the charming setting of a 17th-century fort on Berlenga Island, this hostel (not a youth hostel, however) is run by the Friends of Peniche Association. It offers 20 rooms, open from June to mid-September. Guests who stay here should be prepared to bring their own linen and their own food (unless they eat at the island's only other hostelry — see below). Reservations should be made through the tourist office (phone: 62-72271) in Peniche. Ilha Berlenga. Very inexpensive.

Pavilhão Mar e Sol – Also on Berlenga Island, this comfortable, 5-room residence is run by the Peniche municipal government. Open from June through mid-September, it has a pleasant restaurant — the only one on the island, in fact. Ilha Berlenga (phone: 62-72031). Very inexpensive.

EATING OUT: *Praia Mar* – On the beach, this place specializes in fish and seafood and has windows looking out to sea. Open daily. No reservations. Molhe Leste, Peniche (phone: 62-73106). Moderate.

Marisqueira Mili – A typical restaurant near the fishing port, it, too, specializes in seafood. Open daily. No reservations. Rua José Estevão, Peniche (phone: 62-72278). Inexpensive.

En Route from Peniche – Head east on N114, passing through Atouguia da Baleia, an interesting little town with a 13th-century Romanesque-Gothic church and, in front of the church, a Manueline pillory. In the square in front of another church — a massive baroque one — are the rough stone remains of a bull stall built by King Pedro I during the 14th century — evidence that bullfighting is very old in Portugal. Continue east on N114, turning north onto N8 to the beautiful walled town of Obidos, 15 miles (24 km) from Peniche.

OBIDOS: This small town set on a high hill is rightly called a "museum town." Its medieval atmosphere remains intact, and so many of its houses and other buildings are of historic or artistic significance that it has been declared a national monument. A picture-postcard town today, with flower-covered balconies, whitewashed houses, and narrow cobblestone streets — all surrounded by Moorish walls and dominated by an equally old castle — it was evidently just as pretty during the Middle Ages. The Saintly Isabel admired it so much during a 13th-century visit with her new husband, King Dinis, that he gave it to her as a wedding present. Obidos later became the property of Leonor Teles, wife of King Fernando; Philippa of Lancaster, the English wife of King João I; Leonor of Portugal, wife of João II; and Catherine, wife of King João III. Thus it became known as the Casa das Rainhas (House of Queens).

Pass through the double-arched gateway to the town (Porta da Vila) and follow the narrow main street, Rua Direita, to the Praça de Santa Maria, where there are a few tree-shaded parking spaces. The Igreja de Santa Maria is a beautiful 17th-century church (on the foundations of a Visigothic temple that later became a Moorish mosque), virtually paved with blue-and-white *azulejos* inside. The paintings over the main altar are by João da Costa, while those of St. Catherine over the altar in a chapel to the south (right) were signed by Josefa de Obidos in 1661 (the great 17th-century painter, born in Seville, lived most of her life in Obidos and is buried in another town church, São Pedro). Note, too, the large paintings of biblical scenes, attributed to her father, Baltazar Gomes Gigueira, as well as the exquisitely carved Renaissance tomb of a Governor of Obidos. More works by Josefa de Obidos are in the *Museu Municipal,* in the same square (phone: 62-959263; open from 9 AM to 1 PM and from 2 to 6 PM, closed Mondays and some holidays; admission charge, except on Wednesdays), along with other paintings, sculpture, furniture, archaeological artifacts, and exhibits devoted to the Peninsular War. In the center of the square is a 15th-century pillory donated by Queen Leonor, the wife of João II. It bears the royal coat of arms and the *camaroeiro* (shrimp net) that became her symbol after her son drowned in Santarém and his body was recovered in a fisherman's net.

Proceed on foot to the Igreja de São Tiago, where a path on the left leads to the ramparts. Built by the Moors, the walls enclosing the town are nearly a mile in circumference, with a wide walkway along the top that makes it possible to circumnavigate the crenelated battlements and take in a spectacular view of both the town and the countryside. There are only two interruptions in the circuit: one at the town gateway, the other at the castle, which began as a fortress, was turned into a royal palace during the 16th century, and has now been transformed, in part, into a *pousada,* or inn (see *Checking In*).

Outside the walls, there are several churches and chapels, but the most noteworthy is the unfinished hexagonal church of Senhor da Pedra, which sits alone in a field to the north of town via N8; inside the 17th-century baroque building is an early Christian stone cross. To the south of town is the 16th-century aqueduct, a nearly 2-mile structure of double arches ordered built by Queen Catherine to feed water into the town's various fountains. The tourist office is on Rua Direita (phone: 62-959231).

 CHECKING IN: *Pousada do Castelo* – A rustically elegant, government-owned inn in the castle of Obidos, complete with medieval armor in the decor. There are only 9 rooms and suites, some of them in the towers, plus an excellent restaurant and a bar. Given its size, advance reservations are essential. Paço Real, Obidos (phone: 62-959105 or 62-959146). Very expensive.

Do Convento – Just outside the walls, it was built during the early 19th century to cloister nuns, and it has been delightfully converted into an *estalagem* offering every modern convenience while maintaining its character. There are 24 rooms, a bar, and a beamed restaurant with a stone fireplace (and a garden patio for summer dining). Rua Dom João de Ornelas, Obidos (phone: 62-959217). Expensive.

Josefa d'Obidos – An *albergaria* (inn) in an old house just outside the walls at the entrance to town, it has 42 nicely furnished rooms with bath, a typical restaurant, a bar, and a weekend discotheque. Rua Dom João de Ornelas, Obidos (phone: 62-959228). Moderate.

Rainha Santa Isabel – Another *albergaria,* on the main street of Obidos. Formerly a private home, it's decorated with tiles and has 20 rooms with bath, as well as a bar and several lounges. Rua Direita, Obidos (phone: 62-959115). Moderate.

EATING OUT: *A Ilustre Casa de Ramiro* – The shell of this building outside the walls is very old, but the interior was designed with an Arabic motif by the contemporary architect José Fernando Teixeira. Among the specialties are *arroz de pato* (rice with duck) and grilled codfish; wines are from the Obidos region. Closed Wednesdays. Reservations advised. Rua Porta do Vale, Obidos (phone: 62-959194). Expensive to moderate.

Alcaide – On the main street in the center of town, with lovely views of the countryside. Try the tuna fish, Azores-style. Closed Mondays and the month of November. No reservations. Rua Direita, Obidos (phone: 62-959220). Moderate.

CALDAS DA RAINHA: This sprawling agricultural town, 4 miles (6 km) north of Obidos on N8, has two claims to fame: hot springs and ceramics. The town's name means "the Queen's hot springs" — referring, in this case, to the 15th-century Queen

Leonor, wife of João II. Passing through on her way to Batalha, she noticed peasants bathing in some local pools and, upon learning that the waters were good for rheumatism, did the same. So effective was the therapy for her own ailments that the queen pawned her jewels to establish a hospital and lay out a park, both of which still bear her name (and it's still possible for visitors to steep themselves in the sulfurous waters at the Rainha Dona Leonor Hospital Spa). The Church of Nossa Senhora do Pópulo, which was the chapel of the hospital, is a Gothic and Manueline structure noted for its *azulejos* and a fine 16th-century triptych.

Caldas has been a pottery making center since ancient times. The ceramics fair that takes place here each July draws thousands of visitors, but for those who miss it, the local pottery (the cabbage leaf bowls are a typical item) and other crafts can be seen at the Saturday market on Praça da República, the main square. One of the most famous Caldas potters was Rafael Bordalo Pinheiro, a 19th-century ceramist, cartoonist, and painter who established a studio here and created brightly colored caricatures of people that are still copied today. The *Museu José Malhoa* (in the park; phone: 62-31984; open from 10 AM to 12:30 PM and from 2 to 5 PM; closed Mondays and holidays; admission charge, except on Sunday mornings) displays a fine collection of ceramics by Bordalo Pinheiro, along with paintings by the late-19th- and early-20th-century artist after whom the museum is named. More ceramics can be seen at the far end of the park in the *Museu da Cerámica* (phone: 62-23157; open from 10 AM to noon and from 2 to 5 PM; closed Mondays and holidays; admission charge, except on Sunday mornings), which has a tiled garden, and more of Bordalo Pinheiro's work can be seen nearby at the Faianças Artísticas Bordalo Pinheiro (Bordalo Pinheiro Faïence Factory), which maintains a small museum (closed Saturdays and Sundays). For more information on Caldas da Rainha, contact the tourist office (Praça da República; phone: 62-34511).

 CHECKING IN: *Malhoa* – There are 113 rooms with bath in this modern hostelry, whose amenities also include a swimming pool, sauna, restaurant, and discotheque. 31 Rua António Sérgio, Caldas da Rainha (phone: 62-35011). Moderate.

Dona Leonor – A *pensão* with 30 rooms, each of which has a private bath, TV set, and telephone. There is a bar, but no restaurant. 6 Hemiciclo João Paulo II, Caldas da Rainha (phone: 62-35511). Inexpensive.

 EATING OUT: *Pateo da Rainha* – Good regional cooking and good service prevail. Specialties of the house are rice with monkfish, codfish, and *cozido à portuguesa,* or Portuguese boiled dinner. Open daily. No reservations. 39 Rua de Camões, Caldas da Rainha (phone: 62-24672). Moderate.

En Route from Caldas da Rainha – Take N8 north 7½ miles (12 km) to Alfeizerão and then turn west onto N242. São Martinho do Porto, on a quiet bay, with some interesting 19th-century buildings among the more modern ones of a beach resort, is only 3 miles (5 km) from the turnoff. After São Martinho, N242 heads north to Nazaré, 18 miles (29 km) from Caldas da Rainha.

 CHECKING IN: *São Pedro* – This is a small *albergaria* (inn) with 13 rooms and a bar, located near the beach. 7 Largo Vitorino Frois, São Martinho do Porto (phone: 62-98327). Expensive.

Apartamentos Turísticos São Martinho – A tourist complex offering 160 apartments with kitchenettes, a restaurant, a bar, and a swimming pool. It's near the beach, with water sports available. 31 Rua Dr. Rafael Garcia, São Martinho do Porto (phone: 62-98335). Moderate.

 EATING OUT: *O Viveiro* – A good seafood restaurant near the quay. Open daily. No reservations. Rua Cândido dos Reis, São Martinho do Porto (phone: 62-98691). Moderate.

NAZARÉ: This fishing village has recently become a very popular, rather touristy beach resort, but some of its quaint customs remain, including the wearing of traditional costumes — full skirts with up to seven petticoats for the women, and long, black, plaid-lined capes and black stocking caps for the men. There are two parts to Nazaré. The Praia quarter, along the beach, is the lower, newer part of town, while the older Sítio, or Upper Town, is atop a cliff to the north, reachable by car or by an old funicular. The sea once covered what is now the Lower Town, but it suddenly receded during the 17th century, after which fishermen from Sítio built huts on the beach and eventually made Nazaré the premier fishing town along the coast — an impressive feat, since it has no natural harbor and, until very recently, had no real port facilities. The fishermen launched their boats from the beach and used oxen and, later, tractors to pull the nets back to shore. Given the strong currents, it was a dangerous occupation, but today there is a new sheltered port for the boats — which are long and narrow, with bright eyes painted on the pointed prows, highly suggestive of the Phoenicians from whom it is believed the people of Nazaré are descended. The Praia area is now full of hotels and restaurants and the other trappings of a seaside resort, but visitors can still see women drying fish and men mending nets, even though only a few fishermen remain on the beach.

Before the fishermen spread to the lower town and before the advent of tourists, the Sítio quarter was all there was to Nazaré. There is a spectacular view from the belvedere here; it takes in all the town below, the beach tents and umbrellas, the boat shelter at the far end of the beach, and the distant coastline. On the main square is the Nossa Senhora da Nazaré church, rich in marble and gilt carving; the church's little black image of the Virgin, said to have been brought from the Holy Land after the death of Emperor Constantine, is carried down to the sea during the annual *Romaria da Nossa Senhora de Nazaré,* a festival held in early September. The tiny, white Capela da Memória, built into the side of the cliff by the square, commemorates a 12th-century miracle performed by the Virgin. According to the legend, Dom Fuas Roupinho, a very religious man, was hunting on the cliffs when his horse jumped over the edge after a deer. Dom Fuas prayed to the Virgin, who miraculously set him and his horse back on terra firma, after which he built the chapel on the very spot. The present chapel, dating from the 17th century, is covered with 17th-century *azulejos.* A remaining Sítio landmark is the São Miguel fort, built during the 16th century to protect the town from pirates and now turned into a lighthouse. The tourist office in Nazaré (23 Rua Mouzinho de Albuquerque; phone: 62-52194) is in the Praia section of town.

CHECKING IN: *Dom Fuas* – This new hotel has 32 well-furnished rooms, all with TV sets, as well as a restaurant, bar, and snack bar. It's at the southern end of the Praia section, open from April to mid-October. Avenida Manuel Remígio, Nazaré (phone: 62-51351). Expensive.

Praia – Modern, with 40 rooms with bath, air conditioning, and TV sets, this is on a main street near the beach. It has no restaurant, but there is a breakfast room, a bar, and a disco. 39 Avenida Vieira Guimarães, Nazaré (phone: 62-51423). Expensive.

Maré – Small (36 rooms) and convenient, it's in the heart of the Praia, about a block from the beach, with a restaurant and bar. 8 Rua Mouzinho de Albuquerque, Nazaré (phone: 62-51122). Moderate.

Da Nazaré – In a little square several blocks back from the beach in the Praia quarter, it has 52 rooms with bath, a bar, a restaurant, and a nightclub, and there is a place next door — *Mar Alto* — to take in some folk music and dancing. Largo Afonso Zuquete, Nazaré (phone: 62-46311 or 51311). Moderate.

EATING OUT: *Mar Bravo* – This very elegant place, serving good regional food, some French dishes, and seafood, has a panoramic view of the sea. Open daily. No reservations. Praça Sousa Oliveira, Nazaré (phone: 62-46180). Expensive.

***Paulo Caetano* –** Named after a famous Portuguese bullfighter and decorated with bullfighting pictures and posters, this Sítio restaurant specializes in seafood. Open daily. No reservations. Largo Reitor Baptista, Nazaré (phone: 62-52011). Expensive to moderate.

***Ribamar* –** In a *pensão* on the beach in the center of town — a white building with yellow balconies and windows — it has a lovely view of the sea. Fish, seafood, and typical regional dishes are the specialties. Open daily. No reservations. Avenida da República, Nazaré (phone: 62-51158). Expensive to moderate.

***A Petisqueira* –** Run by three brothers, this yellow, glassed-in restaurant, at the far end of the beach by the fishing boat shelter, serves nine different variations of *caldeirada da Nazaré* (fish stew). Open daily. No reservations. Avenida Manuel Remígio, Nazaré (phone: 62-51594). Moderate.

ALCOBAÇA: Only 8½ miles (14 km) southeast of Nazaré via N8-4, this small town at the confluence of the Alcoa and Baça rivers is completely dominated by the enormous white limestone Cistercian abbey — the Mosteiro de Santa Maria — in its midst, once the home of Portugal's most prosperous religious community and still one of the country's most important architectural landmarks. In thanks for his victory over the Moors at Santarém in 1149, King Afonso Henriques granted land to St. Bernard of Clairvaux, the influential French Cistercian who had championed the Portuguese cause against the Moors. The monks began to build in 1178 and, on the Cistercian model, set to work farming their vast domain, recruiting lay brothers to help them and introducing new agricultural techniques (which accounts for the fact that the Alcobaça vineyards and wines are still some of the best in the country).

The style of the monastery church, the largest church in Portugal, marks the transition from Romanesque to Gothic, although the façade, with its rose window and two bell towers, is a result of 17th- and 18th-century baroque alterations. Inside, the spacious church is, in accordance with Cistercian austerity, devoid of adornment — with two notable exceptions: the exquisite, intricately carved 14th-century Flamboyant Gothic tombs of King Pedro I and his beloved mistress, Dona Inês de Castro, the most famous lovers in Portuguese history. As a prince, Pedro had fallen in love with the beautiful Spanish aristocrat, but his father, fearing Spanish interference with the Portuguese throne, ordered her murder (which took place in Coimbra in 1355). Dom Pedro had his revenge when he ascended the throne. Besides executing some of Inês's murderers, he exhumed her body, dressed her in royal robes and a crown, and forced all of the nobility to kiss her hand. Whether the monastery church at Alcobaça was the scene of this "coronation" is open to question, but both Pedro and Inês are buried here, in tombs placed on opposite sides of the transept, so that their first sight upon opening their eyes on Judgment Day will be of each other.

Behind the ambulatory of the church is the sacristy, preceded by an ornate, 16th-century Manueline doorway, and just off the church nave is the beautiful 14th-century Claustro do Silêncio (its upper story, added later, is Manueline). Around the cloister range other monastic spaces, including the Sala dos Reis (Kings' Hall), an 18th-century addition with terra cotta statues of the Kings of Portugal surmounting an *azulejo* frieze, and the impressive kitchen, totally covered in pale tiles. Not only does the kitchen have a huge fireplace and chimney big enough to roast several oxen at once, it also has a branch of the Alcoa running through it — an early labor-saving device that allowed the monks to catch fish for their dinner and to wash the dishes, too. The monastery (phone:

62-43469) is open daily from 9 AM to 7 PM (to 5 PM from October through March; closed *Christmas* and *New Year's Day*). Admission charge, except on Sunday mornings. Alcobaça's tourist office is in Praça 25 de Abril (phone: 62-42377).

 CHECKING IN: *Santa Maria* – This modern white building with a tiled roof sits in gardens directly in front of the monastery. There are 31 rooms with bath (some of the rooms have balconies), plus a nice, wood-paneled bar. Rua Dr. Francisco Zagalo, Alcobaça (phone: 62-43294). Moderate.

 EATING OUT: *Frei Bernardo* – Behind the Art Nouveau exterior is a nice bar and a very large dining room specializing in *frango na púcara* (chicken in a pot), *chanfana de borrego* (lamb stew), grilled fish, and *açorda de marisco,* a stew or "dry" soup made of seafood and other ingredients. Entertainment is a show of folk dancing and singing and a band that plays Portuguese music. Open daily. Reservations advised. 17-19 Rua Dom Pedro V, Alcobaça (phone: 62-42227). Moderate.

***Trindade* –** The region's most typical dishes are the specialties — *frango na pucara, açorda de marisco,* and fish. Besides the restaurant, there's also a snack bar and a small bar; original 18th-century tiles are part of the decor. Closed Saturdays in winter and from mid-September through the first week in October. No reservations. 22 Praça Dom Afonso Henriques, Alcobaça (phone: 62-42397). Moderate.

En Route from Alcobaça – The town of Aljubarrota is 4 miles (6 km) north along N8, not far from the place where the armies of two pretenders to the Portuguese throne — one Portuguese and one Castilian — faced each other on August 14, 1385. The Portuguese pretender, whose forces were vastly outnumbered, vowed he would build a great monastery if he defeated the Spaniards. The battle was brief and won by the Portuguese, thereby assuring the country's independence and the right of João I to occupy its throne. The enduring monument he constructed is farther up the road, 6 miles (10 km) along N8 and then 2½ miles (4 km) along N1, in Batalha.

BATALHA: The monastery that João I raised to the Virgin Mary in thanks for his decisive victory at Aljubarrota is probably the most beautiful monument in Portugal, despite the discoloration and pollution damage inflicted by passing traffic. Begun in 1388, worked on by several architects throughout the 15th century, and left unfinished early in the 16th century, the Mosteiro de Santa Maria da Vitória (Monastery of Our Lady of Victory) is a masterpiece of Portuguese Gothic, often cited as an example of how the country's builders were able to absorb various foreign influences to forge their own national style. Outside, it's trimmed with gargoyles, flying buttresses, pinnacles, and lacy balustrades (the west front is particularly suggestive of the English Perpendicular style, which is not surprising since the founder's wife, Philippa of Lancaster, was English). Inside, while the church nave is stark and soaring, cloisters and chapels are richly decorated with the delicate curves of Flamboyant Gothic and the florid details of the transitional, Gothic-to-Renaissance, Manueline style.

Be sure to see the Capela do Fundador (Founder's Chapel), off an aisle to the right, where King João I, Queen Philippa, and their children (including Prince Henry the Navigator) are buried beneath a star-shaped vault. The tomb of the king and queen is topped with reclining figures of the pair, their hands joined. The Claustro Real (Royal Cloister), on the other side of the church, mixes Gothic with Manueline (note the pearls, shells, and coils carved on the columns). Just off it is the Sala do Capitúlo (Chapterhouse), which has a vaulted ceiling without intermediate supports — accomplishing this was such a dangerous engineering feat that condemned criminals did the actual work. Another cloister, the Claustro de Dom Afonso V, is beyond the Royal Cloister, after which the visitor can walk around to the Capelas Imperfeitas (Unfinished

Chapels): seven chapels radiating around a rotunda that was meant to be topped with a dome. The incomplete pillars, which serve no purpose now, are nevertheless encrusted with Manueline carving, and the doorway to the chapels is a Manueline tour de force. The Batalha monastery (phone: 44-96497) is open daily from 9 AM to 6 PM (to 5 PM from October through May; closed *Christmas* and *New Year's Day*). Admission charge. Batalha's Tourist Office is on Largo Paulo VI (phone: 44-96180).

 CHECKING IN: *Pousada do Mestre Afonso Domingues* – Formerly a privately owned *estalagem,* it's now a government-owned *pousada,* although unlike most of the chain, it's of modern construction. In the square by the monastery and named after the first of the monastery's architects, it has 20 rooms with bath, a small bar, and a good restaurant. Largo Mestre Afonso Domingues, Batalha (phone: 44-96260). Expensive.

***São Jorge* –** A motel up the hill on the road to Lisbon. Besides the 10 rooms, there are tennis courts, a large swimming pool amid lawns and trees, and a regional-style restaurant. On N1, Batalha (phone: 44-96210 or 44-96186). Moderate.

 EATING OUT: *Mestre de Avis* – A large restaurant upstairs above a café near the monastery square. Decorated in blue and white, it has bay windows offering a good view of the monastery, as well as a terrace for summer dining. Open daily. No reservations. Largo Dom João I, Batalha (phone: 44-96427). Moderate.

En Route from Batalha – Leiria is only 7 miles (11 km) north on N1, but for those with time to spare, the will to face the road (very bad and full of curves), and an interest in the phenomenon that made it famous, Fatima — in the mountains 12½ miles (20 km) east of Batalha along N356 — is worth a side trip.

FATIMA: On the 13th of May, 1917, a vision of the Virgin Mary, standing above a small oak tree, appeared to three peasant children who were tending their sheep here. The apparition returned five more times — on the 13th of each succeeding month — and by the time of the last appearance, a crowd of 70,000 people had gathered at the spot. They saw the sun break through a stormy day and appear to spin toward earth, but only the children saw the Virgin. Fatima has since become a world-famous Roman Catholic shrine, and to this day, pilgrims arrive — some crawling on their knees for miles — to hear mass on the 13th of each month from May through October. On the anniversaries of the first and final apparitions, the crowds are particularly large, and on special occasions they have been known to number a million. The visitor sees a huge esplanade, where the mass is celebrated and torch-lit processions take place, edged by a neo-classical basilica containing the tombs of two of the children, Francisco and Jacinta Marto, who died of influenza in 1919 and 1920 (the third child, Lúcia dos Santos, still lives as a Carmelite nun in Coimbra). The Chapel of the Apparitions, marking the spot where the oak tree stood and the Virgin appeared, is at the far end of the esplanade.

Those who decide to visit Fatima should note that roads leading to it are jammed to capacity on the 12th and 13th of pilgrimage months, and that while hotels are not in short supply, they are equally jammed on those days, since they cater mainly to pilgrims who make reservations months in advance. The Fatima Tourist Office is located on Avenida Dom José Alves Correia da Silva (phone: 49-531139).

 CHECKING IN: *Dom Gonçalo* – A 43-room *estalagem,* with a TV set in each room, a good restaurant and bar, gift shops, and a disco. 100 Rua Jacinta Marto, Fatima (phone: 49-97262). Inexpensive.

 EATING OUT: *Grelha* – One of only a few independent restaurants in Fatima, it specializes in Portuguese cooking, especially grilled meats. The dining room has a fireplace, and there's a good bar. Closed Thursdays. Reservations advised. 76 Rua Jacinta Marto, Fatima (phone: 49-97633). Moderate.

En Route from Fatima – Backtrack to Batalha and from there take the road north to Leiria. Alternatively, return to Batalha by making a circuit southwest of Fatima via N360 and N243 and the towns of Mira de Aire and Porto de Mós. Several caves — *grutas* — are located in this area, among them the São Mamede, Moinhos Velhos, Santo António, and Alvados caves. Of these, the last two — the Grutas de Santo António and the Grutas de Alvados — are probably the most interesting. At the former (phone: 49-84876), there is an enormous chamber of nearly 5,000 square yards, plus rooms of dramatically lighted stalactites and stalagmites. A restaurant and snack bar are also at the site. The latter contain a succession of halls with giant columns and lakes, all well lighted. The caves are open daily year-round. Admission charge (a combined ticket can be bought for both caves).

LEIRIA: An attractive, clean town at the confluence of the Liz and the Lena rivers, Leiria consists of an old medieval quarter and a new town of pleasant gardens and wide avenues. Crowning the whole is a dramatic hilltop castle, which was wrested from the Moors during the 12th century. An Iron Age *castro* and a Roman fortress preceded the castle, whose Moorish foundations are still visible, even though the structure was rebuilt by King Sancho II during the 13th century and later by King Dinis, who, with Saintly Queen Isabel, used it as a residence. Inside the castle walls are the ruins of the Gothic chapel of Nossa Senhora da Pena, roofless but with tall arches; the royal palace of King Dinis, which has an arched loggia with a good view; and the keep of the castle, built by the same king and affording an even better view (open daily from 9 AM to 7 PM, 6 PM in winter; admission charge). Other monuments in the town include the 12th-century Romanesque Church of São Pedro and the Sé (Cathedral), a large, 16th-century building in pale stone.

On the hill opposite the castle's is the Santuário de Nossa Senhora da Encarnação, built during the 17th century and full of tiles from that period. Dedicated to the patron saint of Leiria, it is approached by a staircase of 172 steps. Leiria's Tourist Office (phone: 44-32748) is in the Jardim Luís de Camões, a large park in the center of town graced with cafés and beer gardens. Here, too, is a statue of a man and a woman, representing the two rivers that meet and fall in love in Leiria and continue as one. An open-air market takes place in Leiria on Tuesday and Saturday mornings.

CHECKING IN: Dom João III – Modern, comfortable, and conveniently located, with 64 rooms (with TV sets and telephones), a bar, a restaurant, and gift shops. Avenida Hérois de Angola, Leiria (phone: 44-33902). Expensive.

Euro-sol – A modern high-rise, nicely landscaped. Together with its sister hotel next door, the *Euro-sol Jardim,* it offers 92 rooms with bath, an enticing outdoor swimming pool on a terrace, a top-floor bar and restaurant with a view, a discotheque, and a shopping center. 1 Rua Dr. José Alves Correia da Silva, Leiria (phone: 44-24103). Expensive.

Lis – Attractive and in a renovated building, it has 42 rooms with bath and a bar. Largo Alexandre Herculano, Leiria (phone: 44-31017). Inexpensive.

EATING OUT: Tromba Rija – An eatery in regional style, typically decorated with onions and garlic hanging from the ceiling and located in a village 1¼ miles (2 km) north of town. The codfish and steak dishes are delicious. Try one of the homemade desserts and an almond liqueur. Open daily. Reservations advised. Marrazes (phone: 44-32072). Expensive to moderate.

O Casarão – Located 3 miles (5 km) southwest of town via the road to Nazaré (N1), this is an excellent regional restaurant with a cozy fireplace. There's a garden for summer dining. Closed Mondays. Reservations advised. Cruzamento de Azóia (phone: 44-27980). Moderate.

Jardim – A good, modern place, especially recommended for outdoor dining in summer. Open daily. No reservations. Jardim Luís de Camões, Leiria (phone: 44-32514). Moderate.

Tia Elvira – Regional food is served in this rustic place — to the accompaniment of *fado* music on Fridays and Saturdays. It's about 2 miles (3 km) from the center of town. Open daily. No reservations. 14 Rua do Pinhal Grosso, Marinheiros (phone: 44-31171). Moderate to inexpensive.

En Route from Leiria – Figueira da Foz is 34 miles (54 km) north on N109, but a side trip to the coast from Leiria (a 15-mile — 24-km round trip) is worthwhile to visit the famous old glassmaking town of Marinha Grande and the beach resort of São Pedro de Moel. Take N242 west, passing through the Pinhal do Rei, the pine forest that King Dinis planted almost 700 years ago to control the shifting sands; it later provided timber to build Portugal's fleet. Marinha Grande, 7½ miles (12 km) from Leiria, has more than 40 crystal and glass factories, but the oldest is the Real Fábrica de Marinha Grande, established in 1748 by an Englishman, John Beare, and taken over later in the century by two more Englishmen, the Stephens brothers, who willed it to the state. It became one of the most prestigious glassworks in the world and still uses traditional methods demanding a high degree of skill on the part of its craftsmen. The factory, in an old, pink mansion in the center of town, is open to visitors, who can watch the whole glassmaking process and visit the *National Museum of Glass* on the premises (open Mondays through Fridays from 9 AM to noon and from 2 to 5 PM; no admission charge). São Pedro de Moel, an ancient fishing village turned charming resort, is another 6 miles (10 km) west. It boasts a wide, sandy beach set between cliffs below the pine woods and an enormous saltwater swimming pool by the sea (which is fairly rough here).

Return to Leiria and head north on N109 to Figueira da Foz. Just to the west about 8½ miles (14 km) up the road is Monte Real, a spa with a ruined castle and Belle Epoque houses set in shady gardens. Beyond, the road continues north through beautiful pine forests, skirting Atlantic beaches, only 6 or 7 miles (10 or 11 km) away.

FIGUEIRA DA FOZ: The most popular bathing resort and one of the most important fishing ports on the Portuguese Atlantic is endowed with an exceedingly long, wide sandy beach, plus a full complement of hotels, restaurants, and discos, a Belle Epoque gambling casino, a bullring, and facilities for golf, tennis, and water sports. The town is on a flat plain at the mouth of the Mondego River (which flows into the sea here from Coimbra), its estuary forming a wide inland lagoon. Rice paddies and salt pans are nearby. Cross the soaring new bridge, turn left, and follow the Centro (Center) and Praias (Beaches) signs to the tree-lined esplanade along the seafront. Here there are modern hotels and shops facing the beach and turn-of-the-century houses decorated with tiles and wrought-iron balconies; the old Santa Catarina Fort (with a lighthouse on top) guards the river's mouth.

Most visitors to Figueira spend their time on the 2-mile-long, approximately 1,600-foot-wide beach; indeed, the town has little to detain sightseers, but the enormous *Casa do Paço* (Rua 5 de Outubro), built by a bishop during the 17th century, is well worth the time spent away from the sun. The walls of this old house, now a museum, are decorated with several thousand tiles, many of them Delft, constituting the largest collection in Portugal (open from 9 AM to noon and from 2 to 5 PM; closed Mondays; admission charge). Another museum, the *Museu Municipal Dr. Santos Rocha* (Avenida Calouste Gulbenkian), contains archaeological artifacts, ceramics, coins, furniture, sculpture (religious and African), and contemporary Portuguese and other paintings (open from 9 AM to 12:30 PM and from 2 to 5:30 PM; closed Mondays and holidays; no admission charge). Figueira's Tourist Office (Avenida 25 de Abril; phone: 33-22610 or 28895) has information on other sights, which include the parish church of São Julião and the Misericórdia and Santo António churches. The fish auction, held in the port in the morning when the fleet comes in, is worth getting up early to see. As in other fishing towns, seafood of all kinds is on local restaurant menus, and Figueira has its own typical *caldeirada,* or fish stew.

The old fishing village of Buarcos, 1¼ miles (2 km) along the coast northwest of Figueira (in the direction of Cabo Mondego), represents a change of pace from its larger, more worldly neighbor. Very rich during the 17th century, but always subject to attacks by pirates, the town has a ruined castle and long, sandy beaches with colorful *bateiras* (flat-bottomed fishing boats) drawn up on shore.

CHECKING IN: *Atlântico* – This very tall tower is an apartment-hotel with 70 fully equipped units with living room, bedroom, bath, kitchen, telephone, radio, as well as a bar, TV lounge, and shopping center. The rooms have spectacular views of the beach and the Mondego. Avenida 25 de Abril, Figueira da Foz (phone: 33-24045). Expensive.

Clube Vale do Leão – A luxurious tourist complex on a hill above Buarcos, on the road to Vaís. It has 22 apartments and villas furnished with antiques and endowed with lovely views, in addition to a host of amenities such as a pool by the sea, a restaurant serving international and regional food, a health center, piano bar, cinema, disco, boutique, and hairdresser. Vaís, Serra da Boa Viagem (phone: 33-23001). Expensive.

Grande Hotel da Figueira – The best in Figueira da Foz, situated on the seafront, next door to the Olympic-size swimming pool it shares with the *Estalagem da Piscina* (see below). There are 91 rooms with bath (those on the front have balconies), an excellent restaurant, and a piano bar. Guests enjoy free admission to the casino's international floor show. Avenida 25 de Abril, Figueira da Foz (phone: 33-22146). Expensive.

Da Piscina – Named for the Olympic-size swimming pool that's next door and shared with the *Grande,* this 20-room *estalagem* is modern and comfortable, with a restaurant overlooking the pool and the beach. Closed from November through April. 7 Rua de Santa Catarina, Figueira da Foz (phone: 33-22420). Expensive.

Costa de Prata – There are two modern hotels by this name, *Costa de Prata I* and *Costa de Prata II,* with 66 and 61 rooms respectively, close to each other and both close to the beach. No restaurant. 1 Largo Coronel Galhardo, Figueira da Foz (phone: 33-26610), and 59 Rua Miguel Bombarda, Figueira da Foz (phone: 33-22082). Moderate.

Tamargueira – Modern and functional, with 69 rooms and suites, a grillroom, and a panoramic restaurant and bar. It's on the harbor in the village of Buarcos. Marginal do Cabo Mondego, Buarcos (phone: 33-22514). Moderate.

EATING OUT: *Sereia do Mar* – Good seafood complements this modern place, decorated in blue and white, on the esplanade near the sea. Open daily. Reservations advised. 59 Avenida do Brasil, Figueira da Foz (phone: 33-26190). Expensive to moderate.

Teimoso – Though the owners also rent rooms, this place is better known as a fish restaurant. It's located just outside Buarcos, on the road to Cabo Mondego, and is as good a place as any to try the *caldeirada.* Open daily. Reservations advised. Estrada do Cabo Mondego, Buarcos (phone: 33-22785). Expensive to moderate.

Caçarola II – Right in front of the casino, with a snack bar downstairs and a restaurant upstairs. The seafood is especially good. No reservations. 85 Rua Bernardo Lopes, Figueira da Foz (phone: 33-22522). Moderate.

O Pateo – Decorated in typical regional style, this eatery is in an old part of town above the beach. There is a patio with fruit trees for summer dining, and *fado* music on Saturday nights. Open daily. No reservations. 31 Rua Dr. Santos Rocha, Figueira da Foz (phone: 33-26657). Moderate.

Quinta da Santa Catarina – On the edge of town, in a tree-filled garden with a pool. The food is good, and there is folk dancing on Saturday nights. Open daily. No reservations. Rua Joaquim Sotto Maior, Figueira da Foz (phone: 33-22178). Moderate.

En Route from Figueira da Foz – Take N111 east along the Mondego. The road descends into a valley and then climbs through forests of pine, chestnut, and oak trees, passing water mills and little white churches. After 10 miles (16 km), one of the biggest and most beautiful castles in Portugal is seen standing dramatically above the little town of Montemor-o-Velho. Although the site has been fortified for more than 4,000 years, the castle dates mainly from the 14th century; the church within, Santa Maria da Alcaçova, built during the 11th century, is now mostly Manueline in style. Continue along N111 the remaining 18 miles (29 km) to Coimbra.

COIMBRA: Portugal's most romantic city came into its own during the 12th and 13th centuries as the newly independent country's first capital. Though the capital moved to Lisbon in 1260, the famed *universidade* that King Dinis founded here in 1290 assured the city's continued importance as a cultural and artistic center. Coimbra is still known for its university and for the special brand of Coimbra *fado* that grew out of the student custom of serenading the local girls and singing on the steps of the Old Cathedral at night. For a detailed report of the city, its sights, hotels, and restaurants, see *Coimbra,* THE CITIES.

En Route from Coimbra – Before continuing north toward Aveiro, take a short detour to visit the Roman ruins of Conímbriga, 9½ miles (15 km) southwest of town. Cross the bridge over the Mondego and take N1 south to Condeixa, then follow the signs.

CONÍMBRIGA: The most important Roman site in Portugal, Conímbriga was probably inhabited as far back as the Iron Age, but it was the Romans who made it a monumental city, with an aqueduct, forum, temple, public baths, shops, and houses with beautiful mosaic floors. Situated along the Roman highway between Olisipo (Lisbon) and Bracara Augusta (Braga), the city was at its height during the first part of the 3rd century. Unfortunately, barbarian invasions began during the latter part of the century, forcing the inhabitants to build a new defensive wall, which encompassed only half of the city (stones from buildings outside, funerary stones, bits of statuary, and the old wall were used to construct the new one). The Suevians captured it during the mid-5th century, and the Visigoths later moved to the nearby, more easily protected Aeminium, also Roman in origin. Aeminium grew at Conímbriga's expense and eventually took its new name — Coimbra — from Conímbriga.

Visitors can see remains of the old wall and the aqueduct before entering the site via the main gate in the new defensive wall. On the right are the ruins of the 3rd-century House of Fountains, which was partially destroyed to make way for the wall and in which the layout of the rooms, several with mosaic pavements, is clearly visible. Beyond are other houses, shops, and public baths; the 5th-century House of Cantaber, with private baths beside it; and the forum, including the temple, market, and tribunal. The *Museu Monográfico* at the site (phone: 39-94177) displays objects unearthed here — coins, pottery, cloth, lamps, games, jewelry, sculpture, murals, and mosaics. The museum is open from 10 AM to 1 PM and from 2 to 6 PM, June through September (to

5 PM the rest of the year); closed Mondays and holidays. The site itself is open daily from 9 AM to 1 PM and from 2 to 8 PM, June through September (to 6 PM the rest of the year). There are admission charges to both the ruins and the museum; there also is a restaurant with a panoramic terrace.

En Route from Conímbriga – Return to Condeixa and take the A1 toll highway 37½ miles (60 km) north (bypassing Coimbra) to the junction with N235, which leads to Aveiro. Along the way, watch for turnoffs to points of interest such as Luso, a very ancient spa town on a mountainside (for a description of Luso and its hotels, see *The Beiras* in DIRECTIONS), and Curia, another spa town, famous not only for its waters, but also for its bairrada wines, among the best in Portugal. The bairrada wine producing area extends all the way north from Coimbra to Aveiro.

CHECKING IN: *Palace Hotel da Curia* – This was the most elegant and fashionable hotel in Portugal when it opened in 1922, and it's still a beautifully kept, Old World hostelry, surrounded by lovely woods and formal gardens. Besides 122 rooms, it has an Olympic-size swimming pool, tennis courts, a deer park, bar, and restaurant. A stay here among the stained glass windows, marble statues, and Art Nouveau tables will be memorable. Closed from October through March. Parque da Curia, Curia (phone: 31-52131). Expensive.

AVEIRO: Intersected by several canals, Aveiro was once a port on the Atlantic, at the mouth of the Vouga River. But ocean currents built up a coastal sandbar and the river deposited silt in the estuary, so that by the time a giant storm in 1575 closed the natural channel through the sandbar, Aveiro was left occupying the eastern side of an enclosed lagoon. The ancient port that had traded with the Phoenicians, and from which only a short time before ships had set sail on voyages of discovery and on fishing expeditions to the cod banks of Newfoundland, was left without an outlet to the sea. Only early in the 19th century was a canal cut through the sandbar (stones from the town's 15th-century walls were used in the construction), restoring a measure of prosperity.

Aveiro's shallow saltwater lagoon — the Ria de Aveiro — stretches nearly 30 miles from north to south, though it is only a few miles wide. The lagoon is productive, providing fish, salt, seaweed for fertilizer, and, in the parts above sea level, fertile farmland. It is picturesque, too, dotted with islands, bordered by salt flats, and full of impressive conical mountains of white salt, as well as a variety of boats. Of these, the most beautiful are the seaweed gatherers' flat-bottomed, square-sailed *moliceiros,* their high, curved prows brightly painted with Ria scenes. Their numbers have dwindled, but they can still be spotted throughout the lagoon or gathered together on special occasions, such as Aveiro's *Festa da Ria,* which takes place in late July and early August. A *moliceiro* regatta (departing from Torreira, a fishing village to the north, and arriving in Aveiro 2 days later) and a race of *moliceiros* and other boats are part of the festivities.

Aveiro itself is a lovely town, with more to see than many cities farther south, because the devastating earthquake of 1755 did not reach here. Its canals are crossed by interesting bridges, and in the middle of town, the Central Canal is lined with charming, colorful houses. The former Convento de Jesus, at Praça do Milenário, now the *Museu de Aveiro,* is the first stop for most sightseers. Founded during the 15th century, but mainly baroque following later remodeling, the convent was for almost 2 decades the home of the daughter of King Afonso V, Infanta Dona Joana, who entered it to lead a saintly life after having refused marriage to several kings. She died here in 1490, and her marble tomb, supported by angels, can be seen in the convent church, which is decorated with 18th-century baroque woodwork so intricately carved and gilded it looks like filigree. As a museum, the convent contains valuable collections of sculpture, gold and silver work, vestments, and paintings (the most famous is one of Princesa Santa Joana in 15th-century court dress) — works of art gathered from churches and monasteries throughout the region after the expulsion of religious orders during the 19th century, as well as works originally made for use here. The museum is open from 10 AM to 12:30 PM and from 2 to 5 PM; closed Mondays and holidays. Admission charge, except on Sunday mornings.

Across from the convent is the church of São Domingos, founded during the 15th century as a monastery church but now serving as the Sé (Cathedral) of Aveiro; its baroque door is the result of an 18th-century renovation. Not far away, in Praça da República, is the Misericórdia, a 16th-century church covered with *azulejos* inside (from the 17th century) and out (19th century). The 17th-century Igreja das Carmelitas, to the south (near the post office) is worth a stop to see more *azulejos,* as is, beyond it, the 16th-century Santo António, known for its interesting barrel-vaulted ceiling and carved gilt work. On the north side of the Central Canal, near the fish market, is the chapel of São Gonçalinho, the patron saint of salt workers. Still farther north, not far from the railroad station, is the 18th-century chapel of Senhor Jesus das Barrocas, an octagonal building with a rectangular chancel; magnificent woodcarvings adorn the interior, along with modern paintings of the lives of the saints, commissioned by the devout fishermen of Aveiro.

A variety of water sports — sailing, windsurfing, water skiing, and swimming — can be practiced in the Aveiro area, and there are several excursions that can be made in the vicinity. From mid-June to mid-September, a boat tour of the Ria leaves from Aveiro daily at 10 AM, stopping for lunch at Torreira, and returning to Aveiro at 5 PM. The tourist office (Praça da República in Aveiro; phone: 34-23680) can supply information. Some suggested driving routes taking in more of the colorful Ria towns are given below. Visitors should also make an effort to visit Vista Alegre, about 4½ miles (7 km) south of Aveiro via N109. The world-famous Vista Alegre porcelain factory (Fábrica de Porcelana de Vista Alegre), founded in 1824, is located here, with the *Museu Histórico da Vista Alegre* on its grounds (phone: 34-322365; open from 9 AM to 12:30 PM and from 2 to 5:30 PM; closed Mondays and holidays; no admission charge). The museum has a large collection of the stoneware and crystal that the factory produced in its early years, plus vases, lamps, and porcelain dinnerware from all periods, including examples of valuable pieces made for European royalty. A further attraction is the showrooms, where porcelain can be purchased.

CHECKING IN: *Afonso V* – In a quiet residential district not far from the canals and monuments, it has 80 rooms with private bath and all the modern comforts, a pub-style bar, a discotheque, and the *Cozinha do Rei,* one of the best restaurants in town (see *Eating Out*). 65 Rua Dr. Manuel das Neves, Aveiro (phone: 34-25191). Moderate.

Imperial – A big, modern hotel (107 rooms) in the center of town, with views over the canals and river. There are 3 bars, a solarium, and a very good, very big restaurant, with windows all around. Rua Dr. Nascimento Leitão, Aveiro (phone: 34-22141). Moderate.

Arcada – This lovely old hotel is right in the center of town, on the Central Canal. All 52 rooms have TV sets and telephones; 48 of them have private baths. There is a good bar. 4 Rua Viana do Castelo, Aveiro (phone: 34-23001). Moderate to inexpensive.

EATING OUT: *Cozinha do Rei* – In the *Afonso V* hotel and unquestionably the best restaurant in town. Fountains, plants, and the pink-and-white decor make the large dining room a pleasant place, and the *sopa do rei* (king's soup), with fish and lobster, really is fit for a king. Open daily. Reservations advised. 65 Rua Dr. Manuel das Neves, Aveiro (phone: 34-26802). Expensive to moderate.

Cozinha Velha – Typically Portuguese, with blue-and white tiles on the walls, long tables with benches, and an open kitchen. The specialties are grilled meats and regional dishes such as eel stew. Open daily. No reservations. 7 Travessa da Rua Direita, Aveiro (phone: 34-20392). Moderate.

Taverna Dom Carlos – Attractive, oak-beamed, with old bairrada wine bottles around the walls and even old wine bottling machinery on the premises, it serves good grilled meats and seafood. There is *fado* music after 10:30 PM Thursdays, Fridays, and Saturdays. Closed Sundays. No reservations. 46-48 Rua Dr. Nascimento Leitão, Aveiro (phone: 34-22061). Moderate.

En Route from Aveiro – Porto is 42 miles (67 km) north of Aveiro via the A1 toll highway, but for a closer look at the Ria, the salt pans, and the *moliceiro* boats, take N109-7 west 5 miles (8 km) to Barra. The canal through the sandbar is located here, as are two beaches and houses with pointed roofs, tiled fronts, and brightly painted doors. Turn left and drive south along the Ria to Costa Nova, where there are rows of houses with red-and-white, green-and-white, or blue-and-white stripes, as well as little beaches, cafés, and restaurants. Farther south, at Vagueira, travelers may see trawlers launching their boats into the Atlantic and pulling back the nets with yoked oxen. Retrace the route to Aveiro or return by way of the opposite margin of the Ria.

To visit the northern part of the Ria, take N16 east out of Aveiro, turn onto N109 toward Estarreja, and then onto N109-5 to Murtosa. (The roads are not very good and full of trucks.) Murtosa has an interesting 18th-century parish church, but its port — Cais do Bico — with *moliceiros* gathering or unloading seaweed is what should be seen. Continue on N109-5 and, at the end of the causeway, turn onto N327 to Torreira, where a *moliceiro* race is part of a local festival, the *Romaria de São Paio da Torreira,* held from September 6 through 8. Still on N327, continue south through sand dunes and pine forests to São Jacinto. On the right is the Reserva Natural de São Jacinto nas Dunas, a nature and wildlife preserve in pine-wooded dunes. Paths, elevated walks, and observation towers have been built so visitors can see the birds and animals, and there are two marked trails, one beginning by the preserve headquarters (phone: 34-29752) at its southern end.

Return north 14 miles (22 km) to the turnoff for Ovar, a town famous for its *pão de ló* (sponge cake); its yearly carnival enlivened by masked revelers, flower battles, and allegorical floats; and its *Holy Week* processions. The tile-faced parish church and two chapels (Calvário and Nossa Senhora da Graça) are worth a visit.

Ovar is at the northern tip of the Ria, about 28 miles (45 km), via the A1 toll highway, from Porto, Portugal's second largest city. To reach the highway, take N327 east for 4 miles (6 km). Or, if one last dip in the sea is desired, take N109 to Porto, passing through the popular, modern Costa Verde beach resort of Espinho.

CHECKING IN/EATING OUT: *Pousada da Ria* – This beautiful, waterside member of the *pousada* chain has verandahs where guests can sit and watch the Ria boats, and its 19 rooms have private balconies overlooking the water, too. There is also a pool set in lawns and a restaurant with a terrace and a panoramic view. Fish and seafood are served — fishermen deliver the catch to the *pousada* at 8 every morning. Open all year, but very full from April through September; make reservations at least a month in advance. On N327 between Torreira and São Jacinto (phone: 34-48332). Expensive.

Riabela – A modern, 35-room *estalagem* at the water's edge. It has a very good restaurant, glassed in on three sides with views of the Ria, as well as a swimming pool, tennis courts, and a bar. Torreira (phone: 34-48137). Moderate.

The Minho

The Minho — the northwest corner of Portugal, bordered by the Minho River and Spain to the north, the Douro region to the south, the Atlantic Ocean to the west, and high mountains to the east — is the emerald in Portugal's crown. Of all the Portuguese regions, Mother Nature was most generous with the Minho, gracing it with an eternally green and varied landscape, dense forests, fertile valleys, rolling hills, majestic peaks, golden beaches, and thermal springs. People, in turn, went on to decorate it with picturesque granite villages, fortified castles, elegant manor houses, and a green mantle of vines. With time, this fair land came into its own and gave birth to the Portuguese nation.

The Minho is a fairy-tale land shrouded in mist. Lush and verdant, it has the highest level of rainfall in Portugal during the winter. Clouds coming in from the Atlantic are blocked from the interior by mountain ranges, or *serras,* such as Peneda, Gerês, and Padrela, and are forced to unload their precious cargoes before reaching the high plains of the neighboring Trás-os-Montes region. The temperature is mild, the air somewhat humid, the light soothing to the eye.

Signs of human habitation have been found dating as far back as 5,000 years. Vestiges of fortified granite hamlets, or *castros,* built on high ground by Celtic tribes who settled here about 3000 BC, still dot the landscape. The Phoenicians and Greeks, attracted by the area's rich metal deposits, traded actively with the inhabitants during the Bronze and Iron Ages. The Romans encountered stiff resistance during the 3rd century BC and never totally subjugated the Minho, but they did manage to introduce vine growing techniques and an extensive road system. The Suevians, a Germanic farming tribe, replaced the Romans and introduced the iron plow and the practice of cultivating small land holdings detached from villages. The Visigoths, who arrived next, embraced Catholicism. The Moors invaded from North Africa during the 8th century, but they, like the Romans before them, encountered resistance and were forced out — after several generations.

The region claimed its independence during the 12th century when Afonso Henriques of Guimarães, ruler of an entity known as the county of Portucale and as such a vassal of the King of León and Castile, broke away from his feudal lord and had himself crowned King of Portucale. The Portuguese nation was thus born in the Minho, which continued to provide leadership until Portugal's New World discoveries shifted the political focus south to Lisbon. Even then, it continued to play a large economic role, and today, it is one of the principal cattle raising, wine making, and textile manufacturing areas of the country.

Modernity has made inroads into the Minho, with some ugly results; but a large part of it, particularly the rural interior, retains much of its original beauty and charm and many of its age-old traditions, including a strong community spirit. During the harvest, for example, neighbors help each other husk the corn, singing elaborate traditional songs and drinking wine liberally as they work. This is also an occasion for the young to meet prospective partners, and for maidens who find a rare red ear, the *milho rei* (king corn), to kiss their young suitors. The *minhotos* are friendly, hardworking, and devoutly religious. Unlike most northern workaholics, however, they also know how to play — witness their lively folk dances, the *viras* and the *malhão,* and their colorful traditional clothing. The character of the region is best summed up by its symbol: the heart — a symbol that is as warm and hospitable as its people.

The food in the Minho is diverse. There are game, kid, and pork dishes in the mountain areas, lamprey and trout in the river valleys, fish stews, shellfish, cod, and sardines in the coastal areas, and steaks in major livestock centers around Braga and Guimarães. Meals are accompanied by *pão de milho,* delicious, rich corn bread, and the region's *vinho verde,* or green wine. The wine, drunk chilled, takes its name from its relative youth and the Minho's verdant vegetation rather than its own color (which is usually white). The British, who began importing green wines during the 16th century, called them "eager wines" because of their natural effervescence. The best are the whites from estates such as Palácio de Brejoeira and Solar das Bouças, which have a slightly higher alcohol content than the more common wines such as casal garcia and gaitão. The vines are trained aboveground on concrete *pérgulas,* or trellises, and *cruzetas,* or crosses, and cling to wires strung over roadways and telephone poles — sometimes at heights of 30 to 40 feet. This frees the land for other crops and keeps the grapes from overripening on the warm soil. The result is a wine that is low in alcohol, not too sweet, and extremely refreshing, but one that doesn't age well. Green wines should be drunk within the first 2 years after bottling.

Allow 9 to 10 days for the leisurely tour outlined below. The route begins in Guimarães, the cradle of the nation, and moves on to Braga, the religious capital of Portugal, famous for its *Holy Week* processions and pilgrimages. It then proceeds north into the heart of the Minho to Ponte de Lima and from there follows the bucolic Lima River past monasteries, Roman bridges, manor houses, and rustic farms, crossing paths with oxen whose highly decorated yokes are carved with Celtic inscriptions. The itinerary includes a visit to the Peneda-Gerês National Park before cutting across an impressive mountain pass into the spa-haven of Monção. From there, it makes its way west along the picturesque left bank of the Minho River, past a string of fortresses guarding Portugal's border with Spain. The region's Atlantic coast is explored during the final leg of the journey, as the route moves south past multicolored fishing villages, stops off at Viana do Castelo (known as the capital of Portuguese folklore), detours briefly inland to Barcelos for a dazzling display of pottery, then returns coastward for a final swing through the beach resorts of Póvoa de Varzim and neighboring Vila do Conde.

During July and August, the main roads become congested with tourists and Portuguese workers on vacation from jobs in northern Europe. Try to avoid traveling on weekends, and move from town to town between 1 and 3

PM, when most of the population is eating, working, or at the beach. Better yet, schedule a visit for late May and early June, or mid-September and the first 2 weeks of October, to catch the grain and grape harvests. At all times, try to avoid driving at night, particularly on mountain roads. They tend to be winding and not well marked.

Whenever possible, reserve rooms in advance for the summer season, which runs from June through September. In addition to choosing from among hotels, *pousadas,* and other types of accommodations, travelers in the Minho can opt to stay in a variety of private houses that take in paying guests as part of Portugal's *Tourism in the Country* program (see *Accommodations,* GETTING READY TO GO), which is particularly active in the area. A great many of the participating properties along the route are the manor houses and other stately homes of *Turismo de Habitação,* while a few are the simpler rural houses and farmhouses of *Turismo Rural* and *Agroturismo.* Reservations can be made by contacting the houses directly or, in most cases, by contacting *Turihab, Associação de Turismo de Habitação,* Praça da República, 4990 Ponte de Lima (phone: 58-942729).

Expect to pay from $60 to $120 for a double room in a hotel listed below as expensive, approximately $35 to $55 for one in the moderate category, and $25 or less for one in the inexpensive category. A meal for two with house wine will cost $45 and up in restaurants listed as expensive, from $25 to $40 in moderate ones, and less than $20 in inexpensive ones.

GUIMARÃES: The birthplace of the first Portuguese king and the cradle of the nation lies at the foot of a mountain range 32 miles (51 km) northeast of Porto via N105-2 and N105. Founded during the 10th century, the city came into prominence in 1095, when the King of León and Castile awarded the hand of his daughter, Teresa, to a French nobleman, Henry of Burgundy, who had assisted the Spanish king in driving the Moors out of northern Iberia. The county of Portucale (roughly, the land between the Minho and the Douro, including the city of Porto) was part of Teresa's dowry, and the couple chose Guimarães as their court. Teresa bore Henry a son, Afonso Henriques, and 2 years later, when Henry died, she became regent for the child. She soon incurred the wrath of her subjects, however, by taking up with a Galician count and allying herself with the Spanish overlords. When Afonso came of age, he revolted against Teresa's forces outside Guimarães, in 1128, and in 1139 dealt the Moors a severe blow near Santarém. As a result of these victories, Afonso broke his ties with León and Castile and crowned himself King of Portucale in 1139. Spain recognized the new kingdom in 1143.

Guimarães was also the birthplace of Gil Vicente (1470?–1540?), the founder of Portuguese theater. A goldsmith by trade, he nevertheless found time to entertain the courts of João II and Manuel I with his farces and tragicomedies, and he also wrote religious dramas. Gold and silver smithing continue to thrive today, as do other crafts such as embroidery and linen weaving, but they are less important than the manufacture of textiles, shoes, and kitchenware. The new industries keep Guimarães prosperous, but take their aesthetic toll. The medieval quarter, however, has been rediscovered and is being slowly restored — for the full medieval treatment, be here for the *Festas Gualterianas,* the 1st Sunday in August, when the townspeople dress in medieval attire, a large folk fair with singing and dancing takes place, and all Guimarães returns to the 15th century.

Begin a tour of the city at Largo da Oliveira, a square in the heart of the medieval quarter. On the northwestern side is the Antigo Paços do Conselho (Old Town Hall), an arcaded and crenelated 16th-century building now serving as a public library. On the eastern side is the former convent of Nossa Senhora da Oliveira (Our Lady of the Olive Tree). The convent church marks the spot where the 6th-century Visigothic warrior Wamba was confirmed as king. (According to legend, he said he would accept the charge if his staff sprouted olive leaves when he drove it into the ground, and it did.) During the 10th century, a primitive church was built on the site; virtually nothing remains of the original, but the church's main entrance, where a 14th-century doorway is surmounted by a Gothic pediment, is amusing (it looks like another doorway on top), and the Gothic porch in front is impressive. The convent's 13th-century Romanesque cloister and grounds house the *Museu Regional de Alberto Sampaio* (phone: 53-412465), with a collection of priceless 14th- to 17th-century works from various churches and convents — tiles, paintings by Portuguese masters, tapestries, statues, and a treasure in ecclesiastical plate. Note the Manueline monstrance attributed to Gil Vicente and the magnificent 35-pound silver cross. Open for guided tours from 10 AM to 12:30 PM and from 2 to 5:30 PM; closed Monday and Tuesday mornings. Admission charge.

Walk west along Rua da Rainha to the *Museu Arqueológico da Sociedade Martins Sarmento* (Rua Paio Galvão; phone: 53-415969), housed partly in the cloister of the Church of St. Dominic (São Domingos). Named for the 19th-century archaeologist who excavated the Iron Age cities of Briteiros and Sabroso near Guimarães, the museum contains items from these sites and elsewhere. Most impressive are the stone finds from Briteiros — the Pedra Formosa, a huge carved granite slab that could have been the entrance to a Celtic crematorium, and the Colossus of Pedralva, a 10-foot-high granite idol that took 24 pairs of oxen to drag to its present home. Open for guided tours from 9:30 AM to noon and from 2 to 5 PM; closed Mondays. Admission charge.

Return to Largo da Oliveira and walk north along the cobbled Rua de Santa Maria, lined with handsome 14th- to 17th-century aristocratic residences decorated with coats-of-arms, iron grilles, and statuary. The road slopes upward to the 15th-century Paço dos Duques de Bragança (Palace of the Dukes of Bragança). The massive complex was built by the first duke, Dom Afonso, who was the bastard son of King João I — his status mandated the tilt to the left of the family coat of arms at the entrance to the palace courtyard. The second duke was beheaded by King João II, but the resilient and Machiavellian family returned in style in 1640 when the Duke of Bragança was crowned King João IV, the beginning of a dynasty that furnished Portugal with kings until the country became a republic in 1910. In more recent times, the palace was restored by the late dictator António de Oliveira Salazar, who turned it into an official northern residence for the Portuguese president as well as a museum. To be seen inside are a collection of 15th- to 17th-century Persian carpets, copies of French and Flemish tapestries, Portuguese furniture, Chinese porcelain, paintings by Portuguese, Italian, and Dutch masters, and an armory with 15th-century chain mail. Note the chestnut wood ceilings of the dining and banquet halls, shaped like the hull of a Portuguese caravel in honor of the country's maritime exploits. Guided tours (Portuguese only) take place from 10 AM to 5:15 PM, except on holidays. Admission charge, except on Sunday mornings until 2 PM (phone: 53-412273).

At the top of the hill overlooking the town is the 10th-century castle, with its eight flanking towers and large central keep, the inspiration for the country's coat of arms. Afonso Henriques, Portugal's first king, was born in the castle, which is restored and can be visited (open from 9 AM to 9 PM; closed Mondays; no admission charge); he was baptized, it is said, in the lovely, tiny 12th-century Igreja São Miguel do Castelo, set on the green between the castle and the ducal palace. Besides the baptismal font, the church contains a stone basin where parishioners placed offerings of grain; the floor is covered with the graves of Portuguese grandees.

The Guimarães Tourist Office is in the southern part of town (83 Alameda Resistência ao Fascismo; phone: 53-412450). Nearby, and worth a visit if time permits, is the Igreja de São Francisco (Church of St. Francis), a collage of 15th-, 17th-, and 18th-century architecture, rich in gilt and *azulejos* (phone: 53-412228; open from 10 AM to noon and from 3 to 5 PM; closed Mondays; no admission charge); ask the sacristan for permission to see the fine coffered ceiling in the sacristy. The surrounding countryside is also worthwhile, especially the forested Serra de Santa Catarina southeast of town. The road winds up the mountain to the 20th-century pilgrimage church of Nossa Senhora da Penha (the patron saint of travelers) at the summit, where there are also restaurants, cafés, a simple hotel, and a breathtaking view of the region. Leave the city via N101 east and turn right after Mesão Frio; return to Guimarães via N101-2 by bearing left at the esplanade by the sanctuary.

CHECKING IN: *Casa do Ribeiro* – This large Minho estate with its own woods and streams is a *Turismo de Habitação* participant. About 3 miles (5 km) west of town off N206, it has 2 double bedrooms and a single with bath for rent. Contact Dona Maria do Carmo Ferras Pinto, *Casa do Ribeiro,* São Cristovão do Selho (phone: 53-532881). Expensive.

Fundador Dom Pedro – A modern high-rise hotel, with 63 rooms and suites and a bar. 760 Avenida Dom Afonso Henriques, Guimarães (phone: 53-413781). Expensive.

Paço de São Cipriano – An elegant country manor house with a crenelated tower and a swimming pool, 3 miles (5 km) south of town off N105. Another *Turismo de Habitação* participant, it has 5 double bedrooms. Closed in winter. Contact Dr. João Santiago Sottomayor, *Paço de São Cipriano,* Taboadelo (phone: 53-481337). Expensive.

Pousada de Nossa Senhora da Oliveira – On a quaint narrow street in the heart of the medieval town beside the church of the same name, this is ideal for travelers in search of the service and elegance of old Portugal. Made up of converted townhouses, it has 16 rooms, a cozy bar, and a fine restaurant. Rua de Santa Maria, Guimarães (phone: 53-412157). Expensive.

Pousada de Santa Marinha da Costa – One of Portugal's most luxurious *pousadas,* a favorite of those looking for peace and quiet, it is about 1¼ miles (2 km) out of Guimarães via N101-2. It's housed in a former Augustinian convent on a mountain overlooking the city. Guests have a choice of 50 rooms, ranging from monastic cells to suites furnished with objects from the former royal palace of Ajuda in Lisbon. They can dine in the former kitchen, lined with pillars and arches (see *Eating Out*), and explore the huge garden, which stretches endlessly. Estrada da Penha, Guimarães (phone: 53-418453). Expensive.

Palmeiras – This modern bed and breakfast inn (*albergaria*) with 22 rooms, a pub, a bar, and a small terrace, is located in a shopping center in the newer part of town. Centro Comercial das Palmeiras, Guimarães (phone: 53-410324). Moderate.

EATING OUT: *Pousada de Santa Marinha da Costa* – Simple medieval decor and fine Portuguese cooking, served in the splendor of a former monastic kitchen. Located about 1¼ miles (2 km) from town via N101-2. Open daily. Reservations advised. Estrada da Penha, Guimarães (phone: 53-418453). Expensive to moderate.

Jordão – A lively and popular restaurant with regional decor and some of the best food in town. Closed Monday evenings and all day Tuesdays. Reservations unnecessary. 55 Avenida Dom Afonso Henriques, Guimarães (phone: 53-41498). Moderate.

Solar da Rainha – This typical family-run establishment is ideal for a simple, unpretentious lunch. Closed Mondays. Reservations unnecessary. 133 Rua da Rainha, Guimarães (phone: 53-413519). Moderate.

El Rei – A comfortable, romantic little bistro in the medieval quarter, facing the back of the former Town Hall and the *Pousada de Nossa Senhora da Oliveira*. Closed Sundays. Reservations unnecessary. Praça de São Tiago, Guimarães (phone: 53-419096). Moderate to inexpensive.

Castelo – No frills and home-style cooking make this place a bargain worth the short walk north from the castle. Closed Saturdays. Reservations unnecessary. 47A Rua Dona Teresa, Guimarães (phone: 53-412218). Inexpensive.

En Route from Guimarães – Head 4 miles (6 km) north on N101 to the town of Taipas, renowned for its Roman baths. From here, continue directly to Braga, 10 miles (16 km) away, or take a more scenic and historic route — an extra 8 miles (13 km) or so — and visit the ruins of an Iron Age settlement, Citânia de Briteiros, perched on a 1,112-foot hillock overlooking the valley of the Rio Ave. To reach Briteiros, turn right onto N310 toward Póvoa de Lanhoso, then turn left onto N309 toward Braga. The road climbs to the archaeological site, which is the largest and most important pre-Roman hill town discovered in Portugal, with remains of some 200 granite huts, streets, sewers, and a subterranean cistern. Two of the huts were reconstructed by Dr. Francisco Martins Sarmento, the 19th-century archaeologist who excavated the site. Open from 9 AM to sunset; admission charge; small objects unearthed here can be seen in the *Museu Arqueológico da Sociedade Martins Sarmento* in Guimarães.

Continue climbing north on N309 through a forest of pine, oak, and eucalyptus trees. As the road ascends, the lantern tower of the Sanctuary of the Virgin at the crest of Monte Sameiro (see *Braga,* THE CITIES) comes into view through the treetops; after Sobreposta, the road becomes N103-3 and leads to the sanctuary, which commands a sweeping view of the Minho, over a 1,881-foot mountain pass. Continue on the eastern side of the mountain to the sanctuary of Bom Jesus do Monte (see *Braga,* THE CITIES), shaded by trees, surrounded by fountains, and known for its magnificent staircase. Braga is 3 miles (5 km) away via N203, but be advised that the hotels around Bom Jesus are superior to those in Braga, and the *Sameiro* restaurant (phone: 53-675114) at the Monte Sameiro sanctuary is one of the region's best.

BRAGA: The Minho provincial capital is set in a valley at the junction of three mountain ranges. During the Roman era, it was the intersection of five military roads that crisscrossed northern Portugal and led to Rome. With the establishment of the nation during the 12th century, it became the seat of Portugal's archbishops, who maintained their title, Lords of Braga, into the 18th century, accounting for the city's valuable religious treasures and the unusually large number of its churches. Braga is also the center of baroque art in Portugal, the result of an 18th-century building boom largely directed by two of its prelates and financed by wealth flowing in from the New World. For a detailed report of the city, its sights, hotels, and restaurants, see *Braga,* THE CITIES.

En Route from Braga – Take N201 north and stop at Real to inspect the Byzantine chapel of São Frutuoso de Montélios (see *Braga,* THE CITIES), 2½ miles (4 km) from Braga. Farther along, at Prado, the Cávado River is crossed on an elegant 17th-century bridge, said to have been built by a rich Spanish grandee to allow him to visit his Portuguese lover. The road then begins to climb and, after cresting the pass at Queijada, enters the heart of the Minho. Tiny wood and stone villages and large manor houses dot the landscape, and grape vines on granite crosses follow the contours of the road as it winds down to the valley of the Lima River and the town of Ponte de Lima.

PONTE DE LIMA: When the Roman legions first came upon the Lima, they were so enchanted by its beauty that they mistook it for the Lethe, the mythical river of forgetfulness, and refused to budge until one of their braver generals swam across. Eventually they built a bridge and included the Celtic town on its south bank in the network of roads between Braga and Rome. During the 12th century, the town was an important stronghold against the Moorish-dominated south and provided many of the men who backed young Afonso Henriques when he revolted against León and Castile to establish the Portuguese nation. Today, the river is as enchanting as ever and part of the Roman bridge is in use, but the charming medieval town's martial bent is gone — one of the two medieval towers that used to be a prison is now the town archives, and the 15th-century fortress-palace of the Marquis of Ponte de Lima serves as the Town Hall. The Igreja Matriz (Parish Church), a 14th-century building with 18th-century additions, has an interesting Romanesque doorway, while the 18th-century church of São Francisco, at the eastern end of town facing the river, has been turned into the *Museu dos Terceiros,* a museum of sacred art, containing beautifully carved wood pulpits and altarpieces (open from 10 AM to noon and from 2 to 6 PM; closed Tuesdays; no admission charge).

The main square, with its ornate baroque fountain, is the town's sitting room, a good place from which to admire the river, the bridge, and the church and tower of Santo António da Torre Velha on the opposite bank. (The tiny chapel of São Miguel beside it was used as a stopover by pilgrims on their way to the shrine of Santiago de Compostela in Spain.) Every other Monday, the riverbanks are transformed into the most picturesque of markets, selling farm produce, animals, and local crafts such as linen, wooden furniture, wickerwork, tin lamps, rugs, pottery, and colorful wool blankets. Another good time to be here is during the *Festas de São João* (Feast of St. John), June 23 and 24, or during the *Feiras Novas* (New Fairs), the third weekend (Saturday through Monday) in September; those present are treated to folk dancing and singing by the river and may even be invited to a nocturnal cornhusking party at one of the nearby manor houses. Many of these private properties in the vicinity take in guests, and the headquarters of *Turihab,* the owners' association (phone: 58-942729), is in the same building as the local tourist office (Praça da República; phone: 58-942335).

 CHECKING IN: *Paço de Calheiros* – An impressive 18th-century manor house (a member of *Turismo de Habitação*) perched high amid vineyards a few miles northeast of Ponte de Lima. In the main house, 4 bedrooms face a courtyard and garden; 6 apartments with kitchenettes are in a newer addition. The Count of Calheiros, whose family traces its ancestry back to the founding of the nation, is a charming host who may invite guests to dinner or to visit his textile factory. Contact *Paço de Calheiros,* Calheiros (phone: 58-947164 or 58-941364). Expensive.

Casa do Outeiro – A 16th-century manor house (another member of *Turismo de Habitação*) with a pretty private chapel, across the river from Ponte de Lima. It has 2 double bedrooms with views of a tree-lined courtyard and fountain. Contact Dr. João Gomes de Abreu Lima, *Casa do Outeiro,* Arcozelo, Ponte de Lima (phone: 58-941206). Moderate.

Casa do Pomarchão – Guests can look at the manor house, but they stay in a more modest 2-story house surrounded by orchards and vines. The upper floor (2 double bedrooms, a fireplace, and a kitchen) is ideal for a family; downstairs is more rustic and suitable for a couple. A *Turismo Rural* participant, it's located 1¼ miles (2 km) north of town on N201. Contact Dona Carmen Bernar y Real de Asua, *Casa do Pomarchão,* Arcozelo, Ponte de Lima (phone: 58-941139). Moderate.

Moinho de Estorãos – Another participant in the *Turismo Rural* program, this is a converted 17th-century water mill beside a Roman bridge on a peaceful river nearly 4 miles (6 km) west of Ponte de Lima. It has a double bedroom, a small kitchen, and a living room with a fireplace. Contact Ernesto Martins Pereira, *Moinho de Estorãos,* Estorãos (phone: 58-942372). Moderate.

Quinta de Sabadão – A typical Minho manor house (a *Turismo de Habitação* participant) with an impressive crenelated entrance bearing the family crest. It's just short of a mile (1.6 km) northeast of Ponte de Lima, with 3 large double rooms in the main house. Contact Dona Maria Eulália Abreu Lima e Fonseca, *Quinta de Sabadão,* Arcozelo, Ponte de Lima (phone: 58-941963). Moderate.

 EATING OUT: *Churrasqueria Tulha* – Pleasant and welcoming, it specializes in grilled meats and fish. It's set up in a former grain storage barn, and guests can see the food cooking over a wood fire in the open kitchen. Try the paço do cardido, a fine estate-bottled *vinho verde* from the area. Closed Tuesdays. Reservations unnecessary. Rua Formosa, Ponte de Lima (phone: 58-942879). Moderate.

Monte da Madalena – A great view, classical elegance, gracious service, and well-prepared regional dishes make this a favorite with local dignitaries and aristocrats. Trout with ham and *coelho a caçador* (wine-stewed rabbit) are specialties. It's located on N307 about 2½ miles (4 km) south of town at the summit of a hill overlooking the Lima valley. Closed Wednesdays. Reservations unnecessary. Monte de Santa Maria Madalena (phone: 58-941239). Moderate.

En Route from Ponte de Lima – Take N203 east toward Ponte da Barca, 10½ miles (17 km) away, passing impressive Minho estates, old water mills, rococo monasteries, Romanesque churches, and typical granite farmhouses. At Bravães, 9½ miles (15 km) from Ponte de Lima, is the lovely São Salvador, an intriguing church in a mixture of Romanesque, Moorish, Gothic, and local styles (although the predominant note is 12th-to-13th-century Romanesque). Human and animal motifs are carved in its doorways, and the interior walls show vestiges of Renaissance frescoes.

CHECKING IN: *Casa do Barreiro* – This participant in the *Turismo de Habitação* program, a lovely estate overlooking the Lima 3 miles (5 km) east of Ponte de Lima on N203, is a particularly fine example of a traditional Minho *solar.* It's replete with a colonnaded courtyard, a quaint garden with tiles, flowerpots, roses, and geese, and an adjoining terraced vineyard. There are 7 bedrooms, common rooms, a small bar furnished with Portuguese antiques, and a swimming pool. Contact Gaspar Malheiro, *Casa do Barreiro,* Gemieira (phone: 58-941937). Moderate.

PONTE DA BARCA: The town where the explorer Fernão de Magalhães — more commonly known as Ferdinand Magellan — was born lies on both banks of the Lima. At the entrance to the town, beside an 18th-century bridge, is a pleasant square with a covered market and a *pelourinho* (pillory — a decorative column that served, from the Middle Ages to about the 18th century, as both a symbol of municipal power and a place of punishment). Nearby is the Garden of the Poets, paying tribute to two of the region's most famous men of letters, Diogo Bernardes and Father Agostinho da Cruz. It's said that baptisms used to be performed at midnight under the bridge, with the first passerby acting as the godparent. The tourist information office (Largo de Misericordia; phone: 58-42899) hands out maps with detailed walking tours of the region. Every other Wednesday, the town holds a large crafts fair (on the remaining Wednesdays, the fair takes place in Arcos de Valdevez, a few miles north — see below). The *Festas de São Bartolomeu,* August 23 and 24, is a lively event with music, dancing, and fireworks.

CHECKING IN: *Casa da Agrela* – A handsome 18th-century manor house with garden, a *Turismo de Habitação* property 4 miles (6 km) south of Ponte da Barca off N101. One suite and 2 double bedrooms are for rent. Contact

Antonio Calheiros Fernandes de Oliveira, *Casa da Agrela,* São Pedro do Vale (phone: 58-42313). Expensive to moderate.

Paço Vedro de Magalhães – This baronial 18th-century manor house (a member of *Turismo de Habitação*) belongs to one of Portugal's oldest families. The sprawling grounds — 1¼ miles (2 km) southeast of town off N101 — have views of the surrounding mountains, and the 3 double rooms and 2 suites are furnished with antiques. Contact Dona Maria Constança Corte-Real e Lima, *Paço Vedro de Magalhães,* Ponte da Barca (phone: 58-42117). Expensive to moderate.

EATING OUT: Varanda do Lima – A pleasant spot near the bridge over the Lima, it's very popular during the summer. Regional specialties include *rojões com arroz de sarrabulho,* a pork and rice dish. Open daily. Reservations advised. Ponte da Barca (phone: 58-43469). Moderate.

En Route from Ponte da Barca – Travelers in a hurry should take N101 north 24¼ miles (39 km) to the spa town of Monção. Otherwise, take a 50-mile (80-km) day tour through the Parque Nacional da Peneda-Gerês. The national park, hard by the Spanish border and roughly horseshoe-shaped as it follows the outlines of the Serra da Peneda to the north and the Serra do Gerês to the south, with the Lima River between, contains some of the wildest mountain country in Portugal. Head east out of Ponte da Barca along N203, which accompanies the wooded banks of the Lima, and in 10 miles (16 km) arrive at the park entrance at Entre Ambos-os-Rios. (Since there are no recommendable restaurants along the park route, it's a good idea to pack a picnic lunch for the trip; also, although the road is being widened, night driving should be avoided.) Take the river road into the park toward Lindoso; as it climbs, the terrain becomes rockier — all available land, which is not much, is planted with corn, and cattle graze along the steep slopes.

LINDOSO: The 13th-century castle of this tiny frontier village guards a pass where the Lima River enters Portugal from Spain. Its moat, walls, and towers are well preserved, and some of the original soldiers' quarters have been restored (open May through September, from 10 AM to sunset; generally closed the rest of the year; no admission charge). Look down from the southern end of the castle walls toward the village to see a large concentration of granite *espigueiros* (grain storage huts) on stilts. In the fall, villagers help each other husk corn, and the mountain echoes with their singing.

En Route from Lindoso – To cross the Lima, backtrack a few miles and veer sharply right at the turnoff for Soajo. Descend past a manmade waterfall, cross a small bridge, and climb once again to the tiny village. Soajo sits at the edge of the park atop a mountain overlooking the barren peaks of the Serra da Peneda as they stretch northeast to form a natural border with Spain. Its inhabitants, called *monteiros* (hunters), are known for their independent character, derived from centuries of earning their living by hunting for themselves and the royal house. In turn, they were allowed to govern themselves. King Dinis (1261–1325) went so far as to prohibit the nobility from living here, by ruling that they could not spend more time in the village than it took for a piece of bread to cool down on a spear. This may explain the unusual pillory in the main square, shaped like a spear with a triangle, presumably bread, perched on top. At the eastern end of town, on a large, smooth granite rock, is a large group of *espigueiros.* Cornhusking parties, with singing and dancing, take place on the spot during the fall harvest.

Leave Soajo and the park by heading for Arcos de Valdevez, either by taking N202 directly west or by taking the more scenic route along the Lima. For the latter, leave Soajo by the same road used to reach it and turn toward Ermelo. The cluster of crude, round stone houses seen at the edge of the mountain along the way are *brando* (soft) houses — improvised rock shelters used by shepherds in the summer months. Ermelo itself is a quaint village perched on the steep banks of the river, with a pretty Romanesque church. (To visit the town, park the car on the road and walk several hundred yards on a narrow stone path). Continue to São Jorge, where the road curves north to Vale and Arcos de Valdevez, leaving the river behind.

CHECKING IN/EATING OUT: *Casa do Adro* – A participant in the *Turismo Rural* program, it is in a renovated 18th-century townhouse beside the town square. There are singles, doubles, and suites sleeping 4 to 6 people. Guests have breakfast in the old, rustic kitchen; two cafés next door serve simple meals. Contact Maria or António Enes, *Casa do Adro,* Soajo (phone: 58-47327). Moderate.

ARCOS DE VALDEVEZ: The town, dating from the 10th century, takes its name from the calm Rio Vez, whose banks it graces. It has known better days, but there are several monuments of note, including a Romanesque chapel and a Manueline pillory in the center and the Paço de Giela, a fine example of a medieval baronial house with crenelated tower, about 1¼ miles (2 km) northeast. Arcos de Valdevez can be used as a base to explore the river valley or the mountains (short hikes will turn up a variety of rustic farmhouses, water mills, and *canastros* — wicker containers with thatch covers used to store and dry corn). The tourist office, located at the southern end of town (Avenida Marginal; phone: 58-66001) provides maps and tour information. A crafts fair takes place every other Wednesday in Arcos, alternating with the one in Ponte da Barca, a few miles south.

CHECKING IN: *Casa de Requeijo* – The terraced gardens of this 17th-century manor house (a *Turismo de Habitação* property) have been replaced by a concrete tennis court, a swimming pool, and an outdoor grill, and all available space in the house has been turned into guest quarters, furnished in less than baronial style. The riverside location and sports facilities (including several rowboats and bicycles), however, are an attraction. There are 2 apartments with kitchenettes and 2 suites with double bedrooms on the main floor, plus 2 rustic and slightly cramped suites in the garden. A minimum stay of 5 days may be required from mid-June through September. Contact Alberto and Catherine Pereira, *Casa de Requeijo,* Arcos de Valdevez (phone: 58-65272). Expensive.

EATING OUT: *Adega Regional* – A converted farmhouse in the northern outskirts of town beside the Rio Vez. Dine in a rustic courtyard covered with vines or in a pleasant room decorated with farm implements. The restaurant's grill draws a large clientele — meats and fish are brought in fresh from the river and nearby farms. Closed Mondays. Reservations advised. Located off N101 toward Monção. Silvares (phone: 58-66122). Moderate.

En Route from Arcos de Valdevez – About 9½ miles (15 km) north (N101), the winding but well-paved road begins to climb the Serra de Boulhosa, via a spectacular pass onto whose slopes villages, churches, and vines cling precariously. Once over the top, the valley of the Minho suddenly comes in view and the road descends into the Pinheiros district. It is here that alvarinho, the king of *vinho verde* grapes, grows best, particularly on the estate surrounding the sumptuous 19th-century Palácio de Brejoeira, whose *vinho verde* is the most famous and most expensive of "green wines." (The estate's *aguardentes* — rough brandies — are also coveted.) Peer through the wrought-iron gate into the sprawling grounds; the last King of Portugal spent his final night before exile here, and Britain's Prince Andrew was a recent guest.

MONÇÃO: The Minho forms Portugal's northwestern border with Spain, and this small town on the river's south bank — a spa noted for its hot mineral springs — is one of a string of fortified towns that have for centuries guarded the Portuguese frontier. Legend has it that during the 14th century, a young noblewoman, Deu-la-Deu Martins, saved Monção from a Castilian siege by throwing what was left of the town's bread over the walls, to make the Spanish believe there was bread enough to last a long time. The invaders swallowed the ruse and lifted their siege, and today, a statue of the heroine stands in the town square. Some of Monção's medieval walls and parts of a 17th-century fortress are still standing, and the Romanesque parish church has an elegant 12th-century door. In May or June, *Corpus Christi* is celebrated with a colorful bout between a dragon and a brilliantly clad St. George mounted on a white steed. The tourist office is in the center at Largo do Loreto (phone: 51-52757).

CHECKING IN: *Casa de Rodas* – This elegant 18th-century manor house (a member of *Turismo de Habitação*) surrounded by woods and vineyards is about 1¼ miles (2 km) southeast of Monção. Guests have access to most of the house, which has several drawing rooms furnished with Portuguese antiques, a turn-of-the-century billiard room, and a dining room dripping with chandeliers. There are 4 bedrooms with views. Contact Dona Maria Luísa Tavora, *Casa de Rodas,* Monção (phone: 51-52105). Moderate.

Mané – A simple, clean, 8-room *pensão* in the historic center near the river, suitable for an overnight stay. There is a modern restaurant and snack bar serving tasty food. 5 Rua General Pimenta de Castro, Monção (phone: 51-52355). Moderate.

En Route from Monção – The road southwest (N101) meanders through hills and farm country, playing hide-and-seek with the river. Before entering Valença do Minho, 12 miles (19 km) from Monção, turn left onto N101-1 for a short detour to Monte do Faro, whose 1,865-foot summit provides an impressive view. The Minho Valley and Spain stretch to the north and west, coastal towns and the Minho estuary to the southwest, and the mountains of the Peneda-Gerês National Park to the east.

CHECKING IN/EATING OUT: *Monte do Faro* – A pleasant *pensão* at Monte do Faro, with sweeping views of the surrounding countryside and a fine restaurant. Monte do Faro (phone: 51-22411). Moderate to inexpensive.

VALENÇA DO MINHO: Perched on a hillock overlooking the Minho and, on the opposite bank, the Galician town of Túy, this walled fortress town is another in the series of fortified settlements that have guarded Portugal's northern border from past invasion. Today, the impregnable garrison has become a bazaar, which the Spanish are welcome to plunder as long as they leave their valuable pesetas behind. The old fortified town consists of two 17th-century forts that are linked to each other by a bridge and a manmade vaulted passage and are lined with two sets of walls, a moat, and trenches. Inside are two quaint quarters with narrow, cobbled streets, whitewashed churches, crenelated townhouses, and loads of shops selling linens, leatherware, pottery, wicker, and Portuguese scarves and sweaters. From the ramparts on the northern side of one of the forts, a 19th-century bridge across the Minho, designed by Alexandre-Gustave Eiffel, is visible.

Outside the walls, to the south, is the new town of Valença, devoid of the charm of the old one except for the vintage train museum in the railroad station. On display are a British steam engine built in Manchester in 1875 and an elegant salon car built in France for the Portuguese royal family. (Ask permission from the stationmaster to visit.)

A word of caution: Plan a trip to this area carefully. Valença is on the main road (N103) between Porto and Santiago de Compostela in Spain — a road that becomes congested during the high summer season and on weekends, particularly during July and August. The tourist office (Avenida Espanha; phone: 51-23374) is at the border post by the bridge.

 CHECKING IN: *Pousada de São Teotónio* – An elegant inn at the northern end of Valença's fortifications, with a gorgeous view of the Minho and Spain. Although this is a contemporary structure, the architects cleverly incorporated its courtyard and garden into one of the bastions and ramparts of the fortress. There are 16 bedrooms, a bar, and a restaurant (see *Eating Out*). Valença do Minho (phone: 51-22242). Expensive.

Lara – Modern, with 54 rooms and a reasonable restaurant. Outside the old fortified town, it's suitable for a night if the *pousada* is booked. Rua São Sebastião, Valença do Minho (phone: 51-22348). Moderate.

 EATING OUT: *Pousada de São Teotónio* – The most luxurious restaurant in town is lodged in the *pousada* overlooking the river and Spain. Tasty regional dishes and Portuguese nouvelle cuisine are served by a courteous staff. Open daily. Reservations advised. Valença do Minho (phone: 51-22242). Expensive.

Parque – A cozy, family-run establishment in the Old Town, decorated with tiles and peasant pottery and offering a view of the western battlements. Grilled dishes, particularly chicken, are its forte. Closed Fridays. Reservations unnecessary. Rua Oliveira, Valença do Minho (phone: 51-23131). Moderate.

En Route from Valença – As N13 leads southwest 17 miles (27 km) to Caminha, the rough forested terrain softens. The river begins to widen and a patchwork of orchards and fields of grain, vines, and vegetables spreads quilt-like along its flat embankment. Two tiny islands, Boega and Amores, appear in front of the ancient town of Vila Nova de Cerveira. This is an ideal place to stop and explore the river and surrounding hills, which abound in legends of hidden Moorish treasures and echo with the romantic song of nightingales.

 CHECKING IN/EATING OUT: *Pousada de Dom Dinis* – Built within the ruins of a 14th-century castle overlooking the Minho, it has 29 rooms and suites, terraces and patios, several bars, and a glass-enclosed restaurant. Praça da Liberdade, Vila Nova de Cerveira (phone: 51-95601). Expensive.

Da Boega – An *estalagem* (inn) of 40 rooms lodged in a former 18th-century manor house outside the town of Gondarém in the hills above Vila Nova de Cerveira. Rooms have sweeping views of the Minho; there is a good restaurant, a swimming pool, and a tennis court. Quinta do Outeiral, Gondarém (phone: 51-95231). Expensive to moderate.

CAMINHA: This ancient fortified town guards Portugal's northern border at the mouth of the Minho, at a point where a lesser river, the Coura, flows into the larger one. The tiny Portuguese fortress island of Insua and the Spanish town of Santa Tecla face it. Caminha's whitewashed town square still retains some of its medieval flavor: Of interest here are the loggia and coffered ceilings of the 17th-century Town Hall; the crenelated clock tower; the 15th-century Gothic Pittas Palace, with its neo-Manueline windows; and the parish church, with its beautifully carved Mudéjar ceiling. Inspect the northern exterior of the church to see an amusing gargoyle of a man relieving himself, with his backside facing Spain.

 CHECKING IN: *Casa do Esteiro* – This pleasant country house, a *Turismo Rural* property, is surrounded by gardens and vineyards in the southeastern suburbs of Caminha. Guests can choose a double room or a suite. Contact Dona Maria do Patrocinio de Vilas Boas, *Casa do Esteiro,* Caminha (phone: 58-921356). Moderate.

Ideal – A clean and simple, 30-room *pensão* on a hill overlooking Caminha, about

2 miles (3 km) from town. 125 Rua Engenheiro Sousa Rego, Moledo do Minho (phone: 58-922605). Moderate to inexpensive.

EATING OUT: *Remo* – A modern restaurant sitting on stilts on the wharf of the Caminha sailing club, facing Spain. Both Spanish and Portuguese dishes are served; *arroz de marisco,* Portugal's version of Spain's paella, is a specialty. Closed Tuesdays. Reservations advised. *Posto Nautico do Sporting Clube Caminhense,* Caminha (phone: 58-921459). Expensive to moderate.

***Adega Machado* –** The coziest and most hospitable restaurant in town, on a secluded street southwest of the main square. Discreetly decorated with tiles and wood, it offers a wide selection of typical regional dishes, including *tainha assada no forno* (oven-baked mullet), cold and pickled *savel* (shad), and shellfish. Closed Monday evenings. Reservations unnecessary. 85 Rua Visconde Sousa Rego, Caminha (phone: 58-922794). Moderate.

En Route from Caminha – The road (N13) to Viana do Castelo, 15 miles (24 km) from Caminha, heads south along the Atlantic coast past fishing villages and tourist resorts. Vila Praia de Ancora, set at the mouth of the Rio Ancora, has a small castle, secluded beaches, and good fish restaurants. The river and town apparently received their name after the wife of a local patrician ran away with a Moorish emir, was brought back in chains, and was dropped into the river strapped to an anchor (*âncora*). Afife, nearby, is another small beach resort, with a strange *Lenten* custom: The townspeople burn one of the town's older women in effigy as part of a cleansing ritual. After Afife, the road crosses a flat, windswept marshland and enters Viana do Castelo.

VIANA DO CASTELO: This holiday resort lies at the mouth of the Lima River, with a basilica-topped hill, Monte de Santa Luzia, looming behind it. Legend has it that Viana takes its name from a beautiful woman, Ana, who lived here. Her fiancé, a boatman on the Lima, was so persistent in asking acquaintances encountered on his run whether they had seen Ana — to which they would answer "Vi Ana" ("I saw Ana") — that the name stuck. (Others say the name has something to do with the Greek goddess Diana.) The small city's Manueline and Renaissance houses attest to its prominence during the 16th century when it played a major role in Portugal's maritime discoveries, providing boats, seamen, and explorers such as Alvares Fagundes, who charted the waters of Newfoundland for Portuguese fishermen. Gold from Brazil and an early prominence in the port wine trade with England contributed to a baroque building boom in the 18th century.

The Praça da República and its environs hold some of the city's most impressive architecture. An ornate 16th-century fountain by Viana's master stonemason, João Lopes the Elder, stands in the middle of the cobbled square. Facing it, to the east, is the crenelated Paços do Conselho, the former town hall, a late-16th-century Gothic structure. Next door is one of Viana's most delightful buildings, the Misericórdia; the façade of this 16th-century Renaissance hospice, designed by João Lopes the Younger, is alive with nubile atlantes and caryatids. The adjoining church contains important 18th-century *azulejos* by António de Oliveira Bernardes and his son, Policarpo. South of the square, medieval tradesmen and merchants can be seen resting on the shoulders of the Apostles in the carved portal of the Gothic parish church, which faces a lovely Renaissance house reputed to have belonged to João Lopes the Elder. On the west side of town, the *Museu Municipal* (Largo de São Domingos; phone: 58-24223), housed in an 18th-century palace, contains many treasures, including a valuable collection of 18th-century glazed pottery from Coimbra and a handsome, pre-Roman statue of a Lusitanian warrior. The museum is open for guided tours from 9:30 AM to noon and from 2 to 5:30 PM; closed Mondays and holidays. Admission charge.

Walking tours (Portuguese only) of Viana depart from the tourist office, lodged in a handsome 15th-century palace (Rua do Hospital Velho; phone: 58-22620). Regional crafts are on display here, as well as in several shops around the colonnaded courtyard. Viana is known for its blue-and-white ceramics, table linen, copper goods, gold and silver filigree work, regional costumes and dolls, peasant scarves, and sprays of artificial flowers called *palmitos*. Most conspicuous are the handkerchiefs decorated with hearts that young maidens traditionally give to their boyfriends.

Tradition is indeed strong in this city, which has been called the capital of Portuguese folklore because of the flair and the sheer number of the *festas* (feast days) and *romarias* (pilgrimages) that occur in and around it. The tiny baroque Igreja Nossa Senhora da Agónia (Church of Our Lady of Suffering) is famous throughout Portugal for its annual pilgrimage, probably the most spectacular and lively event of its kind in the north. For 3 days at the end of the third week in August, the city is transformed, with thousands of lights glowing, food and *vinho verde* sold at hundreds of small stalls, and the sounds of singing and dancing echoing through the night. Young women parade in colorful traditional dress, weighed down by intricately carved gold filigree. Mythical giants of the forest — *gigantones* — roam, and a sumptuous procession carries a statue of the Virgin through streets paved with flower petals to bless the fishing fleet. It all ends in a blaze of fireworks at the harbor.

Other events include the *Festas de Santa Cristina,* the first weekend (Friday through Sunday) in August, in the suburb of Meadela, featuring lively folk music and dancing, floats, and religious pageantry — the regional costumes worn by the ladies are a big part of the attraction. In May there are also lavish flower festivals in Viana and its environs. The *Festas da Senhora das Rosas* (Festival of Our Lady of the Roses), early May in Vila Franca do Lima, has young women carrying large baskets woven with intricate rose petal designs of their own making; in the *Festa dos Andores Floridos,* late May in Alvarães, floats covered with roses ride over a carpet of flowers.

Before leaving Viana, don't forget to visit the Basilica de Santa Luzia, on Monte de Santa Luzia (Mount St. Lucy), roughly 2½ miles (4 km) north of town on a well-marked road (or reachable by funicular from Avenida 25 de Abril — it runs from 9 AM to 6 PM, every hour until noon, then at 12:30 PM, 1:30 PM, and every half hour thereafter; from April through September, it also runs at 6:30 and 7 PM). In times of plague or invasion, the people of Viana have always taken refuge in the woods here, and the neo-Byzantine basilica on top of the mountain — a 20th-century copy of the Sacré-Coeur in Paris — is an important pilgrimage church. Those who don't mind narrow passages and a climb of 142 steps will be rewarded at the top of the lantern tower with a panoramic view of the city and its environs.

CHECKING IN: *Do Parque* – A modern, 123-room hotel in a small park on the eastern side of the city, a 5-minute drive from the center. It has a view of the river, a rooftop restaurant, a swimming pool, and a discotheque. Praça da Galiza, Viana do Castelo (phone: 58-828605). Expensive.

***Santa Luzia* –** A turn-of-the-century luxury hotel on Monte de Santa Luzia, with a sweeping view of the region. Recently refurbished in a 1930s style, it has an elegant dining room, salon, and terrace, plus 52 rooms and 3 suites, an outdoor swimming pool, and a tennis court. Monte de Santa Luzia (phone: 58-828889). Expensive.

***Casa do Ameal* –** This *Turismo Rural* program participant is a pleasant townhouse on the Lima River in suburban Meadela; it has 4 double rooms and 2 apartments sleeping four people. Contact Dona Maria Elisa Araújo, *Casa do Ameal,* Meadela (phone: 58-22403). Moderate.

***Casa Grande da Bandeira* –** A *Turismo de Habitação* property, it offers 2 double bedrooms in a large 18th-century townhouse near the center. Contact Dona Maria Meyer de Faria, *Casa Grande da Bandeira,* 488 Rua da Bandeira, Viana do Castelo (phone: 58-23169). Moderate.

Jardim – This quaint inn faces the river and an esplanade near the center of town. There are 20 tastefully furnished rooms. 68 Largo 5 de Outubro, Viana do Castelo (phone: 58-828915). Moderate.

Paço d'Anha – One of the most attractive manor houses in the north of Portugal, it's part of the *Agroturismo* program and is located in a large *vinho verde* producing estate near the beach 3 miles (5 km) south of town. Guests stay in farm buildings converted into apartments (2 double bedrooms, living room, bath, and kitchen). Horseback riding and meals can be arranged. The Prior of Crato was a guest in 1580 when he received the news that he had been proclaimed King of Portugal. Contact António Júlio Alpuim, *Paço d'Anha,* Anha (phone: 58-322459). Moderate.

Viana Sol – Pleasant and hospitable, it's near the city center, with 72 rooms, a cozy bar, discotheque, sauna, a squash court, and an indoor pool. The only weak point is a rather staid indoor restaurant. Largo Vasco da Gama, Viana do Castelo (phone: 58-23401). Moderate.

Alambique – A simple *pensão* of 24 rooms on a quiet side street near the center, it has an adjoining restaurant serving good traditional fare (see *Eating Out*). 86 Rua Manuel Espregueira, Viana do Castelo (phone: 58-23894). Inexpensive.

Dolce Vita – Another little *pensão,* in the center of town across from the tourist office. The 7 rooms are basic and clean (some look out onto medieval streets and Renaissance houses), and there is an adjoining restaurant (see *Eating Out*). This is only for those who don't mind kitchen sounds and don't need parking in the immediate vicinity. 44 Rua do Poço, Viana do Castelo (phone: 58-24860). Inexpensive.

EATING OUT: *Cozinha das Malheiras* – The newest and fanciest restaurant in Viana has a nouvelle Portuguese look to it and its food. It is lodged in the arcades of a medieval building behind the former Town Hall. Try the Paço d'Anha, a white *vinho verde* from a neighboring estate. Open daily. Reservations advised. 19 Rua Gago Coutinho, Viana do Castelo (phone: 58-23680). Expensive.

Casa d'Armas – A waterfront restaurant in an old armory. The medieval decor may be slightly stiff, but the food is good and served by a courteous staff. Try the river salmon or the veal with mushrooms for a main course, and the rich *torta de amêndoa* (almond tart) for dessert. Closed Mondays. Reservations advised. 30 Largo 5 de Outubro, Viana do Castelo (phone: 58-24999). Expensive to moderate.

Alambique – This bistro has good regional food and lively decor. The *carro de caranguejo* (crab stuffed with onions, olives, and egg), lobster with rice, and *cabrito no forno* (roast kid) are recommended. Closed Tuesdays. Reservations unnecessary. 86 Rua Manuel Espregueira, Viana do Castelo (phone: 58-23894). Moderate.

O Espigueiro – A regional restaurant 3 miles (5 km) out of Viana, off the road to Porto. The fine cooking draws a large, regular clientele, so reservations are a must. There's a vine-covered courtyard for outdoor dining. Open daily. Lugar do Santoinho, Darque (phone: 58-322156). Moderate.

Os Tres Portes – The city's most typical Minho restaurant, in an old bakery near the town center, features soft lighting, rustic decor, waitresses in traditional dress, and regional cooking. It's also the place to see and hear folk dancing and singing on Friday and Saturday nights from June through September (Saturdays only during the rest of the year). A fixed-price menu gives guests a sample of various dishes, including such tasty meat dishes as baked kid and *rojões* (pork cooked with pigs' blood). The English owner makes sure the Irish coffee is up to par. Closed Mondays. Reservations are a must in summer. 7 Beco dos Fornos, Viana do Castelo (phone: 58-829928). Moderate.

Dolce Vita – This rustic Italian restaurant done up with checkered tablecloths is across from the tourist office. The Italian specialties, including pizza baked in a large adobe oven, are a nice change of pace from the sometimes heavy Minho diet — and they go well with white *vinho verde.* Open daily. Reservations unnecessary. 44 Rua do Poço, Viana do Castelo (phone: 58-24860). Inexpensive.

Quinta do Santoinho – To experience an *arraial,* the Minho's version of a barn party, head for this lively and colorful barn-like locale where the folk music and dancing go on till the wee hours, with fireworks and *gigantones* to fuel the excitement. For a fixed price, guests feast on grilled pork, sardines, and chicken, and drink to their heart's content out of barrels of wine. Those who last until morning are served a *champorreão* — a powerful punch. The *arraial* takes place at 8 PM on Tuesdays, Thursdays, and Saturdays in August; on Thursdays and Saturdays in July and September (the last two Thursdays of September excluded); and on Saturdays in May, June, and October. The location is 3 miles (5 km) out of town, at Lugar do Santoinho, Darque, but the necessary reservations can be made in Viana at the *AVIC* travel agency, 206 Avenida dos Combatentes (phone: 58-829705). Inexpensive.

En Route from Viana do Castelo – The main road (N13) toward Porto crosses the Lima on a bridge designed by Alexandre-Gustave Eiffel. Stay on the road for 6 miles (10 km), then turn left onto N103 to Barcelos.

BARCELOS: The home of the Portuguese symbol of good luck, the rooster, lies inland 19 miles (30 km) southeast of Viana do Castelo on the Rio Cávado. According to the story, a Galician on his way to Santiago de Compostela was accused of stealing from a wealthy landowner and was sentenced to death by hanging. As his last wish, he requested an audience with the judge, who happened to be sitting down to a meal of roast cockerel when the condemned man was brought before him. The accused pointed to the bird and cried out that as proof of his innocence the cock would get up and crow. The judge laughed and sent the Galician off to his death, but did not touch his meal. Just as the man was being hanged, the cock stood, crowed, then fell back dead again. The judge rushed to the gallows and found the man alive because the knot around the noose had not tightened. A 15th-century monumental cross documenting the miracle, the Cruzeiro do Senhor do Galo (Cross of the Gentleman of the Cock), can be seen in the ruins of the 15th-century Paço dos Duques de Bragança (Palace of the Dukes of Bragança), which have been turned into an open-air archaeological museum (open daily from 9:30 AM to 5:30 PM; no admission charge). Other sights in Barcelos include the Solar dos Pinheiros, a 15th-century mansion directly west of the cross, and, up the street from the house, on Largo do Município, the parish church, which has some interesting capitals and rich interiors. The Igreja do Terço (Avenida dos Combatentes da Grande Guerra), is covered with 18th-century *azulejos.*

Most visitors to Barcelos, however, are drawn by its weekly fair, one of the biggest and most colorful in the country, held on Thursdays in Campo da República. Hand-loomed rugs, colorful straw bags and hats, lace, and other regional crafts are sold, but the main attraction is the pottery — literally tons of it, decorative and utilitarian, in every size and color, made in small cottages and factories in the surrounding countryside. The anthropomorphic animals and large-headed devils playing musical instruments are amusing buys, holdovers of an earlier pagan tradition. The foremost artist of this genre, Rosa Ramalho, who made delightful pregnant goat figures that are said to have inspired Picasso, is no longer living, but her granddaughter continues the family trade. Those who miss the fair can take heart, because many of the goods can be purchased at the *Centro de Artesanato* (phone: 53-812135), the handicrafts shop in the same building as the tourist office (Largo da Porta Nova; phone: 53-811882).

 CHECKING IN: Casa do Monte – An *Agroturismo* participant, it is a large, 2-story house with ivy-covered walls and manicured lawns overlooking a valley about 4 miles (6 km) north of Barcelos off N103. There are 2 double bedrooms per floor. Contact Dona Maria Duarte de Sousa Coutinho, *Casa do Monte,* Abade de Neiva, Barcelos (phone: 53-811519). Moderate.

Quinta do Convento da Franqueira – A former 16th-century Franciscan monastery, now the residence of an Englishman, it stands on 35 acres of pines and vineyards. A participant in *Turismo de Habitação,* it's 2½ miles (4 km) southwest of town off N205, has a swimming pool, and offers a suite and 2 double bedrooms looking onto attractive gardens. Meals can be arranged (the *quinta* produces its own estate-bottled *vinho verde*). Contact Piers Gallie, *Quinta do Convento da Franqueira,* Barcelos (phone: 53-815606). Moderate.

Arantes – Clean and simple, this 12-room bed and breakfast *pensão* is in the center of town, across from the park where the weekly crafts fair is held. 35 Avenida da Liberdade, Barcelos (phone: 53-811326). Inexpensive.

Dom Nuno – Another small bed and breakfast *pensão,* with 27 rooms near the center of town. 76 Avenida Dom Nuno Alvares Pereira, Barcelos (phone: 53-815084). Inexpensive.

EATING OUT: Bagoeira – One of the oldest eating places in town. Wholesome traditional cooking and good service make it a favorite of the old guard. Open daily. Reservations unnecessary. 53 Avenida Dr. Sidónio Pais, Barcelos (phone: 53-811236). Moderate.

Casa dos Arcos – It's cozy and charming, with tasty, authentic Minho cuisine. Ancient stone walls, wood beams, and soft lights provide a medieval touch. Closed Saturdays. Reservations unnecessary. 185 Rua Duques de Bragança, Barcelos (phone: 53-811975). Moderate.

Pérola da Avenida – A modern Portuguese bistro with fine regional cooking and a gracious staff. It faces the park where the weekly crafts fair is held. Open daily. Reservations unnecessary. 66 Avenida dos Combatentes da Grande Guerra, Barcelos (phone: 53-811416). Moderate.

Muralha – Basic regional fare served in a simple, rustic setting beside the tourist office. Open daily. Reservations unnecessary. 1 Largo da Porta Nova, Barcelos (phone: 53-812042). Inexpensive.

En Route from Barcelos – Take N205 southwest 12½ miles (20 km) to the beach town of Póvoa de Varzim and then N13 another 2 miles (3 km) south to the neighboring resort of Vila do Conde. Anyone in a hurry to return to Porto, however, and intending to skip Póvoa and Vila do Conde, should note the existence of a new bypass, which begins about 3 miles (5 km) north of Póvoa and continues for 11 miles (18 km) before connecting again with the main road south (N13).

PÓVOA DE VARZIM: One of the more popular northern beach resorts and the largest fishing town north of Porto is really two towns. The northern side is devoted to pampering visitors, with long, sandy beaches, a casino, tennis courts, water slides, pools, discos, beachside restaurants, boats for hire, and a marina. The southern side contains the fishing port and the picturesque fishermen's *bairro,* where women mend the nets and sell fish while the men tend to the colorfully painted wooden sailboats, or *barcos poveiros.* During the *Festas da Senhora da Assunção* (Feast of Our Lady of the Assumption), August 14 and 15, a large procession of fishermen carries a life-size statue of their patron saint to bless the boats. The event is followed by a lively beachside *arraial,* with music, dancing, fireworks, and a bullfight. The *Museu Municipal de Etnografia e História* (17 Rua do Visconde de Azevedo; phone: 52-622200) has an interesting collection of relics relating to the town's fishing history (open from 10 AM to 12:30 PM and from 2:30 to 6 PM; closed Mondays; admission charge, except on Thursdays).

Póvoa de Varzim is known for its gold and silver smithing. Watch the silversmiths at work on household items such as ornate candelabras at the famous *Gomes* shop (68 Rua da Junqueira; phone: 52-624638). Less pricey but equally beautiful purchases are the hand-embroidered wool fishermen's sweaters sold at shops lining the beachfront Avenida dos Banhos. The beachfront casino (passport identification required for entry to the gambling rooms) is not only a place to try your luck, but also a cultural center where art and crafts exhibits are held.

Several excursions can be made in the area. At A-Ver-O-Mar, 2 miles (3 km) north, seaweed harvesters have built huts on the beach. At Rates, about 9½ miles (15 km) from Póvoa off N206 toward Guimarães, the elegant 12th-century São Pedro church is one of the better-preserved examples of Romanesque architecture in the region. For exact driving instructions, contact Póvoa's Tourist Office (160 Avenida Mouzinho de Albuquerque; phone: 52-624609); the numbering of the buildings along this avenue is confusing, so look for the tourist office near the beach. Another option in the vicinity is the new 18-hole course at the *Estela Golf Club* (phone: 52-685567), located beside the beach at Estela, 5 miles (8 km) north of Póvoa and 2½ miles (4 km) off the main road (N13). Equipment rental and lessons are available throughout the year, and the clubhouse has a restaurant and bar overlooking the sea. The Sopete group, which owns the club, also owns hotels in Póvoa; hotel guests receive discounts on greens fees.

CHECKING IN: *Vermar* – A modern hotel beside the beach, it has 208 rooms, a fine restaurant, grill, bar, sauna, discotheque, and 2 heated pools as an alternative to the cool Atlantic. The service, professional and efficient, doesn't spare the small touches that add up to a hospitable environment. Part of the Sopete group, which also owns the *Estela Golf Club;* guests receive a discount on greens fees. Avenida dos Banhos, Póvoa de Varzim (phone: 52-683401). Expensive.

Costa Verde – This upgraded hotel has 50 rooms, a small garden, and parking space. 56 Avenida Vasco da Gama, Póvoa de Varzim (phone: 52-681531). Moderate.

Grande – Near the beach and the casino, with 99 rooms and a restaurant. Because it's part of the Sopete group, guests receive a discount on the greens fee at the *Estela Golf Club.* Largo do Passeio Alegre, Póvoa de Varzim (phone: 52-622061). Moderate.

Santo André – A pleasant *estalagem* (inn) with 49 rooms right on the beach 2 miles (3 km) north of town at A-Ver-O-Mar. The pool and a restaurant overlooking the water are added attractions. Also a member of the Sopete group. A-Ver-O-Mar (phone: 52-681881). Moderate.

Gett – Simple but welcoming decor and service recommend this 22-room *pensão* near the tourist office. 54 Avenida Mouzinho de Albuquerque, Póvoa de Varzim (phone: 52-683206). Moderate to inexpensive.

EATING OUT: *Casino Monumental* – The most luxurious dining in the area is in the casino. Both Portuguese and international dishes are served, but the *caldeirada de peixe* (fish stew) — Portugal's answer to bouillabaisse — and the *lagosta suada* (steamed lobster) go especially well with the marine decor. There is dancing and a floor show at the cabaret. Open daily. Reservations are a must in summer, advised at other times. Avenida de Braga, Póvoa de Varzim (phone: 52-622112). Expensive.

Chez Tomaz – A friendly place near the tourist office, and also close to the beach. It serves both local and international cooking. Open daily. Reservations advised. 116 Largo do Passeio Alegre, Póvoa de Varzim (phone: 52-620117). Expensive.

Eurocini – Tiny and romantic, this bistro, also near the tourist office, has a good French menu. Open daily. Reservations advised. 29 Avenida Mouzinho de Albuquerque, Póvoa de Varzim (phone: 52-627136). Expensive.

Costa – Unpretentious Portuguese cooking and a rustic decor. Closed Mondays. 104 Rua Dr. Caetano de Oliveira, Póvoa de Varzim (phone: 52-684139). Moderate to inexpensive.

VILA DO CONDE: Only 2 miles (3 km) south of Póvoa de Varzim via N13 is another resort and fishing town. Set on the north bank of the Rio Ave, Vila do Conde was one of Portugal's major shipbuilding and commercial centers during the voyages of discovery, and the shipyards continue to make handsome wooden boats for the country's cod fleet. A tradition of lace making going back to the 17th century also endures. Visitors are welcome at the Escola de Rendas (Lace School), on Largo do Carmo (but scheduled to move to a building nearby), where they can buy bobbin lace — *rendas de bilros* — on the spot. The town's annual crafts fair, beginning on the Saturday of the third week of July and running through the first weekend in August, is another attraction. One of the largest of its kind in Portugal, it features artisans at work, along with folk singing and dancing. The *Festas de São João* (Feast of St. John) on June 23 and 24, another occasion for singing, dancing, feasting, and fireworks, ends with a floodlit procession to the beach.

The town's 16th-century Igreja Matriz (Parish Church) has an elegant Plateresque doorway. The Mosteiro de Santa Clara (Convent of St. Clare), founded during the 14th century but rebuilt during the 18th, has a Gothic church with beautifully carved Renaissance tombs. Note the 18th-century fountain in the cloister — it's fed by an aqueduct that runs from Póvoa de Varzim and was built with 999 arches. (The builders thought that 1,000 would have been too grandiose and might have offended God!) Apply at the convent to visit the church and climb the parvis before the church for a view of Vila do Conde and the surrounding countryside. The tourist office (103 Rua 25 de Abril; phone: 52-631472) can provide further information on the town and its environs, and when the tourist office is closed, the *Centro de Artesanato* (Handicrafts Shop; Rua 5 de Outubro; phone: 52-631497) provides information.

CHECKING IN/EATING OUT: *Do Brasão* – A comfortable, centrally located *estalagem* (inn) with 30 rooms. The restaurant serves good fish dishes such as river trout and shad. Order the *doce de ovos* for a final dose of eggs and sugar. 144 Avenida Dr. João Canavarro, Vila do Conde (phone: 52-632016). Expensive to moderate.

En Route from Vila do Conde – Stop off at Azurara, across the river from Vila do Conde, to inspect the Manueline parish church or do some last-minute shopping. (Azurara is known for its wool fishermen's garments — shirts, hats, socks.) Then continue down N13 to Porto, 17 miles (27 km) from Vila do Conde. For a full report on Portugal's second-largest city, the home of port wine, see *Porto*, THE CITIES.

Douro and Trás-os-Montes

Until recently, the spectacular, rugged scenery of the Douro and Trás-os-Montes regions of northern Portugal eluded most visitors. The natural urge to peer behind the massive mountain ranges east of the country's northern coastal areas was tempered by a lack of suitable accommodations and other facilities for tourists. The situation has improved somewhat lately, and now intrepid travelers in search of a scenic vacation free of crowds and noise can venture into this remote hinterland. The reward is a pioneering look at Portugal's last frontier.

The Douro River flows from Spain clear across the north of Portugal into the Atlantic Ocean at Porto. For some 70 miles, the river is the natural border between the two countries. Its namesake region consists of the Douro Litoral (Coastal, or Lower, Douro), which stretches from Porto and its industrial environs east to the Marão mountain range, and, farther upriver, the Alto Douro (Upper Douro), a dramatic, vine-covered river valley hemmed in by mountains. The river is the backbone of the region, and, before roads, railroad tracks, and dams, it was the region's major highway — called the Rio do Ouro or "River of Gold" because of its golden complexion in certain kinds of light. The real gold mine, however, consists of the grapes that grow on its banks and those of its tributaries — the substance that produces Portugal's famous port wine.

The port wine gold mine begins at Peso da Régua, 75 miles upstream from Porto, and fans out from there to the richest veins in the vicinity of Pinhão, 20 miles farther east. The countryside here is one huge mantle of green and yellow leaves, punctuated occasionally by the white manor house of a grower or shipper. The vines are cultivated on terraces that follow the contours of granite and schist hills, making the riverbanks appear to be edged by gigantic pyramids. There are 85,000 vineyards and 25,000 growers in the port wine zone, the limits of which were set in 1756, making it the world's oldest demarcated zone for wine production. Thanks to the mountains that keep out cold Atlantic winds and rains, this part of the Douro Valley enjoys a semi-Mediterranean climate that is heaven for grapes. (The colder, wetter climate in the coastal areas just over the mountains produces Portugal's lighter, less alcoholic *vinho verde* wine.) It also allows the cultivation of olive, almond, and fruit trees wherever the terrain permits.

In the summer, the Alto Douro is scorched by temperatures up to 104F. A good time to visit, therefore, is during the *vindima* (grape harvest) in September and October, when the region bustles with life and the songs of grape pickers echo throughout the valley. The sheer bravado of the men, women, and children who carry heavy baskets up and down steep slopes can make a visitor not only dizzy, but also fully appreciative of the labor behind a glass of port.

The Alto Douro and the port wine zone are actually part of Portugal's Trás-os-Montes province, which, however, stretches far beyond the river into the northeastern corner of the country. Its name means "beyond the mountains," and much of this land — a plateau sloping up to Spain, surmounted by rocky heights and cut through by deep river valleys — is indeed remote. Only recently have roads and electricity reached some of the tiny villages tucked away in its fertile valleys, so its air remains pure, its waters fresh and clean. Cold, blistering winters and blazing hot summers are the norm, but oases can be found in the valleys where corn, almonds, olives, and citrus fruits thrive. On its high pasturelands, sheep and cattle graze, producing some of the country's best meat.

The area has been inhabited for thousands of years. There are vestiges of Celtic and pre-Celtic habitation in stone *castros* (fortified hamlets) and dolmens, and in the customs and dances of the people. Ancient beliefs such as devil worship persist, and *bruxas* (witches) and *curandeiros* (medicine men) are consulted regularly. Some villages continue to be self-sufficient, leading a communal life. Their inhabitants are friendly and may invite visitors into their granite houses for a taste of rich corn bread, smoked ham, and homemade wine. Don't be surprised to find modern conveniences such as television sets, refrigerators, and gas or electric ovens inside these ancient dwellings, however. They are usually paid for by emigrant members of the family working elsewhere in Europe or overseas. Village elders complain that the appliances are eroding their way of life and that foreign-style houses and modern additions to ancestral homes are altering the harmony of the landscape.

Today, Trás-os-Montes and the Douro Valley are maturing like an ancient bottle of port. A major highway linking Porto and Spain will soon cut through the middle of Trás-os-Montes, opening up the region for development. There are also large iron and coal deposits under the soil of Trás-os-Montes, waiting to be exploited. The Douro Valley is being transformed by hydroelectric dam projects, and there are plans to make the river navigable to the Spanish border by making use of an existing system of locks.

The route outlined below takes travelers east from the Douro capital of Porto, Portugal's second-largest city, to the picturesque town of Amarante. From there, it dips south to Lamego and follows the south bank of the Douro through the port wine region. It returns to the river's north bank at Pinhão and climbs vine-covered mountains to Vila Real, the capital of southwestern Trás-os-Montes. Some 50 miles (80 km) east of Vila Real, a decision must be made either to continue directly to the fortified town of Bragança, at the northeastern tip of Portugal, or to reach the same goal via a less direct swing through the rarely visited southeastern part of Trás-os-Montes, which offers almond-studded valleys, a final view of the Douro before it turns into Spain, and tiny border towns such as Miranda do Douro, renowned for its ancient stick dances and unique dialect. After Bragança, the route perforce turns west, skirting the Montezinho Natural Park on its way to the spa town of

Chaves, graced with a Roman bridge and picturesque wood-balconied houses. Several short excursions are suggested as the route continues west to the spectacular lake region in and around the Peneda-Gerês National Park and into the spa town of Caldas do Gerês. The itinerary ends in Portugal's Minho region, at Braga.

Along the way, look forward to dining heartily on veal, lamb, kid, ham, and sausages, on dairy products such as goat cheese, and on thick vegetable soups such as *caldo verde*. Fish lovers can order trout stuffed with ham in Lamego and Chaves. Wine drinkers will savor real port — now officially known as Porto to distinguish it from port-like wines made elsewhere. As it ages, port is laced with brandy to stop its fermentation and allow it to retain some of its sweetness, but note that the Douro Valley also produces dry red wines. Rosés from the Vila Real area and reds from Valpaços in central Trás-os-Montes are other popular choices.

Hotels and good restaurants in the area are limited, but the dearth of accommodations is relieved by the existence of private homes taking in paying guests under the auspices of Portugal's *Tourism in the Country* program, whose participants range from the manor houses of *Turismo de Habitação* to the simpler houses of *Turismo Rural and Agroturismo* (see *Accommodations,* GETTING READY TO GO). Reservations for all accommodations in summer (June through September) should be made well in advance. Expect to pay $55 and up for a double room in hotels listed below as expensive ($80 and higher for a *pousada*), between $35 and $50 for accommodations in the moderate category, and less than $30 in inexpensive ones. A dinner for two runs from about $45 to $50 and up in restaurants listed as expensive, from $20 to $35 in those listed as moderate, and less than $20 in those listed as inexpensive.

AMARANTE: This old town lies on the banks of the Tâmega River at the foot of the Serra do Marão, 45 miles (72 km) east of Porto via N15. At sundown or in the morning mist, with the wooden balconies of its picturesque houses leaning over the river, there is a dreamy enchantment to the scene. The town is known for its patron saint, São Gonçalo, a 13th-century priest who gained a reputation for helping old maids to marry. Several stories exist to explain the origin of his reputation; in one, he is a frolicsome soul who organized parties for ladies of dubious repute in order to find them husbands. The party tradition has been revived recently as the *Arraiais de São Gonçalo,* open-air parties held Thursdays and Saturdays from June through October. For a small fee, guests eat and drink to their heart's content, dance, and enjoy a lavish fireworks display. The colorful saint is also remembered on June 1 and 2, when, for the semi-religious *Romaria de São Gonçalo* (St. Gonçalo Pilgrimage), single women take red carnations to the Church of São Gonçalo, kiss the statue of him there, pull the red cord of his habit, and pray for a good husband. The lovely 16th-century church, part of the Convento de São Gonçalo, stands by the 18th-century São Gonçalo bridge and contains, besides the remains of the saint, an attractive 17th-century organ case. The museum in the cloister of the church (open from 10 AM to 12:30 PM and from 2 to 5 PM; closed Mondays; no admission charge; phone: 55-423663) contains an extensive art gallery, as well as the town's *demônios,* a pair of devils that are holdovers from the devil worship that once was practiced in the area. A Bishop of Braga took a dim view of this practice and sold the pair to England — causing such a furor that they had to be returned.

Also to be seen in the town is the 18th-century Igreja de São Pedro, which has a baroque façade and an unusual nave decorated with 17th-century *azulejos.* Leisurely repasts on the balconies of the teahouses overlooking the river, scenic walks on paths in the wooded park above the town, and swimming, trout fishing, and boating on the Tâmega are popular local pastimes.

Ask at the Amarante Tourist Office (Rua Cândido dos Reis; phone: 55-422980) for information on excursions in the vicinity. The area is rich in *solares* (manor houses), Romanesque churches, dolmens, Iron Age *castros,* and strange rock formations called *pedras baloiçantes* (balancing rocks). By driving north along N210 and the banks of the Tâmega for 14½ miles (23 km), it's possible to visit Celorico de Basto, a medieval earldom with fine country houses and an 18th-century castle.

CHECKING IN: *Casa Zé da Calçada* – This is a pleasant townhouse overlooking the Tâmega, a short walk from the town center. A participant in *Turismo de Habitação,* it offers 7 double bedrooms, and the owner runs the town's best restaurant, opposite the townhouse (see *Eating Out,* below). Contact José da Fonseca Herdeiros, *Casa Zé da Calçada,* Rua 31 de Janeiro, Amarante (phone: 55-422220). Moderate.

Navarras – A few minutes' drive from the center, this place is modern, with 61 air conditioned rooms, a heated indoor pool, and a large restaurant with a verandah. Rua António Carneiro, Amarante (phone: 55-424036). Moderate.

Amaranto – Modest, it has 35 rooms, a panoramic view of the town monuments, and a restaurant serving regional fare. Rua Madalena, Amarante (phone: 55-422106). Moderate to inexpensive.

EATING OUT: *Zé da Calçada* – The town's best restaurant has an old-fashioned look and serves tasty local dishes. House specialties include cod *Zé da Calçada* style, *cabrito assado no forno* (roast kid), and a variety of fancifully named sweets — *pinhas de ovos* ("egg cones"), for example, and *pinhas de chocolate amarantinos* made with eggs, sugar, and almonds. Several local *vinho verde* wines, such as caves Manuel Pinheiro, moura bastos, and quinta do outeiro, are on the wine list. Open daily. Reservations advised. 72 Rua 31 de Janeiro, Amarante (phone: 55-422023). Expensive to moderate.

Adega Regional de Amarante – A picturesque *tasca* (tavern) in a manmade cave near the river. This is a favorite pre-dinner haunt for tasting regional snacks such as the hams and spicy sausages hanging from the ceiling. The *salpicão,* a sausage cured in red wine and smoked, is a favorite with locals. Open daily. Reservations unnecessary. 57 Rua António Carneiro, Amarante (phone: 55-424581). Inexpensive.

En Route from Amarante – Head southeast toward Lamego on N15 and N101, stopping at Mesão Frio, 14½ miles (23 km) from Amarante, to admire the elegant churches and manor houses in its tree-lined center. At Mesão, take N108 8½ miles (14 km) east to Peso da Régua, at the confluence of the Douro and Corgo rivers. The best port wine vineyards begin here and spread eastward along the Douro and its tributaries. Peso da Régua, also known simply as Régua, is the industry's main administrative and storage center in the Alto Douro, and although the town lacks charm, the surrounding countryside is starkly beautiful. In fact, Régua is the junction of several scenic train routes, including the "Linha do Douro," which runs from Porto up to Pocinho, about 19 miles (30 km) short of Barca d'Alva on the Spanish border. For more information, contact the tourist office opposite the Régua train station, Largo da Estação (phone: 54-22846).

Cross the Douro at Régua and drive south 8 miles (13 km) to Lamego. The well-paved but winding road climbs mountain slopes covered with terraced vineyards and whitewashed manor houses.

LAMEGO: The location of this attractive and peaceful agricultural town — at the edge of a valley surrounded by mountains, vineyards, and orchards — made it an important commercial center in the Middle Ages. Portugal's first *cortes,* a representative assembly of nobles, met here in 1143 to recognize Dom Afonso Henriques as the country's first king. On a hill northeast of town are the partially restored ruins of a 12th-century castle, while the baroque Santuario da Nossa Senhora dos Remédios (Sanctuary of Our Lady of the Remedies) occupies a hill to the south of town. The sanctuary can be reached by car, 2½ miles (4 km) through a lovely wooded forest, or, more dramatically, by climbing an impressive granite staircase decorated with *azulejos* and bristling with pinnacles. During the *Festas da Nossa Senhora dos Remédios,* the largest cultural and religious event in the region and one of the country's biggest fairs, pilgrims can be seen crawling up the steps on their knees. Held from late August to mid-September, the fair also features folk dancing and singing and religious processions with dazzling floats pulled by oxen.

In town, the Sé (Cathedral) has a fine Gothic entrance in which an amusing scene of animal eroticism appears to have eluded the censors of the time. The 18th-century Bishop's Palace next door now houses the *Museu de Lamego* (Largo de Camões; phone: 54-62008), where priceless 16th-century tapestries from Brussels and an early-16th-century painting of the Visitation by the Portuguese master Grão Vasco can be seen (open from 10 AM to 12:30 PM and from 2 to 5 PM; closed Mondays; admission charge, except on Sundays and holidays). Also of interest is the Igreja do Desterro (Church of the Exile), with its sumptuous coffered ceiling depicting scenes from the life of Christ. (Ask at 126 Rua da Calçada for the key to visit). Lamego produces Raposeira, one of Portugal's best sparkling wines. For a taste, visit the Raposeira company's cool cellars carved into the mountainside south of town, reachable via N2 (open Mondays through Fridays from 9:30 AM to 12:30 PM and from 2 to 5:30 PM, but it's best to call *Caves de Raposeira* for an appointment first; phone: 54-62003).

Among the sights in the vicinity of Lamego is the 7th-century Visigothic Church of São Pedro de Balsemão, 9 miles (14 km) east on the banks of the Balsemão River. Besides the elaborate granite tomb of the bishop who remodeled it during the 14th century, it contains a 15th-century stone statue of Nossa Senhora de O (Our Lady of O), depicting a pregnant Virgin. To reach the church, leave Lamego via the popular Bairro da Fonte quarter, where women still bake bread in old-fashioned ovens and blacksmiths still work at open forges. Turn left at the bridge and follow a narrow, unmarked road running north along the banks of the river. The last 100 yards or so is on a dirt road, so begin early enough to avoid driving in the dark.

Another sight is southeast of Lamego. The 12th-century Mosteiro de São João de Tarouca, a former Cistercian monastery (Portugal's first), lies 10 miles (16 km) from town off N226. The impressive church, which was later given a baroque interior, contains exquisite paintings by the 16th-century master Gaspar Vaz, as well as the granite tomb of Dom Pedro, Count of Barcelos and bastard son of King Dinis. (His wife's tomb was taken by a local farmer and used as a wine press before it was recovered and put in the museum in Lamego.) The sacristy has 4,709 tiles, no two alike, and its ceiling has a series of paintings depicting the life of St. Bernard. To visit, apply at the house on the right facing the square. For information on still other sights, contact Lamego's Tourist Office, Avenida Visconde Guedes Teixeira (phone: 54-62005).

CHECKING IN: *Vila Hostilina* – This restored farmhouse, a *Turismo Rural* participant, sits on a hill overlooking the town and the valley, surrounded by gardens and vineyards. Guests are invited to help with the *vindima* (grape harvest) in the fall and to crush grapes the old-fashioned way — by foot. There are 7 rooms with private bath, a rustic bar, tennis court, large swimming pool, and health club with gym, exercise machines, and sauna. Meals are served on request;

reservations are a must in summer. Contact Joaquim Brandão dos Santos, *Vila Hostilina,* Lamego (phone: 54-62394). Expensive.

Do Cerrado – This pleasant *albergaria* (inn) at the entrance to Lamego has 30 balconied rooms. Regional furniture and handmade rugs decorate the common room. Breakfast and snacks are served on a terrace with views of the town and the surrounding countryside. Lugar do Cerrado, Lamego (phone: 54-63164). Moderate.

Parque – A simple, turn-of-the-century hotel of 40 bedrooms, known for its fine restaurant (see *Eating Out*) and ideal location in the gardens beside the Nossa Senhora dos Remédios sanctuary. Nossa Senhora dos Remédios, Lamego (phone: 54-62105). Moderate.

Império – A simple but quaint *pensão,* beside the town's main street and monuments. The look is small-town Portugal; 12 rooms with bath. 6 Travessa dos Loureiros, Lamego (phone: 54-62742). Inexpensive.

Silva – The accommodations are clean but spartan at this 12-room *pensão* on a quiet side street near the cathedral. 26 Rua Detrás da Sé, Lamego (phone: 54-62929). Inexpensive.

Solar – A small, comfortable, and newly refurbished *pensão* with 25 rooms (with bath), in front of the tourist office. 9 Avenida Visconde Guedes Teixeira, Lamego (phone: 54-62060). Inexpensive.

EATING OUT: Parque – By far the best place to eat in Lamego, it has a varied regional menu that includes river trout baked with ham and the chef's award-winning cod dish. Courteous service, an austere old Portugal ambience, and garden views enhance the repast. Raposeira sparkling wines are stocked; have a *bruto* (brut) with the meal and a *meio seco* (semisweet) with dessert. Open daily. Reservations advised. *Hotel Parque,* Nossa Senhora dos Remédios, Lamego (phone: 54-62105). Moderate.

Turiserra – The reward for a 20-minute drive into the mountains north of Lamego is a modern restaurant at an altitude of 2,970 feet, with a spectacular view of the Douro Valley and the atmosphere of a mountain lodge. To reach it, take Avenida 5 de Outubro, turn left onto Avenida Marquês de Pombal, and follow the signs for the Parque de Campismo Turiserra. Open daily. Reservations unnecessary. Serra das Meadas (phone: 54-63380). Moderate.

Mina – A rustic, family-run restaurant with a wholesome regional menu, near the town center, beside the charming Capela do Espiríto Santo (Holy Spirit Chapel). The specialty, *cordeiro assado* (roast lamb), is cooked and served in unglazed black pottery from the region. This is also a good place to try *bolo de Lamego,* or ham pie. Open daily. Reservations unnecessary. 5 Rua Alexandre Herculano, Lamego (phone: 54-63353). Moderate to inexpensive.

En Route from Lamego – To reach Vila Real by the shortest route — 15½ miles (25 km) — return to Peso da Régua and cut north through the impressive gorge of the Corgo River. To reach the city by a longer, more scenic route — 33½ miles (54 km) — through the epicenter of the port wine zone, return to the Douro and take N222 east along its south bank, crossing to the north bank at Pinhão. The road passes some of the larger wine estates along the way, and in Pinhão itself there is a lovely train station with *azulejos* depicting the history of wine making in the area. From Pinhão, take N323 north, climbing steep mountain slopes streaked with terraces and vines and punctuated only occasionally by a lone tree or a white manor house. At Sabrosa, a suitable watering hole with a Luso-Roman cemetery, head west on N322.

About 1¼ miles (2 km) short of Vila Real, the 18th-century Palace of Mateus appears on the left. To many, it will be a familiar sight, because the façade graces the label of the estate's well-known rosé wine. The palace is one of the most elegant examples of the baroque style in Portugal, and although it is a private residence, parts of it, along with the grounds, are open to the public (daily from 9 AM to 1 PM and from 2 to 6 PM from April through September, and from 10 AM to 1 PM and 2 to 5 PM the rest of the year; admission charge). A museum in the palace contains, among other things, a precious collection of fans and letters from 19th-century personalities. Classical music concerts and opera, guitar, and other music courses are given on the premises in August and September. For information, contact the Fundação da Casa de Mateus (Vila Real; phone: 59-23121). Wine tasting takes place at the Sogrape bottling plant nearby, which is open Mondays through Fridays from 9 AM to noon and from 2 to 5:30 PM. An appointment is required. Contact *Sogrape-Vinhos de Portugal* (1159 Avenida da Boavista, Porto; phone: 2-695751).

VILA REAL: The administrative capital of the southwest Trás-os-Montes is a thriving agricultural town on a plateau at the foot of the Marão and Alvão mountain ranges and at the confluence of the Cabril and Corgo rivers. The major road from Porto to the northeast Trás-os-Montes capital of Bragança passes through here, and the scenic "Linha do Corgo" train line arrives here from Peso da Régua. There are also air links with Porto and Lisbon. The main sights are in the town center along the Avenida Carvalho Araújo, where the tourist office (phone: 59-22819) is also located (at No. 94). The cathedral, a former Dominican monastery with Romanesque and Gothic touches, has an interesting statue of the Virgin. Beside the church, at No. 19, is the Renaissance façade of the house of Diogo Cão, the Portuguese explorer of the Congo basin. At the western end of the street is the monumental double staircase of the 19th-century Câmara Municipal (Town Hall). The Old Town behind it has an esplanade encircling the 14th-century Church of São Dinis and a commanding view of the Corgo ravine. Vila Real is a good base from which to explore the Parque Natural do Alvão, which lies to the northwest and is endowed with stone and shale houses, ancient water mills, tumbling waterfalls, and valleys carpeted with flowers.

CHECKING IN: *Casa das Quartas* – A handsome, 16th-century manor house (a *Turismo de Habitação* property), it is surrounded by orchards and flower beds in a southeastern suburb. The sprawling estate, which even has its own private chapel, offers 3 double rooms with private baths and mountain views. Contact José Mourão, *Casa das Quartas,* Abambres (phone: 59-22976). Expensive.

Mira Corgo – Modern, it has 76 air conditioned rooms, a bar, an indoor swimming pool, and a health club. It overlooks the Corgo River gorge. 76-78 Avenida 1 de Maio, Vila Real (phone: 59-25001). Moderate.

Tocaio – This aging hostelry in the center of town has 52 rooms and simple country charm. 45 Avenida Carvalho Araújo, Vila Real (phone: 59-23106). Moderate to inexpensive.

EATING OUT: *Espadeiro* – There's a classic dining room, endowed with a fireplace, and in summer an adjacent smaller room with a terrace overlooking the Corgo River. This is a sophisticated restaurant, well known for regional dishes such as *truta com presunto* (grilled trout with ham) and *cabrito assado com arroz* (roast kid with rice). Open daily. Reservations unnecessary. Avenida Almeida Lucena, Vila Real (phone: 59-22302). Expensive to moderate.

Churrasco – A small, dimly lit restaurant and snack bar decorated with an African motif. Grilled meats are the specialty. Closed Sunday evenings. Reservations unnecessary. 24 Rua António Azevedo, Vila Real (phone: 59-22313). Moderate to inexpensive.

Nevada – The regional menu here features Vila Real's very own *bolo de carne,* a spicy meat loaf. Modern, with a relaxed atmosphere and simple decor, it's beside the *Mira Corgo* hotel. Try a table wine from the Adega Cooperativa de Vila Real. Open daily. Reservations unnecessary. Avenida 1 de Maio, Vila Real (phone: 59-71828). Inexpensive.

En Route from Vila Real – As N15 leads northeast toward Bragança, pine trees begin to alternate with vineyards, olive groves, and fields of grain. The town of Murça, on high slopes above the Tinhela River 25 miles (40 km) out of Vila Real, has an interesting Iron Age granite boar (Porca de Murça) in its main square, one of many such peculiar statues found throughout the region. The agricultural town of Mirandela, known for its 16th-century bridge and a lively fair that runs from the end of July to early August, lies another 19 miles (31 km) east on the banks of the Tua River. Nearby, the rolling hills around Jerusalem do Romeu, 7 miles (11 km) farther east, are covered with olive and cork oak trees as far as the eye can see. Turn right at Jerusalem do Romeu and go about 2 miles (3 km) to Romeu, a typical Trás-os-Montes village that has been restored. The tiny hamlet and its *Maria Rita* restaurant (see *Eating Out*) are owned by a patrician Portuguese family, as is the interesting *Museu das Curiosidades,* which contains family memorabilia such as old sewing machines, photographic and musical equipment, four model Ts, and 19th-century fire trucks. (open daily — the keeper lives on the premises; admission charge).

Return to N15 and continue east 5½ miles (9 km) to the junction with N216. Here a decision must be made. Either continue on N15 28½ miles (46 km) directly to Bragança (through some of the most barren and thinly populated countryside in southern Europe), or take a more circuitous route via a string of old fortress towns running along the Douro and the Spanish border. To follow the latter course, turn southeast onto N216 and drive the few miles to Macedo de Cavaleiros, a neat farming town and favorite hunting spot for northern aristocrats. Then continue on N216 to Mogadouro, 35 miles (56 km) away, known for its woodcrafts and silk, wool, and leather goods, as well as for a ruined 12th-century fortress. If it's spring, take the time to drive up to the nearby Serra da Castanheira and see the countryside covered by a mantle of white from thousands of blossoming almond trees. The tiny town of Sendim, which, surprisingly, can boast one of the most famous restaurants in Portugal (see *Gabriela's* in *Eating Out*), is 17 miles (27 km) east of Mogadouro on N221; Miranda do Douro is another 13 miles (20 km) beyond Sendim.

CHECKING IN: *Do Caçador* – A splendid *estalagem* (inn) and hunting lodge in the former Town Hall of Macedo de Cavaleiros. The 25 rooms are furnished with antiques (room No. 101 has a particularly royal look), the public rooms are rife with wood and leather, and the bar, filled with wicker furniture and hunting trophies, looks like a set out of colonial Africa. (The owner is an avid collector of beer mugs and such oddities as the mahogany lavatory seat of a Portuguese king.) Specialties in the dining room include steaks stuffed with ham and, during hunting season (mid-October through December), game dishes such as partridge and hare. Guests can stroll around a tiny rose garden and swim in a marble-lined pool. Largo Manuel Pinto de Azevedo, Macedo de Cavaleiros (phone: 78-42354). Expensive.

EATING OUT: *Maria Rita* – One of the best restaurants in the region, lodged in a typical Trás-os-Montes house in a tiny village. The large stone fireplaces, antiques, and heavy oak tables set with china and silver add up to an elegantly rustic setting. The regional food features such items as *sopa de alheiras,* a thick and spicy garlic soup, and *espargos bravos,* wild asparagus — not to mention whole turkeys, baby pigs, and lambs for parties calling in advance. Closed Mondays. Reservations advised. Rua da Capela, Romeu (phone: 78-93134). Moderate.

Gabriela's – This 70-year-old restaurant is the culinary pride and joy of Trás-os-Montes. Alice Gabriela, the second-generation owner, has cooked for Portuguese presidents, organized banquets at some of the poshest hotels in the country, and won all sorts of awards, including a much coveted Coq d'Or. The decor is rustic and pure country, as are the smells from the open kitchen, where guests can see Alice in action at a wood fire. Try the *posta a mirandesa a Gabriela,* a large veal steak cooked over a fire of grape vines or olive branches. The sauces are a professional secret. Open daily. Reservations advised. 28 Largo da Praça, Sendim (phone: 73-73180). Moderate to inexpensive.

MIRANDA DO DOURO: This ancient town perches atop the narrow rocky canyon of the Douro that here forms a natural border between Portugal and Spain. It is remote enough to have its own dialect, Mirandes, a mixture of Galician Spanish, Portuguese, and Hebrew, yet during the 16th century it was the cultural center of Trás-os-Montes and the seat of an important bishopric. After several military catastrophes and the loss of its bishop's seat, the town fell into obscurity during the 18th century and is only now coming out of its isolation with the construction of a dam (the northernmost of five on the Douro) and the opening of a border road with Spain. Among the sights to see is the former cathedral, a 16th-century building rich in carved and gilded wood and graced with an unusual little statue — Menino Jesus da Cartolinha — of the baby Jesus sporting a top hat. (It's said to represent a boy who appeared miraculously to help the townspeople resist a Spanish invasion in the 18th century.) The *Museu da Terra de Miranda* (phone: 73-42164) has costumes of the area, rustic furniture, archaeological artifacts, and carved stones from an old synagogue (open from 10 AM to 12:30 PM and from 2:15 to 4:45 PM; closed Mondays; admission charge).

A treat is in store for anyone who visits Miranda during the *Festas de Santa Barbara,* on the third Sunday in August, or the *Romaria de Nossa Senhora de Nazaré,* in early September. These are two occasions to see the town's *pauliteiros,* or stick dancers, perform. Although other ancient and colorful folk dances, such as the *pingacho* (rough ballet), the *geribalda* (a round dance), and the *mira-me-Miguel* (a square dance), are still performed here, the stick dance is the one for which the town is best known. What's involved is a sort of ritual sword dance performed by men in white flannel skirts, aprons, and flower-covered hats, who clash their *paulitos* (sticks) to the tune of a bagpipe, cymbals, and drums. Other components of the local folklore are the coarse wool capes and waistcoats worn by the people of the region and the *facas de palacoulo* — knives with forks attached to them — used traditionally by the shepherds of the area.

CHECKING IN: *Pousada de Santa Catarina* – This simple, modern, 12-room *pousada* sits on a hill overlooking a dam on the Douro about 2 miles (3 km) east of town. The restaurant, which has a fine view of the water and the Spanish plain of Zamora, serves regional dishes such as wood-fired *posta à mirandesa* (veal steaks), *fumeiro* (smoked sausage), river trout, and small game. Estrada da Barragem, Miranda do Douro (phone: 73-42255). Moderate.

EATING OUT: *Mirandes* – A rustic, family-run restaurant in the heart of town. Try the melon with smoked ham or the empanadas (meat-filled pastries) for starters, and then the baby pig done on a spit. The *folares de Páscoa,* or sweet *Easter* cakes, are a local dessert. Closed Mondays. Reservations unnecessary. Largo da Moagem, Miranda do Douro (phone: 73-42418). Moderate to inexpensive.

En Route from Miranda do Douro – Head north on N218 toward Bragança, 52½ miles (84 km) away. Outeiro, 32½ miles (52 km) up the road, has a large church with an ornate Manueline doorway and Gothic rose window. Bragança is another 20½ miles (33 km) ahead.

BRAGANÇA: The medieval walls and castle that dominate this fortified town at Portugal's extreme northeastern corner are the best preserved in the country. Bragança, which occupies a high hill in the Serra da Nogueira, was known to the Celts as Brigantia and to the Romans as Juliobriga. During the 15th century, it was made a fiefdom of the powerful Dukes of Bragança, who became Portugal's royal family in 1640 and ruled until the end of the monarchy in 1910. The town was a major silk center during the 15th century, thanks largely to a thriving Jewish merchant community (which dispersed with the Inquisition, although the area's remoteness allowed some Jews to stay and practice their religion in secret). Today, copper and leather goods and baskets replace silks in the shops around the main square, Praça da Sé, which is outside the walls in the newer (but still old) part of town — Bragança had already begun to expand beyond its medieval walls during the 15th century.

The old walled town contains the 12th-century castle and its tall, square keep, which serves as a military museum. The Torre da Princesa (Princess Tower) beside it was the scene of tragedy when the fourth duke locked up his lovely wife, Dona Leonor, to keep men from laying eyes on her; later, when he moved his court south, he murdered her. In front of the castle is a medieval *pelourinho* (pillory), its shaft driven through a granite statue of a boar said to date (as does the boar in Murça) back to the Iron Age. The 12th-century Domus Municipalis, or Town Hall, is one of the few remaining Romanesque civic buildings in Portugal (to visit, apply at the house in front); it stands next to the 16th-century church of Santa Maria. An interesting museum, the *Museu do Abade de Baçal* (27 Rua Conselheiro Abilio Beça; phone: 73-23242), is outside the walls in the 18th-century Bishop's Palace. Named for the Abbot of Baçal (1865–1945), who spent years recording the history and customs of the region in an 11-volume series, it houses archaeological artifacts, furniture, tools, ancient coins, church plate and vestments, and paintings. The museum (open from 10 AM to 12:30 PM and from 2 to 5 PM; closed Mondays; admission charge, except on Sunday mornings) is on the street that leads to the cathedral, an unimpressive church that was elevated to cathedral status when the seat of the bishop moved here from Miranda do Douro during the 18th century.

Bragança is the ideal spot from which to explore the Parque Natural de Montezinho, whose high plateaus and mountains stretch northeast and northwest of town and contain some of the wildest country in Portugal. Populated with wild boar, wolves, foxes, and other small game, the park is also dotted with tiny, self-sufficient villages where communal life and pre-Christian rituals endure and people still believe in the evil eye, fairies, and witches. The town of Rio de Onor, straddling the border 16½ miles (26 km) northeast of Bragança, has a communal system of ownership and a democratic electoral system that sociologists have studied. Half of the village lies in Portugal and the other in Spain, and the inhabitants, who cross freely from one to the other, have intermarried for centuries. For further information and a map of the park, visit the tourist office in the Câmara (Town Hall) in Bragança (phone: 73-23078), or the small tourism booth at the entrance to town from N218.

CHECKING IN: *Pousada de São Bartolomeu* – A modern, 16-room inn, perched on a hill facing the walled town, its castle, and the surrounding mountains. Guests have a choice of regional or international dishes in the posh restaurant. Estrada do Turismo, Bragança (phone: 73-22493). Expensive.

Bragança – Simple, near the town center, with 42 rooms facing the battlements and castle. Avenida Dr. Francisco Sá Carneiro, Bragança (phone: 73-22579). Moderate.

Cruzeiro – A no-frills *pensão* with 31 rooms near the town center. Travessa do Hospital, Bragança (phone: 73-22634). Inexpensive.

EATING OUT: *Solar Bragançano* – This pleasant, old-fashioned restaurant occupies a palatial townhouse in the main square. A tiled entrance and staircase lead to the formal dining room with wood ceilings, chandeliers, and handwoven rugs. Specialties of the house are *cabrito branco a Montezinho* (white Montezinho kid), cod, and veal steaks *Solar* style. Try the semisweet favaios wine as an aperitif, with *alheiras* (spiced sausages) or some goat cheese. Open daily. Reservations unnecessary. 34 Praça da Sé, Bragança (phone: 73-23875). Moderate.

Lá em Casa – A modern, airy restaurant with pine-paneled walls and rustic regional decor and food. Closed Mondays. Reservations unnecessary. 7 Rua Marquês de Pombal, Bragança (phone: 73-22111). Inexpensive.

En Route from Bragança – The road (N103) to Chaves, 60 miles (96 km) west, sets out running along the edge of and sometimes into the Montezinho Natural Park. Only 3 miles (5 km) beyond Bragança, the Benedictine Monastery of Castro de Avelãs, a handsome building with Romanesque and Moorish touches, sits beside the road; once flourishing, it was abandoned when religious orders were banned during the 19th century. Moving westward, as the high peaks of the Serra de Montezinho and the Serra da Coroa begin to loom majestically, the traveler passes chestnut and oak trees, whitewashed *pombaias* (pigeon houses), trout farms, and grazing cattle. Vinhais, overlooking a valley 19½ miles (31 km) from Bragança, has a castle, a monastery, and churches in a bad state of repair, but its large market is worth attending on the 9th and 23rd days of the month, to see the villagers gather from the surrounding countryside. If the car can endure the bumpy dirt road, take the turnoff, 8½ miles (14 km) short of Chaves, to the Castelo de Montorte, about half a mile (1 km) away. The impressive 14th-century castle sits on a high, windswept hill with views of Spain to the north. Surrounding it are the remains of what is believed to be a Lusitanian *castro* (fortified village) with Roman additions. The castle can be visited daily from 3 to 6 PM (tip the guard).

CHAVES: The spa capital of Portugal, Chaves is on the banks of the Tâmega River in the center of a fertile valley near the Spanish border. The Romans took advantage of this breach in Portugal's northern mountains during the 1st century, when they captured the site, exploited its rich gold and mineral deposits, and built a town called Aquae Flaviae — so named for its warm thermal springs, which are said to cure rheumatism and liver and stomach disorders. When they built Trajan's Bridge over the Tâmega, the town became an important stopover on the Roman road between Braga and Astorga, Spain. The bridge is still in use, but most of the Roman town lies beneath the newer medieval and modern town. Agriculture and textiles are the economic mainstays today, and Chaves is particularly known for its *presunto* (ham).

Most of the sights are found in and around Praça de Camões, the main square. The *Museu da Região Flaviense,* housed in the former palace of the Dukes of Bragança, contains archaeological and ethnographic exhibits, including Roman and pre-Roman relics and old coins. The *Museu Militar,* in the adjacent 12th-century keep, has four floors of uniforms and weapons from various periods of Portuguese history, while the view from the platform at the top embraces the town and the surrounding countryside. Both museums (phone: 76-21965) are open from 9:30 AM to 12:30 PM and from 2 to 5 PM; closed Saturday mornings, Sunday mornings, and Mondays; admission charge.

The manicured keep gardens contain archaeological remains, and its ramparts provide a sweeping view of the river.

Also on the Praça de Camões is the baroque Misericórdia church, its interior embellished with 18th-century *azulejos* depicting the life of Christ; the parish church with a lovely Romanesque doorway; and an ornate Manueline pillory. Note the houses on the eastern side of the square and on the neighboring Rua Direita — they have lovely painted wood verandahs. Nearby, on Rua General Sousa Machado, is the former Jewish Quarter (the chapel at No. 63 is thought to have been a synagogue). Other points of interest in town are two 17th-century fortresses, São Francisco and São Neutal, and the train museum at the railroad station (open weekdays, from noon to 5 PM).

For further information and maps of the Chaves area, contact the tourist office (Terreiro da Cavalaria; phone: 76-21029). Two neighboring spa towns, Vidago and Pedras Salgadas, respectively 10½ miles (17 km) and 18½ miles (30 km) south of Chaves on N2 toward Vila Real, provide most of the region's recreation (swimming, golf, and other sports). Some visitors prefer to stay in Vidago rather than in Chaves, because the former offers better accommodations.

 CHECKING IN: *Aquae Flaviae* – Brand new, with 195 rooms, it's near the 12th-century keep, overlooking the Tâmega. Praça do Brasil, Chaves (phone: 76-26496). Expensive to moderate.

***Trajano* –** This modern, 39-room hostelry stands on top of a Roman bathhouse, discovered while the newer foundations were being laid. It's on a quiet cobbled street near the center of town and is decorated in dark wood and tiles. The dining room is somewhat dim, but the food, particularly the desserts, brightens things up. Travessa Cândido dos Reis, Chaves (phone: 76-22415). Moderate.

***Vidago Palace* –** Set in a lush park and surrounded by gardens, ponds, and fountains, this pink Belle Epoque building in a spa town south of Chaves offers guests a taste of royal Portugal. The hotel was inaugurated by King Dom Luís in 1910 and boasts a royal suite where he stayed. Although the "palace" has lost some luster over the years, a portion of its original splendor is still visible in the carved double staircase and in the large dining room with a white and gold ceiling, marble columns, and ornate lighting fixtures. (The chef cooks a daily fixed-price meal with a choice of regional and international dishes.) Newer apartments, a swimming pool, and a discotheque have been constructed behind the hotel; tennis and rowing on a manmade lake are also available on the sprawling grounds; a picturesque 9-hole golf course nearby may be expanded to 18 holes in the future. All told, there are 123 rooms. Parque, Vidago (phone: 76-97356). Moderate.

***De Chaves* –** Old and austere, it faces the entrance to the old Jewish Quarter. There are 36 rooms. 25 Rua 25 do Abril, Chaves (phone: 76-21118). Inexpensive.

***Flavia* –** A tiny (7-room), simple *hospedaria* (a kind of inn), attached to a typical and inexpensive restaurant opposite the *Trajano* hotel. Be sure to visit the huge wine warehouse of Faustino e Filhos next door for a taste of local color — and wine. 12 Travessa Cândido dos Reis, Chaves (phone: 76-22513). Inexpensive.

 EATING OUT: *Dionisyos* – This bistro-style restaurant serves regional dishes, as well as *arroz de marisco,* Portugal's equivalent of bouillabaisse. It's lodged in a converted house on a medieval square (where lunch can be eaten outdoors) facing the gardens of the keep. Closed Mondays. Reservations unnecessary. Praça do Município, Chaves (phone: 76-23751). Moderate.

***Campismo* –** Homey, family-run, and simply decorated, it has excellent food, including ham-stuffed river trout, *posta de vitela na brasa* (braised veal), and *cabrito de churrasco* (barbecued kid). Try the house white or the wine from the cooperative in neighboring Valpaços. To reach the restaurant, cross Trajan's Bridge to the left bank of the Tâmega and take the first left past the campground. Closed

Thursdays. Reservations unnecessary. Largo de São Roque, Chaves (phone: 76-22912). Inexpensive.

O Pote – Busy and popular, on the outskirts of town on the road to Spain. A large regional menu is offered. Closed Mondays. Reservations unnecessary. Casa Azul, Avenida Duarte Pacheco, Chaves (phone: 76-21226). Inexpensive.

En route from Chaves – The goal is Caldas do Gerês, 71 miles (114 km) away in the Peneda-Gerês National Park. Take N103 west into countryside littered with ancient *castros* and dolmens, as well as primitive granite villages known for their dairy products and handsome, long-horned oxen. At Sapiãos, 12 miles (19 km) from Chaves, a short side trip beckons via N312 to Boticas, 2½ miles (4 km) away, and then via N311 to Carvalhelhos, another 5 miles (8 km) away. Carvalhelhos is known for its spa waters and solitude, Boticas for its wine, which is buried for a year before it is drunk. The practice developed during the Napoleonic invasions, when the villagers hid their wine from French soldiers. Later, when the bottles were dug up, the wine was found to be much improved — and wine bottles ever after have been called *mortos* (dead ones). In summer, tiny villages around Boticas pit their best bulls against each other in the *Chegas de Toiros*. The bull that manages to kill its opponent or force it to retreat is led away triumphantly, a source of great pride to its village. At the end of the season, the champion is rewarded by being put to pasture with the region's cows.

Return to N103 and, some 10½ miles (17 km) farther along, make another short detour, to the town of Montalegre, 5½ miles (9 km) away on N308. The small town is crowned by a 14th-century castle facing the peaks of the Serra do Larouco and an ancient *castro* to the north. To return to the route, follow signs to Vila Nova da Chá and then, back on N103, continue westward along the rocky north bank of the huge manmade lake formed by the Barragem do Alto Rabagão, a dam on the Rabagão River. Beyond the dam, the road crosses the river itself and proceeds along its south bank to another lake, the reservoir of the Barragem de Venda Nova, an ideal place for picnics and swimming.

After the Venda Nova Dam, the Rabagão River flows into the Rio Cávado, and the road weaves along the steep slopes above the latter, passing stone houses, water mills, and churches, with the majestic peaks of the Serra do Gerês looming to the north. About 15 miles (24 km) west of Venda Nova, just before Cerdeirinhas, turn right onto N304; as the road descends past heather and pine trees, the steep Cávado gorge appears, offering one of the most spectacular natural sights in Portugal. (Farther to the west, the power of the Cávado and its tributary, the Caldo, have been harnessed by the Barragem da Caniçada.) After passing Caniçada itself (really only a cluster of houses) and crossing a bridge, turn right onto N308-1, cross a second bridge, and drive along the wooded banks of the Caldo River past the village of Vilar de Veigas and into the spa town of Caldas do Gerês, in the Peneda-Gerês National Park.

CHECKING IN: *Pousada de São Bento* – A topnotch government-run inn modeled after an alpine chalet and located on N304 just a bit less than a mile (1.6 km) after the turnoff from N103. The establishment has 18 bedrooms (being increased to 30 at press time) and a dining room with spectacular views of the Cávado River and surrounding mountains, as well as a swimming pool. Advance reservations are required in summer. Caniçada (phone: 53-647190). Expensive.

De Carvalhelhos – This simply decorated 19-room *estalagem* (inn) surrounded by gardens and forested hills is a pleasant retreat for those in search of something quiet and away from the beaten track. Other attributes are the courteous service and the tasty regional and international dishes available in the dining room. Carvalhelhos (phone: 76-42116). Moderate.

São Cristovão – A modern motel beside the Rabagão just before the town of Venda Nova. The 18 rooms are decorated in pine and marble, and have balconies overlooking a small manmade pond. There are 2 dining rooms, one with a terrace. Venda Nova (phone: 76-659387). Moderate to inexpensive.

EATING OUT: *Santa Cruz* – A typical regional restaurant, family-run and enclosed in glass, where guests can watch their meals being prepared in the large kitchen or gaze down at the Beça River. Dine heartily on stick-to-the-ribs beef, kid, game, and mountain trout, and wash it all down with one of the village's *mortos*. Reservations unnecessary. Boticas (phone: 76-42157). Inexpensive.

CALDAS DO GERÊS: This small resort town, whose mineral springs were known to the Romans, was a fashionable spa in the 18th century and still has several quaint, turn-of-the-century hotels. Tennis, lake and pool swimming, boating, and horseback riding are all available in the area, but since the town lies at the base of a deep wooded gorge just inside the boundary of the Parque Nacional da Peneda-Gerês, it is an important base for park excursions. The 178,000-acre park, shaped like a horseshoe to encompass the Serra do Gerês on its southeastern side and the Serra da Peneda on its northwestern side, runs beyond Caldas up to the Spanish border and contains a wealth of archaeological vestiges — such as milestones and sections of Roman road — as well as waterfalls, wild ponies, rare birds, and 18 species of plants unique to the area. Hiking on marked trails, alone or with a guide, camping, fishing for trout in rivers and lakes, and organized day-long or week-long tours by bus or horseback are all possible. A recently completed *Museu Etnologico,* outside São João do Campo, offers a look at the area's crafts, home furnishings, and farm implements. (Open weekdays from 8:30 AM to noon and from 1:30 to 7 PM; on weekends, it opens a half hour earlier in the morning and closes 2 hours earlier in the evening; admission charge.)

Maps of the park are available at the park's cabin (phone: 53-39181) at the entrance to town or at the local tourist office (Avenida Manuel Francisco da Costa; phone: 53-39133). For advance tour reservations and brochures, contact Paulo Pires, *Trote-Gerês* (Cavalos Cabril, Borralha 5495; phone: 53-659292). The park headquarters, Sede do Parque Nacional (29 Rua de São Geraldo, Braga 4700; phone: 53-26472), also can mail information on the park.

CHECKING IN: *Jardim* – A *pensão* popular with travelers in search of modest accommodations (some of the 57 rooms have TV sets and VCRs, however) and wholesome home cooking. Avenida Manuel Francisco da Costa, Caldas do Gerês (phone: 53-39132). Moderate.

Parque – A turn-of-the-century hotel on the tree-lined main street. The tiled exterior, grand staircase, and carved-wood dining room with waiters in white livery are traces of a more sumptuous bygone era. There are 60 rooms; closed from mid-October to mid-May. Avenida Manuel Francisco da Costa, Caldas do Gerês (phone: 53-39112). Moderate.

Termas – Another *fin de siècle* establishment on the main street. Here, marble baths and the antique common room with fireplace recall a more luxurious era. The dining room of this 31-room hotel faces the Caldo River and the gorge, and the outdoor tables of the busy bar-café face the passing street scene. Avenida Manuel Francisco da Costa, Caldas do Gerês (phone: 53-39143). Moderate.

Geresiana – An aging Belle Epoque *pensão* with 44 rooms and a shaded courtyard. Closed from October through May. Avenida Manuel Francisco da Costa, Caldas do Gerês (phone: 53-39130). Inexpensive.

En Route from Caldas do Gerês – Return to N103 and head southwest toward Braga, 26½ miles (43 km) from Caldas. Beyond Cerdeirinhas, the landscape becomes barren, with round boulders, smoothed by time, teetering precariously on rocky crests. If there's time, take the dirt road that begins about 4 miles (6 km) beyond Cerdeirinhas, barely a mile (1 km) up to the sanctuary of São Mamede. At the summit, there's a tiny chapel and a panoramic view of the region that extends, on a clear day, as far as the Sanctuary of the Virgin on Monte Sameiro, outside Braga. Return to N103; soon the barren landscape gives way to the fertile valley of the Ave River, rich in vines and dotted with tiny hamlets. At Pinheiro, turn left to visit the castle at Póvoa de Lanhoso, about 1¼ miles (2 km) off N103. It was here that the first King of Portugal, Afonso Henriques, imprisoned his mother after defeating her forces in 1128, and here that the wife and father confessor/lover of an enraged Póvoa mayor were later burned. Póvoa de Lanhoso is also known for its goldsmiths and silversmiths, who fashion some of Portugal's famous filigree.

Braga is 10 miles (16 km) beyond Pinheiro on N103, and Porto is 33 miles (54 km) beyond Braga via N14, a road that is narrow, cluttered with towns and factories, and congested with cars and trucks. Allow 2 hours of driving time to reach Porto — avoiding, if possible, the early-morning (8 to 10 AM) and evening (5 to 8 PM) rush hours. As an alternative, the A3, a much faster road, is now available for part of the way from Braga to Porto. Pick it up about 6 miles (10 km) south of Braga. For full details on those cities, see *Braga* and *Porto,* THE CITIES.

The Beiras

Occupying a roughly horizontal strip of Portugal slightly north of the center, between the Douro River and the Tagus, the Beiras region unfolds before visitors like the pages of an age-old romance. In timeworn inns, travelers enjoy the warmth of kindly people and roaring log fires. Ancient crafts endure in picturesque villages that reverberate with the clang of smithies' anvils and the scud of feet on potters' wheels. Shepherds draped in long woolen blankets as protection from the mist and cold move their flocks from pasture to pasture. Medieval castles wreathed in legend cling to the mountains, where visitors can experience the exhilaration of tobogganing down a sunlit, snow-covered slope or hooking a trout from a tumbling river. Unexpected pleasures, like catching the white underbelly of a swooping owl in a car's headlights or the fragrance of almond blossoms on the evening breeze, reawaken a childhood sense of wonder.

The region's inspiring beauty and historical fascination have not yet been undone by mass tourism. Yet the traditional country cooking and fine local wines found in its pleasant hotels and restaurants often rival those of more sophisticated locations, and the friendly welcome surpasses them. Visitors from abroad are usually surprised by the low prices and happy to find themselves far from the madding crowd — although hotels are often fully booked during the peak *Christmas, New Year,* and summer holiday weeks.

The name Beira, meaning "edge," is thought to derive from the region's position on the edge of the central Spanish mountain range that spills over into Portugal as the Serra da Estrela. There are three Beiras. Beira Alta (Upper Beira), in the northeast, is a high plateau capped by the Serra da Estrela range, which forms the country's highest peaks. Beira Baixa (Lower Beira) drops in altitude as it slopes southward to the highlands of the Alentejo. Beira Litoral (Coastal Beira), to the west of both of these, is a lower-lying region reaching down past the city of Coimbra to the Atlantic coast.

The mountains of the Beiras ripple throughout the region. Their granite and schist rocks can be seen in the sturdy village houses and monuments that have withstood the weathering of centuries. Two main rivers, the Mondego and the Zêzere, rise in the Serra da Estrela, cutting deep valleys in the mountains on their way to the sea. High in the *serra,* gorges, glacial basins, and manmade lakes spreading out behind hydroelectric dams provide dramatic vistas; lower down, the contrast between fertile, green river valleys and craggy uplands is striking. The region's climate is relatively temperate. Winter temperatures in the Serra da Estrela are the lowest in Portugal, dropping to between 23 and 59F; in summer, they range from 50 to 68F. Elsewhere in the Beiras, winters are milder and summers hotter, but there are always cooling breezes from the river valleys. Rainfall is considerable in the mountains.

Castles, ramparts, forts, and city walls scattered across the Beiras attest to a history of invasion. Viriatus (Viriato in Portuguese), a shepherd-warrior from the Serra da Estrela, valiantly led a Celtic people known as the Lusitanians in fighting off Roman domination until his assassination (ca. 140 BC). Barbarian tribes — the Suevians and the Visigoths — later overran the province, and the Moorish invasion of Portugal and the subsequent Christian Reconquest also brought heavy fighting. The next wave of invaders came from across the border, when Philip II of Spain seized Portugal in 1580; an uprising in Lisbon in 1640 restored the country's independence, but before Spain formally recognized it in 1668, Portuguese troops had made several stands along the frontier.

Portugal's alliance with Britain against revolutionary, Napoleonic France led to the Peninsular War of 1807–10, when the French invaded three times. They were finally expelled by an Anglo-Portuguese army led by the brilliant military tactician Sir Arthur Wellesley, who later became the Duke of Wellington. Although Portugal emerged the winner, the war ravaged the country, and many treasures were lost to pillaging by both the French and the British. Traces of the military campaigns abound in the region, particularly around the ancient forest of Buçaco, where Wellington achieved his most significant victory.

Like the invasions of the past, the traditional culture of the region weaves through its history in an unbroken thread. In such a rural world, where the earth is often tilled by hand and where donkeys and oxen have not yet been totally replaced by mechanical beasts of burden, life is still dominated by the seasons. Many of the local festivals, while related to the Roman Catholic calendar, have their roots in more primitive beliefs. Spring flower festivals echo pagan fertility rites, and some *Christmas* customs, such as dances around burning *Yule* logs, hark back to the winter solstice. Almost every town and village has its patron saint, and the festivals, or *romarias,* held every year in the saint's honor provide one of the more congenial ways of discovering the region's heart. After the flower-decked statue of the saint or the Virgin is carried in procession, the town is given over to merrymaking. Under a sky brightened by carnival lights and fireworks, couples dance into the night to the sounds of brass bands and local pop groups. Stalls selling crafts and sweetmeats fill the streets, as everyone dines out on chicken and pork, grilled sardines, and flagons of wine.

Beiras farmers cultivate corn and rye in the arable land of the valleys; orchards and olive groves occupy the lower slopes and spill over onto terraces supported by granite stones as the hillsides grow steeper. Livestock is reared in the rich Upper Valley of the Zêzere. But the true wealth of the region is trees. One-third of Portugal is covered with trees, with the Beiras among the most prominent of the forested areas. The scents of pine, eucalyptus, resin, and wood smoke are pervasive. Forests, from productive extents of oaks and aleppo and umbrella pines to the hundreds of exotic varieties at Buçaco, form the backdrop to all the area's breathtaking panoramas. Timber products include resin, pitch, turpentine, and railway sleepers, and the country also has a sizable furniture industry. But wood pulp, used to make paper and cardboard, is the main product of the forests, as well as Portugal's biggest foreign currency earner after tourism and textiles.

Above the forests rise the mountains, the other key to the soul of the Beiras. Where the craggy terrain can no longer support crops, sheep and goats become the mainstay of Portugal's mountain communities, as they have been since time immemorial. The animals provide wool, milk, and, above all, *queijo da serra,* one of Portugal's most sought after delicacies. For hundreds of years, between December and May, this oozy ewe's milk cheese has been made by hand in the farmhouse dairies of the Serra da Estrela — an area of production that is now strictly limited by law. Although an industrially manufactured *queijo do tipo serra* is available more cheaply, it is no match for the real thing. The ewes are milked before dawn and again in the evening. The milk is poured through a cloth bag filled with powdered thistle flowers — a natural coagulant — and a little salt, and is heated over pine logs and broom twigs until it coagulates. It is then patiently squeezed by hand into a wooden press. The round cheeses, bound with a cloth, are cured for 2 weeks to a month until the butter-yellow rind forms; the cheese itself is pale, with a subtle sharp edge to its creaminess. Every restaurant in the region serves *queijo da serra,* and shopkeepers will be happy to help buyers choose a properly ripe one.

The Beiras also produce what many consider to be Portugal's finest wines — the smooth, strong dão reds and crisp dão whites, which take their name from the Dão River, a tributary of the Mondego. The demarcated zone centers on the town of Viseu and includes some 1,200 square miles, although vines can be grown on little more than 5% of the land. The zone's high, forested terrain, rocky granite soil, and climate of hot summers and cold, wet winters are an unlikely combination for wine production, but it is precisely these elements that give Dão reds their distinctive flavor — silky with a slight earthy tang — and their strength, averaging 12% alcohol. The whites have a hard, fresh taste. The best age for a good Dão red is 7 to 10 years, but whites get no better after 3 years, the experts say.

This route, focusing on the heart of the region where the three Beiras meet, begins in the historic university city of Coimbra and winds eastward into the Serra da Estrela mountains (encompassed since 1976 by the Serra da Estrela Natural Park, which seeks to protect the plant and animal life, as well as the environment, culture, and traditions of Portugal's most extensive and highest mountain range). It dips south across the *serra* — detouring to the summit of the 6,532-foot-high Torre, Portugal's highest peak, if desired — to the wool town of Covilhã and then travels along the verdant valley of the Zêzere River to the *serra*'s northeastern tip at Guarda, the country's highest town. A modern highway leads westward to Viseu in the heart of the Dão wine region, from where the route descends through the forested *serras* of Caramulo and Buçaco back to Coimbra.

The round-trip distance, about 500 miles (800 km), can be covered comfortably in 5 to 7 days. Distances between possible overnight stops are short, which allows for leisurely detours to villages and other sights along the way, since many attractions lie off the principal roads and are reached by branching off along the main route or traveling out from the towns. Nevertheless, drivers should be cautious and allow plenty of time for traveling; driving in the Beiras is enjoyable, but it can be taxing. Many of the roads are steep and narrow, twisting up hillsides in sharp hairpin bends, often with a precipice falling away to one side, and some are in poor repair. Allowances should be made for unexpected maneuvers by other drivers — Portugal, unfortunately, has the worst accident rate in Europe. Resist the temptation to enjoy the magnificent views from behind the wheel; instead, use the designated viewing points (signposted *miradouros*). Special care has to be taken in winter, when roads can be treacherously icy and snow occasionally makes it impossible to cross the Serra da Estrela.

Although the region has not been commercialized by tourism, it does not lack comfortable accommodations, which include the luxury of the *Palace Hotel do Buçaco* — among the finest in Europe — and other pleasant hotels, plus government-owned *pousadas* and small, welcoming inns and *pensões*. Also available, under Portugal's *Tourism in the Country* program (see *Accommodations,* GETTING READY TO GO), are rooms in privately owned houses, including the manor houses and other stately country homes that are part of the *Turismo da Habitação* network and the simpler rural houses and farmhouses categorized as *Turismo Rural* and *Agroturismo*. Most hotels are small, and booking ahead is essential for the peak summer and winter seasons, particularly at the *pousadas*. Expect to pay $70 and up for a double room in establishments listed below as expensive, $35 to $70 in moderate places, and less than $30 in inexpensive ones.

Excellent country fare — such as roast mountain kid, trout, and a delicious variety of sausages — is offered at even the simplest of restaurants, accompanied by wines that hold their own against the more famous labels of France and Italy. The majority of the best restaurants belong to hotels or pensions, leaving relatively few independent places in the listings. Most restaurant meals, including wine, will be in the moderate range, meaning from $20 to $40 for two, but there are many small places serving inexpensive meals for under $20.

COIMBRA: For a detailed report on the city, its sights, hotels, and restaurants, see *Coimbra,* THE CITIES.

En Route from Coimbra – Take N17, which leads northeast out of the city to the edge of the Serra da Estrela. You'll soon be climbing steep hills clothed in tall pine trees. Black-clad women balancing baskets on their heads, heavily laden donkey carts (often unlit at night), and terraced plots of vines and fruit trees high on the hillsides are an indication of how the people of the Beiras earn their livelihoods. After about 9½ miles (15 km), turn right onto N236 to Lousã, crossing a small river, the Arouce, which was named after an early king, Arunce, whose court was at Conímbriga. Arouce Castle, with an imposing square watchtower, dominates a nearby hillside. Historians date the fortress to the 11th century, but according to legend, it was built during the 1st century BC, when King Arunce fled to the forests to escape pirate attacks. Most of the present structure is 14th century, although it has been heavily damaged by hunters searching for the treasure the king reputedly buried somewhere inside. Ancient hermitages lie on a ridge below.

LOUSÃ: This small, busy town is deep in the Arouce valley, 5 miles (8 km) from the turnoff from N17. Here, wood from the dense forests of the Beiras is still turned into paper at the country's oldest paper mill, founded in 1718. The town has some fine 18th-century houses of aristocrats, including the white-walled Casa da Viscondessa (Rua do Visconde), whose neo-classical frontage and door were added in 1818. The green wooded hills and bare purple crests of the Serra da Lousã sweep southeast from the town, with small villages and farms dotting the forests. At the western end of the range, not far outside Lousã, is its highest peak, the 3,942-foot-high Alto do Trevim, which rewards climbers with spectacular views over much of central Portugal. Close by the peak are the Real Neveiro, or "royal snow caves," where ice used to be dug out for the court in Lisbon, and the Chapel of Santo António da Neve (St. Anthony of the Snow).

> **En Route from Lousã** – One road from Lousã leads south across the Serra da Lousã to Castelo Branco. But it is a long haul over difficult mountain roads and, despite breathtaking views, offers too few interesting stopping places to make the journey worthwhile. Instead, return to N17, turn right, and continue eastward toward Seia. After about 25 miles (40 km), a turn to the right leads to Lourosa, an ancient village noted for its pre-Romanesque church; built in the form of a basilica in 912, it is one of the rare religious monuments of its era to survive in Portugal. Continue on N17 another few miles to Venda de Galizes, turning right there onto N230 to visit some particularly picturesque Beiras villages. Follow the narrow road as it winds through terraced orchards and vineyards amid magnificent mountain views and turn right at the first crossroads, where the tiered granite houses of the village of Avô, rising from the far side of the banks of the Alva River, can be glimpsed below.

AVÔ: One of the most attractive of the Beiras' many pleasant villages, Avô has a quiet rural charm that belies its somewhat turbulent past. The village, dating back to the 12th century, was part of a line of defense during the Reconquest of Portugal from the Moors, and in the early years of this century, when the country became a republic, it was at the center of a short-lived effort to restore the monarchy. Before crossing the narrow bridge that leads into the village, stop in the courtyard beside the Igreja Matriz (Parish Church). The restored 18th-century church, of medieval origin, has a distinctive entrance with round bell towers rising on each side, linked by a crowning arch; inside is a precious baroque altarpiece. Across the bridge, narrow cobblestone steets, steep alleys, and mossy stone steps weave around Avô's ancient houses, some dating from the 15th and 16th centuries. The sadly dilapidated house of Brás Garcia de Mascarenhas, an early-17th-century poet and adventurer, stands by the water (to the left of the bridge when leaving the village). Modified during the 18th century, it has a beautiful Manueline window at the rear.

> **En Route from Avô** – Return to the crossroads and N230, taking it east a mile or so to the curious Ponte das Três Entradas (Bridge of the Three Entrances), where three roads meet, simultaneously crossing the Alvoco and Alva Rivers at their junction. Turn right from the bridge to climb the Serra do Colcurinho to Aldeia das Dez. (In driving these steep narrow roads with their tight hairpin bends, it is not surprising to learn that one of the toughest stages of the *Portuguese Motor Rally,* considered one of the most grueling rallies in the world, is held at

Arganil, less than 15 miles — 24 km — away.) Just before reaching the village, stop at the Miradouro Penedo da Saudade to take in the exhilarating view.

ALDEIA DAS DEZ: The name, meaning Village of the Ten, derives from the ten houses that gave the settlement its start during the 12th century. Clustered in the folds of the *serra,* Aldeia das Dez is banked too steeply to be traversed easily by streets and is consequently threaded through with cobblestone steps. The stone pillory, a symbol of municipal authority found in towns throughout Portugal, is dated 1661. Most of the village's dwellings are in traditional Beiras style, the lower part built solidly of granite, with wooden balconies sheltered by the roof eaves. Similarly, the life lived here is typical of a Beiras farming village — witness the goatskins hung out to dry, the stacks of pine logs dotted about the streets, and the men returning from the fields with hoes on their shoulders.

En Route from Aldeia das Dez – Return to N17 at Venda de Galizes and, about 3 miles (5 km) farther east, turn left onto the northern stretch of N230, leading to Oliveira do Hospital. In 1120, Queen Teresa gave this small town to the crusading Order of the Hospitalers of St. John of Jerusalem, and several important figures of the order were born here. Today, a statue in homage to Beiras shepherds stands in the tree-lined square. The parish church, built from the 13th to the 14th centuries and reconstructed during the 17th, is noted for the 13th-century funerary chapel of a local nobleman and his wife, whose figures, sculpted in Ança stone, lie above their tombs below a painted altar carved in the same stone.

Return to N17 and continue northeast 10½ miles (17 km), skirting the edge of the Parque Natural da Serra da Estrela (Serra da Estrela Natural Park). Turn right onto N231 at the crossroads signposted Seia. The town is 2 miles (3 km) farther along, inside the park at the foot of the mountains.

CHECKING IN: *Pousada de Santa Bárbara* – This modern member of the government-run *pousada* chain was built in the 1970s. It's set among pines on the western edge of the Serra da Estrela, 2 miles (3 km) along N17 from the Oliveira do Hospital turnoff. Visitors can warm themselves in front of a log fire in the wood-paneled interior and enjoy the view across the hills from the excellent restaurant. There are 16 secluded rooms, plus tennis courts and a swimming pool. Póvoa das Quartas (phone: 38-52252). Expensive.

Casa do Boco – A participant in *Turismo Rural,* this is a large Beiras house in the village of Meruge, on the Cobral River 5 miles (8 km) north of Oliveira do Hospital. Two apartments with double bedrooms are available, for a minimum of 2 nights. Contact Dona Maria da Conceição Antunes, *Casa do Boco,* Meruge, Lagares da Beira (phone: 38-54118). Moderate.

São Paulo – This comfortable hostelry in the center of town has 44 rooms, all with bath, as well as a restaurant. Rua Professor Antunes Varela, Oliveira do Hospital (phone: 38-52361). Moderate.

SEIA: Set at the foot of the Serra da Estrela, Seia is light and airy, with broad streets. The parish church, of Romanesque origin but rebuilt after the Napoleonic wars of the early 19th century, dominates it from a hilltop. The ancient town was captured from the Moors in 1057 and officially recognized as a municipality in 1136. An imposing 18th-century palace, the Casa das Obras, also known as the Solar dos Albuquerques, houses the Town Hall; the future Duke of Wellington used it as his headquarters during the French invasions. Other landmarks nearby are the Solar dos Botelhos, a restored 16th-century granite manor house with three Manueline windows; the 18th-century Misericórdia church; and the pillory. Many of Seia's residents work in the dairy plant in the southern part of the town, and the shops in the streets around the main square

are a good place to buy *queijo da serra,* the ewe's milk cheese that is justly famed among Portugal's cheeses. There are also several handicraft shops here selling sheepskin, pottery, and copper products.

CHECKING IN/EATING OUT: *Camelo* – Fairly new, highly regarded, and decorated with antiques, it replaces a previous hotel that was destroyed by fire. The 57 rooms and suites have wood-paneled ceilings, marble-fitted bathrooms, and TV sets. The restaurant is one of only five in the country distinguished with an award by the Portuguese government; specialties include *sopa à nossa moda* (a vegetable and veal soup), *bacalhau com broa* (codfish with corn bread and almonds), and *requeijão,* a farmer cheese served as dessert. 86 Largo Marquês da Silva, Seia (phone: 38-22530). Moderate.

Seia – This old granite *estalagem,* or inn, has 35 rooms and a restaurant. Avenida Afonso Costa, Seia (phone: 38-22666). Moderate.

Serra da Estrela – A pleasant *pensão* with 21 rooms and a restaurant, where the specialties include *bife com queijo* (steaks with cheese) and *perna de porco com puré de maçã* (roast leg of pork with apple sauce). Rua Dr. Simões Pereira, Seia (phone: 38-22573). Inexpensive.

En Route from Seia – Before penetrating the Serra da Estrela, check the large blue board beside the Misericórdia church. It indicates whether the roads across the mountain — which are sometimes blocked by snow for short periods from November to May — are passable (marked white) or closed (red). If the route is clear, take N339 and climb 7 miles (11 km) for a look at Sabugueiro, the highest village in Portugal, now crowded with souvenir stalls and shops. Then double back toward Seia and turn right at the first crossroads onto N339-1. (There is a more direct route from Sabugueiro to N339-1, along 3 miles — 5 km — of dirt road, but it is recommended only for the adventurous.)

At the next junction, with N232, a right turn leads to Manteigas, but those with time to spare may want to take the left turn to Gouveia, an attractive, ancient town in the hills rising from the Mondego valley. Either way, the road climbs into a desolate landscape where granite crags are strewn with massive boulders, some whipped into strange shapes by the wind and snow. One such boulder, on the right on the way to Gouveia, has been sculpted by the elements into the perfect picture of a toothless old man and is known, fittingly, as the Cabeça do Velho, or Old Man's Head. Mountain flowers blossom among the scrub of grass, heather, and juniper — the latter (*zimbro* in Portuguese) used to brew the fiery white brandy, *aguardente de zimbro,* found all over the Beiras.

CHECKING IN/EATING OUT: *Casa do Sabugueiro* – Part of the *Turismo Rural* program, it offers the chance to stay in a traditional village house, complete with *queijaria,* or cheese dairy, and bread oven. The apartment available has 2 double bedrooms, a living room, kitchen, and bathroom. Contact Dona Teresa da Graça Trindade, *Casa do Sabugueiro,* Sabugueiro (phone: 38-22825). Moderate.

O Abrigo da Montanha – This is a modern *pensão* with 25 rooms, a restaurant, bar, and its own discotheque. Sabugueiro (phone: 38-22394). Inexpensive.

GOUVEIA: The town reputedly dates back to the 6th century BC. Just outside of town, it's possible to climb to a pre-Roman fortification, the *castro* of Alfatima, where Julius Caesar is said to have stayed in 38 BC. (The *castro* takes its name from a later time when Christians and Moors battled over Gouveia, and Fatima, the beautiful daughter of an Arab emir, is supposed to have fled to the mountain with her jewels.) One of the most attractive buildings in town is the Casa da Torre, a late-17th-century manor house with the sculpted ropes of the Manueline style wreathing its windows. The exterior of the 18th-century parish church of São Pedro was renovated in 1940 with blue-and-white tiles depicting religious scenes. The imposing *paço* (Town Hall) was also built during the 18th century, originally as a Jesuit school, although the Jesuits were able to use it for only a few years before they were expelled from Portugal by the Marquês de Pombal. The building became a military hospital during the Peninsular War and later a barracks. An esplanade leading off the small baroque Calvário chapel affords splendid views.

In March, a fair dedicated to *queijo da serra* takes place in Gouveia, but all of the rural trades and crafts around which local life revolves are on display during the *Festas do Senhor do Calvário*, a summer festival held during the second or third week of August. A religious procession and folk dances are the highlights of the festival, but part of the event is devoted to the dark honey of the Beiras — which owes its special flavor to the mountain flowers the bees feed on — and to a competition for Serra da Estrela sheepdogs. As they did in pre-Roman times, these fine dogs still protect their flocks from foxes, wild boar, and, it is said, wolves; a kennel that raises them — the Canil dos Montes — can be visited in the vicinity. It's located at Algueiro, on the southern edge of Gouveia, and welcomes visitors during working hours. (But don't fall in love with the puppies. There usually are waiting lists for all litters. On the other hand, specialists advise smitten visitors not to buy dogs from shops and roadside stands, where they may not be purebreds. All pure sheepdogs should have proof of pedigree.)

CHECKING IN/EATING OUT: *Casa Grande* – Three apartments with double bedrooms are available in the 16th-century manor and adjoining 18th-century house at this *Turismo Rural* participant in Paços da Serra, 5 miles (8 km) south of Gouveia on N232. Extra rooms can be provided for larger families. Breakfast and firewood in the winter are included. Contact Dona Maria Amelia Ribeiro Saraiva, *Casa Grande,* Paços da Serra (phone: 38-43341, or 2-816587). Moderate.

Gouveia – In the center of town, this hostelry has 27 rooms, all with central heating and telephones (4 additional suites also have living rooms and TV sets). Guests have access to the municipal swimming pool and tennis courts. The restaurant serves regional dishes including trout, roast kid, and *fritada serrana,* a fried dish using several kinds of local sausage. Avenida Primeiro de Maio, Gouveia (phone: 38-42890). Moderate.

Estrela do Parque – A 25-room *pensão* with a pretty restaurant that serves regional food. 36 Avenida da República, Gouveia (phone: 38-42171). Inexpensive.

En Route from Gouveia – Retrace the route south on N232, following signs for Manteigas. Not too far after the road bends east, in the vicinity of the junction with N339-1 from Sabugueiro, a signpost indicates the Nascente do Mondego to the right. It is from this spring, at an altitude of 4,462 feet, that the most important of the Portuguese rivers that begin within the country descends, to flow eventually through Coimbra and out to the sea at Figueira da Foz.

Back on N232 to Manteigas, another turn to the right climbs for 2 miles (3 km) to a magnificent view of the Penhas Douradas, a line of three peaks called "golden crests" because they glow in the setting sun. They rise up to 5,471 feet and, like other Serra da Estrela summits, remain capped with snow for all but the three hottest summer months. Continuing to Manteigas, the road begins to descend through 9 miles (14 km) of tortuous bends to the town, which lies at an altitude of 2,362 feet. The scenery is superb: Small waterfalls cascade down the mossy rocks, tumbling through tunnels under the road or freezing into a wild filigree of ice in winter. Tall pines provide green, leafy shade, while ferns, golden and red in the fall, light up the slopes.

MANTEIGAS: This picturesque town is deep in the valley of the Zêzere River. Its white, pink, and beige houses reflect the bright mountain light; the air is crisp and invigorating, the tranquillity refreshing. Viriatus and his Lusitanian warriors are reputed to have used it as one of their last refuges from the Romans during the 2nd century BC. The parish church, with twin bell towers, is of Roman origin, although it betrays no evidence of its beginnings, presenting instead a baroque structure that has been considerably altered over the centuries. The square beside the church has a charming bandstand and offers engaging views over the town's steep, tiled rooftops.

CHECKING IN: *Pousada de São Lourenço* – A 19-room *pousada* of modern vintage, but built of granite high in the hills along the descent to Manteigas from the Penhas Douradas, 8 miles (13 km) north of town. It has wooden paneling, roaring fireplaces, and marvelous views from its balconies and terraces. The restaurant staff, in local costume, serves a wealth of excellent regional dishes and wines. Estrada de Gouveia, Manteigas (phone: 75-98150). Expensive.

***Casa de São Roque* –** At this 3-story townhouse, a *Turismo Rural* participant, visitors can walk out onto the terrace overlooking the valley. A suite and 5 double bedrooms, together with several living rooms, are available. Contact Dona Maria Capelo Ramos, *Casa de São Roque,* 67 Rua de António, Manteigas (phone: 75-47125). Moderate.

***De Manteigas* –** This is a comfortable, restful hotel offering fine views from the mountainside at Caldas de Manteigas, a small spa 2 miles (3 km) south of town. It has 54 rooms, tennis courts, and a good restaurant. Caldas de Manteigas (phone: 75-98514). Moderate.

En Route from Manteigas – Leave town heading south on N338, passing through Caldas de Manteigas, a small spa town with Alpine-style houses, where visitors can take a sauna during the summer months. Cross the bridge over the Zêzere, whose waters splash over the rocks below and operate a nearby water mill. Here it's possible to visit a fish farm, the Posto Aquícola da Fonte Santa (open daily from 9:30 to 11 AM and from 1 to 5 PM; no admission charge), to see trout gleaming in the clear water before they are released into mountain lakes and rivers. A narrow, poorly surfaced road turns off to the left, leading about 4 miles (6 km) up through stirring views to the Poço de Inferno (Well of Hell), where a cataract crashes from wooded heights into a limpid pool below. (In winter, it freezes into a wild weave of ice.)

Continue on N338 as it follows the Upper Valley of the Zêzere — actually a deep trough formed by an Ice Age glacier. Springs and waterfalls tumble down the slopes into the river, and cabins of rough stone, some built in crevices beneath huge boulders, dot the hillsides. As the route climbs toward Torre, the highest point in Portugal (its name, in fact, means tower), snow-covered peaks emerge. At the first crossroads, with N339, a left turn leads to Covilhã; but turn to the right, if there's time, to reach the Torre summit. Pale green moss and lichen lend the strangely shaped rocks an otherworldly appearance as the road rises higher and higher, with the lake of the Covão do Ferro dam below on the left. A little farther on, to the right, a statue of Nossa Senhora da Boa Estrela (Our Lady of the Holy Star) has been carved in relief in the black granite. Stone steps lead up to this sanctuary, where a religious festival marked by a long procession is held each year on the second Sunday in August.

The road continues, well surfaced, sufficiently broad, and not too steep; drivers who branch off left at the signpost can drive half a mile right onto the Torre summit, 6,532 feet above sea level. A stone tower was built to take the peak up to the round figure of 2,000 meters, or 6,560 feet, but this has since been topped by the higher domes of two meteorological observatories. Also known as the Malhão da Estrela (which could be loosely translated as the "High Shot" of the Estrela), Torre is a favorite destination for excursions — the circular road around the top is ringed with cafés and stalls selling regional food, crafts, and souvenirs. The views are magnificent.

Return to N339 and head east for the steep descent to Covilhã, a town tucked into the folds of the mountains at the southeastern edge of the Serra da Estrela Natural Park. The road passes through pine, oak, and chestnut woods along the way, and through Penhas da Saude, a base for skiers that's in full swing from December to May. There are two ski runs with lifts: the 1,246-foot slope at Piornos, between Penhas da Saude and Torre (although for the past several years there hasn't been enough snow for this one to be used), and the 2,590-foot Covão de Loriga slope, which falls away westward from the summit of Torre itself. Ski lessons are available, equipment can be rented, and other activities, such as hiking, climbing, fishing, and camping, are also possible. For further information, contact the *Clube Nacional de Montanhismo* (5 Rua Pedro Alvares Cabral, Covilhã; phone: 75-23364; or the Sede da Região de Turismo da Serra da Estrela, Praça do Município, Covilhã; phone: 75-22151).

CHECKING IN/EATING OUT: *O Pastor* – A small, 8-room *estalagem* with ski equipment and toboggans for hire, and a log fire in the lounge for warmth and atmosphere; there's also central heating. Specialties of the restaurant include both the traditional Portuguese bean-and-pork stew known as *feijoada* and *bacalhau à Pastor,* a dried codfish dish made with grated cheese and cream. Restaurant open daily in the winter and summer peak seasons and closed 1 day weekly (variable) the rest of the year. Penhas da Saude (phone: 75-22810). Moderate.

COVILHÃ: From Torre to this congenial town on the southeastern slopes of the *serra,* the road drops from 6,532 feet to 2,296 feet in only 12½ miles (20 km). Don't drive too fast or your ears might pop! Covilhã is an ancient town, thought to have been founded by the Romans in 41 BC. For centuries, its life has revolved around the flocks of sheep that graze on the mountains, providing raw materials for the town's main industries: dairy products such as *queijo da serra* and wool. But today, much of its livelihood also derives from the winter sports enthusiasts who flock to the area. The intimate relationship with the Serra da Estrela comes as no surprise — almost every street in town offers a stirring panorama of the mountains above and the plains to the south and east.

Covilhã became the center of Portugal's cloth making industry during the 15th century, famed not only for its wool but also for silk, cotton, and linen. From the beginning, the industry struggled against competition from imported fabrics, particularly from Britain. Foreign textiles were outlawed in 1677, but only 26 years later, in 1703, Portugal and Britain signed the Methuen Treaty, which facilitated the entry of British cloth into Portugal while providing a boost for Portuguese exports of port wine to Britain. The agreement dealt a heavy blow to the cloth makers of Covilhã, despite King João V's support in 1710, when he awarded the town a contract to supply his army with uniforms.

Half a century later, in 1755, nature dealt the town a second blow. The earthquake that devastated Lisbon also destroyed many of Covilhã's houses and most of the town walls, with their five gates. The Marquês de Pombal, the prime minister who oversaw the rebuilding of the capital, ordered a textile factory built in Covilhã, using stones from the fallen walls. (The Fábrica Real, on Avenida Marquês d'Avila Bolama, now houses the Beira Interior University Institute.) By the mid-1800s, as many as 7,000 workers were employed in the town's cloth mills; more recently, local cloth makers have again suffered the effects of less expensive foreign imports and the massive artificial fiber industry.

Despite its history, Covilhã, with its trees and gardens, has little of the appearance of an industrial town. The main square, Praça do Município, features a statue of Pero de Covilhã, a 15th-century explorer and adventurer who was born here. The Palacete-Jardim (Avenida Frei Heitor Pinto) is an attractive example of *azulejos,* or painted tiles, and architecture from the turn-of-the-century Art Nouveau period. (The building now houses a regional delegation of the Labor Ministry.) The Capela de São Martinho e Calvário, in the lower part of town, is a simple Romanesque chapel of rough stone housing an 18th-century painting of the Crucifixion and two primitive representations of saints.

 CHECKING IN: *Montalto* – A small *pensão* on the main square, it has 15 rooms, all with bath. No restaurant, but breakfast is served. Praça do Município, Covilhã (phone: 75-25091). Moderate.

***Solneve* –** This 36-room hotel, in an old (but modernized) building, is in the town center. It has a noted restaurant that specializes in regional dishes, including *lingua estufada* (braised tongue) and roast mountain kid. 126 Avenida Visconde da Coriscada, Covilhã (phone: 75-23001). Moderate.

 EATING OUT: *Café Regional* – Although this is a good, modest *pensão* in the center, with 20 rooms, it is especially recommended for its restaurant, which serves regional specialties such as *panela no forno,* a rice dish made with pork. The restaurant is closed Sunday evenings, Mondays, and the first 2 weeks of September. Reservations unnecessary. 4-5 Rua das Flores, Covilhã (phone: 75-22596). Inexpensive.

En route from Covilhã – Take N18 north out of town. The road winds through the green, fertile valley of the Zêzere — the river basin here is a rich farming region known as the Cova da Beira — up to Guarda, 24 miles (38 km) from Covilhã. About halfway to Guarda, make a short detour to the right onto N345, signposted Belmonte. This hilltop town, commanded by a medieval castle, was the birthplace of Pedro Alvares Cabral, who discovered Brazil in 1500; the Romanesque São Tiago church, where he is buried, can be seen. Back on N18, the next right turn, the road to Comeal da Torre, leads to the impressive ruins of what was probably a Roman-Lusitanian inn, known as the Centum Cellas.

GUARDA: High on an exposed hilltop overlooking Spain (the border is only 29½ miles — 47 km — away), this town of granite buildings, lantern-lit alleys, and pillared balconies breathes a medieval atmosphere that brings its history vividly to life. Buffeted by rough winds and winter snow, Guarda, at 3,281 feet, is the highest town in Portugal, and its hardy, hearty character reflects its historic role as the first stronghold against successive invasions from across the frontier. To the Portuguese, the town is known as *feia, forte, farta, e fria,* meaning "ugly, strong, plentiful, and cold." Visitors enjoying its traditional hospitality today are likely to take issue only with the adjective ugly.

Guarda has been settled since prehistoric times, and Julius Caesar is thought to have used it as a military base. The Visigoths and then the Moors took it; after Afonso Henriques, the first King of Portugal, recaptured it, the town was enlarged, fortified, and officially founded by King Sancho I, in 1199. A statue of Sancho stands in the main square, the Praça da Sé (also known as Praça Luís de Camões), to the north of which stands the Sé itself, a magnificent cathedral whose granite stones look almost as pristine as the day they were cut from the surrounding hills more than 500 years ago. To the right is the Paços de Concelho, the Town Hall, and to the left is the charming building housing the tourist office (phone: 71-22251). On the south side is a gallery of shops and houses.

The cathedral was begun in 1390 and completed in 1540, a passage of time that resulted in a mixture of Renaissance and Manueline styles with the original Gothic. The flying buttresses, pinnacles, and gargoyles of the exterior are reminiscent of the monastery at Batalha, a masterpiece of Portuguese architecture that similarly mixes Gothic with Manueline. (The two buildings both feature work by the master architect Boytac and the Mateus Fernandes family.) The cathedral's main doorway, flanked by two octagonal bell towers, is Manueline; inside is a vaulted interior containing a Renaissance altarpiece by Jean de Rouen. It consists of more than 100 figures, sculpted in high relief and painted in gold and white, depicting scenes from the life of Christ on panels that rise to the arched windows. Also of note, through a magnificent Renaissance doorway, is the Capela dos Pinas, which holds the late Gothic tomb of a cathedral founder. He is said to have thrown himself from the roof after he asked the people if the building had any defects — and an old lady replied that the door was too small! The cathedral is open to visitors from 10 AM to 12:30 PM and from 2 to 5:30 PM; closed Mondays. There is a charge to climb to the top of the towers.

From the Praça da Sé, walk through an ancient alleyway to the Torre dos Ferreiros (Blacksmiths' Tower), one of three of the original six gates still standing amid the ruins of the 12th- and 13th-century town walls. (The other two are the Porta da Estrela and the Porta do Rei; the castle keep, or Torre de Menagem, also remains from the original fortifications.) Cross the tree-lined street to the restored 17th-century Misericórdia Church, with its attractive white pediment between two pinnacled bell towers; it has a carved wooden ceiling and a baroque altar and pulpits. Farther along the same street is the *Museu da Guarda* (phone: 71-23460), housed in the 17th-century Bishop's Palace, which has been elegantly modernized and extended. Primitive paintings, sculptures, and ancient town manuscripts are on the ground floor; upstairs are examples of the timeless trades and handicrafts of the region, ranging from linen weaving and silk making to basketry, pottery, and ironwork (open from 10 AM to 1 PM and from 2 to 6 PM, mid-March to mid-September, to 5 PM the rest of the year; closed Mondays; admission charge).

CHECKING IN: *Solar de Alarcão* – A night at this 17th-century manor house, within yards of the cathedral, is a delightful way to experience Guarda. A *Turismo de Habitação* property, it has a covered terrace, a private chapel, and a garden with a belvedere offering views over the Spanish plains. The 3 double bedrooms and suite for 4 people are beautifully decorated with antiques and tapestries. President Mário Soares inaugurated this place as an accommodation for tourists when he spent 8 days in the suite during a presidential visit to the town in 1986. Contact Solar de Alarcão, *Solar de Alarcão,* Largo Dom Miguel Alarcão, Guarda (phone: 71-21275). Expensive.

Filipe – In the town center, this is a comfortable *pensão* with 40 rooms (not all with private bath) and a restaurant. 9 Rua Vasco da Gama, Guarda (phone: 71-22658). Moderate.

Turismo – A sprawling, imposing building with views across the plains, it has 105 rooms and suites, all with private bath, TV sets, and mini-bars. There are 3 bars, a private discotheque, a swimming pool, and a garage. The large restaurant serves Portuguese and international food. Avenida Coronel Orlindo de Carvalho, Guarda (phone: 71-22205). Moderate.

EATING OUT: *A Mexicana* – Less than a mile (1 km) out of town on the road to Spain, this is a good restaurant whose specialties include *tornedós à mexicana,* or tournedos of beef, *lombinho à Beira Alta,* a pork loin dish, *garoupa com môlho de camarão,* or grouper with shrimp sauce, and shellfish. Open for lunch and dinner daily, except for 2 weeks' annual vacation (variable). Reservations unnecessary. Estrada Nacional 16, Guarda (phone: 71-21512). Moderate.

O Telheiro – A bit farther (about a mile/1 km) from the town center on the road to Spain, this large dining room offers panoramic views and good regional cooking, as well as French and Italian dishes. Meals can be served on the terrace in fine weather, or visitors can recover from the winter cold in a bar with deep leather armchairs and a log fire. Open for lunch and dinner daily. Reservations unnecessary. Estrada Nacional 16, Guarda (phone: 71-21356). Moderate.

Casa Reduto – Good home cooking in a small friendly place in the town center. Specialties include kid and *choriçada,* based on a variety of homemade sausages. It's open for lunch and dinner daily but sometimes closes for a month in summer. Reservations unnecessary. 36 Rua Francisco de Passos, Guarda (phone: 71-21879). Inexpensive.

En Route from Guarda – Following signs out of Guarda for Viseu will lead the traveler to the modern highway, IP5, that cuts across the northern tip of the Serra da Estrela some 55 miles (88 km) west to Viseu. About halfway there, in the town of Mangualde, just off the highway to the left, is a 17th-century aristocratic estate, the Palácio dos Condes de Anadia, with some fine 17th- and 18th-century *azulejos* (open daily, from 2 to 6 PM, and occasionally also in the morning; admission charge).

VISEU: A fresh-faced country town set among vineyards, orchards, and pine-forested hills, Viseu exudes life and a long, cultured history. Every Tuesday, crowds jostle amid the colorful stalls of the weekly market on the narrow, medieval streets of the old town. In August and September, people from across the Beiras flock to the annual *São Mateus* fair (black pottery, lace, and carpets are among the traditional crafts to look for). And every June 24, a procession of horseback riders and floats from outlying Vil de Moinhos (Village of the Water Mills) winds through town to the chapel of São João de Carreira. According to tradition, the annual procession began in 1652 as a gesture of thanks from the millers of Vil de Moinhos to their patron saint, John the Baptist, after a dispute with local farmers over the use of water from the Paiva River was decided in their favor. Rich corn bread, or *broas,* baked from flour milled in Vil de Moinhos can still be bought in Viseu's market, while the cakes and sweetmeats found in the local cafés — *ovos moles* (soft eggs), *papos de anjo* (angel's cheeks), and *bolos d'amor* (love cakes), made from eggs, almonds, and lots of sugar — come from old convent recipes.

Walk up the hill from the tree-lined main square, Praça da República, or Rossio, through the Porta do Soar, a 15th-century gate that leads into the old town, and turn right to the Adro da Sé (Cathedral Square), the historical heart of Viseu. On the left, strikingly silhouetted against the sky, is the white façade of the Igreja da Misericórdia, a pure baroque church with twin bell towers and a delicate doorway topped by a balcony. Built during the late 18th century, it now holds a magnificent organ. Across the square are the weathered granite towers of the Sé (Cathedral), which dates from the 13th century but was extensively restored between the 16th and 18th centuries. Inside, its graceful vaulting of knotted ropes reflects the seafaring themes of the 16th-century Manueline style, while its gilded wood altarpiece is baroque. The sacristy has 16th-century tiled walls and a wooden ceiling painted with plants and animals; from the Renaissance cloister, a beautiful late Gothic doorway leads back into the church.

The *Museu de Grão Vasco,* perhaps Viseu's greatest treasure, is housed in the former 16th-century Bishop's Palace next door to the cathedral. Grão Vasco — the Great Vasco — is the name given to Vasco Fernandes (1480–ca. 1543), the founder of a notable school of painting that flourished in Viseu during the 16th century. Two of his masterpieces, a *Calvary* and *St. Peter on His Throne,* are on display in the museum, along with a series of 14 panels, originally from the cathedral altarpiece, painted by him and his collaborators. (One of the kings in the *Adoration of the Magi* from this series is represented in the form of an Indian from newly discovered Brazil.) The collection also contains two paintings — *The Last Supper* and *Christ in the House of Martha* — by Gaspar Vaz, another master of the Viseu school. The museum (phone: 32-26249) is open from 9:30 AM to 12:30 PM and 2 to 5 PM from April through October (opens at 10 AM from November through March); closed Mondays; admission charge.

The remains of the enormous trenches of a Roman encampment can be visited in a park in the northern outskirts of town. The camp, known as the Cava de Viriato (Pit of Viriatus), was originally octagonal, but only two sides remain. It was dug for imperial Roman legions during a campaign against the Galicians in 138 BC, and although it was not used by Viriatus, the Serra da Estrela shepherd-warrior who led the Lusitanians against Portugal's Roman invaders, a bronze monument to him and his warriors stands in the park.

 CHECKING IN: *Avenida* – Comfortable and just off the main square, it has 40 rooms. The restaurant serves regional dishes. 1 Avenida Alberto Sampaio, Viseu (phone: 32-23432). Moderate.

***Grão Vasco* –** Set in attractive gardens in the town center, this spacious hostelry has 86 rooms (with another 24 being added at press time), an outdoor swimming pool, a discotheque, and central heating. The restaurant serves meals on the garden terrace in good weather. Rua Gaspar Barreiros, Viseu (phone: 32-23511). Moderate.

***Maná* –** Some 2½ miles (4 km) from the center, along N16 to the east, this hotel offers television sets, radios, and telephones in its 46 rooms. It also has a restaurant, a garden, and a car park. Via Caçador, Viseu (phone: 32-26143). Moderate.

***Moinho de Vento* –** Here there are 30 modern rooms, with television sets, radios, and telephones, near the main square (Rossio). Breakfast is served, but there's no restaurant. 13 Rua Paulo Emílio, Viseu (phone: 32-24116). Moderate.

***Quinta do Vale do Chão* –** This fine granite house, a Turismo Rural participant, offers a double bedroom, bathroom, and large living room — and the freedom of the rest of the house. It's located 10 miles (16 km) south of Viseu on N231 at Santar, the birthplace of Dom Duarte de Bragança, the man who would be king if Portugal were still a monarchy. The small village has many attractive 18th-century houses. Contact Dona Berta Bebiano Coimbra, *Quinta do Vale do Chão,* Santar, Nelas (phone in Lisbon: 1-765974). Moderate.

 EATING OUT: *O Cortiço* – An excellent restaurant in the medieval part of town, it serves dishes based on old local recipes, whose details are kept secret. Specialties include *arroz caqueirado,* a veal-and-rice dish; *coelho bêbado,* made from wine-fed ("drunken") rabbits; and *bacalhau podre,* a tasty dish worthy of a better name than this, which means "rotten codfish!" Open for lunch and dinner daily except *Christmas.* Reservations necessary. 43 Rua Augusto Hilário, Viseu (phone: 32-23853). Moderate.

***Trave Negra* –** Also in the old part of town, it specializes in traditional dishes, including kid and *espetadas* — kebab-style meat or fish on a skewer. Closed Mondays. Reservations advised. 4 Rua dos Loureiros, Viseu (phone: 32-26138). Moderate.

En Route from Viseu – Take N2 south 15 miles (24 km) through wooded hills to Tondela, then turn right onto N230, following signs for Caramulo, another 12 miles (19 km) away. The N230 highway winds up through the wild pine, oak, and chestnut woods of the Serra do Caramulo, dense with ferns and brambles and interspersed with terraces of olive and other fruit trees and vines.

CARAMULO: This small, well-groomed health resort full of cypress trees and box hedges stands at an altitude of 2,500 feet, basking in crisp air and exhilarating views. The *Museu de Caramulo* (also named after its founder, Abel de Lacerda) features an unexpected mixture of vintage cars and fine art. The automobiles, all in pristine condition, include a 1911 Rolls-Royce, classic 1930s Bugattis, a 1924 Hispano-Suiza, and the suitably sober 1937 armored Mercedes used by António de Oliveira Salazar, Portugal's former dictator. Upstairs, the art collection includes a few lesser known works by Picasso, Dalí, and Chagall, some fine Portuguese primitives, and 16th-century tapestries. The museum (phone: 32-861270) is open daily from 10 AM to 6 PM; admission charge.

Several imposing panoramas are within easy reach of Caramulo. Drive 5 miles (8 km) west along Avenida Abel de Lacerda, which becomes N230-3, to reach the foot of Caramulinho, the highest peak of the Serra do Caramulo. It's possible to climb a steep, rocky path to the summit, 3,527 feet high, for an impressive view. Returning toward Caramulo, branch right to Cabeço da Neve, a 3,264-foot-high peak with a view south over the villages of the Mondego River valley. Pinoucas, a 3,481-foot-high peak offering a magnificent panorama over the *serra,* is 2 miles (3 km) north of Caramulo, traveling first along N230 and then a dirt road.

CHECKING IN/EATING OUT: *Pousada de São Jerónimo* – A modern, government-owned inn with spectacular views from the 6 guestrooms and the dining room. Roaring fires, wooden beams, and an elegant restaurant make this an excellent setting in which to enjoy mountain walks, trout fishing, and seclusion. There also is a badminton court and an outdoor swimming pool. Estrada Nacional 230, Caramulo (phone: 32-861291). Expensive.

En Route from Caramulo – Follow N230 back toward Tondela and turn right onto N2. Santa Comba Dão, a pretty village where the Dão flows into the Mondego, is 10 miles (16 km) farther south. It is best known as Salazar's birthplace, but no statue remains of the dictator, and his abandoned family house has fallen into disrepair. Turn right at Santa Comba Dão onto N234, passing the lovely village of Mortágua on the 16-mile (26-km) journey to the Mata do Buçaco — the ancient forest of Buçaco — and the famed spa of Luso.

BUÇACO: A secluded forest that was tended by monks for more than 1,000 years, the stirring history of a decisive battle, and a romantic summer palace built by a king are all woven into the magic of Buçaco, a 2-square-mile national park atop the northernmost peak of the Serra do Buçaco. Benedictine monks first built a refuge in the primitive forest during the 6th century, and priests from Coimbra cared for the woodland from the 11th to the early 17th century. In 1628, barefoot Carmelite monks began erecting a monastery, ringing the forest with a wall to keep the outside world at bay. The monks carefully tended their domain, adding maples, laurels, Mexican cedars, and many exotic varieties from seeds gathered by their missions around the globe. Earlier, in 1622, a papal bull had banned women from the forest, and in 1643, a second bull prohibited damage to the trees — punishment for either offense was excommunication. (Inscriptions bearing the texts of the bulls can be seen on the walls of the Portas de Coimbra, one of the seven gates in the ancient walls.) Even after religious orders were suppressed in Portugal in 1834 and the care of Buçaco passed to the state, the forest has continued to grow — there are now some 400 native tree varieties and 300 exotic ones, from eucalyptus and oaks to sequoias and evergreen thujas.

In 1888, King Carlos commissioned Luigi Manini, an Italian architect and a set painter at the São Carlos opera house in Lisbon, to build a summer palace and hunting lodge in the midst of the forest. Much of the Carmelite monastery, including the library, was demolished to make way for it, leaving only a small church and a cloister. The building that emerged is a marvelously extravagant pastiche of the Manueline style, with pinnacles, battlements, towers, arched windows, and a magnificent gallery of 12 double arches in the style of the cloister at the Jerónimos monastery in Lisbon. Panels of *azulejos* by renowned Portuguese artists depict scenes from the 16th-century epic *Os Lusíadas* on the outside walls and famous battle scenes in the interior. The palace was completed in 1907, but King Carlos, who was assassinated in 1908, never occupied it, although his son and successor, King Manuel II, stayed in Buçaco in 1910 — reputedly with a mistress — before seeking exile in England. The palace then became a hotel (see *Checking In*), which is well worth a visit as a charming monument in its own right.

Buçaco was the scene of a decisive battle of the Peninsular War, when in 1810, the British general Sir Arthur Wellesley, the future Duke of Wellington, commanding 50,000 Portuguese and British troops, was facing the third invasion of Napoleon's army from Spain. As the French, led by Marshal André Masséna, advanced westward via Viseu, Wellesley concealed his troops along the ridge at Buçaco, spending the eve of the battle in one of the cork-lined monks' cells. (The olive tree where the general is said to have tethered his horse can still be seen.) The French attacked through thick mist on the morning of September 27 and were repulsed during 2 hours of artillery fire, cavalry charges, and bayonet fighting. They lost 4,600 men, while the British and Portuguese lost 626. Although Masséna's army later captured Coimbra, the French defeat at Buçaco prepared the way for the end of the war. Processions on the anniversary of the battle are still held today.

A walk anywhere in Buçaco is enjoyable, particularly if crowded weekends and holidays are avoided. Among the loveliest features is the Fonte Fria (Cold Fountain), where waters that spring from a cave cascade down 144 stone steps into a pool. The path from here leads past a small lake to the Rua dos Fetos (Fern Lane), a 250-yard pathway lined with tall cypresses. The Via Sacra, or Way of the Cross, is a series of 20 small 18th-century chapels in which scenes leading up to the Crucifixion are depicted by terra cotta figures (fashioned in 1938 — sadly, many of them have since been damaged). A few hundred yards outside the Portas de Sula, at the park's southeastern corner, an obelisk topped by a glass star commemorates the Battle of Buçaco and other engagements of the Luso-Britannic campaigns, and offers magnificent views of the Estrela and Caramulo *serras.* Down the hill toward the Portas da Rainha is the interesting *Museu Militar do Buçaco* (phone: 31-93310), a military museum featuring maps, weapons, uniforms, and models from the battle and related campaigns (open from 9 AM to 5:30 PM; 10 AM to 5 PM December through February; closed Mondays; admission charge). One of the trees in Buçaco is an olive tree, the symbol of peace, planted by Wellington after the heavy fighting that led to his victory.

CHECKING IN/EATING OUT: *Palace Hotel do Buçaco* – Now one of the finest hotels in Portugal, it really was built by a king as his summer palace, and it immerses present-day guests in an atmosphere of turn-of-the-century romance and royal luxury. Many of the 80 sumptuous rooms open onto broad terraces, from which guests can watch the stars over the deep green forest. Fine international cooking and local dishes are served under a vaulted, Renaissance-style cupola in good weather. The elegant period charm of the palace and its wonderful setting make it one of the most pleasurable places to stay in the entire country. Mata do Buçaco, Buçaco (phone: 31-93101). Expensive.

LUSO: This attractive, bustling spa on the northwest slope of the Serra do Buçaco is only 2 miles (3 km) from the gate at the northern tip of Buçaco National Park. It's famed for the curative properties of its waters, which rise from a spring in the town center at a temperature of 80F. One of the country's most famous mineral waters, bottled Luso is sold all over Portugal. Here, a pavilion given over to physiotherapy has a heated swimming pool, gyms, mud baths, and other specialized installations, where treatment is given under medical supervision. But Luso is a relaxing and enjoyable place to visit even for those not "taking the waters," and it's a less expensive base for visiting Buçaco than the *Palace* hotel. The town has a splendid outdoor swimming pool and visitors can row on a lake, play tennis, or jog around a special circuit; in addition, there's a cinema, nightclub, and discotheque, as well as several hotels and small pensions.

 CHECKING IN: *Eden* – Modern, with 57 rooms next to the Fonte de São João, the spring where the spa waters rise. There are TV sets in every room, a restaurant, and a disco. Rua Emídio Navarro, Luso (phone: 31-93171). Moderate.

Grande Hotel das Termas – Large and comfortable, it adjoins the thermal baths and is run by the same company that operates them. It offers 173 rooms, a restaurant, indoor and outdoor swimming pools, tennis, squash, miniature golf, and a disco. Rua dos Banhos, Luso (phone: 31-93450). Moderate.

Vila Duparchy – On a hill above Luso, this large 19th-century house was built by a French engineer engaged in the construction of the Beiras railroad. A *Turismo de Habitação* participant, it has 6 comfortable bedrooms with modern bathrooms, 4 living rooms, and a dining room. There is a swimming pool in the spacious garden, which offers a view over the town. Contact *Vila Duparchy,* Estrada Nacional 234, Luso (phone: 31-93120). Moderate.

Alegre – This *pensão* of 20 rooms, a former noble's house, offers a splendid view over the town. It has a good restaurant. Rua Emídio Navarro, Luso (phone: 31-93251). Inexpensive.

Astória – A pleasant 12-room *pensão,* with an English country touch. The amenities include a pub and a restaurant. Rua Emídio Navarro, Luso (phone: 31-93182). Inexpensive.

EATING OUT: *O Cesteiro* – This modern eatery offers regional cooking including *chanfana,* kid cooked with red wine, and *leitão,* roast suckling pig — one of the delicacies of this part of the Beiras. Open for lunch and dinner daily. Reservations unnecessary. Rua José Duarte Figueredo, Luso (phone: 31-92360). Inexpensive.

En Route from Luso – Drive west 4½ miles (7 km) along N234, a mountain road, past Mealhada to join the main N1, which leads south another 13 miles (21 km) to Coimbra or north 60½ miles (97 km) to Porto. Alternatively, return to Coimbra via the smaller N336. Remember to always drive cautiously and be patient on Portuguese roads, where passing is often difficult and inadvisable.

Central Portugal

The Tagus River is Portugal's Mason-Dixon Line. For the sake of convenience, everything above it is lumped together as "The North" and everything below it as "The South." The division, though a fairly sweeping generalization, is remarkably valid. Crossing Portugal's biggest river heading south is indeed like crossing a frontier of some kind. In the space of a few miles the granite of the Beiras fades and a radically different landscape takes its place: terra cotta in color, brilliantly lit, studded with olive, cork, and holm oak trees — unmistakably the landscape of southern Europe. The transformation from North into South is so total, it is as if the curtain had gone up on another set.

The two Portuguese provinces where this intriguing transformation occurs are the Ribatejo and its eastern neighbor, the Alto, or Upper, Alentejo. The latter is the northern half of a region that is not only by far the largest in the country, but also the least densely populated, the hottest, and the driest. It also produces more cork than anywhere else in the world and has what must be the most readily recognized landscape in Portugal. Apart from the São Mamede Range in the northeast, reaching up to 3,382 feet high, and the Ossa Range near Evora, with peaks up to 2,154 feet, there are few outcrops in the Alentejo high enough or rocky enough to be called mountains. The whole region unfolds southward from the Tagus River to the Algarve in a practically unbroken succession of low, rolling hills, bright with wildflowers in the spring, ocher in summer. Providing the car's suspension is youthful enough to handle the sometimes rough roads, it is good driving country — the landscape uncluttered, the roads relatively uncrowded, the little white towns a constant lure on the horizon.

Even though the existence of the Ribatejo has been a geographic and historical fact since medieval times, cartographers have always had trouble drawing its exact limits. That technicality aside, near the town of Santarém the Tagus spreads out and threads through wide alluvial flats before finally flowing into the estuary above Lisbon. This is the quintessential Ribatejo — lonely expanses of grassland where egrets and other wild fowl congregate and where horsemen with long wooden lances herd black fighting bulls. The area has an almost mystical appeal for romantics and aficionados of Portuguese bullfighting and the equestrian arts, but it also has a more prosaic side, as Lisbon's breadbasket and kitchen garden. When the Tagus overflows its banks in winter, the low-lying parts are afflicted by heavy flooding, but the big riverside fields, the *lezirias,* produce large quantities of grain and vegetables when they are not under water, and vineyards in the drier zones away from the river produce much of the country's staple table wine.

Both the Alentejo and the Ribatejo are legendary places: lands of giants, heroic deeds, battles, and chivalry. Very few towns are without a castle or some other reminder of Portugal's long history, and in places the traces of occupation reach back to the Stone Age. During the Iron Age, various Indo-European tribes, probably mostly Celts, drifted across the *mesetas* from Spain, some of them — the ones who were later to become known as Lusitanians — settling the highlands north of the Tagus and elbowing their way into a position of dominance over the whole of the central region. When the Romans turned up during the 2nd century BC, these hillsmen put up fierce resistance under the leadership of Portugal's first truly national hero, the Lusitanian chieftain Viriatus. His death in 139 BC opened the way for the Roman troops and marked the beginning of an occupation of the Ribatejo and Alentejo that lasted some 400 years.

Towns grew up along the Roman roads that crossed the Alentejo plain from Emerita Augusta (Mérida) in Spain and led northward through the Ribatejo. Several of these, notably Ebora (now Evora) and Scallabis (presumed to have been near Santarém, but now lost), were of considerable provincial importance. Archaeological remains from the Roman period are fragmentary but widespread, and most local museums have a collection of Roman pieces.

The Roman period was followed by centuries of invasion and settlement by tribes from northern Europe and ultimately by the Visigoths, who ruled until the arrival of the Moors during the 8th century. Little is left of the Visigothic presence, apart from architectural traces in fortifications, but the influence of their Muslim successors, while almost as fugitive in terms of architecture, was more pervasive, and it is detectable today in such things as place-names (many that begin with "al" are Moorish in origin), language, and local tradition.

Moorish dominance lasted until nearly the end of the 12th century. By that time, the Muslims were weakened by internal power struggles and by frequent raids from the Christian-held north. In 1139, Portugal's first king, Afonso Henriques, won a decisive victory at Oric, which may or may not have been the present-day Chã de Ourique, near Santarém; later, he took Santarém itself and, in 1159, the Muslim strongholds of Evora and Beja. By 1190, the area was in Christian hands, its defense largely entrusted to military orders — the Knights Templars in the Ribatejo and the Knights of Avis in the Alentejo — and the Portuguese turned their attention toward their Spanish neighbors. Both the Ribatejo and the Alentejo lay in the path of any army bent on Lisbon, so fortifications became a major preoccupation. One of the legendary figures of the new nation, King Dinis, who ruled from 1279 to 1325, was prodigious in this respect: He had a hand in building most of the castles encountered along this route.

Marching armies remained a familiar sight until well into the 19th century, as the Spaniards, the French, the British, and, of course, the Portuguese themselves played out their martial chess games with strategically placed Lisbon as the prize. But less bellicose pursuits also managed to flourish, and towns such as Evora, Santarém, and Tomar grew into centers of learning and the arts.

Throughout the military maneuvering, the Alentejo retained the distinctive social structure it had acquired from the Romans and the Moors. North of the Tagus, inheritance laws and custom turned the countryside into a mosaic of tiny properties. The Alentejo is the land of the *latifundio:* the big landed estate where workers are hired (and fired) seasonally and conditions have often been close to feudal. Dispossession of the religious orders and royalty during the 19th-century growth of liberalism merely caused the properties to change hands, but a somewhat successful attempt to change the system was made after the April 25 revolution in 1974. Nearly 3 million acres were confiscated in an agrarian reform program, and many of the big estates were turned into collective farms.

However, don't let this whiff of revolution — tenuous now, in any case — be a deterrent. The people here are as hospitable as any in this hospitable country, and they welcome foreign visitors — for example, at local fairs and festivals, of which there are many. They are skilled in crafts such as pottery, iron working, and weaving, turning out a number of attractive handmade products. Among these, two that have attained international renown and become correspondingly costly are carpets from Arraiolos and woven tapestries from Portalegre, but there are many other hand-crafted articles to buy that carry more modest price tags.

The route outlined below, beginning at Lisbon, follows the Tagus up through the Ribatejo, passing though two towns of great touristic interest: Santarém and Tomar. It then turns inland in the direction of the Spanish border, crossing into the Upper Alentejo. At the spa town of Castelo de Vide, it turns south into the heart of the region, visiting Portalegre, Estremoz, and Evora, one of the most picturesque old cities in Portugal. The return to Lisbon begins as the route proceeds due west from Evora to Setúbal and the Arrábida Peninsula, which actually fall within the boundaries of a third region, Estremadura, although its cultural and geographic affinity with the Alentejo is so close that travelers will hardly note a difference. After a Setúbal-to-Sesimbra-to-Palmela loop around the peninsula, the route heads back to Lisbon via the A2, crossing the Tagus into the city by the impressive suspension bridge.

Apart from two stretches of toll highway, the route follows the regular main highway system, and the roads are good, with two lanes in either direction. Leave the highway to take one of the secondary roads, however, and be prepared for rougher conditions. Even on main roads, in addition to the usual rustic hazards such as slow-moving tractors, herds of animals, and horse-drawn carts, watch out for locals rattling along at night on little motorcycles. Quite often they don't bother about lights — particularly taillights. Last, try to avoid approaching Lisbon from the south on a Saturday or Sunday evening in summer. That is precisely when everybody else will be trying to get back after a day at the beach, and the lineup before the bridge sometimes stretches for miles.

Standard international cooking is usually served in the hotels and better restaurants on this itinerary — probably just as well for weight watchers, as the regional cooking is on the heavy side. Meat dishes such as the typical *ensopado de cabrito* or *ensopado de borrego,* kid or lamb stew, are more prevalent than fish dishes in these inland areas, although the rare and pricey *lampreia* (lamprey eel) and *sável,* a river shad, are Ribatejo delicacies. Even in the dry Alentejo, *bacalhau* (dried salt cod) dishes are popular, and one of the Alentejo's better-known dishes is *carne de porco à alentejana,* a mixture of clams and pork. A superb ewes' milk cheese is made at Serpa, in the Alentejo, and another at Azeitão on the Arrábida Peninsula. Both are becoming regrettably hard to find, but they are worth the search — try them with fresh bread cut from one of the huge, crusty *alentejano* loaves and some of the strong-bodied wine made in the Reguengos or Borba areas.

As predominantly agricultural regions, neither the Ribatejo nor the Alentejo has a highly developed tourist industry. This means that their paths are still relatively untrodden; but it also makes advance planning advisable, because good hotels are not plentiful. That said, it must be added that some of the most interesting accommodations in Portugal are to be found precisely along this route. Expect to pay from $85 to $115 for a double room with bath in hotels listed below as expensive, such as the *pousadas* in Estremoz, Setúbal, and Palmela; from $45 to $75 in hotels listed as moderate; and less than $40 in the inexpensive ones. Dinner for two with wine and coffee will cost $60 and up in one of the few expensive restaurants listed, from $30 to $50 in the more common regional type listed as moderate, and less than $30 in the inexpensive ones.

En Route from Lisbon – Pick up the A1 toll highway on the northern outskirts of town, just past the airport (from downtown, follow signs for the *aeroporto* and the city of Porto). Drive about 24 miles (38 km), passing the Vila Franca de Xira exit and taking the first signposted exit for Santarém. After the exit, turn right onto N3. The town of Cartaxo, center of a wine producing district bearing its name, is 15 miles (24 km) along the road. Ribatejo wines have been known and valued at least since the 12th century, and though more sophisticated ones will be met on this route, the strong-bodied, and fruity cartaxo, with a high alcoholic content, serves as a good introduction. The wines can be sampled and bought at the little *Museu Rural e do Vinho* on the outskirts of town, which also has an interesting collection of traditional wine making implements (open from 9:30 AM to 12:30 PM and from 2:30 to 5 PM; closed Mondays; admission charge). Back on N3, it is 9 miles (14 km) to Santarém.

SANTARÉM: The administrative capital of the Ribatejo and an important market town, Santarém hosts one of Europe's leading agricultural fairs, the *Feira Nacional de Agricultura* (10 days in June, beginning the first Friday of the month), which is accompanied by bullfights and other festivities, and the *Festival Nacional de Gastronomia,* a national gastronomy and handicrafts fair held every November. The city is assumed to stand on or close to the site of the Roman city of Scallabis, an important provincial capital in ancient times that has since disappeared without leaving a physical trace. Its present name comes from Santa Iria (St. Irene), a 7th-century nun who was martyred in Tomar — according to tradition, her body was thrown into the river and washed ashore here. A statue of the saint stands in a riverside shrine on the edge of town, and it is said that if the river ever rises to touch her feet, the final deluge will have come. Winter flooding is a common scourge here and may even have accounted for the disappearance of Scallabis.

Santarém was conquered by the Moors during the 8th century and reconquered by Portugal's first king, Afonso Henriques, during the 12th century. After that, it grew into a town of considerable strategic importance. King Dinis died here in 1325, and it was here, in 1360, that King Pedro I staged the final act in one of history's great tragic love stories by exacting bloodthirsty revenge on the murderers of his former mistress,

Inês de Castro. Several monarchs held court in the city at one time or another, a fact that contributed to its architectural heritage.

In the oldest part of the city, which was once walled and fortified, is the 14th-century Graça church. It has an ornate Portuguese Gothic doorway, but its outstanding feature is a superb rose window above the door, with tracery carved out of a single piece of stone — possibly the finest example of this work in Portugal. Inside is a plain tomb said to hold the remains of the discoverer of Brazil, Pedro Alvares Cabral. The charming little 13th-century church of São João de Alporão nearby functions as a somewhat disorganized *Museu Arqueológico* (open from 9 AM to noon and from 2 to 5 PM; closed Mondays; no admission charge). Its collection includes several Roman pieces, Moorish architectural fragments, and, notably, the beautiful Gothic tomb of Dom Duarte de Meneses, a knight who died in battle against the Moors in 1465. All the tomb contains is one tooth — all that could be found after the ferocious contest. The church's original Romanesque bell tower was knocked down to make way for the royal coach of Queen Maria during a visit in 1815, but standing opposite is another tower, the 15th-century Torre das Cabaças, so called because of the gourd-shaped pots (*cabaças*) placed around the bell on top to give it greater resonance.

A short distance beyond is the little tree-lined Avenida 5 de Outubro, which leads to an ornamental garden, Portas do Sol, set within the old castle walls. From here, there are panoramic views of the Ribatejo countryside, with the Tagus River and the 4,000-foot-long 19th-century Dom Luís Bridge in the foreground. On the way back to the center, stop in at the Igreja da Marvila, founded by the Knights Templars during the 12th century after Afonso Henriques retook the city from the Moors. This church has a wonderfully ornate Portuguese Gothic porch and, inside, three lofty aisles covered with fine 16th-century *azulejos.* Two more churches, Santa Clara and Santa Cruz, can be seen as the road winds down to the river on the way out of Santarém. Santa Clara, its interior stripped down to its 13th-century bones, is a fine example of early Gothic, with another superb rose window. The early Gothic doorway of Santa Cruz, also founded during the 13th century (by King Dinis), was uncovered during restoration work in the 1960s.

 EATING OUT: *Pateo d'Al-Meirim* – This restaurant, in an old Ribatejo house on the outskirts of the town of Almeirim, 4½ miles (7 km) southeast of Santarém, is famed for its *borrego assado no forno de lenha* (lamb roasted in a wood oven), but it's also the place to try any of the regional specialties. Closed Mondays. Reservations advised. 10 Rua das Cancelas, Almeirim (phone: 43-52836). Moderate.

Castiço – A popular regional-style restaurant at the cattle fairground on the outskirts of Santarém. The decor is heavily rustic — the chairs are tree trunks — but the food is good. Try the *caldeiradas* (fish stews) and the grilled steaks. Closed Sundays. Reservations advised. Campo da Feira, Santarém (phone: 43-23891). Inexpensive.

O Mal Cozinhado – One of Santarém's most popular eateries, and the one with perhaps the strongest regional flavor. It has wooden walls, bullfight posters, a bull's head over the bar, and a husband-and-wife team running a kitchen that produces some of the best dishes in town, including *lombinho com coentros* (pork tenderloin with coriander) and *magosto de bacalhau,* the house codfish dish. Open daily. No reservations. Campo da Feira, Santarém (phone: 43-23584). Inexpensive.

Portas do Sol – Unpretentious but good regional cooking is served in this small place, which has an outdoor terrace for summer dining. It's inside the Portas do Sol garden, so the surroundings and view are attractive. Closed Mondays. Reservations advised. Jardim das Portas do Sol, Santarém (phone: 43-29520). Inexpensive.

Toucinho – A favorite of Ribatejo cooking fans in search of authenticity rather than comfort. Helia, the owner, presides over her open country kitchen and the brick oven where the restaurant's famed bread is baked. Try the various grills or the local specialty, *sopa de pedra* — stone soup, literally — a soup made of beans and a variety of meats and vegetables, and served with a small stone in the bowl. (It doesn't taste the same without it, they say.) Closed Wednesdays and the month of August. No reservations. Rua Macau, Almeirim (phone: 43-52237). Inexpensive.

En Route from Santarém – Those who haven't already driven over to Almeirim should take N114 across the Dom Luís Bridge and, about 1¼ miles (2 km) beyond it, turn left onto N368 for Alpiarça. (Those already in Almeirim should take N118 to Alpiarça.) Both Almeirim and Alpiarça are little towns that have been favorite country haunts of Portuguese royalty at one time or another — an abundance of game and excellent wines were the attractions. In Alpiarça, stop at the *Casa dos Patudos,* once the country residence of José Relvas, a prominent political figure and patron of the arts at the beginning of the century. When he died in 1929, he left his house and his sizable art collection to the town as a museum. The oriental rugs, porcelains, and tiles are outstanding (open April through September on Thursdays, Saturdays, and Sundays only, from 10 AM to 12:30 PM and from 2 to 5:30 PM — only afternoons on Thursdays; open the rest of the year on Saturdays and Sundays only, from 10 AM to 12:30 PM and from 2 to 5 PM; admission charge). After the visit, take N118 north 11 miles (18 km) to Chamusca, which is worth a stop, then continue north about 2½ miles (4 km) and take N243 across the river — those with an eye for engineering will like the iron bridge the French built in 1905 — another 3 miles (5 km) into Golegã.

CHAMUSCA: Scarcely anything remains from medieval times, when Chamusca was an important port on the busy thoroughfare of the Tagus, but the town still has a few sights to see, and the old part, with its typical Ribatejo houses, is a pleasant place to stroll. Those who appreciate early Portuguese tiles should not miss the 17th-century interior of the parish church of São Bras or the charming little church of Nossa Senhora do Pranto, from which there is also a magnificent view of the surrounding countryside. The *Casa Rural Tradicional,* a museum (Largo 25 do Abril; no admission charge), is an interesting reconstruction of a typical Ribatejo farmhouse of 50 years ago, with some fine pieces of rustic furniture and other household items. (To visit, ask for the keys at the tourist office, on the same square.)

GOLEGÃ: For the first 2 weeks of November each year, when one of Europe's most important horse fairs, the *Feira Nacional do Cavalo* (also known as the *Feira de São Martinho*), takes place here, this town becomes horse lovers' heaven. The event attracts breeders and dealers from all over the world, principally because of the high-stepping Lusitanian and Andalusian breeds for which the Ribatejo is famous. At other times of the year, the main attraction is the Igreja Matriz (Parish Church), toward the center of town on the road from Chamusca. Founded by King Manuel I during the 16th century, the church has a magnificent doorway in the Manueline style (the Gothic-to-Renaissance transitional style named after the king himself). In front of it stands the town's *pelourinho,* or pillory (in the old days, both a symbol of municipal power and a whipping post). A block away, off Largo Dom Manuel I, is the *Museu Municipal de Fotografia Carlos Relvas,* which is well worth a visit even for those who are not photography buffs. Carlos Relvas, the father of José Relvas (responsible for the *Casa dos Patudos* in Alpiarça), was a wealthy landowner, art collector, and statesman, as well as a passionate amateur photographer, and his studio and splendid Victorian house have been preserved as a museum (open from 11 AM to 12:30 PM and from 2:30 to 6 PM; closed Mondays; admission charge).

EATING OUT: *Central* – This restaurant is in the restored house of one of Portugal's best-known bullfighters, Manuel dos Santos. No great flights of fancy, but the regional fare is good, including the specialty, *açorda de sável,* a sort of "dry" shad soup in which the river fish is mixed with bread and other ingredients. Open daily. Reservations advised. Largo da Imaculada Conceição, Golegã (phone: 49-94345). Inexpensive.

En Route from Golegã – Take N365 north to the junction with N3, 4½ miles (7 km) away, then turn onto N110, following signs for Tomar, 12 miles (19 km) from the crossing. About 1¼ miles (2 km) along, the road passes the church of Nossa Senhora da Assunção (Our Lady of the Assumption) in Atalaia. The church is an interesting example of Renaissance architecture, with an impressive portal at the center of a very imposing but oddly shaped façade; but its most beautiful feature is the yellow-and-blue-tiled interior — a must-see for tile fans. Another 4 miles (6 km) along, off the road to the right, is the village of Asseiceira, the center of a once-important earthenware pottery industry. Though the use of these traditional pots has declined, some of the family potteries are still in business after 200 years or more. Asseiceira is also known for its cast-metal cowbells, *chocalhos,* considered by some collectors to be the best in the country.

TOMAR: Founded during the early 12th century on the Nabão River, near the site of a Roman town and a later Visigothic and Moorish settlement, Tomar is intimately linked with what is often termed the heroic period in Portuguese history — encompassing the founding of the nation during the 12th century, the Christian Reconquest, and then the great maritime expansion of the 15th century. The first sight to see is the Convento de Cristo (Convent of Christ), the extraordinary convent-castle of the two military orders that made Tomar their headquarters. Begun by the Knights Templars on a hilltop overlooking the town during the 12th century, it was continued by the Knights of Christ, who replaced the disbanded Templars during the 14th century, and was finished only during the 17th century. The Templars had been entrusted with the defense of the Tagus Valley after the recapture of Lisbon from the Moors in 1147, and they used their crusaders' knowledge of the military architecture of the Holy Land to build a state-of-the-art castle, with double walls protecting a towering keep. The design proved its value in 1190, when Moors attacking the castle breached the south gate, only to be trapped between the two lines of defense and massacred. To commemorate the carnage, the gate became known as the Porta do Sangue (Bloody Gate).

Besides the fortifications, the Charola — a circular oratory, or temple, modeled after the Holy Sepulchre in Jerusalem — is also part of the convent's 12th-century nucleus (the painted decorations and figures in it are from a later period, however). From the outside, this too looks fortress-like, and it is said that when the knights were at prayer, they would leave their horses standing behind them in the passage surrounding the altar. The early-16th-century Manueline nave attached to the oratory is one of many additions to the original convent. Its exterior is decorated with splendidly ornate tracery full of allusions to Portugal's seafaring past — not surprising, since the Convento de Cristo had been closely linked to the epic voyages of the 15th century, and the square cross that Prince Henry the Navigator's caravels bore on their sails was in fact the emblem of the Order of Christ, of whom Prince Henry himself was a Grand Master. Among other buildings, the maze-like complex contains seven cloisters, including a magnificent mid-16th-century Palladian structure, the Claustro dos Filipes (Cloister of the Philips), in which King Philip II of Spain is supposed to have been proclaimed King Philip I of Portugal. The convent was sacked and pillaged by the French during the 19th-century Peninsular War, but just for the buildings alone it remains one of

Europe's great historical sites (open daily from 9:30 AM to 12:30 PM and from 2 to 6 PM, 5 PM in winter; admission charge).

Also to be seen in Tomar is the little church of Nossa Senhora da Conceição, perhaps the best example of early Renaissance architecture in Portugal. It's on the way down the hill from the convent, but arrange the visit with the tourist office in town (address and phone below), because the church has been stripped practically bare by thieves and is now kept locked. In the Old Town between the foot of the hill and the river is the country's oldest surviving synagogue (73 Rua Dr. Joaquim Jacinto; open from 9:30 AM to 12:30 PM and from 2 to 6 PM, 5 PM in winter; closed Wednesdays). Built during the 15th century and square in plan like a mosque, it was probably used only briefly before the Inquisition was introduced into Portugal — by a monk named Baltazar de Faria, who happens to be entombed in one of the cloisters in the convent.

Just across the river is the lovely and historic Santa Maria do Olival (St. Mary of the Olive Grove), once the mother church for all of Portugal's churches overseas. Historians date it to the mid-13th century, but popular tradition holds that it was founded a century earlier by the celebrated Grand Master of Portuguese Templars, Gualdim Pais, whose bones are interred here along with those of other Templar worthies. Restoration has ruthlessly stripped away the decorative accretion of centuries, but two little stone images of the Virgin and some very pretty tiles relieve the starkness inside. Another church worth a visit is São João Baptista, the parish church that dominates the main square in the center of town, Praça da República, with its imposing bell tower and Manueline doorway. The pulpit in the central nave is a masterpiece of Gothic stone carving.

Near the weir in the town's riverside gardens is a huge waterwheel, of the sort once used for irrigation purposes in the Tomar region. Another water-related sight, the Aqueduto dos Pegões, built between 1593 and 1616 to bring water to the convent, is about 3 miles (5 km) out of town (almost 2 miles — 3 km — on the N113 in the direction of Fatima and Leiria, then left onto the road for Pegões). Over 3 miles long, with 180 arches, the structure was a remarkable piece of engineering for its time and is impressive even now. It is also fairly close to one of Tomar's best restaurants, *Chico Elias* (see *Eating Out*), so a visit to both can be combined.

One of Portugal's most spectacular traditional festivals, the *Festa dos Tabuleiros,* takes place in Tomar. During the festivities, which were probably pagan in origin but later became associated with the alms-giving activities of the saintly Queen Isabel, young girls in white parade through the streets, balancing on their heads enormous crown-like contraptions, the *tabuleiros,* made of loaves of bread interwoven with flowers. The celebration takes place 50 days after *Easter,* but it is not a regular event (at one time it was held more or less biennially), so it should be confirmed first at the tourist office, on Avenida Dr. Cândido Madureira (phone: 49-313237).

CHECKING IN: *Ilha do Lombo* – This exceptionally pretty *estalagem,* or inn, is located about 10 miles (16 km) east of Tomar, on an island in the reservoir upstream from the Castelo de Bode dam (Portugal's biggest dam). There are 17 rooms with tiled terraces looking onto the water. There is also an outdoor pool, and boating and fishing are available. To reach the inn, take N110 north for about half a mile (1 km), then turn right onto the road to Serra and Barreira for the remaining 9½ miles (15 km). The road is narrow and poorly paved, but it winds through pleasant scenery; from Barreira, a small, closed cabin boat called the *Zêzere* ferries guests out to the island — about a 5-minute trip. Bookings for the summer should be made at least 2 months in advance. Ilha do Lombo, Serra de Tomar (phone: 49-371128). Moderate.

Pousada de São Pedro – On the Zêzere River, right beside the Castelo de Bode dam, 8 miles (13 km) southeast of Tomar. A quiet and comfortable government-run inn, with genuine antique furnishings and old prints on the walls, it has 8 rooms in the main building and another 7 in an annex. The picture window in the air conditioned restaurant looks out onto the dam. Take N110 south for 4½ miles (7 km), then turn left onto N358. Castelo de Bode (phone: 49-381175). Moderate.

Templários – A regional favorite combining modern comforts with small-town tranquillity, it's set in a pleasant garden by the river and has 84 rooms, an excellent restaurant, an outdoor pool, and tennis courts. From the balconies of many of the upper rooms, guests can look across to the convent on the hill. 1 Largo Cândido dos Reis, Tomar (phone: 49-312121). Moderate.

Trovador – The best of several pensions in Tomar, it's modern, clean, and located in the newer part of town, near the bus station. The 30 rooms all have private baths and TV sets. No restaurant, but there is a breakfast room and a small bar that's open at night. Rua Dr. Joaquim Ribeiro, Tomar (phone: 49-31567). Moderate.

EATING OUT: *Bela Vista* – One of the oldest restaurants in Tomar and regarded as the most traditional in culinary terms. The combination of old-fashioned decor and good home cooking — including *cabrito no forno* (roast kid) and *caldeirada* (a fish stew prepared with different kinds of fish) — plus a nice riverside location have turned it into an obligatory port of call. Closed Mondays at lunch and all day Tuesdays. Reservations advised. 6 Fonte do Choupo, Tomar (phone: 49-312870). Moderate.

Chez Nous – It has a French bias, but it's also noted for excellent local fare — *bacalhau com natas* (dried cod with a cream sauce), for example. In the old part of town, with an agreeably cozy ambience, it's a popular place and seats only 30, so reserve before going. Closed Saturdays. Reservations advised. 31 Rua Dr. Joaquim Jacinto, Tomar (phone: 49-312294). Moderate.

Chico Elias – This stands apart among the handful of top restaurants in Tomar not only because of its food, but also because it cooks only to order. Phone first and tell them what you want to eat. Among the choices — prepared by Dona Ceu, wife of the owner — are *coelho na abóbora* (rabbit served in a pumpkin), *bacalhau assado com carne de porco* (dried cod baked with pork), *couves a Dom Prior* (a spicy cabbage dish), and *leite creme* (a creamy milk-based dessert that Dona Ceu is reputed to make better than anyone else). The decor is not entirely successful pseudo rustic, but the food makes up for it. Closed Tuesdays. Reservations essential. The restaurant is in a small village about 1¼ miles (2 km) out of Tomar. Estrada de Torres Novas, Algarvias (phone: 49-311067). Moderate.

Marisqueira de Tomar – Large, air conditioned, and pleasantly decorated with rural scenes painted on glass, this is the place to sample the famous Nabão River lamprey. Try the *arroz de lampreia*, a Ribatejo specialty in which the eel is cooked with rice, wine, and garlic and served in a black earthenware pot. The restaurant also has a good seafood bar next door. Closed Mondays. Reservations unnecessary. 9 Avenida Norton de Matos, Tomar (phone: 49-313903). Moderate.

En Route from Tomar – Take N110 south 4½ miles (7 km) and turn left onto N358. The pleasant country road winds through hills and woods for 10 miles (16 km), crossing the Zêzere River via Portugal's biggest dam, at Castelo de Bode, until it reaches Constância. A pretty, quiet little town nowadays, Constância has known busier times, thanks to its strategic position at the confluence of the Tagus and Zêzere Rivers. During the Peninsular War in the early 19th century, the future Duke of Wellington mustered his troops here before marching against the French at Talavera, Spain. The town can even boast the not very impressive ruins of a house where Portugal's greatest poet, Luís de Camões, is said to have written some of his verses in 1546. The steps beside the ruined house afford views of Constância's narrow, whitewashed streets as they climb up to the 18th-century parish church that sits atop everything.

Almost 3 miles (5 km) west of town, and definitely worth the short backtrack, is the Castelo de Almourol. The castle hasn't seen much real action since the Knights Templars built it on top of earlier fortifications in 1171, but it has made up for that by accumulating legend — a process to which its remarkably romantic appearance on an island in the Tagus has contributed enormously. A boatman will row travelers across during visiting hours, daily from 9:30 AM to 5 PM (no admission charge, but pay the boatman). East of town, N3 leads away from the river through wooded countryside and then back to it again at the old town of Abrantes, 10 miles (16 km) from Constância.

ABRANTES: The town stands on the north bank of the Tagus, and its castle, which commands a wide circle of the surrounding land, is worth visiting. Abrantes has been fought over repeatedly during its long history. King Afonso Henriques took it from the Moors in 1148 and then successfully fought off a recapture attempt in 1179. The castle was restored and enlarged, most notably by King Dinis, who finished the walls in 1279; afterward, it was frequently used as a royal residence; several Portuguese princes were born in it. (Some of the halls that once formed part of the residential quarters have been restored to reveal their fine brickwork vaults.) It was here, too, that King João I assembled the army that won the celebrated battle of Aljubarrota against the forces of Castile on August 14, 1385, thus assuring Portugal's continued independence. Later on, in 1807, during the Peninsular War, the French took Abrantes for Napoleon, only to be chased out shortly after by the British. (The French general was named Duke of Abrantes for his pains, however.)

On the hilltop with the castle is the 13th-century Church of Santa Maria do Castelo, inside which is installed the *Museu Regional de Dom Lopo de Almeida* (open from 10 AM to 12:30 PM and from 2 to 5 PM; closed Mondays; no admission charge). It contains an interesting collection of Roman statuary, 15th- and 16th-century church carvings, and some very fine early Mozarabic tiles from Seville. The church was badly damaged by an earthquake in 1492 and was then reconstructed as the pantheon of the Almeida family, Counts of Abrantes, whose elegant Gothic tombs are part of the collection. Information on other sights in town is available at the tourist office on Largo da Feira (phone: 41-22555).

CHECKING IN: *Turismo* – A modern, comfortable hostelry of a standard not usually found in the provinces, it has a privileged and convenient hilltop site on the edge of town, gardens, a pool, and tennis courts, as well as a good restaurant (see *Eating Out,* below). Most of the 50 rooms and suites are air conditioned. Largo de Santo António, Abrantes (phone: 41-21261 or 41-21271). Moderate.

EATING OUT: *Casa do Pastor* – This is a 7½-mile (12-km) drive away, but worth considering for its rustic lodge decor and classic regional dishes such as *ensopado de borrego* (lamb stew), as well as more international standbys such as steaks. Before noon it doubles as a cafeteria for snacks, and after 10 PM as a pub-style bar. Closed Mondays. Reservations advised. Take N244-3 north 5 miles (8 km), then turn right onto N358 for Mouriscas. The restaurant is about 2 miles (about 3 km) down this road on the right, between Cabeça das Mos and Mouriscas (phone: 41-95255). Moderate.

Turismo – The best choice in town, serving very good local and regional dishes in addition to more standard hotel fare. The dining room is large, with pleasantly panoramic views from its big picture windows. Reservations advised. Largo de Santo António, Abrantes (phone: 41-21261 or 41-21271). Moderate.

En Route from Abrantes – At Rossio, just after crossing the bridge going south (there are ruins of an old Roman bridge over the Tagus), turn east at the signposted crossing onto N118 for Portalegre. The road climbs away from the river as it moves toward the Alto Alentejo. At Alpalhão, 37 miles (59 km) from Abrantes, turn left onto N246 in the direction of the Spanish frontier and drive the 10 miles (16 km) to Castelo de Vide. After a visit, continue on N246 another 5½ miles (9 km) to the turnoff (left) to Marvão, which is another 2½ miles (4 km) up a winding road.

CASTELO DE VIDE: This spa town on the slopes of the Serra de São Mamede is of considerable historical interest and one of the prettiest towns in the region. Its waters are said to do wonders for sluggish digestive systems, and for this reason, as well as because it escapes the fierce Alentejo heat, Castelo de Vide has long been a popular summer resort for the Portuguese middle classes. Like virtually all Alentejo border towns of any size, it grew up around a castle — 60 families, in fact, still live within the walls of this one. Portuguese occupation of the site, originally fortified by the Romans, dates to the beginning of the 13th century; early in the following century, King Dinis strengthened it. Since then, the castle has been the object of numerous sieges, during one of the last of which, in 1704, it was badly damaged when the Spanish tried to wrest it from its Portuguese and English defenders.

Most of this small town can be seen on a morning's stroll. Begin in the central square, Praça Dom Pedro V, which is bordered by two fine 18th-century buildings — the Town Hall and the big Church of Santa Maria da Devesa — and by several handsome 17th-century mansions. Head down from the northwest corner of the square to the 16th-century *fonte da vila* (village fountain), in a square at the foot of the oldest part of town. The fountain, one of the prettiest in Portugal, consists of four marble columns supporting a pyramidal roof set over basins that have been worn into undulating curves by centuries of use. From the square, walk up to the castle through the enchanting medieval alleys of the old Jewish Quarter. On the way up, on Rua da Judiaria, don't miss the tiny 16th-century synagogue, which is partly restored and open to the public daily; and note the original medieval details, such as doorways and windows, on the houses on the same street. Not to be missed in the castle itself are the superbly vaulted Gothic hall in the tower and the fine main hall with its brick tunnel vault ceiling. There are stunning views of the surrounding countryside from the ramparts. The castle can be visited at any time — a caretaker will open sections that are closed off. Castelo de Vide's Tourist Office is at 81 Rua Bartolomeu Alvares da Santa (phone: 45-91361).

CHECKING IN: *Jardim* – This 20-room *albergaria* (inn) doesn't have the spaciousness or the modern sophistication of the town's main hotel, the *Sol e Serra,* but it makes up for it by being more homey. Old hands sometimes prefer it to its smarter competitor. 6 Rua Sequeira Sameiro, Castelo de Vide (phone: 45-91217). Moderate.

Sol e Serra – Modern, comfortable, and conveniently situated near a park at the edge of town, it has 51 rooms with balconies, most with an agreeable view. The restaurant specializes in Alentejo dishes (try the *cachafrito de cabrito,* a casserole of kid). The hotel has its own game reserve across the border in Spain, where guests can hunt partridge, pheasant, deer, and wild boar in season; fishing and tennis can also be arranged. Estrada de São Vicente, Castelo de Vide (phone: 45-91301 or 91337). Moderate.

EATING OUT: *Dom Pedro V* – On the central square, it serves excellent, classic Portuguese dishes, as well as some regional ones. Apart from those attached to hotels, it's considered the best restaurant in the area. Closed Mondays. Reservations advised. Praça Dom Pedro V, Castelo de Vide (phone: 45-91236). Moderate.

Casa do Parque – This cheery, attractive restaurant attached to a *pensão* of the same name serves good regional fare without putting on any airs. On the menu are *ensopado de cabrito* (kid stew), a regional and house specialty, and *pezinhos coentradas* (pigs' trotters cooked with fresh coriander). Closed Tuesdays. Reservations advised. Avenida da Aramanhã, Castelo de Vide (phone: 45-91250). Inexpensive.

MARVÃO: This beautiful little walled town 8 miles (12.5 km) east of Castelo de Vide perches on a mountaintop overlooking the Spanish border, only 5 miles (8 km) away. After the turn from N246, the road winds up into the mountains right to the town walls; squeeze through the gate and find a parking space — driving is naturally limited in these tortuous cobbled streets. Because of its strategic position, Marvão has played a part in a great many wars. Afonso Henriques captured the town in 1116, and at the end of the 13th century King Dinis fortified it, building up the walls and the tall castle keep. From then on, it became a vital piece in the military chess game played out on the Iberian Peninsula. The views from the castle, which can be visited at any time, are surely the most impressive in the Alentejo — the only place where "you can look down on eagles," as one Portuguese poet put it. The tourist office is on Rua Dr. Matos Magalhães (phone: 45-95236).

CHECKING IN/EATING OUT: *Pousada de Santa Maria* – A state-owned inn in a converted 17th-century mansion. Very comfortable and very popular, it's in a beautiful spot; because it has only 9 rooms, it's necessary to book well ahead. The excellent restaurant (reservations necessary), which has a spectacular view of the surrounding countryside, is the best eating place in town. The house specialties are regional ones such as *sopa de sarapatel*, a richly flavored, heavy, gruel-like soup of giblets, almost a meal in itself, and *robalo com amêijoas* (turbot cooked with clams and flavored with fresh coriander). Marvão (phone: 45-93201). Moderate.

Dom Dinis – The rooms are tiny in this *pensão*, but they're attractive; some have delightful views, and all have private bathrooms. The restaurant (reservations necessary) serves plain, regional home cooking. Rua Dr. Matos Magalhães, Marvão (phone: 45-95236). Inexpensive.

En route from Marvão – Heading 13 miles (20.5 km) south to Portalegre, N359 crosses the Serra de São Mamede, which contains the highest peak (3,382 feet) in the Alentejo plain. The landscape is pretty, with cork and olive trees beginning to predominate and small farms disappearing as the route enters the domain of the large estate.

PORTALEGRE: The capital of the Alto Alentejo is a busy city and one of the few centers of industry in the region. The cathedral, in the old part of town, is an impressively large edifice, mostly from the 18th century, although it was founded 200 years earlier. It has three vast naves, a wonderfully elegant dome crowning the transept crossing, and some fine 17th-century *azulejos*. Also worth visiting is the church of the Convento de São Bernardo. Founded for the St. Bernard sisters in 1530, the convent is now a barracks, but visitors are escorted in to see the church. Worth noting are the fountain in the courtyard and the superb 16th-century carved doorway, in marble quarried in nearby Estremoz. The history of the order up to its dissolution by the Marquês de Pombal during the 18th century has been poignantly recorded by the nuns on the backs of the stalls in the upper choir.

Portalegre has a famous tapestry factory, located in the center of town in a 16th-century Jesuit convent on Rua Guilherme Gomes Fernandes. Founded in 1947, it specializes in tapestries designed by Portugal's leading artists. All are handwoven, by girls who sit at two long looms running the length of the workshop, surrounded by beautifully dyed wools. The factory can be visited on weekdays from 9 to 11 AM and from 2 to 4:30 PM. Information on other sights in town can be obtained from the tourist office, in the Convento de Santa Clara, near the cathedral on Rua de Elvas (phone: 45-21815).

En Route from Portalegre – Take N18 south through a characteristic Alentejo landscape of dry, open expanses, cork trees, and distant clusters of low, white houses. About halfway to Estremoz, which is 36 miles (58 km) from Portalegre, is the village of Monforte, with Roman excavations nearby and several fine old country houses.

ESTREMOZ: A magnificent 13th-century fortified tower, surrounded by battlements and 18th-century palace buildings, looms majestically over the medieval summit of this attractive and interesting old town. A full 89 feet high, with corner balconies from which boiling oil could be conveniently poured on attackers, the tower was the main defensive feature of what was once one of the Alentejo's most formidable castles, and it is generally considered to be among the finest surviving pieces of medieval military architecture on the Iberian Peninsula. The imposing structure is known as the Torre das Tres Coroas (Tower of the Three Crowns), because three kings are said to have had a hand in its construction. However, it seems to have been mostly the work of King Dinis, who finished it shortly before the end of the 13th century. Dinis also added a royal palace to the fortifications, and this became one of the favorite residences of his wife, Queen Isabel. Unfortunately, most of the original palace was destroyed in 1698 in the explosion of a powder magazine. The present palace, which adjoins Dinis's tower and is now a state *pousada* (see *Checking In*), was built on the same site during the 18th century by King João V. All that is left of the royal residence of Dinis and Isabel is a lovely little arcade of Gothic arches, known as the Gallery of the Audience Hall, as well as the room where the sainted queen died in 1336, which was later turned into a chapel decorated with scenes from her life. Access to the chapel, the tower, and the gallery is through the *pousada* (all three are open to non-guests).

In the Lower Town, which is partially enclosed by a second set of walls (17th century this time), the focal point is the great central square, the Rossio (in full, the Rossio do Marquês de Pombal). Among the interesting buildings surrounding it is the Câmara Municipal (Town Hall), built during the 17th century as a convent; inside is a superb marble staircase decorated with 18th-century tiled panels depicting the life of St. Philip Neri. Another is the Misericórdia Church, with lovely Gothic cloisters. The *Museu Rural da Casa do Povo de Santa Maria,* also on the square, contains a small but extremely interesting collection of local crafts and costumes (open from 9:30 AM to 12:30 PM and from 2:30 to 5:30 PM; closed Mondays; admission charge). The market held on the Rossio every Saturday is a good opportunity to see the earthenware pottery for which Estremoz has been famous for centuries. The traditionally shaped jugs and cooking pots and the charming little painted figures are becoming collectors' items, although they remain inexpensively priced here. Estremoz's Tourist Office is on Largo da República, south of the Rossio (phone: 68-22538).

CHECKING IN: *Pousada da Rainha Santa Isabel* – One of the most highly rated of Portugal's string of state-owned *pousadas,* it's installed in the former palace of King João V, adjoining the Tower of the Three Crowns, and the views are spectacular. The 23 rooms are beautifully furnished with genuine 17th- and 18th-century antiques, and there is a restaurant specializing in regional cooking (see *Eating Out*). Largo Dom Dinis, Estremoz (phone: 68-22618). Expensive.

Alentejano – For all its enchantments, Estremoz is lamentably poor in accommodations, and the gap between the *pousada* and this rickety old commercial hotel is abysmal as far as modern comforts go. Nevertheless, the place has a certain character, and for those who don't mind walking down the hall to the bathroom, it is worth considering. Breakfast is the only meal served. 50 Rossio do Marquês de Pombal, Estremoz (phone: 68-22717). Inexpensive.

EATING OUT: *Pousada da Rainha Santa Isabel* – The best choice in town — in addition to the food (regional cooking, with particularly noteworthy game dishes in season), there are panoramic views from the dining room windows. Try the various lamb (*borrego*) dishes or, during hunting season, the *javali assado* (roast wild boar) or *coelho ao caçador* (a richly flavored rabbit casserole). Open daily. Reservations necessary. Largo Dom Dinis, Estremoz (phone: 68-22618). Expensive.

Aguias d'Ouro – A comfortable, air conditioned restaurant on the main square. The *borrego assado no forno* (roast lamb with onions and bay leaves) is reputed to be the best in the area. Open daily. Reservations advised. 27 Rossio do Marquês de Pombal, Estremoz (phone: 68-22196). Moderate to inexpensive.

En Route from Estremoz – Go directly to Evora, 28½ miles (46 km) from Estremoz, by driving west on N4 for about 4 miles (6 km) and then picking up the southbound N18. Or first make a short but worthwhile detour to the lovely royal town of Vila Viçosa, 11 miles (18 km) from Estremoz, by taking N4 east for 9 miles (14 km) and then turning right onto N255.

VILA VIÇOSA: During the 15th and 16th centuries, this town was the seat of the Dukes of Bragança, who continued to maintain a residence here even after the family became Portugal's last ruling dynasty — in 1640, when the eighth duke became King João IV. Be sure to visit the Paço Ducal (Ducal Palace), whose gorgeous marble façade fills one side of the Terreiro do Paço, the spacious main square. Begun during the 16th century, although dating mainly from the 17th century, the palace has been turned into a museum — the *Museu Biblioteca da Casa de Bragança* — containing furniture, tapestries, paintings, ceramics, and other works of art, as well as many of the possessions of the last Portuguese king, Manuel II, who died in exile in England in 1932 and left behind an important library of 15th- and 16th-century Portuguese books. There is also a small *Museu dos Coches* (Coach Museum). The palace is open from 9:30 AM to 1 PM and from 2 to 6 PM (5 PM in winter); closed Mondays. Admission charge.

In the same square is another good 16th-century Renaissance building, the Convento das Chagas, where the Duchesses of Bragança are buried. The Bragança dukes are buried apart from the ladies, in the church of Santo Agostinho nearby. The *tapada,* the family's walled hunting preserve, the largest in Portugal, has remained intact and is now a nature reserve. For additional information, contact the tourist office on Praça da República (phone: 68-98584).

EVORA: The encircling walls of this remarkable and lovely old city have evidently protected it very well over the centuries. Few cities of Evora's age can boast a standing record of their past quite so neatly encapsulated. Evora was a Roman town of some importance in Julius Caesar's days and became one of the foremost cities on the peninsula during the Moorish occupation from the 8th to the 12th centuries. After the Moors, it was at various times the seat of Portuguese monarchs and was the object of numerous sieges and battles. Today, the city is an important agricultural and university center with a burgeoning tourist industry. For a full description, see *Evora,* THE CITIES.

En Route from Evora – Heading west, N114 leads back to the N4 at Montemor-o-Novo, 20 miles (32 km) from Evora. Anyone who has admired the Arraiolos carpets seen in shops, museums, and some of the better hotels throughout

Portugal, however, is advised to take a short detour to the town where they are made, 10 miles (16 km) north of Evora on N370. Arraiolos has been producing these famed woolen carpets since the beginning of the 18th century, and while there is actually no price advantage in buying straight from one of the factories, it is possible to ask to see the workshops and watch the carpets being made. The oldest established of the factories is *Kalifa*, 44-46 Rua Alexandre Herculano (phone: 66-42117).

Montemor-o-Novo, 15½ miles (25 km) west of Arraiolos on N4, has the picturesque remains of a Moorish castle at the top of the Old Town, but it's notable mainly as the birthplace of João de Deus (John of God), the founder of the Order of Charity, who was declared patron saint of hospitals throughout the Christian world 350 years after his death in 1550. Continue 23 miles (37 km) west of Montemor to Pegões, where there is a crossroads with two possible routes to Lisbon. Be sure to take the one going left, toward Setúbal.

SETÚBAL: This busy, ancient port town sits on the estuary of the Sado River, at the edge of the range of hills known as the Serra da Arrábida. Hans Christian Andersen, who visited Setúbal in 1866, called it a terrestrial paradise. It is now the hub of the most important industrial area in the south of Portugal, with shipbuilding, chemicals, automobile assembly, and fishing its major activities, but it has nevertheless retained a lot of the charm that delighted Andersen over a century ago. On Praça Miguel de Bombarda is the late-15th-century Igreja de Jesus, "one of the prettiest little churches" Andersen had ever seen and the earliest example of the Manueline style of architecture, which was to reach its zenith in the Jerónimos Monastery in Lisbon and in Tomar (open until 5 PM). Across the river on the Tróia Peninsula — a dune and pine-backed sandbar blocking the estuary — is the big Torralta tourism development, with apartment-hotels, a golf course, and miles of good white sand. In a quiet creek near the apartment complex are the excavated ruins of a Roman fish processing factory (which may have been part of the once important Roman town of Cetóbriga) and a fascinating little 8th-century Christian church. The site is open to visitors daily from 9:30 AM to 5:30 PM, from June through September; no admission charge. A regular car ferry service connects Setúbal to Tróia. Information is available from the tourist office on Largo do Corpo Santo (phone: 65-24284) in Setúbal.

CHECKING IN: *Pousada de São Filipe* – Unquestionably Setúbal's best accommodation, this government-run inn is about half a mile (1 km) west of town, overlooking the Sado estuary. It's installed in a fortress built during the late 16th century by King Philip II of Spain (Philip I of Portugal) to defend the "invincible" armada he had assembled in Portugal against a possible English attack. There are 14 rooms (ask for one on the waterfront) and a panoramic restaurant (see *Eating Out*). Castelo de São Filipe, Setúbal (phone: 65-23844). Expensive.

***Apartamentos Turísticos Torralta* –** There are three high-rise apartment-hotels in this development: the *Magnóliamar,* the *Rosamar,* and the *Tulipamar.* On the Tróia Peninsula, a 20-minute ferry ride across the Sado River estuary from Setúbal, they're worth considering as an alternative to something in town, because guests have access to all the facilities of the residential resort complex — a golf course, tennis courts, seawater pools, a supermarket, restaurants, and a disco. The three buildings, each with 129 spacious rooms and suites with kitchenettes, stand close to the beach, surrounded by lawns and flowerbeds; views from the upper-floor balconies are superb. Each hotel has its own telephone number (*Magnóliamar:* 65-44361; *Rosamar:* 65-44151; *Tulipamar:* 65-44201). There also is a central booking office for information and reservations (phone: 65-44221). Expensive to moderate, depending on the season.

Esperança – A comfortable, no-frills hostelry conveniently situated in town. It has 76 small but well-furnished rooms with private baths, plus a restaurant of some repute. 220 Avenida Luísa Todi, Setúbal (phone: 65-25151). Moderate.

EATING OUT: *Pousada de São Filipe* – The inn's dining room serves very good regional dishes, along with a good view. The fish is especially recommended: Try the *cherne grelhado com frutas do mar* (grilled turbot with a seafood sauce) or *amêijoas na cataplana* (clams with tomatoes and onions, steamed quickly in a covered copper pan — the *cataplana*). Reservations necessary. Castelo de São Filipe, Setúbal (phone: 65-23844). Expensive.

Rio Azul – Big, with an open kitchen, this is a prime place for lovers of seafood — fresh crab, lobster, shrimp, prawns. Remember, however, that seafood can be astronomically expensive by local standards (although it's sold by weight, so diners can control what they spend). Try the sea spider (*sapateira*) — it's cheaper than crab or lobster, and just as good. Closed Wednesdays. Reservations advised. 44 Rua Guilherme Fernandes, Setúbal (phone: 65-22828). Expensive to moderate.

A Roda – This small place produces some of the best regional cooking in Setúbal and serves it up with a certain amount of cosmopolitan dash. Like most of the local restaurants, it specializes in fish dishes, but the *lombinho de vaca ao moscatel* (filets of beef braised in wine from nearby Azeitão) is a non-fish specialty. Or try the *espadarte na cataplana,* swordfish cooked in a covered copper pan. The house wine is the local pedras negras. Closed Sundays. Reservations advised. Near the ferryboat station for Tróia. 7 Travessa Postigo do Cais, Setúbal (phone: 65-29264). Moderate.

Retiro da Algodeia – No frills, and they aren't needed. Big, informal, noisy, and very enjoyable, this is the destination of fish lovers for miles around. *Caldeiradas,* or fish stews, and open-fire grills are the specialty. Try the *salmonete* (red mullet) or the *peixe espada* (blade, or scabbard fish), both of which lend themselves wonderfully to grilling. The local pedras negras wine is a good accompaniment. Closed Mondays. Reservations advised. 30 Estrada de Algodeia, Setúbal (phone: 65-27095). Moderate to inexpensive.

Bocage – A popular dining spot where the traditional regional food is prepared simply but well. The establishment doesn't aspire to gastronomic heights or surprises, but it does offer good value. The *costeletas de vitela ao moscatel* (veal cutlets braised in wine with potatoes and onions) are a good choice. Closed Monday evenings and Tuesdays. Reservations advised. 5-8 Rua Marquesa de Faial, Setúbal (phone: 65-22513). Inexpensive.

En Route from Setúbal – The Serra da Arrábida, on the Arrábida (or Setúbal) Peninsula, is one of Portugal's loveliest and most distinctive regions. This range of hills rises out of the Sado River estuary west of Setúbal and forms a high ridge of limestone along the peninsula's southern coast. The whole area, comprising the *serra* itself, which is a national park, and the region around it, has a character of its own, with its own wines, its own cheeses, its own microclimate, and its own flora and fauna. Because of its geographic situation, plants survive here that long ago disappeared elsewhere in Spain and Portugal. Two roads lead west from Setúbal through the range: N10-4 follows the coastline, while N379-1, more spectacular, traverses the spine of the hills, offering stunning views along the way. About 7½ miles (12 km) from Setúbal along N379-1, a signposted left turn winds down to a little harbor, Portinho da Arrábida, where there is a marvelous, crescent-shaped beach protected by a high escarpment. (Lack of space makes parking problems formidable in summer.) High on the mountainside above the harbor is the Convento de Arrábida, a Franciscan monastery founded in 1542. A close view of the lovely old monastic building, rising in cellular form like a terraced wasp's nest, can be had by driving a little way along N10-4 from the road leading down into Portinho. About 4½ miles (7 km) beyond the Portinho turnoff from N379-1, the road branches left to the fishing town of Sesimbra.

SESIMBRA: A popular holiday resort and consequently very crowded in summer, Sesimbra is a center for big-game fishing. Tuna, shark, and swordfish are all caught here. Unfortunately, uncontrolled development has blighted the outskirts of what was once an attractive little fishing village, but there is some charm left in the old village core. The remains of a fine 13th-century castle stand guard over the town from a high hilltop (the castle is empty now, but visitors can walk around it for the superb view). Sesimbra has plenty of fish restaurants where it is easy to get a good meal — although, oddly enough, given all the fish available, no really outstanding restaurant has emerged. The meal to try here is swordfish, because it's difficult to find on menus elsewhere; it's usually prepared as a steak (*bife de espadarte*). Also a delicacy is *peixe espada,* which translates literally as "swordfish" but is, in fact, blade, or scabbard fish. Sesimbra's *caldeiradas,* fish stews made with six or seven varieties of fish, are also particularly good.

CHECKING IN: *Mar* – In a good position overlooking the sea, this is an excellent, modern hostelry offering 120 rooms with private baths and balconies, as well as a restaurant, disco, and swimming pool. 10 Rua General Humberto Delgado, Sesimbra (phone: 65-223-3326). Moderate.

EATING OUT: *Ribamar* – There is no "best" seafood restaurant in town, but this is typical of the better eateries. Try any of the Sesimbra specialties. Closed Mondays. Reservations advised. 6 Largo da Fortaleza, Sesimbra (phone: 65-223-3107). Moderate to inexpensive.

En Route from Sesimbra – Returning eastward, an 9-mile (14-km) drive along N379 leads to Vila Nogueira de Azeitão, at the foot of the Serra da Arrábida. The most notable of several fine buildings in this attractive old village is the early-16th-century palace of the Dukes of Aveiro, still used as a family residence. Here also are two wineries that should be visited. On the main street of town are the old cellars of José Maria da Fonseca (phone: 65-208-0002), where the once widely appreciated moscatel de Setúbal is made. Little known outside of Portugal, it is nevertheless a superb dessert wine that many experts place among the finest of Europe's sweet wines. The cellars are open Mondays through Fridays, from 9 AM to noon and from 2 to 5 PM, and members of small groups can ask to see the small wine museum that the firm maintains here. Around the corner, on the main Lisbon–Setúbal road, is the big, ultramodern winery belonging to J.M. da Fonseca International (phone: 65-208-0227), which makes several classic table wines that are highly regarded in Portugal — but is best known abroad for Lancers Rosé. Visiting hours are the same as those of the old cellars.

Continue eastward from Azeitão, taking N10 in the direction of Setúbal for about 1¼ miles (about 2 km); then branch left onto N379 and follow the signs for Cabanas, Quinta do Anjo, and Palmela.

CHECKING IN/EATING OUT: *Quinta das Torres* – This very comfortable 12-room *estalagem* is in a 16th-century mansion, approached by a tree-lined driveway and surrounded by delightful gardens. A natural pool for swimming graces the grounds, as does a fine ornamental irrigation pond with a little classical pavilion in its center. The style of an old country house extends to the dining room, which serves simple but good Portuguese fare, and to the service. Two dishes to try are the *bacalhau dourado,* fried dried cod, and the *carril de gambas,* curried shrimp. This is also one of the few places where the exquisite and increasingly rare azeitão cheeses — small, creamy sheep's milk cheese with a flavor rather like good brie — can still be found. (The restaurant is closed Saturdays; reservations necessary.) The entrance to the inn's driveway is on the right side of N10 just after leaving Vila Nogueira de Azeitão in the direction of Setúbal. Quinta das Torres (phone: 65-208-0001). Moderate.

PALMELA: The massive castle towering over this little town, at the northeastern end of the Serra da Arrábida, is worth the climb for the views alone. Constructed by the Moors, it was reconstructed after the 12th-century Reconquest, but was partially demolished by the 1755 earthquake that laid waste to Lisbon. Many of the 18th-century houses in the narrow streets below the walls were built with stones salvaged from the disaster.

CHECKING IN/EATING OUT: *Pousada de Palmela* – This 27-room, air conditioned inn is installed in a monastery (Convento de São Tiago) that was built within the castle precincts during the 15th century. The marvelous location and handsome appointments make it one of the flagships of the state-owned *pousada* chain, and the restaurant, occupying the old refectory, offers not only delightful decor, but also the best cooking to be found around Palmela. When game is in season in the fall and around *Christmas,* this is a good place to try partridge or quail casseroles in red wine (*perdiz* or *codorniz estufado*). At other times, try the various lamb dishes, especially *borrego assado no forno,* an oven roast with onions, garlic, and bay leaves. This is also another of the few remaining places where azeitão cheeses can be found. The restaurant is open daily; reservations necessary. Castelo de Palmela, Palmela (phone: 1-235-1395). Expensive.

En Route from Palmela – The signposted access to the A2 toll highway is about 1¼ miles (2 km) away. From there, it is a 20-mile (32-km) drive to the Tagus bridge — the Ponte 25 de Abril — which leads into Lisbon. The world's third-longest suspension bridge, it offers what is probably the finest view of the capital, as a reward for homecoming travelers.

The Algarve

From the wild and windy headlands of Cabo de São Vicente (Cape St. Vincent) to the tranquil estuary of the Guadiana River on the Spanish border, Portugal's Algarve coast is as replete with history as it is with the good things of modern living. Like many southern European coasts, the Algarve has been marred by over-commercialization, but anyone with a spark of imagination who explores beyond the resort condominiums will find rich treasures, products of an exotic mix of Europe with Africa. Sipping an aperitif at sunset on a chalky-white poolside terrace facing Africa, a visitor won't quite be able to see the Moroccan coast, but as the red disk of the sun slips down to the horizon, the spiritual affinity is evident. And if the African heat of the coast seems too harsh, there is the traditional option of Algarve-dwellers — taking to the hills of the Monchique mountain range, which offers the best of both worlds.

In 1927, a Portuguese travel writer lamented the fact that the Algarve women's custom of wearing veils — a last trace of pure Arab influence — had almost given way to Paris fashions. But he noted that in some parts of the region the women — described as "healthy, full-fleshed women with red mouths and great, dark eyes . . . veiled by long, silky eyelashes" — still bore traces of their heritage, bringing to mind "the purest of Arab types." The young Algarve woman of today is more likely to be wearing a bikini than a veil, but the writer reminds us of how culturally different the Moorish-influenced Algarve is from the rest of Portugal, a point borne out by a glimpse of the white rectangular houses with flat roof terraces characteristic of the region and the many Arab waterwheels that can still be seen here.

The Algarve's natural setting is also different from that of the rest of Portugal. While the Alentejo region, just to the north, shares the Algarve's sunny disposition, its undulating landscape is sparsely vegetated and spotted with cork oaks and olive trees. By contrast, the Algarve has distinctive vegetation, its roads and byways lined with almond trees (a delight when they blossom in spring), lush spreading fig trees, olive trees, and the carob bean tree (*alfarrobeira*), which is the basis of a thriving local industry. Unfortunately, development for the tourism industry has destroyed much of this natural growth on the main highway that traverses the coast for about 100 miles, but the back roads of the Algarve open up another world. Here the traveler may share the road with only a plodding mule cart and breathe in the beauty of a landscape uncorrupted by neon signs.

And there are wide variations in the landscape, even within this relatively small coastal province of Portugal. The area between Sagres and Lagos — known as the Costa Vicentina, at the western end of the Algarve — is characterized by dramatic bluffs and promontories and has been declared a protected zone because of the special value of its flora and fauna. To the east, near Faro, is the Ria Formosa marshland, where the coast is paralleled by long sandbanks enclosing seawater lagoons. This is quite a different kind of geography, teeming with interesting birds and marine creatures and considered unique in Europe.

The marked Moorish character of the Algarve derives from the fact that the Islamic occupation lasted longer here than it did elsewhere in the country. Before the Moors and Christian crusaders fought their final battles, however, the Algarve shared with the rest of Portugal a history of invasion by Phoenicians, Romans, and barbarians. The original inhabitants of the area — known to the ancient Greeks as the Cunete tribe — played host first to the Phoenicians, a Semitic seagoing people from the eastern Mediterranean who, around 1300 BC, founded cities at Tavira, Faro, Portimão, and Lagos. The most obvious trace they left was the exotic form of the local fishing boats, which are graced with sweeping Oriental prows and sometimes have a mystical-looking eye painted on either side. (They can still be seen in Albufeira, Portimão, and Faro.)

The Romans then had their turn. Their road system on the Portuguese side of the Iberian Peninsula ran south from Lisbon through Alcácer do Sal to Beja (which was their southern capital) in the Alentejo, then on through Mértola to emerge in the Algarve at Castro Marim, just north of Vila Real de Santo António on the Spanish border. Castro Marim, a fortress town of humble, whitewashed houses that commands a view into Spain over the Guadiana River, imparts a sense of this long, long history. The salt pans that lie below the battlements were worked by the Romans, too.

The Moors conquered the Iberian Peninsula in 711. The Portuguese nation was forged and founded in the Christian crusaders' struggles to oust them, which began in earnest with the reconquest of Porto during the mid-9th century and was broadly won at the Battle of Ourique, near Santarém, in 1139. However, the Algarve did not come back into the fold until 1249. The inland city of Silves, on the Arade River, was then known as Xelb and was the capital of Moorish Algarve. At its height, it was considered an Arab city of great luxury and nobility, a place where fleets loaded oranges, figs, and olives for distant lands. The river has long since silted up, but the rich orange groves and an imposing castle with subterranean cisterns testify to its role in this period. Many Algarve towns still retain their Moorish names — Faro, Tunes, Odeleite, Odeceixe, Odiáxere, Odeleuca, Alcoutim, Aljezur, Alvor — as does the name of the Algarve itself, which comes from the Arabic *Al-Gharb,* meaning "the West," referring to the land west of their territory in Andalusia.

The Algarve has been attracting European vacationers for years, but only recently have Americans begun to discover its beaches — fine, pale sand in long stretches, as well as tiny coves — and year round sunshine (the best time to visit is from the end of January through October, however, or from mid-May to the beginning of October for swimming). Luxury and lesser hotels and resort complexes abound in the more developed parts of the coast, offering excellent opportunities for fishing, boating, water skiing, windsurfing, golf, tennis, and riding. Yet development notwithstanding, there are also simple towns and small fishing villages.

Seafood is, naturally, the basis of traditional Algarve cooking. Clams (*amêijoas*) are the prize coastal produce, and they are presented at their best as *amêijoas na cataplana,* a dish named after the sort of Moorish copper pressure cooker in which it is prepared, using, in addition to clams, ham, local salami, garlic, and coriander — a taste sensation. Lobster, crayfish, and crab (*lavagante, lagosta,* and *sapateira,* respectively) are also featured, as is squid (*lulas*), cooked in a variety of local styles. No visit to Portugal would be complete without trying the humble but tasty sardine, and the recommended place to do this in the Algarve is at the *Portimão Sardine Festival,* held in August on the waterfront, under the town's picturesque iron bridge. Umbrella-shaded tables are set out in the blazing sun, and the sardines are served from the charcoal grill accompanied by boiled potatoes and fresh green salad. They can be washed down with sparkling *vinho verde* — "green," or young, wine — or a cold beer.

The town of Sagres, at Portugal's southwesternmost point, is a logical starting place for a visit to the Algarve, although reaching it may involve retracing steps, because the main road from Lisbon meets the coast's trunk road (N125) at Ferreiras, near Albufeira, 50 miles (80 km) east. An alternative is to use the poorer-quality coastal road from Lisbon, passing through Odemira and Aljezur and picking up N125 at Vila do Bispo, a few miles north of Sagres. Those arriving by plane at Faro, toward the Spanish border, can work their way east or west, but they, too, will have to cover some ground twice, since there is only one main road along the Algarve coast. And note that it is not a coastal route — it's necessary to turn off it to reach beach destinations. Because the entire road is little more than 100 miles (160 km) long, repeating part of it is easily done; one journey can be slow and exploratory, the other a more rapid return, checking on sights missed along the way. (One suggested alternative, for those working their way west from Faro with the intention of then following the route west to east as outlined below, would be to take the back road to Silves from Faro, through the Algarve's rural hinterland. Leave the main highway 5 miles (8 km) west of Faro and go to Loulé, turning left at the main city square, near the bus terminal, and heading north to Salir, 9½ miles (15 km) away. Turn left there and go another 9½ miles (15 km) to the delightful town of Alte, immortalized by James Michener in his book *The Drifters.* Continue in the same direction, through São Bartolomeu de Messines, to Silves. When returning east from Sagres, proceed straight on N125, dispensing with the need to detour to Silves and Loulé as described below.)

Expect to pay $100 and up for a double room in a hotel listed below as expensive — up to $250 a night at places commanding oil sheik rents such as the deluxe resorts of Vale do Lobo and Quinta do Lago. Medium-quality establishments, such as the *Baleeira* at Sagres, are listed as moderate and run from about $50 to $75. Inexpensive hotels and pensions can cost less than $50 — much less in the low season — but none have been included below because such establishments are generally not up to the standards of the foreign pleasure traveler. All hotels listed have air conditioning and are open year-round; for accommodations in July and August, it is advisable to book well in advance. Eating out needn't be costly. With resourcefulness, it is possible to have a good meal for two with wine for $20 to $30, marking the inexpensive end of the spectrum. Moderate means $30 to $70 for two; at restaurants listed as expensive, allow $70 to $100.

SAGRES: This dramatic promontory (Ponta de Sagres in Portuguese) and Cape St. Vincent (Cabo de São Vicente), 4 miles (6 km) away, form the southwestern tip of Europe, a wild landscape where rugged cliffs plunge down to clear blue waters alive with sea life — as the many local fishermen who perch precariously on the rocks bear witness. Popular belief stemming from prehistoric times held that the gods met here, and to the ancients, here was the end of the known world, beyond which the setting sun fell off the face of the earth. The gods aside, the area has played an important role in Portuguese history. It was here during the early 15th century that Prince Henry the Navigator, son of João I of Portugal and his English wife, Philippa of Lancaster, established a school of geography and navigation — a community of scholars who pooled their knowledge of map making, ship building, and mathematics. Under his leadership, Portugal's first voyages of discovery were planned and undertaken, preparing the way for the epic voyages of later men such as Vasco da Gama, Bartholomeu Dias, and Christopher Columbus (the latter was an Italian, of course, who sailed under the Spanish flag after being snubbed by the Portuguese). Although Prince Henry, known in Portuguese as Infante Dom Henrique, did not sail himself, the contributions he made to the advancement of navigation and exploration during 40 years in the area (he died in 1460) provided the basis for the rise of the Portuguese colonial empire and allowed the country to maintain naval supremacy for almost 2 centuries.

The village of Sagres, set on the cliffs, came into the news again in 1597, when it was razed by the British fleet under Sir Francis Drake, then at war with the Spanish (Portugal was subordinated to the Spanish throne at this time). Today it is a bit of an eyesore, but redeemed by the area's spectacular views. Within walking distance of the village is Cabo de São Vicente, where the lighthouse can be inspected at the keeper's discretion daily, between 10 AM and noon and 2 and 5:30 PM (a tip is expected). Between the two, on a windswept bluff, is the Fortaleza do Beliche, dating from the 15th century, but largely reconstructed during the 18th century. An enormous mariner's compass etched into the ground here was presumably designed by Prince Henry. The fort (always open; no admission charge) has climbable ramparts, and its main building houses a youth hostel. Also within the walls is the Sagres Tourist Office (phone: 82-64125).

CHECKING IN: *Pousada do Infante* – This government-owned inn has a stylish setting on the cliff top; there are 23 rooms, with private terraces overlooking the sea. Sagres (phone: 82-64222). Expensive.

Baleeira – Also on the cliffs, it offers quality service and a tasteful, well-maintained interior. Dining here at sunset as migratory swallows swoop around the bluff is an experience in itself; the 120-room hotel also has its own tennis court, swimming pool, and bicycles for hire. Fishing excursions can be arranged. Sagres (phone: 82-64212). Moderate.

EATING OUT: *Tasca* – Set on a cliffside beneath the *Baleeira,* this is a wonderful place to dine alfresco on a summer day. Shellfish is the specialty (the restaurant has its own lobster pools), the salads are fresh, and the wine list is good. In addition, the service is quietly efficient and prices are very reasonable. (Guests at the *Baleeira* receive a 10% discount upon presentation of their check-in card.) Closed Saturdays and from mid-January to mid-February. Reservations unnecessary. Sagres (phone: 82-64177). Inexpensive.

En Route from Sagres – The road to Lagos (N125), 20½ miles (33 km) away, is in poor condition and has little traffic, heightening the feeling of otherworldliness at the Algarve's western tip. The road runs inland from the coast — here called the Costa Vicentina — but a series of good beaches (*praias*) can be reached by turning off N125. All signposted, they include Praia do Martinhal (the sign reads *Martinhal Motel Restaurant*), Praia da Salema, Praia do Burgau, and Praia da Luz, which is a popular resort center.

LAGOS: An attractive harbor town, this, too, holds memories of Henry the Navigator. It was from this port in the mid-15th century that the ships sailing under Prince Henry's authority actually embarked, setting their course south to explore the west coast of Africa. It was also from Lagos that the doomed, fanatically religious King Sebastian sailed in 1578 to fight the Moors at the historic battle of Alcázarquivir in Morocco. He died on the battlefield, leaving the throne to his elderly uncle, the childless Cardinal-King Henrique, who reigned for 2 years. An illegitimate member of the royal family, the Prior of Crato, claimed the throne next but was bested by the superior force of another claimant, Philip of Spain. Because Sebastian's death in North Africa had not been confirmed, his countrymen persisted in the belief that he would one day return to rule again. Thus, a legend was born. In the centuries since, fake Sebastians have "returned" to Portugal — even today claimants show up in small villages — and the term Sebastianism came to be used to describe the belief in a returning redeemer. The legend is remembered in Lagos with a controversial statue by modern sculptor João Cutileiro, who depicts Sebastian as a visionary adolescent gazing out to sea. The statue is in the central Praça de Gil Eanes (named after one of Prince Henry's explorers, born in Lagos), where young travelers with backpacks congregate nowadays, as a starting place to explore the town.

As a result of the voyages to Africa, Lagos had the dubious privilege of being the site of Europe's first slave auctions. The arcaded building where they were held, the Mercado de Escravos (Slave Market), still stands near the waterfront in the Praça da República, opposite the Church of Santa Maria, although there is no plaque to mark its significance. Another of the town's highlights is the 18th-century baroque Igreja de Santo António (Rua General Alberto da Silveira), with a breathtaking ornate altarpiece, gilt cherubs, and antique tiled surfaces. The *Museu Regional* (open from 9:30 AM to 12:30 PM and from 2 to 5 PM; closed Mondays; admission charge), adjoining the church, contains a strange mix of works, from local handicrafts to Roman statuary and a mid-16th century diptych showing the Annunciation and the Presentation in the Temple, attributed to Francisco de Campos. Parts of the old city walls remain; built by the Moors and fortified by their Christian successors, they were largely destroyed by the 1755 earthquake that devastated most of Lagos. Outside the walls is the 17th-century Forte do Pau da Bandeira, built as a defense against pirates. For more information on this historic city, capital of the Algarve from the late 16th to the mid-18th century, stop in at the Lagos Tourist Office (Largo Marquês de Pombal; phone: 82-63031).

 CHECKING IN: *Meia Praia* – Located a bit over 2½ miles (4 km) to the east of Lagos, it has 66 rooms and its own pool, gardens, and tennis courts facing a good swimming beach. Meia Praia (phone: 82-62001). Moderate.

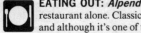 **EATING OUT: *Alpendre* –** A stop in Lagos would be worthwhile for this restaurant alone. Classic Portuguese cooking and service have made it a legend, and although it's one of the few restaurants in Portugal to serve a Caesar salad, its best dishes are distinctively local. Try the clam-based *cataplana* or the *amêijoas à bulhão pato,* clams cooked in a garlic and coriander sauce. For dessert, the crêpes suzette are a rich delight — the restaurant uses a rare, expensive, aged brandy, *adega velha,* for the flambé process. There is also an impressive list of the best

Portuguese wines. Open daily. Reservations advised. 17 Rua António Barbosa Viana, Lagos (phone: 82-62705). Expensive.

En Route from Lagos – The road improves between Lagos and Portimão, 11 miles (18 km) away. Between the two, off the main road, are several good beaches and rocky coves, among them Praia da Dona Ana and Praia dos Tres Irmãos, besides Meia Praia. Browse through Portimão, then turn north (N124 and N266) to the Monchique mountain range.

PORTIMÃO: This is one of the fishing capitals of the Algarve — a modern commercial fishing center rather than a picturesque village, however. Set on the estuary of the Arade River, Portimão was largely destroyed by the 1755 earthquake, but after rebuilding, it has grown into the second-largest town along the coast (after Faro). It has a relaxed Mediterranean atmosphere and a host of sidewalk cafés, bars, restaurants, and shops; its August sardine festival is an optimal occasion to sample the Algarve's *sardinha assada* straight from the charcoal grill. A little over a mile south of town, on the western side of the river's mouth, is Praia da Rocha, a seaside resort on one of the best (but unfortunately overcommercialized) beaches on the coast, noted for its majestic rock formations. On the opposite side of the river is Ferragudo, a small waterfront hamlet with a ruined 16th-century castle.

CHECKING IN: *Bela Vista* – At Praia da Rocha, this is an oasis of quality in a desert of tourist hype. An old-fashioned, privately managed, 14-room hotel, installed in a former mansion, it is something of a Victorian folly, with spires, dark woodwork, and stained glass windows. There is direct access to the beach. Avenida Marginal, Praia da Rocha (phone: 82-24055). Expensive.

EATING OUT: *A Lanterna* – This simple place on the outskirts of Portimão, near the bridge over the Arade, serves fish and seafood, as well as other basic but tasty Portuguese dishes. Closed Sundays and from early December through late January. Reservations unnecessary. Estrada N125, Cruzamento de Ferragudo, Portimão (phone: 82-23948). Moderate.

Safari – An unpretentious place with good, fresh seafood and a beachfront view. Open daily, except for a few weeks in January or February. Reservations unnecessary. Rua António Feu, Praia da Rocha (phone: 82-23540). Moderate.

MONCHIQUE: The eucalyptus-scented and lushly wooded heights of the Monchique Mountains are a pleasant change from the landscape of the coast. The Serra de Monchique, along with the Serra do Caldeirão to the east, forms a natural barrier between the Algarve and the rest of Portugal — which explains not only the coastline's flawless weather, but also why the Moors were able to hold out longer here than elsewhere in the face of advancing Christian armies. In bygone days, the Monchique hills were also a fashionable retreat from the Algarve's searing heat, the medicinal springs bursting from volcanic rock deemed beneficial for a variety of ailments. The springs, located at Caldas de Monchique, a leafy spa town about 11 miles (18 km) north of Portimão, were known to the Romans; King João II, who reigned from 1481 to 1495, was said to have been treated for dropsy here (to no avail — he died soon after). The spa's more recent heyday was around the turn of this century, when the *Grand Hotel* and its casino were in full swing. Today, the charm of Caldas still lies in its old-fashioned cafés banked with potted palms, its walks and views, and the cool town square, where the old hotel has been restored (not the casino, however). The town of Monchique proper, 4 miles (6 km) north of Caldas, has a parish church with a Manueline doorway, but the town itself is less an attraction than the drive to the summit of the nearly 3,000-foot Fóia, the highest point of the Serra de Monchique. Take N266-3 west out of Monchique, and in a few miles the view opens up to the coast and the sea and seems to stretch almost to Africa. The whole Monchique area is known for its handicrafts, including colorful rugs and furniture — the folding wooden Monchique stools are derived from a Roman design and are a good bargain (quite portable, too).

CHECKING IN: *Abrigo da Montanha* – An *estalagem* (inn) of only 8 rooms, it sits a mile or so southwest of Monchique, along the way to Fóia. Given its size, it's advisable to book well in advance, but even those not staying here can sit under the umbrellas amid the cool hydrangeas of the terrace restaurant and enhance the famous Fóia view with good food and wine. Estrada de Fóia, Monchique (phone: 82-92131). Moderate.

Do Lageado – This is a pleasant *albergaria* (another category of inn) with 21 rooms and its own swimming pool, in the main square of Caldas. It's open only from May through October, and note that it doesn't take credit cards. Caldas de Monchique (phone: 82-92616). Moderate.

EATING OUT: *1692* – The restaurant's name comes from the date the stone building it occupies was constructed. At first owned by the Catholic church, then converted into a hotel — the *Grand* — the building has been restored (the *Grand* is now the *Albergaria Velha,* but it's fairly spartan and unattractive). Local dishes are served in a wonderfully green, shady setting. Be sure to try the traditional hot bread, baked with *chouriço,* the spicy Portuguese sausage; it comes from the village's restored bread oven. Open daily. Reservations unnecessary. Caldas de Monchique (phone: 82-92205). Inexpensive.

En Route from Monchique – Return to Portimão and take N125 east 5 miles (8 km) to Lagoa, a market town of some charm that is the junction for the road to Silves, 4½ miles (7 km) north, and Carvoeiro, 3 miles (5 km) south.

SILVES: The sleepy, sunny inland town gives few clues to its former importance as the capital of the Moorish kingdom of the Algarve, although its combination of cypresses, orange groves, and the red stone Moorish castle do impart the flavor of an Arab city. Known as Xelb in Moorish times, Silves sits on the north bank of the Arade River, which is now silted up but at one time made the town a flourishing river port. The castle (open daily from 8 AM to 5:30 PM; no admission charge) has enormous underground cisterns and provides a sweeping view of the Algarve coast. Next to it is the 13th-century Gothic cathedral, the Sé, built on the site of the former mosque. With its gargoyles and cleft windows offset by the same rich, reddish local stone as the castle, the church holds considerable architectural interest. The Cruz de Portugal, an unusual 15th-century limestone sculpture about 10 feet high showing Christ crucified on one side and in the arms of the Virgin Mary on the other, is at the town's eastern exit (on N124 toward São Bartolomeu de Messines). The tourist office in Silves is on Rua 25 do Abril (phone: 82-42255).

CARVOEIRO: This little fishing village has become the favored Algarve playground of northern Europeans — Germans, Dutch, and Scandinavians (and British, too, although their stamping ground tends to be the zone farther east, from Albufeira to Faro). Fishermen's white houses on the cliff tops set the tone, and Carvoeiro remains picturesque, despite the modern resort villa complexes that encircle it, with tennis courts, pools, and their own bar and restaurant facilities. The town has a small but pretty beach.

En route from Carvoeiro – Pick up N125 east once again and continue to Ferreiras, where a right turn onto N395 leads to Albufeira, 16 miles (26 km) from Lagoa. A few miles beyond Lagoa, on the right side of the road, is the *Porches Pottery,* just before the village of the same name. Founded by the late Irish artist

Patrick Swift, who was well known in Portugal as an illustrator, the pottery sells hand-painted ceramics, many bearing his distinctive designs. The pieces are not as authentically Portuguese as other local products — they have a style of their own — but traditional Portuguese techniques have been used in making them, along with superior glazes, which makes them chip less easily in everyday use. A book on Portuguese birds, with illustrations by Swift, is also available at the shop.

ALBUFEIRA: This large resort town was the last Moorish stronghold in the Algarve. At one time, it was a picturesque fishing village, but in recent years it has suffered from the onslaught of development and become the heart of the tourist's Algarve. Set on a cliff, it has steep, cobbled streets that are thronged in summer, and its main beach, reached via a tunnel carved through rock, is wall-to-wall flesh at the height of the season. (There are beaches nearby where it is possible to find space, however — just walk along in either direction.) Little of historical value remains in Albufeira, but a walk through town is a pleasant experience, since there are multitudes of shops, small bars, and restaurants to suit every taste. Albufeira's Tourist Office is on Rua 5 de Outubro (phone: 89-52144), the main street.

CHECKING IN: *Boa Vista* – A cut above average in the Albufeira area, mainly because of its tasteful decor and its site on the cliff face a little away from the center of town. It has 93 rooms and a swimming pool. 6 Rua Samora Barros, Albufeira (phone: 89-52175). Expensive.

EATING OUT: *A Ruína* – Good fish and seafood are served in the pleasant setting of an old fort overlooking the main beach. Open daily. Reservations unnecessary. Cais Herculano, Albufeira (phone: 89-52094). Moderate.

En Route from Albufeira – Return to N125 and continue east to Almansil, where roads lead north to the town of Loulé and south to the hotel, resort villa, and golf course complexes of Vale do Lobo and Quinta do Lago, while the main road presses on to Faro. A must stop in the vicinity is the Igreja de São Lourenço, in the village of São Lourenço, a mile (1.6 km) beyond Almansil. A small church, this is nevertheless one of the most noteworthy in the Algarve, because its walls and barrel-vaulted ceiling — even the underside of the dome — are entirely covered with blue-and-white 18th-century *azulejos* depicting the life of St. Lawrence. The nearby *Centro Cultural São Lourenço,* set up in restored, 200-year-old buildings, is a privately run establishment that maintains its own art gallery and sponsors classical music concerts in summer. Among the regular exhibitors at the gallery are Portuguese artists José Guimarães and João Cutileiro (creator of the statue of King Sebastian in Lagos), whose works can be bought here for prices that are reasonable by the standards of the international art market.

CHECKING IN: *Dona Filipa* – A luxury hotel in the Vale do Lobo resort complex, it has a fine dining room, direct access to the beach, a swimming pool, and tennis courts, as well as 27 holes of golf next door. Most of the 129 rooms have balconies; reserve well in advance. Vale do Lobo, Almansil (phone: 89-394141). Very expensive.

Quinta do Lago – The luxury hotel of the Quinta do Lago resort offers 150 rooms and suites on an extensive, pine-clad, beachfront property. All rooms are air conditioned, with oceanview balconies; there are two restaurants, two swimming pools (three if you count the private pool that goes with the presidential suite), tennis courts, and a health club, in addition to the resort's 27 superb holes of golf nearby. Quinta de Lago, Almansil (phone: 89-96666). Very expensive.

LOULÉ: This old market center with tree-lined streets is in the hills only 3 miles (5 km) up a back road from Almansil. The market, in the center of town and open mornings only, daily except Sundays, used to be the place to buy traditional, hand-crafted wooden toys. Alas, they've given way to the plastic variety, but there are other bargains to be had: rough terra cotta plates hand-painted with exuberant peasant designs in the pottery section; figs, almonds, mountain cheeses, and juicy local oranges in the produce section; and, in the surrounding shops, excellent baskets and raffia hats at ridiculously low prices. Decorative bridles and cattle bells that make good wall hangings can also be bought at local saddleries.

En Route from Loulé – Take the road to Faro, 10 miles (16 km) southeast of Loulé in a direct line. The junction halfway between the two, where N125-4 rejoins N125, should be approached with caution — it has a reputation as a dangerous intersection.

CHECKING IN/EATING OUT: *La Réserve* – Off the road between Loulé and Faro, this is an elegant, modern, and luxurious establishment (a member of the prestigious Relais & Châteaux group — the only one in Portugal). It offers 20 suites (all with bedroom, bath, and living room, plus a verandah with a sea view); grounds that include a swimming pool and a tennis court; and a highly praised restaurant, that has earned a Michelin star. Closed from early September to mid-December (restaurant closed Tuesdays; reservations advised). Note that credit cards are not accepted and that this hostelry is not on the coast, which is 6 miles (10 km) away. Santa Bárbara de Nexe (phone: 89-90234). Expensive.

FARO: Although the airport for the Algarve is located here and the city teems with tourists, there is nevertheless a very attractive quality about Faro, which is the modern-day capital of the Algarve and, with about 29,000 inhabitants, the largest town on the coast. It has streets paved with white cobblestones, cafés set in parkland, and, despite having been reduced to nearly total rubble in the earthquakes of 1722 and 1755, an Old Town partly enclosed by defensive walls. Enter the old section through the 18th-century Arco da Vila, an archway just south of the Manuel Bivar Gardens bordering the harbor (*doca*). Not far away is the Sé (Cathedral), in Largo da Sé, a square noteworthy in itself for its harmonious lines. The cathedral, first built during the 13th century at the time of the Christian victory over the Moors, was rather clumsily restored during the 18th century after the earthquakes. Little of the original remains — just a 13th-century Gothic tower — but its main body is lined with 17th-century *azulejos*. The *Museu Municipal* (Municipal Museum), near the cathedral in the 16th-century Convent of Nossa Senhora da Assunção (which has a very fine cloister), is made up of two sections: an archaeological collection containing rare Roman objects unearthed in the area, and the Ferreira do Almeida collection of sculpture and painting, including 14th-century jasper statues (open Mondays through Fridays, from 9 AM to noon and from 2 to 5 PM; admission charge). Faro's Tourist Office (8-12 Rua da Misericórdia; phone: 89-803604) is near the Arco da Vila, while several blocks north is the interesting Igreja do Carmo. A baroque church of some beauty, it has a gruesome Capela dos Ossos — a chapel paneled in bones and skulls dug up in the adjacent cemetery.

A completely different Faro can be discovered by taking a boat excursion through the rare Ria Formosa marshlands, which form a sort of coastal apron south of the city. As planes drone regularly overhead to and from the airport runway nearby, it is possible to see — with the help of a guide — fiddler crabs, gray herons, egrets, storks, gannets, plover, terns, oystercatchers, and, on a good day, the rare purple gallinule. The day trips, available from *Miltours* (14 Rua Verissimo de Almeida; phone: 89-802040), include a simple Portuguese lunch on a deserted island; bird watching books and binoculars are provided. Faro's beach, Praia de Faro, also occupies an island, Ilha de

Faro; this long and narrow coastal sandbank, about 3 miles (5 km) south of the center, is connected to the mainland by a bridge and also by a ferry from the harbor.

EATING OUT: *Roque* – Popular with the locals for its fresh sea fare and low prices, it is on the Ilha de Faro, a short drive from town on the airport road and then across a long, low bridge. The restaurant faces the beach on the marshland side of the island, with a large area for dining outside. Closed Wednesdays in winter. Reservations unnecessary. Ilha de Faro, Faro (phone: 89-817868). Inexpensive.

En Route from Faro – From here to the east, almost to the Spanish border, the coast is paralleled by a series of sandbars. Like the Costa Vicentina of the western Algarve, the eastern extremity has special charms. Nature has not been spoiled by development, and it is less crowded in summer. Take N125 about 5 miles (8 km) to Olhão and then another 14 miles (22 km) to Tavira.

OLHÃO: A pretty fishing port, Olhão is known as the "Cubist" village, because of its cube-shape white houses with terraced roofs. The peculiarity of its architecture gives it a Moorish appearance, although the town was founded during the 18th century, long after the Moors departed the Algarve. A good local market sells fresh produce and some handicrafts.

TAVIRA: A leading Portuguese weekly has described this as "one of the few places in the Algarve that tourism hasn't corrupted and urban development hasn't disfigured." Happily, the town council has banned construction that might affect the historic qualities of the old town center, which is well worth a stroll. Another fishing port, straddling the Gilão River, Tavira is of ancient origin — the foundations of the bridge across the river date from Roman times. There are remains of an old Moorish castle, and the houses have an Eastern touch to them, with Moorish-influenced roofs.

CHECKING IN: *Eurotel Tavira* – This sprawling 80-room hotel is among the better places to stay in the eastern Algarve. It's set in a tourist complex with its own sports facilities and pools, along the main highway almost 2 miles (3 km) east of town. Quinta das Oliveiras, Tavira (phone: 81-22041). Moderate.

En Route from Tavira – Continue east on N125; after Conceicão there is a turnoff for Cacela Velha, a small village reconquered by the Moors in 1240 and featuring an 18th-century fort. Another tiny coastal settlement, almost within sight of Cacela Velha, is Fabrica, reached from a road leading off from the Cacela Velha turnoff. Both places have restaurants — little more than local taverns — that make a good stop for a meal. Or stop for a swim or a meal at Praia da Manta Rota (reached by another turnoff from N125), a beach offering a long stretch of white sand (although it is pretty packed in summer). Alternatively, press on along N125 past Monte Gordo — a fishing village turned resort, with pale blue houses and a wide, pine-backed beach — to Vila Real de Santo António, where the Algarve coast comes to an end at the Spanish border.

EATING OUT: *O Estábulo* – On Manta Rota beach, it offers a cross section of traditional Algarve seafood dishes and a good wine list. Reservations unnecessary. Praia da Manta Rota (phone: 81-95246). Moderate.

Cacela Velha – A simple, pleasant place catering to a very local clientele (don't expect anything but Portuguese to be spoken). Chicken, pork, and fresh fish cooked on the charcoal grill are the stock in trade, and the fresh oysters are a bargain. No reservations. Cacela Velha (no phone). Inexpensive.

Costa da Fabrica – Another very simple place, with a large rush verandah providing an outdoor dining area facing a lagoon-like strip of water busy with swimmers, boaters, and windsurfers. The menu includes *caldeirada* (seafood stew), *frango com amêijoas* (chicken with clams), *ensopado de enguia* (stewed eels), and *arroz de marisco* (rice with shellfish), as well as more fresh, steamed oysters. No reservations. Fabrica (no phone). Inexpensive.

VILA REAL DE SANTO ANTÓNIO: This town provides a fitting farewell to the Algarve. When Lisbon was destroyed by an earthquake in 1755, much of the Algarve was also affected, and Vila Real de Santo António was razed. It benefited from the national reconstruction plan drawn up by the Marquês de Pombal, whose classical buildings with minimal exterior decoration were laid out in an austere grid pattern. The old center, an example of a pure Pombaline town, imparts the sense of harmony inherent in this style, but the town's unique flavor also comes from the strong Gypsy influence here. Vila Real looks out on the great expanse of the Guadiana River, across which is Ayamonte, Spain, reached by a car ferry across the river. A whimsical but interesting museum, the *Museu Manuel Cabanas,* in Praça Marquês de Pombal, the main square, specializes in wood engravings, but it also has material on the history of the town (open from July through September, from 4 to 6 PM and from 9 to 11 PM; the rest of the year, from 11:30 AM to 12:30 PM and from 2 to 7 PM; closed Mondays; no admission charge). The Vila Real de Santo António Tourist Office is on the riverside Avenida da República (phone: 81-43272).

 CHECKING IN/EATING OUT: *Vasco da Gama* – One of the better places to stay at this far eastern end of the Algarve, it's set among pine trees in the seaside resort of Monte Gordo, a bit less than 2 miles (3 km) west of Vila Real. It has 164 rooms, a restaurant, bar, tennis courts, and its own swimming pool, as well as access to a long strip of sandy beach. Avenida Infante Dom Henrique, Monte Gordo (phone: 81-44321). Moderate.

En Route from Vila Real de Santo António – Car ferries for Spain depart from Vila Real de Santo António. Travelers remaining in Portugul can cut roughly 125 miles (200 km) north across the Alentejo via Beja to Evora (see *Evora,* THE CITIES) and from there return to Lisbon, or they can retrace their path along the Algarve coast to Albufeira and pick up the trunk road back to Lisbon. Before leaving Vila Real, however, one last Algarve excursion can be made to the historic fortress town of Castro Marim, 2½ miles (4 km) north on N122.

CASTRO MARIM: Possibly Portugal's oldest town, it has an unbroken history of settlement going back many centuries before the birth of Christ — neolithic implements found here are believed to have been hewn by the original Portuguese tribes. The Phoenicians arrived during the 9th century BC, and the Romans and the Moors followed centuries later, until the Christian reconquest in 1242. Most of the walls of the original castle-fortress, an accretion of centuries of building, have collapsed, but the whitewashed houses that now constitute the town once all nestled within it. The remaining castle nucleus houses a small historical museum run by the same government agency that administers a nature reserve in the triangle formed by Monte Gordo, Vila Real de Santo António, and Castro Marim. Postcards and posters of the protected wildlife, which includes the white stork and the black-winged stilt, are on sale in the museum (open Mondays through Fridays, from 9:30 AM to 12:30 PM and from 2:30 to 5:30 PM; admission charge). The castle ramparts provide a wonderful view of the Guadiana and the Spanish town of Ayamonte, as well as the Castro Marim salt pans (worked since Roman times) and Vila Real de Santo António.

The Azores

Dreamers and rebels quickly appreciate places like the Azores, which continue to resist the inevitability of progress as the civilized world has come to know it. Rising from the depths of the mid-Atlantic (Lisbon lies about 900 miles to the east, New York 2,300 miles to the west), they are a land apart in pace and setting. Although there has been substantial economic evolution during the past decade, the nine volcanic islands of the archipelago retain a simplicity and cohesiveness that have been erased elsewhere by the frantic tempo and complex demands of modern times. Anyone despairing of finding a place of escape as "unspoiled" as the travel brochures claim it is will find that, in the case of the Azores, the word is apt.

Of the nine islands in the Azores chain, São Miguel, the largest, and neighboring Santa Maria are easternmost. Between 90 and 160 miles to the west are Terceira, Graciosa, São Jorge, Pico, and Faial, clustered in a central island grouping. Flores and its tiny companion, Corvo, are approximately another 150 miles to the west. That they are today an autonomous region of Portugal (linked to the mainland, but fiscally and operationally independent) is a result of settlements established soon after Portuguese explorers came upon them in 1427 or 1431, 8 decades or so after the islands first appeared, misplaced by several hundred miles, on a Genoese map of 1351. While 14th-century Italians (or Italians sailing for Portugal) may have preceded the 15th-century Portuguese, it is also thought that the Carthaginians, consummate seafarers of ancient times, may have preceded them both by nearly 2,000 years, although no remains of Carthaginian settlements have been found.

The Portuguese, who named the islands after the goshawks (*açores*) seen here, proved more committed to these mid-ocean outposts than their possible Carthaginian predecessors. In the century following the Azores' discovery, the Portuguese empire extended to Africa, Asia, and South America, and the islands provided an anchorage and resupply point for voyages of exploration, settlement, trade, plunder, and conquest. Colonization of the Azores themselves began almost immediately, in 1439, with farmers and herdsmen the first settlers. Where soil was ample, large pastures soon replaced the native forest. Where the land was more rock than soil, rock removal followed the cutting away of trees and brush, and the rocks became the walls that today etch the landscape with thin lines of black. Towns developed both in the countryside and along the coasts. Wealth flowed through the ports, where merchants reprovisioned ships or exported barley or maize. By the 18th century, Ponta Delgada (on São Miguel), Angra do Heroísmo (on Terceira), and Horta (on Faial) were large and architecturally distinguished townships, a factor that still weighs in their favor.

Land grants provided a basis of wealth for missions established by Jesuits, Franciscans, and other Catholic religious orders. Beautiful churches and chapels were built in thanks for safe passage or for profits anticipated or gained. Their interiors were gilded and richly detailed, their treasuries stocked with valuable gifts. Although the religious orders are long gone (expelled during the 18th century for religious, political, and economic reasons), the churches they left behind are still in use. Easily accessible and remarkably well preserved, they are a fundamental element of the Azorean lifestyle.

In the late 1700s, after the fortunes of empire had waned, a new armada — American whaling ships — discovered the Azores. Many of the thousands of Azorean men who signed aboard American vessels during the better part of the following century ultimately settled in the United States, forming sizable communities in New England, California, and Hawaii. Others headed to Canada, South Africa, and South America. By local reckoning, today's quarter million Azoreans are outnumbered by emigrants and their descendants four to one.

During World War II, the islands served as a staging area for Europe-bound American forces, a factor that strengthened the already existing commercial and family links to the United States. (The American presence continues in the form of the American-run NATO airfield maintained at Lajes, Terceira.) After the war, but before the advent of the jet plane, the Azores served as a refueling point for airplanes crossing the Atlantic. Otherwise, in the 20th century, with whaling, treasure seeking, and the discovery of new worlds all in the past, the islands settled into the time warp that today is their greatest asset. Outside of Ponta Delgada on São Miguel, the largest city in the islands, there are no traffic jams in the Azores, no contemporary chic, no franchised homogeneity. There is also no mass tourism to thwart authenticity and clutter the landscape with high-rise hotels. Few cruise ships come to call, although several hundred sailboats in transatlantic runs between the Caribbean and the Mediterranean do drop anchor off Faial and Flores.

In the villages, where donkeys and horses share the road with cars and pickup trucks, it is the former that set the pace, moving to the rhythm of a pre-industrial clock that ticks in concert to the rise and fall of a temperate sun. Even in Ponta Delgada, and in the other large town, Angra do Heroísmo, on Terceira, the scale remains human, with buildings rarely more than 4 stories high, and even on these two most heavily populated islands, windmills and church towers still dominate the rural skyline. Surrounding them is an intricate web of fields that provide most Azoreans with a livelihood. Farmland — wheat and maize are the main crops — and pasture — mostly for dairy cows — occupy the lowlands and the foothills. Only higher up on the mountains are there remnants of the original forests.

The landscape attests to the volcanic origin of the Azores, although once-fiery craters and cinder cones are now dressed in a carpet of green. On most of the islands the largest craters house lovely, steep-walled lakes that reflect the passing clouds and a nightly display of moonglow and shooting stars. Steam vents and hot springs evince the molten fires that still burn beneath the surface calm. Almost all of the islands have experienced either volcanic eruptions or major earthquakes within the past 50 years.

Wrestling with nature in mid-ocean isolation has made pioneering self-reliance a definitive part of the Azorean temperament. The climate may be benevolent, avoiding extremes of hot and cold and the worst of the earth's storms, but life still exacts its toll, as the weatherworn features of the old reveal. Homes must be built and kept in good repair. Vineyards must be planted and tended, their grapes turned into wine. Cows must be herded and milked, the milk carted to cooperatives that make flavorful Azorean butter and cheese. Boats must be built and repaired, nets woven and mended for fish to be caught.

Yet because many Azoreans have spent time overseas or have family settled elsewhere, there's a casual sophistication, an awareness of the world beyond that seems incongruous with their rural isolation. English is widely spoken, even in remote villages. Something like "Yeah, I spent 12 years in the States" usually explains it. Some expatriates return to the islands at retirement, when there's an American pension or savings to bankroll land, a house, and the good life. Like mainland Portugal, the Azores are relatively inexpensive, a feature attractive to visitors, too.

The Catholic church plays a crucial role in communal life, dominating the spiritual as well as the terrestrial landscape, as can be seen in the baroque façades on the churches that grace every village, their bells chiming the passing hours to those at home or in the field. The full measure of belief surfaces during the long festival season that runs from spring through early fall, with the largest, most impressive processions and displays held soon after Easter. Week after week, different villages celebrate and affirm family bonds and religious fraternity, some villages creating giant street tapestries made of countless flower petals in extravagant design. On Terceira, the festival season ends with the running of rope-tethered bulls through the narrow streets of the larger towns.

Some people believe the Azores are all that remains of the lost continent of Atlantis. Certainly few places offer such easy access to their magic, which makes them both wonderful to explore and vulnerable to the impact of discovery. Winding two-lane roads circle the islands and challenge their volcanic heights. Sometimes views are panoramas, encompassing the mountains, cliffs, and sea. At other times, the attention is drawn by details: the sweet smell of native cedar, the pink brilliance of roadside lilies, the harmony of forest birds. Island to island, nature runs rampant, providing justification for hyperbole and the real opportunity to get away from it all.

SOURCES AND RESOURCES

TOURIST INFORMATION: The Regional Tourism Board for the Azores is headquartered on the island of Faial (Rua Marcelino Lima, Horta; phone: 92-23801). Branch tourist offices are found in Horta, Faial (Rua Vasco da Gama; phone: 92-22237); in Ponta Delgada, São Miguel (Avenida Infante Dom Henrique; phone: 96-25743); in Angra do Heroísmo, Terceira (47A Rua Rio de Janeiro;

phone: 95-23393); and at Santa Maria Airport (on the island of Santa Maria; phone: 96-82155). There is also a tourist office representative at the *Aparthotel Caravelas* (Rua Conselheiro Terra Pinheiro, Madalena, Pico; phone: 92-92500).

Local Coverage – An English-language booklet, *Azores: Guide for Tourists,* revised annually and distributed free at tourist offices, provides excellent information on all the islands. Also worth reading and available in English editions are pamphlets on the individual islands, each containing useful maps of the island and its main town. The Azorean Emigration Center (11 Praça 5 de Outubro, Ponta Delgada, São Miguel) produces a monthly tabloid that includes some features in English. It is available at the center or at the tourist office in Ponta Delgada.

TELEPHONE – The area code for the islands of São Miguel and Santa Maria is 96; for Terceira, Graciosa, and São Jorge, 95; for Pico, Faial, Flores, and Corvo, 92. If calling from a different area code within the Azores, or from mainland Portugal, dial 0 plus the appropriate area code before the local number. Remember that time in the islands is 1 hour earlier than in mainland Portugal all year long.

CLIMATE: The Azores are not tropical isles. Palm trees are not abundant, beaches are almost nonexistent. The waters of the Gulf Stream modify the islands' maritime climate, and temperatures average a very comfortable 55 to 77F from the coldest to the hottest months. There are, nevertheless, four distinct seasons, with a change of flowers from spring through autumn. At times, the air can be quite humid, exaggerating summer's warmth or winter's chill. Because the islands lie beneath a mid-ocean convergence of high altitude winds, they have earned a reputation for quickly changing weather and frequent rains. The rainfall that keeps them green occurs mostly from October to April, but weather can be changeable in any season. Frequently heard advice: "Get out there when the sun's out; you never know when it'll change on you."

GETTING THERE: To serve the numerous Azoreans who have settled in New England, *TAP Air Portugal* flies nonstop (once a week) between Boston and Ponta Delgada (São Miguel); there are also (once weekly) nonstop flights between Los Angeles and San Francisco and the international airport at Lajes, Terceira. Most inbound traffic arrives aboard *TAP* flights from Lisbon to Lajes, Ponta Delgada, and Horta (Faial). Once a week, a *TAP* flight departs from Porto to Ponta Delgada. *TAP* also flies to Ponta Delgada from Madeira.

Inter-island service for all islands except Corvo (which is reached by boat from Flores) is provided by *Serviço Açoreano de Transportes Aéreos* (*SATA*). Local weather conditions may result in flight delays or cancellations, and it is advisable to travel to remote islands such as Flores and Corvo only if there's time to absorb a possible delay of several days or longer. Advance reservations are suggested as flights are often sold out, particularly during winter, when frequency is reduced substantially. En route stopovers are allowed without additional charge; at press time, a multi-stop round trip cost about $200, with several such trips required to visit all of the islands. *TAP* offices in Lisbon can provide ticketing and information for *SATA* flights.

No ferries connect mainland Portugal with the islands, and there is inter-island ferry service only among the islands of the central group (Terceira, Graciosa, São Jorge, Pico, and Faial). The service is operated by *Transmaçor* (29 Rua Nova das Angústias, Horta; phone: 92-23334), and if the ferry schedule fits your itinerary, it's a relaxing, scenic, inexpensive way to travel. The shortest run links Faial to Pico in about a half hour. Faial to São Jorge takes about 2 hours, São Jorge to Terceira about 4 hours, and Terceira to Graciosa about 3 hours. For travel between Flores and Corvo, it's possible to rent a boat, with or without a captain.

SPECIAL EVENTS: Religious festivals held in one village or another fill the calendar year, but are most concentrated from *Easter* through August, so it's worth planning an itinerary to include one. The largest include elaborate processions and tapestries, or mosaics, of flowers laid down in the streets. Particularly noteworthy are the *Festas do Senhor Santo Cristo* (Lord Christ Festivities), held on São Miguel the weekend of the 5th Sunday after *Easter,* in honor of a 16th-century image of Christ in a local church. Two weeks later, on *Whitsunday* (7 Sundays after *Easter*), all the islands begin to hold *festas* in honor of the Holy Spirit, which go on for successive Sundays as village after village puts on its own version of a celebration that goes back to the Middle Ages. The festival lasts throughout the summer on Terceira, where offerings are collected in little chapels called *impérios* and where *touradas à corda* — bullfights in which the bull is tied to a rope and teased but not killed — and the running of bulls through the streets mark the end of the season. The same bullfights, along with folk singing and dancing, are part of the *Festas de São Joaninhos* (St. John's Festivals), held in June on Terceira. From the first to the second Sunday in August, the island of Faial celebrates *Sea Week,* a secular event stressing water sports and other water-related activities, with accompanying folk music, band concerts, and parades. Another water-related event is the *Festa dos Baleeiros* (Whalers' Festival), the last week in August on Pico; although whaling is a thing of the past in the Azores, this religious procession, followed by music and dancing, still fulfills a vow made by local whalers in the 19th century. Also during August, Santa Maria holds the *Maré do Agosto* (August Tide), a music festival of contemporary artists that often features international names.

 SPORTS AND FITNESS: In addition to the options below, tours with a focus on sports (fishing, golfing, hunting, and others) can be arranged through *Freitas Martins,* 14 Rua Açoreano Oriental, Ponta Delgada, São Miguel (phone: 96-26415).

Deep-Sea Fishing – Local waters provide not just sustenance but big-game sport fishing and some world records. From August through October, the catch is marlin; from September through November, swordfish and tuna; shark, barracuda, bonito, and others are in season all year. Contact *Pescatur* (1 Largo Francisco Tavares, Ponta Delgada; phone: 96-24757). Inland waters on São Miguel and Flores offer a limited season on black bass, pike, perch, and trout. The required licenses can be obtained from *Direcção dos Serviços Florestais* (38 Largo de Camões, Ponta Delgada).

Diving – On Terceira, contact the *Clube Náutico de Angra do Heroísmo* (Estrada Gaspar Côrte Real, Angra do Heroísmo; phone: 95-23300) and rent a boat and driver for a run to the nearest reefs. On Faial, contact *Clube Naval da Horta* (Cais de Santa Cruz, Horta; phone: 92-22331). The *Estalagem de Santa Cruz* (Rua Vasco da Gama, Horta; phone: 92-23021) also handles water sports equipment rentals. On São Miguel, the *Caloura Resort* (Agua de Pau, Lagoa; phone: 96-93240) can provide information regarding equipment, rentals, and locations. Wet suits prevail for much of the year.

Golf – The *Clube de Golfe da Ilha Terceira* (Terceira Island Golf Club; Fajãs Agualva; phone: 95-25847) has an 18-hole course, clubs and caddies for hire, a clubhouse bar and snack shop, and 2 tennis courts. It's closed Mondays except those that fall on holidays (including American holidays, thanks to the air base nearby). São Miguel has a beautiful 9-hole course at the *São Miguel Golf Club* (phone: 96-54141) near Furnas, 45 minutes to an hour from Ponta Delgada. Both offer a setting that emphasizes the relaxation of the game.

Hiking – Hikers can set out on scores of walks in the countryside with no cause for concern. On Pico, the hike to the summit comes with some precautions (see *Pico,* "Special Places").

Tennis – There are courts at the *Clube de Tênis* (Avenida Cecília Meireles, Fajã de Cima, São Miguel; phone: 96-33647). On Terceira, visitors can play at municipal courts or at the tennis courts of the *Terceira Island Golf Club* (see above). There are 2 courts at Horta's *Clube de Tênis* (at the *Fayal* hotel; phone: 92-22181), and another 2 at Pico's *Clube de Tênis* (Externato da Madalena; phone: 92-92145).

Swimming – Rocky coasts make swimming difficult. Among the few beaches are Praia Pim, a half-mile stretch of sand on the outskirts of Horta, Faial; the Praia do Populo, near São Roque, and the Praia da Agua d'Alto, both some miles east of Ponta Delgada, São Miguel; and a nice carpet of white sand at São Lourenço Bay, on Santa Maria. In addition, swimming is possible in the freshwater crater lakes of São Miguel, particularly the easily accessible Sete Cidades, although the shoreline entry is muddy and coastal waters shallow. Cool winters make swimming a summer-only sport.

SÃO MIGUEL

The largest island of the archipelago and the most heavily populated, São Miguel extends approximately 38 miles from east to west and 10 miles from north to south. It is also widely considered to be the most beautiful island, thanks to luxuriant vegetation, a series of magnificent crater lakes, and a landscape that seems to glow with vibrant color. In the eastern part of the island, at Furnas, the still-active volcanic depths surface in sulfur-fumed steam and boiling water. Not the first of the islands to be discovered, it was, with Santa Maria, one of the first to be colonized, and it has maintained its importance ever since. Ponta Delgada, on the south coast, is the island's capital, the capital of the Ponta Delgada district (one of the three political districts into which the archipelago is divided), and the largest city in the Azores. It's a lively town, with much of architectural note, shops that add a touch of unexpected sophistication, and a distinctive charm. Ribeira Grande, Vila Franca do Campo, and Povoação (the first settlement on the island) are other towns of historical and architectural merit.

It takes a day in the countryside to understand why São Miguel is also called the *ilha verde* (green island). The landscape is a rock-veined patchwork of greens, amply accented with blue-purple hydrangeas, azaleas, and other flowers that scent the air for 8 months of the year. Gently sloping lowlands are punctuated by rows of graceful cinder cones, and dark patches of forest crown the heights. From lookouts atop its tallest mountains, the views are spectacular — but the same could be said about almost any drive on the island.

 GETTING AROUND: It takes 2 to 3 days to begin to do justice to São Miguel. Excellent roads circle the island, cutting through the mountains at several places.

Airport – *TAP Air Portugal* arrives daily from Lisbon and less frequently from Porto and from Funchal, Madeira. *SATA* flies in from the other islands. São Miguel's Aeroporto de Ponta Delgada (also called Nordela) is 3 miles (5 km) from the heart of town. Rental cars are available, and a taxi ride into town costs about $3. Offices of both *TAP Air Portugal* (phone: 96-26201) and *SATA* (phone: 96-27221 for information, 96-22311 for reservations) are on Avenida Infante Dom Henrique in Ponta Delgada.

Bicycle – The countryside provides some excellent biking possibilities, although flat, open stretches alternate with hilly terrain that can prove tiring on cross-country rides. Contact *Logo* (Avenida Kopke, Ponta Delgada; phone: 96-25795) for bicycle and motorbike rentals.

Bus – Local bus service is available around the island. Sightseeing tours by bus are offered by *Agência de Viagens Ornelas,* Avenida Infante Dom Henrique, Ponta Delgada (phone: 96-25379).

Car Rental – The local Avis affiliate, *Ilha Verde Rent-a-Car* (19 Praça 5 de Outubro, Ponta Delgada; phone: 96-25200; and at the airport; phone: 96-27301) has the largest fleet. As a rule of thumb, here and elsewhere in the archipelago, expect a rental car to cost anywhere from $65 to $100 a day, including gas and taxes. Watch out for traffic jams in Ponta Delgada around 9 AM and between 5:30 and 7 PM. Azorean drivers can be aggressive, so drive carefully.

Taxi – Taxis are available, and most offer car-and-driver day rates. As on other islands, hiring a car and driver for a day of touring usually costs less than a rental car, with most taxis available at $40 to $65 for an 8- to 10-hour day. Hotel personnel are usually helpful in securing a car and driver if a taxi is not readily at hand. Be on the lookout for newer, plusher Mercedes (like the one driven by Vasco Guadencio; phone: 96-97119), if you're going to spend the day touring. They're not necessarily more expensive than some of the more basic models seen around town.

SPECIAL PLACES: Ponta Delgada – Capital of São Miguel since 1546, Ponta Delgada is a flat town that stretches nearly 2 miles along a bay on the island's south coast. The seafront promenade — the Avenida Infante Dom Henrique — is fed by narrow streets that invite wandering. Highlights of any tour of the town are several old churches, including the parish Church of São Sebastião, built in the 16th century, altered in the 18th century, and noted for a Manueline façade and two baroque doorways as well as for a high altar of carved cedar; the Igreja do Colégio, or former Jesuit church, founded in the 15th century, although the present building, an exercise in baroque geometry, is later; and the Church of São José, decorated with blue-and white 18th-century *azulejos* (glazed tiles). Also of note are the 18th-century town gates and the Santa Ana Palace, a 19th-century building decorated with intricate woodcarvings and tilework. The *Museu Carlos Machado* (Rua João Moreira) is the city's museum of ethnographic interest, art, and natural history; it's open Tuesdays through Fridays from 10 AM to 12:30 PM and from 2 to 5:30 PM, Saturdays and Sundays from 2 to 5:30 PM;; no admission charge. Ponta Delgada began as a fishing village, and boats still unload their catches at sunrise at the western end of the harbor. An equally colorful sight for those who like sleeping past dawn is the open-air market near Largo São João, which runs through the morning.

Caldeira das Sete Cidades – About 20 minutes by car northwest of Ponta Delgada, this is perhaps the single most spectacular sight in the Azores. In the crater of an extinct volcano lie two lakes, separated by a land bridge only a few yards wide. One lake is green, the other blue, and the panorama from the crater rim is worthy of several visits, since it changes dramatically with the quickly changing Azorean weather. Two roads lead to the crater rim and the charming lakeside village of Sete Cidades. According to legend, one of the seven cities of Atlantis is buried in the crater, thus the name.

Vale das Furnas – The volcanic past comes to life in the steam vents, hot springs, thermal pools, and boiling mud of the Furnas Valley, about an hour east of Ponta Delgada. Also here are a lake (Lagoa das Furnas), a botanical garden (Parque Terra Nostra), and the spa town of Furnas.

Ribeira Grande – Granted a charter in 1507, this town on São Miguel's north coast has many fine 16th- and 17th-century buildings. The church of Nossa Senhora da Estrela, consecrated in 1517, is the oldest; inside, the Santos Reis Magos chapel contains various paintings, including a 16th-century Flemish triptych.

SHOPPING: Ponta Delgada is the island's shopping center. Some very high-style European fashions can be found, but on the whole, the town caters to the local population, meaning more basic clothing, housewares, and other necessary items.

Caleche Design – High-fashion leather goods, some made regionally. Largo da Matriz, Ponta Delgada (phone: 96-22523).

A Central dos Moveis – The furniture may not be worth considering, but the imported Chinese porcelain and bric-a-brac are another matter. 47 Largo Manuel da Ponte, Ponta Delgada (phone: 96-22403).

Jame – The place to head for camping gear. 42 Largo de Camões, Ponta Delgada (phone: 96-27309).

Radiante – An interesting collection of small gold charms. 46-51 Rua Machado dos Santos, Ponta Delgada (phone: 96-24696).

CHECKING IN: Hotels, pensions, and the occasional inn (*albergaria* and *estalagem*) provide accommodations for visitors. On the whole, on all the islands, even modest rooms are clean and comfortable; at better hotels, they generally come with private baths, telephones, and television sets. As on the Portuguese mainland, breakfast is almost always included in the price. Advance reservations are suggested, particularly during the summer, when limited space may well sell out. Rates are anywhere from 20% to 30% lower in low season, from November through April, but even at their highest, they are quite reasonable compared to mainland Portugal or other tourist destinations. For that reason, almost all of the hotels below fall into one of only two categories, moderate or inexpensive. Expect to pay $75 and up for a double room in the rare hotel listed below as expensive, from $50 to $70 for a double room at hotels listed as moderate, and from $20 to $45 at those listed as inexpensive.

Açores Atlântico – A brand-new, pink marble hostelry on Ponta Delgada's main seafront avenue, it's an exercise in island-style architecture with modern flair. There are 140 air conditioned rooms and suites with private balconies, plus a restaurant, a heated indoor pool, sauna, and gymnasium. Avenida Infante Dom Henrique, Ponta Delgada (phone: 96-29300). Expensive.

Avenida – A modern, 80-room hotel in the heart of town, it's clean and well kept, with up-to-date facilities. Rua Dr. José Bruno Tavares Carreiro, Ponta Delgada (phone: 96-27331). Moderate.

Caloura – On the southern coast of São Miguel, about a 20-minute drive from Ponta Delgada, this contemporary resort offers 40 rooms, a sauna, and a workout room, as well as a swimming pool and an oceanfront setting. Boating, scuba diving, and horseback riding are other options for guests. Agua de Pau, Lagoa (phone: 96-93240). Moderate.

Gaivota – An apartment hotel, its rooms (27) with kitchen facilities are a prime asset; another is a harborfront setting that offers panoramic views from flower-decked balconies. 103 Avenida Marginal, Ponta Delgada (phone: 96-23286). Moderate.

São Pedro – This would be a find anywhere in the world, which makes it all the more exceptional in as unexpected a place as Ponta Delgada. An elegant, early-19th-century private home — it originally belonged to Thomas Hickling, first American consul in the Azores — has been turned into the finest hotel in the archipelago, with 26 spacious rooms, antique furnishings, excellent service, and a quiet setting just on the edge of downtown. Advance bookings are heartily recommended. It also has a good restaurant (see *Eating Out*). Largo Almirante Dunn, Ponta Delgada (phone: 96-22223). Moderate.

Terra Nostra – Adjacent to the hot springs in the spa town of Furnas, and permeated with the spirit of the 1930s, when it was built. Staying here is a good idea for those who want to explore the eastern part of the island without the hour's drive from Ponta Delgada. Guests can play golf nearby, stroll in the lovely botanical gardens, soak in the outdoor thermal pool or the newer indoor pool, or otherwise take the waters. There are 74 rooms, including 40 in the same wing that contains a gymnasium. Advance reservations are necessary. Rua Padre José Jacinto Botelho, Furnas (phone: 96-54104). Moderate.

América – This modern, 22-room residential *pensão* is centrally located and well maintained. Friendly service adds a personal touch; no restaurant, but there is a small bar. 58 Rua Manuel Inácio Correia, Ponta Delgada (phone: 96-24351). Inexpensive.

Central – The oldest residential pension in Ponta Delgada benefits from charm, a friendly atmosphere, and a central location. No restaurant. 82 Rua Machado dos Santos, Ponta Delgada (phone: 96-24491). Inexpensive.

EATING OUT: On São Miguel and the other islands, restaurant fare tends to be grilled fish or meat rather than local specialties such as *caldo de nabos* (turnip soup), *arroz de lapas* (limpets with rice), or *linguiça com inhames* (spiced sausage with yams). Dorado is the most common catch of the day; squid, octopus, shrimp, lobster, and crab may all be on the menu of the better restaurants of Ponta Delgada or Angra do Heroísmo. Cheeses, usually tangy, are made in many rural districts; those of São Jorge are the best known. São Miguel's pineapples, grown in greenhouses, are prized. Verdelho wines from Pico are the islands' finest; those of Graciosa and Terceira are also highly rated. The Azores are not the place for haute cuisine, although a few of the better restaurants come close. Happily, the cost of dining in such restaurants is not a great deal higher than eating in more modest establishments, and because the span from most to least is not great, the restaurant listings below dispense with an expensive category. Expect to pay anywhere from $15 to $30 for dinner for two, without drinks or wine, in restaurants listed as moderate, and less than $15 in those listed as inexpensive.

London – The place where many local VIPs like to have dinner, it has good service and a varied menu. The location is central. Closed Sundays. Reservations advised. 21 Rua Ernesto do Canto, Ponta Delgada (phone: 96-22500). Moderate.

São Pedro – The dining room of the best hotel in the islands. Tables are elegantly laid with linen, the waiters are equally well attired, and the food matches the setting. Grilled dorado, shrimp, and spider crab are all worth a mention. Open daily. Reservations unnecessary. Largo Almirante Dunn, Ponta Delgada (phone: 96-22223). Moderate.

Boavista – Seafood specialties range from lobster to barnacles, all prepared to taste. This is in the newer part of the city, above the downtown area. Closed for lunch on Saturdays and all day Sundays. Reservations unnecessary. 12 Rua Ilha São Miguel (upstairs), Ponta Delgada (phone: 96-24272). Moderate to inexpensive.

O Fervedouro – Regional dishes include *caldeirada de peixe* (fish chowder) and *polvo guisado em vinho* (octopus cooked in wine sauce). This is a good lunch stop for those touring the island. Closed Mondays. Reservations unnecessary. 3 Rua do Passal, Ribeira Grande (phone: 96-72820). Moderate to inexpensive.

White Shark – A small place with maritime decor on the west side of town, specializing in shark and beef steaks cooked over a lava stone grill. Closed Sundays. Reservations advised. 95 Rua de Tavares Resendes, Ponta Delgada (phone: 96-27663). Moderate to inexpensive.

O Corisco – Casual and in the heart of town, it offers regional specialties and seafood. Closed Mondays. Reservations unnecessary. 28 Rua Manuel da Ponte, Ponta Delgada (phone: 96-24444). Inexpensive.

John's Pub – Piano, guitar, and violins provide the mood for sandwiches or cocktails. Closed Sundays. Reservations unnecessary. Rua Diário dos Açores, Ponta Delgada (phone: 96-24741). Inexpensive.

A Lota – Fresh seafood is the specialty, with a sea view the bonus. Open daily. Reservations unnecessary. 13 Largo do Porto, Lagoa (phone: 96-92595). Inexpensive.

SANTA MARIA

Probably the first of the Azores sighted by Portuguese explorers, Santa Maria is 55 miles south of São Miguel and is the southernmost island in the archipelago. Along with São Miguel, it was also one of the first to be settled, and by 1472 its main town, Vila do Porto — but then known simply as Porto — became the first town in the islands to receive a charter. Christopher Columbus dropped anchor here in 1493 on his return from the West Indies; members of his crew are said to have prayed in a tiny church that still stands at Anjos, on the north coast. The island measures approximately 11 miles from east to west and 6 to 7 miles from north to south, yet its terrain ranges from hilly in the northeast to flat in the southwest and encompasses sheer coastal cliffs, deeply indented bays, and pastoral villages. The large airport outside Vila do Porto is a still-used reminder of the role the Azores played during World War II as a forward base for American troops and in Allied antisubmarine efforts. Today, jets make use of its long runway on flights linking the islands with South America.

 GETTING AROUND: *SATA* flies between São Miguel and Santa Maria (*SATA*'s phone in Vila do Porto: 96-82497). The island's Aeroporto de Santa Maria is just short of 2 miles (3 km) northwest of Vila do Porto.

Car Rental – Rental cars are available from *Rent-a-Car Mariense,* at the airport (phone: 96-82880). Two-lane roads crisscross the island, which can easily be seen in a day. More time can be utilized by slowing down to appreciate things at an Azorean pace.

SPECIAL PLACES: Vila do Porto – Whitewashed walls and red tile roofs define Santa Maria's main town, located on a bay in the southwestern corner of the island. Among its landmarks is the 19th-century parish church, built on the site of a ruined 15th-century church, of which a chapel with a Manueline ceiling remains. The Convent of São Francisco, built in the 17th century, then destroyed by pirates and rebuilt in the 18th century, has lovely chapels, including one decorated with 17th-century glazed Portuguese tiles.

Pico Alto – Santa Maria's highest peak (almost 1,950 feet), in the center of the island, provides wide-angle views.

Baia de São Lourenço – On the northeast coast, São Lourenço has, besides the bay itself, a beach of white sand — a rarity in the Azores. Off the beach is an islet, the Ilhéu do Romeiro, which has an interesting cave and can be reached by boat.

Anjos Chapel – This small chapel on the north coast is a beautifully detailed 15th-century gem that is probably the oldest church in the islands. It has associations with Columbus, some of whose crew gave thanks here in 1493 for their safe return from the voyage that resulted in the European discovery of America.

 CHECKING IN: *Aeroporto* – The only choice. Luckily, this 47-room hotel at the airport is clean and well run, and has a pretty good restaurant (see below). Reservations advised. Estrada do Aeroporto, Vila do Porto (phone: 96-82211). Inexpensive.

EATING OUT: *Praia* – A simple place in a village on a south coast beach; the menu leans toward fish and seafood. Open daily. Reservations unnecessary. Praia Formosa (phone: 96-82635). Moderate.

Aeroporto – This comfortable restaurant with fish, seafood, beef, and chicken specialties is at the *Aeroporto* hotel. Open daily. Reservations unnecessary. Estrada do Aeroporto, Vila do Porto (phone: 96-82211). Moderate to inexpensive.

TERCEIRA

The most heavily populated island in the Azores' central group is 90 miles northwest of São Miguel. Measuring approximately 19 miles by 11 miles, it received its name as the third of the islands to be discovered. The first settlers, who arrived in 1450, were Flemish rather than Portuguese — Flanders was linked by marriage to the Portuguese crown. Vasco da Gama made Terceira a port of call on his return from India and buried his brother on the grounds of the Franciscan friary. Thanks to a central location, the port at Angra (the word means "bay"), in the middle of the island's south coast, soon became the largest in the Azores. Raised to the status of town in 1534, it prospered from the 16th to the 18th centuries and was embellished with beautiful churches, mansions, and government buildings. In the 19th century, Queen Maria II added the honorific *heroísmo* to its name in recognition of the role the island played on behalf of the liberal Regency during the Portuguese civil war. The city is the island's capital and the capital of the Angra do Heroísmo district, the second of the political districts into which the islands are divided.

The Terceiran landscape ranges from starkly volcanic to lushly pastured to meticulously divided into walled fields known as *cerrados*. In contrast to Angra's relative sophistication — and despite the presence of a US-manned NATO air base that also serves as the island's commercial airport — the countryside remains remarkably rural and untouched, much as on the more remote islands.

GETTING AROUND: Airport – *TAP Air Portugal* (25-27 Rua Rio de Janeiro, Angra; phone: 95-24489) flies in from Los Angeles and San Francisco (once a week from each) and several times weekly from Lisbon; *SATA* (2 Rua da Esperança, Angra; phone: 95-22013 for information, 95-22016 for reservations) flies in from the other islands. Lajes Airport is 15 miles (25 km) northeast of Angra, about 25 to 30 minutes by car (rental cars are available). The local buses that stop near the airport entrance take about an hour.

Bus – Public buses provide scheduled, though infrequent, service to outlying villages. Sightseeing tours by bus are arranged by *Empresa de Viação Terceirense* (*EVT*), 15 Rua Dr. Sousa Meneses, Angra (phone: 95-24101).

Car Rental – Several firms operate, including *Rent-a-Car Angrauto* (14-16 Rua Frei Diogo das Chagas, Angra; phone: 95-25585), *AçorAuto* (27B Rua Gervásio Lima, Praia da Vitória; phone: 95-52305), which also has an office at the airport; and *Ilha 3 Rent-a-Car* (22 Rua Direita, Angra; phone: 95-23115), which picks up and delivers anywhere on the island.

Ferry – Ferry service connects Terceira with the other islands of the central group: Graciosa, São Jorge, Pico, and Faial.

Taxi – Taxis are available for full-day and half-day touring, as well as for point-to-point service.

SPECIAL PLACES: Angra do Heroísmo – Named for the sheltered bay that made it a commercial port, Angra was planned in the 16th century but built largely in the 17th and 18th centuries. Although it grew to be one of the two largest cities in the Azores, the mansions, churches, and residential and commercial core retain their architectural integrity, and the old part of town has been recognized by UNESCO as a historic monument of international significance. Unfortunately, many of the city's oldest buildings collapsed and many others were badly damaged when an earthquake struck in 1980. Restoration continues, but much remains to be done.

Among Angra's old buildings, which line narrow streets that wind their way uphill from the port, are the 16th-to-17th-century Colégio church, which has an elaborately carved and gilded altar and a collection of 17th-century Dutch glazed tiles; the 16th-century church of São Gonçalo, also with a carved and gilded altar; and the 17th-century Palácio Bettencourt, a baroque mansion now the repository of extensive archives. The *Angra Museum* (Ladeira de São Francisco; phone: 95-23147), housed in the former Convento de São Francisco (where the remains of Vasco da Gama's brother are supposed to lie), contains paintings, ceramics, coins, and weaponry (open Mondays through Fridays from 9 AM to 12:30 PM and from 2 to 5 PM; no admission charge). The 16th-century castle of São João Baptista, at the western edge of town, is still used by the Portuguese military; it stands at the foot of Monte Brasil, an extinct cinder cone that guards the approach to the port and provides panoramic views of the city and surrounding countryside — it's a favorite picnic spot.

Biscoitos – On the island's north coast, this coastal plain is dotted with unusual formations of black volcanic rock. Walls of lava rock enclose fields of black soil planted with grapes, the harvest used to make the local Biscoitos wines.

Mata da Serrata – These forested hillsides on Terceira's west coast, 45 minutes to an hour from Angra, offer expansive views that take in the neighboring islands of São Jorge and Pico. The sight is particularly impressive at sunset.

Algar do Carvão and Furnas do Enxofre – Ten miles (16 km) and approximately 25 minutes from Angra, in the island's central highlands, are caves with stalactites and stalagmites, usually open on weekends only (more frequently during the summer). Nearby are the steam vents known as the Furnas do Enxofre.

SHOPPING: The best buys are island crafts, particularly embroidered items.

Luís Brandão – A well-priced selection of handmade embroidery, including appealing children's clothing and high-quality table linen. 84A Rua Rego, Angra (phone: 95-23284).

Casa Ilha Lilas – Hand-embroidered goods and other regional handicrafts. 40A Rua de Santo Espírito, Angra (phone: 95-22436).

Direcção Regional dos Assuntos Culturais – The best selection of crafts in the Azores — handwoven wools, appliquéd wall hangings, embroidery — all reasonably priced. Palácio dos Capitões Gerais, Largo Prior do Crato, Angra (phone: 95-25024).

João Pimental e Companhia – Another source of embroidered items and other handicrafts. 24 Rua de São João, Angra (phone: 95-24315).

CHECKING IN: *Angra –* A popular 86-room hotel in the heart of the Old City — which means both a central location and a noisy stay if your room faces the busy Praça Velha (formerly Praca da Restauracão), the city's main square. Praça Velha, Angra (phone: 95-24041). Inexpensive.

Beira Mar – This 15-room *pensão* in the Old City looks out on the harbor and Monte Brasil. Rooms are comfortable and quiet, with small balconies and modern facilities, while the restaurant on the ground floor (see *Eating Out*) is one of the best in the Azores. 1 Rua São João, Angra (phone: 95-25189). Inexpensive.

Cruzeiro – A modern *albergaria* (inn) with 47 rooms in a quiet setting only a short walk from the heart of town; no restaurant. Praça Dr. Sousa Junior, Angra (phone: 95-24071). Inexpensive.

Monte Brasil – In a lovely setting overlooking the harbor in the Monte Brasil residential section of Angra, this *pensão* has 32 modern rooms (but those facing the street tend to be noisy on weekends). The dining room offers wide-angle views. 8-10 Alto das Covas, Angra (phone: 95-22440). Inexpensive.

Teresinha – A best bet for those who want to stay outside Angra, in smaller Praia da Vitória on the island's east coast, about 10 minutes south of the airport. A residential *pensão* with no restaurant, it offers a homey atmosphere and 27 rooms with private bath. 45 Praçeta Dr. Machado Pires, Praia da Vitória (phone: 95-53032). Very inexpensive.

EATING OUT: *Adega Lusitânia* – Regional dishes are served in a setting reminiscent of a candlelit wine cellar. This is a favorite with local cognoscenti. Closed Sundays. Reservations unnecessary. 63 Rua de São Pedro, Angra (phone: 95-22301). Moderate.

Beira Mar – A restaurant that is better known than the *pensão* to which it belongs and is considered one of the best in the islands. Both continental and regional specialties — fish, seafood, beef, chicken, and pork — appear on the menu. The interior is contemporary Portuguese, with plenty of tile to add to the decibel level of a convivial mix of natives and visitors. Closed Mondays. Reservations unnecessary. 1 Rua São João, Angra (phone: 95-25188). Moderate.

A Ilha – In a village east of Angra, steaks are the specialty of the house. Closed Tuesdays. Reservations unnecessary. 49 Rua da Igreja, São Sebastião (phone: 95-94166). Moderate.

Bomina – A very popular pastry shop and ice cream parlor. Open daily, throughout the day. Reservations unnecessary. 3 Alto das Covas, Angra (phone: 95-25611). Inexpensive.

Café-Pastelaria Athanasio – The best sandwiches and pastries in town. Open for breakfast and lunch only. Reservations unnecessary. 130 Rua da Sé, Angra (phone: 95-23702). Inexpensive.

GRACIOSA

Only 10 miles by 4 miles in size, this island 60 miles northwest of Terceira is the smallest of the central group. Its proper name means "gracious" or "graceful" in Portuguese; it is also often called the *ilha branca,* or "white island," because of numerous place-names derived from that color, from Barro Branco to Serra Branca. Among its first settlers was Pedro da Cunha, brother-in-law of Christopher Columbus. By 1486 a charter had been granted to Santa Cruz da Graciosa, which is today the island's main town. Given its isolation from the other islands of the group to the south, Graciosa attracted few ships and developed a predominantly agricultural economy, exporting barley, wine, and brandy to Portugal via markets on Terceira. It retains its agricultural focus, as is evident in the lowland pastures and fields surrounding centrally located Pico Timão, only about 1,320 feet high but still the highest point on this least mountainous of all the Azores. Windmills, added in the 19th century to grind grain and draw water from subterranean depths, dot the landscape. Some are still in use, for this is also the driest of the Azores.

GETTING AROUND: *SATA* (phone in Santa Cruz: 95-72456) flies in several times a week, more frequently in summer than in winter. Ferry service links the island with Terceira. Taxis can be hired for island touring. There is also public bus service on the island.

Car Rental – Rental cars are available from *Auto Turístico Escobar* (Pensão Santa Cruz, Largo Barão de Guadalupe, Santa Cruz; phone: 95-72345), and from *Quedina e Filhos Limitada* (Rua Visconde Almeida Garrett, Santa Cruz; phone: 95-72278).

SPECIAL PLACES: Santa Cruz da Graciosa – Set on the northeast coast of the island, this picturesque town of red-roofed white houses is Graciosa's chief port, but it feels like no more than a rural village. The 16th-century parish church and the three small 18th-century chapels at Monte da Ajuda are typically Azorean in style and detail, containing Flemish paintings, carved wood altars, and glazed tiles. The *Ethnographic Museum* (Rua Alexandre Herculano) is a typical old residence displaying artifacts of Graciosa's agricultural past (open from 10:30 AM to 12:30 PM and from 2 to 5:30 PM; closed Mondays; no admission charge).

Praia – Narrow streets lined with 16th- and 17th-century homes make for interesting browsing in this small port and fishing village 5 miles (8 km) south of Santa Cruz. A boat takes visitors to nearby Praia islet for views of the town and surrounding countryside.

Furna do Enxofre – This sulfur cave, also called the Furna da Caldeira, since it's located inside the island's summit crater, is a rare volcanic phenomenon in the southern part of the island. A 300-foot natural tunnel burrows through rocks into a 250-foot high underground cavern, the roof of which is covered with stalactites that hang over a lake of sulfurous water. A stone stairway leads to the lakeshore. Visit between 11 AM and 2 PM, when the sun enters the cave from a narrow opening above and creates dazzling visual effects. Outside, a trail following the crater rim offers sweeping views of the island and, on a clear day, of neighboring, but distant, Terceira, São Jorge, and Pico.

CHECKING IN: *Ilha Graciosa* – A recent adaptation of a historic old home, this residential *pensão* has 15 rooms with private bath. There is a snack bar, but no restaurant. Avenida Moniz Albuquerque, Santa Cruz (phone: 95-72675). Moderate.

Santa Cruz – A centrally located *pensão* with 19 comfortable rooms (with private bath) and an at-home ambience. There is a restaurant (see below). Largo Barão de Guadalupe, Santa Cruz (phone: 95-72345). Inexpensive.

EATING OUT: *Santa Cruz* – The dinner menu at this pension dining room includes fish chowder, parrot fish (when available), and chicken and beef dishes. Open daily. Reservations unnecessary. Largo Barão de Guadalupe, Santa Cruz (phone: 95-72345). Moderate to inexpensive.

SÃO JORGE

This island is, in fact, a long, narrow, steep mountain range surrounded by the sea: 33 miles long from end to end, but only 5 miles across at its widest point. Despite its central location, 60 miles west of Terceira, 20 miles north of Pico, and 30 miles east of Faial, it is more often seen from a distance than visited. As was the case with most of the other islands in the archipelago, its fertile lowlands were first settled in the middle of the 15th century; subsequently, aside from an invasion (repelled) of French corsairs in the early 18th century, its history has been uneventful. While farms dominate the lowlands, pasture covers much of a central plateau — São Jorge is particularly noted for its dairy products, especially cheese. The island peaks at the nearly 3,500-foot Pico da Esperança. Up-country views are memorable, encompassing not only broad vistas, but also the sight of blue and purple hydrangeas lining the roads in summer. There are several nature preserves, including the small lagoon of the Caldeira do Santo Cristo and the tiny Ilhéu do Topo, an islet off the village of Topo that attracts masses of seabirds. Topo, at the far southeastern tip of São Jorge, was the island's first settlement, but its two main towns today are Velas and Calheta, two ports farther up the south coast.

 GETTING AROUND: *SATA* (Rua de Santo André, Velas; phone: 95-42125) flies into the airport outside Velas. Ferry service links the island with others in the central group.

Car Rental – Rental cars and cars with drivers are available from *J. N. Moura* (Avenida do Livramento, Velas; phone: 95-42292). A single road runs the length of the island, with several roads climbing upward from it to the central plateau.

SPECIAL PLACES: Velas – Houses with whitewashed walls and red tile roofs make up São Jorge's largest village. The church of São Jorge, built in 1460 with funds donated by Prince Henry the Navigator (but rebuilt in the 17th century), was one of the earliest in the Azores. Also of interest are the 17th-century town hall and small museums dedicated to religious art and island ethnography.

Urzelina – Several miles along the coast south of Velas, at Urzelina, is an isolated bell tower, all that remains of a church destroyed when Pico da Esperança last erupted in 1808.

Belvederes – The lookouts at Ribeira do Almeida and Fajã das Almas, both southeast of Velas on the road to Calheta, provide impressive views of Faial and Pico. The lookout at Fajã dos Cubres, on the north coast near Norte Pequeno, takes in the small lakes of the island's summit crater.

 CHECKING IN: *Solmar* – The best bet for those staying in Calheta, it has 9 clean, comfortable rooms with private baths. No restaurant, but there's a bar. Rua Domingos Oliveira, Calheta (phone: 95-46120). Moderate.

Das Velas – The island's largest hostelry is an *estalagem* (inn) of 24 rooms, featuring private baths and verandahs with views of Velas and of neighboring islands. A restaurant and lounge are on the property. Rua Machado Pires, Velas (phone: 95-42632). Inexpensive.

Neto – A *pensão residencial* offering 16 rooms with private bath and a seawater swimming pool. No restaurant. Largo Conselheiro Dr. João Pereira, Velas (phone: 95-42403). Inexpensive.

EATING OUT: *Beira Mar* – Seafood specialties include octopus and the catch of the day. Open daily in summer; closed Sundays the rest of the year. Reservations unnecessary. Largo Conselheiro Dr. João Pereira, Velas (phone: 95-42342). Moderate.

Continental – The menu ranges from seafood to beef, pork, and veal. Closed Mondays. Reservations unnecessary. Rua Padre Joaquim Moreira, Calheta (phone: 95-46200). Moderate.

PICO

The volcanic peak that dominates the landscape also gives Pico (peak) its name. At just over 7,750 feet, cloud-shrouded Pico Grande is the tallest not only in the Azores, but in all of Portugal. The island is the second-largest in the chain (measuring approximately 30 miles from east to west and 9 miles from north to south). Its northern coast falls to the sea in a series of steep cliffs; its southern coast, where the descent to the sea is more gradual, hosts numerous fishing and farm villages. Pastureland exists, but most of the farming done on rugged Pico is fruit growing and the cultivation of the vine, particularly on the fertile volcanic soil of the western part of the island. Several small lakes are also found on the western side, and throughout there are unusual formations of lava rock, called *mistérios,* caused by 18th-century volcanic eruptions, as well as several caves. Native laurel and cedar line the roads.

Settlement began in 1460 on the island's southern coast, near the village of Lajes do Pico. By the 19th century, Lajes had emerged as a major whaling port, and today the town has a small museum, the *Museu dos Baleeiros* (Rua da Pesqueira), documenting its whaling history (open daily from 10:30 AM to 12:30 PM and from 2 to 5:30 PM, Sundays from 2 to 5:30 PM; no admission charge). The *Festa dos Baleeiros* (Whalers Festival), which takes place the last week in August, continues to fulfill a vow made by local whalers in the late 19th century, even though whaling is now a thing of the past in the Azores. Besides Lajes, Pico has two other main towns: São Roque do Pico, on the island's northern coast, and Madalena, on its northwestern coast, directly across from Horta, Faial. Either Lajes or Madalena can make a good base for touring, although Madalena is better prepared to serve visitors.

 GETTING AROUND: *SATA* (phone in Madalena: 92-92411) has daily flights to and from Terceira in summer, less frequently in winter. Ferries connect the island with others in the central group.

Bus – Public buses circle the island.

Car Rental – Cars can be rented from *Manuel Pereira do Amaral Rent-a-Car* (Largo Cardeal Costa Nunes, Madalena; phone: 92-92253), and from *Colômbis Rent-a-Car* (Avenida Machado Serpa, Madalena; phone: 92-92601). The island can be seen in 1 day, although side trips to explore all its villages and caves and perhaps to hike to the summit can easily absorb 3 days.

Taxi – Taxis are available for car-and-driver hires.

 SPECIAL PLACES: Pico Grande – Pico's summit caldera can be reached by trail. While the hike is not too demanding, it can be dangerous if bad weather suddenly sets in, which frequently happens. During the winter, hiking is complicated by snows that cover the upper slopes. Guides are recommended (check with the tourist office representative at the *Aparthotel Caravelas* in Madalena). The ample reward is a 360° perspective that includes Pico and neighboring Faial, São Jorge, and Terceira.

CHECKING IN: *Açor* – A 13-room *pensão residencial* in a private garden setting, on a quiet street within easy walking distance of both the port and the center of town. Rooms have private baths, and there are wonderful views of the sea; no restaurant. 5A Rua D. João Paulino, Lajes (phone: 92-97243). Inexpensive.

Aparthotel Caravelas – This modern 67-unit hotel, including 17 apartments with kitchens, is within walking distance of Madalena's small harbor. Rooms have balconies and views of the coast; the hotel has a restaurant, gymnasium, sauna, and a solarium. Rua Conselheiro Terra Pinheiro, Madalena (phone: 92-92500). Inexpensive.

Montanha – A *pensão residencial* in a scenic wooded area that offers a panoramic view over Pico to the island of São Jorge. There are 16 rooms with bath; no restaurant, but there is a snack bar. Rua do Capitão-Mor, São Roque do Pico (phone: 92-94699). Inexpensive.

Pico – Conveniently located on the outskirts of town, this *pensão* has 32 modern, comfortable, quiet rooms and a friendly and helpful staff. The restaurant is perhaps the best on the island (see below). Biscoitos, Madalena (phone: 92-92392). Inexpensive.

EATING OUT: ***Pico*** – The dining room of the *Pensão Pico* offers an extensive menu of well-prepared fish and meat specialties as well as alfresco dining in summer. Open daily. Reservations unnecessary. Biscoitos, Madalena (phone: 92-92392). Moderate.

O Moinho – Fresh catch of the day is the specialty of the house. Just outside Lajes, with spectacular coastal views from the outdoor patio. Open daily. Reservations unnecessary. Miradouro do Arrife, Terras (phone: 92-97292). Moderate to inexpensive.

O Cadete – Regional dishes and specialties fresh from the sea are served here. Open daily. Reservations unnecessary. Poço, São Roque do Pico (phone 92-94595). Inexpensive.

FAIAL

The westernmost island in the central group, measuring 15 miles by 10 miles, Faial is in part scarred by the eruption of an offshore volcano that took place in 1957, lasted a year, and left the island slightly larger than it had been. Elsewhere, typically flourishing green pastures dominate the landscape, providing a foreground for magnificent views of the towering summit on neighboring Pico, 5 miles away across the Canal do Faial. The island takes its proper name from the forests of beech that once covered it, although it is the ubiquitous blue hydrangeas that grow here today that have earned it the nickname "blue island." Horta, in the southeast corner of the island, is an important port, the island capital, and capital of the third of the Azores' three political districts.

The earliest settlers on Faial were Flemish farmers and herdsmen who arrived in the mid-15th century under the auspices of a Flemish nobleman, Josse de Hurtere. The parish of Flamengos, which lies in a picturesque valley, is a reminder of those times, as is the name of the town of Horta itself. Several centuries later, with the island heavily settled by Portuguese, Faial became a popular port of call for American whalers, who took advantage of Horta's sheltered waters to reprovision their ships. During World War II, the Allies used it as a way station for troops en route to the invasion of Normandy. In 1919, Horta also served as a stopover for the first airplane flight across the Atlantic, and at one time it was the relay point for every cablegram sent across the ocean floor. Today, particularly in April, May, September, and October, it provides refuge for yachts in transit between the Mediterranean and the Caribbean.

GETTING AROUND: Airport – *TAP Air Portugal* (28 Rua Vasco da Gama, Horta; phone: 92-23911) flies nonstop from Lisbon 2 days a week in winter and 4 days a week in summer. *SATA* (Rua Serpa Pinto, Horta; phone: 92-23911) flies in from the other islands. The island airport, Aeroporto da Horta, is about 6 miles (10 km) west of town, at Castelo Branco.

Bus – Local bus service links Horta with other island villages.

Car Rental – Contact *Auto Turística Faialense* (12 Rua Conselheiro Medeiros, Horta; phone: 92-22308), or *Ilha Azul* (14 Rua Conselheiro Medeiros, Horta; phone: 92-31150).

Ferry – There is direct ferry service between Horta and Madalena, Pico, and between Horta and Velas, São Jorge; service to Terceira and Graciosa is indirect.

Taxi – Island taxis are available for touring as well as for individual trips. Try *Fraga* (phone: 92-25575), *João Duarte* (phone: 92-98270), or *Gilberto Dutra* (phone: 92-23921).

SPECIAL PLACES: Horta – This is a tranquil town set on gently sloping land surrounding a sheltered harbor and still graced with the scale and architectural detail of its 16th- and 17th-century origins. It is hard to imagine it as a battleground, but that is indeed what it became in 1583, when the Spanish fleet attacked the Portuguese garrison at the Fort of Santa Cruz; in 1597, Sir Walter Raleigh attacked the same fortress. Horta's harborside jetties are most interesting: They're covered with graffiti — that is, signatures, dedications, and hand-painted murals done by sailors throughout the years, their artistic efforts memorializing long journeys and adventures shared. Also see the 17th-century parish Church of São Salvador, with carved choir stalls and two notable panels of tiles, and the 17th-century São Francisco convent, which has a magnificent gilded altar, paintings, and more glazed tiles. The *Horta Museum* (Largo Duque d'Avila e Bolama; phone: 92-23348) includes religious art, wood sculptures, and a collection of intricately carved figwood miniatures that are something of a local tradition (open weekdays from 9 AM to 12:30 PM and from 2 to 5 PM, weekends from 2 to 5:30 PM; no admission charge). The *Café Sport* (see *Eating Out*) houses an interesting scrimshaw museum.

Ponta dos Capelinhos – The lava- and cinder-scarred landscape here at the westernmost point of the island is a result of the Azores' last major volcanic eruption, which took place in 1957 when a submarine volcano emerged from the sea. Multicolored cinder cones add beauty to a scene of silent devastation, with half-buried houses protruding from hardened ash and the burned-out skeleton of the towering lighthouse that once stood on a coastal cliff now several hundred feet inland.

Caldeira – In the center of the island, Faial's summit caldera is more than a mile in diameter and filled with a crater lake. The highest point is reached at 3,500-foot-high Cabeço Gordo, and the road leading up to it provides magnificent views of the islands of São Jorge and Pico. En route, some of the few remaining windmills on the island can also be seen.

CHECKING IN: *Fayal* – Set on a hillside overlooking Horta, this is as close as Faial gets to a resort hotel. It offers modern conveniences, 84 comfortable rooms, a nightclub, restaurant (see *Eating Out*), and bar, as well as quiet, landscaped grounds that include a swimming pool and tennis courts. Rua Consul Dabney, Horta (phone: 92-22181). Moderate.

Santa Cruz – A contemporary 25-room *estalagem* (inn) built atop the 16th-century fortress of Santa Cruz. It's graced with a historic setting, a central location, Portuguese decor, and across-the-harbor views of the summit on Pico. Facilities include a bar and restaurant. Rua Vasco da Gama, Horta (phone: 92-23021). Moderate.

São Francisco – In the heart of town, this 32-room residential pension offers friendly service, quiet rooms, and something of the feel of a monastery. No restaurant. 13 Rua Conselheiro Medeiros, Horta (phone: 92-22957). Inexpensive.

EATING OUT: Fayal – This hotel dining room serves well-prepared dishes such as pork chops "American-style" (grilled) and scallops of beef in madeira wine. Open daily. Reservations unnecessary. Rua Consul Dabney, Horta (phone: 92-22181). Moderate.

Vista da Baia – American Mary Vargas moved to Faial years ago with her Faial-born husband, Frank. Now they run a restaurant that overlooks the bay at Varadouro, on the island's west coast. Barbecued chicken is the specialty of the house, but this is also a great place to drop by for a drink and some small talk. Closed Mondays. Reservations unnecessary. Estrada do Varadouro (phone: 92-95140). Moderate.

O Tripeiro – By reputation, the best restaurant on the island. A short walk past the harbor, the setting is simple, and the seafood and fish are fresh and delicious. Closed Mondays. Reservations unnecessary. 24 Avenida Marginal, Horta (phone: 92-23295). Moderate to inexpensive.

Café Sport – The "in" place for the at-anchor yacht crowd, this is also known as "Peter's café," or simply "Pete's," and it's known in sailing circles far beyond the shores of the Azores. It also attracts its share of locals, which makes for an interesting, high-energy mix when the drinks are flowing, as they usually are after 5 PM. The menu of fish and meat dishes is okay, but the bar and the crowd (and the interesting scrimshaw museum upstairs) are the real attractions. Open daily. Reservations unnecessary. 9 Rua Tenente Valadim, Horta (phone: 92-22327). Inexpensive.

FLORES

The remotest islands of the Azores are Flores and Corvo, and of these, Flores, about 150 miles from Faial, is the westernmost island in the archipelago and the westernmost point of Europe. The island (11 miles long and 9 miles wide) offers surprisingly diverse beauty within its modest boundaries: rugged terrain, dramatic shoreline cliffs, lovely crater lakes, waterfalls, and everywhere the abundance of wildflowers that eventually gave it its name. Some visitors consider São Miguel the most beautiful of the Azores, but Flores has equally enthusiastic advocates. After its discovery in 1452, early attempts to colonize the island by Flemish settlers were unsuccessful, so that actual settlement did not begin until 1528, when farmers and herdsmen from northern Portugal arrived. During the 16th and 17th centuries, English privateers encroached on the island's serene isolation by using its waters as a base to attack Spanish galleons returning with treasure from the New World. In 1862, the Confederate privateer *Alabama,* outfitted by the British, used it as a base to attack American ships. Today the island's small population (about 4,350), engaged in agriculture and fishing, lives as peaceably as ever, mainly in two towns: Santa Cruz das Flores, in the middle of the island's east coast, and the smaller Lajes das Flores, in its southwest corner.

GETTING AROUND: Until recently, the only way to reach Flores was by boat. Now the only way to reach it (except from Corvo) is by plane: *SATA* (phone in Santa Cruz: 92-52425) flies to the island's recently built airport. Infrequent service, however, combined with stormy weather during winter months, makes a quick visit risky. Although the island can easily be seen in a day, it's not unusual for visitors to be stranded for a week or longer.

Car Rental – Rental cars are available from *Rent-a-Car Vila Flor,* Travessa de São José, Santa Cruz (phone: 92-22190).

Taxi – Taxis provide car-and-driver service for sightseeing out of Santa Cruz.

 SPECIAL PLACES: Santa Cruz das Flores – Churches from the 16th through the 19th centuries provide this charming village with architectural significance. Among them are the parish church, Nossa Senhora da Conceição, a 19th-century building with an imposing façade, and São Pedro, an 18th-century rebuilding of a 16th-century structure, notable for its carved and gilded high altar.

Enxaréus Grotto – Boats take visitors along the deeply indented, cliff-lined coast for a visit to this dramatic sea cave about 3 miles south of Santa Cruz.

Vale da Fajãzinha – On the western coast of Flores, this is a valley with lovely waterfalls cascading to the sea and lush vegetation to give it a feel of the tropics. It's reached by a winding road that makes its way down from the main road leading from Santa Cruz to Lajedo, a 10-mile (16-km) trip that takes about 45 minutes.

Lagoa Funda – The prettiest of the seven crater lakes on the island is surrounded by hydrangeas. It's about a half-hour drive inland from Santa Cruz.

 CHECKING IN: *Toste* – A 10-room *pensão residencial,* basic, but comfortable. Breakfast is served, but there's no restaurant. Rua Senador André de Freitas (phone: 92-52119). Inexpensive.

Vila Flor – This 9-room *pensão* is clean and comfortable, with a homey atmosphere and a restaurant (see below). Rua Senador André de Freitas, Santa Cruz (phone: 92-52190). Inexpensive.

 EATING OUT: *Vila Flor* – A *pensão* restaurant serving a simple menu of fish, octopus, beef, and pork dishes. Open daily. Reservations unnecessary. Rua Senador André de Freitas, Santa Cruz (phone: 92-52190). Moderate.

CORVO

The smallest of the Azores has a population to match its size: Only about 370 people call Corvo home. The island lies 15 miles northeast of Flores and was discovered the same year (1452), although it was settled later (1548). Its name dates back to days when both it and Flores were known jointly by one name, Ilha dos Corvos Marinhos, or "Island of the Sea Crows." Only about 4½ miles long and 3 miles wide, Corvo, like its sister islands, packs a great deal of natural beauty into a very small space. In the north is the Caldeirão, the extinct volcanic crater that formed the island, now carpeted in green and filled with two lovely lakes. From 2,200-foot-high Monte Grosso, atop the crater rim, the panoramic views are magnificent. In the south are the islanders' cultivated fields and pastures, and at the very southern tip, their only settlement, Vila Nova do Corvo, a typically picturesque town of red-roofed white houses laid out along narrow

streets called *canadas*. The only way to reach Corvo is by boat from Santa
Cruz das Flores. There are no rental cars, but a few taxis are available
— and a taxi should be sufficient, since the island has a single road, about
5 miles long, linking the town in the south to Caldeirão in the north.
There are no hotels or other hostelries. Camping out is one possibility; by
asking around, you may find someone to put you up, pension-style. As for
eating out, you're on your own.

Madeira

Lying nearly 400 miles off Morocco's Atlantic coast and nearly 600 miles southwest of the Portuguese mainland, Madeira rises from the sea in an angular assault of mountains, valleys, ravines, and cliffs, the result of millions of years of volcanic activity and erosion. On coastal lowlands and on steep hillsides, terraced fields and rustic homes replace the anarchy of once primeval forest with the geometry of human settlement. Only in a few places, where mountains and sea cliffs proved too vertical and too inaccessible for even the hardy Madeirans to colonize, can fragments of the dense forest that once dominated the island (Ilha da Madeira means "island of wood" in Portuguese) still be found, along with stark evidence of its volcanic past.

Madeira shares its oceanic isolation with a small fleet of neighboring islands that make up the Madeira archipelago. Porto Santo, 27 miles to the northeast across occasionally choppy seas, is comparatively low lying and the only other inhabited island in the group. It serves as a summer getaway for residents of the main island, thanks to sand dunes, beaches, and some of the islands' sunniest weather. To the southeast lie the rugged, unsettled Ilhas Desertas, often visible from Madeira in sharp-edged silhouette on the southeastern horizon. Still farther south, not far from Spain's Canary Islands, is a cluster of equally barren islets, the wild Selvagens.

Until 1964, when a jet airport finally was built on Madeira, visitors arrived aboard passenger ships that made Funchal, the only community on Madeira large enough to be called a city, a standard port of call on transatlantic and around-the-world cruises. Cruise ships still drop anchor at Funchal, which is built around a bay along the island's sheltered south coast, but it was the coming of the jets that opened Madeira to the European holidaymakers who have been arriving in increasing numbers ever since. With 100,000 people, more than a third of the island's population, and a year-round flow of visitors, Funchal is a bustling city that also serves as the capital of the archipelago, which is, in turn, an autonomous region of Portugal. Portuguese law applies, although the local legislature plays a significant role in administration, planning, and budgeting. As with most islands, where isolation establishes a reality that is somewhat different from life on the mainland, here, too, a well-defined individuality encourages consideration of full independence. It is a scenario, however, that practically no one takes very seriously.

For winter-weary Europeans, Madeira's climate is its primary attraction. Winter temperatures rarely dip below 50F, and average a comfortable 60F when most of Europe is 20 to 30 degrees colder. North Americans expecting a Portuguese version of the Caribbean, Mexico, or Hawaii, however, may find such temperate weather a surprise — and something of a disappointment. Summer temperatures are no more extreme, seldom topping the 70s. Indeed, springtime plots a 12-month course here, with one flower or another —

bougainvillea, hibiscus, begonias, birds of paradise, anthuriums, orchids, morning glories, hydrangeas — blooming and one fruit or another — mangos, papayas, figs, oranges, pears, avocados, guavas, passion fruit — ripening throughout the year. Few are indigenous; Madeira's subtropical climate and rich volcanic soil proved a hospitable habitat for plants brought by trading ships from all parts of the globe, tropical and temperate.

Because the island rises so precipitously from sea level to mountaintop, it has distinct zones of vegetation, and visitors can climb from sugarcane to pines and heather in the course of only a short drive. Madeira's steep rise from the sea is the cause of another peculiarity that may disappoint: its lack of sandy beaches. There are a few stretches of gravel or pebbles along the shoreline, and Porto Santo is well endowed with sand, but in the main, swimming on Madeira is confined to hotel pools or to small coves developed with cabana facilities. Thus, for an American visitor, it is the charm of Funchal and the dramatic beauty of the landscape, not the lure of a tropical getaway, that makes a visit worthwhile.

Oblong in shape, roughly 35 miles from east to west and 13 miles from north to south, Madeira is traversed by well-maintained, well-marked roads. Panoramic vistas are a part of any drive, even within the confines of Funchal, where city streets climb 2,000 feet or more above sea level before surrendering to farmland, forest, and the jagged mountains seen from lookouts such as that atop 6,104-foot Pico Ruivo, the island's highest point. More than half of Madeira's inhabitants still live out in the countryside, particularly in the southern part of the island, where their terraced fields — called *poios* — create what seems a vast agricultural suburb extending nearly the full length of the south coast. Funchal itself retains the feel of a large village, with open markets, narrow streets, and a 17th-century scale, while actual small villages such as Ribeira Brava and Machico, west and northeast of Funchal respectively, and São Vicente, on the north coast, retain the atmosphere and scale of traditional Madeira, with whitewashed, tile-roofed houses and the distinctive square bell towers of Madeiran churches dominating the skyline. Yet growth has been explosive for the past 25 years, fueled by expanding tourism that has brought casino gambling, high-rise resort hotels, and condominium apartments in its wake, and by agricultural exports and the money sent back to families by citizens living and working overseas.

Madeirans have been shipping out to parts unknown for several centuries, first drawn aboard as sailors and later enticed by opportunities offered in places as far afield as New England, Hawaii, South Africa, and Australia. Although legend credits the shipwrecked English adventurer Robert McKean (also spelled Machim) with the island's discovery in 1346, better-documented evidence reserves that honor for João Gonçalves Zarco, a Portuguese explorer who, with his fellow sailor Tristão Vaz Teixeira, first spotted the island of Porto Santo (in 1418) and then Madeira (in 1419), and claimed them on behalf of Prince Henry the Navigator, who had sponsored the expeditions.

Many other explorers followed, along with settlers, as Madeira became a popular port for ships heading off across the mysterious Atlantic during the age of exploration, and the first of a string of colonies that would make tiny Portugal a major world power by the mid-16th century. What had been a wilderness was soon home to tens of thousands of Portuguese drawn to this new mid-ocean frontier as sailors, fishermen, farmers, herdsmen, and tradesmen. They established ports, cleared most of the forest, and built the extensive network of irrigation ditches (called *levadas*) that still carry water from the cloud-banked interior and the rainy north coast to the drier south, where settlement was heaviest.

Although Spain controlled Madeira from 1580 to 1640 (when Spanish kings sat on the Portuguese throne), it was the British who ultimately provided a more lasting influence. Links to Britain were forged in 1662 when Catherine of Braganza married King Charles II of England and granted favored status to English settlers on Madeira. British traders strengthened those links, shipping large quantities of sugar, the crop that had brought the island its first taste of prosperity, and wine, which still contributes to Madeira's wealth. The British then took advantage of the commercial links when, in the guise of protector during the Napoleonic era, they sent troops to occupy the island, first in 1801, and then again from 1807 to 1814. Napoleon himself anchored off Funchal in 1815 — as a prisoner en route to exile on the isolated south Atlantic island of St. Helena. The British consul in Madeira, the only visitor allowed the emperor, presented Napoleon with a gift of madeira wine.

Sugarcane, imported from Sicily early in the 15th century, was Madeira's original cash crop. Today, bananas and grapes dominate, the former exported fresh, the other fermented to produce the distinctively rich-flavored wines that have a centuries-long reputation. The first vines, brought to Madeira from Crete during the 15th century, produced sweet wines of the *malvazia*, or, to the British, malmsey type. They were known early and well in England — a 15th-century Duke of Clarence, brother of King Edward IV, was rumored to have been drowned in a cask of madeira, and madeira wine is mentioned in Shakespeare's plays. English wine merchants soon set up shop on the island, and began to export wine to the mother country and the colonies so extensively that by the 18th and 19th centuries, the English, with the Americans, were Madeira's major customers.

George Washington, John Adams, and Thomas Jefferson were all enthusiasts, but the wine they drank was not like the earliest madeira. Over the years, it was discovered that fortifying the local wine with brandy not only increased its alcoholic content, but also made it less likely to spoil during long ocean voyages. Then it was noticed that the heat to which the wine was unavoidably subjected during long months at sea resulted in added body and shelf life. Eventually, the heating stage (called *estufagem*) was made a part of the basic fermentation process. Today, the results can be tasted when visiting the São Francisco Wine Lodge in Funchal, where the four classic types of madeira, named for the grape variety used to produce each — dry sercials, semi-dry verdelhos, semisweet boals, and sweet malmseys — are fermented and stored. Storage racks still hold bottles dating from the 1830s, their contents still drinkable, evidence that madeiras are among the longest lasting of all wines.

The British, again, are credited with creating a market for Madeiran embroidery and building a reputation for quality that continues to this day. In 1856, Elizabeth Phelps, daughter of a British wine merchant, set up a workroom on the island to turn out the embroideries that were so prized by the ladies of the Victorian era. The enthusiastic British response soon had thousands of Madeiran women embroidering for export. An estimated 70,000 still carry on the craft today, as the abundance of embroidered tablecloths, napkins, nightgowns, and other clothing in Funchal's well-stocked shops confirms.

And it was the British, late in the 19th century, who first made Madeira a favorite getaway for sun seekers. That was the era when the legendary *Reid's* hotel, built by a Scot, opened, bringing a touch of Victorian Britain to Funchal. Wealthy British, particularly those in search of a salubrious climate to nurse frail health, soon turned Madeira into something of a private country club, an outpost of the British Empire rather than of the Portuguese. Today, the hotel, which hosted Edward VII while he was Prince of Wales, Winston Churchill, and others, remains the quintessence of British gentility (and still serves afternoon tea), though dozens of other hotels and rental condominiums have opened their doors over the years to accommodate the sharp increase in visitors.

Luckily, the island seems to have absorbed the growth in the number of visitors while maintaining its authenticity. This is due largely to the fact that most Madeirans retain family ties to the land, still hand-tending the terraced fields that have been built and expanded over the centuries as the population has grown. Man and nature do mix surprisingly well on Madeira, as can be seen in precisely this green, terraced sea (a match in scale and beauty for the terraced farmlands of Bali and the Philippines, which are perhaps more familiar). It can also be seen in the seemingly random placement of what look like miniature houses, sprinkled over the dramatic, flowing landscape. The addition of other manmade details make each vista an image of harmonious juxtaposition. Some of the details are hard to bring into focus. Take Madeira's ample population of cows, for instance. A traveler could spend a week in the countryside without ever suspecting they were there, unless he or she happened to look into one of the thatch-roofed huts, called *palheiros,* that dot the hillsides. The terraced fields may provide enough fodder for the cows' feed, but they offer too little space for free grazing and too much risk that a stray might tumble off the edge.

Other images of this amply flowered island complete a picture of great serenity: the brilliant afternoon light on the boats and harbor at the fishing village of Câmara de Lobos; a misty afternoon in the forest near the highland village of Camacha; Funchal at dusk, with city lights serving as a glowing highlight against the sun's last traces. Madeira is a rare travel fantasy come true, and it lingers in the memory like the sweet aftertaste of a sip of madeira wine.

SOURCES AND RESOURCES

TOURIST INFORMATION: The Regional Tourist Office of Madeira has its headquarters (and a well-supplied street-level office) in the heart of town (18 Avenida Arriaga, Funchal; phone: 91-29057); smaller branches on the island are in Machico (Edifício Paz; phone: 91-962712) and at the airport (phone: 91-52933).

Several informative tourist publications are available, including the *Madeira Tourist Guide, Madeira: Somewhere Special,* and *Madeira Tourist Information,* in addition to maps of Funchal and Madeira. Free visitor publications, including the *Madeira Island Bulletin,* a monthly tabloid, are also available at most hotels. *Madeira Holidays,* a magazine with text in English, French, German, and Portuguese, contains a useful "Information and Shopping Guide" and costs about $2. Note that Madeira Tourist Radio broadcasts in English between 5:45 and 6:30 PM daily except Saturdays (1485 on the AM dial).

Porto Santo's Tourism Office is in Vila Baleira, the island's main town (Avenida Vieria de Castro; phone: 91-982361). Maps of the island and town are available; in addition, most guides to Madeira include a few pages about Porto Santo.

Local Coverage – The *Diário de Notícias,* Madeira's daily newspaper, provides a sense of local concerns, as well as information on special events.

Telephone – The area code for all of Madeira (including the island of Porto Santo) is 91. If calling from mainland Portugal (or Porto Santo), dial 091 before the local number.

 CLIMATE: A spring-like climate makes Madeira a year-round destination. Fahrenheit temperatures range from the 50s and 60s in winter (November through April) to the 60s and 70s in summer, with warm periods pushing up into the 80s. December through February are the coolest and rainiest months. July and August are the "season," drawing large crowds of vacationing Europeans.

 GETTING THERE: *TAP Air Portugal* flies nonstop daily from Lisbon, and less frequently from Porto, the Azores (São Miguel and Terceira), Spain's Grand Canary, and several European capitals. Once a week, the *TAP* flight from Lisbon to Funchal continues to the island of Porto Santo, 20 minutes away. Porto Santo is also served by daily flights from Funchal aboard the smaller, non-jet planes of *Linhas Aéreas Regionais* (*LAR*), a domestic carrier whose flights can be booked through *TAP* offices. *TAP*'s main office is in Lisbon (3A Praça Marquês de Pombal; phone: 1-544080); they also have an office in Funchal (8-10 Avenida das Comunidades Madeirenses; phone: 91-30151). While there is no scheduled boat service to Madeira, numerous cruise ships make calls at Funchal. Porto Santo can be reached by ferry from Funchal, but during the winter, when the seas around these islands are prone to be rough, boat service can be canceled.

 SPECIAL EVENTS: Funchal is the prime focus of the special events calendar, setting things going with a magnificent fireworks display over the city on *New Year's Eve.* See the spectacle from land or head out to sea for a deck-top view. *Carnaval* arrives in February or early March and features several parades complete with extravagant floats, musicians, and dancers in costume. The *Festa da Flor* (Flower Festival), lasting 3 days in April, celebrates the island's botanic abundance with flower-decked floats and a parade of 2,000 children carrying blossoms pieced together as a floral Wall of Hope. The festivities have a heavy folk flavor, with plenty of Madeiran music, singing, and dancing. The grape harvest begins in late August, and late September sees the *Festa do Vinho* (Wine Festival), when local wine cellars are open, *fados* are sung, folk dances are performed, and traditional Madeiran foods are served. In late October, brass bands from villages all around the island hold forth in a good-natured competition — with a parade that is an important part of the revelry.

 SPORTS AND FITNESS: Deep-Sea Fishing – Blue marlin, tuna, bonito, and barracuda are some of the fish that can be caught in Madeiran waters, where world records have been set. The *Madeira Game Fishing Centre–Turipesca* offers charter services for up to four sportsmen. Prices, including crew, insurance, tackle, and bait, vary between $500 and $565 per charter depending on the season. Inquire at the entrance to the town pier (Marina) or call 91-31062 or 91-42468. In Machico, contact *Turipesca* at the *Dom Pedro* hotel (phone: 91-962751). Big-game fishing excursions aboard the *Missil* are another possibility; capacity is four to five people and the price is $120 per person for the day. Contact Captain Laquai (phone: 91-933414).

Golf – Madeira's single golf course (outside the village of Santo da Serra, near the airport, a 30-minute drive from Funchal) has 9 holes at present, but another 18 holes are being added and should be completed in 1992. The old clubhouse has a bar, lounge, and changing room; golf club rentals and caddies are available (phone: 91-55139).

Hiking – The tourist office can supply information on a number of recommended trails, which range in difficulty from relatively flat walks following the course of the island's irrigation canals (*levadas*), suitable for almost anyone, to strenuous walks in the vicinity of Pico Ruivo, suitable only for very experienced walkers accustomed to heights. Note that it takes only about half an hour for total darkness to fall, so any walks should be timed accordingly. *Savoy Travel,* at the *Savoy* hotel (phone: 91-31151), offers a half-day *levada* walking tour for those who prefer not to go alone.

Horseback Riding – The facilities of the *Associação Hípica da Madeira* are 5½ miles (9 km) from the center of Funchal at Quinta Vale Pires, accessible via Caminho dos Pretos. About 50 horses are here, as well as two open riding areas and a covered one. Horses can be rented for rides through the countryside at about $7 per hour including insurance. Make reservations through the *Dorisol* (phone: 91-32658), *Estrelicia* (phone: 91-36131), or *Buganvilia* (phone: 91-31015) hotels.

Snorkeling and Scuba Diving – Equipment is available from *Manta Raener Madeira* (phone: 91-93241) at the Tourist Center Galomar in Caniço de Baixo, several miles east of Funchal, and also at the *Madeira Carlton* hotel (formerly the *Sheraton;* phone: 91-31031)).

Swimming – Except for a small one at the eastern tip of the island, sand beaches are lacking on Madeira, and since the coast is generally too rocky for easy ocean access, most swimming is done in hotel pools or in one of several rock-sheltered, manmade pools just to the west of Funchal. These offer cabanas, lounge chairs, food, and drink. The *Lido* (Rua do Gorgulho; phone: 91-62217), the *Clube Naval* (235 Estrada Monumental; phone: 91-22253), and the *Clube de Turismo* (179 Estrada Monumental; phone: 91-62559) attract a mix of Madeirans and visitors. Both guests and non-guests can rent cabanas at the *Savoy* hotel's swimming pools. The island of Porto Santo makes up for the lack of beaches on Madeira with its 4-mile-long strand.

Tennis – The best public facility is at the *Quinta Magnolia* (Rua do Dr. Pita; phone: 91-64013), where the courts have been placed in a garden setting swept by cool breezes. In addition, the *Madeira Palácio* (phone: 91-30001), *Reid's* (phone: 91-23001), the *Savoy* (phone: 91-22031), *Casino Park* (phone: 91-33111), and *Duas Torres* (phone: 91-30061) hotels all have tennis facilities, and most provide court time for non-guests. Few are equipped for night play.

Windsurfing – Lessons and equipment can be obtained in Funchal at the *Savoy* hotel (Avenida do Infante; phone: 91-22031), and in Machico at the *Dom Pedro* hotel (phone: 91-962751).

MADEIRA

Funchal, the island capital, is set on a bay on Madeira's south coast, and attracts by far the greatest number of visitors, although Machico, east of Funchal on another bay, is fast becoming a second tourist center. A chain of mountains stretching across the island — from Ponta de São Lourenço, a low, rocky spit of land at its easternmost tip, to Ponta do Tristão at its northwestern corner — effectively divides Madeira in two. Compared to the north, the mountains slope more gently to the sea in the south, although there are some stunning exceptions, as at Cabo Girão, a headland just west of Funchal. In the more rugged northern half of the island, the mountains come to an abrupt, cliff-hanging halt high above the surf. At points, the road west from São Vicente to Porto Moniz, Madeira's most northwesterly town, follows a narrow shelf that was picked out of the rock by workers who were lowered in baskets from the cliff tops above. Dark tunnels alternate with stunning views, spectacular to most but not recommended for those suffering from vertigo. The northern half of the island is not only more rugged than the southern half, but also windier and wetter, since the chain of mountains blocks northerly winds and traps the clouds and rain — providing the sheltered south coast, Funchal included, with generally sunny skies.

Visitors to Madeira who can be pried away from poolside have much to see around the island. Besides Funchal's museums, churches, and gardens, there are coastal and highland villages and a wealth of spectacular scenery, visible along the road or from lookout points set on the island's highest peaks and at other beautiful spots. With either Funchal or Machico as a base, a week's worth of day trips should be enough to see it all, although it is possible to see the highlights in even less time.

GETTING AROUND: Madeira may look small on the map, but narrow, winding roads make for slow going. Most roads consist of only one lane each way, and pedestrian traffic and carts occasionally reduce even these to just a single lane for both directions. Fortunately, roads are well maintained and well marked. Route 101 circles the island; although segments of it follow the coast, much of the time the road runs anywhere from a few hundred to a couple of thousand feet above the seashore, with panoramic views all the way. Similarly scenic main roads cross the island from south to north. Driving in Funchal, while equally scenic, is complicated by a maze of narrow, slippery, cobblestone, one-way streets. The city cannot be seen entirely on foot, however, although the downtown area is walkable (but leave high heels at home).

Airport – Flights land at the island's Aeroporto de Santa Catarina, at Santa Cruz, 14 miles (23 km) northeast of Funchal. Several car rental firms have offices at the airport (see below). The airport-to-hotel taxi fare usually comes to about $18 to $20.

Bus – Most city buses travel along Avenida do Mar, and intercity buses heading to all parts of the island leave from curbside locations along the same avenue. Detailed information on routes and schedules is in the *Madeira by Bus* brochure, available at the tourist office. Bus stops are marked by signs reading *Paragem.*

Car Rental – Rentals are readily available at unlimited-kilometer rates averaging $60 to $100 a day (including tax and gasoline), depending on the model and the amount of driving done. Local firms charge about the same rates as the major ones; advance booking is recommended, particularly during the summer crush. Firms with airport locations include *Hertz* (12 Rua Ivens; phone: 91-23332; and at the airport; phone: 91-52360); *Avis* (164 Largo António Nobre; phone: 91-64546; and at the airport; phone: 91-52392); and *Rodavante* (Edifício Baía, Estrada Monumental; phone: 91-47448; and at the airport; phone: 91-52718). Also try *Atlantic Rent-a-Car* at the *Duas Torres* hotel (239 Estrada Monumental; phone: 91-22888 or 91-61711); *Hansa Rent-a-Car* at the *São João* hotel (74 Rua das Maravilhas; phone: 91-46122); or *Europcar* (306 Estrada Monumental; phone: 91-28116; and Caminho Velho da Ajuda; phone: 91-62406).

Taxi – Metered taxis can be hailed while they are cruising or picked up at hotels or at designated cabstands in town, including a convenient one near the tourist office (Avenida Arriaga; phone: 91-22500). There is a base rate, after which fares increase by the kilometer, with a typical 10-minute trip coming to about $2.50 to $5. (Add a 5% to 10% tip if service has been good.) Fares for travel outside Funchal are determined by distance, and there is a published list of rates. Many drivers provide day-tour service at prices (about $65) likely to be less than the daily tab for a rental car.

Toboggan – Once upon a time, this was a major means of transportation on Madeira, used for carrying both goods and people down the island's steep slopes. Now primarily run for the fun of the experience, the *carro de cesto* ride down steep, timeworn cobblestone streets from the suburb of Monte (see below) to Funchal is Madeira's most distinctive activity. The vehicle is a wicker-sided sled on wooden runners, powered by gravity and guided and steadied by a team of two people working ropes. From the starting point of this one-way trip, Monte's Nossa Senhora church, take a 10-to-15-minute ride for about $7 per person (each sled holds up to three); the entire 25-to-30-minute trip costs about $11. The sled handlers appreciate a small tip.

Tours – Half- and full-day motorcoach tours of the island depart from Funchal and Machico, picking up and dropping off participants at their hotels; most guides speak some English. Tour desks and travel agents in the larger hotels can handle bookings. Among the itineraries are a half-day excursion to Monte and Eira do Serrado or to Camacha and Pico do Arieiro, a full-day visit to Porto Moniz and Cabo Girão, and a "Madeira by Night" tour including dinner and a show, all offered by *Companhia Automóveis de Turismo* (*CAT;* 52 Avenida Arriaga; phone: 91-25294). *AB Tours* (177 Rua dos Ferreiros; phone: 91-25134) operates out of both Funchal and Machico and offers a day trip to Porto Santo in addition to Madeira island excursions. *Savoy Travel,* at the *Savoy* hotel (phone: 91-31151), *Windsor Travel* (254 Estrada Monumental; phone: 91-31057), and *Abreu* (22 Avenida do Infante; phone: 91-31077) also offer tours.

Excursions by boat are offered by *Costa do Sol* (contact *Turipesca,* phone: 91-31063), which operates seven different day tours visiting the principal ports of Madeira aboard the *Tamisa.* An exciting day watching shark fishing some miles distant from the coast, with lunch aboard the vessel, is also available. Prices vary from $15 to $50 per tour; ask about departure and arrival times and whether lunch is included. Another possibility is the *Pirata Azul* (phone: 91-27020), a riverboat once used as a passenger ferry between Madeira and Porto Santo and now offering half-day excursions (about $20) from April through October (phone: 91-27020). The *Albatroz* is a sailing yacht departing at 10 AM daily for a cruise along the shoreline, a typical Madeiran lunch at anchor, an exhilarating sail accompanied by treacle cake and madeira wine, and a 5 PM return. The full-day price is about $40 ($15 for a half day); contact Robert Wyntje (phone: 91-66532).

SPECIAL PLACES: Funchal – Thanks to its fine natural harbor on Madeira's south coast, where hillsides were once covered in wild fennel (*funcho* in Portuguese), Funchal, founded in 1428, quickly became a port of call for Portuguese ships bent on discovery and the acquisition of a prosperous overseas empire. Old engravings show it as a village tightly clustered around its port; today, while the port remains active handling cargo, pleasure craft, and cruise-ship visitors, the modern city surrounds the old one and ranges far into the mountain foothills, bringing a sense of the country to within a short vertical drive of the Old City's commercial bustle. Something of the overall layout can be seen from the belvedere at Pico dos Barcelos (about 2 miles — 3 km — west of town), which presents the city against a backdrop of coastal cliffs. Another view, from Monte, a hillside suburb above central Funchal, takes in the 1,800-foot drop down the mountainside to the port below. Still another vantage point, at sea level this time, is the Potinha, the breakwater for Funchal harbor built nearly two centuries ago. Make it to the end and climb the steps up the retaining wall (ask permission of the port authorities first); the reward is a panoramic view of the harbor, the towers of the Old City, and a heavily populated mountainside that ultimately surrenders to wilderness.

The Old City of Funchal is east of the hotel zone, stretching roughly between two forts, São Lourenço to the west and São Tiago to the east. Running along the waterfront between them is the Avenida do Mar, a seaside promenade intersected midway by the small town pier. Funchal's main thoroughfare, Avenida Arriaga, is behind Avenida do Mar and parallel to it, with a statue of the island's discoverer, João Gonçalves Zarco, at one end and the Sé, Funchal's 15th-century cathedral, at the other. This, the heart of the Old City and the first Portuguese cathedral to be built "overseas," combines elements of Manueline and baroque design. Built of lava rock and stucco, its interior highlights include a wonderful ceiling of cedar inlaid with ivory, the 17th-century chancel woodwork, the beautiful Flemish paintings above the 16th-century altar, and the gilded wood of the Chapel of the Holy Sacrament.

The city's best shopping streets are near the cathedral, as are alfresco cafés at which to sip richly flavored Brazilian coffee and watch the passing scene. Before taking it easy, however, take a tour of the *São Francisco Wine Lodge* (28 Avenida Arriaga; phone: 91-20121), run by the Madeira Wine Company, the largest exporter of madeira wines. After an informative film, the tour visits the lodge's wine cellars and aging rooms, where still-capped 19th-century vintages are to be found, and ends in the tasting room, where numerous brands are sold. The lodge is open weekdays from 10 AM to 1 PM and from 2:30 to 6 PM (Saturdays by appointment); tours (1 hour) take place at 10:30 AM and at 3:30 PM; (bookings are necessary for groups, and there is a charge for the tour). On the same street is the *Museu Cristovão Colombo* (48 Avenida Arriaga; phone: 91-36192), a new museum and library with nearly 500 titles relating to Columbus and other rare pieces, including a great number of books on Madeira and a fine collection of old prints (open Mondays through Fridays from 10 AM to 1 PM and from 2 to 7 PM; admission charge).

Among several other museums of interest is the *Museu de Arte Sacra* (Museum of Sacred Art; 21 Rua do Bispo; phone: 91-28900), only about 10 minutes on foot from Avenida Arriaga. Housed in the former Episcopal Palace facing Funchal's mosaic-covered Praça do Município, it contains paintings from the 15th to the 18th centuries — Portuguese and Flemish painters are well represented — as well as gold and silver plate, ivory sculpture, and gilded wood ornamentation. Another 10 minutes away is another museum, set in the *Quinta das Cruzes* (1 Calçada do Pico; phone: 91-22382), a 15th-century *quinta* (country house) built by the explorer Zarco, but now dedicated to the decorative arts. Portuguese furniture of the 16th century, Chinese porcelain, and French enamel are displayed in rooms that were once the villa's wine cellar; 1 flight up are French and English furniture and a collection of ivory carvings. The building is surrounded by a botanical garden of several acres of tropical and subtropical flowers. Both museums are open from 10 AM to 12:30 PM and from 2 to 6 PM; closed Mondays. Admission charge. Still another museum, near the *Quinta das Cruzes,* is the *Museu Frederico de Freitas* (Calçada de Santa Clara; phone: 91-20578), displaying art objects, furniture, and a unique collection of Madeiran watercolors in an 18th-century house (admission information is the same as for the two museums above, except that this one closes at 6:30 PM). The Convento de Santa Clara, founded by two of Zarco's grand-daughters on the site of a church he had chosen as a burial place for his family, is on the same street. Now it's run as a kindergarten by nuns, but visitors are welcomed at the door to the right of the church, whose interior, beautifully covered in *azulejo* tiles, contains Zarco's Gothic-style tomb. Not far away is the *Museu Vicente* (42 Rua da Carreira; phone: 91-25050), formerly a leading island photographic studio and now a repository of over 100,000 glass negatives constituting a history of the island and those who have visited it (open Tuesdays and Fridays from 2 to 6 PM; no admission charge).

Nothing typifies Funchal's authenticity better than the *Mercado dos Lavradores* (Workers' Market) at the eastern edge of the Old City. It's best in the morning: Arrive between 7 and 11 AM (closed Sundays) and see the market come alive with the animated dealings of farmers, fishermen, and price-conscious local shoppers. Flower vendors stationed at the door wear traditional Madeiran garb (cap, red vest, ruffled white blouse, and full skirt). The produce arrayed inside (everything from carrots, onions, chestnuts, and papayas to scabbard fish, tuna, swordfish, and eel) serves as an introduction to the fare available at local restaurants. Plan to spend an hour or two wandering about (and note that several blocks farther east is the Barreirinha district, a still-proletarian fishermen's quarter where upscale restaurants provide alfresco dining).

The Jardim Botânico, in the hills at Caminho do Meio, in the Bom Sucesso district (about 15 minutes by car from Avenida Arriaga), is another must see, open from 8 AM to 6 PM; closed Sundays; admission charge. Just about every flower, plant, or tree that grows on Madeira is represented here, laid out on terraces surrounding an old country house. The noteworthy views of the city and harbor are an added attraction. Close by, and also well worth seeing, is the Jardim dos Louros, home to more than 500 tropical birds from around the world (open from 9 AM to 6 PM daily; admission charge). More of Madeira's floral abundance can be seen in the gardens of the Quinta do Palheiro Ferreiro, a private estate 5 miles (8 km) east of the center, open to the public from 9:30 AM to 12:30 PM weekdays (except public holidays); admission charge. Orchids in particular are at Quinta Boavista (27 Rua Albuquerque), 5 minutes from the center and open from 9 AM to 5:30 PM Mondays through Saturdays; no admission charge.

ELSEWHERE ON THE ISLAND

Monte – This hillside community, nestled amid towering trees and an abundance of flowers, is about 3 miles (5 km) and 1,800 feet above the Old City. Once popular as a country retreat, it is now more a suburb of Funchal, but its cool climate, luxuriant vegetation, and panoramic views still attract visitors. The Nossa Senhora do Monte church, built late in the 18th century, provides an unexpectedly sophisticated baroque façade preceded by a steep staircase. Inside, the silver tabernacle above the main altar houses a small statue of Our Lady of the Mount, found in the 15th century at the very spot in Terreiro da Luta where the Virgin Mary is said to have appeared to a young shepherdess. Since that time, Our Lady of the Mount has been Madeira's patron saint, and the church is the object of pilgrimage every *Assumption Day* (August 15), when some of the faithful climb the stairs on their knees. The church also contains the tomb of Charles I, the last of the Austro-Hungarian emperors, who died here in 1922. The famous toboggan ride (see *Getting Around*) begins near the steps of the church.

Câmara de Lobos – Drive 5½ miles (9 km) west of Funchal along Route 101, passing terraces dense with bananas, to reach this picturesque fishing village of whitewashed, red-tile-roofed houses built around a cliff-sheltered harbor and a rocky beach. Named for the seals once abundant in coastal waters, the village was a favorite of Winston Churchill, who often set up his easel here during visits to Madeira. A roadside viewpoint overlooks the harbor and its colorful array of fishing boats, with the dramatic sea cliff of Cabo Girão as a backdrop. Arrive by 8 AM and you're likely to see fishing boats being unloaded after a night at sea. By midday, the scene is more tranquil, as fishermen cluster amid their boats to play cards and women do their wash in the Ribeira do Vigario. The walk along the harbor breakwater provides additional panoramic views.

Cabo Girão – The 1,900-foot headland, the second-highest promontory on earth, lies 7 miles (11 km) west of Câmara de Lobos. Follow Route 101 as bananas give way to vines, then turn left onto the clearly marked road to the lookout at the summit. The view down the almost sheer drop to the pounding sea is magnificent; even here, several hundred feet below, small patches of terraced fields cling to the cliff edges wherever possible.

Serra de Agua – Continue west from Cabo Girão and turn inland at Ribeira Brava. About halfway between the island's north and south coasts is this rustic riverside village, which benefits from a wonderful setting of sharply eroded mountains rising precipitously from terraced hillsides that are often shrouded in mist and clouds. Bamboo and weeping willows line the river, adding a romantic touch to what is otherwise a workaday farm settlement. The road climbs from Serra de Agua to the 3,304-foot-high Encumeada Pass, where new panoramas take in the descent toward the north coast and São Vicente.

São Vicente – This small town on Madeira's north coast, about an hour's drive from Funchal, is set where a river of the same name meets the sea. The views as the road winds its way down from the mountains into town are particularly beautiful, although there is little to see in São Vicente itself, apart from a small cluster of shops. The town does, however, provide a midday stop for a number of motorcoach tours of the island, as well as for sightseers touring on their own. More views are in store as Route 101, which makes a complete circuit of the island, leads west of São Vicente, climbing to cliffside heights and offering sweeping views of Madeira's north coast. Because portions of the road are narrow and unpaved, careful attention to driving is necessary, as is an occasional bit of maneuvering when confronting oncoming traffic.

Porto Moniz – A sheltered anchorage formed by a narrow peninsula that points toward a picturesque islet, Ilhéu Mole, is the setting for this charming fishing village on the northwest coast of Madeira. A further attraction, besides the scenery, is the large natural ocean pool set amid lava rock that attracts swimmers during the summer months. (Winter weather and rough surf can make a swim uninviting and dangerous.) At Porto Moniz, the around-the-island road turns inland to wind its way south and eventually back east to Funchal.

Eira do Serrado – This 3,385-foot lookout point is about 8 miles (13 km) northwest of Funchal, reached by taking the Pico dos Barcelos road and driving approximately 20 minutes through countryside rife with eucalyptus trees and native forest. The lookout sits atop the sawtooth crater of one of Madeira's great formative volcanoes, and the view down into the crater encompasses, surprisingly, not only farmland, but also the whitewashed village of Curral das Freiras. The name of the village means "nuns' shelter," because it was to this spot that the sisters of Funchal's Convento de Santa Clara escaped in the 16th century, in retreat from French pirates who had attacked and pillaged the city. Eventually, the settlement became permanent, and only recently was its isolation infringed upon by more than a footpath. Now there is a road, but the trip from the lookout down to the village is worthwhile only if you've time to spare. At the lookout, vendors sell well-priced handicrafts, and a path leads to additional panoramas.

Pico do Arieiro – No place on Madeira reveals its volcanic nature better than its second-highest peak, 14 miles (22 km) north of Funchal — on a clear day, that is. Often, while the rest of the island is basking in sunlight, this 5,939-foot peak may well be covered in clouds, mist, and rain. When skies clear, the summit lookout reveals a landscape covered in volcanic debris and the eroded mountains that have been created in the millions of years since Madeira surfaced from the sea. Fortunately, the road goes right to the top of Pico do Arieiro, so no mountain climbing is necessary to see the view.

Pico Ruivo – At 6,104 feet, this is Madeira's highest peak, a prize to be gained only by those who make the effort; unlike Pico do Arieiro, no road leads to the top. There is a 4-mile (6-km) trail from Pico do Arieiro that takes about 3 hours of hiking and entails a few treacherous stretches without the benefit of safety rails. Otherwise, a trail from Parque das Queimadas (at the end of a 3-mile/5-km road from Santana, a village on the island's northeastern coast) leads to the heather-covered summit. From here, Madeira's tallest mountains rise all around, and long-distance views take in the valleys of the island's north coast, Ponta de São Lourenço at its easternmost tip, as well as Santana and the village of São Jorge at its northeastern corner. The trip is worthwhile for those with the stamina and the time, and — provided arrangements have been made with the tourist office in Funchal beforehand — it's possible to spend the night in the rustic refuge — *casa de abrigo* — a few minutes' walk from the top.

Camacha – The quiet highland village is just 6 miles (10 km) northeast of Funchal, at an altitude of almost 2,300 feet. The surrounding groves of willows provide the material for making the wickerware that is the village specialty; the wicker shops are worth a visit even for those who don't intend to buy. Try to come to town on a Sunday, when it's buzzing with residents of the area gathered to socialize and promenade.

Machico – It was here, 16 miles (26 km) northeast of Funchal, that the Portuguese explorer João Gonçalves Zarco and his crew made their first landfall on Madeira, in 1419. Thus, the bay fronting the town is known as Zarco's Bay. According to legend, Machico was also the place where the Englishman Robert McKean (or Machim) was shipwrecked with his bride, Ana d'Arfet, in 1346. The young couple died, but the unlikely story has other survivors of the ship taking to sea in a raft and ending up in Morocco, after having been captured by Arab pirates. Eventually, word of Madeira's existence is supposed to have reached Portugal, resulting in the voyage of discovery led by Zarco, along with Tristão Vaz Teixeira, a fellow sailor, who became governor of this part of the island. Machico's parish church and the Capela São Roque both date from the 15th century. At the Capela dos Milagres (Chapel of Miracles), rebuilt in 1829 after having been destroyed by a flood in 1803, a framed cross is said to be the one originally left on the graves of the ill-fated McKean and his wife.

SHOPPING: Embroidery, wine, and wickerware are Madeira's most distinctive products, but a shopping spree on Madeira (and that, for the most part, means Funchal) can also turn up good prices on tooled leather, handmade shoes, and high-fashion European clothing. The best browsing is along Rua do Aljube and the cluster of streets bordered by Avenida Zarco, Rua 5 de Outubro, and Avenida do Mar. Shops are generally open Mondays through Fridays from 9 AM to 12:30 or 1 PM and again from 2 to 6 PM, Saturdays from 9 AM to 1 PM. The lunchtime closing is an 11th commandment, so make shopping plans accordingly. Outside Funchal, shopping is likely to be limited to wicker, another island specialty. The village of Camacha, about 6 miles (10 km) from Funchal, is the center of this activity.

An Englishwoman established Madeiran embroidery during the Victorian era, and today thousands of Madeiran women embroider under contract to makers and retailers of table linens, children's wear, women's lingerie, and other fashions. Prices vary considerably, so shopping around is warranted, but since Madeirans know what the market will bear, don't expect fantastic bargains. Prices, in fact, can be surprisingly high, with a large, intricately embroidered Irish linen tablecloth (napkins included) topping $2,500. But there are lovely things for far less.

Artecouro Leather Shop – The leather is from Portugal, but the bags and belts that are the shop's specialties are made on Madeira with great skill and style; there are also wallets, sandals, and children's boots. 15 Rua da Alfândega, Funchal (phone: 91-37256).

Bazar do Povo – Inexpensive odds and ends, sold in something like a five-and-dime store from another era. 1 Rua do Bettencourt, Funchal (phone: 91-26833).

Camacha Wickerworks – Room after room of things made of wicker, from giraffes and other animals to furniture. Items too large to be carried can be shipped home. Largo da Achada, Camacha (phone: 91-922114). There is also a showroom and shop at the *Centro Comercial do Infante Shopping Center*, 75 Avenida Arriaga, Funchal (phone: 91-34586).

Casa do Turista – A showcase for Portuguese crafts — crystal, porcelain, ceramics, wickerware, dolls, and more, including embroidery — displayed in an old mansion. 2 Rua Conselheiro José Silvestre Ribeiro, Funchal (phone: 91-24907).

Cloe Leather – Everything from shoes to bags to high-fashion accessories in calf, mustang, and more exotic skins. 13 Largo do Phelps, Funchal (phone: 91-27711).

Hélio – The source of well-priced Charles Jourdan shoes — the shop is Madeira's exclusive Jourdan agent. 65 Rua do Aljube, Funchal (phone: 91-23447).

Jabara – Madeiran embroidery; opened in 1908, the store is a downtown landmark. 59 Rua Dr. Fernão de Ornelas, Funchal (phone: 91-29500).

Lãs Voga – An old-fashioned, abundantly stocked yarn shop. 60 Rua Dr. Fernão de Ornelas, Funchal (phone: 91-22336).

A Loja Nova – Sophisticated European women's wear. 45 Rua do Aljube, Funchal (phone: 91-20322).

Nova Minerva – It bills itself as "creative shirtmakers," with a very nice collection of shirts for men. 31 Rua da Alfândega (phone: 91-37627). The shop for women is at 40 Avenida Arriaga (phone: 91-28264).

Oliveiras – One of the widest selections of embroidery in town. The workroom on the floors above is one of a couple of dozen such factories in Funchal. Ask to visit, and see what it takes to create a finished tablecloth or negligee (and ask for the 25% factory discount). At two adjoining downtown locations: 22 Rua dos Murças, Funcha (phone: 91-29340) and 11 Rua da Alfândega, Funchal (phone: 91-20245).

São Francisco Wine Lodge – Run by the Madeira Wine Company — the place to go for seven of the better-known labels, including Leacocks, Blandys, and Cossart Gordon. 28 Avenida Arriaga, Funchal (phone: 91-20121).

H. Stern – Brazil's ubiquitous gemstone jeweler has shops in three Funchal hotels — the *Madeira Carlton* (formerly the *Sheraton*), Largo Antonio Nobre; the *Madeira Palácio,* Estrada Monumental; and the *Casino Park,* Avenida do Infante.

Teixeiras – Still more Madeiran embroidery. This is the place for something special; the prices are a bit higher, but the quality is a bit better, too. 13 Rua do Aljube, Funchal (phone: 91-36616).

NIGHTCLUBS AND NIGHTLIFE: *Fado* is popular here, as it is in Lisbon. If you like its soulful sound, head to *Bar Marcelino* (*Pão e Vinho;* 22A Travessa das Torres; phone: 91-34834). Also check with the major hotels — *Madeira Carlton, Savoy, Casino Park, Madeira Palácio, Reid's* — to see if *fado* or folk performances are scheduled. The *Savoy* hotel (Avenida do Infante; phone: 91-22031) has a rooftop nightclub, *Galaxia,* with panoramic views and its own band (folk dancing on Tuesdays and Thursdays); *Safari* (5 Rua do Favila; phone: 91-20455) follows a disco beat. The *Prince Albert* (86 Rua da Imperatriz Dona Amélia; phone: 91-31793), a pub with Victorian ambience, is quieter, allowing conversation. *Bar on the Rocks* (7 Rua Carvalho Araújo; phone: 91-29087) and *Joe's Bar* (1 Beco Imperatriz Dona Amélia; phone: 91-29087) both offer nightly piano music and an outdoor setting. The former is intimate and comfortable, set on the rocks with a view overlooking the sea; the latter is intimate and charming, with a lovely terrace. *Salsa Latina* (101 Rua da Imperatriz Dona Amélia; phone: 91-25182) has live (quiet) music and serves light meals; *Berilights* (23 Rua do Gorgulho; phone: 91-62535) is a bar and meeting place for young people.

The *Casino da Madeira,* adjoining the *Casino Park* hotel (Avenida do Infante; phone: 91-31121), is open daily from 4 PM to 3 AM (jackets required after 8 PM). Slot machines, craps, blackjack, and American and French roulette are played in the three gaming rooms — an American Room, a European Room, and a private room (Salle Privée), reserved for the casino's best customers. There is a nominal entrance fee for the gaming rooms, and foreigners are expected to present a passport. The casino also offers a nightly floor show at the *Zodiac* nightclub, but those accustomed to Las Vegas and Atlantic City will find it somewhat modest.

CHECKING IN: Although there are several small hotels in outlying towns such as Ribeira Brava, most visitors stay in either Funchal or Machico. Funchal offers elegant high-rise hotels clustered to the west of the port, a few condominiums, and a range of lovely small hotels and pensions on the narrow streets of the Old City. Machico is Madeira in a resort mode, with a number of large hotels. Expect to pay $150 or more a night for a double room at properties listed below as very expensive; $75 and up in a hotel listed as expensive, from $40 to $70 in a moderate one, and $35 or less in an inexpensive one. As on the mainland, breakfast is included; any establishment designated as "residential" does not have a restaurant and usually serves breakfast only. Hotels, large and small, are generally well maintained and well managed, catering primarily to European visitors from Great Britain, Germany, France, and Scandinavia.

FUNCHAL

Casino Park – Part of the casino–conference center–hotel complex designed by Oscar Niemeyer, the architect of Brasília, this is ultramodern in style: simple yet elegant. The 400 rooms offer sweeping views of the sea and Funchal's harbor; facilities include a large pool with landscaped lounging areas, a children's pool, a health center, tennis courts, shops, and more than 1 dining room serving good food. Of the top hotels, this is also the closest to the center of town, a 10-minute walk away. Avenida do Infante (phone: 91-33111). Very expensive.

Madeira Carlton – Formerly the *Sheraton,* the stylish decor, rooms with panoramic ocean views, 2 large swimming pools, tennis, sauna, water sports, and a central location within walking distance of downtown (it's not much farther out than the *Casino Park*) describe this high-rise, which has 372 rooms and is the island's largest hotel. Largo António Nobre (phone: 91-31031). Very expensive.

Madeira Palácio – On the outskirts of town, on a hillside that affords beautiful views of the 2,000-foot sea cliffs at Cabo Girão. Friendly service by a well-informed staff is a major plus, as is the decor in the 260 rooms (comfortably contemporary). There's fine dining, and other facilities include tennis courts, water sports, and an oversize pool with Madeira's dramatic landscape as a backdrop. A free shuttle bus links the hotel to several downtown locations, a 10-minute drive. Estrada Monumental (phone: 91-30001). Very expensive.

Reid's – The quintessential colonial hotel, an outpost of 19th-century propriety in a 21st-century world, where guests still linger in the lounge or parade through the lobby in tuxedoes and evening gowns. Built in 1891, the hotel has been beautifully maintained and, where necessary, modernized. It offers sweeping coastal views from many of its 150 rooms, 10 acres of florally landscaped grounds, 2 lovely heated oceanside swimming pools, water sports, tennis, some of Madeira's best dining options (see *Eating Out*), and a central location within walking distance of the Old City. The price for such pleasures is the highest on Madeira. 139 Estrada Monumental (phone: 91-23001). Very expensive.

Savoy – Kitsch says it all for this 350-room oceanfront property, which is even older than *Reid's* and is its traditional rival. Actually, beyond the garish grandeur of the lobby, it tones down considerably. Poolside is the *Savoy* at its best, however — there are 2 large pools and plenty of space for lounging. Water sports, tennis, and miniature golf are available on the property. Avenida do Infante (phone: 91-22031). Very expensive.

Quinta do Sol – Mid-size at 116 rooms, it offers friendly service in a park-like setting within walking distance of downtown Funchal. It's adjacent to the grounds of the *Quinta Magnólia* (see *Eating Out*), and benefits from easy access to the facilities there. 6 Rua do Dr. Pita (phone: 91-64151). Expensive.

Eden Mar – A nice new apartment-hotel set about 50 yards from the sea. It's located west of the center, in the heart of the tourist zone that surrounds the *Lido* swimming pool complex, and it has 37 studios and 68 junior suites with kitchenettes. 2 Rua do Gorgulho (phone: 91-62221). Expensive to moderate.

Quinta da Penha de França – A large townhouse has been converted into an inn of 35 rooms, with lots of local character, a restaurant and snack bar, gardens, and a swimming pool. It's set in quiet surroundings, close to the *Casino Park* and the other leading hotels. 2 Rua da Penha de França (phone: 91-33083). Expensive to moderate.

Windsor – A middle-of-the-road choice in more ways than one, since this is neither large nor small (67 rooms), quite nice, reasonably priced, and the only one of its category in the center of town; rooftop pool. 4C Rua das Hortas (phone: 91-33083). Expensive to moderate.

Monte Carlo – It occupies the crest of a hillside in the Old City, so there are breathtaking views of ocean, mountains, and red tile roofs from the balconies, dining room, poolside, and many of the 45 rooms — about 20 of which are in the main house, a rococo palace that is something of a landmark in its own right. A friendly atmosphere prevails; reserve in advance, especially during peak seasons. 10 Calçada da Saúde (phone: 91-26131). Moderate.

Reno – An apartment-hotel overlooking the heart of the Old City, within a short walk of Funchal's shops. Studios and 1-bedroom units are available, all with kitchenettes. 15-25 Rua das Pretas (phone: 91-26125). Moderate.

Santa Clara – A wrought-iron gate and a walkway lined with hibiscus lead to this 16-room *pensão residencial* (residential pension), only a block away from the *Quinta das Cruzes* museum and gardens. Inside, the house has a turn-of-the-century, Victorian feel, which means a bit stuffy, but by no means unfriendly. The view from the dining room, swimming pool, and rooftop solarium is particularly beautiful, embracing sea, city, and mountains. 16B Calçada do Pico (phone: 91-24194). Inexpensive.

ELSEWHERE ON THE ISLAND

Atlantis – One of the island's top properties, this high-rise was originally built as a *Holiday Inn*. Set on Zarco's Bay, about 35 minutes from Funchal by taxi or bus, it has 312 rooms, all with balconies and sea views. Guests also appreciate the indoor and outdoor pools, rooftop grill, nightclub, gamerooms, cinema, tennis courts, and shops. Agua de Pena, Machico (phone: 91-962811). Expensive.

Dom Pedro Machico – A self-contained resort overlooking Machico's Bay. It has 218 rooms, a heated saltwater pool, a discotheque, tennis courts, and other amenities, including the necessary equipment for windsurfing and deep-sea fishing. Estrada São Roque, Machico (phone: 91-962791). Expensive to moderate.

BravaMar – Those in the mood to stay in a smaller Madeiran town should try this 36-room hotel. The decor is simple, in fact a bit spartan, but there's privacy, a quiet setting, and plenty of exploring to do in the surrounding countryside. Rooms have ocean views and kitchenettes. Rua Gago Coutinho, Ribeira Brava (phone: 91-952220). Moderate.

Pousada do Pico do Arieiro – A comparatively new member of Portugal's *pousada* chain, it's set on top of the second-highest mountain on the island. Fireplaces and winter gardens contribute to the inn's atmosphere, and the 22 rooms have terraces from which to admire the superb view. Reserve through *Enasol*, 2 Rua da Sé, Funchal (phone: 91-24707), or directly through the inn. Pico do Arieiro (phone: 91-48188). Moderate.

Pousada dos Vinháticos – This woodsy 12-room inn, opened in 1940 as the first *pousada* in all of Portugal, is on the mountain-rimmed road that leads to the scenic

Encumeada Pass. It's a great place to stay for those who want to go hiking (there are numerous trails nearby), and then spend the night in magnificent mountain quiet. Reserve through *Enasol*, 2 Rua da Sé, Funchal (phone: 91-24707), or directly through the inn. Serra de Agua (phone: 91-952344). Moderate.

EATING OUT: There are perfectly acceptable restaurants in all of the large hotels, clusters of restaurants taking advantage of the island's natural beauty spots, even fast-food restaurants; most of the better places are in Funchal, although there are eating places in many towns around the island. Note that Funchal Marina, to the west of the town quay, offers a string of moderate and inexpensive restaurants within a short distance of each other — the area is pleasant and frequented by people of all ages. Madeiran specialties include *sopa de tomate e cebola* (tomato and onion soup), *caldeirada* (fish soup), *bife de atum e milho frito* (grilled tuna steak with fried corn bread), *espada* (black scabbard fish) prepared a variety of ways, and *espetada* (skewered beef, fragrant with laurel and garlic, grilled over charcoal). Pastries may look better than they taste, but *bolo de mel* (honey cake) is an exception. Expect to pay $35 to $45 for a meal for two without drinks at restaurants listed below as expensive, from $20 to $30 in those listed as moderate, and under $15 in the inexpensive ones.

FUNCHAL

Arsenio's – A favorite with Madeirans and visitors. Fine food (local seafood and continental specialties) is complemented by *fado* singers and Brazilian rhythms. Reservations necessary. 169 Rua de Santa Maria (phone: 91-24007). Expensive.

Caravela – Many Madeirans consider this Funchal's best. The menu is mainly continental, but includes local seafood and fish dishes as well. The setting combines casual, contemporary decor with views of the harbor. Open daily from noon to 10 PM. Reservations necessary. 15 Avenida do Mar (phone: 91-28464). Expensive.

Casa dos Reis – For candlelit dinners in a mahogany- and brass-accented setting that still manages to be warm and friendly, this spot is only a short walk from the *Casino Park, Madeira Carlton,* and *Savoy* hotels. Fish, lamb, and specialties of the charcoal grill are the fare. Open for lunch and dinner daily. Reservations necessary. 101 Rua da Imperatriz Dona Amélia (phone: 91-25182). Expensive.

Casa Velha – A 19th-century Madeira residence redone as a restaurant with gently revolving ceiling fans, lace curtains, and blue tiles. Both local and international dishes are served. Open for lunch and dinner daily. Reservations necessary. By the west entrance of the *Casino Park* hotel. 69 Rua da Imperatriz Dona Amélia (phone: 91-25749). Expensive.

Golfinho – The nautical decor matches the menu of this restaurant in the Old City: catch-of-the-day fish and seafood. Reservations necessary. 21 Largo do Corpo Santo (phone: 91-26774). Expensive.

Reid's Grill – Madeira at its most elegant. The tab pays for swank surroundings, quality service, delicious continental fare, and an oceanfront view. Open for dinner nightly, from 7:30 to 11:30 PM. Reservations necessary. *Reid's Hotel*, 139 Estrada Monumental (phone: 91-23000). Expensive.

Solar do F – Portuguese regional cooking is served in this bar/grill/restaurant, where there's also dining on a garden terrace. The surroundings are pleasant and secluded, only 250 yards from the *Madeira Carlton* hotel. Open for lunch and dinner daily. Reservations necessary. 19 Avenida Luís de Camões (phone: 91-20212). Expensive.

Gavina's – Always crowded, lively, and enjoyable, this oceanfront eating place serves fish and seafood — shrimp, lobster, octopus, sea bass, *espada, sargo* (sea bream), *bodião* (parrot fish), *salmonete* (red mullet), and others are all on the menu. A free shuttle van picks up diners and then drops them off at Funchal's major hotels, just 5 to 10 minutes away. Reservations necessary. Rua do Gorgulho (phone: 91-26908). Expensive to moderate.

Jardin – One of several good restaurants in the Old City specializing in seafood and continental dishes. Dine alfresco or inside, amid Victorian decor. Open for lunch and dinner daily. Reservations advised. 60 Rua Campo Dom Carlos I (phone: 91-22864). Expensive to moderate.

Vagrant – Once a yacht owned by the *Beatles,* it's now a restaurant anchored on the east side of the town quay. A large selection — from seafood to sandwiches — is offered. Open daily. Reservations advised. Avenida das Comunidades Madeirenses (phone: 91-23572). Expensive to moderate.

Atlantic – Within the *Lido* swimming pool complex west of town, this is a panoramic place offering fish and shellfish specialties and selected meat dishes. Open for lunch and dinner daily. Reservations advised. Rua do Gorgulho (phone: 91-62212, ext. 59). Moderate.

O Celeiro – Madeiran cooking is served here, in the middle of town, just off the main street, and the atmosphere is pleasant. Open for lunch and dinner daily. Reservations advised. 22 Rua dos Aranhas (phone: 91-37322). Moderate.

Portuguese Grill – Smart, quiet, and near the *Lido* pool complex west of town. Open for lunch and dinner daily. Reservations advised. 21 Caminho da Ajuda (phone: 91-27605). Moderate.

Quinta Magnólia – Don't let the fact that this is a hotel-school restaurant serve as a deterrent. The food is some of the best in Madeira, the service (by a staff in training for coveted jobs in the food and beverage field throughout Portugal) is exceptional, and the setting, an elegant old mansion amid botanical gardens — the former *British Country Club* — is perfect. Since the restaurant serves lunch (a set menu, at 1 PM; bar opens at noon), not dinner, spend the morning at the estate's pool or tennis courts or simply walking the grounds, and make lunch the big meal of the day. Reservations necessary. Otherwise, stop by for tea (at 4 PM); reservations unnecessary. Closed Sundays. 10 Rua do Dr. Pita (phone: 91-64614 or 64013). Moderate.

São José – The menu features local specialties such as *galinha regional* (chicken in tomato sauce), as well as duck *à l'orange* and tournedos Orsini. The decor, with entry via a Moorish arch, is as eclectic as the menu. Good value for the money. Reservations unnecessary. 11 Largo do Corpo Santo (phone: 91-23214). Moderate.

O Almirante – A central location, a casual atmosphere, good food, and good prices are the lure. Fish and grilled meats are the specialties. Reservations advised. 1 Largo do Poço (phone: 91-24252). Moderate to inexpensive.

ELSEWHERE ON THE ISLAND

O Galo – A coastal restaurant facing the sea in a small village 7 miles (11 km) east of Funchal. The fish specialties make it worth the trip. Open for lunch and dinner; closed Mondays. Reservations advised. Caniço de Baixo (phone: 91-932123). Expensive to moderate.

Lagoa – Frequented by lots of locals, this seafood restaurant is near Madeira's golf course, half an hour by car from Funchal. Open for lunch and dinner daily. Reservations necessary. Santo da Serra (phone: 91-55118). Expensive to moderate.

Orca – Set in a picturesque village at the northwest corner of the island where there is bathing in rock pools by the sea, this spot serves Madeiran specialties, as well as international dishes. Open for lunch and dinner daily. Reservations advised. Porto Moniz (phone: 91-852359). Expensive to moderate.

A Rede – Fresh fish and other seafood, plus rice with lobster, crab, shrimp, limpets, clams, and octopus are the draw; located on the coast 7 miles (11 km) east of

Funchal. Open for lunch and dinner daily. Reservations necessary. Caniço de Baixo (phone: 91-933425). Expensive to moderate.

Roca Mar – Also on the east coast, this is a country restaurant facing the ocean and serving regional and international specialties. Open for lunch and dinner daily. Reservations advised. Caniço de Baixo (phone: 91-932999). Expensive to moderate.

Xadrez – Popular and packed with Madeirans, it's a 5-minute drive from the *Dom Pedro Machico* hotel. Open for lunch and dinner; closed Mondays. Reservations necessary. Caramachão Machico (phone: 91-962889). Expensive to moderate.

Café Relógio – A great place to stop while touring the eastern part of the island. Those in the mood for a sandwich or a good cup of espresso can stay downstairs, where the scene is alive with local color on weekends. Upstairs, there's a restaurant serving regional specialties. Reservations advised. Largo da Achada, Camacha (phone: 91-922114). Moderate.

O Facho – Regional cooking, with fish and seafood specialties, make this Machico's best. Reservations advised. Machico (phone: 91-962786). Moderate.

Quebra-Mar – Set on a rocky shelf along the coastal road on Madeira's northern side, with panoramic views and exceptional seafood — fresh shrimp, lobster, squid, and octopus. A prime stop for cars and buses touring the island, it can become quite crowded despite seating for several hundred. Reservations advised. São Vicente (phone: 91-64338). Moderate.

A Seta – Head for the hillside town of Monte for a 7-course meal of regional specialties including *espada, espetada,* roast chicken, cod, and *bolo do caco,* the delicious Madeiran country bread made with sweet potatoes. Dinner is followed by folk music and dancing that ends with audience participation. Reservations advised. 80 Estrada do Livramento, Monte (phone: 91-47643). Moderate.

PORTO SANTO

In contrast to mountainous Madeira, which is 27 miles to the southwest, Porto Santo is a low island — its highest point, Pico do Facho, rises little more than 1,600 feet above sea level. Set in the lee of the clouds attracted to Madeira's higher peaks, it is also far drier and several degrees warmer, on average, than Madeira. The island's limited rainfall and chalky soil result in a further stark contrast: its sparse vegetation versus Madeira's green exuberance. Within the 16 square miles of Porto Santo, however, there is one feature of the landscape that Madeira cannot claim: A 4-mile-long sandy beach attracts not only visitors from abroad but also the Madeirans themselves.

Though it may lie low on the horizon, Porto Santo was the first island of the Madeira archipelago to be discovered. That was in 1418, when Zarco and Teixeira, sailing for Prince Henry the Navigator, found refuge here during a raging Atlantic storm. In honor of the sanctuary it provided, they named the island Porto Santo, or "Holy Port." Settlement began the following year, with farmers using windmills to draw water to irrigate sugarcane, grains, and grapes. Christopher Columbus, who married Isabel Moniz, the daughter of the island's governor, lived here for a brief time before heading off on the voyages that would make him famous.

Today, 5,000 people call Porto Santo home; Vila Baleira, roughly in the middle of the south coast, is both "capital" and the largest town. Most islanders continue to till the soil, harvesting tomatoes, watermelons, figs, grapes, and grain — the few windmills still to be found are a reminder of the difficulties of island agriculture. Other islanders set out to fish, although fewer than before seem willing to put in the time and effort needed to make fishing a career. Summer brings an influx of visitors, but not enough to crowd the beach. Off-season has its appeal, but with temperatures generally in the 60s, it's a bit chilly for swimming. Some visitors arrive on day trips from Madeira. Others, who appreciate Porto Santo's away-from-it-all pace and mood, stay a while.

GETTING AROUND: The island is small, only 7½ miles long and 4 miles wide, so getting around is easy. For those who prefer to leave the arrangements to others, full-day excursions from Madeira are offered by *AB Tours,* 177 Rua dos Ferreiros, Funchal (phone: 91-25134).

Airport – Flights arrive daily from Funchal and land at the Aeroporto de Porto Santo, 2 miles (3 km) from Vila Baleira; taxis are available.

Car Rental – Rental cars are available from *Avis* (phone: 91-982260) and *Atlantic Rent-a-Car* (phone: 91-982630), both on Avenida Vieira de Castro in Vila Baleira. If you're staying in Vila Baleira, however, a rental car is not really necessary, because taxis can be hired for sightseeing excursions.

Ferry – Ferries link Funchal and Vila Baleira; in winter, service is frequently canceled because of rough seas.

Taxi – There are taxi stands in the center of town (Largo do Pelourinho; phone: 91-982160; and on Rua Dr. Nuno Teixeira; phone: 91-982118). *AB-Tours* (7 Rua João Gonçalves Zarco; phone: 91-982175) and *Blandy Brothers* (Avenida Dr. Manuel Pestana Junior; phone: 91-982114) both offer sightseeing tours of the island.

SPECIAL PLACES: Vila Baleira – Also called simply Porto Santo, the island's main town lies toward the center of the 4-mile-long beach. Besides the beach, several pensions, restaurants, facilities for changing money, and the local tourist office (on Avenida Vieira de Castro), its attractions include the small, white Piedade church and the adjacent town hall. Nearby, on Rua Cristovão Colombo, but not open to the public, is the house in which Columbus is said to have lived.

Portela – This lookout point, on a hillside north of Vila, offers an island-wide panorama.

Pico do Castelo – A road lined with cedar trees leads north from Vila almost to the top of this 1,445-foot peak, the island's second highest. The views include most of the island and Madeira's distant mountains.

Ponta da Calheta – The island's southwestern extremity; a lookout here takes in the desolate Baixo islet.

CHECKING IN: The choices are limited to two hotels and several pensions. Advance bookings are necessary in summer, although those who want to take a chance might be able to find an empty room without one. Prices are a bit lower than on the main island of Madeira. Expect to pay $65 or more for a double room in the expensive category, $35 to $60 for a moderate one, and $30 or less for an inexpensive one.

Porto Santo – This 2-story hotel, a bit over a mile (1.6 km) southwest of Vila Baleira, offers 100 rooms with private bath, a beachfront setting, a swimming pool, and a tennis court. Campo de Baixo (phone: 91-982381). Expensive.

Palmeira – A 25-room *pensão* on Vila Baleira's beachfront avenue, it has a pleasant setting and a friendly staff. Avenida Vieira de Castro (phone: 91-982112). Moderate.

Praia Dourada – Nicely maintained and well operated, it has 35 rooms, all with private bath. It's in Vila Baleira, a short walk from the beach. Rua Dr. Pedro Lomelino (phone: 91-982315). Moderate.

Zarco – A small, homey *pensão residencial* of 22 rooms, within a short walk of the beach in Vila Baleira. Rua João Gonçalves Zarco (phone: 91-982273). Inexpensive.

EATING OUT: Fish and seafood predominate. Although many restaurants open only in summer, there are several to choose from throughout the year. Expect a meal for two without drinks to cost $10 to $20 in a moderate restaurant, under $10 in an inexpensive one.

Estrela de Calheta – Fish and seafood specialties are served in this restaurant by the beach, near the end of the road to Ponta da Calheta. Reservations advised. Calheta (phone: 91-982145). Moderate.

Teodorico – Traditional skewered and grilled beef — *espetada* — is the specialty. The restaurant is in the hills in scenic Serra de Fora, northeast of Vila. Reservations advised. Serra de Fora (phone: 91-982257). Moderate.

Baiana – A café–snack bar–restaurant in the center of Vila, it serves the catch of the day, plus regional dishes. The covered outdoor patio is a pleasant place to dine alfresco. Rua Dr. Nuno Teixeira (phone: 91-982209). Moderate to inexpensive.

Index